the World and South East Asia

*In the production of this book
the co-operation of the Governments
of the various countries
of South-east Asia,
the Governments of
the Commonwealth of Australia
and the other Pacific Basin Economic
Council countries,
Canada, New Zealand, Japan and
the United States of America
is gratefully acknowledged.*

First Printed November 1972
Reprint January 1973

Published in Australia 1972
Editor: **Oswald L. Ziegler**
Layout and Production: **Alan D. Ziegler**
Printed by **Times Printers Sdn. Bhd.—Singapore**
© Oswald Ziegler Enterprises 1972
Library of Congress Catalog Card No. 73.183940
ISBN 0 909586 039

PRODUCED AND PUBLISHED BY

Registered in Australia for transmission by post as a book.

the World and South East Asia

OSWALD ZIEGLER ENTERPRISES PTY. LTD., SYDNEY, AUSTRALIA

Foreword

The Hon. E. G. Whitlam, Q.C., M.P.,
Prime Minister of Australia

Despite all the suffering, turbulence and deprivation of our region, I find myself, as head of Australia's new Government, deeply confident of a better future for the region.

The tragedy of Vietnam still hangs over us all. And yet it is still not too late to pluck from the ashes of Indo-China the seeds of a new beginning for us all. It depends on whether we in this region and the four great powers of the United States, Japan, China and Russia have learned the lesson of 1954.

In 1954, after Korea, after Geneva, there was a chance for a new settlement in our region. We lost that opportunity.

Now we have another chance. It must not be thrown away this time, because the price of failure now would be absolute disaster. We must all steadfastly resist any efforts by the great powers to make our region the area for ideological confrontation.

The great task ahead—and one in which the great powers should be encouraged to play their part—is the reduction of the poverty, illiteracy and starvation which keeps the region back and lessens all of us as human beings. Australia is a medium power but a wealthy nation. We menace nobody. My Government stands ready to accept its responsibility on behalf of the Australian people to play a leading role in the real and crucial war of our time—the war on want.

Soon after taking office I broadcast this message to the people of South East Asia:—

> *"There will be no next international war in our region in our time. Let us all use this unparalleled opportunity! Let us make this our objective—that every child now born in our part of the world shall have a chance for a life without fear, without want, without war. Is this an impossible goal? Perhaps—but why, in the name of reason, in the name of humanity, should we set our sights at less?"*

A new start for the new generation will be the next objective of the new Australian Government.

January 1973

E. G. WHITLAM
PRIME MINISTER OF AUSTRALIA

Preface

The World and South-east Asia *is one of a series of volumes in which seven major sectors of the world will be identified and described. Geographic proximity has been the chief criterion in determining which countries should be included in each sector, but other factors have also been taken into account.*

Thus, when The World and South-east Asia *was being planned, considerable thought was given to the inclusion of a Chapter on The People's Republic of China. Though, in terms of geography, China is in many respects part of South-east Asia its position a few years ago was one of relative isolation in world affairs.*

It was therefore decided that The People's Republic of China should find a prominent place in a later volume in the series, in the hope, now perhaps nearer fulfilment, that opportunity would be afforded for a more adequate coverage of that great and ancient country.

The troubled history of the area known for so long as Indo-China, of which the war in Vietnam and Cambodia constitutes a continuing chapter, again has made especially difficult the task of carrying out the purpose of this volume. The sections on Cambodia (Khmer Republic), Laos and Vietnam are presented, however, in the knowledge that, to whatever extent political and economic conditions may change in this area, the basic way of life of its people is not likely to be altered.

The conflict between Pakistan and India during 1971 with its tragic sequel in East Pakistan, came to an end as the Year 1972 was ushered in. With the proclamation of the new People's Republic of Bangladesh substantial revisions had to be made to the Pakistan story and a new Chapter added to the book.

The scope of "The World and South-east Asia" is so wide that even in the planning stages the publishers realised the inevitability of changes taking place before the final release of the volume. This realisation prepared them to cope with relevant problems as they arose.

In the overall compilation of The World and South-east Asia the co-operation of the various governments has been marked and spontaneous, and very substantial support has been accorded by the many leading commercial and industrial organisations in the chapters of their respective countries. This encouragement and support is gratefully acknowledged.

THE PUBLISHERS

Contents

FOREWORD
　　The Hon. E.G. Whitlam, Q.C., M.P.,
　　Prime Minister of Australia

7　PREFACE

8　CONTENTS

10　THE ASIAN NATIONS
　　　Alberto da Cruz

26　THE ECONOMIC EXPLOSION
　　　Derek Davies.
　　　Editor Far Eastern Economic Review

42　UNESCO IN ASIA
　　　W. J. Weedon, O.B.E., M.A., Dip. Ed.

46　THE SIGNIFICANCE OF SEAMEO
　　　South-east Asian Ministers of Education Secretariat

50　THE MIGHTY MEKONG PROJECT
　　　Dick Wilson

56　THE ASIAN HIGHWAY
　　　M. S. Ahmad
　　　Director of Asian Highway

62　ASIAN GODS AND CREEDS
　　　Alberto da Cruz

68　THE NOMAD TRIBES OF ASIA
　　　Peter Hinton, B.A., M.A.,
　　　Professor of Anthropology, University of Sydney

72	Kingdom of BHUTAN	572	Republic of VIETNAM
80	Sultanate of BRUNEI	580	THE PACIFIC BASIN
92	Union of BURMA	582	PACIFIC BASIN CO-OPERATION The Hon. Sir Edward Warren, K.C.M.G., K.B.E., M.S.M., O.M.S.T., R.S.G.C., M.L.C.
100	CEYLON (Republic of SRI LANKA)		
110	Republic of CHINA	586	Australia's Role in Asian Development
142	Commonwealth of AUSTRALIA	589	New Zealand and PBEC
228	HONG KONG	590	The Nation Builders
264	Republic of INDIA	594	British Overseas Banks
292	Kingdom of SIKKIM	598	Canadian Involvement in the Development of Asia
294	Republic of INDONESIA	602	Japan's Economic Aid to Developing Countries
320	JAPAN	606	Partnership Pacific
372	KHMER Republic (CAMBODIA)	607	The Asian Broadcasting Union
380	Republic of KOREA	608	The U.S.A. in Asia
392	Kingdom of LAOS	612	ACKNOWLEDGMENTS AND CREDITS
400	Federation of MALAYSIA	615	INDEX
428	Kingdom of NEPAL		
436	NEW ZEALAND		
448	Islamic Republic of PAKISTAN S. Amjad Ali		
478	People's Republic of BANGLADESH		
486	Republic of THE PHILIPPINES		
518	Republic of SINGAPORE		
550	Kingdom of THAILAND		

History of the Asian Nations

The Beginnings
"Europe and America are the spoiled child and grandchild of Asia, and have never quite realised the wealth of their pre-classical inheritance......
We shall be surprised to learn how much our indispensable inventions, our economic and political organisations, our science and our literature, go back to the Orient."

So wrote Will Durant, the philosopher, but his were not original thoughts. Long before him, the Romans used to say *Ex Oriente Lux,* by which they meant all light came from the East, the Orient—not merely the literal light of the rising sun, but also the illumination resulting from the ascent of knowledge.

Indeed, in Asia began all the world's religions, the art of cultivation of the soil, the oldest irrigation systems, the production of tea and wine, handicrafts, structures of brick, linen, glass, silk, gun-powder, and the compass.

The idea of the village community, notions of courtesy and etiquette, the cry for social justice, and the plea for human brotherhood, were all Asian in origin. Out of the East came the calendar, medicine, music and simple numerals. It was in the East that the subtleties of hypnotism, psychology and metaphysics first stirred the imagination, and fancy created the basis for most of the world's fables.

Five thousand years ago, among the reedy swamps and marshes where the Tigris and the Euphrates empty into the Persian Gulf, a people known as the Sumerians developed, from roots extending far back into pre-history, the world's earliest true civilisation.

It was Mesopotamia that saw the rise of man's first urban centres with their thriving, complex life. At last political loyalty came to embrace the community as a whole, rather than the tribe or a clan. Temples pushed towards the sky, lofty ziggurats that gave architectural expression to the need for God. Art and technology, industrial diversification, and commercial enterprise stopped being haphazard, and the discovery of organisation paved the way for development and expansion.

In Mesopotamia's cities, a profound breakthrough was the invention of writing, making possible the preservation of thought and the handing down of tradition. Ideas and techniques begun by the Sumerians, and nurtured by the Babylonians, the Assyrians and others, were diffused east and west to leave their mark on practically all the cultures of antiquity, and even on those of our own day.

Yet Mesopotamia's key role as the cradle of civilisation is only one facet of the many-splendoured enormity known as Asia, the largest continent in the world and the home of more than half the human race. Its 18.5 million square miles stretch across mountains and steppes, desolate wildernesses, overpopulated basins of great rivers, and the tundras of the Arctic. There is the luxuriance of tropical vegetation and the unsullied majesty of the highest peaks on earth, monastic states and kingdoms only now beginning to lose their isolation, relics of vanished races uncovered in the desert or the jungle, and the continuation of exotic cults and customs.

A third of the continent is more than 3,000 feet above sea level. Continuing the Alps and the Balkan mountains, the ranges of Turkish Armenia rise to Mount Ararat south of the Georgian Kura Valley, and to Mount Elbrus in the Caucasus to the north. The tableland of Iran is dominated by the Elburz mountains, with the snow-capped peak of Mount Demavend.

In Afghanistan where the capital, Kabul, lies at an altitude of 5,800 feet, the Kuh-i-Baba range continues into the Hindu Kush. From the Pamirs, the Himalayas and the Kwen Lun mountains branch off towards the interior, while to the north, the Tien Shan and the Altai mountains spread eastwards and north-eastwards.

In between lie the plateaux and depressions of Mongolia, Dzungaria, the Tarim Basin and Tibet. In the east, these great mountains fan out into the still partially unexplored marginal ranges that run from Indo-China into the Arctic, between which spreads the Chinese plain with its huge population.

Looking towards
the Himalayas from the
slopes of Kathmandu.

The enormous mountain ranges that divide the continent into a southern and a northern half belong for the most part to formative periods of the earth's crust. They are great folds that, at some time in the tertiary, rose from the sea between the ancient land masses of the summit of the world in the north and the south Asian Gondwanaland, a movement believed to be still continuing.

Three peninsula sub-continents project southwards. In the west, Arabia with its deserts and oases, its repository of man's beginnings, leads from the tableland of Iran and Mesopotamia to the African continent. In the centre, lies the triangle of India, with its frontiers of mountains and the ocean. Two basically different racial groups, speaking dissimilar tongues, occupy the north and the south. To the south-east, the Malay archipelago curves like a bow round the Indo-Chinese mainland, the remnant of a land bridge to Australia now half submerged beneath the sea. Also in the east, the edge of the continent splits up into peninsulas and islands before the earth's crust plunges 26,000 feet below the surface of the Pacific Ocean.

In the depressions to the south and east of the central mountain ridges, a fraction of the total area of the continent, live more than nine-tenths of Asia's teeming millions. Here developed those civilisations that played such an important part in human affairs. Here occurred the migrations and intellectual movements over thousands of years—each leaving traces of itself in ruined cities, temples, and the material and ephemeral essences that permeate existence.

THE NATIONS OF ASIA

S i b e r i a
Yenisey
Lake Baikal
Manchuria
MONGOLIA
JAPAN
SEA OF JAPAN
Tokyo
Kamakura
Shenyang
KOREA
Jehol
THE GOBI
Seoul
Tottori
Osaka
Kyoto
Nara
Pekin
Suwon (Suigen)
Himeji
Ordos
Great Wall of China
Tai-Shan
Sinkiang
YELLOW SEA
Hwang-Ho
Yun-Ho
Emperor Canal
Lanchow
Sian
Loyang
Shanghai
C H I N A
Hangchou
EAST CHINA SEA
Tibet
Yangtse-Kiang
Tatsienlu
Tseliutsin
Kung-ka Shan
Chungking
O-Mei-Shan
Lhasa
Gyangtse
Mt. Everest
Amoy
TAIWAN
NORTH PACIFIC OCEAN
BHUTAN
Nuptse
Darjeeling
Gauhati
Kweilin
Kunming (Yünnan)
Hong Kong
BANGLA-DESH
Luzon
Hanoi
Baie d'Along
Calcutta
Mandalay
Pagan
BURMA
Manila
PHILIPPINES
Salween
Mekong
LAOS
Prome
Hué
SOUTH CHINA SEA
Rangoon
Sawankhalok
THAILAND
VIETNAM
Mindanao
OF BENGAL
Bangkok
Angkor
KHMER Republic
Saigon
Sabah
BRUNEI
CELEBES SEA
SARAWAK
Penang
M A L A Y S I A
Kuala Lumpur
Borneo
Celebes
SINGAPORE
Kalimantan
Nias
Sumatra
I N D O N E S I A
JAVA SEA
Djakarta
Bogor
Java
Borobudur
Bali

But precisely because of such a flux within the vastness of a gigantic continental canvas, nothing like a truly Asian culture has emerged. The Arab, the Indian and the Chinese differ in so many important respects that to apply one label to them all collectively runs the risk of being correct only in a geographical sense.

The Races
To talk of Asia as an anthropological unit distinct from adjacent areas is not possible without introducing artifice. A broad view turns Europe properly into only a western peninsula of Asia. At the isthmus of Suez, Africa is linked with Asia. From the eastern cape of Siberia, the American mainland may be seen, and the islands of Indonesia and Melanesia lead, like stepping stones, from south-eastern Asia into Australia and Polynesia.

The result of this geographical propinquity is that the peoples of Europe, Africa, America and Oceania display, in varying degrees, physical, linguistic and cultural affinities with those of Asia. In addition, within itself Asia contains the widest variations in physical types and cultures of all the continents, and a diversity of languages apparently exceeded only in the Americas.

Intensive anthropological studies of the continent make it clear that Asia must have been the scene of a large-scale dispersal of early members of the natural order, the primates, to which man belongs. A previous view that he in fact emerged there is now no longer generally held. He is believed to have originated in Africa instead, but Asia is still the home of the Java man and the Peking man, whose remains are not only definite hominids, but must, by the ordinary canons of zoological classification, also be included generically among the human race, *homo sapiens*.

The majority of the inhabitants of Asia are *Mongoliforms*, to use a modern nomenclature with a termination originally proposed by Martin Gusinde. They occupy most of the northern, central and eastern parts of the continent. The *Mongoliform* races in Asia are the Mongolian, divided into Aralian, Tungusian, Sinian and Pareoean subraces; the Himalayan, with two main branches; and the Nesiote, or Indonesian. The *Europiform* races in Asia from west to east and north to south are the Uralic (Voguls and Ostiaks), between the Urals and the Ob basin; the Ainu in Sakhalin, Hokkaido, and one of the Kurils; the Pamirian, from Anatolia to Sinkiang; the Mediterranean, with one subrace, the Heberian, in the Levant and Arabia, and another, the Caspian, in Iran, Afghanistan, western Pakistan, and the Indo-Gangetic plain; and the Chersiote, often called Dravidian, of peninsula India and Ceylon.

The Veddian, whose members are occasionally known as pre-Dravidians or proto-Australoids, is the only *Australiform* race in Asia. It comprises the Veddas of Ceylon and the Kadirs, Kurumbas, Paniyans and Irulas of southern, and the Bhils, Gonds and Chenchus of north-central India. In Baluchistan, in the Hadhramaut, and in the Yemen in southern Arabia, small pockets of Veddoids have been identified. The Asian *Negriforms* are wholly pygmies of the Negrito race who generally inhabit refuge areas. They include the Andamanese of the Andaman Islands in the Bay of Bengal, the Semang of the Malayan jungles, and the mountain-dwelling Aeta of the Philippines. In southern India, the Kadars and the Pulayas display clear Negritoid traits, which recur in eastern Sumatra.

From the evidence of archaeology, it would seem that the earliest inhabitants of the Near East belonged to the Mediterranean race, with wavy hair, long head, and brown skin. Different regional varieties of this race have evolved—the small-boned, gracile type near the Mediterranean shores, the more robust and rugged *Eurafrican* stock of Arabia, and the tall, long-faced variety with hooked noses distinguished as the Iranian Plateau race.

The Indian peninsula as a geographical unit contains an agglomeration of inhabitants constituting nearly a fifth of the world's population, and representing every stage of culture from forest-dwelling food collectors to the most sophisticated city dwellers. The Negrito survives in the Andaman Islands. The pre-Dravidian type was at one time very widely distributed, and is still strongly represented among the lower strata of both Hindu and Moslem society.

The civilisations and languages of southern India seem to be more ancient than those of the north. Ziggurat-like temples, fire-walking and quasi-religious prostitution recall Mesopotamia and Asia Minor in antiquity. Into the cultures of Dravidian-speakers have intruded later elements with Aryan languages from the north-west, while at one time or another Mongolian peoples have entered from the north and the north-east.

South-east Asia has been peopled by successive migrations resulting in populations of much variety and culture, but Mongoloid elements predominate. The Negrito pygmy survives in the Malay forest and in some of the islands of the Philippines. The Mawkhen tribes occupy the Mergui archipelago, the Punan of Borneo seem to live entirely off the jungle, and the Igorot of the Philippines cultivate in irrigated terraces. In the hills of Burma, Thailand and Indo-China, the basic element composition of numerous tribes seems to be proto-Malayan.

The Chinese are believed to have come from Egypt, Babylon, but it is more probable that they have immigrated at different times from different directions. This inference is supported by the dissimilarity of appearance and character between the slender, quick, excitable Cantonese and the more heavily-built, stolid and urbane northerners. All, however, have straight black hair, broad face and nose, though slightly aquiline noses are not uncommon, pale skin, and the Mongolian fold of the eyelid.

The origin of the Japanese is ascribed to Malaya and the Indonesian islands, and to the Asiatic mainland via Korea. The similarity of prehistoric pottery, stone axes, arrowheads and so on, found both in Japan and Korea, points to the latter as the chief source.

Japanese legend attributes their creation and that of all the Japanese islands to the union of the deities Izanagi and Izanami, and their first identifiable emperor, Jimmu Tenno, is said to have been descended from the sun-goddess Amaterasu through her grandson Nin-iji-o-mikoto, whom she had sent down to rule the Japanese then living in the southern island, Kyushu. Hence the divinity of all Japanese emperors, until General Douglas MacArthur stripped the Emperor Hirohito of it in 1945.

Western Asia

The three great southern and eastern lowland areas are paralleled by three great zones of civilisation in the west, the south, and the east—each a world in itself with its own peoples and empires, religions and distinctive attitudes towards life.

Western Asia belongs to the Mediterranean sphere of influence. In its historical development, it has been most intimately linked at one time with Europe, and at another with Africa. On the banks of the Euphrates and the Tigris, and in other valleys and coastal regions lying like overgrown oases in a landscape consisting mostly of arid waste and mountains, there developed in the centuries before Christ the empires of the Babylonians, the Assyrians, the Hittites and the Persians.

Because they lacked the natural defences of contemporaneous kingdoms such as that of the Pharaohs on the Nile, they could not endure. Again and again they had to defend their fertile soil against the intrusions of other tribes, and in the end they faded from the scene.

The Yangtze Kiang is about 3,100 miles long. As China's most important waterway it carries a great deal of goods traffic from the thickly-populated plain watered by its lower reaches to the province of Szechuan.

Europe first entered the contest for hegemony in Western Asia when Alexander the Great inspired his Macedonian soldiers in the onslaughts that eventually brought about a union of Hellenic civilisation with that of the East. A unity of another sort was achieved as a result of the administrative political genius of the Romans. Even as ruins, the temples and theatres of their garrison towns remain impressive as evidence of a brief season of organised rule.

In contrast to these material, though marginal, achievements of the Graeco-Romans, the Semitic peoples of the Middle East created a world movement of another kind. The Olympic deities crumbled before the one stern God of Israel.

After the death of the Nazarene on a Cross on Calvary, Paul of Tarsus spread the message of redemption with such apostolic fervour that towns in Asia Minor and Greece took to Christianity. The destiny of the West was to absorb this religion, though on Asian soil it took root only among the Armenians and the Georgians.

For the people of this corner of Asia, the teachings of the Prophet Mohammed proved vastly more persuasive. He appeared in Arabia six centuries after the birth of Christ. By combining the monotheism of the Jews with the promise of another, better, brighter, more pleasurable world, he appealed irresistibly to the pristine instincts of the desert people. The Koran, his holy book, provided instructions for daily living with such remarkable clarity and reasonableness that it became a breviary for conquerors.

Within a century of Mohammed's death, the empire established in his name embraced the whole of the Near East as far as Central Asia and India. Victorious Arabs bore the green banner of the Prophet along the north coast of Africa as far as Spain, even threatening France. The Mohammedans placed European Christianity in danger a second time when, in a later age, the Turks ruled the Caliphate for four centuries, advancing to the capital of the Holy Roman Empire itself.

The East offered far less resistance to Islam than Europe, and as a result it spread far beyond the realms of the Caliphs to the very limits of the continent. It became the chief religion in damp and tropical Indonesia. In China, a group of several million Mohammedans persists to this day. In the Soviet Union, despite the official non-religious nature of the government, concessions have been made in domestic and foreign policies to the Muslim faith of the Turki peoples of the Central Asian republics. In the 1940's in defiance of all geographical logic, the state of Pakistan was carved out of the Indian subcontinent so that 80 million people could worship Allah in the way enjoined by the Prophet.

In almost the whole of western and central Asia far down into the south-east, Islam has produced in the last 1,000 years, on the soil of older civilisations, a uniform religious architecture. At Damascus, the Omayads erected the Great Mosque over the skull of John the Baptist, and at Jerusalem, they built the Mosque of Omar on the site of the ancient temple of the Jews. Only a single minaret is left of the Caliphs' buildings at Baghdad on the Tigris, but something of the spirit of Haroun al-Rashid and the fairy-tale world of *The Arabian Nights* still haunt the courtyards of later mosques and noisy bazaars.

In Samarkand, the monuments of the greatest Mohammedan capital of Inner Asia, the residence of Timur, continue to delight the eye. In Ahmedabad, Ajmeer, Bijapur and Golconda, this architecture was transmuted into manifold forms such as ornamental facades, audaciously constructed cupolas, and slender minarets. The Great Moguls and the Indo-Mohammedan princes of the 16th and 17th Centuries raised to their own personal glory famous tombs that are numbered

The Taj Mahal, one of the most beautiful structures in the world. It was built at Agra by the Shah Jehan as a mausoleum for his wife. Both have their resting place within.

today among the most perfect works of art, ranging from the domed island tomb of the Afghan Sher Shah, founder of the first Islamic empire on Indian soil, to the shimmering white marble cupola of jewelled Taj Mahal.

The Indian Triangle
A glance at the map defines the Indian triangle, with the Deccan plateau in the south sloping gently eastwards, and the river zones of the Indus, the Ganges and the Brahmaputra in the north, as a self-enclosed world. The Indian lowlands have been inhabited since time immemorial by highly civilised nations. For the peoples who dwelt in the inhospitable highlands of western and central Asia, these lowlands must have seemed a kind of beckoning, attainable paradise, so that the barrier wall of mountains in the north-west was breached again and again by eager invaders.

On the Khyber Pass, the historic route into India, a traveller still encounters long caravans of merchandise between Afghanistan and the Punjab. Sentinels continue to keep watch at frontier posts of modern armies, and the militant Afridis, whose farmsteads stand like fortresses amid the inhospitable landscape, are also always on the alert. Here and there along the roadside, fragments of Graeco-Buddhist sculpture recall the aftermath of Alexander's campaigns.

The Afghans, the Persians, and the Turki peoples, carrying with them the banner of Mohammed, finally constructed in the Mogul Empire one of the largest and most enduring states in India. In monuments dating from Asoka, there is an echo of motifs belonging to Persian art, such as the lions on the famous capital of the Sarnath columns. The Sanskrit literature of the Vedas and Upanishads points to a prehistoric immigration, linking the classical language of north India with the tongues of Europe.

The most important empire of Indian origin was established by Asoka, grandson of the mighty Maurya King Chandragupta in 249 B.C., under the sign of Buddha, The Enlightened One. In the middle of the unrecorded rise and fall of dynasties, races and sects of protean Brahmanism, Asoka set up his pillars, carving imperishable edicts on them to impress his people. In their simplicity, they embody the confessions of a striver after Truth along with the admonitions of an apostle:

The Nomadic tribes of Central Asia erect villages of tents such as these between journeys in search of better grasslands. The shelter affords protection against howling winds and blinding sandstorms.

"Heed thy mother and father. Heed the venerable *guru* (teacher). Do no harm to any living thing. Speak the truth. Pay regard to the attributes of *dharma* (religion). Let the exalted and the lowly exert himself in monastic devotions."

Behind this emperor-apostle, rises the figure of the Buddha himself. The founder of one of the great religions was born of the Sakya clan in 560 B.C. in what is now Nepal, at the foot of the Himalayas. After seven years of a search for the light with his mind in a turmoil, the Truth suddenly became clear to him as he sat beneath a fig-tree near Gaya. A flash of illumination pointed the path out of the dismal earthly cycle, the requisites being only renunciation and pity.

The Nepal of those days was full of anchorites and ascetics with their own followers. They founded sects and enjoyed great local reputations, but unlike the Buddha, their fame died with them. The Buddha provided the world with one of its religious enigmas when he survived his sojourn on earth, and his radiant, transcendent message achieved a continental universality.

His chief lesson was that suffering is inseparable from existence, which is an evil. The principal cause of suffering being desire, the suppression of desire means the suppression of suffering. This can only be obtained by discipline. The ultimate reward is the attainment of *nirvana*—or the extinction of the self by absorption into the Supreme Spirit.

In its land of origin, Buddhism did not overcome the resistance of Hindus who sought a more luxurious destiny for the soul. But as it spread from India, it proved by far the most effective means by which the land's own spiritual and religious tradition could be made to influence other people. Gently but firmly, not behind the standard of a conqueror, but through the peaceful persuasion of the mind, the Buddha's teachings gained acceptance across the whole eastern zone of the continent.

During this progress, the message took on different forms. As the *Hinayana*, or the Lesser Vehicle, it is personified in Ceylon, Vietnam, Cambodia, Burma and Thailand by the saffron-clad monk on his daily search for alms, with a begging-bowl in hand. There are simple rules for this primitive Buddhism, and for the young neophyte who accepts it by residence in a monastery or a temple compound, it is a testing time. For some, because the doors are always open, the call of the world beyond is eventually heeded, but for others, the compound becomes a permanent dwelling place.

In its *Mahayana* form, or the Greater Vehicle, Buddhism reached China in the first century before Christ, then central Asia and Japan. In the Tantric Buddhism of the Himalayan countries, the message of The Enlightened One is mingled with strange animistic spells. In the Zen Buddhism of Japan, it rises to the pellucid wisdom of learned monks. But at all times, and among all peoples who invoke the name of Buddha, statues of stone, wood, iron and gold are suffused with the glow of a contemplative, benign countenance symbolising an extraordinary man's triumph over the world and the flesh.

Burma, Tibet, Malaya, Thailand, Cambodia and Vietnam could not fail to be partly influenced in their development as independent kingdoms by this transcendental Indian message on the dissolution of all earthly ties—but, materially and politically, they have always had to contend with the overpowering reality of China.

The Potala, former palace of the Dalai Lama in Lhasa, dominates the capital of Tibet. The country, once one of the 'mystery' regions of Asia, is presently under the political influence of Peking.

The Chinese Influence

In 481 B.C., the lord Szu-ma Niu was driven by rival barons from his demesne, one of the many walled towns of north China. As a result, he set forth on a long journey to the south in search of a new fief. His destination was the state of Wu near the mouth of the great Yangtze—a region he considered scarcely civilised. To him, the centre of the world was a cluster of little city-states in the flood plain of the Yellow River and its adjoining foot-hills. He did not call this homeland China, because that alien name was still to be invented. Instead, he saw himself as a man of Hua, of the Middle Kingdom in the Chou dynasty, a native of Sung.

The civilisation to which he belonged in the 5th Century B.C. had its roots deep in the Stone Age, more than 1,000 years earlier, when Chinese history first began. Szu-ma Niu's unknown remote ancestors, the first farmers of China, had valued jade, and had used tripod cauldrons of earthenware designed exactly like those on the altars of the gods. But Szu-ma Niu had only the haziest notions of that prehistoric era and its primordial culture. He was better informed about ancestors who had ruled the Yellow River plain from 1,500 to 1,000 B.C., more than 500 years before his time.

They were the Kings of Shang, overlords of an agricultural nation with a rich religious and ceremonial life. Theirs had been an era comparable in spirit to the heroic age celebrated by Homer in the West. But they had been defeated by the warlike Chou people from the west, though the new masters had themselves been quickly assimilated into the old agricultural theocracy. When in the fullness of time the authority of Chou began to decay, the realm was divided among petty city-states that came and went like the seasons. Szu-ma Niu himself had been involved in an unsuccessful insurrection, and his present journey was the sequel.

No doubt he endured some agony of the mind as his chariot took him to a new life among the barbarians of the south. As a Hua man, the Middle Kingdom was a beacon of civilisation to the outlandish heathens who inhabited shadowy territories above and below. The ancestors of the Turks, Manchus and Mongols in the north were kept out of good lands of millet and wine by a system of defensive walls that later became jointly the nation's famous Great Wall. But they were "barbarians", a derisive epithet. So also were the non-Chinese in the south, the Man people—sometimes called Miao, Mao, Min or Mang, who spoke tongues related to Thai, Burmese and Tibetan. These were the "dog" people.

The term "dog" came from an ancient myth that the Man were all descended from a wonderful dog, P'an Hu. The story went that a king had offered his daughter in marriage to the hero who would bring him the head of an enemy. One dog carried out the dangerous mission successfully, and the king was obliged to yield his daughter. The triumphant canine then carried her off to a new home in a southern cave where she bore him a dozen sons and daughters. From these half-human hybrids sprang all the non-Chinese races of the south.

In mediaeval times, centuries after Szu-ma Niu's journey, some of the southern aborigines accepted the legend of their ancestry, and in fact offered sacrifices to their unusual ancestor. P'an Hu is still remembered by the modern Miao, and is especially revered by the Man tribes of northern Vietnam.

The 200 years following Szu-ma Niu's trip to the south were bitter years for the homeland. The struggle among the city-states became intensified between the 5th and 3rd centuries B.C., and the smaller ones were swallowed up by the larger. But the Chinese world itself was expanding out of the Yellow River basin, conquering, absorbing, eliminating, and in any case ultimately dominating the tribes it encountered. It was inevitable that these barbarians should evolve into Hua men. There was little visible physical difference between them and the new arrivals. To become a Chinese, it was only necessary that a Man tribesman learn to speak the language, write the script, and accept the rule of the king, along with the social and moral doctrines that prevailed in the Middle Kingdom.

Dynasties came and went. Through the centuries, China's influence on neighbours such as Japan, Korea and Tibet grew incalculable. Its contributions ranged from mechanical clocks and fireworks to porcelain and poetry. In turn, it owed much of its own richness and diversity to connections with other cultures.

A by-product of this era of contact was the name China itself, which caught on in the Indian and Persian lands where a stylistic designation like *The Middle Kingdom* had no meaning.

China became the altered form of the name of the Ch'in Empire. It remained current as the preferred synonym for the Middle Kingdom among the nations of south Asia long after the empire itself had passed away. In the twelve centuries separating the journey of Szu-ma Niu and the rule of the great Emperor Li Lung-chi at the height of T'ang power, China flowered into a wonder of the world.

During the T'ang dynasty, its people knew prosperity, freedom, gaiety. Its ruling class undertook unique experimentations in art, music, literature and gardening. Security and confidence followed upon successful wars against the Koreans in the north, the Vietnamese in the south, and the Tibetans and Turks in the west. It was during this age that the empire became a colossus, a greatly-desired country.

Here Persian merchant princes repaired their great seagoing vessels with the fine wood of the *schima*, a relative of tough southern oaks. The new tropical south made available for the table exotic fruit such as the banana, the tangerine and the lychee. Furniture evolved from the skilful use of the tangled liana forest vine.

Gardens grew bright with red and yellow hibiscus. Peacock feathers were transformed into luxurious fans, and green turtles captured in phosphorescent seas dissolved into an exquisite soup for royal banquets.

Foreigners marvelled at a system of literary examinations that allowed every peasant's son to rise to the power and dignity of a viceroy. A universal script, based on characters representing not words but ideas, made understanding possible between various parts of the empire. The emperor, as the Son of Heaven, formed a link between the human world and the invisible forces of the divine, combining in one man holding one office the highest power and the profoundest humility. Three times a year he went to the Temple of Heaven to provide an account of his rule. At the same time, he also implored a favour, since it was his responsibility to see that the national life proceeded in accordance with celestial wishes.

Such a development of national identity at the height of the T'ang, with its welding of incompatible external elements into a magnificent cohesive internal whole, was on a scale unique in the history of the world. Driving southward in his chariot twelve centuries earlier, Szu-ma Niu could not have foreseen how the Middle Kingdom was eventually to spread, how the people of Hua would assimilate everything and everybody on a horizon that kept falling back, and back.

The strange thing was that this power of expansion did not stop with the arrival of modern times. At a moment of paralysis and prostration following the collapse of the old imperial order, a million hard-working Chinese peasants were settled in the previously-nomadic territory of Manchuria. Other expatriates exercised their industry and ingenuity with such remarkable persistence in foreign shores that they changed the structure of cities and countries in the Malay archipelago.

In the first quarter of this century, the population of China was estimated at 400 million. Today, it is believed to exceed 700 million. Such figures make the Chinese the largest ethnic group in the world, destined, from the pressure emanating from this factor alone, to play a decisive role in the future of mankind.

The Great Wall of China, the Wang Lee Chang Cheng, is the world's biggest structure. It measures up to 53 feet high and is 15-26 feet thick. It is interspersed with towers and gateways and extends along some 1,880 miles over the bare loess mountains of the North-west frontier. It was intended to protect the Empire against invading nomad tribes of North and Central Asia.

Land of The Rising Sun
Of the lands on the margin of Chinese rule, the only country that succeeded in evolving a civilisation of its own was the island realm of Japan. The Land of the Rising Sun is a curving chain of volcanic islands larger in area than Great Britain, but smaller than France. On its four main islands of Kyushu, Shikoku, Honshu and Hokkaido, most of the land is mountainous. But among the peaks and forested crags are several fertile plains of considerable size, many flat-bottomed river valleys and innumerable smaller patches of arable soil. It is a beautiful land. But because it lies squarely in the path of annual hurricanes and is subject to active volcanoes and earthquakes, violence is frequent and almost a way of life. Since ancient times, the Japanese have ranked among the world's most ferocious warriors, but no other people have given more elaborate attention to courteous conduct, or more loving devotion to flowers, poetry and art.

The strait of Korea, separating the westernmost island Kyushu from the Asian continent, is 100 miles wide. There are sizeable foothold stepping-stones, but the crossing is difficult and was dangerous in early times. Such a barrier allowed Japan the boon of semi-isolation, placing it within the Chinese cultural area and at the same time setting it apart.

During certain periods, a broad stream of knowledge, literature, art and religion flowed from China to Japan. At other times, the flow was shut off from one side or the other, and Japan developed on its own. But whether in isolation or not, Japan was always itself. Everything that came from China, from household arts to philosophy, was reshaped to suit national tastes and needs.

The country's past, from pre-history through the classical centuries, is fascinating because of the light it casts on modern Japan, many of whose distinctive and contrasting characteristics are traceable to similarities far back in antiquity. The emperor, for example, is treated in much the same way today as he was fifteen centuries ago.

Almost equally ancient is the Japanese trait of eagerly courting foreign ideas so as to adapt them for the benefit of the nation as a whole. The consequences of superior Western technology upon the political face of the southern Asian states were so apparent in the 19th Century that the mediaeval Shogunate was swept away in 1867 under the personal leadership of the Emperor Meiji. No one could have foreseen that only 100 years later the country would play a leading role among the world's select group of industrial giants.

Central Asia
The Gobi desert, the Tarim Basin, the lowlands of Turan and Bukhara, the Kirghiz steppe and the inhospitable mountains lying between them, together form the broad tracts of Central Asia that even today are only sparsely peopled by herdsmen. This was the unknown hinterland out of which nomadic tribes sallied forth on nimble ponies to ravage Europe, Persia, India and China. Among the Huns, Scythians, Turkis and Dzungars were leaders of exceptional stature like Attila, Genghis Khan, and Timur. They shook the foundations of ancient empires with the vigour and mobility of their hordes.

But of their reigns nothing is left except what has fortuitously merged into the civilisations of Europe, Persia-Arabia and China. The tracts of land themselves are firmly in the grip of the two great continental powers, China and Russia. As early as the Middle Ages, merchants from Novgorod had begun to penetrate eastwards into the Siberian lowlands sloping down to the Arctic circle. This opening up of vast tundras and forests by Russian settlers was one of the great colonial enterprises of the white race. In the first half of the 19th Century, the Russian Empire occupied the ancient Caucasian territories of Georgia and Armenia, and a little later it annexed the lowlands of Bukhara with their Mohammedan population.

A colonial enterprise of another sort began in the 16th Century when first Portugal and Spain, then Holland, Britain and France acquired overseas possessions on Asian soil. For the first two, the impulse was a curious desire to convert natives to Christianity mixed with a greed for the monopolisation of the spice trade. The Dutch, the British and the French were motivated mostly by the search for external economies that could be adjusted to the needs of mother countries about to be engulfed in the throes of rapid industrialisation. All came to Asia to exploit her, but in the process did some good.

In tropical countries with despotic forms of social organisation, they set up administrations that made an independent economic and political life possible for the first time. They took steps to safeguard security and order, built roads and railways, combated high mortality rates with modern hygiene, and created the basis for practical, utilitarian, large-scale education. By research and the printed word, they restored to the conquered peoples of ancient civilisations a new confidence in their own magnificent intellectual and artistic traditions. The widespread diffusion of European political ideas, with their emphasis on freedom, democracy, and the right to self-determination, meant that eventually their advocates would be hoist by their own petard.

The Khyber Pass, traditional 'invasion' route into India. The camel remains even today the chief means of transport and the goods it carries range from Japanese wrist watches to contraband hashish.

Mount Fuji, 12,467 feet, is Japan's loftiest and holiest volcanic mountain. In summer, when the summit is free of snow, it is climbed by thousands of pilgrims. The volcano was last active in 1707-08.

This eventually happened in the last few decades, and the profound metamorphosis that has occurred in the political map of Asia is far from over. It remains to be seen to what final extent the principles of democracy and self-determination, invoked in the struggle for independence from colonial rule, will be applied by the Asian peoples and racial groups among themselves. Urbanisation is advancing, and the ubiquitous concept of functionalism is changing the face of the bazaar.

The Asian Outlook

Since 1945, a sense of Asianism, an Asian consciousness has been suggested in the United Nations by spokesmen for 1,000 million human beings, though this is more a reaction to long years of alien domination than the valid expression of a genuine historical concept.

Pindar used the term *Asia* for the first time in his poetry 2,500 years ago. Ever since, a hope has been misunderstood for a fact. In most of Asia until only a few decades ago, it was the village alone that enjoyed autonomy. It had its own order and hierarchy, its own crude system of self-government. The Japanese *buraka*, the Philippine *barrio*, the Indian *panchayat*, and the Chinese *hsien*, had only occasional contact with the court or the central government of the day, so that a continental outlook was inconceivable.

Government officials were regarded almost as aliens. Villagers were usually unaware of the extent and nature of the state to which they belonged, let alone the continent in which their state happened to be placed. Within this context, it became second nature for the ordinary man that the chief goal of his life should be the promotion of his own interests. If he was a decent man, schooled in the Koran, or the sutras, or the analects, he would help his immediate family and himself. If he graduated from this to serve the clan or the village, a kind of local sainthood would be conferred upon him. It would not occur to him to strive for a national or a continental objective, since beyond the extension of his village and his province his vision could not penetrate. But Ba Maw, a Burmese nationalist, reflected an early, still not entirely comprehended aspiration of millions when he told a conference of Greater East Asia in 1953:

"My Asiatic blood has always called to other Asiatics. In my dreams, both sleeping and waking, I have heard the voice of Asia calling to her children. Today, I seem to hear the same voice of Asia gathering her children together. It is the call of our Asiatic blood. This is not the time to think with our minds. This is the time to think with our blood."

The task of thinking with the blood is immense, and figures alone make it seem virtually unrealisable. Britain, France and Germany have separately an average area of 150,000 square miles each, and a population of 60 million each. China is almost 30 times larger than that, and 13 times as populous. India is eight times bigger in area, nine times larger in population. Both Pakistan and Indonesia could embrace two or three European nations of consequence in terms of area and population. The single Indian state of Uttar Pradesh is larger than Britain. The Chinese province of Kwangtung is comparable in size to Spain, and Szechuan is bigger than Thailand.

Surveying this plethora of cultures and traditions, and the awesome magnitude of any attempt to fuse these immensities into a true coherent political unity, Anil Seal, the historian of Indian independence, says:

"By the side of the vast swell of aspiration and rivalry which has hurled it forward, the political readjustments of independence seem of small account. These nationalisms have been merely the swirling surface of the waters. Below the impulse are tides of social change, pulling Asia no man knows where."

He is reinforced by Sutan Sjahrir, the Indonesian socialist revolutionary, who wrote:

"We must extend and intensify life, and raise and improve the goals towards which we strive. This is what the West has taught us, and this is what I admire in the West, despite its brutality and its coarseness. I would even take this brutality and coarseness as accompanying features of the new concept of life that the West has taught us. I would even accept capitalism as an improvement upon the much-famed wisdom and religion of the East. For it is precisely this wisdom and religion that make us unable to understand the fact that we have sunk to the lowest depths to which man can descend: we have sunk to slavery and to enduring subjugation. What we in the East admire most in the West is its indestructible vitality, its love for life and for the fulfilment of life. Every vital young man and young woman in the East ought to look toward the West, for he or she can learn only from the West to regard him or herself as a centre of vitality capable of changing and bettering the world. The East must become Western in the sense that it must acquire as great a vitality and dynamism as in the West. Faust must reveal himself to the Eastern man and mind."

But Jawaharlal Nehru, discussing in his will how he wanted his funeral arranged, provides a lyrical yet significant summation of the manner in which the past continues to influence the Asian mind, and to which, for better or worse, it finds itself captive:–

"My desire to have a handful of my ashes thrown into the Ganga at Allahabad has no religious significance. The Ganga is the river of India, beloved of her people, round which are intertwined her racial memories, her hopes and fears, her songs of triumph, her victories and her defeats. She has been a symbol of India's age-long culture and civilisation, ever-changing, ever-flowing, and yet ever the same Ganga. Though I have discarded much of past tradition and custom, and am anxious that India should rid herself of all shackles that bind and constrain her and divide her people, and suppress vast numbers of them, and prevent the free development of the body and the spirit; though I seek all this yet I do not wish to cut myself off from that past completely. I am proud of that great inheritance that has been, and is, ours, and I am conscious that I, too, like all of us, am a link in that unbroken chain that goes back to the dawn of history in the immemorial past of India. That chain I would not break, for I treasure it and seek inspiration from it. And as witness of this desire of mine and as my last homage to India's cultural inheritance, I am making this request that a handful of my ashes be thrown into the Ganga at Allahabad to be carried to the great ocean that washes India's shores."

Tomorrow

The Asian nations do have this in common. They are all in the process of modernisation, of transforming the material, technological, social, intellectual and organisational bases of their societies. Most of them are involved in turbulence, a direct result of the traumatic events of the 20th Century. There is widespread recognition that the continent's future is bound up with its capacity to evolve afresh, with industry providing the key for the door into the millenium.

The People's Daily of Peking, in an article on the inaugural day of China's first five-year plan, puts it like this: "Industrialisation provides a guarantee that our people shall no longer be exposed by imperialism to treachery and humiliations, and shall no longer live in poverty."

For India, China and Japan, industrialisation is not exactly new. Dwarkanath Tagore, grandfather of the poet Rabindranath, acquired India's largest coal-mine in 1836, and Jamsetji Tata opened his pioneering modern cotton mill in Nagpur on the same day in 1877 that saw Queen Victoria proclaimed the Empress of India.

Japan's first modern textile mill was founded in 1867 by the Lord of Satsuma, while her first modern steel mill, the government-owned Yawata Iron Works, was commissioned in 1901. The Tata steel mill at Jamshedpur in eastern India began seven years later, and steel has been made in Wuhan in Central China since the end of the 19th Century.

The Tien Tan, in Peking. Here it was that the Emperor annually invoked the blessings of heaven upon his country and his people.

But the early enterprises were few and isolated. When India shook off the British connection in 1947, Indian factories were producing only 6 per cent of the national income, and employing less than 2 per cent of the working population. It was only in the 1950's that comprehensive industrialisation schemes began to be pursued, and the serious story of industry in Asia is less than 20 years old.

In those two decades, very long strides have been made. According to United Nations figures, industrial output in Asia expanded almost tenfold during those 20 years. If only heavy industry is considered, the development was even faster. The average annual industrial growth in the developing countries of Asia during the 1960's has been about 8 per cent, which means that industry has been expanding more than twice as fast as the other sectors of the economy. Steel output stood at little more than 12 million tons at the beginning of the 1960's, but has now reached some 20 million tons. Japan's production in 1968 was 67 million tons, more than either Britain or Germany, but that is left out of the calculation. India and China now supply a very large proportion of their own steel needs, with the exception of certain alloys and social products, and both have begun to export the metal.

Machinery and manufacture has grown by leaps and bounds, and both India and China are now able to send abroad for prestige and profit complete industrial plants. The government in Peking says the country has developed by its own techniques, without the aid of foreign advisers, a 12,000-ton hydraulic free-forging press, several 10,000-ton ocean-going liners, large electron microscopes, transistorised electronic computers and full sets of automated metallurgical and chemical industrial plants.

In the last three years, India has sold her railway wagons to the Soviet Union, refrigerators to Hungary, machine tools to West Germany, steel pipes to New Zealand, telecommunications equipment to Africa, and tyres to the United States. Tiny Hong Kong is today the world's 26th leading industrial producer.

In 1970, Japan reached an agreement with the Soviet Union to build a port in Siberia for the Russians according to Japanese design. So there is hope for a better, a more unified tomorrow.

The novelist Lao She, writing of an Asia that has been dead for many decades, projects with blunt lucidity the mental upheaval that is involved:

"In the old days, the Chinese people specialised in the son covering up for the father, and the father covering up for the son. So everyone covered up, and truth and justice were hidden away beyond the hope of discovery. Today, the father-son relationship can no longer bury the truth beneath it."

No one can tell what new Asia will emerge from this schism between painful separation from the past and an optimistic, trade-based faith in the future. But the continent needs to be assisted. Bertrand Russell, addressing himself to the West on this point, argued many years ago:

"I think if we are to feel at home in the world......we shall have to admit Asia to equality in our thoughts, not only politically, but culturally. What changes this will bring about I do not know, but I am convinced that they will be profound and of the greatest importance."

Asian culture, to be intelligible, must be broken down into its component parts, since the elements of which it is chiefly composed, the orthographic, the linguistic, the philosophic, and the religious, are elusive and disparate. But if the unity of the world itself is seen as inescapable, there can be no doubt that this continent, with its immeasurable cultural heritage, will have a singular, congenital role to play in the future destiny of mankind.

The Economic Explosion

WHEN PEACE RETURNED to Asia and the Pacific Basin in August 1945, a new era opened for the region. Those countries which had been occupied by Japan had suffered several years of oppression, plunder and famine under the rule of fellow Asians who had launched their expansionist war with promise of establishing a "Greater Co-prosperity Sphere". Japanese occupation had proved to be a form of economic constriction tighter than that of the Western colonialist powers. Equipment had been removed, factories stripped, plantations allowed to run down. Asian experience of Asian colonialism, however, in no way inspired—except perhaps in Malaya—any desire for a return of the Western variety. The struggle for independence, particularly in Indonesia, Indo-China, Burma and in South Asia, began to be waged again in real ernest with the return of peace. In most cases, however, the West re-established its rule.

The economic problems facing the region as a whole in 1945 were appalling. Throughout South-east Asia the war had brought disorder (in Malaya it had exacerbated relations between Malays and Chinese), destruction (the region had been the battlefield for one of history's most bitterly contested conflicts), starvation and disease. The region's economies were in a desperate plight.

Japan itself, the only nation in Asia which had enthusiastically opted to copy Western patterns of development in a singleminded pursuit of prosperity via industrialisation, also lay in ruins, its cities bombed flat and the American army in occupation. Japan, together with Thailand, had been the only major Asian country to escape being colonialised, either by the West or by an Asian neighbour. It was thus free to make its decision to modernise, while other countries were condemned to wait until independence, until they could begin the long haul towards industrialisation.

The restoration of the Meiji Emperor in 1868 had begun the progress. Japan was fortunate in its Royal Family which led the fight against those social forces which wished Japan to keep its doors closed against the outside world, rejecting the challenge of the "black ships" despatched by America to force Japan to open up to international trade. At the same time, China had the misfortune to be ruled by emperors of the decadent and alien Ching dynasty, who steadfastly tried to refuse or limit admittance to the foreigners, condemning China to a century of humiliating rape by the West, Russia and Japan.

The Meiji Emperor awarded imperial "franchises" to the country's aristocrats, who laid down the foundations of huge industrial, trading and banking consortia —the Zaibatsu. Others were despatched to Europe and America to bring back the new technology—and incidentally to advise Japan on the establishment of a modern army and navy.

The era was a traumatic one for the Japanese because an important part of their cultural tradition exalted the virtues of unworldliness, of abstemiousness and discipline. The Emperor's decision to start his people along the road towards industrialised capitalism, the consumer revolution and Western-style materialism involved a difficult re-orientation of national values. The resulting ambivalence is still a feature of the Japanese national character, although it must be said that the traditional virtue of discipline, together with Japan's racial and social homogenity, its proud nationalism and its people's capacity for hard work, was one of the main ingredients of Japan's economic success.

These virtues contributed to Japan's growth until in 1905 it defeated the European power of imperial Russia (the first concrete proof to early Asian nationalists that the "white man" could be defeated). They manifested themselves further in subsequent progress during the early years of the century when Japan founded its empire and became strong enough to eject the Western powers from East

Asia and to challenge the Pacific supremacy of the United States itself. They were strongly evident in Japan's fantastic recovery since 1945—a quarter of a century in which a nation rose from the ashes of defeat to become the world's third strongest economy, its Gross National Product smaller only than those of the United States and the Soviet Union.

Although the Western powers returned to reclaim their colonies after World War II, Japan had proved that the British, the Dutch, the French and the United States were not insuperable. Although most Asian nationalists aided their Western allies in resisting Japanese occupation, Japan's military successes had provided an inspiration to challenge the restored colonial regimes. In some countries, such as Vietnam and Indonesia, the return of peace prompted unilateral declarations of independence by Asian leaders, gestures which were promptly squashed by the returning French and Dutch.

For the Indian subcontinent, the end of the war had brought a new Labour Government to power in Britain and following a series of protracted negotiations it was decided to hand over power to two successor states—Indian and Pakistan—on the basis of respective Hindu and Muslim majority populations. Pakistan gained its independence on 14th August, with India following on 15th August 1947; Burma on 4th January 1948 and Ceylon a month later.

Elsewhere, the struggle to expel the colonial powers was longer and more bloody. Indonesians did not oust the Dutch until 1950; the French left Indo-China after a long war against the Vietminh in 1954; Malaya gained independence in 1957, in the midst of a communist revolt, while Singapore did not become self-governing until 1959.

Even had Asia escaped both the exploitation of colonialism and the ravages of World War II, the task of giving its citizens a chance of prosperity would have been staggering. After a quarter of a century of developmental effort, the countries of Asia and the Far East in the early 'seventies contained about 40 per cent of the world's population—a proportion which does not include over 700 million mainland China. This 40 per cent accounted for nearly two-thirds of the population of the developing world. The people of the region were crowded together, occupying only 11 per cent of the world's total land area, and only 17 per cent of the land area of developing regions.

Of total world production, it accounted for about 28 per cent in agriculture, 5 per cent in construction, transport communications and services and less than 4 per cent in manufacturing. It made about half of the gross domestic product of the developing world, but because of its huge population its per capita income was the world's lowest. The region as a whole had been able to achieve only a 4 per cent economic growth rate throughout the 'fifties, rising slightly to just under 4.5 per cent during most of the "First Developmental Decade" of the 'sixties. However, in the late 'sixties, new strains of rice seeds, improved irrigation and greater use of fertilisers had ushered in the "Green Revolution", marking a dramatic improvement in what was still the basis of the region's economy—agriculture.

This factor pushed up the growth rate closer to the 5 per cent target set for the First Development Decade. Asia as a whole entered the Second Development Decade—the 'seventies—with hopes of even better growth and with the spectre of famine, which had still periodically haunted countries such as India and Indonesia during the 'sixties, fading away. The Green Revolution, however, also brought its own problems—the threat of glut, of falling cereal prices, shortage of space and drying facilities, while new varieties of seeds were demanding even heavier investments in irrigation and fertiliser production. But at least famine had been defeated.

The limited successes in pushing up growth rates were partially neutralised by increases in population. Children have always been one form of investment for poor agricultural communities, sons at least providing some promise of support during old age. Countries have had to wait for prosperity to cut down population growth rates. Other poorer nations have spent much effort on birth control and family planning programmes, but shortage of funds, ignorance and religious barriers have limited their effectiveness.

No country has gone to the lengths of communist China in deliberately delaying marriages and imposing official limits on the size of families. They have had to settle for less Draconian methods—such as India's widespread distribution of contraceptives and its attempts to popularise sterilisation by means of cash incentives and presents of transistor radios. Thus India's Gross National Product rose throughout the 'fifties and 'sixties by about 3.3 per cent annually, but population went on growing by at least 2.5 per cent reducing the growth of per capita income to 0.8 per cent.

Population growth—at least until the late 'sixties—ensured that malnutrition continued to plague the region. Even at the beginning of the 'seventies up to one-third of all households in India did not receive sufficient protein, while only a few countries in the region—Japan, Hong Kong, South Korea, Taiwan, Malaysia and Singapore, were able to boast an average individual daily intake of calories of over the desirable minimum—2,300 calories.

Food and people were the basic problems, but the economic planners of post World War II Asia had to grapple with many others, all vital for balanced and continued economic progress. The region needed enormous efforts in the fields of education, medical and health and sanitation services, social services, housing, transport and communications. The planners had to find the funds to provide these and other basic elements of their countries' economic infrastructures.

By the early 'seventies some remarkable achievements had been recorded. Education had expanded: in many countries primary school enrolments had reached 90 per cent, while tertiary education had grown significantly. But the planners failed to provide enough jobs for the school-leavers. Unemployment was as high as 40 per cent. The incidence of unemployment was often highest among young people and those with good educations. In health and sanitation, great progress had been made in the eradication of diseases, the reduction of mortality rates and the increase of life expectancy. However, millions of Asians were still living in appalling conditions of poverty, particularly in the cities. It was estimated that while sewage and garbage disposal facilities were unsatisfactory and in many areas non-existent, only 11 per cent of the region's population had access to a supply of piped water. Capital was needed and aid programmes from the developed countries were not sufficient.

When India launched its first plan in 1951, it was receiving an annual average of US$90 million in aid. This figure rose to US$809 million by the early 'sixties and rose further to a peak of $1,824 million in the mid-'sixties, falling off again to an average of $1,031 million in the late 'sixties. Of this aid 56 per cent came from the U.S.A., and of the rest 7 per cent each from Britain and West Germany, 5.5 per cent from the Soviet Union, 4.5 per cent from Canada and 6 per cent from fifteen other aid donor countries. The balance of 14 per cent came from the World Bank and the IDA (International Development Association).

The basic problem of the region's economic planners was thus to squeeze funds out of poor agricultural communities in the form of taxes and savings. They had to cream off sufficient quantities to finance the improvement and expansion of the basic economic infrastructures, to create the desperately needed jobs, to iron out some of the enormous economic disparities (as between India and Pakistan) which provided fertile breeding grounds for social and political unrest, and further to provide the capital needed to push their countries along towards industrialisation.

Faced with problems of these proportions, one might have expected that the newly independent nations of Asia would have lost heart. In fact, the various independence movements had believed that colonial exploitation was the main reason for the poverty of Asia. Both the people and their leaders expected an appreciable improvement in living standards with the attainment of independence, which came amid a region-wide revolution of rising expectations.

The region's leaders were naturally generally inclined towards socialistic theories of economic development. Asian communist parties had played a prominent part in the wars of independence, and Asian nationalists had found the warmest support for their aims within the ranks of the left-wing parties of Western Europe. India's Congress Party, under the leadership of Mahatma Gandhi and his political heir, Jawaharlal Nehru, had established close ties with the British Labour Party. Ho Chi Minh had returned to Indo-China as a card-carrying member of the French Communist Party. Similarly, Senanayake's United National Party and Bandaranaike's Sri Lanka Freedom Party in Ceylon, the "Thirty Comrades" of Burma, Lee Kuan Yew's People's Action Party in Singapore, Sukarno's Nationalist Party, and even Prince Sihanouk's Sangkum in Cambodia, all fell heir to socialist principles. The ruling Pakistan Peoples Party in West Pakistan declared its adherence to a policy of Islamic Socialism, to which Mohamed Ali Jinnah had made reference in a public pronouncement following the creation of Pakistan.

There was much in the economic dogma of Marx to appeal to the masses of Asia. First it taught them that "to rebel is justified" (as Mao Tse-tung put it). Marx provided a persuasive explanation for Asia's poverty: the countries had been exploited by the powers of colonialism and imperialism, who had extracted from them the commodities and raw materials for their factories on which they had thrived. It provided a promise of material prosperity, based on the expropriation of foreign-owned firms, and on nationalisation of the major sectors of the economy, for the sharing out (to each according to his needs) of national wealth instead of its concentration in the hands of a few.

The Western objections to communism—lack of democratic freedoms and authoritarian methods of government—were not so distasteful to Asian minds, formed within societies and cultures which emphasised collective and communal activities at all levels of society and within religions which praised the Confucian, Hindu, Buddhist and Islamic virtues of discipline and respect for authority. The worldliness of dialectical materialism was just as alien to Asian traditions of astheticism and self-denial as capitalism had been to Japan's traditions. But Asian bellies were empty, and self-denial is only a virtue when temptation exists to be rejected. Communism offered much hope for the region's masses.

Other Asian parties rejected the absolutes of Marx but adopted instead the doctrines of Western socialism. The post-colonial leaders of Asia were idealistic men, determined to build new vibrant societies free of foreign exploitation and of the inequalities which appeared to be endemic to Western-style capitalism. They wanted progress without the untold human misery which industrialisation had brought to Western Europe and America.

No country embraced the visions of prosperity through planning with greater enthusiasm than India. During the early years, while Nehru provided a unifying leadership and the philosophical rationale for socialism at home and nonalignment abroad, it appeared that the planners were succeeding in mobilising resources and imparting a very real sense of direction. Gradually, however, momentum was lost. To a great degree this was the result of non-economic factors.

In 1962, India's armies clashed with the People's Liberation Army of China in a major border war in which India lost territory it claimed, and which resulted in more of its national resources being devoted to defence. Bigger defence budgets also followed the war with Pakistan which broke out in 1965 after years of quarrelling between the two countries over the still-undecided fate of Kashmir. In the mid-'sixties, the strong centrifugal political forces which had always threatened to pull India apart began to gain in momentum. Communist governments had achieved power in various states while other opposition parties flourished in states such as Madras. Problems of language and education grew more embittered, while minority peoples (including the Nagas and the Mizos) launched armed rebellions against New Delhi's rule. The centre s hold began to weaken; states began to refuse to obey the edicts of the planners, refusing to deliver grain surpluses to other deficit states, for example. In the late 'sixties, the monsoon failed twice. The grain harvest slumped and prolonged famine affected several regions.

But political and climatic setbacks were not the only reasons for the failure of the planners. In 1967 the brilliant Stockholm economist Gunnar Myrdal published his masterpiece "Asian Drama: An Enquiry Into The Poverty Of Nations". The result of a decade's work, this book examined the way in which economists and planners had mistakenly applied to the developing countries of South and Southeast Asia the theories and concepts imported uncritically from the industrialised nations. Myrdal established that while economic factors could be identified and manipulated in the West, in Asian countries they could not be isolated from the rest of life, from social structures, institutions and religions which did not readily respond to economic decisions and which tended to perpetuate poverty.

Nevertheless, although his book constituted a massive indictment of planning, the Professor stopped short of the obvious conclusion, and argued that the techniques of planning should be improved, after a much more careful scrutiny by practical planners and social scientists of the complex inter-relationships of Asian societies. His book pointed out, for example, that the economic statistics on which the planners base their estimates of resources and their future projections are most unreliable in all fields. But this did not invalidate the planners' tools; statistics had to be better, he argued. His book also failed to explain how planners could budget for political factors, such as those which had undermined New Delhi's authority and for such tragedies as regional wars.

But the planners persisted, and some of their achievements were undeniable. India entered the 'seventies, after two decades of independence, with a vastly improved economic infrastructure, with 60,000 kilometres of railways, 325,000 kilometres of roads, with more than 2 million tons of shipping and a thriving international airline. Food grain production was nearing 100 million tons, after four successive years of good rains. New dams, irrigation schemes, an annual production of over 1.7 million metric tons of chemical fertilisers, the widespread use of new high-yielding varieties of seeds, the growth of storage facilities and a growing programme to educate farmers in modern agricultural techniques had gone far to ensure that, even if the rains failed, or some other disaster struck, the harvest would not fall catastrophically short of India's needs.

In industry, the expensive and not fully-utilised steel mills had nonetheless provided a basis for new factories and products and India had begun to sell not only commodities, but sophisticated manufactured goods, including machine tools and radio-active products, to markets all around the world.

The planners argued that they had laid down the infrastructural and industrial base to ready India for economic take-off.

On the political side, the prospect was brighter too. Nehru's daughter, Mrs Indira Gandhi, had become impatient with the compromises of the old leaders of her Congress Party. She challenged them, and won. She also lost patience with the leaders of the leftist parties with which she had to enter coalitions. In 1971, she took her case to the country which voted her an overwhelming two-thirds majority, enabling her to alter the Constitution should it be necessary. Indira still believed in planning, and determined to enlarge the public sector and to bring larger areas of international trade and the operations of the banking system under New Delhi's control. At last she had restored to India the strong leadership which a planned economy needs.

A remarkably similar pattern of development has characterised the post war history of Ceylon, which has, however, seen the peaceful transference of power from one political party to another after democratic elections. The problems—of poverty, of population pressure, of disparate economic development, of racial and communal tensions, and of modernising a basically agricultural economy—were the same as India's. The politics was the same: towards socialism.

After Mr. Dudley Senanayake's United National Party government of the late 'sixties had failed to keep its election promises, 1970 saw a massive popular vote for Mrs. Sirimavo Bandaranaike's Sri Lanka Freedom Party. South Asia thus saw another woman assume political dominance on a left-wing ticket. Mrs. Bandaranaike had stepped into the shoes of her socialist premier husband, assassinated by a Buddhist priest (Mrs. Gandhi had fallen heir to her father's job; Nehru had seen the father of modern India, Mahatma Gandhi, assassinated by an extremist Hindu). Mrs. Bandaranaike had attacked the Senanayake Government for its supinely pro-Western stance, for its encouragement of foreign investment and its acceptance of aid from the West and from the World Bank. Certainly economic performance had been disappointing. Despite reducing its imports, Ceylon had become increasingly reliant on short-term loans to finance them and on foreign aid.

Exports (mostly tea, rubber and coconut products) had stagnated at around Rs2,000 million due to competition from other producers, the emergence of substitutes and over-production of tea. The contribution of industry to the national product had continued to fall (it employed only about 400,000 people).

Of the population of about 12.3 million, nearly three-quarters of a million were unemployed in 1970. The cost of living was rising, and the economic planners were plagued by sudden fluctuations in the prices fetched by Ceylon's commodities, and in the prices Ceylon had to pay for rice, sugar, and by increased shipping freight rates.

Ceylon had pushed up its growth rate to over 6 per cent a year during the late 'sixties from a less than 4 per cent average rate for the first half of the decade—partly a function of increased foreign aid which rose from a level of US$15.7 million in 1965 to over US$46 million in 1967. But the country had failed to climb out of the slough of poverty, per capita income remained at a low average of less than Rs800 a year per head.

Mrs Bandaranaike's government attempted to tackle these ingrained problems with a mixture of doctrinaire socialism and of pragmatism (the Trotskyite Finance Minister, N.M. Perera, balanced his budget, trying to contain inflation and encourage exports). Ceylon's dwindling private sector protested against the policy of expanding state sector activity in commerce and industry. The Chamber of Commerce pointed out that, according to official statistics, public sector productivity was lower than in the private sector and quoted Dr. Perera's own admission that public sector operations had not even given a 1 per cent return on investments of Rs3,000 million. The businessmen community called for a greater role for private enterprise, lower taxation and cuts in social welfare benefits, which the country could scarcely afford. They attacked the draft of a new Constitution for Ceylon which did not recognise the right to private ownership, discouraging indigenous and foreign investment.

Mrs Bandaranaike's government had been in power less than a year when it was faced with a major revolt, not mounted by the right-wing opposition but by extremist left-wing elements. The communists had previously joined the Sri Lanka Party in coalition governments and they resented the vote which had made the Prime Minister independent of their support. Apparently aided and instigated by North Korean diplomats in Colombo, the rebels rose up in protest against the failure to improve the economic situation and provide more jobs.

The emergence of violent opposition for her left was undoubtedly an unwelcome surprise to Mrs Bandaranaike, and it underlined the extent to which the basic poverty of South Asia, regularly expressed at elections or in violent demonstrations by the 'have-nots', were pushing the area's politics towards the appeal of extreme socialism and communism. After order had been restored in the spring of 1971, Mrs Bandaranaike's government began a process of reaction to the rebellion and began to give encouragement to the private sector.

Businessmen were told that they would have to play a major role in pushing up Ceylon's exports of manufactured goods (then standing at only Rs19.4 million—about 1 per cent of the value of Ceylon's total exports) up to the ambitious target of Rs500 million by 1975. With more government incentives, it appeared possible that foreign investors, who had lost interest in Ceylon, would again be encouraged.

But the country still needed almost Rs500 million to finance its imports—which meant at least US$80 million in foreign aid. It was obvious that production had to be boosted—there was no quick or painless remedy for the island's poverty and unemployment.

Pakistan is the third country in South Asia which provides another tragic example of the failure of politicians and economists to solve the basic problems of poverty, and the consequent plunge into revolutionary politics and violence. In September 1948 the death of M.A. Jinnah, popularly known as Quaid-e-Azam (the Great Leader), the founder and first Governor-General of Pakistan, deprived the young nation of the one leader who was capable of giving it the basic structural foundation of a viable modern state. This national calamity was followed three years later by the assassination of the first Prime Minister, Liaquat Ali Khan, dealing a second drastic blow to Pakistan. The succeeding political leaders and economic planners of Pakistan acquired a reputation for venality and incompetence. No coherent methods were taken to raise agricultural production.

By 1958, the country's balance of payments was in bad shape, and the mounting deficit led to heavy government borrowing and rapid inflationary rises in the cost of living. In October 1958, General Mohammed Ayub Khan seized power and, under martial law quickly re-established confidence. Price controls were instituted and land reforms were implemented to limit individual holdings to 500 irrigated acres of land or 1,000 non-irrigated acres of land. Gold and foreign exchange reserves rose, imports of foodstuffs dropped, production of cotton, yarn and cloth, jute and sugar rose while industrial production rose.

Pakistan launched its second five year plan in 1960 with much greater confidence in the future. With the launching of the third plan in July 1965, prospects had improved even further, the Gross National Product having risen by almost 30 per cent in the previous five years. The rice crop had risen to a peak of about 11.5 million tons, cotton to about $2\frac{1}{2}$ million bales, while industry had made Pakistan self-sufficient in a large number of consumer goods. By 1965, the industrial production index (1960 equals 100) had risen to 165, with tea, vegetable oils, paper, steel rolling, sugar, jute and fertilisers all doing well. The Gross National Product was growing at a rate of about 5.5 per cent a year. Aid was flowing in, totalling US$523 million in 1965—equal to 35 per cent of the country's goods and services.

Then came the first major blow to progress with the outbreak in September 1965 of the war with India. The conflict was short and sharp, and in 1966 the Tashkent Agreement, orchestrated by the Soviet Union, marked an end to the violence. But from this moment on, things did not go so well for Pakistan, although the Gross National Product went on growing—by more than 9 per cent during the late 'sixties. Despite this, however, internal strains began to affect the country—particularly resentment by East Pakistan of the political domination by the Western wing of the country. East Pakistan produced the country's principal exportable raw commodity, jute, but claimed that the profits were expropriated by the West.

The West also dominated the civil service and the army and controlled business enterprises, a disproportionately large part of the country's wealth being in the hands of the "Twenty-two families" which virtually imposed an economic plutocracy over both wings of Pakistan. Resentment in the East erupted in violence against President Ayub Khan's military government. Even in the Western wing the Baluchis, the Sindhis and Pakhtoons, inhabitants of the three outer provinces, became increasingly restless. On 25th March 1969, power passed from Ayub Khan into the hands of General Yahya Khan.

In the two years of his presidency, the country's economic condition further deteriorated. Yahya Khan imposed martial law and dissolved the national provincial assemblies, but he always hoped to reinstitute civilian rule. In December 1970, he organised a general election. In the East, over 98 per cent of the votes went to the Awami League, led by Sheikh Mujibur Rahman, who was demanding regional autonomy based on a six-point formula. In March 1971, after talks between Yahya Khan and the Sheikh in Dacca had failed, the President ordered his army into the eastern wing.

Accounts of the following violence vary, some claiming that the West Pakistan army acted ruthlessly, destroying villages, massacring the population, raping women, and executing intellectuals. These claims are strongly refuted by West Pakistan authorities, who affirm that whatever happened was brought on and aggravated by Indian Army attacks on West Pakistan inciting mutiny in the East. The fact remained, however, that millions of refugees fled over the Pakistan border into India. The East's agony lasted for about nine months. Tensions between India and Pakistan grew and full-scale conflict erupted in early December 1971. The Indian army moved into East Bengal and only twelve days later a new country was proclaimed—Bangladesh.

In the West, Yahya Khan fell and was replaced by Ali Bhutto. He released Sheikh Mujibur Rahman, who had been imprisoned in Rawalpindi. The Sheikh flew back to Bangladesh via London and New Delhi. The new country was recognised internationally. When it became obvious that Britain was about to extend recognition, President Bhutto removed Pakistan from the British Commonwealth.

The end of the armed conflict presented the politicians of India, Pakistan and Bangladesh with huge new problems. Pakistan had lost its source of raw materials, foreign exchange and markets; India had forfeited friendship with the United States (Washington having accused India of having been the aggressor in the conflicts) and had replaced this major source of past aid with a treaty of friendship with the Soviet Union; Bangladesh faced the enormous task of rebuilding its war-torn countryside and re-establishing its jute and tea industries. Between India and Pakistan the festering sore of the disputed State of Kashmir still lay unresolved. Optimists still hoped that the conflict, as a bloodletting, might open the way to co-operation. In January 1972, Indian Foreign Secretary Triloki Nath Kaul urged political and economic co-operation between the countries of the subcontinent, pointing out that Pakistan could cut its coal bill by two-thirds by buying from India, which itself was paying twice as much for jute because of its ban on trade with Pakistan. Certainly, co-operation had much to recommend it. The Green Revolution in wheat production on both sides of the Punjab, the supply of West Pakistan cotton for the hungry mills of India, of fuel and electricity to power-starved Bangladesh, the reuniting of the jute economy of Bengal—all these and many other advantages could stem from a currency settlement agreement, a customs union and eventually, perhaps, a common market, which could even attract other peripheral countries—Ceylon, (now Sri Lanka) Burma and the Himalayan states of Nepal, Sikkim and Bhutan—into a subcontinental confederation. But the subcontinent had, in the early 'seventies, a long way to go before such idealistic dreams came within reach. In the meantime, the subcontinent remained divided by economic inequalities, religious intolerance, linguistic differences and frontier disputes, all of which formed barriers to progress and walls within which millions of people were imprisoned by poverty, malnutrition and over-population.

The Burmese economy, too, suffered many of the stresses exhibited in Pakistan. The Burmans, who form the bulk of the population, have found themselves facing almost continually since dependence not just communist-inspired insurgency, but rebellions by minority groups such as the Shans who bitterly resent Rangoon's control. A large part of the country has never been effectively administered by the central government. To add to the country's woes, the destruction of the industry and the economic infrastructure in the bloody campaign against the Japanese during the Pacific war took almost a decade and a half to rebuild.

An upsurge of nationalism and a desire by the Burmese to control their own fortunes through a national government led to the decision not to remain within the Commonwealth. But the socialism of the politicians plus pressure from Burma's giant neighbour, China, restricted Rangoon's ability to maintain normal commercial relations with the outside world. The emigration of Indian and Chinese communities who had a key role in economic life, has not been compensated by indigenous talent; access to foreign aid and expertise has been severely restricted. The training of a local elite is still at a very early stage.

The doctrinaire socialism of the military rulers—now being replaced by a Buddhist socialism—had pushed nationalisation to extreme lengths regardless of economic consequences. Peasants were freed from the domination of their landlords and offered such aids to modernisation as tractors. These policies favouring the farming community have so far had limited success. But the military were not entirely to blame. Their rulers did try to change the policy of their civilian predecessors: of freezing rice prices which had discouraged peasants from producing a grain surplus. This surplus had formerly been the most important source of the country's foreign exchange. The normal pre-war annual export of 3 million tons of rice dwindled away in the 'sixties until the government was hard-pressed to find even a million tons a year for overseas export markets.

Indonesia went through a similar sorry experience. The destruction of war, the battle for independence, the socialist notions of Sukarno which turned increasingly into ambitions to dominate the southern corner of the region, led to economic collapse. Sukarno extended national frontiers by forcing the Dutch out of their last toehold in Asia—West Irian. But this addition to Indonesia offered no prospect of contributing to the country's prosperity. On the contrary, so backward and primitive was West Irian that Djakarta found it a new hole through which funds needed for economic growth were being drained off.

A quarrel with Malaysia involving Indonesian territorial ambitions also hit the economy hard, cutting Indonesia off from legal traffic with Singapore, one of its key doors to the outside world. The last days of Sukarno were marked by rampant inflation. The country's printing presses churned out paper money in an attempt to cover the budget deficits. An abortive communist coup in 1965 gave the army an excuse to step in and seize control. Slowly, inflation was reduced, the massive overseas debts rescheduled, and foreign capital encouraged to return to the country. The swollen bureaucracy and the over-sized army remained heavy burdens on national resources, but the more pragmatic economics of the new government gave Indonesia its first real hope of progress by 1972. Exports which had been rising by a mere 1 per cent annually from 1960-68 started to increase by more than 10 per cent. Consumer prices which soared by almost 200 per cent a year from 1960-68 had settled to an inflation of about 7 per cent a year. Foreign aid, which amounted to less than US$50 million in 1965 by 1968 shot up to almost US$300 million.

The Philippines seemed drawn steadily over the years towards imitating the less desirable policies of its neighbours. This nation, rich in natural resources, only began to shake off the effects of its domination by the former colonial power (the United States) in 1969. Unfortunately, by this time, so much effort had been lost by a succession of inefficient administrations, that economic nationalism and its calls for the expulsion of foreign capital represented a serious danger to future growth.

The country found itself with an acute balance of payments problem in the early 'seventies as export growth dwindled from the annual rate of over 6 per cent throughout most of the 1960's to virtually nothing in 1969. Agriculture grew by more than 5 per cent through most of the decade, but dropped to 2 per cent in 1970 —a matter of enormous significance for the nation's future since the bulk of the population and its chief industries are dependent on farm production for their development.

The Philippines suffered from a climate of social and political frustration which during the 'fifties and 'sixties showed itself inimical in many ways to economic health. Land reform proved a failure. The family alliances between the rich and the politicians produced grave barriers to the emergence of a dynamic and adventurous middle-class. The attempt to run the sprawling country through a tightly centralised administration meant the remoter areas lacked even law and order. The movement of population from crowded Luzon to the southern islands which would have provided a stimulus for take-off was left to the sporadic and inefficient forces of population pressure.

By 1972 the country appeared to be reaching a crisis. Economic nationalists were calling for an end to the special relationship between the Philippines and the United States which, while giving Manila valuable access to the U.S. market, also allowed Americans special economic privileges within the Philippines. A committee was appointed to draft a new Constitution which could provide some much-needed stability. Filipinos became increasingly critical of the politicians'

failure, especially after an explosion killed and injured many people attending a Liberal Party rally in Manila in August 1971. In the Philippines also, a major political crisis had been brought about by the increasing disparity between the wealthy few and the hungry millions.

Thailand, faced with many of the problems of both Burma and the Philippines, had a much better record than most of the other nations in the region. The country escaped from the ravages of war. Despite racial minorities of some political danger to Bangkok, most of the country was united by ties of religion and strong loyalty to the monarchy. The peasants suffered from little exploitation, and the Government devised a sensible mechanism for taking advantage of the country's rice surplus during the years of Asian hunger.

Some experiments in state industry were tried in the 1950's, but basically the economy was left in private hands and showed considerable capacity for growth. The problem of foreign domination was tackled by a vigorous policy of integrating the Chinese into the Thai population and stern controls over this community's attempt to perpetuate its cultural distinctiveness. The Thais also benefited by an influx of American cash during the Vietnamese war, though this had become an embarrassment by 1971. Bangkok showed considerable acumen in moving towards less intimate U.S. relations and renewed links to Peking and Hanoi.

The success of Thailand in creating the conditions for growth came through strongly in the 'sixties. National income grew at more than 7 per cent in the first half of the 'sixties, with expansion pushing up to more than 9 per cent in the latter half of the decade. From 1960-68, farming increased its output at almost 5 per cent a year but the rate shot up to an average of 7 per cent in the three following years. Inflation was non-existent during the decade, and the ordinary Thai enjoyed a reasonable measure of growing prosperity. However, 1970 and 1971 saw the beginnings of a check to the upward surge as exports began to tail off, and general performance indicated some overheating of the economy. A certain lack of confidence was created by the prospect of an American military withdrawal from Indo-China, by continuing communist insurgence in the north and north-east provinces of Thailand and by the failure to establish a dialogue with Peking. In November 1971 Thailand's Prime Minister Thanom Kittikachorn ended a three-year experiment in parliamentary democracy by suspending the Constitution and putting power in the hands of a Revolutionary Council headed by Thanom and largely formed of personnel from the armed forces and the police. The Council expressed some doubts about the loyalty of the country's 3 million Chinese citizens and instituted harsher measures against crime and a stepped-up military campaign against terrorism. The move took place smoothly and appeared to restore some of the wavering confidence. By the beginning of 1972 it could still be said that on the whole Thailand had laid a firm basis for continued expansion for the future.

Malaysia was one of the best examples of the innate capacity of Asian countries to create prosperous societies, given governments of reasonable efficiency. Despite communist terrorism still not completely checked, the Chinese minority—almost equal in size to the Malay community—the strain of absorbing the new territories of Sabah and Sarawak into the federation, external aggression by Indonesia under Sukarno, racial tensions which reached fever pitch in 1969, and an economy heavily dependent on rubber and tin exports, Malaysia chugged along very happily. Sensible policies for the vital rubber industry allowed the productivity of plantations to rise sufficiently to remain competitive with synthetics. Diversification of economic activities seems to have been more successful in Malaysia than in any other Asian country, with dependence on primary products dropping by almost one-third between 1955 and 1966.

The fundamental lesson of Malaysia was apparently that while the population believes it has some hope of enjoying a decent slice of a growing economic cake, the ordinary citizens will suffer the discomforts of subversion and racial tension and allow the government the opportunity to find solutions to its problems. This promise of prosperity has been more than honoured in Malaysia's case. In 1965, the national income per head was M$928. The government planned to raise this figure by 9 per cent by 1970. United Nations experts believe that once the final statistics are compiled, the growth rate might well exceed this target.

In the middle of the last decade, the authorities forecast trouble ahead for rubber and tin whose exports amounted to a quarter of the national income. In practice, both industries managed to maintain expansion. The government's attempts to spread its export risks by encouraging palm oil and timber have paid off handsomely. These two products were expected to grow by 32 per cent in the latter half of the decade. In fact, their export earnings almost doubled. This resilience and capacity to switch successfully to new lines without abandoning valuable industries is a mark of the latent strength of Malaysia.

The war in Indo-China, which has continued at varying degrees of intensity in the last fifteen years, has made the two Vietnams, Laos and Cambodia into entirely artificial economies. Cambodia under Sihanouk had some independent momentum but was never free from the shadow of the fighting. The governments involved are maintained by foreign aid. Their economies have had to adjust to the ebb and flow of ground combat and bombing. The population's normal life has been disrupted by the demands of conflict. To add to the woes of the four countries, the ordinary destruction of war has been intensified by the use of chemicals whose long-term effects seem totally unpredictable.

The final group of countries consists of four mini-states with the best records of growth in Asia (except for Japan), and who share a common philosophy of total dedication to material advance and a heavy reliance on foreign trade. Hong Kong and Singapore are two Chinese cities with the second and third highest living standards in the region. They began life as entrepôt ports and then expanded into manufacturing. Hong Kong was the first to make the switch and was aided by the well-developed financial and commercial services which had grown up around the port. Singapore in the mid-1960's began to travel the same path. In terms of population, the two together account for a minute proportion of Asia—a mere 6 million.

The other two countries in this category are South Korea and Taiwan. Both were formerly under Japan, both have managed to switch from peasant economies to cash cropping and manufacturing as their main source of prosperity. South Korea, despite its separation from the rest of the peninsula and the havoc wreaked by war, recovered well—thanks to massive injections of American aid followed up by foreign capital. In the first half of the 'sixties, its national income in real terms was growing at 7 per cent a year; in the latter half, expansion was running at 13 per cent. Taiwan functioned equally well, with its breakthrough (as in South Korea's case) coming only after the United States decision to stop subsidising the economy. Real growth in national income was 10 per cent a year throughout the decade. However, Taiwan suffered from far less severe inflationary pressures than South Korea.

In the early 'seventies South Korea faltered in its progress, appearing to lose confidence (as had Thailand), when faced with the prospect of a declining American military commitment to the region. Protectionist forces in the American market, which imposed quotas on South Korea's textile exports (along with those of Japan, Taiwan and Hong Kong in the autumn of 1971) also served to remind South

Korea of its dependence not only on the U.S. military umbrella but on its markets. Contacts with the ever-threatening power of North Korea, ruled by Premier Kim Il-sung who had personally vowed to reunite the country under communism, were tentatively established under the auspices of the Red Cross. But abruptly and unexpectedly President Park Chung Hee of South Korea followed Thailand's example. In December 1971 he declared a state of emergency, claiming that North Korea was prepared to launch a full-scale war on the South and that recent changes in the international situation (specifically the admission of China into the United Nations), had intensified the danger on the Korean peninsula. The President's action nevertheless came as a surprise, since his nation had achieved remarkable progress and appeared to be increasingly confident.

The shock of the UN vote and the prospects of an American rapprochement with Peking fell most severely on Taiwan, whose government still claimed to represent the whole of China. The Taiwan economy had also prospered and its economic breakthrough (like South Korea's) had been achieved after the United States decision to stop direct economic aid. Taiwan's national income grew in real terms by 10 per cent a year throughout the 'sixties, with the island suffering less inflationary pressures than South Korea. Many economists, however, did not believe that the loss of prestige incurred by the UN China vote would necessarily mean a slowdown in Taiwan's economic advance. Even if negotiations between Washington and Peking resulted in an agreement to run down the American military commitment to the island, Taiwan still had access to America's markets, and was continuing to attract investments. Perhaps the greatest threat to its economy (and to that of South Korea) was contained in the Four Principles enunciated by Chou En-lai, designed to discourage Japanese firms from trading with and investing in those countries. But although throughout the last half of 1971 and in early 1972 Japanese firms announced that they would accept Chou's strictures, there was every sign that money was finding its way into the island's prosperous economy.

Some observers argued that the strain of maintaining an increasingly unrealistic claim to be China had been a millstone around Taiwan's neck and that, freed of of this burden, the ruling Kuomintang party would be more prepared to contemplate liberalising political life and giving more power to the native Taiwanese, instead of concentrating it in the hands of those who had fled from the mainland after the communist takeover. Non-membership of the United Nations had not proved to be of economic disadvantage to West Germany, it was pointed out, and there was no reason why it should prove so in Taiwan's case.

Since World War II Asian countries, backed in most cases by powers outside the region, have made several attempts to set up international organisations devoted to the promotion of international cooperation, such as ANZUS, SEATO, ASPAC and ASEAN, and some success has been achieved in the joint marketing of Asian commodities and products, which has helped to stabilise quality and prices. The best hope for short-term co-operation, however, has been stated by such local economists as Dr. Sumitro, Indonesia's Minister of Trade to be in the joint marketing of other Asian commodities, like rubber, tin, tea, sugar, spices, copra.

The Green Revolution, and the prospect of cereal gluts certainly rendered such co-operation desirable for rice. Already in the early 'seventies, the balance of payments of such rice-exporting countries as Burma and Thailand had been affected by the bigger crops, and it appeared likely that international agreement was necessary to stabilise production, build up stockpiles, and plan future agricultural activity if the region's farmers were not to be hard hit by a disastrous drop in prices.

In the long term the best hope for regional co-operation appeared to centre around the huge economy of Japan, which by the early 'seventies was providing such a large market and such a valuable source of investment, aid and technical know-how in the region that critics accused Tokyo of re-creating by peaceful economic means the "Greater Asian Co-Prosperity Sphere" it had failed to impose on the region by military methods in the 'forties. But even those worried by Japan's success had to admit that its wealth was a regional strength and offered the best opportunity to trigger off similar industrial growth in the region, as well as providing a market for Asia's products.

The region thus entered the 'seventies with mixed feelings. Economic development was proving to be a slow and painful process. Too many of its countries were still down at the bottom of the world league when per capita incomes were calculated. Burma came fifth from the bottom (ahead of only Haiti, Ethiopia, Nigeria and Malawi) with a per capita share of the GNP of only just over US$70. Just higher came Nepal, Laos, India, Indonesia, Pakistan and Ceylon with per capita products varying just between US$70 and US$130. The picture for South Asia was gloomy; India was growing at about 1 per cent per year per person.

Higher on the list were Thailand, South Korea, South Vietnam and the Philippines (varying between per capita products of US$170 and $220). Then came a big jump to Malaysia and Taiwan (at about the $320 mark) and an even bigger gap to the real success stories of Singapore and Hong Kong (both around $800). Japan of course led the Asian field with a figure of over $1,400. Even here it must be remembered that Japan, although boasting the world's third largest GNP, was only 19th on the world list of per capita incomes.

But the pressure of population was continuing. Asia had a population of about 2,000 million. If growth rates continue unchanged, the region can expect a population of nearly 5,000 million by the end of the century—a nightmare prospect which brings in its train the threat of a revival of the region's traditional scourges: massive epidemics, disease, famine and even more grinding poverty. Those countries which had taken real and meaningful steps to limit population growth had by and large put up the best economic performances. Japan legalised abortion in 1948 and cut its population growth rate to less than 1 per cent, while Hong Kong, Taiwan, South Korea and Singapore began thorough family planning schemes in the late 'fifties or early 'sixties.

On the other hand, plenty of grounds for hope existed at the beginning of the Second Development Decade (the 'seventies). Asia included some of the world's highest growth rates, as well as some of the lowest. According to the World Bank, Japan during the 'sixties had been growing at nearly 10 per cent a person a year, Hong Kong at over 8 per cent, Taiwan at 6.5 per cent and both North and South Korea at between 5.5 per cent and 6 per cent. The Bank also placed Thailand and Malaysia, Singapore and North Vietnam in the 'affluent club', as far as growth rates went, with per capita of 4.6 per cent, 4.3 per cent, 3.8 per cent and 3.3 per cent respectively.

Asia thus appeared to be splitting in two economically. Historians or sociologists might argue that the rift followed cultural lines, dividing the peoples which had historically fallen under Indian or Hindu influence from those in the Sino-Japanese spheres. Politicians or economists might see the split as one between the socialism of South Asia and the rising capitalism of East Asia. Whatever the basic cause or causes, a rift—a poverty line—running roughly down the culturally-divided and war-torn peninsula of Indo-China was developing.

If the world is viewed as being divided into markets, then North America is probably the most developed and integrated. Then comes Europe, highly developed and well along the road towards integration. Then, possibly come the socialist nations. But the next free market region, already partially developed and exploring the possibility of greater integration, boasting the world's third strongest economy in its midst, is East Asia and the Pacific Basin. The other developing regions—the Middle East, Africa and Latin America—have a long political and economic road to travel before they can rival Asian potential. It has already achieved good growth, it has enormous natural resources (and certainly no shortage of labour), it has already acquired many skills, and a significant level of technological experience.

Possibly the greatest single barrier to progress is not to be found within the region but—in view of the importance of outside markets, foreign investment and aid—the reputation Asia as a whole has acquired as being a region of violence and insecurity. The image has been fostered by Pearl Harbour, the continuing war in Vietnam, by China's (largely unearned) image of belligerence, by confrontation, by the conflict between India and Pakistan, the civil war between the two wings of Pakistan, and by innumerable other quarrels, border disputes, territorial claims, coups d'etat and violence which have characterised the headlines dealing with Asian news over the last half century.

But looking at the region, the long-run pattern of economic and political performance still seems to be determined by the same basic triangle which has shaped its fortunes since 1945. The United States' hostility to China was relaxing in 1971, but the strain between China and Japan—built up after the outbreak of the Korean war as part of the American containment of China—was intensifying. The Japanese economy had emerged from the Korean war with all the resources needed for a massive thrust into the league of advanced nations. During the 1960's, its exports quadrupled to US$16,000 million. Manufacturing capacity had trebled. Monthly household income rose by around 60 per cent to some US$300. National income also rose 300 per cent over the decade. But the Japanese were busy rethinking their relations with the rest of the region and the outside world.

After sticking hard to protectionist policies on both imports of goods and capital, 1971 saw Tokyo feeling self-confident enough to relax restrictions on the entry of foreign goods and overseas firms. But at the same time, the Japanese were bringing to the boil their push into Asian markets such as Thailand, Indonesia and the Philippines. Tokyo found itself faced with denunciations from Peking over its commercial success, and as part of the price for better trade—and diplomatic contacts—with China, was showing signs of severing previously close economic ties with South Korea and Taiwan.

The Chinese for their part were emerging as a new economic influence in Asian affairs. In Bangkok a debate took place on the possibility of trade with China. Chinese rubber purchases helped buttress the Malaysian economy. Ceylon benefited from a substantial trade agreement with the Chinese, while Manila sent a trade mission to Peking. The race between the two giants was on in earnest: Japan the world's third largest economy in terms of national income; China the world's largest nation in terms of population. The pull of cash versus people was starting to have its impact on the rest of Asia as it entered the second development decade.

1971 thus proved to be a watershed year in the history of Asia's development. The first hint of great changes in the pattern of the balance of power in the region had come in 1969 when President Nixon enunciated his Guam doctrine. This foreshadowed a running-down of the American military presence in Asia and policies which required that Asia should shoulder more of the responsibility for its defences and for the fight against subversive movements. It became increasingly obvious that Nixon was determined to run down America's involvement in the Vietnam war prior to his campaign for re-election in November 1972. After he had taken several measures liberalising American embargoes on trade with China and on travel by American citizens to China, the world was astonished to learn on 10th July 1971, that Nixon's Special Advisor on National Security, Henry Kissinger, had flown secretly to Peking and that President Nixon himself planned to visit the Chinese capital—probably early in the following year.

By this time China's post-cultural revolution, pragmatic policies had succeeded in re-establishing old friendships and in winning Peking new friends. Diplomatic recognition by Canada led the way and a queue of countries willing to establish diplomatic relations had formed—even if it meant their cutting links with Taiwan. China's new international success culminated on Monday, 25th October 1971 with a vote by the United Nations General Assembly granting membership to Peking and ousting Taiwan.

World opinion generally hailed this historic vote as a step towards reality, although the U.S.A. itself had made great efforts in the UN to promote its "Two-China" policy, designed to retain membership for Taiwan. Nevertheless, the vote came as a shock to some of America's Asian allies, who had committed their national policies to a strong anti-communist stance. Nations such as Australia, New Zealand, Thailand, South Korea and Japan had already begun reassessing their China policies in the light of the possibility of a détente between Washington and Peking.

Japan was particularly shocked. Washington had persuaded Japan to co-sponsor the vote in the UN designed to retain Taiwan. This blow came as the fourth in a series of set-backs to the prestige of Japan's Prime Minister, Eisako Sato: the sudden announcement of Nixon's trip to Peking, the equally shocking measures taken by the U.S. President to improve the U.S. economy and protect the U.S. dollar (a 10 per cent import surcharge and a temporary cessation of the gold convertibility of the dollar); and thirdly the imposition of quotas on America's imports of synthetic and woollen textiles from Japan. Mr. Sato had firmly identified his policies with those of the U.S.A. and based them on the continuance of the U.S.A.—Japan Security Treaty, which provided Japan with a U.S.A. nuclear umbrella. Mr. Sato had been particularly anxious to negotiate the return to Japan of the Ryukyu Islands (Okinawa) but the price he had to pay for this, including the restraints on textile imports, weakened the support he received from Japan's big commercial and industrial interests, which traditionally form the power base for Japan's ruling Liberal Democrat Party.

Throughout 1970 and 1971 China had mounted a virulent anti-Japanese propaganda campaign which succeeded in reviving many of Asia's bitter memories of World War II. It became evident that China had emerged from the violence and isolation of the Cultural Revolution to discover that Japan (representing successful Asian capitalism) was posing just as great a threat to China and the revolution of Mao Tse-tung as had the military threats posed by the "Soviet revisionists" to China's north and the "American imperialist" presence in Vietnam, supported by its ring of military bases throughout East and South-east Asia. In this sense, China's "New Look", its willingness to establish a dialogue with the U.S.A. and its desire for membership of the UN could be seen as being largely a response to the Japanese challenge—a diplomatic and political campaign waged to counter Japan's growing economic strength and the dominating role it was beginning to play in Asian trade and investment.

It remained to be seen how China would use its membership of the UN—whether it would be disruptive or co-operative. It seemed likely, however, that UN membership and particularly representation in the specialised agencies of the world body would enable China to make a bid for leadership of the "Third World"—as the champion of the developing countries in their campaign to improve the terms of world trade in such forums as the United Nations Conference on Trade and Development (UNCTAD). China probably would attempt to unite the "have-nots" in a rejection of what China termed "Superpower Blackmail".

On 21st February 1972 the long awaited rapprochement between China and the United States began to materialise. President Nixon, accepting an invitation from the People's Republic to visit China, stepped from his plane at Peking Airport. He was met by Premier Chou En-lai. Unexpectedly, during the afternoon Chairman Mao Tse-tung arranged to see the President, and from that first, tense unscheduled meeting a friendly feeling grew between the two leaders and this spirit continued in the talks between the President and Premier Chou En-lai throughout the week.

The final meeting lasted several hours, and both Nixon and Chou showed signs of strain as they carefully phrased their communique. Nixon, referring to Chiang Kai-Shek's island as "Taiwan" and not "The Republic of China", promised to progressively reduce the U.S. forces in Taiwan "as tension in the area diminishes". The Chinese met this concession by refraining from using the statement as a medium for Communist revolutionary propaganda and, in agreeing tacitly to "a peaceful settlement of the Taiwan question by the Chinese themselves", undertook not to use force in regard to the island.

Couched in diplomatic language these promises in themselves may not prove to be as far reaching or as binding as they imply. The significance of the visit, however, was the bridging of 12,000 miles and 22 years of non-communication and hostility between China and the U.S.A., which undoubtedly indicated "progress toward the normalization of relations" to the ultimate benefit of all countries of the world.

UNESCO in Asia

Above and below right:
For some years now new teaching methods have been making their appearance in Asia. In place of the traditional blackboard, diagrams and models are being used. Presented in an attractive manner these teaching tools serve the dual purpose of being amusing and instructive.

MORE THAN ELEVEN centuries ago, in Central Java, a magnificent temple—the Borobudur—was built in honour of the Buddha. Now, the monsoon rains of a thousand years have washed away much of the earth around its base and attempts are being made in many countries to raise funds to restore it.

In May 1971 a Conference of Asian Ministers of Education and Ministers concerned with Economic Planning was held in Singapore to examine the problems of providing by 1980 free and compulsory education for all Asian children. By that time there may be some 520 million children under the age of fifteen in Asia.

For centuries the Indian Ocean has brought life, in the form of food and regular rains, to the countries of southern Asia. Also it has often brought to them death, from shipwrecks in storms and devastation by floods. Only recently have serious attempts been made to explore this vast expanse—one-seventh of the Earth's surface—scientifically. And the link between the efforts to restore the Borobudur, the meeting of Ministers in Singapore, and the international scientific study of the Indian Ocean is UNESCO—the United Nations Educational, Scientific and Cultural Organisation—whose headquarters are in Paris.

UNESCO is 25 years old. It is an organisation of countries, founded in 1946, to promote peace through international co-operation in the fields of Education, Science and Culture. By 'peace' is meant not just the absence of war but something much more positive—the improvement of the quality of life and the raising of living standards.

How does an international organisation, in a quarter of a century, affect a continent in which half the world lives and with civilisations stretching over thousands of years? The answer must surely be: very slowly!

How does half the world, living in Asia, affect UNESCO? The answer here must be that Asia's influence on UNESCO, so far, has perhaps been small in relation to its enormous population.

Let us look at these two influences, and first, at UNESCO's influence on Asia. UNESCO activity in Asia is in fact considerable, whether in Education, Science, Culture or Communications. Each of the nineteen Asian member countries of UNESCO has some UNESCO projects.

How does the Organisation in fact work?

Above: University construction—a priority in spite of difficulties. Many developing countries have been able to put up some exceptionally well-designed buildings with modern facilities. These attest to the importance attached to advanced education.

Education is an immensely wide field in which a great many organisations and bodies are working. UNESCO's aim is to concentrate on certain basic or pilot projects which will give a lead in their field and set the stage for a gradual improvement in the educational systems of all the countries concerned.

In 1952, for instance, a conference of educationists from countries in South-east Asia decided that education at the primary level should not be available only to the privileged; every child should not only be given the opportunity to attend school but should be compelled to do so. But then a series of follow-up meetings led to the realisation of a number of problems: firstly, that the immediate effect of such a decision would involve astronomical costs; furthermore, that neither the schools nor the teachers were yet available to put it into practice; and—by no means least—that secondary, technical and tertiary education for large sectors of the population were just as important as primary education. So the original plan, later known as the Karachi Plan, was revised from time to time and the Meeting of Ministers, mentioned at the beginning, is just one of the steps in the process.

UNESCO helps by providing experts and expert advice in curriculum-building, in teacher training and in many other ways from pre-school to what used to be called 'adult' education but is now usually referred to as 'continuing' or 'life-long' education. It is evident that adults who have never learnt to read need material quite different from schoolchildren and the emphasis now is on what is termed 'functional literacy'—namely the ability to read and write about the kind of things they need to make them better and more efficient farmers, or cooks, or businessmen or industrial workers.

Afghanistan offers an admirable example of the kind of assistance UNESCO is able to provide: an Academy of Teacher Education was set up in 1964 to train the staffs of teachers' colleges. With assistance from experts from many countries, including Australia, provided by UNESCO, nearly 130 teacher educators had been trained by the end of 1969 and many scholarships had been awarded for others to study in foreign countries. Moreover, the work done in the Academy has greatly influenced the development of educational broadcasting and films and the use of audio-visual aids. There is also a college in Kabul, working under UNESCO auspices, which trains teachers in 'functional literacy' and which has already turned out some 400 graduates. It now boasts an enrolment of about 1,000. This institution, like many others in the area, serves a whole region. Other examples would be the agricultural training provided in the Philippines, and the Child Study Centre set up in Bangkok. In every case the international expert or experts provided by UNESCO, having trained nationals within their own country has been able to leave the institution in the hands of those local people.

In India UNESCO has been conducting a Secondary School Science Teaching Project in which scientists from many countries helped to draw up new and more suitable syllabuses for secondary schools. Workshops were set up, suitable equipment mass-produced, new topics introduced and suitable textbooks devised.

Science teaching is only one of the many aspects of UNESCO's scientific programme. In Malaysia, for instance, UNESCO has provided experts to train skilled tradesmen as well as professional and scientific workers to carry out an extensive programme of highway engineering.

There are two UNESCO Regional Science Offices in South-east Asia—one in New Delhi and another in Djakarta—as well as six Science Documentation Offices, which link scientific workers in the region and circulate and publicise scientific information.

Two of UNESCO's biggest scientific projects have been concerned with water—or the lack of it: the Arid Zone Project covered countries like Australia, Israel and Turkey and parts of India and Pakistan which suffer from drought or near-drought, while the Indian Ocean has provided vital information for the oceanographical researches being carried out under UNESCO auspices. In the Indo-China area tremendous projects are in progress to tame the waters of the 2,500 mile long Mekong River which passes through no less than five countries from China to Vietnam.

The third of UNESCO's components is Culture, a term which again embraces a multitude of different activities. One of the most important is the task of making the literature and civilisation of the East better known to the West as well as bringing the output of the Western world within reach of a vast, often newly literate public. UNESCO has sponsored translations of many works into and

Open-air schools are conducted with a certain measure of success. Though the means at the disposal of the children are somewhat rudimentary the solution is infinitely preferable to one where they would have to walk several miles to school.

Right: The popularity of books is no simple catch-phrase to these girls.

Below: A pony-cart library from Thailand-UNESCO Fundamental Education Centre regularly visits all the villages. Here, the cart has just arrived in Gan Pa-ow.

Bottom: A new world opens up for a person able to read. A book can be a teacher, a companion and a source of intense satisfaction

from the languages of South-east Asia and has promoted centres for Book Development in Tokyo and Karachi. Here people from the region are trained in such activities as the production and sale of books.

Up to now twelve of the countries of South-east Asia have adhered to the UNESCO Convention which abolishes tariffs and customs dues on literature and the arts, a Convention initiated at the General Conference in Florence, 1950. Again, UNESCO provides assistance to several governments in the restoration and preservation of ancient monuments and works of art, like the Borobudur Temple in Indonesia, already referred to, for which UNESCO is sponsoring an international appeal.

Another field in which the organisation has been active is in the mass media—press, radio, television and film—where it has helped to set up institutes, granted training fellowships and sponsored comparative studies of the most effective use or the impact of the different media.

How much has Asia influenced UNESCO? In some ways a great deal, in others not so much. Among the significant influences was one at the Organisation's beginning when an Asian delegate proposed that the "Educational and Cultural Organisation" should be enlarged to include Science. Scientific activities are now second only to Education in UNESCO's programme.

Another significant influence arises from the rich and varied cultural inheritance of Asia, now far better known to other world continents as a result of UNESCO's activities.

But Asia, as a continent, consists of countries so diverse that its influence on the politics of UNESCO, and even on the organisation's programme, has been much less than might have been expected. This is partly because mainland China has not been a member of UNESCO and also because the delegations (and probably the governments) of Asian countries have less in common than have delegations (and governments) from other continents such as Europe, Africa or South America. Is this a source of strength or of weakness? In any event it adds to the variety of UNESCO.

It is clear that UNESCO's work can have a profound influence on almost every aspect of the life of the individual citizen, even if that influence is only an indirect one. UNESCO is an institution designed to help not only the developing countries but also the more developed ones and above all to promote the exchange of ideas and knowledge between countries at every level of development and progress. It is only by sharing such knowledge and applying it for the progress and betterment of the people that peace can be built on secure foundations for future generations.

Left:
Darakarn Building in Bangkok, the home of the South-east Asian Ministers of Education Secretariat.

WITH THE COMING of Europe's colonial powers to the ancient kingdoms and scattered tribal villages of South-east Asia, hitherto vaguely marked boundaries were arbitrarily established and divergent populations were fused and moulded into embryo nations. Local interests were steered towards the "mother-country" and between even closely neighbouring states attachments other than those necessary for trade were deflected. Historical, cultural and language differences, accentuated by the forces of colonial rule, made regional co-operation difficult, sometimes even impossible.

Many physical types make up South-east Asia's teeming populations: Mongoloids, Negritos and Nesiots. Several dialects of the two main language groups—Sino-Tibetan and Malayo-Polynesian—may be spoken in any one city or rural area. The upland regions of many countries are peopled by tribal groups who view their more advanced lowland neighbours with suspicion if not hostility. Later immigrants such as the Chinese and Indians are often ostracised in countries they have helped to develop and where they represent a sizeable proportion of the population.

In the period after World War II, the newly independent countries of South-east Asia concentrated on nation building—the acquisition of a Western technology and its accompanying changes in the social structure. With this came both a spirit of nationalism and the awareness of the insanity of nationalism's extremes: a world shrunk by modern communications and made insecure by the atom bomb has little use for isolationism or for exaggerated displays of power.

The Significance of SEAMEO

Above:
INNOTECH, the Regional Centre for Educational Innovation and Technology, is temporarily located in Singapore.
It is to be moved to Saigon in August 1972.

Left:
BIOTROP Headquarters, the Regional Centre for Tropical Biology, at Bogor, Indonesia.

Through the mutual concern of people who realised the need for co-operation and understanding between countries which transcended national boundaries, the great international and regional organisations were founded, UN, SEATO and others. One of the youngest but most potentially significant of these is the South-east Asian Ministers of Education Organisation—SEAMEO.

In 1965, at a meeting in Bangkok of the Ministers of Education of Laos, Malaysia, Singapore, Thailand and Vietnam with Mr. Eugene R. Black, special advisor to President Johnson, and a number of other officials, it was unanimously agreed to form this body. SEAMEO's charter, signed in February, 1968, was formally ratified and came into force in October of the same year. The purpose of the Organisation, as stated in the Charter, is to "promote co-operation among the South-east Asian Nations through education, science and culture, in order to further respect for justice, for the rule of law and for the human rights and fundamental freedoms which are the birthrights of the peoples of the world".

The current members of SEAMEO are Indonesia, Khmer Republic, Laos, Malaysia, Philippines, Singapore, Thailand and Vietnam. The Organisation may be looked upon as international in the sense that many countries outside the South-east Asian region are actively involved in its various activities, particularly in regard to its training and research programmes and the financing of its Secretariat and project centres.

SEAMEO implements its objectives through the following media: The Council, comprising the eight Ministers of Education of the eight member countries, which approves the programmes, policies and budgets of the Body; The Secretariat, recruited on as wide a base as possible, which administers Council decisions, organises studies, seminars and research and helps to secure financial support; and lastly, the Regional Project Centres which conduct training courses and research.

With the view of ensuring the optimum use of local and regional resources and of accelerating educational development in the area, the Organisation has established six regional centres for specialised training and research in such fields as the teaching of English as a second language; science and mathematics; agriculture; tropical biology; tropical medicine and public health; and educational innovation and technology. The establishment of these centres, it is hoped, will increase the number of trained personnel to deal with some of the critical manpower shortages that hinder social and economic development of South-east Asia. The centres will also provide much needed opportunities within the region for professional growth through research and study, the lack of which is an important factor in the region's 'brain-drain'.

Although the balance of the environment has long been of the greatest concern to scientists, it is only in the past two or three years that "ecology" has become a topic of urgent popular discussion. Businesses and governments alike have come to realise that the balance of nature is easily upset and difficult and expensive to restore. BIOTROP, SEAMEO's regional centre for tropical biology in Bogor, Indonesia, has been created in order to investigate and solve some of the biological problems of South-east Asia. Research programmes and training schemes are being carried on in such areas as tropical forests, pests, marine and fresh water biology, man-made lakes and coral reefs, and ecological studies on the development and preservation of human and natural resources.

Top left:
Field work at SEARCA, the Regional Centre for Graduate Study and Research in Agriculture, at Los Banos in the Philippines. Experiments are being carried out on non-wilting vegetables.

SEAMEO's other centres are also studying problems and establishing programmes highly relevant to the future needs of its member countries. The Regional Centre for Educational Innovation and Technology, INNOTECH, aims to identify and solve basic educational problems through the imaginative use of television, radio, programmed instruction and auto-instructional devices. RECSAM, the Regional Centre for Education in Science and Mathematics, has already conducted a number of courses in the teaching of biology, chemistry, physics and mathematics for nearly 300 key-educators from South-east Asia.

In Singapore, the Regional English Language Centre, RELC, has conducted seven 4-month training courses in the teaching of the English language. Its most recent seminar, attended by 450 participants, attracted distinguished scholars, not only from the South-east Asian area, but also from Australia, Canada, Hong Kong, Germany, India, Japan, New Guinea, New Zealand, Soviet Russia, The United Kingdom and The United States of America.

Another SEAMEO project of vital importance is the Regional Centre for Graduate Study and Research in Agriculture, SEARCA. Its research programmes include an assessment of the region's manpower needs; a study of agricultural degree-equivalencies; and investigations into methods of bringing scientific knowledge to the peasant-farmer.

Unlike the previous five centres, TROPMED, the Regional Project for Tropical Medicine and Public Health, is carried on in seven national centres, each one specialising in a different field. Nutrition, the use of radio isotopes, public health, parasitology, entomology, rural and urban medicine, family planning, tropical paediatrics, plague, enteric infections and communicable diseases are some of the subjects researched at centres in Djakarta, Vientiane, Kuala Lumpur, Manila, Singapore, Saigon and Bangkok.

Although capital development and operational costs of these projects are shared by the host country and The United States of America, the cost of programme participants, including training and research scholarships, research fellowships and grants, seminars and conferences, has to be funded from other sources. It has been estimated that project requirements could be met from the 8 to 10 per cent yearly interest on an endowment of US$20 to 25 million, and such a fund has been established by SEAMEO for this purpose. Countries, companies, institutions, foundations and private individuals previously unable to offer donations can now make funds available to the Organisation for a specified number of years, after which the gift is returnable. Only the income generated by the donation will be used to meet fund requirements. Binding instructions on SEAMEO may be given for the gift to be used in a particular field.

In the next decade, the social, economic and political tasks to be faced by South-east Asia are enormous. In a period of rising expectations, the common people hope to make more of their lives—to have more and to be more. To be effective, education must strip itself of its 19th Century European bias and extend to meet the peculiar problems of South-east Asia in the 20th Century: on a 'grass-roots' level, agriculture, particularly food production, must be made efficient and this can only be done by communicating technology to the peasant; on this same level, family planning seems the only effective long-term solution to the population pressures and social ills of the region. Through regional co-operation, in these and other areas of vital concern, SEAMEO has done much to provide effective and practical answers to the area's problems. But these problems and their answers are not only the concern of South-east Asia, but the responsibility of the world, and the hope of future generations lies in the world's response to organisations such as SEAMEO.

Above:
The office of
the Central Co-ordinating Board
of TROPMED,
the Regional Project for Tropical
Medicine and Public Health,
in Bangkok, Thailand.

The Mighty Mekong Project

THE MEKONG RIVER is the eighth longest in the world and one of the most international and at the same time least accessible of the world's rivers. It rises among the snow-capped mountains of the Tibetan plateau, on the borders of the Chinese province of Chinghai—by one of the curiosities of geography, only a few miles from the source of those other two giants, the Yangtze Kiang, which flows through China to Shanghai, and the Salween which flows down through Burma to enter the Indian Ocean at Moulmein.

The Mekong takes a middle course between these two neighbours, flowing through southern China into Laos, the Khmer Republic (formerly Cambodia), and South Vietnam to reach the sea near Saigon. It forms for a few miles the border between China and Burma and is the only frontier between Burma and Laos. It marks the southern half of the border between Laos and Thailand, and it washes past the capitals of both Laos and the Khmer Republic—Vientiane and Phnom Penh. It is 2,800 miles long, and its energies until recently have been almost entirely untapped.

Despite its length there are virtually no bridges across the Mekong, whose width and topography make it a barrier dividing South-east Asia. When the mountain snows melt floods rage uninhibitedly down the river's course, and hundreds of tributaries become swollen. Most of the Mekong's waters are unnavigable except by very small craft. No electricity was generated until a few months ago by the torrents of the Mekong, which for millenia has been only sometimes a friend, too often an enemy and almost never a servant to the 30 million poor farmers living on or near its banks and within its basin.

Yet this mighty stream could bring unprecedented riches to the riparian countries if tamed, channelled and harnessed. One of the early international surveys commented: "Even a cursory examination of the available hydrological and topographic data, meagre as it is, has convinced us of the great potential... Since it is snow-fed, the Mekong has a perennial flow. The possible hydro-power sites are easily accessible... Wise conservation and utilisation of its waters will contribute more towards improving human welfare in this area than any other single undertaking."

That part of the river which goes through China is virtually inaccessible for substantial construction work. But the four countries through which it flows between China and the sea—Laos, Thailand, the Khmer Republic and South Vietnam—could benefit immensely from a number of feasible projects within their territory. This, the project region of the Lower Mekong Basin, comprises about 80 per cent of the drainage area of the river, the total being larger than all of France, or nine times the size of Tasmania. For the past twelve years the United Nations has undertaken the exploitation of the Mekong as a regional co-operation project.

The total discharge of the river flowing out into the South China Sea is 400 million acre feet per annum, a flow of water about 100 times greater than that of the Murray River at the Hume Reservoir, Australia. When the amount of irrigation development that has been successfully carried out on the Murray is considered, and the benefit accrued to Australia, the tremendous potential for development in the Lower Mekong Basin can be readily evaluated.

In spite of the fact that Vietnam and Laos have been engaged throughout the past twelve years in bitter civil war, that relations between Cambodia on the one hand and Thailand and Vietnam on the other have been extremely strained with periods of diplomatic non-recognition, and that each of the four countries has some kind of quarrel with each of the others, the idealism of the United Nations has combined with the funds and expertise which its members can produce to create a viable co-operation project against all hazards of political suspicion.

There is now a slowly dawning appreciation of the enormity of the potential. It is realised that this great water and power resource is vastly under-utilised: less than 3 per cent of the entire lower basin is now irrigated, and vast extensions are possible; no hydro-electric power is drawn from the mainstream, and the four countries of the region are struggling to meet the rising demand for power for industrial development; floods ravage the river valleys, and opportunities for navigation have not been developed. The objective of the project is to bring these tremendous resources under control for the comprehensive development of the region and the benefit of all the people of the region.

The project is directed by the Mekong Committee comprising one plenipotentiary from each of the four riparian countries. It operates under the aegis of the United Nations Economic Committee for Asia and the Far East (ECAFE) which is based in Bangkok, and it is serviced by ECAFE and other UN bodies. More than 25 other UN member countries are helping the project, along with sixteen UN agencies, four private foundations and numerous private firms. Help for this imaginative international scheme has come not only from the relatively well-off Western countries such as the U.S.A., Britain, Australia, France and Holland—and Japan—but also from less affluent Asian neighbours such as India, Taiwan, Pakistan, the Philippines and Indonesia.

The chief architect of the project for its first eleven years was Dr. C. Hart Schaaf, who in 1969 handed over to a Dutch engineer, Mr. Willem J. van der Oord. A total of more than 70 individual projects have been identified within the Mekong Scheme—dams, power stations, experimental farms, soil surveys, bridges, irrigation canals, flood control systems, transport schemes etc. At the beginning of 1971 resources to the tune of more than US$200 million had been pledged, but the total eventual cost of the entire project is impossible to forecast.

So far three dams have been completed, two in north-east Thailand and one in southern Laos. Both of the Thai dams, at Nam Pung and at Nam Pong, include power stations with 6,300 and 25,000 kW capacity respectively. The first one, financed and built by the Thai government itself with Japanese and French technical supervision, is used to pump water from the Mekong to irrigate nearby farms. The second and larger dam will eventually facilitate the irrigation of 53,000 hectares of farmland. This project was mainly financed by Thailand itself, together with a German loan and small gifts from Pakistan and Taiwan. German, Italian and Swiss companies collaborated on the construction work. Fishing in the dammed area is estimated to be almost as valuable as the power generated.

The Lower Se Done dam in the southern part of Laos, financed by France and Laos, has a power output of only 2,000 kW and cost about US$3 million.

There are five other important tributary projects under construction, while preinvestment surveys have been carried out for several much larger power or multi-purpose projects on the mainstream, and financing is being sought for two mainstream bridges—one joining Thailand and Laos, and the other in the delta of South Vietnam.

New farming techniques are already being tested on experimental farms, fisheries are being developed, mineral resources and their processing facilities are being investigated and a comprehensive framework for long-term development is being prepared.

In 1966 the committee for Co-ordination of Investigation of the Lower Mekong Basin (to give it its full name) was the recipient of the Ramon Magsaysay Award for International Understanding. It is, in the words of ECAFE's Executive Secretary, U Nyun, an "international undertaking...for the benefit of all the people...not only for the present generation, but for future generations, without regard to race, class or politics". Many UN observers hope that Communist China will join the construction work of the committee at the appropriate time.

Meanwhile the international spirit of the Mekong project was demonstrated in 1968 when Thailand's Nam Pong hydro-electric scheme was linked to Vientiane, the Laotian capital, across the Mekong River. Power will flow from Thailand to Laos through this first international transmission line in the region. And when the $30 million Nam Ngum dam and hydro-electric station some 40 miles north of Vientiane is completed at the end of 1971, electricity from Laos will be exported to Thailand in repayment.

Eight countries, including Australia and New Zealand as well as Canada, Denmark, France, Japan, Holland and the U.S.A., have contributed nearly US$28 million for the Nam Ngum project in the form of grants, and Thailand has lent the cement on the basis of being repaid later in the form of electric power from the 135,000 kW hydro-electric station.

Nam Ngum will provide power for use in Vientiane as well as a reservoir of 7,000 million cubic metres to help local farmers at times of drought. In spite of the extension of the civil war into areas near to the project, notably in 1969, the Committee urged all concerned, "whether governments, parties or individuals", to recognise its non-political character and not to interfere with it, and U Nyun was able to report subsequently that "there was in fact no interruption".

The progress of the Nam Ngum dam during that period was remarkable in the circumstances. The surrounding countryside was subject to periodical ambushes by the pro-Communist Pathet Lao forces, and the road from Vientiane was not secure at any time. The Laotian government asked that a demilitarised zone be declared extending for six miles round the site, but the Pathet Lao refused. Attacks continued in the area and there were even some deaths. At one stage the twenty Thai technicians walked off the job and went home because of the lack of security, but they returned later. Meanwhile approximately 150 Japanese engineers and technicians, several Canadians and hundreds of Laotian labourers worked round the clock to keep the project as little behind schedule as possible, in spite of flooding problems, the rapid turnover of workers, guerrilla sniping, a shortage of carpenters and the scores of daily technical problems presented.

THE MEKONG RIVER PROJECT

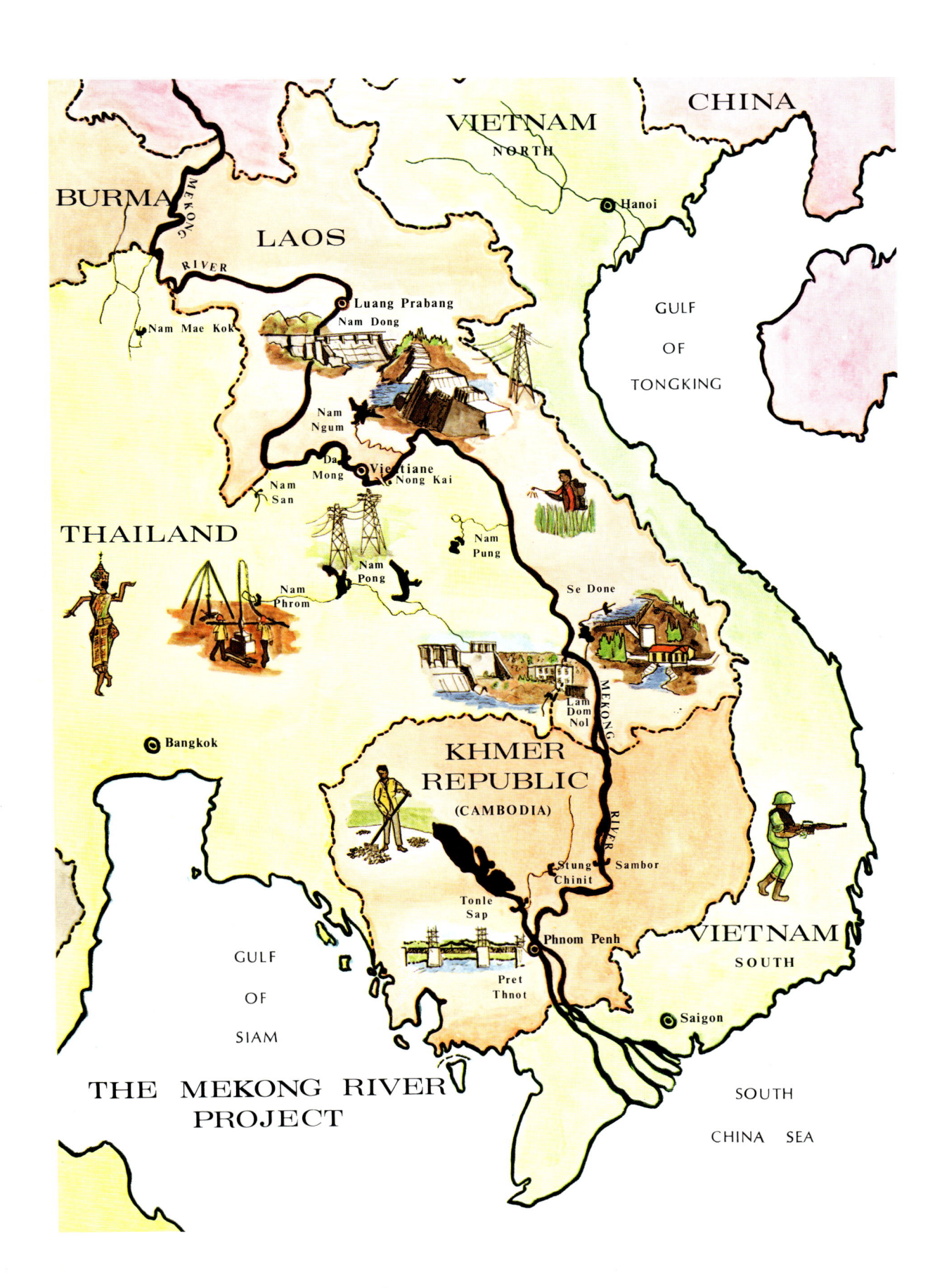

The four other projects under construction are at Prek Thnot in the Khmer Republic, at Nam Dong in Laos and at Nam Phrom and Lam Dom Noi in Thailand. Prek Thnot, about 40 miles west of Phom Penh, comprises one main dam and five auxiliaries with an 18,000kW power station costing in total approximately US$27 million. No fewer than fourteen countries are helping to finance this scheme, while four international organisations or companies are responsible for the surveying and construction. The Australian Snowy Mountains Hydro-Electric Authority is supervising the building of the works; Maeda and Toyomenka of Japan are the principal constructors; the Israeli company Tahal is designing the irrigation scheme; and the Philippine company Certeza Surveying has been commissioned for some of the follow-up work.

In June and July of 1970 this scheme was threatened by security problems arising out of the internal fighting within the Khmer Republic, and U Thant, the United Nations Secretary-General, made a statement on July 2nd in the following terms:

"The Prek Thnot project is international not only in terms of its benefits but also in terms of its sources of financing, as it is aided by contributions from twelve member countries of the United Nations and by the United Nations itself.

Recent developments have threatened progress of the work, and, in view of this, I would like to appeal for the co-operation of all concerned to ensure that there be no interruptions, so that it may be possible for the United Nations, on behalf of the international community, to make this project available to the people of the Mekong Basin for their benefit."

There are six other projects for which the early paper work is complete. These are the Pa Nong, Sambor, Tonle Sap, Stung Chinit, Nam San and Nam Mae Kok projects. The Australian Snowy Mountains team has contributed a feasibility report for the first and a geological survey for the second of these projects. The Pa Nong project is a mainstream dam with subsidiary dams to create a huge lake and power station with irrigation facilities. The Tonle Sap scheme is a particularly important one. When the Mekong rises, the waters washing down from the mountains flow back up the Tonle Sap river, reversing its flow—while at the same time the waters flood the delta and make millions of acres of land unusable from Phnom Penh down to the South China Sea. It is proposed to construct a gated barrage to control the flow from the Great Lake at Tonle Sap, and it is hoped that electric power from the Sambor hydro-electric dam will enable the "Plain of Reeds" in South Vietnam to be reclaimed. The Great Lake has enormous fisheries potential.

Another four projects have been identified but are awaiting funds before preliminary work can be done. These are a multi-purpose flood control, power and irrigation scheme at Battambang in Western Cambodia, near the ancient ruined temple of Angkor Wat; a similar irrigation-power scheme at Upper Se San in Vietnam; a bridge at the My Thuan ferry across the Mekong in Vietnam, at a point where more than a thousand vehicles cross every day, but where ships also pass so that the bridge has to be 150 feet high; and a bridge across the Mekong to connect the Laotian capital of Vientiane with the Thai border town of Nong Khai. This last bridge must carry both a road and railway and will cost more than US$20 million.

There are more than 50 other projects which have not yet been named, lines or dots or blobs on the map which in the years and decades to come will become towns, dams, bridges, canals, roads, new factories, new farmland……

But all this activity is still only the beginning of the realisation of the full potential of the basin, which is on a scale to dwarf such mammoth projects as the Tennessee Valley development in the United States. The final plans may take a further twenty years of investigation, design and construction, and cost some 3,000 to 5,000 million dollars. The total benefits include the irrigation of some 20 million acres of land and an annual power output of some 50 thousand million kilowatt hours per annum. The benefits are substantial, and in many cases are so high in relation to costs that the funds involved could be re-paid in a relatively few years.

The project as a whole is an extremely valuable investment for the peoples of the region.

The politics of the Mekong projects are worthy of Ian Fleming. American and South Vietnamese aircraft occasionally bomb areas within the overall scheme, there is migration of people from one area to another, political refugees traverse the countries involved, and there are many tribal peoples whose position remains obscure and difficult.

The Mekong Committee is also finding finance much more of a handicap. At a recent meeting with the World Bank, one speaker complained that the overall scheme was really at a stage where it required "thirty, forty, fifty times" the amounts of money currently being pledged. But until the political, military and legal aspects of the scheme are a little clearer and quieter, it will remain difficult to persuade bankers to put money into it.

Meanwhile gifts continue to pour in from almost every source—a shipload of fertiliser or cement, a team of geologists or engineers, the supply of steel or even hard cash without strings.

Although the cost of 3,000 to 5,000 million dollars appears high in relation to current levels of expenditure in the region, except, unfortunately, for military expenditure, this cost is not a large amount for a 25-years public works programme for 50 million and more people in the riparian countries, particularly as the Mekong Project is likely to be the foundation for further development of these countries for decades thereafter. The work from now till the completion of the project will take a generation, and it is the young people of the region, with rising aspirations and expectations, who will carry the responsibility for the realisation of the full potential of the Mekong River and its tributaries.

Eventually the harnessing of the river by the mutual agreement of the countries which share it will open up not merely a new prospect for agriculture and fishing in the whole of Indo-China and north-east Thailand, but also the possibilities of exploiting untapped timber and mineral resources, which in turn could be processed on the spot by the use of the hydro-electric power generated from the dams. Plans for a bauxite-aluminium plant are already prepared.

Processing factories could in turn form nuclei of new towns and vastly accelerate the modernisation of the lives of millions of people. If the plan does succeed, even in part, it will probably go down in history as the most ambitious and imaginative single international development project of the 20th Century.

Ten years ago the Mekong Project seemed but a dream yet already much has been achieved. In a region saddened by conflict, the Mekong Project is a shining example of international co-operation and understanding, and a most reassuring promise of a better future for the people of the region.

The Asian Highway

THE FOUNDATIONS of the Asian Highway were laid thousands of years ago when camel caravans began their long, exhausting journeys from Egypt, Phoenicia and Lydia into Persia and on to India and China. They established the first principles of trade and helped develop primitive agriculture and animal husbandry, raising flocks of sheep and goats. They were the channels through which knowledge was spread and the concepts of civilisation were broadened.

Asia's geography, its physical configuration, its vast deserts, towering mountain ranges and long stretches of plains and rivers—placid and turbulent—have had a decisive influence on the development of caravan routes and the movement of peoples. To penetrate the Himalayan ranges in the north of India, flanked as they are by other mountain ranges, the trade routes of pioneers naturally sought out the mountain passes, most of which are still in use, and followed the rivers. Where they proved to be practical, caravan routes were preferred to the sea, avoiding the greater hazards of the elements and all too frequent piracy.

There is little doubt that the establishment of the great kingdoms of the Middle and Far East from the second millennium B.C. helped in providing and ensuring some measure of security to the trade routes that were gradually developed, but the extent of this security was dependent upon the power of the ruler. The establishment of the Assyrian Empire in the Middle East, the Han Dynasty in China, the rise of Cyrus and of Alexander the Great, the Mauryan Dynasty in India and the large-scale missionary efforts of Asoka, all helped toward stabilising the caravan routes and the trade pattern.

These early routes were further developed during the period 266 B.C.-476 A.D. when the Romans built roads which extended over three continents. They provided good communications and security of travel and thus gave a considerable impetus to trade and commerce. Exchange of commodities was facilitated through Greece and Syria, and the merchant caravans wended their tedious way across the Middle East, over the Khyber Pass, following the road via northern India and the Ganges plain to China.

During the time of the Byzantine Empire, caravan trade with the East continued to flourish. The imperial power of Baghdad improved the trans-territorial routes and provided facilities, such as caravanserais or inns, and relays of mounts for traders, pilgrims and official couriers. Thus they established the great trade routes that joined the East and the West.

Frequent contacts between the countries of Asia resulted in the interchange of knowledge and new techniques. Europe owes many of its technological abilities to Asia: the taming of fire, the baking of pottery, various methods of cultivation and irrigation, weaving, the use of the compass and gun-powder and the rudiments of the rocket. Asian scientists studied the interior of the atom and the infinity of the heavens; they developed the principles of calculations (the decimal system was used in China during the reign of Tsu-Chia, more than 3,000 years ago), the esoteric science of medicine and the use of herbs as drugs, the exploration of the universe and profound systems of philosophy, art and literature.

Even Renaissance Venice was proud to call herself the window to the East. It was only after the Industrial Revolution in Europe (1750's-1850's) that the West gained the material and technical supremacy which completely changed the economies of Europe and North America.

The Industrial Revolution in Europe also brought in its wake unprecedented advancement in transport techniques. The discovery of internal combustion led to the development of the automobile engine and the manufacture of motor vehicles. Simultaneously road building methods were evolved. These discoveries

The above scene is typical
of the construction hazards
constantly encountered
in the mountainous regions
over which the Asian Highway
is being built.
This vast project
is an example of development
which depends upon co-ordinated
action by countries within the area.
Four United Nations
regional economic commissions
afford the opportunity
for working out co-operative
approaches to common
economic problems.

and inventions were gradually extended to the East; the old caravan routes were replaced by modern roads and faster and more comfortable modes of transport began to replace the slow-gaited camel. His tracks gave way to surfaced roads.

During the last few decades both Europe and America have been developing trans-continental arterial ways. The Pan-American Highway which is nearing completion—a 29,000-mile network from Alaska all the way to South America—is a unique example of an international road link in the true sense of the term. This road extends from the Arctic to the Antarctic and crosses the Tropic of Cancer, the Equator and the Tropic of Capricorn. It winds over mountains to a height of some 15,000 feet above sea-level and threads its way through the green jungles of the tropics and across mighty rivers.

The Asian Highway project was initiated in 1958 by ECAFE. It aims at modernising and linking up existing roads into a 34,000 miles network that will span Asia from Turkey and Iraq to the Republic of Vietnam, Singapore and Indonesia. It will service an area of some 2,500,000 square miles with a population of over 600 million.
The picture on the right shows a section of the A-1 route of the Asian Highway, some fifteen miles from Kabul. Construction of this road began about twenty years ago, virtually without any mechanical help.
The road leads to the Khyber Pass.

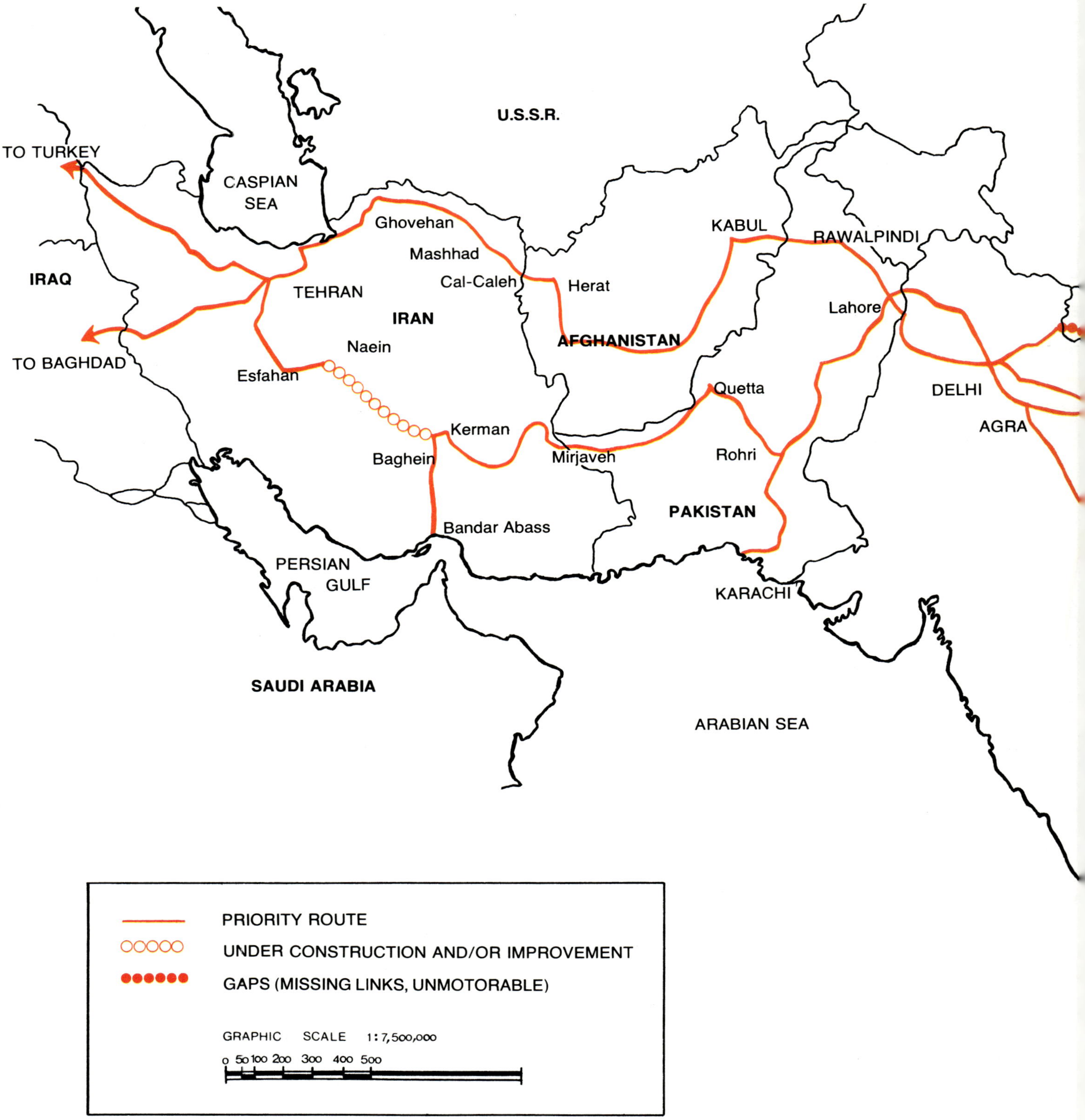
U.S.S.R.
TO TURKEY
CASPIAN SEA
IRAQ
TO BAGHDAD
Ghovehan
Mashhad
Cal-Caleh
TEHRAN
IRAN
Herat
KABUL
RAWALPINDI
Lahore
AFGHANISTAN
Naein
Esfahan
Quetta
DELHI
AGRA
Kerman
Baghein
Mirjaveh
Rohri
PAKISTAN
Bandar Abass
PERSIAN GULF
KARACHI
SAUDI ARABIA
ARABIAN SEA
PRIORITY ROUTE
UNDER CONSTRUCTION AND/OR IMPROVEMENT
GAPS (MISSING LINKS, UNMOTORABLE)
GRAPHIC SCALE 1:7,500,000
0 50 100 200 300 400 500

ASIAN HIGHWAY NETWORK

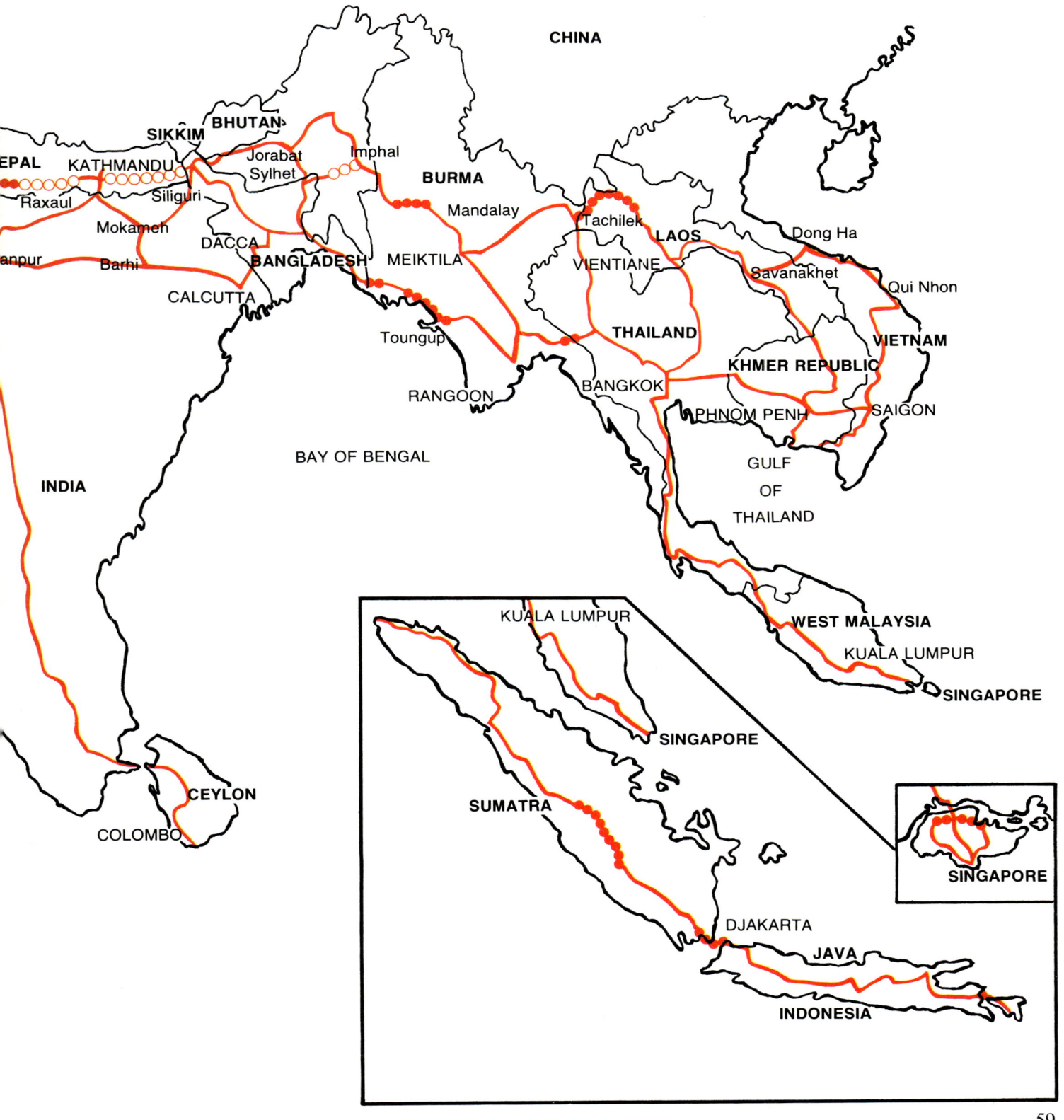

59

After World War II, most countries in Asia emerged as independent nations, and the establishment and development of adequate surface communications for international trade and social and cultural progress was acknowledged as a vital necessity. In the case of landblocked countries such as Afghanistan, Nepal and Laos, it was felt that an international highway network would provide the best means by which trade and commerce might be mutually developed.

The Asian Highway project was therefore drawn up to connect the capitals and important seaports of the countries of Asia and at the same time to provide access to places of historical and religious significance. This project, calling for a network of 60,000 kilometres, covering fourteen countries, grew out of a 1959 decision of the United Nations Economic Commission for Asia and the Far East (ECAFE) and the co-operation of the governments of Afghanistan, Burma, Cambodia (Khmer Republic), Ceylon, India, Indonesia, Iran, Laos, Malaysia, Nepal, Pakistan, Singapore, the Republic of Vietnam and Thailand. The proposal was to establish an international highway system linking the existing main roads all the way between Vietnam, Indonesia and Iran; connecting it to the European Highway network at the border of Iran and Iraq; and then filling in the gaps and bringing the entire route to at least the ECAFE standards laid down for this purpose as the immediate objective. The higher stages of development should follow as traffic increased and funds became available.

The target for the first stage, which coincided with the end of the First United Nations Development Decade in 1970, was to provide at least one through-route from east to west, connecting as many countries as possible and equipped with suitable links to other countries which do not lie along the route. This target has almost been achieved and it is now possible to travel freely from Teheran to Dacca in the western section and from Vientiane to Singapore and beyond to Denpasar in the eastern section by using a sea-ferry service between Singapore and Djakarta.

During the second stage, coinciding with the Second United Nations Development Decade, the main emphasis will be on filling remaining gaps, upgrading substandard sections, and improving road services sufficiently to make highway transport beneficial. Besides good roads, it is important to provide the necessary facilities along the way—such as fuel distribution stations, hotels, workshops, first-aid posts, telecommunication facilities—and to ease the frontier formalities at the borders.

The Role of ECAFE
In 1965, ECAFE set up the Asian Highway Co-ordinating Committee at ministerial level to assist in the development of the project. Three years later, UNDP provided institutional support to the Asian Highway Committee in the form of a Transport Technical Bureau (TTB). ECAFE formulated a plan of action to generate interest and promote financing for the Asian Highway project, which will have far-reaching effects in improving the economic well-being of the peoples of Asia. From 1961-70 an estimated US$900 million was spent on the system by the countries concerned, using their own resources and aid on a bilateral basis. As traffic increases, another US$1,900 million will be needed to build more bridges and upgrade the routes to meet higher standards.

Faster, Better Roads
As has been shown, throughout history, the economic and social development of all continental land-masses has been directly related to the development of its transportation and communications systems.

Most of the movement between Asia and Europe has been by circuitous sea-routes through the Suez Canal, and more recently, around the Cape of Good Hope. The Asian Highway provides a faster and shorter route. Even from the point of view of distances to be traversed, it would be far more economical for commodities to be moved by land-routes between Europe and western parts of Asia than by sea, via the Cape and would also avoid a number of transhipments.

National arterial routes and feeders in each country will assist the expansion of agriculture that is necessary to make the nations of Asia self-sufficient in food-stuffs, give access to the untapped wealth of each country's resources and increase productivity and trade. Provision of the missing links will facilitate the movement of commodities that could not hitherto be profitably transported, and will also open up currently unknown sources of traffic generation. It will permit movements of masses of people in the lower income group. Pilot studies being conducted in Iran and Afghanistan are likely to confirm their feasibility.

In addition, the Asian Highway is helping to develop regional co-operation and creating better understanding among the nations. International contacts are being re-established; closed national doors are being opened.

The routes used in the project were selected by a group of experts representing each member country. From the planning stages just ten years ago, the overall network is now 89 per cent useable by motor vehicles in all weather. Priority route A-1, which stretches from Iran to the Republic of Vietnam and is considered one of the most important routes in the network, is 94 per cent complete.

Links still to be joined are in Burma and Bangladesh, where about six major bridges are to be constructed. Priority Route A-2 which connects Iran and Iraq through to Singapore and, after a ferry-crossing, Indonesia, has missing links only in Nepal, Burma and a short section in India and is nearly complete.

New super-highways are not being built. Existing highways are used where possible. During the past ten years, member countries have given special attention to the Asian Highway routes, incorporating most of the work in their own national plans. Sub-standard portions are being upgraded and missing sections completed. The TTB organises training for highway officials who will pass on their knowledge to the engineers in their own countries. It also helps the countries to develop their testing and quality control laboratories for ensuring economy and quality in building and maintaining roads.

Asian Highway Motor Rallies
Without the improved roads of the Asian Highway the 1970 London to Sydney Marathon would not have been possible. Motor rallies over the completed sections of the Highway will encourage countries to improve their roads and roadside services. Many of the easements to frontier formalities arranged for recent rallies have continued to be in force to benefit international traffic.

Vast Potential
In a recent evaluation of the role of the Asian Highway in regional development and co-operation, ECAFE Executive Secretary, U Nyun commented:

"The Asian Highway will contribute to the expansion of national and international trade, stimulate economic development, promote tourism and, above all, facilitate exchanges among the people of the region. By making it possible for the common man and his family to journey to other countries, it will help to establish close contacts among the peoples of all countries in the region and beyond. The system has thus a vast potential for the betterment of the peoples and for bringing them together in a brotherhood of nations."

On the more level stretches along the Asian Highway route, graders have a simple task preparing the surface for traffic. This picture shows a segment of Priority Route A-2 in the area of Dhonburi, Thailand.

Asian Gods and Creeds

MAN SEEMS ALWAYS to have been preoccupied with the belief that there is an escape from present suffering into a permanent future happiness beyond this world. Religion is the expression of this belief through a system of organised thought and action. Sometimes the system has called for a God, or gods, or for no god at all. But if religion implies the inculcation of precepts generally contributing to the common good and the creation of a gentler human being concerned to lessen the burden of inflicted pain, then the Asian in his setting has never ceased to point the path to virtue.

The living religions divide themselves into two distinct types, the prophetic and the mystical, and all have their origin in Asia with the exception of Mormonism. The first is represented by Judaism, the religion of Israel, and the two great faiths that derive from it, Christianity and Islam. Zoroastrianism arose from the teachings of a prophet in the eastern provinces of ancient Persia, but is professed today by only about 126,000 faithful.

Christianity, the heir to Biblical Israel, has expressed itself more fully in Europe and the West, and now belongs to the Western tradition. Indeed, as it developed through the centuries on the basis of the historical story of God's dealings with a chosen people, it became utterly strange to Asians with their lack of consciousness of God as an external reality. It made little progress to the east of Asia Minor, and the missionary effort in southern and eastern Asia from the 16th Century onward achieved only moderate success.

The mystical tradition has its roots in India. Its non-prophetic, primal form is early Hinduism, from which arose Jainism, and then Buddhism in all its manifestations. Shintoism has intimate ties with Buddhism, but has developed into the national religion of Japan. The final subsidiary streams in the mystical, or immanentist tradition, Confucianism and Taoism, are China's contributions. Taoism certainly represents the same type of religion as the main Indian stream, but Confucianism stands alone, for it is a way of conducting one's worldly life rather than a religion or a belief.

The Buddha is seated cross-legged on a lotus throne with his hands in the teaching gesture. Below is the Wheel of Dharma that he set rolling. The sculpture is from Sarnath, India.

Islam

Islam is the proper name of the religion traditionally called *Mohammedanism* in the West. It is based on the revelations uttered by the Prophet Mohammed in Arabia in the seventh century of the Christian era, and collected shortly after his death in the volume called the *Koran*.

From this work, supplemented by statements and rulings traced back to the Prophet, a system of law and a theology were derived in the following centuries. These combined with elements from other sources to create a distinctive Islamic civilisation, which has continued into modern times. The term *Islam* is applied in the *Koran* to denote the characteristic attitude of its adherents in "committing themselves to the will of Allah." They are Muslims or "Believers."

The religion of Islam was spread by the conquests of the Arabs in the 7th Century A.D. over Western Asia and North Africa, and in the 8th Century A.D. into Central Asia, Sind and Spain. In the 14th Century A.D., it became politically dominant in the Balkans under the Ottoman Turkish sultans, and in India under the sultans of Delhi, and spread, largely by missionary endeavour, into Indonesia and China. On the other hand, it was receding in Spain, from where it was finally expelled at the end of the 15th Century A.D. The total number of Muslims in the world today is estimated at about 493 million.

Refugees from the Chinese invasion of Tibet, these Tibetan Lamas are living in camps set up by the Indian Government.

Mohammed was an ordinary human being charged with a special mission from God, to which he unremittingly devoted himself. He denied supernatural qualities, admitted himself to be liable to error, and disclaimed the power to work miracles.

The *Koran* itself was the sole miracle which demonstrated his prophetic mission, and he was no more than the mouthpiece of its revelation to men. Orthodox Islam has consistently maintained this humanity, and formally rejects any kind of worship addressed to him.

The *Koran* in its finished form is a book of medium size, divided into 114 chapters, called *suras,* and arranged roughly in order of length, from chapters containing more than 200 verses to chapters of three to five short verses at the end.

The first, called The Opening, *al-Fatiha,* is a brief invocation, widely used by Muslims in diverse circumstances, and held by many Muslim divines to encompass all the essentials of Muslim belief;

> In the name of the One God, the Compassionate One, the Merciful.
> Praise be to God, the Lord of the Universe,
> The Compassionate One, the Merciful,
> The Ruler on the Day of Judgement,
> Thee do we worship, and from thee do we seek aid.
> Guide us into the straight path,
> The path of those to whom thou hast shown mercy,
> Not those who have incurred thine anger, nor those who go astray.

Most of the other 113 *suras* are a mosaic of passages of revelation, uttered by Mohammed at different times and on different occasions, somewhat unevenly compiled from oral and written records. When the verses are quoted, they are introduced by the phrase "God has said"—in this way making clear that the Prophet's part has been wholly passive.

The themes stressed in the early passages are God's mercies to man, man's ingratitude and misuse of God's gifts, the evidence of God's creative power in nature, the resurrection of the dead and the Judgement, the joys and bliss of Paradise, the terrors of Hell, the missions of former prophets, and the punishment that followed their rejection by their fellow citizens. Later revelations expand these themes in greater detail.

The religious obligations of prayer, alms, fasting, and pilgrimage are laid down, the basic social institutions of marriage, divorce and inheritance are defined in detail, and a general structure of law explained.

Hinduism
There are probably more than 438 million Hindus in the world, most of them in India. Though they form a large and important religious group, their faith is indefinable in a few words. The Muslim is a man who attempts to follow what he believes to be the teachings of Mohammed, but Hinduism has no such single founder, no prophet.

The Hindu bases his beliefs and way of life on a complex system of faith and practice which has grown up organically in the Indian sub-continent over a period of at least three millennia. So Hinduism is a very ancient religion. It maintains that all living things have souls, which are essentially equal, and are only differentiated through *karma,* or the effect of previous deeds, which conditions the integuments of subtle and gross matter imprisoning the souls, and thus leads to their successive re-births in different types of body. This doctrine of *samsara* has given a distinctive character to much Hindu thought and philosophy.

With the spread of the belief in transmigration, thoughtful Hindus took to leaving their homes and dwelling in austerity in huts in the forests, where they meditated on the problems of the universe, disputed with one another, and often subjected themselves to severe self-mortification in the belief that in this way they might escape from the bonds that tied them to the cycle of birth and death and re-birth. Records of their teachings and discussions are contained in a series of texts called the *Upanishads*.

These texts differ in many particulars, but contain one chief theme, the unity of the individual soul, *atman,* with the one impersonal and absolute world-soul, *Brahman,* which pervades and underlies the cosmos. From the time of the earliest *Upanishads,* perhaps about 600 B.C., to the present day, this has been the basic doctrine of the most important school of Hindu mystical philosophy —the unity of all things in the one Absolute Being, and the necessity of fully realising this unity within the soul of the individual in order to escape from *samsara,* the round of birth and death, and to achieve the highest bliss, in which personality is lost in that which both underlies and transcends it.

In practice, Hinduism is not merely a matter of belief but also of action. For a Hindu of the old-fashioned type, the whole of existence is punctuated at frequent intervals by ritual acts incumbent upon him if he is concerned to maintain the *Dharma,* as his traditional way of life is called. His most important religious acts are performed within the home—with the temple, in Hinduism, not as important as the church in Christianity, the mosque in Islam, or the synagogue in Judaism. In orthodox Hinduism, there is no corporate worship or liturgy in which a congregation takes part. Indeed, domestic ritual is supreme.

Below:
A view of the great temple of Jagannath, Puri, Orissa, built in the 12th Century. It is one of the ceremonial places of worship of Hinduism.

The rites of the Hindu continually remind the devotee that he is a member of an ordered society, in which each member has a part to play. As the family is more important than the individual, and the individual is not a whole man except as part of a family, so families are subsumed in *castes.*

The idea that all men are fundamentally equal is to be found in Buddhism and in the work of mediaeval hymnodists, but is foreign to classical Hinduism. Aryan society is divided into four classes, which were established at the creation of the world, and are absolutely immutable. At the head, the *Brahman* studies and teaches. The *kshatriya,* or nobleman, maintains law and order and preserves the land from foes. The third class, the *vaisya,* comprises the merchants and peasants, and the fourth, the *sudra,* are menials and labourers who serve the three higher classes. This division of function has usually been ideal rather than real, and there are records even of *sudras,* the untouchables, becoming kings—but the system of the four classes has set the tone of Hindu society for as long as three millennia. The four classes are absolutely separate species, normally neither intermarrying nor having meals together. Until well into the last century, no influential body of Hindu opinion seriously criticised such a stratified order of society, but in the last 100 years a new spirit has appeared.

Many of the more effete aspects of the old beliefs have vanished—for example, immolation of the widow, child marriage, and temple prostitution. Animal sacrifice and untouchability are disappearing. Divorce and widow-remarriage are fully legalised, and polygamy is forbidden. Millions of young Hindus are growing up in families where the old taboos and ideas of ritual impurity are unpractised and unknown. Yet they remain true to the ancient wisdom as defined by Mahatma Gandhi, who wrote:

"Some men cling to the forms of the past and the memory of the dead, and they live like the dead. Others hurl themselves into foolish novelties until they plunge into the void. I go forward without losing my way, for I am always coming back to the most ancient traditions through a complete revolution, as with a spinning wheel, a total but natural reversal, willed by God, and coming at its appointed time."

Above:
In this silk painting from the Ming dynasty, Confucius is depicted as a teacher. The painting is one of the treasures in the National Palace Museum, Taiwan.

Buddhism
Buddhism is a name given comparatively recently by the West to the vast synthesis of teachings, now 2,500 years old, attributed to Gautama, the Buddha, sage of the Sakyan clan, and to much that later grew out of them as they spread from India to other lands.

In his own day, the Buddha's teachings were known as *Dharma*—what is right, and as it ought to be. They were also described as *Buddha-vacana,* the word or speech of the Buddha, and again as *Buddha-sasana,* the message, instruction, or dispensation of the Buddha. From its origin down to the present day, this teaching of peace, inner and outer, has made a triumphant appeal, and now probably numbers 177 million followers throughout the world, most in South-east Asia.

"Religion" is perhaps not a very good term to use in connection with Buddhism since it recognises no god, or godhead, no *Isvara* or Brahman in the *Upanishadic* sense. For the Buddhist, life is not a preparation for eternity, but a discipline for governing man's attitude to the here and now, the present condition. If properly and diligently carried out, it will lead on gradually but surely to what is best, the highest good. The "beyond," where it is his aim to arrive and abide, is the supreme form of super-consciousness.

When a meditator achieves this condition of the mind and is deeply and utterly absorbed, the material things are so completely transcended that they cease to attract, or repel, or even impinge on the senses. There is no reaction to them— and final freedom is realised, the only true peace in life.

The Buddha was born about 563 B.C. in the foothills of Nepal into a family called Gautama which belonged to the proud republican clan of the Sakyas who were *kshatriyas,* nobles or warriors, and traced their descent from the Sun. His mother died when he was a week old. Until he was 29, the Buddha lived in luxury, a rich young man, possessed of radiant health and adept in all manner of manly sports. He married, and his wife bore him a son. These bonds might have held him to the world except that he was seized with the urge to seek an escape from man's cycle of birth, age, decay, sorrow, stain and death. He renounced all ties, and went forth on a quest for Enlightenment. He imposed a regime of austerity upon himself, and one night, sitting under a spreading Bo-tree, he felt the wisdom that he sought had come to him.

After a period of hesitation, he was prompted to give his *Dharma* to all who wanted to hear it, and disciples began to form. The yellow robe of the order of monks was adopted. But four centuries were to pass before his sayings, utterances, and discourses came to be written down, the verbal transmission persisting because of an absence of writing material in the India of those days.

Mahayana, or the Greater Vehicle, is the name generally given to those ideas which dominated the latter stages of Buddhistic thought. The Buddhists speak of a "vehicle" because their doctrine, the *Dharma,* is conceived as a raft, or a ship, carrying them across the oceans of this world of suffering to salvation beyond, that is to say, to *Nirvana.* Its adherents call it "greater" in praise of the universality of its tenets and intentions, as opposed to the narrowness of the other Buddhistic schools, which they describe as the *Hinayana,* or the Lesser Vehicle.

At present the *Mahayana* is confined to the northern half of the Buddhist world, and the Buddhists of Nepal, Tibet, China, Korea, and Japan are nearly all *Mahayanists.* The South, on the other hand, is entirely dominated by the *Theravadins,* one of eighteen traditional sects of the *Hinayana,* and their form of Buddhism is the national religion of Ceylon, Burma and Thailand.

Chinese Buddhism evolved as an expression of India's cultural expansion between A.D. 150 and 1000 when contacts between China and India were significant.

It began with the study of the *Sutras,* the collected aphorisms of the Buddha, translated into Chinese from the original Sanskrit.

It was a long time before the radical differences between Buddhism and the native Taoism were clearly understood, and Chinese sects emerged when various groups selected different *Sutras* to represent the *Dharma* in quintessence. The devotees of Chinese Buddhism have exemplified the varieties of religious experience on a wide scale. It counts many saintly men among its followers, both past and present. Its monuments in literature and art are imposing. It is both the most distinguished offshoot of Indian Buddhism, and the parent of Vietnamese, Korean and Japanese Buddhism.

A Buddhist monk, Khantipalo, is collecting his early morning food from a generous alms-giver in Bangkok.

Above:
Crowds attend a ritual ceremony of the Shinto religion at a temple in Japan.
Below:
The monument in the centre is the Ka'ba, sacred to Moslems everywhere. It is the dominant feature of the Sacred Mosque at Mecca.

Shinto, Confucianism, Taoism

Shinto is the national religion of Japan, and adherents around the world number about 70 million. Neither its age nor origin is known. It began as a form of nature worship, and even today the chief deity is Amaterasu, the Sun Goddess.

The highest virtue in Shinto is to obey the deity. Early Shinto was gradually absorbed and superseded by Buddhism which reached the country by way of China.

In the 18th Century, Shinto was made into the religion of the state, and the cult of the emperor as a direct descendant of the Sun Goddess became its chief feature.

State Shinto was banned at the end of World War II when General Douglas MacArthur stripped the Emperor Hirohito of his divinity, but Sect Shinto, the old form, still exists.

What is called in the West "Confucianism" is not a religion, but the traditional view of life and code of manners of the Chinese gentry for 2,000 years up to the revolution of 1911. Confucius was a philosopher who lived between 550 and 478 B.C. He was not the founder of a religion, merely a gentleman whose sense of what is done and what is *not* done has been taken as standard by his countrymen ever since.

Confucianism is the system of cosmology, politics, and ethics derived from the sayings of Confucius, and solidifying during the Han dynasty between 206 B.C. and 220 A.D. It regarded the emperor and the hierarchy of officials as divinely appointed, and social relations as governed by set rules of conduct. The Chinese who asked deeper questions than how to behave as a filial son or a loyal minister, and who required a mystical philosophy or a religion, turned to Taoism or Buddhism.

This did not mean that they ceased to be Confucian. Unless they retired from the world, they continued to direct their public lives as Confucians, and their private lives as Taoists or Buddhists. Such a condition would seem surprising if one imagines that it was like being a Christian or a Muslim at the same time. But it was much more like being both a Christian and a gentleman.

Confucianism has no official place in China today, but Chinese who continue to follow the teachings of the Sage, in so far as they can be applied within People's China, Hong Kong, Macau and Taiwan, number about 371 million.

Taoism is both a religion and a philosophy, with 54 million devotees. It came gradually to the fore in China during the period of the warring states between 453 and 221 B.C. The religion was originally a system of conduct based on the writings attributed to the philosopher Lao Tse, who lived in the 6th Century B.C. Later it came to be invested with magical beliefs and a large pantheon.

It will probably always be an integral part of the Chinese way of life—like Confucianism—despite the indifference of irreligious governments. The reason is that Taoism makes a direct appeal to the innate love of the Chinese for the beauty of their landscape, and the spirit of veneration which the reflection of this beauty calls forth in the soul.

In its fundamental conception, Taoism was a worship of Nature outside and within man, and an attempt to bring both into harmony with each other. Perfection, according to the ancients, was not to obstruct the way of Nature, but to give oneself completely to it. In this manner, it reached a very high ethical standard, and brought out the best qualities in the Chinese character.

The Nomad Tribes of Asia

TOURIST BROCHURES are often misleading. The South-east Asia they so often depict is one of colourful temples in cities swarming with people; of green paddy fields, of elaborate state ceremonies and broad streams lined with ramshackle buildings providing passage for long strings of heavily laden barges. Yet this impression is true of only a part of South-east Asia. A glance at any relief map confirms that virtually all of Laos, a large part of Burma, and most of the northern provinces of Thailand are coloured brown and yellow, indicating country elevated up to 10,000 feet above the green of the plains. In this territory the land is too rough for paddy fields, the streams too narrow and rapid for the passage of commercial traffic, and the only settlements are small bamboo villages perched high above steep valleys. The rest is silent except for the calls of wild animals and birds.

The hills of mainland South-east Asia begin abruptly at the margins of the wide alluvial plains of the Irrawaddy, Salween, Ping and Mekong Rivers. They extend all the way north to the mighty peaks of the Himalayas, through northern India, Tibet, and southern China.

Over a millennium ago the Thai and Burmese peoples moved slowly southwards over these hills, finally settling in the alluvial valleys of the great rivers, displacing less forceful people than themselves, founding kingdoms and cities and establishing traditions. The people who now live in the hills, like the Thai and Burmese before them, migrated slowly southwards through the hills. Their migrations were compelled by their practice of slash and burn agriculture—and by countless wars and revolts in which they have been involved.

These people belong to a score or more of different ethnic groups, or tribes as they are sometimes called: they are the Chin, Kachin, Karen, Meo, Yao, Lahu, Lisu and Akha. Many live out their lives entirely in the hills, seldom venturing to dusty market towns in the lowlands. When they do, to sell the produce of the hills—animal skins, rope bark, honey and wild nuts—and to buy manufactured goods like flashlights, fabrics and enamel bowls, they are immediately distinguishable from the lowland Thai, Burmese and Laotians with whom they rub shoulders. The contrast lies in their colourful dress. But remove their elaborate costumes and substitute the "black pyjamas" characteristic of the lowland folk, and it would be difficult to tell which were the Thai and Burmese, and which were the Karen and Meo among the crowds thronging the market place. For in physical character there is little to identify the hill men: the uplanders are a little stockier, perhaps, but then that is to be expected, for lifetimes of trudging up and down steep paths, often carrying heavy loads, tend to develop broad shoulders and muscular calves.

The uplanders one occasionally finds in the market places of the valleys speak Thai, Lao or Burmese only haltingly, for these are not their native languages. They have their own tongues, often as different from one another as Turkish is from English. Some languages are cognate to the major Chinese languages; others are more closely related to either Thai or Burmese. Others again remain a taxonomical puzzle for linguists. Even if one is equipped with ability to speak one of the tribal languages, communication remains difficult in the villages of other linguistic groups—and one might encounter several of these in the space of a short day's walk. The difficulty is partly resolved by the existence of linguae francae of narrower or wider currency.

The most strikingly obvious badges of tribal identity, however, are the costumes, which are as diverse as the languages of the hills. Pwo Karen women wear a red ankle length skirt which distinguishes them from their unmarried sisters, who are attired in a long white smock; Akha women wear thigh high skirts and elaborate headpieces decorated with silver rupee coins and tufts of gibbon fur.

In a Karen village a white chicken is sacrificed to appease the spirit of the rice fields.

Meo men wear black skull caps topped with red pom-poms, while Lahu men wear a simple turban. Chin and Karen men are elaborately tatooed while Yao men prize an unblemished skin. The variety would stock the wardrobe of the costume manager running quite a large theatre.

In their customs, too, there is diversity. Meo men often have several wives at once, while among the Karen, not only is monogamy the norm, but remarriage following the death of a spouse is not usually permitted. The Yao have elaborate rites to celestial and ancestral spirits, patterned on the Chinese model, in which delicate paintings and carefully inscribed prayer books, scarcely the product of a barbarous folk, are used. Other peoples placate the spirits of the earth, fire and water for bountiful crops, and cure sickness by luring wandering souls back with offerings of rice whisky and the aroma of simmering stew, made from the carcasses of sacrificial chickens and pigs.

Although the mythology of the Ramayana, and concepts about cosmological order which are peculiarly Indian are faintly echoed in the folklore and religious philosophy of the hills peoples, Buddhism, the faith of the lowland Thai and Burmese, is not a widespread influence. There are none of the intricately decorated temples nor saffron robed monks, common emblems of South-east Asian culture, to be found in the bamboo villages of the hills.

Despite the tremendous diversity of language, dress and custom, the rough terrain of the hills compels a similar livelihood upon all who live in them, a livelihood which separates them as a whole from the lowlanders. The lowlanders flood their riceland each year, using dykes and canals to control the flow, plough the soft mud and then transplant rice seedlings from nursery beds. The waters carry mineral-bearing silt, and harbour algae which release nutrients to the crop.

This technique permits the lowlanders to plant the same field year after year—but it is not available to the hills peoples. Their domain is too rough to be irrigated: one cannot flood steep hillsides. Consequently they clear and burn their fields in the forest, sowing rice seeds on the hard, steep ground and harvest when the monsoon rains cease. This technique, called "shifting" or "slash and burn" agriculture but now referred to as "swidden agriculture" (from the old English meaning a burnt clearing) in the specialist literature, has been condemned in the past by some conservationists.

Foresters have claimed that millions of acres of valuable timber are destroyed annually by swidden cultivators. Soil scientists have argued that the technique causes loss of topsoil through erosion. Legislators, particularly in colonial Burma, tried to contain swidden cultivators in specified zones; yet, ironically, enforcement of such laws accelerated the loss of soil and timber by interfering with customary methods of field rotation: swidden cultivation requires a lot of land before it can be productive to the farmers and sparing of natural resources.

Normally, swidden cultivators move to new areas as soon as yields start to decline and before soil damage occurs. Over-cropping only accelerates weed growth and loss of soil nutrients—which affects the swidden cultivators more directly and severely than anyone else. The viability of swidden agriculture depends on long periods of fallow between successive croppings, for regenerating forest restores nutrients to the soil in much the same way as the silt and algae provide sustenance for the rice of the lowland farmer.

Research is now showing that swidden agriculture need not have the disastrous consequences formerly attributed to it. Nevertheless, it is a technique which will support only a low density population. In parts of upland north Thailand the population is now around twenty persons per square mile, yet hunger is being experienced. Flying over such country, it is sometimes hard to believe

A feast of chilli and beef stew is prepared over a wood fire prior to the arrival of visitors to a Karen village.

that a state of overpopulation exists. Yet it does, and while the population is increasing at an explosive rate, the hard truth remains that the hills peoples have no alternative means of livelihood.

In the past, such a state of affairs would have prompted further migration to new tracts of forest. But the hills are now virtually all occupied by one tribe or another, and there can be little further migration; at the same time, the dense population of Thai and Burmese in the valleys rules out most possibilities of settlement in the lowlands.

Most hills peoples are subsistence cultivators, selling very little of their produce. The trails which wind over the hills are steep, allowing passage for only a man with a load on his back, or at the most a pack laden pony. And it is a long way from the high bamboo villages to the crowded lowland market towns. Thus many of the avenues which are open to the Thai, Lao and Burmese for selling cash crops are closed to the uplanders. Tobacco, peanuts, vegetables and surplus rice are too bulky and heavy for the hills peoples to carry to market.

Nevertheless, there is one crop for which parts of the uplands are uniquely suited, which is at once profitable and easy to carry—opium. In November the crests of the ridges at between 3,500 and 5,000 feet altitude, inhabited usually by Meo, Yao, Lisu, Akha or Lahu are covered with the white and red blooms of painstakingly cultivated opium poppies. When the petals start to drop it is time for the harvest, and groups of brightly costumed women and children work through the fields, carefully slitting the pods of the plants, returning the next day to scrape the sap—raw opium—which has oozed from the slits.

Raw opium gathered in this fashion in north Thailand alone is estimated by the United Nations to total around 150 tons annually. And the amount tapped in the whole upland area we are considering is estimated to aggregate a staggering 1,000 tons per annum. Opium cropping is illegal in Thailand, but prevention

A proud Meo mother wears many silver neckbands to signify the wealth of her family.

A bamboo and thatch Karen village nestles in a sheltered valley in northern Thailand near the Burma border.

is impossible in the inaccessible hills. It has been claimed that the whole economy of Laos would collapse if production ceased. The Burmese authorities do not have sufficient control over the upland areas to implement any restrictive policy.

From the grower, opium passes to Chinese traders, who have developed a far flung marketing network over the hills. By devious routes the product finds its way into the world market and may ultimately—in one of its refined forms, as morphine or heroin—be consumed by a drug addict in New York, Sydney or Hong Kong. The Meo or Yao farmer in the hills of Thailand may profit by US$15 per kilogramme of raw opium: by the time the drug has reached New York in the form of heroin, it may be worth more than US$50,000 per kilogramme.

This may seem but small profit to the tribesman, yet it is sufficient to allow Meo, Yao, Lahu and the other opium cultivating peoples, to live at a standard above that of the tribes who grow only rice. Most profits are invested in beaten silver neck pieces, worn by both men and women, the number of neck pieces adorning an individual being an index of his prosperity. He may use his ornaments in many transactions, ranging from paying for his son's bride, to the purchase of livestock.

Nevertheless, in the hills of South-east Asia, as elsewhere, opium exacts its toll. Addiction rates in some villages are in excess of 30 per cent of the population, violence between rival traders is endemic, and corruption of government officials frequent. As one commentator aptly remarked, "the only attractive things about the opium business are the fields of flowering poppies".

The peoples of the hills are often referred to as the "tribal minorities" of Thailand, Burma and Laos, yet this label is misleading in at least two respects. Firstly, although no embracing census has ever been carried out, it is certain that the uplanders constitute a sizeable proportion of the South-east Asian population. In Laos they dominate the Laotians in numerical, if not in political terms. In Burma they are about 40 per cent of the nation's population. In Thailand they are only about 3 per cent of the total population, yet occupy about 60 per cent of the northern area of the country, which is mainly upland.

A second consideration is that talk about "minorities" often connotes inferior status in relation to a dominant "majority" as much as a purely statistical fact. The Aborigines are, in these terms, a minority in Australia, as are the Indians in the United States.

The hills peoples of South-east Asia simply do not fit into such a category. They are proud, independent people who consider national frontiers of little consequence, and who generally resist the efforts of national governments to assert their authority. They are not warlike people, and are at first inclined to move deeper into the hills when confronted with a direct military threat. Yet although divided among themselves, they have at various times in the past been able to muster enough men and arms to become a force to be reckoned with. At various times in Burmese history, hills peoples have brought oppressive lowland dynasties to their knees. More recently, Karen forces almost took Rangoon immediately after World War II, and the Meo have been involved in bitter fighting on both sides of the present Indo-China conflict. At the same time, the Naga are in full revolt against the Indian Government across the Burmese frontier. The lowland civilisations, for their part, have not always handled the uplanders gently, and revolts have often been ruthlessly crushed.

Yet despite chronic antagonism between hill and valley peoples, there have been long periods of peace in which connections between the two have flourished, when trade developed, and intermarriage occurred. Such contacts have contributed a great deal to the diversity and richness of South-east Asian culture.

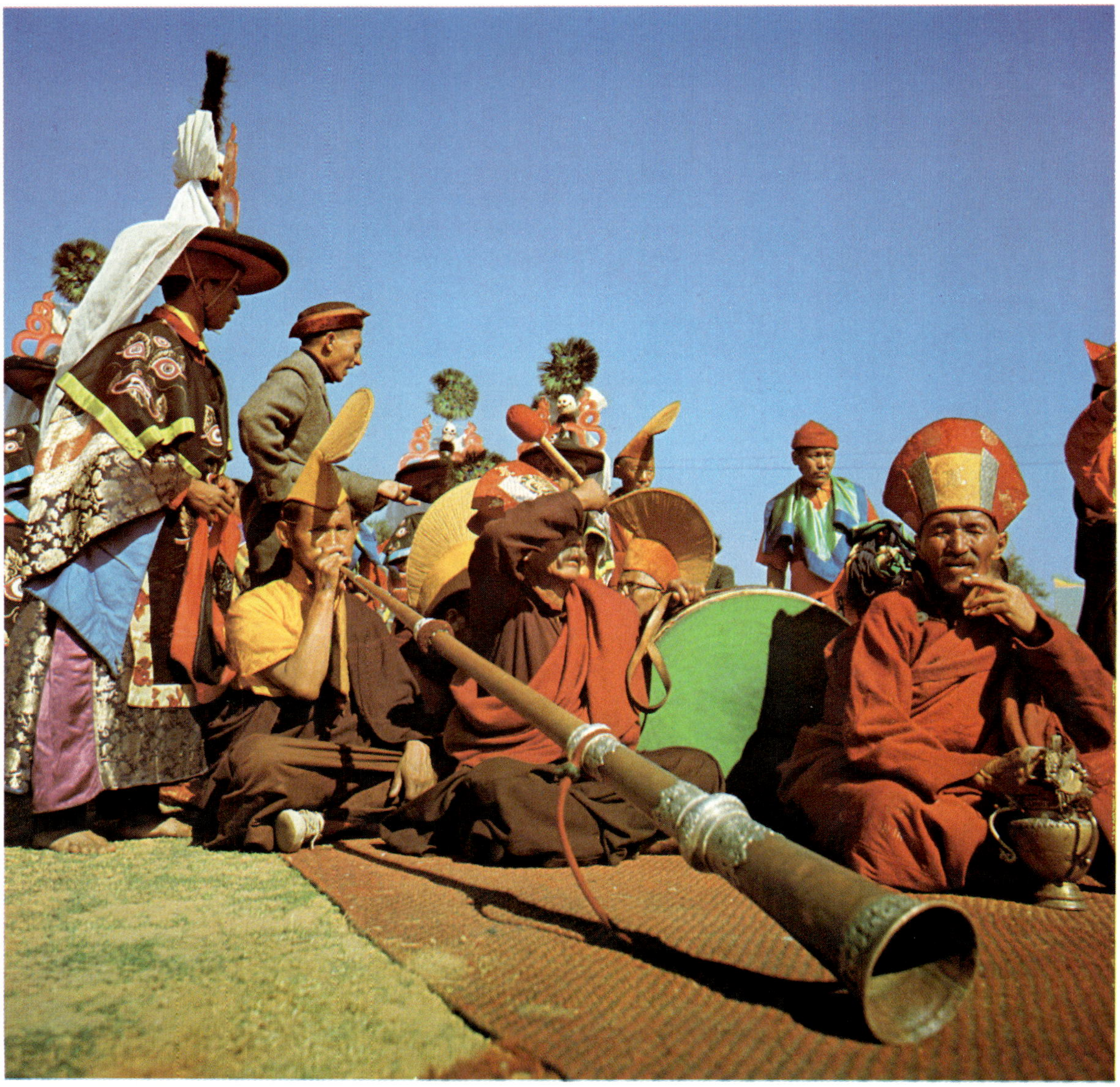

Kingdom of
BHUTAN

LEGEND

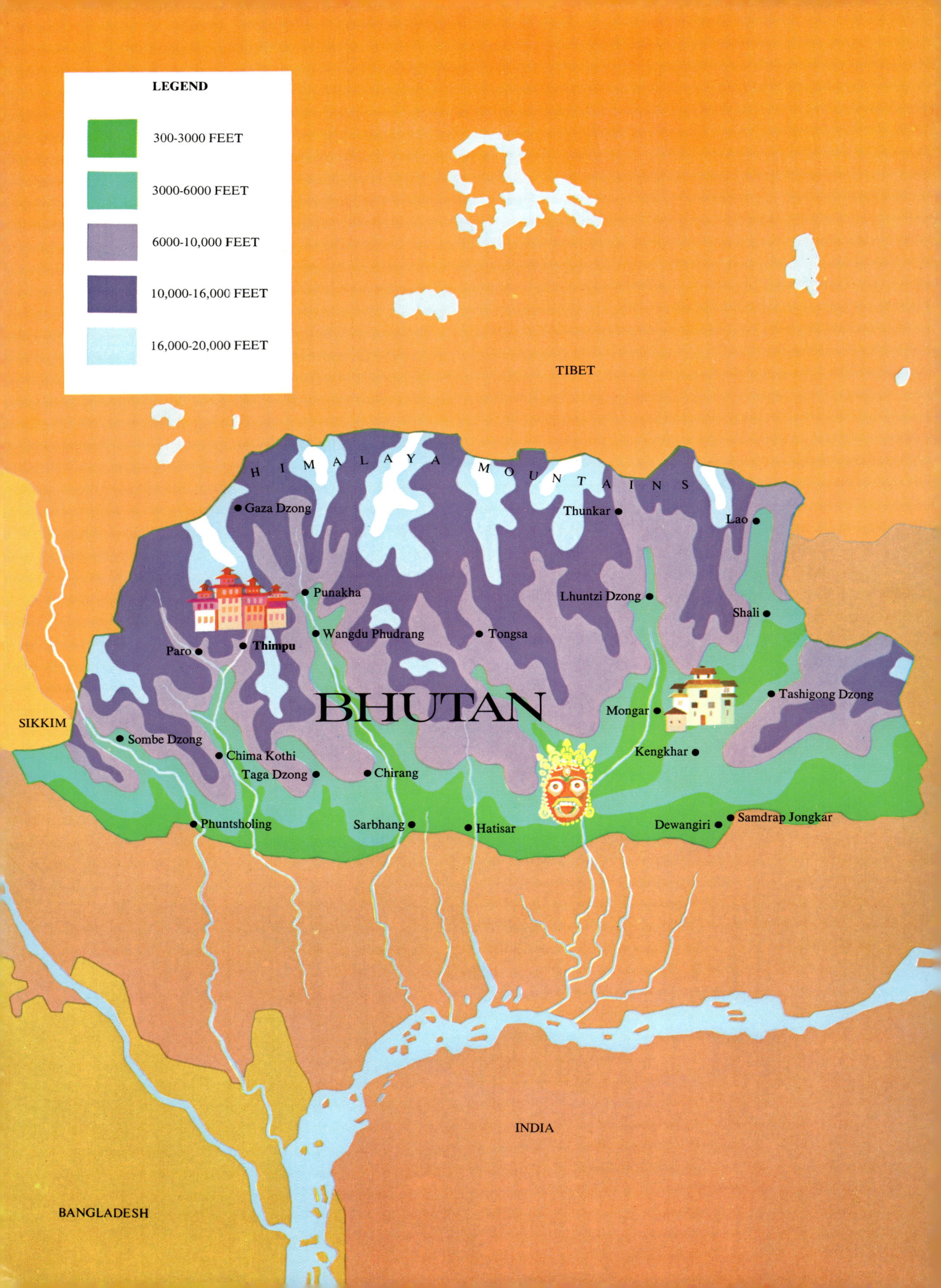

- 300-3000 FEET
- 3000-6000 FEET
- 6000-10,000 FEET
- 10,000-16,000 FEET
- 16,000-20,000 FEET

TIBET

HIMALAYA MOUNTAINS

- Gaza Dzong
- Thunkar
- Lao
- Punakha
- Lhuntzi Dzong
- Shali
- Paro
- Wangdu Phudrang
- Tongsa
- Thimpu

BHUTAN

- Mongar
- Tashigong Dzong
- SIKKIM
- Sombe Dzong
- Kengkhar
- Chima Kothi
- Taga Dzong
- Chirang
- Phuntsholing
- Sarbhang
- Hatisar
- Dewangiri
- Samdrap Jongkar

INDIA

BANGLADESH

Bhutanese women carrying wood for the family fires.

Bhutan

AREA:

18,000 square miles.

LOCATION:

Between 26°45' and 28°00' north latitude and 89°00' and 92°30' east longitude. Bordered on the north by Tibet, on the west by Sikkim and the Chumbi valley of Tibet, and on the east and south by the Indian states of Assam and West Bengal.

TOPOGRAPHY:

The southern zone comprises plains and abrupt mountains between 3-8,000 feet above sea-level; flat, wide valleys and more gradual slopes in the central section; in the far north, the fir and pine forests and snow-capped mountains of the Himalayas rising between 11 and 24,000 feet. Bhutan is a land of many rivers, notably the Amo-chu, Wong-chu, Ma-chu and Manas. A north-south spur of the Himalayas, the Black Mountain Range, divides the country both climatically and ethnographically.

CLIMATE:

The southernmost zone is hot and humid. The middle sector is cooler and in the high Himalayas temperatures rarely rise above freezing point.

RAINFALL:

Annual rainfall up to 300" in the south. In the east, the monsoon currents extend as far as the snow-line; in the west, rain is confined to the southern and central zones.

THE PEOPLE:

To the east the people have greater affinity with the Assam hill-dwellers, a stocky, dark-coloured race, while to the west they retain many more of the Tibeto-Mongoloid features.

POPULATION:

Last census, 1963: 850,000. The figure is now thought to be around the one million mark.

Valleys of Seclusion

BHUTAN is an independent state in the eastern Himalayas, lying between Tibet and India. It is about 18,000 square miles in extent, and its high southern valleys and the Tibetan plateau to the north have made it one of the most difficult countries to reach. The King, Jigme Dorji Wangchuk, (which translated means "Wielder of Fearless Thunderbolt Powers") is making determined efforts to end its isolation.

The country is divided into three distinct tracts, the first being about 30 miles broad, consisting of outer hill ranges rising from the plains of India. They are subject to a heavy rainfall of about 300 inches annually, and dense vegetation is the result.

The second, or central tract, is about 40 miles in width comprising a number of valleys lying at an elevation of between 3,500 and 10,000 feet above sea-level. The slopes of the mountains are gentle, large areas are under cultivation, and there the bulk of the population lives.

The third, or northern tract, is made up of rugged mountains and snowy peaks rising to 24,000 feet. These are part of the great Himalayas. Alpine valleys at heights of 18,000 feet are frequented only by graziers and their herds of cattle.

As is natural in a country rising from low valleys, through central highlands to perpetual snow, every variation of climate is encountered. The lower areas are saturated with moisture, and are hot and steamy.

Sunshine bathes the central districts, and there is a temperate coolness, but the extreme north is inhospitably held in the grip of frost and ice.

Bhutan has a population of about 1 million. The chief race consists of the Bhotias, who come from Tibet. The name Bhutan itself is a derivative of the Indian name Bhotanta, meaning "the end of Bhot": that is, Tibet.

The people speak a dialect of Tibetan, and their religion is a form of Buddhistic lamaism that used to be practised in Tibet.

In certain areas, the Bhotias have been supplanted by Nepalese immigrants who are such thrifty cultivators that they take up wastelands and convert them to tilth. But they are not allowed to carry their industrious labour beyond an agreed point, to avoid bringing the grazing lands of the Bhotias under the plow. Some of the population appear to have affinities with the Assamese and eastern frontier tribes.

Their stature is smaller, their complexion darker, and their features more diminutive than those of the Bhutanese to the north, who are big, burly men with the typical physiognomy of the Mongolian. The chief places and centres of population are Thimpu, Punaka, Trashi-chod-zong, Tongsa, Paro, and Ha.

The lamas or priests are the religious chiefs and temporal authorities under the King. They are regarded with reverence by the people, most of whom used to consider them endowed with supernatural powers. There are nine provinces under eight such chiefs. They live as feudal barons, and have retainers armed with helmets, swords and shields made of leather, which is plentiful in the country. Their forts are like mediaeval castles, dominating the valleys. Called *jongs,* they are sometimes so vast as to be out of all proportion to the humble little huts belonging to the peasantry clustered below them.

The monasteries are also of great size, and frequently picturesquely situated. The Tatsang monastery, for example, is built on the face of a perpendicular crag more than 2,000 feet high, and appears literally to be clinging to the rock. A distinctive feature of the main altars in the chapels of monasteries is that they are supported by a pair of elephant's tusks.

The ordinary houses have a quaint resemblance to chalets in the Swiss Alps, with wooden walls and roofs, and projecting eaves. No ironwork is used, and even the doors turn on wooden hinges.

Due to fire and accident, little evidence remains of Bhutan's early history. Even places, names, dates and events of periods as late as the 16th and 17th Century are disputed by various sources. It is a difficult task, therefore, to outline with detail and precision its early history.

Although Bhutan achieved some political unity during the rule of the exceptional Shabdung Nawang Namgyal in the 16th Century, the country was again divided by warring factions after his death. At this time, the state was ruled by both a temporal head (the Deb Raja) and a spiritual head (the Dharma Raja). The election of the Deb Raja, who was supposed to be chosen by vote of the principal officers of the nation, became more and more a matter of the nomination of the stronger of the country's two provincial governors or penlops. Thus a country already divided by its geography was again divided by the question of its leadership. The ruling powers of the Deb Raja lasted only as long as the powers of the penlop who appointed him.

Above: A young Bhutanese girl with bright, characteristic features.

Left: A musical performance with traditional musical instruments.

Opposite page:
The Bhutanese are famous for their prowess with bow and arrow.

Thus Bhutan was already approaching a state of political chaos when the first British officials made contact in 1772, with the aim of assessing her potential markets and exploring a route from Bhutan to Lhasa. A number of missions followed, their frequency increasing after the border-disputes of the Anglo-Burmese War in 1826. Each successive visit elicited a more negative response from the Bhutanese than the one that went before.

India assumed the political and military protection of Bhutan as a legacy from its own era as a British colony. The Bhutanese, always a warrior race, used to descend on India to plunder, massacre and carry away British subjects as slaves, and it was not until the first half of the 20th Century that Bhutan was finally compelled to abandon these tactics. A treaty in 1865 provided that disputes between Bhutan and Sikkim or Cooch Behar should be referred to the British *raj*. These provisions were amplified by a treaty concluded in 1910 by which the Bhutanese Government agreed to be guided by the advice of the British *raj* in regard to its external affairs, while the British in India undertook that they would not interfere in the internal affairs of Bhutan. An annual allowance of Rs. 100,000 a year to be paid to Bhutan by Britain was then agreed upon.

This treaty disposed of claims advanced by China, and provided Bhutan with a safeguard against Chinese aggression. In the same year, the Chinese Government formally claimed Bhutan as a feudatory, but was informed by Britain that Bhutan was independent of China and that its external relations were under the British *raj,* who would not permit China to exercise influence in Bhutan.

India stepped into Britain's shoes after her own independence, and in 1949 concluded a treaty with Bhutan by which the annual subsidy was raised to Rs. 500,000, and ceded to Bhutan the territory known as Dewangiri.

In 1970, the country's relations with India became closer following visits to the Kingdom by the President of India and the Indian Foreign Minister. President V.V. Giri's trip was the first to Bhutan by an Indian head of state. The King, Jigme Dorji Wangchuk, used the occasion to dispel a widely-held Bhutanese suspicion that India was blocking the country's efforts to join the United Nations. His Majesty noted that India was not only in full agreement with these efforts, but had also decided to sponsor Bhutan's application. Three ranking Bhutanese officials then joined the Indian delegation to the United Nations, a move designed to secure support for the application. It was presented at the 1971 sessions of the General Assembly, and Bhutan was admitted as a member nation.

There have been no incursions by the Chinese army from across the border in Tibet, but in some quarters the threat is regarded as real. For this reason, the King is committed to keeping his army well-trained and equipped.

The Indian Border Roads Organisation (DANTAK) has completed more than 625 miles of roads through strategic areas, a vital contribution as there are no trains and no air travel to Bhutan, but only one main road. The best way to reach the Kingdom is to fly 300 miles from Calcutta to the Indian town of Hashimara, just south of Bhutan. From the border, 760 feet above sea-level, it is seven-hour winding jeep ride up and around lofty Himalayan peaks and clouds to Thimpu, the misty 7,500 ft. high capital.

The road, completed in 1962, is a major improvement over the old mule trails that took seven days to negotiate. Before the road was built, the only wheels said to have turned in Bhutan were the Buddhist prayer wheels.

The hardest part of any journey to the country is obtaining permission—both from Bhutan and India—to enter it. Most requests for visits are placed before the Ruler himself, and he is rarely in a position to give approval for ordinary tourists.

During a visit to New Delhi in April 1971, the King said he was personally anxious to welcome tourists, but at the moment his country lacked facilities to accommodate them. Moreover, he feels that for the time being, rather than build hotels that could bring in more foreign exchange and tourists he would prefer to construct schools.

The Indian Government has the final veto, since it must give clearance for visitors to travel along its militarily-sensitive north-eastern border, normally barred to foreigners, which remains the only passageway to Bhutan. But the opening up of the country to the rest of the world is one of the King's objectives, and membership of the United Nations is regarded by him as a manifestation of approval of such a policy.

The King has a reputation in India, and among his own people, as an enlightened ruler intent on reducing his once absolute powers and the modification of the lamasery system so as to enable it to fit in more with the tempo of modern life. Since he succeeded his father to the throne in 1952, he has abolished serfdom, started a national education system, formed an eight-member royal advisory council—to which the King nominates only one member—and set up a national assembly that now has the power to dismiss him with a two-thirds vote.

The King is concerned that the teeming animal life in the east of the country shall be preserved, for here is the haunt of the elephant, the rhinoceros, the tiger, the leopard, the bison, the mythun, the sambur, the cheetah and the barking deer. The snow regions are the habitat of the bears and musk deer. Pheasants, jungle fowl and other small game abound throughout the Kingdom. Bhutan has also been long famous for its small but sturdy and strong horses or ponies, about 13 hands high, which are admirably suited for rough mountain work. They are called *tanghan*, probably from a Tibetan name for this kind of horse, and are mentioned in the *Ain-i-Akbari* of the 16th Century. In the treaty of 1774 between the East India Company and Bhutan, it was stipulated that the King should pay an annual tribute of five "Tangan horses".

The chief industries of Bhutan are metal-work, the weaving of strong and durable cloth, fine basketwork and matting. The Bhutanese are expert joiners, and excel in working silver, iron, copper and brass.

A five-year development plan was carried out from 1966 to 1971 at an estimated total expenditure of Rs. 200 million. About 95 per cent of all external trade is with India, with the main exports in 1963-64 consisting of timber worth Rs. 1.25 million, and coal Rs. 220,000.

Bhutan has only one source of foreign exchange: its colourful stamps that earn about US$130,000 a year.

Bhutan is a Buddhist Kingdom and everyday life is closely bound to religious beliefs.

Every district has a monk centre and each village has a monastery. Each district holds a traditional festival called the *"Tsechu"* conducted by the monks. It lasts three to four entire days and all the villagers take part. As part of the celebration the people go to monasteries to worship and burn butter lamps. Every month the day of the full moon and the day of the empty moon (when no moon is visible) are observed as holy days, and on these days the old men and women again go to the monasteries to worship and burn lamps. Sometimes the worshipping and lamp-burning is done at home because each Bhutanese home has a special room set aside for this purpose.

In addition to the special ceremonies the old men and women count their beads every

Above:
Bright colours and ornate head-dresses are a feature of
Bhutan ceremonials.

morning and every evening. They repeat the sentence "Om Mani Padme Hung" which means, in Sanskrit, "Jewels in the lotus".

Great respect is shown towards monks, educated persons, officials and elders. When a person who considers himself inferior meets one of these superior people he faces him and bows down towards the ground with his two hands placed side by by side, palms upwards—a ritual which signifies "you are so great and holy that I am touching your lotus feet". If an inferior person meets a superior whom he does not know he will stand at the side of the road until the superior has passed by.

When a child is born in a Bhutanese home there are no visitors allowed for the first three days. On the third morning the head of the household invites a monk to the house. The monk conducts prayers which last about two hours. He sprinkles water all over the room and surroundings and blesses the child with a drop of holy water.

All things which the holy water touches are considered to have been blessed.

When the priest has finished his service, friends and relatives come to see the baby and bring gifts. The householder offers visitors buttered tea, sweetened rice and drink. The drink is prepared three to four months before the birth of the child and is called "mother's medicine wine". The next day, or on the earliest convenient day, an astrologer is called in to read the child's horoscope and to give predictions about his future. He gives the child a name according to his date of birth.

In the Bhutan calendar there are twelve years: the year of the Rat, the Bull, the Tiger, the Rabbit, the Dragon, the Serpent, the Horse, the Sheep, the Monkey, the Bird, the Dog and the Hog. These twelve years make a round of five cycles which total 60 years and have for the Bhutanese the same significance as a century. It is part of Bhutan's tradition that whenever possible the monks give the child his first haircut and a religious name will be given to him on that occasion. The significance of this is that when the Lord Buddha ran away from his palace in search of peace he first cut his hair and then sought a teacher.

Bhutanese children commence their schooling at five to six years of age. They may be admitted to either English language schools or the traditional monastery schools. In the monasteries the monks teach traditional dancing, customs and manners, reading, writing, grammar, literature and religion.

Instruction is free as are all the services provided by the monasteries.

The most popular sport in the country is archery, which is an essential part of every festival. Competitions are usually held between districts and they last for at least two days. The competitions may be purely for entertainment or sometimes betting takes place. During archery matches the women of each competing district perform a great variety of dances and sing songs, hoping thereby to spur the men on to greater efforts. The bows and arrows are made of bamboo painted in many colours. A great variety of food is served by the women on the sports ground. Discus throwing, with a discus made of stone, is another popular game, especially with children and monks.

Marriage is a very simple ceremony arranged by the parents or, sometimes, by the couple themselves. Similarly, a divorce is fairly easily obtained but the husband must support the children and pay compensation to his wife. If a woman leaves her husband for another man then the second husband must pay compensation to the first husband, according to the number of children and the years of the first marriage.

With the permission of his first wife, a man may take a second wife.

There are ten members in the average family. The young married couple usually settle in the home of the parents of either the wife or husband. In either case, the children in a family are entirely responsible for their parents' well-being, although the parents choose which child they want to look after them. In one of the provinces of central Bhutan there are 60 to 100-odd members in one family but they are segregated into groups of fifteen to twenty.

These groups live a nomadic existence but each in turn stays in the home of the parents for four to five years to look after the property and conduct any official business which may be necessary. At change-over time the entire family of up to 100 gathers in the parents' home to worship together and to take part in the handing over of the property to the new householders. The departing group holds a reception and the new residents give a farewell party to which all friends and neighbours are invited. Each family group presents something to the new householders. Occasionally members of a group die before it is their turn to be householders and this is regarded as being very unlucky.

Bhutanese women are very hard working. They do all the housework, look after the cattle and weave their own textiles. The men work in the fields and are fine carpenters, wood workers and bamboo craftsmen. Most farmers do not wear shoes but bamboo hats are normal.

Agriculture is the main industry. Many crops are grown but the staple food in Bhutan is red rice, the most popular variety grown in the country. With the rice, at least one curry, a curd or *Dau* salad is served. The country people do not like powdered spices. The chilli, which is absolutely essential with every Bhutanese dish, should be unground. Homemade beer is brewed from rice, wheat, barley and other grains. Villagers have four meals a day: two light and two heavy, which they eat from the traditional bamboo plate, "bangchung", and drink from a wooden cup or "phob". When wine is being served, a bamboo container called a "palang" is used.

Sometimes a buffalo horn is used for this purpose. It is customary for a Bhutanese to carry a cup, wrapped in a cloth, and a dagger, for an ancient proverb is "Gida Phoshu lala sha, Chungda Thama Gachemey" which means that one should be ready with a cup when wine is flowing and a dagger when a fight is brewing.

The dress of both men and women is made of colourful and finely patterned cloths of silk, wool or cotton, woven in the homes.

Left and below:
Bhutanese stone masons working at their craft; A typical scene in a Bhutan town.

LAGU KEBANGSAAN BRUNEI

Moderato (♩.=90)

YA AL-LAH LAN- JUT KAN LAH U-SI-A DU-LI TU-AN- KU YANG MA-HA MU-LI-A A-DIL BER DAU-LAT ME NAUNG-I NO-SA MEMIM-PIN RA'A-YAT KE KAL BAHA-GI-A HI-DUP SEN-TU-SA NE-GA-RA DAN SULTAN I-LA-HI-SE-LA-MAT KAN BRU-NEI DA-RUS-SA-LAM

O Allah long live
His Highness the Sultan,
To reign and rule justly the nation
and lead the people to lasting happiness.
May the State and Ruler enjoy peace.
O Allah, save Brunei Darus Salam.

Sultanate of
BRUNEI

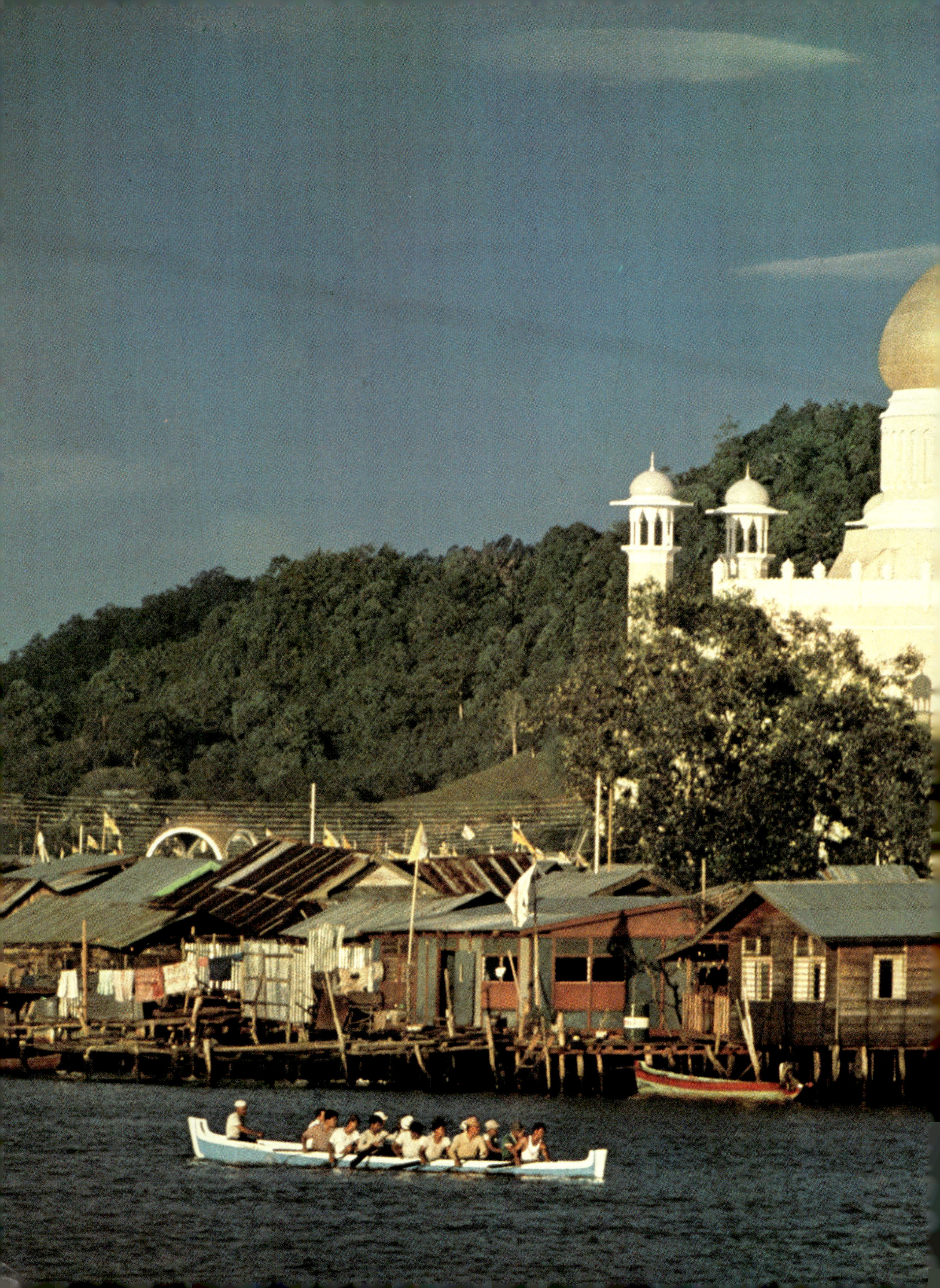

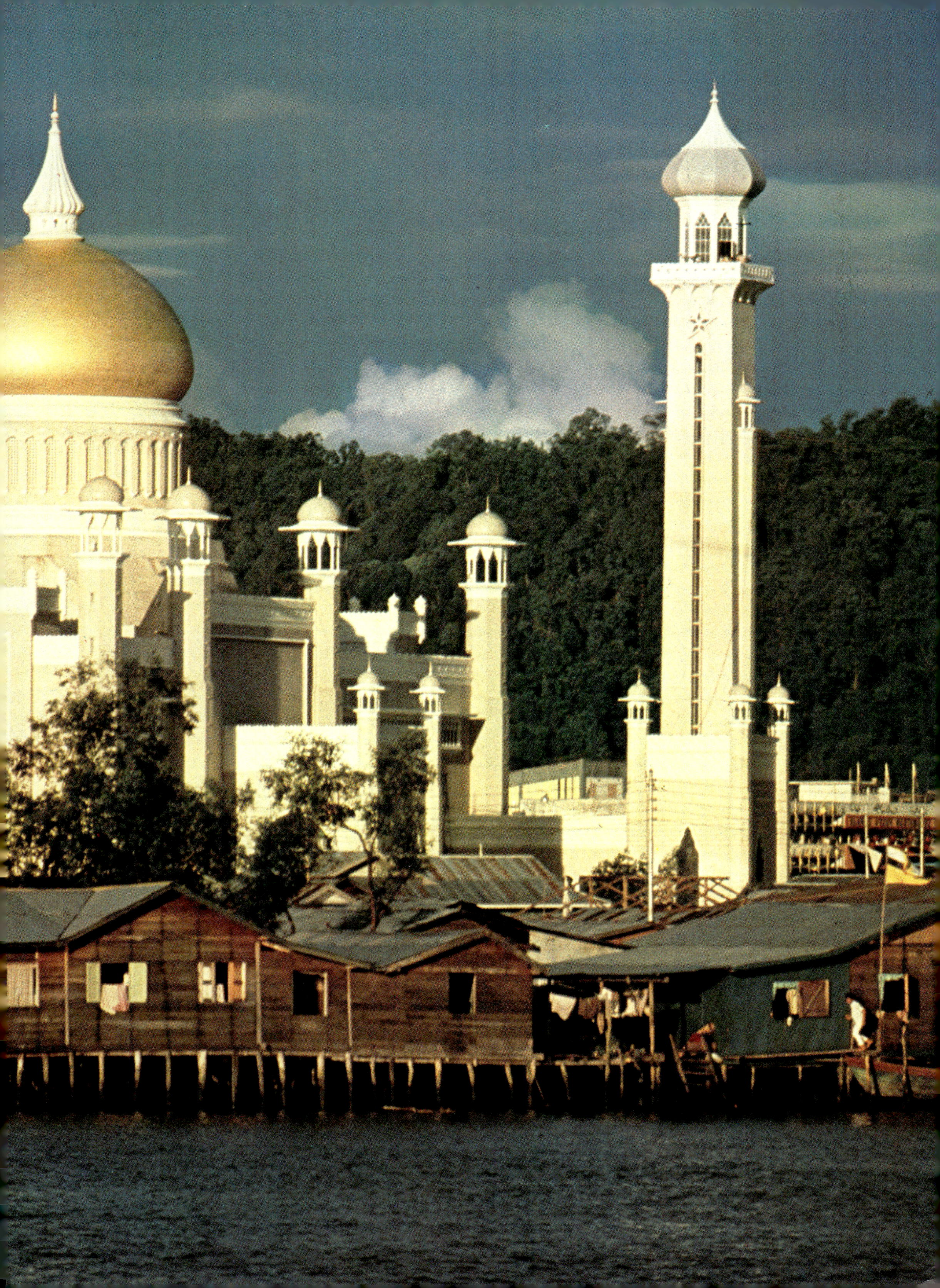

LES ISLES DE LA SONDE,

entre lesquelles sont SVMATRA, IAVA, BORNEO, &c.
Par le Sr. Sanson d'Abbeville Geographe du Roy.
Auec priuilege pour 20 ans. 1652.

Mille Pas Geometriques	60	120
Lieues commu. de France	25	50
Lieues grandes de France	20	40
Lieues com. d'Alemagne	15	30
Degrés de Longit. et Latit.	1	2

Brunei

LOCATION:
On the north-west coast of Borneo.

LATITUDE:
Between 4° 2' and 5° 3' north.

LONGITUDE:
Between 114° 4' and 115° 2' east.

AREA:
2226 square miles.

POPULATION:
Upwards of 140,000.
Approx. 50 per cent Malays
25 per cent Chinese.
Balance comprising other races.

VITAL STATISTICS
(rate per 2000) 1967:
Births   29.0
Deaths   4.3
Infant Mortality 36.7

CLIMATE:
Tropical.
Average temperatures between 76° F and 86° F.

ANNUAL RAINFALL:
Varies from 100 inches coastal to above 200 inches inland.

Illustration on previous pages:
The Sir Omar Ali Saifuddin Mosque, seen from the Brunei River, is one of the most beautiful Islamic buildings in South-east Asia. It was designed by an English firm of architects, Messrs. Booty, Edwards & Partners.

An old Map of South-east Asia.

An Eastern Sultanate

LITTLE IS KNOWN of Brunei's early history but it is believed that centuries ago it was a vassal of China. Some time later it came under Hindu influence through allegiance to Java.

By the early 16th Century the State had thrown off all allegiance and had risen to be a considerable power with *sovereignty* over the whole of Borneo and many smaller islands of the Malay archipelago.

Towards the end of that century, however, Brunei's power began to decline and by the beginning of the 19th Century it included only what is now Sarawak and part of Sabah.

In 1841 Sarawak was ceded by the Sultan of Brunei to the Englishman James Brooke in return for his services in quelling an insurrection at Kuching, and five years later the island of Labuan was handed over to Britain as a base for anti-piracy measures.

The Sultan then entered into a treaty with Britain to extend mutually profitable commercial relations and to secure co-operation in the suppression of pirate ships that plundered the northern coastal villages and traders of Borneo.

By a further treaty in 1888 Brunei was placed under the protection of Britain and in 1906 the Sultan agreed to accept a Resident to represent the British Government under a High Commissioner (at that time the Governor of the Straits Settlements and later the Governor of Sarawak).

The entire economic pattern of Brunei was revolutionised when oil was struck at Seria in 1929.

During World War II the country was occupied by the Japanese from 1941-45 but Civil Government was once more established when Japan capitulated and peace was restored.

Administrative separation from Sarawak was proclaimed in 1959 and a British High Commissioner for Brunei appointed in a new agreement, replacing the pact of 1906. Brunei's first Constitution was published in the same year.

Under it elections were held in 1962 and the Partai Ra'ayat (People's Party) led by A.M. Azahari was appointed to govern the country. But things did not move along as smoothly as expected and on 8th December 1962 a revolt led by the T.N.K.U. (Tentera Nasional Kalimantan Utara) broke out and the State was placed under emergency law. The uprising was eventually put down by British forces called in under the 1959 agreement.

The first direct elections to the Legislative Council were held in March 1965 and life in Brunei continued along an even tenor until on 4th October 1967 His Highness Sultan Sir Omar Ali Saifuddin abdicated from the throne to be succeeded by his eldest son, Pengiran Muda Mahkota Hassanal Bolkiah. The Coronation took place on 1st August 1968 and the jubilant people celebrated the occasion amid pomp and colourful pageantry.

The young Sultan soon assumed his place as President of the Executive Council, the Governing body appointed under the Constitution. The Council comprises the High Commissioner, seven ex-officio members and seven unofficial members and a Legislative Council with the Mentri Besar (Chief Minister), appointed by the Sultan at its head, and consisting of six ex-officio members, five nominated members appointed by the Sultan and ten elected members.

Under the 1959 agreement the British Government is responsible for defence and external affairs and the High Commissioner advises the Sultan on these matters, on internal security and generally on matters other than those affecting the Moslem religion and Malay customs.

In 1965 the former Executive Council became the Council of Ministers, consisting of the six ex-officio members of the Legislative Council, the High Commissioner and four Assistant Ministers, two of whom are appointed from the ten elected members and two from the five nominated members of the Legislative Council.

His Highness the Sultan presides at the Council of Ministers.

The Sultanate of Brunei goes back in history more than 400 years and the present ruler, His Highness Hassanal Bolkiah Mu'izzaddin Waddaulah, D.K., P.S.N.B., P.S.P.N.B., P.S.L.J., S.P.M.B., P.A.N.B., C.M.G. is the 29th Sultan of Brunei. When he succeeded to the throne on 4th October 1967 he was only 21 years of age.

His Highness began his education under private tuition at the Istana school and then entered the Sultan Muhammad Jemalul Alam Malay School in Brunei Town. Later he went to Kuala Lumpur and attended the Gurney Road School to further his studies.

He qualified and in January 1961 entered the Victoria Institution, the premier secondary school in the capital of the Federation of Malaysia.

In 1963 he returned to Brunei to join the State's own premier secondary school, the Sultan Omar Ali Saifuddin College in Brunei Town.

His Highness went to England to study and on 4th January 1966 qualified for admission as a Cadet at the Sandhurst Royal Military College. He left Sandhurst in October 1967 to succeed to the throne.

His Highness is a devout Muslim and practices the teachings of Islam in his everyday life. He meets and mingles freely with his

Ceremonial spear-bearers marching in the Coronation procession, a highly impressive and spectacular event that took place on 1st August 1968.

subjects but holds the greatest respect for his elders, particulary his brothers and sisters who also give him the respect due to an elder brother.

His Highness takes a deep interest in the progress and development of the country especially in social, economic, language and religious matters.

As a Ruler who has been equipped for his office he is loved by the *ra'ayat*.

Following the promulgation of the Constitution of 29th September 1959, a red crest was added to the State flag of yellow, white and black, which had been in use since Brunei became a British protectorate in 1906. The flag is flown on all State occasions. His Highness the Sultan has a personal standard of yellow, incorporating the Royal crest of two golden cats on a red background at the centre of the standard. Her Royal Highness the Raja Isteri, the Sultana of Brunei, has a light yellow standard which also incoporates the Royal crest.

Soon after His Highness Sir Omar Ali Saifuddin was crowned Sultan in 1951 a national anthem was officially adopted. It is played on all official State occasions and at Royal ceremonials the "Nobat Diraja" or Band of Royal Musicians performs the honours. The words and music of the Anthem are reproduced on the first page of this Chapter on Brunei.

LIFE IN BRUNEI

The State capital, Brunei Town, was renamed in 1970 as Bandar Seri Begawan (town of the former Ruler) in honour of the former Sultan, Sir Muda Omar Ali Saifuddin III. The site is twelve miles up the Brunei River from the sea and has been for more than 400 years the main settlement of the Brunei people. Today it has a popula-

Above: His Highness Sultan Hassanal Bolkiah sitting on the Royal throne at the Coronation ceremony.

Left: A view of the Sir Omar Ali Saifuddin Mosque from the air, showing the circular lagoon and the broadwalk approach from the Brunei River. Note the clusters of houses in the Kampong Ayer. These are individual communities of Malay and Chinese river dwellers.

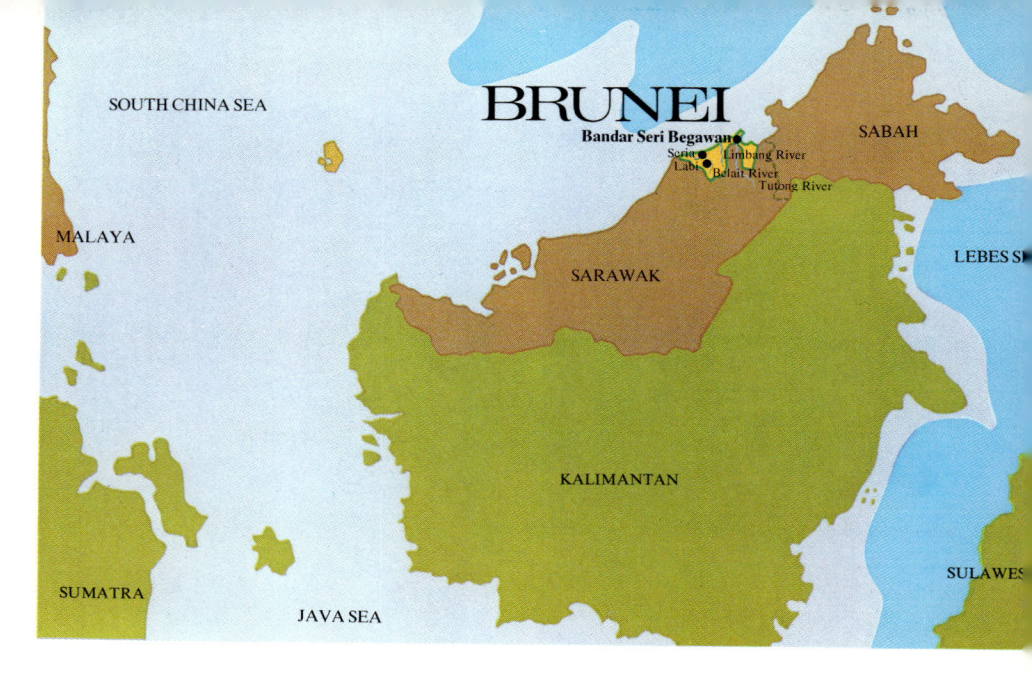

A map showing the Sultanate of Brunei, partly divided by Sarawak.

Below: Inside the Royal Mausoleum showing the headstones marking the graves of minor Royalty. The Sultans' tombs are more elaborate monuments in marble.

tion of upwards of 30,000. Traditionally fishermen, pirates and brass-founders, the inhabitants of the Kampong Ayer (Water Village) live on the Brunei River itself in stilted houses connected to each other by wooden catwalks. The Kampong Ayer, in reality a cluster of smaller villages holding some 15,000 people, is served today by a network of potable water mains and a series of electricity mains running along the west bank. In other parts there are communal generating plants to provide electric current to groups of houses.

The town on the river bank is rapidly expanding and since World War II it has grown from a large village of *attap* houses to an imposing township with modern buildings, the most famous of which is the Sir Omar Ali Saifuddin Mosque (built in 1950's). Other fine structures are the new Lapau (State Assembly Hall), Dewan Majlis (Legislative Council Chamber), the Religious Affairs Department, the new Language and Literature Institute, the Department of Broadcasting and Information and shortly to be opened, the Churchill Memorial. Outside the town is the Brunei Museum, recently constructed on a hilly site overlooking the river and the old Kota Batu (Stone Fort) which was the State capital in the 15th and 16th Centuries. Modern water supply and sewerage systems are now being installed in Bandar Seri Begawan and several other towns. An international airport with a 12,000 ft. runway is under construction and a new deepwater harbour at the mouth of the Brunei River is almost completed.

Several new hotels have recently opened and the lure of tourism is inevitable, particularly when the new airport is opened for international jet services from Europe and Australia. Brunei is normally included in the itinerary of visitors to the Borneo territories of Sabah and Sarawak which can be reached from Singapore and Hong Kong by daily air services.

Geographically, Brunei lies within the tropics on the north-west coast of Borneo. It forms two enclaves in eastern Malaysia, separated from each other by the valley of the Limbang River, and has a coastline of about 100 miles. In the west are the valleys of the Belait and Tutong Rivers, mainly series of swamps broken by ridges, covering more than half the area of the State.

Right: Part of the Kampong Ayer showing the wooden cat walks which connect the houses built on stilts, just as roads connect villages on land. Boats are part of the public transport system where there are no cat walks.

The Labi hills, in the extreme west, reach a maximum height of 1,300 feet. The district of Temburong, on the east side of the Limbang, is hilly, becoming mountainous as it approaches the main Borean range near the border of Sarawak.

THE BRUNEI PEOPLE
The majority of the population, Malays, have strong ties with the Malays of Malaysia and Indonesia. Subject to local variations, they speak the same language, practice the same religion and customs and have similar physical appearance and features. Other sections of Brunei's population comprise Chinese, Ibans, Indians and other races. The principal religions are Islam, Buddhist, Christian and Pagan. Large numbers of migrant workers have been brought into the State because of labour shortages arising from the many development schemes now in progress. In 1970 immigrant workers numbered about 16,000, mostly from other parts of Borneo, Singapore, Hong Kong and Taiwan.

Brunei enjoys one of the highest living standards in South-east Asia and remains one of the few countries in the world without personal income tax. Free enterprise is encouraged and is widely active throughout the State.

Most of the population is self-employed in agriculture, fishing or the harvesting of jungle produce. Some workers are employed in oil mining, by the Government in its Public Works Department, and by sawmills, wood-working industries and rubber estates.

Labour legislation covers such matters as hours of work, health conditions, age of admission to employment, medical treatment and workmen's compensation. There is little unemployment and industrial disputes are rare.

BRUNEI OIL
In the mineral rich, south-western coastal area of Brunei are the oilfields of Seria and S.W. Ampa (land and marine wells) which provide the wealth which the State earns from petroleum. Brunei is the third largest producer of petroleum in the British Commonwealth; in 1970 its wells yielded over 5 million tons of oil for shipment to many parts of Asia and Australia. Until recently the natural gas which accompanies the oil when exploited has had little or no commercial use but a contract has now been signed with Japanese companies to purchase liquefied natural gas as fuel. The elaborate plant required for the liquefication and shipment of this product is now in course of construction at Lumut, a site on the shore some twelve miles from the main oilfields. On completion it will be the largest of its kind in the world. This new industry will increase the revenue obtained from oil production and will also provide more jobs for the local inhabitants. It is expected to be in production in about three years' time.

HEALTH
In the overall picture the health of the population is generally good. Oil revenues have brought relative prosperity and the territory's small geographical area has facilitated the provision of medical services and the control of disease.

Above: An itinerant boat vendor serves the needs of the people of Kampong Ayer who wish to save themselves a trip ashore for marketing.

Malaria, so disastrous in former years, has been reduced to negligible proportions as a result of an eradication campaign begun in 1954, with technical assistance from World Health Organisation staff. A school feeding programme of free mid-day meals and milk, has been put into operation to counter malnutrition among young children and a school dental service has been started.

The infant mortality rate is high but steadily falling. Some 80 per cent of the population now has piped water supplies and water borne sanitation is being gradually introduced.

Two State hospitals (322 beds), one oil company hospital (93 beds), two district dispensaries, five travelling dispensaries, nine maternity and child health clinics, two tuberculosis units and a Flying Doctor Service take care of the health of the people.

EDUCATION

In the year 1968 Brunei had 90 Government Malay-medium primary schools, three Government English-medium preparatory schools, eight aided Chinese-medium primary schools (four of them with preliminary kindergarten classes), seven unaided mission English-medium primary schools (each with kindergarten classes) and one unaided primary school (with kindergarten) run by the Brunei Shell Petroleum Company. Total enrolment in these schools was 27,276 (14,282 boys and 12,994 girls).

There were nineteen secondary schools in the State, of which eight were run by the Government (five in the Malay medium and three in the English medium), and the remaining eleven consisted of three aided Chinese-medium schools, seven unaided mission English-medium schools and one unaided private school. Total enrolment in these schools was 6,521 (3,795 boys and 2,726 girls).

The only vocational school in 1967 was an Artisan Training School run by the Brunei Shell Petroleum Company for the training, mainly of its own artisans, in mechanical and electrical trades, with an enrolment of 106 male trainees.

The Government Teacher Training College had an enrolment in 1967 of 354 students (254 male and 100 female). 195 of these (157 male and 38 female) were receiving training in the Malay medium and 159 (97 male and 62 female) in the English medium.

A total of 224 students (171 male and 53 female) were studying abroad on Government scholarships in 1967; 157 of them (117 boys and 40 girls) in secondary schools, and the rest (54 men and 13 women) in institutions of higher education, teacher training or nursing.

There were also 160 non-Government scholarship holders, (87 male and 73 female), seven (five boys and two girls) in secondary schools, and the rest (82 men and 71 women) in institutions of higher education, teacher training or nursing.

A total of 3,858 adults (1,249 men and 2,609 women) were enrolled in Malay medium adult classes in 1967, the majority in literacy classes and the remainder in Malay language, secondary education, commercial and domestic subjects classes. 1,297 adults (963 men and 334 women) were enrolled in English-medium adult classes ranging from primary to School Certificate/GCE "O" level and including commercial subjects classes.

SOCIAL SERVICES

It is seventeen years since a State non-contributory pension scheme for old people and the disabled, and dependants of the blind, lepers and the insane came into operation in 1955.

The government-owned Brunei Broadcasting Service operates services in Malay, English and Chinese.

There is one weekly newspaper (the Borneo Bulletin) and for five years there was one daily, (the Daily Star), which has since ceased publication.

Radio telegraph and telephone services connect Brunei with Singapore and Malaysia. Air services to Singapore via Kota Kinabalu, Sabah, are provided daily by the national airlines.

BANKING AND FINANCE

In 1967 Brunei issued its own notes and coins and the parity of the Brunei dollar was fixed at .2990299 grammes of fine gold. Before the devaluation of the pound sterling, the Brunei dollar was equivalent to 2s 4d but since devaluation in 1967 it has a value of 2s 8.667d.

Generally speaking the US dollar is worth B$3 and the pound B$7.20.

There are five private enterprise banks operating in Brunei and a Government Post Office Savings Bank which at the end of 1967 had 1,807 depositors with deposits amounting to B$340,935.

The main sources of Brunei's revenue are income tax (applicable to companies only), mining rents and royalties payable by the oil industry, and customs duties. Surplus revenues from the oil industry have been invested and the accumulated funds totalled some B$673.8M in 1968. In 1969 national revenue reached B$157.9 million compared with expenditures totalling B$130.5 million, (the latter figure excludes development expenditure).

A development plan begun in 1962 aims to raise the gross national product by 6 per cent and per capita income by 4 per cent per annum. Overall expenditure is envisaged at B$150m.

This plan is directed towards the diversification of the economy by the development of its agricultural and forest resources and the introduction of secondary industries, the provision of a comprehensive national system of education, improved health and welfare services and the encouragement of recreational facilities and cultural development.

Left: One of the latest marine drilling platforms used for offshore oil production by the Brunei Shell Petroleum Co. Ltd. Note the helicopter pad on the left. These marine drilling platforms are serviced by the helicopter operated by the oil company which also has executive jet aircraft.

Left page: A group of smiling boys greet visitors to the Kampong Ayer (Water Village) where more than half the population of Brunei's capital live.

Below centre: A Hovercraft belonging to the Royal Brunei Malay Regiment takes on passengers on the beach in Brunei.

Below: A basketball match in progress. Sport is a popular outdoor pastime in Brunei in which people of all ages participate.

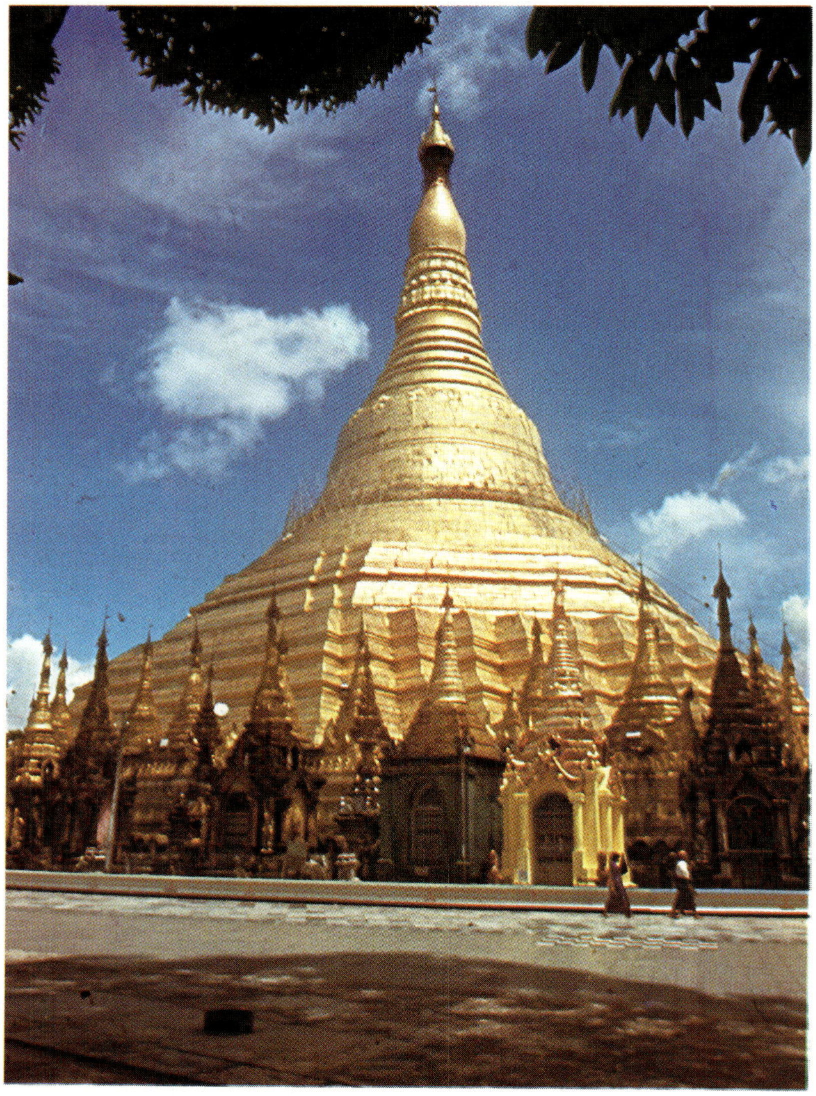

Union of
BURMA

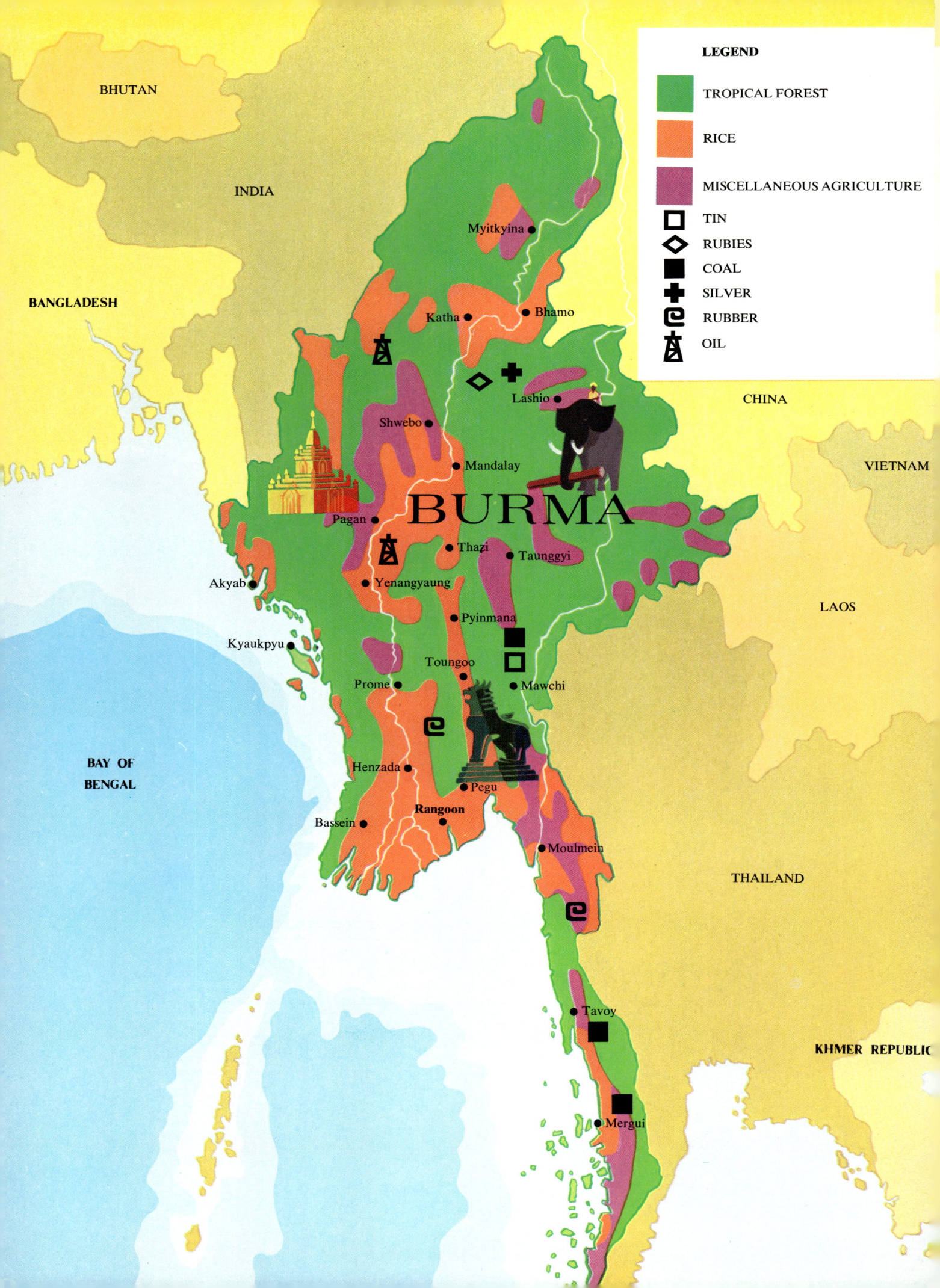

BURMA

LEGEND
- 🟩 TROPICAL FOREST
- 🟧 RICE
- 🟪 MISCELLANEOUS AGRICULTURE
- ☐ TIN
- ◇ RUBIES
- ■ COAL
- ✚ SILVER
- ℮ RUBBER
- ⛽ OIL

Countries: BHUTAN, INDIA, BANGLADESH, CHINA, VIETNAM, LAOS, THAILAND, KHMER REPUBLIC

Cities: Myitkyina, Katha, Bhamo, Lashio, Shwebo, Mandalay, Pagan, Thazi, Taunggyi, Akyab, Yenangyaung, Kyaukpyu, Pyinmana, Toungoo, Mawchi, Prome, Henzada, Pegu, Bassein, **Rangoon**, Moulmein, Tavoy, Mergui

Bay of Bengal

Fishermen from one of the picturesque coastal villages in Burma.

Burma

AREA:
  261,228 square miles.

LENGTH:
  1,300 miles.

WIDTH:
  575 miles.

LOCATION:
  Between 10° and 28½° north latitude and 92° and 101½° east longitude. Extends from the north and north-east near Tibet and the Yunan Province of China, to the Mekong River region near the borders of Laos and Thailand in the east, to the Indian Ocean in the south, and to the borders of Bangladesh and India in the south-west and west.

TOPOGRAPHY:
  Divisible into three geographical units: The western mountain range includes the Patkai, Naga, and Chin Hills and the Arakan Yoma, which respectively decrease, north to south, from summits of 12,000 feet to densely-forested, serrated ridges of 3-5,000 feet; The eastern mountain systems continue from Kachin State through the Shan and Karenni Plateaux into upland Thailand and are dissected by deep gorges, cut by many rivers, notably the Salween; The vast alluvial lowland region of central Burma is drained by the mighty Irrawaddy, and forms the great rice-bowl of the nation.

CLIMATE:
  Tropical-monsoonal. In most areas mean average temperatures are around 80°F, sometimes reaching 100° during the southern summer. December and January are the coolest months but the thermometer rarely falls below 60-65°F.

RAINFALL:
  The south-west monsoon brings heavy rain between May and October. The delta region averages 100″ annually, while up to 200″ may fall along the coast or in the north. Less than 40″ is the rule in the rain-shadow area or Dry Zone behind the mountains of the Arakan Yoma.

ETHNIC GROUPS:
  The indigenous races of Burma are of Mongoloid stock and comprise the Burmese, Karens, Shans, Chins, Kachins, and Kayah. Large immigrant groups include Chinese and Indians.

RELIGION:
  Theravada Buddhism, Animism and Christianity.

POPULATION:
  27,500,000. Population Density: 100 per square mile.

POPULATION GROWTH RATE:
  2.3 per cent annually.

The Road to Mandalay

Left:
The Shwedagon Pagoda in Rangoon,
covered in gold leaf
and encrusted in precious stones,
is the largest temple of its kind
in the world.

Below:
Development of health services
by the Government of Burma
is reaching into the villages.
Anti-malaria mobile teams,
part of a nationwide campaign
to eradicate malaria,
are assisted by
the World Health Organisation
and the UN Children's Fund.
In this photograph,
Dr. Ba Sein is examining
some of the children in the
village of Ywama.

Right:
A scene on beautiful Inle Lake
in the Shan State.
It is sometimes called
the "Venice of the East"
and has many floating islands
and temples on its shores.

THE FIRST WESTERNER to kindle interest in Burma was the famous Venetian explorer Marco Polo. Nearly 700 years ago he passed through northern India and Burma on his way to visit the great Kublai Khan in China and wrote in glowing terms of the wonders of Pagan's 4 million Buddhist temples. Later reports of the mystical land filtered through from time to time until in more recent years Rudyard Kipling wrote of the unforgettable "road to Mandalay".

Kipling's description of the East was typical of the imperial Briton of the time, attracted by its splendours but seeing the people as

"....fluttered folk and wild,
Your new-caught, sullen peoples,
Half devil, half child."

Today Kipling's Far East is Australia's and New Zealand's near north and the antipodeans have a new and more easily accessible view of its ancient cultures and the gracious traditions of the Asian societies which the West has largely lost.

Like other Asian nations Burma has learned much from the West. It learned some of the principles of government from

the British. Its own revolutionary government, set up in 1962, borrows the terminology of left-wing socialism but its modus operandi is tempered by the gentle Buddhist outlook of the mass of the people; a Ministry of Religious Affairs conducts programmes to promote Buddhism, a religion which sets little store by worldly goods. Burmese temples are often encrusted with gold and jewels and in this sense the precious shrines remain communal property. The kings of the Pagan dynasty left no elaborate tombs of self commemoration but they did leave many thousands of pagodas. The "Burmese way to socialism" maintains that "social justice demands that the gaps between incomes are reasonable and correct measures will be taken to narrow these gaps as much as possible".

Plans to modernise the country are aimed at improving the lot of the peasant at village level rather than accumulating profits through urban-based industries, although manufacture is at the present time being developed. This follows the trend of a long-established tradition of Buddhist education. Every village maintains a monastery, where the monks teach the children to read and write, along with the fundamentals of Buddhism. It is a short step for the government to add modern village amenities—a dispensary, reading room, consumers' shop—and to provide instruction in new agricultural techniques. At the same time there is little need for government welfare services since traditional Buddhist charity and family custom make them unnecessary.

Thanks to the pervasive Buddhist education the people of Burma have a common language but there is a diversity of subcultures and costumes reflecting the different origins of the three main migrant stocks which entered Burma from Tibet and Indo-China. The most ancient were the Mon-Khmers who spread to Indo-China, closely followed by groups of Tibeto-Burmans, one of which now constitutes the main Burmese stock. The third migration, the Thai-Chinese, came into Burma from the Chinese Kingdom of Nanchao in the 13th and 14th Centuries.

They shared the Buddhist culture of the inhabitants. In recent times colonial experience under the British, which began in 1885, and wartime occupation by the Japanese, gave new impetus to nationalist feeling.

The heartland of Burma, where most of the Burmese are concentrated, is the Dry Zone, taking in the river valleys of the Irrawaddy, the Sittang and the Salween, which run roughly parallel towards the Andaman Sea. The hilly parts are occupied by other descendants of the main stocks: the Chins, Kachins and the Kayah (Tibeto-Burmese) and the Karens and Shans (Thai-Chinese).

Burma is not densely populated with the teeming millions of the Western stereotype. In the thickly populated Dry Zone there are about 200 people to the square mile but most of the population is dispersed in rural villages.

The staple crop of the country is rice, generally grown under irrigation. The British established a wet-rice industry in the Irrawaddy delta, mainly for export, and this area was severely damaged during World War II.

Rice, timber (including teak), non-ferrous metals and gems (rubies, sapphires and jade) are the main exports. Some industries and commercial enterprises are nationalised, namely rice and timber exports, inland waterways, pawnshops and distilleries. The Government now owns the Burma Oil Company, and also controls banking and insurance. The aim is to free Burma from foreign economic dominance and to keep profits within the country. Since the War local steel and pharmaceutical industries have been established, greatly benefiting Burmese building and agriculture.

Increasing numbers of towns and villages are being served by hydro-electricity from the Lavpita and Baluchaung Falls. Scientific research is enabling agriculture to be more economically developed. One project, partly sponsored by the United Nations, is investigating river systems, particularly those subject to floods, a major factor in a rice economy. The general aim of the research is to improve productivity through technical means and changes in policies of land tenure. Irrigation projects are also under way, the aim being to increase the acreage under rice. Villages are being run as co-operative organisations.

Despite much industrial progress since independence was granted in 1948, the oxcart still sets the pace in Burma, most of which is not served with modern transport. The traditional method of transport is by river, which is also used to float teak logs to the ports. There is a good British-built railway system but it was severely damaged during the War and is still in the process of reconstruction. A modern air network has been established as a practical means of overcoming the difficulties of Burma's jungle-covered and mountainous terrain.

As in mediaeval Europe, life in Burma is centred upon religion. The many colourful festivals are celebrated as holidays and as every pagoda has its own festival one is sure to take place at least every month.

The well-known Water Festival is held at New Year when people are either sprinkled or drenched in playful processions. Literature, drama, ballet, music and all forms of art are taken up with religious themes and pagodas are still being built by the willing hands of hundreds of workers, unaided by technology and less disposed than Western people to make a virtue of industrialised efficiency.

The ancient city of Pagan contains many examples of traditional architecture and art, dating from the days of the Anawrahta dynasty in the 11th Century, a high point in Burmese civilisation. King Anawrahta unified the diverse Burmese peoples for the first time. At Pagan, architecture, sculpture and mural painting express episodes in the life of the Buddha and other Buddhist themes. It was also a famous centre for national music, which

Above:
Rangoon is blazing with lights
on Independence Day
(January 4th).
On the left is the City Hall,
the Independence Monument
is in the centre of the picture,
and the Sule Pagoda
on the right.

Right:
Exquisite bamboo-and-silk parasols
in colourful designs
are made in Bassein.

Opposite page, top:
Kachins, dressed in their
national costume...
and below are some examples of
carved pagodas for which the
Burmese craftsmen are famous.

is still performed during pagoda ceremonies. Classical drama and ballet depict the Buddha's life.

The Burmese people enjoy a long tradition of fine handcraftsmanship; gem-cutting, weaving, lacquerware making, gold- and silver-smithing, wood-carving and furniture making. The art of jade-engraving, well established 1,000 years ago, links Chinese art with Burmese; the jade stone of Burma is the finest in the world. The ancient skill of Burmese metalsmiths is well demonstrated in the bronze Mingun Bell of the Mingun Pagoda near Mandalay. It is the largest hanging bell in the world and weighs nearly 100 tons. It is 12 feet high and 10 feet in diameter.

The largest extant image of the reclining Buddha is to be seen at Pegu, inland from Rangoon, found hidden among jungle undergrowth last century by a British surveyor. The Shwedagon Pagoda in Rangoon is the largest temple of its kind in the world—Kipling's "winking, blinking wonder", covered in gold leaf and encrusted with precious stones. It dates back 2,500 years and is said to have been built over hair relics of the Buddha. It is essentially a vast platform 326 feet high on which dozens of pagodas have been built on a series of three terraces rising to a golden spire.

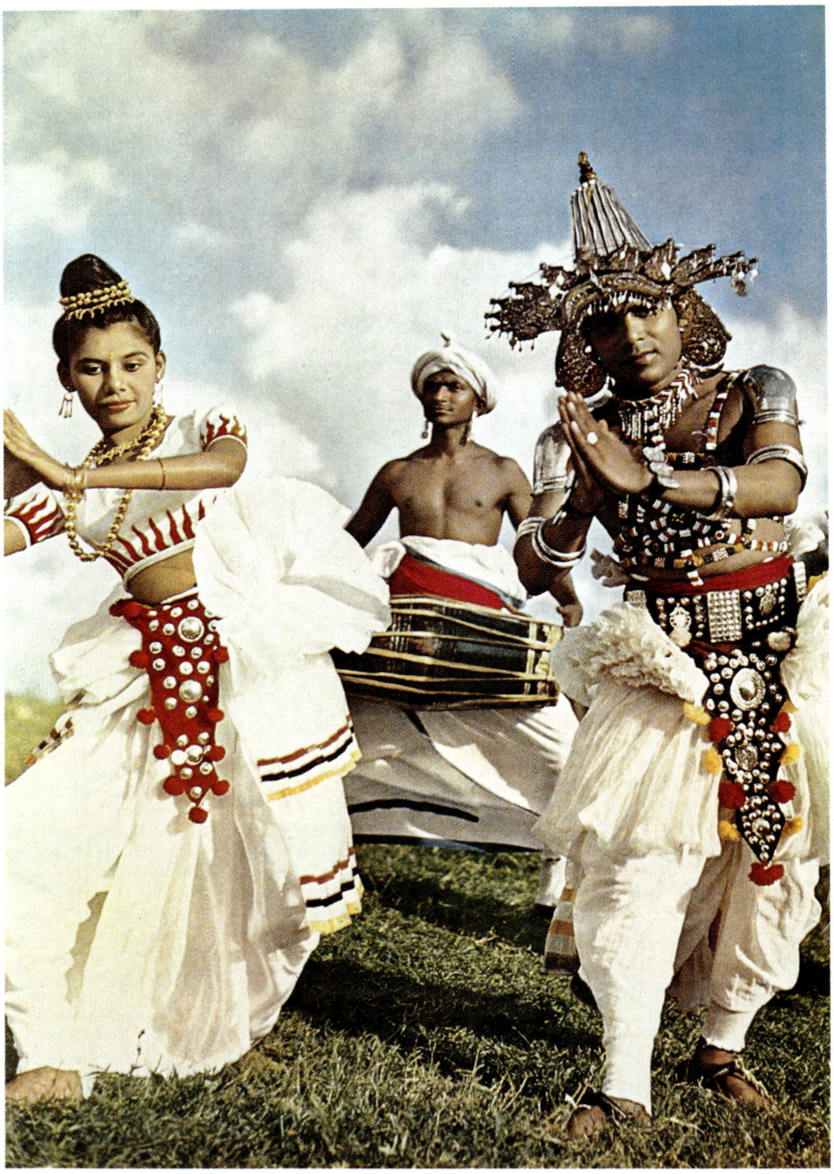

Republic of
SRI LANKA
(Ceylon)

Republic of SRI LANKA (Ceylon)

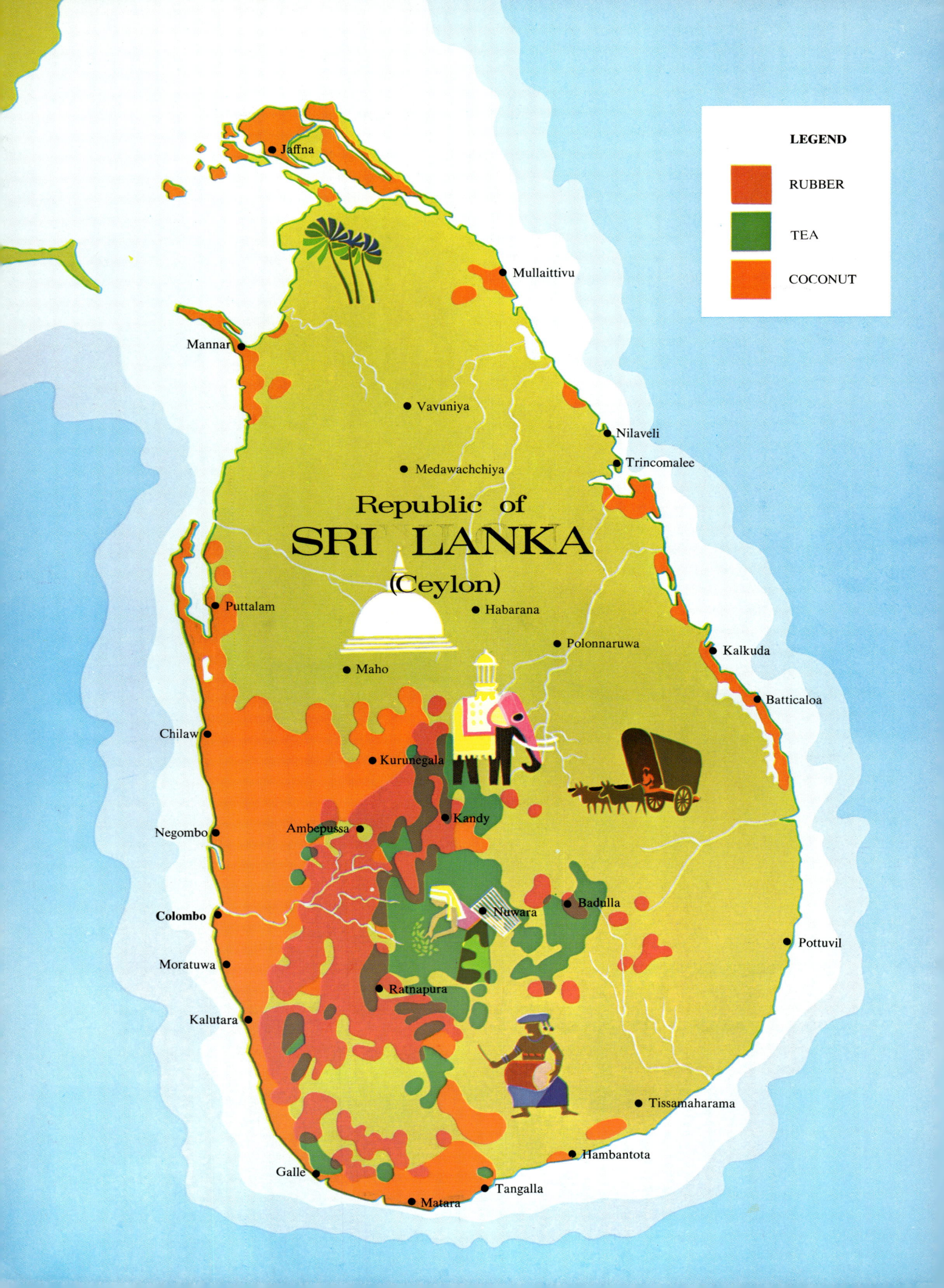

LEGEND
- RUBBER
- TEA
- COCONUT

- Jaffna
- Mullaittivu
- Mannar
- Vavuniya
- Nilaveli
- Trincomalee
- Medawachchiya
- Puttalam
- Habarana
- Polonnaruwa
- Maho
- Kalkuda
- Batticaloa
- Chilaw
- Kurunegala
- Negombo
- Ambepussa
- Kandy
- Colombo
- Nuwara
- Badulla
- Moratuwa
- Pottuvil
- Kalutara
- Ratnapura
- Tissamaharama
- Hambantota
- Galle
- Matara
- Tangalla

The Raja Maha Vihare, the ancient temple of Kalaniya, which legend tells was visited by the Buddha.

Sri Lanka

AREA:
25,332 square miles.

GREATEST LENGTH:
270 miles.

WIDTH:
140 miles.

LOCATION:
Between 5° 55' and 9° 50' north latitude and 79° 42' and 81° 52' east longitude.

CLIMATE:
Tropical — two monsoons (from May to September, from the south-west and from November-December to the end of February from the north-east), modify the heat and bring cooling rains. Average temperatures range from a maximum in the mid-80°s F. to a minimum of around 60° F.

RAINFALL:
A mean annual rainfall of 40 inches in the driest zones to over 200 inches on the south-west slopes.

THE PEOPLE:
Sinhalese, over 70 per cent; Tamils, about 20 per cent; descendants of the Moors, about 7 per cent; descendants of the Dutch (Burghers), Malays, Eurasians and Europeans, about 1 per cent.

RELIGION:
Buddhism is the major religion; Hinduism (the faith of the Tamils), Catholicism, Mohammedanism and Protestantism are also practised.

POPULATION 1972:
13,334,000.

GROWTH OF POPULATION:
2.1 per cent in 1970.

PROJECTED POPULATION 1983:
Between 16 and 18 million.

PROJECTED POPULATION 2003:
Between 24 and 32 million.

The Resplendent Island

RUINS OF TEMPLES, water reservoirs, irrigation systems, monasteries, palaces and great stone statues of the Buddha are imperishable evidence of the energy, technology and imagination of the people of early Ceylon. According to Muslim legend Adam and Eve, on expulsion from the Garden, lived out their lives on Ceylon, next to Eden the most beautiful place on earth. Cosmas, a Greek trader in Egypt, recorded the reports of another Greek, Sopater, who visited the island in the 6th Century. In his time "ships from all parts of India, Persia and Ethiopia" carried Ceylon's gems, spices, woods, aromatic drugs, pearls and shells to the markets of the ancient world.

A chronicle of early Buddhist culture, the "Mahavamsa", tells the story of Aryan migrations from north India to Ceylon and of the great kingdom set up at Anuradhapura in the north-eastern section of the island. These settlers brought with them a comparatively well-developed culture, built around a stable alliance of villages. With the conversion of the King and his subjects to Buddhism, almost 250 years before Christ, a great 'temple culture' evolved around the reservoirs or 'tanks' of Anuradhapura. Under the benign influence of Buddhism the agrarian civilisation of the Sinhala Kingdom flourished producing surpluses of rice which became the nexus of a burgeoning export trade as well as the envy of the poorer classes and marauders of south India.

Ceylon has been known by various names through the centuries. It has long been a significant mercantile nation for its rich and ancient civilisation has held a special attraction for the merchants, wayfarers and vagabonds of the East. Its first recorded name, Taprobane, reported by Alexander the Great's officers, is believed to be derived from the Sanskrit, meaning "pond covered with red lotus". Other sources suggest it refers to the copper-coloured earth of northern Ceylon and is derived from Pali, a Vedic Aryan dialect. Sir Richard Burton, the famous translator of Asian literature, also thought its name came from Pali but meant Sihalan—"the place of jewels". Ptolemy called the island Simundu—"head of the sacred law"; the Moors spoke of it as Tenerism—"the isle of delight"; to the Muslim traders, who once dominated the Indian Ocean, it was known as Serendib; and to the Chinese—Pa-ou-tchow—"the island of gems". Its early Sanskrit name was Lanka—meaning "the Resplendant" —a name still used by the islanders today.

The political history of old Ceylon is mainly a record of reoccuring invasions from India, the benevolent, weak or sometimes ruthless behaviour of its rulers and the bitter, internecine conflicts which repeatedly broke out between the northern and southern kingdoms and the smaller local "clans". By the 16th Century Ceylon was divided into three separate monarchies.

Intent on securing Ceylon's spice trade as a monopoly the Portuguese became, in 1505, the first European power to establish itself on the island. Few lasting impressions were made by their stay: some of the coastal inhabitants were converted to Catholicism and various fruit trees such as the guava and the chillie, planted by the Portuguese, thrived in the tropical climate. For 150 years the Portuguese remained on Ceylon until the Dutch, impelled by similar interests, replaced them. The Dutch exported cinnamon to Europe, elephants to India and arecanuts and whorled chank shells to other parts of Asia; they also made an attempt to control the island's internal trade. But despite their weight of arms the Dutch made many of the mistakes that marred their other colonial ventures and in 1815, following several bloody campaigns, they were expelled by the British. The Dutch left behind them little more than the Portuguese. Their chief contributions to the country were their system of law (still in use today) and the commercial group known as the Burghers.

Whereas the Dutch and the Portuguese had been content to exploit Ceylon's trade the island under the British underwent many radical changes: its 'plantation-economy' was firmly tied to European demand; its food-self-sufficiency was subordinated to cash-cropping; schools were built; villages grew into towns; roads and railways connected all parts of the country. The proud Sinhalese, however, refused to leave their traditional occupations to work on the plantations for a wage so the British brought into the country the Tamils of southern India who were quite willing to pick tea and tend the rubber trees.

In addition to the ever-present pressures of the caste-system another source of friction were the landless poor who, used as an easily mobilised work-force and cut off from the language and education of the English rulers and the established Ceylonese elite, had no vote, little chance of establishing themselves in the growing public service and no real opportunity of becoming part of the new order.

The activity of Ceylonese politicians, such as the two Senanayake brothers—one of whom was to become the nation's first prime minister—the effects of World War II on colonialism and the growth of a national political awareness involving the extension of the suffrage during the period from 1920 to 1931, the introduction of universal Adult franchise in 1931, the formation of Ceylon's own political parties and new Marxist inspired movements, finally achieved independence for Ceylon in February 1948. Its form of government was modelled on the British parliamentary system with the Queen, represented by the Governor-General, at its head and the Senate and particularly the House of Representatives as its governing bodies.

Mrs. Sirimavo Bandaranaike, wife of the former prime minister and member of the Sri Lanka Freedom Party, was elected Prime Minister in 1960 during a period of crisis for Ceylon. The population explosion, severe food shortages, friction between the Tamils and the Sinhalese and a general lack of confidence in the economy were some of the problems inherited by her Government. The defeat of Dudley Senanayake in 1970 and the return of Mrs. Bandaranaike raised hopes that the Sri Lanka Freedom party might be able to press forward with many of the reforms it had commenced in the 1960's.

Today the people of Ceylon are engaged, like many other former colonies in Asia, in

Opposite page:
Gaily caparisoned elephants are a feature of the Esala Perahera, one of the world's most dramatic and spectacular festivals.
It takes place at Kandy every year for ten nights between July-August.

Below: Buddhist priests preparing for a temple ceremony.

a struggle to free themselves from the encumberances of the traditional past and from the out-moded political and economic forms imposed on them by the imperialist powers and to gain sufficient prosperity to enable the common man to lead a life of freedom and dignity.

CULTURAL HERITAGE

Buddhist Art

Just as Europeans constructed many fine buildings to the glory of Christ so also the ancient Sinhalese built magnificent temples in praise of the Lord Buddha. The single most impressive achievement of Buddhist architecture in Ceylon is the "dagaba" which consists of a terrace with a screen or gateway at each cardinal point. It surmounts a massive dome topped with a square platform from which rises a conical spire, finished in gold or rock crystal. A typical temple consists of a dagaba, a "vihara" (Image house), a "bana maduva" (Preaching hall) and a "pansala" (Manse).

Near the temple often grows a holy tree, the "bo", under which the Buddha sat when he first achieved enlightenment.

Artificial reservoirs, dams and canals are found in almost every valley of the island. In the old city of Anuradhapura the two elements of ancient Ceylon, the irrigational and the religious were combined. The essential idea behind this city's construction was its sacredness: it is to the Sinhalese as Jerusalem is to the Jews or Lhasa is to the Tibetans. One of Anuradhapura's many ruins—of temples, palaces and gardens complete with artificial rivers and pavilions —is the Brazen Palace, a primordinate skyscraper, once topped with a copper roof. A single detail of its interior must suffice to show the splendour of the building and the magnificence of this "holy city". The Mahavamsa describes it thus: "...a white parasol with a coral foot, resting on a mountain crystal and having a silver staff. On it, depicted in the seven gems, the eight auspicious figures ...... and rows of little silver bells hung upon the edge".

Secular Art

Secular art is not absent in the Sinhalese tradition. The frescoes of Sigiriya (5th Century A.D.) are the earliest and best-preserved examples of non-religious painting in Ceylon. Here, sheltered in pockets high on the face of a massive stone monolith (rising abruptly from a gentle plain), are more than twenty, three-quarter length figures of women. These murals, painted in brilliantly-luminous colours, are so fresh and alive that it seems that the artist has only just laid aside his brush. The mystery surrounding these beautiful women—do they represent cloud maidens, princesses, devotees with offerings of flowers, or the love-torn courtesans of the parricide King, Kasyappa?—has continued to enthral visitors from early times.

Kandyan Dance

The Kandyan dancing of Ceylon evokes the ritual splendour of the Kandyan areas which remained independent of foreign domination longer than any other portion of the island. Gorgeous costumes, magnificent head-dresses of beaten silver and musical anklets complete the regalia of the dancers. It takes over eight years for both the dancers and the musicians who accompany them on drums and cymbals to become fully-fledged—gesture, rhythm, footwork and movement are so intricate and well co-ordinated.

ECONOMIC STRUCTURE

Ceylon's economic existence depends largely upon three agricultural exports: tea, rubber and coconut. Of the island's 16 million acres about 7 million are cultivated and 1 million are under pasture. Tea, the most important crop, represents nearly three-fifths of the country's exports and about a third of the world's consumption.

Higher-altitude plantations, from 3,000 to 7,000 feet, are the least productive but generally grow the best quality tea-buds.

The final product, made from dark green, glossy young leaves and buds, is processed in up-country factories by withering, rolling, fermenting and firing. All Ceylon tea is black and is sorted into the various grades and flavours of "Broken Orange Pekoe", "Pekoe", "Pekoe-Souchong", "Fannings" and "Dust".

If the present ratio of land planted with tea, rubber and coconut to land devoted to food-crops continues there will be insufficient of the latter to meet the demands of an anticipated rise in population. At the present time only a third of the farming community plants rice and it is necessary, therefore, to import a large proportion of the island's requirements. Realising the importance of increasing domestic food production the Government has encouraged farmers to use their land for this purpose to experiment with new, high-yield varieties of

Above: A street corner in Colombo.

Opposite page: Ceylon women on the outskirts of Colombo.

Right: Ceylon brushes are good value.

rice and other cereals and to make use of modern techniques of fertilisation and multiple-cropping. Other commercial crops include cacao, cinnamon, arecanut (used in the preparation of betel for chewing), citronella, pepper, nutmeg, papain (an enzyme used in medicine and as a meat tenderiser), cardamons, cloves, tobacco, hemp, turmeric, ginger, chillies, sesame, kapok and cashew nuts.

The full extent of Ceylon's fishery resources, a potentially valuable supply of protein, is being evaluated by the Fisheries Corporation of Ceylon. The warm tropical waters around the island carry a great variety of edible fish, including tuna, sardines, pomfrets, horse-mackerel, garfish, shark and a species which resembles the herring.

Secondary industry plays only a minor role in the economy but some steps have been taken towards the establishment of industries which exploit the island's own resources; for example, tyre manufacturing and fish and fruit canning. In 1969 manufacturing and processing contributed 13 per cent of the Gross National Product. Ceylon's factories are mostly state-owned but some are private enterprises and others again operate as joint ventures, receiving their capital from both Government and private sources. The island's more successful industries include leather products, cement, textiles, salt, sugar, paper, chemicals, ceramics, rutile-processing, tyres, plywood and certain steel products.

Among Ceylon's more interesting sources of revenue are its large deposits of gemstones. According to legend the jewels King Solomon presented to the Queen of Sheba were obtained from Ceylon. Many fine specimens are frequently found: blue, yellow, milky-white and golden-brown star sapphires; the beryls—cats-eyes and alexandrites; rubies; spinels; aquamarines; topazes; tourmalines; amethysts; zircon and moonstones.

To assist its foreign exchange balances the Government is pursuing an energetic tourist drive. The programme envisages a total of around 4,500 new hotel rooms and comprehensive resort facilities, to be distributed throughout Ceylon by 1976. Meanwhile, existing accommodation is inspected and classified at regular intervals to maintain standards. Improvements and modernisation of hotels and resthouses has been encouraged by the provision of import duty exemptions and tax relief to hoteliers who improve their establishments.

Although the machine has supplanted manual labour in most trades the Sinhalese craftsman still continues to turn out his exquisite cottage-crafts using techniques handed down through generations from father to son. The craft-industries find their biggest market amongst the island's tourists and are a significant source of foreign exchange.

A FARMER IN CEYLON

To the monotonous chant of a "kavi", a musical verse, the buffaloes yoked to the wooden plough kept lumbering on, trampling the wet soil underneath them. It was just before the monsoon and the seed had to be sown in readiness for the rain-bearing winds of May. Sirisena, his back bared to the noonday sun, was hard at work pushing the plough through the lumps of soil. Rivulets of sweat ran down his back which shone like burnished ebony. It was hard work. Sirisena's hoarse voice flung rude but affectionate curses at the buffaloes. While his hands were busy turning the plough this way and that his mind was plagued by many thoughts, most of them not very pleasant. A silent prayer passed through his mind: "O, God! let the harvest be plentiful and let not the rains spoil it as they did last year. I cannot go through another gruelling period and I have to pay to the credit society at least a small portion of what I have borrowed: otherwise I will not be able to buy my seed paddy for next year. Grant me and my family a happy New Year and if the harvest is good I will give a portion of the new rice to the temple!......" Suddenly, coming across the field, a figure appeared. It was his wife Somawathie bringing his mid-day meal.

Sirisena lived in the village of Malpitiya. His life was full of the typical hardships of the farmer in Ceylon. Situated in the tropics and dependent on the monsoons for rain Ceylon is essentially a rice-cultivating country. Rice is the staple food of the people and over 1,200,000 acres are cultivated with paddy, often for two crops in the year. Because of the fast growing population, coupled with the scarcity of foreign exchange to finance imports of food, a great national effort is being made to extend the area under rice and to improve its yield. The Co-operative Societies and the Agrarian Service Department play important roles and farmers like Sirisena are helped greatly by them as they place within the farmers' reach what they may require in the way of manure, ploughs, barbed wire and cattle. Cash loans are granted and the farmer is also offered assistance in the control of pests.

But loans must be paid back at some time and this is the burden of Sirisena's life. If

Left:
Tea plucking on a hillside plantation. Tea is the most important industry in Ceylon.

Below right:
The snake charmers of Ceylon are a never failing source of interest to the tourist.

there is drought—as there often is—in the growing period the plants will not thrive and rain last year during the harvesting time ruined his crop. However, he does not allow these pessimistic thoughts to deter his physical labour. His muscular body, clad only in a span cloth, courses along the muddy furrows. Next week he must sow his seed paddy and when the new shoots are a few inches high his wife and her friends will do the transplanting.

The farmer in Ceylon gets up at the crack of dawn. A cacophony of sound disturbs the stillness—the chorus of all the cocks in the neighbourhood—and when a streak of light first appears in the grey morning sky Sirisena and his wife rise and light the kerosene oil lamps; when their village is in close proximity to the town some farmers have a single electrical light in their little brick two-roomed cottages. While his wife prepares the morning meal of rice or flour steamed into little cakes and a preparation of coconut and hot chillies and a plain cup of tea, plentifully sugared, Sirisena goes to the well and washes his face; then eats his breakfast, slings his mammoty on his shoulder and walks to the field.

From dawn to dusk his toil is endless, except for the interruption to eat. Usually his wife brings him his tea at mid-morning and his noonday meal of rice, a fish curry, maybe a vegetable curry and the inevitable "pol sambal" (a preparation of shredded coconut and chillies).

The sowing of the seed is done by Sirisena but during the harvesting time his friends rally round and help him in his labours. The transplanting and the reaping are mainly the work of the women. When the twilight is beginning to fade Sirisena wends his way home and takes a refreshing bath in the well, dons his sarong and shirt and goes to the village to relax with his friends over a chew of betel, a smoke and a plain cup of tea. The conversation covers a wide range of subjects because the Ceylon peasant is an interested observer, not only of the island's affairs but also those of the world. Having covered the news from space travel to the price of seed paddy, Sirisena returns home fairly early in the night, has his dinner of rice and curry and goes to sleep to be ready for the next day's tasks.

Sirisena's wife Somawathie plays an important part for she is responsible for her household—that is, her husband and her two children Sarath and Leela who go to the village school. She is usually up at dawn to contend with the day's work. She prepares the early morning meal for her family after which Sirisena sets out to work and the children go to the village school. Life this year has been hard and Somawathie finds it difficult to make ends meet: clothes for the growing children, school books for study, fish and vegetables all cost money but she is hopeful that times will improve.

When Sarath and Leela were young it was difficult to get out into the fields. Her old mother used to come and look after them but now her friends leave their children in a creche run by a voluntary social organisation. Somawathie has her share of work in the fields, sowing and reaping when harvest time comes. She and the other women cook the meals for the men and bind the bundles and carry them to be threshed. In her little garden at home, too, Somawathie is kept busy. Around the coconut palm she has trained a betel vine because Sirisena loves to chew the fresh betel leaf. She has planted a few other vegetables and what her family cannot eat she sells in the local market.

When she has time she tries to supplement her income by weaving bags or mats or by needlework, lace or coil-rope making. She is busy all day. Not only has she to cook the meals but she has to mill the paddy for rice, boil the water for drinking and pour it into a pot which has been placed over the hearth overnight.

Sirisena and Somawathie lead a hard life. Although the farmer is the most important member of the community his work is not an enviable one. The battle with the elements is never-ending but a good harvest brings to the family a sense of achievement and great pleasure.

At the end of the harvest comes the New Year—a festival of great rejoicing and thanksgiving if the harvest has been plentiful. Except for the festival days life is quiet and uneventful. Somawathie and Sirisena are religious and on "Poya" days (quarter-moon days, the Ceylon equivalent of the Christian sabbath) all four of them dressed in white go to the temple to worship. Hus-

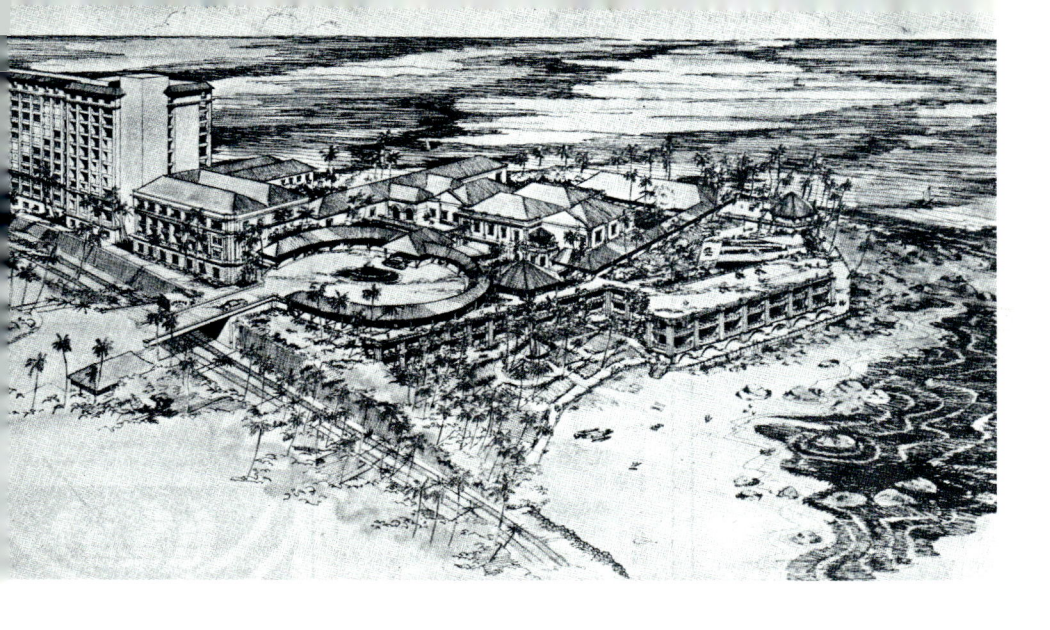

Left: Colombo's expanding tourist trade is being boosted by several new hotels of top standard. The old show-place Mount Lavinia is being developed into a modern hotel complex

band and wife in particular feel at peace with the world after laying at the shrines of the Buddha all their doubts and difficulties, giving thanks with offerings of flowers and incense.

COLOMBO

A city of churches, temples and mosques, Colombo is not merely Ceylon's capital but one of the great ports east of Suez. It is normally a clean city, with main streets flanked by flower-bearing trees—jacaranda, gold mohur and royal poinciana. A few tall commercial buildings tower over high-arched, old-world houses and colonial Government blocks, narrow alleys run parallel with broad highways; carts drawn by bullocks are as much part of the traffic's stream as the latest American convertibles; hawkers squat outside department stores and the clothes of the citizens range from the latest fashions of the West to the traditional garb of centuries past.

The Fort is the heart of Colombo and its shopping centre retails local crafts, Western foods and clothing, and all the more exotic goods expected of a busy Eastern port. Its hotels and restaurants serve modestly-priced Ceylonese and Western dishes, wines, beers, liquers and the locally-distilled potent arrack.

Gems are the most ancient and the most famous of the island's products and Colombo offers jewellery, not only on handsome modern settings but in ornate and authentic antiques as well. Lacquered walking-sticks, powder bowls and lampstands, ornamented brass vases, grotesque wooden masks, ebony elephants, coir mats, "galle" lace and batiks, ivory paper-knives, trinket-boxes, and figurines are some of the wares sold in the shops and market-places of Colombo and other towns of Ceylon. But it is not advisable to buy anything of value before first applying to the Tourist Board for a list of approved jewellers and other stores.

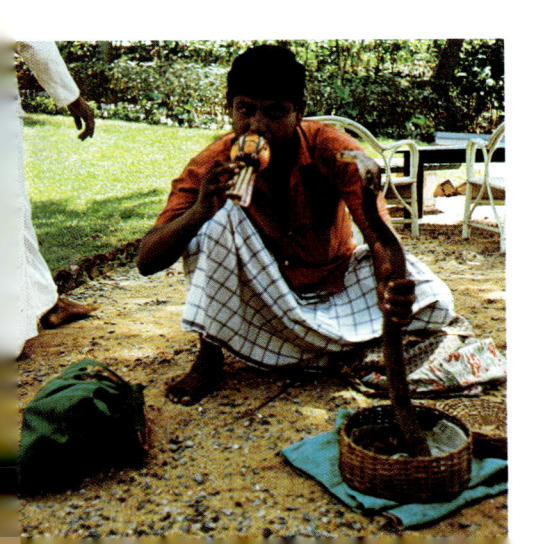

Only a few hours away from Colombo by car or train is Kandy, the ancient hill-capital of Ceylon. Set amidst tea gardens, terraced paddy fields, towering hills and misty waterfalls, it is almost encircled by the island's largest river, the Mahaweliganga.

At night its lake, built by the last King of Kandy in 1807 and known as the Milky Sea (Kiri Muhuda) reflects the myriad lights of houses on the hillsides. In the centre of the lake is an islet which once held the harem of the king.

Today the city is ruled by a gentle sovereignty, Buddhism. At dawn one is awakened by the throb of drums from the Temple of the Tooth, for the faithful from many countries flock here to pay homage to this relic of the Buddha. During July or August of every year, a replica of the tooth is carried through the city's streets in one of the world's most dramatic religious festivals, the Esala Perahera. By the last night of the celebrations, the braying conches re-echo from the hills, pious cries of "sadhu" lift thanksgiving to the sky, dancers leap and whirl in frenzied crimson, white and silver and rank upon rank of elephants, caparisoned in velvet, satin and silk, loom up and dwindle in the distance. For the people of Kandy, the Perahera fuses religion in one week of joyous release which justifies every effort spent in preparing for it.

SPORTS AND RECREATIONS

In addition to modern sports such as cricket, tennis and golf, traditional sports still surviving today are elephant and hackery racing (a hackery is a light two-wheeled cart drawn by racing bullocks). Popular village games include wrestling, racing and acrobatics.

EDUCATION

Ceylon has one of the highest literacy rates in Asia: over 82 per cent. Education is free from kindergarten to university and involves the Government in the yearly expenditure of about 5 per cent of the Gross National Product. Ceylon has four universities, three situated in Colombo and its environs and one at Perandeniya, close to Kandy.

THE FUTURE

Despite Ceylon's economic ills—its over-reliance on plantation-economy coupled with under-production of food and its small internal market—the nation has several resources it can use to its advantage: large deposits of gemstones, commercial quantities of rutile and other minerals, a well-developed transport and communication system, coral reefs, ruins of ancient cities, and other tourist attractions, and a large pool of educated manpower, the first requirement for efficient industry. As a positive step towards establishing a stable economy, early in 1972 Parliament brought in a new Constitution. The old Dominion of Ceylon ceased to be and the Republic of Sri Lanka was proclaimed. Today the people of Sri Lanka are engaged in a struggle like many other former colonies in Asia, to free themselves from the encumbrances of the old-style economies and from the out-moded political and economic forms imposed on them by the colonial powers, and to make workable a society which values the freedom and dignity of the common man.

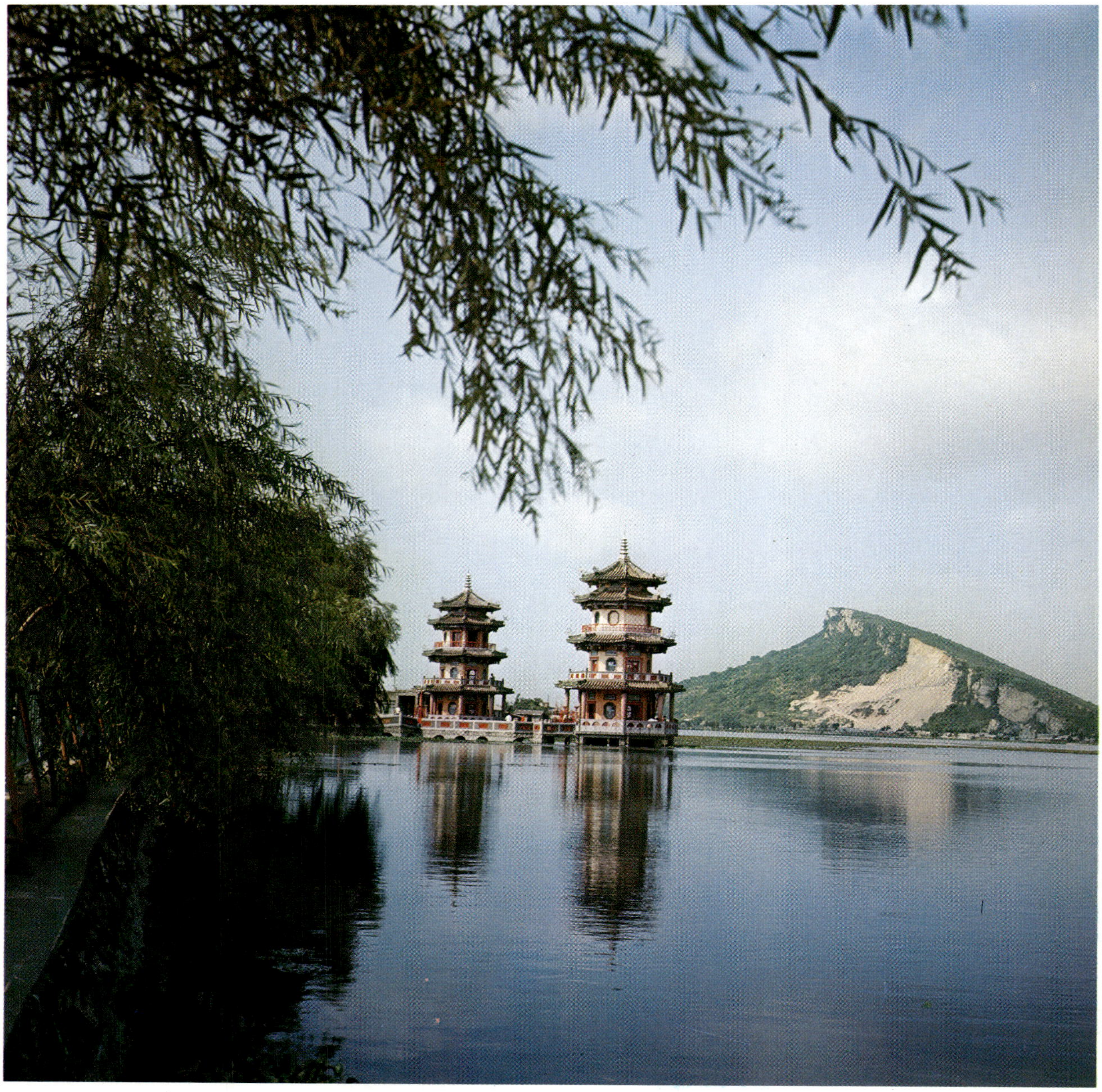

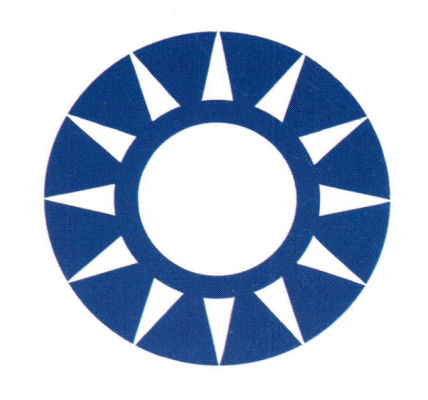

Republic of
CHINA

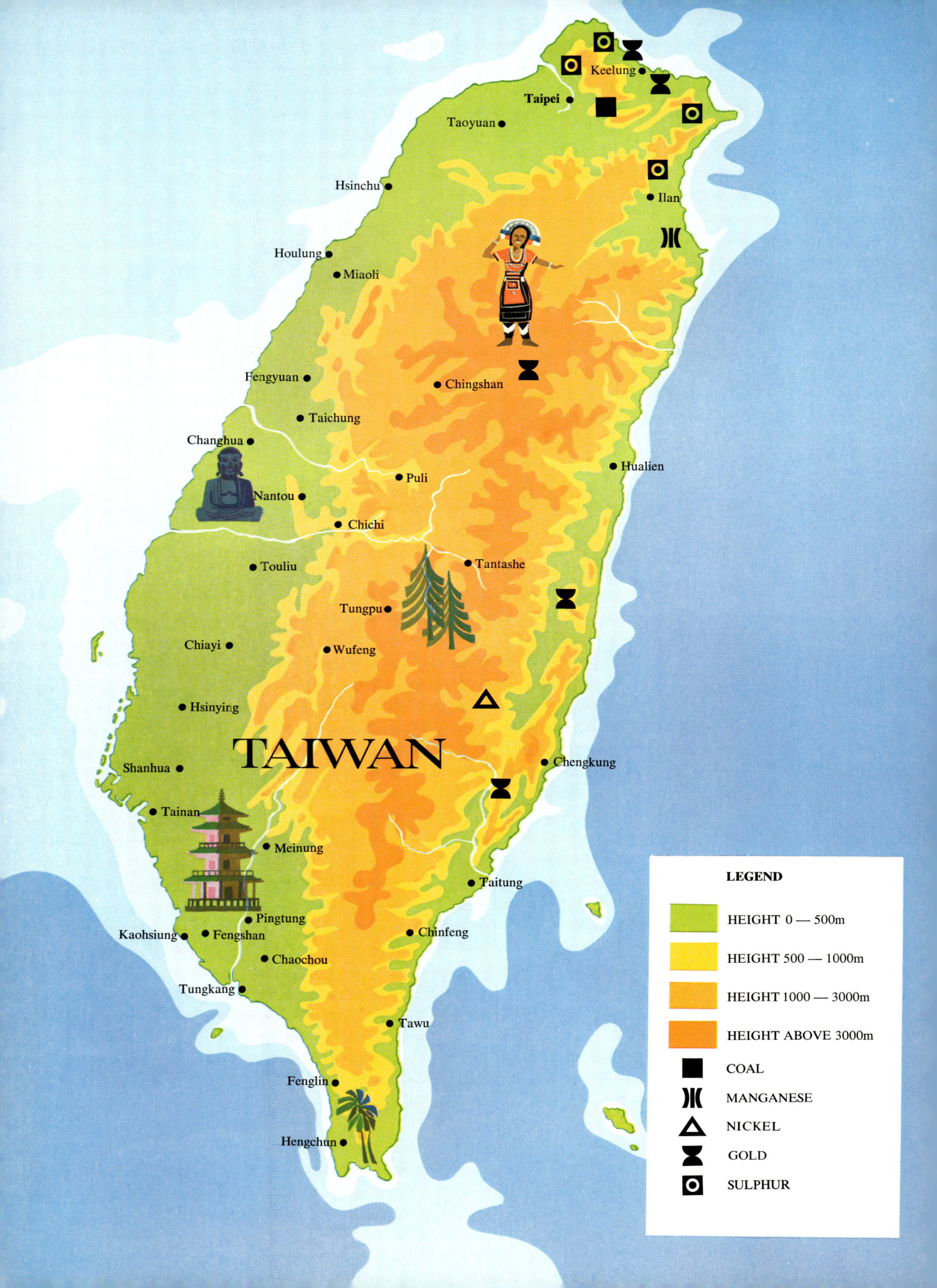

TAIWAN

- Keelung
- Taipei
- Taoyuan
- Hsinchu
- Ilan
- Houlung
- Miaoli
- Fengyuan
- Chingshan
- Changhua
- Taichung
- Nantou
- Puli
- Hualien
- Chichi
- Touliu
- Tungpu
- Tantashe
- Chiayi
- Wufeng
- Hsinying
- Shanhua
- Chengkung
- Tainan
- Meinung
- Taitung
- Pingtung
- Kaohsiung
- Fengshan
- Chaochou
- Chinfeng
- Tungkang
- Tawu
- Fenglin
- Hengchun

LEGEND

- HEIGHT 0 — 500m
- HEIGHT 500 — 1000m
- HEIGHT 1000 — 3000m
- HEIGHT ABOVE 3000m
- ■ COAL
- ⋈ MANGANESE
- △ NICKEL
- ⧖ GOLD
- ⊙ SULPHUR

Taiwan

LOCATION:

Between 21°45' and 25°38' north latitude and 119°18' and 122°6' east longitude. 100 miles (160.93 km) off the South China coast, flanked by the Taiwan Strait in the west and the Pacific Ocean in the east. 225 miles (362.1 km) north of The Philippines and 665 miles (989.75 km) southwest of Japan.

AREA:

Shaped roughly like a tobacco leaf, Taiwan, a province of the Republic of China, covers an area of 13,885 square miles (35,961 square km). Included in the province is the Penghu Archipelago. Kinmen and Matsu, are part of Fukien Province.

AVERAGE LENGTH:

Two hundred and forty miles, from north to south.

BROADEST WIDTH:

Eighty five miles from the coast west of Shanhua to the coast west of Chungkung.

CLIMATE:

Sub-tropical. A comparatively lengthy summer from May to September and a mild winter from December through to February. Average yearly temperatures range from 70.9°F (21.6°C) in the north to 75.7°F (24.3°C) in the south. Temperatures rarely exceed 97°F (38°C), even in the mid-summer months.

RAINFALL:

Yearly average 101.57 inches. More rain falls in the north than in the south. The northern-most port of Keelung is the most rainy city in the world: 238 inches annually.

POPULATION:

Just over 15 million at mid-1971. Average annual natural growth is 2.2 per cent.

PROJECTED POPULATION AT PRESENT RATE OF INCREASE:

Year 1980: 20,800,000
Year 2000: 34,800,000
(These figures do not allow for changes to the present rate of increase and as such are only approximate.)

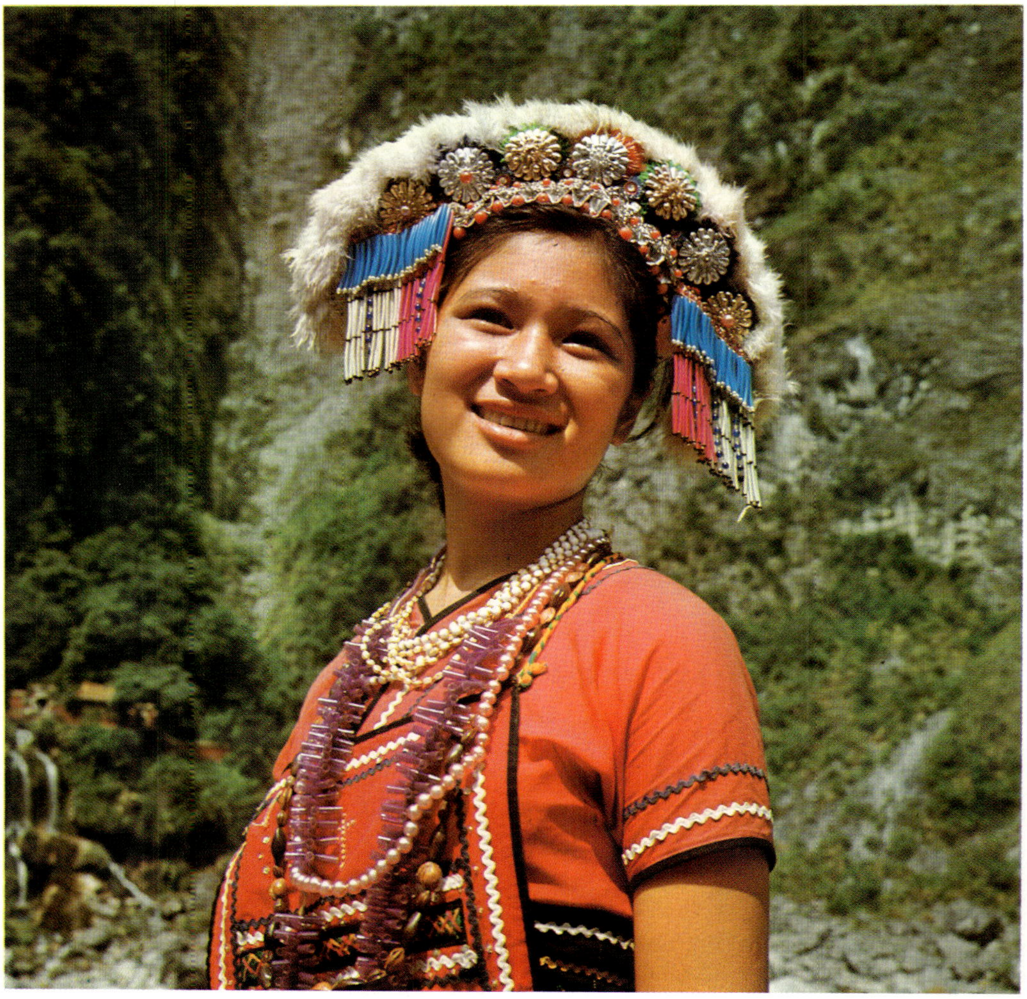

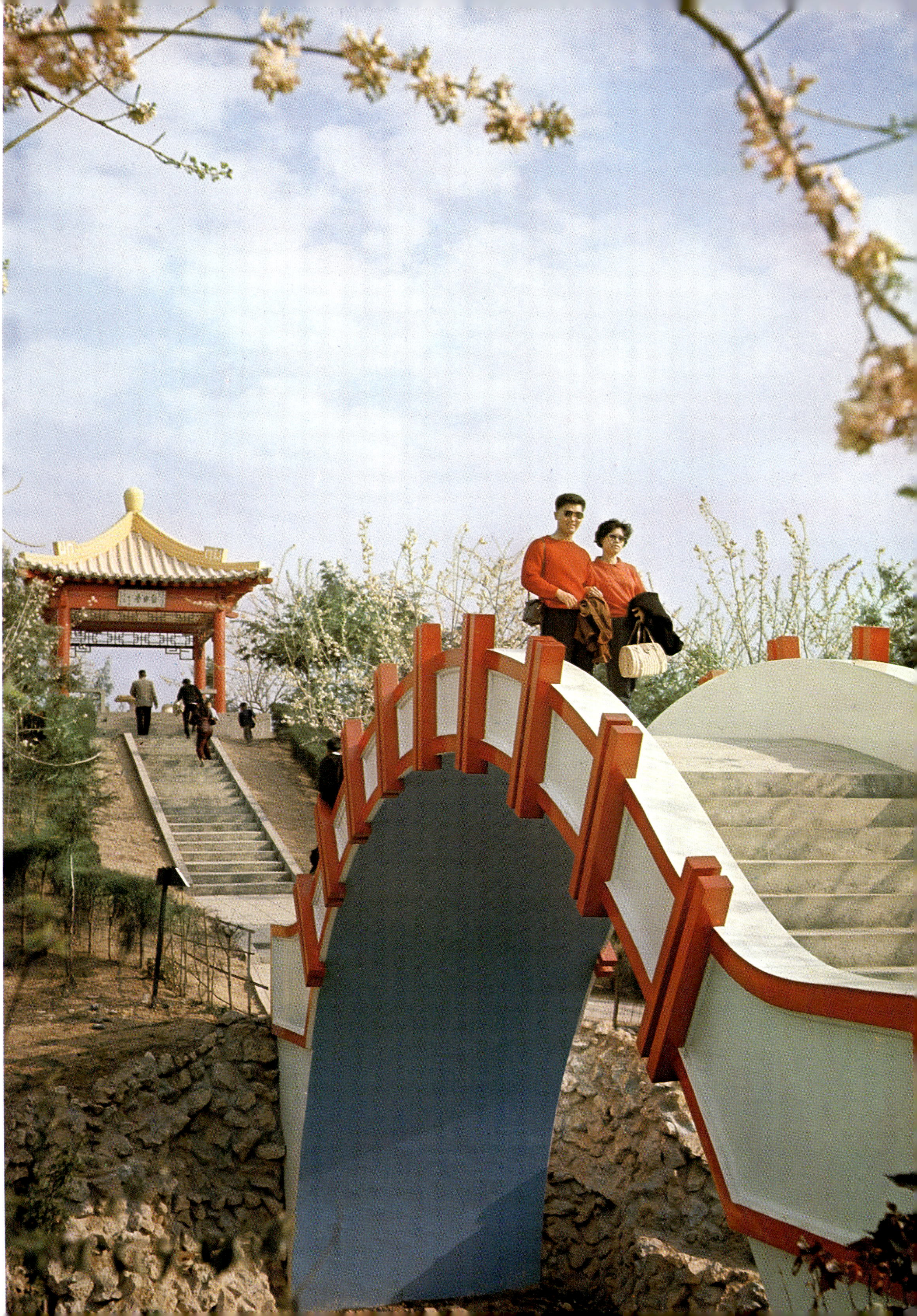

The dragon and peacock are traditional guardians of fortune and happiness.
These symbols are frequently used on the roofs of Chinese temples.

TAIWAN'S PRESENT SIGNIFICANCE in the world and particularly in Asia can only be grasped by examining the forces which have moulded each period of its history; the migrations during a volcanic pre-history, the invasions of the 17th, 18th and 19th Centuries and its more recent propulsion into industrialised modernity.

The island of Taiwan sits in the middle of the Hong Kong-Japan sea lane with the expansive Pacific Ocean to the east and the Taiwan Strait to the west.

Although the climate is temperate the island is often buffeted by typhoons blowing up from the South Pacific, and shaken by earthquakes and volcanic disturbances.

The early migrants (1-600 A.D.) who dared the crossing from China and chose to remain on an inhospitable island, cut off from their homeland, were tough and tenacious, although the fact that many were either social outcasts from Southern China or landless poor from depressed areas of the Fukien province meant that their homeland held little future for them and the island promised land and the right to farm it, unhampered by any pre-constituted authority.

The descendants of these oppressed people were to display the same tenacity and love of freedom under the Dutch and the Japanese, against whom they constantly rebelled.

Authority in this society was shared between the tribal chieftain and the hereditary priestess. The chieftain had jurisdiction in such matters as the cultivation and use of land, whereas the priestess exercised her power over marriage and religion and held the final word in any dispute. The migrants selected land, driving before them northwards and inland the earliest inhabitants—descendants of Proto-Malays—and, hampered by geographic hazards and the consequent difficulty of travel, set up tribes separate from one another, thus losing much of their ethnic unity and forming individual legal systems and customs. Each agricultural group devised laws to cover inheritance, land, marriage and property rights.

These earliest settlers brought with them, in their boats, seeds and cuttings of sugar cane, rice and tea, while migrations during the 13th Century introduced larger-scale farming of millet, cucumbers, melons and pumpkins and the primitive manufacture of silks and dyes. Despite the obvious wealth of the island, China displayed no interest in her rule or exploitation. The eunuch-scholars who advised the emperors, particularly during the Ming and Manchu dynasties, believed China to be the one and only land favoured by heaven and the physical possession of another state, the way of the uncivilised barbarian. This attitude, called tsung chu ch'uan (Sovereignty) by the Chinese, was the other extreme from bloody Western colonialism.

During the 17th Century Taiwan assumed importance as a way-station between the Dutch East Indies and Japan, whilst the Dutch, Spanish, Portuguese and English developed trade ties with the Far East. The Dutch seized control of south and central Taiwan in 1624 and dispossessed the Spanish—who had occupied the northern part of the island since 1626—seventeen years later. In an attempt to force their culture upon the Taiwanese, the Dutch taught their language and religion in missionary schools and attempted to repress Chinese traditions and culture. Sweated labour was used in Dutch factories and, in the sugar plantations, the Dutch East India Company employed the islanders as virtual slaves. Licence fees were required for hunting and fishing and these and other measures reduced the luckless Taiwanese to poverty.

In 1661-2 Cheng Cheng-kung,—better known to Westerners as Koxinga—a warlord and trader, wrested control of the island from the Dutch and built up a military base in the hope of resisting the Manchu rulers who at that time held sway on the entire Chinese mainland. Eventually, however, the Manchus conquered the island in 1683 and after six years it was incorporated as a county of Fukien province across the Taiwan Strait. In 1885 an Imperial decree elevated it to the status of a separate province.

Liu Ming-ch'uan became the first Governor, reforming the transport system, defence and industry. Modernisation was a generation ahead of the mainland: railways were in use, cable communications were established and industries on the western model were functioning. In 1891, however, the Mainland Manchus compelled the Governor to retire, as bitter opposition to reform still existed in a China whose officials resisted all change.

The last half of the 19th Century saw Chinese defeats at the hands of foreign powers: the French and the English at Peking, the Russians in the northwest and the Japanese in Korea. After being overcome in 1895, China signed the treaty of Shimonoseki in which she ceded Taiwan and the Penghu Islands to Japan and recognised the independence of Korea.

Chinese and aboriginal patriots on Taiwan revolted and declared the island a republic. Japan responded by crushing the revolutionaries with over-whelming military force and time and time again, during their rule, put down similar local uprisings. During the Japanese occupation heavy taxes were imposed on the farmers and, when it was

The Island of Taiwan

not possible for them to make payment, they were forced to give up their land to the invaders and work as tenants to pay off their debts. The farmer worked to produce sugar and rice for Japan, while feeding himself and his family on sweet potatoes. The Japanese education system was forced on the Taiwanese, while official posts and higher education were reserved for the invaders.

Repeated defeats by foreign powers, the weakness and incompetence of the corrupt Manchus, plus the example of the Meiji reformation in Japan, stimulated the disillusioned Chinese to respond to the call of the revolutionary, Dr. Sun Yat-sen, whose followers rose against the Manchu Government on 10th October 1911. The nation rallied to the revolutionaries and succeeded in overthrowing the Emperor.

The Republic of China was established on New Year's Day 1912 bringing to an end the last of the Chinese dynasties which had ruled from 1644. The anniversary is known as the Double Tenth because the Manchu dynasty was overthrown on the tenth day of the tenth month of 1911.

The establishment of the Republic, however, did not mark the beginning of stability for China: the task of constructing a new order, based on Dr. Sun's principles of nationalism, democracy and social wellbeing, was almost impossible in the chaotic period which followed the fall of the Imperial Government.

Dr. Sun Yat-sen died at Peiping in 1925 and the mantle of leadership then fell on Generalissimo Chiang Kai-shek, who is currently serving his fifth six-year term as the first constitutional President of the Republic of China. This term began in May 1972. (Chiang, who was born in 1887, was 84 years old on his last birthday, 31st October 1971. By Chinese reckoning a person is a year old at birth so the birthday was celebrated as his 85th.)

A period of disorder in the south and outright warfare in north and central China, led by counter-revolutionary war-lords, left the Government unable to implement their socio-economic plans, until the country was reunified and relative peace was established in 1926 under Generalissimo Chiang's leadership.

This new period of progress towards independence and prosperity was, however, short-lived. Fearful that a strong China might impede its imperialist ambitions in the East, Japan engineered a series of incidents, including the Mukden incident, which led to the occupation of Manchuria and culminated in the Marco Polo Bridge incident of 7th July 1937 which marked the beginning of an eight-year war between China and Japan.

The Chinese, led by Generalissimo Chiang Kai-shek, engaged the stronger, better equipped and better trained Japanese. However, with the help of her allies, (particularly the U.S.A. and Britain) China emerged victorious in 1945. Taiwan was returned to the Republic of China and Chinese nationality restored to the people. The anniversary of the restoration, 25th October, is known as Taiwan Restoration Day and is observed as a national holiday. Japan renounced all rights, title and claim to Taiwan and Penghu in Article II of the Peace Treaty it signed with the Republic of China in 1952.

The Communists, taking advantage of wartime chaos, were quick to stimulate unrest and later, nationwide rebellion. Despite attempts by the Nationalists to hold peace talks, the revolution spread. With the fall of Nanking in 1949 Chiang ordered the evacuation of troops and military equipment, as well as the removal of US$300 million of gold reserves and foreign currencies, to Taiwan, there to establish a base for national recovery. When the Government of the Republic of China moved to Taiwan its headquarters were located at Taipei; the Communists then adopted the name People's Republic of China for their own Government. Aided by evacuated troops, repatriated civilians and guerilla groups, Chiang marshalled a respectable force of 600,000 troops, a fifth of whom were stationed on Quemoy and Matsu, a few miles off the Chinese mainland.

After the outbreak of the Korean War in 1951, Taiwan's new importance to the U.S.A. was reflected in the signing of a mutual defence pact and the provision of large amounts of financial aid for the island's economic development.

The Nationalists, once established on Taiwan, were determined to institute social and economic reforms. They successfully implemented a three-stage land reform programme and thereby fulfilled Dr. Sun's "land to the tiller" ideal.

An economic resurgence began in 1953 when the Government launched the first of a series of four-year economic development plans. Despite immense difficulties the programme was so successful that the United States terminated all grant and concessional aid in mid-1965.

In 1970 Taiwan's international trade reached US$3,070 million with a favourable balance of US$34 million. Exports amount-

Above: A traditional ritual followed in the celebration of the birthday of Confucius.

Left: This ancient gate was erected in memory of Taiwan's past. It is one of two city gates of an ancient wall. It has been preserved at the front of the Presidential Building at Taipei since the wall was demolished many years ago.

ed to US$1,562 million, up 40.6 per cent over 1969, and imports to US$1,528 million, an increase of about 26 per cent. This compared with international trade to the value of US$2,300 million in 1969 which had resulted in an unfavourable balance of US$94 million. Industrial products accounted for 78 per cent of the 1970 exports.

It is forecast that the Republic of China's international trade will overtake and surpass that of Communist-held mainland within the next few years. This would be an outstanding achievement considering that the mainland is about 270 times larger than Taiwan and has almost 50 times the population.

According to liberal estimates the mainland's international trade reached about US$4,200 million in 1970 or the same level as it was eleven years ago. Thus the mainland's per capita trade in 1970 was only US$5.60 compared with US$213 in Taiwan, which enjoys the highest living standard in Asia after Japan.

The inflow of private foreign capital to Taiwan has risen substantially over the years. Approved inflow rose from an average of US$2.5 million before 1960 to about US$41.6 million in 1965 and US$138.9 million in 1970. About one-half of the investment was made in electronics and chemicals. 44 per cent of the 1970 amount was spent in the expansion of plants.

"WEN"

The Taiwan of today is the custodian and preserver of artefacts of the world's oldest culture—brought from the mainland 23 years ago.

Except for about 250,000 aborigines the people are Chinese, originating from mainland China. Full freedom of religion prevails, Buddhism predominates over some 600,000 Christians, divided evenly between Roman Catholics and Protestants, and about 40,000 Moslems.

The island, Taiwan, which literally means "Terraced Bay", is also known as Formosa, an unofficial name which derives from enraptured 16th Century Portuguese mariners who, on sighting Taiwan from the Pacific, exclaimed "Ilha Formosa! Ilha Formosa!" (Beautiful island! Beautiful island!).

Apart from its legendary beauty Taiwan has been developed into an economic showcase. The country is not richly endowed with natural resources and only about one-quarter of its area is arable. Yet it produced not only enough food to feed its inhabitants but also an increasingly substantial surplus for export. Considering the various factors involved, industrial development of the island has been phenomenal.

In the last four years of World War II Taiwan suffered from heavy bombing of factories established by the Japanese. Both factory and farm production fell to an all-time low. Post war reconstruction moved ahead very slowly in the early years and it was not until 1952 that agricultural and industrial production regained their pre-war levels.

The ancient Chinese believed that what distinguished them from the barbarians was the spirit of "wen"—pre-eminence in literature and the arts, ceremonial splendour and the many other things which contributed to a life of refinement, whether that of the city bureaucrat or the rice-growing peasant.

The value of human life, underlined in the teachings of Confucius, formed the basis of Chinese culture. Calligraphy, a daily task of the educated, became a traditional art.

Calligraphy is a specialised form of handwriting displaying originality, style, strength and personality. Script writing may be neat and ornate, but it never involves the intricacies of calligraphy. Chinese characters or ideographs present an infinite variety of forms to challenge the artist's imagination and ingenuity. The theme in prose or verse is unimportant; it is the beauty of form that matters. If the calligrapher feels the need to enhance the artistic value of his work, some of the characters may be distorted and even rendered unrecognisable. Lin Yutang has put it this way: "In appreciating Chinese calligraphy, the meaning is entirely forgotten, and the lines and forms are appreciated in and for themselves...A painting has to convey an object, but a well-written character conveys only its own beauty of line and structure".

To the Chinese, painting—and more especially landscape painting—is the mistress of the arts. Although Chinese painting is impressionistic, in that the artist feels free to omit objects or hint at movement—the flowing lines of a fish through water—a degree of realism is always present. Two main objects of Chinese philosophy are the understanding of the universe and the harmonisation of man's actions with its workings. In almost every Chinese painting an attempt is made to present the forces of nature—"yin" and "yang"—sweet and bitter; acid and alkaline; storm and calm; feminine, dark and negative; masculine, bright and positive, interwoven into a visual orchestration of life, in which man's part is shown as harmonious and essential. This is a unique style which contrasts delicately with the bolder, more factual works of European painters such as Van Gogh and Gauguin and the heavy abstracts of the moderns.

From his detached viewpoint the Chinese artist hints at the truth; his delicate and sometimes spare brush strokes offer a suggestion rather than a picture of his subject. The themes of Chinese painting are those considered spiritually refreshing; they rarely deal with violence and are never crude.

"...subtly mould the breathing bronze..." (Virgil, 70-19BC)

The Chinese of the Shang era were subtly moulding bronze wares thousands of miles from Rome and more than a thousand years before Virgil wrote this line in the Aeneid. Many of the greatest specimens were buried and forgotten for centuries, before they were excavated and acclaimed as masterpieces. Very little survives of the ancient Chinese civilisations that cast these bronzes.

In more recent times a number of inscribed bronze vessels were unearthed by Western archaeologists and the world learnt that this highly sophisticated craft dated back between one and two thousand years before Christ. The Shang bronze artisans made their pieces in striking design and structural perfection; even the most elaborately decorated utensils show no imperfections, a feat that has been rarely duplicated by other workers in metal.

The story of Chinese pottery begins in the pre-dynasty neolothic era. The great Sung and Ming porcelains, which led to the rage for Chinoiserie in Europe during the Eighteenth Century, were then more than four thousand years old. Although the Chinese were probably not the first to develop pottery for household and funerary use, they produced wares of such fineness that the English called porcelains "chinaware" and named the principal raw material, "china clay". The delicate white Ting porcelain of the Sung dynasty inspired the potters of Limoges in France. Blue and white ware of the Ming dynasty became the prototype of the Dutch Delft porcelain.

The Manchu dynasty was marked by a general deterioration of the potter's art. The intrusion of Western taste and the mass production of porcelain needed to supply the European market led inevitably to imitative and stilted designs. Taiwan, however, witnessed a minor revival of ceramics in the late 1950's and 1960's. Peitou, just north of Taipei, is the pottery centre.

Chinese music reflects the traditional regard for ceremony and moral righteousness of the old China. The Confucian way of life emphasises the proper order of things, and the playing of music as providing necessary discipline in conformity. The Book of Changes of pre-Confucian times declared: "There is nothing better than music in reforming people's manners and customs".

Chinese music had disciplined, mathematical connotations from the very beginning.

Many melodic lines were based on mathematical change, and not mere improvisation. In ancient times, it held an important place in the affairs of the state and was considered an essential part of the education system. Buddhist or Taoist music consisted of a droning chant of the scripture to the accompaniment of percussion instruments.

Confucian rituals were marked by slow and stately choral music accompanied by percussion and flutes.

The instruments utilised in Chinese music are not entirely strange to western eyes: the "hu chin" which has two silk strings and is played with a horsehair bow is something like the violin; the "yueh chin" resembles a moon-shaped guitar; the "pi pa" belongs to the lute family; the "ti tzu" is a bamboo flute; and the percussion section contains an assortment of drums, clackers, gongs and cymbals.

Folk music is an important part of the Chinese heritage. Even today workmen sing songs to cheer themselves at their work.

Farmers sing to celebrate the harvest or to accompany the movements of sowing.

Such melodies are still heard on the island of Taiwan; like the folk songs of other nations, they are simple and rhythmic.

A unique aspect of Chinese music is its close association with the language. Chinese is an inflected tongue, and it is difficult to distinguish the point at which speech ends and song begins. In shops, clerks sing of the good quality and reasonable price of their wares. In restaurants, orders are called from waiter to chef in a loud but melodic recitative.

China's popular music is more generally associated with the theatre. It is loud, raucous, and sometimes shrill. Opera music also belongs in this category. Because the appeal is to the general public, accent has been placed on simplicity. Melodic lines are limited to twenty or thirty tunes, with variations and embellishments added to suit the occasion.

"Ching hsi" or traditional Chinese opera is brilliantly colourful to the eye as well as to the ear. Combining music and dance, it contains stylized pantomime and strenuous acrobatics. Costumes are jewelled, brocaded and bright with reds, golds, greens and blues. Colour is used to indicate rank, status and personal character. Heavily painted faces are a distinctive feature, fulfilling much the same function as masks in Greek drama.

Every player must be adept in specialised sleeve, hand and foot movements. This produces a symbolised drama very foreign to that of the West: a door is closed symbolically, the actor merely bringing his two hands together at arm's length; a girl may dispose of her lover in the same way; for a cavalry charge, the riders wave the tasseled sticks they carry as symbols of horses.

The operas are concerned with the whole range of human emotions, but lean toward themes associated with royalty, wars and romance. The best known stories are several hundred years old, although Taiwanese writers are now beginning to incorporate contemporary themes in their works.

Chinese literature contains many features which are not paralleled in the literary tradition of the West, whose greatest poets have drawn much of their inspiration from religion—for example Dante's "Inferno" and Milton's "Paradise Lost". Chinese poetry and drama derived from ritual, but the primary function of Chinese literature, which evolved over the centuries, was to praise virtue and to condemn evil. Although

Above:
Typical modern apartments which have been built in Taipei and other cities of Taiwan in recent years.

Left:
Reserve servicemen performing a lion dance in the celebration of Chinese National Day.

Right:
The National Museum in Taipei houses more than a quarter of a million treasures, handed down from dynasty to dynasty.

many writers rejected this Confucian ethic, few succeeded in avoiding it altogether.

It is almost impossible to discuss Chinese poetry without dealing in depth with the differences between Chinese and Western languages. More than any other poetry, it is prone to distortion and clumsiness in translation.

Chinese poetry, like traditional painting, uses the imagery of nature:

"Bamboo leaves rustle by the southern window,
The moon's light shines on the eastern wall."

It hints at meaning through the use of this delicate imagery and has a restful tone uncommon to much of Western verse.

The Chinese novel and drama sprang from the tales traditionally told by the public story-tellers who made their living by narrating the legends of history or religion in the city market places.

In the 1920's a new generation of young Chinese writers, all of them open to influence from abroad, set out to create a new literature of the people. This movement is continuing today on the island of Taiwan. The old Chinese novel is almost extinct through its failure to adapt itself to a changing society. The drama, however, is as vital as ever and draws large local audiences despite competition from the modern cinema.

In the last twenty years, Western artists, poets and musicians have looked to the East and to China in particular, in search of its all embracing view of nature and that sense of repose which characterises its traditional arts. The Chinese are also looking outside their own culture for new forms in which to experiment and for, perhaps, a sense of urgency and passion which their art has never manifested.

Today on the island of Taiwan, two cultures are merging, the involved ever-changing West is blending with the detached, changeless culture that is the old China. If history takes a middle course, the tempering of these extremes may produce a culture which combines the technology of the West with the ability of the Chinese to use these techniques to humanity's advantage.

POPULATION CONTROL

At the end of 1970 Taiwan had a population of 14,633,241 (excluding the armed forces). The mortality rate was 0.516 per cent and that of infants 2.05 per cent. The average life expectancy was 64.62 years for males and 69.06 for females.

The population density of the island is 407 persons per square kilometre, the highest in the world. In terms of arable land, the density of 1,638 persons per square kilometre is also first in the world, ahead of Japan's 1,489.

The Government and the people have been aware of the population problem for at least two decades. But Taiwan was dominantly rural until the 1960's and the ideal of the big family lingered on until more recent years.

Family planning activities are carried out by both the Taiwan Provincial and Taipei City governments. Both loop and pill have been used to space children and limit the size of families. Information booklets urge later marriages and delaying first child.

The rate of Taiwan's natural increase was nearly 3.7 per cent annually in 1956. The figure in 1970 was decreased to 2.2 and the goal is 2.0 per cent by the end of 1973.

Public opinion indicates that the Taiwan "ideal family" now averages 3.8 children while the actuality is 4.2 children. The target is two children which family planners hope can be reached by 1988. If this is achieved the population growth would continue for another 50 years and then level off at about 26 million.

Family planning was introduced in schools for the first time in the spring of 1971. Graduates of high schools and junior colleges received copies of a booklet entitled "Repair Your Umbrella Before It Rains". Longer schooling, later marriage and small families are advocated.

THE EDUCATION SYSTEM

The education system as established by the Government of the Republic of China in Taiwan is intimately linked with Dr. Sun Yat-sen's principle of Ming Sheng—the people's livelihood. Thus education should not be aimed at producing a new privileged class; rather, in the words of President Chiang Kai-shek, it should enable students "to cultivate their personality and develop their talents...to engage in productive work and dedicate themselves whole-heartedly to the promotion of social progress..." In effect education should be spiritually, socially and economically practical.

In 1968, the basic period of schooling throughout Taiwan was extended from six years to nine. Graduates of primary school now enter junior high school without prior examination. Primary school is free and only minor fees are levied for more advanced grades. Secondary education is completed to senior levels in six years but vocational training may be undertaken as well, in conjunction with secondary school education.

Professions such as nursing and kindergarten teaching may be studied at special secondary schools. Vocational and social education provide for adults who may have been unable to attend school during their childhood; subjects taught include acupuncture, massage, music, sewing, barbering, printing and handicrafts.

There are now 91 universities, independent colleges and junior colleges on the island.

As the student population at these institutions approaches the 200,000 mark, demand for entrance far exceeds classroom space.

To co-ordinate academic research with the practical needs of the community, research centres in agriculture, physics, chemistry and other sciences were set up in 1965.

Chinese education is not confined to the study of academic subjects. Choong Kowkwong, former Minister of Education of the Republic of China once stated: "In accordance with the 2,500 year-old Confucian practice, teachers add to the moral and ethical guidance of parents. Special stress is placed on the Confucian ideals of "jen", the love of mankind, and "i", the concept of righteous conduct for its own sake."

The Republic of China is aware that in choosing a policy of rapid industrialisation it risks the loss of its traditional values. In other words, it risks becoming heir to a materialistic hedonism which could break down its family-centred society and nullify its ideals of patriotism and obedience to authority. As President Chiang points out of modern Western youth: "... many have fallen into degeneration... many have lost their moral courage."

In the shadow of the Communist mainland, Taiwan is shaping an education system centred around the Confucian ethic of discipline. Cut off, as the islanders are, from the continent which is the source of their culture, the Republic of China looks to the values of this culture as a means of maintaining the national identity.

THE POLITICAL SYSTEM

The guiding principles of free Chinese government were laid down by Dr. Sun Yat-sen, the Republic's Founding Father, who guided the new China from the moment of the Revolution of 10th October 1911 until his death in 1925. His political philosophy is based on what he called the "Three Principles of the People". These are Nationalism, Democracy and the People's Livelihood (social welfare). His system, like that of the United States of America, provides the basis for government of the people, by the people and for the people.

Many of Dr. Sun Yat-sen's political ideas are embodied in the Chinese Constitution, which was adopted by the National Assembly in 1946, promulgated by the National Government on 1st January 1947 and became effective on 25th December of that year. The Constitution assures democratic rule and extensive civil rights.

Structure of the National Government follows the five-power system originated by Dr. Sun. Under the President are five Yuans (branches of government): Executive, Legislative, Judicial, Control and Examination. The Examination Yuan safeguards and implements a civil service that has provided persons of merit for government employment for 2,500 years.

The President and Vice President are elected for six-year terms by the National Assembly, which is chosen by universal suffrage.

Normally there is a limit of two presidential terms, but this has been waived due to the Communist takeover of the mainland.

The Executive Yuan resembles the cabinet of Western countries. The Executive Yuan President (Prime Minister) is nominated and appointed by the President of the Republic with the consent of the Legislative Yuan.

Deputy Prime Minister and ministers are appointed by the President of the Republic upon recommendation of the Prime Minister. The Executive Yuan is responsible to the President of the Republic. There are eight Ministries (Interior, Foreign Affairs, National Defence, Finance, Education, Justice, Economic Affairs and Communications), three offices (Information, Comptroller General and Personnel Administration) and one Commission (Overseas Chinese Affairs).

The Legislative Yuan has 446 members elected by direct suffrage. The 73-member Control Yuan has power of consent, impeachment, censure and audit. Under the Judicial Yuan are the Council of Grand Justices, the Supreme Court, the Administrative Court and the Committee on the Discipline of Public Functionaries. The Examination Yuan supervises Ministries of Examination and Personnel.

Because of the Communist occupation of the mainland no elections of National Assembly, Legislative Yuan and Control Yuan members have been held since the late 1940's. Elections in Taiwan were held in 1969 as a result of the 1966 amendment of the Temporary Provisions of the Constitution. Under the Constitution the National Government is empowered to delegate large grants of administrative power to provincial and county governments. The Taiwan Provincial Government comes into close contact with the people in their daily lives. There is a Provincial Assembly of 71 members elected every four years.

Self-government at the lowest levels has been implemented in Taiwan since 1951. Elected by universal, equal, direct suffrage and secret ballot are mayors, county magistrates, city and county councillors and chiefs of townships and villages. The level of government which deals most directly with the people is not only of their own choosing but made up of those from their own communities.

Taiwan has four municipalities and sixteen counties. Taipei became a Special City on 1st July 1967 and is equal in status with Taiwan Province.

Opposite page: A terrace of private homes in modern Taipei.

Opposite page: Fu Jen University.

Left: Primary school children sketching in one of Taipei's many parks

Right: Primary school education is compulsory in Taiwan. 2,445,400 students attend primary schools, representing more than 97 per cent of children at school age.

presence by the melodious notes of flutes; the kitchen gods are sent heavenward with their lips sweetened to encourage favourable reports of the families with whom they are domiciled.

Here are all the glories of the Chinese cuisine that developed so largely from the experiments of master chefs seeking to tempt the sophisticated palates of bygone emperors; and here, too, in abundance are the food stalls in the street, some with electric lights, some illuminated by carbide lamps, but all providing dishes cooked in the traditions of the Old China—Peking duck, barbecued pork, crisp-skin chicken.

Here in Taiwan genuine, uncorrupted Peiping opera is performed at the theatre—or on stages erected in open lots by travelling troupes. Here also, flourishing as never before, are puppet shows that never fail to attract the fascinated village folk. Crowds flock to open spaces to gaze at the moon on the Mid-Autumn Festival and children are held spellbound by the story of the beautiful Chang-O, banished eternally to the Luna planet for stealing an elixir of immortality for her husband.

TAIWAN IS FOR THE TOURIST

THE SURVIVAL of age-old rites and traditions, manners and customs and other facets of a 5,000-year-old culture is one of the reasons that Taiwan is such a fascinating place to visit.

Here all are to be found, ranging from the same deep-rooted veneration for ancestors to the same high regard for filial piety and other virtues extolled by the illustrious sage, Confucius, about 25 centuries ago.

Here in Taiwan the deities in the Chinese pantheon—Huang Ti, the First Emperor; Kuan Yin, Goddess of Mercy; Matsu, Goddess of the Sea; and others of the great assemblage—are honoured as they used to be in mainland China.

Scholars consider Taiwan the repository of the Chinese cultural heritage: art collections formerly housed in Peking and Nanking were removed to the island in 1949 and are now on display in the fine National Palace Museum built in Taipei.

Here, too, thousands of people attend the ceremonial birthday bathing of Buddha; here the city gods are paraded through the streets on their anniversaries; the noodle vendor wails his midnight cry and blind masseurs tap their way, announcing their

Opposite page:
A bridge on the east-west
cross-island highway
which was cut through marble
mountains. This is one of Taiwan's
tourist attractions.

Opposite page, below:
There are almost 300,000 aborigines
in Taiwan.
The young ones
have been assimilated into a
modern population.
The colourful costumes shown here
are worn only on
special occasions.

Above:
The giant Buddha
at Changhua. Tourists may climb
to the head of this great statue
and view the whole of the city
through the eyes, 72 feet
from the ground.

Left:
Peacocks in the Taipei Zoo,
a picturesque and popular park,
particularly for children.

Here, finally, are the terraced paddy fields, water buffaloes in the custodianship of youngsters, the cheerful bazaars, the colourful festivals, the conviviality of dinner parties, the exchange of toasts in Shao Hsing wine.

The Times of London, in a recent article entitled "Tourism Leaps Ahead", said: "One of the brightest facets in the economic development of Taiwan has been the evolution of the tourist industry into a leading export, as it is classified because of the foreign exchange it earns". This fact is all the more remarkable because it was

Above:
Yangminshant Park is famous for its cherry blossoms. From February to the end of March, thousands of people visit this picturesque spot every day.

Below:
A vegetable market in Taipei. Chinese eat more than 50 varieties of vegetables.

Opposite page:
The Tamsui Golf Course is one of the finest in the Far East. This picture shows the restaurant on the country golf course.

Right:
The foreground of Litshan Hotel in a famous summer resort midway on the east-west Taiwan highway.

not until the last decade that organised efforts were initiated to develop the island's tourism potential. The industry's significant role since then is evidenced in the constantly swelling number of visitors and volume of revenues: in 1962, 52,304 visitors; revenue US$3 million;—in 1970, 504,398 visitors; revenue US$89 million.

Marketing experts forecast that in 1976 Taiwan will entertain more than 1 million visitors who will spend more than US$200 million. Matching progress in other sectors of the economic field is accepted as a foregone conclusion.

BANKING IN TAIWAN

THE TAIWAN BANKING SYSTEM. In 1945, when the island of Taiwan was retroceded by Japan to China, the economy was near collapse due to wartime bombings of strategic communication links and factories, the departure of 40,000 Japanese officials, 10,000 professional personnel and severe inflation. The Nationalist Government who established control in 1949, had the task of building a stable economy from the ashes of an agrarian, semi-feudal society which had not managed its domestic affairs since the Japanese take-over in 1895.

New currency was issued by the Bank of Taiwan on 15th June 1949, and through the necessary process of changing its parity several times the value of the monetary unit, the New Taiwan Dollar, was fixed at 40 New Taiwan Dollars ($NT) to the US$1.00 on 30th September 1963, a ratio which still exists today.

Between 1952 and 1968, four 4-year plans were launched to increase production and develop export industries. Without trade ties with their former major importer, mainland China, Taiwan was forced to become an independent trader on the world market.

There no longer exists a generally accepted definition of the term "bank". This is not surprising in consideration of the multiplicity of functions performed by modern banking institutions. The wide range of financial activities carried on by both Government-owned and privately-owned banks in Taiwan illustrates this tendency. Together with national banks there also exist commercial banks, credit unions, agricultural co-operatives and various specialised financial institutions such as development banks.

The Bank of Taiwan is the fiscal agent of the Republic of China. It carried out central functions before reactivation of the Central Bank and still acts as agent of the Central Bank in issuing New Taiwan Dollar notes. Together with these activities, the Bank of Taiwan engages in commercial banking, provides a substantial share of credit extended to public enterprise and deals in foreign exchange.

After eleven years of inactivity, the Central Bank of China was re-established in July 1961. Its functions are the regulation of the money market, management of foreign exchange, issuance of currency, and fiscal services for the Government. Reserves are kept against bank deposits, interest rates are regulated and the Central Bank acts as a lender of last resort and supervises the activities of all financial institutions. Its clients are government agencies, banks, credit institutions and international financial organisations.

Government banks are established in Taiwan under charter and some of these have private shareholders. Many government banks tend to specialise as either savings banks, foreign exchange banks or as lending institutions. Some limit themselves to granting loans to specific sections of the community: either to agricultural or fishery enterprises on the one hand or to industry, including mining and transportation, on the other. Bank loans have encouraged the development of promising new industries, such as mushroom growing and canning. By 1970, this industry, started as late as 1957, had contributed US$34,000,000 in export earnings and Taiwan had become the largest exporter of mushrooms in the world. The value of this product per hectare of land is 30 times that of rice, Taiwan's major crop.

Although the Taiwan banking system does permit some specialisation by individual banks, the broad spectrum of finance, such as savings deposits, loans and insurance, is comparable to that of Western countries.

In co-ordination with the Government's economic policy, the largest commercial banking organisation in the Republic of China, the First Commercial Bank of Taiwan, has enlarged the scope of its credit service by extending loans to firms with sound management and to international traders with expanded volumes of business.

Founded in 1899, the First Commercial Bank now has 93 branches throughout the Republic of China. In order to handle its increasing amount of business, this bank has installed ledger machines to enter deposits and teletypewriters to speed up inter-office communications. Scientific planning and analysis has enabled the First Commercial Bank to improve its business performance, despite a tightly controlled money market and rises in interest rates on fixed term deposits. Senior managers have been sent to individual branches to study local business situations. The First Commercial Bank invited Mr. Henry J. Ralph, a distinguished retired American banker, to help them modernise

Opposite page:
An architect's impression of the new Head Office building of the First Commercial Bank of Taiwan.

Right: The Banking Chamber of the Yuan-Shan Branch.

banking management in 1970. Several new facilities have been added to the ever efficient commercial bank, and a "Small Business Service Centre" has been set up to inform small and medium-sized traders of the nature of banking services, export procedures and the techniques of business management.

Loans extended by the First Commercial Bank in 1971 increased 33.5 per cent over the previous year. The principal borrowers were agricultural, manufacturing and mining industries, followed by businesses engaged in consumer goods and major commodities marketing. The consumer credit service was introduced during 1970 to encourage people with increasing incomes to buy durable goods. Moreover, "Loan for purchase of U.S. goods and services" supported by the Relending Credit programme of the Export and Import bank of the U.S. and pre-export loans of low interest rate schemed by the Central Bank of China have also been brought into effect to enhance the export and import business of this country.

The years between 1954 and 1971 witnessed a steady expansion in both exports and imports. Whereas total trade was equivalent to only slightly more than 20 per cent of the Gross National Product in the early 1950's, it has now grown to more than 52 per cent of a GNP that has more than tripled.

Although the Government first authorised the First Commercial Bank to operate foreign exchange business as recently as 1967, this bank now provides a full range of comprehensive banking services such as commercial letters of credit, purchase of export bills, financing facilities for exports and imports, foreign exchange transfers, foreign currency loans and deposits, and credit information. By 1970 a network of close co-operation had been established with nearly five hundred major world banks. With a view to helping domestic firms promote their foreign operations, data on foreign market situations and the financial status of individual firms is regularly provided.

This added assistance to Taiwan's export programme contributed to an increase of US$451,029,000 in the total value of principal exports between 1969-70. Taiwan marked up favourable balances of trade to the amount of US$34 million in 1970 and of US$186 million in 1971 a huge increase.

The Bank of Taiwan, as the Government's instrumentality, has maintained tight control over the net currency, yet the quantity of note issue rose fifteen fold between 1953 and 1970 because of the increased demand for money to cover business transactions, the increase in loans granted to expanded productive enterprise, such as cement, textiles, electronics and plastics, the increase of exports, and the enhancement of assets in foreign countries. Since this is a natural consequence of sound economy, no ill effects were apparent in the life of the community.

In the monetary field, the Government has taken several retrenchment measures in an attempt to stabilise commodity prices and discourage undesirable speculation in real estate. These measures have included the national savings campaign. The success of the Government's plan is reflected in rises during the years 1969-70 of only 2.8 per cent in the wholesale price index and 4.4 per cent in the consumer price index. The steady growth of economy coupled with the less expensive but fast-learning local labour forces made the country a paradise for investment by many foreign interests.

Because of increased savings, good harvests of rice and soya beans, as well as non-traditional crops such as mushrooms and sugar, the growth of established industries —textiles, fertilizers and motorcycles, and the newer industries, petrochemicals and machinery—a high rate of capital formation, a sustained inflow of foreign investments and a flourishing export sector, the economy is expected to continue to grow vigorously. The 1971 rate of rise of the Gross National Product of about $11\frac{1}{2}$ per cent reflects the confidence in the future of the Republic of China held by the people of the island and, with few exceptions, by the world as a whole.

The First Commercial Bank of Taiwan has fostered, by the granting of credit and the provision of export advice, the Government's policy of support for private enterprise. In this atmosphere the Republic has developed an economy, which in 1972, featured industry to a greater degree than it did agriculture. This is quite a metamorphosis considering the fact that for thousands of years the island's commercial welfare depended on the success or otherwise of the harvests gleaned from the various crops.

The establishment of sophisticated and basic industries is a main target in the Government's economic plans. The ultimate goal is a modern industrialised nation with every citizen living in the freedom and prosperity first visualised by Dr. Sun Yat Sen. Taiwan's role today is that of an independent trader on the world's markets and its freedom and future prosperity lies in its extension of this role.

Above: The Yuan-Shan Branch building on the main street of Taipei City.

Below: The Staff Training Centre located at the rear of the Peitou Branch.

Left:
The Taiwan shipping industry has followed the modern trend of containerisation for sea freight.

Below:
A supermarket in Taipei — the modern development of retail trading.

MANUFACTURE

Since the middle 1950's the Government has adopted a policy of expanding Taiwan's industrial potential through diversification, and promoting export markets to earn foreign exchange for the import of raw materials and capital goods. While many developed countries cry for industrial protection and promote trade wars, the Republic of China has relaxed restrictions on the import of more than one hundred and fifty different items. This liberalising action has been adopted because the Republic's adverse trade balance is shrinking and it can now afford to be more lenient. At the same time, the Chinese in Taiwan are developing one of the most stable economies in Asia. The Government's fifth four-year plan calls for a growth rate of not less than 12.5 per cent in export marketing and not less than 9 per cent in industrial expansion.

Manufacture's share of net domestic production rose from 10.8 per cent in 1952 to 23.5 per cent in 1969. The growth rate was fastest in electrical machinery and appliances, petroleum refining, basic metals, chemicals synthetic fibres and motor car manufacture. The trend towards increased profitability and growth is mainly seen in industries characterised by a higher level of technology and processing.

The 1960 Statute for the Encouragement of Investment provides a five year income tax exemption for industries with special significance to the economy. Taiwan's social, economic and political stability has combined with these incentives to attract external investment, totalling more than US$440 million in the seventeen years since 1953. A quarter of this total was invested in 1969. In recent years, investors have favoured electronics, plastics, metals, precision instruments and other sophisticated industries.

FOREIGN TRADE

During the past decade the Republic of China has made a strong impact on international trade, the country's turnover for 1970 reaching US$3,070 million, with a favourable trade balance of US$34 million.

Export advances were led by textiles, small motors, sewing machines, electrical machinery and motorcycles. Import gains were paced by industrial raw materials and machinery.

Textiles topped export volume at US$450 million, followed by machinery (including electrical) US$273 million; plywood and furniture, US$125 million; basic metals, US$84 million; fish, US$50 million; sugar, US$45 million; bananas, US$35 million; canned mushrooms, US$35 million; petroleum products, US$34 million; canned asparagus, US$30 million; canned pineapple, US$20 million; cement, US$20 million; fresh fruits, US$14 million: and glass, US$12 million.

Electrical machinery led the import list at US$198 million, followed by machinery and tools, US$196 million; basic metals, US$164 million; chemicals, US$160 million; transportation equipment, US$122 million; cotton and man-made fibres, US$102 million; soybeans, US$60 million; timber, US$58 million; crude oil, US$46 million; wheat and barley, US$45 million; maize, US$35 million; canned foods, beverages and tobacco, US$31 million; pharmaceuticals, US$19 million; wool, US$17.5 million; and chemical fertilizers, US$7 million.

Major trading partners were the United States and Japan. Exports to the United States totalled US$567 million and imports were US$454 million. Taiwan sold US$231 million worth of goods to Japan and purchased Japanese goods to the amount of US$567 million.

Hong Kong was in third place at about US$160 million. Then came West Germany, Australia, Indonesia, South Korea, Malaysia, Singapore, the Philippines, South Vietnam, Thailand, the Ryukyu Islands, Italy, the Netherlands, Britain, Canada, the Ivory Coast, Nigeria and Brazil.

TAIWAN SHIPBUILDING

BECAUSE of its relatively small size and mountainous terrain, the Republic of China in Taiwan is inevitably subjected to economic pressures created by limited natural resources which are generally little more than adequate to supply the needs of the domestic market. Its future viability is therefore largely dependent on its ability to build up secondary industries through the import of raw materials, and so expand its already growing export markets. A healthy local ship building industry can play a vital part in the future of the Republic. This was foreseen by the Government in the very early stages of its establishment on Taiwan, and in 1945 it built its own shipyards on Peace Island, near Keelung, the principal port. Under the ownership and control of the Taiwan Shipbuilding Corporation, it has enjoyed a steadily expanding career. After twelve years confined to meeting local demands, the entire plant was leased in 1957 to the Ingalls Company of the U.S.A. for the building and servicing of American ships. It reverted to the Government in 1962 and is now jointly managed by the Ministry of Economic Affairs and the Taiwan Provincial Government. In addition to the construction and maintenance of ships, TSC has diversified its activities into the field of industrial machinery manufacture.

Extending over an area of 200,000 square metres and equipped with two dry docks of 100,000 and 25,000-tons respectively, one 100,000-ton building dock and a 32,000-ton building berth, TSC's shipyard is one of the largest in the Far East. Ships built on Peace Island include one 100,000

Left: A 32,000-ton ship
being overhauled in Keelung dockyard.
A new shipyard,
which will be one of the largest in Asia,
is planned for construction
at Kaohsiung.
At the Keelung shipyard
several 100,000-ton tankers
have already been built.

Above: The urea section
at the Hsinchu plant,
50 miles from Taipei,
one of the Taiwan Fertiliser Company's
complex of eight units.

Right:
An interior of the
Taiwan Aluminium Corporation's
aluminium sheeting section.

DWT tanker, one 58,000 DWT bulk carrier, two 36,000 DWT tankers, six 28,000 DWT bulk carriers and 36 other vessels of various types. In the 26 years since its foundation, TSC has maintained a total gross tonnage of 10 million tons. To facilitate cargo loading it operates six incoming piers from 4.5 to 8 meters in depth.

The Taiwan Shipbuilding Corporation is equipped for steel material treatment and for the assembly and fabrication of almost every type of sea-going vessel. Its shipbuilding berth and dry-docks are capable of building ships up to 120,000 DWT and its maintenance facilities have similar accommodation. One of the recent assignments of TSC was the construction of the 27,000 DWT bulk carrier M.V. "Tai Corn". It is the largest of the fleet owned by the Taiwan Navigation Company.

As an industrial machinery manufacturer, TSC forges crank shafts, cuts gears, grinds and mills various metals and casts iron and steel up to ten tons in one piece, as well as producing alloys to meet specific needs.

CHEMICAL FERTILISERS

THE USE of chemical fertilisers and the application of scientific methods to the traditional forms of agriculture have been major factors in the reform of Taiwan's primary industry since 1952.

The Taiwan Fertiliser Corporation (TFC) was inaugurated in 1946, taking over from the Japanese the three plants ravaged by the war. As the result of renovations and improvements and continued expansion over the past 25 years, TFC today owns a complex of eight units including factories at Keelung, Lotung, Nangkong and Hsinchu and a coal mine near Munan. In addition, TFC bought the foreign shares of Mobil China Allied Chemical Industries Ltd. in 1970 and incorporated the latter's Miaoli plant into its own complex.

TFC's main products include ammonium sulphate, ammonium phosphate, calcium super phosphate, compound fertiliser and nitrochalk and urea, with a total annual production of 1,133,000 tons. By-products from the manufacture of these chemicals include: acetylene black, aqueous and anhydrous ammonia, argon, carbide, coal, ferrosilicon, hydrogen, limestone, nitrogen, oxygen, quick and slaked lime, sodium, silico-fluoride and gypsum.

More than three-quarters of TFC's total production is sold on the home market. In order to improve Taiwan's foreign exchange balance and to extend its own markets TFC has been searching for export avenues for its products which are in excess of local needs. These include carbide, calcium cyanamide, argon, slaked lime, liquid ammonia, urea and ferrosilicon. In addition to these, compound fertiliser and horticultural fertiliser are believed to have export potentials. At the present time TFC's markets extend from Vietnam and Thailand through to Singapore and Australia and as far as the U.S.A.

Because of its competitive prices, top-quality products and prompt delivery, TFC enjoys a high reputation among overseas buyers. Advice on the techniques of scientific cash-cropping provided by TFC, has enabled farmers on Taiwan and in many other parts of South-east Asia to improve their yields and cultivate the available land more economically.

TAIWAN ALUMINIUM

THE TAIWAN Aluminium Corporation (TALCO) is a wholly-owned Government enterprise under the direction of the Ministry of Economic Affairs. It has the responsibility of supplying Taiwan with its aluminium requirements in refined metal and in the semi-fabricated forms of sheets and plates, foil and extruded shapes. TALCO also produces some end-products, but its role in this field is generally limited to the demonstration and the promotion of aluminium in its various forms and uses.

TALCO was established in May 1946 and began production in the following year at an alumina smelting complex originally built in 1935-36. At the end of World War II these plants were heavily war-damaged and output paralysed. During the past 25 years, TALCO has expanded and modernised the complex, rebuilt and expanded the smelting plant, set up rolling and extruding operations, and brought them to a high and efficient stage of production.

With its existing facilities, TALCO is capable of an annual production of 76,000 metric tons of alumina, 38,000 tons of primary aluminium, 24,000 tons of aluminium sheets, 2,100 tons of plain and paper-backed aluminium foil, and 3,600 tons of aluminium extrusions.

As bauxite is not available in Taiwan, the raw aluminium ore for the TALCO plants is imported under long-term contracts, partly from Johore, Malaysia and partly from Weipa on the Cape York Peninsula of Australia. About 150,000 metric tons are brought in every year.

The construction of an unloading pier, begun during 1971 at TALCO's own water front, was completed early in 1972. It is planned to accommodate ships in the 25-30,000-ton class and the unloader has a maximum rated capacity of 300 tons of ore per hour. Although primarily constructed for handling bauxite, the pier can also be used for other bulk commodities.

Aluminium is produced commercially from alumina, a white powdery form of aluminium oxide. TALCO's present smelting plant, equipped with a line of smelting pots (electrolytic cells), commenced operations with a capacity of 20,000 metric tons of primary aluminium. Since then the output has almost doubled. The metal emerges from the pots as commercially pure aluminium, but to conform to modern practice it is conveyed to a cast house to be combined with other metals in various proportions to form alloys.

The construction of a 90-MW diesel engine power plant next to the potline, completed in April 1972, generates sufficient power to feed the electrolytic cells. New constructions started during 1971 and early 1972 include the setting up of an aluminium can plant, an aluminium shipping container and a truck body kit plant. TALCO is also proceeding with plans to produce aluminium alloy wire, roll-bond aluminium products and super-purity aluminium.

To meet the rapidly growing demand for aluminium, the Taiwan Aluminium Corporation proposes the implementation of a large capital investment plan, which involves the construction of a second smelting plant with an initial capacity of 32,000 metric tons per year. This will ultimately be raised to 100,000 tons, and will parallel the expansion of existing plants. Through a process of improved techniques and advanced management principles TALCO is up-grading the already high quality of its products. The Corporation is a practical example of what can be achieved by positive thinking and diligence in a region of the world lacking in secondary industry.

Above: Chingshan Hydro-Electric Power Station, will be the largest in Taiwan. The first two 90 MW units were completed in 1970, the remaining two will operate from August 1972.

Right: Chinese Petroleum Corporation's imposing refinery at Kaohsiung.

DEVELOPMENT OF ELECTRIC POWER

THE RECENT industrial growth in Taiwan has been largely responsible for the increased demand on the island's electricity supply. Taiwan today owns 37 power plants in a network that has boosted the total installed capacity to 2,720,000 kilowatts. Of this capacity one-third of the power output has come from hydro-electric plants; the remainder is generated by thermal stations.

Although Taiwan's rivers provide a source of power adequate for present requirements, this may not be so as the demand increases in the near future. With abundant supplies of natural gas Taiwan is concentrating, therefore, on the installation of thermal stations, which also have the advantage of being quicker and cheaper to build than hydro-stations.

In order to provide adequate power for the island's burgeoning industries, the Government-owned Taiwan Power Company (Taipower) has aggressively engaged in power development programmes, four of which were completed before the end of 1970. A ten-year, long-range programme was begun in 1971 with the aim of bringing the nation's total installed capacity up to 8,707,000 kilowatts by 1980. A brief outline of some of the projects involved in this plan is as follows:

1) The *Linkou Thermo-Electric Project* has undertaken the installation of the second generating unit in the existing Linkou Thermo-electric Plant. This will produce power by the use of a 350,000 kilowatt turbine generator.

2) Installation of four hydro-powered generators of 90,000 kilowatts each has been planned for the *Chinshan Project*. During the first stage, two of the four units were completed. The scheme should be fully operative by the end of 1972.

3) The *Talin Thermo-Electric Project* calls for the construction of a large-scale thermo-electric plant which will utilize oil as fuel. This station is planned to meet the increasing load in the export processing centre of Kaohsiung as well as ensuring continuity of supply throughout the island.

4) The key to the *Tachia River Development* lies in a projected dam which will be located in the Tehchi valley. It will be a concrete, double-curved dam rising to a height of 180 metres. This undertaking, commenced late in 1970, calls for the installation of three turbine generators of 78,000 kilowatts each.

5) In order to develop peaceful application of nuclear energy and to lower the cost of electricity, Taipower has commenced work on the *Northern Island Nuclear Power Project*. Scheduled for completion in 1976, this project will consist of a nuclear power plant equipped with two generators of 636,000 kilowatts each.

Through the successful completion of these schemes, the Taiwan Power Corporation plans to provide the nation with a cheap, dependable power supply, adequate for its future industrial and private needs.

CHINESE PETROLEUM

THE Chinese Petroleum Corporation (CPC) was founded in 1946 as a Government-owned enterprise to engage in the import of crude oil for refining into petroleum products. The Government has undertaken this enterprise: in order to ensure adequate sources of energy; to explore, develop and make use of oil and natural gas resources; and to promote Taiwan's petrochemical industry. Over the past 25 years, CPC has undergone continued expansion to keep pace with the increasing demand for power from the Republic's growth industries. Today, CPC runs a complex of operating units including the Kaohsiung Refinery, the Chiayi Solvent Works and the Taiwan Petroleum Exploration Division.

Following a steady expansion of facilities, CPC today boasts a refining capacity of 138,000 barrels daily. In anticipation of increased demand for petroleum fractions, two projects are now under way. One is the sixth topping unit in the Kaohsiung refinery with a daily capacity of 100,000 barrels and the other is a new refinery in northern Taiwan. By 1974, CPC expects to raise its total refining capacity to more than 300,000 barrels daily.

CPC has carried out oil exploration surveys and geological field work in Taiwan for more than ten years. Rich natural gas fields have been spotted in many areas, including Chinshui and Chingtsao Lake and unexploited resources on the island are estimated at 27 billion cubic metres of natural gas and 2.7 million litres of crude oil. CPC has started work on a joint project with five foreign oil companies, exploring off-shore resources north of Taiwan.

CPC's role in the Republic's petro-chemical industry has been to supply intermediate materials for manufacture into various organic compounds. In southern Taiwan, a naptha pyrolysis plant has been built in the Kaohsiung refinery which yearly yields 120 million pounds of ethylene—the basic compound in the production of polyethylene plastic. Additionally, CPC has co-operated with the Taiwan Alkali Company, Taiwan Fertiliser Company, Kaohsiung Ammonium Sulphate Works and Korean concerns, manufacturing DMT, nylon and other petro-chemical products.

Four-fifths of CPC's products are consumed by the domestic market and the balance is sold throughout the world. These include gasoline, diesel oil, aviation fuels, kerosene, natural gas and asphalt.

Increased local sales have made it necessary for the Corporation to import mass volumes of crude oil in their own fleet of tankers. Sales outlets include over two hundred gas stations throughout the island, stations at every harbour and major fishing port and numerous bulk plants.

In conformation with the nation's economic plans, CPC has been moving in the direction of diversified operations and has successfully established itself as one of the biggest government-owned businesses in the Republic of China.

AGRICULTURE

TO IMPROVE the livelihood of the rural masses the Chinese government launched one of the world's most successful land reform programmes in 1949. By 1963 all Taiwan tenant farmers who had purchased land under the system had paid their last installments, and since then owner-tillers have increased from 36 per cent of all farmers in 1949 to more than 80 per cent, while tenant farmers have decreased from 39 per cent to 9 per cent. The remainder either own or rent the land which they work and the standard of living has improved.

The Government began a land consolidation programme in 1961 to bring together small, scattered plots to save the farmer's time and make agriculture more efficient. Other improvements have included better road networks, access to irrigation water and better drainage. By the end of 1970 about 230,000 hectares of farmland had been consolidated, production increased and production costs lowered.

Land reform, primarily aimed at social justice, has given impetus to economic development. The farmer's net share of the farm yield—i.e. what he could keep for himself after various payments had been made in kind—has been substantially increased and productivity raised. In 1948 the per hectare yield of paddy rice (on a two-crops-a-year basis) was 3,894 kg. of which 47 per cent was retained by the farmer. This reached 8,142 kg. in 1970 and the farmer kept as much as 76 per cent.

The series of four-year plans has made possible the long range programming of agricultural development. As the topography of Taiwan precludes any notable increase in arable land, intensive farming has been persistently promoted. Fortunately the subtropical climate of the island makes this feasible. New farming techniques were introduced, new and better varieties, crop rotation, multicropping, intercropping, increased and more efficient application of chemical fertiliser, intensification of plant disease and pest control and improvement of irrigation and drainage. Farm mechanisation has been encouraged and locally-made power tillers are replacing draft cattle.

Between 1952 and 1970 unit yields of such crops as bananas and pineapple more than doubled. The output of all major crops, except those with reduced acreage, has

Right:
Sheep are raised
on the fertile pastures of Taiwan.
In the mountainous regions in the south,
Angora goats are bred to make use
of the more rugged land.

Below:
African farmers learning progressive
methods of agriculture
from Taiwanese teachers.
Here they are seen studying
vegetable growing.

increased substantially. Some 2.46 million metric tons of rice, the key crop, was produced in 1970, a gain of more than 60 per cent over 1952, although the acreage virtually remained unchanged.

Efforts also have been directed to the diversification of crops and the development of rural sidelines. Choice varieties of new crops have been tested and introduced into areas favourable to their growth. Examples are soybeans, mushrooms and asparagus which have augmented the income of thousands of farm families. Taiwan is the world's largest exporter of canned mushrooms and pineapple and a leading exporter of canned asparagus.

Hog raising has been promoted. As a result of improved breeding, better feeding and disease control, the hog population has increased steadily. The number of hogs slaughtered increased from 1.26 million head in 1952 to 3.92 million in 1970. Pork is the main source of protein for the Taiwanese who now export it in quantity.

A local dairy industry has been established and good progress made with the Government's encouragement. Use of slopelands, which constitute three-quarters of Taiwan's terrain, is under study for the raising of cattle and sheep.

Among primary enterprises fisheries have been forging ahead at the fastest pace in recent years. Production reached 613,000 metric tons in 1970 compared with 121,700 in 1952. The rapid increase is attributable to dieselisation of fishing craft and the improvement of methods and gear. Deep-sea fishing fleets have been enlarged and now cover waters from Guam to the Atlantic.

As more than half the island is forested, timber is an important resource. Since 1953 logging has been carried out under an overall development programme. Logging methods and transportation facilities have been improved. Timber production increased from 448,570 cubic metres in 1952 to 1,080,000 in 1970.

The Government recently initiated a new programme to lower costs of farming, to spur farm mechanisation, to commercialise farm production and set up agricultural research.

The target for agricultural growth under the fifth economic plan is 4.4% a year.

TECHNICAL CO-OPERATION

In December, 1961, 15 Chinese farmers from Taiwan arrived in Liberia to help African farmers grow rice. Within three months, they had covered what formerly had been wasteland with a carpet of green. That was the beginning of a farm demonstration programme which has won world recognition and overwhelming African approval. As of late 1971, some 1,000 free Chinese farmers were working with Africans of 22 countries to grow bigger and better crops of grain, vegetables and varieties of fruits.

The idea for this programme was born in 1960, when officials of many newly independent African countries visited Taiwan. They were impressed by the rural prosperity of the island and noted similarities between the Taiwan and African climates and other aspects of the environment.

Responding to expressions of interest, the Republic of China sent demonstration teams to Liberia and then to Libya. In the latter country rice was grown in saline and previously barren soil on the desert's edge.

Africans were surprised to learn that their soil was remarkably fertile and that labour-intensive agriculture could produce bumper harvests. Rice yields were raised many times.

In the years since, teams have gone to these other countries: Botswana, Central African Republic, Chad, Congo (Kinshasa), Dahomey, Gabon, Gambia, Ghana,

Ivory Coast, Lesotho, Malagasy Republic, Malawi, Mauritius, Niger, Rwanda, Senegal, Sierra Leone, Swaziland, Togo and Upper Volta.

The techniques adopted are simple but effective. The Chinese demonstrators prepare the soil and install irrigation systems when necessary. Then they grow rice and other crops and invite local farmers to observe. Subsequently the programme is transformed into a training system. Advisers are sent out to help as many farmers as they can reach. The use of heavy or expensive machinery is avoided, because few African countries can afford it.

Ivory Coast farmers were raising one crop of rice a year with an average yield of 900 kilogrammes a hectare. Two crops are now yielding 6,574 kilos. Togo's single crop provided only 800 kilogrammes. Three crops are now grown with an output of 16,128 kilos, an increase of more than 20 times.

In ten years, the free Chinese have transformed 42,000 acres of former wasteland into lush paddy and built 5,260,000 feet of irrigation and drainage canals. They have trained 38,000 farmers and 3,000 agriculture officials.

In addition to farm demonstrators, the Republic of China has sent veterinarians and edible oil technicians to Chad, handicraft specialists to Madagascar and the Central African Republic, sugar mill engineers to Rwanda and seed multiplication and supply experts to the Ivory Coast.

Chinese agricultural missions are also working in South Vietnam, Thailand, the Philippines, Dominican Republic, Peru and Panama. Programmes have been completed in a number of other countries in both Africa and Latin America.

African agriculturists are trained in Taiwan, too. Twelve five-month seminars have been held for 583 trainees from 31 countries since 1962. Instruction is in French or English; classroom work is in the field.

THE SUGAR INDUSTRY

The largest industry in Taiwan is sugar refining. Although sugar cane has been grown on the island for over four hundred years, modern refineries were not established until the Japanese occupation in 1895. After World War II, sugar from Taiwan lost the monopoly position it had enjoyed in the Japanese market. In addition, because of heavy population pressure, much of the land previously planted with sugar cane was used to grow rice and sugar crops were relegated to less fertile areas. The survival of the sugar industry depended upon some means of revitalising it. It was this challenge that prompted the Taiwan Sugar Corporation (TSC), a monopoly with joint Government and private capital, to undertake a series of innovations to increase the yield and make full use of the by-products.

A new South African variety of sugar cane, introduced in 1949, increased the yield of sugar from seven to ten tons per hectare. More recently, the Corporation's laboratory and experimental station developed new strains that have resulted in even higher yields.

TSC now owns 25 sugar mills that produce nearly 900,000 metric tons of white sugar a year. Some 22,000 metric tons are sold on the domestic market, the remainder being exported.

As one of Taiwan's largest enterprises, TSC has contributed greatly to the overall development of the nation. It operates its own railways and provides much of the island's inland transportation. The Corporation initiated modern agricultural techniques long before they were popularly accepted in Taiwan: deep well irrigation; mechanised farming; water and soil conservation; compound fertilisation; and collective farm management. Technical aid has also been given to other developing nations. Experts in animal husbandry, farm management and sugar refining have been sent to African, South American and South-east Asian countries.

Besides its agricultural contributions to the economy, the sugar industry has also made a greater use of its by-products through the establishment of several, new inter-locking industries. Residual mollasses provides the basis for the manufacture of alcohol, yeast and monosodium glutamate. The latter, a flavouring essence, is an essential ingredient in Chinese cooking and is now

Right: Raw sugar crystals, fine superior white crystal sugar and superior white crystal sugar are standard grades of the Taiwan Sugar Corporation's production.

Above: Roses under cultivation in a Taipei nursery. The climate of Taiwan is well-suited to many beautiful flowers.

Opposite page: Modern highways have been built to accommodate the growing number of vehicles in Taiwan.

exported. The Corporation uses its sugar wastes to make bagasse boards and particle boards (heavily compressed cane fibres), which are used by the furniture and building industries to replace wood and bricks.

The Taiwan Sugar Corporation has also stimulated the growth of other industries such as pineapple and mushroom canning.

Furthermore, TSC's fuller use of the island's under-employed manpower and under-utilised land has helped to make agriculture a dynamic element in the development of Taiwan.

COMMUNICATIONS

Difficult conditions of roadbuilding are an old story in Taiwan as three-quarters of the island is mountainous. From the broad plain in the west, mountains rise to 13,000 feet, then descend precipitously to a narrow valley in the east. A lesser range separates this valley from the Pacific.

Two cross-island highways have been built in northern and central Taiwan. A southern road was completed towards the end of 1971. All three routes open up scenic high country routes for tourism, lumbering and the development of many varieties of the temperate crops of sub-tropical Taiwan.

Most mountain road construction has been carried out by retired servicemen. The Vocational Assistance Commission for Retired Servicemen is Taiwan's largest construction agency and one of the most versatile enterprises in Taiwan.

Highways of Taiwan exceed 15,000 kilometres. There are 43 kilometres of road for every square kilometre of land. An expressway costing about US$500 million is under construction between Keelung at the island's north tip and Kaohsiung on the south-west coast. More than 1,000 kilometres of broad gauge railway lines have been laid, the main line stretching from Keelung to Kaohsiung. Plans are under consideration to join the east coast line to that of the west, with north-bend and south-bend links through the mountains. This would give Taiwan an around-the-island railroad.

The railroads are carrying 150 million passengers and 15 million metric tons of cargo annually. Dieselisation has taken place on most lines and electrification is expected during the current decade.

Taiwan's two major ports, Keelung and Kaohsiung are undergoing expansion. The shipping capacity of Keelung is limited by its geographical situation, but Kaohsiung can be enlarged to any conceivable size. A new harbour entrance now under construction will give this southern port an annual capacity of 25 million tons or more by the mid-1970's.

As of 1970, Lloyd's Register of Shipping showed that the Republic of China, with 172 vessels totalling more than a million tons, ranked 23rd in the world. Counting vessels owned by overseas Chinese but flying flags of convenience, the Chinese merchant fleet totals about 7 million tons to rank among the world's top 10.

Approximately 90 per cent of the Republic of China's merchant fleet operates on international sea lanes, 47 ships are in scheduled service and 101 are on non-scheduled routes. There are many new vessels, and all ships average 12 years old.

Taiwan is on the main route between Tokyo and Hong Kong the most heavily travelled air corridor in Asia. In 1970 international flights arriving and departing at Taipei's Sungshan airport averaged 50 a day. The Chinese flag carrier—China Airlines—flies to Singapore, Kuala Lumpur, Djakarta, Saigon, Bangkok, Hong kong, Manila, Okinawa, Seoul, Osaka, Tokyo, Honolulu, San Francisco and Los Angeles.

CHINA AIRLINES

FROM MILITARY CONTRACT carrier to internationally acknowledged top-ranking trans-Pacific airline within twelve years this is the enviable record of China Airlines, more familiarly known as CAL.

During the year 1959, a group of retired China Air Force officers decided that rather than spend their time at leisure, they could be of better service to their country by putting their wartime experience and knowledge to practical use. They gathered around them a staff of 26, bought two World War II Catalina flying boats, and formed a company which they called China Airlines. Now the flag-carrier of the Republic of China, CAL has grown to a fleet of 26 aircraft, including four Boeing 707's, three Boeing 727's, one pure-jet Caravelle and a YS-11A turbo-prop. The capital of the Company has risen to over the US$50 million mark and the original staff of 26 has grown to more than 3,500.

Domestic passenger flights were begun in 1962 and an international service to the Asian area commenced operations in 1966. Today the former routes link Taipei with Hualien, Taichung, Tainan, Kaohsiung and Makung in the Pescadores Islands. Regional services reach to Seoul, Tokyo, Osaka, Hong Kong, Manila, Saigon, Bangkok, Kuala Lumpur, Singapore and Djakarta. Service to Los Angeles via Tokyo and Honolulu was begun in early 1971 and the Hong Kong-Taipei-Tokyo-San Francisco route was opened in 1970.

The crude, inadequate terminal facilities of the late 1950's have been developed into a modern, 100,000 square feet maintenance base at Taipei International Airport. A large pool of internationally-qualified engineers and technicians, working with contemporary equipment in the workshops and testing units, spend 200,000 man-hours a month servicing the aircraft of many international airlines as well as those of the U.S. Air Force and the Company's own fleet.

China Airlines service and safety have been key factors in the organisation's success, and the attention given to the selection of experienced pilots and to training their hostesses is equalled only by major international airlines. All pilots employed by CAL must be veterans with records of not less than 10,000 flying hours. Chipao-clad hostesses on international flights speak all the principal Chinese dialects, as well as English, Japanese, French, German and other languages.

Brightly decorated in motifs of ancient China with red and gold panelling and delicate wood carvings, CAL aircraft cabins create an atmosphere of oriental opulence. Chinese cuisine is the airline's specialty. Dishes ranging from crisp-skin chicken and ham rolls, spicy pork in crab-meat sauce and stuffed fish in black-bean sauce, and rice, noodle and vegetable courses more familiar to Western travellers are served during flights, on chinaware inspired by the patterns of the Ming dynasty. Wines of selected vintage are served, particularly the popular Shao Shing, the piquant white wine of Taiwan. Hot beverages include select Chinese green and black teas.

At Taipei, CAL lands at the Sungshan International Airport; the area has been doubled since 1964, and a new, efficient air-conditioning plant and direct loading ramps, enlarged aprons, and a lengthened landing strip for the safe accommodation of Boeing 747 jumbos have been added. Sungshan, which also accommodates ten other international airlines and the domestic flights of CAL and Far Eastern Transport Corporation, is only ten to fifteen minutes from downtown Taipei and most of the more popular hotels. The Government's V.I.P. Grand Hotel, the largest in Taiwan, is barely five minutes away.

An air terminal and extended airstrip have been completed at Kaohsiung, Taiwan's second largest city, about 200 airmiles south of Taipei. CAL has commenced international flights to and from Kaohsiung and other carriers are expected to join, thus making southern Taiwan more accessible to tourists without additional costs. It is anticipated that the effect on the area's tourism will be comparable with the opening of Osaka to international air traffic by the Japanese Government.

Looking towards the era of supersonic aircraft, the Republic of China has completed plans for a gigantic international airport on the island's west coast at an estimated cost of US$100 million. It is hoped that with the availability of funds construction may begin in 1973 and that the airport will be completed in 1975 or early 1976.

From its original few short-haul charter flights, the China Airlines route map has spread long fingers across Asia and the Orient—reaching out to span the Pacific to San Francisco and Los Angeles via Tokyo in the north, or Honolulu in the central Pacific. Future plans include new routes to Australia and Europe which will finally link up in a round-the-world network.

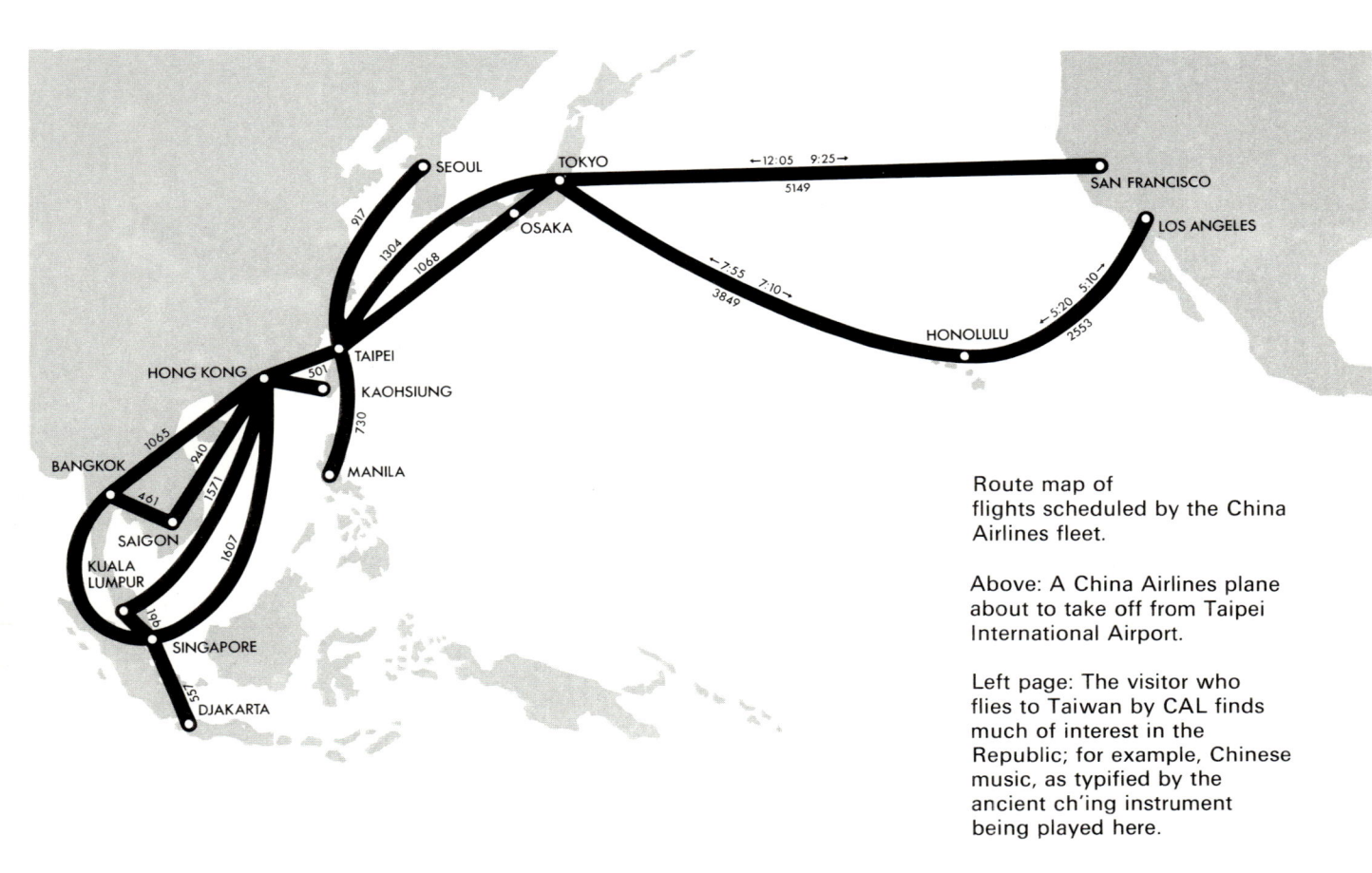

Route map of flights scheduled by the China Airlines fleet.

Above: A China Airlines plane about to take off from Taipei International Airport.

Left page: The visitor who flies to Taiwan by CAL finds much of interest in the Republic; for example, Chinese music, as typified by the ancient ch'ing instrument being played here.

TELEVISION IN TAIWAN

Opposite page, below: Baseball is one of the popular sports in Chinese primary schools. Taiwan has twice won the world championship in the Little League at Williamsport, Pennsylvania, U.S.A., in 1969 and 1971.

Opposite page: A national dance being performed in front of the Presidential Building on 10th October, Chinese National Day.

Below: A drama based on the foundation of the Republic of China being filmed at a television studio in Taipei.

TELEVISION is a vital factor in the changing image of Asia. Like radio broadcasting, television is used as a medium of education, entertainment and keeping the people up-to-date with the news.

The people of rural Taiwan have been alive to modern techniques of hygiene, child welfare, dental care and scientific methods of cultivation for no more than thirty-five years, and the knowledge they have gained has been limited and sporadic. By visually demonstrating to farmers the newest ways of increasing their yields and by making their children part of the "universal television kindergarten", television has brought the 20th Century-world right into the home of the ordinary working man and every member of his family.

In October 1962, the first commercially-owned television network, Taiwan Television Enterprise (TTV) commenced transmission. Now on air for more than twelve hours a day, TTV's typical daily programmes include locally-produced dramas, educational sessions, children's sessions, American films of general interest, television series such as "Combat" and "The Ed Sullivan Show" and local variety shows.

The most popular of these programmes are the locally produced dramas. Chinese operas, Mandarin dramas, plays spoken in the Taiwanese dialect, puppet-theatre and 'soap-operas' adapted from famous novels make up the wide range of theatrical formats of TTV's studio productions. In order to raise the standard of music appreciation and to encourage talents, TTV invited more than 50 musicians from various parts of the world to form the TTV Symphony Orchestra which now appears on the air in regular performances every week.

TTV has a large news department whose editors and analysts prepare three daily newscasts. Use is made of satellite transmissions and live relays, as well as the regular world press-agency-news received via teletype and radio-photo, to keep the public up-to-date on world happenings. There are also daily and weekly "in-depth" examinations of current happenings, for example: "Meet the Newsmaker", a programme which spotlights people of both national and international interest; "News Analysis", a discussion of the causes and effects of recent events; and "Municipal Issues and Answers", an examination of local problems and possible ways and means of solving them.

In order to further develop Taiwan's television industry, to train specialist personnel and to exchange ideas and people from other countries, TTV is in the process of setting up a television training centre. The first subjects expected to be taught in this school are singing, dancing, acting and television techniques.

There are more than three-quarters of a million television receiving sets in use on Taiwan through which the average man is kept aware of daily happenings in all sectors of the globe.

From mundane events in the life of his own tiny community to the epoch making telecasts of man's adventures, a quarter of a million miles away on the moon, television has brought to the average man a new appreciation of the values and wonders of the universe.

RADIO

Radio broadcasting has had a marked influence on the lives of the Taiwanese. In terms of general programming, the system established by the Government is comparable with that of many of the larger Western countries, although more airtime is given to news and news commentaries. The 84 radio stations have combined transmission periods totalling more than 1,913 hours daily.

The Government owns and operates the B.C.C. network, its major function being to beam programmes to the Chinese mainland and foreign countries. Overseas programmes are broadcast to the U.S., the Near and Middle-East, North-eastern Asia and Africa. News and commentaries occupy half the air-time, and music, entertainment and special educational programmes make up the remainder.

There are several commercial radio networks on the island; the largest is operated by the Cheng Sheng Broadcasting Company with six stations throughout the Republic. Although the main function of commercial Taiwanese radio is entertainment, broadcasting stations cooperate with the Government in disseminating agricultural, public health, traffic safety and civil defense information.

In the general field popular programmes are: "Our Family", a typical family life series; "Market of the Air", which deals with daily market reports; "Selected Novels", reviews of recently published books; and "I Sing for You", a session of popular music, light classics and operettas. At the end of June 1969, it was estimated that in Taiwan every ten listeners had at least one receiving set; on a per capita basis this was one of the highest ratios in the world, a striking indication of the significant part played by radio in the daily life of the islanders.

141

Commonwealth of
AUSTRALIA

LEGEND

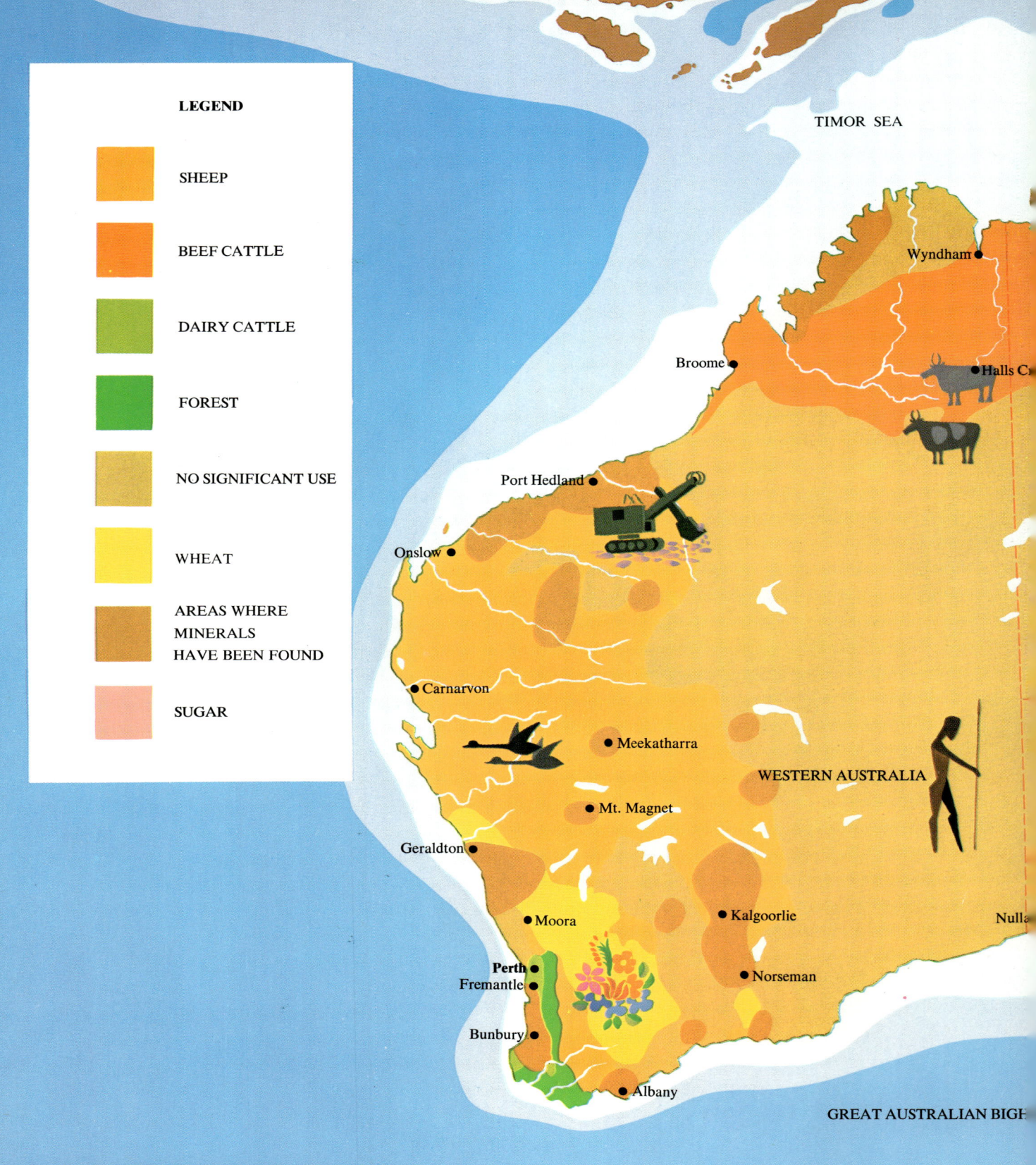

- SHEEP
- BEEF CATTLE
- DAIRY CATTLE
- FOREST
- NO SIGNIFICANT USE
- WHEAT
- AREAS WHERE MINERALS HAVE BEEN FOUND
- SUGAR

TIMOR SEA

Wyndham
Broome
Halls C
Port Hedland
Onslow
Carnarvon
Meekatharra
Mt. Magnet
Geraldton
Moora
Kalgoorlie
Perth
Fremantle
Norseman
Bunbury
Albany

WESTERN AUSTRALIA

Nulla

GREAT AUSTRALIAN BIGH

AUSTRALIA

INDIAN OCEAN

Melville Island
Darwin
Katherine
Groote Eylandt
GULF OF CARPENTARIA
Banks Island
Thursday Island
GREAT BARRIER REEF
CORAL SEA
Cooktown
Wellesley Island
Cairns
Croydon
Tennant Creek
Townsville
NORTHERN TERRITORY
Mount Isa
Cloncurry
Charters Towers
Hughenden
Mackay
QUEENSLAND
Alice Springs
Longreach
Rockhampton
Birdsville
Charleville
Maryborough
Toowoomba
Brisbane
SOUTH AUSTRALIA
Cunnamulla
Inverell
Grafton
Bourke
Coff's Harbour
Tamworth
Broken Hill
NEW SOUTH WALES
Port Augusta
Ceduna
Port Pirie
Dubbo
TASMAN SEA
Newcastle
Orange
Sydney
Mildura
Port Lincoln
Adelaide
Wollongong
Kangaroo Island
Goulburn
Wagga Wagga
VICTORIA
Canberra
Wangaratta
Horsham
Bendigo
Cooma
Ballarat
Mount Gambier
Melbourne
Warrnambool
Geelong
Launceston
TASMANIA
Hobart

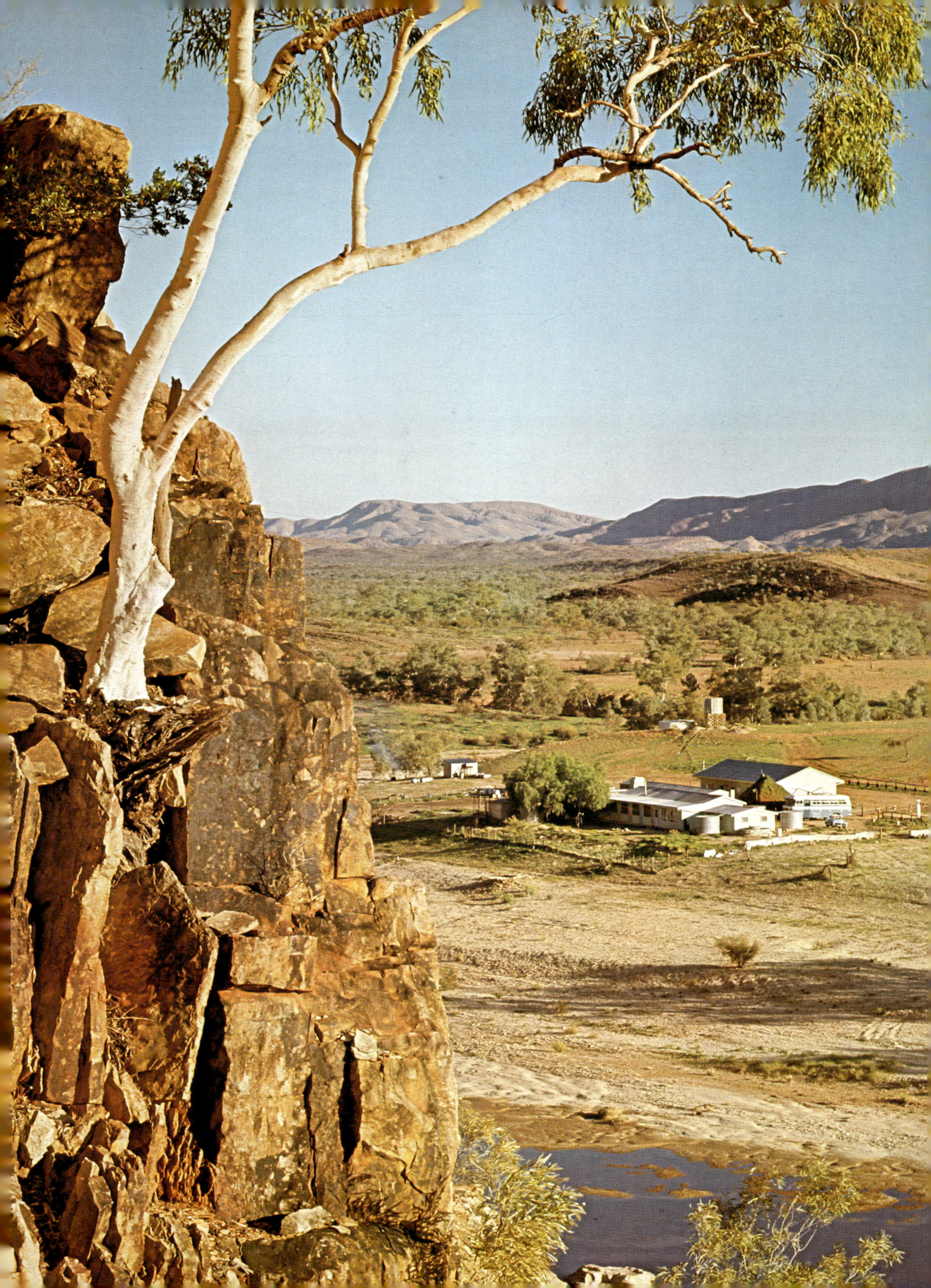

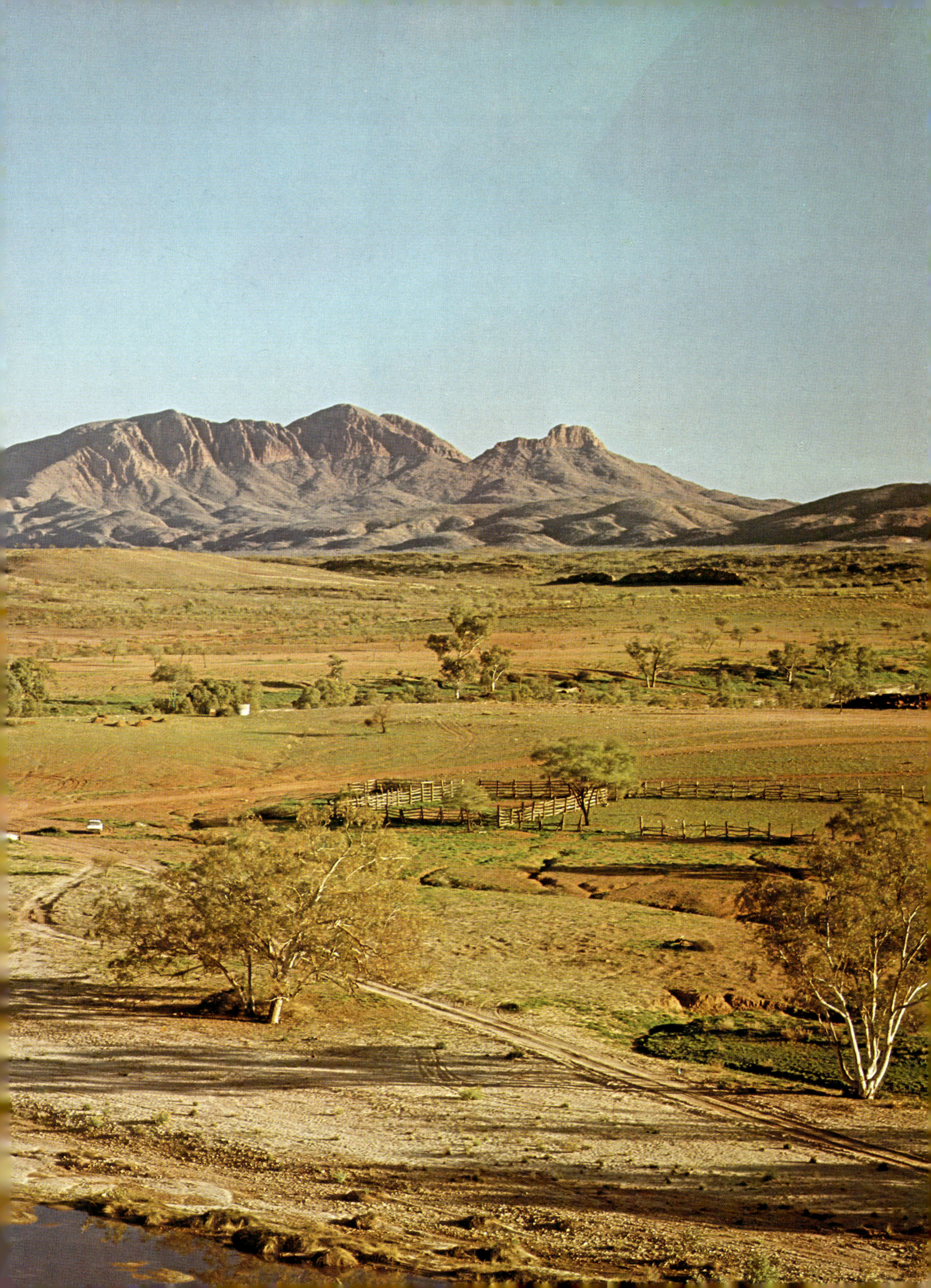

The Wakening Land

IN FAR DISTANT TIMES the Australian Continent was visibly joined with Asia but over millions of years the links disappeared, isolating "the great South Land" and its plants and animals from the rest of the world; they developed in their own fashion in their natural sanctuary, the latter protected from predatory carnivorous creatures which would have come down the land bridge if it had not broken into the chains of islands now separating Australia from the Asian continent. Even so, all traces of the bridge have not disappeared. It would require only a change of 100 feet in the sea floor to re-unite Australia with Papua New Guinea.

In this unique "zoo" at the world's end, as it seemed to the first people from the Northern Hemisphere, strange forms of life developed from the ancestral types.

Among them are the monotremes, or egg-laying mammals, the best known being the platypus, a furred creature which lays eggs, suckles its young, has webbed feet and a duck-like bill. It inhabits streams and rivers. Another is the echidna, or spiny anteater, somewhat of the appearance of a small hedgehog. Nearly half the 230-odd species of mammals recorded in Australia are marsupials, or pouched mammals, the most familiar being the kangaroos, some of which grow to more than 6 feet in height. As might be expected the bird population is much more international.

The Aborigines, the brown-skinned people who preceded the Europeans, are themselves comparative newcomers on the time-scale of the monotremes and marsupials. It is thought that they migrated to Australia some 18,000 years ago, crossing the breaks in the land bridge by canoes or rafts.

They are classed as Australoids, as distinct from the main European, African and Asian groups. It is possible that they emerged as a type in South-east Asia and the Malay Archipelago. There are isolated groups elsewhere with physical resemblances to them, including some aboriginal hill tribes of southern India, the Veddas of Ceylon and the Sakai of Malaysia. The Aborigines brought with them the dingo, thought to be related to the pariah dog of India.

As the arid nature of the Australian continent influenced the development of plant life, so the Aborigines adapted themselves to survive in an often harsh environment, hunting and fishing, for there were no animals which could be tamed and bred or crops which could be cultivated. So they evolved a simple pattern of life, with the primitive economy of nomads, in the centuries before other people came to Australia.

The Aborigines were the true discoverers of *Terra Australis*. Preceding the years of colonisation there is much legend and speculation. The Chaldeans, the Arabs and the Chinese are all thought to have had some knowledge of Australia and the Portuguese too may have sighted part of the coast before 1542. Spaniards were acknowledged visitors and the Dutch made many notable voyages which brought them to the shores of the continent. The first English contact was made by William Dampier in 1688 when his ship *Cygnet* dropped anchor off the north-west littoral near the present port of Derby.

Today's Australia is an island continent of nearly 3 million square miles, almost as large as the United States of America. Its relatively small population of 13 million is accounted for by the fact that it has been occupied by civilised peoples, mainly of European origins, for less than 200 years. The Aborigines had always been a backward race and had done nothing to develop the country. Moreover, Australia is the world's driest continent, lacking the great mountain and river systems of other lands.

Its more fertile parts are in comparatively small sectors and here the bulk of the population has concentrated, largely in the south-eastern corner. Scientists are working on the plan that some day atomic power may be generated to develop vast irrigation systems and so open up tens of thousands of square miles of land now desolate and unproductive. That would completely change the population picture. Already the great Snowy Mountains Hydro-Electric Scheme has shown what can be done by harnessing and damming countless volumes of water that hitherto flowed to waste into the sea.

The story of modern Australia begins on 23rd August 1770 when Captain James Cook, R.N., the great English navigator, took possession "in right of His Majesty King George III" of what are now the

Opposite page:
The Hartz Range in Central Australia, like Mount Sonda, was a favourite subject of the famous Aboriginal painter, the late Albert Namatjira.

Right:
Aborigines in the heart of Central Australia cooking kangaroo — a native-style barbecue.

eastern parts of New South Wales and Queensland, thus adding another territory to the British Empire (now the British Commonwealth of Nations). The 200th anniversary of this event was celebrated in Australia in 1970 in the presence of Her Majesty Queen Elizabeth II, H.R.H. Prince Philip, The Duke of Edinburgh, H.R.H. The Prince of Wales and The Princess Anne. New South Wales, in particular, made it a memorable occasion.

At various times subsequent to Cook's advent the rest of Australia was annexed.

He had not purposely sailed to the continent to colonise it; he was on his way home to England from Tahiti where he had been sent to make astronomical observations.

He landed at Botany Bay—now in the Sydney area—which he named for the large variety of botanical specimens found there.

Cook's account of Australia, or as much of it as he had seen, created interest in England but it was not until 1787 that a fleet of eleven ships set sail under the command of Captain Arthur Phillip, R.N.

who was to be the governor of a new colony called New South Wales. The British Government had two motives for this rather belated settlement. The American Colonies had been lost in the War of Independence and an overseas base was needed for prisoners sentenced to deportation for various crimes. The ships reached Botany Bay on 18th January 1788 but Phillip was not impressed with the site and eight days later he sailed into Port Jackson, twelve miles north along the coast, and established his settlement in Sydney Cove.

Despite great difficulties from lack of supplies and skilled labour the colony was firmly established and exploration of the interior began. Tasmania, formerly known as Van Diemen's Land, the southernmost island of the continent received its first settlers from Sydney in 1803.

It became a colony in its own right in 1825 and Western Australia, a huge area of nearly 1 million square miles, had its first settlement in 1827. South Australia was created a free colony in 1836. During this

time Victoria and Queensland were part of New South Wales politically but in 1851 and 1859 respectively they became separate colonies.

In 1901 all the colonies federated under the title "The Commonwealth of Australia" and from then on they were known as States. A separate territory was set aside from New South Wales as the Federal Capital and in 1913 it was given the name Canberra.

In 1907 control of the sparsely populated, largely barren and undeveloped Northern Territory of South Australia was passed to the Commonwealth which has since administered it. Even now, in more than half a million square miles the Territory has a population of only 73,000.

While all this was going on the lot of the Aborigines was far from happy. The taking over of hunting grounds by white settlers and the clashes which resulted make a dismal chapter in Australian history. For many years it was believed that the Aborigines were doomed to extinction. But in more recent times much more enlightened policies have ruled; there has been wide recognition of the true values of Aboriginal culture and a sincere effort has been made to assimilate into Australian life those Aboriginal people whose old tribal background has been lost.

In the official definition "the policy of assimilation seeks that all persons of Aboriginal descent will choose to attain a similar manner and standard of living to that of other Australians and live as members of a single Australian community —enjoying the same rights and privileges, accepting the same responsibilities and influenced by the same hopes and loyalties as other Australians". The success of some individual Aborigines as public servants, clergymen, artists and sportsmen—and more recently an outstanding politician— has demonstrated their latent potential for embracing a culture different from their own. Of these the best known are probably the late Albert Namatjira, painter; Harold Blair, singer; Lionel Rose, the first Aborigine to win a world sporting championship, the world bantamweight boxing title in Japan in 1968; Evonne Goolagong who had a meteoric rise as one of the greatest woman tennis players the world has produced, reaching the finals at Wimbledon in 1971 on her second attempt and by defeating the reigning champion, Australia's Margaret Court, became the Queen of world tennis at the age of 19. For her outstanding efforts, Her Majesty The Queen awarded her the M.B.E. in the 1972 New Year's Honours and the Australia Day Council proclaimed her "Australian of the Year." Another fine Aborigine, Neville Bonner, was elected to the Queensland Senate in 1971. Figures compiled in 1966 record a population of 44,605 Aborigines, 77,459 part Aborigines and 8,000 Torres Strait Islanders, a total of 130,100, the majority of them living in Queensland.

Australia today is a technologically advanced nation, enjoying a high standard of living. The old picture of Australians as a people of rural occupations—wool-growers, dairyfarmers, wheatgrowers and fruitgrowers—no longer reflects the true nature of the population. For, although these primary industries are still of vital importance to the economy of the country, modern methods of production enable them to be conducted by relatively fewer and fewer people. The majority of Australians are now city dwellers engaged in secondary and tertiary industries and most of them are concentrated in the south-eastern littoral of the continent in a strip running south from the steelmaking city of Newcastle, through Sydney—population 2,780,000—and a second steelmaking centre at Port Kembla in the metropolitan area of Wollongong, to Melbourne — population 2,425,000.

The other State capitals — Brisbane (Queensland), Adelaide (South Australia), Perth (Western Australia) and Hobart (Tasmania) — do not approach Sydney (New South Wales) and Melbourne (Victoria) in size. Canberra, the Federal Capital, although barely 60 years old, already has a population of about 150,000.

This lopsided development has both historical and physiographic bases. Sydney was the first settlement. The States of New South Wales and Victoria are by Australian standards fertile and between them runs Australia's most considerable river, the Murray, whose tributaries are sources of both irrigation water and hydro-electric power. Newcastle is the port of the northern coalfields of New South Wales; hence the establishment there of the steelworks. Port Kembla is likewise the port of the southern coalfields of N.S.W.

The imbalance of population was a greater cause for concern in the past than it is today for world experience from New York to Tokyo clearly demonstrates that it is impracticable to limit the growth of metropolitan aggregations. Nevertheless Australia is learning by the experience of older cities to tackle such problems as traffic congestion, the decay of downtown areas and the incidence of smog and other forms of pollution before they become too bad. Despite the gravitational pull of Sydney and Melbourne there are many Australians who are very well satisfied to live in other comely cities which offer a wide selection of climatic conditions and natural advantages. Brisbane is subtropical; Hobart can be chilly when snow lies on the slopes of Mount Wellington towering over the city and harbour. Adelaide is temperate. Perth, on approximately the same latitude as Sydney but 2,000 miles away on the other side of the continent, is by many people accounted to have the best climate in Australia.

For many years the overall picture of Australia remained much the same—most of the population and secondary industry on the south-eastern seaboard, with a pastoral hinterland in New South Wales and a varied primary production in Victoria.

Up the Queensland coast ran the sugar belt in a strip of high rainfall. Inland were the great sheep and cattle stations, spreading across the continent through the Northern Territory to Western Australia. South Australia grew wheat and wine. It was customary to say that Australia 'rode on the sheep's back', a reference to the importance to the economy of the fine merino wools which Australia exported to many parts of the world.

From time to time, however, minerals had been found in great quantity. As long ago as the 1850's the Gold Rush in Victoria had transformed the Australian economy and indeed influenced the growth of the old British Empire. Other gold discoveries were made later in the century in Western Australia but today gold mining is a languishing industry. At the present price of gold it scarcely pays to mine it.

In the late 19th Century also came the discovery of the great silver-lead-zinc field of Broken Hill in far western New South Wales, which continues in vigorous production to this day. There had also been important discoveries of copper and tin in Tasmania and, in more recent times, Mount Isa in far western Queensland became a leading producer of copper, lead and zinc.

But in the 'sixties and 'seventies of this century mineral discoveries, or developments, came in sensational succession— the gas and oilfields of Bass Strait, the huge bauxite deposits of Queensland and the enormous iron ore resources of Western Australia and Tasmania—to mention only a few.

Thus the early day picture of Australia has dramatically changed. Queensland is no longer a country only of cattle and sugar; Western Australia from being a vast and somewhat neglected outpost has suddenly found millions of dollars pouring in from Britain, the United States, Japan and other countries to dig newly discovered ore and build railways, harbours and whole new towns. There is a new and exciting vision and if the population imbalance has not been altered the spotlight once monopolised by the eastern States is now shared with the booming West and with the North where American interests are busy revitalising the cattle industry.

Left:
Australia's Great Barrier Reef is one of the coral wonders of the world. Starfish and birds — both predatory and otherwise! — attract tourists in their tens of thousands throughout the year.

Opposite page:
Breaking wild brumbies is part of the daily life of the Australian stockman and he has many opportunities to show his skill at local rodeos and agricultural shows.

Australians are well aware that, with limited resources, they cannot do all these things themselves. They therefore welcome international participation and the names of great corporations which are household words in their own countries have become household words in Australia too.

Despite these cosmopolitan aspects Australia is unique in one respect—it is a continent with a single language, English. Just as English is spoken with different accents and vowel sounds in various parts of Great Britain itself, so Australian English differs in some respects of intonation from English English and American English. But all these varieties are interchangeable although an American is immediately recognised as an American, just as an Australian in England is immediately recognised as an Australian.

It is a good life which Australia offers, not only in the cities and bigger towns but in the countryside itself. Even in the far "outback" remote from the big centres of settlement, modern technology has abolished the hardships, loneliness and much of the hazard of pioneering life. Aircraft and radio have been the great instruments of change. The light aircraft makes the remotest station (sheep or cattle ranch) accessible. A "flying doctor" service gives prompt medical aid in the remotest places. The station owner may summon help on his transceiver radio, just as his wife may talk with distant neighbours. Radio serves another purpose: by transmissions from "the school of the air" special teachers of the Education Departments can give regular lessons to children in isolated places in which schooling would otherwise be impossible.

For all the lure of factories and mines and the glamour of the cities the country is still part of the background of a large proportion of Australians. The city dweller is reminded of it in the Agricultural Shows (sometimes called Fairs or Exhibitions in other parts of the world) which are held annually in all the capitals and in many rural centres. In these Shows the produce of the countryside is put on exhibition at special showgrounds, perhaps for a week or more—cattle and sheep, horses and pigs, poultry, fruits, vegetables and many other commodities, plus all the equipment that the countryman uses: farm implements, tractors, cars, milking machinery, pumps and the varieties of modern domestic appliances he and his family need for their homes. The Shows are great occasions—opportunities for farmers and graziers to see the best that is offering and to meet socially and for discussions with their fellow producers. For the city man and his wife and children the Show offers "the fun of the fair" and constitutes a thoroughly enjoyable family outing. At all Shows the principal feature is the Grand Parade of prize stock in which magnificent animals are paraded around the Show ring. Most celebrated of all Australian Shows—and perhaps the finest in the world—is the Royal Easter Show in Sydney which in its scope, organisation and quality and variety of exhibits offers a spectacle which is truly magnificent.

Side by side with material advances, Australians have seen a worthwhile development in the arts. European Australians, however, cannot claim to have introduced them. The Aborigines, primitive though they were, had already done that with a great wealth of songs, dances, painting and carving, much of it unfortunately not understood by Europeans until it was in danger of perishing. The Aboriginal corroboree, for instance, has much that anticipates modern ballet. Ballet in Australia has drawn largely on the European tradition and is a flourishing art form; the Australian Ballet Company's performances have been applauded in many parts of the world. Sir Robert Helpmann, the noted Australian choreographer-dancer-actor, and Dame Peggy van Pragh are leading figures in the international ballet scene.

Australia has produced a surprising number of singers of world repute. The first of these was Melba, the dominant singer of her time—around the turn of the century—and the tradition has been continued by a host of internationally acclaimed singers down to Joan Sutherland today. Sydney's new Opera House, already famed by name and due to be opened early in 1973, will give a great fillip to ballet, opera and other classics. Theatre has had many vicissitudes. Today, apart from top professional performances, its most vigorous manifestations are in productions by small companies of the repertory type interested in techniques and social problems.

In painting Australians have made their mark; those whose works are essentially Australian such as Russell Drysdale, Sidney Nolan and Arthur Boyd usually have gained more recognition in other lands than the followers of various fashionable international styles. In literature it may be claimed Frederic Manning wrote what was perhaps the only great book to come out of World War I—and indeed one of the great books of the century—*The Middle Parts of Fortune*. Internationally Australia's best known writer today is probably the novelist Patrick White.

Australia in the 1970's is a country of the young. More than half the population is under the age of 29. The predominant

Right:
Australian Aborigines make excellent stockmen. A group of them is shown here mustering cattle at Hall's Creek.

Opposite page:
Many overseas visitors to Australia prefer to see something of the vast inland and less frequented spots unique in this island continent. In the red heart is strangely eroded Ayers Rock, the largest monolith in the world. Its vast size dwarfs the trees below.

impression of anyone who walks the streets of an Australian city is one of exuberant youth—all those girls and young men who now put the middle aged and elderly in an obvious minority. Like the youth of most countries they are outwardly to some extent internationalised. Fashions from "swinging London and Paris" and American youth styles made familiar by films and T.V. have replaced the sombre clothes of former years. For the girls, dresses vary from minis to maxis according to the trends of the moment with diversions to "hot pants" and always comfortable, colourful slacks. Here also are the ubiquitous blue jeans for both sexes and for some the "way-out" fashion extremes and hippie gear.

This is indeed a sartorial revolution. The young Australian male once prided himself on an aggressive—perhaps over-aggressive —masculinity. Haircuts were "short back and sides" and anyone who deviated from the norm risked public disapproval. Today in Australia, as elsewhere, the sexes are sometimes hardly distinguishable— long hair and slacks. Certainly most of the people so dressed are students or are engaged in occupations where anything can be worn. The majority conforms to some degree, extravagance perhaps being confined to sidewhiskers and beards and brightly coloured shirts and ties. Underneath all this Australian youth, despite being swept by international trends— student "revolt" for instance—is probably much as it has always been.

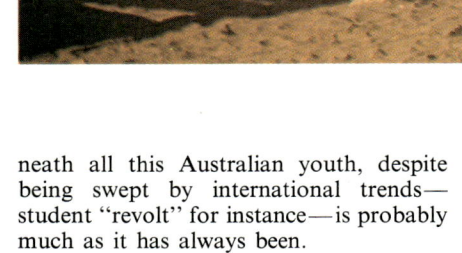

Australia is fortunate in its climate which makes physical recreation easy. There are magnificent beaches within easy reach of all the capitals and snowfields within reach of some of them. Sun, sand, surf and snow are part of the Australian background. Surfing, yachting and boating, golf and skiing are the recreations of the active Australian.

There is a change in emphasis here. In other years when people had to find their amusements close to their own homes, spectator sports, football and racing in particular, dominated the recreational scene. The coming of the motor car and a much greater public affluence, with mobility for all, changed that. Golf, angling, boating, formerly recreations of the rich, became open to everyone. Attendance at spectator sports relative to greatly increased populations has fallen conspicuously—the exceptions being Australian Rules Football in Melbourne, which draws huge crowds exceeding 100,000 in the finals and such important race meetings as the Melbourne, Sydney and Doomben (Brisbane) Cups. Generally it requires an international contest of notable excitement to bring the crowds back to the stadia.

Otherwise in the weekends people will load up their cars and be off to relax and enjoy themselves as the mood moves them.

In international sports, in spite of her small population, Australia has had remarkable success. In tennis and swimming she has dominated the scene on many occasions and in golf and athletics she has produced many record-breakers. Australians, too, have been notably successful cricketers but the international field in this game is limited almost entirely to British Commonwealth countries. In football interest is fragmented between the four codes—Rugby League, Rugby Union, Soccer and Australian Rules—the most notable being Australian Rules which is not played by any other nation. In recent years, with a large migration from Europe, efforts have been made, with some success, to raise the standards of Soccer. In sailing Australian crews have distinguished themselves in Britain's Admiral's Cup and have shown that even the America's Cup is not beyond them.

Among the amusements of the young, pop concerts still rank high although perhaps some of the glamour has worn off since the days when the Beatles had almost hysterical welcome. Nevertheless guitars and excessive noise are still much esteemed and the various international pop groups

The diningrooms and restaurants of the better class hotels and motels generally provide the quality of food obtainable all over the world. But the larger cities also have many restaurants specialising in national cuisines. The Italians, in particular, have made very important contributions to Australian dining. French, Greek. German, Swiss and Dutch are a few other foods which innumerable small restaurants feature with pride.

Chinese cooking (for the most part Cantonese) has enjoyed high popularity in Australia for many years. It stems from the immigration of Chinese to the Australian goldfields 120 years or so ago.

Although most of them returned to their homeland many remained to become permanent parts of Australian life. In addition there are now restaurants specialising in Japanese, Indian and Indonesian foods as well as those of various Arab countries. In this sense Australia is truly cosmopolitan.

In the entertainment field a wide variety of American and British films are always being screened in modern cinemas and drive-in theatres. French, Italian, Greek, Swiss and films from other countries are also shown in special theatres for non-English speaking students and visitors. There is a flourishing professional theatre and, in Sydney in particular, a wide variety of nightclubs.

Australia has often been described in the hackneyed phrase "land of sunshine and opportunity" and many intending migrants — particularly from Britain — have accepted this in its most literal terms. Sunshine, yes. Opportunity, yes—but with qualifications. There is plenty of work available in Australia in almost every walk of life: the percentage of employment in relation to population is one of the highest in the world and anyone who is prepared to work conscientiously will build up a sound and comfortable future for himself and his family. There are opportunities that few other countries can offer.

But those who expect an easy life and immediate high returns will quickly be disillusioned—unless they are lucky enough to strike a big win in a State Lottery or stumble on a rich mineral deposit!

still tour the country with great financial success.

Visitors to Australia find a flourishing country of friendly people with all the amenities expected in a technologically advanced community. Two major domestic airlines provide a network of internal communication of high standard and contemporary rail travel is provided notably by two interstate expresses, the Southern Aurora, which runs between Sydney and Melbourne, and the Indian Pacific, linking Sydney and Perth. All states have their own interstate and intrastate railway systems and the Highways and Main Roads Boards have built modern highways connecting all capitals and roads to all towns throughout the Commonwealth.

Hotels and motels in the cities and suburbs and rural provinces provide excellent accommodation. Health conditions are very high. Diseases once endemic, such as smallpox, cholera, typhoid, diptheria, whooping cough, tuberculosis and poliomyelitis, have been totally or almost totally eliminated. Visitors from countries in which smallpox and other diseases are endemic are advised to ascertain the Australian innoculation requirements before leaving. As a point of interest Australian water is some of the purest in the world and may be drunk straight from the tap.

PAPUA NEW GUINEA, on the outer perimeter of Asia, is preparing to take its place among the nations of the world. It has already reached an important milestone on the road to self-government and independence. In 1971 its House of Assembly agreed to recommendations by its Select Committee on Constitutional Development which the Australian Government accepted. In effect the recommendations set, for the first time, an approximate timetable for constitutional developments. They require the Australian Government to prepare a programme for full internal self-government in the period 1972-76—the lifetime of the third House of Assembly.

That programme will have regard to the state of opinion as it develops after the 1972 House of Assembly elections and to the policies of the political leaders of the day. The interval between the attaining of self-government and independence will also depend on the wishes of the elected leaders. During the Select Committee's two fact-finding tours majority opinion in Papua New Guinea favoured internal self-government during a later period—1976-80—but changes have led the Select Committee to believe that the people might ask for internal self-government within the next five years.

Papua New Guinea has already been launched into the international arena. Through Australia's representations it is an associate member of ECAFE and a full member of the Asian Development Bank. Its flag has been flown at meetings of both these bodies.

It is a member of the South Pacific Conference and a recipient of aid through the South Pacific Commission. It already receives considerable assistance from the World Bank Group and the United Nations Development Programme. A number of international agencies, such as the World Health Organisation, also provide assistance in various ways.

Many Papuan and New Guinean leaders themselves have travelled to other countries. In 1971 a delegation of House of Assembly members toured Indonesia under the leadership of the Speaker, Dr. J. Guise, and other elected members have travelled widely throughout the world, particularly in developing countries. Members are also taking part in educational and business tours of Papua New Guinea's Pacific and Asian neighbours. In October-November 1970 a delegation went to Britain and the six countries of the European Economic Community to continue earlier Australian representations aimed at gaining recognition for Papua New Guinea's special problems.

Geographically Papua New Guinea is diverse. It lies wholly within the tropics. Its climate, for the most part, is hot and humid. Nevertheless there are mountain peaks that sometimes carry snow and in the highlands, where a large proportion of the population lives, the climate is temperate. There are large river systems like the Sepik and the Fly and vast areas of swampland. There are numerous active volcanoes. In addition to large islands like New Britain, New Ireland and Bougainville there are scores of smaller islands.

The People. Papua New Guinea's 2.5 million people are as diverse as the country they live in. They are settled in isolated communities, living an integrated pattern of life based on subsistence agriculture.

There have been tremendous changes in little more than one lifetime. The people are in different stages of advancement ranging from many who are still subsistence farmers to some who are relatively prosperous copra, cocoa, coffee, tea and palm-oil planters; local government councillors; university graduates; and businessmen in varying commercial activities.

The indigenous population can be divided into three groups within the economy. Those engaged wholly in monetary sector activity, about 20 per cent; those engaged wholly in the subsistence sector, slightly above 40 per cent; and those in the process of passing from subsistence to monetary activity who grow crops partially for cash and partially for their own consumption, approaching 40 per cent.

The Economy. Agriculture is the basis of the economy of Papua New Guinea. Major exports are still copra, coffee, cocoa, timber and rubber but exciting new industries are being developed. Production of tea, pyrethrum and palm-oil will reach significant quantities by 1973.

The people of Papua New Guinea have made it clear that they look for rising standards of living, better food and housing, better education for their children, health services and security. The achievement of these aims depends on economic advance-

Above: One of the important industries of Papua New Guinea is coffee growing. Plantation workers are shown picking the ripe berries containing the beans for drying. Left: Aerial approach to Port Moresby, capital of Papua New Guinea. Below: A native fisherman at Rabaul mending his nets.

PAPUA NEW GUINEA LOOKS TO ITS NEIGHBOURS

ment. The Australian Government has strongly supported the economic development of the country as the essential basis for increasing social welfare and meaningful self-government.

Development. The development of Papua New Guinea is at present geared to a five-year development programme begun in 1968. This programme envisaged an expenditure of nearly $A1,000 million by the Administration over the five-year period.

The programme has the following main objectives: maximum increases in production consistent with financial and manpower resources and market capacity; maximum participation by Papuans and New Guineans at all levels; maximum practicable progress towards financial self-reliance; maximum practicable contribution to meeting social needs and contributing to the level of living of the people.

The programme has now been revised to incorporate the impact of the Bougainville copper project and a new development programme to commence in 1973-74.

Non-market primary production and subsistence income grew at an annual rate of only 2½ per cent from 1960-61 to 1969-70 as the emphasis on traditional subsistence activity declined in favour of commercial agriculture and other forms of monetary employment.

Between 1960-61 and 1968-69 purely monetary sector production (Gross Monetary Sector Product at market prices) rose by 14 per cent per annum. Then, largely as a result of the impact of private investment in the Bougainville copper project, GMSP increased by over 30 per cent in 1969-70.

Bougainville, which will be one of the world's largest copper mines, is a growth factor of great importance to Papua New Guinea. Expenditure on this project will be about $A400 million. Depending on the price of copper, the project is expected to double export income in 1972-73, the first year of Bougainville production, exporting concentrates valued at $A140 million in that year. In the following year exports from the Bougainville project will rise to almost $A200 million, a level which should be maintained while sources of higher grade ore are readily accessible. The direct contribution to Gross Monetary Sector Product, at market prices, should be about $A125 million in 1972-73 rising to $A170 million in 1973-74.

Exports. Between 1965-66 and 1969-70 exports of produce from Papua New Guinea increased from $A42 million to $A71 million. The main buyers in 1969-70—based on preliminary estimates—were: Australia 44 per cent; the United Kingdom 16 per cent; the United States 12 per cent; Japan 9 per cent; and West Germany 8 per cent.

Visible imports into Papua New Guinea between 1965-66 and 1969-70 increased from $A110 million to $A214 million. The main suppliers in 1969-70 were: Australia 53 per cent; Japan 12 per cent; the United States 11 per cent; the United Kingdom 6 per cent; Hong Kong 3 per cent; and Singapore 3 per cent.

Trade. Australia remains Papua New Guinea's main trading partner but its dominance has declined slightly in recent years, as has the United Kingdom share, while Japan in particular has played an increasing part in PNG trade. In 1960-61 Papua New Guinea's exports to Japan were valued at $A1.5 million. By 1969-70 they had increased to $A8.6 million. Papua New Guinea's imports from Japan increased at a faster rate, from $A3.5 million in 1960-61 to $A26.3 million in 1969-70.

Papua New Guinea's trade with other Asian and Pacific countries is also increasing. Papua New Guinea competes with other Pacific countries for markets for its coconut and timber products. At the same time it is buying increasing quantities of consumer goods from China, Hong Kong, Malaysia and Singapore.

Reciprocal Education. Papua New Guinea is extending its links with its Pacific neighbours through various political and educational programmes.

Several Papua New Guinea students have trained at the East West Centre in Honolulu and some of its dental and medical students have studied in Fiji. Other Pacific Island students are attending various tertiary institutions in Papua New Guinea. Papua New Guinea is also sending an increasing number of its people to the Pacific to provide technical assistance for its neighbours.

Tourism is another field in which Papua New Guinea is being increasingly involved with the peoples of Asia and the Pacific. The 40,000 tourists expected in 1970-71 are expected to increase to 56,000 in 1972-73. These people are likely to spend $A17 million in Papua New Guinea in 1970-71 and more than $A20 million in 1972-73.

The Past 65 years. These developments illustrate that Papua New Guinea has come a long way since 1906, when Papua became an Australian territory. German New Guinea, as it was then called, was occupied by Australian troops in 1914 and in 1921 was placed under Australian administration by mandate from the League of Nations.

In World War II New Guinea became a battleground and this brought about the suspension of civil administration in Papua New Guinea until the war was over. After the war Australia voluntarily placed the Mandated Territory under the United Nations as a Trust Territory and on 13th December 1946 a Trusteeship Agreement between Australia and the General Assembly of the United Nations designated Australia as the Administering Authority. At the same time provision was made to link the Trust Territory in an administrative union with the Australian possession of Papua.

The 1949 Papua and New Guinea Act provided for common legislative, administrative and judicial systems. The Territory of Papua and New Guinea came into being. Australia has now provided more than $A1,000 million in economic assistance to Papua New Guinea since 1945-46. Aid to the territory forms the major part of Australia's foreign aid programme and the Australian Government has pledged continued assistance when Papua New Guinea is self-governing and independent.

The timing of self-government and independence will be greatly influenced by the policies of the leaders who have emerged from the February-March House of Assembly elections in 1972. In their hands lie the pace and nature of future constitutional development in Papua New Guinea.

A MIGRANT NATION

MIGRANTS have been at the centre of Australian life throughout almost all of her entire history. They founded her, they brought their hopes of better living conditions and saw them nurtured here. In the last twenty-five years they developed her; they made her a nation.

The Pacific War of 1940-45 forced Australia to face ultimate reality for the first time in her brief history. The heavy losses of her young men in World War I had been grievous, the Great Depression of the early 1930's a painful and scarring experience, but the 1940's really brought home to her how easily she could be annihilated. The Japanese had bombed Darwin, their midget submarines had entered Sydney Harbour, their soldiers had almost won New Guinea as a springboard for a land assault on the mainland. The shock was decisive, the resolution made. The 7½ million population had to be boosted—urgently.

To the Rt. Hon. Arthur A. Calwell, the Labor Member for Melbourne in the House of Representatives, went the post of Minister for Immigration and Information in the Chifley Government and to him was given the complex task of formulating a migration policy and then developing a practical and acceptable programme.*

Since those first days some 2.8 million settlers have come to Australia and with natural increases the total population has been built to over 13 million. But the significance of the figures is not in numbers but in the contributions made to the economic and technological base on which the national security depends so much.

Looked at objectively in statistical and economic terms one gains no insight into the great social changes wrought nor the near-miraculous smooth absorption of such proportionately high numbers of varied culture backgrounds by what was —by all standards—an insular society.

---

*NOTE: The Calwell migration plan has been an outstanding success. The Minister held his portfolio until December 1949 when his Party was defeated at the polls. The original Calwell plan has been followed in basic principle by each successive Minister for Immigration and, with certain modifications from time to time, has proved to be sound and practical.

To glean some appreciation of this it is necessary to outline the story of immigration from the earliest days of Australia's founding.

In 1788 the First Fleet brought to Port Jackson, New South Wales, 859 men and women and these persons under Governor Arthur Phillip founded the first colony in Australia—a name that was not to appear for many years later. Subsequent arrivals of free settlers over the next thirty years brought the total to 38,543. By 1855, following the Gold Rush, the population had grown to 793,200 of whom the majority were not Australian born.

Until the middle of the 19th Century there was no restriction or control over immigration. The opening up of grazing lands brought settlers from the British Isles. It was the age of the squatter—the grazier who drove his flocks of sheep on until he found "free" land and then stayed and made it his own. In New South Wales the population nearly trebled. A class of people was being evolved—a class that was to build up the legend of the Australian bush which, with the reformist ideals of the working class movement, was later to fuse a unique form of nationalism.

Then in 1851 gold was discovered in New South Wales and in quick succession further fields were tapped in Victoria. To these colonies were attracted the adventurous from all over the world and in the ten year span from 1850 until 1860 the total population had risen from 400,000 to 1,100,000.

Included in the migrants were an extraordinary number of Chinese. In the primitive conditions existing on the gold fields, grievances were not hard to find.

The European miners with the bond of a common language and culture—for the most part seeing in this new land their future home, feeling the stirrings of pioneering—resented those who remitted abroad all their winnings from the fields and who showed every indication of following their money home as soon as their field was worked out. Resentment flared into rioting and the Governments of New South Wales, Victoria, South Australia and later Queensland, were forced to introduce measures which restricted the entry of Chinese. That this was to meet the current abnormal situations is shown by the fact that as soon as conditions subsided the measures were dropped.

After the gold fever had passed, industry began to get established. Even in these days of comparatively ideal conditions manufacturing was not easy, being disadvantaged by the perennial problems of fragmented markets, long hauls and small population. It is thus not hard to imagine the difficulties in the infinitely worse conditions of the last century and the workers' problems in finding good jobs. Besides, the working class movement had firm ideas about securing for themselves a far more meaningful place in production than had been the case in industrial Britain until that time.

Thus local workers resented competition for jobs and they would have no part of any group of people who did not share their precepts about betterment of working conditions. They therefore tolerated European workers—although reluctantly since they were job competitors—because coming from industrial nations they could be presumed to sympathise with the hopes of the labour movement.

But non-European countries had not developed industrially and therefore could not produce the type of radical worker so necessary for the movement. The Australian saw in this type of migrant not only a person from whom he would get no support in his drive for better conditions but, in fact, one of the very opposite kind—one who would weaken the workers' side by accepting lower pay and worse conditions.

The N.S.W. Trades and Labour Council, founded in 1871, gave expression to these sentiments by taking a firm stand of opposition to immigration, particularly non-European. This policy was reinforced by two current events, the influx into Queensland at the time of the Cooktown gold strike when Chinese outnumbered the local miners, and the seamens' strike brought about by Chinese seamen accepting lower rates of pay. Ironically enough, British opposition to the Queensland Government's restrictive measures fanned rebellious fires, helped develop a nationalistic spirit and so brought in other States not otherwise affected. Immigration then became a common link between the Labor Parties of the various States and this in turn directed the Party's interest towards Federation. In this way restricted immigration slowly became one of the main reasons for the Labor Party desiring Federation. So much so that by the time of Federation (1901) not only the Labor Party but all political parties had adopted the exclusion of non-European's as basic immigration policy.

It was in this historical context that the Labor Government, under Prime Minister Ben Chifley, framed its immigration programme in 1945; a mass movement of people that in recent history has only been exceeded by the flow of migrants to Israel—this, at a time when a massive war effort had strained every aspect of the economy. Consumer goods, raw materials, plant and machinery, housing—almost everything, in fact—were in seriously short supply. But there are rare moments in history when the future course of a nation depends heavily upon a single decision and this was one such moment.

In deciding the composition of the migrants Minister Calwell's recommendations were approved by the Government, basically following the practice of every other nation and selecting those who would be most likely to preserve the security, the social and economic well-being of the nation. It was on this basis that the decision was to maintain the homogenity of the Australian community by assisting the migration (the new settler only paid a small nominal amount for his passage) of those of European and particularly British stock.

Migration agreements were signed with Britain (1947), Malta (1949), The Netherlands, Italy (1951) and Germany (1952).

Refugee camps in Europe were full following the 1939-45 war and Australia had given strong and consistent support to the resettlement of these displaced persons. By March 1969 335,000 of these people had come to Australia.

The target figure for the first year was 70,000—1 per cent of the population; this was raised to 150,000 after 1947. In the period 1945-50 the net migration gain was 353,084; in 1951-55 413,824. By then the economic battle was won—the shortages disappeared and the economy had entered its take-off phase.

The initial years brought many social problems. Australians freely admit that their isolated geographical position, an obstacle to ready contact with other nationalities, had developed in them an insular attitude. This torrent of people from different cultures—some of whom had to learn the language—naturally gave rise to tensions and resentment. Yet, reviewing those years now, the absorption process was remarkably peaceful. The average Australian, even if in some instances narrow-minded, is essentially fair and has a long tradition of supporting those worse off than himself. This trait was given expression by the formation of a number of special organisations and the encouragement of community participation in the assimilation of new settlers.

The needs of these organisations continues and Australia has been uniquely served by its Immigration Planning, Advisory and Publicity Councils, Good Neighbour Movement and Citizenship Conventions. The range of interest and skills of these consultative bodies has been one of the great strengths of the immigration programme.

The vast social experiment that this programme was has been successful. The migrants have broadened the previous narrow outlook, enriched Australia's living by the infusion of their cultures, brought a diversity of skills that have widened the base of Australian industry and commerce; their numbers have boosted production.

But a nation's way of life—like life itself—is always changing. It may be that this happens more quickly in Australia than elsewhere because the country is young and growing. At this stage of her history the immigration policy has shifted in emphasis and direction. The change is not as dramatic as that of 1945 but in the long run it may prove far more significant.

By the late 1960's the annual intake of migrants had exceeded 180,000 but for 1971-72 there was a cut-back to 140,000 in the immigration programme for economic reasons. For some period before that there had been building up a climate of public opinion that favoured a lessening of the migrant intake. The thinking now was that the nation's objectives could no longer be expressed in solely material terms—if indeed they ever were. Rising material standards had made new objectives. For many, "environment" and "conservation" are replacing "development" and "economic growth" as priority objectives. Numbers of migrants, as such, had never been the main consideration of the immigration programme—quality of skills was always stressed—but they had, nevertheless, been an important factor. Now the situation was altered. It was officially announced in 1970 that investigation would be undertaken to determine the desirable future levels to which immigrations should contribute. Even more importantly, the investigations would also seek to establish the desirable structure and distribution of that population.

Earlier shifts in immigration policy occurred in 1964 and 1966 which meant that greater numbers of settlers from Asia would be permitted to enter Australia.

First, the Government decided that people of mixed descent would be considered for entry on an entirely different basis. The skills, present circumstances of applicants and, wherever appropriate, the presence of relatives in Australia would be the determining factors.

In March 1966, following a comprehensive policy review, the Government announced that non-Europeans could be considered for settlement in Australia on the basis of their general suitability, their ability to integrate readily and their possession of qualifications positively useful to Australia. The announcement said that the number of non-Europeans to be admitted would be somewhat greater than previously. However, the changes were not intended to meet general labour shortages or to permit the large-scale admission of workers from Asia but, nevertheless, the widening of eligibility would help to fill some of Australia's special needs.

In 1966 changes also meant that non-Europeans who initially had been admitted as temporary residents but authorised to remain indefinitely could become permanent residents and citizens after five years' stay instead of fifteen years as previously required.

Non-Europeans are allowed into Australia under two categories and during the calendar year 1970 5,657 people of mixed descent were admitted for permanent residence. These included 822 for family reunions and 1,609 with qualifications for positions not adequately filled by local residents. In addition there were 970 people who had come to Australia on temporary residential permits but were given permanent residential status. These included a number of students. In the words of a statement issued in 1971 the policies laid down by the Government are "based on the belief that all Australians want Australia to be an essentially cohesive society notable for economic opportunity and social mobility and without self-perpetuating enclaves and indigested minorities". They try to avoid a situation where there are "substantial groups of ethnic origin very different from the host community proud of difference and determined to perpetuate it and ready to dispute the efforts of the national Government to encourage integration".

AUSTRALIA—THE MODERN MECCA

SINCE THE END of World War II the face of Asia has undergone many changes, politically, economically and socially, to a large extent brought about by the modernisation of transport services by air and sea.

Australia, only 25 years ago a little known continent located on the map somewhere south of South-east Asia, has emerged as a nation of vital importance in the expanding Asian scene. More and more people are visiting its capitals to discuss business projects, more and more tourists are making their plans to include Australia in their itineraries. And in most cases their first port of call is Sydney, the oldest, largest, most picturesque of Australia's beautiful capitals.

To paint a word picture of Sydney is a simple task—small craft dancing on the Harbour to the endless rhythm of the blue Pacific; sails billowing against the massive backdrop of the Harbour Bridge and the unique beauty of the Opera House framed by an ever upward stretching skyline.

But this is a mere fragment of the city, distinctively Australian and yet richly cosmopolitan in character: bustling, boisterous, brash and bawdy, vibrant with life and energy.

In past decades many Australians have travelled the world and been enthused by the wonders they have seen, particularly the colour and mysteries of Asia. They have returned by ship or airliner, only to fall victim to the charm and fascination of their own homeland. This reaction is not peculiar to Australians. It is a common one even among sophisticates from other lands, because Sydney has an aura, a sense of authentic character which makes it one of the

Above:
Inside the Great Hall
of Melbourne's Art Centre.

Left Page:
One of the architectural wonders
of the 20th Century,
Sydney's unique Opera House
is due for completion at
the end of 1972.

It is interesting to recall Phillip's observation as he sailed his tiny fleet through the massive Harbour Heads: "This is the finest Harbour in the world", he wrote in his logbook, "in which 1,000 Ships of the Line may ride in the most perfect security". He might have added that it is also a Harbour of matchless beauty, with harbours within the Harbour proper, and despite its present status as the busiest port in the Southern Hemisphere, Sydney has retained this beauty in remarkable fashion.

The visitor who arrives by ocean liner glides right into the very heart of the city past a shoreline devoid of the unsightly structures and commercial agglomerations which mar so many major ports; he ties up at wharves which once knew the footsteps of Joseph Conrad and resounded to the shanties of the sailors of every maritime nation.

It was from here that the famous wool clippers of the 19th Century set out on their epic voyages to England and Europe, sketching in indelible ink a classic chapter in the history of sail.

Today, in this age of steam and diesel oil the world's biggest ships now berth casually where once the *Cutty Sark* rode at anchor, a mere 'stone's throw' from the compellingly beautiful structure of the Opera House, already acknowledged to be one of the architectural wonders of the 20th Century. In the background, towering office blocks serrate the skyline and around them lies suburban Sydney, stretching in all directions over an area of nearly 700 square miles. This is Sydney as first glimpsed from the sea; from the air the vast panorama is literally breathtaking.

Although each of Australia's capitals has its own individual appeal Sydney has an almost limitless number of attractions and entertainments from the highly sophisticated to the simplest most carefree varieties. The newcomer feels immediately at home in this city.

But like all large cities Sydney also has its seamier sides; and it is true that here, as elsewhere in the world, fools can quite easily be parted from their money. But there are few places where the average citizen may run the risk of injury or theft in the course of sampling the life of the metropolis.

Those who want to learn something of "historic" Sydney will find many opportunities to do so. Some of the public buildings, Government offices, churches, libraries, museums and stately harbourside mansions date from early periods of Australia's history and are built of sandstone blocks laboriously cut by the convicts who were transported here to found the colony.

world's most exciting capitals. By European and Asian standards it is young and very new but many contend that this is more an advantage than otherwise. Certainly it has carefully nurtured the seeds of its history and the Australian character is in evidence in the preservation of the better aspects of its early years and the introduction of new, progressive ideas in its contemporary planning.

Since the time when Australia was founded as a penal colony by its first Governor, Captain Arthur Phillip, in January 1788, Sydney has grown rapidly from a desolate bushland tract to a thriving metropolis of almost $2\frac{3}{4}$ million.

SUMMIT TALK

The streets are sometimes narrow and twisting, the relics of primitive early planning, but large parks and recreation areas and the newly designed Martin Place Plaza right in the centre of the city relieve any sense of constriction. And always there is the Harbour and the multitude of small bays round which the natural bushland has been jealously preserved.

Within the metropolitan area there are 34 ocean beaches and on warm weekends they are alive with life and colour. Surf patrols are constantly on duty to rescue inexperienced swimmers who may get into difficulties. Australia is one of the great swimming nations of the world, as it has demonstrated so often in international competition, and in the specialist field of surfing it yields no nation pride of place.

Surf carnivals are exciting spectacles and are well-known as programme 'stoppers' for visiting dignitaries, who almost invariably stay far longer than the short time allocated in their usually tightly arranged schedules.

Of the other capitals Perth, Hobart, Brisbane and Melbourne have the dual natural advantages of ocean beaches and river waterways. Adelaide has its Torrens Lake in the heart of the City and five miles away are the sheltered beaches of St. Vincent's Gulf. Canberra's still new, man-made Lake Burley Griffin has done much to enhance what is already one of the most beautifully landscaped capitals of the world.

Just as Australia's equable climatic conditions lend themselves to wide indulgence in sporting activities, so also is there an ever-pleasant atmosphere for evening entertainment: theatres presenting drama and ballet, symphonic concerts and opera, drive-in theatres, cinemas, nightclubs, discotheques, entertainment centres and uninhibited variety shows common to all major cities, cater for the divers tastes of residents and visitors.

Annual festivals are held in every capital city and the large rural centres. Sydney's Waratah Spring Festival in October means a week of civic gaiety and pageantry. The Moomba Festival in Melbourne, the Adelaide and Perth Festivals of Art, Brisbane's Warana Festival and Hobart's Blue Gum Festival are all highlights of the year.

For the gourmet, interesting bills of fare are always able to be discovered in numerous restaurants and leading hotels with dishes ranging from Sydney's famous rock oysters, crayfish and prawns, to exotic imported dishes of almost every nationality. And to accompany them Australian wines are available—of wide variety, excellent quality and relatively low cost.

Much thought has been given by enterprising restaurateurs to atmosphere and in every capital and many provincial cities are to be found eating places from the lavishly appointed dining rooms of the big hotels to the small, intimate restaurants and nightclubs, fascinatingly conceived in unusual decors. But of them all Australia's most famous venue of gourmets is the Summit, perched 500 feet above the city of Sydney on the 47th floor of Australia Square. As a restaurant offering fine foods and fine wines it is equal to the best in the world; this revolving eyrie high above one of the world's most exciting panoramas has no peer.

On a clear day—which one may expect to find, with few exceptions, during any month of the year—the Summit buffet or à la carte luncheon is a happening to be experienced in no other city, from London to Seattle, from Tokyo to Timbuktu. As the restaurant revolves in a complete circle every 105 minutes, the sky-scraping City of Sydney—interspersed with green parks and gardens, the sparkling waters of the Harbour stretching from the Heads of Port Jackson past its many bays and inlets, across the Bridge to Lane Cove and Parramatta Rivers, and the Blue Mountains Range 50 miles to the west—is an unforgettable sight. Dinner at night is a dual feast—a feast of food and wine and a feast of a myriad lights. The neoned strips of George and Pitt Streets, William Street, soon to be a magnificent new boulevarde pointing the way to the night spots of King's Cross, the gleaming gliding ferry boats on the colour-splashed waters of the Harbour, the darkened silhouettes of tall commercial buildings and apartments on the skyline, the delicately floodlit Opera House, the illuminated ships in Woolloomooloo Bay, Circular Quay and Darling Harbour—all combine in a thrilling cyclorama made even more memorable by the soft rhythm of a cool combo.

The express elevator from the Square podium literally rockets to the 47th level where the head waiter greets his guests and hostesses check hats and cloaks. A drink at the cocktail bar conditions diners to the atmosphere of the restaurant, revolving so slowly one scarcely realises the movement until the city panorama imperceptibly changes. They are then seated at the table

Opposite page:
Viewed from across the Harbour,
the City of Sydney at night
is one of the great sights of the world.
The cylindrical building in the centre
of the picture is Australia Square;
from the Summit Restaurant
on the 47th floor
the view is breathtaking....
The scene at mid-day, no less exciting,
is pictured above, on this page....
The Summit cocktail bar is shown
on the left.

161

THE LAND OF "THE SOUTHERN CROSS"

previously reserved, where the drink and food waiters take charge. Comfortable swivel chairs give the guests ample scope to take in every angle of the passing scene...... On special occasions international festivals are held and menus of Italian, French, Hungarian or Swiss foods and wines are served at the Summit and products of the countries are displayed in the foyer. Sundays are family days and a special buffet luncheon of dozens of appetising dishes is prepared to appeal to the younger members of the family.

Changing the scene to another city: Melbourne, Victoria's elegant capital, built on the banks of the Yarra River and bordered on its south-eastern angle by the beautifully landscaped, green-lawned Domain and Alexandra Gardens and Fitzroy Gardens. In the warmer seasons the Myer Bowl draws tens of thousands to the Alexandra Gardens to hear free concerts given by the Melbourne Symphony Orchestra, celebrity artists and pop groups. Nearby is Melbourne's new Arts Centre, housing famous paintings, rare ceramics, historic pieces of art and other valuable possessions of the City. In the Fitzroy Gardens are hundreds of huge shady trees, ornamental shrubs, a heated glass house where begonias and many other seasonal floral specimens are displayed. Set among the trees on a widespread lawn is a replica of Captain Cook's cottage—his home in Marton in Cleveland, Yorkshire, England. Within a short distance of Fitzroy Gardens is Exhibition Street with its landmark, the Southern Cross Hotel, a member of the internationally famous Inter-Continental Group and one of the finest hotels in Australia.

Back in the swinging 1800's this was the site of what was known as "Paddy's Market", a great open area where anything could be bought from fruit and vegetables, live rabbits or dead, poultry, second-hand books, ironmongery, groceries, second-hand household utensils—ad lib. It was also an arena for political speeches and in July 1865 there was an all-in brawl between the congregations of four rival preachers. In those days Melbourne was a wild old town. Paddy's Market was replanned in the 1870's as a great tin-roofed building known as the Eastern Market. Not many Australian's remember that it had a somewhat lurid history. Madame Tingara Lee, a mountain of a woman, had a small booth where she told fortunes for a shilling (10 cents); Frank Cartwright, a vaudeville artist, was shot by Professor Medor, an astrologist who was declared insane after a verdict of murder. There were peep-show machines that our present permissive indoctrinated censors would hesitate to approve. There also was born the inspiration for "The Sentimental Bloke", a masterpiece of one of Australia's most loved poets, C.J. Dennis.

Although much water has flowed under the bridge since then, the Southern Cross Hotel has honoured the memory of "The Bloke" in a bronze plaque fixed on the Bourke Street side of the Garden Plaza.

The Southern Cross Hotel was opened by Australia's former Prime Minister Sir Robert Menzies on 24th August 1962. It's fifteen storeys are set on $2\frac{1}{2}$ acres—almost a miniature city within a city. It has an interior shopping Plaza of more than 70 boutiques and specialty shops grouped around an open-air courtyard and a fountain designed in the form of a pair of boomerangs.

Like all top class international hotels the Southern Cross has to feed large numbers of people with widely differing tastes and limitations of funds. The Southern Cross caters for them all in its nine restaurants and bars—from Royalty and Heads of State, international celebrities of the political, entertainment and commercial worlds to the ordinary man-in-the-street, his wife and family. One of the most popular retreats for businessmen at lunch time is the Club Grill, in a rich warm club atmosphere with an open rotisserie from which succulent Australian steaks are served on sizzling platters. The Mayfair Room is a truly elegant restaurant, where one may dine and dance in romantic surroundings and enjoy the finest wines with a gourmet cuisine. The decor reflects Victoriana in the grand manner in colours of plush burgundy, with gold velvet, graceful trellis arches and the soft glow of gasoliers.

The Coolibah Coffee Shop is the place for informal meals at modest prices and quick service well into the early hours of the A.M. It got its name from the tree made famous by the Australian bush ballad "Waltzing Matilda". A mural of aboriginal folk lore dominates the length and breadth of one wall. Happy conversation and a drink in an intimate atmosphere go together in the "Wilawa" Cocktail Bar built of Australian blackwood panels and decorated with aboriginal bark paintings and a didgeridoo. Other popular meeting places are the Ice Cream Parlor, the Tavern Bar, the Stable charcoal grill and the Public Bar. All these are located in the Garden Plaza and ground floor areas.

The Hotel has 435 bedrooms and suites all with private bathrooms, individually controlled air-conditioning, dial-out telephones, radio and television. On the 15th floor is a Penthouse Suite offering the ultimate in luxury, with a panoramic view of the entire city and the Port Philip Bay shoreline. There are nine Convention Rooms to seat from ten to 700, catering for business and social functions; five are named after the Stars that make up the Southern Cross Constellation — Alpha, Beta, Gamma, Delta and Epsilon. The Ballroom will accommodate a fully televised conference or a formal dinner. Services available include translation equipment for all languages, microphones, tape recording, projectors, lighting control, music, bands and platforms. The car park will accommodate 300 guests' cars.

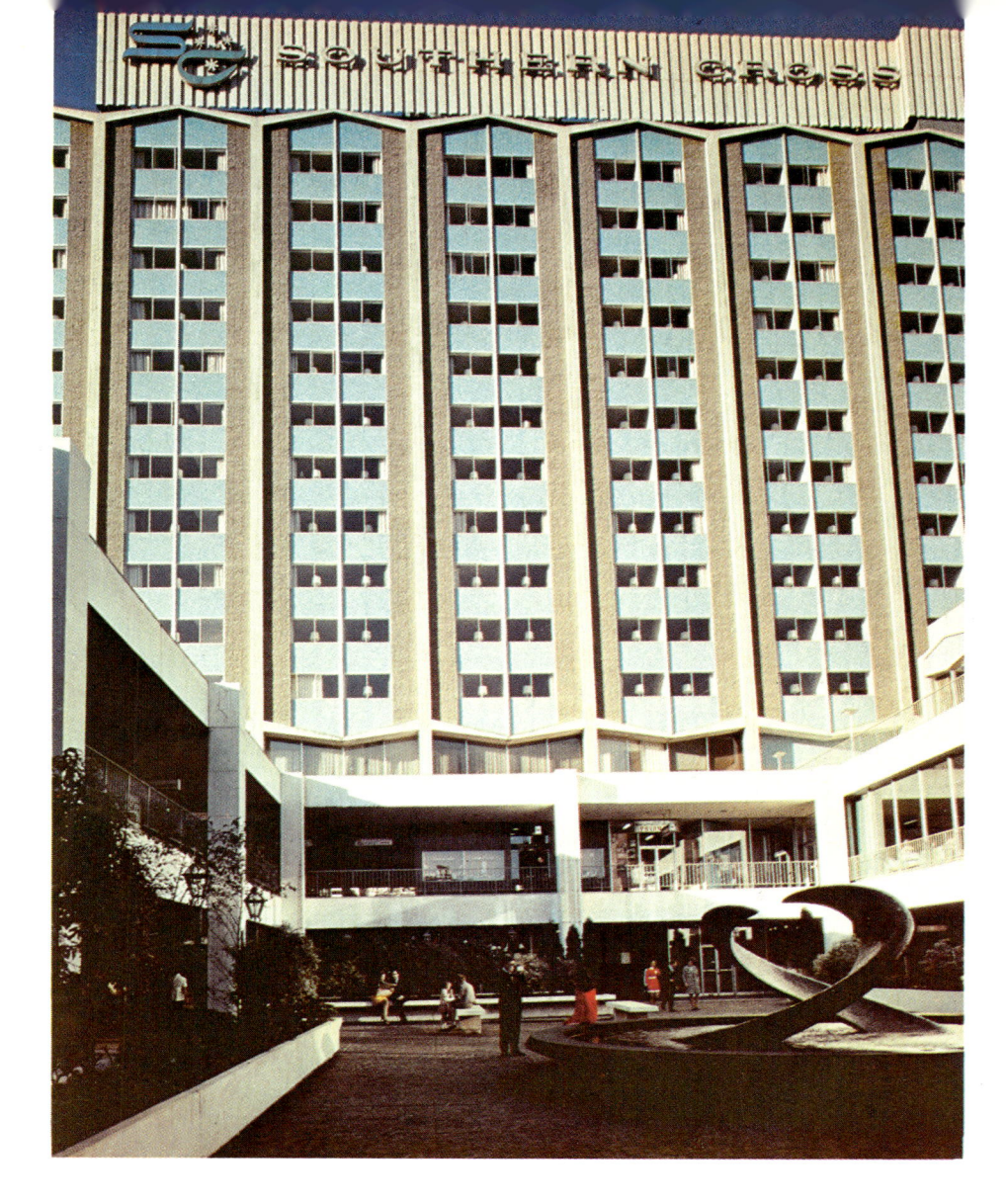

In the next decade the face of Australia's capitals will see many changes. Plans have been announced for the development of Sydney's historic Rocks Area, an ambitious scheme to cost $A500,000,000; the transformation of old Woolloomooloo into a modern commercial centre on a grand scale involving another $A100,000,000 and private enterprise skyscraping office blocks and hotels worth still another $A100,000,000.

Australia is the newly emerging Mecca of the south-west Pacific: the conference room for the keen businessman searching for new and more profitable ventures, a haven for the jaded globe trotter and for the wanderer looking for a happy time in a peaceful, yet fresh and ever exciting atmosphere.

Above:
The Garden Plaza of the
Southern Cross Inter-Continental
Hotel with its
Boomerang Fountain
in the foreground.

Left:
The Mayfair Room,
one of Australia's sophisticated
restaurants.

Opposite page:
The City of Melbourne viewed from
the River Yarra.

AUSTRALIA is a tough, hard country. Its economy is relatively young and its population relatively small by comparison with those of most major nations of the world.

It is isolated geographically and until the recent discoveries of rich mineral deposits described further in this Chapter, it was not considered to be very well endowed with natural resources.

Despite all this, Australian living standards have for long ranked amongst the highest in the world. This has been due in some part to the manner in which its banking and financial systems have been able to assist in the growth of gross national product.

There are not many banks in Australia but most of them are characterised by large numbers of branches. Indeed, the branch system of banking, which has been operating in Australia for about 140 years, still appeals to Australians today as being at least as suitable to modern conditions as it was when the nation was emerging from a state of being completely undeveloped.

There probably has never been a nation which, for such a large proportion of its history, has been so well served by its banks. This may be dramatically illustrated by reference to Australia's first bank, the Bank of New South Wales, which today, in addition to being highly computerised, has a staff which numbers virtually as many people as there were settlers in Australia when the bank was established in the year 1817.

The Bank of New South Wales may be cited as being symbolic of the stability of the banking system in Australia. Although some commercial banks failed last century, none has done so in the 1900's. In well over 150 years the Bank of New South Wales has never had to close its doors on any business day, nor has it failed in any year to pay a dividend to its shareholders.

The legal structure of the Australian banking system centres around the Federal Government's "Reserve Bank of Australia". The Reserve Bank has authority to implement Government policy over all those banks which operate nationally in Australia. But its powers over State-owned institutions whose branches do not extend beyond the borders of any one State, are of the nature of persuasion rather than of legal direction. The Reserve Bank's powers over the nationally-operating banks are exercised through interest rate controls; by requiring the banks to maintain certain liquidity ratios; and by making them surrender some of their liquid assets to the trusteeship of the central banks.

Head Office of the
Bank of New South Wales,
Martin Place, Sydney.

THE BANKING SCENE

There are some seven commercial (or "trading") banks operating across the nation and coming within the direct influence of the Federal Parliament. These are generally known as "the major banks".

Another seven commercial banks either limit their operations to within single States or have very few branches. Of the fourteen commercial banks in Australia, seven are public corporations, one is entirely owned by the Australian Government, three are owned by various State Governments and three by foreign governments.

Of the twelve savings banks in Australia seven are owned by associated "major" commercial banks, three are owned by States, whilst the remaining two are trustee banks with limited spheres of operation.

The incidence of Reserve Bank controls, which have applied exclusively to the nationally-operating banks, has led to the very rapid growth in Australia of a wide range of financial institutions other than banks. In the belief that these could not be controlled federally under the Australian Constitution a hot-house atmosphere developed. As the authorities continued to impose controls on the "true" banks, the newer "fringe" banks grew rapidly.

In these circumstances the true banks have been very energetic in diversifying into what may be traditionally regarded as "non-bank" areas. As well, they have expanded their branch networks into many new areas not only within Australia but also in other places. For example, and to refer again to the oldest and largest commercial bank, the Bank of New South Wales has recently established branches throughout the Pacific area in places where it has never before been represented. It has gone beyond New Guinea and Fiji, where it has been for many years, and now has branches in Nauru, Tarawa (in the Gilbert and Ellice Islands), Kieta (on Bougainville), and Vila in the New Hebrides. The Bank has established representative offices in New York, Tokyo, Hong Kong and Singapore. It also maintains three branches in London being the first foreign bank set up there.

The Bank of New South Wales has also invested in several non-bank undertakings, prominent amongst which are Australian Guarantee Corporation Ltd., which is the largest non-bank finance house in Australia.

The Bank's share of the capital of this corporation is 43 per cent. It has set up an international finance organisation "Partnership Pacific Limited" in joint ownership with The Bank of Tokyo Ltd. and the Bank of America. It also has made capital investments in sundry mining ventures of a major nature and within its own structure has established the largest travel service in the south-west Pacific area and one of the largest investment management services. Through the latter it conducts unit trusts and superannuation funds for the general public. It provides a most comprehensive investment portfolio management service which both local and overseas investors find extremely useful, and profitable.

The Australian banking industry as a whole is as solid and reliable as any in the world and Australians are amongst the greatest per capita bank users in the world.

Because of the great trading propensity of Australia and because of its geographical isolation the commercial banks 'down under' are expert in all the techniques of financing international trading and money flow operations. The range of services available to investors in, and traders with, Australia leaves nothing to be desired.

Main Queensland office
of the Bank of New South Wales
at Brisbane.

Below:
A typical Bank of New South Wales
branch office at Feilding, New Zealand.

Above: The first departmental store to be built in the Colony stood at the corner of George and Barrack Streets, opposite the Sydney Post Office. It was opened in 1838 by the late David Jones, the founder of what is now the oldest and one of the largest retail organisations in Australia. Operating in all States of the Commonwealth, it includes suburban shopping complexes such as that at Brookvale, N.S.W., (illustrated left), the Mount Gravatt Shopping Centre, eight miles from Brisbane, comprising 80 stores and speciality shops (below), and the Adelaide city departmental store (opposite page).

AUSTRALIAN RETAILING

RETAIL TRADING in Australia had a somewhat unsavoury beginning. All food, clothing and other necessities for the young Colony in the early years of settlement, from 1788 till the beginning of the 19th Century, were commandeered by the officers of the New South Wales Corps as soon as they arrived and sold at extortionate prices. This unsatisfactory situation continued for thirty or forty years and it was only when Governor Macquarie arrived and replaced the New South Wales Corps with his own Highland regiment that the worst aspects of the developing Colony were corrected.

Small businesses began to emerge and responsible citizens took active parts in legitimate trading. Among them was a Welshman named David Jones. In 1838 he opened an unpretentious one-storeyed General drapery store opposite the first Post Office in George Street. Jones was a man of ideas—he bought land near his store for Sydney's first "parking station", where shoppers and agents could leave their horses, carriages and bullock waggons; as the Colony extended inland he set up Australia's first mail-order service for country customers—delivering goods by the well known Cobb & Co. coaches.

David Jones was one of the few retailers whose store could always be relied upon to stock sound quality goods. Following his principles of fair trading and high integrity, his business flourished, and continued to do so throughout the formative years of the 1800's.

In 1906 the David Jones business was established as a Public Company with three of the founder's grandsons as Directors. One of the latter was Charles Lloyd Jones, later to be knighted by Her Majesty the Queen for his outstanding services to Australian retailing. His son, Mr. Charles Lloyd Jones, is the present Chairman of the Company. Sir Charles made history when he brought the famous French couturier Pierre Balmain and his fashion collection to Sydney in 1956 and since that time similar importations from Paris, London, New York and Rome have become regular features of David Jones' stores. Annual promotions displaying the latest products of Asia, Britain, Europe and the United States of America have gained international recognition for the Company. In its 134 years of trading, David Jones has grown to 23 stores throughout the mainland of Australia, employing 13,500 people. At the Company's annual meeting in October 1970 the Chairman predicted that by the end of the 1970's the David Jones establishments would be doubled. By March 1971, six new stores were already either under construction or on the drawing boards. Since its establishment as a Public Company, the annual financial results of its operations and the profits derived have continued to increase, and as at the 31st July 1971 it had accumulated assets totalling $A141,352,000. Its net profit had risen to a record $A5,966,000.

The changing shape and rising population of Australia's capitals and bigger provincial cities has brought about the development of large suburban community shopping centres, containing branches of major stores. These modern retail complexes, air-conditioned for summer comfort, and providing ample parking space for the ever growing number of customers' cars, bring shopping facilities within easy reach of out-of-city housewives.

David Jones Limited has three such centres in Sydney. They are also established in the $20 million Garden City complex in the Brisbane suburb of Mount Gravatt, which provides parking space for 2,000 cars and has a municipal library, baby minding centre, scores of small shops and three major department stores. They are established in similar centres in Perth, W.A., Canberra, A.C.T., and in another in Brisbane. In addition, the Company plans to participate in two more centres in widely separated but equally fashionable shopping areas of Sydney; one complex alone is budgeted to cost its developers $A40 million.

This is the new approach to the enlivenment of the social life of the community; a new facet to modern Australia's development in which David Jones plays so notable a part.

NATURAL GAS

HUGE NATURAL GAS discoveries and developments have led the Australian gas industry into an era of the most rapid change and expansion in its 130 years' history. This new gas age is certain to be of great significance in improving the material comforts and economic well-being of both the peoples of Australia and Asia.

Natural gas is generally believed to have been formed over millions of years by the action of heat, pressure, chemicals and bacteria on the remains of minute marine organisms and plants which collected in beds of sediment laid down by the large oceans and inland seas of former geological times. The gas became trapped in huge reservoirs of porous rock formed beneath the ground by movements of the earth's crust.

In chemical terms natural gas is described as a colourless, odourless gas consisting mostly of methane—CH_4, a compound of hydrogen and carbon, the simplest and lightest member of the paraffin series of hydrocarbons. Ethane, propane and butane are also present in small quantities, varying according to the source, and other possible constituents are carbon dioxide, hydrogen sulphide, nitrogen and, more rarely, hydrogen, oxygen and helium. Natural gas has a calorific or heating value of about 1,000 *Btu per cubic foot, approximately twice that of manufactured gas, better known as Town Gas. Natural gas deposits so far discovered in Australia have a negligible sulphur content and are virtually free of hydrogen sulphide. For this latter reason it is termed a "sweet" gas.

Known reserves of natural gas in Australia now exceed 20 trillion (million million) cubic feet. Development and utilisation of this cheap, easily transportable, easily usable and indigenous form of energy is changing the gas industry. From its former fully-contained look, in that it both manufactured, distributed and marketed gas on an individual basis in cities and major towns, it is now three separate but related and fully interdependent sections, comprising producers, pipeline operators and gas distributors.

This combination of modern enterprise involving large capital investment and sophisticated technical and marketing skills will lead, in this decade, to a vast interconnected pipeline grid linking gas resources with Australia's capital cities, country cities and towns. It will lead, also, to natural gas taking over a steadily increasing share of the primary energy market. From 1968 to 1980 natural gas for energy is forecast to rise from 20.2 million therms* to 3,200 million therms.

*FOOTNOTE Btu, British Thermal Unit is defined as the quantity of heat required to raise the temperature of 1 pound of water through 1° Fahrenheit. As it is an inconveniently small unit quantities of gas are often quoted in therms, (1 Therm = 100,000 Btu).

Above: Model of The Australian Gas Light Company's proposed new two-building Head Office in Sydney. Plans for this striking project include the use of a natural gas "total energy" system to supply electricity and air-conditioning.

ITS MULTIPLE USES

Natural gas is now in Melbourne, Brisbane, Adelaide and Perth. By 1973 it will be piped to the most heavily populated and industrialised centres of New South Wales —the great Sydney-Newcastle-Wollongong complex. It will come in a 30-inch diameter, 850 mile long pipeline from Moomba-Gidgealpa area in the north-east corner of South Australia. The pipeline will be constructed and operated by The Australian Gas Light Company through its subsidiary, East-Aust. Pipeline Corporation. As far as possible it will follow a direct route and will supply country cities and towns on the way. Spur lines will serve major rural regions to the north and south.

In line with the experience of the United States, Canada, Russia, France, Italy, Holland, Britain and other countries, the coming of natural gas could bring about something of an industrial revolution in New South Wales and enable it to maintain its position as the prime manufacturing State of Australia.

Above right: Flaring Off operation at Gasfield Cooper Basin, South Australia.

Below: The raincoat worn by the model is made of synthetic fabric processed from natural gas derivatives.

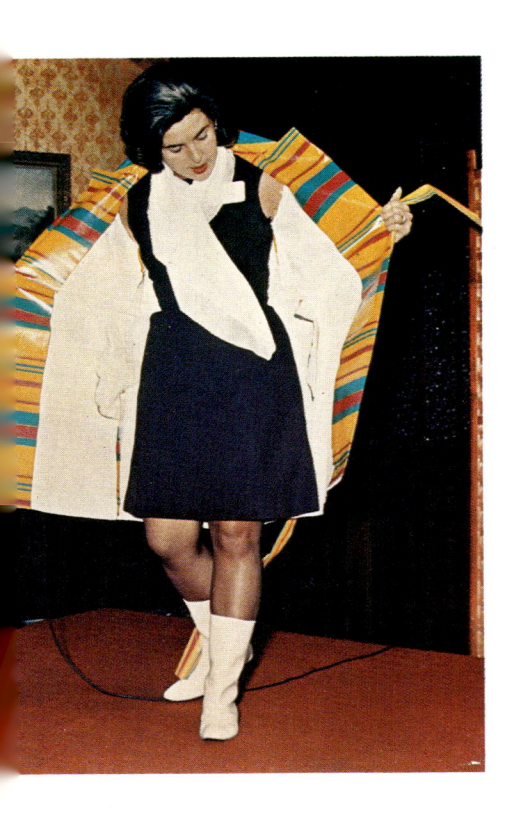

While the inherent properties of natural gas—cleanliness, non-toxicity, convenience and ready sensitivity to precise thermostatic control—earn it acceptance for cooking and heating in domestic and commercial uses, its greatest impact is in industry because of performance and low cost considerations. Its pollution-free qualities alone could make it the most desirable form of energy for the future; carbon dioxide and water, natural ingredients of the atmosphere, are its only residues.

In industry, natural gas is used for forging, cutting, hardening, galvanising, drying and other tasks. It plays an increasing role in making steel, textiles, plastics, tiles, cement, glass, chemicals and paper.

The uses of natural gas as raw material are myriad. Natural gas and the valuable liquid hydrocarbons extracted from it are combined with other substances to make plastics, synthetic rubber, a wide range of miracle fibres, fertilisers, insecticides, medicines, explosives, detergents and solvents.

The Australian Gas Light Company's proposed new $A25 million Head Office will be the first office block in Sydney to use a natural gas "total energy" system. With this type of system natural gas is used to supply electric power, lighting, heating and cooling.

The virtue of such systems is that full use is made of all the energy, with the exhaust heat providing space heating, water heating, absorption air-conditioning and process heat.

The emergence of a low and stable priced energy in Australia, a country with vast primary food and raw material resources, will rapidly up-grade the nation's development of secondary industry. In turn this will assist the Asian countries because Australia will be able to increase its ability to supply them with a wide range of processed foods and goods as well as light and heavy industrial equipment for developmental needs.

Australia's natural gas is now assisting those Asian countries faced with a shortage of primary energy resources. Associated with natural gas production from Bass Strait fields are very large tonnages of liquefied petroleum gases. Up to June 1971 330,000 metric tons of LPG have been exported to the Pacific Islands and Asia, particularly Japan.

Presently consortia of Asian business interests are engaged with Australian producers in feasibility studies into the liquefaction* of the huge gas discoveries in remote areas for export in tankers.

This latter instance is typical of the many opportunities available for the pooling of resources and knowledge in the building of greater friendships and co-prosperity throughout Asia and Australasia.

*FOOTNOTE Liquefied natural gas is a liquid form of the gas which is obtained by chilling it to minus 258°F. Liquefying natural gas reduces its volume by a 600 to 1 ratio, permitting storage of large quantities in compact spaces. When required, LNG is drawn from storage tanks, changed by vapourisation into a gas, odourised and fed into gas mains.

Left: A general view of the opal fields at Coober Pedy, South Australia.

IN ALL DIRECTIONS, hundreds of miles of sunburnt stony ground, red dust rising from the road in choking clouds, the monotony of the red plain relieved only by sparse patches of dry yellow grass, grey-green saltbush and mulga and the shimmering white of salt-lakes ...... This is the route from Port Augusta to the rich opal fields of Coober Pedy.

At the Coober, about 500 miles north-west of Adelaide, the landscape is pitted and scarred by the mullock heaps of scores of claims. The lunar-like desolation is broken only by water-tanks, jeeps, a few fibre-board and corrugated iron shops and an equally unpretentious hotel or two. The miners' homes, dugout shelters cut into the hills, are almost invisible from a distance. Some are decorated with beer-bottle and concrete steps and terraces, some have front gardens of plastic flowers—the only variety suited to the climate—others are distinguished only by the piles of cans and scrap wire outside the door.

The gold-rushes of the 1850's first labelled Australia as a land of promise. Today is the age of functional metals and vast fields of mineral deposits are being developed by mammoth industrial enterprises and their bankers. Only the search for gemstones—and opals in particular—is still the province of the fossicker and the adventurer forever hoping to strike it rich, his only requirements being a capacity for backbreaking work, a belief in his own good luck, and his gambler's optimism.

Italians, Greeks, Czechs, Swedes, Englishmen and Australians have caught the 'opal-fever' and they battle together in the most primitive conditions. On many fields, dugouts serve both as kitchen and bedroom; the local iron-roofed hotel is the miners' only meeting-place and drinking their only entertainment. The work is hard and tedious; the hours are long; their tools, the miner's pick and shovel and a plug of gelignite. Only in recent times has some automation come to the diggings: jack-picks, power-winches and electric drills to speed up the heaviest work. But there is still the oppressive heat of the outback; the flies; the isolation; the lack of even the simple comforts and the danger of an underground collapse.

Why then do men still flock to the opal fields? The primary answer to this question must lie in the money to be won: prices for high-quality white opal found at Coober Pedy and Andamooka range from $A600 to $A1,200 an ounce. Quality black opal from Lightning Ridge will bring anything from $A100 to $A700 per carat. A secondary answer and the reason why so many choose to remain on the fields, even after their luck and money have run out, is that this is one of the few remaining environments where 'men can be men'. Women do go to the fields and some are miners themselves, but most men leave their girl friends and wives at home.

An opal miner leads a life of great freedom and little care. All his aspirations hinge on the finding of "colour" (quality opal). After six months of hard work he may make enough to spend the next year or two in the city or even take a holiday in Hong Kong or Japan. Some men, the lucky ones, have been known to retire before the age of thirty.

Opal is rarely found far below the surface, generally not deeper than about 85 feet. The miner blasts and burrows a shaft into a promising site and digs tunnels in the hope of finding sandstone, the rock in which opal is formed. When a tunnel reaches opal-bearing rock, the miner proceeds carefully, digging with a small pick, for opal is easily cracked and rendered worthless. Promising deposits are carried to the surface either by hand or machine-operated hoist. The painstaking work does not stop with the finding of opal. Long nights must be spent in grading and cutting to present the stones in the most attractive forms to obtain the highest prices from the buyers. After a mine has been worked for some time, the

Right: A home dug out of the sandstone on the Coober Pedy opal fields.

AUSTRALIAN OPALS AND OTHER GEMSTONES

A collection of opals mined in Australia: the dark opal at the top right corner, although basically blue in colour, is known as black opal, the most highly prized of all. The red fire in it adds value to the stone.

surface area becomes piled high with mullock (waste rock). Aborigines, children and tourists spend hot hours "noodling" (sifting) the heaps searching for overlooked stones.

Apart from opals, other gemstones have been discovered in commercial quantities in Australia. Chrysoprase is found in north Queensland and more particularly in Western Australia and a strong export market for these stones has been developed in Asia. Although its quality varies, the best chrysoprase is being rapidly accepted on world markets as a substitute for green jade, which it closely resembles. Another popular gem is the sapphire, found in a range of colours from dark blue to green at Inverell in northern New South Wales and parts of Queensland. Gold sapphires are also found and are reputed to be the finest in the world, an outstanding example being the "Golden Queen" which weighed over 100 carats. Although pearls are not classified as gemstones they are one of the most popular items of feminine adornment. The cultured pearl industry has become big business in northern Australia where some twenty farms are producing excellent pearls. A fourteen millimetre pearl choker was recently sold in the United States for US $100,000.

But opals remain Australia's most profitable gemstones and Australia is the largest opal-producer in the world. The value of gemstone-quality opal depends on the depth and variety of its colours. It may come in many sizes and forms ranging from small scintillating "pin-fire" opal to fist-sized, broad-banded, opalised shells or wood deposits. The range of colour, pattern and intensity displayed by these stones has been the subject of much scientific research.

White light is diffracted or split up into its spectral colours by the action of various silica particles within the stone, and this everchanging play of colours gives opals their distinctive appearance: peacock blues, yellows and reds fan out into variegated ripples; flashes of dark greens spring from deep within the gem. Patterns may resemble landscapes, animals or even faces!

The colours of high quality stone are vibrant and clear. Opal is one of the few gems that have not been produced synthetically with any great success.

Precious opal is mined commercially in Australia in five main areas: Coober Pedy and Andamooka in South Australia; White Cliffs and Lightning Ridge in New South Wales and scattered fields in Queensland. Solid black opal from Lightning Ridge is the most valuable but the lesser stones are much more plentiful at Coober Pedy. If an

Right: A blue enamel and gold brooch and a magnificent Australian cultured pearl.

Below: Finely mounted chrysoprase gemstones and pearls: an example of Prouds' craftsmanship.

opal displays solid colour, it may be cut into a single solid piece. So much of the stone, however, comes in thin seams and broken nodules that it must be sliced thin for cementing together with non-valuable material such as quartz, to make what is called a double or triplet. These techniques are intended to conserve valuable opal and not to deceive, but unscrupulous dealers have been known to take advantage of the unwary. It is wise, therefore, to deal only with jewellers and dealers of repute.

In this, Australia's most prosperous era, ornaments and precious stones delicately fashioned by the world's top ranking goldsmiths and silversmiths are being displayed in the more exclusive jewellery stores. The largest in Australia, and one of the biggest in the world, is the Proud Group. Since its establishment in Sydney nearly 70 years ago, Prouds has extended to most of the capital cities and to many provincial and suburban centres—even to remote parts of the Pacific, Suva, Lautoka, Nadi, and Norfolk Island.

Australian gemstones are featured in much of Prouds' jewellery: golden sapphire rings, chrysoprase brooches and ornaments and cultured pearl necklaces in shades varying from pink to silver white. Opals are available at all Prouds' stores in both traditional and modern settings. The value of these gems has risen to such a peak in recent years that stones are now cut to conform to their original form and colour rather than to any pre-planned shape. As well as saving precious opal, this method has resulted in many beautiful and unusual designs. One of the finest collections of Australian opals is to be seen at the headquarters display centre of Prouds Pty. Ltd. on the corner of Pitt and King Streets, Sydney, where experts are available to advise on the best quality stones within the price range of the purchaser.

Right: A magnificent golden sapphire displayed by Prouds. Australia produces the finest golden sapphires in the world.

Australia's oldest city and biggest capital is Sydney. Its sound economic development has largely resulted from the foresight and enterprise of such nationwide organisations as The Mutual Life and Citizens' Assurance Company Limited.

SAFEGUARDING PROSPERITY

THE FOREGOING PAGES of this Chapter have told of an ancient uncivilised land that in less than two centuries has become a rich Commonwealth, holding an honoured place among the great nations of the world.

It has fine cities and prosperous towns and homes for 13 million people; its economy is stable and its Gross National Product is worth more than $A27,000 million.

This land is Australia.

Its people are enjoying the fruits of the labours of their forebears and the foresight that prompted them to secure their holdings against the innumerable hazards that were bound to beset them: floods, fire, drought, sickness, death by accident and death from natural causes.

These precautions have saved Australians untold millions since the first insurance company came into being in the 1830's, only 50 years after the First Fleet under the command of Captain Arthur Phillip sailed into Sydney Cove.

Today there are 48 life insurance companies operating in Australia with assets totalling $A5,443 million. This huge store of savings is the result of investment in commercial and industrial enterprises, enabling important developments to be carried out far more rapidly than would otherwise be possible.

This aid to Australia's progress has been a major contribution but it ranks second to the benefits bestowed upon individual members of the public and their families in the form of payments to policy holders. In the single year 1970 no less than $A300 million was paid to holders of life insurance and $A523 million to persons and companies insured against loss by fire.

With such vast sums involved, strict legislation was introduced soon after World War II to control the activities of life insurance companies. This is administered through the office of the Insurance Commissioner, who operates within the framework of "The Life Insurance Act, 1945-1965". At the present time fire insurance companies are not subject to surveillance by an Insurance Commissioner, but similar legislation to that relating to life insurance is currently being contemplated.

Australia's experience in this important field has been recognised abroad. In 1962 the Malayan government co-opted Mr. Arthur Gray, Assistant General Manager of the Mutual Life and Citizens' Assurance Co. Ltd., one of Australia's largest insurance companies, to advise on the setting up of similar legislation in Malaya. Mr. Gray's plan was adopted and also used as a model for the regulation of insurance companies in Singapore.

The growth of the insurance industry in the last two decades, and its contribution to the economic development of Australia have both been enormous. Current indications are that this trend will continue and that insurance will be a major contributing factor to the flourishing future forecast for the Commonwealth.

Left:
A rear view of the antenna at the O.T.C. Ceduna (South Australia) earth station which carries telecommunications between Australia, Great Britain and Europe via the INTELSAT III Indian Ocean satellite. The cable wrap is located inside the conical support tower of the antenna.

Below: The cable wrap connecting the 97 ft. parabolic antenna with the ground equipment at the Overseas Telecommunications Commission (Australia) Ceduna earth station for satellite communications.

COMMUNICATIONS GATEWAY FOR SOUTH-EAST ASIA

DURING THE LAST DECADE or so Australia has become the communications gateway to the world for many South-east Asian countries. Her geographical position, straddling the Indian and Pacific oceans and within easy striking distance of most parts of South-east Asia, makes the island Continent a convenient stepping off point for communications links to most points of the world.

The COMPAC coaxial cable submarine system, which stretches across the Pacific from Canada via New Zealand, terminates in Sydney, Australia, where it interconnects with the SEACOM cable system through South-east Asia. Australia is also ideally placed as far as satellite communications are concerned in that it can "see" both the Indian and Pacific ocean satellites of the INTELSAT global system.

As each of these satellites has a coverage of approximately one-third of the earth's surface it is potentially possible for Australia to set up direct communications links via satellite with almost any part of the world, excepting the Atlantic Ocean area.

Communications through Australia are soundly logical for another reason—they save time. Because of world time differences, the peak demand for communications to and from each country tends to occur at different periods.

International communicators in South-east Asia have been quick to realise Australia's strategic position and consequently telephone calls, telex messages and telegrams from many South-east Asian countries stream through Australia on their way to other parts of the world throughout the 24 hours of the day. Similar communications from Europe and the United States come to Australia before being distributed to their destinations in South-east Asia. Many of these are effected through what are known as "hard-wire" connections; that is, permanent connections between fixed points via a transit terminal. Various other communications are carried through switched connections.

The Overseas Telecommunications Commission (Australia) at its Paddington, Sydney, international telecommunications terminal provides automatic facilities for the switching of communications traffic transiting Australia. These include a $2 million computer-controlled message relay system for international telegrams, which also handles telegrams terminating or originating in Australia, and large modern automatic telephone and telex exchanges.

Australia operates transit telephone services for New Zealand, Hong Kong, Papua New Guinea, Japan, Malaysia, Singapore and the Philippines which can be switched from Australia to such varying destinations as Canada, Britain, Europe, East Africa, Jamaica, Nigeria, Zambia, Hawaii and the U.S.A.

Transit switching arrangements in the telex and telegram services are similar although not necessarily with the same countries. As an example of the volume of transit traffic carried through Australia, some 25,000 telegrams a day pass through the message relay system at Paddington, originating from and destined for other countries. To ensure that facilities are constantly available for traffic switching, the Overseas Telecommunications Commission (Australia) has embarked on a number of short and long-term network planning studies. Complex computer programmes have been drawn up which take into account world

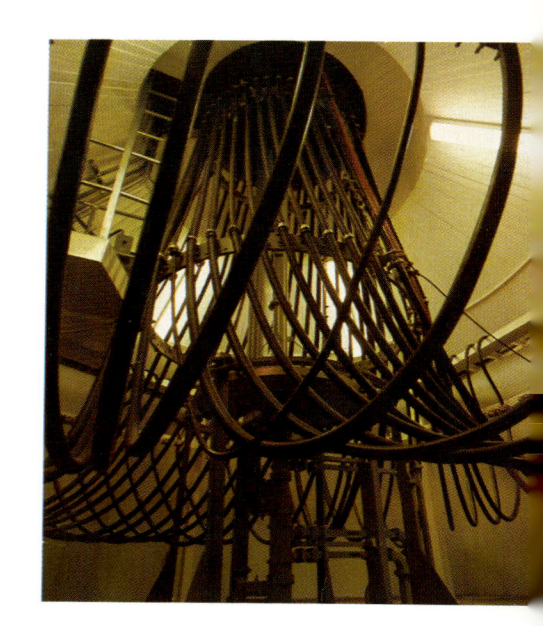

The intricate intertwining of innumerable cables in O.T.C. communications equipment has its counterpart in modern arterial highway communication systems, an example being an overpass complex on the Sydney-Newcastle expressway shown on the opposite page.
Plans have been prepared for an amenities area to be built over one of these complexes affording extensive views of the Hawkesbury River, N.S.W. It will cater for motorists and tourists and incorporate a restaurant, cafeteria, food bar and petrol and service stations.

time differences, present and projected demand for communications between countries, available alternative routes and the availability of terminal and transit switching equipment.

Through these studies, among the first of their type in the world, OTC hopes to be able to continue to provide a high standard of communications despite the rapid escalation in demand for transit-switched traffic from South-east Asia.

SEA, LAND AND AIR

BECAUSE AUSTRALIA is an island, the sea was the determining influence in the location of its early settlements. All its State capitals are ports or are linked with ports closely adjoining them. The distances between them run to hundreds of miles.

In the course of time the sea lanes were augmented by roads and railways and in more recent years by air routes, and these means of communication have all played vital parts in the life and development of the nation.

At Sydney, Australia's greatest port, 4,500 ships aggregating 20 million net tons enter the Harbour every year. Melbourne, the second largest receives 13 million tons, and Brisbane, Adelaide, Perth and Hobart and the many other major and minor ports together handle their share of the 16,000 ships that enter Australia annually, representing a total of 83 million net tons.

Harbour and dock facilities have been highly developed to deal efficiently with conventional shipping, with tankers, bulk ships of all kinds and container ships.

Australia's first train was inaugurated in 1854, running between central Melbourne and Port Melbourne. It was privately owned but in due course it was taken over by the Government. Almost all of Australia's railways are now run by the States or the Commonwealth.

The railway system, which girdles a large part of Australia and strikes inland to many key centres, has never lost its economic importance but as a passenger carrier it was for a time surpassed in glamour by air and road. In recent years two long-distance passenger trains have come into operation which in luxury and amenities are not surpassed by any in the world: the Southern Aurora which runs nightly from Sydney to Melbourne, and vice versa, and the Indian-Pacific travelling 2,500 miles from Sydney to Adelaide (by-passing Melbourne) and thence to Perth.

Progress of the railways has seen the steady rise of diesel-electric locomotives for long-distance haulage and the decline of steam. The suburban systems in Sydney and Melbourne are electrified. An underground system operates in Sydney and a start has been made on the construction of an underground in Melbourne.

Roads and highways in Australia have passed through several phases. The first were little more than bush tracks, serving the needs of bullock teams and pack horses. The American-inspired coaching firm of Cobb and Co., using American horse-drawn vehicles, became part of the legend of the Australian "outback".

The coming of the motor vehicle opened up a new era, taking over from the railways a large part of passenger transport in luxury parlour coaches and certain types of freight transport. Since then Australia (with New Zealand) has become the most highly motorised country next to the United States and Canada.

The total length of main roads, highways and lesser roads in Australia is more than 130,000 miles.

Not only do the highways—such as those linking Brisbane, Sydney, Melbourne and Adelaide—carry a great volume of normal passenger, tourist and commercial traffic, but those in the outback are of vital importance to the cattle industry and to the newly developing mining towns. Semi-trailers roar for hundreds of miles in a continuous procession to the iron ore projects and the ports of north-western Western Australia. "Road trains"—a succession of vehicles drawn by a prime mover—carry cattle and sheep to ports for shipment or to sale yards and abattoirs.

In the more highly developed areas of the eastern States of Australia a network of freeways and tourist roads makes easily accessible the pleasures of beach and snowfield, rugged mountain scenery and gentle vineyard country.

THIRTY-EIGHT YEARS AGO Djakarta was known as Batavia and the Republic of Indonesia was the Dutch East Indies. Singapore was one of the Federated States of Malaya. For thirteen years Australia's northern sector, embracing Queensland and the Northern Territory, had been the only part of the Continent linked by air routes. These were operated by the Queensland and Northern Territory Aerial Services with two World War I aircraft, of which one was a 504K biplane, small and primitive by today's standards but the first step towards what is now a vast network of services reaching from Cooktown to southern Tasmania, from Sydney to Perth, from the Snowy Mountains to the rich mineral fields of north-west Western Australia and to all major countries of the world.

Thirty-eight years ago Queensland and Northern Territory Aerial Services joined forces with Britain's Imperial Airways and forged the first air link between Australia and England. It shed its lengthy, cumbersome name and became QANTAS. The British Airline is now known as BOAC.

Qantas took over the responsibility for the Brisbane-Singapore sector and in February 1935 its first specially designed DH86 aircraft made the inaugural flight that was to establish Australia's overseas airline as one of the top-ranking services in the world.

Scheduled travelling time for the Brisbane-Singapore flight, with Batavia as one of seventeen intermediate stops including three overnights, was $3\frac{1}{2}$ days which seems incredibly slow by today's jet-speed standards, but at that time it was the fastest overseas commercial air service in the world.

Since then the Qantas network of routes has stretched around the globe and its list of ports of call in the South-east Asian area has grown accordingly.

The fall of Singapore in February 1942 suspended the Australia-England service, but Qantas reopened the route in 1943 by starting bi-weekly flights from Perth, Western Australia, across 3,513 miles of Indian Ocean nonstop to Colombo in one of the most remarkable operations in the airline's history. From then on the Qantas Catalina flying boats kept the route open for the carriage of essential mail and high priority passengers, and in operating the "cats" with up to $3\frac{1}{2}$ tons overload of fuel, Qantas operational staff evolved new techniques in long-range flying and developed the expertise which was to be the foundation for the Company's post war expansion into "round-the-world" operation.

Flying by dead-reckoning and astro-navigation, and in radio silence, Qantas made more than 800 Perth-Colombo crossings, then the longest regular ocean flight, and it was at this stage that the name "Kangaroo Service" was originated, because of the long hop involved, and also gave Qantas the inspiration for its aircraft symbol.

A Qantas flying boat was the first civil aircraft to land at Singapore after the War in October 1945, carrying staff to reopen the civil air service.

During the course of its rapid expansion in the post war years, Qantas has added half-a-dozen other South-east Asian ports to its network. In December, 1947 it began flying to Manila, in 1948 to Tokyo, in 1949 to Hong Kong. In 1950 Djakarta, after a long break, once again became a Qantas port of call. In 1953 came Bangkok,

in 1961 New Delhi, in 1965 Kuala Lumpur and in August 1969 the most recent addition to the network, beautiful Bali.

Today Qantas services link all these ports with the rest of the world through four different "round-the-world" routes: from Australia north and west to Europe through either Singapore or Hong Kong with other South-east Asian ports included in both routes. From London the return trip may be completed either through New York, San Francisco, Honolulu and Fiji, or through Bermuda, Nassau, Mexico and Tahiti.

From Australia a variety of special low-cost tours of the fascinating South-east Asian countries is available. Most travel agents offer a wide choice and Qantas itself has a long list of inclusive-price tours. On one of these, Singapore lies only a dinner and a few drinks away from departure time in Sydney, and tour parties usually arrive in the early evening, with the option of spending a quiet few hours at a hotel or going 'out on the town'.

Next day the traveller may tour Singapore and cross the Causeway to Johore Bahru on the mainland of Malaysia, take some time for the sights and sounds of the "Lion City", then fly on to Kuala Lumpur, Penang or Bangkok—depending on how much time is available. Exciting days may be spent in Bangkok, visiting the floating markets, the Royal Palace, or perhaps watching the unique spectacles of Thai boxing and dancing, and at least one day wandering around Thailand's colourful capital, shopping for Thai silks, cotton and jewellery.

From Bangkok the jet flies to Tokyo where moderate cost hotels serve as a base for exploring the world's biggest

GO NORTH-WEST, YOUNG MAN

city; sightseeing and shopping are highlights of the visit to this amazing capital of Japan. Then to cool and graceful Nikko, where temples and tree- and shrub-filled parks are living evidence of ancient Japanese culture and art.

Most tourists travel in groups, and with the help of Japanese guides spend eight days or so touring the country.

They call at lakeside Hakone, in the foothills below towering snowcapped Mount Fuji, then by coach down the age-old Tokaido way to Kyoto to see the pearl-divers bring in their baskets of pearl-bearing oysters.

From Osaka, the second largest city in Japan, is another jet hop to Hong Kong, the shopper's paradise of the Orient. This is truly one of the world's most fascinating cities. From colonial Hong Kong Island to the mainland-side twin city of Kowloon, to the Portuguese gambling isle of Macao, to the New Territories on the edge of China, Hong Kong offers a never-to-be-forgotten week of sightseeing. At Kai Tak airport the Qantas V-Jet waits to return to Australia, with possibly a stopover in Manila to explore the Philippines.

The plane which Qantas first flew to Singapore was a four-engined biplane, a DH86 with a crew of two—the First Officer doubling as Steward to serve thermos coffee with a box luncheon—the refinement of "a toilet room and, as an additional convenience for passengers, a looking glass and wash basin with running water from a tank". There was seating for ten passengers, though it could carry barely half that number on the Timor Sea crossing from Darwin to Kepang. The aircraft had an all-up loaded weight of 10,000 lb.

Since those days Qantas has introduced many new services and a variety of progressively more modern aircraft: recently, the Qantas fleet of Boeing 707 V-Jets.

On 17th September 1971 a new era in flying service began with Singapore as the first destination port for the Qantas Boeing 747B Jumbo Jet.

Like the DH86 of 1935, the Boeing 747B is a four-engined aircraft. But there the comparison ends. The 747B is a monoplane with the swept wings that have become the symbol of the jet age. Its four engines are monsters, each developing 45,500 lb. thrust, compared with the DH86's six-cylinder, 200 h.p. counterparts. It has a cruising speed of 570 m.p.h. compared with the De Havilland's 145 m.p.h. It has a crew of seventeen, including thirteen cabin hostesses and stewards to "pour the coffee". It has fifteen toilets complete with "looking glass", hot and cold running water from a 320-gallon tank, and innumerable other amenities. There is roomy seating for 56 first class and 300 economy passengers. The maximum take-off weight is 735,147 lb. (328 tons), and the maximum payload 146,420 lb. (65 tons). One engine of a 747B alone weighs more than one-third as much again as an empty DH86.

One thing common to both the first DH86 into Singapore and the first 747B—besides four engines—was the name "Canberra" after Australia's national capital.

The nature of the Qantas long-range routes demanded a jetliner just a little different from the others, and the answer was an order for a fleet of five 747B's, the long-range and more powerful version of the earlier 747. Incorporating the latest technological developments in the aviation industry, this aircraft has made it possible to operate very long-range sectors such as Sydney-Tokyo direct, Sydney-Hong Kong and Sydney-Honolulu.

In addition to being a technologically more advanced machine, a number of new design features have been incorporated in the Qantas version of the 747B. It has the largest 747 lounge in the world, full-length feature movies, top-class musical entertainment and a downstairs galley with elevators to carry food. The Captain Cook Lounge is reached by walking up the aircraft's spiral staircase and, with its twenty windows—fourteen more than the standard 747—it is a more spacious, brighter and quieter spot where passengers may relax. The two large galleys can produce more than 400 meals on any flight sector.

Altogether, in the 747B, Qantas has a new aircraft tailor-made to its own special requirements.

Left page, above:
The DH86—the first aircraft which Qantas flew to Singapore when the airline began overseas operations 35 years ago.

Left page, below:
Full-length movies and top-class musical entertainment are featured throughout the Qantas 747B.

Above: A Qantas 747B on the tarmac at Sydney International Airport.

Left:
The Qantas 747B's Captain Cook Lounge which, with twenty windows instead of the standard six, is a more spacious, brighter and quieter spot for passengers to relax.

AUSTRALIA'S AIR NETWORKS

AUSTRALIA'S SUCCESS in the tough competitive international scene derives from the fact that her people are amongst the most airminded in the world. They welcomed the advent of commercial aircraft with an enthusiasm backed by a sound insight into its ultimate potential. Fast cheap air transport helped Australians to overcome one of their biggest problems, the vastness of the country.

Centres of population are very widely separated. In their earlier days many were isolated by under-development and bad weather that halted surface transport. This geographical problem of distance created a need for air travel more urgent in Australia than in other countries, so it was inevitable that Australians should take to the air.

Heroic qualities displayed by aviation pioneers endeared the thought of flying to the Australian heart. In some of the most difficult country in the world, war aces like Pard Mustar and Ray Parer opened up New Guinea with aircraft, where no surface transport, not even the elemental pack-mule, could operate. Parer especially, with his qualities of resource and improvisation, appealed to the Australian temperament and became a hero to Australian youth.

His countrymen also loved Bert Hinkler, the Bundaberg boy who set up world records, flying in a bowler hat, and accomplished the first South Atlantic crossing without a prior word to anyone.

He landed in Darwin on 22nd February 1928, only sixteen days out from London, with new records for solo flight and light aircraft. The country took him to its heart.

Australian isolation made the records more momentous here. A few months after Hinkler landed in Darwin, Charles Kingsford Smith flew westwards across the Pacific, the world's most hazardous barrier at the time, and continued with a series of other world record-breaking flights.

The first scheduled flights within Australia were made between Geraldton and Derby in Western Australia under the terms of an air mail contract. Similar contracts soon resulted in regular services in each State and then in interstate flights and established aviation as an accepted and integral part of Australian life. The number of passengers grew steadily until Australian airlines carried a combined total of nearly 100,000 people during 1939. World War II brought tremendous progress in aircraft design and performance and these advances were quickly incorporated in civil airliners when hostilities ended.

At this stage some fifteen airlines were maintaining regular services within the Commonwealth of Australia, the great majority confining their activities to intrastate, sometimes to a single service.

In 1945 the Chifley Government introduced legislation to nationalise airlines but the High Court of Australia, approached by the then largest company, Australian National Airways Pty. Ltd., ruled that the legislation was invalid. Three years later the company was still carrying half of the Australian passenger total.

In August 1945, however, an Act of Parliament established the Australian National Airlines Commission which now operates under the name of Trans-Australia Airlines. The Act provided for "the establishment and operation of national airline services by the Commonwealth". Amended in 1947, it authorised the Commonwealth to establish and maintain interstate services and gave the National Airlines Commission sufficient control to minimise the possibility of interference by political groups.

In September 1946 TAA's first flight was authorised. Two years later the first pressurised airliners, the Convairs, augmented the DC3's and DC4's that began the service.

In 1947 freighter aircraft were introduced and the routes began to lengthen into the impressive network that now provides service for most parts of Australia and Papua New Guinea. In 1948 TAA acquired the route between Adelaide and Darwin that Guinea Airways had established some years before. In the following year it took over all the inland routes that Qantas had pioneered.

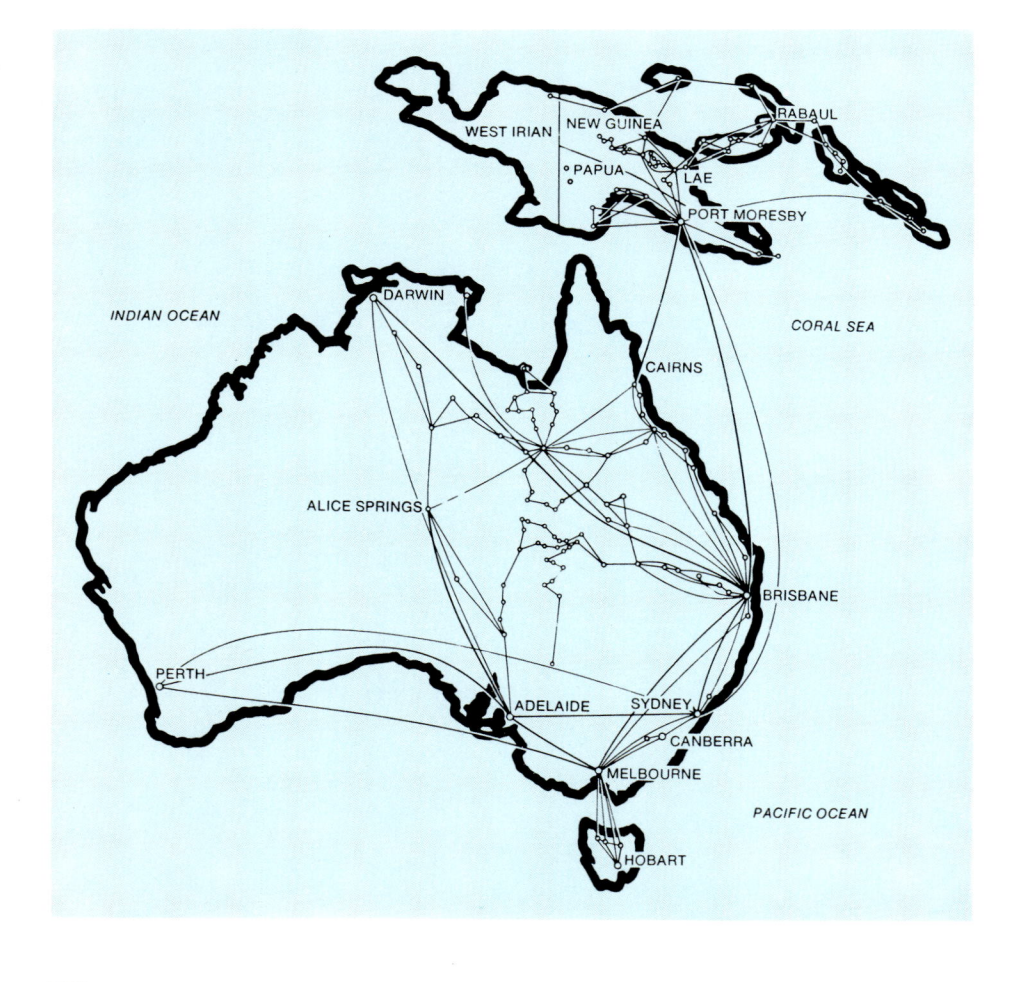

TAA introduced the first turbine-powered aircraft to commercial Australian use with the prop-jet Viscounts in 1954. It became the first airline outside Europe to use turbine-powered aircraft.

Commercial jets did not arrive in Australia until late in 1964 but today the major domestic air routes are served mainly by pure jet Boeing 727's and DC9's. While the sophisticated equipment operating these services is equal to the best in the world the airlines maintain supplementary flights to small isolated communities and homesteads in the lonely outback. TAA uses propjet Twin Otter aircraft for this work.

Airline pilots serving these pioneer communities also provide station owners with weather forecasts, reports on such urgent matters as flood patterns seen from the air and frequently the location of stranded herds of cattle during times of emergency.

Today scheduled interstate services are provided by two airlines only, TAA and a private enterprise airline, Ansett Airlines of Australia. All principal routes are competitive and the Airlines Equipment Act 1958 establishes the machinery for the achievement and maintenance of comparable but not necessarily identical fleets. Both airlines operate routes to Papua New Guinea and non-competitive intrastate routes. TAA competes within Papua New Guinea with another private enterprise service and also operates regular flights between Darwin and Portuguese Timor under charter to Transportes Aeros de Timor.

Additionally, smaller charter companies provide many air services, commuter services from small settlements, aerial surveying, taxi services and cropdusting.

Above: A TAA Boeing 727 T-Jet flying Australia's skies; just one of a fleet of twenty-two rear-engined pure jets now in service, or on order for TAA, to keep up with the industry's 10% growth rate over the past few years.

Opposite page: Looking a little like a population density map, TAA's network throws a 50,000-mile web of routes across the continent and Papua New Guinea. In 1969-70 TAA's passenger miles amounted to over 1,400 million.

Left: The Fokker Friendship is used by TAA in Papua New Guinea, on services to many important provincial cities in Australia and in the outback. The airline has a number of quick change versions of the Friendship which are used to carry passengers on some flights and containerised cargo on others.

THE MARITIME REVOLUTION

TINY RAFTS, CANOES, catamarans, wooden sailing ships, iron steamers, diesel-powered ocean liners, container freighters and steel tankers of enormous proportions —that is the evolution of man's way of harnessing the oceans to transport him over the globe.

Shipping today is a modern, enterprising and resourceful industry geared to meet the challenge of a fast-changing age. Revolutions in ship design, construction and operation have confronted the companies whose business lies in sending ships to carry trade across deep waters.

Out of these revolutions is emerging a shipping industry strengthened through rigorous self-analysis and re-assessment of values.

In the forefront of this change is the P & O Group. To maintain the leadership it has enjoyed through many decades, its fleet is being modernised with the introduction of specialised vessels: container ships, bulk carriers, tankers, off-shore service craft, chemical carriers, roll-on/roll-off ferries and long hatch steel carriers. The Group has also diversified into many other fields including road haulage, air freighting, resort development and the study of cargo-handling techniques.

The progressive management approach of the P & O Group is reflected in the major reorganisation which has followed the Group's diversification. All the various companies within the Group have been merged into five operating divisions: Passenger, Bulk Shipping, General Cargo, European and Air Transport and General Holdings.

Much of P & O's progress is particularly related to Asia and Australia, countries with which the Company has had a long and deep involvement. The great shipyards of Japan have built many of the new, highly specialised ships of the P & O fleet—supertankers; speedy, open-hatch cargo liners and bulk carriers. The new "Strath" class cargo liners were built in Japanese yards and these are the core of the P & O fast freight service between the United Kingdom and Japan.

The first of the Company's ships to be seen in Japan was the *Azof,* a steam-powered vessel of 700 tons with auxiliary sails, which arrived in Nagasaki in September 1858, at the time when Japan was opening its gates to the Western world. One of P & O's Hong Kong representatives, Thomas Sutherland —who later became Chairman of the Company and remained in office for 34 years— visited Nagasaki to prepare a report on the opportunities for trade and shipping.

Following his report, the new P & O cargo and passenger service inaugurated a thriving tourist traffic. As early as 1861 passengers began to travel to Japan on sightseeing tours to take in the little known wonders of the East. These were the forerunners of the popular Pacific and Far East cruises to be planned by P & O one hundred years later. Now the Company's liners sail on more than 35 cruises a year from Australia alone, opening the Pacific and Asian ports to wave upon wave of new travellers.

The Company also forged important trade links between Japan and Australia, through the longest established shipping company trading between the two countries, the Eastern and Australian Line (E & A), whose two passenger/cargo ships *Cathay* and *Chitral* are now part of the P & O Passenger Division. E & A began operations in 1873, carrying the mails from Singapore to Brisbane, Australia, and, seven years later, extending the service to Japan. Soon the Company had a fleet of cargo and passenger liners maintaining a regular schedule between Australian ports and Japan.

Many exciting incidents were associated with E & A's early days:

In the 1880's, the *Bowen* (1,509 tons) sailed from Hong Kong for Singapore. After departure, the Captain heard that a number of pirates had slipped on board as passengers and were planning to take over the ship in mid-ocean; they would then rendezvous with two pirate junks packed with cutthroats. Acting quickly the ship's officers seized the pirates while *Bowen* clapped on

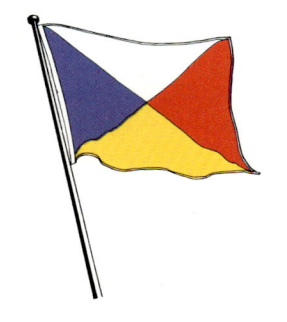

The flag of the P & O fleet.

speed. She left the waiting junks wallowing in her wake as she passed them at two knots better than her designed speed.

Today, the beautifully appointed, yacht-like, 14,000-ton liners *Cathay* and *Chitral,* sail on alternate months from Australian east coast ports to Port Moresby, Manila, Hong Kong, Keelung, Kobe, Nagoya, Yokohama and Rabaul. Cargo services formerly operated by E & A have been taken over by the Australia-Japan Container Line.

One of the fleets now forming the P & O General Cargo Division is that of the British India Steam Navigation Company Limited — popularly known as B.I. — which has had an interesting and romantic history since its formation in 1856. The origins of B.I. go back to the time of the East India Company with a contract to carry mails between Calcutta and Rangoon. B.I. has been closely associated with the development of trade on the Indian coast, in Burma, on the Iranian Gulf, in East and South Africa, Australia and the Far East, Britain and the Continent.

Today Asia and Australia continue to be linked together by modern P & O liners and, through the Company's world-girdling routes, these continents are connected with North America, South Africa and Europe. The Company's fleet of passenger liners and superliners provides a travel experience unique in its service, shipboard entertainment and opportunities to visit numerous ports of call.

The shipping industry is one of the basic necessities to mankind. It transports his agricultural products and manufactured goods; his loved ones and his ambassadors; his minerals and his armies. Through its long-learned expertise and technical innovations, P & O is playing an important role in today's shipping revolution and is continuing to be a leader in maritime trade and commerce.

Left: The P & O Liner *Oriana* is an impressive sight berthed at Sydney's Overseas Terminal, Circular Quay, particularly at night time with the floodlit Harbour Bridge in the background.

Opp. page: The 14,000-ton P & O Liner *Cathay* on one of its scheduled runs between Australia and Japan.

181

Australian manufacture covers a range of products as wide as any country in the world.
From great ocean going ships to the tiniest electronic components, Australia has attained the highest level of workmanship.
Far from the realms of modern mechanisation, on the little island of Timana, off the north coast of Queensland,
two young Australians earn their livelihoods weaving woollen tapestries, like the sample above.

THE GROWTH OF INDUSTRY

WHEN WESTERNERS first settled on the edge of the vast island continent of Australia over 200 years ago they had little conception that this apparently harsh and inhospitable land would some day give birth to one of the world's greatest trading nations, drawing immense wealth from its pastures, grainfields, orchards, mines and factories, and, through trade, sharing this wealth with the rest of the world.

Equally, they could not know that the toil of the first pioneers—so many of them convict-exiles from the bitter injustices of 18th and early 19th Century Britain—would lead to a society in which social, political and economic egalitarianism was a functioning reality long before it occurred in the lands from which they had formerly come.

For about 150 years, Australia, almost literally, lived off the land: the economic base of prosperity was the farms which produced wool, meat, dairy products and grains which the world wanted and which the country poured forth in abundance.

Manufacturing industry was then primarily oriented to making what the farmer and those who served agriculture needed to increase the land's bounty. Sophisticated or complex manufactured goods, and particularly the machinery of production itself, were largely imported from Europe and North America. And at that time Australia itself was not a unified state but a collection of six British colonies, economically and politically.

Even when Australia became a federated independent member of the British Empire in 1901 "economic colonialism" still held sway in matters of industry and international trade.

Industrialisation on a substantial scale is generally conceded to have been sparked by World War I, a period when Australia was denied many of its former imports of manufactured goods which were diverted to or destroyed by war activities in Europe and elsewhere.

The list of products, which Australia then began to manufacture and continued to make after the War, extended greatly in the next twenty years and World War II provided another and even more vital impetus to the manufacturing of a greater volume and diversity of both consumer and industrial products.

Today there are few manufacturing fields in which Australia cannot match the skills and technological processes of the most advanced industrial nations in the world, although the comparatively small domestic market—only 13 million people—limits the scope in certain areas and in these cases the country continues to rely on overseas imports to fulfil its necessary requirements.

Small though the population is, the Gross National Product of Australia—the value of all goods, services and wages—totals more than $A27,000 million. Of this the manufacturing sector is responsible for nearly $A8,000 million a year. Manufacturing investment in terms of fixed capital expenditure is running at the rate of nearly $A1,000 million a year and more than 1,400,000 of Australia's 5.6 million labour force are directly employed in manufacturing activities—a notable contribution to the economic and social wealth of the country.

Australian manufacturers are responsible for almost 20 per cent of the country's overseas export income—over $A800 million a year.

Ranging from motor cars to electronic equipment, from processed foods to textiles, steel to chemicals, and sports equipment to cosmetics, these exports have helped in large measure to offset diminishing prices and contracting markets for Australia's traditional exports of agricultural products.

For many decades Australia rode "on the sheep's back". In bad seasons for the pastoralist the economy fell drastically. Today the sheep industry is still of prime importance but the expansion of manufacturing has proved a sound stabiliser. Allied to enormous increases in exports of basic minerals with which the Commonwealth is so richly endowed, these manufactured exports have become, in less than ten years, critically important to the country's international trading balance.

Indeed, Australia has entered into another era of historical importance, at least equal to the agricultural pioneering period of last century: that of exploiting a manufacturing and mineral potential on which it is almost impossible to place a limit.

It is Australia's intention that this wealth shall be shared with the world in general and in particular with the countries and peoples of Asia with whose future Australia and her people are indissolubly linked.

Australia seeks the friendship and co-operation of the peoples of many lands to help develop her economic wealth. Her farmers, manufacturers and miners will not only supply her Asian neighbours with the manufactures, foodstuffs, minerals and fibres they need to improve their own economies and standards of living but will increasingly seek avenues of investment and in other ways help the underdeveloped nations of Asia to develop and exploit their own resources for mutual benefit. And already Australian money and technical skills are beginning to play a substantial part in this process.

AUSTRALIA AS A WORLD TRADER

AUSTRALIA has been described as a nation on the move. In every State there are signs of growth and expansion. In two decades the traditional image of a basically rural society has been erased and great strides have been made industrially, particularly in the exploitation of her newly discovered, enormously rich mineral fields.

This expansion symbolises Australia's prosperity: the key to it is trade.

Since the early days of the colony external trade has been a vital part of Australia's economy and income from exports has become an essential aid to financing current major projects.

Initially her exports were channelled toward the "mother country" and this "favoured nation" policy persisted for 160 years, until, in the past two decades, Australia has shed her reliance on a European market and re-orientated her product outlets.

Her rapid development during this period has largely been made possible by well planned export promotions, so successful that she now stands as a major world trader; to be precise, thirteenth on the list. When considering the value of trade on a per capita basis, however, Australia's position in seniority is fourteenth. For some commodities such as wool, veal, beef, mutton and lamb, wheat, preserved and dried fruit, sugar and some minerals, her exports rank among the first two or three in the world.

Asia is already one of the Commonwealth's major trading partners. During 1970-71, and for the first time, more than one-third of Australia's total exports went to Asian countries, Japan being her biggest customer and one of her principal suppliers.

This emergence of the Asian market has been a gradual process. Twenty years ago the total value of mutual trade between the two continents was $A158.5 million, but by the end of the 1970-71 financial year it had risen to almost $A1,900 million.

On the present world scene Australia's total trade is worth more than $A8,500 million a year, representing an increase in imports of 7 per cent over the 1969-70 figure and a rise in exports by more than 6 per cent.

Despite the fact that the direction of Australia's trade has been drastically altered Europe still remains her most important single trading area. More than 40 per cent of her imports come from Europe and the region takes over 5 per cent of her exports.

Up to 1971 the Commonwealth relied upon Britain as the major buyer of her farm products. It had taken about two-thirds of her butter exports, two-thirds of her canned fruit exports, 39 per cent of her dried fruit exports and one-fifth of her sugar exports.

Because of this dependence Australia was concerned when Britain joined the European Economic Community. It meant a drastic reassessment of her future export potentials and plans are now under way to channel her export commodities in other directions Asia, the United States and the Pacific Islands are assured of greater importance.

Although Australia's exports of farm products have grown in total terms, they have declined as a proportion of total exports from 91 per cent twenty years ago to 50 per cent in 1971. Conversely, exports of manufactures and minerals during the same period have increased from 7 per cent of total exports to 45 per cent.

Further change has been apparent on the import scene. Australia has traditionally been an importer of producers' material and capital equipment for development in the manufacturing industries, but greater industrialisation has meant substantial increases in import replacement, particularly in consumer durables and transport equipment.

Meanwhile the value of exports of manufactured goods has increased by more than 1,500 per cent since 1948-49.

Australia is still very dependent on overseas capital, machinery, equipment and know-how for the continuing growth of manufacturing industries and for exploitation of her new mineral discoveries.

The latter will undoubtedly play an increasing part in adding to Australia's export income, estimated to be three-fold in the coming decade.

There appears little doubt also that in spite of the international financial crises of 1971 the upward trends of the Australian trade pattern will continue. The nation will rely less on farm products, more on manufactured goods—goods which will meet the requirements of many of the developing countries in Asia and in other parts of the world.

It is a far cry
from the days of the old
paddle steamers —
the means of carrying cargoes
of wheat, sheep, wool and other
primary products
from the inland areas of Australia
to the principal shipping ports —
to the great container ships of today.
Each has had the same major objective:
developing and facilitating
Australia's trade.

THE AUSTRALIAN motor industry had its beginning at the turn of the 20th Century when the first primitive body was built in Melbourne to house a foreign automobile engine.

From then onwards the embryo industry crawled slowly until in 1917 Holden Motor Body Builders Ltd. made an all-Australian car chassis. Six years later a pact was signed with General Motors Corporation of America to build exclusively all G.M. motor bodies for the Australian market. This resulted in a merger between the two companies and General Motors-Holdens Ltd. was formed in 1931.

In the mid-1940's the Australian Government invited all automotive companies then operating in Australia to submit proposals for manufacturing an Australian vehicle.

Of the four companies which responded to the Government's invitation, only GMH elected to design and build vehicles completely within Australia. This was a bold decision in view of the small Australian market for motor vehicles, and the limited scope of the existing components industry. The venture has been of great significance in the industrial development and economic growth of Australia. In fact it is generally accepted that the establishment of automobile manufacture by GMH in 1948 was primarily responsible for the introduction of the techniques of quality, high volume production to Australia.

However it was necessary simultaneously to establish adequate local supply sources for the very wide range of raw materials and components used in automobile manufacture. To this end GMH provided supplying companies with technical advice and assistance helping them to increase the quality and volume of their existing production, and in many cases to undertake new fields of manufacture. Many of the techniques thus acquired have subsequently been used by supplying companies for purposes totally unconnected with the automotive industry. An indication of the extent of the resulting stimulus to the Australian economy is that in 1948 there were some 300 companies supplying components to GMH. Today the company's suppliers number more than 4,000—many of them having been established solely to fulfill GMH's requirements. Holden entered the export field in 1954 with shipments to New Zealand. The quantity and range of shipments have increased with the establishment of new markets.

Although Holdens are now exported to 71 territories around the world, the company's major interests are in the growing markets of the South-east Asian, Pacific and African areas. Statistics for 1970 provide striking evidence of the growth in export performance, and the development of the company as a major manufacturing base for the Asian-Pacific motor markets.

In following this trend, General Motors, late in 1970, established the area headquarters for this part of the world in Australia. This regional office is responsible for the co-ordination and development of GM activities in the area.

Building on previous years' gains, total export revenue for 1970 rose 49.4 per cent to $42 million. This rise brought to $217 million the cumulative value of GMH exports since the first shipments in 1954.

It is indicative of the rate of growth in the company's export business that it took twelve years to reach the first $100 million and less than four years to achieve the second $100 million.

The export of vehicles in component sets or "completely knocked down" form for assembly in overseas plants has shown an especially strong growth. The seven overseas plants assembling Holden vehicles from Australian manufactured components are located in Pakistan, Malaysia, Indonesia, the Philippines, New Zealand, South Africa and Trinidad.

The increasing sales of Holden vehicles in Asia have been largely attributable to their size, economy and reliability. This particularly applies to the six cylinder Torana range which is being assembled in Malaysia and Indonesia: compact size and durability are factors essentially suited to the Asian terrain. All models undergo extensive and tortuous testing at the GMH proving ground to prepare the vehicles for use on the varying roads and the changing, sometimes drastic, weather conditions.

Holden's long standing reputation for reliability has been a major factor in its success against competition within Australia and in the many countries to which it is exported.

As the most advanced motor vehicle company in the immediate region in terms of basic engineering resources and manufacturing facilities, GMH is ideally placed to continue to play a leading role as a supplier of complete cars—and, more significantly, of components for overseas assembly.

AUSTRALIA'S AUTOMOTIVE INNOVATOR

Left: A Holden Torana in Hong Kong, with the famous floating restaurants of Aberdeen in the background.

Below: An "H.Q." Holden Kingswood sedan.

Left Page: An Australian Holden on the assembly line in Malaysia.

Bottom left: Unloading Holden component parts in Malaysia.

Bottom right: The prestigious Statesman de Ville.

AUSTRALIAN TECHNOLOGY HELPS ASIAN INDUSTRY

THE INCREASING INVOLVEMENT in Asia of The Broken Hill Proprietary Coy. Ltd. underlines the extent to which Australia's world-ranking steelmaker is able to contribute to the region. During 1971, BHP —the name by which the Company is widely known—gave valuable help to Asian industry by making available the services of its highly competent experts in science-based steel technology.

BHP is no stranger to Asia. For many years it has marketed steel products at competitive prices in the region and has established offices in Singapore and Tokyo. Currently the Company is acting as consultant to several Asian governments in assessing the steelmaking potential of their countries and is developing a number of enterprises in joint ownership with Asian interests.

BHP has established a wholly-owned subsidiary in Taiwan and has a substantial minority equity in a rod and wire mill in Malaysia. It is also investigating several other opportunities for the export of its expertise into industrial projects which it will own jointly with Asian companies.

BHP was originally incorporated in 1885 to mine the silver, lead and zinc deposits discovered at Broken Hill, New South Wales. The mine which gave the Company its name was closed down in 1939 for economic reasons. BHP's first blast furnace went into production at Newcastle, N.S.W. in March 1915 when the Company decided to extend its interests to the making of steel. In its first year its output of steel was 7,000 tons.

Today BHP has the distinction of being Australia's largest company, employing a work force of 56,000 people, and having an annual production capacity of 8.6 million tons of raw material. It operates from four iron and steelworks centres, and maintains three major laboratories which keep it to the forefront of world steel technology.

The Company has fast adapted new steelmaking techniques. It was one of the first to use the basic oxygen steelmaking process; a continuous casting machine is in operation and sophisticated computerised rolling mills have been installed.

BHP produces almost without exception the entire range of sizes, shapes and grades of steel required by the Australian economy.

It is one of the world's most highly integrated steelmakers, controlling virtually all its raw materials supplies, their transportation, and the marketing and distribution of the finished products. In addition to steel and steel products the Company also supplies a major part of Australia's gas and oil requirements, and is a leading world producer of manganese ore and other raw materials for steelmaking. Located on Asia's doorstep, Australia's BHP is technologically advanced and large enough by world standards to successfully combine with Asian interests in mutually beneficial industrial projects.

Opposite page:
Whyalla's B.O.S. cycle can produce 100 tons of steel in 45 minutes.
The furnace is shown being tapped.

Above:
A general view of the hot strip mill installation of the Flat Products Division at Port Kembla.
The three slab reheating furnaces are on the left;
on the right the vertical and horizontal scale breakers, broadside mill;
on the far right the indicator of the 86-inch, 4-high reversing mill.

Left:
An ingot coming out of the soaking pit at Whyalla.

IN THE CHAPTERS of this book are stories of crises that have threatened the downfall of Governments and spelled economic disaster for more than one Asian country. In averting complete collapse and particularly in effecting recovery of balance, the part played by the greater private enterprises has been a major contributing factor.

Stabilising old markets and building up new for increasing volumes of primary products and manufactured goods has needed skill, courage and readily available funds, the acquisition of which has been made possible, in many instances, by tapping hitherto hidden natural resources and converting them into tangible national assets.

In the past century her broad acres of agricultural and grazing lands and rich gold fields attracted the attention of the world to Australia; here was a potential source from which dwindling larders might be replenished. But Australia herself was dependent upon these primary products and it was not until the middle of the present century that her manufacturing industries began to rival and augment the rural products.

Over past decades both branches of industry have had to fight for survival against their natural enemies, drought and flood, and the stringencies imposed by wars and depressions.

Not only have they survived but they have lived to see Australia reach the threshold of an exciting future of prosperity, unprecedented in the history of the country and private enterprise has played a dominant part in creating this happy situation.

Just as Japan has its "Big Ten" Australia has its group of powerful companies whose driving force and vision have influenced the Commonwealth's modern development

Above:
An ore stacker at Port Hedland, Western Australia.
Iron ore is brought 265 miles by rail from Mt. Newman and held in stacks, ready to be reclaimed and loaded into ships.

Opposite page:
Synthetic alcohols plants at CSR Chemicals, Rhodes, N.S.W. CSR has a 50.3 per cent interest in CSR Chemicals and ICI Australia has the remainder.

Below:
Part of the large pilot plant at the CSR Research Laboratories, Roseville, N.S.W., and some pilot plants in operation.

ENTERPRISE IN INDUSTRY

One such company is the Colonial Sugar Refining Company Ltd., which began in 1855 when Australia was experiencing the first flush of gold fever.

Its principal shareholder and member of the Board was Edward Knox, who was born in Denmark of Scottish parents. He was the guiding light of the company in its early years and was primarily responsible for the sound basis on which it was founded.

The northern rivers area of New South Wales was considered at the time an ideal environment for the growing of sugar cane and from initial plantations in the Port Macquarie and Clarence River regions more suitable areas were later planted in the north of Queensland.

In its earlier years the sugar industry suffered a severe slump on the world markets and throughout the 1860's Edward Knox led a great struggle to keep his refining company solvent. His efforts brought their reward when the market recovered and CSR built three big raw sugar mills on the northern rivers of New South Wales. They began crushing in 1870.

Through the turn of the century until the 1930's industrial development in Australia was slow. CSR remained a sugar company and a distiller, using molasses as the raw material. The Great Depression of the 1930's was the worst in Australia's history and when it began to wane in 1936 CSR built a pilot plant at Macknade Mill, north Queensland, for the manufacture of building board from the cane by-product bagasse. This was the forerunner of the diversification into many fields of industrial activity which has since made the Colonial Sugar Refining Company Ltd. one of the largest and most influential among Australia's leading enterprises.

Following the Macknade experiments CSR began the manufacture in 1939 of an insulating softboard known as Cane-ite.

It built a plaster factory at Concord, Sydney in 1942. The end of World War II found a pent-up demand for housing and CSR moved further into the building materials industry. In 1959 it acquired the assets of the Masonite hardboard factory and bought a substantial interest in the insulating plants of the Bradford Insulation group in Queensland, New South Wales, Victoria, South Australia and Western Australia. CSR's hardboard interests are now combined with those of Australian Pulp and Paper Mills in an associate company, Hardboard Australia Limited.

Even this range of building materials was not complete as housing took on the character of the age and became more sophisticated in its requirements. CSR began to manufacture vinyl asbestos floor and wall tiles and pioneered the making of particle board (Pyneboard), a product that has helped to revolutionise the cabinet and furniture making trades. In association with Australian Paper Manufacturers Ltd. CSR now operates three Pyneboard factories—at Oberon and Tumut in New South Wales and at Rosedale, Victoria.

The increasing trend to specialisation in Australian industry has influenced CSR's diversification into chemicals. For many years the company had produced ethyl alcohol from molasses and in 1939 it became more closely involved in the production of chemicals when it bought into a plant at Lane Cove, New South Wales.

It is now joined with ICI Australia Limited in CSR Chemicals Ltd.

Products include acetate flake and moulding powders, synthetic alcohols, butanol and iso-butanol, iso-octanol, phthalic anhydride, beta napthol and plasticisers.

In the 1960's, when Australia entered her new phase of vigorous development in mining, CSR ventured into iron ore production and the development of large bauxite deposits. A subsidiary, Pilbara Iron Ltd. was formed. This company owns 30 per cent of the $450 million Mt. Newman mining operation, a vast project that is transforming the silent loneliness of a part of Western Australia into a bustling community. Another subsidiary, Gove Alumina Ltd., owns 30 per cent of a $A310 million development of bauxite deposits in Arnhem Land, believed to be the largest single project ever undertaken by private enterprise in Australia.

In its early stages in the present century Australian industry had sometimes been criticised for a lack of conclusive research.

CSR has been conducting research since the time it began raw sugar milling. A central Research Department was formed by CSR in 1923 at Pyrmont, Sydney and the expansion of its activities resulted in the construction of the more extensive CSR Research Laboratories at Roseville, New South Wales, in 1963. CSR conducts the David North Plant Research Centre at Brisbane, which has the world's only phytotron (a large series of glass houses in which plants can be grown under controlled conditions) devoted solely to the sugar cane plant.

The company has agricultural experiment stations in Queensland, New South Wales and Fiji and large building materials research laboratories at Concord, also in New South Wales.

Australia, still a young country by world standards, is discovering and proving herself in a wide range of activities and enterprises.

It is to such companies as CSR that she owes much of the progress she has already made and the prospects that look so promising for the future.

THE SCIENCE OF ELECTRONICS and its practical applications to industry and commerce, and its influence on the lives of people, has been one of the most significant happenings the world has known in recent times.

The first positive step in this direction was taken in Australia when the world-wide Philips organisation built a factory at Newcastle in the 1920's for the making of electric lamps.

Since that time the company has ventured into many other fields of electronics, benefiting from research carried out in its Australian laboratories and in the factories of members of the Philips group in many other parts of the world.

Today Australia is one of the leaders in the complex sphere of telecommunications, and as the Commonwealth's largest manufacturer of electronic devices Philips has made the greatest contribution.

If a taxi is called in Hong Kong, it is almost certain that the driver will be summoned over a radio-telephone made by Philips-TMC in Melbourne. It is a similar story from Taiwan to Singapore.

In Rabaul, the Central Volcanological Observatory is using Philips Australian-made VHC FM transmitters and receivers for the volcano surveillance systems.

The Malaysian Federal Agricultural Marketing Authority uses Philips mobile radio-telephones, the Singapore Telephone Board cable terminations are made in Melbourne and Australia's Overseas Telecommunications Commission has installed Philips high-speed telegraph units on its circuit to Hong Kong.

Schools in some Asian countries use audio-visual teaching aids, developed and made by Philips in Australia—teaching aids which are so advanced that orders for sets

The ant in the picture on the right, in real life less than half an inch long, is carrying in its mouth a Philips integrated circuit chip only 1/16th of an inch (approx. 160 microns) square. The integrated circuit, a marvel of miniaturisation, contains in micro-circuitry all the electronic components shown in the photograph on the top of the opposite page. The tiny integrated circuit chip, made at the Philips Hendon, South Australia, Facility, replaces the 87 transistors, two capacitors and 67 resistors shown in this picture.

have been received from Europe, the United States and Canada. At Hendon, in South Australia, there is a $A1 million facility for the manufacture of integrated circuits—tiny silicon chips containing many miniaturised transistors, resistors and diodes—which replace many of the conventional circuits for radios, television sets and computers.

The past decade has seen a tremendous growth in communications and trade between Australia and Asia. One result of this has been an increasing number of multi-national conferences, for which Philips has been called upon to provide simultaneous interpretation systems. One conference held in 1971 involved more than 1,000 delegates, speaking seven different languages.

But Australia's links with Asia involve more than talks and trade. They also involve the export of management and technical skills. Since August 1969, Philips Australia has been responsible to the Singapore Government for the management and operation of the former Electronics Facility at the Singapore Dockyard—some 90,000 square feet of workshops containing all the measuring apparatus and the test and repair devices needed to maintain sophisticated electronics including radar, sonar, communications and control systems. Employees of Philips

THE WORLD OF ELECTRONICS

Australia are working on this project in Singapore and others are contributing their skills to projects in Port Moresby, Bougainville, Kuala Lumpur, Bangkok and Bandung.

Other countries in Asia—notably Japan—are vitally interested in the development of Australia's mineral deposits, and here, too, Philips is playing a major role.

Computer-controlled X-ray spectrometers are widely in use as part of the new analytical technology needed in the mines. One of them was installed at the Australian National University to analyse rocks brought back from the moon by Apollo II. A development of world-wide importance in the field of mineral analysis was announced by Philips in June 1971. This was the breakthrough in the automation of mineral processing plants. The new process uses radio-isotope probes and makes possible the on-stream analysis of minerals which is expected to save Australian mining companies millions of dollars a year.

The process was developed as a result of co-operation between the Australian Atomic Energy Commission, the Australian Mineral Development Laboratories, the Australian Mineral Industries Research Association, the Zinc Corporation and Philips.

Mining interests in other countries have been quick to investigate the possibility of buying these analysers.

The world of electronics and telecommunications continues to expand. To make this expansion possible—and for Australia to maintain the high standard of its technology—constant research and development are vital.

Because of its world-wide ramifications, its international research facilities and its considerable resources, Philips is playing a major role in Asia and Australia.

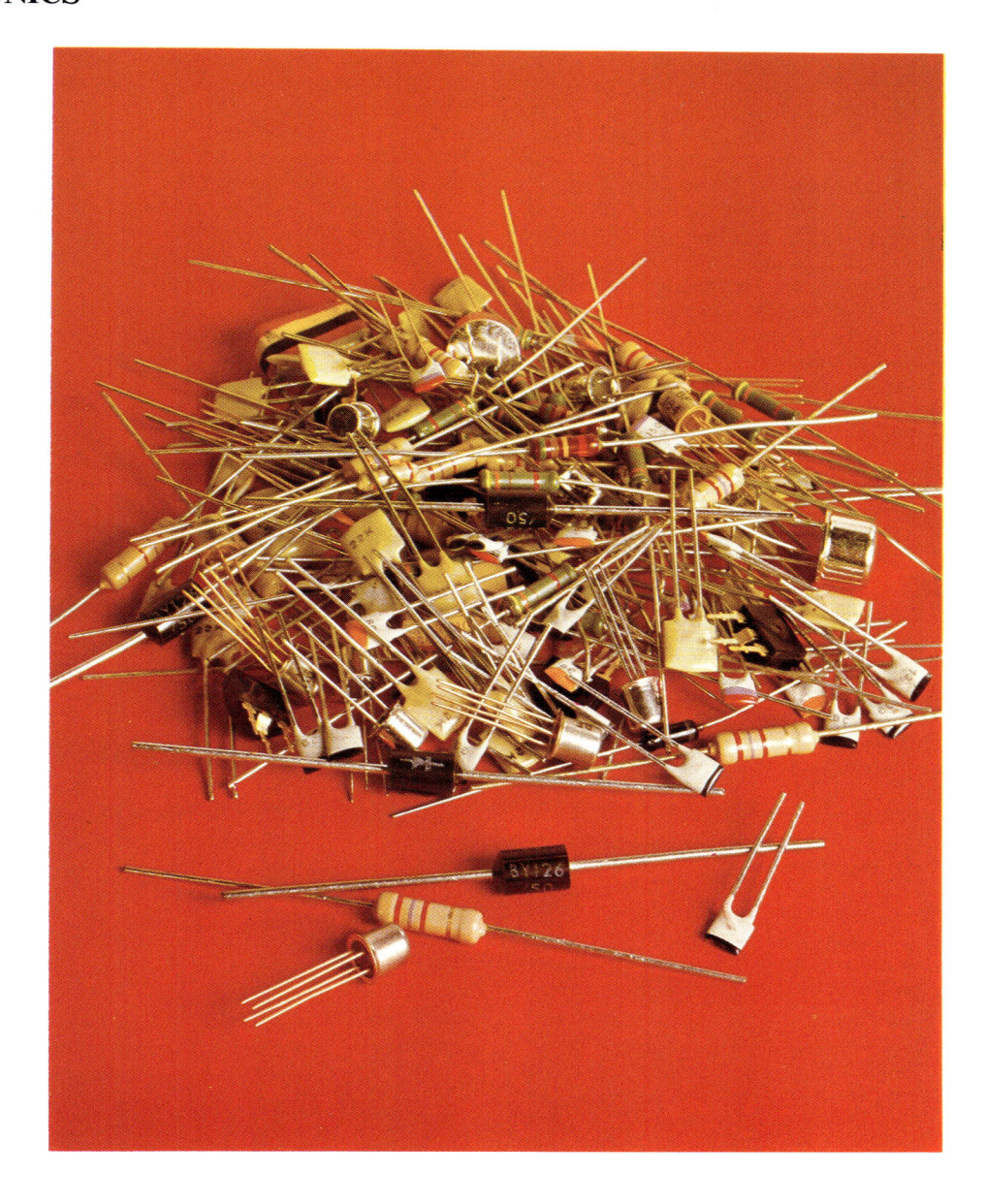

Left:
The Philips Closed Circuit Television System in the Qantas Terminal at Sydney's International Air Terminal at Mascot, shows the Qantas operational control position.
On the television monitor screens the controller can watch the activity on the tarmac parking bays and control the service vehicles. Other cameras enable him to observe incoming and departing aircraft on the taxiways and runways.

INDUSTRIAL CHEMICALS IN THE MODERN WORLD

IN AUSTRALIA, as in other parts of the world, chemical products are of vital importance to all sections of industry. It is also an area of continuous change, for about 70 per cent of the chemicals made today were not known 25 years ago.

With such a large number of new items being introduced each year, only intensive research and the closest attention to cost and quality can enable the Australian chemical industry to compete successfully with overseas firms.

Although Australia has produced chemicals of various kinds for many years, it is of interest to note that the fast rate of growth of the past three decades started at the time of World War II, when the Government realised how vulnerable an isolated country such as Australia could be, with the long sea routes from Europe to America under constant attack and many valuable cargoes being lost due to enemy action.

ICI Australia Limited is Australia's largest chemical company, producing a wide range of products.

With its large investment in people and equipment, this organisation is able to carry out research relating to products and processes of particular interest to Australia and to nearby markets. Researchers have to be continually looking ahead to determine the types of products likely to be in demand in the next five or ten years. By anticipating the future trends in local markets, the Company is able to make best use of its own research facilities and the continual flow of knowledge from associated companies overseas.

In addition to the 170 or so people employed at the Central Research Laboratories at Ascot Vale, Victoria, ICI Australia also maintains a staff of about 100 at the Merrindale and D'Aguilar Biological Research Stations and on the many field trials organised by the Company.

In Australia, ICI research teams already have an impressive list of discoveries to their credit, many of them in relation to farming. One recent development in this section of industry is the production of levamisole for the treatment of parasites in animals.

In 1964, a Belgian firm discovered the drug tetramisole, an anthelmintic for the control of worms in farm animals. The elimination of these parasites improves the health of the animals and gives better and larger yields of both meat and fleece.

Although tetramisole was proved to be a most efficient drug, the first discoverers had no way of making it at an economical price. It was in this field that ICI research workers in Australia made the first major breakthrough, by establishing an economically viable process for its manufacture. Although, in time, others also found answers to the problem, the early patents in Australia gave ICI valuable lead time, not only at home but also overseas. The process is now used in South-east Asia and in other parts of the world.

However, this was only the start, for tetramisole consists of two types of molecules, identical in composition except that structurally they are mirror images of each other. Further work by veterinarians showed that only levamisole, the left-hand molecule, killed worms; the right-hand one was inactive. Chemists at the ICI Ascot Vale Laboratories made their second discovery through an ingenious process by which the two kinds of molecules could be separated. This was of tremendous importance, because, by discarding the inactive molecules and retaining the active ones, it was possible to halve the dosage.

The value of this reduction in dose size becomes apparent, when it is realised that the comparative levamisole dose is now 7.5 units per beast, compared with the 600 units of phenothiazine required some 30 years ago.

This now allows the treatment of animals to be carried out by an injection, instead of using the clumsy drenching gun which had to be forced down the animal's throat and the animal held until it swallowed the drug. Because of the time saving alone, this is a matter of considerable importance.

Further work by the chemists resulted in another advance, with a process which allows for the conversion of the right-handed, otherwise useless, molecules, into the active left-hand form.

This is only one of the inventions developed by ICI in Australia; there will undoubtedly be more to come, for some 600 chemicals are tested in the various laboratories each year to determine if they can be used in the rural industry.

Rural products make up only one field of ICI's research activity. Others include explosives, plastics, industrial chemicals, dyes and pigments, artificial fibres, anaesthetics and other drugs, pharmaceuticals—all likely areas for the development of new products or new equipment and processes or for the improvement of existing plants.

The Polymer Section of ICI's Research Laboratories deals with the wide range of applications of plastics raw materials, including the ways in which the final properties of plastics can be given new characteristics by means of artificial irradiation. Its functions also include studies of the production and properties of artificial fibres such as nylon and "Terylene" and of plastic films.

The major interest of the Organics Section lies in the heavy organic chemicals such as the chlorinated hydrocarbons, olefines and ethylene oxide, and includes production of special chemicals and formulations for use as solvents, detergents, brake fluids, etc.

The Inorganic Chemicals Section deals mainly with the production and uses of chemicals made by the caustic/chlorine and ammonia/soda processes—caustic soda, soda ash, bicarbonate of soda, chlorine and other related items. It is also involved in the manufacture of explosives and in mineral beneficiation processes.

The experts in these and other fields collaborate with specialist teams trained in the designing and building of pilot plants to test processes and to produce supplies of chemicals for full-scale evaluation. In many instances these plants are subsequently translated into designs for large-scale production. This often includes the design of special instrumentation for process control—most important in this day and age of automation.

Several technical laboratories which provide a wide range of services for customers, buying plastics, dyestuffs, pigments, surfactant materials and the many other products supplied by ICI, are located at the Central Research Laboratories. The close proximity of technical services and research activities permits continuous consultation between the two groups of people, thus bringing the problems of research and marketing much closer together.

A modern technical information service enables researchers to keep in touch with the activities of others operating in similar fields in associated companies—in the universities, the C.S.I.R.O.—Commonwealth Scientific and Industrial Research Organisation, and similar research organisations in Australia and overseas.

Special attention is paid to patent rights, particularly in the regions of rapid innovation such as fibres, plastics, pesticides, drugs and petrochemicals. Not only does this help the scientist to keep in touch with inventions in other parts of the world, but the fact of obtaining patents quickly often gives the company valuable lead time in the development of new products and processes with the attendant financial rewards.

Above:
The ICI research laboratories have provided simpler and quicker methods of treating worm parasites in sheep.

Opposite page:
Small pilot plants designed and built by research engineers and scientists form the basis of full-scale factories.

193

AUSTRALIA stands at one of the apices of the Pacific Basin triangle formed with the other two principal industrial countries of the region, the United States of America and Japan. Within the Basin lie South-east Asia, a major part of Asia proper, and the islands of the Pacific— all areas with some standards of living low by western comparisons but rising rapidly.

In proximate terms, Australia and Japan lie closest to this region of increasing purchasing power, but Australia is unique in being almost Asian geographically and western culturally and economically. On these bases it is in a favourable position to service the Basin countries with products of its own manufacture and to take advantage of the rising standards of living demanded by all people within the area.

In achieving this goal Australia has at its command an almost unlimited source of indigenous raw materials, coupled with a well-developed technology capable of utilising these raw materials both for its own benefit and for the benefit of the other countries concerned.

It is conscious of its ability to assist in volume and quality of export commodities and in technical "know-how", and more particularly in co-operating with the peoples of the region to improve their living standards. A veritable power-base of technology has been developed within Australia over the past decades. It has been created by investment in its manufacturing industries, for the purpose of acquiring the associated technologies upon which those industries depend.

Laporte came to Australia some 40 years ago and since the early 1930's it has had a continuing history of investment in this country. Just as Laporte in the United Kingdom — the parent Company — long ago recognised the development potential of Australia, Laporte in Australia recognises the development potential of the neighbouring countries to the near north, and because of its own background of development it is in a knowledgeable position to assist others.

Laporte Australia Limited manufactures hydrogen peroxide, organic and inorganic peroxides and titanium oxide, chemical compounds which are in constant demand in countries of growing economies and industrial sophistication. Hydrogen peroxide is used in the textile, paper and food industries; organic peroxides are essential catalysts in the manufacture of plastics and titanium oxide is the basic white pigment used in virtually all types of paint.

CHEMICAL TECHNOLOGY AND KNOW-HOW

Experience in other regions of the world shows that as living standards rise so does the demand for textiles, paper, plastics and paint. To an increasing extent, therefore, the peoples of the Pacific Basin area will require the end products of the Laporte manufacturing processes. And if industries are to be established and developed within the Pacific Basin region, local manufacturers will need, to a continually increasing extent, aid and counselling in the use of chemicals such as those manufactured by Laporte.

Australian industry, and its chemical industry in particular, is in a position to provide this service. Because of the heavy investment in Australian industry over the years, the technology of Australian manufacturers is of world standard, and technically Australia has the ability to satisfy the demands of the region. Laporte in Australia recognises this, and is aware of the role it is able to play. It has an active programme of contact with people and companies in the area; members of its staff make regular visits and are well acquainted with the individual needs of the multitude of countries within the Basin. These visits enable the Company to assist in solving the problems of Asian companies, thereby making a valuable contribution to the industrial development of the region.

Conversely, to strengthen its own potential, Laporte also brings to Australia men of experience from other parts of the world. The ability of the average Asian manufacturer is widely acknowledged but the specialised research and development facilities that exist within the Laporte organisation are not normally within his reach.

Technicians and technical executives from other countries have already been brought to Australia to avail themselves of these facilities, to work alongside Laporte's technical staff in the solution of problems to each other's mutual benefit. In many cases new techniques and new or modified equipment have been the subjects of demonstrations.

While tangible benefits are of obvious importance, it is the interchange of ideas and methods of approaching various problems that has been a highlight of these visits. The return of the visitors to their own environment has brought technical progress in modified instrumentation, quality control methods, and other significant directions. Thus the interchange of technical facilities and expertise has benefited the individual, his company, his country and the region as a whole.

Opposite page:
A section of the
N.S.W. chemical complex of Laporte
at Banksmeadow.

Above: An aerial view of the
Laporte Titanium Oxide Plant
in Western Australia.

MAKERS OF MODERN LIVING

THE MODERN WAY OF LIFE in the western world is fundamentally efficient and simple. The ornate and complicated designs and processes of past centuries have given way to streamlined sophistication.

The exotic architecture and furnishings of the East still fascinate westerners but many ancient cities are losing something of their flamboyance—their alcazars, khans and bazaars are yielding to the demands of space conservation and economic structure. Modern hotels, huge department stores and fashion boutiques are rising almost cheek by jowl with temples and mosques that have stood the tests of time for hundreds of years.

Where stained-glass oriels once gave meagre light for dim-lit sanctuaries, plastic-coated, steel-framed, glass windows gleam from multi-storeyed, high-rise offices and apartment buildings.

The modern scene is ever changing and competition brings a flood of innovations every year. The current vogue and status symbol in the home and in the office is the wall-to-wall carpet; a carpet that harmonises with the furniture, furnishings and room settings and gives an appearance of comfort and unobtrusive affluence. This vogue began in Australia in the mid-1920's when a Company now known as F & T Industries Limited began making woollen felt floor coverings. From this traditional fibre was evolved an all-wool floor felt called "Feltex". It was cheap and it was durable and, although restricted to a small colour range, it was priced within the reach of the average home and office.

Until the outbreak of World War II most of Australia's pile carpets came from the United Kingdom, but with the imposition of import restrictions local manufacturers were given the opportunity of increasing their output and improving the range and quality of their products. In 1936 F & T had manufactured Australia's first woven carpet and from the success of this venture the Company pioneered the first broadloom tufted carpets in 1955. Eight years later it introduced the first carpet printing equipment in Australia.

Today F & T Industries is the largest maker of carpets in the Commonwealth.

Moreover, the Company's mills are producing carpets for export to many overseas countries including Japan, Malaysia, Singapore, Thailand and even the ancient home of carpets, the Middle East. The range includes Wilton, Spool Axminster, Tufted and rubber-backed carpet varieties and accessories such as non-pile needled carpets and floor felts.

The Company's brand "Redbook" is to be found on the carpets covering the floors of the new headquarters building of Australia's Broken Hill Proprietary Company and the Shell Company of Australia in Melbourne, the Reserve Bank, the Australian Mutual Provident Society's Head Office and Gold Fields House in Sydney.

Beyond Australia F & T carpets have won their place against world-wide competition and are seen in the Hong Kong Hilton Hotel, Bangkok's Rama and President Hotels, Singapore's Imperial, the Federal and Merlin Hotels in Kuala Lumpur. The Tunku's palace in Kuala Lumpur and most of the palaces of Sultans throughout the Malaysian States are all carpeted with "Redbook".

Some of this carpeting has been manufactured at the F & T Wilton carpet mill at Kuala Lumpur. Before opening this mill Malaysians were trained at the F & T factories in Australia where they learned the techniques of carpet manufacture and installation.

The Company's tufted carpet mill in New South Wales is Australia's largest and newest. Two other mills have been built near Melbourne—a woven complex for making Wiltons and Axminsters at Tottenham and a tufted carpet plant at Footscray. (Axminster spools on one of the broadloom machines at the Tottenham mill are shown in the picture on the right.)

Since it began operating 50 years ago F & T has undergone many changes. From its textile origins in 1921, a field in which it still dominates, it has diversified its activities and become one of the largest manufacturers of plastics in Australia. These take the form of P.V.C. (polyvinyl chloride) sheet, film and coated fabrics, as well as moulded plastics, including a wide range of electrical accessories.

In this period of Australia's growing affluence, the skylines of her capital cities are being pierced by surges of high-rise office and apartment buildings. Plastic-coated steel window frames for these new and imposing structures, and services for complete glazing are being provided by F & T.

Self-service stores are spreading throughout Australia, and shopping is becoming a more personal and unaided choice—a phenomenon already popular throughout Europe. Among them are the vast "super markets", offering all kinds of food and merchandise displayed in fittings ranging from open shelves to delicatessen units. F & T's factories are providing the components—truly "makers of modern living."

The picture
on the top of the left page
shows a "Redbook" carpet
installed in the loungeroom
of an Australian home.

Above:
Spool Axminster weaving machines
at F & T Industries' Melbourne mill—
the largest woven carpet production
centre in the Southern Hemisphere.

AUSTRALIA'S PHYSICAL ENVIRONMENT

DURING THE PAST two decades the interest of many countries of the world, particularly those of Asia, has been drawn to Australia. From a land of little international significance it has become a focal point of attention, particularly in relation to its natural resources. For this reason it is important to understand the physical environment of this island continent, its liabilities—mainly in lack of water—and its almost unlimited assets.

Australia covers an area of nearly 769 million hectares. Geographically it is an old country, containing large regions of eroded plateaux with some steep escarpments but few high mountains. The highest point is Mt. Kosciusko, 2225 metres above sea-level. Very little land rises above 1500 metres, but there are large areas between 400 metres and 800 metres, including the Great Western Plateau—about 450 million ha.—and the Eastern Highlands.

A third of the continent, including the west and north-west coast, most of the Great Western Plateau and large tracts in the central plains, receive less than 250mm of rainfall a year. Evaporation on the other hand, is extremely high, ranging from 1,700 mm to 3,300mm a year in these areas.

Although Australia is about 20 times the area of Japan, only 7 per cent or slightly less than 54 million hectares receives more than 1,000mm of rain annually. Half of the continent has a rainfall of less than 320mm a year, while the average is little more than 400mm, or approximately one-quarter that of Japan.

Generally, rainfall in Australia is lower and more variable than in any other continent. Long periods of drought are experienced from time to time in many parts and severe flood damage sometimes results from short periods of very heavy rain over large areas of the country, including many places where droughts are common.

As a result of such climatic problems, cropping of the soil is impossible over three-quarters of the continent. In the remaining quarter much of the land is mountainous, and the variability of rainfall in other areas makes the growing of crops extremely risky.

The areas where both climate and terrain are suitable for cultivation comprise about 8 per cent (roughly 65,000 million hectares) of the total, but parts that can be used continuously for intensive cropping are even smaller. Nevertheless, the full potential for agricultural development has still not been realised and the opening up of new areas is continuing, for example, the Esperance region in Western Australia and the Brigalow in Queensland.

The area available for agriculture has been extended by irrigation, but irrigation must remain limited because of the overall scarcity of water. In total, some 0.6 million ha. of crops and 0.9 million ha. of pastures are irrigated, about 0.5 million ha. of this having been added in the past seven years, partly as a result of additional water from the Snowy Mountains Scheme.

RURAL INDUSTRIES

Rural industries contribute an important part of Australia's gross national product and 10 per cent of all occupied males are engaged in farm activities of some sort throughout the Commonwealth.

In spite of the growth of manufacturing in recent decades the Australian economy is still heavily dependent on rural industries which earn about half of the foreign exchange revenue from merchandise exports. Moreover, overseas purchasers of many rural commodities rely on Australia as a responsible source of supplies. Almost 45 per cent of world exports of raw wool come from Australia and a large proportion of world trade in meat, wheat, butter, canned and dried vine fruits is provided by Australian producers.

This involvement in world trade implies that Australia has a vital interest in developments in international markets. In terms of the absolute value of total trade Australia ranks about thirteenth; as an exporter of agricultural products she ranks among the first four, being surpassed by the United States and on occasions by France and the Netherlands.

The average combined annual flow of all Australian rivers is exceeded by about fifteen of the world's major rivers and is rather less than that of the Amur River in Far Eastern Asia. The average annual depth of run-off is only 45 mm if spread over the whole country but there are large areas where any run-off evaporates long before it can reach the sea.

In spite of these limitations it has been proved that if ways and means can be found to provide water present useless areas can be made highly productive.

Rural Holdings. The physical environment described in the preceding column has naturally shaped the development of rural industries. Although most farms are owned by individual families freehold tenure predominates only in the southern and eastern areas of good rainfall. Land in the north and in the dry interior is leased by the Government in large blocks for relatively low rentals.

About one-third of Australia is not suitable for economic development with techniques at present available. A small portion of the remaining two-thirds comprises cities, state forests, industrial areas etc. but most is used for some form of rural activity. There are just over 250,000 rural holdings covering 480 million ha., about 70 million ha. being freehold and 410 million ha. leasehold. Practically all the leasehold land and nearly half the freehold is used primarily for rough grazing of sheep and cattle and much of the leasehold land can be used for this purpose only in favourable seasons. The area of arable land is about 36 million ha., fairly evenly divided between sown pastures and crops.

Most of the rough grazing land in the drier areas is divided amongst a small number of big "stations". Some 2,870 of them are larger than 20,000 ha. and together they cover 70 per cent of the area of all rural holdings. A further 6,260 large holdings—between 4,000 ha. and 20,000 ha.—account for 12 per cent of the area, leaving 18 per cent of all the land in rural holdings (i.e. 86 million ha.) divided among about 241,000 holdings of less than 4,000 ha. in area.

The median area of Australian farms is about 135 ha., the smaller ones being near the coast and large cities. Unlike the mean area the median is not distorted by the few very large holdings with low production potential.

Major Rural Industries. Australia extends from the tropics to cool temperate regions and is capable of raising most agricultural products. The principal livestock are sheep, beef cattle and dairy cattle and the main livestock yields are wool, beef and milk. Wheat is by far the major Australian crop although a wide variety of cereal, industrial and horticultural crops is also grown.

The distribution of agricultural production is illustrated in the land-use map on the opposite page.

Most crop growing in Australia is carried on in association with livestock grazing. The grain crops of wheat, barley, oats and sorghum, which together occupy 70 per cent of the area cropped, are grown mainly in the wheat-sheep zone.

Wheat production expanded rapidly in the decade ended 1968-69 but subsequent marketing difficulties have led to production being regulated to bring about a better balance between supplies and market opportunities. Plantings of other cereal crops, particularly barley and sorghum, are expanding to supply the growing demand of the livestock industries of Western Europe and Japan for feedingstuffs.

LAND USE

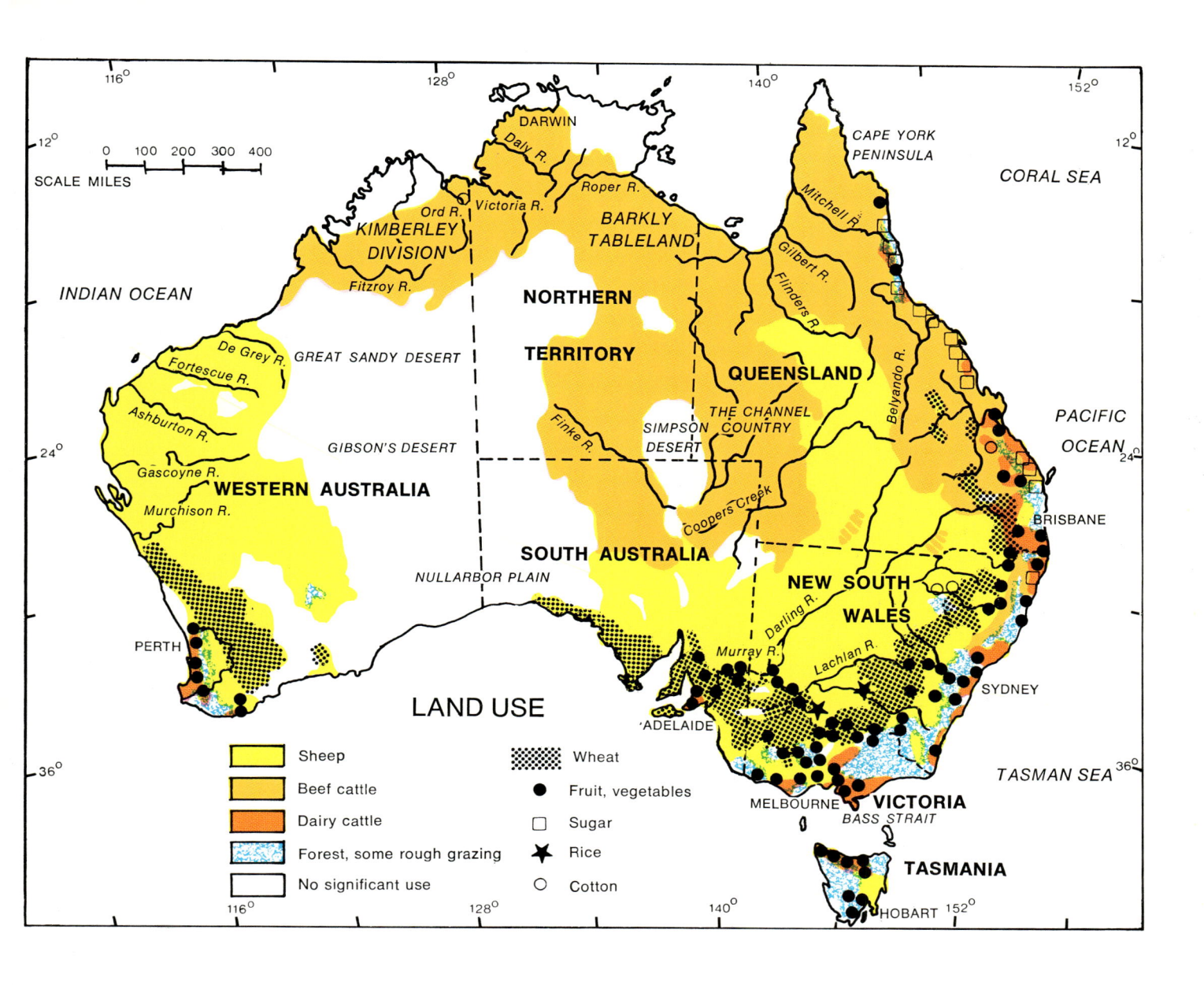

Legend:
- Sheep
- Beef cattle
- Dairy cattle
- Forest, some rough grazing
- No significant use
- Wheat
- ● Fruit, vegetables
- □ Sugar
- ★ Rice
- ○ Cotton

Non-cereal crops occupy only 5 per cent of the area under cultivation and are not usually associated with livestock. These include fruit, vegetables and a wide range of industrial crops such as sugar cane, tobacco, cotton and oilseeds. Sugar is an important industry in northern Australia and it is a significant earner of foreign exchange. Production is strictly controlled in accordance with the availability of markets and Australia's commitments under the International Sugar Agreement and the British Commonwealth Sugar Agreement. Although fruit occupies less than 2 per cent of the total area cultivated for crops, major communities, particularly in Victoria and Tasmania, are heavily dependent on the fruit growing industries.

All commercially produced rice in Australia is grown under irrigation and the area planted is limited by the availability of water. Individual acreage allotments are determined each year by the irrigation authority in consultation with producer, processor and marketing interests. In this way production is kept in line with market prospects and a reasonable return to growers is maintained.

Wool has long been Australia's leading rural product with some 95 per cent of output being exported. In general, sheep in the drier inland areas are used for wool production. In the higher rainfall altitudes towards the coast and near the large urban centres sheep meat production is important but even here wool is the major source of producers' incomes.

Beef production is distributed through wide areas of northern and southern Australia. In northern Australia—Queensland, the Northern Territory and the Kimberley region of Western Australia—extensive open rangeland grazing is the most common form of land use, while in southern Australia cattle are raised under more intensive conditions and usually in association with some other enterprise, mainly sheep.

The dairying industry is concentrated in areas with higher rainfall and introduced perennial pastures along coastal river valleys and lowlands, in inland irrigation areas and near the main centres of population. Areas close to metropolitan centres supply liquid milk; areas further away supply milk or cream for processing and for local urban requirements.

Pig raising has long been an adjunct to dairying where cream is separated for delivery to butter factories, the remaining skim milk being fed to the pigs. In recent years, however, there has been less dependence on skim milk supplies and grain feeding has become more important with the result that the pig industry has acquired an identity of its own.

Commercial production of poultry is mainly around the capital cities and larger urban centres.

While aggregate rural output in Australia has fluctuated from year to year, according to prevailing seasonal conditions, there was a significant increase of about 4 per cent per annum over the ten years ended 1968-69. The principal sources of this increase were substantially larger crops of wheat and sugar and of several of the less important such as cotton, rice and fruit. Beef prices were inclined to encourage increased production but expansion was restricted by droughts and by the time taken to build up breeding herds.

The volume of rural output rose to a peak in 1968-69 but declined in 1969-70 and again in 1970-71. In part the decline was due to adverse seasonal conditions but also to difficulties in marketing the increased volume of products accumulated from more bounteous earlier years. Such problems have led to restraints on wheat production, to a tightening of restrictions on sugar crops and to producers being obliged to change their programmes to meet variations in marketing procedures. Thus the production of meat, barley, sorghum and oilseeds is expanding at a faster rate than in the past and markets will need to become available for the additional supplies if prices are to be sustained.

Marketing. A high proportion of farm output is sold on overseas markets which have a tendency to be less certain than those at home and also present problems of distance, freight rates, different currencies etc. The structure of rural industry generally is individualistic and competitive but farmers have strengthened their selling potential by entering into a variety of orderly marketing arrangements, some administered by statutory boards others by voluntary boards or co-operatives. Most of the major farm products are subject to some degree of statutory marketing control, particularly in the export field.

Statutory bodies to control marketing have been established at both Commonwealth and State levels. The former are largely concerned with exports and the latter, with several exceptions, concentrate on domestic fields. There are also voluntary or co-operative marketing schemes. Commonwealth statutes provide for eleven commodity boards for the following industries: wool, meat, dairy produce, wheat, tobacco, dried vine fruits, canned fruits, apples and pears, eggs, wine and honey. In addition the Australian Wool Commission has been set up to administer the marketing of the Australian wool clip.

Primary producers are represented on all Commonwealth boards. In the case of dried fruits, meat, apples and pears, honey and wheat, where the commodity undergoes little or no processing before marketing, the producers' representatives are in the majority. In the case of dairy produce, canned fruits and wines the manufacturers have the largest vote. However, as there are separate nominees for co-operatives who, to an extent, have a common interest with producers, the latter generally command an equal hearing with other interests on these boards.

The functions of the boards vary according to the needs of the industry they serve. Most are regulatory in nature although the Wheat Board is a full-scale trading authority and the Dairy Produce and Egg Boards exercise limited trading powers. The Wool Board is concerned primarily with the promotion of wool but it has power to inquire into and report upon matters connected with marketing. The Australian Wool Commission has been set up to administer the marketing of the Australian wool clip and may buy wool when this is necessary in the operation of its reserve price scheme.

All the boards, excepting the Wheat Board, spend a proportion of their income on publicity and promotion and eight concerned with food products—including the wine industry—are members of the Overseas Trade Publicity Committee. The Australian Wool Board provides a large part of the budget of the International Wool Secretariat. Many of the boards endeavour to increase the total demand for their products by engaging in domestic promotion. Nearly all undertake research, with finance from their own funds often being matched by Commonwealth contributions. The costs of administration are met in various ways, the most usual being a levy on exports or a levy on production. Trading operations are usually financed by an advance from the Reserve Bank guaranteed by the Commonwealth Government.

Each State has a number of marketing boards set up under State legislation to control the internal marketing of primary products. Queensland in particular has built up a comprehensive system with almost twenty separate marketing authorities. While most of the State boards are concerned solely with marketing within Australia, often confined to the particular State itself, some also conduct export operations, e.g. the Sugar Board (Queensland), the Australian Barley Board (South Australia and Victoria) and the Central Queensland Grain Sorghum Marketing Board. Another feature, especially in Queensland, is that State authorities sometimes enter the processing field operating as full trading bodies, e.g. the Queensland Peanut Marketing Board sells most of the peanuts grown in the State and has its own storage facilities.

There are also several voluntary pooling arrangements, some with statutory backing and some without. Examples are the Western Australian State Voluntary Oats Pool (which has statutory backing) and the Victorian Oatgrowers Pool and Marketing Co. Ltd. (with no statutory backing).

There is no set pattern in this complex of trading or regulatory controls, statutory or voluntary authorities, Commonwealth or State Boards. In general, marketing methods have evolved to meet the differing requirements of particular rural industries and the attitudes of the producers concerned. The farmers have been trying to reduce the commercial hazards in marketing, just as they have been trying, by management practices and the conservation of fodder and water, to reduce the physical hazards in production.

Rural Exports. The rural industries have always provided a large proportion of Australia's total exports and the continuing increases in production have been sufficient to meet an expanding domestic demand as well as making possible an increase in the volume of rural exports. But falling world prices have meant that foreign earnings from this source have not kept pace with the volume exported.

The aggregate value of exports of rural origin tended to rise until 1963-64 when it reached a record of $A2,147 million. Subsequently it has fluctuated without showing any clear trend while the value of non-rural exports has continued to rise. Thus the share of Australia's total export earnings contributed by rural exports has fallen to just under 50 per cent from more than 70 per cent before 1964-65.

There is very little export of some of Australia's rural products, such as potatoes, but a high proportion of many products is sold overseas; for example about 90 to 95 per cent of the wool clip, 60 to 80 per cent of the wheat and about 65 per cent of the sugar crop are normally exported.

Australia supplies almost half the total volume of wool in international trade and wool contributes the greatest share of the total value of Australian rural exports. Beef and veal have increased in relative importance since pre-war, as have sugar and cereals other than wheat, but dairy products and mutton and lamb have declined.

Considerable changes have taken place in the geographical distribution of Australia's agricultural trade. Outstanding among these is the diminution of reliance on the United Kingdom as an outlet for Australian farm products. It has now been surpassed in this role by Japan and by the United States. Mainland China has been an important market during the past decade owing to heavy purchases of wheat.

In recent years increasing attention has focused on the South-east Asian region and on Japan as markets for many of Australia's rural commodities. However, so far the main diversion increases in rural exports from the United Kingdom to the United States and Asia has involved only a few farm products such as meat, wheat, wool and sugar. Small quantities of fresh fruits also have been sold in Asian countries and sales of dairy products, especially cheese, have been increasing. Nevertheless the United Kingdom and Europe remain important markets for many export commodities, e.g. dairy products, sugar, dried, canned and fresh fruits, cereals and wool.

NOTE: In this story metric units have been used and the relevant data may be converted to English units by the use of the following approximate equivalents:

    1 hectare (ha) = 2.5 acres
    25 mm   = 1 inch
    1 metre   = 3.3 feet
    1 ton   = 0.984 long tons

Opposite page:
A scene on a typical Tasmanian timber plantation.

Below:
A stockman and his sheep on a property near Bathurst, N.S.W.

AUSTRALIA'S WOOL IN ASIA'S FUTURE

OVER the past 25 years Asian countries have been developing closer and firmer commercial and cultural links with Australia.

In both continents, governments and people have come to realise that as the more recent years have brought an acceleration of these interests and attachments the process will be further intensified in the years ahead.

Whether the issues are economic or political, cultural or humanitarian, of defence or military strategy, it is abundantly clear that if this sector of the globe is to progress it must do so through greater regional co-operation.

The formative process will entail an assessment of the basic products each country can supply that can be of use and benefit to the sector as a whole.

Australia's richness in primary and secondary products will enable her to play a continuing, valuable role. But, in both the short and long term, one of the most important contributions Australia can make to the nations of the Asian area is her uniquely traditional one—wool.

Despite many changes in Australia's industrial and economic landscape over the last 25 years her wool industry still remains an important one.

Today her sheep population totals 185 million, 30 million more than ten years ago. In 1970 these sheep provided a record clip of 2,043 million lb. of greasy wool—25 per cent more than the figure of ten years ago and almost double that of 1950.

Despite price fluctuations, strategic changes and effective economies now being made throughout the industry indicate the confidence of the Australian Government, wool producers and the public in general in the industry's soundness, value and continuing future importance.

COMPETITIVE STRENGTH. Since 1956 auction prices for Australian wool have fallen by about 20 per cent, in a world where most other commodities have also suffered. This decline has resulted partly from growing competition from synthetic fibres. But it has not removed wool from the vital position it holds in the overall Australian economy.

In 1970 the country benefited by $A825 million from wool exports, representing 21 per cent of the value of all merchandise exports and 45 per cent of all rural export commodities.

It was exceeded only by the $A1,067 million received from mineral exports and was $A125 million higher than the return for manufactured exports.

Australia's wool industry is today well prepared to enter the battles of competitive trading that lie in the years ahead by the knowledge and the assurance of careful future projections that world demand for fibres of all kinds must increase.

This applies particularly in countries where development will require a greater need for textiles.

The Australian wool industry has improved its structures and planned new objectives. Previously there had been little or no unified control over the product once it was sold. Other minds and hands took up the different tasks of distribution, manufacture and marketing of finished products made from wool.

But now, under some pressure from competitive trade influences and profiting from the experiences of other industries, today's producer will increasingly participate in decisions on what happens to his wool, sometimes up to the finished product stage and its marketing.

Asia is already an important market for Australian wool. In 1969-70 Japan's purchases were valued at $A257.9 million, making it the biggest single buyer.

Purchases by other Asian countries were: India $A18.7 million; Taiwan $A12.4 million; Republic of Korea $A10.9 million; Hong Kong $A7.4 million; Peoples' Republic of China $A2.7 million.

In the cases of Japan and Hong Kong these values were approximately equal to the annual purchases over the five years since 1965. But the amount sold to India was three times the value of five years earlier.

Taiwan's purchases have been rising consistently and have doubled since 1966-67. Korea's imports were almost three times the level of 1965-66 following similarly consistent increases.

Mainland China's purchases have fluctuated considerably in recent years, rising at times to more than $A7 million, with the 1969-70 figure the lowest for several years.

But it is clear and significant that for each country the sales figures are at least constant and in most cases growing annually. All predictions indicate that the growth pattern will continue.

Asia represents the world's largest and most heavily populated developing area. Mainland China and India have a combined population of about 1,300 million and both of them, like all Asian countries, are rapidly increasing their populations every year.

All Asian countries operate their own textile industries and in most cases textile operations are expanding in line with their economic growth. An exception is Japan, where heavy industry is expanding more rapidly. But, on the other hand, Japanese capital is at present helping build Indonesia's, Hong Kong's and Taiwan's textile industries.

Throughout all Asian countries living standards are rising just as populations are growing. Even slight increases in either or both of these factors can mean a significant rise in demand for wool in terms of total consumption.

MARKET DEVELOPMENT. Aware of this, the International Wool Secretariat has already made healthy progress in the development of markets throughout Asia with the support of the Australian industry. One of its tasks has been to remove from many peoples' minds the thought that wool must always be associated with cold weather.

At present, for purely climatic reasons, colder areas such as Korea show a greater need for wool than warmer countries such as Malaysia. But developments in lighter weight wool and the manufacture of lightweight wool fabrics, possibly in association with some synthetic fibres, are seen as important assaults on the ancient barriers against better sales of wool in warmer climates.

New methods of textile production, particularly knitting, are continually making it easier for wool to establish itself in countries developing multi-fibre textile processing.

Woolmark—the international symbol for pure new wool.

Right: A typical group of world-famous Australian merinos.

Below: Shearing is still a manual operation, even in this highly mechanised age.

United Nations development and assistance programmes lay heavy emphasis on the introduction of chemical industries into developing countries. Part of the reason for this is to extend the output of fertilisers so that local food production may be increased. But another part, and an important by-product from these industries also, will be the setting up and expansion of synthetic fibre industries.

This development can be seen as offering new opportunities for these countries to take larger quantities of wool, the most durable natural fibre, to be mixed with synthetics in the textile manufacturing process. Once these industries are soundly established their output need not be confined purely to local markets. Just as India's large and profitable carpet-making industry works mainly for the export trade so countries expanding their textile operations can look forward to selling in other parts of the world once these operations become fully functional.

Japan, with a growing population and consistently improving standards of living, provides an example of the potential growth of wool requirements throughout all of Asia in the years ahead. From 1966 to 1969 net domestic consumption of wool per head of population rose from 3 lb. to 3.4 lb., meaning a total increase in demand from 305 million lb. to 350 million lb. Even if Japan's economy is growing at a faster rate than that of other Asian nations these figures signify the sort of advance that the Australian wool industry anticipates in coming years throughout all countries of Asia.

In the year ended June 1970 Japan's total wool imports were 8.4 per cent higher than for the previous year. Her imports of Australian wool were up 9.6 per cent. Despite the advances made by synthetic fibres the average man's suit in Japan contains 94 per cent wool.

Present wool marketing methods are aimed at increasing sales of casual jackets, slacks and lightweight summer suits so that the demand for wool in these garments continues to rise.

Techniques such as permanent creasing of wool fabrics, first developed by the C.S.I.R.O. in Australia, are among the special aids the wool industry can offer its customers.

Made in Hong Kong. Hong Kong enjoys a warmer climate than Japan; it also enjoys a lucrative export trade in manufactured woollen goods. In the first six months of 1970 her total export of wool products was valued at $A23.7 million. This included such wool items as wigs, which have reached extraordinarily high production figures, and sales of all kinds of goods to countries as remote as Scandinavia.

Korea's textile industry has shown rapid growth in recent years. In 1966 it had 78,000 spindles handling worsted materials. By 1969 the number had grown to 271,000.

Demand for wool is expected to increase at a yearly rate of 10 per cent to satisfy both local needs and an expanding export trade in wool products, particularly to the United States.

Taiwan's current G.N.P. rate is increasing at 10 per cent per annum with a parallel growth rate in the wool textile industry.

In 1970 she had 90,000 spindles working on wool textiles. In a few years this number is expected to grow to 200,000. Wool yarn production has more than doubled since 1964, with wool fabrics showing a similar trend. Imports of wool have more than doubled since 1965, the average rate of increase being 28 per cent.

Singapore's textile industry uses wool and synthetics to make 274,000 lb. of yarn a year. In *the Philippines* production of carpets and woollen yarns has increased dramatically.

While prospects for expanded usage of wool in all these countries seem clearly evident *mainland China's* future development and interest in wool remain as yet unknown. But among several prevalent factors it is known that China is increasingly enlarging her contacts with foreign nations and extending her trade as well as her political and cultural contacts with them.

Since the Cultural Revolution China's industry has been consistently expanding, especially in the fields of chemical production—with fertilisers as one product—and textiles. She remains a fluctuating, but ever-growing, buyer of Australian wool.

And a recent debate in the Australian Parliament indicated awareness that China's requirements for a greater part of the annual Australian wool clip were expected to increase in proportion to the needs of her expanding textile operations.

China is also among several countries anxious to buy Australian Merino sheep, the main producers of fine quality wool, to improve their own flocks. But by comparison with the rest of the world she is probably the last major nation to remain under-developed as far as wool is concerned. Her growth graph in this regard can show only a gradual upward curve.

Once China can satisfy her home market with her production she will naturally seek to expand into an export one. And it is to be assumed that she would continue to use Australian wool in increasing quantities to facilitate this expansion. It was Japan's awareness of such a probability that was behind the decision to extend her textile operations to the establishment of a foreign base in Indonesia. There is little doubt that China will become a new competitor in the Asian textile business in coming years.

The comparatively low cost of establishing textile industries favours their introduction into developing countries, often with outside financial help, and the inevitable increase in demand for textiles will have to be met by improved technologies and marketing methods. In the ensuing competition for markets the quality of finished products must also rise.

All these factors point to an increasing use of wool in the goods coming out of this major expansion.

Today, almost half of all the raw wool entering world trade is produced in Australia. It is only natural that Australia's

Above left: Wool bales being dumped—a process to compress the 300-pound packs to half their size before shipping.
Below: The conventional method of loading wool aboard a ship. About 95 per cent of Australia's wool clip is shipped overseas.

Right, and foot of page: Australian designers create world-class fashions from pure new wool, as shown in these two outstanding examples—one from Maglia and one by Prue Acton.

Below: Pure new wool travel rugs which can be washed and spun dried. New technological processes are making wool easier to handle and more attractive to customers.

geographic proximity to Asian markets will bring these markets some keen price advantages over markets in more distant centres because shipping involves lower transport costs.

Cohesive Trade Links. In the medium term, under GATT and other agreements, many developing countries should be able to export greater quantities of their textiles to developed countries. Already some developed countries are moving to grant tariff reductions on their imports from developing countries and this process should continue.

Obviously the potential for special trading relationships with Asia will be explored more deeply by developed countries in other parts of the world. Just as textile manufacturers will become increasingly important as suppliers to home markets and for export trading with most Asian nations the availability of high quality Australian wool at competitive prices will be an increasingly essential ingredient in what might be called the "fabric of the future" for the people of Asia.

Above: Australian butter and cheeses find their place on thousands of tables throughout South-east Asia.

Opposite page: The promotion of Australian processed cheese is a frequent happening in the supermarkets of Tokyo.

PROTEINS FOR THE PEOPLE OF ASIA

WHEREVER milk, cheese and butter are enjoyed throughout Asian countries, the chances are that they were produced in Australia.

With its reputation as a dry continent, Australia's lush, green, highly-productive, dairying areas—situated in all States, but chiefly down the plains of the south-eastern seaboard—surprise many people. About 50,000 dairy farms produce more than 1,600 million gallons of milk a year. About 70% of this goes to the 328 modern factories responsible for this great, export-orientated industry. Australia is one of the world's principal exporters of dairy produce. This is made possible because her dairying industry is operated at relatively low cost and her products are competitive on any world market.

The Australian dairying industry is also a trendsetter in manufacturing techniques. An example is the production of cheddar cheese by mechanisation, pioneered by the world famous Australian research body, the Commonwealth Scientific and Industrial Research Organisation, and now used in many of the world's foremost dairying countries. This mechanisation lowers the cost of large-scale cheese manufacture and allows production of a more uniform cheddar cheese, popular wherever it is tasted.

Less well-known abroad are Australia's other 40-odd varieties of excellent cheese. Production of these kinds is expanding rapidly and exports are increasing. Just under 20,000 tons of cheese, mainly cheddar, is now exported to South-east Asian countries each year—most of it to Japan and the Philippines, with substantial quantities to Ceylon, Hong Kong, Malaysia, Singapore, New Caledonia and Papua New Guinea.

Efficiency, hygiene and quality are important considerations in the Australian dairy industry's modern factories. Most milk is collected from the farm in refrigerated bulk-milk tankers and has to satisfy rigid quality tests in the factory laboratory.

The most modern stainless steel equipment is used to process the milk into butter, cheese, dried milk, condensed milk or one of the many other important by-products of milk. The resultant products are then submitted to stringent quality tests by the Department of Primary Industry and, if they pass these tests, they are exported. The Japanese, among the most quality conscious in the world, have realised this and Australia is a major supplier to the Japanese market.

Australia's marketers also endeavour to supply products in the form most useful to the importing countries. Mild cheese is supplied to Japan's large processing companies, who can then process, pack and market cheese in the form most acceptable to the consumer. In the same way, the Australian industry has joined with commercial interests in a number of Asian countries to manufacture various types of condensed milks and other dairy products, utilising Australian anhydrous milk fat and non-fat milk powder (the components of whole milk in dried form).

The Australian Dairy Produce Board holds equities in all these operations and also provides finances on liberal terms for the importation of Australian raw materials.

Australian technicians and scientists supervise the construction and installation of the most advanced equipment available. Standards and quality guidelines are laid down to ensure that the products manufactured by these operations conform to the very high standards required in Australia. Initially, a number of Australian technicians are required to manage operations. They then provide specialised training to Asian technicians who progressively take up as many responsible positions as possible, thereby reducing the number of Australians required.

A third of Australia's butter and butter oil exports are sent to the Asian area. Australian exporters realise the importance of this growing market and it is carefully catered for. Japan has a taste for unsalted butter and this is the variety that Australia supplies for the Japanese people. The choicest butter is exported to other tropical and semi-tropical countries, and because modern refrigeration makes transport time negligible, the products arrive in perfect condition.

Australia is aware of the great need in the Asian market for not only traditional products, such as Westerners eat, but also for new products that will bring to the Asian people the benefits of improved diets and, where milk products are concerned, protein.

EARLY in the 1960's the Australian Dairy Produce Board set up a subsidiary company called Asia Dairy Industries (H.K.) Ltd.

Above: Cartoned liquid pasteurised milk is manufactured by P.T. Australia-Indonesian Milk Industries.

Right: Cans of Mali brand sweetened condensed milk at the Thai Dairy Industry Company's factory in Bangkok.

Below: Koala brand evaporated milk is manufactured by Marikina Dairy Industries Inc. at the Australian-Filipino joint venture recombining plant at Manila.

With headquarters in Hong Kong, it was formed for the management and liaison between the Board and joint venture manufacturing and marketing companies in various countries of South-east Asia. The company is also responsible for the provision of technical know-how on manufacturing and for arranging supplies of raw materials from Australia. The companies established in this enterprise include: Marikina Dairy Industries Inc. in Manila, the Philippines; The Thai Dairy Industry Co. Ltd. in Bangkok, Thailand; P.T. Australia-Indonesian Milk Industries in Djakarta, Indonesia; and Sokilait, S. A. (Societe Khmere pour L'Industrie Laitiere) in Phnom Penh, Khmer Republic.

A milk plant jointly owned in Singapore was sold in 1968 although Australia still continues to supply it with skim milk powder and anhydrous milk fat for processing for the Singapore market.

At the present time the four joint ventures employ some 900 people—most of them Asian nationals. It is Asia Dairy's policy to train local people to operate the milk factories and Australian personnel are kept to a minimum in order to give the people of the country every opportunity to use their talents. Their main products are sweetened condensed milk and evaporated milk, both marketed in cans. In the Khmer Republic, Thailand and Indonesia, however, recombined butter is being made and the milk plant in Indonesia also manufactures recombined liquid milk which is sold in cartons. Recently this product line was expanded to include flavoured milk, which has proved extremely popular with consumers throughout the Indonesian territories.

It is anticipated that the joint venture plants will soon undertake the manufacture of other foods made from Australian dairy products, such as ice-cream, infant-formula milk powder and special foods based on those regularly eaten throughout Southeast Asia.

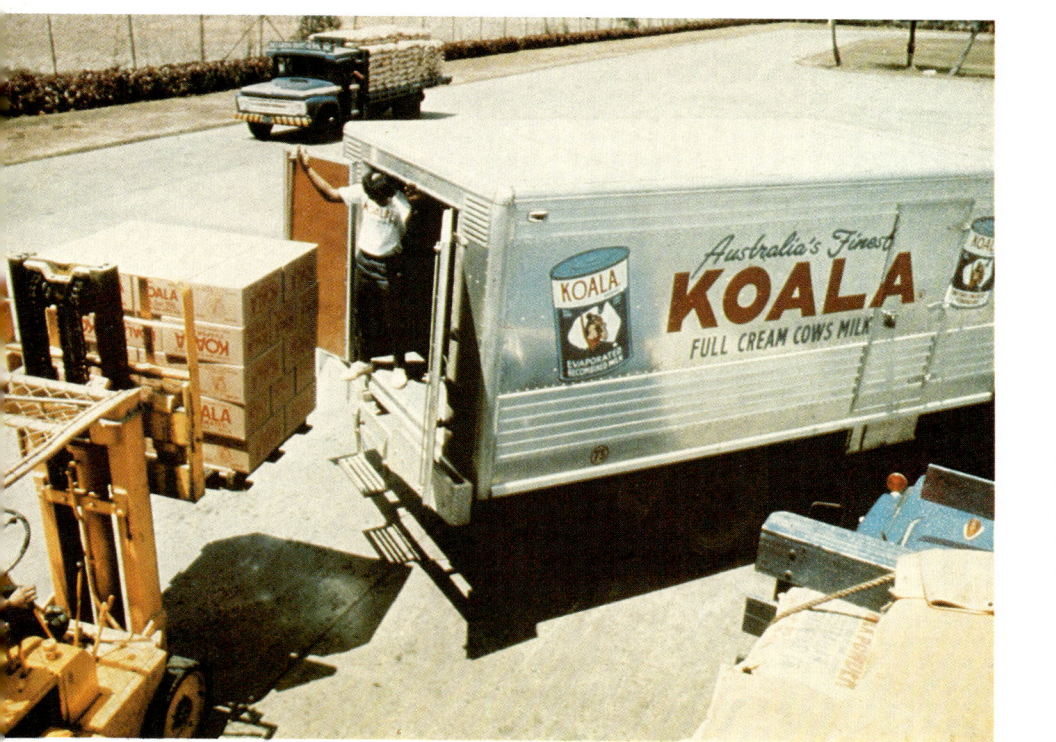

Australia has been associated with this enterprise since 1962 and in that time has shipped almost 110,000 tons of skim milk powder and anhydrous milk fat to its joint industries. These plants also use local sugar, tin plate, labels and packing cases, as well as other raw materials not related to Australian dairying, thus assisting the development of local industries.

Not only do they use local materials but they employ local labour and give training in such skills as food technology, manufacturing, engineering and marketing. They also keep down consumer prices of products —otherwise imported—and save valuable foreign exchange by purchasing raw materials rather than finished products.

Establishment of such plants is therefore a decided two-way benefit.

AUSTRALIAN WHEAT

DESPITE man's vast and evergrowing scientific knowledge, his new inventions and new way of life, he is dependent upon nature to provide the essentials for his existence: the basic products of the good earth. In Australia the greatest of these is wheat.

The Australian wheat harvest ranks seventh in the world; it is one of the most highly mechanised industries.

More than 50,000 farmers produce around 400 million bushels a year from an average planting of 22 million acres over a wheat belt stretching 2,500 miles through the five mainland states.

The marketing of the crop both domestically and abroad is the sole prerogative of the Australian Wheat Board. It has the huge task of selling the bulk of the harvest overseas, for the local market accounts for only 60 to 70 million bushels. International politics, overseas crop failures or successes, the continuing universal trend to greater acreage of plantings are all part and parcel of the Board's problems. Its efforts have been successful, for Australia rates as the third largest exporter after the United States and Canada.

Wheat is the second highest income earner among the Commonwealth's primary products, averaging, with flour, $334 million a year for the last three years, or approximately 10 per cent of the nation's total export revenue; sales are made to more than 50 countries, including most parts of Asia.

Australia has earned a reputation for producing a white, bright, clean and dry sample of wheat. The grain is low in unmillable material and free from insect infestation. As a result of technical and scientific discoveries in the last two decades—especially in breeding new, more suitable and better quality varieties—Australia produces a wide range of wheat qualities. Careful segregation of the different classes and grades enables the grain to be marketed to the best advantage. This is especially important as buyers' demands are becoming more sophisticated and specific.

There are four basic categories of Australian wheat. First is the Prime Hard class, the high protein content of which gives it breadmaking qualities equal to the best in the world. The Hard wheat class is of intermediate quality and next is Fair Average Quality, segregated on a geographical basis, a medium to low protein wheat possessing ideal attributes for blending and wide utility use. Finally, there is the Soft wheat class, specially selected for biscuit making.

Australia has a long history in growing this age-old cereal, beginning when the first colony was founded at Sydney Cove in 1788. It is truly part of the fabric of the nation, and notwithstanding the extensive and spectacular development of mineral deposits and the growth of other industries, wheat will inevitably remain one of the major essential products of the nation.

Above:
Flour made from Australian wheat is the basis of many foods throughout the world.

Left:
A typical wheat harvest scene in Australia.

IN ASSESSING the importance of Australia's primary products pride of place for more than a century has been given to wool. In more recent years other industries have made great strides and the yardstick of progress points in many directions.

Sugar, for example, earned overseas income of $A120 million in 1970. It has a history going back to the early 1820's when the first trial plots of cane were grown at the convict settlement at Port Macquarie on the coast of New South Wales just north of Newcastle. Today Australia is one of the largest producers of raw cane sugar and the world's second exporter after Cuba. But its importance to the Commonwealth goes beyond its high commercial status. Sugar cane has been the means of developing the far north coast of Queensland and over 250,000 people in the sugar districts are directly or indirectly dependent upon the industry for their livelihoods. They live in a discontinuous strip of some 1,300 miles stretching from Maclean, near Grafton in New South Wales to Mossman north of Cairns on the far north Queensland coast. Many Queensland towns exist solely because of their association with sugar mills.

For such socio-economic reasons the Federal and Queensland Governments exercise strict marketing control over the industry. Domestic wholesale prices are fixed and refining and distribution are in the hands of two companies—the Colonial Sugar Refining Co. Ltd. and the Millaquin Sugar Company. Exports from Australia are governed by three international covenants, each relating to particular markets —the British Commonwealth Sugar Agreement, the United States Sugar Act, and the International Sugar Agreement. About two-thirds of the Australian crop is exported under these Agreements. The latter aims at promoting the expansion and orderly development of the world free market at reasonably remunerative and stable prices.

The basic objective of price regulation is to control the flow of sugar on to the market by means of export quotas and to limit price fluctuation around a "pivot" price of 4c(U.S.) per pound.

Sugar cane needs a warm moist climate with an annual rainfall of at least 40 inches, or an adequate irrigation system. The Australian farms average about 90 acres although there is a tendency for this size to increase by beneficial amalgamations.

The cane takes from twelve to eighteen months to mature before the crop is ready to be harvested. Prior to cutting, the cane is burnt to remove weeds and trash from among the stalks and although this does not affect the sugar content immediately delays in harvesting and crushing at the mills will cause deterioration of the sugar. More than 90 per cent of the Australian crop is harvested mechanically, a significant factor in keeping costs at an economically low level.

After harvesting, a new generation of stalks will grow from the roots left in the ground. This is called a ratoon crop and may be repeated two or three times. A new crop is planted by placing cuttings of the stalks, known as setts, flat in a furrow and covering them with soil.

One acre yield averages 30 tons of cane which produces about 4 tons of raw sugar. Efficient agronomy and management techniques and improved varieties of cane have all helped to increase farm yields which have risen by almost 100 per cent over the past 60 years.

As sugar cane is highly perishable when harvested it must be milled as soon as possible. For this reason and because of its bulk the raw sugar mills are located within the cane-growing areas. There are 34 of these mills—31 in Queensland and 3 in New South Wales—of which 12 are co-operatives and 7 owned by the CSR.

Organising the harvesting and the transport of cane to maintain supplies to enable the mills to work at full capacity and avoid deterioration of the cane is a large-scale

Top of page: Cane lands near Gordonvale, Queensland.

Above: The bulk terminal at Cairns, Queensland, one of six in Australia.

Right: Research workers inspect cane seedlings at the Queensland Bureau of Sugar Experiment Stations' establishment at Mackay.

AUSTRALIAN SUGAR

management operation. During the harvesting and crushing season, which lasts for six months, a detailed timetable of cane burning, harvesting and transport schedules is laid down. Most of the transport is by rail and the mills own, maintain and operate more than 2,000 miles of permanent light gauge railways. In the six months' harvesting and crushing period more tonnage is carried than the Queensland State Railways transport system is able to handle in a full year.

At the mill the cane is weighed and sampled for sugar content and this forms the basis of payment to the farmer. The cane is then chopped, shredded and crushed between a series of heavy rollers to extract as much of the juice as possible. Then follows a complex process of boiling under vacuum which is repeated many times. In this way the juice is concentrated and crystallised into a mixture of raw sugar crystals and syrup. High speed centrifugal machines spin off the syrup—known as molasses—which is sold to distilleries to make alcohol and other chemicals, to farmers for use as fertilizer and to graziers as stock feed.

The crystals remaining are dried by tumbling through hot air in revolving drums and then conveyed to bulk bins for transport by rail or road to bulk handling installations at six ports on the Queensland coast: Cairns, Mourilyan, Lucinda, Townsville, Mackay and Bundaberg. Each port is capable of handling ships from 7,000 to 30,000 tons, loading at rates up to 1,000 tons an hour. Mechanised loading has reduced the period in port from three weeks in the days of hand loading to less than 24 hours.

This system is part of the sugar industry's continuing up-dating to increase performance and cut costs.

Industries based on world markets for commodities have always had problems and sugar in the 1970's faces another with the probable eventual loss of at least 335,000 tons when Britain joins the European Common Market. The industry, however, is realistic and progressive. Already it is looking ahead to 1975 when Australia will be phased out of the U.K. market if that country joins with Europe.

Meantime its research programme involving an expenditure of some $2 million annually, subscribed by the industry, will be continued. Research is carried out in cane agriculture and sugar-milling at a centre recognised as a world leader in sugar technology.

The Australian sugar industry, in preparing to meet the marketing problems of the 1970's, is also preserving the livelihood of 8,000-odd growers and hundreds of thousands of others living in the sugar districts.

WINE FOR THE ORIENT

THE ENJOYMENT of alcoholic beverages is as old as civilisation; the ancient Egyptians, the Greeks and the Romans all held their feasts, their bacchanalia and their carousals long before the Christian era began. In more modern times fermentations of fruits and grain and distillations have given variety to the popular taste. Until the British and other European settlers came on the scene the Asian peoples were content with their own national liquors, the Indians had their arrack, distilled from the coconut palm, the Japanese and Chinese their sake rice wine and varieties of rice spirits. Beer and whisky and gin had little impact on Asian life until the establishment of European colonies introduced spirits and beer.

Even today the cheaply produced national beverages are still drunk by the masses and the imported varieties are confined to the tables of the more privileged, higher salaried groups. The taste for wines was not cultivated because none were made in any of the South-east Asian countries until the Japanese began to grow grapes a comparatively few years ago. Only connoisseurs and the more affluent families could pay for the French and German wines which were and still are subject to high import duties. Australian wines were rarely exported to Asia because they did not enjoy the reputation of the European product and yet were as heavily restricted by customs tariffs.

Long before World War II Australia had been a heavy producer of wines, some of which were of very good quality, but Australians generally had never been appreciative of table wines and there was insufficient demand to encourage the vignerons to make more than a limited quantity of unfortified wines.

When the Australian Government embarked upon an intensive programme of immigration (q.v.) the wine industry underwent a dramatic change. The influx of tens of thousands of European families, to whom wine had always been a way of

From the Penfold vineyards (top right) to the crushing of the grapes and fermentation processes;
from the making of the wine and storing for maturation (left)
to the sampling of the vintage (top left),
Penfolds wines always find themselves in the best of company.

life, brought a ready, more extensive market for table wines of many varieties.

Among the new Australians were many of discerning tastes who wanted something better than the average wines of the immediate post war period. The vignerons were encouraged to improve their vintages by the importation of new grape varieties and with the introduction of better quality wines so the demand grew. Today the best of Australian wines are accepted by connoisseurs as being equal to—and in many instances better than—top quality European wines. And there is no reason why this should not be for the most noted of Australia's vineyards were originally started with cuttings from the vines of famous vineyards of France and Germany.

Today Australian wines are finding their way into many of the top class hotels of the Orient. On the wine lists of Singapore, Malaysia, India, Indonesia, Hong Kong and Japan the Penfold brand takes its place with the best from France and Germany—for Penfolds wines are acknowledged in Australia as being the finest produced in the Southern Hemisphere.

The Penfold family began making wine in South Australia in 1844 when the founder, Dr. Rawson Penfold, settled at Magill on the outskirts of the city of Adelaide.

Through four generations the Penfolds have extended their wineries from Magill to the famous Barossa Valley and Coonawarra in the south-east of South Australia to the equally famous Hunter Valley, Minchinbury and Murrumbidgee Irrigation Area of New South Wales and to the North Island of New Zealand.

With the rapid westernisation of most Asian countries have come a liking for western foods and a gradual taste for wines with meals. No longer have the wines of France and Germany a monopoly; Australian wines are high in demand. The Chinese know that white wines go well with any of their foods; a sweet table wine like Penfolds Sauternes or a slightly sweet like Riesling or Moselle or a less sweet like Penfolds Hock. These wines are ideal with all forms of poultry and fish. Similarly, with Indian and Pakistani curries the well chilled white wines or the very light red wine known as rosé are most palatable.

The red wines are more often favoured with red meats—steaks, lamb and mutton or beef—and Penfolds reds are quoted among Australia's finest: Grange Hermitage, Dalwood Claret and Dalwood Burgundy, to mention only a few. For weddings, which are of significant importance in the lives of Asian families, and other special occasions Minchinbury Champagne and Minchinbury Sparkling Burgundy have no peer. Thus another link is being forged in the chain that is bringing Asia and Australia more closely together.

MEAT FOR ASIA'S MILLIONS

AUSTRALIA'S PROSPERITY has been substantially based on its rural industries, with animal products playing a vital part.

Exports began early with wool, hides and tallow from the livestock enterprises that developed soon after settlement. These were later supplemented by exports of meat when commercial refrigeration became a reality.

Today, Australia is one of the world's major meat exporting nations, supplying beef, mutton and lamb to all corners of the globe.

Geographically, Australia is in an ideal position to supply beef and sheep meats to the countries of South-east Asia, and already has important markets in this region.

Having a big potential for increased production, Australia is constantly watching changes and developments in the area leading to increased trade in meat products.

The Livestock Industries. There were no domesticated meat-producing animals in Australia until the first settlers arrived. There were, however, wide expanses of country suitable for grazing. The sheep and cattle brought to the new land adapted quickly and, today, the nation's flocks and herds number more than 185 million sheep and over 20 million cattle.

Only healthy livestock survived the long sea journeys under sail to form the nucleus of today's sheep and cattle industries.

Strict quarantine in more recent years has maintained Australia free of most serious animal diseases, while year-round grazing in a sunny, open-air environment means Australian livestock are among the world's healthiest. This relative freedom from disease is one of the industry's greatest assets.

As a supplier of meat to the market-places of the world since the introduction of refrigeration, Australia has gained a wealth of experience that today enables her to meet the requirements of any country.

Beginnings of the Meat Export Industry. In the earliest days of the colony, barrels of salted meat, and quite a few live animals, left Australian ports, but these were mainly for use en-voyage.

An economic and effective means of preservation was needed before any significant trade in meat could be developed.

In the mid-1800's, the canning of meat began on a limited scale, and on 2nd February 1880 the steamship *Strathleven* steamed into London, nine weeks out from Sydney, Australia, with what is acknowledged to have been the world's first commercial shipment of meat under refrigeration.

This was a notable Australian technical achievement that ushered in the era of enormous world trade in perishable foodstuffs.

Loaded aboard *Strathleven* late in 1879 were 40 tons of beef, mutton and lamb. It was frozen down, and carried safely, in a specially constructed refrigerated hold, installed for a group of enterprising Queensland graziers. That was the beginning. Since that time canned meat has become a very important export from Australia, 21,300 tons in 1970. In 1970 some 530,000 tons of fresh meat was exported under refrigeration.

Producing Meat for Export. All Australian meat for export is produced in modern establishments, under hygiene standards equal to the most demanding in the world.

Inspection by officers of the Commonwealth Government's Department of Primary Industry begins with the live animals as they arrive at the meatworks, follows the carcass through to the boning rooms, and the product right into the hold of the ship.

Many modern techniques of meat production and handling have been developed in Australia. Apart from the pioneering work with shipboard refrigeration, the Australian export industry led in the production of boneless meat cuts and carton packaging suitable for economic and efficient handling in freezer, warehouse, wharf and ship's hold.

Customers for Australian Meat. Australians themselves are among the world's most enthusiastic consumers of meat, eating about three-fifths of the country's total production. Beef, mutton or lamb provides the basis of most 'square' meals in Australia.

Red meat as a basic food item in the diet is a Western tradition, but one that is being accepted by the people of Asia, just as Eastern foods have proved popular in the West. The nutritional advantages of a high quality protein diet are also being realised.

Australia's meat export industry is well placed to supply the product needed, at competitive prices.

Increasing tourist activity in South-east Asian countries means a steady demand for high quality meat cuts by restaurants and hotels serving the tourist trade. The Australian industry is also developing its capacity to serve this requirement.

These, then, are factors which Australians see as auguring well for expansion of its trade in red meats to South-east Asia.

Traditionally, Australia's main meat markets have lain further afield, on the other side of the globe. For many years, virtually all exports went to the United Kingdom. More recently, large quantities of manufacturing grades have been sold to meet the great North American demand for hamburgers and sausage products.

Most recently-developed as a major market for a broad range of Australia's meats has been Japan, while Malaysia, Singapore, Okinawa, the Philippines, Hong Kong and various Pacific Islands all feature on export lists.

Iran, Kuwait and the Gulf States also buy Australian meat and, more recently, significant numbers of live sheep. These are slaughtered in accordance with religious rites within the importing country, although Australia can and does supply meat thus prepared.

A Trade Develops. The pattern of Australian meat exports to Japan in recent years has been a classic example of a trade developing in a South-east Asian country to the advantage of local consumers and Australian producers.

Close and growing contact with the western world has introduced many new features to the Japanese way of life, features which have been adopted alongside the ancient customs. Habits of dress, social customs and eating habits reflect notable changes from those of the 1930's. For example, meat, once used only in small quantities, more for flavouring than as a source of protein, has now become an important food item for many Japanese people. Japan is, of course, the home of world famous Kobe beef. It is, however, produced only in limited quantities and price has placed beef of this quality beyond the reach of the average citizen. Moreover, limited land availability has prevented large scale expansion of beef production in Japan.

The solution to growing demands for meat, at prices the consumer can afford, has been found in imports. Officials of the Japanese Government and the meat distribution trade have visited most parts of the world where meat is in surplus production. The nearest and largest source was found to be Australia.

A recent development in Australian meat exports to Japan has been associated with "container" shipping which now allows a regular, quick transit of self-contained refrigerated units. These can be loaded under ideal conditions at a meatworks, readily maintained at correct temperatures during the voyage and remain unopened until unloaded, again under ideal conditions, at destination.

Because the journey to Japan is completed within two or three weeks it is unnecessary to hard freeze a meat cargo. Instead it can travel at "chilled" temperature, just above freezing point. Under these conditions the meat will "age" and improve in flavour and tenderness. This "chilled" beef is already proving extremely popular in Japan and meets a requirement for good quality beef cuts.

Increasing quantities of manufacturing grade meats, particularly mutton, are also being sought by Japan, much of it from Australia, for use in sausage and other processed red meat foods.

As Australia's livestock and meat industries expand, more of the product will be available for export to world markets. South-east Asia is seen as a collection of markets, each having its own specific requirements but, as a whole, an area of increasing importance to Australia as a market for meat, the complete protein food.

Above: Australian meat in its many forms is widely used in dishes popular among the Asians. The delicate flavour of Australian mutton is well suited to oriental cooking.

Prime beef is reared on open range grazing across wide areas of Australia. Pictured on the left page is a group of Hereford cows with cross-breed calves at foot, in good pastures in south-eastern Australia. The Hereford is one of the most popular breeds throughout all Australia's cattle regions.

THE SNOWY MOUNTAINS SCHEME

IN THE SNOWY MOUNTAINS of eastern Australia construction is drawing to a close on the Snowy Mountains Scheme, the combined hydro-electric and irrigation complex that ranks as the largest civil engineering project undertaken in Australia.

Within an area of 2,000 square miles, the individual projects of the Scheme divert and regulate the headwaters of three major rivers rising in these mountains to generate peak load electricity and increase the supplies of water for irrigation.

The harnessing, diversion, and regulation of the rivers of the Snowy Mountains had been frequently proposed by early statesmen, economists and engineers to counteract the repeated heavy droughts and to bring hydro-electric power to the growing industries of Australia. But the means of bringing these proposals to fruition were fragmented until 1947 when the Commonwealth-States Technical Committee was established to review all earlier proposals and examine the whole potential of the waters of the Snowy Mountains. From these studies developed a scheme wherein the Murray and Murrumbidgee Rivers, which flow inland for hundreds of miles through dry but fertile plains, would be fed directly with the waters diverted and regulated from the coastal-flowing Snowy River; in their passage from east to west these waters would produce electricity for the industries and cities established and developing in south-eastern Australia.

Today this has been achieved. The waters of the Snowy River and its tributaries are collected high in the snow-capped ranges to be turned through tunnels driven under the mountains to the two inland rivers. The surface and underground power stations located along the diverted route will possess a capacity of 3,740,000 kilowatts and each year, through the tunnels, pipelines, aqueducts, reservoirs and man-made lakes, pass 2,000,000 acre feet of water to supplement the summer flows of the Murray and Murrumbidgee Rivers for irrigation.

In 1949 the Snowy Mountains Authority was established as the organisation responsible for the investigation, design and construction of the Scheme. The work has involved sixteen large dams and many smaller structures, seven power stations, a pumping station, over 90 miles of tunnels and some 50 miles of aqueducts, and

Below: Construction nears completion on the Tumut 3 Pumped-Storage Project, the last and largest project of the Snowy Mountains Scheme.

Above: A road location survey party moves along the selected route of the Lom Sak-Chumpae Highway, the Thai link of the future Asian Highway.

hundreds of miles of transmission lines interconnecting the power projects and the load centres of New South Wales, Victoria, and the Australian Capital Territory.

The only work now remaining to complete the Scheme involves the 1,500,000 kilowatt Tumut 3 Pumped-storage Project, the largest in a chain of four power projects located along the Tumut River, a major tributary of the Murrumbidgee on the west of the range. By 1974 the last of the pump-generating units of the Tumut 3 station will have been commissioned and the work of 25 years will be complete.

Completion of the Snowy Mountains Scheme will not mean the dispersion of the engineering and technical expertise which made construction of this large enterprise possible. In June 1970, the Commonwealth Government established the Snowy Mountains Engineering Corporation from the Snowy teams to retain their knowledge and skills for the continuing benefit of Australia and countries overseas, in the consulting fields of hydro-electric and irrigation engineering and associated studies.

Transfer of engineers, technical officers and administrative staff from the Authority to the Corporation is proceeding as work on the final stages of the Scheme diminishes and the calls on the consulting services continue to grow.

The assignments overseas, some of which are being undertaken on behalf of the Department of Foreign Affairs under the Colombo Plan, fall into four main categories: (1) Major projects carried out through all stages from feasibility studies up to the final construction—for example, the Lom Sak-Chumpae Highway Project in Thailand; (2) Engineering design, preparation of contract documents, and contract supervision of a specialised kind lying within the Corporation's specific range of competence—for example, the Prek Thnot Hydro-electric and Irrigation Project in Cambodia; (3) Feasibility studies, sometimes followed by the design of structures and preparation of contract documents by the Corporation—for example, the Andong Dam Multi-purpose Development Project in South Korea; (4) the supply of experts with particular qualifications for aid assignments—for example, the establishment of a stream gauging network in Sabah and the training of local technicians.

Nearer to its base in Cooma, New South Wales, the Corporation has been responsible for the investigation, design and preparation of specifications for such Projects as the Shoalhaven (Sydney) Water Supply Scheme and for the design, preparation of contracts and construction advice for the civil works of the Eastern Suburbs (Sydney) Underground Railway.

In its Engineering Laboratories the Corporation is able to assist in solving a wide variety of problems, carrying out work ranging from the investigation for and testing of construction materials to hydraulic model studies.

The experience and knowledge gained in a quarter of a century's work in the Snowy Mountains has therefore not only created an $A800,000,000 development project but has firmly established an engineering consulting body with proven ability to operate in any part of the world for Australia's future benefit and the benefit of all who call upon its services.

AUSTRALIAN MINING — ITS INFLUENCE ON ASIA

FROM THE ONSET of the gold rushes in the middle of the 19th Century Australia began to undergo changes which were to entirely alter her image in the economic world. Mining gradually played an increasingly important role in an economy hitherto based overwhelmingly on agriculture. Migration from a number of countries caused a rapid increase in population and diversity of interests.

These factors combined to encourage the growth of secondary industries.

The pace of mutation, however, was slow. Until the middle of the 20th Century Australia was still primarily dependent upon the land. Her exports were predominantly wool for British and European mills, and wheat, meat and dairy products for which, again, the United Kingdom was the principal market.

The pattern of Australian trade had, in fact, become more firmly settled by the formal exchange of preferential tariffs with Great Britain and other members of the British Empire in the Ottawa Agreement of 1932.

But great changes were soon to come. World War II emphasised Australia's remoteness from Europe and the dangers of excessive dependence upon an economy based on only a few main products.

Most of all, it emphasised what should have been obvious all along—that Australia could not escape from its geographical relationship with Asia.

In the second half of the 20th Century Australia embarked upon a policy of deliberate expansion of its population and greater development of secondary industries. At the same time the spread of natural desires for independence, particularly evidenced in many colonies of European nations, led to a complete re-orientation of the outlook of many countries in Africa and South America, as well as Australia. Old loyalties, based principally on sentiment, rapidly disappeared and Australia, in company with many other developing countries, began to re-assess her place in the world.

While this evolution was taking place the Japanese economy was rising from the ashes of World War II. Whereas in earlier years Japan's industrial structure was, at best, a second-hand imitation of the more advanced countries of Western Europe and North America, it began to exhibit a dynamism which rose to challenge its former masters. But it lacked almost every raw material upon which the secondary industries of other nations were based. In its time Australia had been a significant supplier of gold, tin, lead and zinc to the world's markets and its mining industry, after its early impetus, had become stabilised around these few key minerals.

The rise of Japan as a potential consumer, the disillusionment of many international mining companies with developments in Africa and South America and the birth of a more international outlook in Australia, paved the way for a sharp increase in the level of mineral exploration in Australia.

In 1955 substantial deposits of bauxite had been discovered and, shortly afterwards, the twenty-years-old embargo on the export of iron ore was lifted.

The natural consequence of these events was the realisation that Australia was able to provide the key raw materials which Japan essentially needed for its industrial revolution.

The parallel development of Japanese manufacture and the Australian mining industry is well illustrated by the fact that, in the financial year which ended in June 1970, Japanese purchases of Australian minerals amounted to about $A575 million, or almost 55 per cent of the latter's total mineral exports and more than half of its total exports to Japan.

More particularly, the trade is a reflection of the unprecedented growth of the Japanese steel industry in recent years. Almost three-quarters of the Australia-Japan mineral trade was in raw materials for the steel industry. At the head of the list was iron ore to the value of $A245 million followed by $A155 million worth of coal. Significant quantities of pig iron and manganese made up the balance.

Less spectacular, but nevertheless important results were achieved over a wide range of minerals. Bauxite, alumina and aluminium metal sales are growing rapidly as Australia moves into a position of a major world supplier of this group of products. Copper is another major, and growing, item in the trade. The shopping list is completed by smaller quantities of the whole range of the mineral exports—lead, zinc, mineral sands, nickel, salt, opals and other products.

The rise in Japanese mineral purchases from Australia—virtually all of it in the last decade—could not have come at a more opportune time for Australia. Rural products, always the backbone of the export trade, suffered a progressive weakening of markets in the 1960's, brought about by a variety of causes.

Some of the contributing factors have been rising domestic costs, increasing self-sufficiency in many traditional consumer countries, dumping on the part of many exporters and the swing from natural to synthetic fibres. All of these trends seem likely to continue and, indeed, to be added to by Britain's entry into the European Economic Community. Australia's growing mineral trade was facilitated by two new features: the willingness of the buyers to negotiate long-term sales contracts and the development of giant bulk carriers.

The first of these provided the assurance of sales which enabled huge sums of money to be raised on the world's loan markets for economic scales of production.

The second helped to overcome one of Australia's inherent weaknesses — distance—by reducing transport costs to an extent which would not have been thought possible a few years ago.

Although the mineral trade has been so clearly beneficial to both Australia and Japan problems will inevitably arise from time to time.

One area in which differences may appear is in the degree of processing which should be applied to mineral exports. Put in the most direct way it is natural for both countries to want to carry out as much processing as possible within their own shores in order to bring about the maximum degree of industrial development, and simultaneously, achieve the greatest benefit to their balance of payments.

No country can be content to be a quarry supplying crude materials on which its trading partners base their industrialisation. From its earliest days the Australian mining industry has processed a high proportion of its output.

There is no doubt that Australia will continue to expand mineral processing in the future and this must have an impact on the pattern of its mineral exports.

Aluminium metal and alumina must feature more prominently than bauxite; the steel industry will expand further and metallised agglomerates are already on the horizon; production facilities for the other main metals can be expected to expand in the same way.

But we must not become irrational about this. Australia cannot expect other countries to gratify her desire for more local processing by closing down their own facilities. No-one actually says that they should but this is the effect of demands that Australia should export steel rather than iron ore and aluminium products rather than bauxite.

Increased processing must, therefore, be fitted into the context of expanding world markets. Both the Japanese and the Australians are realistic enough to recognise each other's legitimate needs in this area.

Trade and investment usually go hand in hand and it is common for industrialists to endeavour to guarantee their raw material supplies as far as possible. For these reasons the growing mineral trade between Australia and Japan has been accompanied by Japanese investment in our mining industry. To date equity interests have been taken, or announced, in three iron ore ventures, two coal developments and one bauxite-alumina project. Several Japanese companies are engaged in mineral exploration in Australia. This interest is certain to increase as time goes on.

Japan's industry will continue to grow as will Australia's ability to supply a wide range of minerals in a wide variety of forms. Further growth in the Australia to Japan mineral trade is therefore certain.

The rise of Australia's mining industry has itself provided a useful market for Japanese heavy industry. A wide range of products, ranging from mining equipment and treatment facilities to railway and shiploading equipment, has been incorporated into the rapidly expanding mineral development in the north and west of Australia.

Apart from Japan, Australia's mineral exports to Asia are fairly limited. Aluminium products are exported to Hong Kong and the Philippines while lead and zinc form a significant part of our trade with India, the Philippines and China. The Australian steel industry has significant markets in the Philippines, Hong Kong, Malaysia and Singapore, while substantial quantities of opals are exported to Hong Kong.

Nevertheless, the extent of this trade in total is only about one-tenth of Australian mineral exports to Japan. At the same time, Australia's experience with Japan illustrates the potential which exists for mutually beneficial trade with the rest of Asia.

In the first instance Australia is in a position to utilise her expertise in mineral exploration and development to assist Asian countries in developing their own mineral industries. This has already been commenced by the activities of some of the larger Australian mining companies which have extended their exploration activities into South-east Asia. This is a trend which should continue as long as the Australian experts are made welcome.

At the government level Australia has extended training facilities to its Asian neighbours in the fields of professional training of potential geologists and mining engineers and also by conducting training courses for government administrators in fields related to mining.

In the longer term closer integration of the Australian mining industry and the developing economies of Asia should be possible for many decades to come.

Initially this may take the form of the supply of semi-finished products for conversion into consumer goods in the importing countries. Later on, as their economies develop, Australia is in a position to supply them with raw materials for almost every type of mineral processing.

The recent establishment of the South-east Asian Iron and Steel Institute provides an excellent example of regional co-operation. In this Institute six developing countries in South-east Asia, together with Japan and Australia, have come together to foster the development of the iron and steel industries throughout South-east Asia. The Institute will examine raw material supplies, available technology and potential markets throughout the region and will endeavour to co-ordinate the development of industries in the respective countries, to their mutual benefit.

There might well be scope for an extension of this type of organisation into other fields, for example, aluminium and copper.

Australia is fortunate in that it possesses supplies of industrial raw materials currently in excess of any foreseeable demands from its own industries. In Asia the large populations which, at present, have relatively low standards of living nevertheless have potentials for industrial expansion which could provide a ready market for these raw materials.

Australia is in a position to assist in the development of these countries through the provision of capital and technology and, at the same time, to provide the raw materials on which any worthwhile industrial expansion must be based. The complementary nature of the respective economies and the realisation that Australia's trading future lies more and more with Asia should ensure that this potential development becomes a reality.

COAL was the first mineral to be found in Australia. It was officially discovered by the explorer George Bass at Coalcliff, south of Sydney, in 1797.

Later in the same year when Lieutenant John Shortland sailed up the coast on the lookout for convicts who had escaped from the settlement at Sydney Town he returned with news of the Hunter River (Newcastle) and the black mineral found there. That was the beginning of what is now one of Australia's most vital industries. In 1799 the first export cargo reached India.

Following development of the trade the Newcastle coal mines, which had been operated by the British Government, were handed over to private enterprise and more efficient mining methods were adopted.

The pioneer in this venture and in the opening of new mines was the firm of James and Alex Brown, who, in 1858 sent its own vessel with a coal cargo to Java. Between 1860 and 1914 about one-third of the coal produced in New South Wales was exported.

Australian coal has always been a prime factor in the development of trading relations with Asia, particularly in the early years of the export trade, from the 1860's. This has continued since the beginning of the post war period and exports are currently being made to Japan, Pakistan, Taiwan, Korea and Ceylon.

During 1969-70 exports of coal were stepped up by about 25 per cent to 17.7 million tons. The eastern States are the main producers and export markets are becoming increasingly significant in the planning of Australia's future. Exports from New South Wales have risen to an annual total of 12 million tons and Queensland coal showed a gain of 40 per cent to reach 5.7 million tons in 1969-70.

The principal types of coal exported from Australia are coking coal for furnaces of the great steel foundries and steam-raising and gasmaking coals and in these respects the industry is fulfilling an important function in helping to provide a major source of energy for the fast developing industrialisation of Asia.

In 1969-70 Australia's overseas coal exports absorbed 40 per cent of the combined coal output of New South Wales and Queensland and earned income of more than $A165 million.

A significant development during that year was the commencement of coal shipments from New South Wales to Europe. The first two cargoes were sent from Newcastle to Hamburg and Rotterdam at the end of 1969 and, in the twelve months to 27th March 1971, the port shipped over three-quarters of a million tons of coal to European destinations. A further half-million tons went to the United Kingdom during that period.

Japan, Australia's most important customer, accounts for a major part of the coal exports and further soundly-based expan-

Timbering is essential where mining operations extend into very thick coal seams. All working sections of the mine have to be made safe during mining operations. This high timbering machine is pictured at the Aberdare No. 7 colliery of Coal & Allied Industries Ltd.

The following figures are relevant to Australia's coal production:

BLACK COAL ('000 TONS)

Year	N.S.W.	Vic	Qld	S.A.	W.A.	Tas	Total
1949-50	11,293	140	2,181	308	785	186	14,893
1959-60	17,076	89	2,722	765	939	310	21,901
1969-70	34,766	0.4	9,318	2,115	1,154	120	47,473

COAL EXPORTS FROM AUSTRALIA ('000 TONS)

Year	N.S.W.	Qld & W.A.	Total
1951-52	67	—	67
1955-56	204	—	204
1960-61	1,849	47	1,896
1965-66	6,201	1,714	7,916
1969-70	12,028	5,651	17,679

THE SIGNIFICANCE OF COAL IN THE FUTURE OF ASIA

sion of this trade will undoubtedly take place in the years ahead. In 1969-70 Japanese buyers purchased 16.4 million tons or 92.6 per cent of the total Australian coal exports.

It was reported by the Bureau of Mineral Resources that, in the same year, coal represented 15.5 per cent of the total Australian export income from mineral products, including processed minerals. It also believes that, in the next ten years, coal's contribution to Australian export income will increase even further and that it will be surpassed amongst the minerals only by iron and aluminium.

The current rate of investment by coal producers in New South Wales in new machinery and plant and in new mines is about $A60 million a year and it is believed that annual production in this State could reach 80 million tons by 1980. About one-half of this would be coal for export.

Most of the coal produced in New South Wales comes from underground mines and 99 per cent is extracted by machine — one of the world's highest levels of mechanisation. During 1969, 88 per cent of the underground coal was mined by continuous mining machines.

Queensland operations are being concentrated on the development of large open cut mines in the central district, primarily to supply the export market.

Geological investigations by government authorities and coalmining companies are extending the known areas of coal reserves available for mining. These studies are revealing that Australia has reserves of coal extensive enough to supply the world markets.

Efficient port installations are of vital importance to the development of exports and government-operated facilities have been provided at Newcastle where coal can be loaded at the rate of 2,000 tons an hour. Port Kembla has a similar loading capacity and the Port of Sydney is able to handle 1,000 tons an hour. A privately-owned loading installation of 5,000 tons an hour capacity is under construction at Hay Point, south of Mackay, in Queensland.

Attention is now being given to doubling the existing shiploading facilities in Newcastle and to building near Newcastle and Port Kembla high capacity off-shore loading installations capable of accommodating vessels of 100,000 tons or more.

Future development of export trading in coal will also involve the use of unit trains operating between the mines and high-speed shiploading equipment on the seaboard.

Australia's trade with Asia, covering a wide range of commodities, is growing fast and now accounts for about 35 per cent of our total overseas transactions.

The international committees of businessmen, which are energetically developing trade and cultural relations in the Pacific Basin area, are convinced that the future will demand the closest collaboration between all countries in this area in order to achieve maximum welfare and security.

An aerial view of the Newcastle Coal Shiploading Plant.

MINERAL DIVERSITIES

MORE THAN a hundred years ago when coal was well established as an important Australian industry the Newcastle Wallsend Coal Company Ltd. was formed, and for nine decades it functioned as a major producer of anthracite in the Newcastle area. In 1961 the Wallsend Holding and Investment Company Limited, which owned the Newcastle Wallsend Coal Company Ltd., merged with Peko Mines Ltd. to become Peko-Wallsend Ltd.

Peko came into existence when gold was discovered at Tennant Creek in the Northern Territory. For five years it struggled along with little to show for its efforts and, as Peko Gold Mines N.L., it created only a minor impact on the mining industry. In 1954 operations were diverted to the production of copper concentrate containing gold and within seven years the company was on a sound enough footing to join forces with the Wallsend organisation.

From then on Peko-Wallsend Ltd. has made its mark as one of Australia's top mining companies operating in diversified fields from its original gold, copper and coal to interests in bismuth, tungsten, rutile, zircon, monazite, ilmenite, iron, uranium, bauxite and pyrites.

As the result of scientific exploration over a broad territory radiating from Tennant Creek, three new satellite mines have been brought into production: Orlando, Ivanhoe and the rich gold-bismuth bearing Juno.

By June 1972 another big mine, Warrego, is to begin production with a projected output of 500,000 tons of ore per annum.

Towards the end of this year another mine, named Gecko, will be operating. A Finnish type flash smelter capable of handling 25,000 tons of copper per annum is being installed. This modern installation will smelt all the copper concentrate from the field in addition to producing bismuth bullion from flue dust. It is forecast that Tennant Creek will be capable of producing at least 1,000 tons of bismuth metal a year and will become one of the world's major sources of supply.

From its underground operations at Tennant Creek, and its Pelton and Gretley coal mines near Cessnock in the Newcastle area of New South Wales, Peko-Wallsend moved into the open cut field by taking over Mount Morgan, Australia's largest, and also one of its oldest operating, metalliferous open cut mines.

Since that time, January 1968, the company's total production of copper and gold has been increased and its new acquisition has contributed large resources of pyrites.

A modernisation programme in mining equipment, in the mill and in the smelter, was completed in 1971 and by this means the operations of the big cut have been made more efficient and capable of coping with the pressures of mounting costs.

Above: Pouring a bar of Juno gold at the Peko Mines, Tennant Creek, Northern Territory.

Right: The typical red sunset of the Northern Territory silhouettes the Peko mines skyline at Tennant Creek.

The Mount Morgan mine at Mount Morgan, Queensland, Australia's largest and one of its oldest operating metalliferous open cuts.

In January 1969 Peko-Wallsend added King Island Scheelite Ltd. to its growing list of properties. King Island is situated to the north-west of Tasmania and is the greatest source of calcium tungstate, or scheelite, in the Commonwealth. From this mineral tungsten is produced, a metal of strategic importance in the production of certain types of steel. As in the case of Mount Morgan, and as an interim measure, the King Island plant was modernised and production stepped up. In the meantime a totally new 450,000 tons per annum concentrator, together with supporting complex, is scheduled to be built late in 1973.

From this King Island Scheelite will emerge as one of the most important tungsten mining areas of the world.

Still further afield Peko-Wallsend has ventured into the beach sand industry with the formation of Rutile & Zircon Mines (Newcastle) Ltd. in equal partnership with Kathleen Investments (Australia) Limited. Since it began operations in 1963 this project has developed into one of the outstanding beach mining operations on the east coast, treating some 15 million tons of sand per year to recover rutile, zircon, ilmenite and monazite. Associated with these activities is Chlorine Technology Ltd., by which a large scale research programme is being carried out on the beneficiation of ilmenite with pilot plant work at Mount Morgan. Progress in this project has been so encouraging that the feasibility of establishing a large commercial plant is contemplated.

At Gove, in the Northern Territory, the Group has an eighth interest in the Australian equity of the vast project which is already shipping bauxite overseas and plans to produce alumina by mid-1972.

In spite of these current multiple interests Peko-Wallsend is looking to further prospects in the near future. In a joint venture with the Electrolytic Zinc Company of Australasia Ltd., the development of the Ranger Uranium project 140 miles east of Darwin is already on the planning boards for 1976. Ranger has forecast a reserve of some 70,000 metric tons of uranium oxide, which would make it one of the major uranium deposits of the world.

In association with Coal and Allied Industries, deposits of 120 million tons of coking coal have been secured at Bargo near Bowral, New South Wales. It is proposed to develop a large underground mine on this site.

To perpetuate the Peko-Wallsend Group's identity with mineral discovery, an exploration subsidiary was formed in January 1963. This highly scientific organisation undertakes all exploration and mine geology for the Group. Registered as Geopeko Ltd. it has bases in Sydney, Tennant Creek, Darwin, Mount Morgan, King Island and Newcastle, where its personnel of 130 scientists and field assistants operate with an annual budget of more than $2,000,000 at their disposal.

To consolidate the technical forces of Peko-Wallsend, an Australian manufacturer of metallurgical equipment and supplier of design services was acquired in 1969. The operations of this organisation, known as Warman Equipment (international) Ltd. centred at Artarmon, a suburb of Sydney, have been expanded to include an induction furnace alloy foundry of world standard.

A manufacturing base has been established at Madison, Wisconsin, U.S.A. to improve service to the American pump market.

As a strengthening link in the long industrial chain envisaged by the Peko-Wallsend planners, the minerals transport business of A.F. Toll Transport Ltd. was acquired in 1961. This old established Newcastle company has since been expanded with operating units and extra loading and terminal equipment. To further complement these facilities the transport business of H.H. Chadwick Ltd. was bought in 1969.

This case study of Peko-Wallsend is typical of Australian mining pioneering—whether early or recent—and the confidence that this often harsh and forbidding continent has much to yield.

SHAPING A CONTINENT

SINCE THE FIRST SETTLERS arrived in Australia mining has been the hard core of the continent's history. Mining influenced her immigration laws, initiated her only rebellion and gave her soldiers a unique name by which they are known all over the world—"Diggers". Today, mining is the greatest single factor perpetuating the Australian legend of the pioneer, as communities and towns rise up in remote areas to mine the amazing mineral discoveries of the past decade.

In the 19th Century men came from all parts of the world in search of gold and gave the first real boost to Australia's population. This century, and particularly in the last twenty years, mining has attracted capital from overseas countries and the resulting developments have given Australia its first taste of real wealth in the shape of expanded overseas reserves—massive skyscrapers have added sophistication to commercial life.

Conzinc Riotinto of Australia Ltd. is a company in which the expertise and capital of international mining is blended with the accumulated experience of the long established local miner. In its story can be found vivid chapters of Australia's struggles to discover and develop her mineral wealth, some of the ebb and flow in her progress, her major successes and minor failures.

Although C.R.A. was comparatively recently constituted in its present form it has been linked with the Australian mining industry since 1905. It was formed in 1962 with the merging of The Rio Tinto Mining Co. of Australia Ltd. and Consolidated Zinc Pty. Ltd., a company founded at the turn of the century. Before the merger the mining interests were connected primarily with lead/zinc, aluminium, uranium and iron ore. The lead/zinc interests consisted of two of the four mining companies on the famous Broken Hill line of lode. These

An aerial view of Broken Hill, New South Wales.

companies were The Zinc Corporation, Ltd. and New Broken Hill Consolidated Ltd. The concentrates from these mines were smelted by Sulphide Corporation Pty. Ltd. at Cockle Creek near Newcastle and The Broken Hill Associated Smelters Pty. Ltd. at Port Pirie.

During the 'fifties exploration had discovered the vast bauxite deposits centred on Weipa in the Cape York Peninsula and a certain amount of development work had been done.

Mary Kathleen Uranium Ltd., Australia's largest uranium producer, was brought into production in 1958 and in Western Australia geologists were soon to delineate massive iron ore deposits which, in the early 1960's, impressed the world with their size, richness and the enormous potential they represented.

The merger in 1962 set the stage for further rapid expansion which in ten years has made C.R.A. the largest and most diversified mining group in Australia.

Comalco Ltd., 45 per cent owned by C.R.A., has become a large integrated aluminium complex operating in the international field. Bauxite drawn from the Weipa deposits is exported unprocessed to Japan and other markets. Shipped to the plant of Queensland Alumina Ltd. at Gladstone, it is processed to alumina which is also sold overseas or sent to Bell Bay in Tasmania or Bluff in New Zealand for smelting to aluminium metal. The metal is further processed in most of the state capital cities of Australia where numbers of large factories have been established.

The extensive iron ore deposits in the Hamersley Ranges are being mined by Hamersley Iron Pty. Ltd., 54 per cent owned by C.R.A. Mining operations are currently based on Mt. Tom Price and the iron ore is railed to the port of Dampier where it is either shipped overseas or made into iron oxide pellets for export abroad. The operation was originally designed with a production capacity of 5 million tons a

An aerial view of Hamersley's Dampier East Intercourse Island port complex, Western Australia and in the centre of the picture, the town of Dampier.

year. Such has been the demand for the product that by 1972, only six years after operations started, Hamersley can now produce at the rate of 22.5 million tons a year and planned expansion will increase capacity to 37½ million tons a year. The ore is shipped to steel mills in Japan, Britain, many European countries, and the United States of America.

The latest and by far the most momentous C.R.A. project is the mammoth development of the copper deposits at Bougainville Island which will in time rank among the largest copper mining operations in the world. The ore was discovered in 1964 by a C.R.A. exploration team and by March 1970 experimental drilling had disclosed that ore for open pit mining was available in quantities up to 900 million tons with an average grade of 0.48 per cent copper. Production started in 1972 and by that time some $A400 million had been spent. The operation is unique in that it is the first large scale mining project to employ indigenes, with the Administration holding a 20 per cent share in trust for the whole of the population of Papua New Guinea.

C.R.A. is working on a scale in keeping with the new dimensions of Australian mining and in a range of minerals that shows the diversity of this country's wealth under the ground. In carrying out its immense tasks it has to face the human challenge of creating environments suitable to the needs and aspirations of its employees. In so doing it is building communities, a new society and a new Australia.

IRON ORE COUNTRY

DEEP in the Australian consciousness from the beginning of the 20th Century there has been the urge, sometimes muted, sometimes blazoned forth as a desperate cry, "Develop the north!". It was more than a desire, it was a need in the nation's very existence; it became a dedication towards a goal of future greatness.

Agricultural and pastoral visions came, but faded. Others more real, more related to Australia's industrial world, took their place.

In some of those isolated parts in the north of the continent, by reason of mysterious foldings and primeval processes in the formation of the earth's crust, there have been found some of the world's richest mineral deposits. And of all these areas none more vast in size and splendour exists than the Pilbara region in the north-west of Western Australia where, in the Hamersley Ranges, are to be found some of the greatest iron ore deposits in the world. The development of these deposits has been swift and thorough.

Discoveries were made as late as the early 1960's and now three major mining projects are in production with others planned or under construction. Five years ago iron ore exports from Australia were virtually nil; in 1970 they approached 35 million tons. By 1975 it is expected that more than 80 million tons a year will be shipped overseas. This extraordinary progression has been made possible by two main factors; one is the buying policy of the Japanese steel mills which, by introducing the concept of long-term contracts, enabled the necessary massive capital to be mobilised; the second is the modern and efficient mechanisms of the Australian mining companies.

No iron ore mining project has caught the interest of the Australian public as that of Hamersley Iron, better known as Hamersley, which is 100 per cent owned by the public company Hamersley Holdings Limited. Its initial operations were of such magnitude that it was immediately promoted to the top line of Australian companies. Hamersley entered into contracts that were big even by world standards. It commenced a saga of development, establishing two towns in the wilderness, building 180 miles of railways through the loneliness, constructing a port, a feat that still grips the imagination. The initial challenging and lofty objectives it had set were achieved within 20 months.

Some idea of Hamersley's rapid growth in iron ore production in the Pilbara can be seen from its expansion from a project with output capacity of 5 million tons a year in 1966, the first year of production, to a capacity of 22.5 mty in August 1971, and planned expansions will raise this to 37.5 mty. Capital requirements are correspondingly huge, and when announced plans have been implemented Hamersley will have spent more than $A700 million which has been provided by shareholders, U.S. banks, debentures bought by the Australian and European public and an Australian bank, the Bank of New South Wales.

The rail transportation of millions of tons of iron ore is in itself a big undertaking. Currently 26 mainline diesel electric locomotives and 1,488 ore cars of 100-tons capacity are used, and to handle 37.5 million tons a year of product, 36 locomotives and 1,881 ore cars will be required. The 1,000th ore carrier sailed from Dampier in August 1971 in just over five years of operations; it is expected that the next 1,000 carriers will be loaded in about two and a half years.

At present the iron ore is being mined from the mighty Mt. Tom Price which had a pit production in 1970 of 28.4 million tons. Some 62 miles away by rail the new mine of Paraburdoo is being opened up and with this a town of some 600 homes is being constructed. Only when one sees the extent of the towns being created is the reality and permanent nature of the development fully appreciated. By 1974 Hamersley will have built about 2,500 houses and flats. Obviously, the key to all major projects is 'people' and the basis of all development in this vast area is 'people'.

Hamersley has already built the towns of Tom Price and Dampier and Paraburdoo is under construction. Karratha is being built in conjunction with the W.A. Government. All the ancillary services are the responsibility of Hamersley—power, water, sewerage, roads, shops, schools, hospitals, community centres, playing fields and swimming pools. Total infrastructure expenditures, of which townships represent a considerable part, have amounted to no less than $A276 million since the inception of the company.

In spite of the great strides made by Australia's mining industry within a short span of years, a sector of the community has strongly expressed the view that overseas financed companies such as Hamersley are a liability, in that dividends and interest repayments regularly leave the country to fill the coffers of foreign investors. The annual report for 1970 of Hamersley Holdings refutes this view, pointing out that since its inception the huge sum of $A435 million has been expended in developments in Australia.

Moreover, it emphasises that at least 70 per cent of Hamersley's cash receipts will be spent in the Commonwealth. Up to the end of 1970 Hamersley had contributed $A390 million to Australia's balance of payments and even if it had been necessary to pay in full all its overseas borrowings and the overseas shareholders their full share of retained profits, its contribution to the balance of payments would still amount to the very substantial sum of $A223 million.

Whilst these figures are in themselves significant, the prime point of emphasis lies in the fact that the development of this fierce, harsh, formerly apparently worthless land in the north of Australia has started. Moreover, this is the development for which so many Australians have been clamouring for many years, and it is on a scale that even the most visionary never anticipated. Thus companies such as Hamersley are playing vital roles in the fulfilment of Australia's national destiny.

SYSTEMS OF GOVERNMENT

THE COMMONWEALTH of Australia is a Federation of six States which in its 72 years of existence has taken courses that its founding fathers could scarcely have envisaged. The desirability of federation had long been discussed between the six Colonies before it became a fact in 1901. Some functions which were formerly the prerogatives of the individual Colonies could obviously be performed better in common: defence, the conduct of the post office, immigration, health (where there was a mutual interest such as quarantine) and customs, involving a range of policies from protection to free trade among the Colonies.

The States, as they became, relinquished their powers in these matters to the Commonwealth but retained control in those spheres which most directly affected the lives of the people—health, insofar as they were responsible for local hygiene and the conduct of hospitals—education, transport and police and courts. The States retained the vital power of levying direct income tax.

This system worked well enough until World War I, when the demands placed upon the Commonwealth Government required the imposition, as a temporary measure, of Federal income tax over and above the State taxes. The war ended but the Federal tax remained.

With the extraordinary demands of World War II the Commonwealth assumed control over the whole field of direct income taxation, the States being reimbursed by the Commonwealth in accordance with budgetary requirements. This system is still maintained.

Today Australia has seven Parliaments—one Commonwealth and six State. The former, in addition to those duties specifically conferred upon it, has another function which was of little significance at the time of federation—the conduct of foreign affairs, including foreign trade. In its early years, Australia blindly followed British policy; it found itself committed without consultation to participation in World War I. The events of this period forced Australians to realise that they must evolve a policy based on their own economy and conscience rather than that of London—or, in more recent years, Washington. This was one of the vital functions of the Ministry of External Affairs, whose title, in 1970 was changed to Ministry of Foreign Affairs.

The Parliament of the Commonwealth of Australia consists of two Houses, a Senate or States' House, designed to protect the interests of the former smaller Colonies, and a House of Representatives, elected on an overall population basis. These are echoes of the American system but only lately has the Senate begun to take on some of the functions of public inquiry which distinguish the United States Senate. Both Houses are elected on a universal franchise, the Senate with 60 representatives of the various political parties—the present ruling party is a coalition of the Liberal and Country Parties and the Australian Labor Party is the Opposition. The Democratic Labour Party is also represented and, at the present time, there is one Independent member. The House of Representatives is composed of 66 members of the coalition government and 59 of the Australian Labor Party.

The Parliamentary Party of the Liberal-Country Party coalition or the Caucus of the Labor Party—whichever is in power at the time—chooses its leader who becomes Prime Minister. The Prime Minister then chooses his ministers, twelve of whom constitute the Cabinet. The Prime Minister is always a member of the House of Representatives and all his ministers are members of one or other House. The acts of the Government, if they are alleged to be unconstitutional, may be challenged in the High Court, the interpreter of Australia's written Constitution. The Australian system is thus a mixture of the British and United States systems.

The titular head of the Nation is the Governor-General, the personal representative of The Queen of England in her capacity as Queen of Australia. His duties are largely formal. Although he is appointed by The Queen he is in practice the nominee—or one of a panel of nominees—of the Australian Government. The situation is complex and anachronistic but no-one has demonstrated any strong wish to alter it.

Each State also has its own Parliament and its own Governor. Once the Governors-General and Governors were always British; now they are more often Australian.

The developments which have led to Australia's greater participation in foreign affairs have also led to a greater realisation of her responsibilities toward the peoples of her neighbour nations, especially when positive aid can be given. This is based on an objective assessment of the world scene.

For example, the average income per head of population in the United States is currently the equivalent of $A3,300 per annum. Two-thirds of the world's people receive less than $A500 per year and in Indonesia, India and Pakistan the average income per head is less than $A100 a year. In Australia it is about $A1,700.

Australia's programme of aid to developing Asian countries in 1969-70 was estimated to amount to approximately $A162.4 million, (See Pacific Basin Chapter) and towards this Australians contributed about $A13 per head, as part of their yearly taxation assessment.

Parliament House, Canberra: Seat of Government of the Commonwealth of Australia.

HONG KONG

CHINA

LO WU

LOK MA CHAU
(Border Post)

FANLING GOLF CLUB

PING SHAN

YUEN LONG

KAM TIN WALLED VILLAGE

PO TOI MONASTERY

CASTLE PEAK

NEW T

TAI LAM CHUNG RESERVOIR & OPEN PRISON FOR DRUG ADDICTS

LUNG KWU CHAU

CASTLE PEAK BAY

BROTHERS PT.

MA WAN ISLAND

TSUEN WAN TOWN

TSING YI ISLAND

TUNG CHUNG BAY

CHEK LAP KOK IS.

PENG CHAU IS.

TUNG CHUNG FORT

TRAPPIST MONASTERY

LANTAU ISLAND

SILVERMINE BAY

SUNSHINE ISLAND

PO LIN MONASTERY

HEI LING CHAU

SHEK PIK DAM

SHEK KWU CHAU IS.

CHEUNG CHAU IS.

ROBIN'S NEST

KAT O CHAU IS.
STARLING INLET
NGO MEI CHAU IS.
DOUBLE HAVEN
WONG WAN CHAU IS.
ANCIENT BRIDGE
PLOVER COVE PROJECT
PORT ISLAND

PLOVER COVE RESERVOIR
TAP MUN CHAU

TOLO CHANNEL
LONG HARBOUR
TAI PO MARKET STATION
TAI PO KAU STA.
TOLO HARBOUR
SHARP PEAK
THREE FATHOM COVE

CHINESE UNIVERSITY OF H.K.

TEMPLE OF 10,000 BUDDHAS
FLYING DOCTOR SERVICE

TORIES

FONG SHAN
SHA TIN STA.
AMAH ROCK
SHAN HA WAI

HIGH ISLAND
BEACON HILL
KAU SAI CHAU
LION ROCK TUNNEL
HEBE HAVEN

PORT SHELTER
JIN ISLAND
HAM SHUI PO
LAND
HONG KONG AIRPORT
KWUN TONG
HIGH JUNK PEAK
BLUFF IS.
BASALT IS.
KOWLOON
QUARRY BAY
JUNK BAY
HARBOUR
LEI YUE MUN
JUNK ISLAND
CLEAR WATER BAY
TIGER BALM GARDEN
CHAI WAN
PEAK TRAM
NINEPIN GROUP
HONG KONG ISLAND
POTTINGER PEAK
BERDEEN
BIG WAVE BAY
LAM TONG IS.
DEEP WATER BAY
REPULSE BAY
TAI TAM BAY
SHEK O BAY
STANLEY
SOUTH BAY
SOUTH CHINA SEA
ISLAND
CAPE D'AGUILAR

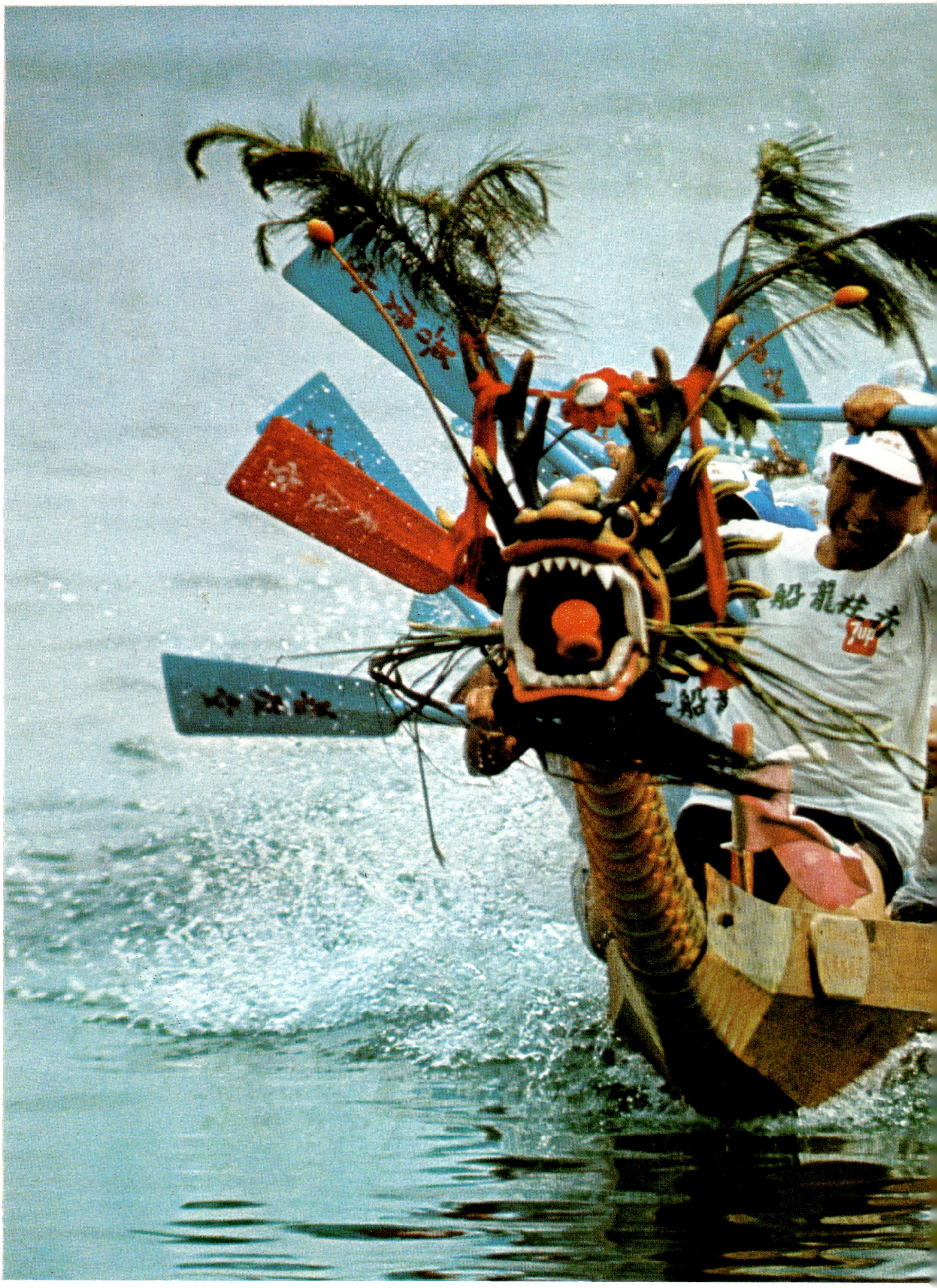
7up

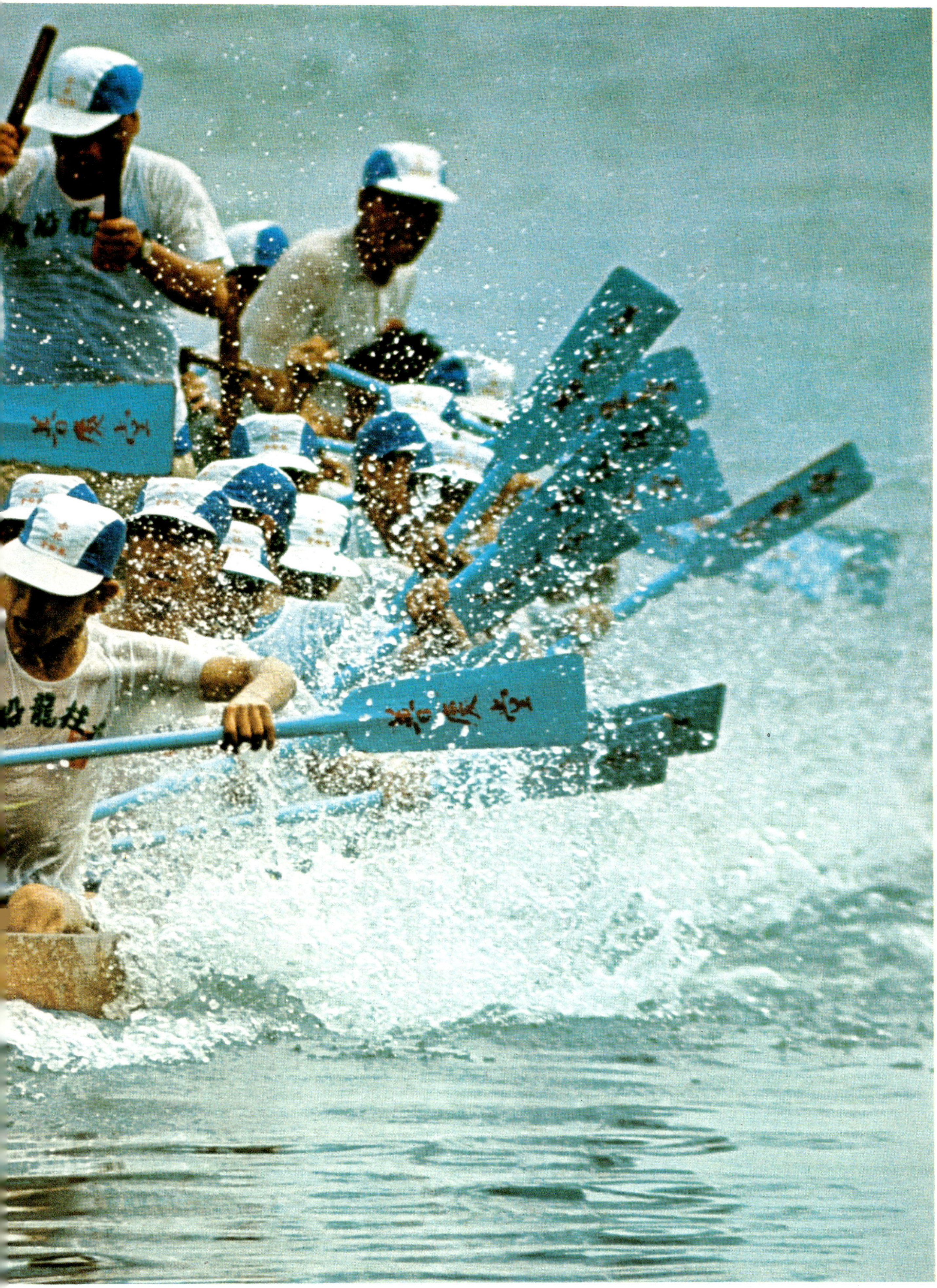

HONG KONG STORY

THE IMPACT OF HONG KONG on Asia—and on the world at large—is out of all proportion to its size. It covers just under 400 square miles, numbers just over 4 million people, lacks any natural resources and achieves an annual growth rate of 17 per cent in domestic exports which, for 1970, totalled HK$12,347 million.

Although a British colony, Hong Kong has derived relatively little material benefit from its colonial patronage. Like a late child precociously independent almost from birth, Hong Kong was largely left to its own devices by an anxious parent preoccupied with the problems of less self-reliant and less progressive progeny.

As a result, Hong Kong has never weighed on the pocket of the British taxpayer or developed anything like the complicated love-hate relationships experienced by other members of the Commonwealth family.

And yet, when most of the parental obligations have been discharged, and a half-relieved, half-anxious Britain looks around a strangely silent and empty household, what does she still discover standing by her side but tiny Hong Kong, not hanging on to any apron strings but there simply because there is nowhere else to go. Hong Kong's relationship with Britain, unusual from the outset, is hardly less so now, in an age when the entire colonial concept is regarded as an anachronism.

It sprang from the growing determination of British merchant adventurers, in the early 19th Century, to secure a firmer foothold on China's unfriendly doorstep. The toe they had poked over the threshold at Canton chafed under the pressure of a door that could close at any moment.

In their Canton "factories", they were collectively quarantined for dealings only through a consortium of middlemen appointed by a remote Imperial Court, suspicious of their motives and unresponsive to their overtures. It was like conducting business at the tradesmen's entrance, while the master watched through drawn curtains at an upper window. Such a state of affairs did not suit the proud temperament of East India traders accustomed to dictating affairs of state.

The suspicions of the Imperial Court were justified. Opium was a commodity which figured increasingly in the foreigners' wares. Special Commissioner Lin Tse-hsu, directed by the Emperor to stamp out the opium traffic, besieged the Canton factories and demanded the surrender of all opium supplies for destruction. When the traders refused to comply with what they felt to be an unreasonable demand that threatened their already weak position, they were driven from Canton and compelled to take refuge in the surrounding island waters. The dispatches from Superintendent of Trade, Captain Charles Elliot, RN., were read with concern by Britain's Foreign Secretary Lord Palmerston. Pressured by commercial interests in Parliament and burdened with the conduct of a colonial empire that already seemed to be growing out of hand as a result of adventures in distant parts of the world, he had to weigh the repercussions and allow for those irritating delays in communication, enforced by the long sea voyage, which could so often be used to advantage by the man on the spot. Past experience prepared him for the possibility that by the time his decision arrived some surprise *fait accompli* might already have been effected.

It was not unusual at that time for the supposed policy makers in Whitehall to be informed, months after the event, of some new acquisition in a remote corner of the world which would require hasty consultation of the most recently revised Atlas. And the global map was changing very rapidly.

Palmerson decided that the time had come for a settlement with China. He demanded either a treaty which would put commercial relations on a satisfactory footing or the cession of a small island where the British community could live free of restrictions. Backed by an expeditionary force which arrived in June 1840, Elliot negotiated the preliminaries of a treaty which would cede Hong Kong to the British. And allowing for the customary delay in the mails, he anticipated the formal acceptance of this treaty known as the Convention of Chuenpi, by occupying the island with a naval party on 26th January 1841.

But neither side accepted the terms. The Chinese were shamed and angered by the cession and Palmerston rejected Hong Kong as a "barren island with hardly a house upon it". Elliot was replaced by Sir Henry Pottinger and hostilities were renewed, to end in August 1842 with the Treaty of Nanking, which not only confirmed the cession of Hong Kong but also opened four additional ports on the mainland to trade.

Palmerston had to back down. Despite his strictures, development had pushed ahead so rapidly in the infant colony that ratification of the Nanking Treaty in June 1843 was a foregone conclusion. Though her name was conferred upon the settlement, and its main throughfare was designated Queen's Road, Queen Victoria shared her Foreign Secretary's doubts. Hong Kong was one topic upon which she declared herself to be amused.

But at this stage events began to be influenced by a factor which nobody had fully foreseen. The Chinese themselves, with their intuitive ability to sense success, invested in the Hong Kong gamble. Their unsolicited participation certainly received no blessing from the Chinese Government and little encouragement from the British colonists, but without it Hong Kong's fate would undoubtedly have borne out Palmerston's worst misgivings.

As it was, a strange alliance was formed in Hong Kong between British administrative ability and the new technology of the Industrial Revolution on the one hand, and, on the other, Chinese initiative and capacity for sheer hard work. Below the solid pillars of the foreign mercantile houses came the supporting structure of the smaller Chinese "hongs", which were themselves founded on trading practices far older than any Britain had known. History has produced few examples to rival the effectiveness of this combination.

THE SWITCH TO INDUSTRY

Additions to the colony were made in 1860, with the cession of Kowloon and Stonecutters Island, and in 1898, with the lease, for a period of 99 years, of the New Territories, comprising an area of the mainland north of the Kowloon hills together with more than 230 islands and islets.

Otherwise there was little to interrupt the passage of the hundred years during which Hong Kong prospered along the path chosen more in a surfeit of optimism than in any calculated certainty of success. Until the Japanese invasion in December 1941.

The effects of the Pacific War were too deep to be erased with the reoccupation of Hong Kong in 1945. More than its own setbacks, it was the change that had occurred in China, its prime customer and the entire *raison d'etre* of its entrepôt existence, which shook the colony to its foundations.

The neighbouring mainland was in a state of political turmoil which drove refugees across the border into Hong Kong at the rate of nearly 100,000 a month. The colony's population, which had been reduced to 600,000 under the Japanese occupation, rose to 1,800,000 by the end of 1947. A further three-quarters of a million arrived during 1949 and the spring of 1950, when the Chinese Nationalist Government was defeated by the Communists.

Trade with China was seriously disrupted, and clearly would never return to its traditional pattern. Any lingering illusions in this regard were finally dispelled with the embargo on export of strategic goods to China, resulting from the Korean War. Hong Kong suffered widespread unemployment as a direct consequence of this embargo and it was obvious that mere survival was dependent upon rapid reconstruction of the entire economy from the ground up.

As has so often happened in Hong Kong's history, this process of adaption was instinctive more than planned. It began in the tin sheds of makeshift settlements that proliferated on the hillsides because of the critical shortage of accommodation. And it ended in massive factories equipped with the most up-to-date industrial machinery.

Everywhere in Hong Kong, people applied their skills and resources to the making of various goods, both simple and complex.

They made whatever was in their means to produce, from aluminium pans to knitted woollens. Whatever was new, whatever was different, whatever was likely to sell anywhere in the world, they studied, absorbed and duplicated.

In the forefront of this industrial transformation were the new immigrants, including shrewd businessmen who had salvaged their wits and their skills, if not their fortunes, from their lost investments in Shanghai and other China ports.

Opposite page:
Government House is
a famous and picturesque
survivor of Hong Kong's early
colonial days.

Above:
The imposing Supreme
Court building.

Left:
Hong Kong's
Legislative Council
in session.

The colony's administration, well acquainted with the Chinese propensity for squaring up to, and patiently overwhelming, the most formidable of challenges, gave them as much latitude as possible. Free enterprise was the governing spirit of Hong Kong, hopefully reflected but seldom reciprocated in negotiations with the countries importing Hong Kong goods. Where the Emperor of China had once regarded with suspicion the affairs of the foreign factories at Canton, overseas industrialists now regarded with mistrust the emergence of a newly industrialised Hong Kong.

Concerned at the inroads into their markets, they began a campaign to denigrate Hong Kong products, resorting to convenient labels such as "sweat shop labour" in condemning Hong Kong methods. The reality of conditions in Hong Kong was something they never cared to investigate, preferring instead to preserve their convenient prejudices.

The trade tariffs against Hong Kong goods, which were erected as a result of their efforts, served more to stimulate than frustrate the colony's manufacturing growth. A more serious deterent to this expansion has been the shortage of labour. Today 589,505 people are employed in 17,239 registered factories, more than 11 times the figure for 1947. Vacancies number 16,714 representing 2.84 per cent of total employment.

As a result of this shortage, workers are mobile and hard to win. And the economic forces of supply and demand, instead of legislated minimum levels, dictate the wage structure and keep it moving upward. Since 1964, wages in the manufacturing industries have shown an overall increase of 77 per cent. Employers compete for labour with such additional incentives as free medical treatment, subsidised meals and transport, good attendance bonuses, paid rest days and, in some cases, subsidised or free housing. Government legislation has reduced maximum working hours for women and persons under eighteen years to eight hours a day and 48 hours a week.

The Chinese are world famous for the exquisite workmanship displayed in their jade carvings. The illustration above is just one of the treasures available to the visitor in Hong Kong.

Right page: An interior of a small factory where furniture is being made.

Below: An interior section of a textile factory in the industrial area of Tsuen Wan.

Manual workers are entitled to four rest days a month. Most have a statutory entitlement to six paid annual holidays and sickness allowance up to twelve days a year at half pay.

It was generally accepted in 1959 that Hong Kong's industrial wage rates were third highest in Asia after Japan and Singapore. They are now believed to be second only to Japan.

THE POPULATION PRESSURE

While the pressing problem of earning a living was tackled by individual initiative and private enterprise, public resources were applied to the massive social needs of housing, schooling and health.

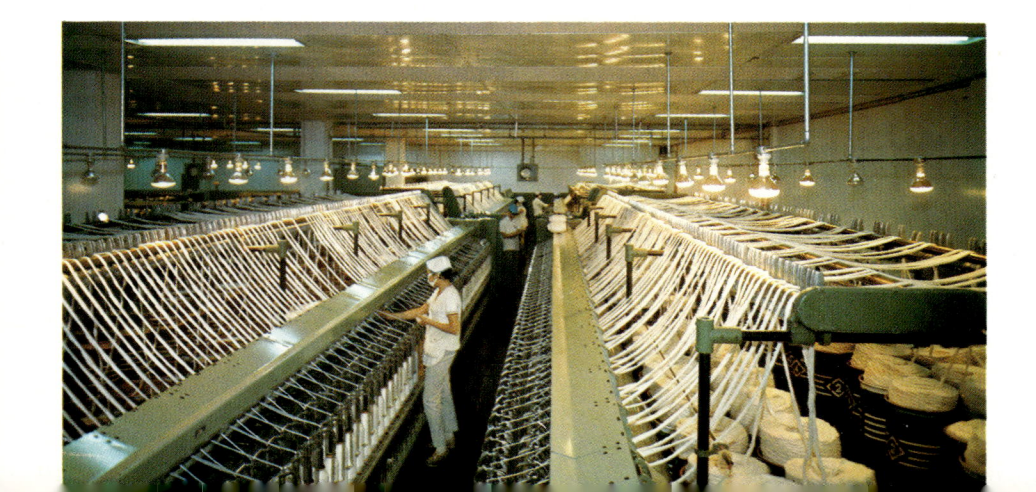

By 1954 there were 2.5 million people living in a colony whose proper housing facilities, largely in pre-war tenement buildings of which many were already obsolete, could reasonably cope with a good deal less than half that number. The overspill took to the roofs and to the hillsides in makeshift structures of their own devising, built of tin, timber or any material that came to hand.

Disastrous fires ravaged these overcrowded settlements and made thousands homeless. Others lost their property, and sometimes their lives, in the floods and landslides resulting from typhoons and rainstorms.

But 1954 also saw the start of a public housing programme under which the Government has since housed 1,339,665 people or 32.4 per cent of the population. These government housing estates comprise blocks up to 16-storeys high, and the largest are virtually self-contained townships, with their own shops, schools, clinics, post offices, banks and bus terminals. Rents are fixed at the lowest possible level to cover reimbursement of capital over 40 years at $3\frac{1}{2}$ per cent interest. For standard accommodation they range from HK$18 to HK$34 a month respectively in the older and newer blocks.

Other low-cost housing programmes have been tackled by government subsidised agencies such as the Housing Authority and Housing Society who, between them, have housed 321,457 people.

Education was another aspect of administration in which accepted practice and existing blueprints had to be discarded overnight to meet an unexpected crisis situation. Primary education was the most urgent priority and absorbed much of the new development.

Public works architects and designers found themselves grappling with social amenity needs, in contexts novel not only in Hong Kong but anywhere in Asia. If your high-density housing estate started out as a township, where could you possibly put the school? Their answer was—the roof, playground and all. The early designs were full of improvisation, because the planning had to proceed apace with the doing. With experience, there have been changes, adaptions and many improvements. New estate schools, for instance, no longer go up to the rooftops but occupy annexe blocks of their own.

By 1970 there were 1,240,540 students attending all educational institutions in the colony, some five times the number in 1954 and representing 30 per cent of the total population. The first steps have been taken towards free primary education, with a school place available for every child of primary age. Two universities, the University of Hong Kong and the Chinese University of Hong Kong, have a total enrolment of 5,401.

The number of hospital beds has trebled in the past fifteen years, totalling 16,471 by 1970, or four beds to every 1,000 people. Outpatients clinics are liberally distributed throughout the colony on the basis of one to every 100,000 people in urban areas and one to every 50,000 in rural areas. Treatment is provided at less than the cost of national health subscription in countries such as the United Kingdom. A visit to a government clinic costs HK$1, including medicine as well as any X-ray examinations and laboratory tests that may be necessary. Hospitalisation in a general ward costs HK$2 a day, all-inclusive. Even these fees are waived if the patient cannot afford them. A decisive factor in planning has been a shortage of land which necessitated extensive, and expensive, reclamation projects. Again, there was no time to calculate how much development one could accommodate to the acre. Clearly the development had to be accommodated there whatever the calculations might reveal as the ideal density. Whole tracts of urban area, where an accepted style of architecture had developed over decades to meet specific needs, were demolished and rebuilt upwards to five and six times their previous levels because those needs had been entirely superseded. Storeys were multiplied and multiplied again to densities that no-one would have thought possible before; and with such speed that those involved were unaware at the time of the full extent of the experiment upon which they were engaged—Asia's first introduction to really high-density urban development.

Hong Kong's superb land-locked harbour has been a magnet ever since the first trading vessels dropped anchor there. Extending over 23 square miles, and varying in width from one to three miles, it rivals San Francisco, Rio de Janeiro and Sydney as one of the four most perfect natural harbours in the world. The addition of the New Territories at the end of the last century did little to detract from this focus of attention, so that a striking contrast developed between an increasingly sophisticated, increasingly concentrated metropolis and its largely undisturbed rural environs.

More than three-quarters of the population live in the area bordering the harbour, so that the average population density of the Kowloon peninsula, and the north shore of Hong Kong Island, is 300,000 to the square mile—one of the highest figures in the world.

Over the past two decades the government has made increasing efforts to correct this imbalance with a policy of establishing satellite towns. Tsuen Wan and Kwai Chung, on the south coast of the New Territories hinterland, already accommodate 300,000 of their projected million residents. Further west along the coast, Castle Peak is accepting its first settlers, while the groundwork has been laid for the next development at Sha Tin, just north of the Kowloon hills.

Industrial development is the lever for this expansion into the New Territories. Tsuen Wan and Kwai Chung have absorbed a large share of the textile factories which continue to account for 45 per cent of the colony's domestic exports. Their workers in all forms of manufacture represent 13 per cent of the colony's total industrial labour force.

THE SYSTEM OF GOVERNMENT

Not least of the many factors which distinguish Hong Kong from other Asian territories is its unique relationship with China, which precludes the accepted pattern of transition from colonial administration to self-determination.

But in practice Hong Kong has been responsible for its own affairs, employing administrators picked for their ability to put the colony's interests before any other consideration, as they have proved many times in trade and financial negotiations, such as the re-assessment of the Hong Kong dollar in relation to sterling following Britain's devaluation of the pound in 1967. The Governor presides over both the Executive and Legislative Councils. The former fulfils a role similar to that of the Cabinet and Privy Council in Britain, while the latter concerns itself with legislation and financial control. The Executive Council has six official and eight nominated but unofficial members. The Legislative Council has thirteen official and thirteen nominated unofficial members.

Elections are confined to the process of selecting Urban Council members, whose responsibilities range from the running of markets and inspection of food premises to the licensing of hawkers and provision of recreational facilities. Ten of the Urban

Council's twenty unofficial members are elected and the remainder are nominated. In addition to the unofficials there are six official members.

One of the most important links between government and people is formed by city district offices, which are a recent urban equivalent of the rural district office system so familiar in colonial administration in former years.

Unlike their rural counterparts, city district officers deal not with close-knit and self-contained village communities but with densely populated metropolitan areas whose thousands of residents come from different origins and backgrounds and speak many different dialects.

The traditional Chinese attitude towards administration is one of disinclination to tamper so long as it functions properly, so that the city district officers had initially to work hard to attract interest. They were helped in this by the clansmen's associations which had assisted the administration for over a century by representing public interests. Today the public has come to accept city district officers as their most direct means of communication with a government which they discover functions better for knowing their needs and desires.

CULTURES—OLD AND NEW

Hong Kong offers easy access to the cultural inheritance of the world's oldest surviving civilisation. Here the creeds and customs of the Chinese, dating back many thousands of years, are practised more freely than they are in their homeland. In the New Territories, intermingled with fast growing satellite townships and market centres, village communities continue to occupy ancestral grounds dating back at least 800 years, and their ceremonies have altered little if at all. In the urban areas the ceremonies have been adapted to conform with a radically new way of living, but they continue to flourish.

Children are still reared on Chinese opera, staged in huge bamboo-frame, tin-roofed theatres which are assembled for these performances in a matter of days, usually on sites cleared for reconstruction. They become familiar with the traditional plots, so that they can identify the development at any stage, in spite of the acceptable hubbub of conversation and crackle of peanuts in the audience.

Factory and office workers get up early so that they can practice the ritualised, ballet-like postures of shadow boxing in the liberal acres of public parks and gardens scattered all over the city by a recreation-conscious Urban Council. Mahjong is still their favourite pastime.

There are numerous clubs and associations teaching the ancient arts of self-defence, scroll painting, calligraphy, music and other civilised pursuits, developed centuries ago by men who recognised the need for disciplined and dignified activity.

But quiet pride from the preservation of tradition goes hand in hand with tolerant acceptance of what is new and worthwhile from the west. So that football, pop art symphony concerts and "soul" singers all have their following.

Hong Kong's City Hall seemed a risky venture when it was due for inauguration in 1962. It replaced one which had been demolished in 1933 to make way for a bank; an act regarded by cynics as a fitting epitaph for the colony's pretensions to culture. Within five years of its opening more than 3 million people attended the new City Hall's concerts and theatrical events alone, while at least 6 million visited its art, photographic and other displays. Some 10,000 functions were held there during this period, including stage performances, film shows and exhibitions.

Opposite page: Hong Kong's famous Happy Valley Race Course in one of the most picturesque settings in the world.

Above: Typical of ornate Chinese architectural design, this is the gateway to the throughfare leading to Sha Tin floating restaurant.

Left: The Chinese junk is a familiar sight on Hong Kong Harbour.

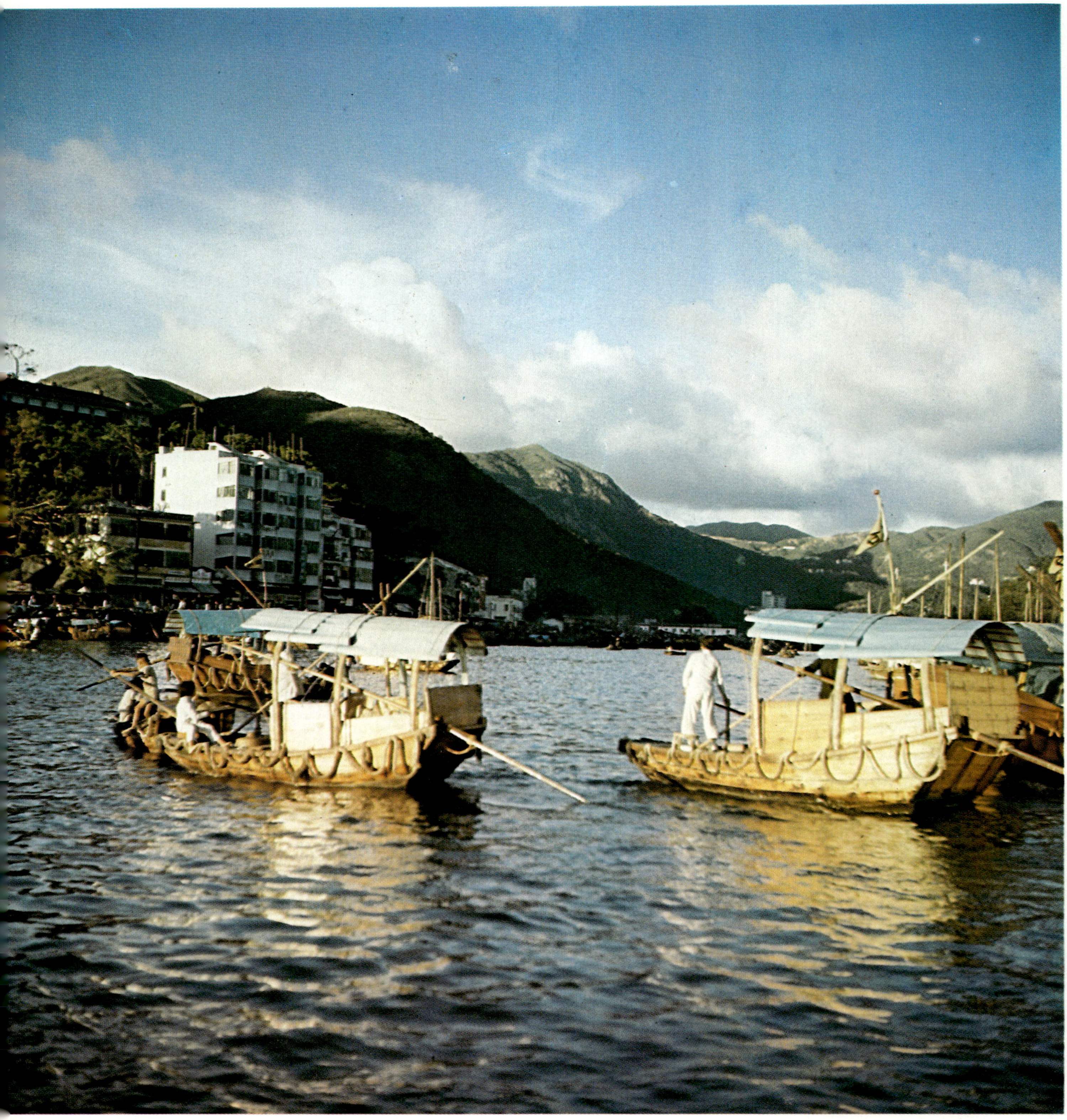

Television has done much to stimulate cultural appetites. There are two television stations providing separate English and Chinese services, one of them broadcasting in colour. A third station, devoted to educational television, is due to start operating shortly. It is conservatively estimated that more than 2 million people—half the population—are regular television viewers. Radio licensing was abandoned some years ago, owing to the impracticality of enforcement in view of the very considerable numbers involved, but it is estimated there are 1.5 million radio receivers in use. Hong Kong has two radio stations and a wired sound service.

Hong Kong people are very conscious of their involvement in Asian and world affairs. Because of their dependence upon overseas markets, their nerves lie close to the surface, ready to react swiftly to repercussions which may stem from any remote event in another corner of the globe. This acute sensitivity to international relations makes them avid readers of newspapers and followers of all other news media. With 70 dailies to choose from including four in English, one out of every three people in the colony buys his own newspaper. Television news coverage includes relays of important international events through Hong Kong's first earth satellite; a second station is now under construction.

CHANGING ATTITUDES

Historically Hong Kong's free admission policies did little to encourage a feeling of belonging. In the early days, when Chinese immigrants poured through to seek their fortunes wherever a deck passage might bear them, the colony was looked upon less as permanent home than convenient staging post. Its tiny size and its geographical location in the mainstream of the Far East trade routes both conspired to give it the feeling of a comfortable foothold secured on a stepping stone to a distant shore.

This transient feeling persisted into the postwar years, deterred only by the growing realisation that if Hong Kong's door was still ajar, others were firmly closing or already barred. And eventually the sheer pressure on its resources forced Hong Kong to limit the flood of new arrivals to more controllable proportions.

Since the tailing off of the massive influx in the early 'fifties, attitudes have changed. In proportion to resident population, Hong Kong may still see more comings and goings than just about any other territory on earth, but the transients nowadays are nearly all tourists.

The great majority of Hong Kong people have come to accept that, for better or worse, Hong Kong is their home. 57 per cent of the urban population have known no other, for they were born there.

Age is the major factor influencing the search for identity. Just over half the population are under 21. Their growing interest in the colony's affairs and their concern for their role in its destiny are unprecedented in Hong Kong's history. Assisted by voluntary organisations, the Government is doing much to sponsor and encourage these newly awakened sensibilities. A good example is a programme of creative activities which caters for over a million youngsters a year.

Rising living standards and increased leisure time have carried Hong Kong people well past the point where all their energies were preoccupied with the needs for survival. The quality of life is something to which they are now giving greater attention.

Below: Raising ducks is a profitable business in Hong Kong where these birds are a favourite delicacy on Chinese menus.

Beautiful Deep Water Bay, pictured opposite, was the setting for several scenes in the film version of Han Su Yin's famous book "Love is a Many Splendoured Thing".

THE FAMILY OF WING-KUN.

IT WAS VERY HARD for fifteen-year old Tam Wing-kun to follow the political debates and disputes that surrounded him. He was told that the armies of Chiang Kai-shek were being defeated and that Nanking and Shanghai would soon fall to the armies of Mao Tse-tung. The villagers were undecided whether to stay or not. Many of the older men pointed out that Canton had been a stronghold of the Kuomintang; they feared reprisals would be taken against the people. Other minds counselled patience; they suggested that danger is greater when it has not been faced. Many of the people stayed but some left their farms on the Canton River. In 1949 Wing-kun followed those who moved down the river of the pearl.

Wing-kun's flight from uncertainty took him to a squatter settlement at Kowloon Tong. The Pearl River had brought him to the Pearl of the Orient, as Hong Kong is known to many. And to ride on the tramway to the peak of Victoria Hill is to believe this poetic reference. But Wing-kun did not reach the peak that year. His first pressing tasks were to find employment and accommodation.

Though his skills with rice and cattle were useless in the city he persuaded a master carpenter to apprentice him to his trade.

Wing-kun slept on a mattress in a corner of his master's factory and he was given regular, though hardly luxurious, meals. He worked at least ten hours each day, receiving little money for his labours. But when his apprenticeship finished Wing-kun was paid HK$25 each week for his work. Much of this he saved carefully for several years to buy the tools needed for his trade; for Wing-kun was determined to become his own master.

In 1956 Wing-kun and another carpenter from Canton, Kai-tung, began to make furniture in their own factory in Kowloon Tong. Their factory was their home and at the end of the small shed they had a double bunk where they slept when they were not working. Often the oil lamps would burn as they toiled slowly and diligently to complete an order for a chest.

It was pleasant to be able to draw water from the tap outside, as a break from planing and sawing. Still, Wing-kun was sometimes depressed by his squalid surroundings for cleanliness was his habit: but a community of refugees working and living in one overcrowded site would rob even the brightest pearl of its lustre.

Their business grew, and even if it did not make them prosperous its success encouraged them to think of marriage. As Wing-kun was the first to take a wife Kai-tung agreed to move out of the shed.

For four years Wing-kun's family lived in the small shed, his goods out front on fine days to provide more working space. Wing-kun realised that his time as an apprentice had not been nearly so hard after all.

A son, the first born of his children, grew healthy and strong, playing inside the shed with toys made by his father or outside with the children of other squatters. But the second child, a girl born a year later, was sickly. Wing-kun's wife and her mother tended the child lovingly but neither Chinese nor Western medicine helped her. She died in 1965.

Moving because you have decided to act is comforting, moving because the government has decided to act is discomforting.

Below:
A familiar scene at Aberdeen, where hundreds of Chinese live on their tiny boats. Their principal food is fish.

Foot of page:
One of the low cost estates built by the Hong Kong Government to house families like the Tams.

The Tams were initially distrustful of the Resettlement Department's plans to move them out of Kowloon Tong. How would his regular customers find him? Would there be enough customers in this new industrial estate to which his business was being transferred? Was it true that his flat was not near his work? Surely it must be very expensive to have a house in one place and a factory in another? Wing-kun remembered the advice he had ignored when he was younger and the family awaited their new home with hope as well as fear. In 1966 the Tams moved from Kowloon Tong to a huge residential estate at Tsz Wan Shan, the Mountain of the Benevolent Cloud.

The estate at Tsz Wan Shan is one of the largest in Hong Kong: it now houses 130,000 people in massive blocks of flats. The estate contains all the services needed for daily living: there are shops, schools, restaurants, clinics, buses and play areas. But there are no factories in the estate. Wing-kun's wife walks to the shops for the duck, beans, soya sauce, fish, crab, jam, shark fins and rice that she buys from time to time. Wing-kun's boy walks to the elementary school nearby. But Wing-kun rides in a special bus to his workshop. Since their arrival in 1966 his business has expanded. His original 200 square feet has been increased to 1,000 square feet. In this space ten men make camphor-wood chests under his direction so he is well able to afford the rental of HK$70 a week. However, he confides to Kai-tung when they meet, it is more expensive to have apprentices these days as they are not allowed to sleep in the factory.

Wing-kun now has more time to enjoy the brilliant robes and classical singing of the Chinese opera, which he loves and which tourists come to hear, though rarely to appreciate. Sometimes the family cross by ferry to Victoria to the Chinese shops hidden from the hard-bargaining tourists in Nathan Road. They have visited the Tiger Balm Gardens, where the children frolicked near the seaward-looking statue of the Buddha. They have taken the tram to the peak and walked through the park at the reservoir and the beauty of the island filled their hearts, for this was part of their lives and their home.

It is natural that the family looked back toward Kwang Tung Province when they were on the peak for there lies the home of their ancestors. It is natural too that they did not travel as far as Chaiwan on the island, for there lies a reminder of days of hardship in Kowloon Tong. But the adult Tams speak carefully of these things to their children. For, though not all refugees are lucky, they feel that fate has been benevolent. To their children they speak most about the present, sometimes of the troubled past and occasionally of the good fortune their parents wish for them in the years to come.

Above:
A comfortable room in the type of home where Wing-kun and his family lived after his business became well established.

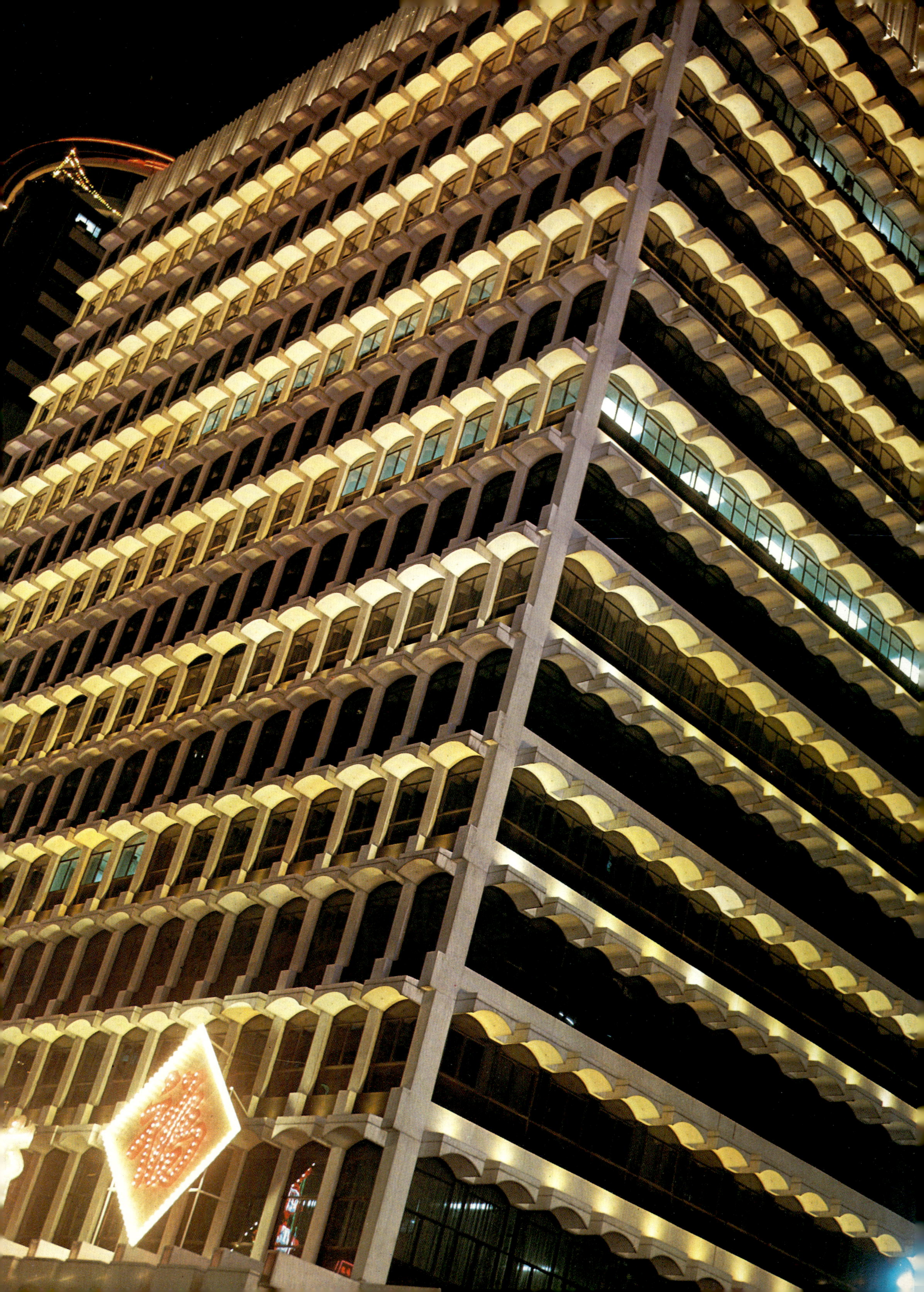

THE HONGKONG AND SHANGHAI BANKING CORPORATION

DURING THE 19TH CENTURY it was customary for a foreign firm in China to be given a shortened name in addition to its straightforward translation into Chinese. Such names usually had some meaning that was attractive in the Chinese language. For example, Dent and Company, one of the earliest firms to be established in Canton and Hong Kong and one of the original consortium which founded the Hongkong Bank, was given Chinese characters which translated as "Precious and Compliant Firm". The Hongkong Bank's abbreviated name is "Wayfoong" meaning "Abundance of Remittances". It was conferred about 1880.

The descriptive characters first appeared on the Hongkong Bank's currency notes in 1881 and are still in use on its cheque books and bank notes. Today the Bank is still familiarly known to all who speak the Chinese language as "Wayfoong". It has become one of the most powerful financial institutions in Asia with branches and representative offices in many parts of the world. Its modern name is The Hongkong and Shanghai Banking Corporation but the shorter title, Hongkong Bank, is still in more frequent use.

The Bank was established in 1865, with branches in Hong Kong, Shanghai and later, London, which became the head office during World War II. Apart from that brief period Hong Kong has always been the Bank's headquarters. In 1875 a branch office was opened in San Francisco; another in New York in 1879 and in Hamburg in 1889. Still another branch was opened in Lyons, France, in 1881. The Hongkong Bank is the oldest British banking company still operating in Japan, Thailand and the Philippines.

At the time the Bank was founded, trade between Europe and the Far East was beginning to expand. Western traders were entering China through many gateways other than Canton, the first large port in China to be opened to foreign trade; Hong Kong had been established as a trading centre since 1842. Although banks had operated in China for the past several hundred years, they had never directly financed foreign trade nor dealt in foreign exchange.

For this reason, the banking needs of the commercial community were mainly handled by the merchant houses themselves. Some British banks had extended their activities to Hong Kong from India, but being controlled either from India or London, their branches were unable to provide the services the merchants of Hong Kong required. Thus, when business gained impetus after 1850, the overall banking facilities of Hong Kong and surrounding areas proved to be inadequate.

A group of merchants in Bombay, in an endeavour to remedy the situation, decided to establish a bank to be known as the Bank of China. When news of this proposal reached Hong Kong, several local merchants determined to form their own bank. The result was the founding of The Hongkong and Shanghai Banking Corporation.

The provisional committee, which included representatives of the mercantile community from Britain, America, Germany, France and India, met in summer 1864.

For the next ten years or so the new Bank went through some difficult periods, particularly in 1874 and the first half of 1875, but, from then onwards, its fortunes steadily improved.

Throughout the second half of the 19th Century and the beginning of the 20th Century, The Hongkong and Shanghai Banking Corporation was principally engaged in financing trade and local investment. It also raised substantial loans to assist the Japanese and Chinese Governments to reorganise their finances, and to provide funds for the construction of railways in China.

Until the outbreak of World War II, the Bank's policy was one of steady development in South-east Asia. It took an active part in the financing of trade between its eastern branches and those which it had established in Europe and the United States, India and Ceylon, all of which were connected to some degree with trading with Hong Kong and China. The Bank also built up connections with leading banks in many other parts of the world.

During World War II, most of the Corporation's branches in Asia and those in France and Germany were occupied and it was left with large reserve funds in England and America but with only six offices operating under its control. Later in the war the Chief Manager was interned and died in Hong Kong.

His place was filled by Mr Arthur Morse, Manager of the London Branch, who became Acting Chief Manager. When the war ended he returned to Hong Kong and was appointed Chief Manager.

Mr Morse had undertaken that when the Bank reopened in Hong Kong it would assist public utilities to renew their normal functions and pre-war business houses to re-establish themselves. In honouring this commitment the Bank was taking a considerable risk, as many companies had lost all their assets during the hostile period.

Brilliantly illuminated
for the lunar new year,
the Hongkong and Shanghai Bank's
Branch in Mongkok,
one of the busiest industrial areas
in Hong Kong.
This ultra modern 18-storey building
which includes such features
as a column free floor plan,
was completed in 1969.

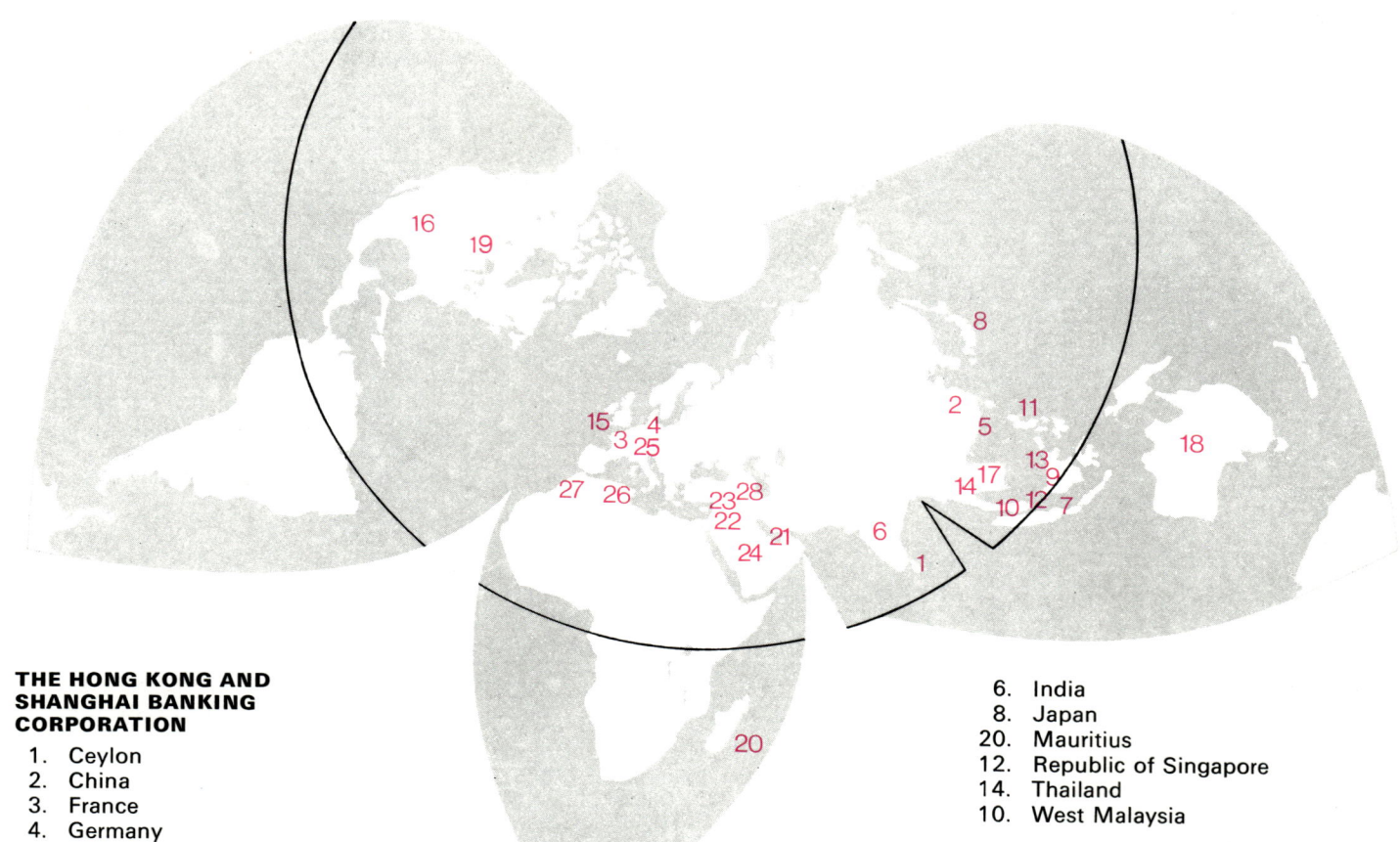

THE HONG KONG AND SHANGHAI BANKING CORPORATION

1. Ceylon
2. China
3. France
4. Germany
5. Hongkong
6. India
7. Indonesia
8. Japan
9. East Malaysia
10. West Malaysia
11. Philippines
12. Republic of Singapore
13. State of Brunei
14. Thailand
15. United Kingdom
16. U.S.A.
17. Vietnam
18. Australia
19. Canada

MERCANTILE BANK LIMITED

15. United Kingdom
1. Ceylon
5. Hongkong
6. India
8. Japan
20. Mauritius
12. Republic of Singapore
14. Thailand
10. West Malaysia

THE BRITISH BANK OF THE MIDDLE EAST

21. Arabian Gulf
6. India
22. Jordan
23. Lebanon
24. Saudi Arabia
25. Switzerland
26. Tunisia
15. United Kingdom
27. Morocco
28. Iran

Left:
A section of the Bank's EDP Centre housing computers which serve the Group's offices in the Colony. These now exceed 80 in number.

The Bank also honoured notes which it had been forced to issue under duress during the war, totalling some £7.5 million. This action greatly enhanced its reputation. Changing circumstances in the Far East in the late 1940's meant that the area would never again return to conditions approximating those which had prevailed before the war. By its own efforts, however, and with considerable assistance from The Hongkong Bank, Hong Kong's economy recovered and, despite a lack of natural resources, quickly regained its former sound footing. For his valuable contribution to the rehabilitation of the Colony, a knighthood was conferred upon Arthur Morse by Her Majesty the Queen.

When the entrepôt trade between China and Europe declined in the 1950's, Hong Kong had to take new measures to ensure its survival. With limited natural resources and agriculture restricted by its small area of available arable land, Hong Kong's main asset was a large labour force, augmented by some 2 million Chinese refugees who had arrived from the mainland.

Manufacturing industries were set up with the Bank's financial backing and these have since become the mainstay of the Colony's economy. Large quantities of textiles, electrical goods, plastics and toys are produced. Ship-breaking is another major industry and there are many others, all contributing to the industrial expansion which continues to make headway at a very satisfactory rate. Low taxation, a free foreign exchange market and minimum control by the government have all helped Hong Kong's progress.

Once the economy had been firmly re-established, The Hongkong Bank began to extend beyond the areas in which it had operated for the previous 90 years.

A subsidiary company was set up in California, where the Group now has ten branches. In 1959 the Bank gained control of the Mercantile Bank Ltd. and, in the following year, The British Bank of the Middle East, which itself has subsidiary and associated companies in Morocco and Iran. In 1965 a controlling interest was secured in the Hang Seng Bank Ltd. of Hong Kong. Interests have been acquired in many other banking and finance firms and hire purchase companies in Hong Kong, Malaysia and Singapore, as well as the usual ancillary services of trustee and nominee companies, which have been added to the fold. The Bank also has interests in shipping and aviation.

Representative offices are now established in Sydney, Australia, and in Vancouver, Canada, where the Bank has a controlling interest in finance companies.

In 1865, when The Hongkong Bank was established, its paid-up capital was HK$5 million. By 1922 this had been increased to HK$20 million and was raised to HK$25 million in 1955. The Bank's progress in the last sixteen years can be gauged from the fact that in March 1972, when shareholders approved the latest of several capital increases, paid-up capital was HK$463 million (stg. £31.8 million). The Group's reserve fund then totalled HK$474 million (stg. £32.6 million). At 31st December 1971 the total assets of the Group exceeded stg. £2,000 million.

Above:
The mosaic mural
which decorates the
barrel vault ceiling of the
banking hall in the Head Office,
Hong Kong. It was designed by
Russian artist, Poudgoursky,
and Professor Dal Zotto of Italy,
where the tiles were made.
It was completed in 1935.

THE HOUSE OF HEAVENLY PROSPERITY

"TEEN CHEONG YEUNG HONG"—The House of Heavenly Prosperity". This is typical of the quaint names the Chinese people bestowed upon foreign trading companies when they first began operating in the Far East during the middle years of the last century.

A company gains greater 'face' in the eyes of the Chinese by adopting a classical, high-sounding title like "Teen Cheong", than by using a direct translation of their proper name. This practice of naming enterprises has prevailed right up until the present day.

The Chinese appellation, "The House of Heavenly Prosperity", was given to the British trading firm of W. R. Adamson & Co. when it first established itself in Shanghai in the 1850's, to begin a business enterprise that was later to become one of the largest and longest-established trading houses in the Far East today—Dodwell & Co. Ltd.

The "Heavenly" part of the name was certainly very apt at the time, although its influence on the company's prosperity might be argued. Were it not for the highly suspicious nature of the Chinese merchants at the time of Adamson's initial visit to Shanghai, the future of Dodwell & Co. might have been very different. Adamson was not welcomed by the Chinese when he first arrived. It appeared that they were not at all willing to have any dealings with a 'barbarian', and he was forced to embark and set sail for home. On the night of his departure, however, a strong typhoon blew up and his ship was forced ashore. The following morning, much to his surprise, he was approached by a group of Shanghai elders and merchants whose attitude towards him was totally changed. Apparently they were convinced the typhoon brought a message from the "spirits of the air" who were angered by their hostility to the foreigner, and their revised attitude was necessary to appease the wrath of these "spirits". The immediate future of the company was thus assured.

W. R. Adamson & Co. was registered in London in 1858, and this year is officially recognised as the year of the founding of Dodwell & Co. Ltd. Records tell of the progressive expansion of the company, which opened branches in Shanghai, Hankow, Foochow and Hong Kong, and later in Japan after the country had concluded trade treaties with a number of foreign governments.

Trading was brisk and profitable, the mainstays being such items as tea and silk, together with general import-export practices. Later, shipping interests were to see the formation of a Pacific steamship route linking Vancouver, Canada, with China, from which the famous Canadian Pacific Line was born.

With the joining of a new partner, the Company name changed to Adamson, Bell & Co., and the backbone of this new-named company was made up of a group of energetic and determined men who were later to rescue it from a financial crisis and takeover all its business interests and branch offices. Among these were Messrs. George Benjamin Dodwell and A. J. H. Carlill, who lent their names to the reformation of the company—an event which marked a new phase of growth for the organisation and added considerably to its status.

Dodwell, Carlill & Co., as it then became known, established its head office in Hong Kong and maintained the company's policy of expansion by opening branches in Ceylon, Canada and the United States, as well as extending its existing operations in Japan.

London, however, was rapidly becoming the focal point of Far Eastern trade, and in the late 1890's, the head office was transferred there. The company was registered as a Private Limited Liability Company, and in 1899 became Dodwell & Co. Ltd., the name it still continues to use at the present day.

Right:
Dodwell operate their own chain stores in Hong Kong.
This shows part of their largest store situated in the Ocean Terminal—one of the most extensive shopping areas in Asia.

Dodwell continued to expand. The company now has branches and associate companies not only in Asia—in Hong Kong, throughout Japan, in Singapore and Taiwan—but also in Canada, the U.S.A., West Germany, India, East Africa and Australia. Business activities are more varied and diversified, although the basis of operations is still general import-export trading. The company has retained its keen shipping interests and actively participates as agents for both lines and tramp-ships and in the engaging of Chinese crews. It also has interests in air freight forwarding, insurance and tour operations.

In Hong Kong, the company's export department handles an immense range of domestic produce, and is one of the tiny island's leading exporters of manufactured goods. Imports, too, cover a wide field, varying from heavy machinery, building supplies, telecommunications equipment and business machines to groceries, pharmaceuticals, medicines and wines and spirits. The company also operates its own retail stores in Hong Kong which have the exclusive franchise for the well-known St. Michael brand of merchandise from the famous United Kingdom Company of Marks and Spencers.

Above:
The Hong Kong office
of Dodwell and Co. Ltd.
is situated in the Hongkong and
Shanghai Bank Building
in the heart of the
Colony's business community.

CABLE AND WIRELESS
LINKS ASIA WITH THE REST OF THE WORLD

TELECOMMUNICATIONS means, simply, communication from a distance, by cable or radio, by the use of electrical or electronic signals. Through these means millions of people all over the world are kept in touch with one another.

Over a century ago Cable and Wireless originated the world telegraph cable system and developed the global radio and telephone cable networks so well known today.

The Group now operates the largest single international telecommunications system in the world and is one of the pioneers of communications by satellite—a present-day marvel of modern science.

This latest and most wonderful way of sending an electronic signal from one side of the world to the other is to 'bounce' it from an earth station to a satellite in space and back again to another earth station.

Each signal goes up 22,300 miles—and comes down again the same distance.

Every word spoken on the telephone, every message sent, makes this journey and covers the 44,600 miles in a split second.

MEN ON THE MOON. Cable and Wireless operated one of the first earth stations of all time—on Ascension Island in the Atlantic. This helped put the first astronauts on the moon and is still a vital link in the U.S. space programme.

In the near future Cable and Wireless and its associates will have no less than eight earth stations in different parts of the world. And each single one of them can send signals across a third of the earth's surface!

THE MOST MODERN SYSTEM FOR THE FAR EAST. The communications satellites are in orbit in fixed positions relative to the earth. They revolve as the earth revolves.

There is a series of satellites positioned over the Indian Ocean, the Atlantic and the Pacific. One of the most important Cable and Wireless earth stations is in Hong Kong and has been operational since 1969. A second Hong Kong station, of equal importance, became operational in 1971.

Hong Kong I, the first of these stations, beams signals up to the Pacific Ocean satellite. Hong Kong II works with a satellite over the Indian Ocean.

In this way the countries of the Far East benefit from the most up-to-date scientific techniques.

Hong Kong is the centre of a complex network of Cable and Wireless radio and cable links serving Far Eastern centres, and the addition of two earth stations has made this country one of the most modern communications centres in the world—even more important than it was before.

INSTANT TELEVISION NEWS. As well as telephone conversations, telegrams and the telex used by commercial firms, television pictures can be transmitted and received by satellite. T.V. news from Asia can be beamed direct to the U.S.A. and Europe in full colour or into the area from global centres. In the past, film had to be flown from the area concerned to the point of transmission—a time consuming process involving many hours that greatly reduced the immediate value of the news.

CABLES COVER THE OCEANS OF THE WORLD. Cables on the sea bed—the method of linking continents pioneered by Cable and Wireless—are still a highly efficient way of carrying telecommunications traffic.

Cable and Wireless maintains a vital cable link in South-east Asia by linking the operations of the Eastern Extension Company of Manila in the Philippines with Hong Kong through the medium of the Seacom cable.

The latter connects Australia, New Guinea, Guam, Hong Kong, Malaysia and Singapore and links with the trans-Pacific and trans-Atlantic cables also owned and operated by Commonwealth Partner nations. Cable and Wireless maintains the greater part of this world-wide network, together with its own cables, inspecting cables across the seven seas with a fleet of cable ships.

273 MILLION TELEPHONES. There are more than 273 million telephones in the world today and every year this number increases dramatically. So does the use of international telephone systems—the ones which link country to country.

New techniques are making this vast number of calls easy to handle. Instead of each call being 'plugged in' by an operator, calls are handled automatically at a switching centre which is able to link national systems with international ones.

The Cable and Wireless Group's first international switching centre came into service in Hong Kong in 1966.

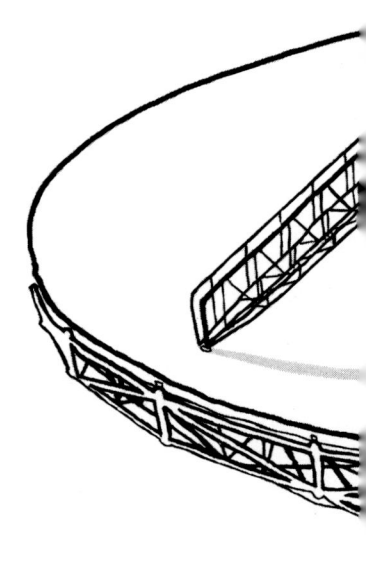

RADIO: AN ADAPTABLE MEDIUM
Telecommunication closely resembles aircraft communication. There are long hauls and short hauls and each type has its own specialist system. Radio by satellite is a long-haul system. Tropospheric scatter radio is a specially developed high-quality short-haul system widely used by Cable and Wireless in the Far East, Arabian Gulf and Caribbean.

Giant Cable and Wireless tropospheric scatter aerials in Hong Kong transmit all forms of messages to Manila.

The Cable and Wireless global radio system is the most comprehensive and

This giant aerial at the Cable and Wireless Hong Kong earth station sends and receives signals via a satellite in space.

Ninety-feet tropospheric scatter radio aerials at Hong Kong transmit and receive high-quality messages over distances up to 400 miles.

advanced international network. The Group has engineered and operates every type of radio system—using 40 radio stations in key world centres. One of the most important of these centres is in Hong Kong where the Group's computer based message switching centre is situated. At Kai Tak Airport in Hong Kong, Cable and Wireless installed the radar systems, which they maintain, and also the air-to-ground radio.

ORGANISED TRAINING AT LOCAL CENTRES. Most of the people working for Cable and Wireless are citizens of the countries in which they work. Training in the most modern techniques is carried out at Cable and Wireless training colleges all over the world. Technical courses at the Group's college in Hong Kong cover a wide variety of subjects, including all aspects of radio. At the Cable and Wireless engineering college in Britain, students from more than 40 countries have been trained in the most modern techniques with the most up-to-date equipment.

There are always interesting careers in Cable and Wireless for keen, intelligent young people. It is on them that the future of the Group depends.

251

252

THE HONGS OF HONG KONG

Left page, below:
Taking shape beside the Hong Kong harbour at Hung Hom, these giant tubes will form a tunnel across the harbour floor to Hong Kong. Each of these units, when cased in concrete, out-weighs any other objects launched in Hong Kong to date.

Right: The Lloyd Boeing 707 loads in Kuala Lumpur.

Left page: The tunnel construction proceeds 24 hours a day against the spectacular background of Hong Kong by night. When completed it will run in a straight line from its southern entrance adjoining the Royal Hong Kong Yacht Club, below the harbour to its northern entrance in Hung Hom.

AMONG THE "NOBLE HOUSES" or "Hongs" of Hong Kong a handful of names have already been recorded in history. They constitute the solid foundations from which the Colony has risen. Many of them were established shortly after Hong Kong became a Colony of Great Britain and they have seen tremendous growth since the turn of the last century.

Among the "Hongs" more recently established in Hong Kong is the Wheelock Marden Group which embraces some 300 companies with offices established in four continents, and operating in widely varying fields. They may be divided broadly into the categories of aviation, computers and engineering, finance and investments, insurance, manufacturing, merchandising, real estate, shipping, ship-breaking and metal-rolling, and travel.

The Head Office of Wheelock Marden and Company Limited is in Hong Kong. The Group's operations began in Shanghai in 1932, when the firm was incorporated into a limited company to acquire, by exchange of shares, the whole of the capital of G. E. Marden and Company Limited and the Shanghai Tug and Lighter Company Limited, both of which were then public companies quoted on the Shanghai Stock Exchange. G. E. Marden and Company Limited, formed in 1925, had acquired substantial interests in warehousing, forwarding, general transportation and ship-owning.

The new "Wheelocks" greatly expanded the activities of the old companies—steelwork, insurance, real estate and investment trust management—under the leadership of the Founder President, the late Mr. G. E. Marden, and in 1930 a branch was established in Japan. When war broke out with Japan and business activities in Shanghai came to a halt, the principal companies were transferred to the United Kingdom and from there Mr. G. E. Marden, who was repatriated, was able to operate the shipping interests of the Group, as well as some of its insurance activities, using temporarily registered United Kingdom companies.

After World War II, much of the Shanghai operation was transferred to Hong Kong, as were the temporary U.K. companies at a later date, but during the intervening period the Group acquired interests in Britain which have since been developed into a substantial group of their own.

When the Head Office was firmly established in Hong Kong, in addition to revising and enlarging former activities, expansions were made into the fields of property development and management, general finance, bullion and share dealings, insurance broking and manufacturing.

Today the most substantial and important part of the Group's business is in real estate, the Group having a controlling interest in Hongkong Realty and Trust Company Limited, which in turn has major holdings in Realty Development Corporation Limited and China Emporium Limited, all quoted public companies in Hong Kong.

The real estate group is associated with Crawford Realty Limited which will be redeveloping the site of the well-known building called Lane Crawford House in which is housed the Head Office of the Group. The combined assets of this real estate group, which today has a number of projects in hand, includes revenue-producing assets estimated at approximately HK$400,000,000 (Stg.£27,500,000).

In addition to the real estate group of companies in Hong Kong, Wheelock Marden has a controlling interest in Lane Crawford Limited — the managers and operators of the well-known and very old established department store of Lane Crawford, Metal Industries Corporation Limited and also the Group's associate company, Allied Investors Corporation Limited. These three organisations are all public companies quoted on the Hong Kong Stock Exchange.

Shipping is still a very substantial and important part of the Group's business and in addition to the fleet of twelve directly owned ships representing a deadweight tonnage totalling 306,283 tons, the Group

253

Left: Fine furniture and furnishings from Turning Furniture Industries Limited's showrooms grace some of the Colony's luxurious apartments. The view overlooking the harbour from the island is breathtaking and the furnishings of these flats provides the right setting for appreciating this view.

Below: The arcade on the third floor of Lane Crawford House leads to I.D.L. European Antiques, recalling memories of the old world.

Right: One of the six galleries of I.D.L. European Antiques.

254

also has a 20 per cent investment in World Maritime Bahamas Limited, a company jointly owned by Wheelock Marden and Company Limited, World-Wide (Shipping) Limited and The Hongkong and Shanghai Banking Corporation. The World Maritime Bahamas fleet now consists of 25 vessels afloat and some 14 others on order, totalling 3,750,000 deadweight tons.

As a measure of the Group's strength and its pride and trust in the future development of Hong Kong, it holds a substantial interest in The Cross-Harbour Tunnel Company Limited, presently constructing a tunnel under Victoria Harbour to link the mainland at Kowloon with the island of Hong Kong. To date all of the fifteen units which comprise the tunnel's tube have been launched and have been lowered into the prepared trench on the harbourbed. The opening date for the tunnel is scheduled for September, 1972.

Overseas, the Group has extensive interests in the sophisticated fields of computer distribution, data processing and, through Wheelock Marden Engineering Limited, is developing and co-ordinating the various engineering and technical agencies of the Group throughout the Far East.

In the United Kingdom, in addition to a number of active trading companies, the organisation has a substantial interest in Lloyd International Airways which currently owns three Boeing 707's and four Britannias employed on the international charter market.

In Japan, Cornes and Company Limited, which was formed in the late 19th Century, is the senior overseas corporation to be established in Japan. A further merchant company is operating in Thailand. In Australia the Company's interests are in real estate, mainly in the area surrounding Sydney, and its latest expansion is into Indonesia where a factory has been constructed for the manufacture and packaging under licence of well-known brands of pharmaceuticals and toiletries.

SEEING HONG KONG

HONG KONG, 236 islands of rugged hills forming a protective ring around the peaceful waters of Victoria Harbour, has proved itself an edifying source of inspiration for myriads of painted landscapes on pieces of silk and satin and bamboo scrolls.

Travel over extensive distances is non-existent in this British Crown Colony for it covers an area of only 398 square miles jutting off the coast of mainland China into the South China Sea. But there is more than enough variety to fill a different and unique seven days of the week.

Hong Kong's extensive stretches of coastline in a sub-tropical climate invite almost every variety of aquatic sport. Popular Repulse Bay is one of twelve accessible beaches on the southern coast of Hong Kong Island, which lies just off the tip of Kowloon Peninsula.

Hong Kong Island, 29 square miles in area, rises to a hilly ridge affording the visitor a superb panoramic view of the Harbour and the mainland on the one side and the South China Sea on the other. The highest point of the Island is The Peak, accessible by road and by The Peak Tramway. It overlooks the clean, geometric structures on both sides of the Harbour.

The city of Hong Kong curves around the urban tip of Kowloon Peninsula with busy ferries and a tunnel, to be completed in 1972, linking them together. Victoria Harbour, one of the most beautiful and naturally perfect in the world, presents a constantly changing scene. Ships from every country lie at anchor with busy satellites of tugboats, barges, junks, pilot launches and an occasional sampan or pleasure yacht dotting the blue sea.

Large ocean cruisers berth at the Ocean Terminal on the tip of Kowloon Peninsula where shops, stocked with duty-free goods of every description, proliferate around the many sophisticated hotels in the area. The visitor arriving by air lands on the runway of Kai Tak International Airport stretching out into the harbour at Kowloon Bay on the eastern side of the peninsula. The aerial view of the harbour by night is truly memorable. Coloured neon signs flash amidst sparkling millions of individual lights in the twin cities, and diamond-like clusters stud the tall skyscrapers and groups of great housing blocks.

In Causeway Bay and Wanchai on the Hong Kong side and Tsimshatsui, the "Golden Mile" on the tip of Kowloon Peninsula, lively diversions abound in the numerous bars, discotheques and night clubs billing top international show-business personalities. For the ecstasy of the gourmet, famous chefs from all over the world create exotic

To see Hong Kong at night is one of the world's most exciting experiences. In the Harbour ply ships from all corners of the earth but the most picturesque of them all are the Chinese junks. When the Chinese celebrate their festivals in the Lunar New Year and the Mid-Autumn Moon, the Dragon Boat and other occasions on their calendar, the quaint customs and colourful pageantry of an ancient civilisation run riot.

dishes in the internationally known restaurants of Hong Kong. Culinary artists from overseas must excel themselves because competition for the discriminating palates is kept at a high level by the local Cantonese chefs.

North of Kowloon Peninsula, beyond the Nine Dragon Hills, lie the New Territories, leased from China until 1997. Duck and fish farms formed by inundated fields, and vegetable patches as neat as any show case garden, can be seen in these rural areas.

The undulating roads through the central part of the New Territories often cross or run alongside the tracks of the Kowloon-Canton Railway. It starts from the tip of the peninsula with a check-point at the border to ensure that China watchers without permits into China merely do their watching visually from outside the Bamboo Curtain.

Along the coast, 85 secluded beaches await discovery among the many hidden coves, bays and promontories of the New Territories and outlying islands of Lantao and Cheung Chau. For those lacking the compulsion to get away from it all, there are 36 accessible beaches maintained by the Urban Services Department.

Scheduled ferry services leave the Outlying Districts Ferry Pier in the Central District of Hong Kong Island for the islands of Lantao, Cheung Chau and Lamma, with harbour cruises and excursions to popular spots on weekends during the summer. Daily water-tours in junks and converted ferries with lunch, dinner or tea provided are available throughout the year.

The visitor with a good pair of walking shoes will find excellent hiking weather during the dry and relatively mild winters of Hong Kong. Easily discernible paths, marked by dotted lines on maps, wind through rugged terrain to vantage lookout points, or weave through the forested hills around some of the many water reservoirs of Hong Kong.

For the time-conscious businessman there is a helicopter sightseeing service that also makes commuter flights to Kai Tak International Airport from Hong Kong Island. This airborne facility is typical of the quick, efficient travel services available in Hong Kong.

Hong Kong is a free port
and goods from all over the world
are available tax free
at fiercely competitive prices.
Textiles, watches, cameras,
antiques, jewellery, model fashions,
perfumes—
all available at the Ocean Terminal,
the boutiques,
custom tailors and modistes
in the arcades of hotels,
or at the little shops
in Kowloon.
Above is an architect's conception
of Peak Tower,
Hongkong and Shanghai Hotels'
new restaurant and shopping complex
at the Peak on top
of Hong Kong.

The interior of the Hotel still reflects the days of gracious living, but air-conditioning and other modern amenities have since been added for the comfort of guests. Now it is primarily a resort hotel, away from the bustle of the city, where water skiing, fishing, golf, skin diving and tennis are only yards away and a glorious beach is just outside the front door. The view of the Bay from the Hotel is magnificent, with a panorama stretching beyond the beach to distant islands, and in July when the flame trees burst into brilliant flower the gardens are a blaze of colour.

The most famous of Hong Kong's hotels is the sumptuous Peninsula. Built on 63,500 sq. ft. of reclaimed land in Kowloon with a glorious view over the ever-busy harbour, The Peninsula was completed in 1927 in the days when Kowloon was still a sleepy little village of tree-lined avenues; the nine storeys of the Hotel towered over the surrounding small dwellings and shops. The Peninsula stands just opposite the site of the old railway station where travellers alighted at the end of journeys from the vast reaches of China and Russia. From there it was only a one minute walk to the portals of the Hotel.

Soon after the completion of the building England sent over more troops to safeguard her interests in China, and shortage of accommodation forced them to use the new Hotel as a billett. After some years of peaceful existence World War II broke out.

Hong Kong fell to the enemy and The Peninsula was once more used as a billett— this time for Japanese officers. When Peace was declared again repairs and re-

The beautiful Bauhinia Blakeana shown above is the national flower of Hong Kong.
The picture below is Repulse Bay, with the red roofs of the Repulse Bay Hotel in the left centre. The calm, quiet beach draws its thousands of bathers in the warmer months of the year.

HISTORY IN THE MAKING

NO TALE OF HONG KONG would be complete without mention of The Peninsula and The Repulse Bay hotels, both of which have long been landmarks in the colony.

The earliest pictorial records of The Repulse Bay Hotel date back to 1918 when Hong Kong was a base for European military excursions into China and the occasional pirate still menaced shipping. Since that time, the exterior of the fine old colonial building has changed little, though a new wing was added in 1928, and the young saplings shown in the early photographs are now sturdy veterans in the beautifully landscaped gardens.

decorations were carried out and the Hotel was restored to its normal state.

1962 marked the beginning of a programme of extensive modernisation which lasted six years and cost HK$26 million (about $US4,000,000.00). The result is a magnificent blend of occidental and oriental decor and a happy marriage of traditional and modern in an atmosphere of quiet luxury. On the plate glass doors of the front entrance to the Hotel the Chinese Door Gods keep watch to ensure that no evil enters, while the interior is graced by the ultra-modern artistic works in metal of the Hong Kong sculptor Van Lau, and beautiful murals in porcelain and gold leaf by Casadei.

In March 1970 The Peninsula bedrooms were increased to 350 by incorporating the old Peninsula Court across the road by way of a covered aluminium bridge on the second floor level to link the two buildings.

The Hotel has four fine restaurants, encompassing a variety of tastes, the most famous being Gaddi's, internationally acclaimed for its superb French cuisine. The main restaurant is The Verandah, shaped as its name suggests to make the most of the magnificent, constantly changing harbour scene, while next door through a heavily carved wooden door is the Chesa, a restaurant authentically Swiss in food and decor. In the Marco Polo Restaurant a luncheon buffet is served where the dishes symbolise the countries through which that intrepid traveller passed. One of the latest additions to the Hotel is The Scene, a sophisticated night spot in the basement, which first introduced Hong Kong to the age of the discotheque. The Peninsula and The Repulse Bay are both owned and operated by The Hongkong and Shanghai Hotels Limited.

While The Peninsula has become a second home for itinerant royalty, diplomats, tycoons and stars, The Hongkong Hotel has more recently been added to the Hongkong and Shanghai Group. The original Hongkong Hotel was demolished in 1954 after more than 80 years of service, and in 1969 the new building was opened with 800 pristine new rooms providing first class accommodation. The new Hongkong stands right at the harbour's edge adjoining The Ocean Terminal, the largest most exotic indoor shopping complex in Asia.

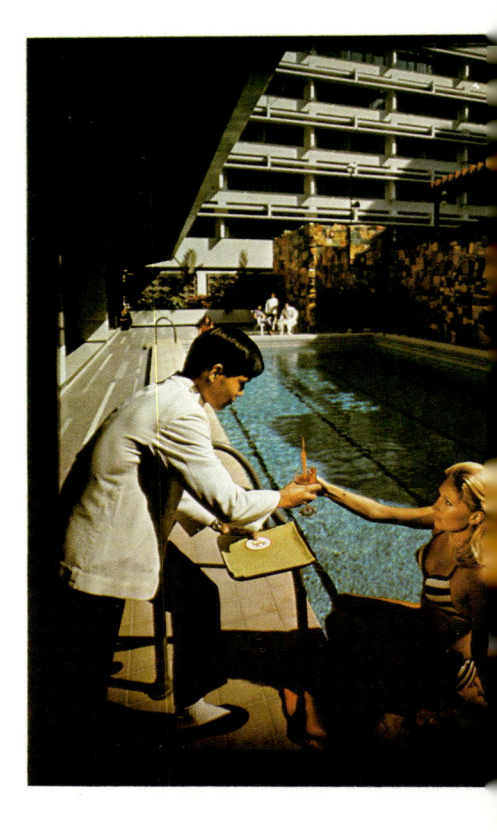

The sixth floor of the Hongkong Hotel is the hub of social activity. The decorative roof garden is the venue for barbecues and fashion shows, and the Poolside Lounge overlooks the swimming pool. The Bauhinia Room, the main restaurant, where excellent Chinese and Western foods are served, is named after the Bauhinia Blakeana, the delicate pink orchid which is Hong Kong's national emblem. The decor of the Tai Pan Grill room is reminiscent of Hong Kong in the 1860's and is true to its name in providing sustenance worthy of any "tai pan"—the colloquial Cantonese for "big boss". On the ground floor a cheerful Coffee Shop sits opposite the Gun Bar, which itself recalls old Hong Kong with its rattan chairs and colonial-style decor.

On the walls famous French cartoonist Zabo (author of the hilarious pictorial commentary on Hong Kong titled "Sweet and Sour") has sketched the funny side of life in the Colony.

The Hongkong and Shanghai Hotels Group embraces the best from the gracious days of old Hong Kong without sacrificing modern luxuries. The Peninsula has recently acquired a fleet of seven Rolls Royce limousines for transporting guests, and this is a symbol of the hotel Group's policy to provide nothing but the best.

In the Poolside Lounge of the Hong Kong Hotel visitors may relax in the cool surroundings and enjoy a swim in the blue-tiled pool shown on the opposite page.

The international Buffet rooms at The Peninsula and Hong Kong Hotels are popular meeting places for business luncheons and social gatherings. The chefs are famous for their foods of many nations which they serve in wide varieties and mouth-watering displays. Special dishes are prepared by the head waiter at the guests' table ... The picture above shows the great colonial-designed foyer of The Peninsula Hotel.

THE AIR-WORLD OF ASIA

IN THE QUARTER CENTURY since the end of World War II there has been amazing progress in almost every field of human endeavour. Nowhere is this more in evidence and more dramatic than in air transport. The aeroplane of the 1940's made its mark as the inevitable medium of future travel; the jet of today more than confirms the wildest predictions. Air travel is an accepted part of the modern mode of living, and is particularly obvious in South-east Asia.

The quickened tempo of air transport is paralleled by the explosive economic expansion of every major country in the area, and the converse result has been dynamic growth in airline operations. One airline company began at the dawn of the post war era, making flights from Hong Kong to neighbouring Asian countries. Its name, Cathay Pacific, is now a household word in every Asian nation, even as far south as Australia.

On 24th September 1946 an Australian, Syd de Kantzow and Roy Farrell, an American, two World War II pilots, each produced one Hong Kong dollar as the initial paid-up capital of a new airline company which they called Cathay Pacific.

Work was where it could be found; air freighting manufactured goods from Australia to China and other newly-opened markets in the Far East, carrying migrants from India and Burma to Australia— charter work of all kinds. The aircraft were war-surplus Dakotas, the famous DC-3's, the most honest craft of the post war period. Hard work, initiative in opening services to Macao, Manila, Bangkok, Rangoon and Singapore made the small company prosper. In a few years the fleet had grown to seven 'planes.

By 1948 governments recognised that controls would have to be introduced to regulate the rapidly expanding air transport. It was the end of a hectic period of freelance activity. Cathay Pacific was licensed to operate south of Hong Kong and steps were taken to allow it to expand on a bigger scale. The company was taken over by Butterfield and Swire and Australian National Airways, (now Ansett Airlines of Australia), reorganised and recapitalised.

The record of Cathay Pacific's purchase of aircraft since its inception is the story of its growth and the development of technology in the aircraft industry. The company purchased its first DC-4 in 1949, and DC-6 and DC-6B aircraft were introduced in the 1950's. In 1959 two Lockheed Electra jets were added to the fleet to operate

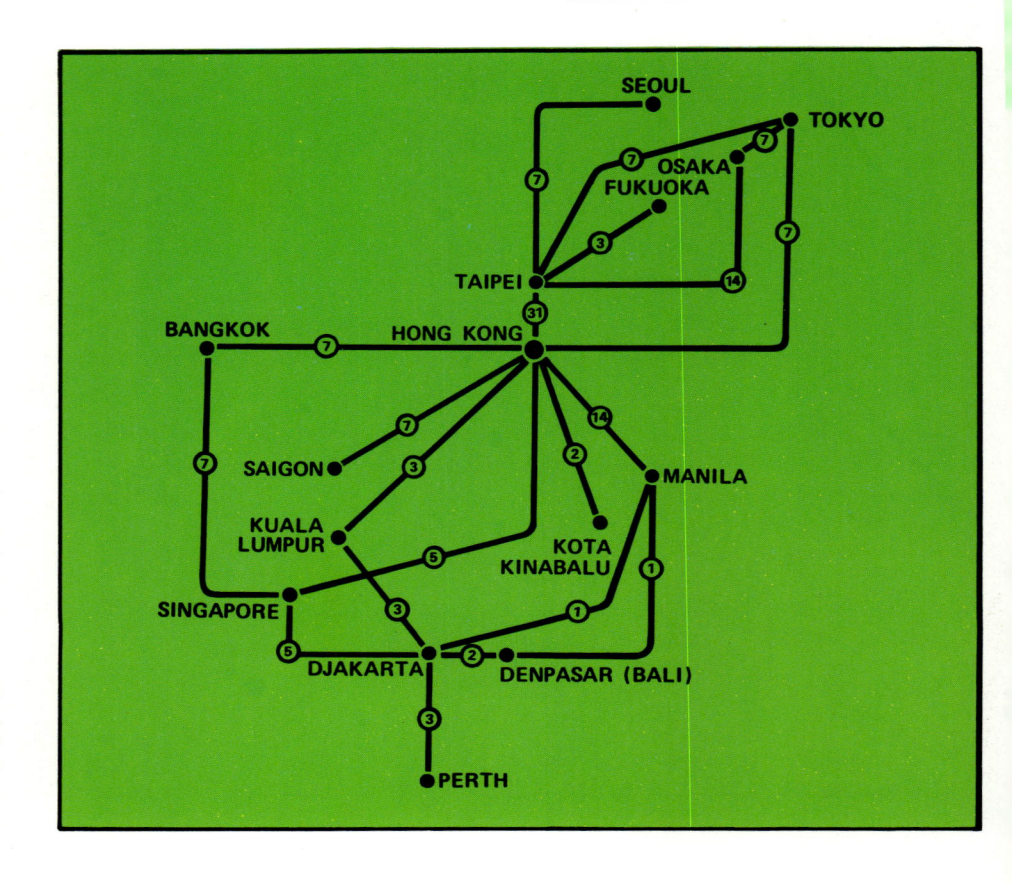

Above:
Hong Kong's Cathay Pacific frequency route map. The figures indicate the number of flights operated on each sector per week. There are many through and connecting services in all directions through Hong Kong.

Below:
Passengers board a Cathay Pacific flight at Kai Tak International Airport, Hong Kong.

The famous "Lion Rock" can be seen in the background. Cathay Pacific has 152 scheduled flights a week into and out of Hong Kong.

Right page:
One of Cathay Pacific's Convair 880 jetliners flying over Hong Kong Harbour; the Island and busy Central District are seen in the foreground.

between Hong Kong and Sydney but in 1961 other carriers introduced pure-jet equipment on this route and the Electra service was suspended. In the same year it was decided to order a Convair 880-22M jet from General Dynamics, a move that proved so successful that further Convairs were commissioned each subsequent year and older equipment phased out. At the end of 1970 Cathay Pacific was operating a fleet of eight Convair 880-22M's.

It was the post war recovery of Japan, probably more than any other factor, which gave air transport its spectacular impetus in Asia. Growth in the 1950's had been steady but in the 1960's, with the lifting of foreign currency controls by the Japanese Government, increasing numbers of the Japanese people began to travel abroad. Cathay Pacific had prepared for this eventuality; in 1959 it had absorbed Hong Kong Airways which some ten years earlier had been licensed to fly north of Hong Kong. The company now stepped up its sales operations and by the end of 1970 it had scheduled 21 flights weekly from Hong Kong to Tokyo, 14 to Osaka and 2 to Fukuoka. At the present time it operates thirteen offices in Japan.

The need for world-wide representation of airline companies is well recognised and, although only a regional operator, Cathay Pacific has established offices in eight North American cities, and off-line offices in London, Paris, Frankfurt, Beirut, Sydney and Melbourne. This complements the international flavour of the airline itself. The flight deck crews are from Australia, New Zealand and Britain, the aircraft from the United States and the cabin crews from nine different Asian countries.

Air transport has moved into the sphere of big business and many major companies have acquired interests in associated industries. Cathay Pacific, for example, holds a controlling shareholding in Air Caterers Ltd., whose flight kitchens prepare an average of 3,000 meals a day for ten other passenger carriers in addition to Cathay Pacific. In Hong Kong the company provides traffic handling facilities for almost 40 per cent of the flights into Kai Tak airport.

In the fiercely competitive world of air travel, airlines are mindful of the need to maintain reputations they have striven to build up. Cathay Pacific is no exception.

Recently it invested more than $A1 million in a Convair 880M digital flight simulator —one of the most advanced and complex items of precision instrumentation in Asia. The ultimate training aid for modern jet air crews, the simulator is the result of three years' planning and preparation.

In another technological field, Cathay Pacific's computerised reservations system went into operation in June, 1971. Cathay Pacific is the first airline of its size in the world to have installed such a system. In September 1971 Cathay Pacific introduced a twice-weekly service to Bali, increasing to fifteen the number of Asian cities to which it operates. At the same time it added the first Boeing 707 to complement the Convair fleet. This is the first of a series of 707's the airline will acquire, all of which will have a revolutionary "superjet" interior design to provide more room in the aircraft. Initially these aircraft will be used on the Hong Kong-Japan routes.

In the last decade Cathay Pacific Airways has had an annual 20 per cent growth rate—well in advance of the average for the industry. It is confident that this will be maintained throughout the 1970's.

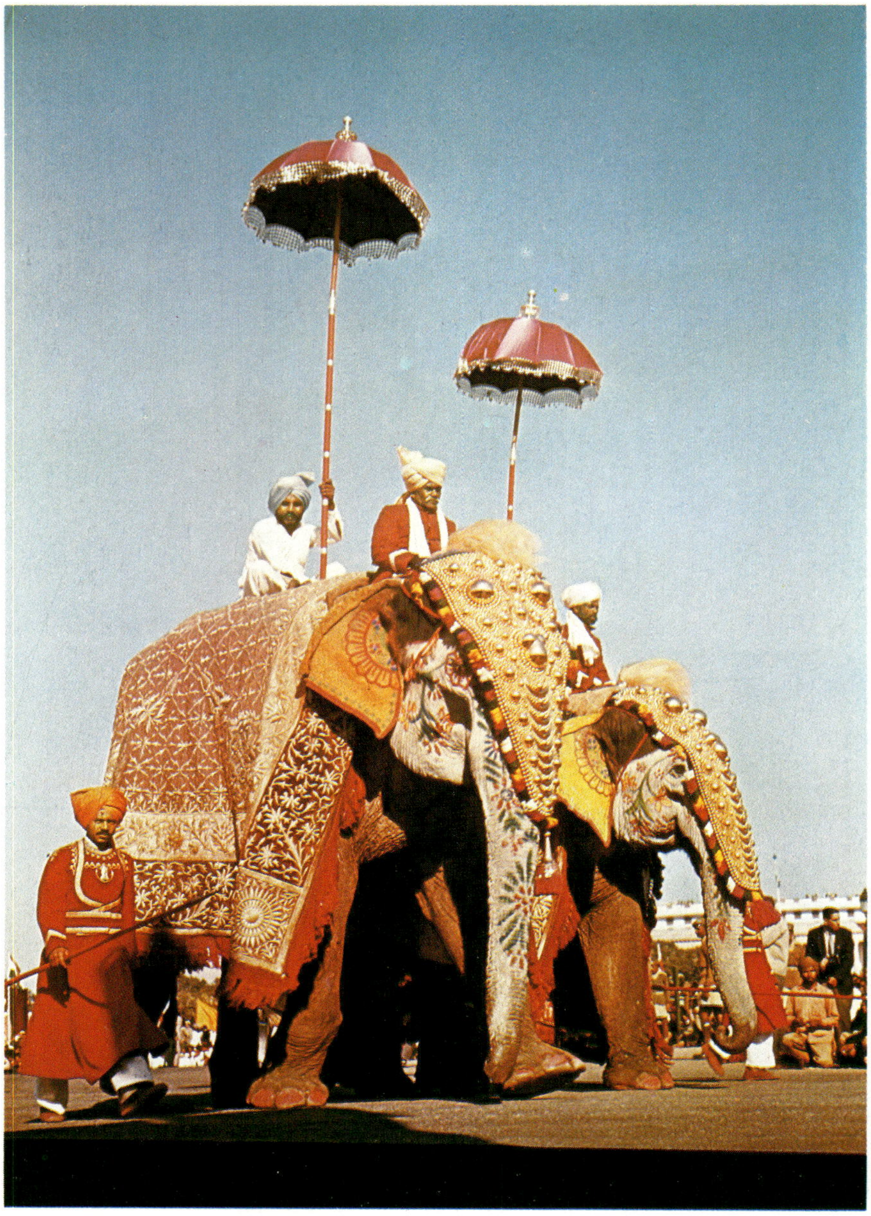

सत्यमेव जयते

Republic of
INDIA

The Kandariya Mahadera Temple at Khajuraho.

This Ancient Land

A CYNIC ONCE OBSERVED: "If you want to write a book on India, do so at the end of your first week in the country. If you don't, you will never do it." This is because the longer you stay the better you will realise the truth of the saying "Everything you say about India, its opposite is also true." Its vastness and diversity are the two predominant impressions of the visitor. With an area of about 3.3 million square kilometres and 547 million people (according to the 1971 census) India is the seventh largest country in the world—a little smaller than Australia—and next to China the second most populated.

India is an ethnological museum with all the principal races of mankind, the Australoid, the Europoid, the Mongoloid and the Negroid represented in it. It has an equal variety of religious persuasions, and followers of all the major religions—Hindus (84 per cent of the population 1961), Muslims (11 per cent), Christians (a little less than 3 per cent), Buddhists, Jews, Sikhs, Zoroastrians, Jains—live there. There are also around 30 million tribals, many of them practising a variety of animistic cults.

The Indian Constitution lists fifteen national languages—almost as many as those spoken in the whole of Europe—each with a script and literature of its own. English, which is widely spoken, is the mother tongue of 150,000 Anglo-Indians. The 1961 census figures give a count of 826 'mother tongues', most of which are spoken but have no scripts. About 80 per cent of the population live in more than half a million villages and the rest in 2,921 cities and towns which include cities bursting at the seams like Calcutta and Bombay. India is a nation of young people, with more than half its population under 25 years of age. One must beware of attempting capsule judgments on a nation of such kaleidoscopic variety.

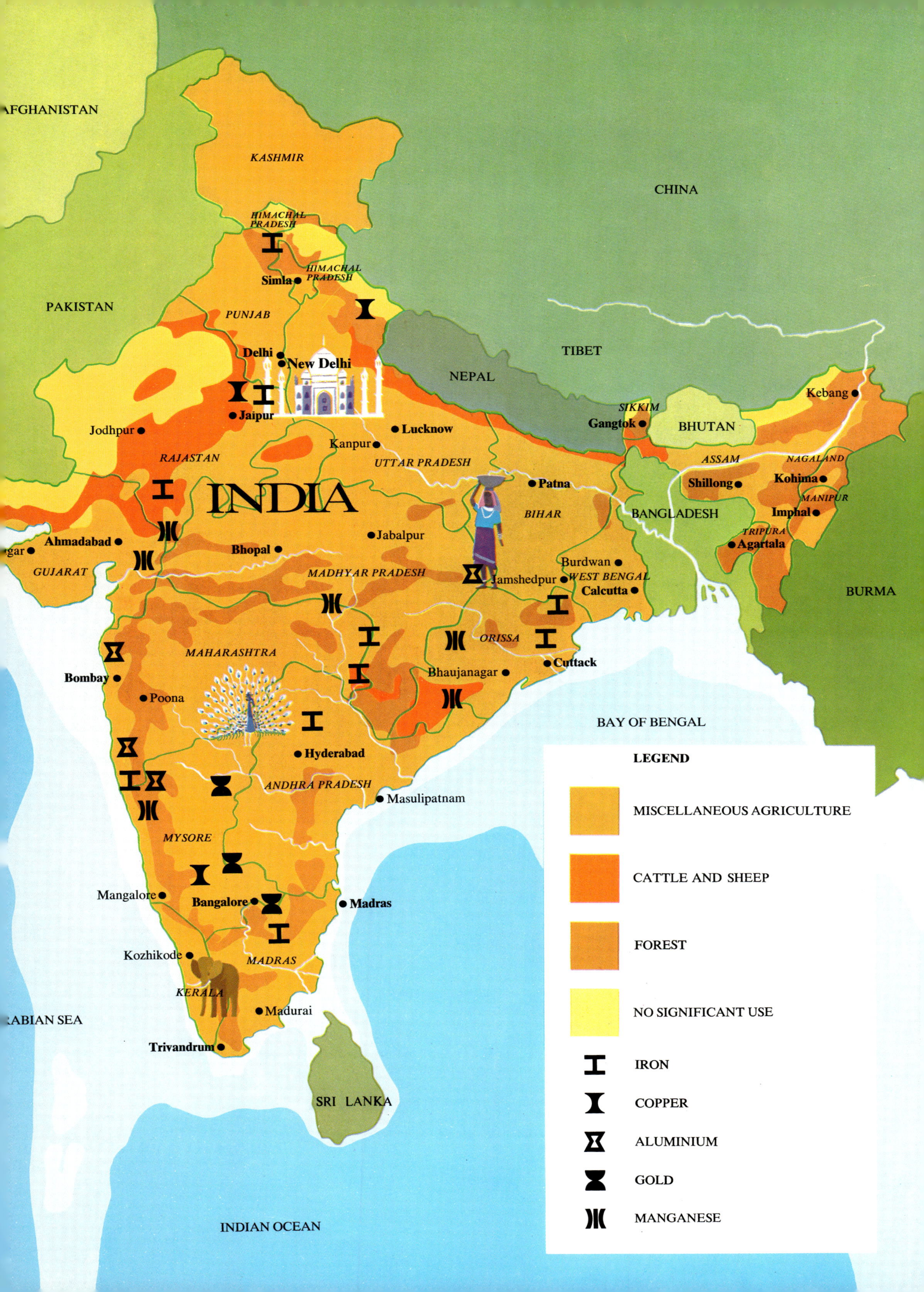

AFGHANISTAN
PAKISTAN
CHINA
TIBET
NEPAL
BHUTAN
BANGLADESH
BURMA
INDIA
KASHMIR
HIMACHAL PRADESH
PUNJAB
RAJASTAN
UTTAR PRADESH
BIHAR
SIKKIM
ASSAM
NAGALAND
MANIPUR
TRIPURA
WEST BENGAL
GUJARAT
MADHYAR PRADESH
ORISSA
MAHARASHTRA
ANDHRA PRADESH
MYSORE
MADRAS
KERALA
Simla
Delhi
New Delhi
Jaipur
Jodhpur
Lucknow
Kanpur
Patna
Gangtok
Kebang
Shillong
Kohima
Imphal
Agartala
Ahmadabad
Bhopal
Jabalpur
Jamshedpur
Burdwan
Calcutta
Cuttack
Bhaujanagar
Bombay
Poona
Hyderabad
Masulipatnam
Mangalore
Bangalore
Madras
Kozhikode
Madurai
Trivandrum
SRI LANKA
BAY OF BENGAL
ARABIAN SEA
INDIAN OCEAN
LEGEND
MISCELLANEOUS AGRICULTURE
CATTLE AND SHEEP
FOREST
NO SIGNIFICANT USE
IRON
COPPER
ALUMINIUM
GOLD
MANGANESE

Above: One of India's many animal celebration days, the Nandi Festival at Mysore.

Top right: Interior architecture of the Red Fort at New Delhi.

Below right: On the anniversary of Republic Day the main highways of Delhi are lined with thousands of celebrants.

The variety of people and their cultures is the legacy of India's long history, but the most significant period, the seed-time of the ideas and ideals which have left their imprint on the ways of living of the people, is shrouded in the mists of prehistoric ages.

Ancient Indians made remarkable contributions to almost all branches of human knowledge—the concept of the zero, for example, is India's gift to mathematics. A sense of history is not a notable Indian trait, but in place of history there is a mystifying collection of myths, legends and fairy tales from which the sedulous investigator can draw his own conclusions. Ancient Indian history is thus largely made up of conjectures based on the interpretation of artefacts left by ancient cultures discovered by archaeologists, and inferences based on conditions as they were known to exist in later times.

Up to half a century ago it was thought that Indian history began with the immigration of Aryan Tribes from Central Asia in the Second Millennium B.C., and that they brought with them the songs and myths, the basis of the Vedic religion which later developed into Hinduism or more precisely the Hindu way of life. But the spade of the archaeologist has pushed the frontiers of proto-history to the Fourth Millennium with the discovery of a highly-developed urban civilisation in the Indus Valley similar to the contemporary civilisations of Sumer and Egypt. Little is known about the people who created this civilisation, for their script has defied every effort to decipher it. Claims have been made for the Dravidian origin of the Indus Valley culture which is supposed to have been destroyed by the Aryan invaders. Its origin, extent and relation to the contemporary and succeeding cultures are still matters of controversy among scholars. Recent discoveries, however, have shown that the Harappan culture was not confined to the Indus Valley but extended to Gujarat in the South and Rajasthan to the East. Investigations might show that it was part of a common civilisation which extended over most of the sub-continent.

The excavations in the Indus Valley sites suggest that the civilisation came to a sudden, catastrophic end. Most scholars think that the Indus Valley cities were destroyed by the invading Aryan tribes who, in course of time, pushed deep into the Gangetic Valley and later further south and established an enduring pattern of civilisation inspired by a common system of religious ideas rooted in a common sacred language, Sanskrit.

This theory, as the origin of Hindu civilisation, is not universally accepted. It is totally rejected by Indians who prefer to acknowledge their ancient traditions. They point out that there is no hint in the most ancient myths or legends that their ancestors had come from outside the Indian sub-continent. Western scholars who have made deep analytical studies of the early Puranas which present historical information along with cosmological myths have arrived at the same conclusion. But this remains a minority view in schools where Oriental origins are studied.

Little can be said with certainty of the political history of the country during the ancient period except in terms of tracing the succession of ruling dynasties. Here the time scale extends over centuries and provides a few landmarks like the birth of Buddha (6th—5th Century B.C.), or the invasion of Alexander (4th Century B.C.) which can be dated with some degree of precision. It was during this period that the contours of Indian culture and the religious ideas which inspired it were evolved and established. In spite of the diversity of race and language, the Hindu population of India has a religious faith which gives them a remarkable cultural unity. It has been likened to the *banyan,* the fig tree of India, "which from a single stem sends out numerous branches destined to send roots to the ground to become trees themselves, till the parent stock is lost in a dense forest of its own offshoots; so has this pantheistic creed of the Vedic times rooted itself firmly in the Hindu mind and spread its ramifications so luxuriantly..."

HISTORY IN PERSPECTIVE

The comparison with the *banyan* is apt. For in spite of ramifications, the identity is not lost. The basic dogma, as formulated by its seers, is *"Ekam Sat, Vipra Bahudha Vadanti".* Though the followers of different sects worship different gods, these are identified with the Supreme Being of which they are regarded as manifestations. Even movements like Buddhism which arose as protests against prevalent religious practices were ultimately absorbed in the popular religion and the Buddha was included among the ten *avatars* (incarnations) of Vishnu. While Buddhism was thus absorbed and disappeared from the land of its birth, it transformed the character of Hinduism, both as popular religion and in its higher metaphysical reaches. The Buddhist period was also marked by the spreading of art and architecture and India owes its most ancient surviving examples to Buddhist piety which was emulated by other religious sects.

During this period there were a number of invasions from the West. The invaders were either ejected, or absorbed within the social framework of the system of castes which has survived to this day. This process of absorption continued until the advent of the Muslims, whose attempt to impose their faith by force set up its own reaction and blocked further efforts at integration.

Though Muslim inroads started early in the 8th Century when Mohammed Bin Kassim raided Sind, now part of Pakistan, in 712 A.D. and established his authority, the rest of the country remained unaffected and probably unaware of the new message. Towards the end of the 10th Century, Sultan Mahmud of Ghazni carried out a number of devastating raids with the object of plundering Hindu temples, and in so doing annexed a considerable portion of the Punjab. But the real beginning of the attempt of Muslims to conquer and establish their authority in India was the expedition of Mohammed Ghori in 1192. Within the next twenty years, his General Kutbuddin, the first Sultan of Delhi, subjugated the entire Indo-Gangetic plain from the Indus to the Bay of Bengal.

A number of Muslim dynasties ruled from Delhi during the period up to the 16th Century when Babar established the Mughal Empire. During this period Muslim power was extended to the Deccan and Hindu resistance became a major factor with the establishment of the Vijayanagar Empire in the south and the Rajput confederacy under the leadership of the Ranas of Mewar in the west. The iconoclastic fury of the early Muslim rulers ensured the destruction of the Hindu temples in northern India, so that it is only in the forests and mountains of central and eastern India and in the south—which, under the Vijayanagar Empire, enjoyed freedom from Muslim domination—that examples of Hindu religious architecture are to be found.

A succession of able rulers starting with Akbar consolidated the Mughal Empire and extended its frontiers by following a broadminded policy of encouraging Hindu culture. This policy was reversed by Aurangzeb. Though he was able to extend the Empire to the far south, he provoked movements of resistance among the Marathas and Rajputs with the result that the Empire began to disintegrate after his death. The Mughal emperors continued to exercise nominal sovereignty from Delhi till the middle of the 19th Century when the last Mughal Emperor was dethroned and exiled to Burma by the British.

The discovery of the sea route to India round the Cape of Good Hope by the Portuguese in 1498 brought India into direct contact with the maritime nations of Europe. The Portuguese were followed by the Dutch, the French and the British who established trading posts on the western and eastern coasts of the peninsula. With the collapse of the Mughal Empire and the breakdown of central authority, British and French trading companies took part in the struggles of the rival local rulers in order to preserve their trading interests. In the course of the struggle the British emerged on top.

With the defeat of the Marathas Confederacy in 1803, the British became supreme over the whole country except for the Punjab, which was annexed in 1848, and the whole of India came under British rule. This was soon followed by the first struggle to throw off the foreign yoke. It began as a mutiny of Indian troops in Meerut and soon engulfed the whole of northern India in 1857. The revolt was suppressed and the government of the country was taken over from the East India Company by the British Crown.

The half century which followed the assumption of power by Britain was a period of administrative unification marked by the establishment of a good system of roads and railways, post and telegraph services, a common currency and the beginnings of local self-government. This period also saw the stirrings of national consciousness and the desire among the educated middle-classes for a say in the governance of the country. They agitated for political reforms from the platform of the Indian National Congress which was established in 1885.

After World War I the spirit of nationalism which had begun to assert itself in the early decades of the 20th Century gathered momentum under the unique leadership of Mahatma Gandhi. His policy of non-violent resistance to foreign rule transformed what was formerly an agitation by the middle-classes for a share of power into a mass movement for freedom from exploitation. Mahatma Gandhi led three mass campaigns, the non-co-operation movement of 1920, the civil disobedience movement of 1930 and the Quit India Campaign during World War II. But the unity which characterised the movement in the early stages was disrupted by the separatist policies of the Muslims who, under Jinnah's leadership, put forth the demand for the partition of the country and on the eve of World War II, the establishment of a separate Muslim State. Various proposals for transfer of power to a united India were wrecked on the rock of deep-rooted mutual suspicion and antagonism between the Hindus and the Muslims. When the British finally and irrevocably decided to quit, they transferred power of government to two independent states, India on the one side and Pakistan on the other. This was brought into effect on 15th August 1947.

Despite the vicissitudes of four major wars, three of them with Pakistan, and many years during which the people suffered from very severe droughts, from national disasters and from poverty bordering on starvation, since then India has had an unbroken record of parliamentary democracy. Within three years of independence, India adopted a written constitution firmly founded on liberal principles. It embodied a set of inalienable fundamental rights and directive principles of State Policy that enjoined the State to promote a social order in which "justice—social, economic and political—shall inform all institutions of national life".

The first general election based on adult franchise under the new Constitution was held in 1951-52. Subsequently India has had four general elections, conducted by an autonomous Election Commission. Over 146 million men and women cast their votes in the elections held throughout India in March 1971.

THE GOVERNMENT OF INDIA

Under the Constitution of 26th January 1950 India, like Australia and the U.S.A., became a Union of States (and some "Union territories") with the legislative powers divided between the Union and the States but with the residuary powers vesting in the Union. As with all Federal Constitutions, there have been endless arguments about the precise degree of centralisation or dispersal of power in practice. Defence, foreign affairs, currency, railways and communications are among the exclusive responsibilities of the Centre. Education, irrigation, power, roads and agriculture are among the exclusive concerns of the States, involving however, some overlapping of responsibilities. Income tax is levied and collected by the Centre but is shared with the States on the basis of the recommendations of the five-yearly Finance Commissions provided for in the Constitution.

There is a Union Parliament of two Houses, the directly elected Lok Sabha and the indirectly elected Rajya Sabha. The Union Executive is headed nominally by the President, resembling the British sovereign rather than the American President in this respect. The actual power is vested in the Prime Minister and the Cabinet both responsible to Parliament. The State Executives and Legislatures substantially duplicate the central pattern. There is a Supreme Court, which is co-equal with the Parliament and the Executive, with binding powers of interpreting the law of the land as it deems fit. The Indian Constitution has worn well during the last twenty years, though it has had to be amended 27 times during that time. Indians are inveterate constitutional litigants, invoking the fundamental rights vigorously (and often successfully) against executive and parliamentary supererogation. A development of some significance during 1971 was the 24th amendment of the Constitution which has in effect nullified a ruling of the Supreme Court that placed the fundamental rights above even Parliamentary abridgment.

POPULATION PROBLEMS

The impact of economic progress, impressive as it is in absolute terms, has been largely neutralised by the growth of population which is India's biggest problem. Extensive public health measures have practically eradicated malaria and controlled killers like cholera, smallpox and tuberculosis. Improvement in public health has raised life expectancy at birth. It was as low as 27 thirty years ago and is 55 at present. The death rate has fallen from 27 to 17 per 1,000. The resultant growth of population is being tackled by a comprehensive family planning programme which aims to bring down the birth rate from 39 to 25 per thousand during the next ten or twelve years. The current annual rate of growth of population is about 2.5 per cent.

EDUCATION

Investment in human capital in the form of education is still below the nation's needs, though heroic in terms of the resources available. Educational facilities at all levels, including that of technical education, have been greatly expanded. The proportion of school-going children in the age group 6-11 is estimated at about 80 per cent. According to the latest census, literacy has improved since 1960 from 16.6 per cent to just under 30 per cent.

THE SOCIAL MILIEU

Under the impact of political and economic changes and social legislation Indian society is going through a period of transmutation. Historic distinctions still exist and the socially underprivileged Harijans—the lowest in the caste hierarchy—and the economically landless labour—often the two kinds of people are the same—still have to win the substance of a good life. The caste system however, is breaking down in social contexts, although political caste affiliations still play their part during elections to

Top left:
Indira Gandhi,
Prime Minister
of India, daughter
of Jawaharlal Nehru,
is following in the
footsteps of her famous
father in endeavouring to
bring peace and
prosperity
to India.

Below left:
Outside a temple a
Buddhist priest is
praying.

legislatures. Here too, with the increasing politicisation of the ordinary people, the last elections showed that the caste factor is becoming progressively less important.

At the micro-level, family and community life styles are changing. Because of the country's extreme diversity, it is difficult to generalise about a "typical" family in India. But two kinds of forces are at work towards the creation of an archetype—or rather two archetypes—of an Indian family: one is the basic religious unity that has held India together for centuries and has created a uniformity of beliefs and behaviour all over the country, despite linguistic and other differences. The other form of unity is that created by rapid urbanisation and industrialisation and a progressive assimilation to the ways of life in the industrialised west.

The first is particularly noticeable among the older generations and in the peculiar institution of the joint Hindu family that has grown up over the centuries. Though breaking down rapidly under the impact of the nuclear families of recent times, it still survives, particularly in rural India and aided by tax laws, among certain business castes. Each family has a *Karta*, like the Managing Director of an old-fashioned Corporation, who exerts his benign authority over the rest of the family. At its best, the Hindu joint family provided a system of mutual obligations and a much needed frame of social security at a time when the State was not providing it. Even more importantly, it supplied a frame in which emotional security was available to the very young and the very old and a medium for the pooling and deployment of all available skills of the family. At its worst, the joint family was a source of endless friction and heart-burn, especially among the women who were jealous of their own talents. Individual initiative and responsibility went unrewarded and were even suppressed, while parasitism was allowed to flourish sheltered by traditional family loyalties.

The kind of privacy and individual freedom prized by modern nuclear families was never available in the Hindu joint family system. But the Hindu joint family, with its less formalised analogues among the Christians and the Muslims, is on its way out under the pressure of an industrialised society. In cities like Bombay or Calcutta, factory workers clock in at eight a.m., leaving their homes early to commute in crowded buses and trains, and their life styles are not very different from those of the working classes elsewhere. The clerical staffs, at a slightly higher level of economic independence have a similar routine. Civil servants, company executives, professional men like lawyers, journalists and university dons in the bigger cities again have a pattern of life very little different from those of their confreres elsewhere. A foreigner meeting an educated Indian professional at his place of work need have no major reservations, though this may not be true of an encounter at his home. Except for a very small percentage of completely westernised Indians who still find themselves psychologically and spiritually uncomfortable in the company of their countrymen, most Indians manage to live with no great discomfort in two worlds. In this they resemble the Japanese.

Centre:
The peacock, graceful and
beautifully hued, has been
adopted as the national
bird of India.

Left:
An Indian bride,
a symbol of ethereal grace,
charm and beauty.

ENOUGH survives of past Indian artistic achievement to testify to its variety and to the creative exuberance of her artists. The whole range of ancient Hindu architecture, sculpture, painting, music, dance and literature manifests a highly developed philosophy of beauty and artistic enjoyment.

Architecture and Sculpture

There are few remaining examples of Indian architecture prior to the 4th Century B.C., presumably because most of it was of wood.

Stone became a medium about this period and there are some interesting specimens still to be found in the *stupa,* a hemi-spherical mound in which relics of the Buddha were placed. In course of time the stupa developed into an elaborate structure with circumambulating balustrades and finely-wrought gateways, such as the Sanchi Complex in Central India. Buddhist cave temples and rock-cut monasteries are exemplified in the famous group in Ajanta. Later cave temples—5-800 A.D.—were mostly Hindu, the best known being the Kailasa temple at Ellora.

Beginning as structures hewn from rocks, the temples of Southern India eventually developed into the soaring *gopuras*—gateway towers—with sculptured figures of all shapes and sizes, and the "thousand pillared" halls which surrounded the central shrine.

The Muslim contribution to Indian architecture was no less impressive. During the Mughal period of 16th to 18th Centuries, forts, tombs and mausoleums—such as the famous Taj Mahal at Agra, became the fashion. Indian architecture, like many other forms of Indian culture, travelled overseas. It inspired the arts of countries like Ceylon, Indonesia and Indo-China. The Buddhist stupa in Borobudur in Indonesia and the temples at Angkor in the Khmer Republic are outstanding examples. In sculpture Indian tradition spans the whole gamut, from 3rd Century Harappan terracotta and sandstone figurines and seal engravings, to modern examples of expressionistic work. The myriad gods and goddesses in Hindu mythology have been cast into beautiful shapes in metal, rock and wood. At Mahabilipuram near Madras, the surface of an entire rock has been turned into a magnificent bas-relief. Other examples include the richly sensuous carvings decorating the Khajaraho temples in Madhya Pradesh and the famous symbolic representation of the four handed god, Mataraja. Nearer the present, modern sculptors like D.P. Roy Chaudhury, Pradosh Das Gupta, Shankho Chaudhury and Dhan Raj Bhagat have experimented in a variety of styles and materials.

Painting

The earliest extant Indian paintings are those mainly depicting the life of Buddha, on the walls and ceilings of cave temples. The "Ajanta Beauty"—after the sinuous and langorous women in the famous frescoes on the Ajanta cave walls—has become the quintessence of feminine form in India's artistic tradition. With the Mughals came other inspirations like the Persian miniature paintings and in time these mingled harmoniously with native themes and styles. But the 19th Century saw the not altogether happy introduction of Western influences, with the heavy hand of Royal Academy art smothering native inspiration.

Since then, however, modern Indian painting has broken loose from the merely mimetic and representational and has acquired immense vitality producing an extraordinary range from the abstract and esoteric to the 'pop' and 'op' art of the 'seventies. Rabindranath Tagore, Jamini Roy and Amrita Shergil were three pioneering Indian moderns.

Dance

Ancient India developed a highly sophisticated aesthetics comprehending not only poetry and drama as in the Aristotlean canon, but also dance and music. The 3rd Century *Natya Shastra* postulates theories about the true nature of aesthetic enjoyment and also discusses the minutiae of the formal and structural aspects of dance. According

Left: Indian legend is perpetuated in late 18th Century paintings...Top left: The Sun Temple of Kanarak has many examples of Indian sculptors' genius... Above: A dancer performing for the Gods Rama, Vishnu and Shiva... Below: An image of the God Ganesha, symbol of good health and prosperity.

to Sanskrit aesthetics, the end of every artistic effort is to make the audience realise one or other of the nine *Basas*, 'emotional essences'—ranging from horror and disgust to compassion and beautific quietude. The gestures or *mudras* that are employed to express emotions or to represent various objects are the vocabulary, as it were, of the classical Indian dance. Though it has an ancient lineage, modern Indian dance forms have grown from local traditions of more recent origin, for example: the *Kathakali* or story-play in Kerala and the *Sadr* or *Bharata Natyam* in Tamil. These and various other forms are actively promoted and attract wide audiences both locally and, more recently, abroad, and many European and American enthusiasts are now striving to master the complex and intricate grammar of this exacting art.

Music

Of all the arts of India, music is probably the most baffling to non-Indians. The simple difference between Indian and Western classical music is that one is melodic and the other harmonic. Also, the Indian musician composes his music in the very act of singing or playing it. Classical texts refer to three aspects of music. The first, *Bhava*, refers to the associative emotions of particular melodic modes. The second, *Raga*, refers to the unique configuration of a specified number of notes—there are 22 notes and microtones within the Indian scale— that are permuted and combined in melodic phrases to the exclusion of any others. Thus, the skill and imagination with which the singer or instrumentalist produces endless mellifluous improvisations within the basic raga, determines his stature as a musician. *Tala*, the third ingredient of Indian music, is the rhythmic discipline provided by the percussionist, to which the set pieces have to submit themselves. Moreover, the percussionist's art has its own autonomous scholarship and modes of enjoyment. Anyone who has heard Palghat Mani Iyer on the *Mridangam* or Alla Rakha on the *Tabla* will agree the experience is an exciting one. The vitality of Indian music is testified to by the great influence it has recently had on Western jazz and pop, and by the vast audiences attracted by Indian classical musicians such as Ravi Shankar.

SPORTS AND GAMES

Organised sports in their many forms are very much a British legacy to India. This is evident in the widely played cricket, hockey and tennis. India cricket is experiencing a surge of popularity, following two victories in a row in test rubbers against the West Indies and England in 1971—by no means flashes in the pan—with world-class spinners in Prasanna, Venkataraghavan and Bedi and some sound batting strength in players like Gavaskar. Indians have always had men like Vinoo Mankad, who could hold their place in a world eleven, but their weakness has been found in a lack of balance as a team, resulting particularly from a dearth of really fast bowlers.

Hockey, in which India's supremacy was unchallenged for three decades following its first Olympic victory in 1928, has become, in more recent years, a Pakistani game par excellence. India lost to Pakistan in the Rome Olympics in 1960, again in Tokyo in 1964 and at the first World Cup tournament at Barcelona in 1971. In tennis, India has produced a wizard of artistry in Krishnan. Football has a passionate following in metropolitan cities, but in this game India is way behind world-class. In athletics and track events she has produced one or two world champions but the rest are not up to world standards. Thus with all the modern craze for speed and power, India still has a battle in front of her before reaching the top.

GROWTH OF INDUSTRY

The "Green Revolution" has created conditions for the rapid growth of industry, catering to the needs of agriculture and the transformation of the rural economy and the standard of living of the rural population.

The Community Development Agency and the co-operatives are playing leading roles in bringing about this transformation. The achievement of economic development with social justice implies the restructuring of economic and social relations. A comprehensive programme of land reform, designed to assure security of tenure to the actual cultivators, which was initiated in 1950 with the abolition of large landed estates, is now nearing the final stage with the fixation of ceilings on individual land holdings.

Indian industry has made rapid progress under planned development and has become more diversified and more broadly based. The production of steel (6.06 million tonnes of ingots in 1970-71) has increased more than four-fold since planning began.

Aluminium production was a bare 4,000 tonnes in 1951 and reached 160,000 tonnes in 1971. Installed capacity for generation of electricity has increased from 2.3 million kW to 16.5 million kW. Power generation is based on coal, water and nuclear energy.

One nuclear power station has been commissioned at Tarapore near Bombay, and two more are under construction at Rana Pratap Sagar in Rajasthan and Kalpakkam in Madras. They will generate an additional 1.2 million kW when commissioned.

The development of oil refineries which began ten years ago has made rapid strides and now aggregates a throughput of twenty million tonnes. Coal production has increased from 32.8 million tonnes in 1951 to over 70 million tons. Industrial production comprises automobiles, diesel engines, bicycles and scooters, railway rolling stock—including diesel and electric locomotives, machine tools, power transformers and various types of industrial machinery. A striking feature of the Indian scene today is the growth of small industrial units, mainly those with a capital investment in plant and machinery of less than Rs.750,000, of which there are more than 190,000 employing around 650,000 persons and accounting for Rs.40.6 billion. 'Cottage industries' employ around 20 million people.

THE ECONOMY

In 1951, soon after independence, India embarked on a programme of planned economic development when the First Five-Year Plan was inaugurated. Three Five-Year Plans were subsequently completed and in April 1969 the Fourth Plan was launched. The main objective of planning is to transform a traditional society of low level production and productivity into a modern industrial state so that the pitifully low living standards of the vast population may be raised in both quantitative and qualitative terms. The total investment in the first three plans was Rs.205,910 million. (At the current official rate of exchange, one Australian dollar is equivalent to about Rs.8.50). The Fourth Plan 1964-74, evisages a total outlay of Rs.248,820 million, and the achievement of an annual rate of growth of between 5 and 6 per cent.

As a result of planned development over two decades, the net national income at current prices has increased from Rs.95,300 million in 1951 to Rs.311,740 million in 1969-70. For about twenty years after achievement of independence, India was dependent on imports to meet deficits in the production of food grains. But with the adoption of a new agricultural strategy based on new high-yielding varieties and the application of heavy doses of fertilisers, the agricultural outlook has been transformed. India is now moving from an era of shortage to one of surplus in foodgrains. Consumption of nitrogenous fertilisers increased from 55,000 tons in 1951 to over 1.5 million tons in 1970-71. Over a hundred thousand tractors and 1.6 million electric pumps are changing the rural landscape.

In spite of these developments the problem of poverty is still very acute. It is recognised that planning for economic development has to be accompanied by measures for ensuring social justice, spreading employment and eradicating poverty, and providing the basic minimum needs of the masses of people. A sustained improvement in the quality of life of the common man is of the essence of development.

EXPORT MARKETS

The growth and diversification of Indian industries has had a massive impact on the pattern of its exports. Agricultural and mineral products, cotton and jute textiles and hides and skins were the major items of export until recently. India was and is still the world's largest exporter of tea and jute goods. In addition it exports sizeable quantities of manganese and mica and iron ore.

But this image of an exporter of essentially primary commodities has changed in the past ten years. The traditioned exports have not been totally displaced from their pre-eminent place in the marketing pattern but a wide range of new products, from ready-made garments to radio isotopes, have become part of India's exports. Reflecting India's growing industrial sophistication, a wide variety of engineering goods now rank third, next only to jute and tea. These include machine tools, railway wagons and equipment, refrigerators, telephone equipment, steel structurals, surgical goods, textile and sugar mill machinery, electric meters, cranes, power cables and heavy transmission cables.

Equally significant is the fact that Indian businessmen have set up, in co-operation with local entrepreneurs, over 100 industrial ventures, mainly in countries of the Afro-Asian world. Twenty-four of these joint ventures have gone into production in Ethiopia, Kenya, Libya, Mauritius, Nigeria, Ceylon, Iran and Malaysia. Even more interestingly, carrying coals to Newcastle, Indian technology is finding its way to the developed world, with Indian entrepreneurs setting up joint venture operations in Britain, Canada, West Germany and the United States of America.

Not only is the product pattern of Indian exports being diversified but their destinations are also spreading. At one time Britain was India's biggest trading partner. In the last ten years Indian trade with the Communist bloc in East Europe has grown remarkably, mainly by the mechanism of self-balancing bilateral trading reckoned in Indian rupees. This is evidenced by the fact that in 1971 the Soviet Union emerged as the largest single market for Indian goods.

This page and opposite page, top: India has developed a vast capacity for the manufacture of all types of consumer products thus reducing imports to a very low level. Chemicals and chemical products are in this category. The hands of the craftsman have created true beauty in the intricate, colourful patterns carved, woven and beaten into Indian objects of art.

Opposite page, left: Harvest time on a wheat farm in India.

275

THE BIRLAS OF BOMBAY

BOMBAY was a quaint "old world" town in 1862 when Seth Shivnarain Birla migrated from his family home in Rajasthan to set up a small trading house in Marwari Bazar. Today, 110 years later, Bombay is a thriving metropolis of 5 million inhabitants, and the House of Birlas has grown to be one of India's industrial giants. Its interests are almost without limit, extending as they do from textiles—cottons, woollens, linen, rayon and staple fibre—textile machinery, linoleum, cement, sugar and confectionary; sugar machinery; paper; electric motors and fans; bicycles; automobiles; ball bearings; non-ferrous metals; light engineering; fertilisers; radio; plastics and heavy chemicals—to running plantations and administering insurance and banking institutions now nationalised.

For 60 years the Birla Organisation has been carried on by Seth Shivnarain's grandchildren, the four brothers—Jugalkishore, Rameshwardas, Ghanshyamdas and Brijmohan, although for the last decade or so the senior members of the clan have gradually yielded place to a younger generation. The oldest surviving son, Rameshwardas, has relinquished many of his responsibilities and his main interest lies in the charitable activities of the Company. Ghanshyamdas Birla, however, at the age of 79, is still the Group's inspiration and moving spirit, and the pride of place in the Indian community held by the House of Birlas today is largely due to the energies and vision of "G.D." as he is popularly known.

Three years after the opening of his trading house Seth's first son Baldeodas was born, and to honour the occasion the name of the little business was changed to Shivnarain Baldeodas. Several new commodities were added to his short list of trading lines. In due course, the firm began to expand and when Baldeodas came of age he moved to Calcutta and opened a new branch which he called Baldeodas Jugalkishore, bringing in the name of his first son. By now he was dealing in cotton and oilseeds, trading in bullion and importing piecegoods.

Soon after the outbreak of World War I, Baldeodas realised one of his ambitions by extending into industry. He set up his first venture, a cotton spinning mill, in 1916, and a few years later the family firm was converted into a public company, Birla Brothers Ltd. At the age of twelve, another son, Ghanshyamdas, had joined the firm, and he soon proved that he had outstanding qualities as an industrialist. In 1919 the traditional Birla reliance upon general trading took a more positive step into the field of production. Ghanshyamdas assumed a leading position in Indian industry and politics. In 1927 he was elected the employers' delegate to the International Labour Organisation (ILO) conference in Geneva, and since that time he has led several important industrial delegations abroad.

Resenting British domination of India, throughout the 'thirties and 'forties G.D. became a noted figure in India's independence movement and a warm friendship grew between him and Mahatma Gandhi. As a member of the Round Table Conference, he spent much time in the United Kingdom while the Government of India Act was on the legislative drawing board. During these and later years he cultivated the friendship and enjoyed the confidence of numerous prominent politicians and statesmen, including Ramsay McDonald, Sir Winston Churchill, Harold Macmillan, U.S. Presidents Truman and Eisenhower, John Foster Dulles, Lord Mountbatten, Dr. Ludwig Erhard and many others.

Inspired by the adventurous spirit of "G.D.", the Birlas have extended their activities, carrying out diversification even in traditional industries and establishing a reputation for technological expertise, one of the most striking examples being the Century Spinning and Manufacturing Company. Incorporated in 1897, this company confined itself to the making of cotton textiles until Birlas took it over in 1951. Under its new management it expanded rapidly: traditional textiles grew in scope and variety and, parallel with this, the company diversified into the manufacture of rayon filament and tyre cord yarns; to these were added caustic soda, sulphuric acid and other chemicals.

Early in 1972 the Company prepared plans to set up a rayon grade wood-pulp project in Uttar Pradesh and a cement factory in Madhya Pradesh. It also has a scheme for the manufacture of seamless steel pipes. Finance for these projects, following the traditional pattern, will be mainly drawn from the Company's self-generated resources.

The Gwalior Rayon Silk Mfg. (Wvg.) Co. Ltd. is an example of the technical versatility of Birla industries. When India attained her independence from Britain in 1948, she lost vast and valuable cotton growing areas to the Pakistanis. To meet the consequent acute shortage Gwalior Rayon was established to manufacture a substitute for cotton from neglected but versatile forest woods.

Subsequently this new Birla unit developed a process—independent of any foreign technical guidance—by which rayon could be produced from indigenous bamboo. For this it received the Indian Chemical Manufacturers Association Award in 1965. Today its activities cover the production of rayon grade pulp, staple fibre and high quality fabrics. Furthermore, it has set up an engineering division where it fabricates its own machinery and equipment.

More than 55 million kilograms of staple fibre is produced every year for use by hundreds of textile mills throughout the land, and the yarn spun from it gives employment to thousands of power loom and hand loom weavers. Staple fibre production during the year ended 31st March 1970 amounted to 57,039 tons, equivalent in

Above:
A display of textiles woven at Jiyajeerao Cotton Mills against the enchanting backdrop of the old Gwalior fort.

Left page, left:
Workers carrying bauxite for the alumina plant of Hindustan Aluminium Corporation.

Left centre:
Gwalior Rayon's bamboo fibre is being used to an increasing degree as a substitute for scarce cotton in India's textile mills.

spinning value to more than 350,000 bales of cotton, a valuable contribution to counteract the country's continuing acute shortage of cotton. Since it began operations Gwalior Rayon has saved the country almost Rs. 2000 million in foreign exchange and boosted the excheqeur by Rs. 590 million. The Company plans to set up a new pulp and fibre complex at Harihar in Mysore State, which will produce initially 100 tons of staple fibre per day from its own pulp.

Another Birla enterprise, Jiyajeerao Cotton Mills Limited, carries the hallmark of G.D.'s spirit of adventure in business. In 1921, the then Maharaja of Gwalior, His Highness Madhavrao Scindia, requested that his friend, Mr Birla, establish a cotton mill to provide employment for his people and to mark the State's first step towards industrialisation. Gwalior was considered a most unsuitable place for a cotton mill.

It was 300 miles from the nearest cotton growing areas, subject to extreme climatic conditions and very dry both in summer and winter. Fearful of these natural handicaps, few outsiders subscribed to the Company's initial capital and G.D. and his friends provided most of the Rs. 3.5 million required.

Any doubts about the success of the vénture have since been proved groundless and for many years the few available shares in J.C. Mills have always been in keen demand. With its jubilee soon to be celebrated, in spite of natural handicaps the Company has made steady progress. The cotton mill has more than trebled its original capacity, and a chemical plant has been established in Saurahstra, on the west coast of Gujarat State, for the manufacture of caustic soda and soda ash.

The Birla units in its customary fields of textiles, jute and plantations have created steady demands both in India and abroad. Exports have not been restricted, however, to agricultural and textile products, for industrial and engineering goods, too, have carved a niche in many overseas markets. To further build up the image of India, Birlas have set up factories to produce a wide range of entirely different products, some of them never before made in India. In the consumer goods field, the Birla Group is pre-eminent: at Hyderabad, the Allwyn Metal Works produces refrigerators and office furniture; at Worli in Bombay, a Birla factory makes bicycles. Hindustan Motors, another Birla project to pioneer an important industry, has proved that Indian made and assembled cars can compete successfully with foreign imports. Starting as an assembly plant in 1945, Hindustan Motors now manufactures Bedford trucks, tankers and buses, and a popular family car, the Hindustan Ambassador.

Aluminium is another significant Birla interest. The Hindustan Aluminium Corporation plant for the making of Hindalco products has been built at Renukoot, at the foot of the Himalayas, only a few motoring hours from the hill resort of Darjeeling. A joint venture in partnership with Kaiser of America, Hindalco is a notable example of Indo-American business co-operation. Starting with a production of 20,000 tons in 1962, the Company has quadrupled its yearly output of aluminium to 80,000 tons when it will have attained the honour of being the largest aluminium plant in India.

It is now extending the factory to increase output by another 40,000 tons to its licenced capacity of 120,000 tons. Hindalco has its own alumina plant where it casts aluminium ingots and fabricated redraw rods, sheets, cords, angles and other end-products. It has also set up a 135 megawatt thermal power plant which last year generated more than 1,000 million units of power, compared with 630 million units in 1968. Plans are under way to install a third generator to meet the Company's anticipated requirements when further expansions become necessary.

Under construction are two important projects: a Rs.243.22 million, 40,000 tonnes alloy steel plant in the northern state of Bihar, named after it as Bihar Alloy Steels Ltd., and a Rs.560 million project, Zuari Agro Chemicals Ltd., a joint venture with United States Steel Corporation, for the manufacture of urea and compound fertilisers in Goa on the western coast.

Birlas have long upheld the noble tradition of Indian culture that private philanthropy should begin with public welfare. In a nation afflicted with mass poverty and illiteracy, education has always been the pinnacle of noble causes, and for this reason the House of Birlas has created a number of educational trusts and foundations.

Here again, Mr G.D. Birla has been the inspiration behind the Company's philanthropy. Institutions supported by the Birlas range from nursery schools and university arts centres, to scientific research and technology.

The Birla Education Trust has promoted the Rajasthan Academy of Sciences; it has liberally endowed the Central Electronics Engineering Research Institute at Pilani, an agricultural college in West Bengal, a planetarium at Calcutta; it conducts an engineering college at Anand, a college of textile technology at Bhiwani and a public school at Naini Tal; it has established hostels in Bombay and Madras.

But the hub of the Trust's activities is the Vidya Vihar (educational centre) in Pilani, the ancestral home of the Birlas, in Rajasthan. Here the educational structure has been raised from a number of primary and middle schools to a higher secondary school for girls, and a multi-purpose higher secondary school and public school for boys. Three colleges offer Engineering, Science, Commerce, Pharmacy and Arts as Courses. A large and well-housed Central Library is stocked with thousands of books, many of them specialising in Rajasthani literature, history and arts; a Central Museum is a focal point for visitors. Serving the welfare of the community are the Birla Hospital and the Dairy and Agricultural Farms.

The Birlas have contributed much to the development of India through the setting up of their numerous industries. Over the years they have devoted much time and energy to the establishment of schools, colleges, libraries and laboratories and, through their humanitarianism, they have helped many thousands of India's sons to accept their birthrights.

Left page, left:
A steel furnace at the foundry of Central India Machinery Manufacturing Company.

Left centre:
Testing tyre cord for tensile strength at Century's rayon division at Kalyan, 45 miles from Bombay.

Top: The fabrication shop of the Hindustan Aluminium Corporation Ltd. at Uttar Pradesh.

Above:
The late Mahatma Gandhi attending the inauguration of the Birla Temple in New Delhi.
Mr. G.D. Birla (centre) is pointing out a feature of special interest.

INDIA'S COTTON TEXTILES

IT IS A CHARACTERISTIC of many great nations that they leave their imprint on specific industries and crafts so that thoughts of one are immediately associated with thoughts of the other—silks with Japan, batik printing with Indonesia, wood carvings with the Philippines, tea with Ceylon and cotton textiles with India. Some are the result of geography, others have been developed because of the ready availability of materials—but all bear the individual stamp of a country's genius and a peculiar relationship to the people and their history.

The cotton cloth weavers of India have been known since the earliest days of recorded history. A fragment of madder-dyed cloth found in the Indus Valley excavation in northern India showed that weaving and dyeing were flourishing arts 5,000 years ago. They were skills that were to increase and diversify down the centuries, attracting wider and more lasting acclaim. The Roman historian, Pliny, bewailed the flight of Roman gold to India because of the Roman passion for Indian fabrics. St. Jerome's Latin translation of the Bible (4th Century A.D.) quotes the ancient Patriarch Job as saying that wisdom was more enduring than the dyed colours of India. Arab travellers in 9th Century India reported that "...they make garments of such extraordinary perfection that nowhere else is their likeness to be seen..."

Marco Polo observed that the art of embroidery, as practised in Gujarat in the 13th Century, was incomparable.

It was not only the technique of dyeing that made India's textiles famous. The fabrics were embellished with scintillating designs which India alone could offer. There were some of which every thread of warp and woof was dyed before being placed on the loom; a design appeared as the weaving progressed and was identical on either side. It was the craft of the individual artist who inherited his skill from his forbears and who gave his own aesthetic conception to the products he made with his own hands.

Then it all changed. The 19th Century brought with it the industrial revolution and the era of mass-produced goods, versatile and cheap but with the impersonality of the machine. Hand-woven products, rich and warm as they were, became costly luxuries. The Indian textile industry—unchallenged for nearly 30 centuries—had to adapt to the new age or perish.

A humble beginning was made in 1818 in Bengal with British patronage but the real foundation of the modern cotton mill industry was laid 36 years later in Bombay. On 2nd February 1854, the Bombay Spinning Mills started functioning with 20,000 spindles. It was the beginning of an era, not only in the sphere of textiles, but in the entire industrial world of India.

Thus the new foundations were firmly laid; there was no looking back and despite upheavals, booms, depressions and all the uncertainties that have marked the last 115 years the industry has gone further ahead, growing at the rate of an average of four mills a year over that period.

The pioneers of the Indian industry were men of purpose, vision, integrity and devotion who were able to graft modern industrial techniques on to the inherent genius of the Indian textile craftsman. In spite of the many challenges they faced—notably from the long established and vigorously promoted cotton textile industry of Lancashire—these men never wavered in their belief that the Indian industry could lead the world. Had they been alive today they would have seen their dreams abundantly fulfilled. The cotton textile industry is the cornerstone of India's industrial progress held in esteem for the superiority of its products the world over.

The use of modern techniques and equipment in the latest processes has made possible increased manufactures of finer fabrics in a variety of mercerised, bleached, dyed and pre-shrunk textiles. With the growing demand from overseas countries —bigger populations, sophisticated ideas— all possibilities are explored to include the widest range of finished fabrics—twills, drills, sateens...prints, drapery fabrics, osnaburgs and ducks...broad cloth, poplins, towelling—the whole range of materials right down to industrial garments.

Today textiles are the largest organised industry in India. It employs nearly 750,000 workers, has 17 million spindles and 207,000 looms. It produces the enormous quantity of 970 million kgs. of yarn and 4,200 million metres of cloth a year, and this not including the 3,600 million metres of cloth produced by the handloom and powerloom weavers. More significantly it is one of India's major sources of foreign exchange, being the third largest exporting industry and accounting for about 8 per cent of the total foreign exchange earnings of the Republic.

Indian textiles are exported all over the world. The traditional grey goods have gradually given way to meet the colourful demands of the modern sophisticate. In fact, the marked increase in the export of finished goods and garments is the most noteworthy and encouraging feature of the Indian cotton industry's emergence on the world's markets.

So a timeless industry continues, taking new shifts in direction but never changing, being as unmistakeably Indian as ever it was in its long history.

Opposite page: The trend of modern youth is towards vivid colours and the dyeing industry laboratories are producing rich hues for shirts and other wearing apparel made in the clothing factories of India.

Above: India's woven textiles are famous throughout the world. Delicate colours and distinctive patterns have been hallmarks of the Indian craftsmen for centuries past; the beautiful cotton materials shown above are typical examples.

THE STATE TRADING CORPORATION OF INDIA

INDUSTRIALLY and technologically India in the 1970's occupies a position between the developing and the developed nations. It is one of the top ten national markets in terms of gross national expenditure and with its sound infrastructure and expanding industries, India is a market with a strongly growing potential.

India has always been the home of the craftsman with rare traditional skills. Today, these skills are being applied to the manufacture of products ranging from complex communications equipment to cosmetics. Many international companies have set up plants in India to manufacture wide ranges of products with world marks and designs. Developed countries are finding it more profitable to import from India products that require considerable labour in mass production but at the same time that maintain top-level industrial techniques and precision. Indian products conform to international standards laid down by the highly reputable Indian Standards Institution, and pre-shipment inspection and testing agencies have been set up to ensure that quality specifications are observed.

The State Trading Corporation of India Ltd., was established in 1956 for the purpose of increasing Indian exports and organising the importation of essential items. Today it is the premier international trading house, with a turnover of over Rs.3,250 million. By 1969 the S.T.C. had opened branch offices in twelve countries and had appointed associates all over the world. In 1970-71 another nine branches were established, many of them pioneering new markets.

S.T.C. has a special relationship with all sectors of Indian industry. An autonomous organisation, run on modern commercial lines, it efficiently markets and services buyers and sellers in India and abroad. Thus, when an overseas buyer is offered a product, it has been selected from a survey of the complete Indian market, with strict observance of fair price, quality and assurance of delivery.

S.T.C. functions as a complete marketing organisation separated into marketing divisions, each dealing with a group of related products and staffed with men specialising in their respective field, backed by advisory and service sub-divisions.

To consolidate its rapid growth, the corporation carried out a major internal reorganisation in late 1971 creating many new and compact marketing divisions capable of further expansion.

CONSUMER GOODS EXPORTS. This newly formed division is involved in pioneering the export of non-traditional consumer items ranging over combs, cufflinks, cosmetics, cigars, paint brushes, batteries, electric bulbs, gramophone records, plastic products etc. Apart from products diversification, the division is also spreading out geographically into Hungary with cigars, Australia with ready-made garments and chippendale furniture, and the U.K., France and Austria with rayon tyre cord. The division aspires to become the "department store" of S.T.C.

DEVELOPMENT EXPORTS. This again is a newly formed division and acts as a reconnaissance and pioneering group to take over entirely new products through the stages of gestation and birth, till they have acquired enough strength to be handed over to one of the 'bread and butter' export divisions. Sports goods, processed foods, fresh meat, vegetables, fruits and flowers, timber, drugs and pharmaceuticals are some of the products covered by this division. Army software forms a separate and special department. South-east Asia, Africa and the Middle East which are India's natural neighbouring markets will be the main regions receiving special attention.

THE ENGINEERING DIVISION. Until 3 years ago S.T.C. operated in a small way in this field, its activity consisting mainly of importing a few engineering items from East Europe. It has expanded its engineering exports considerably since then.

This Division arranges the setting up of collaboration ventures and undertakes turnkey projects. Indian entrepreneurs have now established joint ventures in Ghana, Nigeria, Saudi Arabia, Iran, Ceylon, Nepal, Malaysia, Northern Ireland, Canada, Colombia, Great Britain and other countries. These projects cover a wide range of industries, such as engineering goods, textile machinery, sugar plants, pipes, trailers, electric motors, transformers, hose pipes, sewing machines, bicycles and steel furniture, etc. There are now over 40 such ventures operating abroad, some of their products including: earthmoving equipment, aluminium and steel furniture; pumps; valves; surgical instruments and refrigerators.

RAILWAY EQUIPMENT DIVISION. The Indian rolling stock and railway equipment industry is amongst the largest in the world. Diesel and electric locomotives, freight and passenger cars, signalling and tele-communication equipment, and track material are some of the principal items available for export. The industry is backed by the Indian Railways which is the second largest railway system under one management in the world. It works closely with the Indian Railways' Research, Design and Development Organisation. Contracts for export of rolling stock have been completed or signed with many countries including Hungary, Poland, Sudan, Nigeria, Iran, Ceylon, Burma, Thailand, Taiwan and South Korea. In addition to export of rolling stock, the Railway Equipment Division also undertakes the setting up of railway systems from the initial surveying and assessment work to equipping and final operation.

Left Page:
Interior of a factory building diesel and electric locomotives and passenger and freight cars; one of India's major industries.

Left:
Bicycles, one of the most popular means of transport in India, have developed into an important item of manufacture.

Below:
India's chemical industry plays a pivotal role in the industrial progress of the Republic.

INDUSTRIAL PRODUCTS EXPORTS. This division specialises in the export of bulk industrial products such as cement, salt, molasses, alcohol and benzene which have problems of their own in relation to collection, transport and shipping. It also handles lighter industrial products such as detergents and chemicals.

LEATHERWARE EXPORTS. This is a wholly export-orientated division which consistently develops new markets and introduces new products. It has made a notable advance in the export of leather, leather goods, canvas and a range of plastic footwear.

In addition to its principal activity of exporting shoes to Russia, and cowboy boot uppers and soles to the U.S.A., prospects for obtaining orders for canvas sports shoes, suede, hunting calf leather, wet blues and school shoe leathers and leather sandals are also under investigation from Australian companies.

The human hair export from India which had declined due to stiff competition from China and synthetic hair, is now being gradually revived. The division undertakes service within India to smaller producers in terms of quality control, finance, the acquisition of raw materials, technical assistance or advice and the establishment of appropriate local and overseas markets for their products.

PRODUCE EXPORTS. This division specialises in exports of all traditional and primary products like rice, coffee, opium for medical purposes, castor oil, jute, tobacco and spices. It also expects to act as the safety valve to the agricultural sectors by exporting their surpluses. The division has made significant progress in the export of Indian coffee to France, Switzerland and Yugoslavia as well as to Singapore in the Asian region.

On the import side, the Corporation has been re-organised into divisions for the import of chemicals, drugs and pharmaceuticals, industrial products, oils and fats.

The Industrial Raw Material Assistance Centre which was set up as a service agency about two years ago helps in bulking the requirements of small customers and buying in anticipation of exporters requirements. This centre has been responsible for the development of 31 various items for 30 industrial fields.

The Projects & Equipment Corporation of India Ltd., The Cashew Corporation of India Ltd., The Handicraft Corporation of India Ltd., and the Indian Motion Pictures Corporation of India Ltd., function as subsidiaries of the S.T.C. of India which is the holding company. These companies together constitute the State Trading Corporation of India Group.

INDIA'S WOVEN MIRACLES

FOR MANY CENTURIES, India has been a world leader in the making of cloth: camel caravans once carried fine Indian cottons and riotously-coloured, hand-embroidered and dyed fabrics to far distant countries to the north and west. Today handweavers still make fine silk, cotton and wool materials. But, as elsewhere, the industrial revolution began with machine-made textiles and now, with greater production, fast container ships will carry this much sought cargo to all parts of the world. The largest single exporter of woven materials is Bombay Dyeing and Manufacturing Company whose fabrics and materials are shipped as far afield as Australia and New Zealand, the United States, Europe and the United Kingdom. Their rich colourings and fine textures have become proverbial. During the early years of England's trading with India, the English encouraged the expansion of the Indian textile industry, in order to provide cloth to trade in other parts of Asia for England's needs. Under European management and the use of new production techniques, this scheme proved very successful and soon a booming business in cotton cloth developed. The innovation of bulk trade changed clothing habits in England. Cheap calico, muslin and chintz provided a wider, finer and more versatile range of clothing for the ordinary people than they had ever been able to afford.

In the 1860's many textile mills grew up around Bombay. Today they represent India's largest single industry, employing almost a million workers, and cloth is carrying on its tradition as one of the country's leading exports.

Bombay is still the centre of India's weaving industry and Bombay Dyeing is among the oldest, largest and most efficient of her textile units, producing a wide range of cloth and yarn and manufacturing finished fabrics into shirts and pyjamas and other ready-made articles of clothing.

In order to maintain a growth increase of about 20 per cent each year, Bombay Dyeing has completely modernised its plant and production processes. One of its mills is among the biggest "under-one-roof" textile units in the world and is the most extensive, fully-integrated, self-sufficient plant of its kind in India. Scientific management has ensured continuous maximum efficiency in the running of the mills, with such up-to-date facilities as air-conditioned quality control and standards departments, an ultra-modern laboratory, a miniature spinning plant to continually check the quality of cotton, a training school for staff and supervisory personnel and a fully equipped machine workshop which keeps the vast complex of machinery and equipment humming.

In pace with the progressive introduction of a wide range of finishing machinery and the latest technical innovations, a special design section creates new vogues in woven and printed fabrics to cater to the more fastidious element among the fashion and quality-conscious, buying public.

The production spectrum embraces a wide range of products, at one end household lines such as bed linen, towels and table-linen, furnishings in a permaglaze finish, and jacquard tapestries in a variety of weaves, designs and colours; at the other end there are fabrics for the family, from lightweight, synthetic-blend suitings and shirtings and casual-wear gaberdines, tussores and drills for men, to fine and superfine fabrics for the rest of the family.

From the mills also come fabrics for a wide range of industrial applications: calicos for cable installations, canvas for shoe-making, water-proof cloth, parachute cloth and drills, satins, light canvas ducks for numerous requirements in industry.

With the fast changing face of South-east Asia, the next two decades will be a critical period in India's industrial growth. Companies like Bombay Dyeing will provide the answers to many of the country's present problems. The lone weaver sitting at his loom, his feet drawing patterns in the dust, is no longer the colourful but primitive image of India. His place has been taken by mechanical giants performing their tasks in a fraction of the time and in vastly greater volume. And India has learned that to maintain her status among the greater nations of the world she must build up her exports and the products for which she has become justly famous must retain their high quality and so withstand competition on the leading international markets.

Pictures on these pages
illustrate some of the fine textiles
manufactured by the Bombay Dyeing
and Manufacturing Company:
materials for modern frocks;
curtain materials; bed spreads
and woven floor coverings.

MINING AND MINERALS

THE HISTORY of modern India tells of a nation attempting to do the "impossible": to enter into non-traditional spheres of industry and to compete successfully in the markets of the world. A notable example of achievement in this enterprise is found in the mining and processing of metals and minerals.

Within a few years of the founding of the State Trading Corporation of India, its activities in exporting and importing showed remarkable growth. Paralleling its developments, India's minerals and metals industries also reached peaks of production undreamed of a decade before. So efficient had the mining and processing operations become that certain ores and allied semi-manufactures were fast establishing themselves as top foreign exchange earners—iron ore, iron and steel, coal and coke and non-metallic minerals were some of the most significant.

The Government of India recognised the need to give greater attention to finding export channels for these products. And thus, in April 1963, it was decided to bifurcate the State Trading Corporation to establish a second body, to be called the Minerals and Metals Trading Corporation of India, Ltd. The new Corporation started functioning as a registered company from October 1963 and all work relating to minerals and metals, together with relevant assets and liabilities, were transferred from the parent body to the new organisation.

The fully Government-owned M.M.T.C. has two main aims:-

(I) To organise and undertake exports of minerals ores and concentrates.

Left:
Mining in India, and iron mining in particular, is a vigorous industry today. More than two million tons of ore are produced annually from the Kiriburu mine at Orissa, for export to Japan.

Left: In the development of transport India has taken big strides. Its railway system, covering more than 60,000 kilometres and annually carrying 2,200 million passengers, is one of the biggest in the world. The country now makes its own automobiles, locomotives, electric and diesel trains, ships and some aeroplanes. It has an extensive network of internal and external air services. It supplies wagons and railway equipment to other countries.

(II) To organise and undertake imports of metals including iron and steel and their alloys, semi-manufactures, and industrial raw materials required in processing iron and steel for industrial and domestic uses.

Although India's mineral resources were late developed, (partially because of the 19th Century colonial administration's frustrating laws in this sphere) modern methods and positive State incentives have led to current boom conditions. Encouraged by new long-term export contracts, iron mining is today a particularly vigorous enterprise. For example: the Kiriburu mine in Orissa now produces 2 million tons of ore for export each year to Japan under a long-term agreement which has enabled plans to be formulated for the expansion of the mine's capacity to 5 million tons. The responsibility for the export of the nation's iron ore rests solely with the Minerals and Metals Trading Corporation, with the one exception of the part played by the mine owner/shippers of Goa. During 1970-71, the Corporation exported 20 million tons of iron ore out of a total production of approximately 30 million tons.

Other minerals exported through the Corporation include coal, manganese ore, and ferro-manganese. Total minerals exports during 1971-72 were valued at Rs. 870 million. Important items of import comprise copper, zinc, lead, aluminium and some varieties of iron and steel. The total imports of the Corporation exceeded Rs. 1,800 million during 1971-72 compared with an amount of Rs. 1,450 million the year before. The total trade turnover in 1970-71 was valued at Rs. 2,510 million and is expected to reach Rs. 2,680 million in 1971-72.

COMMUNICATIONS

The growth of industry has been supported by corresponding development of railways, roads, shipping and telecommunications. The Indian railways now run more than 10,000 trains every day. They carry 6.6 million passengers and haul a daily average of 600,000 tons of goods. The network of surfaced roads has been doubled over the past twenty years. It extends over 326,000 kilometres through the length and breadth of the country. Indian shipping has made rapid progress since independence. Starting from zero the Indian mercantile marine now has a tonnage of nearly 2.5 million with another 1.15 million GRT on order. The Hindustan shipyard at Vishakapatnam has a capacity to build four ships a year. A new shipyard is being set up at Cochin.

All important Indian cities are connected by a network of air services operated by the state-owned Indian Airlines with a fleet of modern aircraft including Boeing 737's, Caravelles, Viscounts and Fokkers, besides India's own HS 748's. International services are operated by Air India, which flies to 24 countries with its fleet of Jumbo Jets and Boeing 707's.

Next to Railways, the Postal Services are India's largest nationalised undertaking. There are over 109,000 post offices, 90 per cent of them in rural areas, 99,000 having savings bank facilities. The overseas communications system links India with almost all countries in the world through telegraph, radio, telephone, teleprinter and international telex systems. A satellite communication earth station set up near Poona at a cost of over Rs. 80 million, has become commercially operational since February 1971. The telephone traffic has already increased by more than 100 per cent and about 90 per cent of international calls are now handled over the satellite system. A second station in the northern region is being built.

Broadcasting in India is a State monopoly. The number of radio receivers in 1966 increased from 6.4 million to over 11 million by the end of 1970. All India Radio will have 108 broadcasting centres with 6 auxiliary stations at the end of the Fourth Plan when 89 per cent of the population will be served by medium wave transmission. The 'Transistor Revolution' has thus caught up with India, but at one set per 50 persons this is a pitifully small use of a potentially powerful agent for the dissemination of news and current happenings.

Television is still a virtually untried medium. There is one station in Delhi. Two more will become operational in 1972, one in Srinagar in Kashmir and the other in Bombay. Before March 1974 Calcutta, Kanpur and Madras will also have T.V.

TATA'S REALM

LATE IN THE 19th CENTURY, Jamsetji Tata, the founder of Tata Enterprises, became convinced that India's political freedom would be meaningless without its economic and industrial emancipation. He felt that the making of steel, the generation of electricity and industrial research were the three pillars on which to erect an industrial base for modern India. As a consequence of that conviction, Tata activity in the formative years was confined to pioneering in the basic or heavy industries. Tata planners and managers thus deliberately avoided entering the area of small-scale and consumer goods industries despite the attraction of higher and more rapid profits. Thus came into being India's first integrated iron and steel works, electric power generation, cotton textile factories, cement works, general and life insurance and industrial investment; subsequently Tatas entered the fields of heavy engineering, locomotive construction, trucks and commercial vehicles, earth-moving and materials-handling equipment, heavy chemicals, agricultural inputs, and pesticides, detergents, soaps and edible oils, industrial perfumes, cosmetics, refrigeration and air-conditioning, radios and electronic equipment, and fisheries and processed foods.

In recent years, Tatas have extended their activities into a broad range of consultancy services, including consultancy in engineering and personnel and a computerised service which provides the most advanced techniques as an aid to modern management.

The Tata Companies, however, pride themselves on their deep sense of social responsibility rather than their size and spread into so many fields of endeavour.

Among the Tata manufacturing units is one which was the first in India to have introduced retirement benefits and which drew up rules for payment of accident compensation as far back as 1877, more than 50 years before it was converted into legislation. Tata workers are among the best paid, the best provided and best equipped in Indian industry.

More than 80 per cent of the capital of the founding company of Tata Sons is held by philanthropic trusts endowed by Jamsetji Tata and his two sons, Sir Dorab and Sir Ratan Tata. The grants from the various Tata foundations have established a number of India's public institutions of a pioneering character in the fields of medicine, science, technology, fundamental research in physics and nuclear science, social sciences, rural welfare projects and the performing arts.

The annual output of the various Tata Companies in 1970-71 was almost Rs. 5,825 million (US$777 million). Between them they employed 145,000 people and contributed to the National Exchequer in annual tax payments a sum of Rs. 635 million (US$85 million).

Below:
A shrine outside
a Buddhist temple at Bodh Gaya,
a source of inspiration
to followers of the Buddha
to strive for perfection in
all their endeavours.

WHAT OF INDIA'S FUTURE?

That the Indian society is undergoing profound changes is obvious even to the most superficial observer. The simplest way to describe it is "modernisation". In many ways it is inimical to the modern ideals of equality and freedom and of material rewards won by individual initiative. It is weighted heavily in favour of stability rather than mobility, of acceptance rather than protest. It is being changed by every legislative, political and economic means available to a more or less committed elite schooled in modern ideas.

In the process of changing, the old and the new co-exist in the most bewildering medley. As a perceptive observer once put it, "Indians don't live in space but in time". The traveller in India does not go from one place to another, but from one century to another. Delhi and Bombay can offer practically everything that can be found in New York and London—including protesting hippies. But within miles of Delhi there is a different world. Those who are forever looking for the bizarre will find it in plenty. In India the contrasts can be overwhelming. For example, it is common to see a bullock cart, or one pulled by a human, carrying modern equipment for, say, an atomic power plant.

In their pessimistic moods, Indians are prone to be destructively self-critical. But in their more hopeful moments, they like to quote Milton's apocalyptic vision in Aeropagitica:

"Methinks I see in my mind a noble and puissant nation rousing itself like a strong man after sleep, and shaking his invincible locks. Methinks I see her as an eagle mewing her mightly youth, and kindling her undazzled eye at the full midday beam."

INTERNATIONAL CO-OPERATION

In the international financial and economic contexts, Indian involvement flows primarily from its being a developing nation. Individually and collectively, through forums like ECAFE and UNCTAD, India has attempted to obtain redressal of historic disabilities in international trade. It has been particularly active in seeking to secure a stable market for primary commodities and an expanding one for the simpler manufactures of the poorer countries. India has played its part in securing for the developing world concessions like the generalised scheme of preferences for the manufactures of the poorer nations in the markets of the rich. The pattern for this scheme of non-reciprocal tariff concessions for the products of developing countries was set by the Indo-Australian Agreement in July 1966. India has also played its part in regional co-operation in Asia, working for freer flow of goods within the region and for the establishment of an Asian Payments Union. India is a member of the Asian Development Bank and is the biggest Asian contributor to its capital after Japan and, by a self-denying ordinance, has not been seeking assistance from it for its own development. After twenty years of conscious industrialisation, India is at the interesting stage—which has its awkward aspects—of being at once in need of technology and skills from abroad and in a position to lend them to others. In recent years, India has been as much a donor as a receiver of aid, particularly in the exchange of skills and technical expertise.

Right:
Facade of
Hawa Mahal, the
Palace of the Winds,
which once was the residence
of the Jaipur rulers.

IN RECENT years, India has been making vigorous efforts to ride the flood of world tourism, the now thriving industry of the 'seventies. It expects an estimated turnover of 30 billion dollars by 1975. India is well-endowed in tourist attractions with places of great scenic beauty like the Kashmir valley, and historical and artistic monuments of great interest. The potentialities of its long coastline beaches and other spots of interest to the conventional or off-beat holiday-maker are still to be fully exploited. In 1970, 280,000 tourists came to India, and these figures are expected to grow to 400,000 by 1973. This is by no means a sensational share of the 260 million international tourists that the International Union of Official Travel Organisations (IUOTO) envisages by 1980. Although there is a current shortage of hotels and other amenities of the standard expected by modern tourists, particularly those seeking 'a home from home', there are several "Five Star" hotels in the major cities and many more of a less prestigious kind. The Indian Tourist Development Corporation, a State owned Agency which has six hotels including Ashoka in Delhi is planning expansion. The Hilton and the Inter-Continental are already in business, and Air-India proposes entering the hotel business in a big way.

Above:
Dances in India are
inherited from ages past,
and range from classical forms
to traditional rural
romps.

INDIA—MADE FOR THE TOURIST

Left:
The Lake Palace of Udaipur, a city of lakes and many palaces in Rajasthan, south-west of Delhi.

Below:
North of India is Kashmir, its natural beauty enhanced by snow-capped mountains and picturesque lakes, such as Dal Lake in Srinagar, the capital of the State.

Kingdom of SIKKIM

SIKKIM is the smallest of the Himalayan mountain-kingdoms, with an area of only 2,828 square miles and a population of around 200,000. Its capital is Gangtok. The encircling wall of peaks to the north and east of Sikkim forms its frontiers with Tibet; in the south and west, the mountains divide the small nation from Nepal; to the south-east, the watershed of the Dichu River creates a natural boundary between Sikkim and Bhutan. Its climate is semi-tropical, temperatures varying from a mean of about 40°F in January to about 62°F in July. In the higher altitudes of the Kingdom temperatures are considerably lower. Rainfall is heavy, averaging over 110 inches, most of which falls during the summer monsoon, June to September. Nepalese comprise 72 per cent of the population, the remainder being fairly equally divided among the original inhabitants of the Kingdom—believed to have migrated from the direction of Burma and Assam—the Lepchas, and a people of Tibetan origin, the Bhutias. Small communities of Tsongs—Tibetans from the Tsang-Po Valley—and Indian traders also live in the country. The state religion of Sikkim is Mahayana Buddhism, but a large proportion of the people, being Nepalese, are Hindus.

There has been little study of the geography or history of Sikkim. Information available has not yet been systematized, though Indian economists and scientists are at last making a thorough survey of the Kingdom's wealth. Sikkim's pre-16th Century history is almost unknown, and the little that is known is difficult to separate from legend. Between the 16th and the 19th Centuries the story is one of internal dissension and external conflict. Sikkim came into being as a political entity in 1641 and was ruled by the first consecrated Gyalpo, or King, Phuntsog Namgyal. It was at that time a much larger and more powerful nation than it is today. Its borders extended well into Tibet, Nepal and Bhutan, and to the frontiers of Bihar and Bengal in India. Between the 16th and 19th Centuries, however, family feuds and rivalry for the throne opened up the country to invasion. In successive wars with each of its border nations, it lost much of its power and territory. In 1817, in order to secure its trade routes into China, the East India Company negotiated an alliance with Sikkim which guaranteed British merchants protection and freedom from taxation, in return for which the country was offered British support against its hostile neighbours.

In 1861, following a series of incidents which underlined Sikkim's resentment of the British interlopers, a new, harsher treaty was drawn up which annexed from Sikkim the trade and tourist centre of Darjeeling and gave Britain greater power to intervene in the Kingdom's domestic as well as foreign affairs. After India achieved independence, its Government pursued the same policy, signing a treaty which assumed Indian responsibility for Sikkim's foreign affairs, defence and strategic communications. The present King is His Highness Major-General Palden Thondup Namgyal, who succeeded his father in December 1963. Although the final authority still resides in the King, Sikkim's internal affairs are today in the hands of two main law-making councils and an administrative body, the Secretariat.

Sikkim's wealth is principally derived from agriculture and forests. Rice and maize are the main crops, supported by subsidiary harvests of millet, buckwheat, barley and vegetables. Cardamon is the principal export crop. The cultivation of potatoes is a new and growing industry. Tea, seed-paddy, mustard, citrus fruits, apples and pineapples are also grown. Food processing industries, primarily fruit canneries, are valuable secondary industries.

Bamboo and sal grow in the south; conifers are profuse in the north but lack of transport has prevented their exploitation. Copper, lead and zinc are found in various localities. Copper, the most plentiful, is mined by companies jointly financed by the Sikkimese and Indian Governments.

Sino-Indian border disputes, together with Chinese claims to Sikkim, have led India to regard the Kingdom as an important wedge in her northern defence-perimeter. Realising, however, that military preparedness was not a complete answer to her northern security, India has spent vast amounts on developing the economy of the Kingdom. Roads, hydro-electric schemes, hospitals and schools have been built with Indian aid. Basic surveys and feasibility studies on the setting up of locally-based industries are under way. Model farms and nurseries have also been established throughout the country.

With its varied climate and topography, Sikkim has a richness of flower-life and vegetation that is unique. Forests of rhododendrons cover entire mountain sides and several hundred different types of orchids bloom in its rural areas. Alpine flowers form a colourful carpet over the higher valleys and passes. Sikkim's geography has also influenced the growth of its culture, which has absorbed the diverse ideas and symbols of India, Tibet and China. These three sources are reflected in the religious art and architecture of the country. Within its temples, carved demons and imps grin and snarl. Contrary themes of ferocity and gentleness are portrayed in its sacred statuary: on most altars, Guru Rimpoche is seated to the right of the impassive Buddha, a thunderbolt in one hand, a human skull-cup filled with blood in the other; on the left, Chenresig, Lord of Mercy and patron saint of Lamaism, looks on, one pair of hands joined in devotion, the upper right holding a crystal rosary and the left, a lotus flower. While many diverse peoples enrich Sikkim's cultural fabric, her geographic position at the junction of two great civilizations, China and India, has forced her to seek security through quick economic development. This has brought with it a two-fold problem: firstly, the Kingdom must maintain foreign investment in a political climate of some uncertainty and, secondly, in obtaining aid from India, it must not jeopardise its remaining autonomy and neutrality, which, after economic security, is its best defence.

Despite these considerations, its economic development programme has succeeded—at least to some extent. Because of Indian aid, and the Kingdom's lack of population pressures, its per capita income is now higher than in most parts of India. Between 1960 and 1967, the revenue-earning capacity of the State trebled. Sikkim enjoys the unique Asian distinction of having no problems due to the unemployment of her people; no beggars are found roaming the streets.

Top left:
A man of Sikkim
holding a prayer wheel, rosary beads
and musical instrument.

Above:
A typical Sikkimese girl
dressed in warm clothing
for the cold winter months
in the higher altitudes.

Left:
Dwellings in Sikkim.
Prominent on the right are
grotesque masks carved from native
stone, outside a temple.

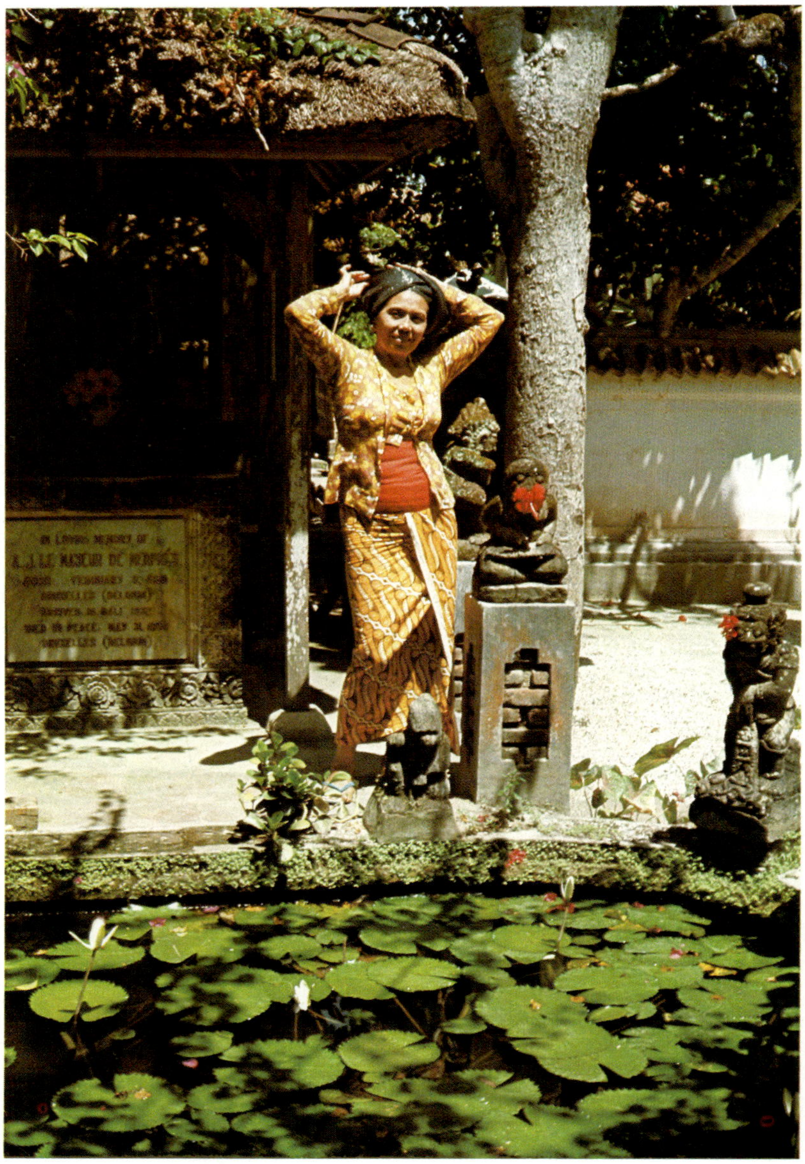

Republic of
INDONESIA

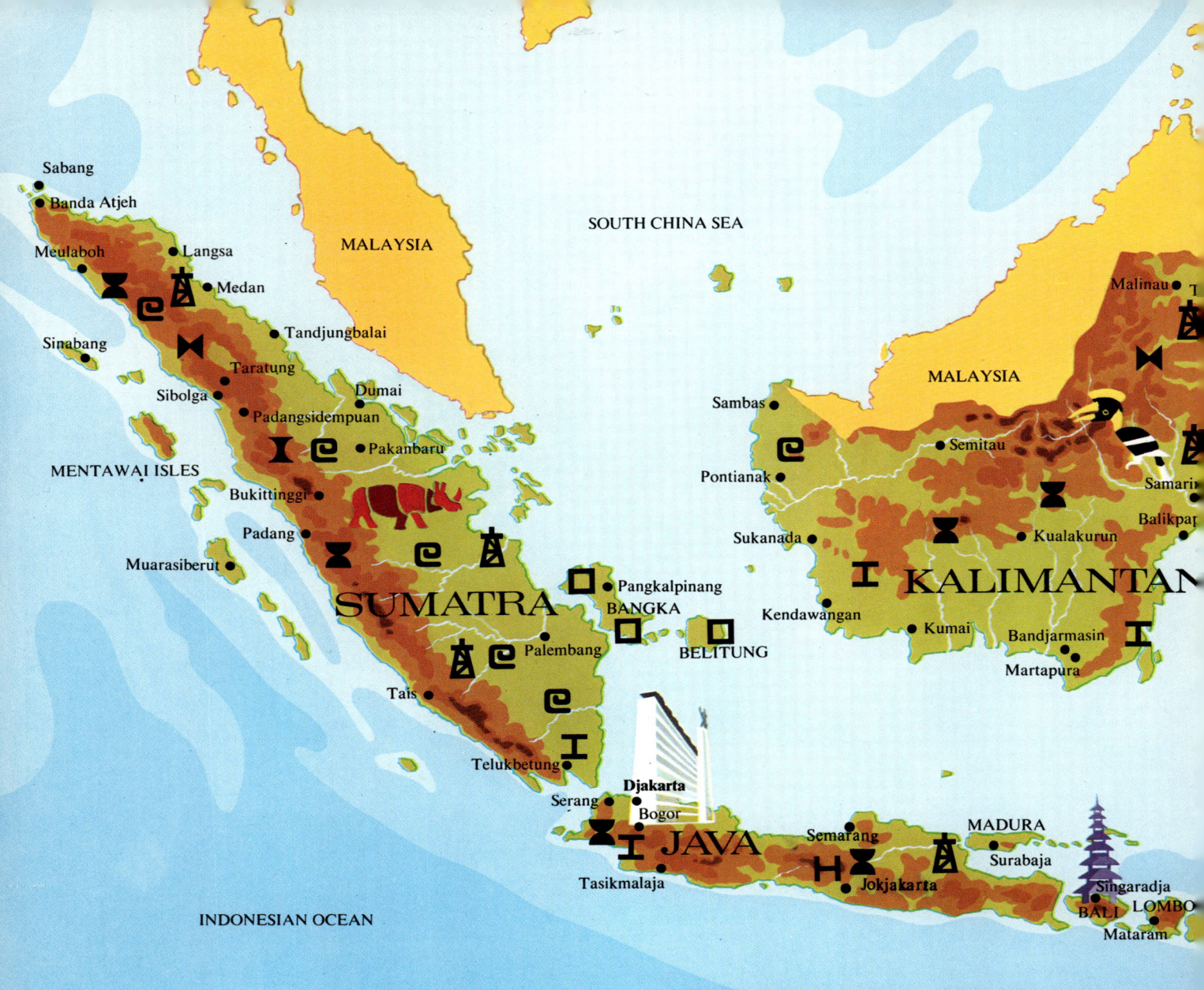

Indonesia

AREA:
735,000 square miles (1,904,345 sq. km.)

LENGTH:
3,200 miles (5,110 km.)

WIDTH:
1,200 miles (1,888 km.)

LOCATION:
Between 6° north and 11° south latitude, Indonesia comprises some 13,000 islands. Malaysia and Australia are two of Indonesia's most significant neighbours.

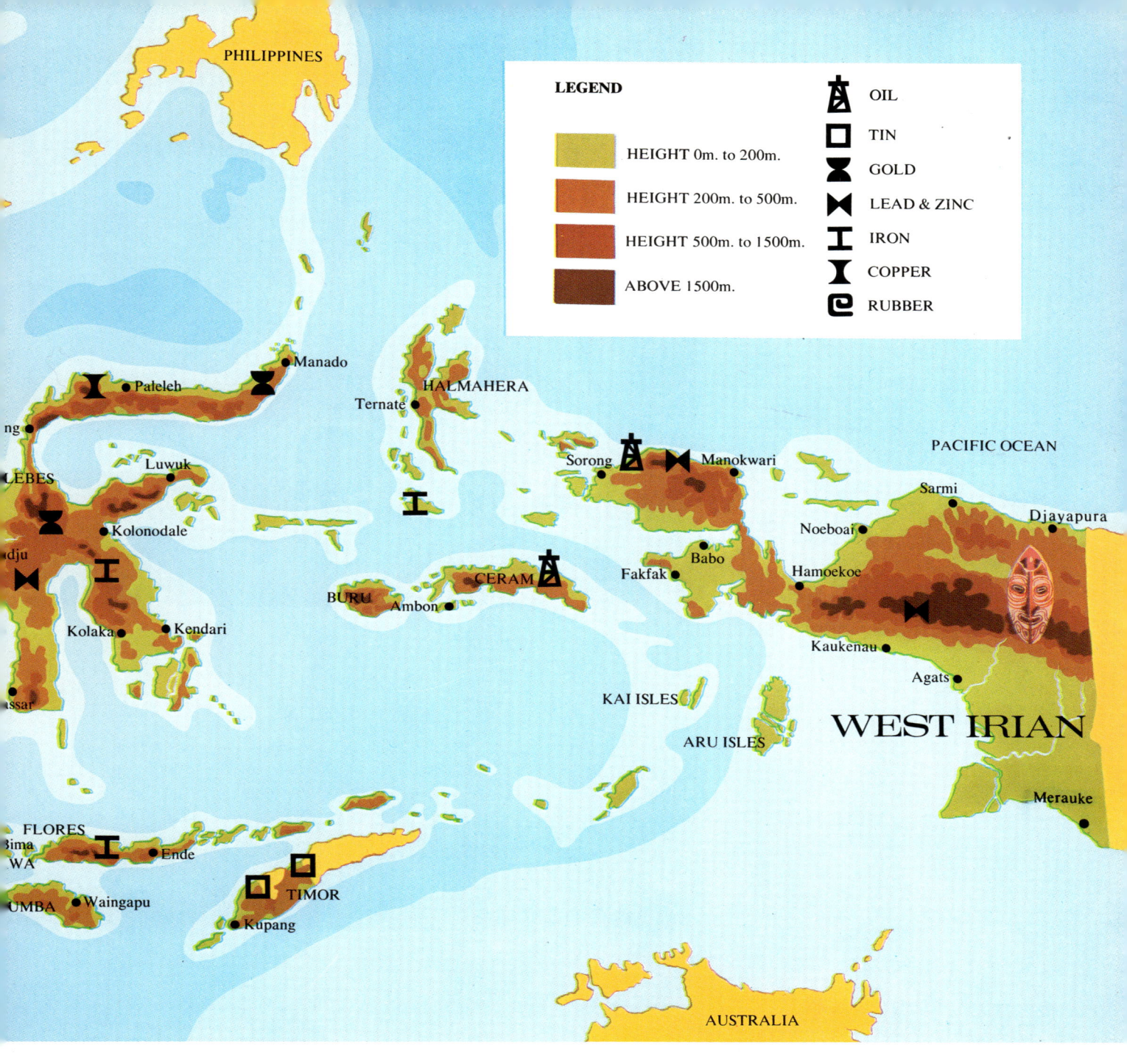

TOPOGRAPHY:
Mountainous, with some 100 active volcanos. Coastal plains and river valleys are relatively narrow. Areas of high plateau country are somewhat more extensive.

CLIMATE:
Maritime equatorial—the "dry" begins in May and ends in October; the "wet" lasts from November to April. Temperatures average near 80°F on the coastal areas, whilst the higher country regions are generally much cooler.

RAINFALL:
Varies from light to heavy—the west coast of Kalimantan averages 126" annually, while the east coast of Java averages only 68".

ETHNIC GROUPS:
Malay, Melanesoid, Australoid together with the non-indigenous groups of Chinese, Arabs and Eurasians.

RELIGIONS:
Mainly Moslem, some Hindus mostly living on the Island of Bali.

POPULATION:
Spreading over the numerous islands of the Indonesian archipelago is a population estimated at 126 million.

POPULATION GROWTH RATE:
Lack of access to many parts of the islands renders census figures difficult to obtain with a degree of accuracy. Average growth rate, about 2.3 to 2.8 per cent per annum, indicates that the population will reach 143.8 million by 1980.

297

THE PEOPLES OF INDONESIA have a cultural history which extends 2,500 years back to Neolithic Times. The celebrated Java Man's skull which was found in East Java in 1890 gave a key to an early stage of human evolution and for a time it was thought to be the "missing link" between man and the higher apes. This species flourished many thousands of years before the Australian Aborigines crossed the landbridges which then linked Australia and Asia, in all probability passing through what is now Indonesia 20,000 or more years ago. Hand axes and flake tools of a Stone Age culture have been found in Central Sumatra. It is possible that the earliest inhabitants came from the same stock as the Australian Aborigines, related to the first known inhabitants of India, and quite distinct from the Mongoloid peoples who began to migrate to the archipelago in about 3,000 B.C. They emigrated from Yunnan province in southern China, pushed their way down through mainland South-east Asia, the Malayan Peninsula and then adventurously sailed their slim riverboats out to the islands of Indonesia. As seafarers, they were more advanced than the Stone Age food-gatherers. Theirs was not any sudden movement of people but a process which probably took some thousands of years. Having arrived in Indonesia they set themselves up in permanent settlements where they built rectangular pile dwellings, developed artificially irrigated rice growing and raised pigs. They made clothing from bark and simple coiled pottery which supplemented the large number of household vessels made from bamboo. They also began producing artistically worked objects in stone, such as beads and bracelets, and later introduced metal-working and weaving. They established the peaceful settled way of village life which has become the basic pattern for most Indonesians today.

During this time the village was a self-contained entity modelled on the universe; political, economical, religious and even magical—everything had some relationship with everything else. The *mana* or living force of the community, which safeguarded and perpetuated it, was controlled by appropriate actions and symbols, which, in time, became highly ritualised. The leaders of the rituals, the *shamans,* were the most respected members of the community for it was only they who could contact the ancestral spirits which were the bearers of the community's mana. The villagers lived according to their own unique *adat* or customs which ordained the ceremonies of birth, marriage and death, the times and methods for sowing rice, building houses, praying for rain, cooking, and other things. Economics, politics and religion all came within adat. It was a legacy from their ancestors and most of their usages and customs are still observed. In such a community, family and village loyalties prevail over all others. Change from within was very slow, and although internal changes did occur, the course of Indonesia's history has been largely directed by external influences.

During the First Century A.D. Indian traders and missionaries brought with them a religion that, though having many similarities with indigenous Indonesian beliefs, was more coherent and refined. What the Indonesians saw as spirits and supernatural amorphous forms, Hindu culture had already endowed with the forms of Gods, systematically ranked and with specific functions in the cosmic relations between man and the heavens. The doctrine of Karma being a very well-thought-out version of the Indonesian mana gave the sha-

Above:
Typical of the Indonesian sculptors' art are the innumerable stone carvings in the equally innumerable temples. Frequently they are decorated with brightly coloured hibiscus blooms. On the right is a further example of native sculpture in this great temple.

The Peoples of Indonesia

mans of the small Indonesian communities the opportunity to reassert themselves in the name of new and all-powerful deities. They were assisted by the introduction of cart transport, plank boats, more efficient administrations and the blessings of Indian advisors.

About 200 years before the Christian era the first trading contacts with South China were established. This marked the beginning of the commercial pre-eminence of the Chinese, which still exists today throughout most of South-east Asia. They dealt in pearls, precious stones, metals, spices and timber, most of which are still important exports today; the spice trade of the Christian era was to change the fortunes of these peaceful islands.

Since early times Indonesian civilisation has been profoundly influenced by India. The first traders and missionaries from southern India settled in the 1st Century A.D. They introduced Indian scripts, versions of which were used until the Indonesian language was transcribed into the Latin alphabet in the last century. Trade was extended to southern India and Arabia. The Hindu influx continued until about 650 A.D. and Hinduisation remained through the centuries, first through Brahmanism and later through its offshoot Buddhism.

The Hindus brought superior cultural attainments and established themselves as aristocrats in feudal kingdoms in which villages were linked by a literate bureaucracy. They were benevolent rulers, not interfering with the local customs and saw themselves as philanthropists and healers with considerable knowledge of medicine.

In the 2nd Century, Chinese travellers observed that the Indonesians had a knowledge of astronomy, navigation, batik painting and the metric system.

Hindu kingdoms known to Chinese historians of the 7th Century included Kantoli (now Palembang) in Sumatra and Malaya in Djambi. The latter was conquered by a Buddhist dynasty in 673 A.D., and developed as a strong naval and commercial power which fostered art and learning. Many scholars from all parts of South-east Asia attended the Buddhist university at Palembang. There are still many shrines extant of Shaivite Hindu and Buddhist origin which date from this period of Hindu influence.

The 10th and 11th Centuries saw the codification of Javanese law, the development in East Java of irrigation systems which are still in use, the translation of the Hindu epic *Bhagavad Gita* and the writing of the Javanese *Adiparwa*.

Arab traders landed in Sumatra in the 1st Century, and introduced Islam when they began to settle there eleven hundred years later. Their trading kingdoms in North Sumatra flourished on the spice trade. Initially they paid tribute to the Hindu kingdoms but gradually they became independent.

The 13th Century saw the rise of the greatest Hindu kingdom, the Majapahit Empire in East Java, which flourished until overthrown by Moslem princes in the 16th Century. This was a golden age of art, literature and law-making, and through it diplomatic and trade relations were extended throughout South-east Asia. Lesser kingdoms of the same era paid tribute to the Majapahit Empire.

The first European to visit Java and Sumatra was Marco Polo, in 1292. The Portuguese arrived in 1509 in search of spices, having first established themselves on the Malay Peninsula. The Majapahit empire was finally overthrown in the 15th Century, to be superseded by Javanese Moslem powers. This represented the end of the period of Hindu feudalism and the beginning of modern political life. In some ways the change paralleled the Renaissance in Europe; the Hindu period stratified society in a caste system and discouraged individualism, while Islam was not only more democratic but was also imbued with a scientific spirit.

As traders, the Moslems extended Islam throughout the archipelago and with it the Malay language, which became the *lingua franca* of the area and ultimately the Indonesian national tongue. Eventually most of the islands were ruled by Moslem kings. In the early 16th Century some Hindu princes fled from Java to Bali, where to this day a Hindu-derived civilisation has been perpetuated. Dutch traders followed shortly upon the Portuguese, in quest of the spices which made mediaeval European food palatable. In 1602 the Dutch East India Company was founded and in 1605 it set itself up in Indonesia, taking control of the spice and coffee exports, and exacting agricultural tribute from the people. Ambon was seized in 1605, to be followed by the Banda Islands in 1623, thus securing a spice monopoly. Trade between the islands and with South-east Asia gradually ceased, as

THE WORLD'S LARGEST ARCHIPELAGO

the Indonesian economy was subordinated to the monopoly. Chinese were mostly used as middlemen.

Some resistance was offered by the local traders. The Sultan of Mataram unsuccessfully attacked Batavia in 1629. The Sultan of Goa was defeated in 1666. There was local opposition followed by punitive expeditions when the Dutch East India Company cut down thousands of clove trees in 1690, to keep prices at a high level. By 1800 corruption or mismanagement had forced the Company into bankruptcy, and control of all its territories passed into the hands of the Dutch Government.

Colonial exploitation continued under a policy of "divide and rule", but generally the 19th Century brought Indonesia closer to the modern ideas of democracy and self-determination. During the Napoleonic wars, the British occupied the Dutch territories, and some abuses were abolished, including the slave trade and forced contributions of plantation produce. National pride was stimulated by the work of Western historians and archaeologists, among whom were Sir Stamford Raffles, who wrote a history of Java. The earliest independence movements were partly inspired by the ideals of the French Revolution, and during the 19th Century a series of rebellions took place.

They were unsuccessful, but by the turn of the century Indonesian leaders started a cultural movement to promote greater interest in the native language and in the rich and diverse heritage of the country. The Budi Utomo (Noble Endeavour) was formed in 1908. Indonesian morale was initially raised when Japan defeated Russia in 1901 and proved that Europeans could be beaten. The Moslem national organisation, the Sarekat Dagang Islam, was formed in 1911. Generally the early 20th Century saw a liberalisation of Dutch colonial policy, and the emergence of an educated elite, drawn from the upper classes of the traditional society, which later turned the European democratic ideals against their masters and mentors. Legal and medical faculties were opened in 1924 and 1927, but technical education was neglected, a factor which was to hold back national progress after indepedence.

The inter-war period was marked by opposition to the government by the nationalist parties. The Indonesian Nationalist Party (PNI) was formed in 1927 with Dr. Sukarno as a member. It adopted Bahasa Indonesia as the official tongue and espoused militant non-co-operation with the Dutch. In 1939 the Dutch rejected claims for a fully fledged Parliament, but this decision was overruled when the Japanese entered the war in 1941.

The defeat of the Europeans by an Asian power was a psychological victory for the Indonesians, even though the Japanese occupation brought suffering and hardship in many forms. After the end of the war, on 17th August 1945, the Indonesians, led by Dr. Sukarno and Dr. Mohammed Hatta, proclaimed their independence. Dr. Sukarno was elected President and Dr. Hatta Vice-President of the Republic of Indonesia. When the Dutch sought to reimpose their rule, large-scale fighting broke out, and continued in various areas until 1949. The situation was brought before the UN Security Council in 1946 and negotiations between Holland and Indonesia began under a British chairman. During this period the tensions between colonialists and nationalists were aggravated by the Communist Party, which attempted a coup in 1948. That same year, the Dutch captured and interned Sukarno and Hatta, but the Republican government continued under an emergency cabinet. It was not until 7th May 1950, as a result of UN pressure, that an agreement was signed ending hostilities and recognising the Republic.

The infant Republic's problems were far from over. The first elections were held in 1955, but the new Parliament failed in its attempts to draw up a constitution. Such a failure is not unusual in under-developed countries without previous experience of democratic forms. President Sukarno adopted a policy of "guided democracy", which resulted in the concentration of power in the hands of the President. Unfortunately, in Indonesia as elsewhere, Communism identified itself with national aspirations, and power in the hands of a national hero led them to attempt a coup in 1965, with results that are now history.

It is no disparagement of a patriot to observe that the older Sukarno not only played into the hands of the Communists but also squandered public money in grandiose schemes and empty nationalist symbols, instead of attempting to solve Indonesia's practical problems. The defeat of the coup ended his regime and a military government with a policy of economic development was set up under General Suharto. The first elections for sixteen years were held in 1971 and the people confirmed their preference for military rule by recording a majority of votes for the newly established regime.

Their judgment has not been misplaced, for in the intervening years, under considerable difficulties, Indonesia has made steady if not spectacular progress and under Suharto's presidency the Republic has regained high prestige and the full respect of the nations of the world.

INDONESIA is the world's largest archipelago, the world's fifth most populous nation, and in Asia, after China and India, it ranks third. Comprising some 13,000 islands of widely varying sizes the Republic of Indonesia is politically divided into Provinces (Propinsi) and Special Districts (Daerah Istimewa). While smaller islands are grouped into a single province larger ones are divided into several.

Of these islands there are five of greater importance than all the others, for they contain more than 90 per cent of the Republic's population. The majority of the 126 million people live on Java, which ranks fourth in size. It is divided into five provinces—Djakarta Raya, Java Tengah, Daerah Istimewa Jogjakarta, Java Timur, and Java Barat.

DJAWA—to use the Indonesian spelling for Java—is one of the most densely populated islands in the world. It is dominated by a backbone fold of mountains which include a long series of 115 volcanic cones; fifteen of them are still active. The highest mountain is Semeru.

When Hindu traders and missionaries came to Java, the Indian World Mountain—Mahameru—was soon identified with certain Javanese mountains where ancestral spirits were thought to dwell. According to legend the *Mahameru* was transported to Java, and when an attempt was made to transplant it in the west the island began to tip; so to put the balance right it was moved eastwards. On the way, pieces kept falling off its lower rim, and thus the mountains of Lawu, Wilis, Kelud, Kawi, Ardjuna and Welirang were formed. On its unsteady journey its top fell off just south of Surabaja, and became Mount Penanggungan.

North of the mountain chain are fertile plains crossed by a number of swift streams of which the Bengawan Solo and Kali Brantas are the longest. Commercially they are of great significance as they bring huge quantities of silt and water to the rice farms on the northern plains. The southern part of the island is flanked mostly by infertile limestone mountains falling away to long stretches of lonely beaches.

SUMATRA, the second largest and the second most populous island in the Indonesian Republic is about three times as big as Java. The western part is dominated by the Bukit Barisan, a line of volcanic peaks which descend eastwards to a flat stretch of country split by several large rivers. In between the mountains of Bukit Barisan lie several magnificent lakes, Toba, Manindjau and Singkarak being the largest. In contrast to the western rivers which are only navigable for short distances, those on the east form a very important means of transport and communications: the port of Pekanbaru (Pekan = market; baru = new) is located 100 miles upstream on the Siak River; ocean steamers can travel 54 miles up the Musi from the Straits of Malacca to Palembang.

KALIMANTAN (Kali = river; intan = diamond) which comprises three-quarters of the island of Borneo, has a central core of tangled mountains flattening out to wide, swampy coastlands. The principal rivers—Kapuas, Barito, Kehajan, and Mahakam—form the only means of transport for most of Kalimantan's population. Although agriculture largely concentrates on subsistence crops, rubber, cloves and tobacco are also grown. Oil is obtained from the island of Tarakan and from the district between Balikpapan and Samarinda. High quality and commercially exploited diamonds are found near Matapura, the Islamic centre of South Kalimantan.

SULAWESI—rugged and mountainous—consists of a north-south backbone off which three arms project in easterly directions. The mountains are flanked by narrow coastal plains over which short unimportant rivers flow. On the upland basins and plateau wet rice and maize crops are grown. Rice, coffee, makassar oil and spices are the island's main exports.

THE MALUKU, long known as THE SPICE ISLES because for centuries they supplied the kitchens of Europe with cloves and nutmeg, are a group of islands between Sulawesi and Irian Barat. Most of them are mountainous and densely forested. Today spices are sent only to Java, and copra has replaced cloves as the group's main export.

The NUSA TENGGARA or Lesser Sundas is a string of islands stretching between Bali and Timor. Shifting cultivation is generally practised although Timor still exports the fragrant, scented sandalwood.

IRIAN BARAT, with a population of less than one million, occupies 22 per cent of Indonesia's total area. It is the least densely populated and the least developed province. Despite large capital outlays and oil investments since "The act of free choice" in 1969, in terms of economic development Irian Barat is still decades behind Java.

Left:
A native village where tribal dancing is a continual attraction to Indonesia's tourists.

Above:
A gaily decorated elephant at the entrance to a village.

CLIMATIC CONDITIONS

The climate of Indonesia is dominated by monsoonal winds which blow between Australia and Asia. From December to February the west monsoon brings rain to southern Sumatra, Java and Nusa Tenggara islands. In June, July and August these areas are affected by the east monsoon coming from the dry interior of Australia. Only areas east of Solo in Djawa Tengah have well-defined dry seasons and their duration increases as they become nearer Australia. In East Java only three months of the year receive less than one inch of rain, but Kupang in Timor has a dry season lasting up to seven months. Sumatra and Kalimantan, close to the equator and far from Australia, experience no dry season. Temperatures on the lowlands range between 65°F and 85°F with lower maxima and minima on the highlands.

NATURAL RESOURCES

Indonesia possesses a considerable range of natural resources. Rich volcanic soils and a warm, wet climate permit the intensive cultivation of a wide variety of food and commercial crops. The largely tropical forests cover roughly 60 per cent of the total land area, 75 per cent of which are located mainly in Irian Barat, Kalimantan and Sumatra, and are under large-scale exploitation by foreign companies. In 1968 timber, after oil, was Indonesia's main foreign exchange earner.

Indonesian fishing resources include more edible species of fish than any other comparable area in the world. They include tuna, shrimp and anchovies in the inter-island waters, carp and prawns in the fishponds along Java's northern coast and "goldfish" (ikan mas) from the freshwater ponds and padi fields of West Java and the Padang Highlands in West Sumatra.

There are substantial reserves of tin, petroleum, bauxite, nickel, building materials, salt, iodine and limited deposits of gold, diamonds and silver. But except for tin, petroleum and bauxite, there has been little exploitation of Indonesia's mineral resources. To date the major sources of oil have been Sumatra and Kalimantan, the proven reserves of which are expected to last for several more decades. Tin is almost wholly produced on the islands of Billiton, Bangka and Singkep. Coal reserves, moderate in quantity and of poor quality, exist in East Kalimantan, in South and West Sumatra at Bukit Asam and on the shores of Lake Singkarak in Ombilin. Bauxite—the country's reserves are estimated at a fifth of the world's total—is mined on the island of Riau and deposits are reported to exist in Sumatra. Nickel is found in south-eastern Sulawesi. Although iron would need to be imported to support any large steel industry, there are considerable quantities of ore in Nusa Tenggara, Sulawesi, Kalimantan and Sumatra. The uneven quality of the mineral, transportation difficulties, and the expense of the refining processes have, to date, deterred their development. Other mineral resources of moderate importance are sulphur, salt, iodine, manganese, copper, lead, gold and silver, which are found in small quantities in small scattered areas. Diamonds, gold and silver are found in Kalimantan; salt is produced in Madura and there are large sulphur deposits in all volcanic areas. Phosphates used in fertiliser manufacture are found in Java.

RESOURCE UTILISATION

The utilisation of Indonesia's natural resources has been limited and as yet of little value to the country. The five year economic development plan, which began in 1969, represents the first serious attempt to program the country's development. Prior to the colonial period the islands produced surpluses of rice, pepper, cloves and other spices together with precious forest products such as the sweet smelling sandalwood of Timor. Trade, and Indonesia's participation in it, was lively. In the 18th Century the Dutch assumed monopoly powers over the resources of the archipelago and fostered or directed their development only so far as it fitted into their own exploitative plans. Some processing industries and estate crops were established in the agricultural, industrial and manufacturing sectors.

AGRICULTURE

First and foremost Indonesians are farmers living in small rural villages. They have a relationship with their land which is far more complex and personal than that of the Western farmer "who rides over his property with an evil-smelling monster of steel, ripping and wounding the soil". The Indonesian farmer does not see his land as an exploitable resource to be used for the purpose of raising his family's standard of living. It is sacred, and when a rice crop is ready for harvesting the good earth must be paid its due respect. For this reason the farmer uses a small semi-circular knife, concealed in his hand so that it will not offend *Dewi Sri*, the guardian goddess of the land. Farming is a way of life that is as traditional as the customs of the village in which the farmer lives and to which he is intangibly tied.

The typical Indonesian farmer is a rice grower, using the grain to feed his family and selling some of it to the government mill, to the itinerant merchant or taking it to market himself. With the money so derived he buys such things as furniture, textiles, kerosene, cooking oil, sugar, fertiliser and the more status-gaining consumer goods such as a radio or a motor scooter, or he perhaps uses it to send his son to high school.

He prefers to live in Java where the rich volcanic soils, the supply of irrigated water and the large amounts of sunshine favour the growing of wet rice. Further, the Indonesian farmer grows rice rather than anything else because, to him, it is the tastiest of all grains. Moreover, it can be stored for up to three years and it is always saleable.

Rice growing and the eating of rice is determined by the *adat* of the area. Thus, in Bali for instance, at every stage of the agricultural cycle appropriate ceremonies are held and offerings are made and passages from holy texts are chanted. Although not obvious to the casual observer, the adat of any village, its dictates and taboos, govern the actions and behaviour of its inhabitants.

As in Java, wet rice or *sawah* is the principal crop in Bali and Sumatra. About 10 per cent of the estimated 6 million hectares under grain is irrigated. In the Outer Provinces large tracts of land are occupied by a relatively small number of subsistence farmers who exist by cultivating *ladangs* or plots of cleared land, planted several times then disbanded. Practiced in Timor, and the mountainous districts of central Sumatra and Kalimantan, shifting cultivation is a system of which the main characteristics are rotation of fields instead of crops, clearing by means of fire, the employment of much human labour and the use of uncomplicated implements such as the digging stick. The ladang farmer's simple routine is burning, clearing, planting and harvesting; his crops are upland rice and corn. In most parts of the world shifting farming always means village relocation. In Indonesia this is not the case. Nearly all shifting farmers live in permanent villages which may be some distance from their ladangs. Although this method of cultivation has been strongly criticised as wasteful it is now coming to be recognised as a well balanced system in which man and environment are well adjusted. Nevertheless in a country whose population is increasing by 2 to 3 per cent every year, a system which requires roughly ten times the area needed for sawah growing is obviously not practical.

Although most Indonesians are subsistence farmers there are millions of rural dwellers who derive their livings from commercial or estate crops; that is, crops for sale and not for private consumption. About 35 per cent of all arable land is devoted to cultivation either on estates or on small holdings. Of the 40 or more commercial crops, only rubber, tobacco, sugar, copra, palm oil, hard fibre, coffee and tea are of national importance. Before World War II Indonesia was a leading supplier of rubber, copra, tea, palm oil and sisal and almost monopolised the world's supply of cinchona, pepper and kapok.

The cultivation of export crops was originally controlled by foreign estates, but to satisfy the ambitions of the small farmer and to ensure better conditions for the people, the government has encouraged ownership and management of plantations by Indonesian nationals.

MANUFACTURING

Manufacturing in Indonesia is mainly of the cottage industry type whereby villagers and urban dwellers produce goods from local raw materials for local consumption. Modern large-scale factory type production is concerned mainly with the processing of raw materials such as the refining of food crops. The production of electrical equipment, machinery and similar complex goods, is small but growing as European and Japanese companies seek opportunities to utilise Indonesia's ample labour force. In this respect it must be added that most foreign countries that take the trouble to unravel the mysteries of Indonesian administrative procedures and business methods invariably make huge profits.

Left page:
Native fishermen
and their decorative boats
on a jungle-lined beach.

Left:
Rice terraces
contoured to take advantage
of the hilly country.

OIL has become a vital factor in the modern machine age. It is the main source of energy for transportation and industry and the raw material from which many products are made for everyday use. Thus oil plays an important role in the building of a nation. In Indonesia the national oil industry has reached such a peak that today it exercises a dominating influence on the economy of the country and is in fact the axis of the National Five-Year Development Plan.

Since the end of the turbulent "Old Order" Sukarno regime, the steady and healthy statesmanship of President Suharto with his "Developing Cabinet" has given every opportunity for the development of serious working enterprises, strengthening the Nation's fundamental economic and social life. This was the chance for which the National Oil Company had long been waiting.

Freed of economic and political influences, oil has become Indonesia's boom industry —the leading earner of foreign exchange. Gross proceeds from oil exports for 1969-1970 reached a target of US$372.8 million, and represented roughly 73 per cent of Indonesia's total crude oil. Exports of crude oil by-products represented another 12 per cent.

A study made in 1969 revealed that Indonesia's current energy consumption is estimated at an oil equivalent of 21.4 million Kl. per annum. Of this, 17 million Kl. is supplied to the domestic sector, mainly for cooking and lighting; 2 million Kl. goes to the transportation sector, about 1 million Kl. to manufacturing industries and nearly ½ million Kl. to military establishments. About one-third of Indonesia's energy comes from petroleum and the rest is supplied by non-oil products.

Oil is the main source of revenue from which Indonesia's urgent Five-Year Development Plan is financed. Indonesia's oil has been an enticement to foreign private enterprises from America, Europe and Asia, and they are already playing prominent parts in furthering Indonesia's all-out efforts to re-establish, stabilise and maintain the economic status of the Republic.

Development of the National Oil Company.
Dating its establishment from Indonesia's Proclamation of Independence, which came very shortly after the Japanese Army's surrender to the Allied Forces on 15th August 1945, the present PERTAMINA organisation originated from the devastated remnants of the "scorched earth" oil fields and installations of the 65-year-old, Dutch-owned "N.V. de BPM" N.V. de Bataafsche Petroleum Maatschappij (N.V. de BPM) at Pangkalan Brandan in North Sumatra.

CRUDE OIL PRODUCTION

000's Bbls.	1966	1970	Second Quarter 1971	Third Quarter 1971
LEMIGAS	546	465	133	149
PERTAMINA	37,957	35,533	8,874	9,629
STANVAC	20,898	17,674	5,355	6,281
CALTEX	111,123	257,887	63,244	68,101
Total	170,524	311,549	77,606	84,160
Thousand barrels per day	467.2	853.6	852.8	914.8

CRUDE OIL EXPORTS

000's Bbls.	1970	Second Quarter 1971	Third Quarter 1971	b/d
By Company:				
PERTAMINA	62,778	14,921	12,737	138,445.6
STANVAC	13,741	3,373	4,147	45,076.2
CALTEX	151,749	38,088	43,100	468,478.2
Total	228,268	56,382	59,984	652,000.0

PRODUCT EXPORTS

000's Bbls.	1970	Second Quarter 1971	Third Quarter 1971	b/d
By Company:				
PERTAMINA	36,267	8,436	8,111	88,163.0
Total	36,267	8,436	8,111	88,163.0

TANKER FLEET

DWT	1968	1970	Second Quarter 1971
Owned	198,765	278,729	354,934
Hire Purchased	168,571	373,209	379,518
Chartered	236,744	212,775	178,535
Total	604,080	864,713	912,987

OIL IN THE INDONESIAN ECONOMY

In this picture,
Lieutenant-General Dr. Ibnu Sutowo,
President Director of Pertamina (right)
explains to President Suharto (left)
about Cinta-1 production.
Extreme left is U.S. Ambassador to
Indonesia, Mr. Francis J. Galbraith.

Below: The oil
refinery at Pladju,
South Sumatra.

In later years, alive to the vital role that oil was playing in the building of nations, its essential functions both in times of peace and war, the Government of the young Republic of Indonesia took over control of the oil industry from the Indonesian freedom fighters, who, lacking the necessary experience and technical know-how, had managed it poorly from 1945 through 1950. Complete control by the Government of the installations at Pangkalan Brandan dated from 15th October 1957, when the Indonesian Army Chief of Staff, General A.H. Nasution, appointed Colonel Dr. Ibnu Sutowo, now Army Lieutenant-General, to establish a limited liability company (P.T.) called P.T. PERMINA (Perusahaan Minjak Nasional). His responsibility was to rehabilitate the oil industry, and to organise the export of its crude product. The "Refining Associates of Canada" (REFICAN) was the only foreign oil company courageous enough to risk purchasing P.T. PERMINA's crude oil, defying the claims of BPM to their pre-war rights to the abandoned oil facilities at Pangkalan Brandan.

The first successful crude oil export to the U.S.A. in August 1958 was an added incentive and paved the way for speedy rehabilitation of the oil installations at Pangkalan Brandan—an historic milestone in the history of Indonesia's national industry. Reconstruction was speeded up and within twelve months P.T. PERMINA concluded an agreement with a Japanese Oil Company "NOSODECO" (North Sumatra Oil Development Company) which provided for long-term credit for the purchase of machinery and the hiring of technicians. Payment was to be made in crude oil produced under the agreement.

On 10th December 1959 P.T. PERMINA was converted into a State-owned enterprise, P.N. Perusahaan Minjak Nasional—P.N. PERMINA.

The fast rate of development of its oil industry made it incumbent upon Indonesia to become a member of OPEC (Organisation of Petroleum Exporting Countries). Her membership took effect in 1962 and since then the Republic has played a significant role in international oil politics.

To stimulate Indonesia's oil export marketing, P.N. PERMINA became allied with some Japanese companies and in May 1965 they established "The Far East Oil Trading Company Ltd." as a 50-50 joint venture. This organisation now serves as a main supply-channel to Japan for most of Indonesia's crude oil and oil products.

On 30th December 1965 the Indonesian Government purchased all the assets of P.T. Shell Indonesia, valued at US$110 million. On behalf of the Government P.N. PERMINA assumed the responsibility of its operations and of meeting instalment payments over a five-year period.

Another State-owned oil enterprise called P.N. PERTAMIN (Pertambangan Minjak Indonesia) was established in February 1961 as sole distributor of petroleum products for the domestic market. Later this company took over the marketing operations of Shell, Stanvac and Caltex throughout Indonesia, including their storage facilities and retail outlets, which the Government purchased on 27th July 1965 at a cost of some US$12.9 million.

On 20th August 1968, P.N. PERTAMIN was amalgamated with P.N. PERMINA and converted into what was firstly called P.N. PERTAMINA (P.N. Pertambangan Minjak & Gas Bumi Nasional). It is now called PERTAMINA, and Lieutenant-General Dr. H. Ibnu Sutowo remains as President-Director.

P.N. Pertamina: An integrated National Oil Company. The merger which resulted in the formation of P.N. PERTAMINA placed both domestic and foreign aspects of Indonesia's oil business under complete Government control. It is the aim of the Company to reshape the whole structure of the oil industry into a national integrated organisation to ensure greater efficiency in administration and maximum productivity.

P.N. PERTAMINA was active in the field of oil and gas mining, involving exploration, production, refining and manufacturing, transportation and marketing. Indonesia's national crude oil production of 1,331 thousand barrels in 1958 steadily increased year by year to a total of 35,533 thousand barrels in 1970.

Exploration/Production. Exploration for oil in Indonesia has embraced sites both onshore and offshore. In the framework of increasing the country's oil reserve potential, an extensive exploration programme has been operating since the end of 1964, in co-operation with some 45 foreign contractors.

The offshore activities are based on a "joint production sharing", a 65-35 per cent arrangement with the ownership and management of the oil under PERTAMINA's control.

It has been announced that a further $198 million or more will probably be invested in the next five years, mainly for the exploration of new fields, on-word and offshore. The widespread hunt for oil beneath the Indonesian waters during the past three years has uncovered some promising commercial fields.

The first offshore oil discovery in the South-east Sumatra Contract Area was the result of the joint effort of Pertamina and IIAPCO. The Cinta-1 well was spudded on 10th August 1970, and reached a total depth of 3,760 feet on 26th August 1970.

Left: An offshore platform being built by Ingram Far East Pte. Ltd. on Batam Island.... Below: A barit-producing "Dresser Magcobar Plant" on Batam Island.

Right: Offshore exploration in East Kalimantan being carried out by Pertamina.

JAPEX (Japan Petroleum Exploration) in the Malacca Straits, SINCLAIR/IIAPCO (Independent Indonesian American Petroleum Company) and ICS (Indonesian Cities Service), both in the Java Sea, and JAPEX-UNION joint exploration efforts offshore in East Kalimantan (Makakam Area), have struck new oil reserves; the Idi in offshore North Sumatra, Cinta-field and E-Structure in the Java Sea and Attaka Field in offshore East Kalimantan are estimated to have produced some 100,000 barrels per day during 1971/72. Indonesia reached an overall oil target of one million b/d in 1971 compared with the 1970 production of 850,000 barrels per day.

Refining and Manufacturing. With the purchase of the Stanvac Sungei Gerong Refinery early in 1970, PERTAMINA now has all the Indonesian refining facilities under its complete control. Refineries are under construction at Dumai and Sungei Pakning in Central Sumatra, with capacities respectively of 100,000 and 50,000 b/d. This will mean increased oil supplies for home consumption and foreign markets and will bring the total Indonesian refining capacity in the hands of PERTAMINA to about 411,000 barrels per day.

Transportation. PERTAMINA's tanker fleet has steadily grown year by year. In 1959 it began to take over the shuttle service in the Pangkalan Brandan area with two tankers of about 2,500 tons d.w.t. Since then the fleet has increased to a total owned-tonnage of some 278,729 d.w.t. in 1970 and 354,934 d.w.t. in the second quarter of 1971. The transportation of crude oil and products for the foreign market is still being undertaken in combination with foreign tankers, but all domestic supplies are carried by PERTAMINA vessels.

Marketing. In the field of foreign marketing since its acquisition of the Stanvac Sungei Gerong Refinery, PERTAMINA has proved its ability to handle greater volumes of crude oil and petroleum products. The domestic market, which has been solely PERTAMINA's responsibility since 1961, is running smoothly, with regular supplies for home consumption.

Aviation. The important task of aviation refueling has been carried on by PERTAMINA's trained employees, giving services to National as well as International airlines at airfields all over Indonesia.

Petrochemical Expansion. The petrochemical industry began in 1919 as an extension of the oil industry, and since 1960 it developed to such a degree that petrochemicals could soon attain the significance of the classical products gasoline and kerosene. PERTAMINA is already producing LPG (Liquefied Propane and Butane gases), oxygen, hydrocarbon, solvents and carbon black, insecticides for home and agricultural purposes, and a variety of plastic articles. A fertiliser plant "P.T. Pupuk Sriwidjaja" (PUSRI) at Palembang, now manufactures some 100,000 tons of urea fertiliser annually; it processes natural gas feedstocks supplied by PERTAMINA. PUSRI plans to raise its production to 480,000 tons per annum, which means more natural gas will be needed. As cheap fertilisers for the farmers are mainly aimed at supporting the "self-sufficiency in food programme"—the top priority project of the Five-Year Development Plan—PERTAMINA has scheduled the construction of a new fertiliser plant, the biggest in Indonesia, in the Cheribon Area of West Java.

In order to research the possible production of other petrochemical products, investigations into further possibilities for the utilising of natural gas or refinery gas in other branches of the petrochemical industry has been initiated; for example, plastics and synthetic fibres.

A polymerisation plant is under construction in Pladju and on its scheduled completion date in 1972 it is expected to reach an annual capacity of 20,000 tons of polypropylene resin.

On Page 304 is a summary of PERTAMINA's extraordinary progress during the period 1966 to the third quarter of 1971.

INDONESIA'S INDOMILK

IN A REGION where the majority of the people have traditionally depended upon rice as the staple constituent of their diet, with fish as the main protein element, the modern pressures of population coupled with relatively primitive methods of agriculture, have led to a general nutritional deficiency. Lack of high-grade protein products, and to varying degrees, apathy and debilitation, can cause devastating physical illness. Thus the many millions in Asian countries who are in fact so affected have little chance of improving their lot. Malnutrition is a major link in the depressing and vicious circle—called by writer Ritchie Calder "the misery-go-round of poverty".

Only through more health-promoting diets can the South-east Asian malnourished peoples build up their constitutions and so take fullest advantage of increasing secondary aids such as education and technology.

Milk has long been recognised as one of the cheapest and most acceptable forms of high-quality protein. Through a joint venture scheme initiated by the Australian Dairy Produce Board and their Indonesian partners, P.D. & I. "Marison" N.V., Indonesia is now processing large quantities of Australian milk products.

The US$1.7 million P.T. Australia-Indonesian Milk Industries plant, built on five acres of land at Gandaria on the outskirts of Djakarta, was opened on 3rd July 1969 by the President, General Suharto.

Right:
The recombining plant at P.T. Indomilk where Australian skim milk powder and anhydrous milk fat are recombined to manufacture sweetened condensed milk and liquid pasteurised milk.

Above:
The quality control officer of P.T. Australia-Indonesian Milk Industries checks a sample of reconstituted canned milk of the "Indomilk" brand.

Opposite page:
The main administrative building of P.T. Australia-Indonesian Milk Industries at Gandaria on the outskirts of Djakarta.

By March 1971, it had produced more than 1 million cases of sweetened condensed milk, each case containing four dozen 14-ounce cans. It is also making combined pasteurised liquid milk in increasingly large quantities and soon will begin the recombining of butter from Australian butter-oil.

Indomilk—as the organisation is locally called—has the most modern dairy installation in Indonesia. It comprises a main factory of 47,000 square feet, a service block with steam boilers and electrical generators with a combined capacity of 1,300 KVA, an amenities block and a two-storey office and modernly equipped laboratory building. The mixing and processing machinery is geared to handle 1,000 gallons of condensed milk an hour, and automatic filling and labelling machinery 250 cans a minute. 18,000 cans manufactured from imported tinplate are turned out from the can-line every hour. Water is supplied by three 300-foot bores on the site and is purified before use.

Indomilk was the first industry to be approved under Indonesia's foreign investment law, which was passed by the Suharto government to aid development and encourage a substantial flow of overseas capital and technical know-how.

Establishment of the plant has meant that valuable Indonesian foreign exchange which would otherwise have been required for importing condensed milk has been saved for important local development programmes. Moreover, the new industry is providing much needed job opportunities for both skilled and unskilled Indonesian workers.

As with other milk plants established by the Australian Dairy Produce Board in Southeast Asia, Australian personnel are employed to assist with administration and train local staff to take over important positions in the fields of food technology, manufacturing, engineering and marketing. P.T. Indomilk provides jobs for 200 Indonesian nationals in the operation of its plant.

The initial requirement of Australian dairy produce by the milk plant was to have been 3,000 tons of skim milk powder and 1,000 tons of anhydrous milk fat a year. However, the rapid expansion of the plant indicates that much more than this will be required to meet the future needs of the people. Locally grown sugar is used in making the sweetened condensed milk, when it is available, and all cans are manufactured at the plant. Cartons and cases which are also produced locally, give added employment to Indonesia's fast growing work force.

Australia's geographical proximity to Indonesia makes co-operation through trade obvious and sensible. The Republic's population of more than 120 million is in need of more proteins in their diet. Thus Australia, with a large, exportable surplus of protein-rich dairy produce, is a natural supplier and this fact is strengthening the friendly ties that already exist between the two nations.

THE FAMILY OF SHAMSUDDIN

THE average Indonesian family is of Malay racial stock. The people are rather short—about 5 feet 4 inches tall—lean, brown-skinned, with closely cropped black hair. Living in the village where they were born, the family, together with their relatives and neighbours, cultivate padi in the *desa's* fields which surround their homes. If the price of rubber on world markets is 'right' they will tap some of the 100-odd rubber trees which grow in a generally untidy smallholding in the foothills of a nearby mountain range.

Shamsuddin—a common Indonesian name derived from Islam—lives with his wife and four children. His house is a small rectangular structure barely ten square yards in area. Its frame consists of a system of wooden pillars and beams, the walls are panels of plaited bamboo and the thatch roof consists of overlapping layers of plaited coconut leaves which are attached to the wooden rafters of the roof frame by thin strips of bamboo. The inside of the house is divided into small compartments by movable bamboo panels. Light enters through large holes in the upper part of the side walls. The family's kitchen is a small room separated by a covered passageway, at the back of the house. A nearby stream provides water facilities for laundry and toilet purposes.

The ages of Shamsuddin's children range from twelve down to four years. His wife's mother, together with an adopted child, make up the rest of the household although relatives from other villages frequently come and stay with them. There are no hotels or other accommodation in the village and it would be considered uncharitable not to offer hospitality to relatives, no matter how distant the blood tie might be.

Shamsuddin owns a little less than one hectare of good padi land. A few years ago he was able to plant only one crop a year, but the completion of a nearby irrigation canal now means a guaranteed permanent water supply and he manages five crops in two years. Moreover, his yields have increased because, besides the irrigation water, the local government agricultural officer—working with the Bogor Agricultural Institute—has supplied Shamsuddin with a new variety of seed—a cross between a Philippine variety and a local grain. The Institute also provides the necessary chemical fertilisers from the Pusri plant in Palembang. All of these improvements have helped Shamsuddin to increase his output by more than 100 per cent, and as a result he has been able to afford a Sanyo transistor radio, a luxury much envied by the rest of the village.

Both he and his wife can read the Indonesian national language (Bahasa Indonesia). Writing it is difficult because they have little opportunity to practise. Even so, they are very fortunate because many of their neighbours have only a scant knowledge of Bahasa Indonesia, which, however, does not really matter much because around the village all conversation is in the local Suku language.

Shamsuddin and his family live well. Besides producing enough padi rice for their needs and earning a little extra money from the rubber to buy kerosene, soap, cooking oil, sugar and salt, at the back of their house there is a fruit and vegetable garden.

Above:
Shamsuddin's wife is a typical attractive Indonesian girl.

Below:
In the sitting room of Sartono, an average middle-class Government employee.

Right: The farming communities raise flocks of geese as a luxury addition to their food.

Here Shamsuddin's wife and children grow sweet potatoes, cassava, long beans, spinach, cucumbers and peanuts, together with bananas, paw-paw, rambutans, mangosteens and mangoes. The family also keeps a dozen or so chickens which are continually foraging around the kitchen door on the lookout for scraps.

As is already apparent, rice is the most important food for the Shamsuddin family. In fact, the three basic meals—taken at 6 a.m., 2 p.m. and 7 p.m.—consist mainly of *nasi* or boiled rice. It is supplemented with a variety of side dishes, some quite mild, others tastily spiced with ginger, pepper, chillies, lemon grass and tumeric. Warm unsweetened tea grown in the cool misty highlands of West Java accompanies all meals. In between snacks are very popular. These consist of fried bananas (pisang goring), fried fermented cassava, a great variety of cakes, some made from rice flour, others from Australian wheat flour, prawn and fish crisps. Whenever they get the opportunity—which is fairly often—they eat a lot of fresh fruits. They are particularly fond of the durian, which is shunned by many Europeans because of its somewhat nauseatingly unpleasant odour. Apart from the radio—which is usually turned up full—Shamsuddin has very little "modern" entertainment. But he does not miss it for he and his wife lead busy social lives—receiving guests, visiting, attending religious gatherings known as *kenduries*, celebrating weddings, circumcisions, births and funerals. Talking and smoking clove spiced *kretek* cigarettes—but never drinking alcohol—and playing with his younger children takes up most of Shamsuddin's leisure time.

Shamsuddin has never been to Djakarta. In fact, he has never been out of his province. The only time he leaves the *desa* is just before *lebaran* when he takes the whole family to the provincial capital. There they have an evening meal at a *padang* restaurant and visit the Peoples' Entertainment Park (Taman Hiburan Rakjat) where they enjoy seeing a Javanese folk drama (wajang wong). Shamsuddin's wife and daughters buy pieces of the much-valued batik cloth which the women wear on Hari Idulfitri, the day celebrating the end of the Islamic fast. This annual spree absorbs most of Shamsuddin's yearly savings but he does not begrudge it because his wife and family always enjoy themselves so much.

Despite his normal contentment there are several things which vaguely worry him. His wife is expecting another child, and as his younger brother has just died—leaving his wife and two small children to fend for themselves—Shamsuddin knows that in the not too distant future he will have to support an extra four people. In such cases the government does not provide any assistance. And as he is both the oldest and richest member of their family the responsibility falls upon him. Even if he had the capital—which he does not—he would find it almost impossible to buy more land because all the village *sawah* is owned jointly by related families—and selling family land for money would be akin to sacrilege. Further, his eldest son—Hadi—will soon have to enrol in the Lower Secondary School (Sekolah Menengah Pertama), and as there is only a primary school in the desa, Hadi will have to continue his schooling in the *kabupaten* capital some 27 kilometres away. Shamsuddin dearly wants Hadi to receive an education but the expense involved might require sacrifices which he does not want to impose upon the rest of the family.

Apart from these economic worries Shamsuddin feels uneasy about the new way of life. Recently a pretty lass from the desa, while staying with relatives in the *kabupaten* capital, ran away with a merchant from another island. Along with the rest of the village Shamsuddin was upset by the girl's total disregard for local adat. They felt that she should have married somebody from their own *suku*. The girl's family was embarrassed by her behaviour and they made a vow never to mention her name again. Other failings of today's youth also irk him. They do not have the respect for age and social standing which was drilled into him when he was a youth. Also, many boys of the village are too ready to question —in a frighteningly frank manner—values and customs which the older members of the village consider sacrosanct.

In fact, when Shamsuddin begins to compare the old village ways with those of the West—imported from Djakarta—he becomes terribly confused. Usually he resolves this confusion by conceding that change there must be but…well, it's best to wait and see.

CITY LIFE

Indonesian city dwellers have been forced to come to terms with the realities of the modern world far more quickly than they are normally able to adjust themselves. Although Indonesian cities now hold about 15 per cent of the total population the trend towards urban living is growing more rapidly than anywhere else in the world. The high growth rate is not only due to the expansion of industry and the establishment of services which provide more job opportunities; rather it is the result of the immigration of landless unemployed to the cities in the hope of some form of employment. Most of them end up becoming betjak drivers, council workers and daily labourers.

Many sections of the cities still have a rural appearance—reflecting the background of their inhabitants—a phenomenon particularly peculiar to South-east Asian cities— the *kampung*. In the kampung or village the people live in wooden houses loosely grouped in a haphazard manner among vegetable plots and fruit trees, and narrow pathways wind about in all directions.

All Indonesian cities have their characteristic markets or *pasars*, huge warehouse type buildings where just about everything can be bought. According to author Clifford Geertz the pasar is the climax of pre-industrial life, "its focus and centre". But in recent times many Western style buildings have appeared and some parts of Indonesia's cities have taken on a more modern appearance. The central business district of Medan, for instance, is like that of any European city. Intermingled with the old and the modern are the Chinese *tokos*— open fronted shophouses—and the many thousands of *warungs* or open-air, stall-type snack bars. The country boasts only one department store, in the heart of Djakarta, and its financial losses are an embarrassment to all associated with it. Modern shopping centres and arcades are non-existent outside Djakarta, which has one of each.

So great is the variety of city dwellings it is almost impossible to describe a typical home. Sartono, a middle class Government employee, lives in one of the ubiquitous *gangs* or side streets that sprout out from the main roads. Most likely it is paved, but badly in need of repair, and so narrow that only two wheeled vehicles can enter. Open drains line the footway, often clogged up despite the efforts of the local residents to keep them clean. His home is one of a row of ten single storey tenements, set about three feet back from the gang. Built of bricks and cement with red roofing tiles, its three small bedrooms could be used by as many as nine people. They are supplied with main electricity of 90 watts. Water is problematical. Sartono is lucky for he has a small manual Japanese pump to draw his water from a self-dug well. Otherwise, his wife would have to spend a lot of time swinging the well bucket. Sewerage disposal presents a constant health hazard because the neighbourhood pipe has rusted away and at various points in the street the effluence rises to the surface. To reduce the health risks he and his neighbours carry

Left:
The betjak is a multi-purpose vehicle capable of carrying up to four adults or considerable loads of rice and other commodities. At the end of 1970, there were almost 95,000 betjaks in Djakarta.

Below:
Sacks of Indonesian rice for local consumption and export.

Right:
Fresh fruits and vegetables in a market place of one of Indonesia's typical villages.

nightsoil to the nearest canal and ditch it there. He knows this is wrong but there is no available alternative.

Sartono is employed as a draftsman by the Department of Public Works. He receives a monthly salary of Rp.4,000 (about US$12), an allowance of 10 kilogrammes of rice which lasts for about two weeks, free medical treatment for himself and his family and free transport to and from the office. He earns some extra money working part-time for a Chinese building contractor. This often takes up more time than his official job and Sartono frequently leaves the office some two hours before he should. But as many of his colleagues do the same thing his conscience does not trouble him. Moreover, until the government increases his salary to at least three times its present level for the sake of his family he must continue to hold down two jobs.

In most Indonesian cities there is a pressing housing shortage. Since 1968 this has become most obvious in Djakarta where good houses are so scarce that foreigners posted there are forced to pay in advance rents of no less than US$500 per month for three years. The cost of building such a house in 1971 was about Rp.9 million or US$24,500. When the average employee receives about Rp.10,000 per month it is obvious that only the very privileged are in a position to afford what Westerners would consider 'normal' accommodation.

Notwithstanding the generally inferior standard of living in most Indonesian cities in recent years (1968-72) there have been many marked improvements and developments, particularly in Djakarta and Surabaja. Fully divided roads, pedestrian crossovers, widened streets and traffic lights have brought some sanity to the chaos of betjaks, pony traps and motorised vehicles that comprise Djakarta's traffic. Fortunately, in the cities outside of Djakarta, Surabaja, Medan, Palembang and Makassar motorised traffic has not yet reached a volume sufficient to constitute a problem. Tempo in the rural cities and towns is still pleasantly old-worldish.

A TOURISTS' DREAM

Indonesians are only just realising that tourism is as good an export commodity as rubber. In the past their attempts to utilise and develop it have been naive and inadequate, and generally speaking the local tourist entrepreneurs have had little conception of the needs and desires of most foreign visitors. They have failed to recognise the simple fact that foreigners go to Indonesia to see and experience Indonesia — not imported Western entertainment. Their pricing policies have been unreasonably high and there has been little or no attempt to exploit the great potentialities of the Outer Islands while they let Bali be spoiled by wealthy but ignorant tourists.

For a people with a largely ill-based knowledge of Europeans this initial reaction to the first influx of visitors is perhaps not surprising. Heartening are the efforts of the responsible weekly press which are stimulating re-assessments of Indonesian attitudes to foreigners.

Perhaps part of the reason for the still relatively low number of tourists (1968-75,000: 1970-100,000) has been the lack of modern accommodation. Only in Djakarta, Denpasar (Bali), Jogjakarta and Pelabuhan Ratu are there hotels of international standing where the tariff for an air conditioned single room without food can vary from US$10 to US$19 plus 21 per cent government tax and service charges. In these and other cities in Indonesia satisfactory accommodation at reasonable rates ($5-$10) is also available although only local travel agents will know the names of hotels in the smaller towns. The travel world at large is abysmally ignorant of travel conditions and tourist facilities in Indonesia.

Ironically, while most educated Indonesians are fairly intent upon Westernising themselves as quickly and as successfully as possible, most foreigners come to Indonesia in the expectation of seeing traditional dances, ancient rituals and experiencing local customs. They do not understand that Indonesia is striving to assume a place alongside the established nations of the world, to be recognised as a nation independent of political and economic ties and of being able to provide its peoples with ample food, freedom, justice and democracy.

That these ideals have not yet been achieved is a reflection of the many problems that face the still-very-young Republic of Indonesia.

HANDICRAFTS

Visitors to Indonesia praise the great variety and quality of local handicrafts—including textiles, woodcarvings, cane, silver and gold work. But today handicraft manufacture is confined to only a dozen or so villages and the number of skilled craftsmen is decreasing. It is a sad fact that the Indonesian elite has little appreciation for the arts and crafts of the indigenous artisan and the production of many traditional handicrafts has long ceased. This has been the case in Sumatra's northernmost province, Atjeh, where intricately engraved copper bowls and elaborate brocades used to be made; now the art has all but disappeared. Nevertheless a few handicrafts have managed to survive. In Jogjakarta and Solo, for instance, *batik* making is thriving but there has been a drift away from the time consuming, painstaking *batik tulis* to the quicker but definitely inferior *batik tjap*.

In addition to the smaller examples of the local craftsman's skill, Indonesia is noted for its traditional monuments. *Tjandis* or sacred monuments and tombs which trace back to Indian cultural influence are found scattered all over Central and East Java. The most famous are those near Jogjakarta—tjandis Borobudur, Mendut, Kalasan and Prambanan. All date from the 8th and 9th Centuries.

The Islamisation of Indonesia during the 15th and 16th Centuries saw the flourishing of arts for which Java remains famous—batik textiles and the not previously mentioned armoury. Although these and other arts were stimulated by the sultans of the new central Javanese Islamic states the motifs and styles used were from the previous Hindu-Javanese eras. European influence on Indonesian art has been limited almost entirely to painting, a field in which Indonesia has no long traditions.

ECONOMIC DEVELOPMENT

A major factor in the rehabilitation of Djakarta has been the strength and stability of the Suharto government. In fact the current government has been the first to actively plan and encourage economic activity in a rational way. "Pelita", the plan instituted in 1969, has received both the financial and moral support of the country's foreign debtors and prospective investors. Undoubtedly this assistance has done much to help restore some of the prestige which Djakarta lost during the period of the Government under the control of President Sukarno.

Serious efforts to improve the economy of Indonesia through planned development were started at the beginning of 1967, when the replacement of former President Sukarno by President Suharto brought about a change in the policies and priorities of the Government.

Indonesia's economy in 1966 was in a desperate state. Hyper-inflation soared to uncontrollable heights: the index figures of 62 commodities stood at 650 per cent compared with the previous year. Prior to 1966, prices went up not year by year, nor month by month, but day by day. This was a disastrous situation not only for workers on fixed salaries but also for virtually every form of business because a favourable climate for healthy business practice was lacking. An absence of sound economic leadership opened the door for speculation and corruptive practices, thus making the chaotic picture complete. Government control had been introduced over practically all economic activities, and state enterprises were established, which because of inefficiency, ended in becoming a burden to the state budget.

Food production, particularly rice, increased only by 2.3 per cent per annum during 1960-66, which was quite inadequate to meet the demands of the natural growth of population. Other basic commodities such as clothes and kerosene were in short supply.

Despite the relative unimportance of mining, industry and manufacture, these sectors of the economy accounted for roughly 15 per cent of the country's GNP in 1966. The often pressing importance of mining and estate cropping lies in their capacity to earn much needed foreign exchange. Conversely, the performance of the industrial and manufacturing sectors reduces the drain of foreign reserves out of the country.

Oil production and exploration in Indonesia is proceeding apace. Foreign investors, attracted by the favourable conditions of investment, have signed 36 production sharing agreements with the state-owned monopoly—Pertamina.

Tin is the country's second biggest mineral export. However, owing to a declining world demand, a reduction in the reserves of the more accessible ores and the obsolete form of equipment, production declined by almost half to 18,000 tons in the period 1954 to 1962. Indonesia has fallen from second to third among the world's tin producing countries.

All Indonesian nickel is obtained from mines in the Pomala district of Sulawesi Selatan. By 1967 the Sulawesi Nickel Corporation of Japan had increased the Republic's ore output from 0.1 million tons to 0.17 million tons. Indonesia—Asia's largest producer of nickel—exports all that it produces to Japan—Asia's largest nickel user.

The export trade also deteriorated considerably in the first part of the 'sixties. In 1960 Indonesia's exports, worth US$840.70 million, went down to US$665.44 million in 1966, including proceeds from petroleum. Several export products decreased in quantity and quality because of inadequate maintenance and care. In the rubber plantations, for example, no new trees were planted, and only old, less productive trees were tapped.

Foreign market prices fell. For Indonesia —like any other predominantly agrarian export-oriented country—the picture was really disheartening, and this was the unhappy situation when the present Suharto administration assumed the task of systematic rehabilitation and economic reconstruction. Lacking capital and skilled manpower, but with the support of experts in various fields, the economic strategy of present-day Indonesia was designed and put into practice in 1966. The first vital steps were to solve the problem of inflation, improve the supply of food and clothing, and rehabilitate infrastructures and production facilities.

To overcome the problem of inflation a balanced budget system and healthier practices in the use of credits were introduced. The mechanism of free market forces and prices was applied under the watchful eye of the Government. Price adjustments were made in certain categories but the Government refrained from direct interference in any field of economic activity. Instead, direction and assistance were given to enterprise together with facilities to bring about free and maximum production. Exports were stimulated through institutional changes, greater incentives were given to exporters and the export production sector was expanded. In this context, Indonesia re-entered the international business world. The Government did everything possible to increase domestic revenues through more balanced taxation and doing away with the inefficient granting of subsidies, etc. To relieve the financial burden the Government sought foreign capital assistance on the easiest of practical terms. Debts made by the previous regime were acknowledged, but ways were sought to repay them on more realistic terms. Beginning in 1966 Bank credits were supplemented by funds from the State budget to carry over the first years of stabilisation, rehabilitation, and reconstruction. Government funds were supplied in the form of investment credits. Domestic capital investments were stimulated, and a new policy was introduced to open Indonesia's doors to foreign capital investments.

By the beginning of 1969 all these measures were beginning to show results, thus justifying their continuance and the establishment of an Economic Development Five-year Plan.

Such a Plan was started on 1st April 1969. It primarily focused attention on the agricultural field, on the production of food and particularly on rice. The main objective was to produce so much rice during the first vital five years, that Indonesia might gradually decrease rice imports and ultimately stop them completely. Foreign exchange saved in this way could be used for other purposes in the context of economic development.

Export production was to be stepped up, particularly in commodities derived from estates and mines, thus establishing a relationship between production exports and imports that would ultimately achieve a sound economic balance.

Rural industries were to be geared to the production of raw materials needed by the

Top left:
Morning prayer on Idul Fitri
on the First Sjawal 1390 Hidjriar
(1st December 1970).
The Indonesia State guarantees freedom of worship to all religions.

Right:
Brightly coloured scarves
with Indonesian printed designs
are sold in bazaars
and villages.

Left:
An Indonesian woman
working a pattern on dress material
for a special customer.

agricultural sector, and fertiliser, cement, pesticides, etc. were high on the priority list. Next was the making of agricultural equipment such as rice grinders and rice mills, crumb rubber machines and so on. Another industrial sector of high priority included the clothing and people's handicraft industries because of their capacity to absorb manpower to a degree second only to agriculture. Textile industries, if developed properly, would have the capacity to save foreign exchange, and therefore received due attention in the Five-year Plan.

Notwithstanding the high merit of these plans it was essential that they be supported by equally significant measures in the field of economic infrastructures. Thus, under the Five-year Plan, a high priority was given to the rehabilitation and further development of roads, bridges, railroads, harbours, airports, irrigation works and electric power generation. Placing the most strategic first, improvements were made in stages, and gradually embraced such other fields as telecommunications.

As planning and progress in the various sectors were closely related, complete success could only be ensured if developments in the social field were paralleled with administrative and institutional advancement.

Essentially, the whole development strategy aimed at creating more employment opportunities for the population of over 115 million (1969). This accounted for the emphasis on the agricultural sector as having greatest potential in absorbing manpower. Next in importance were industry and people's handicrafts. In order to attract new manpower, infrastructural activities and investments were directed to the development of the less populated areas outside Java. Even before the beginning of the Five-year Plan starts were made in Second Level regions and towns throughout the Indonesian Republic.

RISING SOCIETY

In the social field development plans were directed towards education in the improvement of vocational and intermediate technical schools, and higher education in specialised fields; health programmes gave priority to the eradication of contagious diseases and the improvement of health; family planning was to be achieved in a national programme involving 3 million acceptors within five years of operation.

Legal security to all strata of the population, to ensure business stability and zest for economic enterprise were to be effected through improvements in the administration of the law.

Since 1967 the structure of central government services has been simplified and a more efficient relationship with the regional governments has developed.

Foreign trade measures were taken to bring about administrative and institutional improvements such as simplification of procedures, incentives to exporters, indirect targeting and directing to rationalise the composition of imported goods, and to simplify foreign exchange.

Budget appropriations are now made on the basis of programmes, no longer on the basis of departmental requisitions. Thus project planning has assumed prime importance. Taxation measures are being planned to improve the level of government revenues. Improvement in the management of government enterprises has resulted in their being given greater autonomy in their operations. Those that function as commercial enterprises have been corporations or limited liability companies.

In the past it was contended that there were far too many civil servants and that their productivity was low. This was probably due to the low level of salaries. It was therefore proposed to increase salaries as a gradual process based on the current cost of living as otherwise any increase would be ineffective; at the same time the number of personnel employed in each government unit was subjected to review.

By these various means inflation has been halted, as the following percentage indices for 62 kinds of goods on the free market in Djakarta indicate: 1966—650 per cent; 1967—120 per cent; 1968—85 per cent; 1969—10 per cent, and up to November 1970 8.2 per cent. Indonesia's rupiah has become more stable, as is indicated in the recent consistent exchange rates against foreign currencies.

Significantly, the volume of money circulation has shown steady growth since 1966: 1966—Rp. 113,894 million; 1969—Rp. 179,973 million and up to the month of November of 1970—Rp. 249,800 million.

The production of rice has shown spectacular increases; for 1967 it was 9,000 thousand tons; 10,200 thousand tons in 1968; 10,800 thousand tons in 1969; 1970: 11,430 thousand tons. An intensive programme for rice production has been put into operation involving better supplies of irrigation water, timely delivery of fertiliser, and credit loans to farmers through efficient banking systems.

Other farm and estate products have also shown remarkable production increases and the same applies to industries. But really spectacular figures have been recorded in the mining field. Fixing the index for 1960 at 100, the production of crude oil for 1966 was 113, rising to 179 in 1969. Tin stood at 56 in 1966, and at 76 in 1969. The figure for bauxite was 177 in 1966, and at 193 in 1969 was almost double the 1961 index of 106. Nickel ore which had stood at 134 in 1966, increased to 726 in 1969.

The viability of the Indonesian economy continues to depend on her export trade. Despite the chaotic export situation during the old regime, the present Government has managed to simplify retarding administrative procedures and attract industries with export potential, thus increasing the flow of out-going trade.

The rise in export value, according to Bank Indonesia figures which include petroleum, was from 678,532,000 US dollars in 1966 to 831,201,000 US dollars in 1969.

Foreign capital investments in Indonesia since 1967 involved 281 projects up to September 1970, with a planned total investment capital of US$1,250 million.

Summarising, it may be said that the average rate of growth of the Indonesian economy for the years 1960 to 1970 inclusive was slightly more than 6 per cent.

Above:
Recreation parks and sea-shore and lake amusement areas have sprung up all over Indonesia.
This is the children's sector at Bina Ria at Autjol Djakarta a resort complete with swimming pool, yachting, canoeing, restaurants and bars and a drive-in theatre.

Centre:
Young daughters and wives wash their families' clothes in a river near their homes.

Top left:
The local girls in bright costumes join in a community dance.

Left:
An Indonesian musician playing his percussion instruments.

Right:
Hotel Inter-Continental Indonesia at Djakarta with Slamat Datang (Welcome) Statue in the foreground.

Below:
The lobby of Hotel Indonesia.

Below right:
Almost every day some sort of festival or ceremonial is held in Indonesia.

HOTEL INDONESIA

walls of the restaurant, dancers, birds and flowers are caught in endless mime within the mosaic of conflicts, love and hate.

Here, the traditional foods of Indonesian celebrations are served: rijstafel, an appetising array of curried meats, fish and vegetables; nasi goreng, a national dish of rice, fried in coconut oil with egg, meat, tomato, cucumber and chilies; and soto, a popular casserole of chicken, vegetables and dumplings. Built into the atmosphere of the country, the Hotel Indonesia combines modern sophistication with the traditions of a thousand years.

It offers dining and dancing at the "Nirwana Supper Club", Cantonese food at the "Restaurant Orientale", freshly-roasted coffee at the "Java Room", and a large shopping arcade where the thousand-and-one souvenirs, items of tropical clothing, and services expected by the globe-trotting tourist are to be found.

THE MAIN BOULEVARDE of downtown Djakarta is the fast developing Djalan Thamrin.

Endless streams of traffic flow through its length: limousines and sports cars vie with thousands of three-wheeled pedicabs—the betjaks; small jitney buses carrying only eight passengers race past the horsedrawn "delman" carriages. In the midst of the hubbub of sirens, horns and bells is the tallest building in the capital—the 450-room, air-conditioned, fourteen-storeyed Inter-Continental Hotel Indonesia. Its view extends from the Mendeka Palace on the north side of Freedom Square, the suburb of Grogol (site of the vast Asian Games stadium) and the immense grand mosque at Kebajoram, to the older harbour districts of Tandjung Priok, the fish market—Pasar Ikan—and the quaint Dutch houses and wide canals of Chinatown—Djakarta Kota.

The balconies of the eastern aspect rooms look over the great lawn-bordered swimming pool where beach umbrellas and deck chairs beckon the languid visitor in the cool of the evening. The Hotel can accommodate a thousand guests in its great Bali Room where international conventions and State dinners are held.

Each year, at the town of Prambanan, brilliantly-costumed dancers tell the story of the Ramayana, against the floodlit background of a 9th Century Hindu temple. The tale is retold in murals and on the drapes of the Hotel Indonesia's Ramayana Restaurant. It is as old as Homer's Iliad and, like the Iliad, depicts the abduction of a beautiful princess and the furious battles being fought to rescue her. On the

Right:
A Balinese beauty.

Below:
The Hotel Inter-Continental at Bali Beach.

BALI BEACH

ONE OF THE MOST FAMOUS islands of the wide spreading Indonesian archipelago is Bali, a comparatively small tract of forest-covered terrain, some 2,000 square miles in area. Its name is a legend among the tourist spots of the world and since the jet airliner has become the international mode of fast travel, the island has been brought within a few hours' flying time of all the countries in the broad expanse of the South-east Asian area.

Geologically Bali is a volcanic mountain sloping down through green forests and palm groves to white, sandy, reef-protected beaches. And this is the home of 3.5 million Balinese who lead a peaceful, carefree way of life in an idyllic environment.

On Bali there are 10,000 temples, spread all over the tiny island, and the visitor is almost sure to witness at least one religious festival somewhere, anytime of the year. Hinduism is the Balinese faith, and into the people has been inculcated the centuries old Hindu tradition evidenced in their carvings, paintings and weaving. The grace and beauty of the dancing girls has brought them fame all over the world.

There are many places the visitor cannot afford to miss. Mas is where the famous Balinese wood carvings and paintings are to be found; Tjeluk is eight miles from Denpasar, the capital of the island, and here the best of the silverwork is to be seen.

The museum at Denpasar displays examples of all forms of Balinese art from ages past. Ubud is the home of the painters and some 200 dedicated artists live here, both local and many from foreign parts.

These are the traditional interests of Bali, but the 20th Century has created a demand for something more than natural beauty and local colour—a place of comfort and luxury in which one may live whilst enjoying the bounty of nature.

In Bali this is provided by the Inter-Continental Hotel Bali Beach.

On a reef-protected beach near Sanur, ten miles from Denpasar airport, the 300-room glistening white hotel overlooks the tropic waters of the vast Indian Ocean. In it are combined the ancient living cultures of Bali with all the ultra-modern amenities that a sophisiticated civilisation can provide.

Outside the Hotel there is swimming in the great palm-shaded pool or in the rolling ocean, pleasure boating by native proa or motor boat and picnics to neighbouring islands, fishing, water skiing, surfboard riding and skin diving. There is horseback riding along the beaches and in forest glades, tennis, shuffleboard, volley ball and badminton.

Inside the Hotel there are almost as many restaurants as colours in the tropical sunset.

Dining in the crimson and gold Raja Room includes oriental, Indonesian and international cuisine, music and dinner dancing.

Nightly entertainment highlights the rooftop Bali Hai Supper Club. The Baruna Pavilion offers snacks and light refreshment outdoors at the beach and pool. Cocktails are served in the native-atmosphere Baris Lounge, as well as on the breeze-cooled Nu Santara Terrace overlooking the ocean with the mountain, Gunung Agung, reaching its 10,000 feet into the azure Balinese sky. The Bali Kopi Shop menu features "coffee shop" fare.

The Hotel's 300-seat outdoor theatre presents regular performances of classical Balinese dance dramas. Dressed in gold and silver, accompanied by gamelang and gambang (bamboo) orchestras, the dancers weave through traditional movements depicting folk epics. In the tradition of colourful Bali the Ketjak or Monkey Dance is performed every sunset by more than a hundred dancers swaying in the flickering light of torches.

JAPAN

LEGEND

- 🟨 FOREST
- 🟩 MISCELLANEOUS AGRICULTURE
- 🟢 RICE & CORN
- ⊥ IRON
- ⋈ COPPER
- ⋈ GOLD
- ◯ URANIUM
- ⊙ SULPHUR

CHINA

SOVIET UNION

SOUTH KOREA

SEA OF JAPAN

JAPAN

Kanazawa

Hiroshima
Fukuoka
Sasebo
Kitakyushu
Okayama
Kobe
Kyoto
Gifu
Nagoya
Takamatsu
Sakai
Osaka
Hamamatsu
Nagasaki
Kumamoto
Kochi
Wakayama

Kagoshima

EAST CHINA SEA

PACIFIC OCEAN

Senkaku Islands

Map of Japan

Hokkaido region:
- Otaru
- Sapporo
- Asahikawa
- Muroran
- Hakodate

Honshu (northern):
- Aomori
- Hachinohe
- Akita
- Morioka
- Yamagata
- Sendai
- Fukushima
- Niigata
- Nagano
- Maebashi
- Mito
- Hachioji
- Tokyo
- Yokohama

Nansei (South West) Islands:
- Kagoshima
- Tanegashima Is.
- Yakushima Is.
- Amami Islands
- NAZE
- Amami Oshima Is.
- Okinawa Islands
- Okinawa Is.
- NAHA
- Daito Islands
- Miyako Is.
- Sakishima Islands

Ogasawara (Bonin) Islands:
- Tokyo
- Izu Islands

Kazan (Volcano) Islands

PACIFIC OCEAN

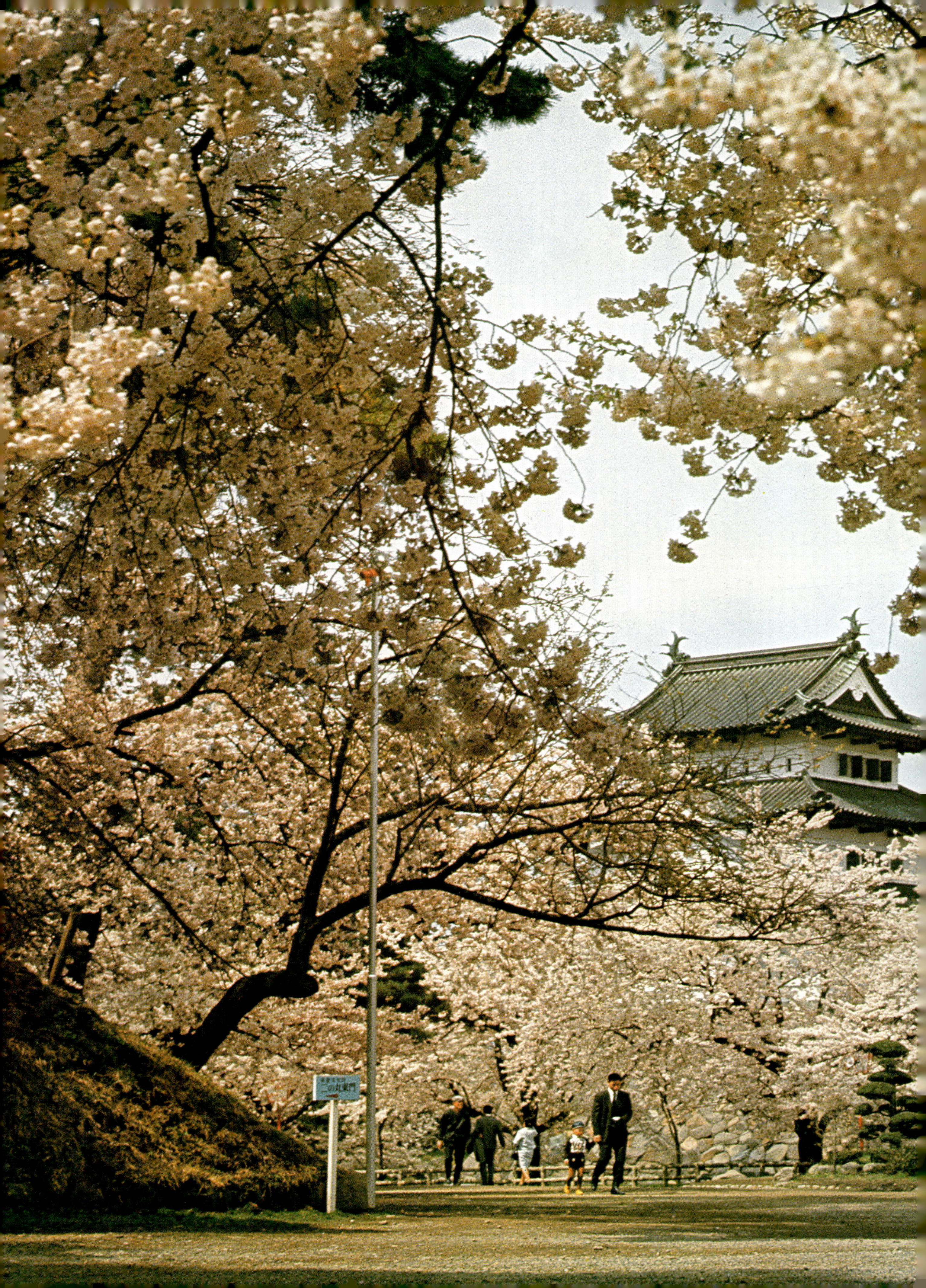

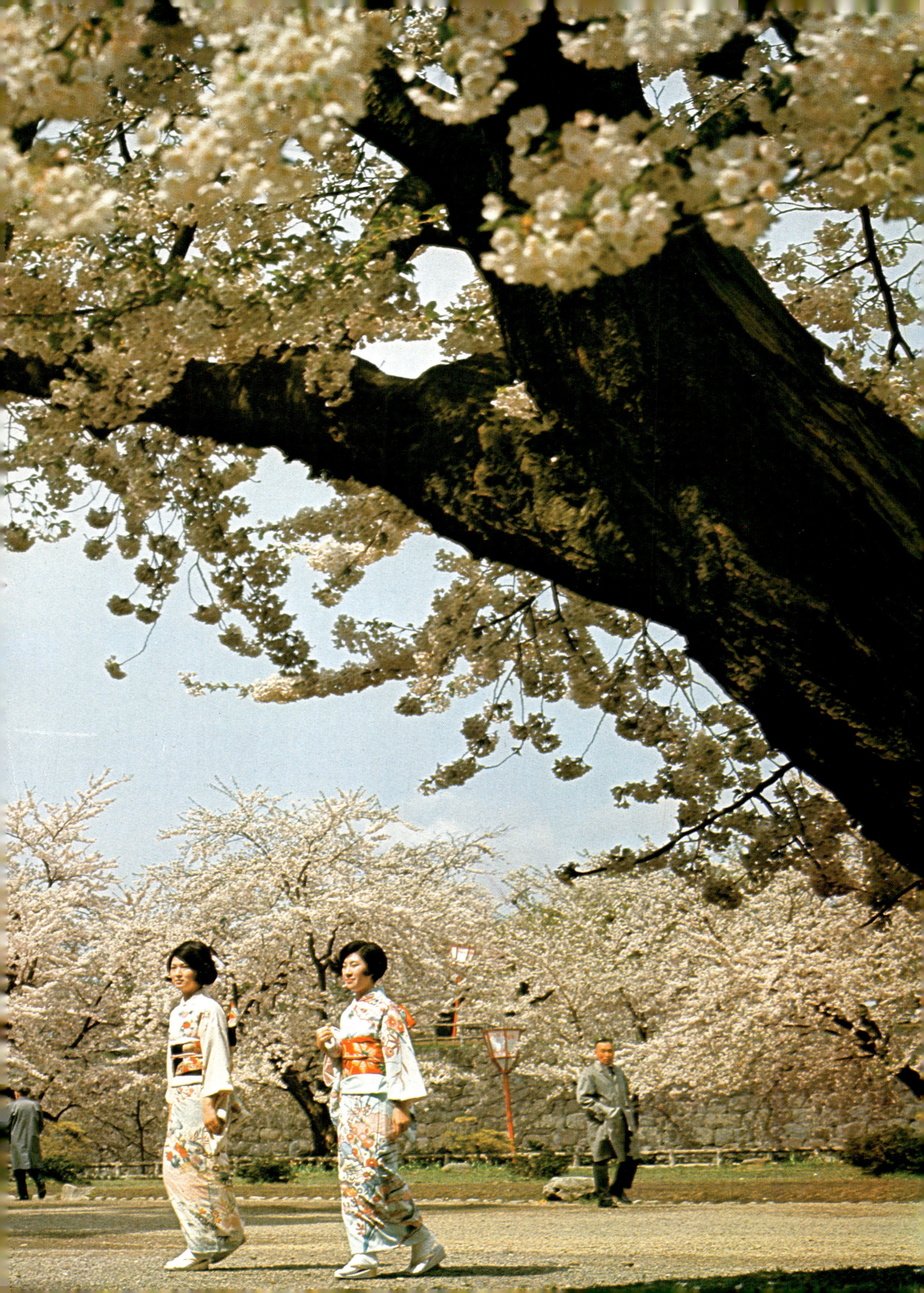

A Country Called Japan

GEOGRAPHICALLY Japan comprises four main islands—Honshu, Shikoku, Kyushu and Hokkaido—in addition to hundreds of other smaller islands and tiny islets. The archipelago stretches in an arc, 3,800 kilometres (2,360 miles) long from north to south off the eastern coast of the Asian Continent, and covers an area of 377,384 square kilometres (145,670 square miles).

At the end of World War II Japan lost all its territorial possessions, which then represented 45.5 per cent of its total area. The land area of Japan today is less than one-twentieth that of Australia, one-eighth that of India and one-and-a-half times as big as the United Kingdom.

The islands of Japan lie in the temperate zone. Rainfall is abundant, ranging from 1,000 to 2,500 millimetres (40 to 100 inches) a year and there is heavy snow in the northern parts of the country in winter.

The climate is generally mild and the seasons distinct. Summer, which is warm and humid, begins after a rainy season (towards mid-June) that lasts for about four weeks. Except in northern Japan the winter is usually mild with long periods of sun. Spring and autumn are the best times of the year with balmy days and bright sunshine. Japan's famous cherry blossoms appear in spring, and in autumn the countryside is filled with the variegated hues of falling leaves.

The mountains, which account for 80 per cent of Japan's total land area, are everywhere in view. More than 580 of them are more than 2,000 metres (6,560 feet) high and the tallest is Mt. Fuji, whose perfect cone reaches 3,776 metres (12,389 feet) above sea-level. Mt. Fuji is a volcano that has been dormant since its last eruption in 1707. In all, Japan has 196 volcanoes of which 30 are still active. They provide the country with mineral hot springs that are tapped mainly for recreational purposes; they feed numerous hot spring resorts which cater to millions of holiday-makers in search of peace and relaxation.

WHO ARE THE JAPANESE?

No-one knows the exact origin of the Japanese people. Some scholars say that the first settlers came from northern Asia and the region of southern China; others believe they migrated from the islands of the South Pacific. As they are today, however, the Japanese have probably emerged from the intermingling of several races.

By the beginning of the 4th Century the organisation of Japan's political society was consolidated after several reforms. It was ruled by the Imperial Family—which continues to rule at the present day—and by members of the nobility.

During these early years Korea and China were the sources from which Japan derived her arts, crafts and learning and these were the foundations on which Japan's own culture was gradually built. Through Chinese scripts the Japanese learned the rudiments of medicine, astronomy and philosophy. In 538 A.D. Buddhism was also introduced through China and Korea. Mahayana Buddhism as well as Shinto, Japan's native religious faith, were the dominating features in building up the Japanese culture.

The ancient capital of Japan, which had been moved from one place to another in the Yamato district (Nara Prefecture), was finally established in Nara at the beginning of the 8th Century. It was then transferred to Kyoto, a few miles north of Nara, towards the close of the 8th Century. Here it remained as the capital of Japan until 1868. During the period from the 13th Century to the middle of the 19th Century the samurai warriors held political power. In 1192 Yoritomo, head of the Minamoto clan, established a military government called the Shogunate at Kamakura and assumed all administrative powers that had previously been held by the Emperor in Kyoto.

The Minamotos were succeeded by the Hojos. Imperial rule was once again restored in 1333 though it was short lived. A new Shogunate was soon established by the Ashikagas at Muromachi in Kyoto. After two centuries (1333-1573) of ruling, the Ashikaga Shogunate was driven out of Kyoto by rival clans. Towards the end of the 16th Century there were continual civil wars as provincial lords battled for supremacy. In 1590 order was finally restored by a great general, Hideyoshi Toyotomi. His aim of uniting the country was achieved by Ieyasu Tokugawa, founder of the Tokugawa Shogunate.

The first Westerners to visit Japan were Portuguese traders who landed on an islet off Kyushu in 1543. They were followed by Jesuit Missionaries and groups of Spaniards. Trade with the Dutch and the British also began. European missionaries made numerous converts, particularly in southern Japan. Being afraid of political interference by the West through religious infiltration, the Shogunate eventually proscribed Christianity and closed the doors of Japan to all foreigners except Dutch and Chinese traders, who were confined to a small island at Nagasaki.

From the end of the 18th Century Japan was placed under increasing pressure to open up her ports to foreign ships. Everywhere at home there appeared signs of

A Haniwa clay figurine of a kneeling man—a valuable cultural relic of the 6th to 7th Centuries.

decay in the feudalistic socio-political structure. Finally in 1854 Japan concluded a treaty of amity with the United States followed by similar treaties with other countries. Thus Japan opened her doors to the outside world ending nearly 300 years of isolation. The impact of these events increased the pressure on social and political currents that were undermining the feudal structure. The shogunate collapsed in 1867 and full sovereignty was restored to the Emperor in 1868. The period that followed was the most significant in Japan's modern history; it was called the Meiji Restoration. Its impact on the country and the world was like the bursting of a dam behind which had accumulated the energies and forces of centuries. Japan set out to achieve in only a few decades what had taken centuries to develop in the West—the creation of a modern nation. She emerged victorious in the Sino-Japanese War (1894-95) and the Russo-Japanese War (1904-05). By the end of World War I, which she entered under the provisions of the Anglo-Japanese Alliance of 1902, Japan was recognised as one of the world's great powers and continued to grow in stature for the next forty years.

After being defeated in World War II Japan came under foreign occupation for the first time in her history. The morale of her people had sunk to the lowest level, their homes in ruins and their country's economy virtually at zero. Nearly seven years of allied occupation passed before she regained her sovereignty in April 1952.

Today this island country stands among the nations of the world as a democratic state, endeavouring to contribute to the well-being of her people and to the growth of a peaceful international community.

Left:
A scene from the traditional Noh play "Matsukaze" or "Pine Breeze".

Above:
The thousand and one images of the Goddess of Mercy in the Myohoin Temple at Sanjusangendo, Kyoto.

On many occasions the Emperor of Japan has generously recognised outstanding services to his country and people. One of Japan's high awards is the Order of Merit First Class Sacred Treasure illustrated below.

In April 1972 the Hon. Sir Edward Warren, K.C.M.G., K.B.E., M.S.M., O.M.S.T., R.S.G.C., M.L.C., became the first non-Japanese to receive this Order, for his long and valuable services to Japanese-Australian relations.

The Emperor had previously awarded to Sir Edward the Order of the Rising Sun with Grand Cordon in 1967.

LIVING IN JAPAN

Japan's population was 103,704,000 according to the last national census held in 1970. Although her birth rate is one of the lowest in the world the population will continue to increase for some time to come as the result of a declining mortality rate.

Japan ranks sixth in the world in terms of population after mainland China, India, the Soviet Union, the United States and the Republic of Indonesia.

The density of population is 280 people per square kilometre, which is exceeded only by the Republic of China, the Republic of Korea, Belgium and the Netherlands, in that order. These figures, however, are misleading. Since Japan's mountains leave scarcely 16 per cent of the total area suitable for cultivation, its population density in proportion to its arable land is the heaviest in the world. More than 40 per cent of Japan's 104 million people are in fact concentrated in only 1 per cent of the country's total land area.

The concentration is heaviest in the Metropolitan Prefecture of Tokyo where about one in every nine Japanese lives today. At the time of the 1970 census Tokyo's population was 11,399,000.

Increasing numbers of Japanese are leaving the land and flocking to the big cities as a result of the steady expansion of the country's industrial economy.

The population of the eight largest cities, according to the October 1970 census were: the Metropolitan Prefecture of Tokyo 11,399,000; Osaka 2,980,000; Yokohama 2,238,000; Nagoya 2,036,000; Kyoto 1,419,000; Kobe 1,289,000; Kitakyushu 1,289,000 and Sapporo 1,010,000.

JAPAN'S DEMOCRACY

Japan has a democratic form of Government. Under its present Constitution, which came into force on 3rd May 1947, the highest law-making body is the Diet, or Parliament, elected directly by the people. The Diet is composed of a House of Representatives with 491 members and a House of Councillors with 252 members. The Representatives are elected for a four-year term of office, although this may be terminated before its usual expiry date if the Diet is dissolved. The Councillors are elected for a six-year term of office with half of the members elected every three years.

All men and women attaining the age of twenty have the right to vote in all elections. The chief executive of the State is the Prime Minister, who is elected by the Diet from among its members; he is usually the leader of the majority party. The Prime Minister usually selects eighteen Ministers of State to serve in his Cabinet. All these Ministers must be civilians and at least half of them must also be members of the Diet. Each Minister heads a government department such as Foreign Affairs, Finance, Justice and so forth.

If the House of Representatives votes disapproval of the Prime Minister and his policies the entire Cabinet must resign at once and the Diet then selects a new Prime Minister. However, the Prime Minister may not resign but may, instead, dissolve the House of Representatives and call for national elections after which the Cabinet resigns and the new Diet selects a Prime Minister.

The highest court of law is the Supreme Court which has a Chief Justice and fourteen other judges. The Supreme Court and all lower courts are completely independent of both the Diet and the Cabinet. The main political parties at present are: the Liberal-Democratic Party (the conservative party in Japan today), the Socialist Party, the Komeito Party and the Democratic-Socialist Party. Minor parties are also represented in the Diet, including the Communist Party.

For local administration Japan is divided into 46 prefectures including the capital district called the Metropolitan Prefecture of Tokyo. All prefectures, as well as cities, towns and villages, have local assemblies, the members of which are directly elected by the voters in the local community.

ART AND CULTURE

Japanese art today is as diverse in its forms as it is long in its tradition. The culture and art of mainland Asia—India, China, Korea—were brought to Japan together with Buddhism in the 6th Century. By the 10th Century these cultural imports had been changed so that they were completely Japanese in form and style. During subsequent centuries, the arts developed under the direction and encouragement of the Buddhist priests and the nobility among whom were included the Imperial Family.

Wooden and bronze sculpture, painting, pottery, lacquer work and woodblock prints have been developed to a high degree of beauty. At all times Japanese art has been based upon the beauty of nature. Thus landscape gardening and flower arrangement are an important part of Japanese life.

In Japanese houses and in modern public buildings the natural colour of the construction materials is usually left untouched; the use of large sliding windows and wall panels allows the interior to be opened directly onto the gardens and outside space. Poetry and music also are expressions of the beauties of nature.

Traditional Japanese drama includes the classic *Noh* plays, the *Bunraku* or puppet theatre and the *Kabuki* theatre with its magnificent costumes and colourful settings. In recent years Japanese films have become very popular in foreign countries and have received many prizes in international film competitions.

All major Japanese cities have symphony orchestras while opera and ballet performances draw large audiences.

Above:
With Mount Fuji
forming an impressive
scenic backdrop, a typical
Japanese farm and
paddy rice field.

Opposite page:
The Diet Building,
or House of Parliament,
in Tokyo. It accommodates
the House of Representatives and House
of Councillors.

Above:
Nijo Castle in Kyoto is one of the finest examples of Japanese decorative architecture.

In the capital city cultural activities are almost a way of life and today Tokyo has its Metropolitan Festival Hall which has become a major centre for all the performing arts. Each year in Osaka the International Music Festival brings visitors from many parts of the world.

Japan was primarily responsible for the formation of the Asian Broadcasting Union, an organisation that is doing much today to assist Asian countries to develop and improve their radio and T.V. programmes. In 1957 the Japan Broadcasting Corporation (NHK) invited other Asian broadcasters to attend a conference in Tokyo to discuss programme exchanges and other activities. From that conference the ABU was born and Japan's initiative is reflected in the greatly improved standard of broadcasting in Asia. Japanese painters and artists enjoy very high reputations and their works are often included in international exhibitions.

The Japanese have long been active in the field of literature and writing. Many novels have been translated into foreign languages.

THE EDUCATION SYSTEM

The standard of literacy among the Japanese people had been almost 100 per cent even before the turn of the 20th Century. Education for Japanese children today is free and compulsory for the first nine years, i.e. for six years of primary schooling and three years of lower secondary schooling.

After these nine years students can enter upper secondary school for a three-year period by passing an examination and by paying a small tuition fee. After upper secondary school, students can continue their studies at various universities, usually for four years. There are also special two-year colleges. Almost all universities and other schools are co-educational.

Throughout Japan there are 379 universities and colleges and 473 two-year junior colleges at which are enrolled about 1,618,200 students, including 9,810 from other parts of Asia and the world.

In addition to schools Japan has many libraries, museums and exhibition halls, and many public auditoriums where all kinds of musical and theatrical performances are held.

Increasing numbers of foreign students come to Japan each year to study in Japanese universities and to receive training in industries and various fields of science and technology.

In 1969 nearly 2,600 Japanese book publishers issued about 26,424 titles and 2,485 magazines dealing with a multiplicity of interests.

Above: A Japanese wood-cut print depicting Emperor Meiji at a display of horses by the farmers of Morioka in 1876.

Above left: A class of Japanese young ladies at one of the many Schools of Ikebana, the art of floral arrangement.

Left: The Empress of Japan attending the inauguration of a girls' school in 1885. Today it is the Girls' Senior High School of Gakushuin in Tokyo.

AN URBAN FAMILY AT HOME

A unique feature of the traditional Japanese house is the use of sturdy sliding panels as windows and doors. There are sliding outer panels of wood with additional panels inside fitted with glass panes or covered with special paper called *shoji*. The floor is also unique being covered with cushioned straw mats called *tatami*.

Rooms are used for many purposes: each can be used for dining, to sleep in or just as a sitting room. One of the reasons for this is maximum utilisation of space. Most Japanese sleep on bedding rolled out on the *tatami* at night, and stored away in closets during the day to permit the rooms to be used for other purposes. The partitions between rooms are sliding doors which may be closed to form smaller rooms or opened to make a larger space.

Furniture is usually limited to low tables and a few chests of drawers; in place of chairs cushions are placed on the *tatami*. These mats are always clean because shoes are never worn in a Japanese house.

Today, with the changing customs, more and more western-style chairs, tables and other pieces of furniture are used and one almost always finds a television set occupying an important corner in the main room. But, as in all countries the world over, it is the family that makes the home.

Take the Hondas who live in the Japanese city of Nagoya; this story is told by one of the family's old friends:

Today was one of the happiest days Shuji Honda had known. After failing four times he had at last passed the second promotion examination in the Nagoya City Government. Shuji is an official in the Foreign Service Sub-Section of the Secretariat Section.

Nagoya is one of the largest cities in Japan with a population of over 2 million and its Government employs almost 20,000 Japanese. In addition to the head office there are fourteen district offices and numerous branch offices. Every ambitious official tries to get an appointment in the head office, particularly in such sections as Personnel, Finance and Secretariat, for these are the nerve centres of the Government and those who are working there have the best opportunities for promotion.

The City of Nagoya has been affiliated with Los Angeles as a sister city and many exchange programmes have been carried out between them. Mr Honda once accompanied a deputy mayor as interpreter when he visited Los Angeles some time ago. As Japan is geographically isolated from the developed western countries, the people usually see a special value in having been overseas.

Although English is practically a compulsory subject in the high schools of Japan, only a small percentage of the people speak it with reasonable fluency. Students are extremely keen to practise English conversation for they know that speaking English fluently can win them a scarcity value.

Shuji Honda and his wife have two children, a two year old daughter, Michiko, and a six year old son called Yoshio. They live in a modern flat in a housing project built by a semi-governmental body. Both the central and local governments in Japan are very actively engaged in building plans to cope with housing shortage; mostly flats in western-style concrete structures of three to five floors. Mr Honda's flat is typical of those built for the middle-class family, and contains 2 bedrooms and a dining-kitchen.

The rooms are separated by sliding doors, which can be closed or taken off when necessary to make a large room on special occasions. The Japanese leave their shoes at the small entrance hall when they step up into a room on a higher level. This helps to keep the inside of the home very clean.

The Honda's dining-kitchen is a western type and the family dine at a high table, sitting on chairs. The bedrooms are of Japanese style and the floors are covered with straw *tatami* mats, although Shuji Honda has put carpets on them in both rooms, now a common practice in Japan.

There are no beds in the bedrooms: when the family sleep they use cotton mattresses and quilts which are neatly kept in a closet during the daytime. Thus, the bedrooms can serve as a lounge for the family and guests when they are not being used to sleep in. In the Japanese-styled rooms everyone sits on cushions instead of chairs.

As a non-university graduate Shuji Honda appreciates the Nagoya system of affording its employees chances of advancement through competitive examinations. Nevertheless it was a great burden for him to study, particularly with a family and the extra work it involved.

In recent years he has been extremely busy at his office for Nagoya frequently acts as a host city for international conferences such as the United Nations Conference on City Planning, the Japan-American Conference of Mayors and the Chamber of Commerce Presidents' Conference. Often he returns home as late as 11 o'clock at night. He commutes to the City Hall by bus which takes him one hour each way. As the office starts at 8.30 a.m. he has to leave home a little after 7 o'clock, and in some weeks he hardly has a chance to talk to Michiko because when he sets off she is still asleep and when he returns home she is already in bed. Mr Honda is sorry about that but cannot help it.

After a day's work he finds it hard to concentrate on study, but when he forces himself to do so, on the following day he finds himself dull and unable to do a good job. He realises that he needs at least seven hours sleep to keep his brain in good condition and whenever he is lucky enough to find a seat in the bus he tries to have a nap to catch up on his rest. The office is open $5\frac{1}{2}$ days a week but on Saturday afternoons he often has to remain to do some miscellaneous jobs. So, Saturday evenings and Sundays are the only times always available for study for his exams.

Mrs Honda is very sympathetic towards her husband and this year she has made it a rule to visit her parents on Sundays so that he can be free from disturbance by the children. Before leaving home, of course, she never forgets to make a delicious and nutritious lunch for her husband.

In previous years Shuji used to drop in at bars and pinball parlours for a little relaxation on the way home from the office as most of his colleagues did, but this year he has scarcely ever done so in the sincere hope that this will see the end of his studies.

After such perseverance and industriousness it was good news indeed to learn that he had finally passed his exam and he lost no time in telephoning his wife from a public telephone in the City Hall. This was the happiest occasion for Mr and Mrs Honda in a long time; they could not stop talking.

After hanging up the telephone Yoko Honda went to the shopping centre for a bottle of sake and a big sea bream. Shuji called at a department store on the way home to buy a pearl necklace, which his wife had long wanted, and a battery-operated talking doll for his little daughter. That night there was a big celebration with Yoko Honda's parents as guests. Everybody was so happy and merry that even the baby's cry sounded like a sweet song.

Opposite page:
An "open field"
tea making ceremony or "nodate".
Above left:
The Honda family have
adopted the Western style of eating
in their home.
Left:
Shuiji and Yoko Honda were
married at the Meiji Shrine at Tokyo
in a Shinto wedding.
Above:
Yoshio has an excellent school
teacher who gives him a lot of
personal help in his studies.

JAPAN AT PLAY

EVERY TYPE OF SPORT, both traditional and modern, has a large following in Japan. In 1964 Tokyo was the host city for the 18th Olympic Games. In 1958 the Third Asian Games were held in Tokyo and in 1967 the Universiade brought competitors and spectators from many countries throughout the world. An even bigger meeting, in terms of participants, is held every year. This is the National Athletic Meet, an amateur event with the participation of more than 18,800 young athletes from all over Japan.

Radio and television have considerably revived the popularity of *sumo*, Japan's traditional style of wrestling. *Judo*, another time-honoured Japanese sport, is today popular not only in Japan but in many other countries.

In addition to their traditional games, the Japanese engage in almost every form of Western sports from track and field events to baseball, rowing and equestrianism.

Many Japanese athletes have taken part in international games at overseas venues and numerous foreign teams and individual athletes have been in turn invited to compete in Japan.

Baseball and swimming are among the most popular sports. Golf is also establishing itself in popularity. There are 560 courses spread throughout the land and it is estimated that about 3.5 million golfers participate in competitions or play the game at irregular intervals throughout the year.

In the 1964 Olympic Games Japanese athletes won gold medals in weight-lifting, boxing, wrestling, gymnastics, judo and women's volleyball, thus ranking Japan third after the United States and the Soviet Union in the number of gold medals.

In April 1966 the International Olympic Committee (IOC) designated Sapporo, Hokkaido, as the site of the 1972 Winter Olympic Games.

JAPAN'S NEWES

SHINJUKU is Tokyo's new exciting day and night area. Shinjuku, which in Japanese means "new lodgings", is located in the north-west part of the world's largest city. In the old days, it was a frontier transfer point where travellers on foot or horse-back would stop to rest on their way in or out of Edo (Tokyo). Then it was just a grassy plain with a few inns and shops. Today it is Japan's busiest centre. More people pass through Shinjuku than anywhere else in the country.

And Shinjuku is the site of a new metropolitan centre—a city within a city—complete with department stores, cinemas, art theatres, turkish and sauna baths and parks, by day; and cabarets, bars, nightclubs and discotheques, by night. And towering above the entire scene is the magnificent white granite and steel earthquake-proof building, the Keio Plaza Inter-Continental Hotel.

Diversity is the keynote of the Keio Plaza Hotel. One American travel writer called it "a city, not a hotel". The Keio Plaza has 1,057 guest rooms, 24 party and convention rooms, 10 restaurants and 9 bars and cocktail lounges. The truly wide-ranging list of amenities includes: a shopping arcade; printing shop; 800-car parking space; house physician; sauna bath; massage rooms; beauty parlour; secretarial service; baby-sitter; baby-food; hotel golf course; dentist; and photographic studio as well as all the expected services of rented cars and buses; safety deposit vaults; barber shop; airline and travel desks; 24-hour room service; laundry; and dry-cleaning.

In the main lobby, above the marble floor, a cobweb of space-borne silvery pipes provides illumination. In the lobby-centre, a twisting contorted creation of four giant mirrors reflects the striking designs of the

MOST LUXURIOUS HOTEL

floor lamps and the boldly coloured armchairs and tapestry, creating a fresh and exhilarating impression. A wide escalator at the east entrance leads directly up to banquet rooms, the capacities of which vary from 20 to 140 persons. For the larger meeting, the Concord Ballroom is ideal. With an elevator stage, carlift, burnished copper network of overhead studio lights, sophisticated illumination and sound controls, booths for simultaneous interpretation into six languages and equipment for live television broadcasts, it is the most professional facility of its type in Tokyo.

Each restaurant and bar has its own personality. Wadakim, the house which made Matsuzaka beef famous around the world, limits its sales to a select group of restaurants around Japan, of which the Keio Plaza's Okahan is one. The Ambrosia, another Keio Plaza restaurant, serves repasts in the Olympian manner—the food of the gods—and, from the 44th floor windows, a god-like view of the city is laid out in a broad panorama below. Two of Japan's classic dishes—*Tempura*, served in the Inagiku Restaurant, and *Edomae Sushi* (raw fish) in the Kyubei—can be sampled at the Hotel.

Bars are plentiful and their atmospheres vary from the convivial psychedelia of the Young Bar and the gay informality of the Aurora Lounge, to the cozy warmth of the Pole Star and the cool restfulness of the Brillant. For the soft-drink set, there are tea-rooms, coffee lounges and a sparkling Soda Fountain on the Top Floor Sky Promenada.

There is none of that stifling, 'shut-in' feeling in the Hotel's guest rooms. Every one of the Hotel's 1,057 rooms has large picture windows that look out on the urban kaleidoscope that is Tokyo.

Above: Keio Plaza Inter-Continental Hotel is almost a miniature city towering 170 metres into the Tokyo sky.

Left: Hana is one of the beautifully planned Banquet Rooms, colourfully furnished and decorated.

Left page, centre: A Kendo contest, one of the traditional sports of Japan.

Left page, below: A huge snow and ice castle at the Snow Festival held every winter at Sapporo.

FOREIGN EXCHANGE—MAINSPRING OF JAPAN'S OVERSEAS TRADE

IN THE SURGE OF EXPANSION and development that occurred after World War II and subsequent to the Korean War, the Japanese Government became increasingly alive to the vital part that overseas trade would play in the country's revival, and so the Foreign Exchange Act was promulgated in 1954. By this legislation a unique type of banking was introduced to specialise in foreign exchange and it proved to be a system ideally suited to Japan's special needs.

In 1946 the Bank of Tokyo was established to perform the new banking functions. Founded in the immediate post war period when Japan was still in ruins, it was destined to carry on the work of the famous pre-war institution, the Yokohama Specie Bank, known all over the world as Y.S.B. This bank began its operations as far back as 1880 and in its sixty-odd years succeeded in building a reservoir of experience and skill in international banking and finance. When the Bank of Tokyo opened its doors it inherited all the Y.S.B. assets together with its large staff of experienced personnel. To gain some conception of the role that banking — and particularly specialised banking such as the Bank of Tokyo plays in Japan's modern world of commerce—it is necessary to look back to the beginning of the Meiji Restoration. Banking and shipping were the first private activities to come on the scene as modern large-scale operations after the Restoration. In both instances their inception was the result of the Government's policy of special protective concessions, so in the strictest sense it cannot be said that they were wholly private enterprises. But their early success opened the way to the development of private large-scale modern industries and thus they made major contributions as pioneering businesses.

The Y.S.B. had been set up by the Government to deal in foreign exchange and by the second decade of the Meiji Era it had established branches in New York, Lyons, London and San Francisco. In the beginning, the main purpose of the bank was to absorb *specie* (money in the shape of coin) rather than help the progress of foreign trade, but by the third decade of the Restoration overseas branches were opened

336

primarily for the promotion of Japan's foreign trade.

The Bank of Tokyo now carries on the former activities of the Y.S.B. as a joint stock company responsible to shareholders. It performs all normal banking operations but its main business is dealing in all aspects of international trade, in which it has unique expertise. So much so that some Japanese commercial banks which could well carry out their own foreign transactions, avail themselves of the facilities of this specialist bank. The Japanese Government uses the Bank of Tokyo for the handling of foreign bond issues and for the settlement of Japanese External Loan Bonds. From time to time it has been designated by foreign governments—especially those in East Asia—to be the sole Japanese bank entrusted with transactions under special trade arrangements with Japan.

The Bank of Tokyo has 39 branches and 20 representative offices in overseas countries, and these give it supreme advantages in carrying out international transactions. It is able to provide financial facilities for all types of international trade, such as direct and indirect financing of exports and imports; financing of foreign-trade-related industries in Japan and overseas; offering services to those requiring exchange and monetary arrangements, both corporate and individual; providing advisory and managerial services to overseas investors in Japanese securities. With the greater flow of overseas capital into Japanese companies and manufacturing enterprises, the Bank of Tokyo finds itself increasingly called upon to fulfil this last service.

As a result the Bank handles a far greater share of Japan's international banking business and related activities than any other financial institution in Japan. It was particularly fortunate in being able to draw upon the Y.S.B.'s skilled personnel whose experience in international trade has ensured that research into this field can be undertaken with confidence and purpose.

The rapid and extensive diversification of so many great Japanese companies—such as those dealt with in this chapter—has brought a corresponding expansion of the foreign interests of the Bank of Tokyo.

In addition to its overseas branches and representatives it also has twelve affiliates and associated banks in the United States, Brazil, France, Switzerland, Luxembourg, Iran, Thailand, and in Australia—Partnership Pacific Limited and Beneficial Finance Corporation Limited. Together with its 33 home offices it employs 6,800 men and women. The authorised capital of the Bank is 30,000 million Yen (US$100 million) and paid up capital 30,000 million Yen (US$100 million).

In spite of the Bank of Tokyo's extensive activities, the sophisticated atmosphere in which it operates and the huge sums involved in its international trade, it still functions as a normal commercial bank, handling all types of deposit accounts, money transfers, collections and payments, both domestic and foreign. Service and information is available to travellers.

The Bank of Tokyo, Ltd., as the country's specialist in overseas trade, has contributed in a significant way to Japan's present high economic status. Projections point to a continuance of operations and the inevitable need for new refinements in financing in this field which is the Bank of Tokyo's speciality.

On the left page is shown the Head Office of the Bank of Tokyo, Ltd., in Tokyo.

Above is the Bank of Tokyo, New York Agency, and the Bank of Tokyo Trust Co. Head Office in New York.

Above:
One of Japan's biggest industries is shipbuilding.
Above is the shipyard at Nagasaki which holds the record for the world's highest output tonnage.

AN INDUSTRIOUS PEOPLE

ALTHOUGH JAPAN'S HISTORY reaches far back into the mists of time, there are few countries belonging so actively to the modern world.

Traditionally a people of vitality and spirit, the Japanese have emerged in recent decades from their former rigid isolationist existence and have successfully adapted themselves to westernised conditions. Today, new and old as well as the East and the West find their meeting point in Japan and are fused in a unique harmony.

The history and geography of Japan have made the Japanese an unusually homogeneous people. Undisturbed by foreign invasions they developed customs and characteristics that gave them a strong sense of national identity and common purpose. They have made fundamental changes in the structure of their society.

Little more than a century ago Japan opened its doors to the outside world and by so doing made itself one of the world's greatest industrial nations, producing high-quality goods for expanding international markets. With this industrial growth has come tremendous advances in the standard of living. Today the people are enjoying better housing, a healthier diet and more leisure than ever before in their history.

Factory-hands in many large industries work in well-lit, well-ventilated buildings, using the finest equipment that modern techniques can provide. White-collar workers commute between their homes and offices in fast, punctual trains and in the evening return to houses which they own themselves or to the blocks of small but comfortable flats which are becoming more common in the larger cities.

In the countryside, television aerials above straw-thatched farmhouses, electric washing machines in the backyards and motor trucks parked ready for the next day's work are concrete evidence of the new prosperity that has reached all sectors of the Japanese community.

Yet, in the midst of these economic achievements, Japan is constantly faced with a major problem—the poverty of its natural resources. To provide adequate shelter, food and clothing for a huge and growing population and to supply the industries by which the people make their living, Japan must rely on an expanding foreign trade. It must import vast quantities of raw materials and, to pay for these imports, it must sell its manufactured goods abroad.

GROWTH OF INDUSTRY

Because of its upsurge in industrial development Japan has become one of the most vital industrial nations in the world today, a country of significant importance in the future economy of Asia.

A few examples may illustrate the point: Since 1959 Japan has been the world's leading shipbuilding nation. In 1969 it produced 9,384,000 gross tons of ships' bottoms, including the world's largest ships of more than 300,000 gross tons each. Japan ranked third in the world in steel production in 1969 with a total output of 82,164,000 tons in terms of crude steel.

Motor vehicle manufacturing, one of the fastest growing industries in Japan, built 4,689,000 units of all types in 1969 to rank second in the world. Aircraft construction has recently been re-established and the industry is producing chiefly small passenger planes for private and company use.

Japan is also the world's top maker of radios with its output totalling 33,807,000 units in 1968. In chemical fibre production in 1969 Japan ranked second in the world with an annual production of 1,321,000 tons.

There has been a great expansion in the production of practically all industrial goods including precision instruments such as cameras, television sets and home appliances like refrigerators, washing machines and vacuum cleaners.

In the year 1968 Japan had almost 56,500 registered trade unions with a total membership of 10,755,000. They represented about 34 per cent of the total number of employees, as compared with 42 per cent in the U.K., 36 per cent in the Federal Republic of Germany and 28 per cent in the United States in 1966. In Japan most labour unions are organised on a single industry basis.

Right: The first steel ship to be built in Japan was the *Yugao Maru,* constructed in 1887 when Mitsubishi acquired the shipbuilding facilities of the Government.

THE MEIJI RESTORATION AND THE ECONOMIC MIRACLE

IN ASSESSING the amazing economic recovery of Japan since World War II there has been a tendency to see the whole of the story as being within that 25-year period. The advantages gained by completely new machinery; the boom brought about by the Korean War and later the War in Vietnam; the industry and skill of the Japanese people; the imaginative and well-calculated concepts of mammoth ore carriers to reduce unit freight costs and long-term contracts—these are some of the popularly held reasons for Japan's business success.

These last 25 years, however, are only part of the story. To find the complete answer one has to go back a little more than 100 years to the accession of the Emperor Meiji when there began the most remarkable period of modern Japanese history—the Restoration Period which lasted some 44 years until 1912.

Those familiar with Japan's present near super-power status will find it hard to accept this picture of 1868 Japan. At that time the population was almost wholly agrarian (80-85 per cent), with the Samurai class (5 per cent), Buddhist monks and Shinto priests (5 per cent) and town people (5 per cent) accounting for the balance. The Tokugawa Shogunate was inept and powerless against the Western Nations who had had the Ansei Treaty revised in 1867. This granted them recognition of consular courts and unilateral rights of extraterritoriality and set custom duties at 5 per cent. Yet in 1912, 44 years later, at the end of the Meiji era the whole picture had changed and Japan was on the way to becoming a modern state.

Some brief history of events at that time is necessary to understand why this change came about. The Western Powers were steadily moving into Asia. The Nanking Treaty in 1842 ceded Hong Kong to Britain, in 1851 Britain occupied Rangoon and began the colonisation of Burma, in 1858 India became a British colony and going further east in 1859 France occupied Saigon and in 1862 made Cambodia a protectorate.

Japan was obviously marked for colonial status and she had the bleak choice of waiting for this to occur or of modernising and meeting the West on its own terms. Inherent in this was the certainty of a period of strain and civil upheaval and the possibility of failure which would leave her still susceptible to colonisation. There are clues to the national character and their estimate of their ability in the decision to industrialise and compete with the West.

The two great reforms at the heart of this change were (1) the development of the country's trade and (2) the total abolition of the feudal system. The first altered the entire economic basis and the latter the whole social system of the country.

The development of international trade encouraged industrial expansion. The overseas markets for silk and tea brought about big shifts in the traditional agriculture while silk processing performed the additional task of playing a pioneering role in Japan's modern factories. The Western demand for porcelain ware encouraged the industry to develop modern scientific technology. On the other hand foreign imports brought the Japanese people in contact with modern Western equipment and methods.

The abolition of the feudal system had one most important consequence. The Samurai tradition of service to their clan—which was placed above personal considerations—was now diverted into service to the nation through the new medium of commerce either as a government official (in the early years the government owned and managed productive industries) or as a private entrepreneur. These entrepreneurs did not regard money-making as a total objective but rather that of service to the nation through industry. It is no coincidence therefore that one of the traditional objectives of the Mitsubishi Corporation—a key member of the giant Mitsubishi Group—is "To Serve the Public".

In tracing the development of the Japanese economy and industry since 1870 it is useful to follow the rise of this organisation—for the name Mitsubishi signifies the most influential group of companies in Japan and indeed is one of the most powerful in the world. Japan's growth and success may be seen paralleling that of Mitsubishi and in the present-day size and composition of the organisation, the depth and diversity of the Japanese economy.

In 1870, the very beginning of the Restoration, one Yataro Iwasaki forsook the life of a Samurai and began a commercial career by founding the Tokyo-Osaka-Kochi shipping service. In 1875 the name Mitsubishi (literally "three diamonds"—the family crest that had come down to the Iwasaki family) first appeared as Mitsubishi Kisen Kaisha, a shipping company that showed its efficiency by winning the race on the Hong Kong and Shanghai service routes against Pacific Mail of the U.S. and P & O of Britain.

In 1885 Yataro Iwasaki died but his family continued to control Mitsubishi. That year marked the first seventeen years of the Meiji era—a period which saw the foundations of a modern state laid but not without its price in social upheaval (the South Western Rebellion in 1877) and in costly government industrial policy mistakes. Some brief mention of the latter is needed.

The original production industries policy of the Meiji Government was chiefly to introduce and administer modern Western large-scale manufacturing and mining industries. But the mere transplanting of industries could not succeed without a sophisticated market and ready availability of capital and technology. These prerequisites were not present in Meiji Japan.

The Government thus decided to reduce the tempo of the introduction of Western large-scale industries, concentrate more on the development of existing local industries and finally to alter the principle of government-run businesses to one of privately-run.

Benefits were offered to help this transfer and the buyers were businessmen of Samurai background. One of these was Yataro Iwasaki and the effects of this new policy are to be seen in the history of the Mitsubishi Group.

In 1886 there is mention that the Iwasaki family had been widening their interests into finance, mining and ship repairs and that the Mitsubishi Company was formed to place all these activities under unified control. In 1887 the government-managed Nagasaki dockyard was released to their ownership and increasing emphasis came to be laid on ship building. From that small beginning emerged the present-day Mitsubishi Heavy Industries Ltd., a mammoth company that, apart from being one of the world's largest ship builders, is also a manufacturer of motor vehicles, aircraft, turbines and a wide range of heavy machinery. Nagasaki itself is now the biggest shipyard in the world.

The second stage of the Meiji Restoration (lasting until 1913) saw the rapid acceleration of the growth and development of a modern economy. The original treaties with the Western powers which had been such a hindrance to development were reformed. Introduction of foreign capital brought new life to industry. The foundation of the modern state had been truly and firmly laid.

It was shortly after this that Koyata Iwasaki (the fourth after Yataro) reorganised the various divisions of Mitsubishi into independent organisations. Thus was formed the Mitsubishi Bank, Mitsubishi Metal Mining, Mitsubishi Trading Co. (now Mitsubishi Corporation which in 1970 accounted for 11.5 per cent of Japan's entire export-import trade) and so on. It was the beginning of the present-day Mitsubishi Group with its 40-odd companies and a combined capital of about US$1,471 million (as at 1st July 1970) employing some 340,000 workers covering such diverse activities as manufacturing, mining, trading, banking, insurance, transportation, warehousing, real estate, research and information services.

Today the Japanese nation is on the threshold of enjoying the benefits of that century-old foundation which has contributed so greatly to the spectacular growth of the last 25 years. But one task remains—that of translating economic success into high standard living conditions. For in spite of a large and rising per capita income and increasing overseas reserves housing development has not kept pace with the progress so marked in other directions, and the country faces a pollution crisis.

Japanese industry always rises to the challenge and this is demonstrated in the reaction of the Mitsubishi Group. In 1970 the Mitsubishi Development Corporation was formed. Acting on the principle that cities of the future must be developed as total systems of rationally distributed energy and space, the Corporation sees the housing industry in the context of the environmental situation, as part of an integral city or community development planning.

The co-ordinator within the Group is the Mitsubishi Corporation, an international trading, investment and venture company. In the 1970 Annual Report the President, Chujiro Fujino, had this to say of his company and his remarks indicate the close meshing of Mitsubishi with the future way of Japanese life, "(the Corporation) will accelerate its advances into new fields of industry such as housing, regional and urban development, the information and knowledge industry and others connected with the prevention of pollution".

OGO (Orbiting Geophysical Observatory) is a large scientific spacecraft for systematic study of the earth and its space environment. It gathers vast quantities of scientific data needed to fill important gaps still remaining in our understanding of the earth and its physical environment. Mitsubishi-TRW, as a system engineering company, is playing its part in space development in Japan.

341

INDUSTRIAL UNITY JAPANESE STYLE

IN THE EARLY DAYS of the Meiji Restoration opportunities for business were unlimited. It was a time when, given sufficient capital and a capable managerial staff, the Japanese entrepreneur could take up a profitable position in any sector of industry. Those who had these requisites were able to succeed even in fields that had no direct connection with their original interests. Others who became rich in their own line of business invested heavily in interrelated giant enterprises. Thus, even as early as the second decade of the Meiji era, was developed the Zaibatsu—a system of management and exclusive ownership of a group of enterprises by a family that formed a financial clique. These large groupings of diverse activities, with their ability to mobilize capital, skills and experience in different fields of business, were a prime factor in the growth and strength of the modern Japanese economy.

Sumitomo was numbered as one of the most important among these Zaibatsu, but whereas the other Zaibatsu did not grow into prominence until just after the Restoration, Sumitomo was already established as the largest copper refiner and trader in Japan well before the Restoration—in fact some 200 years before.

Since those early beginnings Sumitomo has followed its own distinctive pattern of development, basing its growth on the philosophy of its original founder and on its own techniques.

The house of Sumitomo was started by one Masatomo, the son of a minor feudal lord. He renounced his status as a samurai and for some time he sheltered from the arena of war as a Buddhist priest before starting a shop for books and medicines in Kyoto early in the 17th Century. He was a highly principled man and, in accordance with the Buddhist teachings learned while he was a priest, was deeply concerned for the public welfare. His employees learnt an important precept from him: "business is not merely the pursuit of immediate profit—reliability and steadiness transcend profit." And in the best traditions of loyalty to company and founder, this became—and remains—the principle on which the Sumitomo enterprises have been founded.

In the days when the house of Sumitomo began, copper production and copper trading were among the country's most important enterprises, and Sumitomo was induced to enter this field when a relative of the founder perfected a new method of copper refining. The process was acquired by the Company and before the middle of the 17th Century Sumitomo had become the largest copper refiner and merchant in Japan. The discovery of the Besshi copper mine on Shikoku Island was a further addition to the Company's activities and, before the end of the century, Sumitomo was also the leading copper producer in the country. So rich are the deposits in the Besshi mine that they are still being exploited today.

The success of Besshi as a modern capital-equipped mining company ultimately led to the birth and development of other Sumitomo enterprises. It provided the base from which the Company could extend into related activities. Thus was brought about the foundation of the present organisation which is rated one of the top enterprises of modern Japan.

In order to make use of the increasing output of the Besshi mine, the manufacture of electric wires and cables was started to meet the rapidly growing demand for a medium to transmit power for the first electric light bulbs that revolutionised

Above: Copper smelting at the original Sumitomo refinery in Osaka, using the new method by which silver was extracted from copper by using lead.

Below:
The new Sumitomo Building in the heart of Osaka's business centre.

lighting in 1878. Greater production and the necessity for efficient and economic operations led to coal mining, forestry, power generation and machinery. The manufacture of fertilizers, using by-products of the copper mine, was a natural consequence that gave birth to the chemical industry. Along with these activities grew the infrastructure of industry—warehousing, finance, insurance, trading—forming, as it were, an integrated activity of commercial and industrial enterprise that revolved about is own axis.

At present the Sumitomo Group comprises over three dozen independent corporations, each a leading enterprise in Japan — Sumitomo Metal Industries, Sumitomo Metal Mining Co., Sumitomo Chemicals, Sumitomo Electric Industries, Nippon Electric, Sumitomo Shipbuilding and Machinery, Sumitomo Cement, The Sumitomo Bank, The Sumitomo Trust and Banking, The Sumitomo Marine and Insurance, The Sumitomo Warehouse and so forth. Among the members of the group is Sumitomo Shoji, a top-ranking integrated trading company, which acts simultaneously as a promoter and a co-ordinator of all the other member companies.

As Japan's industry became more diversified and grew in economic strength after the Restoration, the Zaibatsu developed and weathered many economic storms. At the end of World War II they faced the most severe crisis of their histories.

Under the Economic Deconcentration Law, enforced by the Occupation Authorities, they were broken up and seemingly liquidated for all time. But they had become too much a part of Japanese commercial life, too much bound up with the history and progress of the nation to disappear so easily and so quickly. When Japan regained independence after the San Francisco Peace Treaty in 1952 its new Government relaxed the restrictions, while continuing to maintain very strict anti-monopoly laws. As a result, many of the splintered companies soon came together again and the component parts merged back into the old industrial or trading companies.

Just as the Meiji Restoration, by almost causing the extinction of the Sumitomo organisation, was actually the means of giving it new incentive and vigour, so too the post war break-up of the Group gave it new, fresh energy to be reconstructed. This was duly accomplished, not as were the former Zaibatsu family-managed and family-owned enterprises, but as an informal consortium of independent corporations with company shares placed on the open market, each company conducting its business individually, but sharing in a common tradition and a common reputation. Thus the Group was built up once again, to greater strength, a wider diversity of activities and a higher level of prosperity. So it was also with other great combines, and the economic recovery of Japan was under way.

Sumitomo today is an example of the power and diversity of these financial and industrial giants. It also typifies the spirit that moves their employees. The Sumitomo companies cover practically all spheres of activity, each one holding a leading position in its respective field. The traditions of reliability and steadiness fostered long ago by Masatomo are maintained and given poetic symbolism by its trade mark of the "Igeta" which represents an ancient well frame, an expression of the effort of Sumitomo to continue as fresh in spirit and substance as the never-ending flow of a fountain.

STEEL—BLUEPRINT OF SUCCESS

JAPAN HAS BEEN REBORN TWICE. The first rebirth of this Far Eastern island nation happened around the 1860's when Japan, or Nippon, opened its shores to foreign visitors after an almost complete isolation of some 350 years.

From an agricultural, backward and feudal society, it has grown to, within decades, a modern nation. The emperor Meiji moved his court from Kyoto to the new capital Tokyo in 1868, and under his energetic leadership Japan became westernised.

The second Japanese rebirth happened in the early years of the post World War II period, which saw an utterly devastated Japan. During and after this period, the Japanese as a nation banded together and, in an amazingly short time, developed a thriving economy. Where cheap and shoddy Japanese goods had been sold on foreign markets Japan now surprised the world by turning out products of high standard and, what is equally noteworthy, at competitive prices. In fact, the quality was generally so high that it equalled, and often surpassed, that of similar products manufactured in the Western countries.

Several factors contributed to this phenomenon but the most outstanding were the technical ingenuity displayed by the Japanese industrialists and the extensive modernisation of plant equipment.

One of the companies indirectly to play a prominent part during this period of transition is Nippon Steel Corporation. It was created on 31st March 1970 from a merger between Yawata Iron & Steel Co., Ltd. and Fuji Iron Steel Co., Ltd.

Japan's first blast furnace went into operation more than a century ago, in 1857. The Yawata Steel Works came into being in 1901. In 1934 the Japan Iron & Steel Co., Ltd. was founded by the merger of several steel manufacturers, including Yawata Steel, but after sixteen years the company was dissolved, and two separate organisations emerged—Yawata Iron & Steel Co., Ltd. and Fuji Iron & Steel Co., Ltd. Both companies flourished and during the past two decades they contributed greatly to the healthy growth of the Japanese economy.

These two steel enterprises, foreseeing the need for higher efficiency of investment in plant equipment and research, for better and more rational utilisation of raw materials, and for eliminating inexpedient cross-transportation, came together and agreed to an amalgamation. The result of this merger was the formation of Nippon Steel Corporation.

In capital and assets, output and exports, Nippon Steel is a gigantic enterprise, not only in the Japanese steel industry, but among the steel manufacturers of the world. The chief foreign sources of iron ore for the Japanese steel mills are Australia, Brazil and Africa. Coking coal is mainly supplied by the United States of America. Nippon Steel imports some 50 million tons of iron ore and 25 million tons of coking coal annually for its nine main steel works established in various parts of Japan, each turning out high-quality steel. Sweeping modernisation programmes have been carried out at all works to meet the continually increasing demand for steel products in the rapidly expanding Japanese economy.

The great variety of Nippon Steel Products includes: heavy and medium plates, hot and cold-rolled sheets and coils, electrical sheets, H-shapes, sections, rails, bars and wire rods, sheet piling, special steels, stainless steels, pipe and tubes, fabricated steel products, and pig iron and semi-finished steels.

With its wealth of technical know-how and operating experience, Nippon Steel is able to meet the most exacting demands of new developments in technology. The company has three main research laboratories, employing more than 2,000 researchers. From their experiments new steel processes and products have been evolved for which a large number of patent applications have been made. Attached to each of the major steel works of the company are additional laboratories for research in industrialisation and production know-how.

Despite obstacles such as labour shortages and spiralling costs, Nippon Steel, since its inception, has gained steadily in production, sales and profits and its employees now number almost 80,000. The company's wage levels and welfare establishments generally rank among the highest and best developed of Japan's industries, resulting in exceptionally stable labour-management relations. Neither labour disputes nor strikes have halted production over more than twelve years—since 1960 in fact.

In the Japanese Fiscal Year 1970 (April 1, 1970—March 31, 1971) the gross sales of Nippon Steel were ¥1,296,991 million (US$3,603 million) of which profit after taxes was ¥26,519 million (US$73.7 million). During the same year the total crude steel production was 32,980,000 metric tons.

Technical co-operation with countries overseas is actively encouraged by Nippon Steel. The company assists developing countries in Asia, Africa and Latin America, and also co-operates with the industrially developed countries of Europe and America in engineering services, plant operation and the granting of patent rights.

Realising their position of responsibility towards society and the world economy, the major steel companies of the non-communist world have joined together to form the International Iron and Steel Institute. Nippon Steel gives full support to all the activities of IISI.

The late 20th Century is a technological age. Industry in all its aspects will see considerable structural changes in the near future, with new industries coming into prominence: space development, oceanic research, nuclear energy, to name a few, will assume increasing importance in industrial enterprises.

Steel will be widely used in these industries of the future, and Nippon Steel Corporation, Japan's largest industrial concern, is expected to play an important role in this new era, for the betterment and welfare of mankind.

Above:
An Electrolytic Tinning Line
at the Yawata works of
Nippon Steel Corporation.

Left page:
Blast Furnaces at the Nagoya Works of
Nippon Steel Corporation.

THE JAPANESE CAR

Left:
Datsun cars
about to leave the Zama factory
on the outskirts of Tokyo.

Right:
Nearing the end
of the assembly line;
Datsun cars
awaiting the fitting of wheels
at one of the Nissan Motor
Company's factories.

JAPAN'S miraculous economic recovery in the relatively short span of 25 years is manifest in many ways, the most striking of which, perhaps, is the evolution of the automobile industry. From being virtually unknown outside Asia in pre-war times it has grown to be second only to that of the United States, producing more than $5\frac{1}{2}$ million vehicles a year.

Today the Japanese car is seen in many major countries of the world, strongly competing with the best of the local products.

From being a minority export of the industry only a few years ago, the passenger car now represents 73 per cent of all Japanese motor vehicles sold abroad. Many are exported as parts and assembled in knockdown factories throughout South-east Asia, Australia and New Zealand.

With the advent of modern freeways and expressways, manufacturers have been able to modify their former predominant emphasis on road-worthiness and durability to give more attention to speed and acceleration, fuel economy, riding comfort and attractive exterior design. These factors have been greatly facilitated by the rising technical skills of the designers and engineers and the efficiency of those working on the assembly and testing lines.

Examples of this new, high performance approach are found in the "Datsun" cars built in several ranges by the Nissan Motor Company, one of the top two automobile manufacturing companies of Japan and the fifth largest in the world. In fact, the Datsun 240Z Sports won Overall First Prize in the 1971 Safari Rally in Africa—one of the most gruelling international tests of dependability, endurance and high speed performance conducted in any part of the motoring world.

The foundation of the Nissan Company dates back to 1933. Despite the stresses of World War II, in the years which immediately followed, Nissan kept pace with the rapid progress of motorisation that paralleled Japan's accelerated post war growth. It now employs some 50,000 and is capitalised at almost US$137 million.

Nissan's holdings include nine manufacturing complexes, four of which are assembly plants. As part of its 1970 expansion programme, the Company opened another plant in Tochigi, some 60 miles north of Tokyo. Together with 19 affiliates and 150 major sub-contractors, these plants form the highly integrated manufacturing organisation known as the Nissan Group. Most of the parts and components needed for the building of the Nissan cars and trucks are made by the Company or supplied by its related firms in the Group. Some of the major items the Company buys from outside include steel, glass, tyres, rubber and electrical equipment. After assembly is complete, cars earmarked for export are transferred to the Company's own Hommoku Wharf, where they are loaded aboard Company ships and chartered vessels for shipment overseas. With a land area of 330,000 square metres, Hommoku Wharf is one of the largest of its kind in Japan.

Nissan's own shipping fleet includes eight auto carrier ships in service over the trans-Pacific route, and two more ships of this type are scheduled to come into service in 1972. Along with these, coastal ships, railway and "haulaway" trucks, and hired drivers are used to deliver domestic models to the Company's 300 dealers across the nation.

Ten years ago the Nissan Company's annual production was 166,000 motor vehicles.

The year 1971 ended with the record production of 1,593,000 units, representing close to a tenfold increase over the past decade, nearly a third of which were exported. Figures for 1971 revealed an increased export of 630,000 vehicles, including Datsuns shipped for assembly in 22 overseas plants. Today Nissan products are sent to well over 100 countries around the world and every year the world demand grows progressively larger. During 1970 Nissan achieved record gross sales of US$2.22 billion, including its non-automotive lines such as textile machinery and space and aeronautical equipment. Technical advances and productivity gains, as well as the rising personal income level which has kept the nation's economy humming, have been prime factors in the growth and progress of Nissan.

One of the major reasons for the international popularity of the Japanese car is its unvarying dependability, which stems from the devoted workmanship of the employee and is evident in all of Japan's manufactured products. In the Japanese tradition of company loyalty, Nissan workers look upon the Organisation as their protector, and their boss as a second father.

In turn, Nissan regards employees as adopted sons and daughters and provides them with social, educational and recreational services and life-long security.

Above:
Tokyo by night.
The Head Office of the
Nissan Motor Company
on Japan's most glamorous street,
the Ginza.

Left:
Datsun cars lined up
at the Nissan Motor Company's
Hommoku Wharf, Yokohama,
ready for export overseas.

ONE FACTOR which has confirmed the universal reputation of Japan as a highly competent, top world-standard manufacturing nation has been her production of heavy machinery. Formerly known as a maker of textiles, light industrial goods and the like, Japan has emerged since World War II, and particularly from the 1960's, as a serious contender in the supply of capital equipment, especially in the heavy electrical field. Japanese manufacturers have won important tenders in development projects all over the world and in doing so have confirmed Japan's status as a leading industrial power.

In the forefront of the manufacture of heavy electrical equipment is Hitachi, Ltd., the largest integrated maker of electrical appliances and machinery in Japan. Starting as a small repair shop in the village of Hitachi where one Namihei Odaira commenced business in 1910, gradually transforming into a thriving corporation which resulted in the establishment of Hitachi, Ltd. in 1920, the company has now grown into a combine of thirty-four extensive plants and the five original employees have become a powerful force of almost 170,000 workers.

It is the practice of Japanese companies to adopt mottoes which express the basic theme of their operation. Hitachi has three such mottoes and the one which fits it most aptly is the pledge to manufacture its products to its own design or, if that is not practical, according to some other essentially Japanese design—but never to a foreign design. The company has spent

MACHINERY—IMAGE OF NEW JAPAN

vast sums of money in thus improving its technological skill and the results have been noteworthy.

Today Hitachi has eight large scale research laboratories employing around 5,000 scientists and assistants. The Hitachi Research Laboratory was established in 1939 primarily to conduct tests on large hydro-electric and thermo-electric equipment, mechanical and metallic engineering. The Central Research Laboratory built in 1942 is engaged in basic research in physics, chemistry and mathematics and the study of electricity, nuclearology and electronics. The Mechanical Engineering Research Laboratory was added in 1966 to develop machines and equipment for industrial materials handling and construction use and for water treatment devices.

These research laboratories have consolidated Hitachi's position as the principal manufacturer of electrical appliances and machinery in Japan. Its invested capital has grown to US$338.72 million and in 1971 sales reached the immense total of US $3,328 million.

Since World War II the production of machinery has grown faster than any other industry, particularly in the building of ships and motor vehicles and electrical machines. It is now Japan's largest industry, accounting for 41 per cent of the Nation's internal revenue in 1967 compared with only 18 per cent in 1955. Between 1960 and 1966 the production of electrical machinery doubled its output.

Machinery accounted for 34 per cent of Japan's exports in 1967 and some specific examples of the wide range of electrical machinery purchased by overseas countries are given in Hitachi's record of foreign sales: a motor manufacturing plant for Poland; eighteen diesel electric locomotives for Iran; seven units of 367,000 h.p. water turbines for Venezuela; a pressure vessel for a 1,100,000 kW atomic power plant for the U.S.A. The pace of industrial development is increasing all over the world and the demand is correspondingly growing for more power and more efficient means of generating it.

Two major projects which have brought fame to Hitachi are Japan's super-express for the New Tokaido Line, in the building of which Hitachi played an important part in co-operation with the Japanese National Railways, and the Haneda Monorail Line running from downtown Tokyo to the Tokyo International Airport. Various types of rolling stock have been manufactured for use in the railway systems of many countries of the world including India, Thailand, Sudan, Bolivia, Egypt, Pakistan, Argentina and Iran.

Detailed and painstaking research, modern methods of manufacture and a very high degree of quality control are becoming the hallmark of Japanese industry and in long range planning the big industrialists of Japan are making every effort to emphasise this fact upon their growing lists of world customers.

Left page: Engaged in basic research in the areas of electronics, information science, communications systems, chemistry, metallurgy, mathematics etc., is the Hitachi Central Research Laboratory in Tokyo .

Left: Japan's world-famous Tokaido super-express in the building of which Hitachi played an important part .

Above: Iron ore is mixed and crushed at Mt. Tom Price in Western Australia. It travels 182 miles by rail to Dampier, where it is unloaded by this remarkable piece of Hitachi equipment. The rotary dumper picks up the cars, two at a time, turns them upside down and returns them to the upright position, empty, in 45 seconds.

TODAY Japan's manufacturing industries are producing an ever increasing range and volume of heavy capital goods and capturing a growing share of the world's markets. But the industry which first brought her to the attention of international consumers was in the field of light electrical appliances and allied products. Radios, tape recorders, stereo and television sets—these were the electronic machines that went directly into homes and publicised Japan's new and growing skills, her industrial capability and her craftmanship.

For there was a real Japanese flavour about these products. Imaginative new designs, neat and precise workmanship, true performance and all of them conceived with the consumer's convenience in mind; these stylish manufactures opened up new vistas of enjoyment and spread sound into areas never reached before. There was seemingly no end to the range of design and variety of products, each with its own particular virtue, that flowed from Japanese factories.

Consumer goods, however, are only a part—although a substantial part—of Japan's large electrical manufactures. The world of tomorrow is the world of electricity. Massive power equipment to satisfy the increasingly voracious appetite for more energy; communications and electronics equipment to meet the need for new, faster and more accurate links across the globe; nuclear equipment to make better use of the forces still locked deep in nature—these are only some of the broad fields in which electrical manufacturers have seen such exciting possibilities.

Japanese industry of the 1970's is in world class in quantity of production, quality and inventiveness. It vies with the U.S.A. as number one producer; repeat orders from overseas speak for its quality and a continual range of new products show its inventiveness. An illustration of this point is found in the record of a Japanese leader in this field, The Tokyo Shibaura Electric Co., Ltd., or as it is more popularly known all over the world, Toshiba.

This now great organisation began in 1875 when Hisashige Tanaka began his small privately owned firm of Tanaka Seisakusho for the making of telegraphic instruments.

He decided on a very simple but effective policy that has remained with the company to this day and has been one of the chief factors in building it to the highly successful concern that it is. That policy was in the tradition of the true craftsman—that whatever product comes from his workshop will be the very best of its kind. By 1893 Tanaka's skills had created a strong demand for his equipment and the former small firm was incorporated as a public company, Shibaura Seisakusho. Today there are 1,200 scientists and engineers in Japan's largest—and one of the world's foremost—research centres, the Toshiba Central Research Laboratory, all bearing witness to an unrelenting emphasis on quality and striving for supremacy.

At present Toshiba is spending 3 per cent of its annual sales revenue on research and developmental work. The investment of such a vast sum has produced a notable crop of successes, impressive in their imaginative concept and in the uses to which they can be put: the "radio-photographic newspaper" referred to as the newspaper of the future; the "clearly visible" television which projects material objects in dark areas on its

Above:
A super-high voltage transformer being tested at the Tsurumi Works.

Below:
Mass production colour television in an exclusively-designed Toshiba factory.

THE ELECTRICAL GOODS INDUSTRY OF JAPAN

screen; the "postal automatic reading system" designed to read hand-written figures; the world's smallest and lightest television camera (weighing about 10 lb.) for industrial, educational and home use; and to illustrate the range of research, a circulation system for use in stimulating an artificial heart in the treatment of patients with heart disease—these are only a few of the achievements of the Research Laboratory.

The work of research is almost limitless in its scope. The scientists of Toshiba are now moving into the so-called futuristic industries such as atomic energy, oceanography and space exploration—fields which by their very nature promise exciting developments.

It is not only in research that Hisashige Tanaka's small workshop has come a long way. Today Toshiba is a giant industrial complex that manufactures nearly 10,000 different products in 30 factories and employs some 134,000 workers. In Australia Toshiba has made notable contributions to the development of some of the country's biggest projects: 600 MW steam turbo-generating sets for the N.S.W. State Electricity Commission at Vales Point Power Station; 350 MW steam turbo-generating sets for the State Electricity Commission of Victoria at Yallourn West Power Station; 285 MW water turbines and pumps for the Snowy Mountains Hydro-Electric Authority's Snowy Mountains Scheme; electrical equipment for industrial use such as rolling mills for The Broken Hill Proprietary Coy. Ltd. and John Lysaght (Australia) Limited; and 40 ultra high voltage power transformers of 100 MVA or more. Contracts for equipment for Australia are currently worth $A75 million. In addition to fulfilling Australian orders Toshiba is now making heavy electrical machinery for many other parts of the world—generating equipment for Canada; 620,000 kW water turbines for the U.S.A.; thermal power plants for South Africa, Lebanon and South-east Asian countries.

On the home market the denki (electrical) boom in the 1950's gave the industry its opportunity to enter the economic 'take-off' phase. Part of this phase harks back to the end of last century when a scientist named Ichisuke Fujioka established a company for the manufacture of Japan's first incandescent lamps: it was titled Hakunetsusha. In 1899 it became incorporated as the Tokyo Denki Co. Ltd. and its field of industry was expanded to include vacuum tubes, meters, radios and wireless communications equipment. A close association developed between Tokyo Denki and Shibaura Seisakusho and in 1939 the two companies joined forces to become the Tokyo Shibaura Electric Co. Ltd. Since those days the continually rising standard of living has given the Japanese people more disposable incomes and although the market for traditional home appliances and consumer goods—washing machines, refrigerators, television sets—has slackened, a constant stream of new products from the inventive research teams, new in use and new in design, has kept the industry operating at full capacity.

A breakdown of the sales of an integrated electrical manufacturer such as Toshiba indicates the high rating of the consumer goods market. In 1970 sales of these products accounted for 47 per cent of Toshiba's total net sales. The importance of new products in maintaining this high figure is shown by the development of inventions such as microwave ovens, a novel design cassette-type tape recorder, a new integrated circuit type radio with excellent reception of FM broadcasts—to name but a few. Heavy electrical equipment contributed 31 per cent of sales, followed by industrial electronic products which accounted for 20 per cent.

This last category is one of the faster growing sectors of production as the fruits of research are increasingly applied to industry. Demand for electronic computers is rising and even greater development is foreseen in this field. System engineering is another area demanding more attention; an example is an order for an air cargo handling terminal system for the new Tokyo International Airport which requires for its completion an unusually high level of technical skills.

Below:
A steam turbine being built at the Nishi Works of Toshiba.

The electrical goods industry has brought quick prominence to Japan and has considerably increased the enjoyment of life—not only for the Japanese but also for the people of many other countries. It has established itself as one of the most important factors in the Japanese economy.

Now, with the advent of liberalisation of foreign capital, trade competition in Japan and overseas will become more intense.

Those firms which have invested heavily in research will find the challenges easier to resist and—such is the effect of competition on those most able to bear it—will be spurred into greater achievements and produce even more imaginative and useful products for the benefit and enjoyment of mankind.

JAPAN IN THE WORLD OF COMMERCE

Opposite page, top:
The Mitsui Kasumigaseki Building in Tokyo.

Opposite page, below:
The Sakawa River Bridge project, completed by Mitsui Construction Co. Ltd. in September 1968, is one of the vital links on the 436 km super-highway connecting Nagoya with Tokyo.

Below: Even the most solidly built and the most beautiful of Japan's ancient castles are subject to the hazards of nature and a Taisho Marine & Fire Insurance policy is the surest protection.

JAPAN'S large trading companies are unique in today's world of commerce. They differ from trading firms in other countries because they undertake a multiplicity of business functions such as participating in joint ventures, financing, engineering, transportation, warehousing, insurance, construction and the promotion of investment projects at home and abroad, in addition to their main business of buying and selling, importing and exporting. The complexity of modern business demands that they perform an increasingly wide variety of services and keep abreast of business trends throughout the world.

Japan's oldest trading firm and one of its largest, Mitsui & Co. Ltd., handles more than 10,000 items covering the entire range of economic life. In one way or another, the company's activities touch on the lives of millions of people around the world.

In addition to the wide variety of business in which it has been engaged for many years, Mitsui is planning for further expansion. It has already moved into systems industries, including the development of space, marine resources, land areas, housing development projects and information.

Because such industries involve a wide variety of activities, Mitsui, as organiser of its large group of industrial enterprises, is active in balancing the diversified efforts of its member companies.

These companies comprise a number of independent industrial firms engaged in diverse fields of business while maintaining close intra-Group co-operation in various undertakings. Mitsui & Co. co-ordinates the activity of the Group members and through their combined efforts can undertake domestic and international projects considered too large for individual firms. With its access to this expert knowledge, negotiations can be made for mammoth projects requiring co-ordination of efforts in many different fields.

The Mitsui network circles the globe with 116 offices in 71 countries, each staffed by specialists and experts in economics and marketing trends the world over; its employees total more than 12,000.

The history of Mitsui traces back some 300 years—a rare distinction among modern trading companies—and its growing prosperity and influence can still be largely attributed to the principles of adaptability and flexible service to fit the needs of individual customers that were introduced by the founder three centuries ago.

During the post war period Japan's industries have had to depend upon both domestic and imported technology for economic and industrial expansion and to meet this situation Mitsui has played a major role in buying and selling techniques and effecting cross licensing agreements with firms throughout the world. In the exchange of industrial technology between Japan and other countries the Company's experience has proved to be invaluable.

A Technical Development Department has been established at head office in Tokyo and in Technical Development Centres in the key cities of Osaka, New York, London, Paris, Dusseldorf, Milan, Madrid and Moscow. These offices maintain highly qualified specialist staffs.

More than 100 joint international business firms in over 80 different parts of the world are now engaged in a veriety of activities. They enable Mitsui to supply Japan's industries with raw materials for manufacture into finished products for sale on the domestic market and for export and also help to boost the economy of host countries. Joint investments in which Mitsui is participating include the production of galvanized iron sheet, fibre, automobile assembly and sales, sugar refining, textile manufacturing and many others in South-east Asia, Africa, Australia, New Zealand, North and South America, Europe and Latin America.

Australia is involved in some of the most exciting Mitsui projects in the Pacific Basin.

In the early days wool amounted to about half of Australia's trade with Mitsui. It is still very big business but after the war the company won important contracts to supply secondary industry. There were turbines and pumps for the Snowy Mountains Hydro-Electricity Scheme, steel rolling mills and ancillary equipment for the Broken Hill Proprietary Coy. Ltd., John Lysaght (Australia) Limited and other companies, rolling stock for the Queensland Railways and the Hamersley project, ship loaders at Gladstone and Port Hedland and electrical equipment of many types for many uses, including the supply of 60 miles of oil-filled electric power cables to transmit extra high voltages around Sydney for the Electricity Commission of New South Wales.

As early as 1958 Mitsui shipped 20,000 tons of Queensland coking coal to Japan and this led to the formation of an international company, Thiess-Peabody-Mitsui, which is engaged in a mining venture at Moura, worth nearly $A70 million. The annual shipping capacity is 4.5 million tons.

At the Cliffs Robe River iron ore project, six Japanese steelmakers will import through Mitsui 87 million tons of pellets over a 21 year period and 72 million tons of prepared sinter fines in 15 years. The total value is expected to be $A1,400 million.

More than 240 million tons of ore will be shipped to seven Japanese steelmakers from Mt. Newman during the next fifteen years. The value to Australia will be about $A1,800 million.

Mitsui is also a major exporter of Australian wheat and other grain. The company has helped Australian farmers to diversify from wheat crops to grain sorghum in order to satisfy the increasing world demand for animal feeds. Australian exports of sorghum exceeded 1 million tons during 1971.

And under an agreement between Tasmanian Pulp and Forest Holdings Ltd. and Mitsui 600,000 tons of eucalyptus woodchips will be exported annually for the next fifteen years—worth $A150 million.

Projects such as these not only assure a steady supply of industrial raw material for Japan's expanding industries but also assist other countries to exploit untapped natural resources.

As an island nation with few natural resources, Japan has to depend on import-export traffic with other countries to nourish her industrial and economic growth. Her large trading companies have assumed this responsibility since the early days of the Meiji Era (1868-1912) and today Japanese enterprises continue the practice of combining with large integrated firms for their imports and exports and taking advantage of their knowledge of available markets.

These big trading companies also have facilities for raising funds from various sources as a result of their special relations with major commercial banks.

Because of their unique position in the business world today Japan's large trading firms might well be regarded as commercial phenomena. They will continue to serve as centres around which the country's industry and economy revolve.

Above:
Japanese goods are exported
to all corners
of the globe
where her cargoes
are a familiar sight
in port.

FOREIGN TRADE

FOREIGN trade is Japan's life-line. With limited natural resources and a large population, Japan must necessarily import great quantities of raw materials from other countries. In order to pay for the imports, it has to manufacture finished and semi-finished products from the raw substances and sell them to foreign buyers. Thus, Japan today is one of the world's great processing countries.

Raw materials, fuel and food are the principal items of import. For example, all Japan's supplies of raw cotton, wool and rubber, up to 99 per cent of its supply of crude oil, 96 per cent of its iron ore and more than 60 per cent of its wheat all come from other countries. Imports of petroleum, scrap iron and iron ore are steadily increasing as Japan's heavy industries continue to grow and expand.

Machinery accounted for 44.5 per cent of Japan's total exports, metal products 18.4 per cent and chemicals 6.4 per cent in 1969. Textiles and textile goods, once major export items, contributed only 14.2 per cent of the total export revenue, while there was a steady increase in the volume of such manufactured goods as ships, cars, cameras, transistor radios and television sets sold to foreign countries.

Japan's biggest single trading partner is the United States which takes about one-third of Japan's total exports. In turn Japan is the second biggest purchaser of American products after Canada. In terms of areas, North America (U.S. and Canada) buys the greatest volume of Japanese exports, followed by Asia; and conversely the largest volume of imports comes from North America followed next by the Asian region. In recent years Australia has become a major trading partner of Japan. In 1969 the Commonwealth was the second largest supplier of commodities—mainly wool and mineral ores—accounting for 8.3 per cent of the total value of Japanese imports during that year.

On the other hand, during the same year, as an export outlet for Japan, Australia ranked sixth in the world taking 3.0 per cent in value of Japan's total exports.

Japan is a member of the General Agreement on Tariffs and Trade (GATT) and is working with many other countries to reduce tariffs and to expand free trading among all nations.

DIVERSIFICATIC

FOR MANY CENTURIES Japan's isolationist existence was at least partially vindicated by the modest needs of her people. With far less millions than she has now, the land and the sea provided the simple foods that formed the staple dietary. When the smaller industries grew to bigger industries the scarcity of raw materials became an obstacle to further expansion and the manufacturers had to look abroad for their needs. To counteract import budgetary imbalances export markets were sought and with the dawn of the 20th Century Japan was beginning to be known among the trading nations of the world.

Today overseas trading is the very core of Japan's existence. Even more deficient in natural resources she is dependent upon a regular inflow of raw materials to keep her industrial machines constantly in motion and thus earn all important foreign exchange. The intermediaries in this immense traffic of materials and goods—the trading houses—have built for themselves a significant place in the commercial life of modern Japan.

Japan's base for her industrial growth was the manufacture of textiles which she commenced soon after trade with the West was established. Textiles earned her money abroad, began her experience in overseas marketing and developed new manufacturing skills which were used to diversify into other fields. She became a major exporter of textiles and in her climb to pre-eminence the raw materials she most urgently needed were wool and cotton.

The first importation of wool was from Australia and the shipment was organised by the firm of Kanematsu, founded by one Fusajiro Kanematsu in 1889. Kanematsu was a remarkable man whose versatility in skills and pursuits were later to be matched by the firm which bore his name. He had played a leading role in establishing the famous O.S.K. Line, one of the foremost shipping companies of Japan, and a little later forming the Mainichi Press, now one of the world's greatest newspapers. During his career he waged a successful campaign to remove the import duty on wool. He was among the world's first businessmen to put corporate ownership in the hands of employee-shareholders.

Today, the trade that began in a modest way with Australia has become global.

COMMERCE

The business once restricted to wool has boundlessly diversified. And the transactions formerly confined to import, export and sales now involve every phase of modern international commerce.

The partner to wool in the initial years of Japan's textile industry was cotton. In the merchant city of Osaka, shortly after Kanematsu was founded, the House of Gosho was established as an importer of raw cotton. From importing Gosho extended its activities to the spinning of cotton yarn and soon became an influential leader among the three prospering textile trading houses in Japan. Like Kanematsu the House of Gosho expanded its trade and spheres of activity far beyond textiles.

In 1967, 70 years after the foundation of these firms, they merged their interests and thus became the company of Kanematsu-Gosho. The original link with the textile fibre industry is still maintained and Kanematsu-Gosho is today one of the foremost buyers of Australian wool. The range of the company's interests now covers the whole spectrum of Japanese trade. Foodstuffs, chemical products, petroleum and lumber, papers and pulp, electronics, general merchandise, metals and machinery are only some of the commodity classifications traded by Kanematsu-Gosho in great volume. There are some 60 representative offices operating in 36 countries of the world.

Cereals imported by Kanematsu-Gosho have supplied Japan's food processors for decades; the company imports more wheat and rice than anyone else in Japan. Their own mills process imported maize and supply feed and fodder for the poultry and cattle industries. A wide range of marine products is also imported and distributed on local markets and exported to Europe and the U.S.A. The company purchases large quantities of Australian beef, mutton, lamb and pork and finds a ready demand in all parts of Japan. It is a leading importer of lumber and plywoods of various grades. By reason of close ties with top lumber yards and plywood fabricators Kanematsu-Gosho is assured of regular exports of plywood sheets and hardboard and in this respect it operates its own ocean-going log carriers thus ensuring regular supplies to Japan's processing centres.

In another related activity the company imports dissolving pulp for Japanese synthetic textile manufacturers. It imports sulphite pulp to meet the demands of Japanese paper mills. All types of paper and cardboard are exported to all parts of the world.

A fast growing interest is the export from Australia of large quantities of minerals and metals for the heavy manufacturing industries of Japan. From this it is an easy step to the exportation of heavy industrial machinery from Japan to European countries and the United States of America.

The widespread activities of Kanematsu-Gosho augment those of the other trading giants referred to in a preceding article in this chapter. Together they are building up a limitless range of commodities to meet any requirement of any community in the world.

The Kanematsu Memorial Institute of Pathology at Sydney Hospital was officially opened on 20th April 1933, as a memorial to the late Fusajiro Kanematsu. The funds to provide this memorial were subscribed by the staff members of his Company. The Institute has gained a world-renowned reputation for its original research, especially in heart, kidney and blood diseases.

Left: The heart of Tokyo, the Ginza.

Loading facilities at Koolan Island, Yampi Sound, Western Australia. From a BHP mine "Yampi Sound iron ore" is loaded and shipped to Japan by Tokyo Boeki.

TRADING WITH THE GIANTS

IN THE UPSURGE OF TRADE that has brought widespread opportunities to the great trading houses of Japan it was inevitable that smaller but more specialised houses would similarly benefit. When the American Occupation Forces proscribed the zaibatsu at the end of World War II the way was open—and a few of the more enterprising stepped in. Among them was Tokyo Boeki Ltd., a company formed in 1947 from the splintering of Mitsubishi Shoji Kaisha Ltd., one of the largest Japanese trading companies in pre-war years and now the largest. Mr. Y. Matsumiya, President of Tokyo Boeki, had served with Mitsubishi in the fields of commerce and marketing. He decided that bright prospects were looming for specialising in supplies for the steel industry and selling steel products. His decision was a sound one for steel has grown into such an enormous industry that Japan is now one of the world's leading steel producing nations.

The founding of Tokyo Boeki was an act of courage, for in 1947 the future of Japan was problematical. Almost completely ravaged by war, her industry was stripped bare of plant and machinery. American loans plus Japan's own strong banking system—and, paradoxically enough, the very destruction of plant, for it meant that up-to-date machinery had to be installed—prepared her industry for the demands of the Korean conflict which proved to be the catalyst to the recovery of the nation's economy.

These conditions were favourable to trading companies and their turnovers increased rapidly. Tokyo Boeki, by concentrating its efforts in specialised fields and adopting a flexible outlook, was able to foresee future trends and establish a sound footing in steel and machinery. Offices were opened throughout Japan and overseas. As industry expanded, more and more raw materials were needed and the inflow into Japan accelerated. Iron ore pellets from Australia; iron ore from Goa; coal from the U.S.A., Australia, U.S.S.R. and China; chrome and manganese ores from the U.S.S.R.; manganese ore from Groote Eylandt, Australia—these were some of the raw materials imported by Tokyo Boeki to feed the furnaces of Japanese heavy industry. By 1965 sales amounted to US$85.6 million. By 1970 they had more than doubled to reach US$183.5 million.

It is difficult for people of the outside world to realise the depths to which the Japanese morale had sunk in the concluding days of World War II. Many of their great cities were heaps of rubble, their homes destroyed and their savings gone. The recovery of Japan in a short span of 25 years is one of the miracles of modern times and a tribute to the race whose centuries-old traditions gave them the courage not only to rehabilitate themselves, but to rebuild their cities and towns—in some respects beyond comparison with the finest in the world, and establish themselves as leaders among the commercial and industrial giants of the day.

This is the spirit of the Tokyo Boekis of Japan, the little traders who have grown to big traders in scarcely more than two decades and who are destined to play leading roles in the future progress of their nation.

TOTAL BUSINESS

From textiles to steel, C. Itoh and Co. distributes, imports and exports literally hundreds of products through its global network. Its annual turnover is reckoned in thousands of millions of dollars. The Tokyo office of the Company is shown on the right.

IN THE WORLD-WIDE sphere of commerce the range and diversity of business experience and activity of the big Japanese trading companies is almost unique. All of them have moved away from straight merchandising into the broader fields of promotion, ventures and joint ventures, business co-ordination and new and exciting industrial project developments. This means that hitherto financially impractical proposals can now be considered by major trading companies with the resources to mobilise skills, experience and capital with confidence in ultimate success.

One of the four largest of Japan's "Big Ten" trading houses, C. Itoh & Co. Ltd., has adopted the phrase "total business company" to describe its involvement in a wide diversity of activities. It has interests in projects all over the world and its ventures in Australia alone typify the many and differing fields in which 20th Century Japan is so thoroughly equipped to enter.

C. Itoh & Co. has a stake in the huge Mt. Newman iron ore mining project with its own geologist to advise on and evaluate developments. It has a 20 per cent equity in a prawn fishing enterprise with a fleet of twelve trawlers based in Darwin. This venture shipped 1,500 tons of frozen prawns to Japan during the year 1970.

In New South Wales the company is planning to participate in a scheme to raise cattle to supply the Japanese market with prime beef. In the remote vastness of north-western Australia, C. Itoh is exploring possibilities of agricultural developments such as the cultivation of grain sorghum. Still another activity is the Eden (New South Wales) wood-chip plant in which Itoh has a 37.5 per cent interest. In 1970, 250,000 tons of wood-chips were shipped from this plant to Japanese pulping mills. In the Bismarck Sea the Company is conducting a shipjack fishing operation with Madang as the base for the fishing fleet. This project is expected to become a joint venture with local interests in the near future. In the Gulf of Papua, Itoh is investigating the possibilities of prawn fishing.

The Company is also active in the field of oil and gas and has taken the initiative in exporting to Japan crude oil from Bass Strait and Barrow Island. It is now working to establish a means of supplying liquefied natural gas and possibly liquefied petroleum gas to meet the growing demand in Japan.

Most of the giant trading houses of Japan began as small and simple concerns. The original founding of C. Itoh dates back to 1858 when Itoh Chubei I established a wholesale business in linen cloth. It thus saw the collapse of the old Shogunate, the restoration of the Imperial rule and experienced the tremendous growth in trade in the era of the Emperor Meiji.

Itoh Chubei II took over his father's business in 1903 and five years later it was transferred from individual to family management. In 1914 it was again re-organised, this time as a partnership corporation, the C. Itoh Gomei Kaisha. Then in 1918, on the basis of this partnership, C. Itoh was founded.

During the 1940's Japan's economic structure underwent drastic changes and in the post war period C. Itoh effected several amalgamations to meet current developments, notably with Marubeni and Co., Ltd., and Kishimoto and Co., Ltd. A few years later Itoh joined with Kureha Spinning Co. and the Daido Trading Co. in the formation of the Daiken Sangyo K.K.

In 1949 the Japanese Government brought in a law prohibiting excessive concentration of economic power and the production and trading departments of Daiken Sangyo were directed to separate. Thus the present company was incorporated under the original title of C. Itoh and Co. Ltd.

In their long history of more than 100 years the Japanese trading companies have survived depressions, wars, domestic and international upheavals. They have survived because they have developed a new mental approach, completely reversing the former isolationist policies of their rulers to the broadest views on international planes. The world is their client and their customer. They need the world; the world needs them.

THE BIG TEN

NISSHO-IWAI is another of the great trading houses that have contributed so much to the growth of Japan since the end of World War II. It is only when the ramifications and resources of these companies are known that one realises the vastness of the Japanese economy and the dominating influence of the Big Ten. By virtue of its size and contribution Nissho-Iwai is one of the first five of this select group of major traders.

Those who are unfamiliar with Japanese commerce can have little conception of the keen competition that exists in all fields. This is particularly in evidence among the trading firms for not only do they compete with each other in a range of interests so wide that their ingenuity is stretched to the limit but they have to watch any developing tendency among manufacturers to undertake their own trading. This means that their service must be progressively stepped up and their administrators constantly on the watch for new fields into which they might profitably venture and so steal a march on their competitors.

A perusal of the Nissho-Iwai activities indicates the specialised world-wide range in which the company operates: a developer of natural resources, an organiser of projects, yet still a trading entity engaged in the ordinary routine of everyday needs. The flood of goods through its 80-odd offices throughout the world includes the highly technical and sophisticated to the mundane and unpretentious. Invoices and shipping documents list aeroplanes, ships, atomic energy plants, industrial plants, chemical plants, steel plants, railway and port facilities, electric power plants and computers, wool, petroleum, coal, ferrous and non-ferrous mineral ores, bauxite, iron sand, zircon, rutile, ilmenite, rare earths, lumber, pulp and paper, foodstuffs (oils, fats, feed and livestock, marine products), synthetic textiles, all kinds of steel products, cement, gypsum....the list is seemingly endless.

Nissho-Iwai acts as sales representative in Japan for the Boeing Company of the U.S.A., the world's largest manufacturer of commercial jet air transports. It holds a sales record of some 30 Boeing 727 jetliners, thirteen 737's and some twenty of the 747 Jumbos. It also holds the agency for the products of McDonnel-Douglas Inc. U.S.A. and was responsible for the successful introduction into Japan of the Phantom F4 fighter plane.

Another first for Nissho-Iwai was the introduction into Japan of the first commercial atomic power plant of Calder Hall type with a rated output of 166,000 kW. The company retains interest in the operation of this plant by importing and supplying the necessary power fuel.

Many of Japan's vital needs emanate from remote, inaccessible areas and the resources of the trading companies are put to the test to surmount such supply difficulties. As Japan's principal power-fuel importer Nissho-Iwai has extensive oil-storage facilities strategically situated throughout the country. It imports liquefied petroleum gas and is the largest supplier of industrial salts, accounting for more than 40 per cent of Japan's requirements, which it obtains primarily from Mexico. Nissho-Iwai is the No. 1 supplier of lumber which it imports from North America and the South Pacific Islands. In conjunction with the Papua New Guinea Development Bank the company is cutting and exporting 25 million super feet of logs and timber from the forests which cover large areas of New Britain.

The rising technical and industrial skills of Japan have been utilised by the developing countries of Asia to build up their own economies. Fertiliser and steel plants have been prefabricated and sent to East Pakistan, cement mills to the Philippines and specialised steel factories to India. Trading houses are called upon to co-ordinate the many stages of these projects and to act as consultants. Extensive organisation is required since everything from market survey, plant site inspection, land and sea transportation, insurance and the purchase of materials to port requisitioning and trial operations has to be carried out with due regard for efficiency.

Nowhere has trade been more highly developed than between Japan and Australia. Great quantities of Australia's newly discovered mineral ores are being shipped to Japan's smelters, refiners and manufacturers. Nissho-Iwai shipments of minerals have been worth almost $A35 million a year over the last three years. Wool—for long the main Australian export—is cargoed by Nissho-Iwai to Japan to the extent of some $A20 million per year.

Nissho-Iwai has co-operated with several Australian organisations in the development of some of her most promising and

Right:
Nissho-Iwai's export trade has grown from $495 million in 1966 to an estimated $1,465 million in 1972.

Below:
Primary production in many fields, including the growing of grain for foodstuffs, is an important part of the sogo shosha companies in Japan—
"the bridge between buyer and seller".

Opposite page:
The Head office of Nissho-Iwai, Tokyo.
This Company was born in 1968 by the merging of the two dynamic organisations Nissho and Iwai, each of which had behind it almost a century-old history of overseas and domestic trade.

ambitious projects. With Comalco, British Tobacco and Colonial Mutual Life Assurance Society, Nissho-Iwai has joined in the formation of Dampier Salt Ltd., which is producing at the initial stage some 1,200,000 tons of salt annually in the northwest of Western Australia. With Elder Smith-Goldsbrough Mort Ltd. and the Electricity Commission of Victoria, Nissho-Iwai has formed Australian Char Pty. Ltd., to produce 60,000 tons of char annually in Victoria. Char is a carbonised form of compressed brown coal briquettes which are used in the chemical and metallurgical industries with further prospects for versatile uses in the field of anti-pollution agents.

In a more recent venture Nissho-Iwai has joined with Japan Petroleum Exploration Co. Ltd. (Japex) to form a new company, Oceania Petroleum Pty. Ltd. Oceania, which has ten major companies as its members, will enter into petroleum exploration in Australia and surrounding areas. The first programme will be a farm-in in the Carnarvon Basin of Western Australia where an extensive geophysical survey has already been in progress during the past year.

In the consortium formed by Nissho-Iwai and Japex are four major refinery orientated companies, three companies with exploration emphasis and three of which Nissho-Iwai is one, geared for extensive distribution. Thus the new company is entirely self-contained and functional and what is of major importance, it has a backing of tremendous capital strength.

The first drilling on the Western Australian leases is expected to be undertaken during 1973-74. Operations will be over a vast area of 28,000 square miles—more than the U.S. State of Kansas or the Japanese Island of Kyushu.

As the world continues to expand its horizons and the pace of development increases, as living standards rise all over the world and people demand new products and new ways of living, the trading houses of Japan will discover a growing need for their services. In the vanguard to meet these demands will inevitably be the Big Ten.

THE TRADING HOUSE SYSTEM

MANY of Japan's modern enterprises developed out of clan, group, home, or family industries, while others rose from the going concerns inherited or purchased from the Meiji Government. The former retained their identification to some degree, while the latter grew into the great Zaibatsu empires of pre-war Japan.

In the former groups lie the roots of Marubeni Corporation. The founders of the original company, in 1858, like most trading houses of the time, were engaged principally in domestic trade prior to the Meiji period. Imports from and exports to foreign countries were handled mainly by foreign companies. Spurred by the encouragement of the government, trading houses turned to foreign business.

Initially trade was in cotton, grain, soy beans, fabric and machinery, and the traders acted as commission brokers. But as trade extended the list of items grew in number and volume, necessitating the creation of more divisions and departments, each specialising in its own particular products.

In its earlier years Marubeni Corporation traded in textiles and fabrics but today the textile department is accounting for only 22 per cent of the business, yielding pride of place to the metal group which leads with 31 per cent; the machinery group and chemical products represent 26 per cent and foodstuffs, paper, pulp and general merchandise make up the remaining 21 per cent.

While the trading houses of Japan were building up their range of products and their financial power was increasing, the technique of trading as such did not alter greatly until the 1950's. By then the domestic economy had become more international, there was improvement in global communication and trading in overseas markets had, to a large extent, lost its mystery. It seemed to the Japanese industrialist and manufacturer that it would not be very difficult for them to do their own buying and selling, thus effecting important savings in commission. For a time there appeared a possibility that the role of the trading house—the simple routing of orders—would diminish.

However, in the increasingly complex world of business it was not difficult for the trading houses to see new functions they could perform. World trade was expanding quickly, development projects of immense size were being spoken of— money and the expertise in handling it, co-ordinating and administrative skills— these were to be the new attributes that international business was seeking. Only the trading houses had the capacity to supply what was needed.

So they widened their roles and became financiers, administrators. They improved their techniques of market research. They became managers and organisers of multi-disciplinary industrial groups which tackled the complex requirements of massive projects. They searched the globe for natural resources and raw materials for their industries and then helped the host country develop these resources. These new tasks they handled competently and with intelligence and imagination.

In addition, the trading houses extended their techniques in buying and selling— such as tripartite deals which promoted trade relations between countries where none previously seemed possible. In Japan they helped streamline the nation's distribution system which was having problems due to the great increase in volume of goods. Distribution centres were established along with chains of supermarkets. Before the first round of capital liberalisation in 1967, trading houses had seen the need to introduce foreign technology into Japan. As they had had long associations with overseas companies, good relationships had been established and they were thus well placed to perform this introduction service. After capital liberalisation, foreign firms found that it was necessary to rely on the trading companies for guidance in the Japanese market. Thus ties with these overseas companies became tighter.

Probably the keynote of the trading companies is their capability of flexible functioning. These Sogo Shosha, as the modern-day giants are known in Japan, with their tremendous financial backing, speedy communications and overall business acumen, have arranged the development of vast tracts of natural resources abroad, constructed gigantic industrial complexes overseas, established countless joint ventures and have organised a number of companies into a group to meet the challenges of new fields in which single companies would be less efficient.

As an example, in the field of ocean development Marubeni was responsible for founding the Fuyo Ocean Development and Engineering Company which was a joint venture of 34 organisations ranging from banks and manufacturers to hardware and relevant training groups.

In Japan there are some 8,117 trading companies of which the Sogo Shosha number about ten. During the period from 1960 to 1968 these ten companies accounted for about 25 per cent of Japan's Gross National Product. They also handled 48 per cent of the export trade and 63 per cent of imports.

Marubeni, now ranking third among the giant traders, was incorporated in its present form in 1949. It has a paid-up capital of US$69.4 million and gives employment to more than 9,500 in its 53 offices and 100 subsidiaries and affiliates within Japan and in 95 cities abroad.

It is a partner in 59 joint ventures with overseas interests. The company's sales for the fiscal year 1970 including export, import, tripartite trade and domestic business grossed more than US$7.2 billion. In August 1971 Marubeni acquired a 12.8 per cent equity interest in the Australian coal mining company of Austen and Butta Ltd., Sydney. One half the purchase price was provided by Mitsubishi Chemical Industries Ltd. The joint enterprise plans to supply coking coal to Mitsubishi Chemical through Marubeni.

Opposite page: An oil refinery plant in Peru built and installed by Marubeni Corporation.... Above: Marubeni Australia Pty. Ltd. loading iron ore from Hamersley, West Australia, for Japan. Left: Cars being shipped by Marubeni Corporation from Yokohama, Japan.

Left:
A section of the Dodwell Export Buying Office showroom in Tokyo.

Below:
Confectionery Section in a large Tokyo department store, displaying goods supplied by the Dodwell Consumer Import Division.

Bottom:
The Dodwell Aircargo Service delivering to Haneda International Airport, Tokyo.

AFTER THE SIGNING of the Treaty of Nanking the principal Japanese ports were opened to foreign merchants and many big traders were quick to take advantage of the opportunity to do business with this great country whose doors had for so long been closed to the outside world.

Among them was the firm of Dodwell & Company. Their activities were first confined to exporting tea, silk and chinaware to Europe and North America and importing general merchandise to Japan.

Following the success of their initial ventures, the Company began to operate as shipping agents and in 1887 Dodwells played a leading part in inaugurating the first regular steamship line across the Pacific, later to become the famous Canadian Pacific Line.

From this it was a short step to the launching of the North Pacific Steamship Company and the linking of ports in the Orient with those on the North American coast.

In 1898 Dodwells was registered in London as a private limited company. Having weathered World War I and the post war slump, and then the depression years of the 'thirties, the Company was operating over a wide international field when World War II was declared. Although this meant the total immobilisation of most of its Far Eastern branches for the duration of the War, the Dodwell branches were again functioning in Hong Kong and Japan soon after hostilities ended. Since then, many new branch offices have been opened and wholly-owned subsidiaries and associated companies formed across the world.

From its early days of "merchant adventuring", Dodwells has developed the characteristics that make the organisation rare among international trading groups. The Company is now deeply involved in the sophisticated marketing of a wide variety of products, while its shipping

MERCHANT ADVENTURERS—WORLD TRADERS

activities are supplemented by participation in the developing field of air freight.

More than 100 years have passed since Dodwell & Company first became established in Japan and their offices, now located in Tokyo, Yokohama, Kobe, Osaka, Nagoya and Fukuoka, carry staffs totalling over 1,300.

The Dodwell Japan Branch operates a complete range of international marketing and shipping services for which it integrates a number of divisions specially equipped to handle the multiple needs of manufacturers, buyers, importers and exporters, and other merchants.

The Japan Export Buying Office (EBO) acts as exclusive buying agent for consumer products for customers overseas—mainly departmental and chain stores. This Dodwell Division has an intimate knowledge of the local manufacturing market and exporting practices. It employs special officers experienced in research, market information, sampling, order placing, inspection, documentation, shipping and financing, thus leaving the buyer free to concentrate on his prime functions of merchandising and buying. When he visits Japan, the EBO prepares for him a fully planned schedule to ensure that his valuable time is well spent.

EBO buys a wide variety of products on behalf of leading stores throughout the world: sound equipment, electrical appliances, calculators, novelty gift items, textiles and footwear, and various types of sporting goods.

Dodwell Consumer Imports acts as agent in Japan for overseas manufacturers of consumer products and provides a complete marketing service and distribution network; the division also arranges advertising and sales promotion campaigns on behalf of the importer.

The products handled by this Division come from many countries and are mostly of a prestige nature to appeal to particular Japanese consumers—wines and brandy from France, Scotch whisky, biscuits and confectionery from the U.K., and pet-foods from Australia.

Another specialist activity of Dodwell Japan Branch is its Marketing Consultants Division which undertakes assignments on behalf of clients overseas, such as carrying out market research surveys, negotiating agreements for the local manufacture of products under licence, and helping foreign companies set up joint venture operations in Japan.

One important field in which the Japan Branch has developed particular expertise is that of marketing business machines and systems through its own direct sales organisation. These include addressing machines, accounting machines, electric typewriters, electronic calculators and computers from famous makers in Germany, Switzerland, the United Kingdom and the U.S.A. Dodwell maintains technical staff for the maintenance and trouble-free performance of these machines. Courses are arranged to train future machine operators up to high standards to ensure maximum efficiency of operation.

The Division also conducts a computer centre in Tokyo, where customers may make use of its services.

In the field of industrial machinery, Dodwell Industrial Divisions act as agents for foreign manufacturers, providing a complete marketing service. They also export Japanese machinery and equipment to overseas clients. The Divisions are all specialists in their own fields. (1) Dodwell Industrial Machinery markets a variety of industrial machinery, including equipment from the U.K. for motor car manufacturing, strapping machinery from Switzerland, and equipment for synthetic fibre spinning from Germany; (2) Dodwell Marine Machinery markets a full range of marine equipment for oil tankers; (3) Dodwell Process Control markets process control devices and nuclear instrumentation equipment; and (4) Dodwell Industrial Exports handles Japanese machinery and equipment: car parts to the U.S.A., and diesel engines, container straddle carriers and crawler cranes to Australia.

Dodwell Shipping Division acts as agents for Liner Services to Europe, America, Canada, the Persian Gulf and many other areas. It is tramp agent for bulk carriers, tankers and special product carriers and acts as broker for ship owners and cargo owners. For example, it is the agent for Scanservice, which currently operates seven express liner sailings between Japan and Europe. Dodwell books cargo for the ships and makes all arrangements for the arrival of Scanservice vessels in port, lighterage, victualling, fresh water supplies and bunkering.

In 1972 it is planned that Scanservice will form a joint service with Ned-Lloyd to become Scan-Dutch, when a container ship service will be inaugurated. Dodwell will then form a joint venture with Royal Interocean Lines, which will be called Eurobridge Ltd, to act as agents for Scan-Dutch.

Dodwell Aircargo Service, together with a world-wide network of agents, arranges deliveries, pick-up, cartage and packing of air freight in Japan for consignment to countries all over the world.

Preparation of schedules and booking arrangements for overseas travel by air and sea, as well as tours within Japan, are each the particular responsibility of Dodwell Travel Service.

Left:
A launch of the
Dodwell Shipping Division
servicing a Scanservice
vessel in port.

Above:
The slim "bullet" train
flashes through the countryside
as it speeds up to 130 miles an hour.
Mount Fuji is in the background.

TRANSPORT

IN JAPAN the principal means of land transport is by railway and in this field Japan ranks first in the world in the number of passengers carried.

The first railway was installed in 1872 over a short distance between Tokyo and Yokohama. By 1930 the total length of railways in operation had reached 25,000 kilometres (approximately 16,000 miles). Today rail services are operated over 27,000 kilometres, very close to those of the United Kingdom, France and West Germany.

Electric locomotives and diesel cars have taken the place of steam trains and the standard of railway transport generally has greatly improved in the past decade. The new Tokaido line completed in 1964, for instance, enables the "Hikari" express to travel the 552.6 kilometres between Tokyo and Osaka in three hours and ten minutes, the fastest rail service in the world.

Motor vehicle transport in Japan has been somewhat retarded because of the well-developed Japanese railway system. However, through the pioneering construction of expressways in the Tokyo metropolitan district, completion of high-speed auto roads between Tokyo and Nagoya, Nagoya and Kobe, and other principal cities, Japan has entered a new era of high-speed road transport. At present a nationwide trunk system of motorways is under construction.

As the result of a remarkable increase in motor vehicle manufacture, the number of Japanese cars had reached 14 million before the end of March 1969—about 5.8 times higher than the 1958 figure. Transport of goods by motor vehicle is also becoming very important. In 1968 the total tonnage of goods carried by trucks was more than 4.2 times as much as in 1958.

Marine transport in Japan developed rapidly after World War I. During the 1930's the United Kingdom, the United States and Japan were the top three sea powers. Although World War II severely crippled Japan's shipping facilities, her merchant marine was soon rebuilt and by 1969 it had reached a strength totalling 12,539,000 gross tons.

Despite forced suspension of activities during the war, Japan's civil aviation has expanded rapidly. In 1968 Japanese air lines carried almost 9 million passengers—nearly fourteen times the 1958 figure—and 89 million tons of freight. At December 1968, the number of aircraft registered in Japan was 952. A new international airport has recently been constructed at Narita, some 50 kilometres from Tokyo. Japan Air Lines, Japan's flag carrier in international air service, together with other domestic companies, operates on various regional air routes.

POST WAR GROWTH

THE TSURU, OR THE CRANE, is the symbol of Japan's national airline, known almost all over the world as JAL. Perhaps instead of the crane the phoenix would have been more appropriate, for the growth of civil aviation in Japan over the last two decades has much in common with that legendary bird. From a single leased aircraft in 1951 to this age of Japan's prosperity, Japan Air Lines has built up its fleet to 61 jet aircraft including three 747 Jumbo Jets, the first of sixteen of these great Boeings; it employs 15,000 staff, and is the sixth largest IATA carrier in the world today.

The rapid growth of civil aviation in Japan has been partly a case of geographical expediency, partly of economics, and partly of what, for want of a better word, one might call "Japanese-ness."

Geographically, as an island nation, the Japanese need to fly to get abroad in the shortest space of time and people need to fly to get to Japan. Domestically, the movement of people in the densely populated Japanese islands on business trips, innumerable visits home and on holiday weekends, has built a remarkable volume of air traffic.

Economically, the growth of the Japanese GNP has run parallel with the extraordinary growth of the civil aviation industry in Japan.

These are the obvious factors. Less obvious is the "Japanese-ness". Undoubtedly the consuming curiosity of the Japanese people has been a strong motivator in the increase of foreign travel; but of even greater significance is the numbers of non-Japanese who consistently fly with JAL.

Competition between the top airlines is growing keener every year. They all fly the best planes the world can build and, in order to maintain a maximum patronage, they must offer something more than a comfortable seat in a fast plane. In its simplest term this is "atmosphere"—the impression imparted to the traveller that the airline is capable of, and eager to fill every required service in a warm, friendly manner. This is the Japanese art of making flying a real pleasure.

In introducing JAL's first 747 to his staff Mr. Shizuma Matsuo, Chairman of the Company, said: "With the introduction of this giant jet, we are suddenly faced with the care and transport of a great many more people at one time. Japan Air Lines has always boasted that every employee treats every passenger not merely as a seat number or an item to be moved, but as an honourable and honoured human being—he is 'more than a passenger, he is an honoured

CIVIL AVIATION IN JAPAN

Below:
The care and attention paid to passengers by JAL stewardesses stems from more than careful training—it is part of their way of life.

Foot of page:
13 Boeing 747 Superjets are on order for JAL to join the three already flying.

guest'. This attitude, practised by every one of you, has been one of the principal reasons why our airline has come so far so quickly. The introduction of our 747 service does not change the attitude of the airline on this point, and I am confident it will not change your aim of putting this corporate attitude into daily practice."

With the introduction of the Boeing 747 the Japanese were confronted with a dilemma somewhat similar to that of a few years previously when they were beaten to the post across the Pacific when the big jets became available. This time they determined to be well out in front. When the 747's were about to be introduced on the same route, JAL made an all-out effort to establish a special "atmosphere" for their new giant planes: they called them the "Garden Jets", and planned each vast interior so that each seating section on a JAL 747 now has its own special design motif in a garden theme. Each conveys the feeling of the beauty of a Japanese garden, a feeling in which everything, down to the last sake cup, is in keeping. JAL's early incursion into the big jet world, and the manner in which the entry was effected, is an indication of the airline's determination to continue to grow, yet still retain the distinctive individuality of its established hallmark. As an extension of this policy, Japan Air Lines recently announced a five-year plan for the expansion of its services world-wide, including a service from Tokyo to Chicago and beyond to New York (JAL daily 747 service to Europe from April 1972). The extension of the current Tokyo-Vancouver route to Mexico (from April 1972), the Djakarta service to Bali, and the Sydney route to Auckland are also part of the total plan. The current Tokyo-Guam service which began to operate during April 1972 now calls at Saipan. Looking still further into the future, Japan Air Lines hopes to commence services to Africa and also to the South Pacific. Flights on the current global network will operate more frequently than formerly.

To meet all these requirements, JAL intends to increase its current fleet of 61 aircraft to 87. A variety of large jets are on order, including two Concorde SST's and, as a long term project, the as yet uncertain U.S. SST. And to fly all these new planes JAL's pilot force will increase from 800 to 1,300.

While the airline has these extensive plans for future development, the essential character of the inflight service—the carefully nurtured feeling of tradition which is JAL's great asset among international travellers—will not be changed.

JAPAN'S MERCHANT MARINE

Below:
S.S. Hakozaki Maru,
a full containership servicing
between Australia and Japan,
loading 1,160 20-foot containers.
It has a speed of 23 knots.

JAPAN has a long seafaring history. Inland, the forested mountains and wide river beds have always made road transport difficult and so most of her population centres have been established near the coast to give them the advantage of transport by sea. The waters, too, have yielded good quantities of the fish that constitute a basis of Japanese diet. Thus the planning of one of the biggest merchant marines in the world has presented the Japanese shipping companies with a challenge which they have readily met.

In the forefront of the rise to pre-eminence is Nippon Yusen Kaisha, the integral part of the N.Y.K. Group which has become the foremost shipping organisation in the world, with ramifications embracing a container terminal and container transport, in line with modern efficiency.

N.Y.K. was established in 1885, the dawn of the Japanese modern state. The Meiji government was struggling to find formulae for a suitable economic system and programme that would enable Japan to meet the challenge of the West. The policy of the Tokugawa shogunate in limiting ship size and restricting voyage distances was reversed. They built ships and encouraged overseas trade. It was the start of Japan as a great maritime nation and companies such as N.Y.K. grasped the opportunities offered and used them to the full.

From small beginnings of purely local character N.Y.K. has developed an operating fleet of 292 ships (7,670,000 DWT) of which they own 166, comprising conventional liner services, containerships and a special carrier service designed to meet the many needs of its clients—ships ranging from tankers, LPG tankers, lumber carriers, chip carriers, special pulp carriers, special ore carriers to autobulk and heavy cargo carriers.

N.Y.K. pioneered containership services by assigning their two specially constructed vessels "Hakone Maru" and "Haruna Maru" to the California-Japan route in the summer of 1968. The company then followed with "Hakozaki Maru" on the Australia-Japan trade and the "Hotaka Maru" on the Pacific-north-west Japan route. At the end of 1971 a service embracing Europe-Japan-Far East was inaugurated and in 1972 New York and Japan were linked. In the near future the Mediterranean-Japan route will be containerised and N.Y.K. will have spread this particular service to the main trading routes of the world.

Research and development are basic features of all major Japanese industries. N.Y.K. is investigating such aspects as greater ship size, increased speed and the application of automation. By 1974 it plans to invest some US$70 million in the construction of new containerships and related facilities, tankers and bulk carriers to further expand its services.

The pace of Japan's growth continues with barely perceptible pauses. New industrial areas are being opened on land reclaimed from the sea and new deep-water harbours are being built. These developments and the new container ports are influencing the pattern of Japan's trade since raw materials from overseas are now going direct to factory rather than being trans-shipped into smaller carrying vessels. As far back as 1965 the Social and Economic Development Plan proposed many innovations to cater for a growing trade in larger ships, much of it carried in containers or needing bulk handling facilities.

With Japan in the process of rapid industrial growth companies such as N.Y.K. must inevitably be called upon to assume greater responsibilities and to play their part in consolidating the nation's fast growing economy.

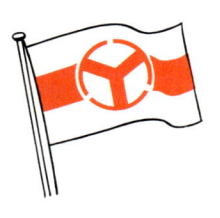

Right:
The Kashu Maru,
a full containership of 16,000 DWT,
servicing the
California-Japan route.

ALL THE GREAT trading nations have found it economically expedient to carry the largest possible proportion of their imports and exports in ships of their own lines. This is the only means by which full benefit can be realised from increased trade and the haemorrhage in a nation's economy—her 'invisibles', of which the biggest is freight paid out to overseas flags—can be stemmed to avoid a burdensome drain on imports, and offset to avoid promotional expenditure on exports. It is a doctrine that Japan has followed since she became a modern state.

Although most of her huge fleet was sunk during World War II, Japan has built up her merchant marine so rapidly since 1945, that today her vessels carry more than half of her own foreign trade cargoes. They are fast and modern—more than 70 per cent are less than ten years old—and her tankers and ore carriers have created a new concept in shipping.

Among the companies participating in Japan's very efficient maritime service is the Y.S. Line or to give its full name, the Yamashita-Shinnihon Steamship Co., Ltd. In contrast to some Japanese companies with long historical backgrounds the Y.S. Line is a comparative newcomer. It was founded a mere 60 years ago. But despite its relative youth and the drastic check it suffered together with so many other companies in World War II, Y.S. is now ranked as one of the largest shipping lines in the world. Its services include ocean liners, trampers, special carriers, bulk carriers and tankers. It is particularly well-known for its tramper fleet, which is one of the best afloat.

Although operating services all over the world the Y.S. Line has attracted attention through its transport links with the U.S.S.R. and various eastern European countries and particularly with Siberia, a unique combination of sea/land transport. When the new Soviet port at Vrangel, near Nakhodka, is completed in 1973 Y.S. will begin further large-scale operations.

Along with other Japanese shipping companies the Y.S. Line is developing the newest phase in sea transport—the container service. Y.S.'s first container route was to Los Angeles in 1968 when "Kashu Maru" inaugurated the service. This was followed in 1970 by the Australia-Japan route with "Tohgu Maru" and the Pacific-north-west Japan route with "Beishu Maru".

Before World War II Japan's merchant marine was the second largest in the world. Although reduced almost to zero by the end of the war she set about building up her fleets once again. By 1970 she had regained her former status—second only to Liberia whose pre-eminent position is due to its being able to offer the flag of convenience facility to shipping all over the world—but to achieve this Japan's tonnage had to double the pre-war figure. The size of some of the maritime companies can be gauged by observing the Y.S. Line. As of September 1971 this company operated 169 ships which aggregated about 5,700,000 DWT, including 67 vessels of its own, totalling 3,300,000 DWT. By late 1972 another five more ships will add a further 600,000 tons to the fleet.

Like all responsible Japanese companies the Y.S. Line is continually searching for ways to improve services and extend into fields not yet fully exploited.

Left:
The Niihata Maru,
an ore carrier of 114,849 DWT,
for the transport of iron ore
between Australia and Japan.

machinery are being used in place of the traditional farming methods.

The production levels of Japanese primary producers are very high for their size. Rice yields per acre, for example, are the highest in the world. Yet Japan is unable to grow all the food it needs for local requirements. It imports large quantities of wheat, sugar and soya beans.

Japan's chief crop is rice followed by wheat and barley. Green vegetables are also high on the list of priority products. In recent years, there has been a steady increase in the growing of many kinds of fruits, the most in demand being mandarin oranges, apples, strawberries and peaches.

Another important change has been seen in the steady development of dairy farms, the largest being situated in the northern island of Hokkaido. This growth has mainly been caused by a radical change in the diets of the Japanese people who today are consuming more meat, butter, milk and eggs than ever before. However, because good pasture land is limited, dairy farming is kept on a small scale.

Above: Japan's climate is ideally suited to apple growing. This picture shows a popular variety being harvested.

Below: Picking young Japanese tea leaf buds. Traditional Japanese green tea is consumed in enormous quantities.

AGRICULTURE

Agriculture is an important part of Japan's economy although the total income from the land represents only 10 per cent of the national wealth and persons engaged in agriculture account for only 19 per cent of the work force. Moreover, this percentage is slowly decreasing as more families are moving from the land to take jobs in industry. Also, many people whose homes are in rural districts hold part-time jobs in the manufacturing and servicing industries.

The area of land that can be used for farming is extremely limited because of Japan's mountainous terrain. Only 16 per cent, or about 60,040 square kilometres of the total land area is arable.

The farms themselves are also very small, the average size being only $2\frac{1}{2}$ acres. Farmers till every possible piece of land, making terraces on the sides of hills and strips along river banks. They use chemical fertilisers extensively and employ the most advanced agricultural techniques. More and more mechanical tillers and other small-size

FISHERIES

For centuries, fish has been the main source of protein in the Japanese diet. The average Japanese eats about 24.8 kg. of fish and 7.6 kg. of meat every year. Fishing is therefore one of Japan's most important industries. The total catch in 1968 was almost 8 million tons, and this was the second biggest in the world, next to Peru. In whaling, Japan retains its place at the top, for its present annual catch totals nearly twice that of its most prosperous pre-war years. The large catches are due not only to Japan's favourable location but particularly to its advanced techniques. Many countries, especially in South-east Asia and South America, are studying these techniques under special agreements with Japan.

The Japanese fishing grounds extend over the Pacific Ocean and into the Indian Ocean where they catch whales, tuna, bonito, salmon, mackerel, herring, sardines, crabs and other shellfish. The fishing fleet numbers some 397,000 vessels consisting mostly of small boats. Almost all the towns and villages along Japan's sea coasts have small fishing fleets of individually-owned boats working for co-operatives. These fleets are confined to coastal waters. For deep-sea fishing large fishery companies operate big fleets of ships, complete with a factory ship equipped with modern machinery to freeze, store and can the fish while the fleet is at sea, thus ensuring freshness on arrival at port. Fish is an important export item for Japan, particularly tinned and frozen tuna and crabmeat.

A new development of Japan's fishery industry is "fish-farming". At present, prawn, sea bream and yellowtail are being bred by the shallow sea culture method and quantities of these fish are seen on the market with increasing frequency.

Production of cultured pearls is another aspect of the industry. The method, invented by the Japanese many years ago, consists of placing a tiny piece of shell in each oyster. The oysters are placed in wire cages which are lowered into the sea. After several years, the oysters form a pearl around the tiny piece of shell.

Above: Japanese cultured pearls are famous throughout the world. Breeding pearl oysters has become a highly scientific process.

Below: Pearl oysters are collected from the sea bed by women divers and placed in floating buckets.

It is at this time that Mount Fuji calls to hikers and skiers from all over Japan—in fact from all parts of the world—for from November to March this beloved symbol of Japan is snowcapped and at its best. Below it Lake Hakone mirrors the glistening cone-like peak and photographers, pleasure cruising or wandering through the surrounding lakeside glens, reap harvests of wonderful pictures.

During the summer months, the seaside, mountain and hot-spring resorts are booming, and the mild evenings lure their thousands to the beaches and to the many landscaped parks that adorn every city throughout Japan.

In Autumn the air is crisp and bracing and the pigmented leaves of the maple and liquid amber blend with the whites, yellows and russets of other ornamental trees in great splashes of vivid colour. Autumn is also a season of many festivals. Shrines and temples, some massive like the Todaiji Temple of Nara, others resplendent like the Toshogu of Nikki, or still others, small and simple, are found in every city, town and country village.

At festival-time brightly coloured lanterns illumine the folk dancers as they move among rows of tiny shops and stalls, in the parks and gardens, and differences in social scales disappear in the gaiety and warmth which the colourful festivals always engender in Japan.

But Japan does not rely entirely upon Nature to draw its millions of visitors. In the past two decades the principal cities—particularly Tokyo and Osaka—have emerged as modern miracles of engineering and civic construction.

Towering skyscrapers which were for many years thought to be impractical in a region

Above: The most famous thoroughfare in Japan is the Ginza, Tokyo's busiest and most glamorous shopping centre.

Right: Autumn at Kegon Falls and Lake Chuzenji in Nikko National Park, a landscape of great beauty in all seasons of the year.

Opposite page, top: No visit to Japan is complete without a night at the exotic Kokusai Theatre, where the visitor sees one of the most spectacular performances in the world.

Opposite page, below: Daimyo Gyoretsu, a grand feudal lords' procession, at Hakone.

JAPAN is one of the famous tourist countries of the world. Nature has endowed it with a special scenic beauty to which each of its four seasons adds its own distinctive appeal.

For almost a week in January gay celebrations usher in the Japanese New Year and from late February to mid-April Springtime is in full swing, climaxing with the glorious spectacle of the Cherry Blossom festival in which both the Japanese and visitors from many countries play a happy part.

The many great parks filled with cherry trees in a profusion of blossoms, pink and white, mark the beginning of a joyful outdoor life which continues through summer until winter comes again towards the end of the year.

UNIQUE TOURIST LAND

prone to earth tremors, are springing up amid the squat buildings constructed in the past.

Hotels to bear comparison with the finest the Western world can offer, with their luxurious suites, colour television, dreamworld shopping arcades, restaurants and night clubs; theatres staging their gorgeous summer dance spectaculars; the traditional Japanese opera, *Kabuki, Bunraki* puppets and *Noh* dramas; the excitement of the myriad flashing lights of the Ginza; the super express train that covers the 460 miles from Tokyo to Okayama in little more than four hours—these are some of the things that are filling the Jumbo jets and the ocean liners with tourists from all points of the globe—destination Japan.

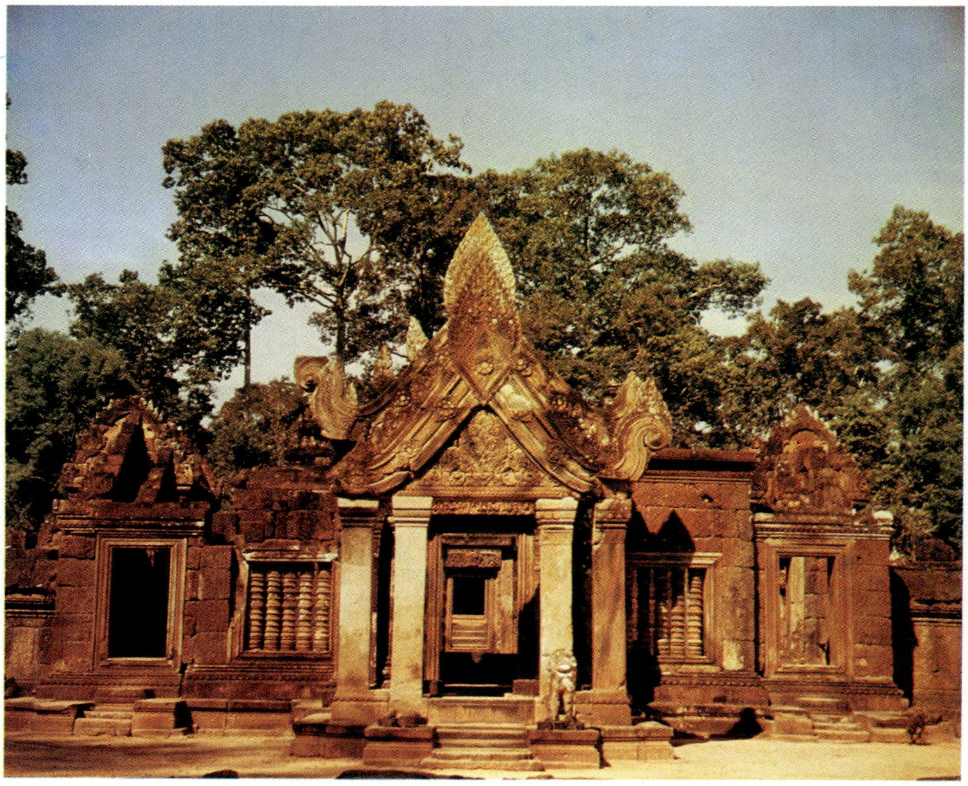

KHMER REPUBLIC

(Cambodia)

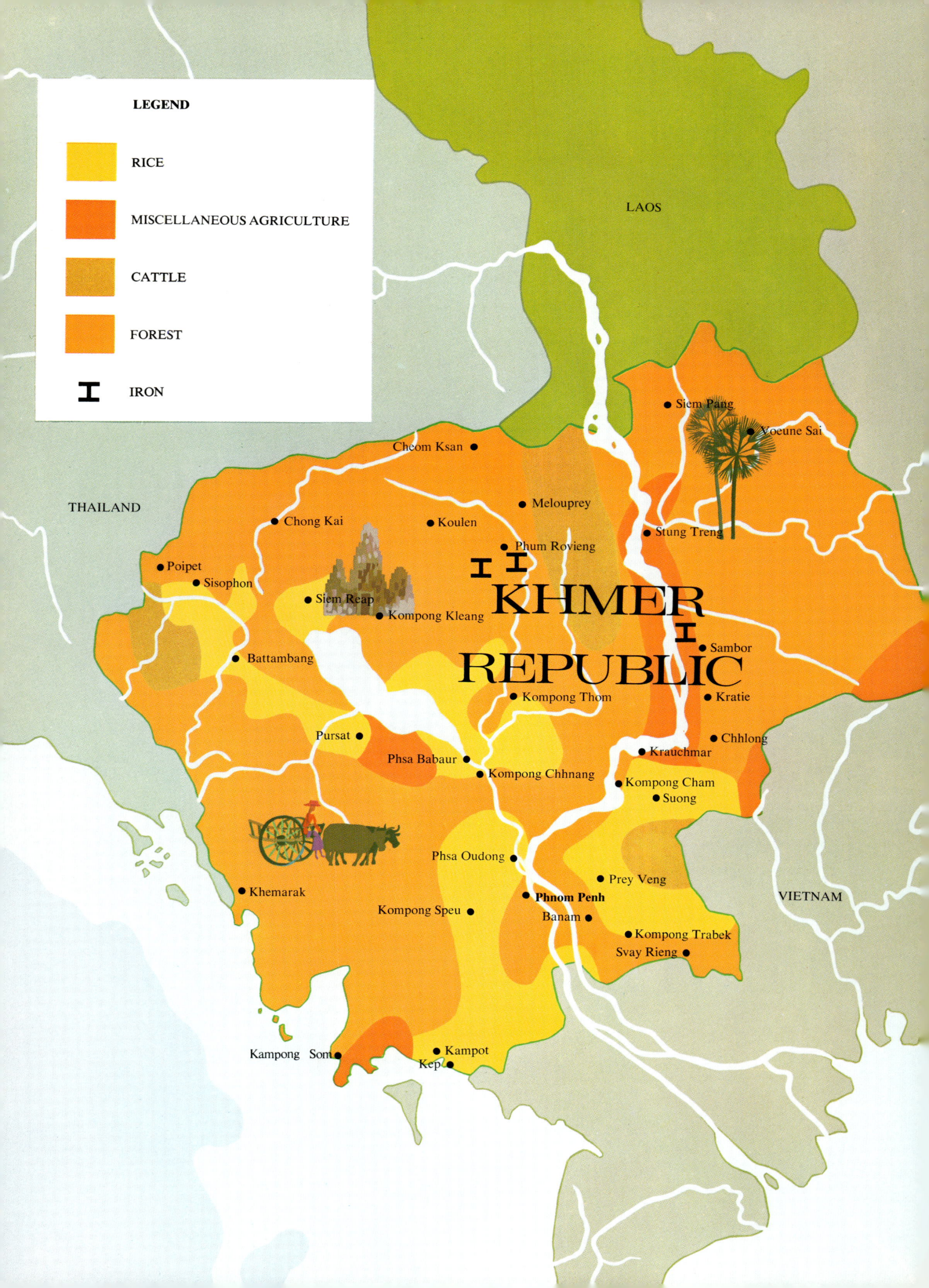

LEGEND

- **RICE**
- **MISCELLANEOUS AGRICULTURE**
- **CATTLE**
- **FOREST**
- **I** IRON

KHMER REPUBLIC

LAOS

THAILAND

VIETNAM

Cheom Ksan
Siem Pang
Voeune Sai
Chong Kai
Koulen
Melouprey
Phum Rovieng
Stung Treng
Poipet
Sisophon
Siem Reap
Kompong Kleang
Sambor
Battambang
Kompong Thom
Kratie
Chhlong
Pursat
Krauchmar
Phsa Babaur
Kompong Chhnang
Kompong Cham
Suong
Phsa Oudong
Prey Veng
Khemarak
Kompong Speu
Phnom Penh
Banam
Kompong Trabek
Svay Rieng
Kampong Som
Kep
Kampot

Among the many spectacles to interest the visitor to Phnom Penh is boat racing on the Mekong River.

Khmer Republic

LENGTH:

North-South, approximately 300 miles.

WIDTH:

East-West approximately 340 miles.

AREA:

69,866 square miles.

LOCATION:

Between 10°15′ and 14°15′ north latitude, and 102°30′ and 107°30′ east longitude. Bounded by Laos to the north, Thailand to the west, South Vietnam to the east and the Gulf of Siam to the south.

TOPOGRAPHY:

Centred in the basin or lowland region which makes up three-quarters of the country, Tonle Sap or the Great Lake is Cambodia's major physical feature. Flooding from the lake, which regularly trebles its size during the wet season, and from the Mekong River and its tributaries, deposits rich alluvial soils throughout the basin.

CLIMATE:

Tropical monsoon — warm throughout the year. Day-time temperatures are usually in the 80's F. Without much seasonal variation. Nights are somewhat cooler.

RAINFALL:

The Lowland region generally receives less than 60″ a year while the highlands, along the northern border, in the southwest and in the eastern plateaux region, generally receive between 60″ and 80″, or more.

ETHNIC GROUPS:

Nine-tenths of the population are Khmer. Vietnamese and Chinese are the next largest groups.

POPULATION:

6,818,200 (U.N. estimate 1970) Density, 94 persons per square mile.

A New-born Republic

CAMBODIA is a country of the Indo-Chinese peninsula, bounded on the north-east by Laos, on the east and south-east by South Vietnam, on the south by the Gulf of Siam, and on the west and north by Thailand. Its area is 69,866 square miles, and its population was estimated in 1970 to be 6,818,200, of which Cambodians make up 85 per cent, Vietnamese 8 per cent and Chinese 6 per cent. The capital is Phnom Penh, with a population of 468,900. The languages spoken in the country are Khmer and French, with all the educated classes speaking, reading and writing fluent French. The religion of the people is Buddhism.

Cambodia's sandstone Dangrek mountains along the Thai frontier in the north fall abruptly to the central lowlands. On the south-western side of these lowlands, the granitic Cardamom mountains rise to more than 4,900 feet, and the calcareous Elephant range runs south-south-eastwards from the Cardamoms, separating the lowlands from the greater part of the coast, which is fringed with little islands.

The great depression of the Tonle Sap is enclosed on two sides by mountain ranges, and there is a broken arc of hills to the north-east, forming the watershed between it and the Mekong. This great river traverses the eastern part of the Republic from north to south, and beyond is higher ground toward the mountains of southern Vietnam. In the extreme north-east, the basins of the Se Kong and the Tonle Srepok converge on that of the Mekong at Stungtreng.

The Tonle Sap, or Great Lake, is the remnant of an ancient gulf. Fed by streams from uplands encircling the depression, it has an area of 100 square miles, and a maximum depth of five feet at the height of the dry season, when its water has been flowing away down the great channel that enters the Mekong just above Phnom Penh. In June, the Mekong rises to 45 feet, and empties its flood waters back through the channel into the lake, which then increases its depth to 48 feet, and spreads to cover 770 square miles, inundating the surrounding marshes, forests and cultivated lands.

The Khmer race appears to be the result of a pre-historic fusion, anti-dating the Hindu migrations, between invaders from the north and the aborigines. The Khmer language, presumably derived from that of the invaders, is related to the Mon of southern Burma, with which it constitutes the Mon-Khmer linguistic family. But the alphabet is derived from Indian models. The men are taller and more muscular than the Thais or the Vietnamese, but the women are small and inclined to stoutness. The face of the typical Cambodian is flat and wide, the mouth large, and the eyes only slightly oblique. The skin is dark brown, and the hair black. Both sexes wear the *sampot,* a copious sort of loincloth. The men supplement it with a short jacket, and the women with a long scarf draped around the figure like a long clinging robe. The wife enjoys a respected status. Divorce may be demanded by either party. Recent reforms discountenance polygamy, which in general has always been a prerogative of the richer classes.

For the Buddhism practised in the Khmer Republic the sacred texts are in Pali, but the worship of spirits or local genii is also widespread. Numerous monks or *bonzes* live by alms and in return teach the young to read and superintend marriages, funerals and other ceremonies. Most young men of higher education take on monkhood during their later teen years as a lesson in righteous living to prepare them for their adult life. Some remain as monks indefinitely. There is no hereditary nobility, but there are superior castes founded on blood relationship. The former court maintained Brahmanism.

Until 18th March 1970 the Chief of State was Prince Norodom Sihanouk, and the country was a monarchy. Because of student pressure, the Government was forced to take action to eliminate North Vietanmese and Vietcong from the border area adjacent to South Vietnam. During a student demonstration, Prince Norodom Sihanouk was requested to return from Paris, where he had been recuperating from ill health. Possibly because the Prince believed that his country's interests would be best served by preserving complete neutrality, and knowing that the Cambodian Army was then very small, he declined to return and face the Government and the students. With all airports closed, the National Assembly met, surrounded by armoured cars. An historic decision was later announced by President Cheng Heng: "The National Assembly and the Council of the Kingdom, meeting in joint session, have withdrawn, conforming to the constitution, in an unanimous vote, their confidence from Prince Norodom Sihanouk in his position as Chief of State."

The Assembly chose Cheng Heng as the new provisional Head of State, a position reduced in status to one of formal significance only. Lieutenant-General Lon Nol continued as Premier. On 5th October 1970 the Cambodian Parliament voted unanimously to proclaim the nation a Republic, effective on 1st November. Thus, after more than 1,000 years the monarchy was ended and Cambodia become the Khmer Republic. Prince Sihanouk took refuge in Peking, where he set up a government-in-exile, composed only of his private staff who had been travelling with him. The Government of Lon Nol took action against insurgents and later the United States and South Vietnamese joined in and war began.

The modern Khmer Republic is an historical evolution of the great Kingdom of Founan, set up in the area by Hindu migrants from India proper in the 1st Century A.D. Its major political competitor was Champa, the Cham Kingdom on its eastern frontier. Though Founan's diplomatic orientation was largely towards China, relations were maintained with India in the 3rd Century, with a considerable immigration from India from the middle of the 4th to the middle of the 5th Centuries. Kaundinya, progenitor of the last Kings of Founan, is supposed to have arrived in the country in A.D. 400. An irregularity in Rudravarnam's accession on the death of Kaundinya Jayavarman, in A.D. 514, seems to have led to the breakup of Founan among rival pretenders in the second half of the 6th Century. Out of the disorder rose the power of Tchen-la, originally one of Founan's vassal kingdoms, on the Mekong River in the Bassac region. The Kings of Tchen-la claimed descent from the mythical couple Kambu and Mera—eponyms of Kambuja, or Cambodia, and of the Khmer people—and the princess of Tchen-la married Rudravarman's grandson Bhavavarman I.

The latter, with his brother Chitrasena, or Mahendravarman, began the process of Khmer expansion at the expense of other remnants of Founan. But after the death of Jayavarman I at the end of the 7th Century, Tchen-la was divided between north and south, the south being itself subdivided among principalities and subject to the Javanese "king of the mountains".

Only in the 9th Century in the period between A.D. 802 and 850 was the Khmer revival inaugurated, with the foundation of the dynasty of Angkor by Jayavarman II. To release the country from alien overlordship, this Prince assumed the traditional cult of the god-king—which had passed from Java to Founan—and settled at Kulen, a holy mountain from which the royal-cum-divine authority was derived.

There followed other dynasties, with the fortunes of the country subject to the consequences of war until Suryavarman II, of the dynasty of Mahidharapura, made war on Annam in 1128 and 1138, on China in 1132, and most successfully on Champa in 1145, subduing the whole of Champa for two years and the northern part for four. It was he who built Angkor Wat.

For hundreds of years afterwards, the Khmers in their kingdom found themselves continuously encroached upon by the Thais and the Annamites. Eventually the rump of the ancient kingdom found itself the vassal of Thailand and Annam. In the course of these Khmer misfortunes, the great temple at Angkor was abandoned, and the jungle crept upon it and concealed it from the world. According to Western history, one morning in 1860 a French naturalist, searching for a butterfly, turned a corner in a forest path and discovered the temple. Looming through gaps in the impenetrable green foliage, he saw the grey towers of Angkor Wat. He halted in amazement, scarcely believing his eyes. Subsequently however, Henri Mouhot's diary was resurrected and published. He stated that he left London bent on visiting the temples of Angkor. With the help of records of other visits by little known Europeans, he was able to plan his journey. Using local guides Henri Mouhot arrived at "Ongcor" around 2nd January 1861. Desperately ill on many occasions, his journey was fraught with danger from marauding natives, attacks by wild animals, poisonous insects and snakes. Henri Mouhot, the naturalist, wrote afterwards that coming upon the Wat in its jungle setting was like being suddenly "transported from barbarism to civilisation, from profound darkness to light".

The first European contacts with Cambodia were made in the 16th Century when Portuguese and Spanish ships visited it. But only after 300 years had elapsed did the Western world exert any influence there. The turn of events in Annam from the beginning of the 19th Century was such as to diminish the threat to Cambodia from that quarter, giving the Thais a free hand. They overran Battambang and Siem Reap, and treated the King of Oudang, as their puppet. But their trespassing on Annamite spheres of influence provoked a reaction, leading to Norodom I's acceptance of a French protectorate status on 11th August 1863. This ended with the 1954 Geneva Convention.

PRIMARY INDUSTRY

Economically, the Tonle Sap, or the Great Lake, is the country's most valuable asset. In the first place, it makes excellent conditions for rice growing—the country's staple agriculture—particularly Battambang at its western end. Secondly, it supports a fishing population of 30,000 and yields an annual catch of 100,000 tons of fish.

Besides rice, the chief crops are maize, rubber—particularly around Kompong Chan, on the Mekong upstream from Phom Penh—and cotton grown on the banks of the Mekong. But the war since 1970 has dealt a severe blow to the rubber plantations, many of which were developed by French expatriates, and the cotton industry has become almost dormant. Other crops are pepper, sugar, tobacco, coffee and tea.

Top, left: A typical Khmer beauty...
Above: These oxen are extensively used on farms as described in the story of Sok Dim...
Below: Pedicabs; a popular, cheap form of transport...
Below, right: A section of the business centre in Phnom Penh.

Silk used to be produced, and still is, but in greatly diminished quantities. Much timber is cut in the forests. Water buffaloes, oxen and elephants are kept as draught animals. In peace time, precious stones are mined in the Pailin area, and there are deposits of iron in Kompong Thom, within the arc of hills separating the Tonle Sap from the Mekong. The people living in the islands off the coast depend on fishing for their livelihood, and great is the jubilation when a bumper catch is brought in.

Above: Holy men gathered at one of the temple entrances to Angkor Wat.

Right: An example of some of the fine stone carvings that decorate the innumerable temples throughout the Khmer Republic.

The picture on the opposite page shows gifts laid at the feet of a huge deity figure in Phnom Penh.

THE ECONOMY
Because the Mekong delta is the Khmer Republic's natural outlet to the sea, most of the foreign trade passes through, or at least used to pass through, the Vietnamese emporium of Saigon. Commerce is largely in Chinese hands. The country's monetary unit is the riel, with a rate of exchange following a devaluation on 18th August 1969 of 55.54 riels to the United States dollar. The budget in 1969, the last year of peace before war, was based on a revenue of 6,250 million riels and an expenditure of 7,565 million riels.

In 1968 imports to Cambodia amounted to 4,060 million riels, with exports at 3,100 million riels. The main import sources were France 31 per cent, Japan 21 per cent, Singapore 10 per cent, Hong Kong 6 per cent and China 6 per cent. Export destinations were principally South Vietnam 17 per cent, Hong Kong 11 per cent, China 10 per cent, France 8 per cent and Singapore 8 per cent. The main exports in 1967 were rice 42 per cent, rubber 25 per cent and corn 5 per cent.

THE LURE OF ANGKOR WAT
The shattering of the economy as a consequence of war resulted in the riel plummeting to more than 100 to the United States dollar. Big rubber plantations were razed by bombings, and earnings from tourism dropped to nil, with the chief attraction of the temples of Angkor closed to visitors, because the North Vietnamese Army had occupied the area as a safe place to hospitalise wounded troops. Knowing that the Government would not destroy any part of the temple, they felt quite secure. Action by the Government, using only small arms and low explosive ammunition is now under way to clear the area. The Government in Phnom Penh is concerned to preserve this masterpiece for posterity.

Of Angkor Wat, Malcolm MacDonald wrote: "Here the jungle, the monuments and wild beasts live in perfect harmony. There are touches of symmetry about the natural forms of the woodland and the architectural forms of the buildings. The Wat is the supreme masterpiece of Khmer art. It is an Asian contemporary of the Notre Dame in Paris, and Ely and Lincoln cathedrals in England. But in spaciousness and splendour it is more ambitious than any of these."

MILITARY AND ECONOMIC AID
The United States Agency for International Development estimated in 1970 that the Government would need US$230 million in outside support to keep the economy functioning through 1971. Late in 1970, President Nixon obtained United States Congress approval for a supplementary appropriation of US$255 million for military and economic aid to the Khmer Republic.

PHNOM PENH AND ITS PEOPLE
Phnom Penh, the capital of the Republic, sprawls beside the Mekong River. In the little city's heart rises a small hill which gives the place one half of its name, for the Khmer word for hill is "phnom", and a Buddhist temple on the summit provides the second half, since it was built there two centuries ago by a pious lady named Penh.

The city is neatly planned, with broad avenues of flame-of-the-forest trees, elegant official residences standing in gardens scented by tropical blooms, narrower streets bordered by crowded rows of native dwellings where banana trees sprout untidily in backyards, and a commercial centre where imposing European shops rise from pavements cluttered with open-air Oriental stalls —all gathered round the little hill with its Buddhist temple among graceful palms.

The capital's inhabitants are idle and inquisitive. They are humble, peaceful folk, content to tackle each day's little problems as they arise, lacking any higher ambition. Most are nearer poverty than wealth, but what they miss in material affluence is compensated by their natural possessions of abundant sunshine and fruitful earth.

Their fields produce plenty of rice, and their huge river holds multitudes of fish. So existence—at least until the start of the war against the Communists—is easy, pleasant and relaxed. For these blessings, they give thanks to the supernatural beings who decide the fates of men.

Like most simple, rustic people in the East, in their hearts, they are still attached to animist beliefs. But their official faith is Buddhism, and religion is the strongest impulse in their lives. Among them priests have great power.

Often, groups of these holy men stroll along the streets holding parasols to shade their shaven heads and golden-brown bodies, swathed in yellow robes thrown across their shoulders like Roman togas.

LIFE IN A FARMING COMMUNITY

Sok Dim is a 32 year-old Cambodian. He is married with four children whose ages are eight, nine, ten and eleven. He lives with his family and his old mother at Chey Chork village in Takeo province. Their house is made of wooden boards, the floor being raised about seven feet off the ground, the roof thatched with palm leaves. Under the house are the fowls, ducks and pigs and the stable, covered with straw for the oxen. Everyday, as soon as the roosters crow, usually about 5 o'clock, Dim gets up from his wooden bed covered with straw matting. He goes down to the bathroom to wash, taking water from a large barrel with half a coconut shell. Behind the two bedrooms is the kitchen, where his wife prepares rice and salty, smoked and dried fish, some cucumbers, salads and other vegetables for his breakfast and lunch. Dim changes from his sarong into his black working clothes and then goes into the sitting room in the centre of the house to have his morning meal. After breakfast he takes a dried sankeo leaf from a box and wraps some tobacco in it to make a cigarette. While his wife makes the bed and rearranges the mosquito net Dim smokes and talks to her about what he will do on the farm.

Dim says good-bye to his wife, goes down to the stable to release the two oxen, yokes them and attaches the cart in which he puts his lunch, a tea pot, a wooden plough with its shining plough-share, a rake and other farming tools. He drives off to one of his three farms, two miles from the house. Dim, like his fellow Cambodians, has complete ownership of his land.

His wife wakes the children, feeds them and sends them to the monastery school, situated in the grounds of the pagoda about a mile away. Then she feeds the animals, does the housework and attends her vegetable and flower gardens. At about 10 o'clock she starts to prepare some food and rice for the Buddhist monks who pass her house every day around 11 o'clock. This is a tradition which is carried on in all the villages.

At the farm, at this time of year when the first rain has fallen, usually early April, the soil is wet and easy to plough so Dim works continuously. Sometimes he takes a break to wipe his face with the cotton cloth he wears on his head, to have a cup of tea or to smoke a cigarette. As soon as the sun is directly above, he stops working and looks for a tree to tie his oxen to while he eats under the shady branches. He always has a big appetite. After lunch Dim has a short siesta and then continues his work. Sometimes he has a chat with some of his friends walking past his farm. Dim goes on ploughing until the sun goes down.

His day's work over, Dim returns home for dinner. He talks to his wife and asks his children about school. After dinner the whole family sits around the petrol lamp. Dim listens to the transistor radio while the children do their homework or ask their grandmother to tell them stories. His wife does some sewing. There is nothing they enjoy more than spending such evenings together as a family. At about 9 or 10 o'clock they all go off to bed, sleepy and happy.

Dim's whole life is greatly influenced by the Buddhist tradition. In every village there is a pagoda—the symbol of this tradition. It consists of a temple in which there is a large statue of Buddha, several monasteries where the monks live, a school house for the children and the student monks, and a communal eating house for the monks and the villagers. Most pagodas do not have a surrounding wall; instead there is usually a moat. Dim's family goes to the pagoda every fortnight to join in the traditional ceremony at which all the villagers offer the monks food. They also pray or listen to the story of Buddha's life and his doctrines by which the people learn to be kind and gentle, to be honest and considerate, to behave decently and to accept life as it is.

In readiness for the three-day New Year holiday, which falls in mid-April, Dim's family, like all the other villagers, buys new clothes, tidies the house, cleans up the yard and prepares large quantities of food to take to the pagoda to offer the monks, who represent God. Nobody works during this festive occasion. Instead, the people pray, listen to the monks and build five small piles of sand, believing this will liberate them from sin. The young boys and girls play traditional games and music, and dance the popular Lamthon.

Late in April it is time to plant the rice. The ground has been prepared and manured. Dim asks about ten or fifteen of his friends from the village to help him plant out the rice seedlings. Each of Dim's two acre farms is divided into six separate fields by a system of dykes. The fields are irrigated by scooping the water from a small pond in one corner of the farm. When the crop is ripe for harvesting, usually in October which marks the end of the rainy seaons, Dim once again calls on his friends to help him. The rice has to be cut, tied in bundles and thrashed against a wooden board to separate the grain. The stalks left in the ground are burnt to make potash for the soil. In return for their help Dim provides food for his friends. He in his turn helps them when their crops are ready to be harvested.

From his harvest Dim keeps enough rice to feed his family for the year; the rest he sells to the local farming co-operative which is run by the Government. He also sells some pigs, fowls, eggs and ducks to the co-operative and with the money thus earned he may save some, buy more stock, some new clothes, pay for entertainment and buy meat and fish.

Dim takes an active part in the life of the village community. He has helped in the actual building of a new monastery and also contributed some money for materials. He participates in the government of other villages as well as his own. When the people of Dim's village wanted additional classrooms for their school, they approached the mayor who governs several neighbouring villages. These people came together to discuss the matter and contributed a sum of money. The mayor appealed to the Phnom Penh Government and more money was provided. Dim helped in the construction of the building along with the professional builders. Thus Dim plays an active part in the affairs of his own community and like the rest of his friends is always ready to give help to neighbouring villages when they need it.

As a typical Cambodian farmer, Dim believes that his duty lies in caring for his family, in living in the tradition of Buddhism and in helping in the improvement and development of his own village and, in turn, his country.

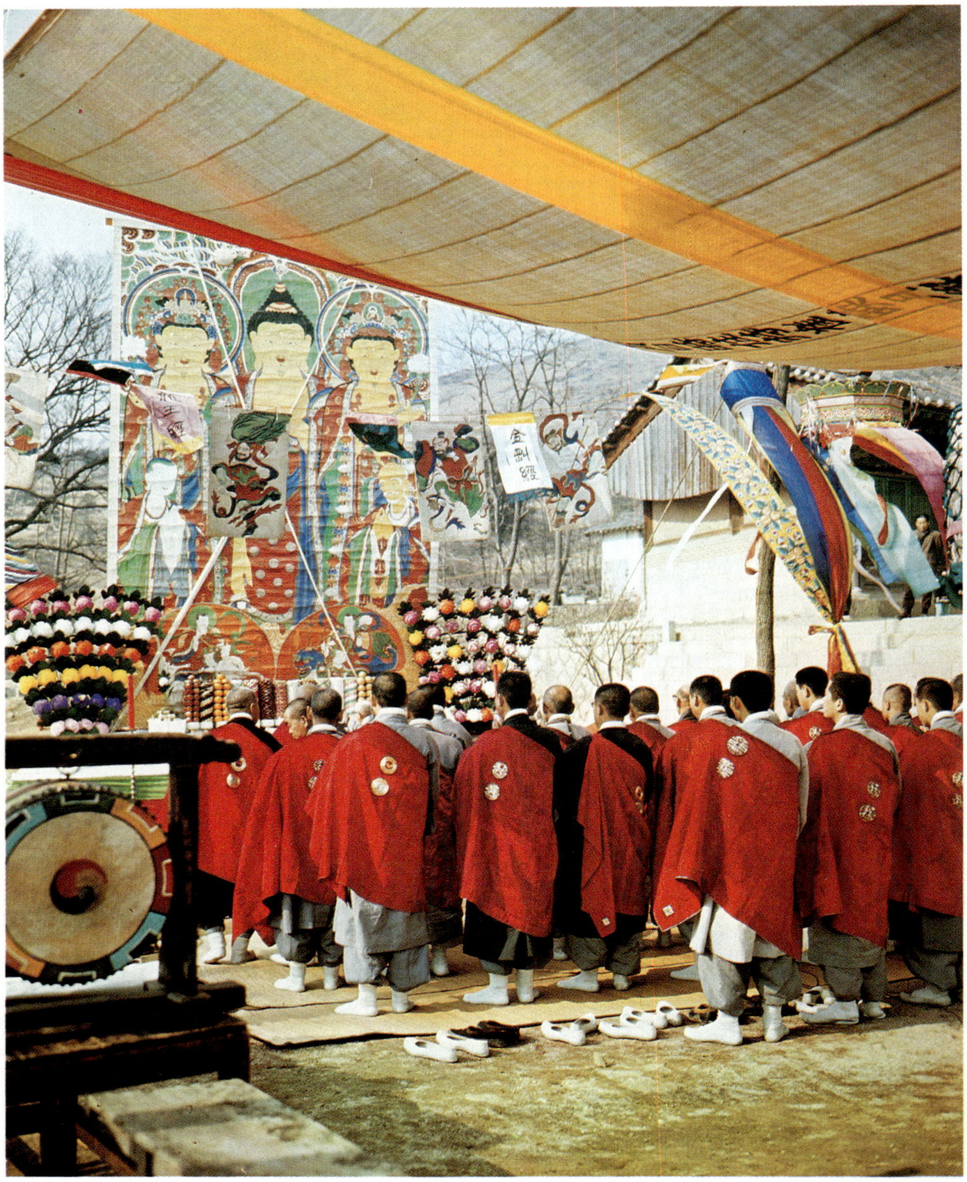

Republic of
KOREA

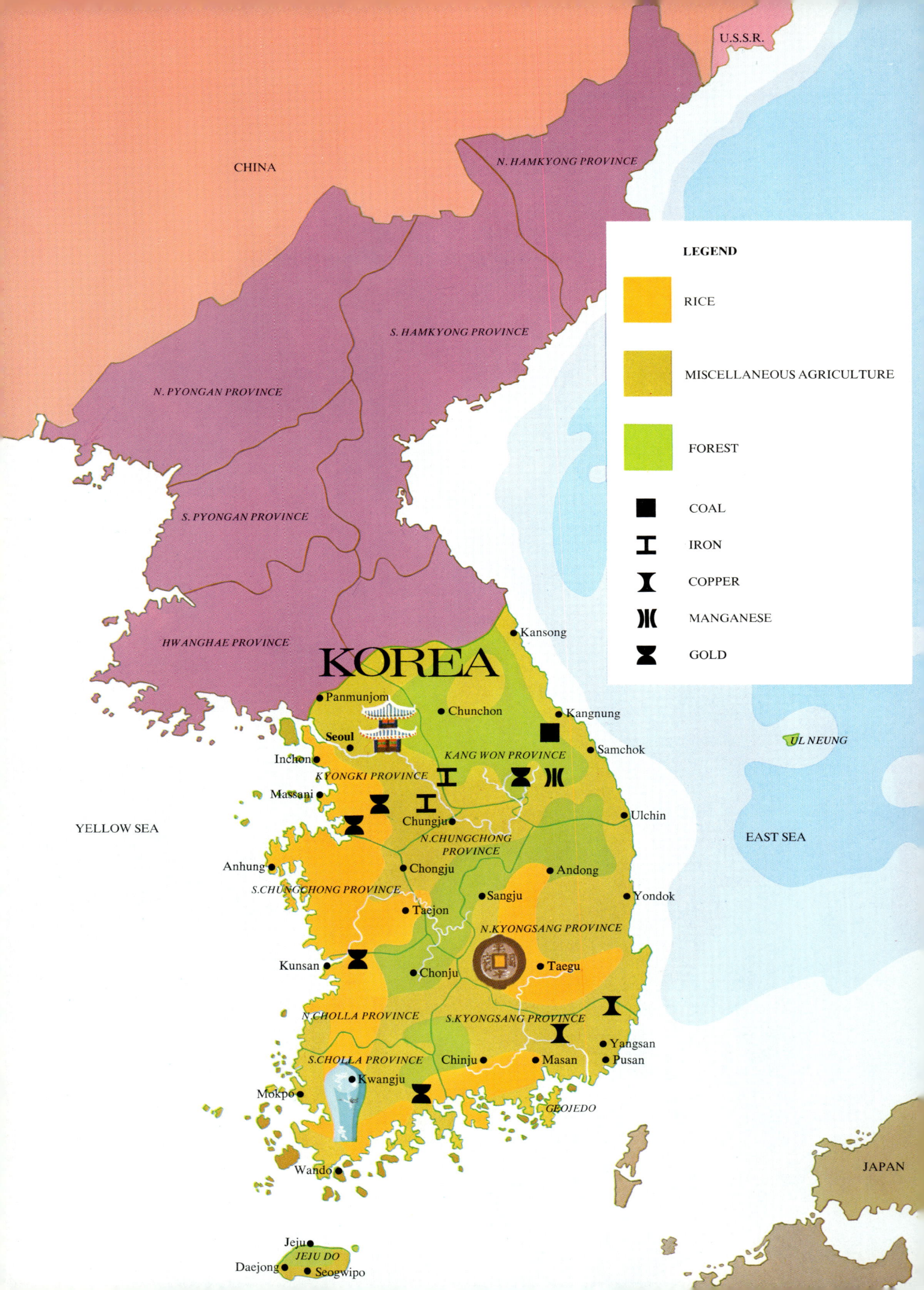

KOREA

LEGEND

- RICE
- MISCELLANEOUS AGRICULTURE
- FOREST
- ■ COAL
- ⊢⊣ IRON
- ⊃⊂ COPPER
- ⊃⊃⊂ MANGANESE
- ⋈ GOLD

Provinces

- N. HAMKYONG PROVINCE
- S. HAMKYONG PROVINCE
- N. PYONGAN PROVINCE
- S. PYONGAN PROVINCE
- HWANGHAE PROVINCE
- KYONGKI PROVINCE
- KANG WON PROVINCE
- N. CHUNGCHONG PROVINCE
- S. CHUNGCHONG PROVINCE
- N. KYONGSANG PROVINCE
- S. KYONGSANG PROVINCE
- N. CHOLLA PROVINCE
- S. CHOLLA PROVINCE
- JEJU DO

Cities and Places

Panmunjom, Seoul, Inchon, Massani, Chunchon, Kangnung, Samchok, Chungju, Ulchin, Anhung, Chongju, Taejon, Sangju, Andong, Yondok, Kunsan, Chonju, Taegu, Chinju, Masan, Yangsan, Pusan, Mokpo, Kwangju, Wando, Kansong, Jeju, Daejong, Seogwipo, UL NEUNG, GEOJEDO

Surrounding Regions

CHINA, U.S.S.R., JAPAN, YELLOW SEA, EAST SEA

Korea

Hyangwon-jong Pavilion in the beautifully landscaped Kyung-Bok gardens.

NEW HORIZONS FOR AN ANCIENT NATION

Korea is a rugged peninsula extending like a finger pointing in a southerly direction from northern Asia toward the Japanese archipelago. Though long influenced by the culture and institutions of the vast neighbouring empire of China, and sometimes dominated by an expansion-minded Japan, Korea has preserved for over 4,000 years her own unique individuality of language, arts, traditions and nationalism.

Today she is seeking new horizons as one of the most rapidly developing emerging nations in the Pacific area.

Korea is only 1,000 km in length and 206 km wide at the narrowest point. Moreover, it is so mountainous that only about a quarter of the land area is arable, supporting an estimated total population of nearly 45,000,000. Of these 31.5 million live in the southern zone, or Republic of Korea, with which this Chapter is concerned.

The remainder are in the Communist northern zone of Korea, sundered from the rest by international partition following World War II and the civil war of 1950-53.

The nation has the fourth densest population concentration in the world; and until recently, a rate of increase surpassing 2.4 per cent per year.

During the 1960's this rate fell to 1.9 per cent as the result of a vigorous family planning programme. It must be further cut to well below 1.5 per cent before the overpopulation problem may be said to have been brought under control.

Korea is historically a rice-growing agricultural area. Despite the rapid expansion of cities consequent upon the modernisation and industrialisation commencing in the 20th Century, over half of the country's people are still engaged in farming or fishing, which produce 30 per cent of the Gross National Product. One of Korea's most urgent needs is for an equalisation of progress and a more even sharing of the fruits of economic success between the more affluent urban populace and the rural citizenry.

National per capita income for 1970 was US$223, a low figure internationally but showing considerable improvement over the US$198 of the preceding year. The figure is expected to rise to US$389 by 1976, the target year of the third five-year Economic Development Plan.

The Korean people are nearly 100 per cent literate, most of them having completed six years of compulsory schooling. School attendance marked 96.1 per cent of those eligible in 1970. Many have attended higher schools, colleges and universities as well.

Koreans have a long-standing respect for scholarship, a residue of the ancient Confucian system of government by scholar-administrators, which continued until near the end of the 19th Century. Recently the ascendancy in education of the arts and humanities over more practical pursuits has been challenged by the increasing need for skills in engineering, technology and management required to run a modern, developing society.

Korea now has 200 college or university-level schools with over 10,000 faculty members and an enrolment approaching a quarter of a million.

Land of the Morning Calm

THE BEGINNINGS of Korean civilisation and culture reach back to the legendary time of Tangun, a mythical divine being who is said to have descended from heaven 24 centuries before Christ to found a Utopian tribal state on the peninsula.

By the 10th Century B.C. a Neolithic (New Stone Age) people of Ural-Altaic stock had established themselves in this territory. Their remains have been unearthed by modern archaeologists. Three tribal groups—Mahan, Chinhan and Pyonhan—flourished in the south, consisting of hundreds or thousands of households.

The language spoken by these tribes was a prototype of modern Korean, resembling Turkish, Hungarian or Finnish more than any Oriental language group.

The 5th Century B.C. saw the dawn of Korea's Bronze Age with the introduction of metal-working skills from China. At this stage, the primitive tribal nations began to expand and evolve. From the 1st to the 3rd Centuries A.D., the first historically documented confederations began to emerge, known as the Three Kingdoms: Koguryo in the north, encompassing southern Manchuria and northern Korea; Paekje, occupying the central Han River basin; and Silla to the south, whose territory extended along the Nakdong River.

These early Kingdoms had adopted Confucian social philosophy and Buddhist religion from China and India by the 4th Century. Paekje in addition maintained close relations with Japan during this period, and passed on many continental influences to the island empire, including Chinese ideographic writing, farming methods, weaving, medicine, painting, music, and religion. Silla, the slowest of the three states to develop an advanced culture, eventually outstripped them all, at the same time coming into conflict with Koguryo, and forming an alliance with Paekje. After several centuries of sporadic warfare Silla—with the help of T'ang China—defeated its old ally Paekje in 661 A.D., and subsequently conquered Koguryo in 668.

The Korean peninsula was thus unified as a single political entity for the first time, and experienced a major cultural efflorescence, mainly under the influence of Buddhism, which became the state religion.

The Kingdom declined rather rapidly, however, because of the decentralisation of power in the hands of feudalistic nobles who often attempted rebellion.

One of Silla's outstanding achievements was the establishment of the chivalric order of highly cultivated warrior-esthetes called Hwarang, or Flower Youth, corresponding to the tradition of chivalry represented by tales of King Arthur and the Round Table in Europe.

But nothing could save the fragmenting state of Silla, which eventually was taken over by one its rebel provinces in 936 A.D., marking the founding of a new dynasty for the nation.

The Koryo Kingdom, from which the foreign name for the country, Korea, was derived, lasted from 936 until 1392. Despite its relatively stable internal organisation, still strongly influenced by Buddhist priests active behind the scenes in politics, the nation was assailed from outside with increasing frequency.

Koryo was harassed by northern tribes such as the Tartars and Mongols. Between 993 and 1018, three major invasions were fought off. But finally, in 1213, the

Above:
Inside the Sukk ram Cave temple a priest is praying to Buddha.

Right:
The Korean game of Ko Saum. According to legend, if the team on the west side wins, it will mean a bumper harvest.

Opposite page:
The Royal Audience Hall at the Kyung-Bok Palace, Seoul.

hordes of the Great Khan swept over the country. The invaders, though they decimated the nation and perpetrated wholesale plunder, failed to capture the Koryo Government, which had prudently taken refuge on an offshore island.

By 1270, a peace treaty was imposed on the King which forced him to take a Mongol princess as bride, and to conduct himself as a vassal of the Mongol empire.

Despite impressive cultural accomplishments—including the printing of a definitive edition of Buddhist texts as an offering to heaven imploring divine protection from the Mongols—the power of the Koryo Kingdom was gradually bled away. Even after foreign occupying forces withdrew, their influence remained entrenched in the Government.

When an anti-Mongol general named Yi Song-gae reluctantly took a stand against the pro-Mongol court, the dynasty rapidly crumbled and Gen. Yi—perhaps somewhat to his own surprise—found himself pressed to ascend the throne as progenitor of Korea's last royal dynasty. This he did in 1392, assuming the title of King Taejo.

The Yi period was characterised by the emergence of an elaborate civil service bureaucracy under the strict Confucian system. All official posts were filled by literati who had completed the stringent national examinations in those Chinese classics which heavily emphasised poetry, propriety, and ritual. It was thus a government of scholars and gentlemen which soon grew into a caste or ruling clique.

Buddhism, previously so influential in royal circles, was disestablished and its temples banished to outlying areas. Never again did this religion regain its earlier influence in national affairs.

The Golden Age of this Kingdom came with the enlightened reign of its fourth monarch, King Sejong (1419-1450), called the Great. This humane, cultured ruler conceived and fostered the development of a simple phonetic alphabet called Hangul, which eliminated the thousands of cumbersome Chinese ideographs in which the Korean language had been written, thus making universal literacy possible. He also initiated important scientific and technological developments.

During the 16th Century, factional feuds in the higher levels of the bureaucracy weakened the grasp of the Government. Between 1592 and 1598, the Japanese warlord Hideyoshi launched two devastating invasions of the peninsula, with the unsuccessful aim of conquering China. These invasions were eventually frustrated by a combination of Japanese logistic difficulties, Chinese troops sent in to help the Koreans, and the genius of Korea's most renowned leader, Admiral Yi Sun-sin, who invented the world's first ironclad warships, and wrought havoc among the Japanese fleet.

However, great damage had been inflicted during the land war, and a Manchurian invasion in 1636 dealt another crippling blow to the already wounded nation.

Through all these trials, divisive factional rivalries within the government increased steadily, thus weakening the dynasty still further.

Korea's reaction was to retreat into a stringent isolationism that surpassed even that of Japan. This period of apathy and decline ended only in 1876, when a reawakened Japan, assisted indirectly by the gunboat diplomacy of Western nations, forced the opening of the hermit Kingdom's ports to foreign commerce.

After Japan emerged victor in the Sino-Japanese War of 1894-5 and the Russo-Japanese War ten years later, she felt strong enough to establish a protectorate over Korea in 1905, and then to proclaim outright annexation in 1910.

The Korean emperor became a figurehead, and when King Kojong died in 1919 he was not succeeded by his son; thus ended the Yi dynasty.

The day of mourning permitted by the Japanese authorities in connection with Kojong's funeral was utilised by Korean nationalist leaders, who had picked up their ideals of political and social reform from knowledge of the Western liberal democracies, to launch nationwide peaceful demonstrations for independence. So carefully organised and concealed was this secret movement that on 1st March 1919—a date the Koreans still observe as their independence day—the Japanese were caught completely off guard. Their police and military reacted with brutality and many thousands of demonstrators were killed, wounded, or arrested and tortured.

From this time on, the Korean independence leaders either went underground or into exile, waging a 25-year battle against the Japanese plan for a calculated, forced cultural and political assimilation of Korea as part of the Japanese empire.

This dark period was fitfully illuminated by many acts of patriotism and self-sacrifice on the part of Korean nationalists, but under the prevailing circumstances freedom was forced to wait for the final defeat of the Japanese military forces by the Western allies in the Pacific War (1941-45).

After this came the unexpected national division, when Soviet forces moved into northern Korea and set up a puppet regime; the resulting fratricidal Korean War and a period of stagnation and political corruption in the 1950's culminated in a student uprising in 1960 and a military *coup d'etat* in 1961.

The two years of military government ushered in many desperately needed reforms, and set the stage for a resurgence of national pride and purpose.

Since the restitution of a democratic, representative civilian government following the elections of 1963, progress and development in all fields have been both remarkable and reassuring. Korea is once more preparing to play the role of an independent, self-determining and influential power in the Pacific area.

THE ARTS, LITERATURE AND MUSIC

Among the earliest surviving arts in Korea are Buddhist architecture, sculpture, painting and poetry derived from Chinese lore. Buddhism is also prominently in evidence in the Japanese arts and the irrepressable Korean is said to have influenced many Japanese figurative painters. Later came the world-famous celadon ware and scrolls, both of Chinese calligraphy and genre paintings. Prized specimens of these arts, together with outstanding royal, civil and religious structures, have been designated as national treasures under the protection of the Government.

During the Koryo Dynasty (918-1392 A.D.) the art of ceramics evolved under the influence of China's Sung Dynasty. Most famous is the celadon or blue porcelain ware. The pictures found on the surfaces of celadon jugs, bowls and vases are examples in delicacy and invention of the finest of Korea's naturalistic art. Water-fowl, trees, reeds, willows, flowers, fish and birds were depicted with feeling and grace.

Korean literature is predominantly poetic, ranging from imitations of Chinese models and themes to purely native works like the "kasa" narrative poems, the brief lyrics called "sijo" and folk epics, chanted in villages to "pansori" or drum accompaniment. Prose fiction has a briefer history: novels and stories in the modern sense were hardly known before the 20th Century. Drama was traditionally found in the form of broadly farcical maskdances in popular folk-style.

Traditional Korean music is divided into "A-ak", court music of Chinese and local origin — "Tang-ak" and "Hyang-ak" — and various types of military, chamber and vocal music. In addition, the older music includes Buddhist chants and the folk songs and farmers' dances of the common people. The court music is stately and complex in its interweaving of long, elaborate melodies, played together in high and low registers in a kind of "simultaneous variation" style. The ancient instruments include flutes and reeds, plucked-string zithers and a variety of drums and percussion instruments.

The dances that go along with the court music are likewise solemn, static and highly-stylised with emphasis placed on the upper half of the body, the image being introduced by shoulder movement and responded to by the arms and the head moving in affirmation.

Folk music is usually fast and lively, in irregular triple beat patterns, with zestful dancing. Some of the court instruments are used but folk music relies more on metal gongs, the hour-glass shaped drum called the changgo and a loud trumpet-like oboe.

Modern Western art was introduced into Korea in the closing years of the 19th Century and today there is an interesting admixture of traditional and modern art in current painting and sculpture. The most important annual event in Korea's art world is the National Art Exhibit which is held every autumn under Government patronage. The modern trend is in evidence in the writings of many of Korea's authors such as Richard E. Kim and Kim Yong-ik. Music, too, has been influenced and stimulated by Western styles and the works of famous composers are featured on programmes performed by Seoul's two symphony orchestras and several opera companies.

SOUTH KOREAN ECONOMY

After the Korean War (1950-53) the nation's nascent industrial development was found to be nearly wrecked and recovery was slow. During the 1960's, however, the growth of the economy, sparked by foreign aid and investment plus mobilisation of domestic resources under two successive five-year plans, was so remarkable as to be dubbed "the miracle of the Han".

The average annual growth rate between 1961 and 1970 was about 10 per cent. To prevent such undesirable side effects as inflation the planned growth rate for the third five-year plan will be held at 8 per cent. By 1976, if the new plan succeeds, Korea will have become completely self-sufficient in both basic manufactured goods and food supply.

Since agriculture still employs more than half the total Korean population no real or lasting progress is possible without taking into account the need for farm modernisation. Methods to achieve this goal include the utilisation of mechanised farm tools, consolidation of paddy fields, use of hybrid and other improved seeds, better breed-stock for animals, the raising of cash-crops for industrial use and the modernisation of the fishing fleet to permit operations over long-distance and increased deep-sea fishing

In a number of aspects ambitious government programmes can make as impressive an impact upon agriculture as they have on manufacturing. These benefits may be visualised most clearly in the elaborate plan for the integrated development of four major river basin areas: the Naktong, Han, Yongsan and Kum rivers. This great project set to continue over a period of eleven years will cost 314,028 million won and require in addition foreign exchange amounting to US$60 million. The plan includes major flood control projects, multi-purpose dams, new irrigation systems, land drainage, urban water supply and reforestation. Newly cultivable land to the extent of 8,700 hectares will be made productive and the annual rice harvest boosted by around 600,000 tons.

During the 1960's the nation built up its domestic infrastructure of railroads, highways, electric power generation, communications and supply of such crucial materials as refined petroleum products, cement and

Opposite page, top:
A Celadon vase of the Koryo Dynasty;
a national treasure.

Opposite page, below:
Traditional folk dancers in weird masks and strange costumes.

Right:
The Children's Centre on Mt. Namsan commands a panoramic view of the bustling city of Seoul.

chemical fertiliser. Consumer goods increased in quantity, variety and quality. All this made possible a reduction in imports and consequent saving of foreign exchange reserves. Exports increased not only in volume but in profitability.

Before 1960 Korea's exports consisted mostly of raw materials, unprocessed agricultural products and mineral ores. Now the lion's share goes to manufactured goods, utilising the high degree of skill and relatively low wage rates of Korean workers for national and individual benefit. Many foreign-invested enterprises have been established and special privileges are extended to attract capital from abroad.

Among the more popular Korean export items are plywood, plastic products, sweaters and other clothing, radios and other electronic goods, leather and handicraft items, wigs and artificial hair, bicycles and musical instruments. Metals produced include iron, lead and zinc ores together with smaller amounts of copper, tungsten and gold. The major food crop is rice. Non-traditional crops which can be profitably sold to manufacturing industries as raw materials are arrowroot, flax, sesame oil, vegetables, cotton, tea and fruit.

SEEING KOREA

During the Korean War and ensuing years nearly three-quarters of a million Americans, Australians, New Zealanders and other Westerners went to Korea but for most their visits to this most beautiful of lands were tinged with unhappy memories. Many thousands are returning but this time under more pleasant circumstances, for the country again displays the gaiety and colourful beauty that only peace can bring to the people.

The last ten years of national reconstruction have brought with them a greater awareness of Korea's potential as a tourist nation.

There are now daily flights from Tokyo to Seoul landing at Kimpo, the city's modern airport terminal. The capital's best hotels are up to international standards and others, while not lavish, are comfortable and comparatively cheap. There are night clubs in the larger Korean cities and gambling is legal in the Monte Carlo-style casinos.

Seoul, although fully modern in its outward appearance, shops and services, still possesses many reminders of older days.

Three extensive Royal Palace complexes, their grounds now open as public parks, recall the time of the Yi dynasty. The Secret Garden of the Changdok Palace is a beautiful example of the sophisticated landscaping and gardening arts of Korea's age-old traditions.

About 60 miles from the south-west corner of the mainland, Cheju Island preserves its own characteristic customs and traditions. Mt. Halla, an extinct volcano and highest mountain of South Korea, towers in the midst of the island's semi-tropical forest. In coastal areas women earn their living the year round by diving to the ocean floor to collect various types of sea-food. For sheer spectacular scenery the Sorak Mountains on the north-east coast of the peninsula probably rank highest. Swimming in summer, hiking in spring and autumn and skiing in winter make this district a sportsman's paradise.

But Korea's beauty is not limited to any one resort or season. Throughout the country the visitor will find rushing torrents, both fragile and thunderous waterfalls, quaint Buddhist temples and decorative shrines and monuments, sometimes framed in the reds and yellows of autumn or the joyous greens of summer, sometimes in the frozen white of winter or the tentative shades of spring.

NATIONAL SPORTS

From the earliest times the people of Korea have developed their own unique versions of archery, wrestling, horse-riding, sledding and tug-of-war. Originally these sports were closely connected with hunting, fighting and religious rituals. Kite-flying, now mainly a children's game, was once a pastime of the nobility. The kite, decorated with grotesque animals and spirit faces, performed a kind of exorcism. Attached to them were lists of evils, which, when the kites were cut loose on a high wind, carried miles from their point of origin. This symbolically freed the flier from his wrong-doings and he considered himself literally "without sin".

No less symbolic, but more easily understood, are the sports of Korea today.

Athletic games and physical culture are part of the school curricula and traditional rivalries in intramural sports always attract lively interest. Baseball, basketball, soccer, volleyball, table tennis, marathon track events, boxing and wrestling are among the more popular games.

Each year a national athletic meet is arranged in which various provinces compete for trophies and local talent is screened for the Korean Olympic teams. Since the 1930's Korean athletes have participated in Olympic Games, Asian Games, World Women's Basketball matches and have been especially successful in track events, weight lifting, boxing, wrestling, basketball and volleyball.

Visiting foreign athletes and teams occasionally come to Seoul for exhibition games or to compete against Koreans. In 1971 Korea hosted the first President's Cup soccer matches for the Asian region when the host country tied with Burma for the top trophy.

A MODERN FAMILY IN KOREA

The modern Korean family lives in a large city—probably the capital, Seoul, a sprawling, mountain-girt megalopolis of 5 million where one out of every six of the country's population resides. The Kim family is in a sense typical, but not by any means average. For one thing, urban income far surpasses rural, so that many poor country people flock to the cities in the hope of better living, only to remain unemployed or underemployed.

The Kims typify the growing edge of the new Korea: the enterprising middle class of professional, managerial, technical or entrepreneurial specialists, so familiar and ubiquitous in highly-developed countries, but still a new phenomenon in emerging nations such as Korea.

Call them the Kims, since this is the most popular family name in Korea, along with Lee, Park, and a few others.

Mr Kim is a college graduate, in his early thirties, and has been employed as a chemical engineer at a large industrial plant for nearly ten years. He was lucky to get a job in his own field just after graduation, for in those days not many did. The factory is in the outskirts of Seoul, and he must commute to work by means of crowded buses in dense traffic every day, since only the rich can afford their own private cars.

Kim shows both ability and initiative on the job, works long hours, and has thus risen to assistant chief of his section.

There is talk about relocating the factory further from the capital, now that the new super-highway which spans the nation makes transport and freight hauling so much easier. This would permit plant expansion, and help alleviate the air pollution problem in Seoul, which is becoming more and more serious.

In that case, the Kims would probably move to a "company town"—rows of new, uniform bungalows provided for managerial-level employees in housing-short rural areas now being developed. At present they live in a private, rented house with a walled miniature garden of their own, in an old part of the city.

Mrs Kim, who retains her family name of Cho, attended high school, but did not graduate because her family needed all their money to put four boys through college. Instead she took a short course in typing, and got a job in the office of the factory where Kim worked. This is how they met; but when they became interested in each other, the rather old-fashioned Cho family insisted that a go-between—an old friend of the family—be called upon to arrange an engagement, after inquiring into the character and prospects of Mr Kim, before the couple could even be allowed to go out together socially. Not many years ago this is how all marriages were arranged, with the fortune teller often called in as consultant to make sure the omens were favourable.

The Kims were married eight years ago, and Mrs Kim still takes part-time jobs in offices despite her busy schedule as a housewife with two small children. She feels she ought to contribute to the family's income, since living costs in the city are high and rising rapidly. Only a few years ago it was very unusual for a woman to continue working after marriage, even though she might have high professional qualifications, but now it is much more common.

The Kims are lucky to be able to rent their home on easy terms from the parents of Mrs Kim, fairly prosperous rural people who used to maintain the house as a city base. Many Korean families must put down large cash deposits instead of, or more often in addition to, paying high rents in order to secure a suitable house or apartment in Seoul, a city which suffers from a severe housing shortage. Hundreds of new apartment buildings have risen to accommodate various income groups—some government-financed, some private ventures. But many Koreans dislike apartment living, since all but the most expensive units are crowded, noisy, and otherwise uncomfortable. Perhaps because of their agricultural past, no Korean seems to feel quite at ease unless he has his own house and plot of land, no matter how small, whether it is owned or rented.

The Kims' house is not large. It consists of three moderate-size rooms, including a cement-floored kitchen on a level lower than the rest. Running water is intermittent, though the power supply is much more dependable than it was a few years ago. The indoor toilet in a lean-to is a recent addition for which the family had to save for a long time.

The two main rooms are for living and dining by day, recreation in the evening, and sleeping at night. Mr and Mrs Kim use one, the children the other, though the separation, by means of paper-covered sliding wood screens, is merely formal.

In order to assure versatility of use, the rooms are sparsely furnished. Everyone sits on the floor, which is made of flat-cemented stones with varnished oil paper glued on top, and is heated in winter by underground stone flues running from the kitchen fire, or from an outside ground-level grate that burns coal briquettes. This ancient heating system, called ondol, is still popular, though the fumes from the burning coal can be dangerous in an improperly ventilated room.

Mr Kim has pasted on the wall a periodical chart of the chemical elements, while his wife—a Christian convert during girlhood—has hung a coloured picture of Jesus over her low vanity stand. An advertising calendar features a discreet Korean pinup girl, and the children keep a bowl of goldfish on the low utility table, next to the tall clothes chest. This is all the furniture, and all the decoration, the house has to show.

Meals are brought in from the kitchen on low serving tables by the little housemaid. Since Mrs Kim is a working wife, she needs a servant to take care of the home and the children, but can afford only a young girl from her father's village, perhaps a distant cousin of the family, who works for little more than room and board, and who will leave as soon as she can find a better job in a factory.

Every meal, three times a day, includes the basic elements: a bowl of white rice; a broth of meat or fish, vegetables, and spices; and one or more of *kimchi,* the national dish, peppery fermented vegetable pickle, stored underground in earthenware crocks over the winter. On special occasions there may be elaborate meat, fish, or egg dishes, or fancy pastel riceflour cakes. But the Kims reserve most such treats for their children.

Time-saving prepared foods are becoming increasingly popular; but many families, either for reasons of economy or preference for their own recipes, still prepare their food from basic ingredients, over the simple one-burner stove. Not many houses have a refrigerator, and Mrs Kim is lucky to have received one as a wedding gift from a prosperous friend of her father, who was also the presiding officer selected for her civil wedding, a Korean ceremony that is a compromise between the Western church ceremony and the old custom.

The normal beverage at meals is an unsweetened infusion of parched barley or rice water. Coffee or tea are imported luxuries for infrequent use. Mr Kim likes to take a drink once in a while, but the good local beer is so highly taxed that he usually settles for a cheap old-fashioned rice wine. Locally produced cigarettes are cheap enough for him to afford but his wife neither smokes nor drinks, though some modern women do.

The Kims are young moderns and so they dress in Western-style clothes nearly all the time. Mrs Kim's extra income gives her enough surplus to buy a fashionable suit or dress from a good dressmaker every year or so; otherwise, she sews her own clothes from patterns that appear in women's magazines. Her husband can get cheap tailor-made suits of Korean woollen or synthetic material; there are no ready-made or rack-job suit stores yet.

Only on important national or family holidays does Mrs Kim don the traditional short, flared blouse called *chogori,* and the long, gracefully flowing skirt known as *chima;* while her husband never wears the old-fashioned ankle-length baggy knickers and loose jackets that may still be seen in the countryside, usually made of cotton or coarse linen.

Years ago, nearly all Koreans lived in clan groups under an extended-family system. Nowadays this type of family structure is seen mostly in rural areas, where the eldest son and his dependents live with the family patriarch until his death. Sometimes the younger brothers also live at the homestead and sprawling additions are built on to the one-storey, clay-walled and thatch-roofed farmhouses to accommodate more and more people.

Mrs Kim's parents are fairly prosperous orchard proprietors living near the central metropolis of Taegu, famed as a fruit-producing area. She sees them several times a year when the elder Chos come to Seoul for pleasure or business, or when she goes down to Taegu on holidays for the simple family ceremony of offering food and wine at the graves of ancestors.

Though she is now a Christian Mrs Kim continues these observances, which are more in the nature of memorial services than religious rites. She does not attach as great a significance to them, however, as do some back-country people who still believe in an uncodified syncretic folk-religion which blends Buddhist ideas with older animistic beliefs. Like nearly everybody, though, she and her family enjoy visiting Buddhist temples in the mountains for picnic and mountaineering excursions.

Mr Kim, who was a refugee from the north during the Korean War, does not know whether his parents or brothers and sisters are alive. The Seoul uncle who raised him is dead and though he seldom speaks of it, Mr Kim feels a deep sense of deprivation in the loss of his entire family, and the inability to render his parents the due memorial rites, though he has no literal belief in any religion.

This sense of loss makes him especially tender and solicitous toward his own children.

Most Koreans of the present generation look toward their children, to an extraordinary degree, as the main justification for their own existence. This is true partly because in the old Confucian philosophy a man must have sons in order to continue the obligatory reverence for the ancestors in the family ceremonies. Only thus could he expect to become a revered ancestor himself someday. This is especially

Left:
A dancing exhibition during the Kyonggi Girls' High School Festival.

Left page:
Children at play in one of Korea's fine kindergartens.
The Kim children, described in this chapter attend such a school.

the case now for nearly every Korean over thirty years of age can look back over a period of twenty years during which his own career and prospects were blighted by the disruptions of the Korean War; by economic stagnation and political corruption; and finally by the financial sacrifices entailed by the recent "decade of nation-building", when stringent economic controls were required. Things are better now, but the lost time can never be made up, and today's Koreans often live for a future that they feel is not really their own, but that of their children.

The Kims have a boy of seven and a girl of five. They plan no more children; the propaganda of the planned parenthood movement has been most effective among the rising middle classes. All their care, all their resources, all their love will be lavished on these two.

The boy, Hyung-joo, has just emerged from pampered babyhood into the stringent rigors of first grade. Henceforward, for his own eventual good, his parents must encourage him to keep reasonably near the top of his class, in order that he may pass the highly competitive entrance examinations for high school and college—the only pathways to advancement in this degree-conscious, vertically-structured, and paper-venerating society.

Keeping up with his peers means that Hyung-joo will inevitably have to enroll for extra classes after regular hours, or take lessons from a private tutor at home. He will have to buy extra books, engage in extra-curricular activities spend long hours in libraries and stay up late for extra study. His family will have to pay for all these extras, and in addition the physical or mental health of many students is often adversely affected by the psychological strain, or the lack of rest. But failure in the examinations is a family tragedy, out of all proportion to a Western observer.

Mrs Kim regretfully feels that the same burdens will have to be placed on the girl, Yoon-sook, when her turn comes. A daughter might not marry, after all; or, like her mother, she might marry into a situation where she would have to work. And in any case, even a rich bridegroom would be looking for a wife with a fashionable degree from a famous college, especially if she had no family wealth or prestige to offer. So there is no help for it.

When Hyung-joo started kindergarten, Mr Kim used up most of his savings to invest in the relative luxury of a television set. The excuse was that its educational value would help the children at school. There is little that is educational to be seen on the set, but it is true that having a TV in the family is a prestige factor of which fellow students, and even the school authorities, are well aware.

Since the television arrived, the Kims go out less than ever for entertainment or recreation, unless perhaps on weekend family outings to the old palace grounds scattered around the city that are now public parks, zoos, and museums. But that again is mostly for the children. The husband and wife still occasionally attend the neighbourhood movie—not the expensive theatres downtown where foreign features are often shown—and afterwards eat out at a modest Chinese or Japanese restaurant.

The Kims love Western classical music, as do many Koreans, but seats for concerts and operas in downtown auditoriums cost several dollars each for admission, and are usually televised later anyway. The radio is full of good music programmes—if you don't mind the ends of songs or symphonies being snipped of for commercials or time checks!

Mrs Kim enjoys raising flowers in the tiny garden in the warm months—and during the steamy summer monsoon rains of July and August it is too much bother to think of going out anyway. More than half the annual rainfall comes pouring down at this period, accompanied by quickly changing temperatures and extreme winds. And inevitably, there is always plenty of mending and sewing to occupy her time.

Mr Kim will occasionally invite a few friends to the house to play *paduk,* a complex Oriental form of chess, while his wife attends meetings of the *keh,* which is an informal neighbourhood financial union whose members pool their small savings for highly speculative investments, and then share the profits, if any.

If Mr Kim were seriously campaigning for a better job, or had a higher position to maintain, or needed to exculpate himself from some legal or professional difficulty, he might be forced to spend considerable time, and money, entertaining people at all-male evening parties in "kisaeng" restaurants, where fancy food and drinks are served by pretty, accomplished and compliant hostesses. Much business is conducted under these informal, but extremely expensive, conditions; getting into the "kisaeng house" habit, or its associative pattern of compulsive gambling, can threaten even a prosperous family.

Luckily, Kim has neither the predilection nor the pressing need for this sort of behaviour. Within limits, he is content to rest on his merits, and to depend upon his professional capabilities to bring him slow if steady advancement. If an emergency of some sort arose, however, he would find himself reverting to the more traditional expedient without thinking twice —except, perhaps, about the expense.

Thus the life of the Kim family, although simple and austere, is secure and stable compared with many earlier periods they can easily remember. They have strong family solidarity, a relatively comfortable living situation, and—most important— cautious confidence in a viable future.

Mr Kim still clearly remembers the long-ago desperate days when he managed to survive only by clinging to the motto: "First one must live". Nowadays he can add a second, less fatalistic line: "Next, one may hope!"

Left page:
Skiing is a popular winter sport in Korea. On several occasions Korean athletes have distinguished themselves in various sports at Olympic and Asian Games.

Below:
The City Hall Plaza, located in the heart of the South Korean modern capital, Seoul.

GOVERNMENT

Korea has been a democracy since its liberation from Japan in 1945. Under the 1963 constitutional revision, the government consists of a single-house, four-year legislature of 204 members elected from all the administrative districts; a president, acting through a cabinet headed by a premier; and a Supreme Court.

The two-party system has begun to take root in Korea, as evidenced by gains made by the major opposition party in the 1971 elections. In those elections, President Park was re-elected to a third term.

Korea's rebirth in the 1960's has been closely associated with Park Chung Hee, who as a reform-minded Army general led the bloodless military coup of 1961. He presided over a much needed house cleaning in government, and then left the army to run for president under the new civilian system in 1963.

Park has not only sparked the vigorous campaign for economic development; he has also served as a personal example to his countrymen of hard work, integrity and modesty. Even his strongest supporters cannot credit him with a magnetic or charismatic personality; even his bitterest opponents cannot seriously accuse him of vanity, venality, or insincerity. His main characteristics are dedication to duty, capacity for hard work, and devotion to long-range national interests.

Though in public he seems awkward and reserved, this down-to-earth son of a poor farming family has been able to catalyze and channel the enthusiasm of a people previously left cynical or apathetic by the paralysing blows of recent history.

Park and his government aim at nothing less than complete national self-sufficiency, independence, and prosperity. This will be the decade in which it will be seen whether they succeed or fail.

Though the problems Korea faces are still many and serious, few Koreans doubt that they can eventually be solved. This is the faith that has kept the nation united in spirit over many centuries, and is its strongest force as it stands almost at the threshold of success in a new era.

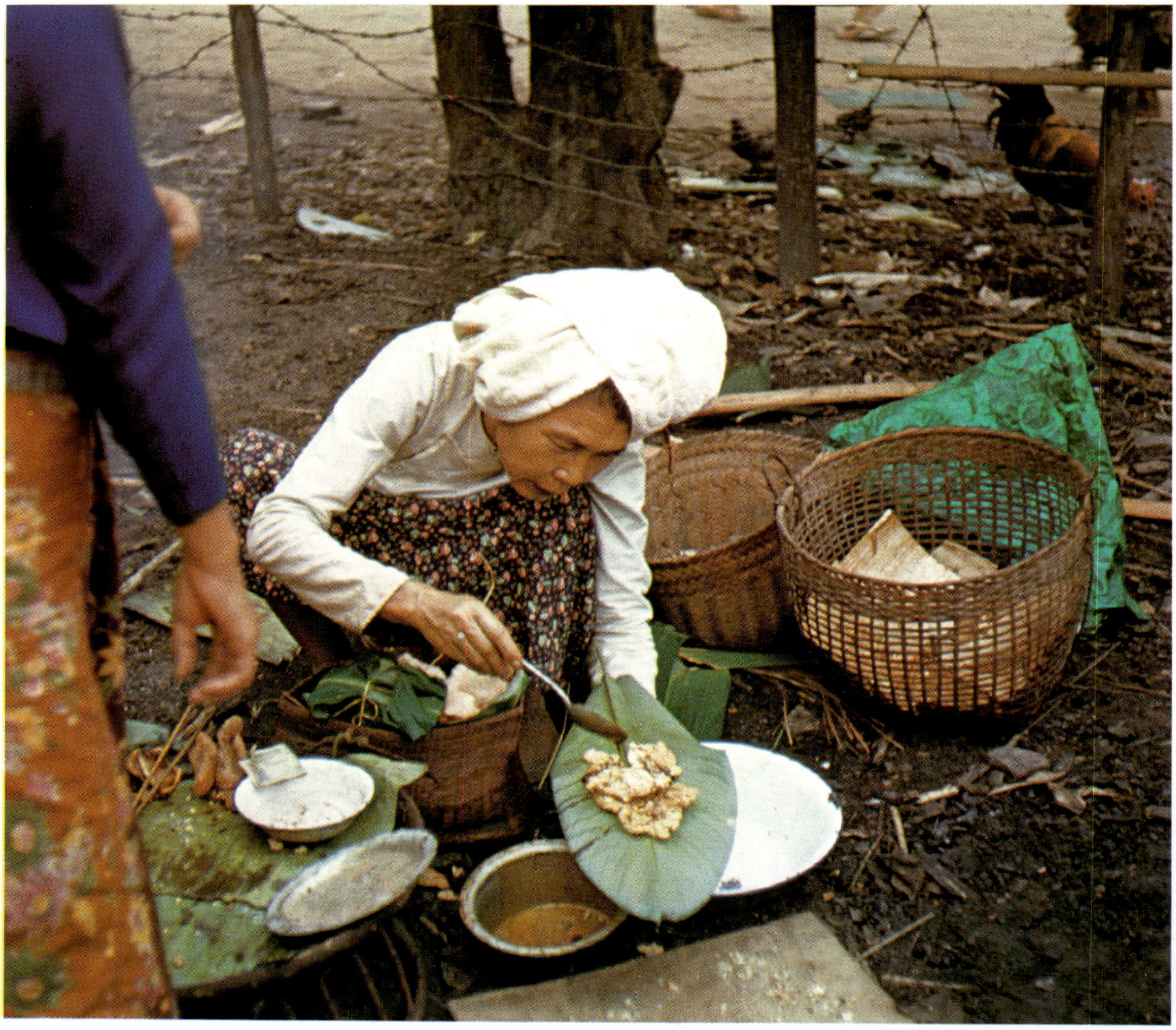

Kingdom of
LAOS

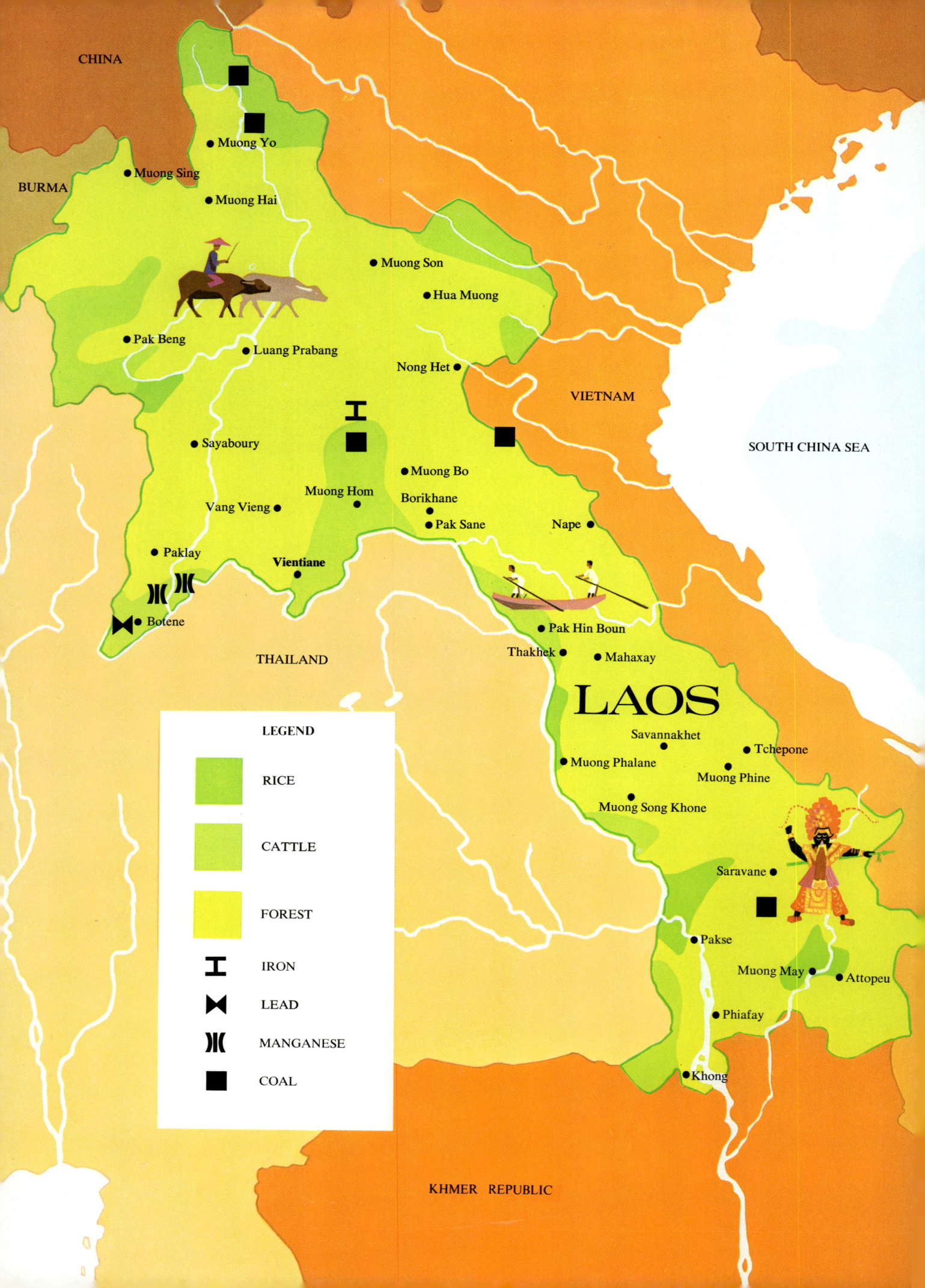

LAOS

Countries: CHINA, BURMA, VIETNAM, THAILAND, KHMER REPUBLIC

Sea: SOUTH CHINA SEA

Cities and towns:
- Muong Yo
- Muong Sing
- Muong Hai
- Muong Son
- Hua Muong
- Pak Beng
- Luang Prabang
- Nong Het
- Sayaboury
- Muong Bo
- Muong Hom
- Borikhane
- Vang Vieng
- Pak Sane
- Nape
- Paklay
- Vientiane
- Pak Hin Boun
- Thakhek
- Mahaxay
- Botene
- Savannakhet
- Muong Phalane
- Tchepone
- Muong Phine
- Muong Song Khone
- Saravane
- Pakse
- Muong May
- Attopeu
- Phiafay
- Khong

LEGEND

- RICE
- CATTLE
- FOREST
- IRON
- LEAD
- MANGANESE
- COAL

A scene in the market place of Vientiane, capital of Laos.

Laos

AREA:
91,428 square miles.

LENGTH:
600 miles.

WIDTH:
Varies from 280 miles in the north to barely 50 miles in some parts of the south.

LOCATION:
Between approximately 14° and 23° north latitude and 100° and 107° east longitude, Laos covers a land-locked, hatchet-shaped area of the Indo-China peninsula, bordered by China to the north, North Vietnam to the north-east and east, South Vietnam to the east and south-east, Cambodia (the Khmer Republic) to the south, Thailand to the west and Burma to the north-west. For its greatest extent the western border follows the course of the Mekong river.

TOPOGRAPHY:
The country is generally mountainous with two-thirds of its area heavily timbered with tropical rain or deciduous monsoon forests. The northern part is transversed by many rivers, which have worn deep and forbidding gorges in the lime and sandstone strata. In the south, numerous short streams drain from the Annamese Cordillera watershed into the Mekong.

CLIMATE:
Tropical monsoon—extremes of temperature may vary from around 60°F in the lowlands and below freezing point in the mountains from December to February, to over 90°F from March to May.

RAINFALL:
The driest part of Indo-China—the province of Luang Prabang—averages only 53" per annum, most of which falls during May-September. From December to February, when the Mekong is at its lowest ebb because of frozen headwaters, there are often droughts.

ETHNIC GROUPS:
The Lao, ethnically of the same stock as the Thais, share the Kingdom with minority groups including the Meo, Yao, Kha and others who live in the high country, Vietnamese, Chinese and some Indian traders.

RELIGION:
Hinayana (Lesser Vehicle) Buddhism.

LANGUAGE:
Lao, with French used as a second language.

POPULATION:
2,893,000 (1969 estimates) Growth of population is 2.75 per cent annually.

KINGDOM OF A MILLION ELEPHANTS

Above:
Two Lao farm workers operating small, hand-driven rotary hoes to cultivate rice.

ACCORDING TO archaeological evidence, the earliest inhabitants of Laos appear to have been Indonesian aboriginals and others of Khmer origin. There is no recorded history of this period, but tradition holds that a Buddhist mission outpost was established at what is now Luang Prabang, some time before the 10th Century A.D. From the 11th Century onwards, a migration of tribes from Yunnan, China, began southwards, the migrants founding chieftaincies in Upper Siam, Burma and along the Mekong river, and freely inter-marrying with the local people.

At the end of the 12th Century, the Khmer Empire—although it already showed some signs of decay—extended as far up the Mekong as Vientiane. The establishment of the Lao State was favoured during the next century and a half by the waning of the Sukho-Siamese Kingdom and the rise of the Kingdom of Ayuthaya. The father of Laos and the son of an exiled Lao chief, Fa Ngum, took advantage of these shifts in power to reconquer the lost lands on the upper-east side of the Mekong and form the Kingdom of Lan Xang or the Million Elephants. This meant that Khmer culture and Hinayana Buddhism, which formerly had reached only to Vientiane, were now introduced to the upper Mekong territories that were loosely unified with the south.

Once King, Fa Ngum surrounded himself with priests, artisans and scholarly advisers, and brought to the royal capital the celebrated golden Buddha, Prabang—hence the town's present name, Luang Prabang.

In the 600-odd years which followed, Laos, like countries in the Western World, was involved in intermittent warfare. From the beginning, there were struggles with bordering kingdoms and principalities. One such war in 1563, when Lao power was at its height and laid claims to large parts of Siam, caused the capital to be moved from Luang Prabang to Vientiane. Today the two capitals are still recognised, the former as the royal residence, the latter as the seat of administration.

Although some degree of unity was restored by King Soulingavangsa during the 17th Century, dynastic quarrels and covetous neighbours again caused the state to dissolve into its constituent principalities. In the late 18th and a great part of the 19th Centuries, Laos, as the buffer state between Siam and Assam, was twice sacked by the Siamese, and finally became part of Siam.

It was during this period that Western civilisation began to intrude into the affairs of Indo-China. In 1858 France entered Annam and revived an old claim to territory west of the Mekong. This brought France into conflict with Siam and resulted in further warfare in Laos. At the same time, there was strong Franco-Chinese hostility which led to frequent Chinese raids into the north of Laos. A treaty signed in 1893, by which Siam agreed to withdraw from territories she occupied east of the Mekong and in the south, established a temporary peace and the country's modern political boundaries which were further expanded by Britain's ceding France part of Upper Burma.

In 1899, Laos became a component of French Indo-China. However, it was still not a unified country, but rather a collection of principalities—the Kingdom of Luang Prabang, being made a French protectorate and the remaining area, a colony. For the first time, the name "Laos" was used officially.

In 1940, the Japanese advanced into Indo-China and overran Tonkin, part of Vietnam, to the north-east of Laos. This led to Siam reviving her claims to the territories of Laos west of the Mekong and fighting between France and Siam followed. In 1941 Japan undertook to arbitrate a settlement in the matter, whereby Siam acquired former Lao territory to the west of the Mekong. Internally this strengthened the Luang Prabang ruler, whose state took on more the appearance of a Kingdom, incorporating all remaining Lao territory, northwards and eastwards from Vientiane. As well as tendencies towards unification, there were also moves, encouraged by the Japanese, towards Lao independence. The Lao Issara, or Free Laotian Party—although forced by the French after the War to temporarily flee to Bangkok—organised strong support for a confederation of chieftains and princes under one King.

Finally, in 1946, France agreed to recognise Sisavang Vong, King of Luang Prabang since 1905, as King of all Laos. The following year a constitution was granted which provided for a National Assembly of elected members responsible to a Council of Ministers nominated by the King.

With the attainment of self-government, negotiations were speeded up for full independence. This was granted by France in 1949 and became effective on 13th April

Top:
A surveyor on the Mekong River Project in a section flowing through Laos.

Centre left:
An old craftsman
in the Royal capital of
Luang Prabang.

Above:
A hippie in Laos.

Left:
A juvenile businessman
selling toy pistols and other items
in the open-air
Vientiane market.

1950, with Laos remaining in the French Union for the next six years. In 1955, the Kingdom was admitted to membership of the United Nations.

CONFLICT OF IDEOLOGIES

The story of Laos, from the early 1950's to the present day, is a confusing one of a three-cornered civil war, aggravated by outside support for the different factions. At times, it has seemed that this small trouble spot in South-east Asia could form the nucleus of a major conflict.

The three factions which developed after independence were: the extreme right pro-Western group, the government party; the neutralists in the middle, who demanded that all outside interference with Laos, including that of the UN, should cease; and the Communist Pathet Lao, at the left. Each group was led by one of the Laotian princes.

As early as 1953, Vietminh forces, with foreign support, invaded Laos and set up a Communist state in the north-east which was named Pathet Lao. The following year they moved further south but were repulsed. At the other extreme, support for the right wing came from the U.S. and France, while the middle faction sought no outside aid. And so the unhappy conflict dragged on.

In June 1962, a serious attempt was made to end the civil war. The three factions signed a pact to cease hostilities and form a coalition government. In November they agreed to integrate their military and police forces, but factional rivalries and ideological differences which carried with them opposing forms of external support were not stilled, and, in the following year, guerilla warfare broke out again.

In 1970 Prince Souphanouvong, leader of the revolutionary forces, took control of the strategic Plaine des Jarres, opposite the two Laotian capitals, and also a strip of territory to the east, bordering the so-called Ho Chi Minh Trail, the major supply route to South Vietnam for the Viet Cong. For a while it appeared that American troops would be sent in to assist the Laotian Government, but the U.S. Congress banned the entry of ground forces. Air support and military aid, however, were given.

During 1970 and 1971 several approaches aimed at settlement of the conflict were made between the Prime Minister, Prince Souvanna Phouma, and Prince Souphanouvong. Up to the beginning of 1972 discussions had broken down, but there were hopeful signs indicating a willingness to find a solution to the unfortunate state of the Kingdom of Laos.

THE ECONOMY

Laos is a poor country. The major part of the population is made up of subsistence farmers living in isolated valley and mountain communities, who cultivate a million acres of paddy rice. Despite the large area under cultivation, however, their methods are so primitive—particularly in the hill regions where their "slash and burn" technique of shifting agriculture has resulted in serious deforestation—that Laos has the lowest average yield in the whole of Southeast Asia. In the mountains opium is grown, but the considerable revenue it produces cannot be brought into national budgetary calculations. Although copper, lead, iron and coal are present in commercial amounts they remain unexploited. Cash crops of spices, oil plants and, more recently, coffee—which was extensively grown before the War but subsequently destroyed almost totally by blight—are cultivated in some areas.

The rivers are of great importance to the economy both for fishing and transport, and lately for hydro-electric power and irrigation schemes. Even the rapids of the Mekong are dared to bring out timber from the mountains. The lumbering industry, despite the vast quantity of teak in the forests, is still in need of development.

As might be expected, Laos has an extremely adverse trade balance. Throughout the 1960's her imports, mainly of foods from Thailand, the U.S., Japan and France, were

Left:
Lao villagers,
and below,
schoolgirls chatting before
classes begin.

many times in excess of her exports, the chief of which were tin ore mined at Phong Tiou, and teak. To offset this, Laos received large foreign aid grants, with the major portion coming from the U.S.

Education is still lagging in Laos, despite Government efforts to raise standards and build schools with overseas help. There are some 1,200 primary schools, but very few are at secondary level.

Aid is also being provided in assisting the Government to build and improve the nation's roads. By 1968, 5,600 kilometres of roads had been built, of which 3,000 had successfully stood the test of improved surfacing, thus opening up the way for heavier economic traffic. Despite the concentration on military vehicles in recent years, bus transport is improving and passenger cars now number about 11,000. While there are no railways in Laos, there has been considerable development in communication by air, with some dozen airports now in operation. A radio network, Radiodiffusion Nationale Lao, has been installed by the Government at Vientiane and broadcasts are given in both Lao and French.

There is much potential wealth in Laos, especially in the timber industry, but the present internal unrest, coupled with the larger warfare around the borders, retains the troubled Kingdom—once called "le pays de sourire", "the country of sorrow", by the French colonists—in the sphere of the world's most underdeveloped nations.

CUSTOMS, FESTIVALS AND ARTS

In general, the Lao is strongly attached to his place of birth and rarely leaves it. Extremely pious, he nonetheless loves music and song, and holidays are often the occasion for joyous parties. He is very attached to local tradition and is particularly strong in his observation of the rules of politeness. The family is at the centre of Laos society. The old are venerated.

In Laos, the sacred and the profane are closely linked. The smallest events of daily life become occasions for religious celebrations the commonest being the *Baci*.

This form of ceremonial can be adapted to express a wish for good health and long life to the new-born infant, to the new mother, to one who has just recovered from an illness or to the soldier going to war. There are New Year's baci and marriage baci, the baci offered to important visitors, to old friends rediscovered, to government officials newly honoured.

One of the most important holidays is the New Year, which is celebrated in mid-April in a strictly traditional form. It takes place in Luang Prabang and lasts for several days.

Another holiday features the traditional Lao sport, Ti Khi and a large fair.

There are many facets to Laotian art which vary according to religion or ethnic group.

The women spin silk or cotton and weave it on rustic looms in the shade under their stilt-supported houses. Shimmering scarves and silk skirts decorated with gold thread are worn by young Lao girls at holiday time. Women of the Meo, Yao and Lu tribes embroider their clothes in multi-coloured patterns.

The most beautiful wood sculptures are to be found in Luang Prabang on the panels of doors and shutters. They are characterised by a stylised representation of the vegetable kingdom which gives rise to skilful and flamboyant arabesques. Bamboo is used to create objects necessary to daily life—traps, winnowing baskets, seats and screens.

Music is everywhere in Laos. The *Khene*, a sort of hipped flute with silver fittings, is made from reeds and adds rhythm to chants sung during courting or during village festivals called *bouns*. *Maykanhiou*, a kind of ironwood, is used to make *lanats*, or small xylophones which, along with single-stringed violins, cymbals, drum and gongs, make up the local orchestras. In each village young girls perform traditional dances in which the lifting of a finger or the fluttering of an eyelid may suggest war or love.

Volcanic outcrops, waterfalls, snow-clad mountains, pleasantly cool plateaux, steaming rain forests and fertile river valleys—all are present within the small area that holds the ever-changing drama of the Laotian landscape. Towns are small, high-class accommodation is rare, but each centre preserves its centuries-old identity.

Temples, museums and ancient limestone devotional caves are found throughout the Kingdom. In Luang Prabang, the Wat Phousi is curiously built atop a rocky lookout on a frangipani-covered hill rising abruptly in the centre of town to overlook the Mekong and the Royal Palace. The potential fertility of Laos can be seen in chrysalis near the market town of Paksong on the Bolovens Plateau. Here, roses, jasmines, laurels and bougainvillia blossom the year round. Here, wild elephants and deer graze on the Plateau, a hunter's paradise, in all seasons of the year.

In fact, despite its troubles, and perhaps because of its resulting lack of organised tourism, Laos remains one of the most beautiful countries in South-east Asia—both scenically and culturally—and the traditional Buddhist openness and tolerance of its people offers at least one hope for the future peace and stability of the nation.

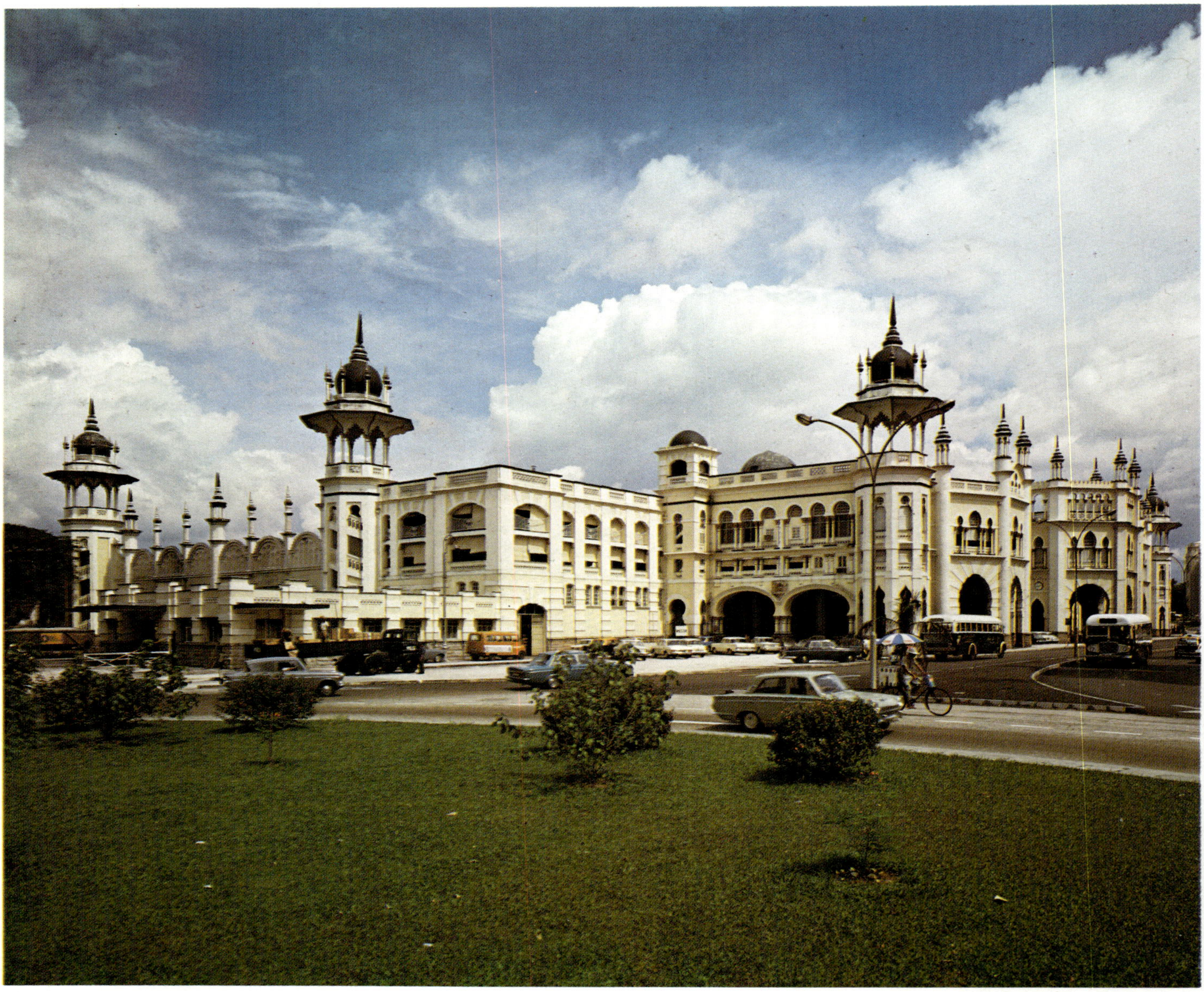

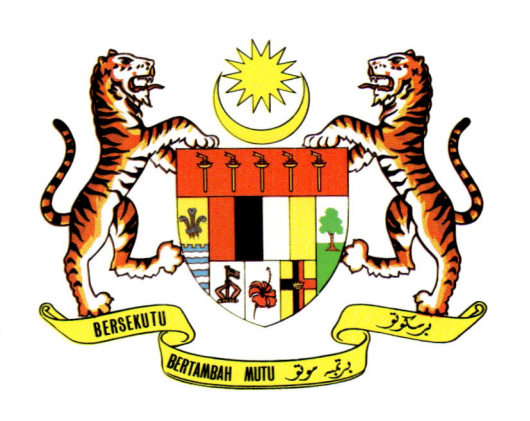

Federation of
MALAYSIA

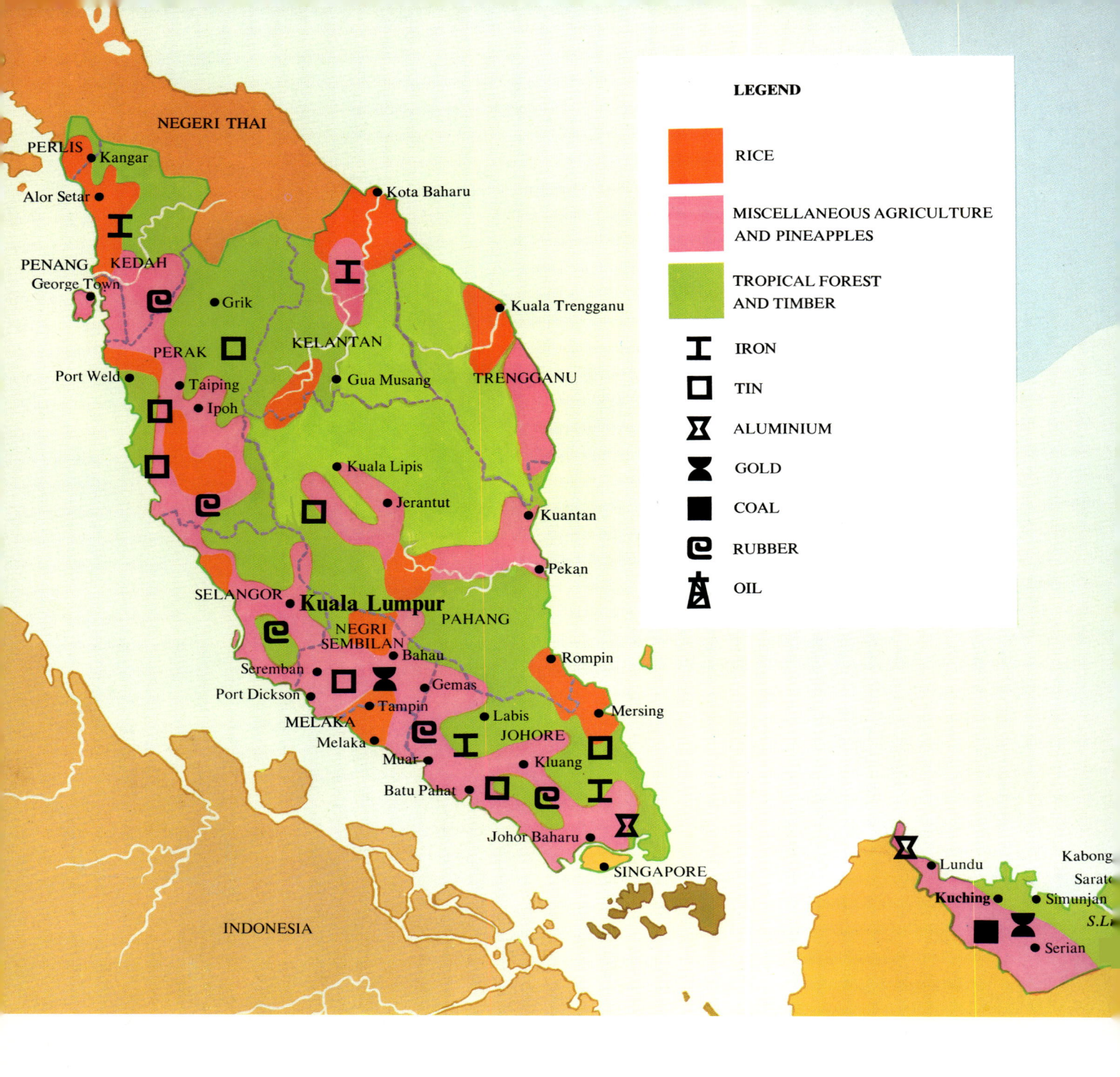

Malaysia

LEGEND

- RICE
- MISCELLANEOUS AGRICULTURE AND PINEAPPLES
- TROPICAL FOREST AND TIMBER
- IRON
- TIN
- ALUMINIUM
- GOLD
- COAL
- RUBBER
- OIL

AREA:
Total area: 128,400 sq. miles. West Malaysia: 50,806 sq. miles. East Malaysia: 76,510 sq. miles, comprising Sarawak 48,050 sq. miles, and Sabah 28,460 sq. miles.

LOCATION:
Between 1° and 7° north latitude, and longitude 100° and 119° east. Thailand forms the northern border of West Malaysia and Kalimantan is on East Malaysia's southern border.

TOPOGRAPHY:
West Malaysia: mountainous interior; more developed, coastal lowlands to the east and west.
East Malaysia: similar but more extreme, rivers are longer, mountains higher, jungles more dense, lowlands wider.

MALAYSIA

CLIMATE:

East and West Malaysia have similar equatorial climates—average temperatures from 70° to 90°; the highland regions are cool. Relative humidity high.

RAINFALL:

The year is divided into Southwest and North-east monsoon seasons. In the peninsula the North-east monsoon prevails from October to February, the South-west monsoon from mid-May to September. Average rainfall, 120 to 160 inches. Heavy rain in Sarawak from October to February. From April to July rainfall occurs in afternoon thunderstorms. Annual rainfall is between 60 to 120 inches.

In Sabah the rainy season is October to April and the drier period from May to August. Rainfall, 60 to 160 inches.

ETHNIC GROUPS:

Malays, Chinese, Indians and Pakistanis, and aborigines of the Peninsula—the Senoi, Sakai, Jakuns and Negritos. The indigenous peoples of Sabah are the Kadazans, Bajaus and Muruts and those of Sarawak are the Ibans, Bidayuhs and Kayans.

POPULATION:

Total Population: 10,452,309

West Malaysia: 8,819,928;
Sabah: 654,943
Sarawak: 977,438.

Density: West Malaysia 173.60 per square mile; Sabah 15.97 per square mile; Sarawak 15.49 per square mile.
Annual growth: 3 per cent.

A Nation Emerging

Right:
Relics of the Portuguese settlement days at Malacca, carvings in the stone Porta di Santiago.

Below:
A carved stone figure, relic of ancient Malaya, is seen in the Museum at Kuala Lumpur.

ARCHAEOLOGICAL RESEARCH has provided evidence of early human habitation in the Niah Caves in Sarawak, before 50,000 B.C. By the beginning of the Christian era, iron age settlements had been established and travellers from Southern China and India had made commercial and trade contacts with settlements at Kedah, Southern Johore and at Santubong in West Borneo. From this period onwards Malaysian history is interwoven with those of the various Buddhist (Langkasuka and Sri Vijaya) and Hindu (Majapahit) empires which held sway over parts of the region. The influence of Islam reached Malaysia through Muslim traders and by the middle of the 14th Century it was established in several centres. Meanwhile, the Malacca Sultanate, founded by Parameswara had flourished and in 1405 Parameswara received the recognition of the Emperor of China. In 1414 Malacca became a major centre for the spreading of the word of Islam. When it was captured for the Portuguese by Alfonso d'Albuguerque in 1511 it marked the beginning of European incursion into Malaysia, and the Portuguese in turn were ousted by the Dutch in 1614. The British began to show a mild commercial interest about this time and over the next two centuries they gradually superseded the Dutch, establishing in 1786, a settlement for the East India Company in Penang.

Nearly forty years afterwards, in 1825, they negotiated the exchange of British Bencoolen in Sumatra for Dutch Malacca. A year later Penang, Malacca and Singapore were combined to form the Colony of the Straits Settlements which was administered from India. Thus, by the beginning of the second quarter of the 19th Century, the greater part of the Malay Peninsula was within the British sphere of influence. In 1867, the Colonial Office assumed the administration of the Straits Settlements.

In this way the lands and waters of Malaysia saw ancient Asian empires rise and fall, explorers and traders of many countries come and go, and was dominated by three successive nations thrusting from Europe.

In 1873, owing to the constant threats to economic progress from civil wars and piracy, the British introduced the Residential system by which British officers were appointed to advise on all matters other than those touching Malay religion and custom. In 1895, Perak, Selangor, Negri Sembilan and Pahang became a Federation with a British Resident-General, under a system of centralised government.

British presence in the Borneo territories began in 1840, when Britain acted to secure the safety of the seas for her commerce and navigation. James Brooke intervened in a dispute in Sarawak and, as a reward for his services, was installed Rajah. The commercial exploitation of North Borneo (Sabah) was undertaken in the 1870's by a British merchant, Alfred Dent, and an Austrian Count, Baron Overbeck, to both of whom were ceded large areas of territory by the Sultan of Brunei.

During World War II, Malaya and the Borneo territories were over-run by the Japanese who ruled there until September 1945. Following the defeat of the Japanese forces and their surrender to the Allies in 1945, British Military Administration was established. In 1946, the Malayan Union was formed and Singapore became a separate colony. Two years later the Union was abandoned, as the result of strong opposition from the Malay nationalists, and a Federation of Malaya was created.

After the Japanese occupation of Borneo, the Rajah resumed administration in Sarawak under the British Crown. In June 1946, Sarawak came under the Crown's direct control and when the British Military Administration ended later in the year, North Borneo, (Sabah) including Labuan, became a Crown Colony. Government was conducted by the Governor assisted by an Advisory Council. In 1950 a new Constitution was drawn up to provide for the establishment of Executive and Legislative Councils, in Sabah.

In July 1948 a State of Emergency was declared in Malaysia, following an armed Communist insurrection in which violent efforts were made to paralyse the nation's economy. After a long and bitter struggle, the insurgents were crushed and on 31st July 1960, Emergency Control was lifted. Even today, however, there is still a small force of hard-core communists along the Thai-Malaysian border.

In 1955 a new Constitution transferred to the elected representatives of the people most of the responsibility for the country's government and, as a result of agreement reached at a conference in London early in 1965, Malaya finally achieved autonomy. The Federation of Malaya Agreement was signed in August 1957 and on 31st August the same year independence was proclaimed.

In 1963, the 1956 Sarawak Constitution which provided for popular representation in the legislature was amended to include electoral and constitutional advances. Elections were conducted the same year. By that time North Borneo (Sabah) had a State Ministerial Cabinet and a State Legislature with a majority of elected members.

REALISATION OF MALAYSIA

Malaysia was created on 16th September 1963 as a Federation of the States of Malaya, Sarawak, North Borneo and Singapore. In August 1965, the constitution was amended to allow for the separation of Singapore from the Federation.

The new Federation, which was hailed as an end to colonialism in this part of the world, was not, however, welcomed by the Philippines and Indonesia. The Philippines deferred recognition of Malaysia and subsequently broke off diplomatic ties with her. Indonesia's opposition took the form of a 'confrontation' against the new nation. In 1966, following the downfall of the Sukarno regime, Indonesia resumed normal relations with Malaysia. At the Ministerial meeting of ASEAN in December 1969, the Philippines agreed to normalise relations with Malaysia forthwith.

After post-election riots in 1969, assumed to have been instigated by extremist communal elements, Tunku Abdul Rahman stepped down from his position as Prime Minister to hand over to his close friend, co-architect and chosen successor, Tun Haji Abdul Razak bin Dato Hussein. Tun Razak, who became Prime Minister of Malaysia, headed the National Operations Council, a body set up during the Emergency to restore and maintain law and order and preserve harmony among Malaysia's various races. The operations of this body have so far proved successful and Malaysia is now enjoying one of the most peaceful and productive periods in her history.

THE COUNTRY AND ITS PEOPLE

Flying over Malaysia, one sees below a land eternally green. Two-thirds of the landscape is virgin jungle, speckled throughout the coastal areas with the orderly contours of rubber estates, coconut and oil palm plantations. The shores, long sweeping bays and wide white beaches, receive the ebb and flow of deep green oceans. Over the centuries, the verdant Malay Peninsula has had a magnetic attraction for the poor and humble of the civilisations of India, Indonesia and China. In the early 1870's Chinese traders came in their thousands to exploit the world's richest and newest tin mines in the Kinta Valley of Perak. When it was found that rubber trees could thrive in the hot and humid jungle regions, large numbers of Tamils, Telegus and Malayalams from southern India, and more Chinese were brought in to work the new plantations. From the time when the British consolidated their hold as 'protectors' of the peninsula in 1863, many members of the Indian Civil Service began to arrive in the beneficent land of the hospitable Malays. One result of this heterogeneous blend was a high rate of intermarriage between the different races. Thus, Malaysia's population today comprises many Eurasians and Asians of mixed Eastern parentage.

The most significant of all the immigrant races, the Indonesians, blood-brothers of the Malays, must not be forgotten. They have always had contact with Sabah and Sarawak as well as the States of Malaya because of the proximity of their homeland. In fact, some of the ruling dynasties on the Malay Peninsula originally hailed from Indonesia.

Apart from the immigrant people, the diversity of the indigenous inhabitants of both West and East Malaysia is quite remarkable. Beside the Malays there are about 50,000 Orang Asli or aborigines, who belong to many tribes but who are generally grouped as Negritos, Senoi, Sakai or Jakuns. In Sabah and Sarawak, the Malays and Chinese are outnumbered by indigenous groups; in Sarawak the Ibans or Sea Dyaks, the Land Dyak long-house dwellers, Melanaus, Punans and other minor communities; in Sabah the rice-growing Kadazans, the Bajau horsemen and the nomadic Murut hunters and farmers.

Three-quarters of the total population live in West Malaysia, where the Malays make up slightly more than half, the Chinese slightly more than one-third and the Indians one-tenth of the population. In Sabah and Sarawak, Chinese are the main immigrant groups.

THE LANGUAGE

Bahasa Malaysia (Malay) is the national language and the lingua franca of the entire region. Since 1967 it has had the status of sole official language of the nation, but in a multi-racial country like Malaysia many other languages and dialects, such as Chinese and Tamil, are spoken. English is widely used in commerce and industry and is taught in all Malaysian schools. Thus the younger generation is growing up to be either bi- or tri-lingual.

RELIGIONS

The diversity of races is repeated in the great variety of religious beliefs. Under the Constitution, the State Religion is Islam—all Malays are Muslim and naturally there are many mosques; but Malaysia abounds in places of worship—Buddhist, Hindu, Sikh and Taoist temples as well as Christian churches of all denominations, for Malaysians of every creed are guaranteed freedom of worship.

FESTIVALS

This intermingling of races and religions brings with it a wealth of festivals throughout the year. The Muslims, especially the Malays, celebrate Hari Raya Puasa, the joyful day of family gatherings which marks the end of the fasting month of Ramadan. They also celebrate Hari Raya Haji, the Prophet's birthday, the Muharram, the beginning of the Islamic Lunar Year. The Chinese commemorate their own New Year with two days of public festivities and family re-union dinners and a further fifteen days of celebrations, culminating in Chap Goh Meh, a time of gaiety, especially for young girls. In this season, the Chinese honour their debts and settle old grudges.

The Indians have Deepavali, the Festival of Lights, and Thaipusam, the occasion for penitence and fulfilment of vows. The Buddhists honour the birthday of the Lord Buddha on Wesak Day, usually with lantern processions, while the Christians solemnise Christmas and Easter with all the rituals common in the West.

In Sarawak traditional Dyak festivals include the Gawai Kenyalang (Festival of Heroes) and the Gawai Antu (Festival for the Dead). On holidays such as these, there are colourful regattas on the great rivers of the State. Every year in Sabah the Kadazans hold a lively harvest festival, the highlight of which is their traditional dance, the Sumazau. The Tamu Besar or Annual Market Day is a country fair with events including blow-pipe contests and dances by Bajau horsemen.

Finally, an event of great importance to Malaysians is the Koran Reading Competition, which was held for the first time on a nation-wide basis in 1960, but now attracts readers from several Muslim countries. This important event is held once every year, first at State level, then at National level, and finally as a forum for readers of many nations, the solemn festivities lasting a whole week.

Left:
The Parliament of Malaysia in session at Parliament House, Kuala Lumpur.

THE SYSTEM OF GOVERNMENT

MALAYSIA is a constitutional monarchy. The Yang di-Pertuan Agong or King is the Supreme Head of the nation. Every five years a new monarch is elected by the Conference of the Rulers of the nine States of Malaysia from amongst themselves.

The King is the Supreme Commander of the Armed Forces. All legislation passes through his hands, although he is obliged, as Constitutional Monarch, to act on the advice of the Prime Minister. The King has the power to appoint a Prime Minister from the majority political party, as well as High Court and Federal judges.

The Parliament of Malaysia, the supreme legislative authority in the country, comprises the Yang di-Pertuan Agong and the two Houses of Parliament—the Dewan Ra'ayat (House of Representatives) and the Dewan Negara (Senate). The former consists of 144 members: 104 from West Malaysia and 40 from East Malaysia, elected for a term of five years. The Senate has a membership of 58 of whom 26 are elected and 32 appointed by the King.

THE INSTALLATION

Malaysia's constitutional monarch is never crowned—he is installed. The installation preserves the ancient splendour and solemn traditions of Malaysia. Customarily held in the Tunku Abdul Rahman Hall, the ceremony proper takes place on a yellow seven-tiered dais, over which hangs a yellow and gold canopy. On the seventh level are two superbly-carved, gilded thrones.

The most important phase of the installation is the taking of the oath on the holy Qur'an which gives the occasion a spiritual, temporal and legal significance. Most of the ceremonial proceedings during and following the oath are in accord with old customs. Among the most traditionally significant is the playing of the Nobat (Royal Orchestra). The important items of regalia are the maces and the kris, the former giving the King temporal and religious powers, and the latter in their various forms symbolising royalty, power and authority.

Along the walls, palace guardsmen hold silver-mounted spears and yellow silk umbrellas. The nine Rulers and their Consorts attend in ceremonial attire adorned with insignia. Bewigged and gowned judges, diplomats in full morning dress, traditionally-costumed Malays, Chinese in brocaded cheong-sams, and Indians in silken saris —all add colour and pageantry to the occasion.

On the left side of the Supreme Head stands the Queen, the Raja Permaisuri Agong, clothed in hand-woven silk ornamented with tiny jewelled stars, necklace and gold chain and crowned with a diamond tiara. His Majesty is dressed in the black and gold uniform of State with a platinum crescent and eleven point star set with 66 diamonds flashing from the centre of his stiff, silk head-dress. His Majesty kisses the long, gold Keris Panjang di-Raja (Dagger of State) and reads the Document of Oath. As he finishes, the first round of a 21-gun salute to the new King booms out. After receiving a message of felicitation and a pledge of loyalty delivered by the Prime Minister, the King reads the responding Royal Message. A prayer, recited by the Chief Imam of the National Mosque, brings the splendid ceremony to an end.

SOCIAL DEVELOPMENT

Social development, especially in the fields of education and health, has accompanied economic growth. Nine years of education is available free to all children in Malaysia.

At higher levels, scholarships and bursaries permit students with the necessary ability to continue studies in either the academic or vocational streams. There are five universities in Malaysia and several teacher training, technical and other colleges. Large numbers of previously illiterate adults are now being taught the basics of reading and writing through a scheme operated by the Ministry of National and Rural Development.

Medical treatment is provided throughout Malaysia by hospitals, dispensaries and clinics, and a network of rural health centres and mobile clinics, using up-to-date techniques, drugs and equipment. Malaysian doctors are being trained at the University of Malaya's Teaching Hospital—a modern centre and one of the best equipped in the entire region. The general health of the population continues to improve and mortality rates due to traditional diseases such as malaria are steadily declining through improved public health measures.

MALAYSIA — EXOTIC SYMBOL OF THE EAST

MALAYSIA is a land of tropical beauty of wide and varying aspects, where equally diverse peoples still retain their traditional customs, festivals and national dress. Among these are Malays, Chinese, Indians, Ibans, Kadazans and Dyaks. Relics of earlier national influences — Chinese, Indian, Arab, Portuguese, Dutch and English—still abound in many of the Malaysian cities, some telling of the lavish ease of colonial life, others of the harsher realities half a world from Rotterdam and Coventry, still others of the indomitable Chinese urge to ornament—in gold leaf, porcelain, wood and brass. The shopfronts and alleyways of every street are stages for human drama and comedy for it seems that the Malaysian city-dweller, better than any other, has learned to squeeze the most joy and sadness from his living-space.

A little over a hundred years ago, Kuala Lumpur was a small tin-mining outpost called Ampang. Today Ampang is a suburb, and Kuala Lumpur, with a population of over half a million, is the fastest growing city in Malaysia and the country's capital. Yet Kuala Lumpur has none of the remoteness and impersonality associated with the average modern metropolis; its people are warm, friendly and often speak two or more languages.

Malaysia's multiform origins can be seen in the styles of the capital's architecture. The dome and minaret-studded Railway Station—a fine example of traditional Moorish architecture—contrasts with the modern design of the National Mosque with its Saracen umbrella-shaped dome dominating the skyline. Contemporary office buildings have grown up by the side of Indian and Chinese temples and adjoining Malay kampongs.

Buses, taxis and trishaws are in their transport element for Malaysia has some of the best roads in Asia. In fact, it is possible to travel most of its length and breadth on tarred and sealed highways.

The cities of Malaysia, unlike many in the West, are never cut off from the countryside by impenetrable stretches of suburbs and industrial estates. Only a short ride from the centre of Kuala Lumpur are the tranquil Lake Gardens and the neighbouring Batu Caves, a remarkable limestone towering outcrop, honeycombed with vast caverns. Situated in a wooded valley, on the banks of a small river, the 42-acre National Zoo is nine miles outside the capital. A few miles further out is Templer Park, a haven of forested hills and tumbling cascades where many examples of Malaysia's most extravagant and exotic flora are to be found. Among the 300 different kinds

Brilliant sunsets are typical of Malaysia, particularly on the East Coast.

of trees growing in the region are screwpines, tree-ferns, rattan, swamp-laurel, the small scarlet-fruiting rambutans and breadfruit. In the green, half-light of the rain forest every imaginable type of creeper grows—some as thin as cotton, others as thick as a man's wrist. From the jungle to the heart of Kuala Lumpur, flowering plants are found in abundance—including over 800 different kinds of orchid and the strange insectivorous pitcher-plant, whose prey falls into the liquid contained in its trumpet-shaped lid and becomes trapped, for downward-pointing bristles prevent its retreat.

In the jungles, the National Zoo and in smaller zoos and reserves—notably the National Park—are many animal species commonly believed not to exist outside Africa or India. In fact, over half the world's total number of mammal, bird and reptile species live in Malaysia. Among them are the elephant, the orang-utan, gibbon and other monkeys, the two-horned rhinoceros—overhunted for its horns which are coveted by the Chinese as an aphrodisiac—the Malayan tapir with its black, grey and white body, the powerful seladang or wild ox, the barking deer, the honey bear, the crocodile, the courageous boar, the wild red dog, regarded as the most dangerous and relentless inhabitant of the jungle, and the harimau or tiger, the aristocrat of them all. In the National Park, jungle lodges equipped with electricity, beds, mosquito nets, cooking utensils and camping equipment have been built for tourists and holiday makers. Short journeys can be made on foot from the lodges or by boat down the Tembeling River. Rod and line fishing is permitted on licence in the Park and jungle rivers teem with fish of many varieties. Outside the parks and reserves, hunting is permitted on licence and professional guides may be hired.

Off the west coast, a short flight by airliner from Kuala Lumpur, is the island of Penang. Its capital, Georgetown, has all the sophistication expected of an Eastern port but retains the grace and friendliness of leisurely Malaysia. Shopping in Penang —partially a free port—is an affair which may last well into the night, when the trishaw drivers pull over to the curb to sleep, curled under newspapers or canvas in their vehicles. Transport on the island is excellent. A funicular railway which ascends Penang Hill (2,722 feet) on a cable, provides a wide panoramic view of the island and the mainland, and a tar road passing through rubber, pineapple and banana plantations and skirting small and large surfing beaches, encircles the island's coastline. Both Buddhist and Hindu temples are numerous in Penang. Each night at the Chinese Snake Temple worshippers place hens' eggs at the alter to feed the temple's numerous green snakes.

Malacca is another city which tells eloquently of Malaysia's past. Established in 1402, it remained subject to Chinese influence until the Portuguese and later the Dutch and British used it as a base for trade and influence in the area. Today the city still holds relics of each nation's presence. The ruined Santiago Gate—all that remains of a mighty fortress—and the ruins of St. Francis Xavier's church are among the few surviving marks of the 130-year Portuguese rule. Salmon-pink houses and public buildings like the Stadthuys, believed to be the oldest Dutch building in the East, bear witness to the solidity of Dutch masonry and woodwork. A local vantage point is the Kim Seng Bridge over the Malacca River where travellers and locals alike spend hours watching the beamy river boats being piloted toward the cargo wharves. Along the river's banks stilted houses stand flush with the water's edge, each with its canoes and rowing boats moored alongside. Seagoing vessels—from barques to Chinese sampans—have been using Malacca for centuries, long before Marco Polo's visit in 1292.

The northern states of West Malaysia, from Perak, the most populous state in the country, to Perlis and Kelantan, near the Thai border, are famous for their silverware and batek. Ipoh, the capital of Perak and centre of the area's tin mining industry, is a modern town with many cinemas and an amusement park. Fifty-three miles north-west of Ipoh, in the town of Taiping, is the oldest museum on the peninsula. Its two large galleries display ancient Malay weapons, silver and brassware, woven fabrics, traditional pottery, wood carvings and implements. Just off the coast of Perlis lies one of the most beautiful tourist resorts in the country: Langkawi, the rugged holiday island of hot springs, fresh-water lakes, marble quarries, a waterfall and a beach of black sand.

On the east coast of the peninsula, the states of Pahang, Trengganu and Kelantan are lined by a succession of beautiful beaches—mile upon mile of palm-fringed sand, often a rich, grainy gold, but sometimes white and powderfine. In the towns and villages of these states cottage industries flourish. In the port of Kuala Trengganu are to be found some of the cheapest and best examples of Malaysian crafts—plaited mats and baskets, hand-woven brocade (songket), brass and silverware.

East Malaysia, which comprises the former British states of Sabah and Sarawak in north and north-eastern Borneo, is a striking change from West Malaysia with its sophisticated night-life and urbanised society. Although East Malaysia is no longer remote, due in part to fast plane travel and the development of its oil resources, the names Borneo, Sabah and Sarawak still conjure up visions of head-hunters, poisoned darts, white rajahs and plundering free-booters. And although most of the blood has been drained from the country's more frightening images, there are still peoples and places in Sabah and Sarawak little-touched by hundreds of years of colonisation, world war, local problems, international trade and environmental pollution.

Kota Kinabalu, the capital of Sabah—called the "land below the wind" by pirates who used its ports as havens from the typhoons of the north—is a leisurely town with several new hotels, just a short trip from Singapore. Its most progressive people are the Kadazans, once headhunters, but today a community of agriculturists with a keen interest in the progress of their country. Other indigenous people of Sabah are the Bajaus, Muruts and Kedayans, who are occupied in farming and fishing in the

Top left:
A romantic beach scene on the coast of Penang Island.

Bottom row, left to right:
Dutch architecture lends charm to Malacca's historic buildings;
A Hindu penitent during a festival in a Malaysian town;
An ornately carved Khoo clan house;
The "garden city" look of Malaysia's capital, Kuala Lumpur, accentuates the Moorish-style architecture of its Government building.

Above: Luxuriant foliage in Malaysia's rain forests.

many villages. Forty-eight miles north of the capital is Kota Belud, where each Sunday at the market-fair, Bajau "cowboys", dressed in embroidered jackets and silk trousers, race their wiry, bell-bedecked ponies in fierce and flamboyant competition. At the market-place the air is filled with the mixed sounds and smells of Sabah, the crowing of fighting cocks, the bells and cries of food vendors and the sweet-sour smell of tobacco, durian and roasted peanuts. Laid out in boxes and stands are the colourful fruits of the tropics—red rambutans, yellow pomelos and gold papayas, purple mangosteens, green oranges and yellow bananas. From Kota Belud can be seen Mt. Kinabalu, the highest peak in South-east Asia—even taller than Mt. Fuji. On the east coast lies Sandakan, trade centre of Sabah and still the haunt of the sea-gypsies of the South China and Celebes Seas. Two miles outside the harbour can be seen Berhala Island, the red of its hills contrasting with the deep blue water of its beaches and lagoons—a perfect spot for fishermen and swimmers.

The interior of Sarawak, like Sabah, is mountainous and thick with jungle. Motor launches form the main means of transportation up its broad rivers. Kuching, the capital of Sarawak, is an old colonial town in which the Astana, the palace of the White Rajahs, still stands. Apart from its beaches, scenery and colonial relics, Sarawak's main attraction is its native peoples—their gaudy dress, ancient rituals and unique styles of communal living. Built on the Sarawak River, Kuching is only half a day's journey up river from numerous Sea Dyak longhouses, some containing a whole village community. Each longhouse has its own headman and houses 30 to 70 families in a series of family rooms with a long "ruai"—communal hall or verandah—all down one side. Each family room serves as a kitchen but the ruai is the centre of most other activities, and in the evenings the families move to it to discuss the day's events or make bamboo baskets, carving or beadwork.

In the late afternoon throughout Malaysia the "wau bulan" or moon kite soars aloft, above cities and peaceful villages. As night falls, the "busar" or bow-shaped device attached to the kite makes a soft humming sound, lulling its owner and his friends to sleep. On a street corner in busy Kuala Lumpur, a Chinese minstrel-philosopher plays a soft and lyrical Cantonese nursery rhyme on the two strings of his battered pear-shaped instrument. Further along the street, a group of boys scuffles for a rattan ball while shoppers drift from one stall to the next, bargaining for Malaysian rambutans, Californian grapefruit, Australian apples and Spanish grapes. Chinese consult the local herbalist: dried beetles for a sore throat, powdered deer antlers for potency. In roadside restaurants, waiters lay out steaming dishes of bean curd and roast duck, stinging curry and subtle shark-fin soup.

A short distance from the bustle of the market is the tranquility of the town mosque, where swallows flash through arched windows to nest between bronze-inlaid pillars and duck-egg blue rafters. This is Malaysia and these are some of its sights, sounds and smells—fecund and splendid, changing yet unchanged, its cities and peoples, growing in the same ordered confusion and tropical beauty as its primordial jungles.

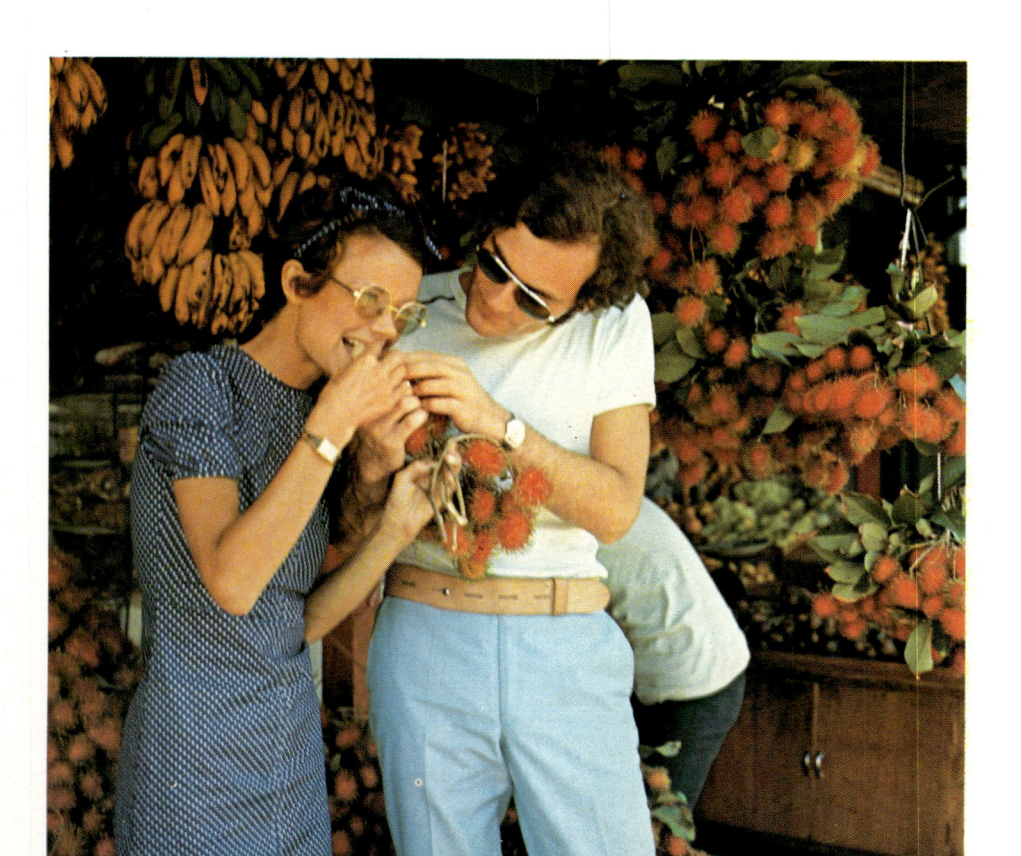

Above:
Bajau horsemen in their picturesque traditional attire.

Left:
One of Malaysia's popular tropical fruits is the scarlet-skinned rambutan.

Right:
The To' Dalang with his puppets of cow-hide; hence the name Wayang Kulit, or "skin play".

MALAYSIAN ART

Malaysia has emerged rapidly into the international art scene. In 1970 the Government sent a touring exhibition to Australia and New Zealand, assembled a representative collection for display in Japan's Expo '70 and in the "Man and His World Exhibition 1970" in Montreal, Canada. Malaysia also took part in the Second Young Artists Exhibition in Vienna and in the Biennial International Exhibition of Prints in Tokyo and Kyoto.

To encourage the appreciation of both the old and new in Malaysian art, the National Art Gallery was founded in Kuala Lumpur in 1958. Today it holds some of the finest exhibitions in South-east Asia.

The pioneers of Malaysian art were the early water-colourists of the 'thirties who painted idyllic landscapes in the tradition of the British water-colour school. They were followed by painters influenced by the Indonesian academic tradition of the Jogjakarta Seni Rupa, a large number of independents during the 'fifties and 'sixties, and a movement led by Chuah Thean Teng, which popularised *batek* art. Today the utility and beauty of this form is exploited not only in the traditional sarong and in wall-hangings, but also in fashion clothes and interior decorating materials.

Syed Ahmad Jamal, Yeoh Jin Leng, Jolly Koh, Lee Joo For, Abdul Latif and Ismail Zain—the abstract expressionists of the 'sixties—responded to the challenge of creating a true Malaysian art by employing evocative colours, shapes, symbols, calligraphic gestures and localised motifs. Today the constructivists Tan Teong Eng, Tan Tuch Kan, Piyadasa, Choong Kam Kow and Suleiman Esa, and socio-political commentators like Ibrahim Hussein and Joseph Tan, who employ pop art imagery, have added new dimensions to the art scene.

Artists in Malaysia are free to explore and to express themselves in any way they wish.

Thus there are the picture-makers, the image-makers and those who concern themselves with a conceptual approach. This reflects the healthy diversity in Malaysian art as well as the changes within the local environment. The growing swing towards a more urban way of life has had a tremendous effect on both art and artists.

DANCE AND DRAMA

Malaysian dances are as old as her games and pastimes. The Mak Inang, a traditional folk-dance depicting courtship, is one of the earliest forms and from it developed many other Malay dances performed today. The *Zapin*, a popular dance performed at many Malay wedding ceremonies, has simple, dignified movements set to music provided by instruments of Arabic origin. Other dances include the *Tarian Sabong* (cock-fighting dance), which mimes the movements of fighting cocks; the Dance of the turtles in which the dancer lets himself fall into a trance and continues dancing until overcome with exhaustion; and the *Kuda Kepang,* an interesting performance in which the gay splendour of Arab horsemen is depicted by dancers dressed in colourful costumes, riding 'horses' made of leather and bamboo. Lion and Dragon Dance teams roam the streets on certain festival days, demonstrating their gymnastic skills.

The acrobats form a human ladder to reach the *ang-pow* (red packet of money) which is tied from the highest windows. The most lively of the European influences, the Portuguese, is still very much in evidence and the folk-dances and music of Old Portugal are often performed.

The glittering world of Chinese opera, with its legendary tales and well-knit plots, still draws large crowds. Chinese, Japanese and Indian sword-fighting movie epics are all-time favourites. But beside the new is always the old, as popular as ever. Penang's Chingay procession, in which teams compete in manipulating giant flags and banners, is unclassifiable as either dance or drama but has all the showmanship and skills of both, together with the excitement of a sporting contest.

GAMES AND PASTIMES

Kite flying demands great skill and strength, and in the East Coast States of Kelantan and Trengganu during the kite season, there is keen competition and all those in the village who can get to the open fields make a point of attending.

Gasing (top spinning) is another favourite pastime of the rural people and is usually played before the harvest when the men have sufficient leisure time and vitality for contests that may continue all day long. At one time an indispensable part of a young man's education was *Bersilat*—the art of self-defence said to have been introduced to 15th Century Malacca from Sumatra. Today it is regarded as an artistic form of physical exercise, demonstrations of which are usually given at weddings and cultural festivals.

SPORTS

Sports are important to Malaysians. In playing fields and open spaces throughout the country, the young and old can be seen playing football, badminton, golf, tennis, *sepak takraw*—the national game, and many other sports. Nearly every State now has a stadium, while playing fields and other facilities are well-developed throughout the country. Football is the most popular game and the Annual Merdeka Football Tournament, in which teams from several Southeast Asian countries compete in Kuala Lumpur every year, is one of the region's best supported events.

Malaysia's national game, sepak takraw, requires agility, speed and split-second timing. Known to be at least six centuries old, it was until recently played between teams of nine players. The modern game, however, is contested by two sides, each with three players, on an area the size of a badminton court and with a rattan ball and a net.

Since the Olympic Games in 1956, Malaysia has been a regular participant not only in Olympiads but also in Asian Games and the South-east Asia Peninsular Games. Malaysia has been the host of many a regional and international tournament such as football, badminton, and basketball. Malaysia also twice hosted the South-east Asia Peninsular Games in 1965 and 1971. In the last games, Malaysians swept the board in the men's badminton events, took many gold medals in athletics and performed splendidly in cycling, hockey, judo and other sports.

THE FEDERATED STATES OF MALAYSIA

JOHORE: The southern-most State of West Malaysia, it is linked with Singapore by the Johore Causeway. Among its attractions is a popular beach at Mersing. Important primary products are pineapples, coconuts, rubber and palm oil.

KEDAH: The northern State is the great rice bowl of Malaysia. The recently completed Muda Irrigation project waters a million acres. This State produces substantial quantities of rubber.

KELANTAN: The eastern State in West Malaysia, bordering Thailand, is one of the largest but most sparsely populated. It is famous for its silverware and cloth of gold (songket); Kelantan batek also has a wide reputation. Kelantan has become an important palm oil producing State. It is known for the giant kites that are almost a symbol of Malaysia, and for its enormous wooden tops. Kelantan produces large quantities of good quality timber.

MALACCA: Steeped in history, the remains of old Portuguese and Dutch buildings still stand. Until recently it was the base for Commonwealth troops. Dampier, in 1768, wrote that Malacca canes had been brought to England. The cane, strong, stout and with long internodes also grows in other States of Malaysia. It is believed that if the internode is as high as its owner, it will bring good luck. The cane is used mainly for making walking sticks and some kinds of furniture.

NEGRI SEMBILAN: The name means "the nine counties". This State has strong Sumatran (Minangkabau) influences and time-honoured matriarchal traditions. It produces rice, rubber and coconut. Port Dickson, perhaps the most popular holiday resort in the country, is on the west coast of Negri Sembilan.

PAHANG: This is the largest State in West Malaysia, with a long coastline bordering the South China Sea. It has a National Park and a great variety of wildlife, from the Malayan elephant to the tiger and *seladang* (wild ox), many species of monkey, the tapir and the rhinoceros. Pahang produces large quantities of high-grade soft and hard woods. The recent opening of the great Jengka Triangle Scheme for pioneer settlement has brought about the development of a million acres. Kuantan, the State capital, is being developed as a secondary port. Pahang has long stretches of beautiful beaches which attract many tourists. Road development in the years since independence has opened the interior of the State which until recent times was virtually virgin jungle. Primary production includes palm oil, rice and quantities of rubber. Mining mostly for tin, is an extensive industry.

PENANG: The island State is a famous holiday resort and a Port of growing importance. Until recent times it was a free Port, but some importations are now restricted. A part of this territory, Province Wellesley is on the mainland. It is linked with the island by regular ferry services. Penang also has the Air Force base located at Butterworth. Recent port developments have made Penang a vital factor in the nation's economy. It has few natural products, however, and its importance to the State lies in its port dues and tourist attractions. Recently a steel industry was established outside the town of Prai and this has given a great boost to the island's economy. Electronics plants have also been set up.

PERAK: This is one of the richest States in the country, producing most of the tin and rubber and a good proportion of rice. Over the past ten years industrialisation has expanded. Together with the States of Kedah and Kelantan, Perak forms the northern border between Malaysia and Thailand. Communications are well established and it boasts two popular holiday resorts—Maxwell Hill and Fraser's Hill. Another important tourist attraction is the holiday island of Pangkor.

PERLIS: The smallest State of the Federation, it is also the northern-most in West Malaysia, bordering Thailand. It is largely an agricultural State producing rice as its main crop. Sugar cane has just begun to be grown extensively.

SABAH: Sabah in East Malaysia earns a great proportion of the timber revenue of the country; it is famous for its medium and hard woods. The State has many places of interest to tourists. Mount Kinabalu, the highest peak in the region, is a challenge to all mountaineers. Another highlight for the visitor is an exhibition of riding by the Bajau horsemen. The rubber industry is fast developing in Sabah and oil exploration is proceeding. The beach at Tanjong Aru stretches along four or five miles of picturesque scenery.

SARAWAK: Sarawak is the largest State in the Federation. Timber is an important industry but Sarawak is best known for its high quality pepper. There is also an important sago industry.

The road system which had been neglected under British rule is rapidly developing.

Bordering Indonesia, the State contains a great variety of wildlife, the most famous being the rhinoceros, the horn-bill and the orang-utang. Recent discoveries at the Niah Caves have shown that a civilisation existed in the region thousands of years ago and indicate that the people were probably participants in a great migration from the mainland of Asia to Australia. There are plans to make Sarawak a vast rice growing State.

SELANGOR: Selangor is the most important State in the Federation for its capital, Kuala Lumpur, is also the Federal capital.

Selangor produces tin and rubber in good quantities and it boasts the biggest opencast tin mine in the world. Recent industrial development in the State has changed the character of the Malaysian economy. Car assembly is one of the recent ventures and building materials are being produced in great quantities. In Kuala Lumpur is produced the famous Selangor pewter ware.

Port Klang is the major port in the country. Kuala Lumpur itself is a city of more than half a million people. Its cosmopolitan architecture is modern and spectacular.

TRENGANNU: This State has a long coastline on the South China Sea, and is famous for its beaches. Its craftsmen excel in silver, brass, cloth of gold (songket) and batek ware. In recent times oil palm has been planted in large areas and the traditional rice farming has been expanded. There is also some tin mining. A famous tourist attraction is the annual visit of the great leathery-backed turtles which arrive in the summer months to lay their eggs on the beaches.

Far left:
Finished batek garments. Fine batek materials from Malaysia are exported to the U.S.A., Europe and Australia.

Top left page:
Making a giant kite in Kelantan.

Above:
One of the most striking buildings in South-east Asia is Parliament House, Kuala Lumpur.

Left:
Among the famous landmarks of East Malaysia is Mount Kinabalu.

413

Right:
A Malaysian Railways train in the station at Kuala Lumpur.

Below:
Kuala Lumpur International Airport, one of the most modern in Asia.

Right page:
Port Klang. International ocean liners call for bulk shipment of varieties of cargos.

MALAYSIAN RAILWAYS

Railway development in Malaya began in 1885, and construction of the network was completed in 1931, with the main line running up the west coast, and a spur crossing over from Gemas to the east coast and on up into Thailand. In recent years the volume of freight traffic carried has shown a steady increase and, though passenger traffic dropped off for a period as a result of competition from private motor cars, buses and domestic airlines, it is now picking up again in response to the tourist boom.

Rail travel affords the tourist opportunity to see West Malaysia in its proper setting, since much of the 1,028 miles of railway line from Singapore to the Border of Thailand passes through characteristic Malaysian landscape—rubber estates, tin mining lands, coconut groves, and acre upon acre of padi fields and oil palm plantations.

With its modern railcars and streamlined diesel engines, through-express services and also air-conditioned or pressure-ventilated sleepers, the Malaysian Railway offers fast, convenient and comfortable travel.

The Malaysian Railway provides First, Second and Third class passenger accommodation. Most of the first-class coaches are air-conditioned and special sleeperette coaches with aircraft-type reclining seats have been introduced for long-distance third-class passengers.

Tourists visiting West Malaysia have an opportunity to tour the East Coast on the "Sumpitan Emas"—Golden Blowpipe—Express, on the line which branches off from the main line at Gemas, 137 miles north of Singapore and which runs thrice weekly between Kuala Lumpur and Tumpat and Singapore and Tumpat. Pressure-ventilated first and second class sleeping coaches are attached to the Golden Blowpipe, on which appetising meals and refreshments are provided in its air-conditioned buffet cars.

Both sea and air travellers have the choice of a stop-over or an overland rail trip to the city of Bangkok on the direct International Express train between Prai (Penang) and Bangkok. Connection with the night express, running to and from Kuala Lumpur, is made at Prai. Travel between Penang Island, the famed "Pearl of the Orient" and mainland Malaysia has been made faster by the extension of the railway line from Prai to Butterworth with a swing span bridge, the only bridge of its kind in Southeast Asia. This was opened on the 10th anniversary of Malaysia's Independence. Malaysian Railway, the nation's principal carrier, is the mainstay of Malaysia's commerce and industry. To facilitate and promote the Government's drive for new business and to facilitate and promote the Government's new measures on industrialisation, Malaysian Railway has geared its services to meet the rapidly growing demands of industries by providing frequent and efficient express freight services at competitive rates. Annually the Railway carries more than 10 million passengers and moves over 4 million tons of goods.

AIR, SEA AND LAND SERVICES

Fast and efficient air transport systems link Malaysia to all parts of the world. The International Airport at Subang, near Kuala Lumpur, can accommodate some of the world's largest jet-liners.

Officially opened in 1965, the Airport's building was constructed for the traveller of the future. Glass walk-ways provide access to the tarmac regardless of the weather; modern baggage-handling equipment ensures a minimum of delay. A wide scenic drive to the Airport, surrounding waterfalls and gardens and spacious interior restaurants and bars create an entertainment environment for both visiting tourists and the cosmopolitan population. The new airport at Johore Bahru in the State of Johore will be ready in 1973.

To cope with the increasing volume of sea trade, extensive development of port facilities are being undertaken. The principal ports are Port Klang and Penang in West Malaysia; Sandakan, Labuan, Kota Kinabalu and Kuching in East Malaysia. A new port is soon to be built in Johore.

Telephone, water and electricity services are being expanded to meet the demands of a growing nation. The telecommunications system in Malaysia is among the most modern to be operated in any developing country, with facilities such as overseas telegraph, telex links with some 70 countries, radio services as well as marine and air communications.

COMMUNICATIONS

The wheels of Malaysian industry are kept turning with notable efficiency by the aid of a steadily developing infrastructure. The country has a network of first class roads which exceeds 13,000 miles and more than 1,340 miles of railway tracks. Although the main means of transport in Sabah and Sarawak still remain the riverboat and the light aeroplane—because of the particularly difficult nature of the terrain—surface transport is gradually being improved and air transport is adding to its routes and the frequency of its services.

EAST-WEST HIGHWAY PROJECT

In West Malaysia, the highway system, already one of the best in Asia, is being extended by the construction of an east-west link between Butterworth, on the west coast and Khota Bharu, in the north-east corner of Kelantan State.

The first phase of the project is the construction of a 66-mile long, 24-foot wide paved road for the missing link between Jeli in Kelantan and Grik in Perak through some of the most difficult terrain ever encountered in Malaysia. The road formation and construction of culverts and bridges are expected to be completed around 1976. The proposed highway is beneficial and is essential for the economic development of the east and north-east region of West Malaysia. This road has already been accepted as part of the Asian Highway System (Route A19), and will link south-east Thailand with the north-west of West Malaysia with the completion of the Golok Bridge, which is being built by the Malaysian and the Thai Governments as an Asean Project.

PORT KLANG

Malaysia's economy is dependent upon exporting and trade in general. For any trading nation cheap, efficient port facilities can spell the difference between competitive and non-competitive exports and this is particularly so with Malaysia. The Port of Singapore has traditionally played an important role as a transshipment centre for Malaysia's goods but with recent developments and improvements in the Port of Penang and Port Klang this role has been vigorously challenged.

Built as a coastal port in the early 1900's to serve the hinterland of the central States of West Malaysia, Port Klang has emerged as a major ocean port. In 1969, over 3.3 million deadweight tons of cargo—an all time high—was handled at this international sea terminal and through it passed almost 20,000 passengers.

Port Klang is 30 miles from the Malaysian capital, Kuala Lumpur. Its wharfage areas have been enlarged and port facilities have been increased under a major development scheme. The North Port, which was recently completed is situated 3 miles north of the old port—the South Port. Both have good national road and rail link-ups.

NORTH PORT

Facilities at the North Port include four ocean berths with a total length of 2,490 feet. Each berth is approximately 580 feet long, has a width of 202 feet and a draft of 30 feet. Each is also served with a transit shed with continuous surface from the wharf, thus facilitating the use of forklift tractors and other mechanical equipment.

Covered storage extends over an area of more than a million square feet and more than a quarter of a million square feet of open storage space is also available. Berth extensions are currently being carried out south of the existing wharves to make a total 2,800 feet of new berths. Of these berths, 2,100 feet are expected to accommodate container vessels in 1973.

OLD PORT

The existing facilities at the South Port comprise three ocean wharves of 1,640 feet, 5 swinging buoys and two anchorages. Other facilities include storage space, cranes and tankage, tractors and prime movers, forklifts, tugs, launches and lighters. The Port Authority plans to construct an additional berth for the handling of liquid cargo and palm oil.

Already there are indications that within a few years Port Klang will become the largest oil palm port in the region.

PORT OF PENANG

PENANG, one of the two major ports in Malaysia, is situated on the north-western coast of West Malaysia. It is a port of call for cargo and passenger ships along the main route from Europe, the Middle-East and South Africa to the Far East, Australia and the American continents. It is also an important port for coastal ships to and from Indonesia, Burma and Thailand.

Penang Harbour consists of an extensive stretch of sheltered navigable water between the Island of Penang and the north-western coast of West Malaysia. Vessels calling at the Port can either work alongside the wharves at Penang Island and Butterworth, on the mainland, or at anchorage in the Roads.

The exports handled at the Port include the principal raw materials produced in the hinterland, such as refined tin, rubber, latex, copra, coconut and palm oil, timber, iron and ilmenite ore. An increasing quantity of manufactured goods, such as plywood, iron and steel pipes and bars, are also shipped through Penang. Imports chiefly comprise engineering and building materials, foodstuffs, machinery for mines and estates, petroleum products and manufactured goods.

The Penang Port Commission operates and maintains at Penang Island a deep-water wharf, 1,200 ft. long, providing berths for two ocean-going vessels up to 32 ft. draught at a time.

At Prai, on the mainland, the Commission operates port installations which are linked to the road and rail systems of West Malaysia. The wharves are 2,600 ft. long and provide berthing for lighters and coastal vessels up to 12 ft. draught. There are a number of godowns of considerable area, and open storage space.

The Commission has constructed deep-water wharves, 2,928 ft. long with berths for five ships, at Butterworth on the mainland, to provide additional berthing facilities for ocean-going vessels. Two of the berths are designed for conversion to handle containerised cargo when such facilities are required, a time which appears not to be far distant.

Left page:
Butterworth wharves
on the mainland, opposite
the island of
Penang.

Below:
An aerial view
of Penang city, showing
the Port facilities.

MAS—MALAYSIAN AIRLINE SYSTEM

THIS YEAR, 1972, MAS—Malaysian Airline System, the National Airline of Malaysia—has taken to the sky in full livery of red, white and blue. The birth of this new National Airline came about with the liquidation of Malaysia-Singapore Airlines (MSA)—once the designated flag carrier of Malaysia and Singapore. The split was the inevitable solution to the widening differences between the two major shareholders, the Governments of Malaysia and Singapore, largely caused by diverging national priorities. Malaysia's National Airline will now be able to concentrate on serving the travelling public of the Federation of Malaysia.

Right:
The new symbol of Malaysian Airline System.

Below:
Giant kites of Kelantan, inspiration for the MAS symbol.

THE SYMBOL OF MAS

The MAS symbol was inspired by a unique Malaysian tradition—the mastery of controlled flight. Indigenous to Malaysia, the Kelantan Kite dates back many centuries. It is a tangible symbol of the mythologies that enrich Malaysia's folklore. It expresses the Malay aptitude for design and artistic handicraft.

Modified to represent MAS, the new symbol has been evolved from a highly stylised design of the Kelantan "bird kite", conveying a great feeling of movement and combining a sense of heritage with modernism.

ROUTES

MAS flies to 38 different destinations throughout Malaysia and Asia—more than any other airline in the region. Careful planning ensures maximum integration of all MAS services; from the Britten-Norman Islanders and the Fokker Friendships to the Boeing 737-200 jets. The Boeing jets radiate from Kuala Lumpur, Malaysia's capital, serving the international cities of

The illustration at right shows 1972 air routes of the newly formed Malaysian Airline System.

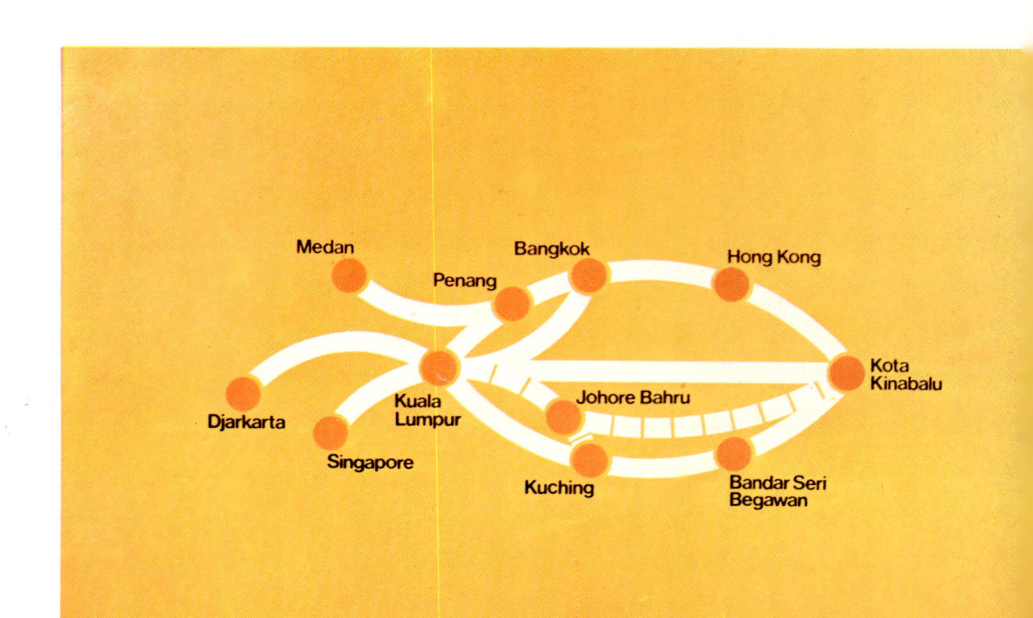

Right:
Units of the MAS fleet with their new red, white and blue colour scheme.

Below:
Attractive MAS stewardesses dressed in sarong kebayas of Malaysian batek.

Hong Kong, Bangkok, Singapore, Medan, Djakarta and Brunei. From these points, convenient connections are effected by air and sea to all other parts of the world.

THE MAS FLEET
To thrust Malaysia into the sky the initial fleet comprises 19 aircraft. Seven latest models of the Boeing 737, the 200 series, form the backbone of the fleet. They operate some domestic and all the airline's international services. The jets are all brand new and have a "plus" point over other Boeings of the same series. They are the stretched version and will incorporate the "jumbo" look interior, with more head room and more stretched out leg room, made possible because the lockers are built-in and out of the way. The decor is distinctively Malaysian in an atmosphere of warmth and comfort. To complement these Boeings will be nine new Fokker Friendships F27-500 which will operate the shorter domestic routes, and the three Britten-Norman Islanders (BN2) which will provide feeder services within East Malaysia.

THE INSIDE STORY
To mount the operations efficiently MAS has a team of highly experienced pilots. Top flight engineers have also been recruited. Malaysian stewardesses are on hand to see to the needs and comfort of all MAS passengers and to extend traditional Malaysian hospitality. The stewardesses are dressed in sarong kebayas of batek in distinctive and unique design enhancing the Malaysian atmosphere which the Airline has set itself out to create.
All these—the symbol; the brand new aircraft; the pilots; the engineers; the stewardesses and the Airline's cuisine contribute to the making of MAS—Malaysia's National Airline.

THE MALAYSIAN ECONOMY

MALAYSIA is a land rich in natural resources, a land where the gifts of nature are mined and felled and then turned into exportable products. A small nation in Southeast Asia, Malaysia stands today as the world's largest exporter of natural rubber, palm oil, tropical hardwoods and tin. Economic development has progressed at a commendable rate. During 1966-1970 the Gross National Product at current market prices (GNP) rose by an average rate of 6.4 per cent per annum, continuing to increase in 1971 to reach M$12,170 million. As economic growth was achieved in an environment of domestic price stability it contributed to rising standards of living. The per capita income, the fourth highest in Asia, rose from M$940 in 1966 to M$1,075 in 1971 and by 1975 it is expected to reach M$1,300.

A series of well-planned development programmes has enabled the Malaysian economy to maintain its growth momentum. Currently being implemented is the Second Malaysia Plan, which covers the five-year period from 1971-1975. It emphasises a more equitable distribution of income, a more balanced growth among ethnic groups and regions in the country, the reduction of unemployment and general improvement in the overall economy.

The process involves the modernisation of the rural sector and more direct government participation in industries. To increase productivity and income in the rural sector, more efficient production techniques, improved marketing and credit, financial and technical assistance will be made available. A new approach to land development is the implementation of large-scale regional schemes where economic and social interests will be integrated.

The Malaysian economy, largely dominated by the agricultural and mining sectors, is also highly export-oriented.

In 1971 the agricultural and mining sectors contributed slightly over 37 per cent of the gross domestic product and provided for over half of the employed labour force. Its contribution to domestic output, however, has declined over the past decade as a result of the economic diversification policy of the government.

In terms of value of production the principal agricultural products are rubber, timber, rice, palm oil and pepper, and the main minerals are tin, crude petroleum and iron-ore. Except for rice, these commodities are export-oriented and accounted for the major portion of foreign exchange earnings in 1971.

Malaysia is the world's largest producer and exporter of natural rubber and tin and the world's largest commercial producer and exporter of palm oil. It is also an important exporter of timber, canned pineapples, pepper, spices, petroleum products and crude oil.

Rubber is by far the most important agricultural commodity in terms of acreage and employment. It is also the country's top foreign exchange earner, accounting for 29 per cent of foreign exchange earnings in 1971. Production of natural rubber increased at an average rate of slightly over 6 per cent per annum during the period 1966-1971.

Natural rubber has been able to more than withstand keen competition from synthetic rubber by reducing the cost of production and improving the quality of rubber.

Malaysia also pioneered the development of technically specified rubber called Standard Malaysia Rubber (SMR) which commands a price premium over ordinary rubber sheet.

A steady expansion in tin production and the slowly rising long-term price trend strengthened the position of tin as Malaysia's second foreign exchange earner accounting for 18 per cent of gross export earnings.

Stimulated by world demand the production of timber and palm oil has increased significantly. Between 1966-1971, output of saw logs increased by an average of 11.5 per cent per annum and sawn timber by 9 per cent. During the same period palm oil production rose by an average rate of 25 per cent per annum.

Since 1960, manufacturing output, concentrated mainly in West Malaysia, has been expanding at an average annual rate of slightly over 10 per cent, representing 14 per cent of the gross domestic product in 1971. Industries are engaged mainly in the production of consumer and intermediate goods.

The Government is vigorously promoting the establishment of labour-intensive industries and industries which have an export demand, in particular wood-based and agro-based industries, electronics, and textiles.

To stimulate industrial investment liberal tax incentives, tariff protection and other assistance are given to investors. Industrial sites and free trade zones have been established, the latter intended specially for export-oriented industries.

Above right: Large sheets of latex foam rubber being made at the Dunlop factory at Seremban. It is popularly known as "Dunlopillo".

Left: A rubber tapper on a Malaysian rubber estate.

Right: The making of rubber tyres in Malaysia was pioneered by the Dunlop company in 1962.

RUBBER IN MALAYSIA

ALTHOUGH rubber planting in Malaysia goes back more than a hundred years it was not until the early part of the present century that the industry became established on economically productive lines.

That was the period when Dunlop became interested in Malaysia and began an association that has since made the scientific production of rubber a vital factor in the country's economy.

Through the work carried out at the Dunlop Research Centre at Batang Melaka valuable knowledge of the growing of rubber has greatly benefited the industry and the company's estates are models on which many other plantations have been based.

As the interest in plantation rubber expanded the international Dunlop Group developed a plan whereby the entire natural rubber requirements of the organisation were to be procured from Malaysia. This was effected by the establishment of a central purchasing organisation which in 1970 took up more than 10 per cent of the entire Malaysian rubber output.

Whilst Dunlop has been primarily associated with rubber as a Malaysian industry it has long been established in trade and commerce as a distributor of its Group products, particularly rubber tyres.

The growing demand for tyres led to the building of a factory at Petaling Jaya, a suburb of Kuala Lumpur, in 1962 and the formation of Dunlop Malaysian Industries Berhad. This pioneered the making of rubber tyres in Malaysia and was one of the first major ventures in the wake of a growing awareness of the need for a greater emphasis on local industry.

In the past decade the Dunlop plant has undergone a succession of major expansions to keep pace with the demands of a fast developing country. In 1968, on the Petaling Jaya site, another new factory building was added and here a wide range of earthmover and tractor tyres is made for local needs and more particularly for overseas markets.

Products from this plant, together with tyres from the main factory, are shipped to Australia, Zambia, Sweden and other countries and contribute substantially to the much needed export earnings of the Malaysian manufacturing industry.

From its earliest beginnings in the industrial field in Malaysia, Dunlop has followed a policy of expansion and diversification. In 1968 another factory was added to the Petaling Jaya complex mainly to serve the vehicle assembly industry with adhesives and sealants. This factory, now firmly established, has expanded into products for use in the laminated plastics and footwear industries and provides a technical and development service available to a wide range of industries. As in other product lines an export business in adhesives is also building up.

In 1970 another factory was constructed to carry out the specialised process of retreading and reconditioning aircraft tyres. In this field the company was fortunate in having access to the considerable experience and technical know-how of other members of the Dunlop Group.

"Dunlopillo", now recognised widely as a product name for latex foam products, was manufactured in Malaysia even before the tyre factory was established and in 1964 production was greatly expanded when a new factory was built at Seremban in the neighbouring State of Negri Sembilan. Recently this factory was re-equipped with new sheeting machinery and at the same time the most modern system of conveyorisation was installed to maintain the high quality standards which "Dunlopillo" has set in latex foam manufacture. Today manufactured products from Malaysia, the home of natural rubber, maintain this tradition in many countries of the world.

The expanding economy of Malaysia and the growing need for an efficient industrialisation programme have given rise to greater opportunities for employment and in this regard Dunlop has made a material contribution. Dunlop Malaysian Industries Berhad has a total employment force of more than 1,600 people in a diversified grouping of industrial ventures and with the rising affluence of Malaysia the scope for further enterprises is increasing year by year. In the development of the country's industry the benefits derived from Dunlop's Malaysian operations are likely to continue through the decade of the 1970's and beyond.

STRAITS TIN

Above:
A bronze axe
and dagger, weapons
made by Chinese craftsmen of
the Shang dynasty in the
15th Century B.C.

Below:
A gang of
tin prospectors
operating a mechanical
Banka Drill to test
ore-bearing country for
mining feasibility.

TIN IS A TIMELESS METAL that has aided man's progress since the Stone Age. Tin ushered in the Bronze Age and has served civilisations over the centuries in ever-increasing quantities and uses. In the present Space Age it has become an indispensable part of scientific, commercial industrial and domestic life. Tin is a veritable gift of Nature. Many millions of years ago molten masses within the earth were squeezed up towards the surface and solidified into rocks. Some of these rocks contained a black or brown substance now known as cassiterite or tin ore. Thus derived, Straits Tin is a product of the Federation of Malaysia, a country whose free enterprise tin industry has led in the production of tin since 1883 and for many years has mined no less than 40 per cent of the world's total output. "Straits" signifies the highest quality of tin, just as "Sterling" is the hallmark of silver. It has long been chosen by industrialists throughout the world because it is a metal of guaranteed purity and high quality.

Tin has played a significant part in the economy of Malaysia. The general high standard of living enjoyed by her people today is founded on the work of the early miners who made tin mining the first of the country's industries and, just as the mines in the gold rushes of the 1850's laid the pattern for the future development of Australia, so in Malaysia tin mining established a sound economic basis for that country.

Roads and railways followed the developing mines, and tiny settlements grew into the present day towns. Small workshops and trading houses set up to serve the needs of the pioneer miners were the forerunners of the flourishing secondary industries and commercial enterprises that now form an important part of the economy.

Tin contributes materially to Malaysia's finances, providing a substantial proportion of the Government's annual revenue and making available millions of dollars in foreign exchange. This revenue has become of vital importance in the implementation of Malaysia's new plans for National development and expansion of essential services.

Important as tin mining is to the country, the outside world is also becoming increasingly dependent upon Malaysia for a constant supply of this necessary and valuable metal. International demand had built up to such an extent that the 1961 production of 56,028 tons of tin from Malaysian mines had increased to 75,069 tons by 1968. In that year the total free world production was 182,100 long tons.

"Straits" tin is the final product of tin ore, which is found in Malaysia in alluvial deposits and primary lodes in the form of cassiterite or tin oxide. It is closely associated with granite, the main rock formation in the country's mountainous backbone. The tin ore is of very high quality, averaging 75 per cent of metallic tin. The world's largest single alluvial tin field lies in the Kinta Valley on the western side of the central mountain range of West Malaysia.

Pioneer miners in Malaysia obtained their tin ore both by panning and by sinking pits, some of which, uncovered by later miners, were 20 to 50 feet deep and up to 7 or 8 feet across. Ground sluicing was also used in hilly areas.

For some years now open-cast mines using gravel pumps have produced over 50 per cent of Malaysia's tin annually; open-casting was the main method of mining prior to the introduction of the first bucket dredge in January 1913. Chinese miners who pioneered open-cast mining in Malaysia ever since the last quarter of the last century continue to operate most of the 900 gravel pump mines which are in production today.

It is possible to set up these mines profitably in smaller tin-bearing areas at a relatively low capital outlay, for instance M$50 to M$250 thousand, compared with the M$10-15 million required to build a large modern dredge.

Early Chinese open-cast workings were about 20 feet deep, the ore being removed by a continuous chain of workers carrying baskets. Steam pumps introduced in Perak State in 1877 for preventing flooding were later modified into gravel pumps for pumping the tin-bearing material from the bottom of the mine to the sluice box or *palong,* where the heavier tin is trapped behind wooden slats, over which the lighter materials are carried away in the constant flow of water. These steam pumps were also converted for pumping water under pressure to be directed at the mine face through gun-like monitors in order to break up the earth and wash the tin ore down to the gravel pump at the bottom of the mine. Many modern gravel pump mines are now employing jigs as well as palongs to recover the tin from the other materials. Hydraulic monitors and elevators were also introduced where mountain rivers could be found to provide the head of water.

A suction dredge from Tasmania was introduced to Malaya in 1906 as the forerunner to the bucket dredge. By 1921 there were 30 bucket dredges in operation and a peak of 105 such active units had been reached by 1929, a similar peak of 104 units being reached again in 1940 when another 19 units were idle, making a total of 123 in all. The first hydro-electric power plant for tin mining in the Kinta Valley was installed in 1906 making use of the country's high rainfall in the mountains of the main range. All Malaysia's dredges are now operated by electricity, as are many gravel pump mines, but diesel power is also widely used by the latter. Total installed horsepower for a large dredge is in the region of 4,300 h.p.

The first dredge could dig to 50 feet with buckets of 10 cubic foot capacity and cost about M$184,000. Bucket dredges being built today have buckets up to 24 cubic foot capacity and, in addition to the capital cost of up to M$15 million, also require another M$5 million for roads, housing, stores and workshops. Dredges are most practical and economical in the vast areas of jungle swamp and alluvial plains where they can dig throughout the year at high through-put and low cost. Bucket dredges traverse the mine face from side to side and dig up the ore systematically, in some cases reaching to maximum depth of 180 feet below the surface, the dredge being moved sideways and forwards by wire ropes operated by winches on the dredge. Digging is by means of an endless chain of up to 135 manganese steel buckets costing up to M$7,000 each mounted on a bucket "ladder" which can be raised and lowered by wire ropes on yet another winch. The complete bucket ladder can weigh up to 1,000 tons. Constructed on pontoons up to 320 feet long, 105 feet wide and 14 feet in depth, reaching a height of up 60 feet, the dredges float on their own ponds, digging their way forward and filling in behind them with the earth from which they have extracted the tin ore.

Many dredges have a workshop on board with lathes, welding plant and all other necessary equipment used in the tin mining operation.

In dredges the ore bearing material is deposited into a dropchute as the buckets turn over and continue their way to dig up more at the working face below water level at the front-end of the revolving bucket chain. The dropchute delivers the material to a revolving trommel screen whence it is evenly distributed to batteries of jigs at the rear end of the dredge, the barren "tailings" flowing out with the water behind the dredge. Similarly, in a gravel pump mine, the tin ore is pumped up to the "palong" or sluice box and frequently to a smaller-scale jig plant for separating the heavy minerals—including the tin ore—from the sand and earth. Before being sent to the smelters the heavy mineral concentrate is further treated, usually in a central plant, by a process which separates the tin ore from the other minerals also present.

Research runs parallel with mineral-dressing practice in Malaysia, and in the dressing sheds new techniques are continually being adapted and evolved to suit local conditions and to deal with individual mining problems caused by the varying nature of the ore.

Shaking tables, classifiers, magnetic and electrostatic separators as well as flotation

Above:
A giant modern electrically driven bucket dredge mining tin in West Malaysia.

Left:
Giant monitors cutting stiff clays containing tin ore.

Right: A "palong" or sluice box to which the ore-bearing material is pumped from the mine below by gravel pumps for separation of the heavier tin from the lighter clay, sand and gravel.

Below: Molten tin flowing from a smelting furnace into a refining kettle.

systems are commonly used to separate and concentrate the tin ore from associated minerals and other materials.

Besides operating the largest tin dredges in the world, Malaysia also has the largest dry open-cast tin mine at Sungei Besi, near Kuala Lumpur; the largest and deepest (down to 2,000 feet) underground lode tin mine in the world, at Sungei Lembing in Pahang and the largest hydraulic tin mine in the world, at Gopeng in Perak.

One of the oldest methods in the world for recovering minerals from the earth is panning. In Malaysia it is known as *dulang* washing and in the western parts of the Federation licences are issued to women and girls—but not to men—to recover tin ore from the river beds and swamps. In this way the dulang washers recover about 5,000 *piculs* of tin concentrate a month. (A *picul* is a Chinese weight equivalent to $133\frac{1}{3}$ lbs.) Dulangs are also used when prospecting, to separate the tin concentrates from other material in the sample taken from the ground. Tin—or gold, as the case may be in other countries—is recovered by scooping up earth and water with the dulang, rotating it in such a way that heavy tin sinks to the centre of the pan and lighter sand and soil spill over the side with the water.

The tin mines of Malaysia are worked by an industrious and loyal labour force of about 46,000 Malaysians of various racial origins. Wages are amongst the highest in the country.

At the end of 1971 there were 1,078 active mines including 63 dredges and 965 gravel pump mines. A number of small dredging units which had exhausted their reserves were replaced during 1970 by larger dredges operating in other areas. Depending upon the size of the dredge and the grade of the ground, dredge production normally lies between 300 and 1,500 tons of tin metal per annum in concentrates form.

In 1971 Malaysia attained its second highest post war production with a tin metal content of 74,253 tons, of which 55 per cent was from gravel pump mines and 32 per cent from dredges, the remainder from underground mining, dulang washing and other methods.

The future of tin mining in Malaysia is dependent upon the price of the metal on the World Markets. The Penang market is operated by Malaysia's two tin smelters: the Straits Trading Company Ltd. and the Eastern Smelting Company in the State of Penang. The price is regulated every day by bids from world tin consumers, according to the laws of supply and demand. The miners do not know the exact price they will get for their product, all metal offered being sold daily at the lowest bid price for the total metal available for sale on each market day.

Malaysia is signatory to the International Tin Agreement and during the last quarter of 1968 and throughout 1969 a modest restriction of the export of tin metal was enforced to keep it to the rate of the 1968 total. On 1st January 1970, when the International Tin Council removed tin export control, the price of tin metal on the Penang Market was $698.50 as compared with the average price for 1969 of $626.10. In 1971 the Malaysian Government collected duty on the export of tin amounting to M$126,464,326 from an export of 75,564 long tons of primary tin worth about M$800 million.

Today tin is one of the world's most important metals; it is used for a multiplicity of purposes: in tinplate for making tin cans, used for foods, beer, and aerosols etc.; for pewter, solder and plumbing metal; for bearing metals, for motor car engines and many other engineering purposes; and for bronzes and gun metals. Tin is also used as an addition to cast iron for vehicle engine cylinder blocks and in the manufacture of float glass.

Tin is used extensively for the making of fusible alloys with low melting points;

dental amalgams; collapsible tubes for pharmaceuticals and for plating household goods and toys. New uses of tin are in the form of chemical compounds for such purposes as agricultural pesticides, wood-preservatives and also as stabilisers for PVC plastics.

OTHER MALAYSIAN MINERALS

Although tin is by far the most important mineral to be found in Malaysia there are others of appreciable economic value.

First on the list is iron. During 1970 Malaysia's largest iron mine at Rompin in Pahang was closed owing to the exhaustion of its paying reserves, and the country's 1971 production fell from 4.4 million to 934,982 long tons. The twelve remaining iron mines are located in the States of Pahang, Kedah, Perak and Johore.

Five bauxite mines in the southern State of Johore yielded 962,497 tons, most of which was exported to overseas countries to be smelted into aluminium.

Exports of ilmenite, an oxide of titanium and iron, amounted to 153,223 tons in 1971. Titanium is a lightweight, strong metal used in the building of space rockets, but the main use of ilmenite is for making titanium oxide for use in paints.

The total raw gold production for the whole of Malaysia in 1971 was 5,671 troy ounces, of which 1,180 ozs. was mined in 4 mines in Sarawak and 4,491 ozs. produced in Malaysia as a by-product of tin mining.

Two new kaolin mines came into operation during 1970 and production of clay in 1971 rose to 11,471 tons.

Like ilmenite, several other mineral by-products of tin mining are being exported or used in Malaysia in relatively small quantities. These include the following: Zircon, the ore of zirconium, a mineral generally used in foundries as a moulding material; xenotime, an ore of ittrium, a virtually unknown mineral until the advent of colour television and microwave radio found important uses for it; monazite, an ore of cerium, thorium and a number of other rare earths which are used in the chloride form as catalysts in petroleum refining. The oxides are used in glass making and the metals in alloys and carbon electrodes for welding.

Scheelite and wolfram are both ores of tungsten which forms the brightly glowing filaments of electric light bulbs. As tungsten carbide it is used in the cutting and shaping of other metals.

Columbite is an ore of columbium and tantalum. The former is mainly used in special steel alloys and in alloys of other metals. Tantalum has its principal value in electronics, chemical processing equipment, high temperature alloys and metal cutting tools.

During 1970 a mine from which quantities of manganese and ferro-manganese had been obtained in past years was temporarily closed down and production ceased.

East Malaysia's copper mine in Sabah situated at the foot of Mount Kinabalu at Mamut is expected to yield 40,000 tons of ore per year when this Malaysian/Japanese venture eventually comes into production. With the initial exploration completed, the processing plant, access roads and port facilities for shipment to Japan, are now being constructed.

CONCLUSION

Tin and its by-products remain overwhelmingly the most important of Malaysia's minerals. By producing another record tonnage at 74,253 tons in 1971, second highest post war production (1968 = 75,069) Malaysia's tin mining industry has continued to show its resilience. Future reserves and production levels are always a matter for speculation, but the inducement of an adequate price will undoubtedly stimulate production and ensure the future of the industry.

Above:
The molten metal is poured into ingot moulds.

Left:
Thousands of tons of pure tin ingots awaiting transport to the wharves for shipment overseas or to local manufacturers.

THE STORY OF SELANGOR PEWTER

On these pages are some examples of exquisite Selangor pewter. Malaysia produces more than 42 per cent of the world's tin, the basic ingredient of fine quality pewter alloy.

PEWTER was used more than 2,000 years ago by the Chinese and the Romans. Since then this attractive tin alloy has spread to most parts of the world. The Americans, Europeans and Australians hold it in high esteem.

It is in Malaysia, the largest source of the world's tin supply, that the startlingly beautiful pewter is manufactured today, a result made possible by its high tin content. Malaysia produces more than 42 per cent of the world's tin and this bountiful supply has been the important stimulus to the pewter industry in this region.

The story of pewter in Malaysia began in the 1880's when a young man from the Swatow province of China came in a sailing junk to make his fortune in what was then called Malaya. Swatow was the home of the famed Chinese pewterers. (Pewter-making is an age-old Chinese handicraft jealously handed down from father to son.)

The young man, whose name was Yong Koon, brought nothing with him except a few tools. His only wealth was his skill in the making of pewter. Yong Koon had heard that tin, the metal from which pewter is made, was plentiful in Malaya and he was confident that with his skill and hard work, he could make a good living there.

Like all Chinese, Yong Koon was a very diligent lad and he toiled day and night to earn a livelihood in the new land. Patiently, he fashioned containers for ancestral worship—incense burners, joss-stick holders, wine jugs, tiny wine cups and so on. Much of his handiwork can still be found today in the stately old homes of the local Chinese community where it is used at the altars, especially on festive occasions.

As the demand for his pewter increased, Yong Koon employed a few apprentices to help him. Everything was done by hand and each piece of pewter received loving care and attention and was faultlessly wrought. Each craftsman took immense pride in his work.

As time went on, more items were added to the range of pewter products—ash trays, beer mugs, vases, pitchers and other pieces. More craftsmen were trained to help.

When Yong Koon grew old, one of his four sons, Yong Peng Kai, carried on his business and the fame of the family's Selangor Pewter Company grew. (Selangor is the name of the Malaysian State in which the pewter company is located.)

From a small, one-man concern, operated in the backyard of a shop-house, it has now graduated to a modern factory with special machinery to help production. But throughout, the original meticulous care and attention which has characterised this particular brand of pewter is still rigidly observed.

During World War II, pewter beer mugs were much in demand and were used to trade for food and cigarettes.

Gradually the range of products was increased and the scope of production widened to encompass special orders for trophies and presentation pieces.

Today Selangor Pewter is being run by the third generation of the Yong family.

Yong Koon's son, Yong Peng Kai and his four children head this flourishing pewter industry with factories in Singapore and Kuala Lumpur and distributing centres in most parts of the world. Australians and people in many other countries have learnt to recognise the distinctive designs and superb craftsmanship which make Selangor Pewter one of the finest in the world.

Tourists who visit Malaysia make a point of taking home with them a few pieces of Selangor Pewter, not only as fitting mementos of their visit to the lovely land of Malaysia but also as elegant objects of art and utility.

Visitors to Kuala Lumpur are invited to tour the Selangor Pewter Demonstration Works where they are shown the different processes of the industry. People are intrigued by the painstaking care which goes into the making of each piece of pewter and the skill displayed by the craftsmen in fashioning such a wide range of beautiful articles.

Pewter is made by melting blocks of Straits Refined Tin mixed with a little antimony and copper in a large cauldron; the exact proportion is 97 per cent tin with 3 per cent antimony and copper. The molten pewter is poured into sheets which are then cut into different patterns and sizes for the various items to be manufactured. These are spun into the required shapes before being polished to a gleaming finish. Some are left plain and others are given a hammered finish by tapping a small hammer on to the pewter by hand. This leaves rows and rows of "dimples" on the article; for instance on a beer mug there may be as many as 3,000 "dimples".

The craftsman responsible for this operation is so skilled that he never misses or forms a crooked row.

To make a beer mug, a flat pewter sheet is first formed into a cylinder by hand and then spun to the proper shape. The inside is polished smooth and the base is soldered on. Later the outside is polished before the handle is attached with solder. A final touch-up and inspection is given before the beer mug leaves the factory for the showroom and ultimately ends up in some far-off pub or home of a great beer drinker.

The skill of the Selangor craftsmen is superb: although various parts are joined together, the soldering is so well done the seams can never be detected. Each craftsman takes great pride in his work. Several have spent their entire lives with the company and now their children are learning the trade too.

The Yong family has made their pewter so world-renowned that every visitor to Malaysia has already heard of it. Foreign dignitaries on State visits or attending conferences are often presented with a piece of Selangor Pewter by Malaysian Government officials. Malaysians who go abroad on official business or for pleasure take with them Selangor Pewter gifts, for they know they will be treasured by the recipients.

Selangor Pewter products are not restricted to items for the home or the office. Trophies and special orders—unique, modern designs—are custom-made to clients' requirements by trained experts of the Design Department. Trophies and medals for international events, for schools sports and exhibitions, are made up to world standards.

So, when in Malaysia, remember to look for Selangor Pewter with its distinctive trade mark—the little man at the anvil—the guarantee of top quality pewter.

An intricate design embroidered on carpet or wall cloth telling a story of a legendary God.

Kingdom of
NEPAL

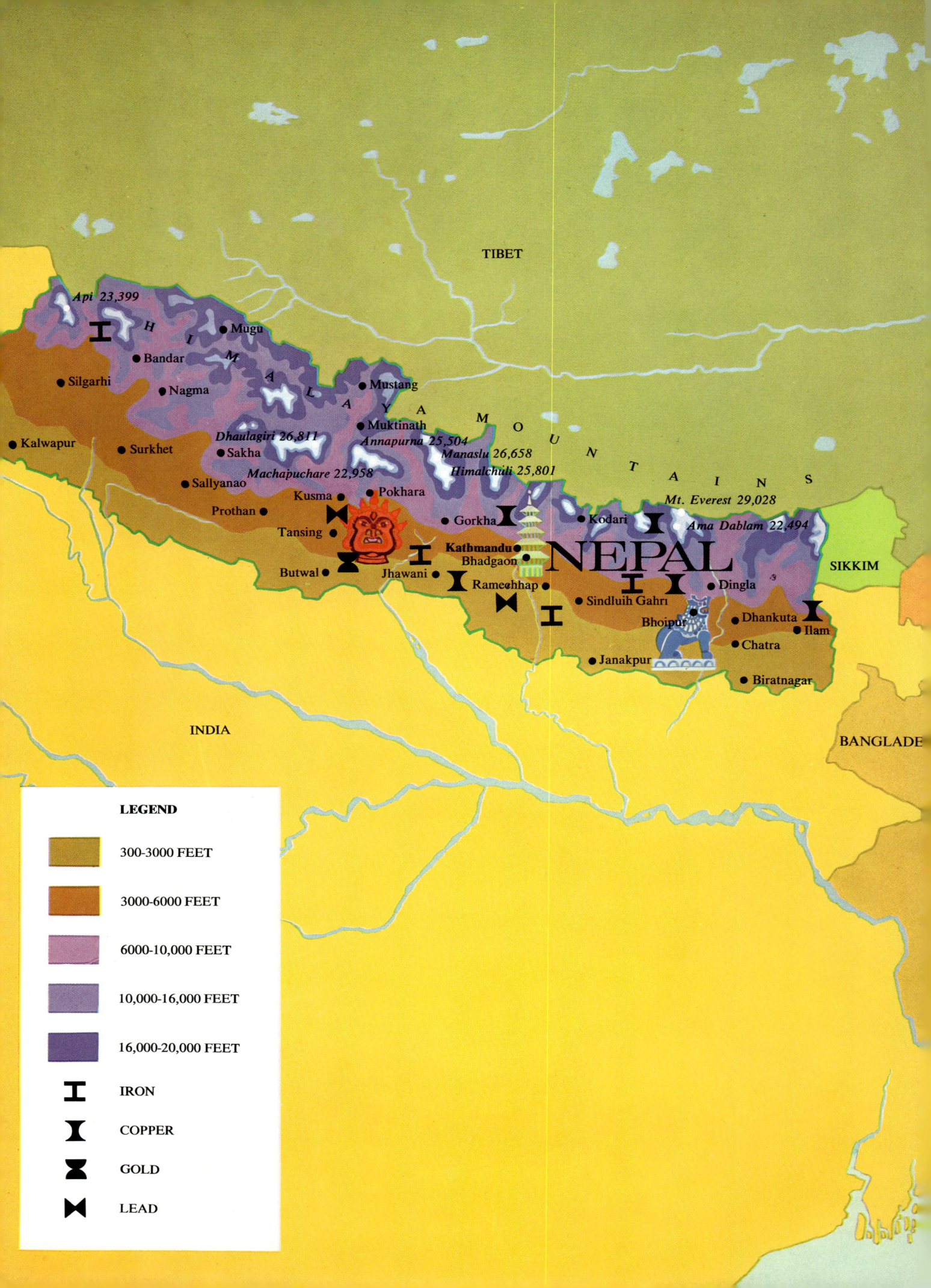

NEPAL

LEGEND

- 300-3000 FEET
- 3000-6000 FEET
- 6000-10,000 FEET
- 10,000-16,000 FEET
- 16,000-20,000 FEET

- IRON
- COPPER
- GOLD
- LEAD

Mountains (feet):
- Api 23,399
- Dhaulagiri 26,811
- Annapurna 25,504
- Manaslu 26,658
- Machapuchare 22,958
- Himalchuli 25,801
- Mt. Everest 29,028
- Ama Dablam 22,494

Places: Mugu, Bandar, Silgarhi, Nagma, Kalwapur, Surkhet, Sakha, Mustang, Muktinath, Sallyanao, Prothan, Kusma, Pokhara, Tansing, Jhawani, Gorkha, Kodari, Butwal, Kathmandu, Bhadgaon, Ramechhap, Sindluih Gahri, Bhoipur, Dingla, Janakpur, Dhankuta, Ilam, Chatra, Biratnagar

Neighboring regions: TIBET, INDIA, SIKKIM, BANGLADESH

Nepal

The Himalayas, like great snow-covered temples, tower over Kathmandu.

AREA:
54,362 square miles.

AVERAGE LENGTH:
550 miles.

WIDTH:
Greatest—150 miles.
Smallest—90 miles.

LOCATION:
Between 26° 15′ and 30° 30′ north latitude and 80° 15′ and 88° 15′ east longitude.

BOUNDARIES:
North—The Tibet Region of the People's Republic of China.

East—Sikkim and West Bengal.

West and South—the Indian States of Uttar Pradesh and Bihar.

CLIMATE:
Extremely cold, below zero in higher altitudes. In June in Kathmandu Valley the temperature can reach 95° Fahrenheit on occasions. In the plains areas in the Terai temperatures can reach over 100° Fahrenheit in summer.

RAINFALL:
Average in Himalayas 20″ annually (precipitations mainly snow). Maximum in Valley up to 150″ annually.

POPULATION:
Approximately 10 million.

GROWTH OF POPULATION:
1.6% annually.

PROJECTED POPULATION YEAR 2000:
15.2 million.

Nepal

Left: Carved wooden architecture on a temple which stands in front of the old Durbar Square in Hanuman Dhoka. Similar work is prominent in front of the police headquarters at Kathmandu.

Below: One of the typical famous Nepalese temples in the city area of Patan.

KINGDOM IN THE SNOWS

THE HISTORY of civilisation in Nepal goes back many thousands of years before the Christian era began. Its modern existence is the result of the integration of a number of former independent Kingdoms, culminating in the foundation of the Kingdom of Nepal in 1769 under Prithivi Narayan Shah, King of the Gorkhas. The ruling King today is His Majesty Birenda Bir Bikra Shah Deva, the tenth King in the Shah dynasty. He succeeded his father, King Mahendra, who died at the early age of 51 on 31st January 1972.

Surviving turbulent periods between 1846 and 1951 when the hereditary Rana Prime Ministers despotically ruled the country, King Tribhuban, with strong support from the Crown Prince, the recent King, and other members of the Royal Family, wiped out the Rana autocracy and established a democratic form of government. Since December 1960 Nepal has made marked economic and social headway under a non-party Panchayat system of democracy.

The Panchayat system is 4-tier, with the Village and Town Panchayats, the executive bodies of the Village and Town Assemblies, as the basis unit. The District Assembly composed of the Village and Town Panchayat members choose from among themselves 11 members who form the District Panchayat and, in turn, constitute the Zonal Assembly. They elect from their ranks 11 members to act in the Zonal Panchayat. The whole system is ruled by a 125 member unicameral supreme legislature known as the Rashtriya Panchayat; 16 members nominated by the King and 109 elected. Its membership is drawn chiefly from the Panchayat hierarchy and various class groups such as peasants, workers, youth and women's organisations. The result of this somewhat complex form of administration has been the freedom of the people from the oppression of the previous

Above right:
The lion idol which stands in front of a temple gate for protection against the devil.

Above:
Offerings to the deities in the capital city.

undemocratic Rana Regime, and the restoration of their inherent right to shape their own destinies within the framework of a democracy—a rare blending of the old and the new in a modern civilisation.

The 10 million people who populate Nepal comprise an assortment of many races and tribes, living in different regions, wearing different styles of clothing and speaking different languages and dialects. As a general principle they are of light to medium complexion, short to medium height and sturdy limbed. In the west and on the southern slopes of Annapurna, Himalchuli and Ganesh Himal live the Gurungs and Magars. They, like the majority of the hill-people, are farmers and virtually self-supporting. They till the soil, raise their herds of sheep, goats, yak, buffalo, horses and mules, spin and weave wool and make it into simple clothes. Sometimes, to earn a little extra money they hire themselves out as carriers. The eastern mountains are inhabited by Rais, Limbus and Sunwars. The famous Gorkhas, belonging to the ancient indigenous Mongoloid communities, also inhabit the mountain areas. In the First World War, when all Nepalese soldiers were known as "Gurkhas", they distinguished themselves as fierce and courageous fighters; 200,000 of them enlisted at the British Army recruiting camps in India. In the Second World War they proved their prowess in battle in almost all the fronts in Africa and Asia.

In the Himalayas are the Sherpas, those "Tigers of the Snow", whose tribal name was given world-wide publicity when Sir Edmond Hillary in 1951 became the first white man to climb 29,028 feet to the summit of Mount Everest, the highest peak in the world. Tensing Norkay, the chief guide of the party, is a Sherpa, born at Khumbu, in the Himalayas. He was actually the first human to reach the peak, only a few steps in front of Hillary. In the Sherpa regions of 15,000 feet altitudes have been found the tracks of "the abominable snowman", that mysterious creature never actually seen by scientific expeditions but thought possibly to be the missing link between the human and the anthropoid. The Sherpas assert that the "yeti", as they call it, walks upright, is extremely aggressive and even is intelligent enough to talk in some strange sort of language.

In the valley of Kathmandu the most numerous race is the Newar. There are Tharus and Dhimals in the Terai Region. Brahmins, Kshatriyas and Thakuris are sprinkled all over the Kingdom and peacefully coexist with the diverse racial stocks of the country to form an integral whole.

THE PEOPLE AND LIFE IN NEPAL

In the less civilised parts live primitive tribes, short, dark Mongoloids. They dwell in caves or in crude huts made of branches. Their diet is the flesh of wild animals, birds and fish, tubers, roots, leaves and native fruits of the forests.

In the valleys and basins the chief source of livelihood is the land, the principal crops being paddy rice, wheat, maize, tobacco and millet, with commercial and industrial off-shoots of agriculture. Other domestic or 'cottage' occupations are ghee making, grazing, weaving, hosiery and paper making, pottery and simple cane furniture, but the life pattern is changing almost from day to day under the impact of 20th Century civilisation.

The people speak many different languages and dialects but Nepali and Newari are by far in most general use. Nepali is the national tongue and is spoken and understood everywhere.

The religions of the Nepalese are mainly divided between Hinduism and Buddhism with a complex blending of both. For many centuries the two sects have cherished a mutual respect and regard for one another. Lord Gautama Buddha was born in Lumbini (in west Nepal) in 560 B.C.

Almost all the infectious tropical diseases are endemic—dysentery, cholera, typhoid, smallpox, jaundice and malaria. And yet the Nepalese are an inherently happy people with a serene self-assurance seldom found in the more advanced countries. They are honest, reliable, polite and loyal and in spite of the alarming spread of banditry and gangsterism in so many other parts of the world the visitor, the explorer and the mountaineer in Nepal is in no danger at all from such terrors.

In recent years many social changes have improved the lives of the people. There are now more than 55 hospitals spread through the country and 121 health centres. Almost 7,500 primary, intermediate and high schools have been built and for higher level education 36 colleges, 13 professional institutions and a university are functioning to a notable degree of efficiency. Education is a real problem to the authorities, for almost 90 per cent of the population is illiterate.

In such a rugged, largely hilly to mountainous country, transport is another problem to be overcome. In many localities travelling by foot is the only way, helped by the traditional beasts of burden, horses, mules and yak. But during the past decade 24 airports have been established, 100 kilometres of railways laid and roadways stretch over more than 3,000 kilometres.

In the mountain regions the 28 miles of ropeways are the fastest and cheapest means of getting from one place to another.

It is only in recent years that tourists have been allowed to enter the country but today they are welcomed, for Nepal, in spite of a growing awareness of the possession of potentially valuable natural resources only waiting to be developed, is still an economically poor nation and the wealthy tourist is a friend in need and he will find his visit most rewarding. Normally he will enter Nepal from the south, crossing the rolling plains of the Terai skirting the foothills, clamber the serried ranks of the mountains enclosing lush valleys and so on to the snow mantled walls of the mighty Himalayas and beyond to the highest peaks in the world: Sagarmatha (Mt. Everest), Kangchenjunga, Makulu, Lhotse, Dhaulagiri, Annapurna, Himalchuli and Gauri Shanker; all of them ranging from 23,000 to 28,000 feet.

Within the confines of hills and valleys rare bright-plumed birds wing their tuneful flights through forests of great arboreal beauty and variety, through glens of rhododendrons, orchids, azaleas, poinsettias and primulas. In the shadowed darkness of wooded hills and plains rustle and roar Nepal's jungle creatures, the massive one-horned rhino, the golden furred tiger, the leopard, the elephant and the wide-eyed leaping fawn.

The swift flowing rivers and the numerous lakes and ponds are filled with rohu, salmon, eel and trout. Over all, the towering majesty of the snowcapped Himalayas weaves a magic spell that is never to be forgotten. The three cities of Kathmandu, Patan and Bhadgaon are virtually open-air museums of art and architecture. A stroll through any of their main thoroughfares and neatly paved alleys will discover exquisite, intricate carvings on the woodwork of the many pagodas, on the latticed windows and balconies of buildings and homes. The cities are landscaped into the undulating swings of the surrounding hills and the architecture is designed to perfect conformity. The pagoda style is still preserved throughout the Kingdom, not only in these principal cities but in towns like Dhulikhel, Biratnagar and Gorkha, and in the amazing 28,000 villages scattered over all parts of the land.

On the glacial fringe of Dhaulagiri is the Muktinath temple; in the midst of Lake Phewa in Pokhara is the Barahi temple; by the sacred banks of the Bagmati river is the Pashupatinath. These and innumerable other treasures bear tribute to the architects and builders of Nepal. To them must also be added the 55-windowed Palace in Bhadgaon, the monasteries of Kwabhal in Patan and Bhagwan Bahal in Kathmandu.

In this peculiarly Nepalese atmosphere, during many months of the year festivals call to the people far and wide and the Kathmandu Valley is the venue of the most colourful of them all. Here the chariot festival of the Machhendra Nath is held in March and April. But whether it be local, regional or national the festival is an unforgettable sight. It is always accompanied by folk dancing, singing and music and the highlight is a rare costume parade. As part of the festival all the noteworthy Bahals are converted into museums in which are displayed amazing collections of bronze statues of great antiquity, with the image of the Dipankar Buddha predominating. During the Indrajatra (vestal virgin) Festival at Kathmandu the Durbar Square comes to life with the solemn beats and gestures of masked dancers performing in brilliant flare-lit traditional tableaux. On 11th June is celebrated the official birthday of the reigning monarch, throughout the land, in a spirit of solemn rededication to the great ideals for which His Majesty stands.

Left: Street singers with their home-made instruments singing to visitors stories of people who have achieved great things.

Below:
Elephants crossing
one of the rivers in the Terai Region of Nepal.

Those who wish their memories to remain with them can buy all sorts of souvenirs: exquisite wooden carvings, miniature buddhas, pashmina shawls, hand-made shoes and slippers, khukuri knives (the favourite weapon of the fighting Gurkha), dolls and masks. The Newars of the Kathmandu Valley are the real craftsmen as their beautifully decorated temples and buildings testify. Their metal and stone work and wood carvings are exceptionally fine. The famous White Pagoda at Peking was built by the Newars at the Time of Kublai Khan as a gift from an artistically talented, friendly neighbour.

For centuries past there has been a lively intercourse of trade and traffic, art and culture between Nepal and its neighbouring countries to the north and south but until as recently as 1950 Nepal was regarded as a backward land. Since the establishment of the Panchayat and the social Revolution of 1950-51 a new era has begun and Nepal's former isolation has broken into a new concept of external relations. A bold and purposeful foreign policy directed by the late King Mahendra gained for Nepal full membership of the international community—a seat among the United Nations. A solid and honourable friendship has been established with India; diplomatic relations have been cemented with the People's Republic of China. Continued efforts are being made to ease the Indo-Pakistan tension and a firm policy of peaceful co-existence has been formulated.

The way is open for extending trade relations with many countries, for the demand for food and raw materials for the more populous and highly industrialised nations is growing every year.

Left page: A typical,
street scene in the Nepalese capital, Kathmandu.

Left: Pashupatinath,
an ancient Hindu Temple,
is the holiest and busiest of all Hindu sacred places in the Himalayas.
It is situated on the river Bagmati, revered by Hindus as a source
of the sacred Ganges River.

435

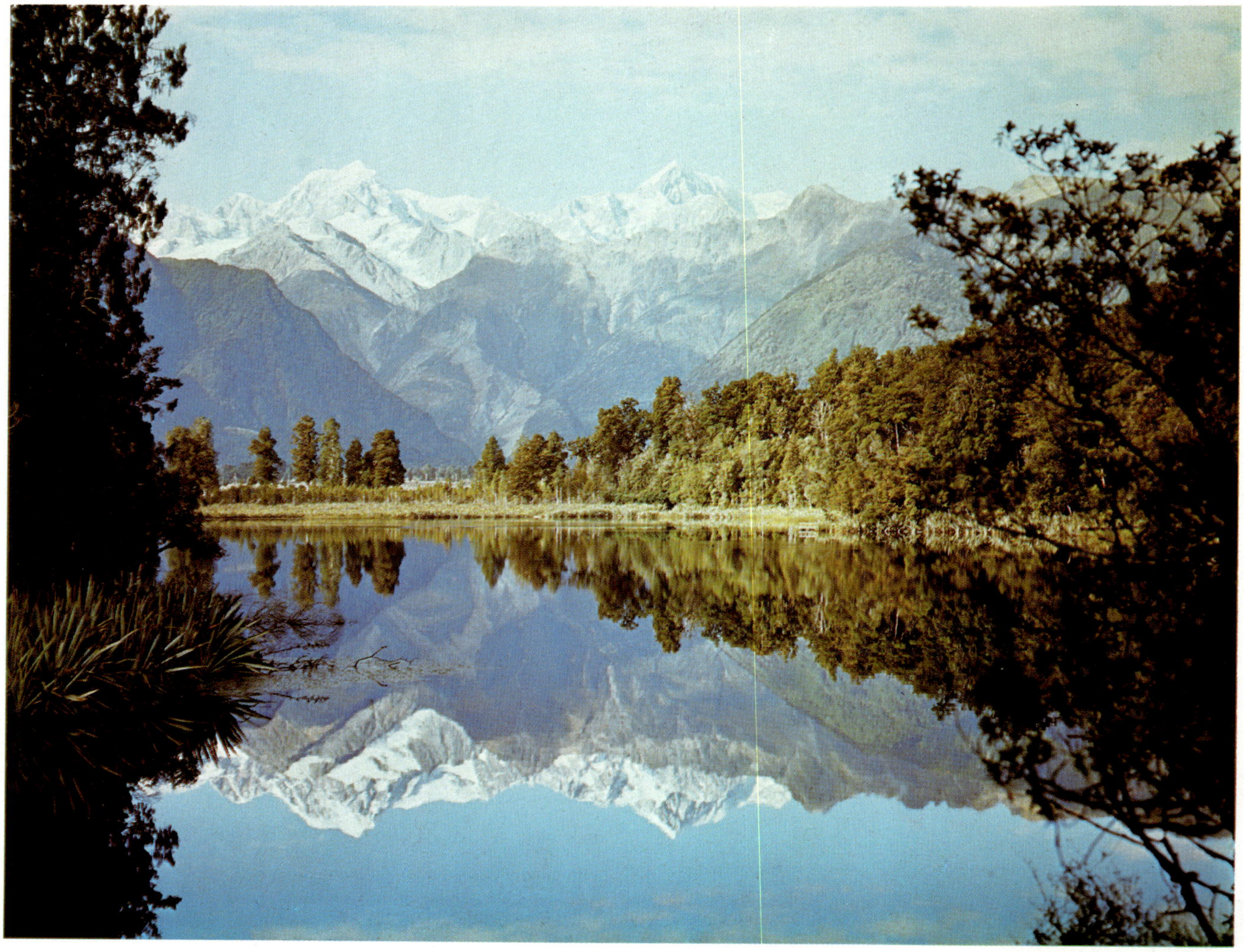

NEW ZEALAND

NEW ZEALAND

New Zealand

AREA:
Total: 103,560 sq. miles, comprising North Island, South Island and Stewart Island.

SIZE:
North-south the New Zealand group stretches approximately 900 miles. No one point in the country is more than 80 miles from the sea.

LOCATION:
Approximately 1,300 miles south-east of Australia, the main islands of New Zealand lie between 34° and 47° south latitude and 166° and 178° east longitude, surrounded on three sides by the South Pacific Ocean, with the Tasman Sea to the west.

TOPOGRAPHY:
Significant physical features include: the north-south chain of mountains, particularly the Southern Alps (Highest Mountain: Mt. Cook: 12,347 ft.); some short, fast-flowing rivers (Longest: Waikato — 220 miles); wide expanses of elevated open country and several lakes (Largest Lake: Taupo— 238 sq. miles); earthquakes, volcanoes, boiling mud-pools, geysers and other thermal phenomena mainly in the Rotorua region.

CLIMATE:
Three main factors influence the climate: 1) New Zealand's situation in the westerly wind belt; 2) the mountains which produce a barrier to the westward moving air-masses create a rainshadow area east of the chain; 3) a general maritime influence produces a low mean temperature range and an evenly distributed yearly rainfall. Average maximum temperature: 82°F. Average minimum: 32°F. Rainfall averages lie between 25 and 60 inches yearly. Below 2,000 feet, snow rarely falls for more than a few days each year, except in the south of South Island.

RELIGION:
Christian denominations.

POPULATION:
2,860,000 (including some 227,100 Maori indigenes).

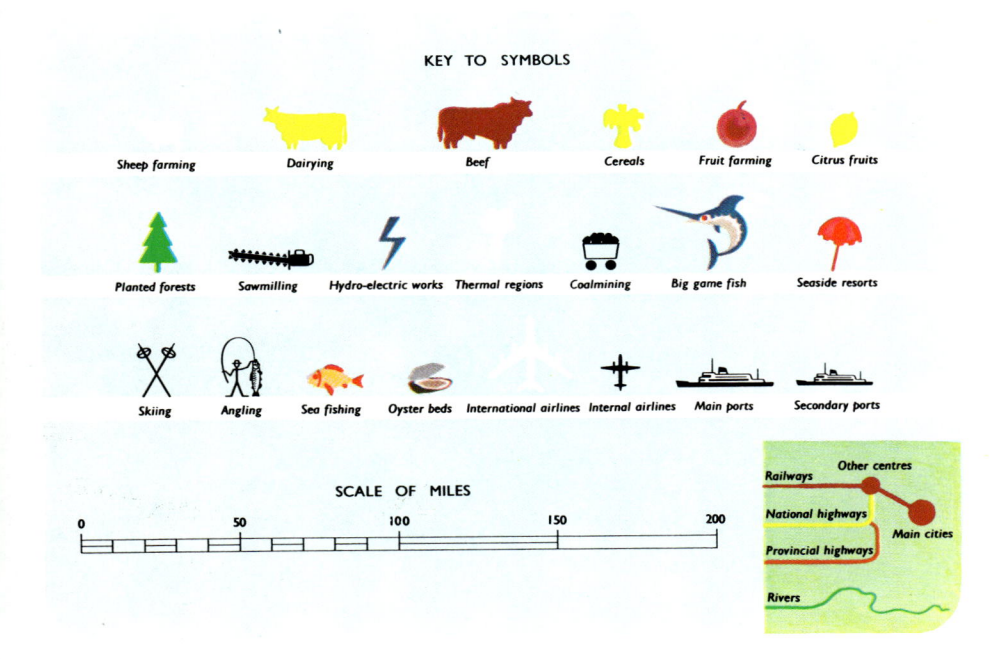

KEY TO SYMBOLS

Sheep farming · Dairying · Beef · Cereals · Fruit farming · Citrus fruits

Planted forests · Sawmilling · Hydro-electric works · Thermal regions · Coalmining · Big game fish · Seaside resorts

Skiing · Angling · Sea fishing · Oyster beds · International airlines · Internal airlines · Main ports · Secondary ports

SCALE OF MILES
0 · 50 · 100 · 150 · 200

Railways · Other centres · National highways · Main cities · Provincial highways · Rivers

The Discovery of New Zealand

WHEN ABEL TASMAN, the Dutch navigator, discovered New Zealand in 1642 it was inhabited by Maoris, a Polynesian people thought to be of southern Asian origin who migrated from the Asian mainland through the islands of the eastern and southern Pacific, which they explored intensively. Most Maori tribes arrived in New Zealand from the Society Islands about the middle of the 14th Century. More than 100 years later, Captain James Cook, of the British Navy, made a thorough exploration of the coastline in a series of three outstanding voyages.

Among the first Europeans to reach New Zealand were sealers and whalers who sailed to the South Pacific early in the 19th Century. But European interchanges with the Maoris were often bitter and eventually the British Government was obliged to establish sovereignty over the islands of New Zealand. In February 1840, Captain William Hobson, R.N., and leading Maori chiefs signed the Treaty of Waitangi, by which they acknowledged British Rule and received for the Maori people full British citizenship. In return, the Maoris were guaranteed protection of their lands, forests, fisheries, as well as other territorial rights.

In 1852, Britain granted self-government to New Zealand. The central New Zealand Government was initially established at Russell, in the Bay of Islands, then at Auckland, and finally at Wellington. A few years later, four seats in the New Zealand House of Representatives were specifically set aside for Maori Members of Parliament to represent their own race. This policy is still in force, and Maoris also have the right to contest European seats in elections.

GOVERNMENT
New Zealand is an independent member of the British Commonwealth; the reigning monarch is represented by a Governor-General appointed for a term of five years. Modelled on British Parliamentary democracy, the New Zealand Parliament has one chamber, the House of Representatives, with 84 members. General elections are normally held every three years when all men and women 20 years and over may vote by secret ballot. Although there is no legal obligation to vote, over 90 per cent of the electorate customarily exercise their voting rights when parliamentary elections are held.

THE OMBUDSMAN
In 1962, following the example of Sweden, the New Zealand Government appointed an Ombudsman to investigate citizens' complaints against decisions or actions of the State administration not actionable in Court or open to immediate redress by the Government.

ADMINISTRATION
Government policy, as established by legislation and Cabinet decision, is adminis-

Above:
This map shows the possible routes of migration of the Maori people to New Zealand.

Right:
An artist's impression of life in a Maori fortified village before European settlement.

Left:
Designed in the shape of a beehive, this addition to Parliament Buildings, Wellington, is to be completed in the early 1970's.

tered by 37 Ministries, most of which are called "departments". Each department has a permanent head responsible to his Minister. Public servants, in departments under the control of a State Services Commission, number more than 70,000. Another 130,000 are employed in such State services as teaching, hospitals, the Post Offices, Police, transport (railways and some road services, the principal airlines, and some shipping), and the staffs of corporations controlling facilities such as broadcasting. There are also more than 13,000 men and women enlisted for various occupations in the New Zealand armed services.

In additional to the Central Government organisations, there are over 600 local authorities—that is, local administrations directed by elected citizens as in Britain. These control the municipalities and counties, and many services and functions including harbours, hospitals, roading, drainage, and the distribution of electricity.

PUBLIC SERVICES

Private enterprise predominates in business, but such essential services as the railways, the main airlines, post and telegraph services, electricity supply and radio and television broadcasting come under public ownership.

The Government owns the railways, including an inter-island road-rail ferry service, and through corporations it operates an international airline (Air New Zealand) and the main internal airline (National Airways Corporation). It also controls about 8 per cent of road transport. Postal, telegraph and telephone systems are State-operated and television stations are run by the New Zealand Broadcasting Corporation. Nearly all New Zealand shipping is privately owned. A Tourist Hotel Corporation, set up by the Government, operates some hotels, largely in the more popular tourist resorts.

More than half of New Zealand's coal output comes from the State mines. Three-quarters of the commercially exploitable native forest, supplying building and paper pulp timbers, is Government owned, as are half the exotic plantations.

Above:
Wellington, the capital city, is the commercial and administrative centre of New Zealand.

441

LIVING IN NEW ZEALAND

Right: A good standard of living is in evidence in the average homes, illustrated here in an Auckland suburb.

Below: Coronet Peak on the South Island is one of New Zealand's many popular ski resorts.

Right page, centre: Typical New Zealand school children. Education is compulsory from the ages of six to fifteen years.

Extreme right: Two typical healthy New Zealanders.

TODAY when the quality of life is becoming more important than the economic facts of a standard of living index, the New Zealander finds himself more than fortunate.

A pastoral, scenic country, full employment, a social system which has eliminated real poverty, and the evolution of a society which while not classless is more nearly so than most others, provide a unique background for the nation to develop.

This security has not stifled the New Zealander's individuality, a keystone of the national life, and it is in the art of living that he excels.

In this context, New Zealanders are well housed. With minor fluctuations, there has been a steady long-term increase in the building of houses and flats to meet the needs of a growing population. Though in the cities the trend towards multi-storey flats and town houses is marked, the New Zealand family prefers to live, as the majority do, in detached bungalows. These are usually wooden, though brick and concrete are becoming more frequently used. A steady extension and improvement of the road network has ended the hardship of rural life. Comparable properties in the country districts tend to be more spacious and are invariably less expensive than those in the cities.

New Zealand children receive compulsory education from the ages of six to fifteen, although they may be enrolled and attend school from the age of five. Younger children attend play centres and kindergartens. As well as the State schools, there are others built and run mainly by churches, with limited Government assistance, but subject to inspection and following curricula prescribed by the Department of Education. In remote areas, the Department's correspondence schools provide full-time primary and secondary education for over 5,000 pupils.

New Zealand has six universities, which are in the main cities of Auckland, Wellington, Christchurch, Dunedin, Hamilton and Palmerston North.

Underpinning every New Zealander is comprehensive social security. The nation was a pioneer in making statutory provision for old age pensions (in 1890) and has a system of benefits providing for general family welfare and for all contingencies arising from sickness, accident, unemployment, death of the breadwinner and old age. The Social Security Act 1938, upon which the present system is based, ensures that all citizens have a reasonable standard of living and that they are safe-guarded against economic ills from which they may be unable to protect themselves. Age benefits for men and women are payable at 60 and at 65 superannuation is universal. Regardless of the income of the parents, a regular weekly payment is given for each child under 16 years of age. Invalids and widows are also assisted.

Interwoven with the social security network is a full range of health services available to New Zealanders through Government agencies. Public hospital treatment and pre-natal, maternity, and post-natal services are free. Normal service by private doctors is subsidised, the Government paying part of each fee for consultation and treatment. A wide range of medicines and drugs prescribed by doctors is also supplied free.

An institution unique to New Zealand is the Plunket Society, which is largely responsible for post-natal care. Its highly-trained nurses pay regular visits on the mothers for the first few weeks of the child's life and its clinics see to the young family's welfare after that.

The Government, hospital boards, municipal authorities and a large number of welfare organisations share responsibility for the aged. A capital subsidy of 100 per cent is available to religious and welfare organisations for homes and hospitals for old people.

With these comprehensive services, the New Zealander's life expectation is 68 years for men and 73 for women.

New Zealand is outstanding as an example of a land where, to a great extent, harmony has been achieved between two races of different colour and background.

While no-one would claim that there have been no instances of injustice and discrimination, relations between the two main groups, the Polynesian Maori and the European *pakeha* have not been marked by any great degree of friction.

New Zealand's Maori population has grown from 80,000 to 228,000 in 150 years. The Maoris have been in no way submerged by the tide of settlement and European culture. They are retaining their race and culture to the extent that they desire, and while keeping this identity, they tend to form an homogenous society with the Europeans especially in sport, politics, administration, and in the professions, and now increasingly in intermarriage. From the earliest days, Maoris have demonstrated their high intellectual potential by pursuing university courses and taking the highest honours. In recent years the most striking development has been the increasing numbers voluntarily seeking further education. The Government has made great efforts, by way of special assistance in training, to ensure that the talents of the Maori people are used to the full.

In recent years, New Zealand's cultural scene has undergone a remarkable change. There was a time when the country's position in the South Pacific cut it off quite drastically from world influences. Now, the arrival of the superjet aircraft, and developments within New Zealand, have encouraged many of the world's leading entertainers and artists to visit. This change from isolation to an acute awareness of the world cultural scene has speeded up the momentum of the arts in New Zealand.

Amateur and professional theatre, music, painting, pottery and literature have been developed to a high degree. Television, although there is no choice of channel, is a vigorous medium, screening, as well as good quality programmes of local interest, a selection of programmes from overseas. The renowned National Film Unit has won many world-class awards and its recent creation, "This is New Zealand", which employs the three-screen technique, is one of its finest achievements.

New Zealand is, above all, an outdoor country and its culture is inseparable from the nation's astonishing performance in international sports. Its success is out of all proportion to its size. Olympic Games gold medal winners Peter Snell and Murray Halberg, golfer Bob Charles, racing driver Dennis Hulme and great rugby players, such as Don Clarke, Brian Lochore, and Colin Meads, are known all over the sporting world.

The equable climate and the open spaces permit year-round sports ranging from swimming, tramping, surfing, boating and climbing in the summer to skiing in winter. Yet, although this choice is wide, there is no doubt that Rugby Union is king. Its players range from primary schoolboys to the famous "All Black" team—the national representatives. The All Blacks tour Great Britain, France, North America, Australia and South Africa and some teams have visited Pacific Islands, Ceylon and Japan.

As a direct result of these increasing international contacts and a growing role in the world, New Zealand has many thousands of visitors annually. With faster air travel, and the advent of the package holiday, the country is rapidly boosting its tourist trade into a major industry. New Zealand combines in a comparatively small area a host of scenic and sporting attractions, any one of which would make another country famous.

In order to cope with the growing influx, New Zealand's hotel industry, once lagging, has embarked on an ambitious programme of building accommodation ranging from motels to top international hotels. Towns and cities have plenty to offer the visitor. Hotels are open until 10 p.m., restaurants cater for late diners with fine food and entertainment and in the larger cities there are stage shows in addition to a wide range of cinemas.

A growing country and a rapidly changing one, keeping pace with the world, New Zealand is nevertheless clinging hard and successfully to its precious kind of living—its unique and special "quality of life."

TRADE AND INDUSTRY

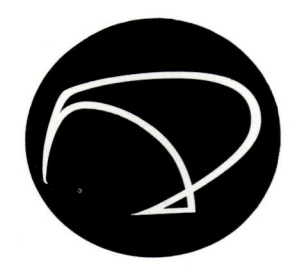

NEW ZEALAND is unusual, if not unique, in the world. A country the size of Britain with a population of almost 3 million, for many years it has enjoyed a higher per capita value of international trade than any other country. Even today very few other countries participate to a greater extent in world trade in proportion to the size of their population.

Trade has long brought New Zealand wealth and prosperity. In other countries wealth is associated with high levels of industrial development. The unusual feature about New Zealand is that this trade and this wealth have been largely based on agriculture and the export of farm products. New Zealand is the biggest exporter of meat and dairy products in the world, and the second biggest wool exporter. There are approximately 60,000,000 sheep and 9,000,000 cattle earning more than eighty per cent of the country's export income in meat, wool, butter, cheese and products derived from them. Already 100 products, including a high protein, flavoured milk biscuit are made from 5.5 million tons of milk produced on New Zealand farms each year. The production of skim-milk powder, which can be recombined to form milk, has been expanded to meet the needs of developing countries.

The success of New Zealand's agricultural industry is due to the country's mild climate and abundant rainfall that encourages the growth of lush pastures. But the New Zealand farm would not be as productive if the farmer did not use machines for every possible purpose. Advanced farming techniques have enabled New Zealand to carry 6-8 sheep to the acre and an acre is nearly sufficient to maintain one cow.

But although New Zealand has always depended on its agricultural produce, many other avenues of wealth from the soil are constantly being developed. Pure wool carpets, finely made leather goods and gourmet foods such as strawberries and asparagus that are flown to restaurants around the world are helping to broaden the base of primary industry.

In the future New Zealand's exports will continue to be largely commodities which have their origin in the land and soil, but of increasing importance will be manufactured goods based on the skills and enterprise of the people.

Forestry: New Zealand has one of the largest man-made forests in the world and this, along with other giant plantations, provides the basis for a rapidly expanding timber, pulp and paper industry. In fact, as the value of New Zealand's forest products continues to climb it has become one of the most important industries.

Manufacturing: As the agricultural industry has developed and grown so has the manufacturing sector. From meeting the simple needs of the early settlers 130 years ago production has become more diversified and more sophisticated to include not only consumer goods but also, for example, plant, machinery and industrial electronic equipment.

Engineers have invented, for the local market and for export, farming and roading machinery. They have also developed the jet-boat that can negotiate tumultuous rivers and shallow rapids. Steel is being made from huge deposits of ironsands found along the western beaches of North and South Islands. In the years ahead, New Zealand will be in a position to make high-grade steels at a cost fully competitive with overseas figures.

Power: Farms as well as industry take full advantage of reliable power provided by

Above:
New Zealand
is the only
country in the world
to base a steel industry
on natural deposits
of ironsands.

Top of page:
Spreading fertiliser
from the air on
hill country in Queenstown,
South Island.

Left:
Auckland is New Zealand's leading industrial centre. This aerial view shows Queen's Wharf on the left and Princess Wharf on the right.

Centre:
Natural steam reserves have been harnessed to generate electricity.

Below:
Natural gas separators at Kapunui in the North Island.

hydro-electric stations. Water power provides 85 per cent of the country's needs and geothermal steam from volcanic regions has also been tapped to provide a boost to the national supply.

The provision of a cheap source of electricity has led to an exciting project to manufacture aluminium. Bauxite, the raw material for aluminium is being imported from Australia and the smelter is using electricity provided from an underground powerhouse at Lake Manapouri. Ultimately the smelter operation will be one of the largest in the world.

Industry: New Zealand has a larger number of domestic meat-producing animals, in relation to population, than any other country in the world. But although farming is the basis of her economy, only about one-ninth of the labour force works on the land. Most people are engaged in industry, commerce, services or the professions.

Mineral Resources: New Zealand's important minerals are coal, petroleum and natural gas, titano-magnetite and ilmenite sands, non-metallics such as halloysite and bentonite clays, dolomite, limestone and high-grade silica.

Communications: New Zealand belongs to the International Communications Consortium and has an earth satellite station for meeting telephone, telegraph and television demands. About 400,000,000 copies of newspapers and magazines are sold each year. New Zealand is rated fifth in the world in newspaper readership.

Internal Travel: Although the total length of New Zealand is little more than 1,030 miles, there are more than 58,000 miles of roads, 3,220 miles of railways, and 7,750 miles of regular air routes.

Research: Ruakura in the North Island is the largest agricultural research centre in the Southern Hemisphere.

TELEVISION AND RADIO IN NEW ZEALAND

THE NEW ZEALAND Broadcasting Corporation covers the entire country with 47 radio stations in 22 towns while four television channels in the main centres provide a service for 90 per cent of the population.

Because of the difficult terrain—New Zealand is a mountainous country with a scattered population—special engineering problems have had to be overcome to give such radio and television coverage.

In both media, the NZBC operates both commercial and non-commercial services. As well, the Corporation runs the NZBC Symphony Orchestra, the only fully professional symphony orchestra in the country, and makes substantial contributions towards the development of the arts.

New Zealand's place in relation to its geographical neighbours is recognised by the NZBC, not only through shortwave transmission and its membership of the Asian Broadcasting Union, but also through the staff training facilities it offers to broadcasters from developing nations.

NZBC radio and television features are now heard and seen in many countries through its programme exchange service. Over the years the NZBC has become increasingly self-reliant in its programming and the larger proportion of its radio output is home-produced. As a recently-established service—it is just a decade old—NZBC television still has to draw to a considerable extent on imported programmes. However, news, documentaries and major dramatic productions are an indigenous element in N.Z. viewing.

Currently, a new television complex is being constructed at the capital city of Wellington and much of the up-to-date, fully transistorised radio and television equipment being installed by the NZBC is New Zealand designed. Although colour television and multi-channel transmission are still in the future for New Zealand, the NZBC already has the operational facilities to meet these developments.

The NZBC is increasing its output of locally produced programmes to reduce its dependence on overseas imports and to foster local talent. The illustration above shows a television musical in production.

Below: The NZBC Symphony Orchestra rehearsing for a festive occasion.

From its elevated position the Hotel Inter-Continental Auckland commands unsurpassed views of the city and harbour.

Below left:
The Captain's Galley Restaurant.

Below:
The Abel Tasman Room.

HIGH LIVING AT THE PACIFIC CROSSROADS

NEW ZEALAND is at the crossroads of the entire South Pacific region: by air, a mere three hours from Sydney and Melbourne, a little further from Samoa and Tahiti, but closer still to Fiji. Sight-seeing in this spectacular country is endless. On every mountainside and riverbank exotic natural wonders abound: like Glowworm Grotto in the eerie Waitomo Caves; Rotorua's awesome geysers and eternal, boiling mud pools; and the mammoth Franz Josef glacier on the South Island.

Among New Zealand's man-made achievements must be counted its largest city, Auckland. Here, around the twin harbours of Waitemata and Manukau, and beneath the shadow of the extinct volcano, Mount Eden, Auckland lies in all its modern complexity and sophistication and all its ancient beauty and tranquility.

And at the centre of this thriving metropolis is New Zealand's newest, most elegant hotel, the Hotel Inter-Continental Auckland. Built to cater for the nation's fast growing numbers of tourists, the Inter-Continental offers the comforts and amenities the international traveller expects when he stays at the finest hotels of the world's most modern cities. Rising twelve storeys over Waitemata Harbour, it has 332 richly-carpeted guest rooms with ensuite baths and toilets, and laundry, valet and 24-hour room services. In the shopping arcade are fashionable boutiques, beauty and barber shops. The Inter-Continental has outstanding facilities for conferences, conventions and other functions. The ballroom accommodates 350 guests for banquets and up to 600 for meetings and receptions. There are three private dining rooms which cater for smaller gatherings of 15 to 55.

The sumptuous Top of the Town restaurant is the rendezvous of Auckland's smart set. In a nostalgic turn-of-the-century setting, superb continental cuisine and in season, succulent national dishes such as venison and toheroa soup, are served overlooking an unsurpassed view of Auckland.

For more casual occasions there is the Captain's Galley, or its adjoining Schooner Coffee Bar for the hurried traveller. There are bars for every mood: the chic rooftop Vista Bar; the Sporting Life with its light meals and newswire service; the Turf Club Bar for racing fans; and, for the carefree, the Saloon Bar's pool tables and cool ale.

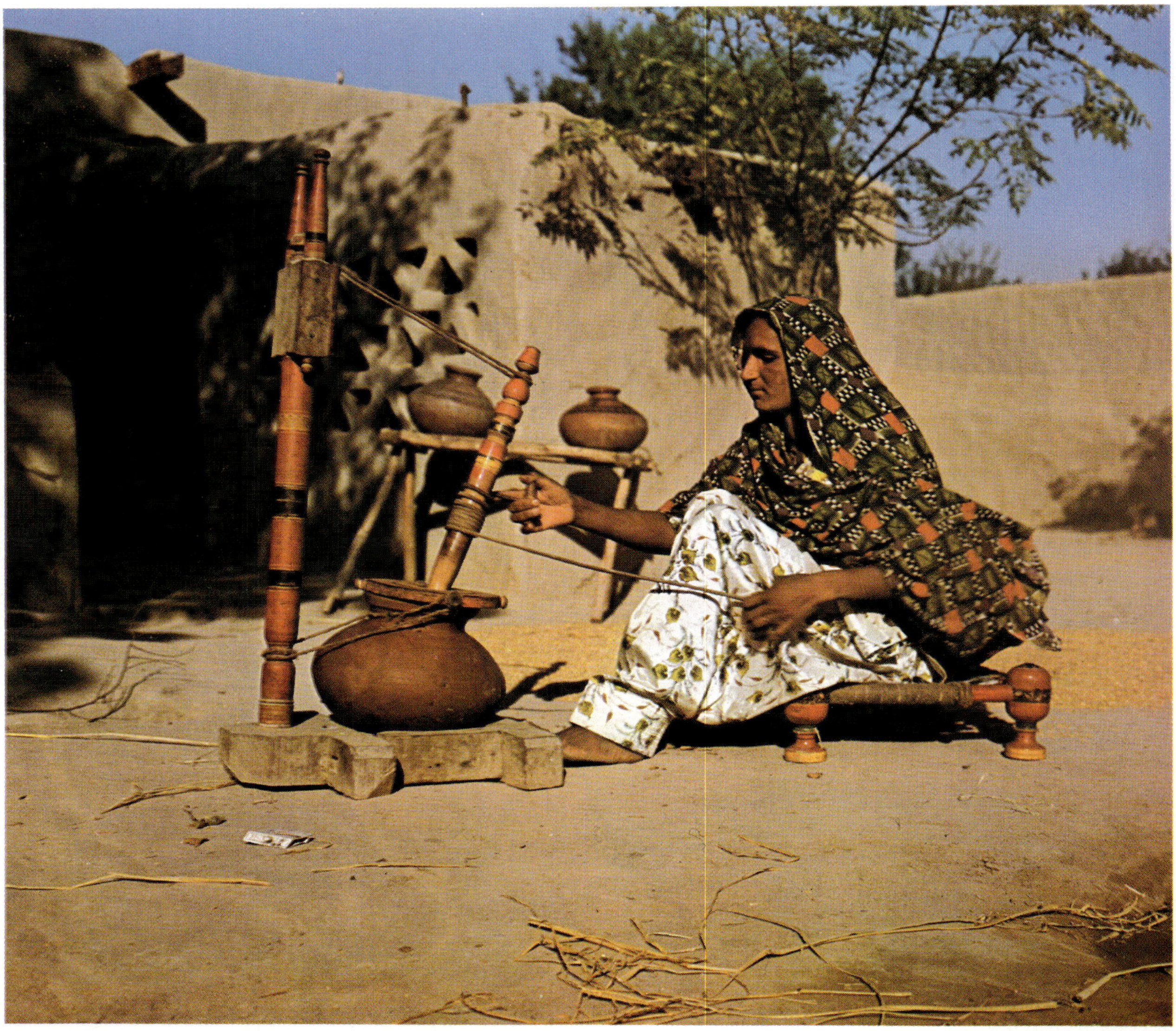

The Islamic Republic of
PAKISTAN

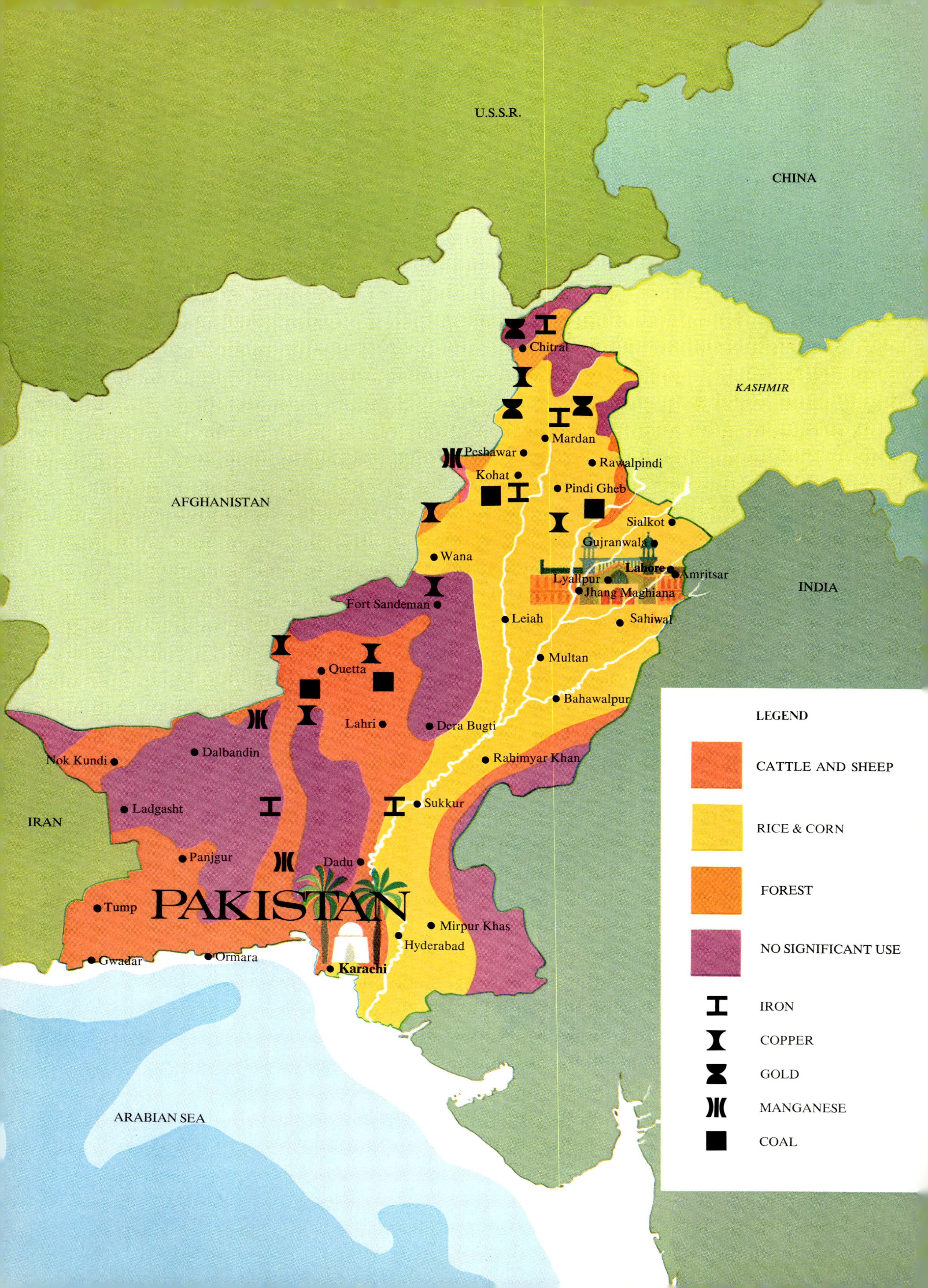
U.S.S.R.
CHINA
KASHMIR
AFGHANISTAN
INDIA
IRAN
ARABIAN SEA
PAKISTAN
Chitral
Mardan
Peshawar
Rawalpindi
Kohat
Pindi Gheb
Sialkot
Gujranwala
Lahore
Amritsar
Lyallpur
Jhang Maghiana
Wana
Fort Sandeman
Leiah
Sahiwal
Multan
Quetta
Bahawalpur
Lahri
Dera Bugti
Dalbandin
Nok Kundi
Rahimyar Khan
Ladgasht
Sukkur
Panjgur
Dadu
Tump
Mirpur Khas
Hyderabad
Gwadar
Ormara
Karachi
LEGEND
CATTLE AND SHEEP
RICE & CORN
FOREST
NO SIGNIFICANT USE
IRON
COPPER
GOLD
MANGANESE
COAL

The Nature of Pakistan

PAKISTAN is a land of great rivers like the Indus, mighty dams like the Mangla, lofty peaks like K2 and Nanga Parbat. It is the nursery of wild elephants and tigers, splendid horses and cattle, famous regiments and crack pilots, champion cricketers and squash players, great jurists, poets and philosophers.

What kind of a land and what sort of people are these that live in Pakistan? Before the East seceded it was in two parts, perhaps the only country in the world separated by a thousand miles of foreign territory. West Pakistan—or to use its full name, the Islamic Republic of Pakistan, is 330,000 square miles in area, lying mainly in the valley of the Indus. It is a land of vast deserts and arid plateaux of mountains with hardly any forests except in the north. Right up in the north the land borders on China and in that part are the famous holiday resorts, the lovely valleys of Hunza, Gilgit, Swat and Chitral. Two mountain ranges form an arch on the northern borders of the Republic, the mighty Karakorums on the north-east and the Hindukush on the north-west. The lofty Karakorums are a welter of glaciers but even here there are passes like the Mintika Pass through which the most remarkable Karakorum Highway has been built by Pakistani and Chinese engineers, making it possible for trucks to go right through. In the Hindukush there are gorges through which the Kabul River enters, while at the lower end of the Hindukush are the Safed Koh (white or snow-covered mountains) where is situated the most famous pass in the world, the Khyber Pass. South of the Karakorums and parallel spread the mighty Himalayas. In between flows the Indus, heading north-west for six hundred miles after issuing from the glaciers in Tibet and then at a point where it joins the Gilgit, it breaks through the Himalayan barrier and storms its way almost at right angles to its previous course, flowing south-west another 1,200 miles to the Arabian Sea near Karachi.

The well-populated plains are the creation of the Indus. This famous river, which flows through Pakistan, emerges from the hills at a place called Darband, some sixty miles above the gorge of Attock. It is joined at Attock by the Kabul flowing in from the west, and by five great rivers coming from the east—the Sutlej, Beas, Ravi, Chenab and Jhelum. The Beas does not enter Pakistan but joins the Sutlej which then flows into Pakistan. The whole vast plain watered by the five great rivers is the Indus Basin, a fertile region where a great civilisation arose as far back as five thousand years ago. The land slopes down from the Himalayas to the foothills in which are many lovely valleys—from the west, Chitral, Swat, Gilgit, Siran, Kaghan. Below is the tableland of Potohar on which are built the towns of Jhelum, Rawalpindi, the capital city of Islamabad, and Cambelpur. Then begin the vast plains of the Punjab, the land of the Five Rivers. It is a vast unending stretch of level land, unrelieved by any hills except for a sudden outcrop of a conical peak at Sangla Hill and the Kirana Hills on either side of the Chenab. Watered by the biggest system of irrigation canals in the world, sap green fields of rice, cotton and sugar spread as far as the eye can see in summer, while in winter tall crops of wheat and barley, gram and the yellow flowering mustard gladden the eye. Every bit of land has been won over for cultivation, forests cut down, marshes drained, and many deserts irrigated. Only copses of trees can be seen here and there along the roads and around the 40,000 villages dotting the countryside. Big cities are few, comparatively speaking, and the most important ones lie along the main railway line and the national highway that skirts the border from Karachi to Hyderabad, Sukkur, Multan, Sahiwal, Lahore, Gujrat, Jhelum, Rawalpindi, Nowshera and Peshawar. Twenty miles beyond is the Khyber Pass and the frontiers of Pakistan which adjoin the country to Afghanistan.

The Punjab plains spread like a Chinese fan, with the base in the south a hundred miles below Multan where the five rivers meet and the plains narrow down, pressed by desert on the east and mountains on the west. Again the plains open out and spread on either side of the life-giving Indus in the plains of Sind. The land is more arid and the vegetation more desert-like, except in the irrigated tracts. Towns in this region are much wider apart and even villages are much fewer.

The camel, the palmgroves, and the ever-present great river, remind one of Egypt. It is a land of ancient civilisations, historical monuments and many saints and shrines. It remains to mention that apart from the Indus basin, there is a vast plateau that stretches out to the south-west towards Iran. Forming the province of Baluchistan, it is a rock strewn arid waste spreading over a hundred thousand square miles and more. Outcrops of bleak mountains with crags and cliffs and contorted shapes, give a fierce and deterring look to the landscape. Water is scarce and the population is about ten to a square mile, but here and there are oases of greenery where some of the most luscious fruits of Pakistan are grown, especially grapes and apples, plums and apricots.

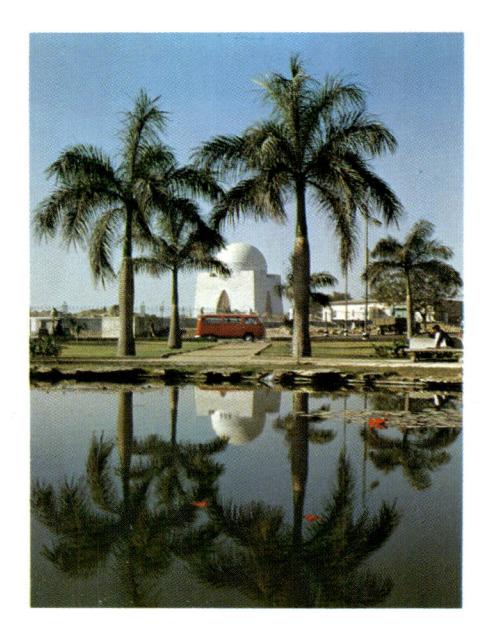

The magnificent mausoleum of Quaid-e-Azam at Karachi.

BACKGROUND TO HISTORY

Left:
Tipu Sultan's last swordstroke, fighting for his life against the British rulers.

Right:
King Akbar the Great, the most famous of all Mughal Emperors.

Below:
The Fasting Buddha, excavated from the Gandhara region, now preserved in the Taxila Archaeological Museum.

THE WORLD'S third oldest civilisation began in the Indus Valley and from 2500 to 1500 B.C. it flourished. Whilst its rural phase has been unearthed in a number of minor sites, it found its fullest expression in the urban phase, in the famous cities of Moenjo Daro and Harappa (one in the Punjab, the other in Sind) dug out of the earth in 1922. These amazing ancient sites have revealed glimpses of the life of a people who could build well-planned cities, make bronze implements, grow wheat and cotton, weave cloth, write a language, and create marvellous sculpture.

Somewhere around 1500 B.C. it is surmised that this rich civilisation came to a violent end at the hands of the Aryans who invaded the region after migrating in mass from their homes in Central Asia. These nomadic people at first destroyed settled habitations but later developed a civilisation of their own. Living in the Punjab, the Land of the Five Rivers, in north-western Pakistan, they composed the religious hymns known as the Rig Veda, one of the oldest books of mankind, and laid the foundations of the Hindu religion. Later they spread out east to the valley of the Ganges, where the Hindu religion developed fully.

In the middle of the 6th Century B.C. great events took place east and west of this region, which exercised a decisive influence upon its history. Cyrus founded the Achaemenian Empire in Persia and Gautama Buddha was born in Nepal round about 550 B.C. Cyrus and his grandson, Darius, invaded western Pakistan and it is learned in the rock inscriptions left by the latter at many places in Iran that he claimed it (Sindhu, land of the Sind or Indus) as his twentieth province. Persian conquests were repeated later in the 2nd and 5th Centuries A.D. and thus Persian cultural influences became an important part of the life of Pakistan, particularly in the matter of civil and military administration, architecture, state ceremonial, and official language (Kharoshti). The Buddhist religion soon spread to this region and by the beginning of the Christian era, Gandhara (modern Peshawar valley), Taxila and Swat had become the strongholds and holy places of Buddhism.

In 327 B.C. Alexander of Macedon invaded the area. The many historical accounts left behind by men accompanying the expedition brought Pakistan into the realms of recorded history.

The Greek rulers left behind by Alexander were overthrown by a local military commander named Chandragupta who set up the Mauryan Empire in 322 B.C. with its capital at Pataliputra, modern Patna. His grandson, Asoka, became one of the greatest kings in history, not only for the extent of his empire but for the benevolence of his rule and his missionary work in the cause of Buddhism. The gigantic rock pillars which he set up all over his great empire were inscribed with the noble moral teachings of Buddhism.

The Mauryan empire soon declined and came to an end after the death of Asoka. From the early 2nd Century A.D., a series of invasions—or rather migrations—rolled like a flood over Pakistan. First came the Bactrians, the Greeks of the Macedonian invasion, who had settled in and around Balkh and Bokhara. Towards the middle of the 1st Century A.D., the Chinese-oriented Kushans, whose greatest ruler was Kanishka, arrived in large numbers. Kanishka became a Buddhist and under his patronage arose the famous Buddhist school of sculpture called Gandhara after the region in which it flourished.

With much rise and fall of fortune, the Kushan empire lasted till 460 A.D. when Pakistan was over-run by the terrible White Huns, and civilised life temporarily came to an end. The power of the Huns was smashed in 528 by the united strength of local rajas led by Yasodharman, King of Malwa.

In the 4th, 5th and 6th Centuries there was no important dynasty of rulers in Pakistan, but in mid-northern India there existed in this period the great Gupta dynasty whose last ruler was the celebrated Harsha (606-647), a Hindu with strong leanings towards Buddhism. The Gupta empire occasionally extended into parts of Pakistan and at other times shrank to the regions of mid-northern India.

For a hundred years after the death of Harsha, northern Indo-Pakistan was in utter disorder and divided up into small warring states. During these very years the world was witnessing the marvellous phenomenon of the spread of Islam from Arabia, where it arose in 611, to the west as far as Spain, and east as far as Sind, both by the year 712.

Led by the young leader Mohammed bin Qasim, the Arabs landed somewhere near Karachi and conquered not only Sind but all the country up to Multan. In the conquered areas twin kingdoms were established by the Arabs, one in the north ruled from Multan, and the other in the south ruled from Mansurah. These two kingdoms lasted till the end of the 10th Century.

At this time another great Muslim conqueror emerged from the north-west, Mahmud of Ghazni. He was one of the greatest generals of history and became the most powerful ruler of Asia in his time. Apart from conquering vast territories in the Middle East, Mahmud led seventeen victorious expeditions into Indo-Pakistan and completely shattered the Hindu power in the Punjab and Delhi. The heterodox Qarmatians who had usurped the Arab Kingdoms of Multan and Mansurah were also destroyed by him. Mahmud's successors ruled north-western Pakistan (or the Punjab) till 1186 when he was defeated by a great new empire-builder, Shahabuddin Ghori.

Ghori went on to meet the confederation of Hindu rajas led by the dread Prithvi Raj of Delhi and defeated them in 1192. His general, Qutbuddin Aibak, spread the conquests as far as Bihar, while another general, Bakhtiyar Khilji, went right up to Bengal in the east, bringing a vast territory under Muslim dominion before Ghori died in 1206.

Muslim rule was now established firmly in the whole of northern Indo-Pakistan and lasted till the British took over in the middle of the 18th Century in Bengal and in the middle of the 19th Century in the west. Worthy of special note is the two hundred years rule by the Mughals who established their sway over Indo-Pakistan in 1526, and ruled till about 1800 in fact, and till 1857 in name. Their rule is marked by a remarkable efflorescence of culture and all round progress and prosperity in every domain. Political organisation, social institutions, art, letters and architecture, and above all the art of living, were developed to the greatest heights. An idea of this progress can be gained by reference to the "Ain-e-Akbari" or "The Institutes of Akbar", which is perhaps the most detailed compendium of information about the daily life of a country for a period as far back as the 16th Century.

Meanwhile the British East India Company had been formed in England in 1600, and established its first trading post in Indo-Pakistan at Surat (near the later site of Bombay) in 1612. Similar trading posts were established at places that subsequently became Madras and Calcutta. The local soldiers whom they recruited to guard their trading stations developed into small well-trained armies, and were soon exploited to

453

Above:
Tombs of Chaukandi
near Karachi.

Left:
The tower known
as "Minar-i-Pakistan"
in Iqbal Park, Lahore.
This 195 ft. tall edifice
marks the place where the
famous Pakistan Resolution
was passed by the
Muslim League on
22nd March 1949.

Right:
The tomb
of Nizamuddin, Makli,
Thatta, Pakistan.

support one or other of the warring nawabs and rajas. Gradually, the English came to a position where they could challenge the Nawab of Bengal himself. With contrived treachery, they defeated him in the Battle of Plassey in 1757, and thus became rulers of the great kingdom of Bengal.

Spreading west, they gradually occupied Delhi in 1803 and took the Punjab from the Sikhs in 1849. Earlier they had advanced from Bombay and annexed Sind in an unprovoked invasion in 1843.

In 1857 the whole of Indo-Pakistan rose against the new Western usurpers but the great war of independence was unsuccessful. The struggle was resumed again after the failure of the 1857 war. This time it was a civil and political fight. The movement grew in intensity after World War I, which the brave soldiers of Indo-Pakistan helped the British to win, in the belief that they were fighting for the ideals of freedom and democracy. At first it was a joint struggle of the Muslims and the Hindus. The Muslims discovered, however, that the Hindus were not prepared to grant them even the minimum demands to enable the Muslims to live in a free united India as a permanent minority. The brief experience of existing under Hindu majority rule from 1937 to 1939, when provincial autonomy was granted by the British, convinced the Muslims that it would be impossible to endure such conditions again if the British handed over power to the larger community. In 1940, the Muslims decided to abandon efforts to obtain assurances from the Hindus and to work for a separate state of their own. This was achieved on 14th August 1947, when the British agreed to give independence to the two dominions— India and Pakistan.

THE PEOPLE

Living in a vast and varied country, the people of Pakistan are naturally marked by diversity in the midst of unity. The diversity adds colour while the unity gives strength to the nation. Take the common factors first, as they are predominant. The vast majority are Muslims, except for a few million Hindus who represent about one-sixth of the population. There are half a million Buddhists, half a million Christians and about 15,000 Zoroastrians. All the regions of Pakistan chose voluntarily to become a part of Pakistan at the time of the partition of Indo-Pakistan, because they valued their common heritage and wanted freedom to continue to live as Muslims, with their distinctive culture and social life. Ceremonials at birth, death and marriage, daily prayers, and seasonal feasts, notions of spiritual life, morality, etiquette and personal hygiene, are basically the same. They are all inspired by the same heroes, they look back to the same history, and above all are linked by a sense of common struggle in winning their new homeland of Pakistan.

Secondly, the overwhelming majority of Pakistanis are countryfolk and mostly farmers. That means they tend to be simple, but with sound common sense; industrious but unhurried; optimistic but resigned to fate; conservative and suspicious of change until fully convinced.

THE CULTURE OF PAKISTAN

In the cultural field, Pakistan has a rich heritage to draw upon. It has been already pointed out that a highly developed way of life was attained by the people of Pakistan in the Indus Valley civilisation of 5,000 years ago. Well planned cities, a well organised society, and realistic sculpture of astonishing maturity, similar to the Greek, were some of the features of this civilisation.

It came to an end in mysterious circumstances around 1500 B.C. Then about 500 B.C. there arose in the north the city of Taxila which became a famous centre of Buddhist learning and culture for a thousand years, drawing people from all parts of Asia. In fact, the entire north-west of Pakistan, particularly Swat Valley and Peshawar Valley (olden Gandhara), was the home of that extra-ordinary Gandhara Sculpture which forms one of the most amazing examples of East-West synthesis.

Apart from sculpture, these regions and, in fact, all of Pakistan became the centre of a flourishing Buddhist culture.

The progress of the arts of peace was rudely interrupted in 460 A.D. by the devastating invasion of the White Huns who about this time, were battering at the Roman Empire.

Buddhist culture in Pakistan received a severe setback. Hinduism reasserted itself and after the combined forces of the Hindu rajas of India defeated the Huns in 528, the Hindu influence spread more and more to Pakistan from north-central India where the Hindu dynasty of the Imperial Guptas had arisen in the 4th Century, and lasted till the 6th. In the 7th Century arose the last great Hindu king of India, Harsha, who died in 647. He was broad-minded and tolerant, and it was during his time that the famous Chinese monk, Hieun Tsang visited Indo-Pakistan, and wrote a detailed account of all he saw during sixteen years of travel.

He described the decline of Buddhism and the many deserted monasteries he saw all over the country. Sesanka, King of Bengal, and a contemporary of Harsha, burnt Buddhist monasteries and even cut down the Bodhi (or Bo) tree at Gaya, under which Buddha had experienced his revelation. The greatest Buddhist monastery of Indo-Pakistan whose ruins have been excavated at Paharpur bears testimony to their patronage of Buddhism. Today Buddhism has been driven out of this sub-continent by the Hindus, and its last refuge is in the Chittagong Hill Tracts.

Buddhist culture dominated Pakistan from the time of Asoka in the 3rd Century B.C. to the invasion of the Huns in the 5th Century. Hindu culture revived and flourished during the next five centuries until the coming of the Muslims in north-western Pakistan and for three centuries in south-western Pakistan, which was conquered by the Muslims in 712. Although Islam came with its own distinctive philosophy of life, it could not help absorbing innumerable marks of Hindu culture which survive today in the music of Pakistan, its poetry, architecture, dress, jewellery, food, festivals, manners and customs, and above all its language, the great repository of culture values. The national language, Urdu, and also the regional languages, Punjabi, Sindhi, Baluchi (but not Brohi and Pushto) are basically Aryan drawn from Sanskrit and Prakrit, products of Hindu culture. Of course, during a thousand years of use they have been heavily overlaid with Arabic and Persian words and ideas.

With the coming of the Muslims, however, the stream of culture flows uninterrupted to the present. During these thousand years or so, a new way of life was developed, based on Islam in a hundred and one ways, drawing heavily on Arab and even more so on Persian culture, but producing a unique synthesis of local and imported ideas and manners which constitute the culture of Pakistan today.

The most important aspects of culture are always intangible, and in Pakistani culture these are preoccupied with religion—if not always spiritually, then at least ritually—martial traditions and love of sport; rigid organisation of society with authoritarian approach in family life, educational life, religious life and political life; love of tradition and strong conservatism; contentedness and a philosophic resignation towards the trials of existence; and good natured informality, friendliness, love of celebration and hospitality.

But these are qualities that are more difficult to observe than the more tangible expressions of culture in the form of the arts. Among the latter, in which the genius of the Muslims of Pakistan has found fullest expression during the last thousand years and in which the most notable successes have been achieved are, in order of importance, architecture, music, painting and calligraphy. Dance and sculpture have not been practised as art forms to any extent, because of religious discouragement.

Ceramics too for some unknown reason have been neglected except in the form of coloured glazed tiles that decorate some older monuments. Among traditional handicrafts, the gorgeous fabrics of Sind were the glories of bygone Muslim culture and the unfailing attraction of the traders.

Carving in wood, stone, ivory and engraving in brass and copper and also embossing or repousse work, embroidery, swords and muskets, gold and silver jewellery, are only some in the long list of articles of daily use that were embellished with skill and turned into objects d'art.

Some remarkable examples of traditional architecture are to be found in every one of the old cities. Only 30 miles from Karachi, at Chaukhandi there are oblong tiered graves, profusely carved with floral and geometrical designs that make them look like fabulous creations in lace. In Thatta, the Jam-e or Chief Mosque built by Shah Jehan, the builder of the Taj Mahal, is covered with the most gorgeous glazed tile work. Beyond, in Multan, there are the grand mausoleums of famous saints like Shah Rukan-e-Alam, Shams Sabzwari and others, dating back to the days before the Mughals. In Lahore are the magnificent Mughal monuments such as the Fort with its numerous buildings, the great Badshahl Mosque built by Aurangzeb, and the tomb of Jahangir.

Another precious heritage of Pakistani culture is classical music, which in its present form is a magical blend of Hindu Indian music with Muslim, Arab and Persian. Many of the *ragas* or modes of musical compositions have been either invented or modified by Muslim musicians like the great Tan Sen at the court of Akbar, the Grand Moghul. The famous raga Darbari, Mian Ki Todi, Mian Ki Malhar together with numerous other compositions are attributed to him. The most versatile instrument of classical music, the stringed Sarangi and the inevitable accompaniment of all classical music, the pair of drums, one for the right hand and one for the left, are both the invention of that remarkable genius of the 14th Century, Amir Khusro, mystic, poet, musician, and minister of six kings.

The art of painting developed into the field of book illustration and was carried on by a long line of early painters, under the patronage of kings and nobles. Later, as a result of the keen interest of Akbar and even more so of his son Jahangir, miniature paintings began to be made on separate sheets to be preserved in portfolios. The favourite subject and one in which the greatest heights were attained was portraiture and court scenes containing multiple portraits. But other subjects too were treated such as flowers, birds, animals, buildings and so on. Almost all the great museums of the world possess one or more masterpieces of Mughal miniature painting.

The art continued to flourish until the coming of the British although it underwent many changes during the last three hundred years.

Calligraphy was the most honoured art among the Muslims, who developed it with infinite love and ingenuity in order to glorify the Word of God and to copy the Holy Quoran. Numerous styles were invented and the highest degree of technical perfection was achieved in rendering each style. Kings and princes were proud to

Left page: Students at the Government Girls' College at Rawalpindi.

Below: A skilled Sindhi craftsman at work.

Right: A sturdy young Punjabi wearing the traditional turban and waist-coat.

become pupils of great calligraphists, and in fact proficiency in the art was the mark of a cultured gentleman. Since painting evolved as a hand-maid of calligraphy, the calligraphist ranked higher than a painter in ancient times.

This art would probably have died out in the modern world but for the invention of lithography which led to the printing of hand-written books in Urdu, Persian and Arabic—all using the same script. In newspapers, those who write the headings and other decorative or special lines, are the master calligraphists who maintain the high traditions of the art. They also write separate panels for framing and display, and special inscriptions such as those on coins, bank notes, book titles, calendars, posters and buildings. The greatest calligrapher of Pakistan today is Ustad (or Master) Yusuf, whose work adorns the bank notes of Pakistan and the Vice regal Lodge and Secretariat buildings in New Delhi (done long before the partition of the sub-continent).

Since Independence there has been a remarkable burgeoning of art in Pakistan, and above all of painting. In 1947 there was only one famous artist in the country, Chughtai, practising an enlarged version of miniature painting, though with a very distinct and individual style. Today there are at least a dozen artists of the first rank and scores of devoted professionals. Every day there is one or more painting exhibitions in the cities of Karachi, Lahore, and Rawalpindi. Among the famous names are the semi-abstract Shakir Ali and the figurative painter Sadequain who has won renown for his many great murals, including a gigantic one at Mangla. There are abstract painters like Parvez, portrait painters like Gulgee and landscapists like Jamil.

Music is a universally loved art in Pakistan. It exists at three levels: classical music of the cultural elite, film music of the city proletariat and the masses in the countryside, and finally folk music, the real expression of the musical genius of the people.

The first has received great encouragement from radio and television, in the absence of the aristocratic patrons of olden times.

There are great artists like the singer Roshanara Begum, "Queen of Melody", Ustad Nazakat Ali and Salamat Ali, Ustad Amanat Ali and Fateh Ali Khan, Umeed Ali Khan, and others. In the field of films the name of Nur Jahan dominates the scene as an outstanding popular singer, and the youthful Kausau Niazi must also be mentioned. Among composers of music for the films the leaders are Khurshid Anwar, who has tried to present classical ragas in a popular form; Mehdi Zaheer, who has combined elements of Arabic and Persian music with that of Pakistan, and Sohail Rana, who has written ragas and other compositions in staff notation. Folk songs echo through all the land. The Pathans have their own distinctive songs and folk instruments; so have the Punjabis and the Sindhis. The *char baitas* of the Pathans, the jovial *dholak* or drum songs of the Punjab and the mystical *kafis* of Sind, each have their distinctive charms.

Handicrafts, both sophisticated and folk, flourish in Pakistan, and every region has its own speciality. Thus in the North West Frontier they make silken handkerchiefs and turbans in rich dark reds, blues and greens; gold embroidered caps and sandals and fine glazed pottery. In the Punjab there is a distinctive craft in every small district, but the handloom coverlets with floral or geometrical designs in one or many colours are bound to appeal to everyone. Silk embroidered coverlets called *phulkari* are no longer made for sale but only for the trousseau. This laboriously produced article is a work of art and old examples are museum pieces. In Sind, the tie-dyed sheet of dark red and blue design called *ajrak*, is a distinctive product, invariably used by the country folk. A peculiar design and a distinctive embroidery for the long frock used by the Sindhi women is another product of Sind. The handicrafts of Sind are, however, too numerous to describe as every article of daily use in the village has some embellishment, even the trappings of the horse and the camel which are the common means of transport in the arid wastes of the countryside. Caps and turbans of men, the fairy-like slippers of women, even baskets and wickerwork of palm leaves, wooden stools and chairs with coloured lacquer work, and of course pottery of gorgeous colours and glazes, are only some of the products of Sind's handicrafts.

EDUCATION IN PAKISTAN

The educational requirements of a nation of 55 million people are bound to be colossal. Much more is being spent on education today (about Rs. 1,000 million every year) than was spent on all the "welfare departments" by the British. And yet there are not enough schools to accommodate all the children in the country. In 1970 there were about 10 million children studying in the Primary Schools (first five classes, 2 million in the Middle Schools (VI to VIII), 575,000 in High Schools (IX and X), and 350,000 in the Higher Secondary Schools. Apart from schools run by the Government (in this case the Governments of the provinces, for education is a provincial subject), there are a very large number of schools conducted by local bodies, religious and charitable institutions and by private individuals. Almost all the good private institutions are aided by the Government, as it is felt that the help of the private sector in solving the problems of mass teaching is essential. The demand for learning has increased manifold since independence, and today everyone is eager to give his child the best education, even if it is available only in expensive private schools.

The most spectacular advances have been made in the field of higher education. There are fourteen universities as against only three at the time of independence.

Of these one in each wing of the country is an agricultural university and in each an engineering university. There are 350 Intermediate Colleges (Higher Secondary Classes, XI, XII) and 315 Degree Colleges (both XI, XII and another two classes for graduation), besides Profession Colleges, which number another 77, including agriculture, engineering, medicine, commerce, law, fine arts, home economics and others. A special feature of the New Education Policy introduced in 1969 is the shifting of the emphasis in secondary education to

Above:
A typical Kalash tribes girl from Chitral wearing the colourful and distinctive dress of the Kalash people.

Above:
A camel caravan led by a Baluchi woman, in the rugged desert country of Baluchistan.

Below:
Primitive life in Sind.

science, technical and vocational education, so as to achieve a predominant ratio of 60:40 in relation to general academic courses. This is mandatory in an age of science and technology, and it is gratifying to note that the number of higher professional institutions has more than doubled in the fifteen years from 1955 to 1970, now numbering 77 as against 34 previously. The lower technical institutions in which enrolment is after Class X and which do not award degrees but diplomas, have increased from 231 to 390 in the same period.

The ratio of enrolment is even higher. Apart from schools, colleges and universities there are scientific research institutes, of which the most important is the PCSIR, the Pakistan Council for Scientific and Industrial Research. It has well-equipped laboratories for research in different fields of science as applied to industry, and it is staffed by highly-qualified scientists. The chief laboratories are at Karachi, Lahore, Rawalpindi and Peshawar. During the last two decades they have made an important contribution to scientific research and industrial progress.

The Pakistan Atomic Energy Commission is another notable research body which has excellent equipped laboratories in Islamabad and also regional laboratories for research in medical and agricultural fields with nuclear aids. The Nuclear Power Station which began functioning near Karachi at the end of 1971 is also the result of the efforts of the Pakistan Atomic Energy Commission.

There are other important research institutions in the fields of the humanities such as the Islamic Research Institute, the Iqbal Academy, and the Nazrul Islam Academy (named after two greatest poets of the Urdu and Bengali languages). There is also the Pakistan Historical Research Society, the Pakistan Asiatic Society, the Institute of International Affairs, two institutes of Educational Research, and many more.

THE CITIES OF PAKISTAN

The recognisable features on the face of a country are the cities and this holds particularly true in the case of Pakistan. The most convenient point to begin a survey of this new Republic is Karachi, as most visitors enter by the international airport.

Little more than a fishing village a hundred years ago, Karachi today is one of the great cities of the world, with its population of $3\frac{1}{2}$ million, a growing industrial complex and booming commerce. Its importance to Pakistan is enormous because it is the only seaport and international airport; everything that goes in or out of the Republic thus passes through Karachi.

At the advent of independence in 1947, Karachi was only one-tenth of its present size, but it acquired sudden importance as the capital of the new country—which it remained until 1960 when the Government moved temporarily to Rawalpindi and then to the new city of Islamabad in the outskirts, a decade or so later. However, Karachi is still the commercial and industrial capital of Pakistan, and intense activity in the spheres of the press, the arts and education made it intellectually the most stimulating place in the country.

As one moves north along the national highway and the railway line that hug the Indus, one comes upon Hyderabad, 113 miles away by train. The ramparts of the old fort on the outskirts of the city indicate its age; it was founded in 1757 by the great Kalhora ruler, Ghulam Shah. This is the heart of Sind, with the full flavour of Sindhi culture—the old world courtesy, the colourful handloom fabrics and handicrafts, and the exotic cuisine. The great Ghulam Muhammad Barrage on the Indus is one of the sights of Hyderabad, while the residential university situated on the other side of the Indus is another prominent landmark.

Three hundred miles north of Karachi, one comes upon Sukkur, where the first great barrage on the Indus was built by the British in 1932, to irrigate vast surrounding tracts of potentially arable land. Since independence, another four barrages have been built and the greatest dam in the world is being constructed right up in the north at Tarbela. Sukkur is a picturesque city lying on the western or right bank of the Indus, while on the eastern lies the ancient and smaller city of Rohri, a great railway junction. The two are connected by two remarkable bridges, one 70 years old and now used only for road traffic and the other new, for the railway only. Between the two cities, in the middle of the Indus, lies the island of Bhakkar with its formidable old fort where the fleeing Humayun, son of Babar, took refuge during the early 16th Century.

The next in sequence is Multan, 578 miles by train from Karachi and the oldest living city of Pakistan. It was flourishing when Alexander besieged it in 326 B.C. and almost lost his life in the attempt. The city proper is built on a mound of considerable height, formed of the debris of ages past. It is surrounded by a wall, outside which are the ruins of an ancient fort. The only remarkable monuments of Pakistan dating anterior to the Mughals are found in Multan, and these include the Tomb of Shah Rukan-e-Alam, one of the finest structures ever built to honour the dead. Some of the most gorgeous examples of glazed tile decoration to be found in the whole of Indo-Pakistan adorns the old monuments of Multan and the art is still flourishing. Modern Multan is famous for its textiles and even more so for handloom fabrics and coverlets of fascinating designs and colours.

Some 757 miles from Karachi is Lahore, the heart of the Punjab and the most beloved city of Pakistan—perhaps because many people in the Punjab spent the happy days of their student life in one of its famous colleges or the old university. Although an ancient city, with the most magnificent architectural monuments of the Mughals, it has a youthful air because of its high student population, its lively sports activities and flourishing film industry. The Horse and Cattle Show, held every year in spring, with its many sensational riding events, tent pegging and night tattoo, is considered one of the most spectacular shows of its kind in the world. Among the lovely gardens of Lahore is the famous Shalimar Garden and the many monuments, such as the Fort and the Badshahi Mosque and the Ravi River which flows nearby, make Lahore a fascinating place for the visitor.

The route now turns north-west along the ancient Grand Trunk Road as we head towards the twin cities of Rawalpindi and Islamabad, some 180 miles away. Situated on a plateau, Rawalpindi has a delightfully bracing climate, where winters are severe and the summers are relieved by constant storms and cloudbursts. The whole region is inhabitated by a handsome, tall people of martial bearing. Because of its central position, Rawalpindi became the headquarters of the army. While the capital of Pakistan is ten miles away in Islamabad, many offices spill over into Rawalpindi and add to its bustle and activity.

The modern capital of Islamabad is situated on the cool slopes of the Margalla Hills, beautifully landscaped with an astonishing variety of trees and shrubs. The main plan of the city was drawn up by the famous Greek architect Doxiades, but the various public and private buildings have been designed by many architects from all over the world, including some from Pakistan itself.

The main Secretariat of the Government of Pakistan and many other Departments and Government offices have been moved to Islamabad, and are functioning in massive blocks built and furnished in ultra-modern style. The garden-like residential area sprawls over many miles and provides comfortable accommodation for every class of government servant. Apart from the Secretariat blocks, the most noteworthy structures are the Sheharazad Hotel and the State Bank of Pakistan Building. The Rawal Dam built nearby, and the lake created by the dammed waters to supply Islamabad is one of the interesting sights of the area.

Within easy reach of Rawalpindi are two other towns of special interest: the ruins of the ancient Buddhist city of Taxila which flourished from the 5th Century B.C. to the 5th Century A.D. and the delightful hill resort of Murree nestling in the Pines at a cool height of about 6,500 feet. The first is 20 miles and the second 37 miles from Rawalpindi.

Proceeding north-west along the national highway the Indus is crossed at Attock, where Akbar, the great Mughal, built a formidable fort on the rocky banks. A drive along the Kabul, a tributary of the Indus, passes through Nowshera, 80 miles from Rawalpindi. Another 27 miles and Peshawar is reached, the last city on the great national arterial road which turns into an international highway as it crosses the Khyber Pass and leads onward into Afghanistan.

Peshawar is one of the ancient cities of Pakistan. Herodotus has referred to it as Paskapuros. Situated in the middle of the green and well-watered valley of Peshawar, the city is famous for its picturesque old bazaars and many turning and twisting lanes that lie inside the old walled city, while the modern quarters called the Cantonment spread outside. The most famous is the street called the Qissa Khwani Bazaar (the Street of Story Tellers) with its rows of shops selling many varieties of colourful handicrafts—the silken handkerchiefs and turbans, gold embroidered caps and sandals, engraved decorative goods of brass and repousse work, utensils of copper for daily use, and of course leather bandoliers and pistol cases for the arms that everyone wears, like people of other countries wear a watch. The ancient fort, the modern residential university, the fine museum and the great Warsak Dam and Power House on the Kabul, are other notable attractions of Peshawar.

Eleven miles away begins the historic Khyber Pass through which have marched the armies of many great conquerors like, Alexander, Mahmud of Ghazni, Babar, the great Mughal, Nadir Shah, the Persian, and Ahmad Shah Abdali, the victor of the Third Battle of Panipat. The Khyber begins at Jamrud Fort and winds through one of the most amazing roads in the world up to Torkhum.

Top left: A view of the city of Karachi.

Below left: A bend in the road of the historic Khyber Pass.

Left: The beautiful gardens of Shalimar at Lahore, immortalised in the Kashmiri Love Lyrics.

Below: The Municipal Corporation Building at Karachi,

THE EAST PAKISTAN CRISIS

FOR MANY CENTURIES the two dominant religious and political groups on the sub-continent of India have been the Muslims and the Hindus. Divided by age-old animosities, a climax was reached in the 1940's as Britain prepared to withdraw from her 'brightest jewel'. It became apparent that there would be a power struggle in the country as each of the two factors sought to fill the position of authority vacated by the departing British Raj. Neither had any intentions of living under the other's rule. Talks were held in 1946 between the leader of the Muslim League, Mohammed Ali Jinnah and Pandit Jawaharlal Nehru of the Indian Congress Party, in an endeavour to heal their differences, but the effort was fruitless. So, in the end, India was partitioned; it seemed to be the only possible course of action to avoid bloodshed and perhaps even civil war. On August 15, 1947, when India became free of British rule the country was partitioned and the State of Pakistan came into being. But even this solution presented its problems: the two halves of Pakistan, East Pakistan and West Pakistan, were about 1,200 miles apart and had little in common. Islamic fervour was the only cementing factor in Pakistan but its utility proved short-lived.

The new State was faced with almost insuperable problems, such as the setting up of a whole government machinery, organising the defence forces whose units had been divided and which received almost no share of ordnance supplies. But above all was the problem of the ten million refugees who had poured out from India to seek asylum in the new Muslim homeland. Economic progress first achieved was considerable and the Korean boom came as a windfall at an opportune time. Unfortunately, however, political institutions could not be developed strongly and the parliamentary system of government in this case produced only instability and even chaos leading to the imposition of Martial Law in 1958.

In 1962 the leadership of the East Pakistan political party, the Awami League, passed from H.S. Suhrawardly to Sheikh Mujib-ur Rahman. Sheikh Mujib had served several jail sentences following convictions based on political offences and when he assumed leadership he immediately began campaigning for greater autonomy for East Pakistan. Despite a large measure of provincial autonomy granted in 1962, there was still a sense of economic exploitation, political deprivation, and cultural subjugation by West Pakistan, and this led to the formulation of the Six-Point Programme by the Awami League in East Pakistan, demanding provincial autonomy in all matters except Defence and Foreign Affairs. In 1966 the President of Pakistan, General Ayub Khan had Mujib arrested and jailed once more for leading violent demonstrations supporting provincial autonomy for East Pakistan. During this period in prison, he became a symbol of Bengali Nationalism in East Pakistan. The Sheikh was finally released in 1969 when West Pakistan political leaders pressed Ayub Khan to call the Sheikh to the Round Table Conference at which the transfer of power by Ayub Khan was being negotiated.

In March 1969 General Ayub Khan was forced to step down in favour of a martial law regime led by General Yahya Khan. The circumstances under which he came to power obliged the General to promise to hand over rule to the people after holding Pakistan's first-ever nation-wide election on the basis of adult franchise. In preparation for this, he lifted the ban on political activity on January 1, 1970, marking the beginning of a hectic and eventful year in the country's history.

After a postponement, the elections were held in December 1970. General Yahya and his aides waited for the results "with bated breath". He had expected that divisive trends, reflected in the multiplicity of parties, would prevent any group from getting a clear majority in its own right. He had thought he would be able to manipulate the Constituent Assembly to decide in favour of a dispensation that left the Armed Forces with the final say in the shaping of the country's destiny. In any event, he had reserved to himself the power to ratify or reject the Constitution.

But unfortunately for him, the Eastern Wing gave an overwhelming mandate to Sheikh Mujib; his Awami League won 167 of the 169 East Pakistan seats in the 313-member Pakistan National Assembly. He was helped by two factors; first the indignation of East Pakistanis over Islamabad's tardiness in providing relief to the millions left destitute by a cyclone of unprecedented ferocity in November 1970; secondly, the East Pakistanis' decision to turn the election into a referendum on the autonomy issue.

In the West, Mr. Bhutto's Pakistan Peoples Party gained almost two-thirds of the remaining 144 seats in the National Assembly. But he was not content to sit in opposition; he told a mass rally in Lahore on December 20 that "majority alone does not count in national politics"—meaning that, in a Federal Government, a purely regional majority cannot rule the whole nation without co-operating with other regions.

The National Assembly was thus deadlocked. The Awami League and the Peoples Party could not agree on a formula. Mujib stood firmly by his Six-Point Plan for autonomy in the East. Zulfikar Ali Bhutto could not agree, believing it would lead to the disintegration of Pakistan's unity.

Bhutto flew to Dacca for a discussion with Mujib and on January 12, 1971, the President himself went. But again talks were of no avail. In fact, they seemed to have made matters even worse, for both the Peoples Party and the Muslim League declared they would not be present at the next meeting of the National Assembly set down for March 3, 1971, unless the Sheikh was prepared to take part in free discussions in the Assembly on constitutional matters. Believing there was no use in convening the Assembly with the two major Pakistani parties boycotting it, President Yahya put off the Assembly inauguration scheduled for March 3.

This precipitated the showdown. The first slogans demanding *Swadhin* (independent) Bangladesh were heard in the streets of Dacca. Sheikh Mujib was clearly not prepared to go that far; he opted instead for a civil disobedience movement to press his demand for transfer of power at the provincial level only. This movement was an overwhelming success; even the Chief Justice refused to swear in the new Governor, Lt.-Gen. Tikka Khan, appointed by Islamabad to replace Admiral Ahsan who had advised against a confrontation with the Awami League.

It was in this atmosphere that the final round of negotiations began in Dacca after General Yahya Khan arrived there on March 15. Compromise proposals were formulated, one envisaging a provisional national government under Sheikh Mujib and the second making over power to provinces even while General Yahya remained in charge at the centre. Mr. Bhutto rejected both.

All the East Pakistan members of Pakistan's armed forces, military and para-military, had been imbued with the Awami League ideology and were secretly preparing for a showdown with the Central Government. Even as the negotiations proceeded, troops in large numbers were being brought across from West Pakistan. President Yahya Khan made an unannounced departure from East Pakistan on March 25. It was a question of who strikes first. On the night of March 25, the Pakistan army soldiers slipped into battle dress and struck without warning with automatic weapons and tanks. Twenty-four hours later, Mr. Bhutto said in Karachi when he flew back from Dacca: "Thank God, Pakistan is saved".

But as he made this comment, a radio station in Chittagong broadcast a proclamation of independence by Major Zia Rahman, speaking in the name of Sheikh Mujib-ur Rahman. The battle was now joined, even though the Sheikh himself had been taken into military custody on charges of treason and his party banned. On April 10, the Bangladesh Government was formally constituted with the imprisoned Sheikh Mujib as President, Syed Nazrul Islam as acting President and Mr. Tajuddin Ahmed as Prime Minister. This was the beginning of the end; the final denouement was however still several months away.

On the 30th March, India called on the United Nations to take the initiative to stop the suppression of democratic principles by the Pakistani Army in East Pakistan and help promote a political solution acceptable to the Bengali people and their elected representatives, so that peace might return to the troubled land, and the refugees who had come to India might return to their homes. The next day, the Indian Parliament passed a resolution demanding immediate cessation of the use of force and the massacre of defenceless people, calling upon all peoples and governments of the world to prevail upon the Government of Pakistan to put an end immediately to the systematic decimation of people which amounts to genocide. Over the next few months, relations between the two nations grew worse as India criticised Pakistan's actions and Pakistan complained bitterly about Indian support for the outlawed Awami League. Greater and greater concentration of troops began to mass on both sides of borders, and Communist China, worried at the thought of Indian intervention on behalf of the "rebels", renewed its pledge of support for Yahya Khan and warned the Indian Government not to meddle in Pakistan's affairs. By this time there were hundreds of thousands of refugees streaming across the border into India to escape the fighting in East Pakistan, and India claimed that this could disastrously affect her economy. Towards the end of April there were over a million refugees in India but even this vast number increased to well over nine million in the ensuing months.

At the beginning of June 1971, at a time when the Pakistan Government appealed to the refugees to come home, cholera broke out in East Pakistan with the result that even more people headed for the border in their frantic endeavour to escape the new menace.

On June 28, General Yahya Khan announced general amnesty to all people who had fled into India. On this date too, Yahya Khan announced a new plan to hand over the Government of the country to civilians, this to be effective within the following three or four months. Soon afterwards, a ban on political activities was lifted and replaced by regulations precluding any action prejudicial to the integrity, security and ideology of the country.

In August, when the establishment of a civilian Government in East Pakistan had already been postponed beyond the promised date, it was announced that Sheikh Mujib-ur Rahman would be put on trial. This further aggravated the situation, especially as nearly two-thirds of the Awami League candidates who had been elected to office had now been disqualified by the Pakistan Government. Also, notwithstanding that the ban on political activities had been lifted, the Awami League itself was still outlawed. Again, ostensibly in an attempt at reconciliation, Yahya Khan renewed his general amnesty to all except Awami League members, and freed some political prisoners who had been taken when the fighting first broke out. In October 1971, Yahya Khan proposed to India a mutual withdrawal from the border regions and called on the United Nations to take constructive steps to ease the threat of war between the two countries. Later, during November at a Press Conference in Paris, the Secretary of Pakistan's Foreign Affairs Ministry emphasised the vast difference between the military strengths of the two countries; India outnumbered Pakistan by five to one. He observed that it would be ludicrous for Pakistan to attack India under these circumstances. Simultaneously, in Rawalpindi, President Yahya Khan offered to settle the differences between his country and India. To this, the Indian Government's reply was that a settlement should be sought not with India but with the legally elected representatives of East Pakistan to the National Assembly.

On November 23, General Yahya Khan declared a state of emergency in Pakistan, because India had embarked on large scale operations against East Pakistan in support of Bangladesh. Speaking to correspondents at Rawalpindi on November 26, he revealed that war was already on and Pakistan was fighting a defensive battle.

On December 3, Pakistan fighter planes launched pre-emptive strikes on a number of Indian airfields and launched heavy ground attacks at a number of points all along the Western border. The President of India proclaimed a state of emergency.

On December 5, the United States put a resolution to the Security Council of the U.N. calling for ceasefire. The Russians, who had signed a friendship pact with the Indians in August 1971, vetoed the move. Another resolution was tabled the next day and although it was accepted by eleven members it was again vetoed by the U.S.S.R. The matter was then taken up to the General Assembly on December 7 where it received overwhelming support, only ten delegates voting against and eleven abstaining, including France and the U.K. Pakistan accepted the U.S. resolution for ceasefire and troop withdrawal, but India refused to approve it since it did not deal with the crux of the problem, the need for a political solution. On December 16, India reported to the Security Council a unilateral ceasefire in the Eastern Sector (East Pakistan) and the prospect of one on the Western border the following day. But no resolution could be passed by the Security Council until the war was actually ended.

Two days after the cessation of hostilities, India's Defence Minister Jagjivan Ram announced that his country was willing to build up a new relationship with Pakistan, based on co-operation rather than on conflict.

On Yahya Khan's shoulders had fallen the responsibility for his country's overwhelming misfortunes, and on December 20 he announced his resignation. The mantle of Pakistan's presidency then fell upon Zulfikar Ali Bhutto.

So the war ended. And just as Pakistan had been created as a result of the disintegration of Indo-Pakistan, so the independent nation of Bangladesh, meaning Bengal Country, was created by secession from Pakistan.

The new State will undoubtedly face the same economic and financial difficulties that beset the young nation of Pakistan 25 years ago. It remains to be seen if its leader, Sheikh Mujib-ur Rahman, will be strong enough to master his country's problems and establish it as one of the honoured nations of the world. The Sheikh was released from imprisonment by President Bhutto on January 8, 1972 and given facilities to fly to London. After talks concerning the future of the new country he returned to Dacca on January 10, 1972.

June 5, 1972

Although Bangladesh has proclaimed itself an independent State, President Bhutto still looks upon it as East Pakistan under a new name. As this book goes to Press the world is awaiting the outcome of a meeting between President Bhutto and India's Prime Minister, Indira Ghandi, expected to take place late in June 1972. On this occasion it is hoped that the two leaders will settle their countries' differences and pave the way for a lasting peace.

Left:
The Pakistan Institute of Nuclear Science and Technology, Nilore, Islamabad, Punjab.

Below:
A grain market place in Okara.

THE NATION'S ECONOMY

Despite many changes in the political scene economic progress in Pakistan has been steady, and even remarkable in some fields like industry. The country has successfully completed three five-year plans of development and has now embarked on its fourth plan (1970-75). While at the advent of independence, there was hardly any industry in Pakistan, except for a few cement factories, sugar mills, and textile mills, today the country is self-sufficient in almost all its consumer goods—cotton, woollen, nylon and jute fabrics; sugar, cooking oils, leather, shoes, paper and cardboard, cement, cycles, sewing machines, electric fans, telephone receivers, electric lamps and other goods, pens, spectacle frames, glass and China crockery, chemicals and medicines, petroleum products, sporting goods, surgical goods, cutlery, and much else.

The biggest industry by far is the textiles industry. There are many cotton textile mills, four woollen mills and a number of silk and rayon mills—using locally produced rayon yarn.

The biggest investment of all is in the oil and gas industry. Natural gas has been discovered at nine sites in Pakistan. One is being used to supply industry for thermal power production, and one to produce chemical fertilisers. There are besides, four oil refineries using mostly imported petroleum.

There is a shipyard in Karachi building seagoing vessels, while railway carriages and wagons are manufactured in Lahore. Cars and trucks are being assembled in Karachi.

More and more attention is being paid to the production of capital goods. A large machine tools factory has been set up in Karachi and a huge heavy mechanical complex to produce a variety of plants, cranes and road rollers has gone into production at Taxila near Rawalpindi.

About one-fourth of all industry is concentrated in Karachi, and there are vast industrial estates in Lahore and all the way from there to Rawalpindi. Lyallpur in the centre of the Punjab is another great industrial centre—the cotton capital of Pakistan, both for growth of cotton and manufacture of cotton textiles.

Most of Pakistan's industry has been developed by private enterprise while the Government has provided the infrastructure, such as cheap power, roads and communications, loans, especially in foreign currency, and so on. The Government has also entered some fields which are reserved for the public sector—such as hydel-power production, ship building, steel production, mining and chemical fertilisers. There is one privately owned chemical fertiliser factory. The Government projects are operated by the Industrial Development Corporation.

AGRICULTURE

Pakistan is primarily an agricultural country with three-fourths of the people actually engaged on the land and many more depending directly or indirectly upon primary activities. Scholars like the late Gordon Childe averred that the art of agriculture was first developed by man in the plateau of Baluchistan, in south-western Pakistan. Certainly, cotton and wheat were found in the excavated ruins of Moenjodaro—the 5,000 years old city in Sind.

Today Pakistan grows bumper crops of wheat (about 6.5 million tons), and some high quality rice—(about 2 million tons).

The major cash crop is cotton (about 4 million bales of 440 lb each).

The total area of Pakistan is about 200 million acres (about 310,000 square miles), of which some 50 million acres are cultivated. Two crops are sown on almost all the land.

About one-third of the cultivated land is under wheat (in winter), one-third under other foodgrains, and the rest devoted to other crops. Cotton (a summer crop) covers about one-tenth of the acreage.

Apart from the undoubted initiative shown by the farmers, a number of important measures have been taken by the Government that have helped in promoting agriculture and in raising the production of foodgrains from 13.5 million tons in 1948-49 to 22.8 million tons in 1969-70. Cash crops (cotton, jute, sugar cane, tobacco, tea, rape and mustard seed) have been increased from 13.7 million tons to 36 million tons.

The most important measure taken to develop agriculture has been Land Reforms. The problem was serious, and no Government could dare to take steps against the powerful landlords until a military regime came into power in October, 1958, and land reforms were enacted by ordinance early in 1959. All land in excess of 500 acres irrigated or 1000 acres unirrigated, were resumed, and distributed among tenants. The second instalment of Land Reforms was introduced by President Bhutto on 1st March 1972, when the upper ceiling of land ownership was reduced to 150 acres of irrigated land.

Four chemical fertiliser factories were set up and fertiliser was distributed to farmers at subsidised prices to popularise its use.

Dwarf varieties of wheat producing twice as much as the old varieties had been developed in Mexico, and 'miracle rice' or IRRI variety in Manila at agricultural research institutes. These seeds were imported and further developed and acclimatised for use by Pakistani farmers.

To advance loans to farmers, an Agricultural Development Bank has been set up, augmenting the many other existing institutions which supply finance.

An Agricultural Development Corporation has been established to distribute better seeds, better implements, and fertilisers. It is also helping farmers to use lift irrigation during winter (when the level of water falls in rivers) and assisting in the installation of tube-wells. There are no less than 60,000 now operating.

The Agricultural Departments of the provincial governments have set up model farms and are spreading the knowledge of modern methods of cultivation.

Above:
Picking the bolls
in a cotton field
in Multan.

WATER AND POWER. Pakistan is an arid land, and some spectacular engineering works have been constructed to provide essential irrigation. The biggest of these is the Mangla Dam on the Jhelum producing hydel power in addition to irrigation. The series of five great barrages built on the Indus deserve special mention—three having been built after independence at Hyderabad, Guddu and Taunsa.

Apart from many other projects, by far the biggest and perhaps without parallel in the world, is the Indus Basin Works, completed during the last eleven years.

The partition of India had played havoc with the irrigation system, cutting rivers and canals into two, leaving the head works on one side and the canals on the other. This led to constant disputes between India and Pakistan regarding supply of water to the canals in Pakistan from headworks in India.

After long negotiations under the auspices of the World Bank, the Indus Water Treaty was signed with India in 1960 under which the three eastern rivers of the Indus Basin (Sutlej, Beas and Ravi) were given entirely to India, to use all the waters as they thought fit. Pakistan was thus faced with the challenge of bringing water from her western rivers to feed the canals which had previously been supplied by the three eastern rivers.

It was a colossal project, many times bigger than the Aswan Dam in terms of square yards excavated and built. Some seven new link canals were constructed of a length of 380 miles, plus five barrages and one dam —the mighty Mangla Dam mentioned earlier.

Pakistan completed the entire project in ten years at a cost of $2.25 billion. The only work still in progress is the Tarbela Dam, the biggest in the world, on the Indus, which will not replace the lost water supply but will provide additional water resources for irrigation and further production of electricity.

Right: The Pakistan Water and Power Development Authority Building at Lahore.

Below: Rasul Barrage near Mandi Bahauddin.

Right: The old system of irrigation in a rice field.

GOOD LIVING IN KARACHI

THE CITY OF KARACHI is a city of contrasts, a busy metropolis of 2 million people, on the shores of the Arabian Sea. On its verge is the Inter-Continental Hotel, like a great oasis—a tall imposing building of modern design influenced by ancient Moslem architecture. Around this central point are lawns, car parks, a shopping concourse and a great swimming pool bordered by arched colonnades, where the weary traveller may relax in a cool and comfortable atmosphere.

A quarter mile away a constant stream of traffic flows: camel carts vie with Cadillacs; veiled women in graceful saris and tightly trousered Westerners hurry through the bazaars; Victorian mansions encompass historic mosques.

Just beyond the hotel street-music fills the air: the quiet prattle of Urdu in the market-place, the rustle of date-palms, the soft padding of feet on pavement, the blare of horns and the rattle of motor rickshaws—an ancient rhythm with a modern upbeat. The Inter-Continental is the largest and most striking hotel in Pakistan. From its rooftop Chandni lounge Karachi stretches out in a broad panorama a hundred feet below—an intriguing scene by day; a gem-speckled, Arabian-Night vista after dark. This vantage point is the meeting place of the indigenous gourmet and the cosmopolitan sophisticate, a restaurant where the finest of Pakistani foods are the specialities of the day. Music from top pop bands and sittarists are in harmony with the varied menus of oriental and western fare served here and in the formal dining-room. The

Right: Entrance to the Karachi Hotel Inter-Continental.

Centre: One of Karachi's most exclusive dining places is the Nasreen Room at Hotel Karachi.

Below: Modern architecture blends with traditional Moorish design in the Karachi Inter-Continental's striking Hotel complex.

coffee shop and snack bar cater for the casual popular taste.

In an eastern atmosphere the entrance foyer to the Hotel is a cool haven from the summer heat and the decors of lounges, coffee shops and restaurants are exciting patterns of a new-old world. Behind the arches of the shopping arcade hide exotic gift shops and boutiques of many types to lure the tourist, the businessman and his wife, and airline offices, travel agencies and banks provide essential services.

Among the hotel's special features are a large and lavishly-appointed ballroom and convention room, a sauna bath and gymnasium. There are 250 bedrooms and suites with furnishings in individual patterns and styles. All in all, the Hotel Karachi Inter-Continental is an international hotel containing many varied features to appeal to the world traveller.

ON THE THRESHOLD OF THE HIMALAYAS

AT THE EDGE OF THE CLIFF we let our packs slide to the ground and gazed in awe. The green slopes of Miran Jani glittered in the sunlight piercing through the stately pine, maple, fir and chestnut trees. In the far distance was the snow-capped Nanga Parbat, thrusting her white cone against a silvery sky. The majestic Himalayas, covered with blue-green forests rose almost vertically. Turning back we saw the hillscape sloping down towards the Pothwar plain under a grey haze hiding Rawalpindi and Islamabad.

From Abbotabad, the neat, small town of spacious green parks, verdant gardens and golf links, we had jeeped up the steep incline to stare in the face of the rocky hillscape. The road, which was being widened, was far from a super-highway. Winding from hill to hill, past precipices, cliffs and steep slopes marked by landslides, it climbed from mountain to mountain.

Before we had time to admire a view to our heart's content, it would disappear, replaced by another in a succession of breath-taking scenes of pristine natural grandeur. The kaleidoscopic panorama was formed by shifting scenes of rocky mountain slopes, covered with laurels and feathery ferns, woodlands of lofty, dark green pines and firs, and terraced fields, on which maize was grown, descending into deep ravines.

This fascinating, multi-coloured panorama unfolded on our twenty-mile journey to Nathiagali amidst a landscape seen only in dreams. It took us an hour and a half to arrive at this, one of the most picturesque hill stations of West Pakistan.

Above: Terraced houses of Murree, known popularly as "Queen of the Hills".

Below: The magnificent work of Pakistan's craftsmen is seen in the murals of the Tomb of Shah Rukan-e-Alam at Multan.

Situated at an altitude of 5,200 feet: and exactly midway between Abbotabad and Muree, Nathiagali lies at the very centre of the beautiful *Galis*—the resorts of the Hills region. Its cool and bracing climate and enchanting scenery makes it a place of dream-like peace and beauty so very soothing and relaxing to strained nerves. Nathiagali is the tourist's paradise, the painter's delight and a health resort for the sick.

Chalets, bungalows and villages perch high above the road or below it, each partially hidden by blossoming flower gardens and towering evergreens. We walked through the paths skirting lush green meadows, overshadowed by huge *deodars*, oaks and chestnuts. We saw an infinite variety of flowers—daisies, myosotis, gentians—spreading their colourful carpets.

The show-piece of Nathiagali is the Government House, commanding a majestic view of the hillscape. It perches on a hillock. On the slopes around it, wild bushes grow. Firs and deodars cast their long, dark shadows on the green meadows that surround it. The building is Alpine in architecture, a style first introduced by the British rulers and later adopted by Pakistanis.

The high peaked roofs, hooded gables and stone walls provide a touch of cosiness and protection against snowfall during winters. This same type of architecture has been adopted for bungalows and villas.

Another interesting place to see is Lalazar. Derived from Persian, the word "Lalazar" means a garden of tulips. A charming cottage nestles here under the shades of stately deodars and fine firs, overlooking a path where holiday-makers sit on chairs in the open, sip tea or coffee and gossip in the sunshine with tulips nodding in the fragrant breeze.

You cannot help comparing Nathiagali with Murree, which Pakistanis lovingly call the queen of the hills. In mountain scenery and bracing climate the two are similar, but the similarity ends there.

In Murree you are never out of sight or sound of man's eternal activity. The whirl of social life goes on within its town limits. Men and women shoulder their way through the crowd or stand talking in groups on the Mall, or buying or selling in the cobbled streets of the lower bazaar.

In Nathiagali there is no crowding. Here peace and quiet reigns supreme. You are virtually in the bosom of nature, hearing the music of wild birds as you walk undisturbed through shaded paths and peaceful retreats. The ubiquitous cuckoo sings merrily in the glens. Rose finches whistle melodiously, flitting about in search of nectar and berries. Yellow-throated sparrows, wagtails and green parakeets wing about gracefully.

Though far from the hustle of city life, Nathiagali is not devoid of basic amenities. You can stay comfortably at modern hotels like the Pines, the Valley View or the New Green. The charges are not very high. The P.W.D. Rest House is cheaper and can be booked in advance. There are some government bungalows which can be hired for the season but they need considerable renovation.

We passed two delightful days and two wonderful nights at Nathiagali. The neat, little houses nestling in the clumps of pines, over the slopes presented a unique sight. The valley was aglow with dim lamps twinkling in all the widely scattered homesteads. It looked like the starlit dome of heaven, inverted.

We left Nathiagali on the third day with unforgettable, happy memories.

After a few minutes' journey, we reached Dunga Gali (7,800 feet) sprawling on the slopes of Makspuri hill (highest elevation 9,232 feet). There was a panoramic view of the wooded spurs descending into the valley through which the river Jhelum flows in its turbulent course. The farflung landscape clothed in green was profusely dotted with the bright and varied colours of wild flowers. Natural springs cascaded down the slopes, their waters tamed in a reservoir which supplies much-needed drinking water to Murree and its suburbs.

The visit to the twin resorts of Ghora Daka and Khanspur was an exciting experience. Their location on a spur projecting towards the river Jhelum offered an unforgettable view of steep precipices and lofty pines. We were told that bears and leopards roam the thick forests covering the slopes.

Ghora Daka and Khanspur, along with two other resorts Changla Gali and Khaira Gali, are being developed into a tourist complex named Ayubia. Modern hotels, restaurants and cinemas are under completion. A lift chair has been installed to provide a commanding view of the picturesque and enchanting valley. People are fast buying land and constructing houses in Ayubia which offers unique opportunities of rest and recreation and summer and winter sports.

Above:
The snow covered mountains of Swat, one of the famous tourist spots of Pakistan.

From Ayubia we drove to Murree.

For four exciting days we had driven, camped and hiked through the forests of the Galis. All along the way there are summer holiday stations, located at altitudes ranging between 7,000 to 10,000 feet above sea level.

Compared to the perpetually snow-capped giants of Nanga Parbat and K-2, these mountains are mere pigmies. All the same, they provide an ideally delightful escape from the heat and dust of the plains and from the din and bustle of the cities. Set amidst green forests and jagged peaks, with a cool, bracing climate, the Galis have been luring the tourists away from the scorching plains of Sind and the Punjab since about a century ago, when the British built barracks and bungalows to provide places of comfort and repose for their battle-weary soldiers.

Thirty years later, the roads linking Rawalpindi with Abbotabad and the Galis were metalled, thus opening the wonderland of this hilly region to the outside world.

Before the British came, the Galis slumbered for ages under the snow-white wings of the towering Himalayas. Battles were fought and won and lost, on the plateaux and plains lying to the west. The Galis formed a part of the Nazara District which was included in the Kingdom of Taxila that Alexander conquered. After the withdrawal, the territory came under the sway of the Mauryan Emperor, and was part of this empire for several centuries.

The Hindu *Raj* continued as ruler up to the 12th Century A.D. after which the territory was over-run by the Muslim conquerors.

It was known as Pakhli Sarkar during the Mughal period. The break-up of the Mughal empire was followed by Sikh rule in Hazara and the rest of the Punjab.

After the Sikhs were defeated in 1846, the territory was handed over to the Dogra ruler of Kashmir, Gulab Singh, from whom the British took over.

The Galis lack the ancient relics of Taxila and Moenjodaro and the historical monuments of Lahore and Dacca, but what they offer is a mountainous wonderland of scenic beauty, invigorating climate and exciting adventure. You get the feeling of limitless space above and the undisturbed milieu of forests, mountains and a wide range of wild flora and fauna all around.

Left: PIA hostesses in their winter and summer uniforms... Above: PIA mechanics carrying out maintenance on a Boeing engine... Below: A PIA hostess welcomes passengers... Right: Meals are a special event on PIA flights.

PAKISTAN'S NATIONAL AIRLINE

LIKE THE YOUNG and vigorous nation to which it belongs Pakistan International Airlines has developed with remarkable speed from modest beginnings. Nearly seven years after the birth of Pakistan as a sovereign state, PIA commenced operations as a department of the Government. Within a year it was converted into a statutory corporation.

In 1955, the year of its foundation, PIA entered the world of international aviation with limited equipment and meagre resources. Its service was from Karachi to London via Cairo and Rome. Its fleet comprised fifteen piston-engined aircraft, three of which were Superconstellations, two Convairs, and ten Dakotas. In 1959, as the first step in a scheme for modernisation, the Corporation's five Convairs were replaced by Viscount turboprop aircraft.

Twelve months later a Boeing 707 was leased from Pan American World Airways, and thus PIA became the first Asian Airline to operate a jet aircraft.

During the next few years it bought its own Boeings for international and inter-wing operations and on the domestic routes it replaced the Dakotas with Fokker F-27's and the Viscounts with Trident 1E's. In 1964-65 PIA was the first non-Communist airline to fly to the People's Republic of China and to operate a service between Asia and Europe via Moscow. It has recently inaugurated a Karachi-London-New York service and is thus the second airline in the world to link Mainland China with the U.S.A.

Internationally, PIA has carried the flag of Pakistan as an ambassador of goodwill. Its services, offices and personnel have helped to make the country more widely known and her people better understood in many parts of the world.

The current PIA fleet comprises nine Boeing 707 340C's, three Boeing 720B's, nine Fokker F-27's and six Twin Otter D HC-6's, with two additional Fokkers on order. The Airline's network now girdles more than half the globe, from New York through London to Tokyo. Its international operations serve 32 cities in 31 countries, and its domestic services cover all the major cities and towns in Pakistan. (Flights to East Pakistan—now Bangladesh—have been suspended since December 1971.)

The interiors of PIA aircraft have recently been redecorated in muted tones of green and gold which blend elegantly with their hostesses' new uniform—a striking and unusual combination of green and gold-trimmed trousers with a stylish draped and hooded tunic top.

Pakistan's airline is now in a position to meet all its own engineering and training needs and to provide services to a number of other Asian and African airlines, including those of Ceylon, Burma, Malaysia and Nepal.

To further improve its already highly rated catering service the Airline opened a new Flight Kitchen early in 1972. It is equipped with every modern cooking appliance and is one of the largest and most efficient Flight Kitchens in the world. It is able to provide 8,000 meals and snacks a day—sufficient to meet PIA's own requirement of 2,000 a day as well as that of all 26 foreign airlines passing through Karachi. Many overseas airlines are availing themselves of PIA's catering service, thus adding considerably to the Airline's foreign exchange earnings.

Through the development of its internal and external services PIA has made a substantial contribution to the promotion of tourism in Pakistan. On the one hand its Special Tours Promotion Unit has publicised the country's tourist attractions abroad and on the other it has helped in the modernisation of tourist facilities and the construction of first-class hotels at home. It has become associated with the building of four large Inter-Continental Hotels at Karachi, Dacca, Lahore and Rawalpindi and a fifth under construction at Peshawar.

PIA is planning to build another fourteen hotels at an estimated cost of Rs. 55 million or approximately US$14 million. The opening of these hotels will go a long way towards meeting the growing demands of tourists from the world over.

During the past decade the unduplicated routes of PIA have more than tripled to an aggregate of 50,000 miles. In 1966-67 alone the route map was extended as much as 48 per cent to 14,000 miles. The passenger mile chart showed a rise of over 500 per cent when PIA's passenger traffic touched the million mark in 1967-68. During the following year it rose further to over 1.2 million. In the light of its past record, PIA's future seems assured.

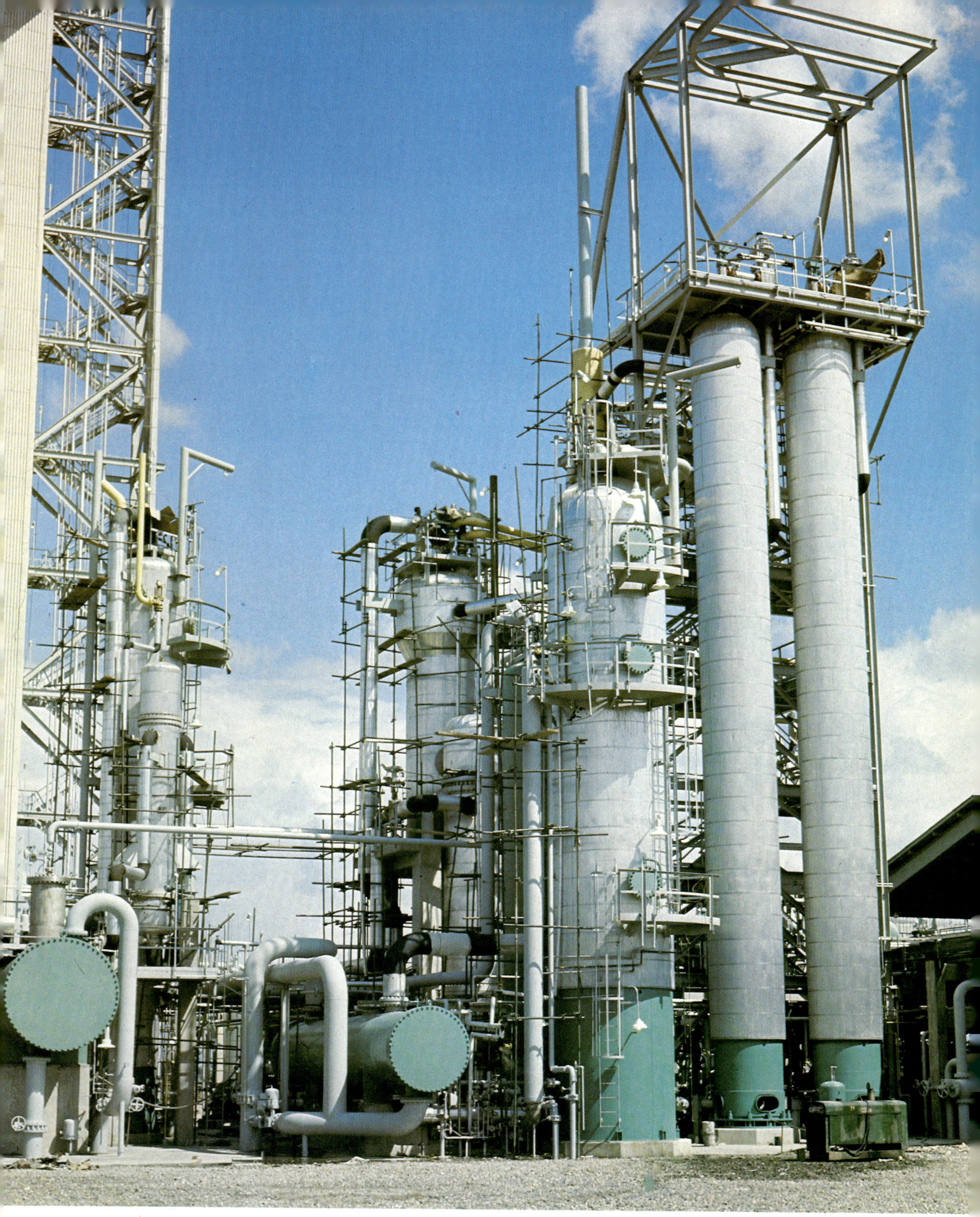

THE DAWOODS OF PAKISTAN

MOST of the world's huge industrial organisations which in time assume almost legendary status are initiated by the collective enterprise of a family, or occasionally by the determined endeavours of a single individual. The Dawood Organisation, embracing under its name a bank, an insurance company, a shipping line, a trio of textile industries, an oil company and six other concerns, is a typical example of the former.

Its impressive diversity, ranging from insurance to the manufacture of paper and fertilisers, has been a high tribute to the entrepreneural skill of the Dawood family. Together, they survived many vicissitudes and their success has reflected the determination and hard work by which it has been accomplished.

The secret of the organisation has been perhaps, the remarkable unity of the family, for in the words of the Chairman, Mr. Ahmed Dawood, the architect of many of their achievements:-

"My greatest wish is that the family stays united".

The implementation of this wish, coupled with undoubted business acumen, has made the Dawoods one of the outstanding private enterprises of the Asian sub-continent.

Until the conflict that ultimately caused the separation of East Pakistan from West Pakistan, the organisation had grown to produce 20 per cent of the country's total cotton exports, 50 per cent of the requirements in woollen fabrics and yarn, 51 per cent of the paper needs, and employed nearly 25,000 people. Yet it had a relatively modest beginning in the fields of exporting and importing.

The Dawood saga began in the early part of this century, when Ahmed, Suleman, Siddique and Ali Mohammed, scions of a reputed Memon family (one of the best known business communities of the sub-continent), joined their father Dawood Yakub, and began trading under the name "M. Siddique & Co." By 1947 the Dawoods—for that was the name family tradition bestowed on all of Dawood Yakub's sons—had established themselves well enough to consider launching a vast textile enterprise near Bombay.

1947 was a time of crises in India; it was also the time of fresh hope, for after many harrowing trials the new State of Pakistan was created. The Dawoods joined millions of others of the Muslim faith in a mass exodus, and committed themselves to the ideology of the creation of a new homeland. The years

Opposite page:
A urea reactor at
Dawood Hercules Chemicals
complex.

Below:
A section of
a control room for experiments
at Dawood Hercules Fertilisers.

following partition were difficult ones; the country started from scratch. Though assets were considerable, industrial facilities to exploit them were almost negligible. The Dawoods, aware of the immense cotton potential of the country, pooled their collective resources and implemented their earlier plan to establish a cotton spinning and weaving mill at Landhi, a few miles from Karachi. This was the nucleus of all future Dawood ventures. Some years later a similar mill was acquired at Burewala and by 1971 the two mills housed 3,181 looms or 8.8 per cent of the total number of cotton looms in Pakistan.

For many years cotton has been one of Pakistan's main exports, ranking third in Asia in textile products and representing 25 per cent of the total output. Of this, the Dawood contribution was 20 per cent, a striking indication of the family's importance to the industry. Over the years of the 'fifties and 'sixties, Pakistan's export of cotton yarn and textiles increased by about 22 per cent annually, compared with a growth of 2 to 3 per cent in world trade in these commodities. Being the largest single contributor, the Dawoods played a leading role in making this achievement possible.

With the acquisition of the Lawrencepur Woollen & Textile Mills in 1961 the Dawood Group entered the woollen textile industry. Starting with 54 looms and 6,700 spindles, it grew to be the largest woollen textile mill in Pakistan, operating 196 looms and 9,248 spindles. Supplying a large proportion of the domestic needs, the Lawrencepur Woollen & Textile Mills Limited manufacture high quality products including woollen cloth, blankets, woollen and worsted yarn, knitting yarn and carpet yarn. With a reputation for high quality at competitive prices, its products have proved very popular on the home market and a sound demand has been created in a number of foreign countries.

The Dawood plan for textile development in natural fibres was completed in 1970, when the group initiated an enormous jute mill project at Chittagong in East Pakistan. This enterprise, involving an investment of Rs. 50,000,000 had 200 broad looms for the manufacture of backing cloth for tufted carpets, one of the principal uses of jute.

In the field of artificial fibres the Dawoods took the lead as early as 1953, when they prepared plans for a rayon and chemicals plant in East Pakistan. The Karnaphuli Rayon & Chemicals Ltd. was established with an investment of Rs. 130,000,000 with a daily production capacity of ten tons of rayon yarn for weaving 400,000,000 yards of art silk per annum.

Relatively speaking, the paper industry constituted a very small part of the total industrial establishment on the Asian scene. In Pakistan, however, its size was considerable in view of the country's Third Five Year Plan which forecast an estimated production of 100,000 tons of paper of various kinds. The Dawoods entered this field in 1959, when they took over the Karnaphuli Paper Mills from the Pakistan Industrial Development Corporation. Under the new management production steadily increased.

Of an estimated 61,000 tons of writing, printing and packing paper manufactured up to 1969-70, Karnaphuli's contribution was 31,712 tons. Although manufacturing two dozen varieties of fine paper, the Karnaphuli Paper Mills had previously been kept from exporting its products because of the pressures of domestic requirements but with the advent of other interests, a progressive export policy was planned.

The Central Insurance Co. Ltd., underwriters of fire, marine and general risks, together with its subsidiary the Central Life Assurance Co. Ltd., were both Dawood ventures. The Group also established what is now called the Asian Co-operative Bank, to extend banking facilities to the people and to promote the interests of the small investor.

The establishment of an oil company in 1966 was perhaps the Dawoods' bravest venture. Entering into a field dominated by well-known international companies, Dawood Petroleum Limited soon consolidated its position as one of the leading oil distributors of the country. Its string of filling stations is a familiar sight on the many roads and newly-engineered highways criss-crossing the territory of Pakistan.

To keep abreast of the changing times and bearing in mind the growing needs of Pakistan, the Dawoods entered into an agreement in 1968 with Hercules Inc. of the United States to set up a fertiliser manufacturing plant in Sheikhupura near Lahore. This plant went into full production in October 1971. It comprises an ammonia plant with a capacity of 200,000 metric tons of ammonia per year, and a urea plant capable of converting this ammonia to 340,000 metric tons of prilled urea.

Stretching from the north-west frontier to the Hill Tracts of Chittagong, the diversified Dawood organisation held together by outstanding co-ordinating ability and high managerial skill. Though the various existing interests are still well defined autonomies, an overall observance of the objectives of the organisation is constantly borne in mind.

For many years the Dawoods have helped materially in the economic development of Pakistan and have also contributed liberally to various charitable causes. The Dawood Foundation, an institution to promote education in Pakistan, was formed in 1961. Its funds today are in the region of Rs. 60,000,000 (about US$12,000,000). The Foundation established the Dawood College of Engineering & Technology at a cost of Rs.6,000,000. Through it, degree courses were made available in chemical engineering, electronics and metallurgy as well as numerous scholarships and grants. Every year the foundation set aside a sum of Rs. 25,000 for literary prizes for the four best books published in Pakistan.

During the 'sixties and 'seventies, the total effective assets of the Group grew to the order of Rs. 1,000,000,000 (US$200,000,000), a fact which gave great satisfaction to its thousands of shareholders, many of them small investors. High dividends have been paid and such is the reputation of the organisation that whenever a new concern is floated, the public issue becomes heavily over-subscribed.

The events of 1971 which split the East and West sectors of Pakistan was a tragedy which affected the lives of all members of the Pakistan community. The Dawood Group with its immense holdings in the Eastern Wing of the country was particularly affected. Though the fate of the holdings of West Pakistanis in East Pakistan has not been finally determined it seems that the Dawoods have lost three of their major projects, Karnaphuli Paper Mills Ltd., Karnaphuli Rayon and Chemicals Ltd., and the Dawood Jute Mills Ltd., in addition to the total East Pakistani assets of their other concerns.

Notwithstanding this severe setback, it is safe to assume that the traditional tenacity of the Dawoods will be asserted in the general replanning of the nation. The family played a big part in the creation and development of a new land; it hopes to play an equally important role in the years to come.

Above:
The Dawood Centre is shown as a land mark in the heart of Karachi. On the left page is the Workers' Hostel and garden at the Dawood Cotton Mills at Landhi.

THE ROLE OF PAKISTAN

What kind of role is the Pakistan nation likely to play in the future world? Apart from offering the greatest challenges to the mountaineers of the world, inviting visitors to some of the loveliest mountain valleys of all, fielding world champions in hockey, squash, cricket, polo and wrestling, maintaining one of the world's finest armies, enjoying one of the richest treasures of folk music and folk art, Pakistan is in the position to make a unique contribution, perhaps only small, perhaps very big, to the world at large. Pakistan was created to be an ideological state. It is, above all, an ideal and like all ideals hard of achievement, not to be judged only by its past but by its present endeavours as well as future aspirations.

It is the only country in the modern world avowedly and specifically created to establish an Islamic state and an Islamic policy for the people.

This may puzzle some Western readers because Islam is not a widely understood religion. And if the Muslims have failed to give the fullest expression to the real meaning of their ideal, Islam is synonymous with tolerance and social justice, with progress and with dominion over nature and all its resources, and above everything else with Godly living.

Just as Islam was among the very first to teach and to practise the complete brotherhood of man, to abolish racial discrimination and give legal status and rights to women, to exhort men to study nature and

Above:
Quaid-i-Azam Mohammed Ali Jinnah, the founder of Pakistan, died on 11th September 1948, only a year after Pakistan's inception.

Right:
The Tomb of Shah Rukan-e-Alam in Multan.

Right page, top:
Floral design is a feature of the inside of Mirs Tomb at Hyderabad.

Right page, below:
The High Court Building at Lahore.

its laws, to teach the world the sciences of astronomy and medicine, the arts of making paper, sugar, many wonderful textiles, and much else—above all to establish the ideals of tolerance and justice and "the middle path", so Pakistan also aspires to deserve the title of "Ummat-ul-Wusta" given to the Muslims by the Holy Quoran—in other words, the Middle Nation, followers of the Golden Mean.

Pakistan has in fact, taken a middle position on the chequerboard of the world, neither to the far left, nor to the far right, befriending both and learning from the experiences of both in economic, political and social matters. The economic system it has adopted is tempered with an overriding sense of social responsibility. In social matters, everyone is equal before God and in the eyes of the law, as can be seen every day at prayer time in a mosque. But combined with this proud individualism is oriental grace in giving respect where it is due—to authority, to age, to learning and to piety. In political matters, the belief and practice is on the side of democracy. But the people tend to entrust more and more functions to the state —to be placed somehow in the public sector as against the private, thus emphasising the strong leaning towards the collective spirit in matters concerning public weal and common good.

While the right to elect the leaders is fiercely asserted, equally strong is the loyalty and devotion the people give to the chosen leader once in office and their confidence in him has been justified.

Pakistan is about to complete a quarter of a century of its turbulent existence, a brief period in the life of a nation filled with many trials.

Carping critics will find a great deal to criticise, and justifiably so, but men of goodwill blessed with insight will see in this performance of 25 years glimmerings of a state which is not so much a piece of land or a mass of people as an idea.

The splitting of East Pakistan from the West early in 1972 was a tragedy in the fullest sense of the word—a tragedy for the people in the East and a great loss for the people in the West.

The resultant birth of two new Republics has opened up new ways of life for the Bangladeshi and the Islamic Pakistanis. It is fervently hoped that the years ahead will see the solving of their individual problems and bring them lasting peace and more prosperous existence.

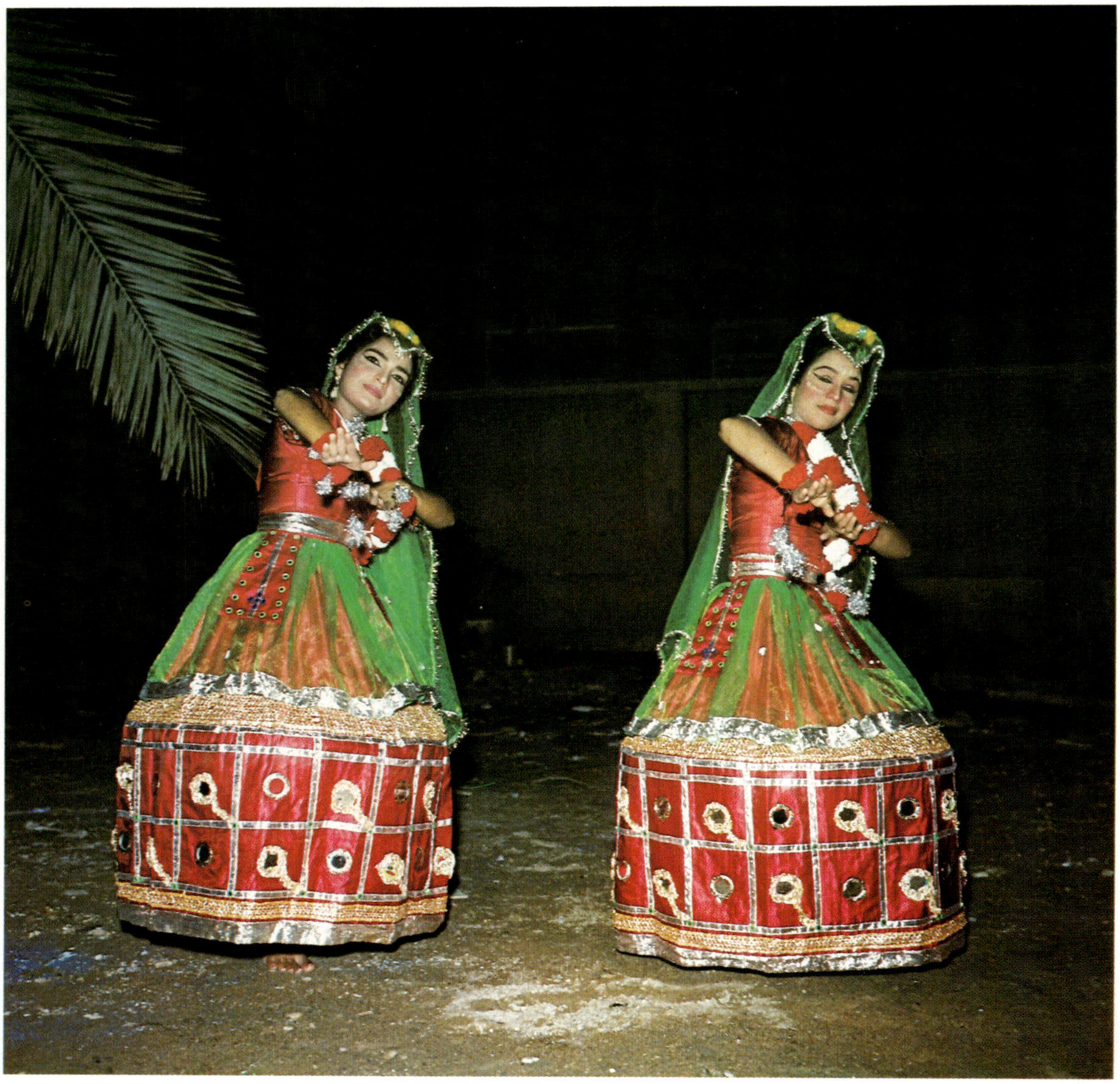

People's Republic of
BANGLADESH

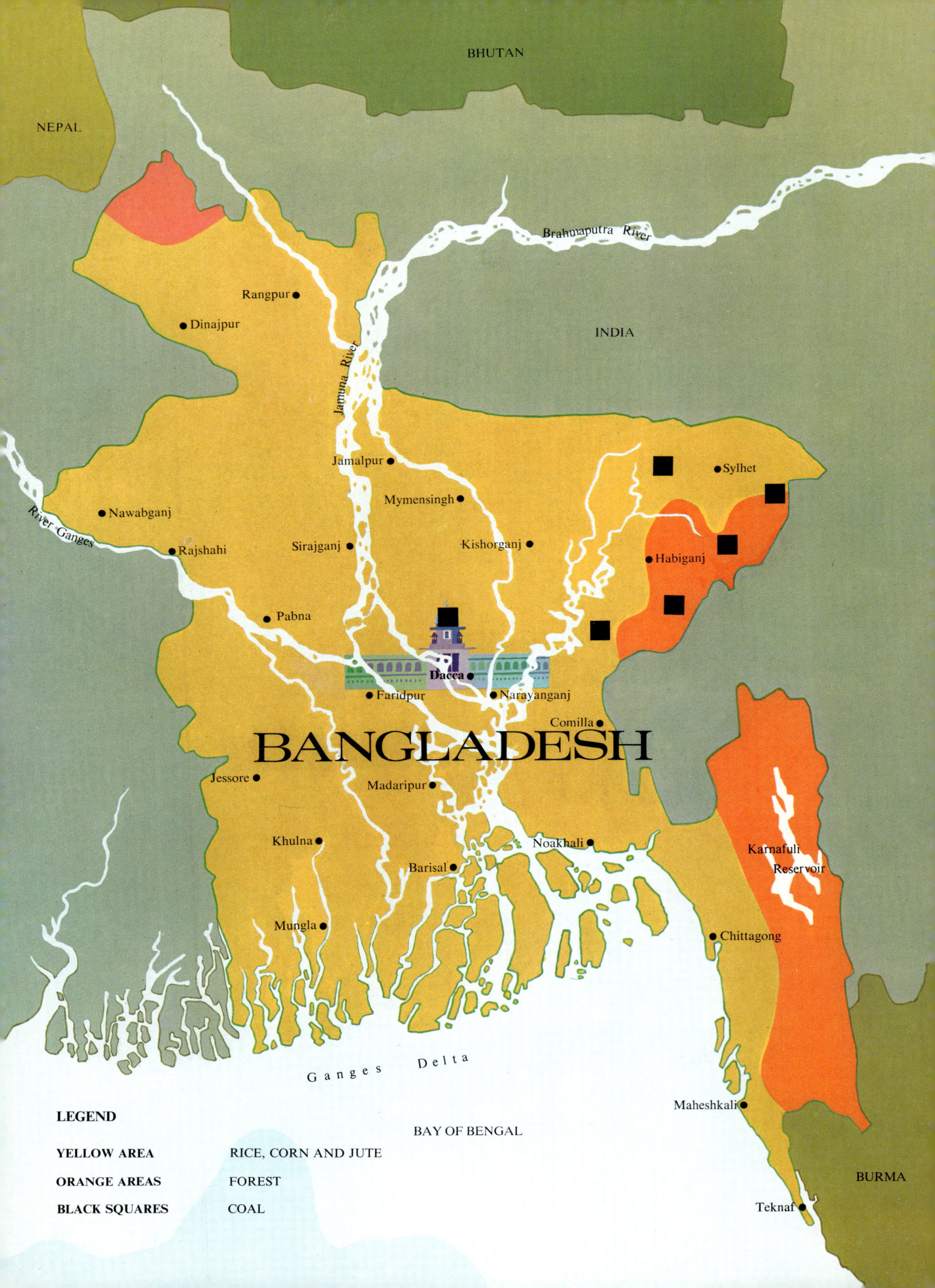

BANGLADESH

LEGEND

YELLOW AREA — RICE, CORN AND JUTE
ORANGE AREAS — FOREST
BLACK SQUARES — COAL

The ancient Seven-Domed Mosque in Dacca, capital city of Bangladesh.

Bangladesh

AREA:
55,126 square miles.

LENGTH AND BREADTH:
315 miles and 216 miles respectively. (Owing to the country's irregular shape and the lack of precise statistics both length and breadth are approximate).

LOCATION:
Between 20° and 27° north latitude and 88° and 93° east longitude. Bounded by the Bay of Bengal to the south, India to the north, west and east, and Burma to the southeast.

TOPOGRAPHY:
Situated in the delta region of the Ganges and Brahmaputra rivers, the country is largely made up of annually-flooded plains. To the east lies the Chittagong hill tracts, an area of steep, rain forest-covered ranges.

CLIMATE:
Humid tropical monsoon. Although there are no real seasons somewhat cooler, dryer weather occurs between November and February (average January temperature in Dacca is 67°F) while the south-west monsoon is associated with warmer, more humid weather (May to September temperatures in Dacca average 84°F).

RAINFALL:
Heavy, mean annual average 74", 75 per cent falling between June and September, the wet months of the year.

RELIGION:
Mainly Muslim, 89 per cent. A minority of 10 per cent of the population still adheres to the Hindu faith.

ETHNIC GROUPS:
The majority group, the Bengalis, are a short, dark people with subdued Mongolian features.

POPULATION:
Approximately 65 million according to 1970 estimates.

POPULATION DENSITY:
1,360 persons per square mile.

POPULATION GROWTH RATE:
Around 2.2 per cent per annum.

Young Nation, Old Country

BORN AT THE BEGINNING of the present year 1972 in the midst of social and economic turmoil, the People's Republic of Bangladesh is the youngest nation in Asia. Yet it has a long and noble history behind it under other names and under other rulers. Beneath the sway of the great Gupta Dynasty, influenced by the successive ebb and flow of Buddhism, Jainism and Brahmanism, and later as part of the Muslim empire in the northern sub-continent after the conquests of Shahbuddin Ghori's general, Bakhotiyar Khilji, the territory later known as East Bengal saw the rise and fall of many civilisations. Beginning in 750 A.D. the Pala Dynasty brought prosperity and stable government to Bengal, where earlier administrations had been described by contemporaries as *matsya nyaya*—chaotic. Dharmapala of this dynasty made himself master of northern India and his influence is said to have extended to Gandhara in West Pakistan.

In the 11th Century Lakshman Sen, overthrowing the Palas, declared himself King of Gaur (Gaureshwar). Despite his first brilliant victories, however, his reign ended with a rout at the hands of the Muslim forces led by Bakhotiyar Khilji at Nadia in 1202. Sen fled to East Bengal to rule there until his death, and then that region, too, fell to the Muslims.

With the coming of the British in the mid 18th Century, Muslim power declined. Supported by Hindu princes and with the recruitment of local soldiers, the British and the Hindus gradually dominated the whole of the sub-continent. They achieved a position where they could challenge the power of the strongest Muslim rulers, even the Nawab of Bengal himself. In the Battle of Plassey in 1757, the Nawab was defeated and the British were thus able to use Bengal as an outpost for new trade and as a base for their drive to the west.

In 1857, the whole of Indo-Pakistan rose in mutiny against the foreign interlopers, and although the bid failed, the stage was set for 90 years of civil and political resistance to British domination. The Muslims of Bengal, who had probably suffered most under British rule, provided leadership in the freedom struggle. In 1906, the All-India Muslim League was formed in Dacca to fight for Muslim political rights. When the British gave a measure of provincial autonomy to India under the Act of 1935, the Muslims of Bengal were sufficiently alive politically to sweep the elections and to capture the government under their great leader, A.K. Fazl-ul-Haq.

Throughout the succeeding twelve years, the Muslims of Bengal played a leading role as the freedom movement gained momentum, and eventually in 1947 they helped win Pakistan from the Indians. The partitioned half of Bengal that came to the share of Pakistan was designated East Pakistan.

Initially optimistic and much more unified than formerly thought possible, Pakistan suffered the first of several blows to its unity with the death in 1948 of its charismatic leader, Mohammed Ali Jinnah. Difficulties in framing a constitution, which many believed would have been resolved had Jinnah lived, continued to arise. After the assassination of his successor, Liaquat Ali Khan, in 1951, further problems developed in evolving a workable national democracy. In 1954, the Central Government dismissed the newly-elected East Wing Cabinet led by the popular Fazl-ul-Haq; riots occurred, and a West Pakistani General was sent to govern the East under special powers. In 1958, in the face of an increasingly corrupt government and a sinking international prestige, the 1956 Constitution—the first ever—was abrogated and a bloodless military coup brought General Ayub Khan to power.

During the next twelve years, the economic dissatisfactions of East Pakistan reached a climax. Specifically these were that: (1) the allocation of foreign exchange earned by the East's jute and that provided by foreign aid disproportionately favoured West Pakistan; (2) that allocation of domestic investment reinforced a great and ever-widening income disparity; and (3) that high tariffs and import quotas raised prices in East Pakistan in order to provide profits and jobs in West Pakistan. According to an independent survey in 1971 by three World Bank officials, Mason, Dorfman and Marglin, "All senior military members of the administration have been West Pakistani, and of the senior officers in the Central civil services 87 per cent were West Pakistani in 1960, and the proportion has not changed much since. The Deputy Chairman of the Planning Commission and the Central Finance Minister, key individuals in resource allocation, have always been West Pakistanis."

Right: The new Dacca stadium with the city skyline in the background.

Below: The High Court of Bangladesh at Dacca.

Although it is no doubt true that the East wing suffered from several great economic disadvantages at the time of the Partitioning of Pakistan, that this disparity should have been permitted to continue without even a partial cure being found was a major contributing cause of the national uprising. Thus it was that when Sheikh Mujib-ur Rahman's Awami League, which advocated economic autonomy for the East, contested the first direct elections in Pakistan in December 1970, it swept to victory, commanding 167 out of 169 East Pakistani seats in the National Assembly. The Party's policy was to transfer control over foreign trade, foreign aid allocation and taxation powers to the provinces. This move was blocked by the major parties in the West who declined to attend a meeting of the Constituent Assembly unless these demands were dropped. The subsequent non-co-operation movement, Yahya Khan's military crack-down, the flight of refugees to India and the birth of Bangladesh are described by Derek Davies in his Chapter "The Economic Explosion" in the early part of this book.

THE LAND AND THE LIVING

Seen from the air Bangladesh appears as a green and watery world, an endless stretch of rice-fields, dotted with meandering groves of trees and criss-crossed by a thick network of rivers, streams and ponds. Here, in its vast alluvial terrain, are nestled the 100,000 villages in which the bulk of the population lives.

There is no simple itinerary which will take the traveller to every important town in Bangladesh, for they are relatively few and scattered at widely divergent points in a great labyrinth of rivers. No more than four or five towns have populations exceeding 100,000 and old-fashioned steamers ply the rivers that flow between them. Dacca, the capital, is a city of mosques. Although the minarets and domes of its temples dominate the scene modern buildings of contemporary architecture are gradually springing up beside them. The shops sell the nation's finest handicrafts, particularly the Dacca muslin for which the country is famous. Silver and conch shell jewellery are also in demand.

The trees of the country range from the splendid mango to the multi-trunked banyan; wild flowers, ferns and weeds cover every unused inch of ground. That cruel beauty, the water hyacinth, chokes the water-ways and ponds and even strangles the young paddy-rice. Not satisfied with mere chaotic beauty around his homestead the Bangladeshi peasant plants the Bengal Rose, the Queen of the Night—Nyctanthis

Above: A student at work at the Dacca College of Arts.

Left:
A market scene—a meeting place in a suburb of Dacca.

Arbortristis, the Jasmine, and—the most loved and painted flower in the nation—the Kamini.

THE ECONOMY

Although the new Bangladeshi economy is basically the same jute-and-rice structure it was prior to the 1971 conflict, the new government has introduced certain basic changes concerning ownership, collectivisation, industrialisation and markets.

Now that peace is restored and Bangladesh has already been diplomatically recognised by most of the world, the immediate task lies in resettling the many millions rendered homeless by the war. To do this Bangladesh will need an enormous amount of aid; it has been estimated that at least US$1 billion will be required to prevent widespread famine, without even considering the vast sums needed to restore agriculture and industry to full productive capacity.

Looking to the future, the big challenge will be to build a viable economy on the ashes of under-industrialised, semi-colonial East Pakistan.

INDUSTRY

Before the creation of Bangladesh, some of the larger West Pakistani industrial concerns set up manufacturing branches in the East Wing; for example: jute mills and a machine tools factory in Dacca; a steel mill and an electrical wire and cable plant in Chittagong, and a newsprint mill in Khulna. All principal industries, including those mentioned, have been nationalised but it is not yet certain how these will operate without the capital and expertise so long injected by the Western Wing.

AGRICULTURE

About five-sevenths of the country's area is under cultivation. Agriculture is intensive; up to three or even more crops a year are grown on most farms. Three-quarters of the land is under rice, one-tenth under jute and a smaller fraction is devoted to tea. Although monsoon rains often flood the country, a properly managed irrigation system to offset lack of rain during the 'dry' season could increase production by as much as 33 per cent. Since the former Western Wing grows a much greater range of crops, including wheat, fruits and vegetables which it once supplied to its Eastern sector, Bangladesh is now forced to sow a greater diversity of food crops, in order to conserve much needed foreign exchange. The importance of jute, too, will have to be re-assessed, as synthetics are now replacing it to some extent.

NATURAL RESOURCES

Bangladesh is a delta region and singularly lacking in mineral resources. Even the limestone for building has to be imported. Without commercial coal-reserves the nation has been fortunate in discovering natural gas in sufficient quantities to keep the country supplied with fuel for years to come.

TRANSPORT

Due to the danger of damage by flooding surface transport by road and rail has been late in developing. Surfaced roads now cover about 12,500 miles and dirt roads extend a further 98,500 miles to serve a considerable area. The latter, however, are not functional during the monsoon. Railways have been improved by dieselisation. Chittagong is the major port, handling 43 million tons of shipping annually. The inland rivers, still mainly used by small private craft and cargo-carrying barges, are capable of being developed into a highly efficient means of transport.

Opposite page, top:
Girl students
in the garden of
Rajshahi University of
Bangladesh.

Opposite page, below:
Timber packs
made ready for
floating down river
to the sawmills, at
Dacca.

Below:
Making dolls
in the national
costume of Bangladesh in
a design centre
at Dacca.

Foot of page:
Assembling motors in
a machine shop of the Machine
Tools Factory at Joyadapur,
near Dacca.

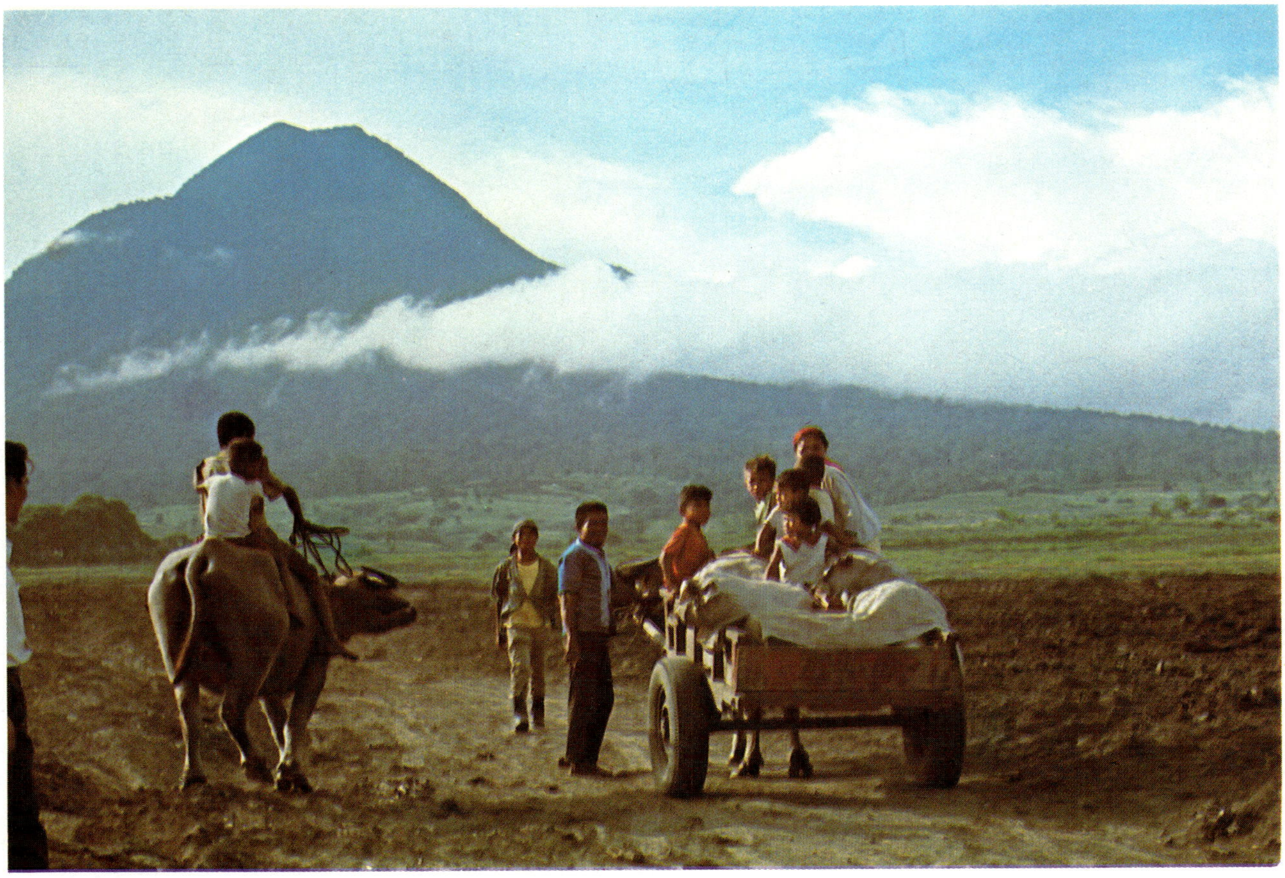

Republic of the
PHILIPPINES

PHILIPPINES

LEGEND

- 🟥 RICE & CORN
- 🟧 MISCELLANEOUS AGRICULTURE
- 🟩 FOREST
- IRON
- COPPER
- GOLD
- MANGANESE
- SULPHUR

FACTS ABOUT THE PHILIPPINES

THE PHILIPPINE ARCHIPELAGO is made up of 7,107 islands covering a land area of 115,739 square miles located between 21°21′ and 4°23′ north latitude and 116°55′ and 126° east longitude. It is about 600 miles off the southern coast of Asia, bounded on the north by Taiwan, on the south by East Malaysia, the east by the Pacific and on the west by the China Sea. The fragmented shape and topographic features of the larger inhabited islands are formidable obstacles to the economic development of the country.

A mobile belt extends longitudinally through Luzon, the Visayas and Mindanao, characterised by earthquake epicentres, numerous active and inactive volcanoes.

In contrast there is a stable region confined to the south-western sections embracing Palawan, the Cuyo Island group, the Sulu Sea and southern Mindoro.

Luzon consists of three ranges with intermediate lowland belts. From west to east are the Western Cordillera and the Cordillera Central—comprising steep slopes, deep ravines, canyons, irregular patterns of ridges and peaks above 6,500 and 8,000 feet—and the Sierra Madre Mountains with peaks ranging from 4,000 to 5,000 feet, throughout their entire length of 350 miles. The lowland areas are the Central Plain and the Cagayan Valley. The Trinidad Valley and the Baguio Upland are the best known of their categories. The southernmost extension of the range is the Bondoc Peninsula where hills are low and rolling.

Many of the islands in the *Visayas* are eroded crests and the mountains are rough and steep. Extinct and active volcanoes are widely scattered.

Mindoro is a broad anticline with extensive lowlands along the east and north-east coasts. The central part is made up of rugged mountains which extend over the entire length of the island.

Palawan forms a chain of mountainous or hilly islands resting on a great reef-strewn bank along the north-west margin of the Sulu Sea. It constitutes an interrupted land bridge about 450 miles long from North Borneo to Mindoro.

CLIMATE

Temperatures in the Philippines are fairly uniform, with little variation between the coldest month and the warmest. In comparison, rainfall variation is great, involving typhoon and other types of tropical disturbances from June to October particularly in the northern half of the Philippines. The southern half is subject to winds and air masses from the northern hemisphere converging with those from the southern hemisphere.

NATURAL RESOURCES

Soils. Fertile alluvial soils in the lowland areas are the most important agricultural soils in the Philippines; heavy textured and difficult-to-manage grumosols are commonly found in plains and hills in the western and southern parts of the country.

Vegetation. The principle vegetation in the Philippines consists of mangrove swamps along the coasts, tropical rainforests covering large areas in lowlands and lower mountain slopes, pine forests in higher mountain ranges, and mossy forests on the slopes of some of the highest mountains.

Grasslands called *cognales* are largely the outcome of continuous *kaingin* or "slash and burn" method of shifting cultivation: the cutting down of trees and brush early in the dry season and then burning them later. The cleared land is used for one or two seasons and then abandoned for a new clearing.

Agricultural Resources. Land suitable for agriculture in the Philippines amounts to about one-third of the total land surface. Approximately 27 per cent is farmlands, including a relatively small area in pastures. Although the total farm area is substantial, cultivated land is relatively small and yields are low.

The favourable combination of topography, climate, soils and natural vegetation has provided the arable land area which man has made productive.

Land with gradual slopes can be readily cultivated, the upper slope limits requiring special farming methods and techniques such as terracing, contouring and strip cropping.

Forest Resources. The large and diverse forests of the Philippines constitute a valuable resource. Slightly over one-fourth of the total land surface is covered by commercial forest stands from which timber is cut. There are important stands of hardwood and other timbers related to the teak family.

74 per cent of the commercial forest lands are found in north-eastern and south-western Mindanao, southern Luzon and adjacent islands, and the Cagayan Valley. The aggregate volume of standing hardwood timber of 55 centimetres or more in diameter, in commercial and non-commercial forests, is over 853,000,000 cubic metres.

However, of the 3,500 tree species known throughout the Philippine islands only 100 are commonly used and 60 are commercially important.

Fishery Resources. The Philippines has an extensive coastline of 11,000 miles with numerous protected anchorages. The islands possess a wide variety but limited quantity of fish.

Opportunities for the development of offshore fisheries are fairly good with the use of advanced technologies developed locally and abroad. Offshore or deep-sea fishing is relatively new and there are very few large deep-sea fishing craft owned by Filipinos. Inland fisheries are capable of much greater development among the 716,000 hectares of swamps and marshes in the country.

Fauna. There are very few species of bird and animal life in the Philippines, mostly found in Mindanao, Sulu and Palawan. The more numerous permanent regional birds are pigeons, parrots, pheasants, doves, quail, cuckoos, jungle fowl and ducks.

Deer, boar, some civet cats and monkeys were once found everywhere throughout the Philippine islands but are now less numerous.

There are various types of squirrels, tree shrews, lemurs, lorises and crocodiles. The tamaraw or wild carabo is confined to Mindoro.

Fuel Resources. The Philippines has problems with regard to fuel resources. Coal reserves are small, scattered and low grade, generally of the non-coking variety. Oil and natural gas in commercial quantities have yet to be discovered. Water, however, as a source of power holds more promise. Mountain topography and high annual precipitation make hydro-electric power development feasible. But large hydro-electric power sites in the Philippines are few.

Metals and Minerals. The metals and minerals of the Philippines are dealt with elsewhere in the Republic of the Philippines' Chapter.

Whence came the Filipino

AS WITH ALMOST every other Asian country, the history of the Philippines provides evidence of thriving social, economic and political life in the islands long before the coming of the Westerner. Although historical records of the pre-Western era are scant, the Filipino's reconstruction of his past reaches far beyond the time of the country's discovery in the middle of the 16th Century.

Pre-Spanish Era. Long before the coming of the Spaniards the Filipinos lived in communities, or extended family groups, that indicated a distinct form of social and political organisation. These communities have since become known as *barangays*, a hispanicised term, because according to one tradition the original settlers on the islands had sailed from Malaysia and Indonesia in ships called *balangay*.

Thus began a society of status based on kinship. Each community was economically self-contained, providing for its needs by means of agriculture, some form of household industry, and trade.

Although contacts between barangays were necessarily limited and occasionally took the form of confrontations, some barangays tended to have a more advanced form of political organisation: a body of literature, a government based on the barangay principle, and a set of written laws—the Code of Kalantiao. There is evidence of lively commercial relations between the Philippine islands and neighbouring countries during the pre-Western Era. The Spaniards in fact found a culture that showed Indian, Chinese and Arabic influences.

Trade relations with China appear to have been established in the 9th Century of the Christian Era. By the middle of the 14th Century, other countries of the Far East, like Cambodia and Champa in Indo-China, had a burgeoning trade with the Philippines, bartering their porcelain products for Philippine wares. A little later, Annam, Siam and Tonkin also began trade with the Philippines. Vigorous commercial exchange lasted up to the Javanese or Madjapahit Empire.

In the 15th Century, following the establishment of the Malaccan Empire, Islam spread to the Philippines, principally in the southern islands of Mindanao. The Filipino Muslims rapidly developed a flourishing commercial trade with Chinese and Indo-Chinese.

Despite this clear evidence of activity in the islands, inter-relations between the different groups of inhabitants remained largely polarised from ritualistic politeness on the one hand, to open conflict on the other hand.

European Discovery and Settlement. By the 16th Century a struggle for control of the lucrative spice trade at its source—the Moluccas—had developed among European nations. This became the motive and impetus for Spanish expansionism in Asia. On 16th March 1521, the Portuguese explorer Ferdinand Magellan, in the service of the King of Castille, reached the Philippines archipelago to prove his theory that the earth was round. Personal glory was short-lived, however, for a month later he was killed on the island of Mactan in a battle with native warriors led by Lapulapu. The survivors of his command continued west and returned to Spain, and with their return commenced the Spanish conquest and colonisation of the Philippine islands.

Five more expeditions were dispatched by the Spanish crown to continue the exploration of the new islands claimed by Magellan for the crown. The first four were disastrous failures, but the last, led by Miguel Lopez de Legaspi from Navidad, Mexico, reached Cebu on 27th April 1565. With him, besides his crew and troops, were six friars.

It was Legaspi who subsequently gave the name "Filipinas" to the entire archipelago, in honour of King Philip II of Spain. The first years of Spanish colonisation were marked by threats posed against Spanish authority in the islands by the Portuguese, the Dutch, the Chinese, and the Filipinos themselves.

None of these threats prospered, but in Mindanao, the Moros, as the Spaniards called the Muslim Filipinos after the Moors in Spain, held fast against Spanish rule and Christianisation. Christian settlements and armed outposts were organised in Mindanao as a brake to attacks by Muslims, but the latter crossed these barriers easily. Nor did the Muslims confine their rebellion against Spanish rule to Mindanao and Sulu. Time and again they carried out lightning raids that reached out as far as Northern Luzon, and this threat to Spanish colonial rule was to persist well into the 19th Century when steamboats finally arrived in the islands and curbed the activities of the Muslim *vintas*.

Yet the Filipino Muslims remained insulated from the colonial designs of the Spaniards, and up to the American occupation of the Philippines, they were to remain relatively free of foreign domination.

The Philippine Revolution. With the Christianised Filipinos, Spanish rule did not sit well. Time and again, pocket rebellions erupted in various parts of the islands, and by the 19th Century there had grown in the country a fully-fledged movement for independence. There were several reasons for this, the principal being the abuses of the Spanish colonial authority and the avarice of the Spanish friars. At the same time, a kind of enlightenment had dawned on the Filipinos, enhanced not only by their bitter colonial experience but also by a growing national and political consciousness, by the influence of the Spanish Cortez, by the opening of Philippine ports to foreign trade, and by the rise of a Filipino middle class.

The inability of the colonial government to satisfy the reformist demands of the Filipinos resulted finally in revolution, launched in 1896 by the Katipunan, a secret revolutionary society, under the leadership of Andres Bonifacio, a labourer and self-taught man.

Leadership passed shortly from Bonifacio to Emilio Aguinaldo, who carried the revolutionary movement to its first tastes of victory and first addressed his countrymen as "the Filipino people".

Events moved fast for the people who had been sequestered for more than 200 years. An armistice was agreed upon between the revolutionaries and the Spanish authorities in 1897, but in May of the following year hostilities resumed. On 12th June 1898 Aguinaldo proclaimed the independence of the Philippines. A constitutional congress met in September and drafted the first republican constitution in Asia. The revolution now had a government, a constitution, a united people, and a national leader. On 23rd January 1899 the first Philippine Republic was inaugurated.

The Philippine-American War. But the Republic was not to survive, for it was launched in the shadow of yet another alien thirst for expansion—American imperialism. War with Spain having been declared over Cuba, the United States sailed from Hong Kong on 27th April 1898 to wage war against the embattled Spaniards. Victory was swift for the Americans, after a mock show of Spanish resistance in Manila Bay, and the Filipino revolutionary movement took a sudden but definite turn. Spain ceded the Philippines by treaty to the U.S.A.

Conflict between the Filipino people and the Americans became unavoidable, and less than a month after the proclamation of the First Philippine Republic, hostilities broke out. Fresh from a costly war of independence, the Filipinos took the front short of ammunition and depleted of troops. The issue was never in doubt, and in 1901 President Aguinaldo was captured. Shortly afterwards the ensuing guerilla resistance likewise collapsed.

The American Occupation. Upon the surrender of Manila, the Americans established a military government. In 1900 the so-called Spooner Amendment was passed by the United States Congress, authorising the President of the United States of America to establish a civil government in the Philippines.

The American occupation, from 1900 to 1946, was a half century of compromise between the claims of jingoistic American imperialism at the turn of the century, and the ideals of Filipino nationalism. A lack of unity back home in America regarding the imperialist adventure resulted in a moderated form of imperialism, manifested by policies of accommodation toward the Filipinos. The resulting sense of participation for the Filipinos in their political affairs quenched what remained of their independent spirit. For the next four decades, life with the American colonisers was to be marked by co-operation and trust. Henceforth, the Filipino people would seek to win their independence at the bargaining table.

In 1934, a Philippine Mission headed by Senate President Manuel L. Quezon secured the passage of a new independence law—the Tydings-McDuffie law.

A Constitutional Convention was held to frame an organic law. The new Constitution, patterned on American lines but unitary in structure, was approved by President Franklin D. Roosevelt on 23rd March 1935 and was later ratified in a plebiscite by the Filipino electorate. In the meantime, a Commonwealth government was instituted to preside over the transition from a colony to an independent republic, and Quezon was elected President.

The Commonwealth of the Philippines was inaugurated on 15th November 1935. The Commonwealth year and Quezon's leadership were marked by an overwhelming concern for social justice and national unity. Yet the orderly transition to full republican status was not to transpire as planned, for on 8th December 1941 the country was invaded by the Japanese forces.

The Filipinos and Americans fought bravely but they were grossly outnumbered, and on 6th May 1942, with the fall of Corregidor, the Philippines passed to Japanese rule. The ensuing three years were a time of great adversity and suffering for the majority of Filipinos. Under conditions of extreme hardship, some maintained a stubborn and effective guerilla resistance that continued until the country was liberated by the American forces.

Three days after the Americans landed on Leyte on 20th October 1944, the Commonwealth government was re-established on Philippine soil with Sergio Osmena as President. President Manuel L. Quezon had died a month earlier while ministering to the government in exile.

The Second Philippine Republic. It was in a setting of desolation that the second Philippine Republic was born on 4th July 1946, as provided for by the Philippine Independence Act of 1934. Crushing problems of rehabilitation and reconstruction faced the Republic and its President, Manuel Roxas. Before he could finish his term and before the country could be said to have truly recovered from the ravages of the war, President Roxas died in office in July 1948. He was succeeded by his Vice-President, Elpidio Quirino.

President Quirino went on to win a presidential term in his own right in 1949, but a graft-ridden administration sent him to defeat in 1953 at the hands of his former Secretary of National Defense, Ramon Magsaysay. President Magsaysay, however, did not live long enough to finish his term and to win almost certain re-election. He died in a plane crash nine months before the expansion of his presidential term. His successor, President Carlos P. Garcia, established himself well enough in the next nine months, but the same inability as experienced by his predecessors to solve the major problems of the country, doomed his re-election bid in the presidential polls of 1961.

Below: A native clay stove, relic of the early days of the Philippines. Many families living in the *barios* still use this type of heater.

The fifth President of the second Philippine Republic, Diosdado Macapagal, launched a programme under the aegis of what he called "the Unfinished Revolution" but a preoccupation with politics left the all-important agenda barely touched. To his credit, he pushed through the Congress the most substantial land reform programme ever launched by the government, but his achievement could not offset the mounting problems of the country.

In the 1965 elections, a new President, Ferdinand E. Marcos, emerged. In his first year he launched an ambitious development programme that gravely taxed the coffers of government. In the long run, however, this resulted in increased rural productivity, growth in industry and development of infrastructures.

In 1969 President Marcos sought another mandate from the Filipino electorate and was re-elected—an unprecedented feat.

Beyond the clearly evident signs of a viable and healthy democracy, however, the marks of a society in transition are apparent. The body politic appears to have a new and pervasive interest in national affairs, exemplified by the awakening of the studentry and the labour and peasant sectors. The Filipino people seem bent on making the system and its various institutions more workable than they have been for the past several decades.

They had an unique opportunity of doing just that in the Constitutional Convention of 1971, the historic meeting at which significant plans were put forward for the future government of the Philippines in the ensuing years.

THE CULTURAL HERITAGE

All Asian peoples have been subjected, to some degree, to the impact of Western culture, but few to the extent of the Filipinos. The commingling of Eastern and European influences has given the Philippines a culture that is truly unique in its diversity and richness.

The Filipino's cultural heritage stems mainly from the Malay, Spanish and Anglo-Saxon, but Chinese, Arabic and Indian cultures have also been introduced.

For all its admixtures, however, Philippine culture is basically and predominantly Malay. The assimilation of Western and Oriental influences is typical of the Malay temperament—eclectic and easy to adjust. Thus, what one sees in the national culture today—in the life-styles of the Filipinos, in their outlook, in their art and literature—has become peculiarly Filipino.

The Cultural Centre of the Philippines. In recent years, there has been a concerted drive to preserve the centuries-old art and literature of the Philippines and promote among the people a greater knowledge and appreciation of their priceless heritage. Among the more significant projects is the Cultural Centre of the Philippines. In an imposing complex of buildings on Manila Bay, the Centre sponsors performing arts, a cultural library, and a fine guesthouse for visiting artists from other countries.

The Cultural Centre is an achievement of private and government initiative, conducted as a private institution. The government's own programmes for the promotion, teaching, and patronage of the arts come mainly in the form of supplementing and aiding the various arts associations, and in supporting with scholarships and giving recognition to local artists and writers.

One of the highest honours bestowed by the nation for cultural and artistic achievement is the annual Republic Cultural Heritage Award, which is conferred upon Filipino artists and writers.

Almost every Filipino university has its own programme for training students for the theatre, the fine arts, literature and other cultural activities.

Painting and Sculpture. In contemporary Filipino painting and sculpture the old is blended skilfully with the modern, an intricate admixture of Spanish and pre-Spanish culture with the complex abstract forms of contemporary art.

Filipino painting is as old as the intricate tapestries and decorations made by the Malays when they first settled in the archipelago. The subsequent conquest of the islands opened this native art to European influences that culminated in the colourful religious art of the Spanish period and the famous paintings of Juan Luna and Resurreccion Hidalgo.

Filipino sculpture has a similar, if not older, history dating far back to the pre-Spanish Era. Before European contact, the Filipinos carved figures of animals, herds, men and women, from wood and stone. The Muslims evolved a unique and intricate metal work. With the arrival of the Spaniards, sculpture acquired a religious theme among the Christian Filipinos and many beautiful carvings were made for churches, particularly scriptural images and intricate designs in masonry.

Today, schools of fine arts abound in Manila, and painting has become one of the more profitable professions to pursue. Many Filipino painters and sculptors have won recognition abroad.

Music. The Filipinos had a strong musical heritage long before the coming of the Westerner, and many musical forms still retain their traditional formats almost free of Spanish influence. True Filipino music is still evident today in the survival of native musical instruments and native composition—largely folk music, descriptive of the Malay's way of life.

Formal musical compositions are now coming from Filipino composers and musicologists, from Abelards and Francisco to Pajars, Kesilag, de Leon and Macedo. The rush of American pop culture has swamped Filipino classical music and folk songs with the sounds of Frank Sinatra, the Beatles and other favourites, but luckily, has not stifled it.

Architecture. One of the most valuable legacies of the Spanish Era is the great wealth of architecture that still survives. It is most evident in the century-old Filipino churches and is often remarked upon for its beauty, design and solidity. A few of these legacies are the worse for wear and tear of the years.

The development of an international style of architecture after the last World War found its way to the Philippines, and much has been influenced by the work of Frank Lloyd Wright. Yet the Filipino tradition is still obvious. Foreigners often remark on the Filipino architect's aptitude for home design.

Theatre. Unlike some other arts in the Philippines, theatre never found a long enduring tradition strong enough to connect the theatre of the pre-Hispanic Filipino to the Hispanic theatre and finally to the stage of today.

Pre-Hispanic Filipino theatre leaned heavily on religious rituals. A partial picture can be reconstructed from the studies of anthropologists who maintained that it consisted of pantomime, chanting and magical drum-beating. Yet, one never gains a clear picture of how much of the

Left:
Nila Cathedral
one of many examples
of Spanish architecture to
be found in the
Philippines.

Opposite page:
An antique
brooch of Indonesian
origin featuring
a garuda.

pre-Hispanic religious drama was lost on contact with the new and aggressive culture of the Spaniards. Since it was barely at its threshold the impact of European culture displaced it substantially.

Since Christianisation was a main objective of Spanish conquest, and pre-Hispanic theatre was rooted in religious ritual, the Spanish priests undertook a real campaign to bring down the spirits which then embodied religion for the inhabitants of the islands. In place of the old rituals, the Spaniards introduced religious theatre which flourished rapidly, and in a short time the Filipinos had their own kind of passion play, *cenaculo,* and their *moro-moro* (dramas on themes of the Victories of Christians over infidels) and *za-zuelas,* (satires on politics and society in the form of revues).

None of these forms have survived today as typical Filipino theatrical presentations, although occasionally one still finds a *moro-moro* being staged during a town fiesta or a *za-zuela* resurrected by some eager lover of Philippine theatre.

Contemporary Filipino theatre, whether in English or Pilipino, is really modern theatre, with all that it implies in terms of dramaturgy and staging; but it still has to find an enduring repertory of Filipino plays. Filipino playwrights are a growing tribe and growing bolder in their writings, and these are shown alongside the European and American plays that at present constitute part of the repertoire of the Philippine theatre.

Literature. Although there is no single literary tradition in the Philippines, there is an abundance of Filipino literary works in other traditions and various other languages that aptly describe the sensibility of the Filipino.

In official languages, Pilipino, English and Spanish, there is a distinct body of Filipino writing. And in at least four of the major dialects spoken in the country, there are likewise strong and enduring literary traditions.

Filipino literature during the Spanish era was largely political in content and in interest. The foremost Filipino novels in Spanish are *Noli Me Tangere* and *El Filibusterismo,* written by the Filipino patriot, Dr. Jose Rizal. They were written in sequel and dealt mainly with Spanish abuses committed against the Filipinos, and represented the thinking of the emergent Filipino during the latter half of the 19th Century. Similarly the most famous Filipino poetry of the period written in Tagalog, *Florante at Laura,* by Francisco Balagtas, was a long epic poem with a political message to and about the oppressed people.

Philippine literature in English has since become dominant on the contemporary scene. While it is concededly young, it has rapidly developed in the various literary forms—novel, short story, poetry, drama and essay. As in the other arts, the Filipino has made use of an alien tool (English) for the literary expression of his sensibility although much effort is being exerted by him to express himself equally in the national language Pilipino. In English he retains a great deal that is uniquely Filipino and mysterious to the foreigner.

A FILIPINO FARMER'S FAMILY

It is a cold, sharp December dawn and Tonio awakens to his mother's call for breakfast. It is the cool, dry season of the Philippines and only scattered clumps of bamboo and mango trees break the chill winds that blow over the farming lands just outside the town. Leaving his bed reluctantly, Tonio is glad he changed into heavy flannel pyjamas the night before. Like most Filipinos, Tonio's family sits down to a breakfast of boiled rice, fried fish and coffee with brown sugar. Sometimes, on very special occasions, they have bread and margarine, topped with cottage cheese. At first light, Tonio's *Tatay* (father) leaves home for the rice fields and the family eats in silence. After the meal, Tonio puts the dishes away while his sisters wash up and clean the wooden table.

Tonio's *Nanay* (mother) wraps the breakfast left-overs in a banana leaf for the childrens' lunches and pours coffee into a clean bottle for Tatay. Before they leave for school—a ten-minute walk across the paddies—the children take Nanay's right hand and touch it to their foreheads as she blesses them in the traditional manner. At 7.15 a.m. the school bell rings and the children assemble in the schoolyard to salute the flag of the Philippines and sing the national anthem. The principal then gives a short speech on the week's topic—responsibility—before the children march into class. Being in fourth grade, Tonio has to work only until 12.30 p.m., while his sisters, in fifth and sixth grade, must stay until 4.30 in the afternoon.

Back at the farm house, Tonio's elder brother, Berto (*kuya*) arrives for breakfast. He drives a motorised bicycle with a sidecar and earns 5 or 6 pesos (about US 80 cents) a day. He does not own the bicycle but drives it in return for a percentage of his earnings. He is only sixteen, and every evening he hands over all his pay to his mother. Nanay is sorry that they cannot send him to high school but she hopes that one day she will have saved enough from his earnings to buy him his own bicycle.

While Berto is eating, Nanay takes rice and fish to the rice field for Tatay's breakfast. He eats it under a mango tree, telling his wife that he will be home for lunch, as he plans to mend the bamboo fence. They sit for a while and discuss the pending harvest. If it does not rain, Tatay tells his wife they will have a wonderful Christmas. Happy with the thought of a good season, Nanay walks back through the fields, where the rice-plants are drooping, heavy with grain. She cheerfully begins the housework: floors are wiped clean; window sills dusted and stairs scrubbed. She takes the clay pots and pans, now black with soot from the wood-burning stove, down to the yard to the artesian well where she washes them in a large iron tub. After refilling the tub with fresh water she gives the baby her daily outdoor bath.

Freshly washed and dressed, the baby amuses herself on the floor, while Nanay measures out three cups of rice into the pot and starts the cooking fire for the noon meal. Hearing the woman fish-vendor's raucous call she walks to the gate and after much haggling, selects the day's supply, about two pesos' worth. A little later Tonio and Tatay arrive home for their usual lunch of rice and fish served with fresh, garden-grown cucumbers. Nanay glows with pride when Tatay comments that her salt and vinegar dressing is very good.

Tonio gets rather tired of rice and fish every day and wonders when they will have beef or chicken again—perhaps at Christmas.

After lunch the children take their usual siesta, while the adults sit sleepily by the window. An hour later Tatay begins mending the fence and Nanay does the washing, scrubbing the clothes and bleaching the linen in the sun. Tonio and his baby sister play until late afternoon when it is time to feed the chickens. The two girls arrive home about half past four. The elder minds the baby while her sister helps Nanay with the evening meal, the same as lunch with some extra vegetables added. At dusk the family gathers around the table. Tonio remembers when the village had no electricity and they had to eat before sundown. But now there is electric light, and after the dishes are put away, they sit around the radio and listen to the news.

Sometimes the neighbours drop in to listen with them and the adults discuss the latest newscast. The current topic is student unrest in the city and Berto relates how a group of students came to town that morning to talk to farmers about their rights under the land reform laws. The three schoolchildren are studying in the kitchen but Tonio listens quietly to what the grown-ups are saying. He begins to wonder if his dream of one day going to the city will ever come true and trembles at the thought of being mistaken for a student rioter. Nanay says the students are being used by revolutionaries but Berto insists that they truly love their country and the common people. Another discussion opens up and Tatay tells of the Philippines he knew as a young boy.

At nine o'clock the visitors say goodnight. Another day is gone. Prayers are said, lights are turned out and soon Tonio and his family are asleep.

THE FILIPINOS

The people of the Philippines both in their culture and their origins, are predominantly Malay, but the impact of more than three centuries of Spanish, followed by American, rule infused into the native culture a wide variety of influences and diversified to some extent the Filipino bloodstream. From their Malay origins alone, in the Filipinos run the strains of the Indians, Persians, Arabs, Thais and the Chinese of the Chou period. To these have been added the blood of the Europeans and the Anglo-Saxons in the aftermath of European discovery and colonisation.

The great diversity of the Filipino strain is mirrored in a culture which has often been described as "hybrid", a term used to describe the curious mingling of Western and Oriental cultures in Philippine life. Yet, the historical evidence indicates that the matrix of Philippine culture preceded the arrival of the Westerner, and the lives of Filipinos today further show that whatever

Right:
Festivities in the Philippines go very much hand in hand with the religious customs of the people, each observance and pageant being a cause of joy.

Below left:
Filipinos bagging a crop after harvest.

they have adopted from Western civilisation they have made peculiarly their own. This is particularly demonstrated by the manner in which the people have interwoven Christianity and democracy into their way of life.

Population. The Filipinos today number 39,102,000 and by 1975 the population is expected to reach 42,743,000. This will mainly be due to the country's 3.5 per cent population growth rate, one of the highest in the world. In Asia alone it ranks third, next to the 7.1 and 4.1 per cent annual population increase of Kuwait and Jordan. A sustained high birth rate combined with a rapidly declining death rate has been the main cause of this accelerated growth. Improved living conditions brought about by better health services, by the advancement of science and technology, and by the country's economic development, have reduced the death rate and given the Filipinos a life expectancy of 52 to 55 years.

The majority of the Filipino population belongs to the group under 25 years of age, roughly 75 per cent of the entire total, and with a computed median age of 16 years, the Filipinos are relatively young among the peoples of the world.

The most populous province is Rizal, with 2,097,000 inhabitants, and Negros Eccidental comes next with 1.88 million. Cebu is third, with 1.87 million. Manila supports 1.6 million. Other populous cities are the suburban cities of Greater Manila, Baguio, Cebu, Dagupan, Marawi, Cavite, Iloilo, Angeles and Quezon City, the capital of the Philippines. The urban areas have an average population density of 1,000 persons per square kilometre.

Religion. Freedom of worship is a right guaranteed and safeguarded by the Philippine Constitution, and in the Filipino milieu, practically every faith is represented. The majority of the population, however, is decidedly Christian, comprising some 94 per cent of the total. Catholics account for 83.8 per cent; Protestants, 2.9 per cent; Aglipayans, 5.2 per cent; and Inglesia ni Kriste, 1.5 per cent. Non-Christian Filipinos make up a little over 6 per cent of the population, foremost among them being the Muslims, 4.9 per cent.

The Muslims are concentrated mainly in southernmost regions of Mindanao and Sulu, and their conversion to the Islamic faith dates as far back as 1380, long before the arrival of Christianity. Their subsequent resistance to Spanish attempts to Christianise them remains a significant page in Philippine history. Today the Muslims are truly a part of the national community and their participation in national affairs has grown considerably in the past decade.

Labour Force. The labour force of the Philippines has steadily increased since the birth of the second Republic. Today, it is estimated to be 11.8 million. The rise in numbers has been generated mainly by the government's intensive work in this area through agencies such as the Department of Labour and its Manpower Development Council.

The urban labour force in 1967 was estimated at 3.4 million, males outnumbering the females by 5 to 3. The rural labour force number 8.3 million, 70 per cent of the total force.

Language. Another indication of the great variety and richness of Philippine life is the 87 different languages and dialects spoken by the Filipinos. The ten major tongues are *Tagalog,* spoken in Manila, Mindoro and most of Luzon; *Cebuano* spoken in Cebu, Bohol and parts of Mindanao; *Hiligaynon,* spoken in Samar and Leyte; *Bikol,* spoken in the Bicol provinces; *Pampango,* spoken in Pampanga and Tarlac; *Ilocano,* spoken in La Union and the Ilocos provinces; *Maguindanao,* spoken by the Muslims; and *Tausog,* spoken by the Muslims of Zamboanga and the Sulu archipelago.

These languages are mainly of Malayo-Polynesian and Sanskrit origin, but many have assimilated words from the Indian, Arabic, Chinese, Spanish and English languages. With the founding of the second Philippine Republic on 4th July 1946, Tagalog was made the national language of the Philippines. English, however, is the primary medium of instruction in the schools. In 1962 the name Tagalog for the national language was officially changed to "Pilipino".

EDUCATION SYSTEMS

The Philippine Constitution and other laws have provided for a free public school system on the grade school level, on the principle that "all educational institutions shall be under the supervision of and subject to regulations by the State. The Government shall provide at least public primary education and citizenship training to adult citizens".

The national government spends about one-third of its annual budget towards the funding of the entire public primary school enrolment and about 86 per cent of the public intermediate school enrolment.

While the public schools serve the greater portion of the elementary school age population (about 95 per cent of the total enrolment), at the secondary and college levels the private schools serve the needs of the population. Of the existing 33 universities all over the country, 27 are private institutions.

There are some 400, mostly private, colleges. The University of the Philippines in Diliman, Quezon City, is the premier State University. Private schools in the Philippines numbered 2,525 in the school year 1967-68, with a total enrolment of 1,666,408.

The educational system closely follows that of the U.S.A. and is open to every Filipino regardless of his station in life. English is the primary medium of instruction. 54,000 foreign students representing 43 countries are presently enrolled in Philippine private and public schools.

Literacy Rate. Because of the high priority placed by the State on education and an ingrained Filipino partiality to learning, the Philippines enjoys a high literacy rate well above the world average. Its 72 per cent literacy rate placed the Philippines 49th in a group of 136 countries studied by the United Nations, and in South-east Asia and the Far East, Manila alone has a literacy rate of 91.4 per cent.

Instruction. In grade school, the Filipino pupil for the first two grades uses his local dialect for all lessons, while at the same time learning English and Pilipino (the national language) as two related subjects. In grade three, English becomes the medium of instruction, with Pilipino still a basic subject for study. Thus the Filipino pupil studies at least three languages during his years in grade school.

In high school, English becomes the primary language for instruction. Pilipino is retained as a main subject up to fourth year. On the college level, all instruction is in English, except in the study of specific languages. A wide variety of study courses covers especially the Sciences, the Arts and the Social Sciences.

Private colleges and universities receive almost 95 per cent of the total enrolment for higher education. In several courses, the government sets a board examination for all graduates before they are allowed to practice their professions.

Teacher-training is a major area of study in the Philippines. To be qualified to teach, the student is required to finish four years of college education and obtain a Bachelor's degree. Most Filipino teachers usually continue their studies on the graduate level.

Present Educational Priorities. Because of the growing problems of the Philippines as a developing nation, Philippine education is in a state of transition. One particular concern is the development of the nation's human resources so as to cope with manpower needs and the demands of social change. Curricula are being orientated particularly to the sciences and vocational training. A manpower Development Programme has been launched by the national government to provide answers to the needs of growing and new industries.

Finally, an intensive effort is being made to apply the resources of modern technology in instruction at both the elementary and secondary school levels. Educational television and radio are fast gaining usage in the development of Philippine education.

THE ECONOMY

The Philippines' economy is still basically agricultural, but industrialisation is rapidly taking place. Moreover, the export trade is expanding as new trading partners are sought and won and more products become available for export. The per capita income is still low (851 pesos), yet in real terms it has grown by about 2 per cent annually over the last decade.

The Spaniards opened the Philippines to foreign trade in 1855 transforming it from a subsistence economy to an export economy, growing primary products such as abaca, sugar, coconut and coffee, in exchange for the finished consumer goods of the West.

At the close of the 19th Century the United States took sovereignty over the islands from Spain. The process of foreign trade expansion set in motion by the Spaniards was continued. World War II rendered the economy of the country a shambles. When political independence came in 1946, the country was faced with the task of rebuilding and rehabilitation. This was accomplished rapidly: production in 1946 was less than 40 per cent of the 1937 level; in 1949 total production increased by 51 per cent over the 1946 level. Exports climbed quickly. Millions of coconut trees survived the war and the country was able to export large quantities of coconut products. A world shortage of fats and oils pushed up prices. Full restoration of the country's production capacity, however, was not accomplished until 1954 when sugar exports finally reached the pre-war level.

One of the problems tackled after political independence was "economic independence". The Philippine economy had become tied to that of the United States because of free trade established between the two countries during the American regime. Arrangements had been devised as early as 1934 to gradually wean the economy from that of the United States, but it was only in 1956 that the first real steps were taken for the reciprocal reduction of preferences. The movement is still going on. Today, although the United States is still the leading trading partner of the Philippines, Japan has become a close second. In fact, imports from Japan already surpass those from the United States.

The main thrust in the 1950's was modernisation in the industrial sector. The results show the extent of progress. In 1949 manufacturing had accounted for only 11.1 per cent of net domestic product; in 1960 it rose to 19.1 per cent. The value of industrial output trebled from 1954 to 1960. The rise of manufacturing tells only part of the story, for the real accomplishment was to turn the face of the economy to the modern world. A native group of entrepreneurs went far beyond merely engaging in the traditional pursuits of trade and

Above:
The modern Administrative Building of the University of the Philippines.

Below right:
Cultivating a paddy rice field before setting the rice plants.

export agriculture; they concerned themselves with the application of modern technology in manufacturing, in the development of the financial sector, the building up of skilled labour, and most important, the fostering of a climate conducive to growth in 20th Century business enterprise —all achieved in less than a decade. The rest of the economy grew along with domestic manufacturing.

In the mid-1960's, the task was modernisation of agriculture so as to increase food supplies and raise rural incomes, thus laying the base for mass purchasing power outside the cities. More resources were devoted to road building and school construction. Existing mileage of roads in 1965 was 55,778 km. This had increased by 17 per cent by 1970.

The story is similar in school building. Expenditure was raised from 13 million pesos in 1965 to over 32 million in 1969.

Similar events were happening in rice production. New and more productive rice varieties were coming out of the research laboratories of the International Rice Research Institute, the College of Agriculture of the University of the Philippines, and the Bureau of Plant Industry. Fertiliser production increased considerably. A Land Reform Code laid the framework for more effective agricultural extension, farm credit, and so on. Modernisation in agriculture was accomplished, again in a short span of time. Whereas in 1965 the index of agricultural production was only 140.4, in 1969 it was 181.4 an increase of 29 per cent.

Another major economic area that has shown tremendous development is mining. Mining had been important in the pre-war period. Gold was the wonder metal in the 1930's and accounted for almost 90 per cent of mineral production. Production in the Philippines surpassed those of Alaska and California, the major gold producing areas in the United States. After the war, however, the gold industry became moribund as the mines were destroyed and the price of gold had become too low to invite immediate and total rehabilitation of the mines.

Expansion in mining of other metals, however, began in earnest in the 1950's, particularly chromite, iron ore, manganese, mercury, and lead. By the 1960's another metal had risen to prominence, far surpassing that of gold during pre-war days. This metal is copper. In 1940 copper production was only 9,100 metric tons. By 1969, production was 131,020 metric tons or 30 times the level of 1950. Exports of copper amounted to $1.73 million in 1950, and $132.8 million in 1969.

For the decade of the 1970's, it is anticipated that the wonder metal will be nickel. A number of mining ventures are being pushed forward in the vast ore deposit in Manec Island off Mindoro and other sites in the country.

PHILIPPINE GOVERNMENT

The Philippines was the first of the Asian nations to become a republic. Three centuries of absolutist government as a colony of Spain ended in revolution and a short-lived republic proclaimed on 12th June 1896, then succumbed to American might. A western type democracy superimposed on age-old institutions developed under American tutelage until the Philippines was proclaimed independent in accordance with the United States Congress' Tydings-McDuffie Law soon after World War II on 4th July 1946. After several years the Filipinos have changed their date of independence to 12th June 1896.

The government is unitary in structure, necessarily because of the fragmentation of the country into many islands. Governmental power is vested in three independent, co-equal and co-ordinate branches: the Executive, the Legislative, and the Judiciary.

The Executive. Executive power is vested in the President, who with the Vice-President, is elected by the people, the former for a maximum period of eight consecutive years, and the latter for any number of terms.

While the legislative and judicial powers are vested in collective bodies or shared by individuals, the powers of the executive are the prerogative of one man. In many respects, the Philippine presidency is stronger than that of the United States. The President appoints department heads, bureau chiefs, ambassadors, ministers, consuls and most of the ranking officials of the national government, and exercises general supervision over the local government. The President may be removed from office only by impeachment.

The Legislative. Legislative power is vested in a bicameral Congress composed of the Senate, the upper chamber, with 24 members, and a House of Representatives, the lower chamber, with a present membership of 107.

Senators are elected for a term of six years; they represent the entire national constituency in the legislative body; congressmen are elected every four years, each representing a congressional district. Their stays in office may run for an unlimited number of terms. The upper chamber is headed by the Senate President and the lower chamber by the Speaker.

Congress, the policy-forming body, has the sole power to make, revise and repeal laws. It may propose amendments to the Constitution or call a convention for this purpose; it has the power to impeach, declare war, impose taxes, and authorise the expenditure of public funds.

The Judiciary. Judicial power is vested in a Supreme Court set up by the Constitution and in inferior courts established by law. The old Spanish system of courts was continued essentially on the same framework, by the American system which instituted a bill of rights, in its earliest organic laws, democratised the laws of procedure, and gradually Filipinised the courts from bottom to top. All the justices and the judges of inferior courts are appointed by the President with the consent of the Commission on Appointments.

THE MANY WORLDS OF THE PHILIPPINES

Check and Balance. Although the legislative, judicial and executive branches of the government are co-equal and independent, the Constitution has wisely provided a system by which each branch may check the other. The President may check Congressional excess through the exercise of his veto power; Congress, on the other hand, may pass a vetoed measure by a two-thirds vote in a joint session. Through its Commission on Appointments, Congress may disapprove a Presidential appointment, and may even impeach the President.

The Civil Service and the General Auditing Office. A Civil Service to insure fair appointments to government posts, and a general auditing office, the government's fiscal watchdog, are other checks.

Political Parties. The two major political parties, the Nacionalista (currently in power) and the Liberal, manifest no significant ideological or sociological differences.

The Commission of Elections is an independent agency which administers all election laws.

Summation; the Constitutional Convention. The Philippine Government has been under foreign sovereigns whose ghosts still remain amidst the people's social unrest and nationalist striving. Beyond retaining the nationalist spirit of the Constitution of 1935, the Constitution now in the making is expected to be responsive to the people's new aspirations.

The Development Bank of the Philippines (DBP) is a long-term financing institution chartered by act of Congress and owned wholly by the Government of the Republic of the Philippines.

The DBP was established "to provide credit facilities for the rehabilitation and development and expansion of agriculture and industry, the reconstruction of property damaged by war, and the broadening and diversification of the national economy, and to provide the establishment of private development banks in the provinces and cities". It is one of the major government-owned development banks in Asia.

The DBP authorised capital stock of 2 billion pesos, fully subscribed by the Government of the Philippines. Funds for operations are obtained from paid-in capital, profits from operations and from borrowing from local and foreign sources. Its legal borrowing capacity is equivalent to ten times its paid-in capital and surplus, such borrowings being tax-exempt and unconditionally guaranteed by the Government of the Republic of the Philippines.

Management of the DBP is vested in a Board of Governors, composed of a Chairman and eight members, four of whom are full-time governors of the Bank. They are appointed by the President, with the consent of the Commission on Appointments, for a term of seven years.

AN OLD WORLD ROMANCE under a coconut tree...The rhythm of an Oriental city whose people speak English...Thatched nipa huts sleeping atop a ricefield...The most fabulous hotels in Asia's swingingest city...A Muslim princess on a sultan's throne...Sea gypsies and g-stringed tribes...Fashion shows and strobe lights...Horse-drawn carriages, cadillacs, sea-shells, pine-trees. These are the many different worlds of the Philippines.

The Philippines is a chain of 7,107 islands 600 miles off the south-east coast of mainland Asia. Only 1,195 of them are inhabited; the rest are little emerald dots, a few of which appear and disappear with the tide. In all, they cover a land area of 115,739 square miles filled with the most charming mixture of different times and different cultures. It can be pre-historic, 12th Century, 1800 or 1972 all at one time. The Philippines can be today, tomorrow, yesterday and forever.

The first step of discovery begins at landing time at the Manila International Airport. The Philippines lies at the very crossroads of the East, a vital air and sea port in the major international travel routes. If you are bound for Hong Kong, Tokyo, Taipei, Bangkok or Singapore, Manila, the main city, is on your way for no extra fare. Once there, you do not need a visa for 21 days.

Wreaths of smiles on many faces will be the first surprise that will greet you. These faces are representative of the 37 million Filipinos—a rather new and interesting breed who have evolved from a varied and rich past.

The Filipino origin traces its roots to the first Indonesian and Malayan migrants who settled on the islands and formed little kingdoms ruled by "datus" in different parts of the archipelago. They either bought or fought for their lands from the aboriginal negritos who were called "Atis" or "Aetas". Through the years and as early as the 11th Century the island people carried on trade relations and mingled with traders who came from neighbouring countries like China, Siam, India and Arabia. In 1521 Magellan, a Portuguese navigator sailing in the name of Spain, paved the way for the beginning of western colonisation of the island. It was also a Spaniard, Ruy Lopez de Villalobos, who gave the Philippines its present name. Spanish legacy to the Filipinos included the acquisition of a new religion, Catholicism, and the latin temperament. After the Spanish-American War, the Americans took over the island for a 30-year rule. From them the Filipinos learned to adopt a second language, English, and a democratic system of government. The Philippines is today the third largest English-speaking nation in the world.

Through all the changes, the Filipino watched, waited, assimilated. Then with his new freedom, he emerged as if from a cocoon—warm, gay, beautiful, easily the most hospitable person you can ever hope to meet.

The Filipinos have the highest literacy rate in South-east Asia, and yet they have retained their heritage of the romantic and the exotic, etched in their souls by the centuries.

A glimpse of the Filipino spirit will come with a strange piece of transportation—the jeepney. This is a renovated American jeep, sporting wild colours, psychedelic patterns, plastic flags and fringes, chrome ponies and gay buntings. If you prefer to go by taxi or car, you can still get a chance to see this circus at the Nayong Pilipino—a park containing replicas of the country's major tourist spots and featuring industries and houses typical of the six major representative regions of the Philippines: the Mountain Province, the Ilocos region, the Central Luzon area, the Bicol regions, the Visayas and Mindanao.

From here, the visitor can decide which of the real things he wants to see. There's quite a choice—the world's most perfect cone, Mayon Volcano, in Albay; the eighth wonder of the world, the Banaue Rice Terraces, in Ifugao; round limestone mounds, Chocolate Hills in Bohol; houses on stilts on Zamboanga seashores.

There is also quite a choice of hand-made products coming from all over the country, like carved wooden statues and tableware, lamps, containers and decorative items made from capiz shells, pineapple fibre handwoven fabrics, all hand-embroidered, multi-coloured straw hats, bags and mats, brass gongs, plates, and swords, carabao horn rings and earrings, bamboo flutes, chairs, nic-nacs, all stamped with the special flavour of the people who made them. And with the present rate of exchange (US$1 = 6.50 pesos), everything is a bargain.

Left page:
Sailing in a Filipino vinta
in Southern Mindanao.

Above:
Rizal Park in the heart of Manila.
On the lawns, amid its beautiful gardens,
are held concerts, and performances
by world famous ballets.

Left:
Tinikling dancers.

Shopping is one of the big tourist attractions in the Philippines.

And then there is Manila, a new-old city nestling by the sea, lit by the most fantastic sunset in the world. In the midst of the hustle and bustle of this cosmopolitan city, echo strains from its Spanish past. This is best seen in Intramuros, the old walled capital. Its Fort Santiago is now a beautiful park with a museum built in honour of the national hero, Dr. Jose Rizal. Here are relics from World War II when political prisoners were held by the Japanese, and an avant-garde, open-air theatre. A few streets away from Intramuros, "calesas" (horse-drawn rigs) clatter on their daily routes, passing by old women selling candles outside the church.

Manila is the centre of arts, culture and business in the Philippines. The Cultural Centre is a must for culture-addicts or just plain admirers of the magnificent. Built against the Manila Bay, this imposing structure is a showcase of Philippine arts. It has an open amphitheatre, a concert hall, little theatre, a music and arts library, a museum and two art galleries. More of the arts are found in the galleries and museums of the Ermita area of Manila.

Business centres are in busy downtown Manila and in sparkling modern Makati. Makati is a fast rising commercial and residential suburb, a few minutes from the city.

If you have a day or two, take a drive to the country. Tagaytay City, just an hour and a half away, is a cool vacation place perched on a ridge and overlooking one of the lowest craters on earth—Taal Volcano. A little lake sits inside the volcano which also sits inside a lake, part of a larger volcano.

Or experience the thrill of shooting 14 rapids in a narrow wooden boat to get to the Pagsanjan Falls. If the excitement of pushing through slimy boulders and rushing waters isn't enough, there is the gorge, decorated with lilies, trees, rocks and rivulets of waterfalls.

With 10,850 miles of coastline, the Philippines is a natural beach country. From its northern tip to its southern end, it is lined with hundreds of white sand and black sand beaches, most of which are virtual paradises untouched by civilisation. Bathing, skin-diving and fishing are enjoyed all year 'round. Except for occasional typhoons it is usually sunny in the Philippines. If you want to find your own Bali Hai easily, the Hundred Islands, a cluster of uninhabited islets, abounds with interesting coral formations.

But the Philippines is more than a grand vacation land. It is also an adventure.

Hidden in the hills and mountains of the north are the hardy Ifugaos who still retain the traditional values and strange ways of their forefathers. Clothed in g-strings or handwoven skirts, they eke out a living by planting rice on terraces carved by bare hands and crude tools on the mountainsides. They have thousands of personal gods which they keep alive in songs chanted during day-long festivities and in carved wooden statues kept in their houses.

The southern island of Mindanao pulsates with a totally different beat. In this land of promise, replete with virgin forests and unexplored lands, live the Muslims of the Philippines. A mixture of the Arab and the Indonesian, they are clad in malongs and chew betel nuts. Their traditional handicrafts are handmade brass gongs, ceremonial jars and swords. The Muslims are great navigators: they sail by the stars in bright and colourful sailboats called "vintas".

The Badjaos, a vanishing breed of sea dwellers, live amidst the islands strewn across Zamboanga and Jolo, making their homes on wooden boats or houses built over the waters.

A great number of the 96 ethnic groups of the Philippines can be found in the exotic land of Mindanao. They are heavily ornamented, beaded and tatooed people with a distinct way of life. Soon time and technology will paint another face on these people.

The best time to visit them would be now. The Philippines has 66 provinces and 60 cities to choose from. Each has a feeling, an atmosphere of its own. One visit can yield a lifetime of memories.

Above:
The jeepney,
a converted American jeep,
is a modern form of public transport
in Manila.

Top left:
Although the
Filipinos are
predominantly Catholic,
the people are free to worship as
they wish. This is one of the
magnificent mosques of
the Muslim faith.

Left:
Banaue terraces
for growing rice form a
picturesque setting for
a mountain village.

THE PHILIPPINE ECONOMY

MINERAL RESOURCES

THE PHILIPPINES is generally considered rich in mineral resources, but development has been limited and slow because of lack of capital.

Among the industrial metals, iron and copper deposits are the most important. Chromite, manganese, nickel and cobalt are also found in different parts of the country. Because of low prices in the world market, lead and zinc deposits have remained untapped. Mercury is being mined profitably in the island of Palawan.

Of the non-metallic minerals, limestone is the most significant. Deposits are found extensively all over the country and demand is great in agriculture and in the iron and steel industry. Sulphur is also widely distributed throughout the country.

Gold production occupies an important position in the mining industry. About 75 per cent of the country's gold is mined in Northern Luzon.

Coal reserves discovered so far are small, scattered and low-grade. Although there are indications of some oil in many inland and offshore sites, no commercial quantities have so far been found. The last few years have seen much exploration and drilling for oil in the country and it may be a matter of time before commercial deposits will be struck.

Other non-metallic minerals that are contributing to the economy are asphalt, asbestos, marble, gypsum and industrial clay.

Water as a source of power for industry holds great promise and several large hydro-electric power plants are in operation.

THE SIGNIFICANCE OF COPPER

The second largest area of production in the Philippines in the period 1971-1972 is mining. Prior to World War II it began to assume major significance in the country's economy; in the 1930's gold was the wonder metal and accounted for almost 90 per cent of mineral production, even surpassing the fabulous gold finds of Alaska and California. After the war, however, the gold industry became moribund (gold production is now only a third of its pre-war yields) as the valuable plants were destroyed during the liberation campaign and the price of gold was too low to invite massive rehabilitation of the mines.

In the 1950's mining of other metals began to expand, particularly chromite, iron ore, manganese, mercury and lead. In the 1960's copper became the glamour metal, its production exceeding that of gold even at its pre-war peak. In 1940 production of copper was 9,100 metric tons; in 1950 still only 10,390 metric tons, but in the next ten years it rose to 44,010 metric tons. In 1971 the output of the copper mines reached 188,500 metric tons—18 times the level of 1950 and 4.2 times more than in 1960. Exports of copper were worth $1.73 million in 1950 and $29.59 million in 1960 but even this substantial increase was minute compared with the jump to $178 million in 1971.

The largest copper mine in Asia is the Atlas Consolidated Mining and Development Corporation of Toledo, Cebu, in the middle islands of the Philippines. Beginning in 1953 with the merging of three pre-World War II gold mines, Atlas, under the initiative and drive of its former President, Andres Soriano, transferred its interests to copper and soon afterwards started the exploration and development of a low-grade copper deposit in the island of Cebu. Its first few years were difficult, but by the early 1960's the future of the mine was more or less assured. In 1969 the daily treatment of ore averaged almost 24,000 tons and Atlas accounted for 36 per cent of the total copper produced in the country. Atlas completed its expansion programme in mid-1971 under Jose M. Soriano, President and Chairman of the Board, and a record of 74,000 metric tons of copper contained in concentrates was produced in that year, as well as by-products of gold, silver, magnetite and pyrite concentrates. The current total capacity of the Corporation's two copper concentrators is 65,000 tons of ore per day.

Increasing productive efficiency and continuous investment have made Atlas, under the management of A. Soriano y Cia, one of the leading copper mining companies, not only in Asia but also in the world.

At present, Atlas Consolidated Mining and Development Corporation contributes the largest share to the foreign exchange earnings of Philippine exports and was the second largest tax payer in the country in 1971.

Atlas has not been the sole progressive copper mine in the Philippines. Together with other mining companies such as Marcopper, Marinduque Mining, Lepanto Consolidated and Philex Mine, Atlas has made copper one of the country's chief export resources.

For the decade of the 1970's it is anticipated that the wonder metal will be nickel, and already a number of ventures in nickel mining are being pushed forward actively, notably the vast lateritic ore deposit in Nonoc Island off Surigao Province in the south, and other locations in Palawan and Mindanao islands. Marinduque's nickel project will be operational in 1975 and Atlas is planning to follow closely thereafter.

PRINCIPAL PHILIPPINE MINERAL OUTPUTS
('000 Metric tons unless otherwise stated)

	1969	1970	1971
Gold (oz.)	571.1	582.1	638.6
Silver (oz.)	1,561.3	1,684.4	1,910.0
Copper	131.5	162.7	188.5
Mercury (flasks)	3.5	4.3	4.8
Chrome ore	469.4	567.4	422.1
Iron ore	1,561.5	1,837.1	2,066.8
Manganese	26.1	6.7	5.1
Cement	2,845.3	2,446.9	2,820.0

Atlas Consolidated Mining Complex showing two open pits and headframe for underground mine; one of two concentrators in the centre; Hospital, Church, Elementary School and High School, Recreation, Housing and Administration buildings in the foreground. To the extreme left, is the 2,800-ft. asphalted air strip.

NATIONAL SCIENCE AND DEVELOPMENT BOARD

Below is a model
of a nuclear power plant
to be built in Luzon sometime
in 1978. Studies have shown that
nuclear power will become competitive
with other sources of
power by that time.

Opposite page:
The Philippines is currently
producing 31 kinds of radioisotopes
and labelled compounds, on one
of which nuclear scientists are shown
working at the Philippine
Atomic Reactor Centre.

FOR MOST of its brief existence, the National Science and Development Board of the Philippines has dedicated itself to serving as the linchpin of the ever-expanding national effort in the vast domain of science and technology. In the exercise of its mission as spelled out in its charter (Republic Act 2067), the Board gives financial assistance for research and development in economic and social fields, and provides funds for science education to ensure that adequate scientific and technological manpower will be available for the country's needs.

The charter of the Board empowers it "to establish a system of priorities for scientific and technological projects". Thus the Board formulates the priorities, but does so in consultation with science agencies and other development planning organisations, both of the government and of private sectors.

In the past few years the Board has been implementing a Research and Development Programme geared to the achievement of two major goals—the development of the nation's science resources and the application of such resources for an acceleration of the economic, social and cultural progress of the Philippines.

By these means, all available skills and techniques are being harnessed and put to work, to modernise agriculture, to diversify manufacturing industries, and improve communications and transportation systems. Vast riches in mineral ores, metals and solid fuels are being discovered and developed. The study of Philippine cultures is being facilitated, and research in the social factors which hasten or impede acceptance of change is being encouraged. While not neglecting pure and fundamental research, the current R and D programme gives priority to the investigation of problems of immediate practical importance in the successful prosecution of the national economic goals. In other words, if the programme gives priority to researches in agriculture and industry, the prime consideration is that the produce of the agricultural areas and other natural resources will directly affect the stability of the Philippines international trade. Thus agricultural production must be improved in quantity and quality parallel with the conservation of relevant natural resources.

The need for a more realistic delineation and periodic review of priorities in industry is an established planning policy of the Board in view of the variegated areas that have simultaneously been expanding as a result of burgeoning industrialisation.

Notable among the agricultural research projects currently being undertaken are the increase and improvement of animal production through breeding; the increase of production and improvement of quality of the principal crops; the increase of fish production through appropriate conservation methods and practices; the efficient utilisation of forest products; and the preservation of natural flora and fauna. Still further studies focus on agricultural engineering and soil and water conservation and utilisation.

In industrial research the Board gives priority to studies on the development of new sources of energy, notably nuclear and geothermal power in order to save on fuel importations. Other projects supported under this category are: studies in chemical engineering processes that could result in new technologies or improvement of known manufacturing procedures; applied and developmental studies in the primary metal, chemical, pulp and paper, and small-scale industries, textile and food technology; the utilisation of the abundant raw and waste materials for the production of substitutes for imported raw materials; and methods of controlling air and water pollution. Complementary to the industrial research programme, provision has been made for assistance to projects and activities relative to the promotion and development of inventions by Filipinos.

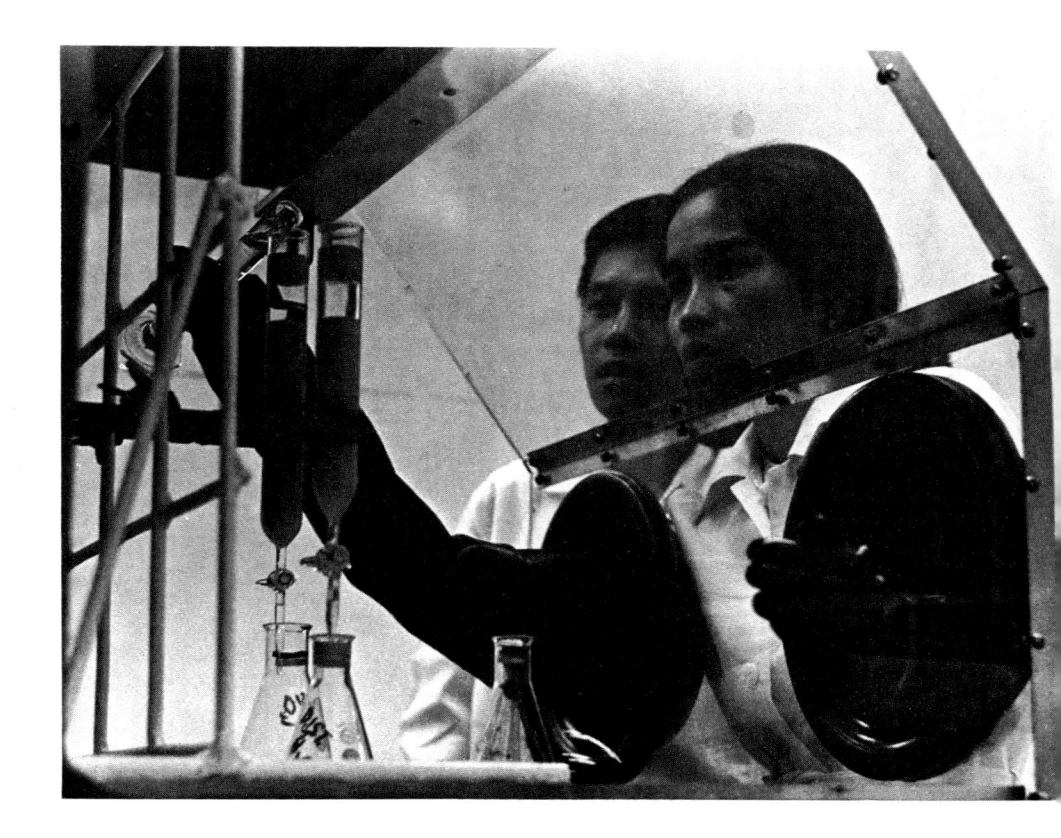

Inasmuch as the progress of any developing country in the attainment of overall national growth is directly related to the condition of health and fitness of its people, the Board has been implementing a wide programme of medical studies covering specific areas of infectious and communicable diseases, particularly those that have been top killers among Filipinos and those that affect Filipinos and Asians more than other races. The programme also encourages a systematic study of such flora and fauna in the Philippines as could possibly yield new and effective drugs and medicinal preparations.

The biggest problem of most developing countries is not so much the paucity of natural resources as the shortage of highly trained manpower to harness these resources for development. Since its establishment in 1958, the National Science and Development Board has been allocating a substantial portion of its funds and other resources to the training and education of such scientific and technological manpower in the Philippines.

In the intervening years the Board has expanded tremendously in size and functions, and it now directly supervises six principal research agencies compared to only two fourteen years ago. These agencies are: the National Institute of Science and Technology, the Philippine Atomic Energy Commission, the Forest Products Research and Industries Development Commission, the Philippine Textile Research Institute, the Philippine Coconut Research Institute and the Philippine Inventors Commission. Three other agencies—the Metals Industry Development Centre, National Water and Air Pollution Control Commission and Philippine Science High School—are also associated with the Board by operation of the laws.

Putting the role of the National Science Development in perspective, Chairman Florencio A. Medina candidly says: "The basic task of science-technology is to help in every possible way in the development of a pattern of economy for the Philippines, wherein the basic essentials in living are produced locally and industrial raw materials are also locally processed instead of exported in raw form. This is a kind of economy that is naturally more prosperous and stable because it will, on one hand, conserve dollar earnings from foreign trade, and at the same time, put to work millions of the unemployed in the numerous processing and finishing industries."

THE PHILIPPINE NATIONAL BANK IN ECONOMIC PROGRESS

THE PHILIPPINE NATIONAL BANK, since its establishment 55 years ago, has been a major contributor to Philippine economic progress. It has met the increasingly diverse banking needs of the economy and has been responsible as well for the development of primary economic institutions supportive of the country's economic development. Emerging as the Philippine premier commercial bank, after itself undergoing a long and difficult evolution, the Bank has become a potent tool in the implementation of monetary and credit policy in the Philippines.

The PNB is unique as a financial institution, having been endowed with institutional attributes which differentiate it from other commercial banks in the country.

Unlike other commercial banks, PNB's operations are largely oriented to public service, rather than to profit as is understandably the case with private commercial banks operating in a free enterprise economy. Such orientation does not derive wholly from the PNB being a public institution but also springs from the political, economic and social environment under which it functions.

Another significant evolutionary hallmark of the PNB is, that prior to the establishment in the Philippines of a central bank, development banks and rural banks, it performed, in addition to purely commercial banking functions, limited central banking (power to issue currency notes), development banking (grant of long-term loans and shared equity) and rural banking functions. And even after the creation of the Central Bank of the Philippines in 1949, PNB remained what might be termed as an "intermediate central bank" in the sense of being at times a secondary banker's bank. An equally historic heritage of the PNB is that its establishment not only broke the dominant hold of foreign interests on the domestic commercial banking system but also brought along major changes in the structure and practices of commercial banking in the Philippines.

The Philippine commercial banking system by 1st January 1972 consisted of 40 banks with combined resources of 15.8 billion pesos, total deposits of 9.4 billion pesos and an aggregate loan investment of 10.5 billion pesos. Of these amounts, PNB's total assets of 4.2 billion pesos accounted for 26.75 per cent of the combined resources of the system; its deposits of 2.6 billion pesos represented 27.3 per cent of the system's total; and its loan investment of 2.8 billion pesos corresponded to 26.8 per cent of the system's aggregate.

BANKING, ECONOMIC GROWTH. The original resources of the Bank when it was established in 1916 stood at only 50 million pesos; these multiplied 85 times to reach 4.2 billion pesos in five decades. Behind this growth, is the multi-faceted and vital role PNB has been playing in the gigantic task of nation-building and economic development.

Corollary to PNB's physical expansion was the development of basic economic institutions which in turn induced changes in the economic habits and attitudes of the Filipino people. The Bank's continuing progress in putting up branches and agencies even in remote frontier areas where prospects of profit are dim, paved the way for the development of branch banking in the Philippines.

As of 1st January 1972, PNB's network of nationwide offices consisted of 20 metropolitan branches and 124 provincial branches and agencies, and overseas offices numbering nine, or a total of 133 offices.

Following PNB's lead, other commercial banks have also established branches and agencies all over the country. These extensions of other commercial banks numbered 534. These offices, as mobilisers of savings and dispensers of capital funds, are now important vehicles of economic and social growth.

AGRICULTURAL DEVELOPMENT.
A more direct and tangible contribution of PNB to Philippine economic progress, however, is its support, through financial assistance, of the development of the country's resources, especially agriculture. The extent of such support is reflected in the Bank's annual loan investment in sugar, palay, coconut, corn, abaca, tobacco, fishing, livestock and poultry, and forestry industries, to mention a few. In 1971, the Bank's total loan investment in agriculture amounted to 902 million pesos or 32 per cent of the Bank's loan portfolio.

PNB's continuing financial assistance to the sugar industry has been a major factor which enabled it not only to modernise productive facilities but also to develop as one of the Philippines' premier industries.

INDUSTRIAL DEVELOPMENT.
PNB's industrial loan investment is no less significant. Although assistance has been extended to all sectors of the manufacturing and utilities industries, outstanding projects assisted by the Bank, either as co-lender or as confirming bank, include the purchase of the Manila Electric Company and the Philippine Long Distance Telephone Company by local businessmen, the establishment of the Private Development Corporation of the Philippines, and the establishment of five new sugar mills in different sectors of the country. In 1971, the Bank's total loans outstanding in manufacturing was 205 million pesos corresponding to 7.3 per cent of its total loan portfolio.

Within the framework of its Charter, PNB established in 1963 an investment subsidiary—The National Investment and Development Corporation—which engages in both long-term and equity financing.

As of year-end 1971, NIDC's outstanding financial assistance in the form of loans, equity financing and guarantees amounted to 978.9 million pesos, of which 19 per cent was for manufacturing projects, 70 per cent for transport, storage and communication projects, and 11 per cent for other industries.

TRADE MOBILISER.
PNB's financial and trade assistance has stimulated not only the trading relationships of the Philippines with other countries but also that of domestic trade. The Bank, in addition to numerous correspondent banks in principal cities of the world, has nine overseas offices: a branch in New York, an agency in San Francisco and in Honolulu, and six representative offices, in Hamburg, Hongkong, Tokyo, London, Singapore, Djakarta. These offices provide business, economic, financial and other types of relevant information and foster closer relationships between Philippine and foreign businessmen and banks.

In 1971, the Bank's outstanding financial assistance to trade amounted to 812.8 million pesos, of which 71 million pesos was extended to foreign trade and 741.8 million pesos to domestic trade. Foreign and domestic trade financing corresponded to 2.5 per cent and 26.3 per cent respectively of the Bank's total loan portfolio in that year.

Government price stabilisation measures have also gained the continued support of the Bank. Extension of credit to the Rice and Corn Administration, the government's marketing arm for cereals, enables this agency to keep prices of rice within the purchasing range of the general public.

Aside from credit extension, PNB operates another subsidiary—the Philippine Exchange Company, established in 1920. The company serves the Bank's insurance requirements and, when necessary, as the trading arm in the procurement and distribution of essential commodities such as rice and sugar. These trading activities assure farmers of ready and stable markets and consumers of adequate supplies at reasonable prices.

FINANCIAL STABILITY. In the monetary field, the Bank has been and is a stabilising force in the foreign exchange market. The PNB also assumes the role of being a secondary banker's bank at times when recourse to the Central Bank is limited.

In its more than half a century of dedicated service to the nation, PNB has been in the forefront of Philippine economic progress. With its rich tradition and heritage, coupled with the stature and prominence it enjoys in both domestic and international banking, PNB is a symbol of Philippine financial stability as well as of Filipino competence in the nationally-significant field of commercial banking.

Above:
An aerial view
of the modern 14-storey Philippine
National Bank Building at the Escolta
—the Wall Street
of Manila.

Left page, above:
The P.N.B. makes a tangible
contribution to Philippine economic
progress in its financial assistance
to the development of primary
resources, of which forestry
industries are an important
part.

Left page, below:
A fast-growing "Miracle rice"
variety developed by the International
Rice and Research Institute
has boosted the rice
production of the
Philippines.

THE STORY OF SAN MIGUEL

IN 1970 SAN MIGUEL BEER celebrated its 80th anniversary. From a small brewery in Manila in 1890, the original company has become a multi-million dollar, multi-product corporation, a symbol of Philippine progress. Today, the San Miguel Corporation (SMC) is one of the major brewery complexes of the world, owning and operating three plants in the Philippines, three in Spain and one in Hong Kong. To better serve the Pacific area, an eighth brewery has recently been established in Guam.

In addition to beer, more than 30 other products are now manufactured by the Company, with distribution centres in many parts of the world, extensively in the Asian and Pacific areas.

From brewery by-products SMC produces poultry and livestock feeds. Its bottle requirements are met by two glass plants, which also service the food, drug and beverage industries in the Philippines, besides producing bottles for export to Singapore, Hong Kong, Okinawa, New Guinea and Australia. In the field of soft drink manufacture, SMC is the authorised bottler of Coca-Cola and also produces and markets its own "Royal" products through a division which operates sixteen plants, strategically located throughout the country. The Company also makes ice-cream and dairy products under the brand name Magnolia, as well as yeast and solid and liquid carbon dioxide. It supplies the needs of its various divisions and other Philippine industries in the manufacture of corrugated board boxes, collapsible tubes, tuboplast polyethylene containers, plastics and metal closures. San Miguel also has a lithographic printing works, which produces its own labels, packaging and brochures, and a commercial printing section.

San Miguel's investments have been largely directed to pioneering the production of such essential items as industrial bags, ramie and synthetic fibres, flour, coffee and canned milk, steel drums and pails, wires and cables, veneer plywood and logs, pre-stressed concrete structures and copper concentrates. San Miguel has also invested in a radio and television network and in a newspaper, the Philippines Herald, which in 1970 was selected the Newspaper of the Year by the Manila Rotary Club.

The Corporation's impact on the country's economy may be gauged by the fact that it contributes four to five per cent of the National Government's total tax revenue, making it the Philippines' highest taxpayer.

Above:
Administrative building of San Miguel's Hong Kong Brewery.

Below: San Miguel's modern Burgos Brewery in Spain.

Opposite page:
The Aviles Brewery is shown in its picturesque setting in Manila, the Philippines.

It employs more than 15,000 people in its plants and offices. An eloquent testimony to one aspect of the SMC national contribution was given by President Marcos, who declared that under the shadow of San Miguel "innumerable businesses have prospered" and hence "it can truly be called the mother of new industries..."

The brewing of San Miguel beer was initiated as a family enterprise in Manila under a Spanish Royal Grant in 1890.

This brewery was the first of its kind in South-east Asia, and it still stands on its original site near the President's Malacañang Palace in Manila.

Today SMC exports canned beer to many foreign cities. In Hong Kong, it supplements the sales of its local affiliate which markets the premium San Miguel pilsener and the lower-priced Ching San in the Crown Colony. Other countries in the Pacific area and the Far East obtain their supplies from the Philippine breweries.

They stretch from Japan to Okinawa, Korea, Taiwan, down to Samoa, Fiji and Tahiti, New Guinea, Australia, Indonesia, Borneo, Malaysia, Singapore—all the way up to Laos, Cambodia, Thailand, Burma, Ceylon, India—and on to Nepal, Pakistan, Afghanistan and Iran. San Miguel is the only one of 52 beers to be marketed nationwide in Spain, where it is sold by the SMC affiliate company. In Central America, the Caribbean and in Africa supplies of San Miguel are obtained from the Company's Spanish breweries. Even in such countries as West Germany, where the local beer has been favoured for centuries, San Miguel has captured a share of the market.

Only top-grade malt from Canada and Australia and the best American and German hops are utilised in the making of San Miguel beer and its claim to quality is backed by the gold and silver medals won in acknowledged beer capitals of the world.

In 1952 it was awarded first prize at the Empire and Commonwealth Bottled Beer Competition in London; in 1958 it gained a silver medal at the Brussels World Fair Prix D'Excellence and in 1962 the silver medal during the Palmares de Olympiades Europeenes de la Bier in Brussels. The Coupe d'Or Du Bon Gout Français in Spain was given to San Miguel in 1966, and to these were added the 1966 Investigation Centre and Sales Promotion Medaille d'Or de la Qualite Biere in Brussels and the gold medal of the 1964 Monde Selection in Paris.

These achievements were largely rendered possible through Don Andres Soriano, who joined the Company's accounting department in 1918 and became San Miguel's guiding genius as president of the Company for 33 years. His business acumen and vision enabled him to create within a lifetime a vast network of industries, stretching the length of the archipelago and beyond.

Since his death in 1964, his two sons, Jose Maria and Andres Jr. have assumed the management of the diverse industries he left as his legacy. With the assistance of his Company officers, President Andres Soriano Jr. is reaching for even higher peaks of performance. Thus, in 1970, the San Miguel Corporation recorded sales totalling 714,449,723 pesos or US$111,025,598 and its assets grew from 286,806,087 pesos in 1964 to 665,326,050 pesos, or US$103,391,772 in 1970.

Plans for expansion are being formulated continuously. SMC's new 35 million pesos Magnolia plant in Quezon City, the biggest automated dairy and ice-cream complex in the Far East, has been operational since early 1971. Barely two years after its start, the Mandaue Brewery in the Southern Philippines was extended, utilising a new concept of vertical storage and fermenting.

In late 1971, the pulp and paper mill of the Paper Industries Corporation of the Philippines began to produce newsprint and other paper needs, an enterprise expected to save the country as much as US$20 million annually.

San Miguel is recognised for its leadership not only in business but also in philanthropy. Following a dictum that what is good for the country is good for business, it has given generously to the cause of vocational education and community development, and most recently took the lead in the formation of a foundation composed of more than 100 business firms dedicated to the solution of the country's social ills.

ELECTRIC POWER FOR NATIONAL DEVELOPMENT

THERE ARE MORE THAN 400 electric utilities operating in different parts of the Philippines and one of them serves more than half of the nation's electric energy to people living within its franchise area. This is the investor-owned Manila Electric Company, popularly known as Meralco.

Meralco's service area covers seven chartered cities and forty municipalities in the island of Luzon, including the Greater Manila area and municipalities in the provinces of Rizal, Bulacan, Laguna and others. Meralco also provides power to many smaller utilities which serve some thirty other municipalities.

The Meralco franchise area covers a little over a thousand square miles and has a population of about 5 million. Although it comprises less than one-hundredth of the nation's total area, roughly 13 per cent of Filipinos and many of the country's business houses and government departments are concentrated within its bounds. The electric energy supplied by Meralco to its industrial customers is almost one-half of all the electricity consumed by industry throughout the archipelago.

The heart of this territory is Greater Manila, embracing, besides the city, a number of contiguous lesser cities and municipalities which together form the country's leading metropolitan area.

The history of Meralco has been intimately interwoven with the history of this metropolitan area during the present century, each playing its part in the development of the other.

This relationship began in 1903, when Charles M. Swift of Detroit was granted a franchise to operate an electric street railway and to furnish electric current for light, heat and power in Manila and its suburbs.

With capital raised in the United States and Europe and equipment obtained from the same sources, Swift organised the Manila Electric Railroad and Light Company, which came to be known as "Meralco", from the acronym formed with the initials of the Company's corporate name.

Right:
Meralco's Gardner and Snyder Thermal Generating Stations located at Barrio Sucat, Muntinglupa, Rizal, as they were in June 1971.

Meralco bought out two Filipino-Spanish firms: the Compañia de los Tranvias de Filipinas which operated a small horse-drawn street railway system and a steam tramway, and La Electricista, a small electric lighting concern. The Company then proceeded to construct and equip a completely new and up-to-date railway and electric system to cover the city. A new powerhouse was built on Isla de Provisor on the Pasig River and, in 1905, a new electric street railway system was formally inaugurated.

By providing Manila with its first rapid, mass-transportation system, Meralco's tranvias helped to spark development not only in the heart of the city, but also in outlying or intermediate areas, hastening their integration with the rest of the city.

Over the years, the system grew and improved as the metropolis expanded. Bigger, better street-cars were added to the fleet; more lines were opened. In 1927, buses were added to supplement the railway system.

Although its transport operations dominated Meralco's early years, the electricity enterprise soon began to grow in relative importance. Each year, from 1895 when La Electricista initiated its service, the numbers of Manilans using the new device to light their homes and business establishments had increased. With the arrival of the Americans a new impetus was given to this development. In 1905, having taken over the former supplier's 3,000 customers during the previous year, Meralco completed the Isla de Provisor generating plant—later naming it Blaisdell Station.

After some months of adjustments, the plant was able to provide the area's total power requirements; it was to remain the city's sole central supplier for the next quarter of a century.

In 1919, the Manila Electric Railroad and Light Company and its affiliate, the Manila Suburban Railways Company, were reorganised into a single new corporation called the Manila Electric Company. This reorganisation was followed by a period of great expansion. By 1924, the Isla de Provisor plant's capacity had been raised from 9,250 to 29,500 kilowatts.

In 1929-30, Meralco added the 16,000-kilowatt Botocan Hydro Station to its system—the country's first major hydro-electric plant. Meanwhile, the Company's electric service area was expanded to include eventually not only Manila and adjacent areas in the Province of Rizal, but also a large number of municipalities in a sizeable portion of Luzon.

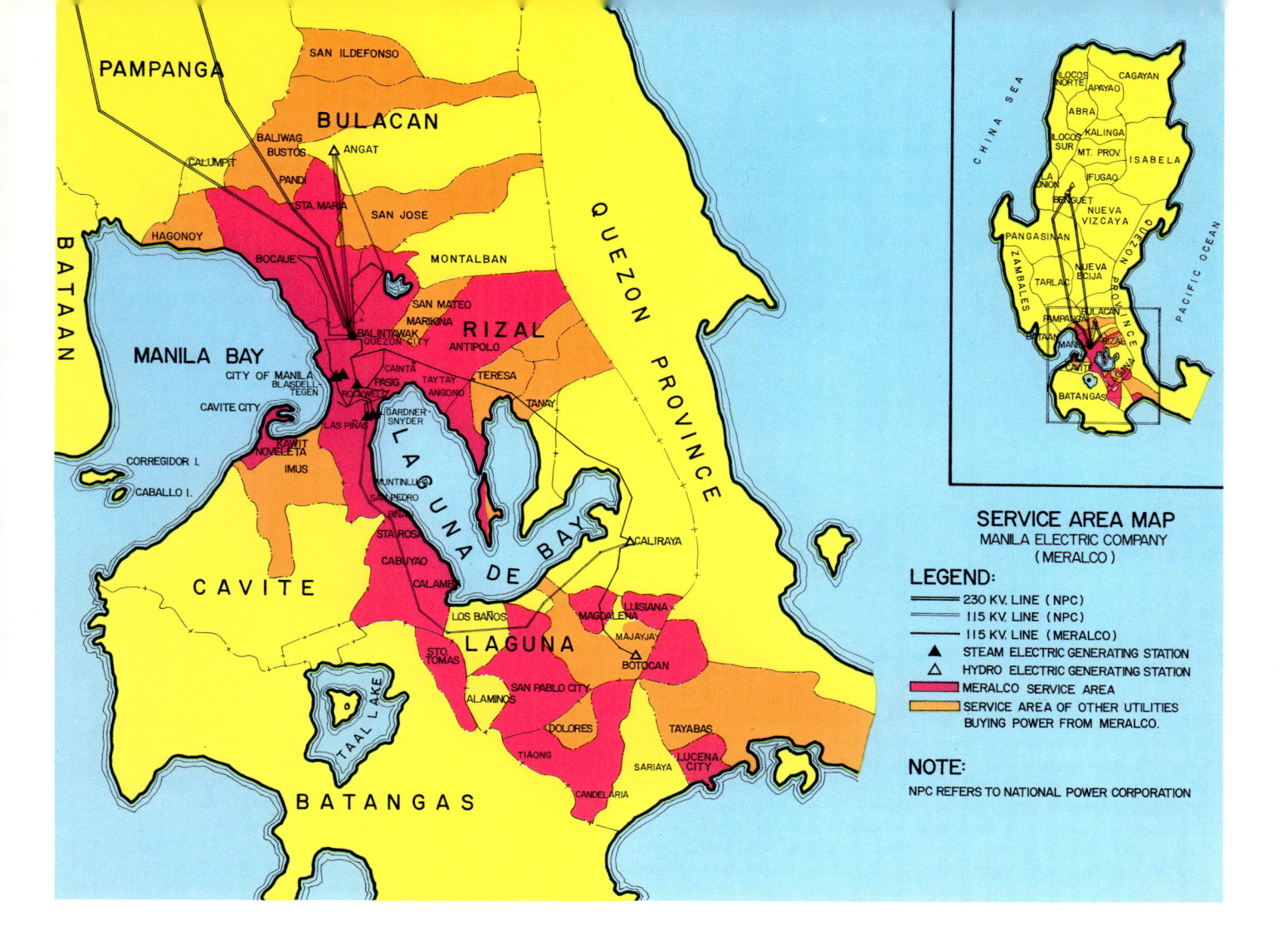

World War II left Meralco in ruins. At the time of the Japanese invasion American authorities commandeered the majority of Meralco's buses for troop transport. Three years later, the heavy bombing, shelling and street fighting in the wake of the Japanese withdrawal, which caused havoc in Manila, also permanently destroyed the Company's street-car system and crippled most of its electric facilities. With the advent of peace came an attempt to restore the bus transportation service but, after three years, this part of the enterprise was sold and Meralco turned its entire efforts and resources to supplying electricity for the people's needs.

From 1945 onwards, the Meralco organisation worked feverishly to re-establish its generating plants and transmission and distribution network. In order to concentrate better on its central system, a considerable number of outlying local franchises were relinquished. The problem was no longer to develop demand for electricity, as in pre-war times, but to keep abreast of a demand which multiplied as the Filipino struggled to rebuild and develop the land of his birth.

By the end of 1948 the peak load on the electricity system was already more than double the pre-war level. It was an uphill battle, but the completion in 1950 of several related works, primarily the large, new thermal generating plant, Rockwell Station, in Makati, was the culminating point in Meralco's post war fight to restore its former efficiency and high standard of service.

During the next decade, with the setting up of new local industries, power consumption mushroomed. The total generating capacity of Meralco's stations was increased from 45,500 kilowatts in 1941 to 318,500 kilowatts in 1961; total energy sales grew from 138 million kilowatt-hours in 1941 to almost 1.7 billion in 1961.

In 1962, after almost 59 years of American ownership, Meralco was purchased by a group of Filipino investors headed by Eugenio Lopez. This group organised the Meralco Securities Corporation which acquired the securities of the Manila Electric Company—then held by General Public Utilities Corporation of New York—in a move hailed in all quarters as a major step in the growth to maturity of the young Republic.

Within the decade ending 1971, since the Company's transfer into Filipino hands, the new management quadrupled its generating capacity to well over a million kilowatts, adding another unit to Rockwell Station and building three more thermal plants, the Tegen, Gardner and Snyder Stations. Two new units, each with a generating capacity of 330,000 kilowatts, are scheduled for operation in 1972 and 1973—these and further developments being justified by the recent acceleration in electricity consumption—for by 1971, Meralco's customers were consuming close to 5 billion kilowatt-hours annually.

In order to keep up with this demand, the Company has accumulated fixed assets devoted to the public service, the net value of which first passed the one billion peso mark in 1969, making Meralco the first, and so far the only, billion peso non-financial corporation in the Philippines.

It is today, in terms of total assets, by far the largest investor-owned enterprise in the whole of the country.

511

SHAPING A NEW FOREIGN POLICY

THE WORLD of the nineteen seventies is vastly different from the world of the 'forties or the decade of the 'fifties. In 1941, at the outbreak of the War in the Pacific, there were 19 million Filipinos. Today there are almost 40 million and numerous changes have taken place on the national and world scenes. Post war reconstruction in many parts of the world has been completed, and prosperity has been achieved in many countries destroyed by the war. Modern technology has vastly improved life in such advanced societies as the United States, the U.S.S.R., Western Europe, Scandinavia and Japan. The People's Republic of China has emerged as a nuclear power. A realignment of forces has taken place in the Western Alliance, and the once monolithic Communist force led by the U.S.S.R. is in disarray. Nationalism is on the rise in the countries of Eastern Europe.

Whereas in 1945, there were only 50 member-states in the United Nations and one nuclear power, today, membership in the United Nations has increased to 127 nations, and the United States no longer has a nuclear monopoly. While the superpowers race to the moon and devote vast sums for the development of weapons for mass destruction, the peoples of the developing countries of Asia, Africa and Latin America are engaged in another race: the race to achieve the good life and to complete the revolution of rising expectations.

Against this background of change in the post war years, the Filipino people have discovered that in the last analysis they must learn to fend for themselves. Having grown to maturity, they now demand fulfilment of their national aspirations and they see in nationalism the driving force or the means by which to achieve them.

The new foreign policy takes into account the realities of our times. It is a foreign policy that emphasises Asian relationships; seeks to readjust the Philippines' political, military and economic relations with the United States consistent with the sovereign interests of each; searches for new markets abroad in addition to those established in years gone by.

The Philippines has begun developing ties with Asian neighbours on bilateral and multilateral bases. Where the objectives for national growth are impeded by lack of resources, it seeks to rely on regional economic co-operations. It is relaxing its relations with Communist countries and allowing trade with them on an experimental, selective, chamber-to-chamber basis. It is exploring the possibilities of expanding its trade with Western Europe. The new foreign policy, then, rests upon the need to secure the peace and well-being of the Filipino people. It is a policy of self-reliance which recognises broadly that a difference in ideologies is not necessarily a barrier to co-operation or co-existence between and among countries. This is the innovative approach to Philippine foreign policy, needed in an age when the alliances of both East and West have become fragmented, when the two superpowers have found it necessary to seek areas of accommodation, when, because of decolonisation, the West has withdrawn from Asia, when new forms of colonialism threaten the independence of countries. In such a situation the Filipino people find it imperative to pursue a policy which realises the truth of the axiom that there are no permanent friends, only permanent interests.

The Philippines has shed off the pretence that the People's Republic of China does not exist. Towards the Socialist countries of Europe it has opened trade relations in an exploratory spirit, hoping to widen such relations if circumstances permit. In the meantime it is unshackling itself from the limiting and self-imposed restrictions which had unduly narrowed its old horizon.

Meanwhile, it has maintained its adherence to the principles of the United Nations Charter. In keeping with the changes in international politics and the demands of scores of nation-states in Asia and Africa, the Philippines seeks a revision of the UN Charter in order to strengthen the World Organisation; it joins a common plea that the developed countries accord the developing countries opportunities for economic growth through non-reciprocal trade preferences and by allowing it to sell its semi-manufactured goods in their markets as well as to commit one per cent of their Gross National Product in assistance to the developing countries. The "Group of 77" of which the Philippines is a member has called upon the developed countries to help the developing countries get on their feet by means which are definitely delineated.

The Philippines continues to promote relations with the new states of Asia and Africa, in the UN and outside and to espouse the causes of decolonisation and economic development, committed as it is to the self-determination of peoples. It has joined the countries of Asia, Africa and Latin America in the struggle against apartheid and all other forms of discrimination based on race and colour. It is committed to the promotion and advancement of human rights, whether it is in South Africa or Angola, in Hungary or Tibet.

The Philippines supports the idea of a United Nations in which the hopes of mankind for a just peace are secured, which has an effective peacekeeping machinery, and which can help effectively in bridging the poverty gap in the world.

The decade of the 'seventies has been aptly described by General Romulo as "a dangerous decade," because of three dangers: "the danger of international respect for human rights becoming unenforceable; the danger of the poverty gap becoming unbridgeable, and the danger of the nuclear arms race becoming uncontrollable." Hence, the Philippines has supported proposals for disarmament and for the rechannelling of the financial resources that go to armament. It has affirmed the UN principle of settling disputes between nations through peaceful means, which, in fact, is President Marcos' reason for proposing an Asian Forum. The Philippines is at the same time an active supporter of the objectives of the Second Development Decade.

But while there are dangers in the 'seventies, it is also a decade of opportunity. The present foreign policy of the Philippines is committed to turning that opportunity into reality. The country is at the crossroads of change; it must make friends with nations which wish the Philippines no harm and which believe like it in the validity of conducting relations on the basis of mutual benefit and respect. In this period of transition and growth, the Filipino people are engaged in a search for national identity. More than ever before, they realise that in the conflicts of these times, there must be shifts in relations among nations, that life can be made better, and that they have it in their hands to make it so.

Right page: Technical progress has evolved to such a degree that complicated electronic products such as T.V. sets are manufactured locally.
Typical Philips chassis are shown below.

Left: The Philips factory with its administrative building at Las Piñas, located 24 km from Manila.

Below: Technical progress has evolved to such a degree that complicated electronic products such as T.V. sets are manufactured locally.
Typical Philips chassis are shown below.

ELECTRONICS IN THE PHILIPPINES

AS THE PROSPERITY of his nation is steadily rising, the average Filipino has become an integral factor in the "revolution of rising expectations". In his daily life he expects to use more sophisticated tools; he has a radio to bring him vital information on the season's weather, so he may plant his crops more wisely; in health he relaxes to the sounds of electronic music; in sickness he has the sophisticated machinery of modern medicine to aid his healing. His children may soon be taught by television. His evenings are no longer spent in the half-light of the kerosene lamp but are illuminated and made productive by the use of electricity.

One of the leading contributors to the improving Filipino way of life and to fulfilment of the average man's dreams is the Philips Group of Industries in Manila.

Philips had its modest beginning in the Philippines in the 1920's when incandescent bulbs were brought to the Islands from its parent company in Holland.

In 1936, when it was well established, it introduced the first shortwave radios, enabling the far-flung sectors of the nation to greatly facilitate communication. From these beginnings an ever-growing range of sophisticated electronic devices has followed, establishing for Philips a permanent and responsible position in the Philippine community.

Parallel with the expanding local industries, the manufacture of electrical goods has grown at a remarkable rate since World War II. In 1958 Philips built the first modern lamp and glass factory in the suburban town of Las Piñas, where today it employs over 500 skilled workers in making a wide variety of quality lamps, radio, gramophone and television sets. The electronics industry has become of vital importance to the national economy. The overall value of its output increased from 145 million pesos in 1965 to 203 million in 1967. In addition to its local products, Philips supplies telecommunications equipment, pharmaceuticals, language teaching facilities, and analytical equipment. Its manufactures include such diverse products as: co-axial cable systems; Plumbicon TV cameras and cinema projectors; oscilloscopes; medical X-Ray and nuclear equipment for therapy and diagnostics; cardiac monitoring devices; cryogenic equipment; as well as a wide range of electronic components.

Complex tools for the factory, university, hospital and home—these are all part of Philips' contribution to the rising standards of the Filipino and to his ambitions for his country's tomorrow.

Right:
In the streets of Manila
the bright colours of many costumes
help to impart a character peculiar
to the Philippines.
In this picture
a Muslim prince walks
with two attendants carrying umbrellas
to shelter him from the heat
of the sun.

Above:
Manila is a combination
of traditional and modern architecture.
While many commercial buildings
feature contemporary designs
in a wide variety of forms,
Spanish and Portuguese influences
are evident in the older structures
such as the National Media
Production Centre.

Left:
The Inter-Continental Manila—
an ultra-modern hotel in
an old world atmosphere.

Below:
Le Boulevardier cocktail lounge,
a glimpse of Paris in Manila,
a gay spot in the Philippines.

Below left:
Prince Albert Rotisserie,
where the finest of vintage wines
are served with gourmet meals
'mid the splendour of
a Victorian Court.

HOTEL INTER-CONTINENTAL MANILA

ON THE TROPICAL ISLAND of Luzon, just beyond the bustle of downtown Manila, a whole new city is mushrooming. This is Makati, the commercial stronghold of foreign millionaires—American, Japanese, British, Australian and Scandinavian; a business city of steel and glass; a pleasure city of bright lights and excitement in the full trend of modern development.

And the hub of activity is the Hotel Inter-Continental Manila, where "mabuhay" is given its full and warmest meaning of "welcome".

Here the atmosphere changes as the occasion dictates: bright, sparkling for the dinner dance and special party; sober, serious for big business conventions, for meetings when mergers are made, contracts drawn up, and big deals clinched.

The fourteen-storeyed Hotel Inter-Continental Manila is in the heart of Makati's new shopping centre, eight miles or ten minutes from Manila International Airport. The Hotel has everything going for the visitor—fully-trained staff, air-conditioned lounges and five great restaurants that serve the widest variety of foods and drinks from the simplest fare to the most exotic dishes, cocktails and wines. Fashion parades, audio-visual light shows and industrial exhibitions are part and parcel of commercial and industrial conventions, where the world sells to The Philippines and The Philippines sells to the world and a thousand people can attend.

A few steps from the Cabana Club is the shimmering blue swimming pool; at the El Castellano supper club, flamencos and gypsy dances bring a new and exciting rhythm while spicy paellas are served nearby; in the Prince Albert Rotisserie, English roast beef and vintage wines are de rigueur. The Jeepney Coffee Lounge, inspired by the colourful Jeepney buses of Manila, specialises in papaya and coconut concoctions and in the French-decored Boulevardier Lounge the native cocktails will impress the most blasé.

Only a short distance from the Hotel are most of Luzon's resort areas. Just south is Matabungkay Beach, a stretch of fine, white sand, ideal for swimming, fishing and skindiving. An hour's ride from Makati is the two-cratered, dormant Taal Volcano which sits in the middle of a wide blue lake, said to be the crater of another volcano—parent to the first—extinct but enormous in size.

After a day of sightseeing, the Inter-Continental Manila offers all the comforts needed for relaxation or entertainment—the beauty and barber shops, comfortable divans and easy chairs, and a 24-hour room service—all combined with the Filipino flair for easy hospitality, and the natural gift of making the stranger a welcome guest.

TO THE PHILIPPINES WITH PAL

THE STORY of South-east Asia since 1945 highlights the emergence of several countries of the region from colonial status to independent nationhood and their struggles to develop and stabilise their economies. Their endeavours have been marked by a deep sense of national pride, manifest in many ways.

In the modern world, commerce, travel and communication have afforded opportunities to display a country's national emblem as an identifying symbol in all corners of the globe.

During the year of proclamation of the Republic of the Philippines, 1946, Philippine Airlines was found by the late Colonel Andres Soriano, one of the country's leading industrialists.

Philippine Airlines took its name from a small airline which Soriano had also established in 1941 and whose planes helped evacuate American air force pilots to Australia early during World War II. It commenced operations with five Douglas DC-3's. A few months later DC-4's were added to the small fleet, beginning scheduled flights to Oakland, U.S.A., and thus PAL became the first Asian airline to operate a trans-Pacific service. In the same year it was elected a member of IATA. In 1948 the Company purchased two other local airlines, making it the only scheduled operator in the Philippines. In the process of financing these purchases the Philippine Government acquired majority shares, although Colonel Soriano remained as President. During the early 1950's PAL expanded rapidly and its international services covered three-fourths of the world. In a period of economic stringency, the Government suspended international services in 1954 for lack of funds to purchase new equipment. By 1957 the crisis had passed and the fleet was modernised with jet-prop Vickers

Viscounts and with Fokker F.27's in 1960. In the early 1960's the board was reconstructed. Colonel Soriano resigned in 1961 and Benigno P. Toda, Jr., joined the Company as chairman and in 1962 he piloted it towards resumption of its international services. June of the same year saw Philippine Airlines operating DC-8's, initially on the trans-Pacific route, with a non-stop service between Manila and Honolulu. The overseas route system has expanded to include Australia, Europe as well as Asia.

Since 1962 annual passenger loads have exceeded one million, giving the Company a ranking in the top third of IATA members in the number of passengers flown annually. In 1965 PAL reverted to private control, with the Government, however, still retaining a 25 per cent interest. The Company experienced its first taste of domestic competition in seventeen years when two other local airlines were given operational permits, a challenge it has successfully resisted by retaining 80 per cent of the market. The status and management strength of the Company were confirmed with the appointment of its chairman, Benigno Toda, Jr., as president of the International Air Transport Association 1967-1968, and first chairman of the Assembly of Presidents of the Orient Airlines Association.

The international scope of PAL is indicated in its services. McDonnell Douglas DC-8 jetliners fly to San Francisco, Honolulu, Sydney, Melbourne, Hong Kong, Tokyo, Taipei, Singapore, Bangkok, Karachi, Rome, Frankfurt and Amsterdam. The trans-Pacific service is daily. Overseas sales offices are located in San Francisco, Honolulu, Seattle, Los Angeles, Chicago, Washington, Miami, New York and Dallas in the United States; Sydney and Melbourne in Australia; Rome, London, Madrid and Frankfurt in Europe; Hong Kong, Tokyo, Osaka, Singapore, Taipei, Bangkok and Saigon in Asia; and Toronto in Canada.

Philippine Airlines plans to acquire high-capacity jets and to further expand its international route system. More pure-jet services will operate on domestic routes.

In ancillary activities it is performing ground handling services for almost all of the foreign airlines calling at Manila, and maintenance of the Philippine and United States armed forces, other carriers and privately-owned aircraft. The airline is certified by the U.S. Federal Aviation Administration as a repair agency for U.S.-registered aircraft.

The Filipino atmosphere on the aircraft and in its terminal offices gives PAL a distinction and sets a standard equalled by few other major international airlines.

Above: PAL uses DC-8's including the DC-8-63 for its international services linking Manila to Europe, the U.S. and principal Asian cities.

Left: The colourful vintas of the Muslim provinces of the Philippines accent the variety of cultures found in the multi-island Republic.

Opposite page, top: The Cultural Centre at Manila, in its solid but graceful lines, is the home of performing and other arts of the Philippines. It holds several galleries and museums.

Opposite page, below: Smart and attractive hostesses help to make PAL one of the most popular airlines in Asia.

517

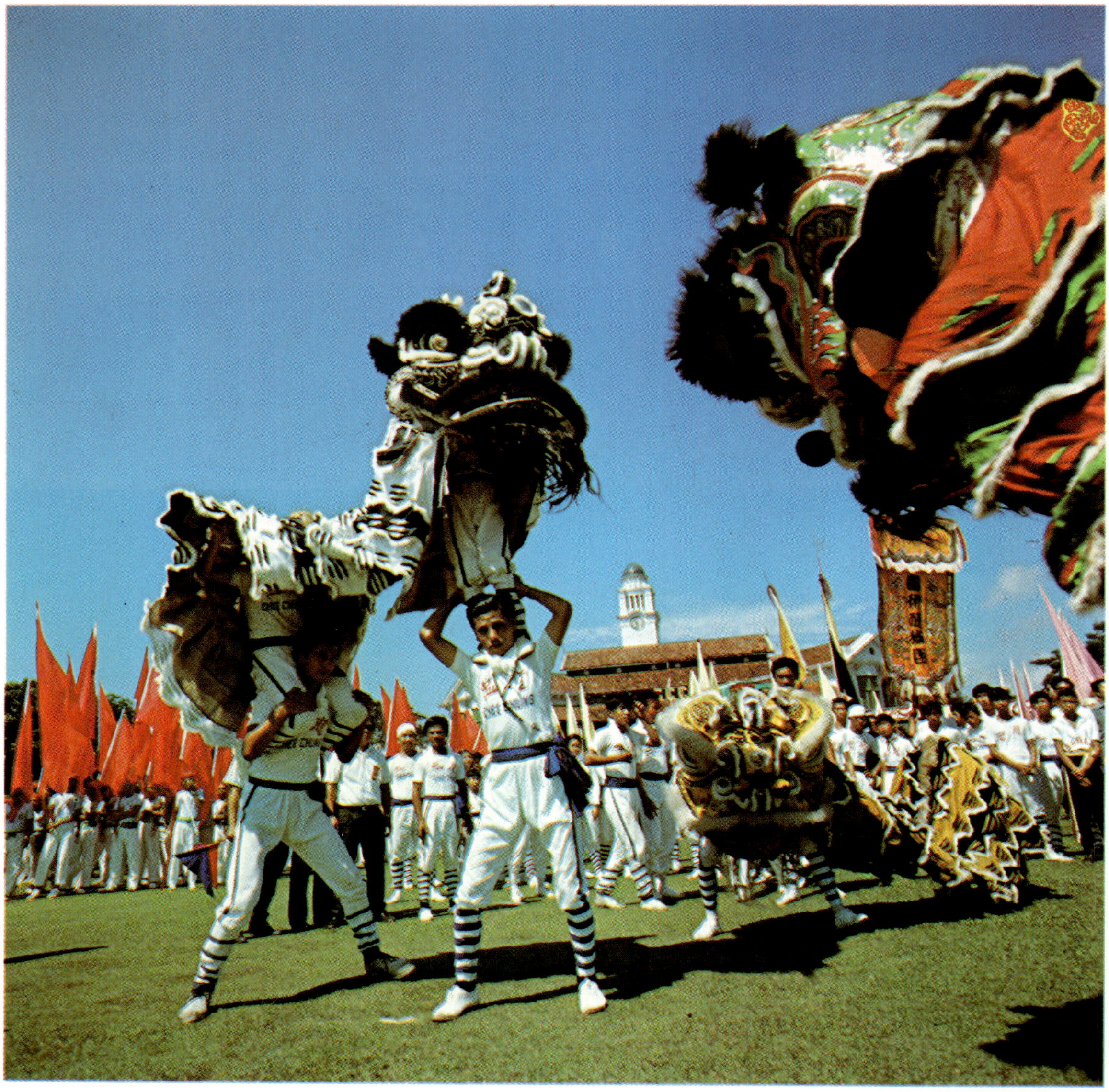

Republic of
SINGAPORE

MALAYSIA

JOHORE

JOHORE BAHRU

SELAT

CAUSEWAY

Woodlands

Thong Hoe

LIM CHU KANG ROAD

MANDAI ROAD

WOODLANDS ROAD

Seletar Reservoir

CHOA CHU KANG ROAD

Bt. Panjang

UPPER BUKIT TIMAH ROAD

Pierce Reservoir

Choa Chu Kang

Jurong

JURONG ROAD

Bt. Timah

UPPER JURONG ROAD

JALAN AHMAD IBRAHIM

HOLLAND ROAD

Tuas

AYER RAJAH ROAD

Pasir Panjang

PASIR PANJANG ROAD

Buona Vista

PULAU PESEK
PULAU MERLIMAU
PULAU SERAYA
PULAU AYER CHAWAN
PULAU AYER MERBAU
PULAU SAKRA
PULAU BAKAU

PULAU BUKUM

SINGAPORE

LEGEND

- MISCELLANEOUS AGRICULTURE
- NATURE RESERVE

Chong Pang
Punggol
Pulau Ubin
Serangoon Harbour
Serangoon
Changi
Airport
Mac Ritchie Reservoir
Changi Beach
Bedok
Clifford Pier
Pulau Brani
Pulau Sentosa
Singapore Strait

Sembawang Road
Upper Thomson Road
Yio Chu Kang Road
Punggol Road
Upper Serangoon Road
Upper Paya Lebar Road
Tampines Road
Upper Changi Road
Bukit Timah Road
Orchard Road
Geylang Road
Changi Road
Mount Batten Road
East Coast Road
Nicoll Highway
Robinson Road
Keppel Road

STRAIT
CITY

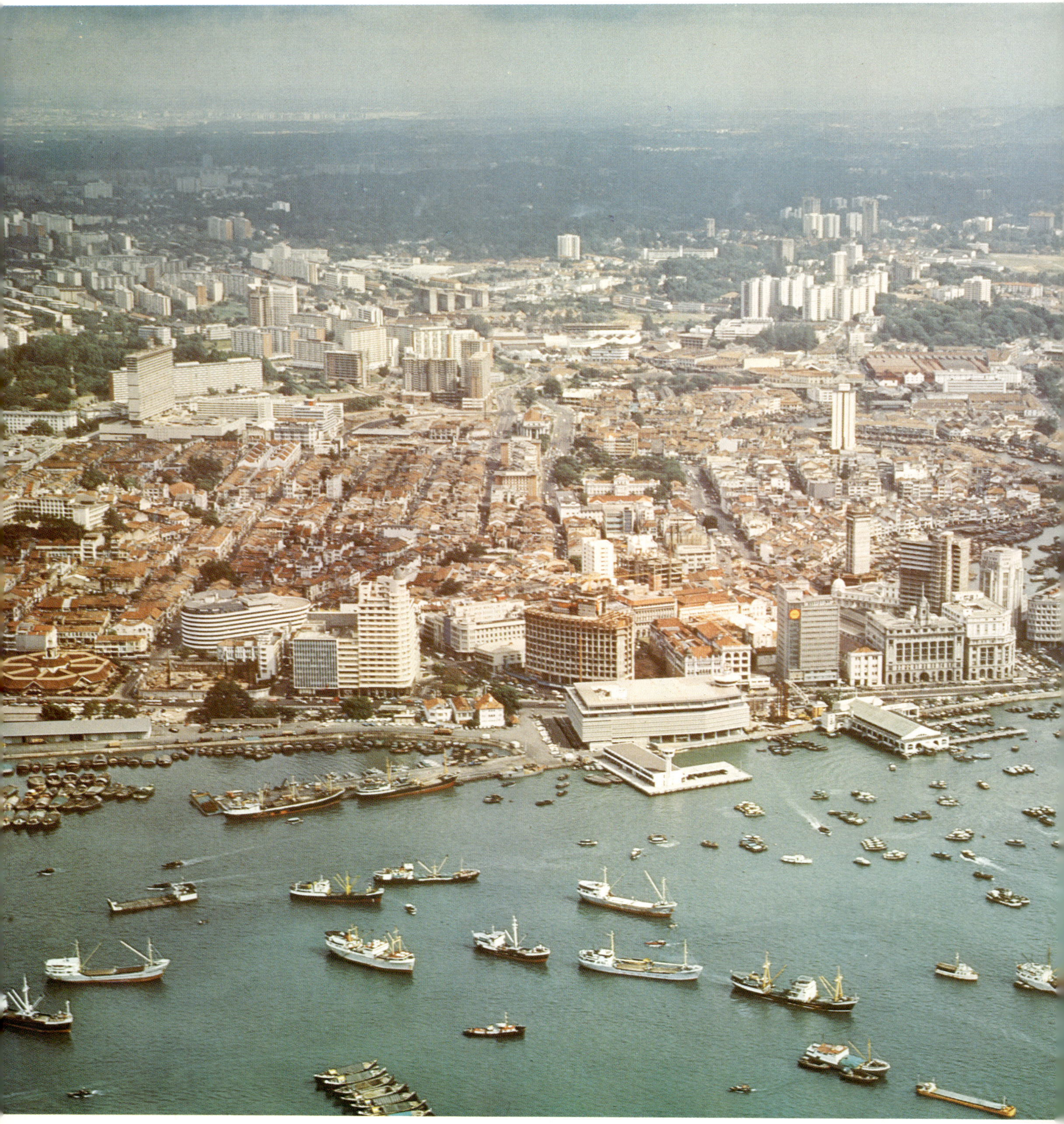

Singapore - Instant Asia

Singapura - Lion City

FOR SEVERAL CENTURIES Singapore existed as a port of call for small coastal traders and a haven for pirates, until Britain began to show interest in the Island as a potential counterfoil to the Dutch presence in Java and Malacca. On 29th January 1819, following the exploration of several possible areas for settlement in the Straits of Johore, Britain's envoy, Sir Stamford Raffles, dropped anchor in the clear, deep waters just off the mouth of the Singapore River. This ideal harbour, at the junction of most of the sea-routes to and from South-east, North and East Asia, to India, to the Middle East and Europe, was the perfect site for Raffles' dream of "a great commercial emporium for trade in the southern seas".

After a few months, during which he surveyed the Island's possibilities, he wrote to a friend: "You may take my word for it, this is by far the most important station in the East, and as far as naval superiority and commercial interests are concerned, of much higher value than whole continents of territory".

In the first 40 years following its European discovery, Singapore more than fulfilled its founder's prophecies. The population rapidly increased and trade expanded. The young settlement soon eclipsed Penang and Malacca in importance, and in 1824 it became the centre of administration for the entire Straits Settlements established by the East India Company. Between 1821 and 1825 the value of Singapore's trade grew from 1.8 million to 12.1 million Spanish silver dollars and by 1829 square-rigged, ocean-going vessels were calling at the rate of more than one a day. In 1867 the Straits Settlements became a colony under the Colonial Office, and when British influence extended into Malaya the Governor assumed additional responsibilities as High Commissioner to the Malay States.

At the turn of the century Singapore functioned as the fulcrum of the modern Malaya whose fame was spreading as a producer of tin and rubber. Financial, promotional and organisational services were provided from the island which became the world centre of distribution for the area's abundant raw materials. Parallel with this growth the port of Singapore was modernised and expanded to handle the exports and imports of the burgeoning economies of South-east Asia. This period of rapid development led to a corresponding increase in population through immigration and natural growth. Along with the rest of the world, Singapore suffered a reverse during the economic crisis of the late 'twenties and early 'thirties, but as soon as the slump began to ease Singapore met the recovering demand for labour with immigration. Previously, men had far outnumbered women but now, in order to avoid a continuing imbalance of the sexes, legislation was enacted to restrict the number of males entering the Colony. The new migrants—and many others who, until this time, had considered their presence on the island to be of temporary duration—now married in Singapore and their children were born there. From these families arose a new national consciousness which led, after World War II, to the fruition of Singaporean independence.

By halting further migration and by destroying much of Britain's former prestige, the occupying Japanese forces engendered a sense of nationalism among the ordinary citizens. During the long years of the War, under the restrictions imposed by the enemy, the people of Singapore had to make their own decisions and work out their own problems. In the free post war world and under the watchful eyes of Sukarno and Nehru, a return to the colonial status quo was virtually impossible. Singapore's Prime Minister, Mr Lee Kuan Yew, described the feelings of the new nationalist when he said: "We decided that from then on (World War II) our lives would be ours to decide, that we should not be the pawn and playthings of foreign powers".

In 1948 Singapore held its first elections for the Legislative Council. The majority of the members were either officials or official appointees until 1955, when the Rendel Commission established a Legislative Assembly of 32 members, 25 of whom were elected from one-member constituencies. 1955 and 1956 were years of Communist activity through the trade unions and Chinese middle schools, but an attempted takeover in 1956 was defeated and the militant leaders imprisoned.

The final state of emergence from the status of a colony to that of an internally self-governing state was smoothly achieved in 1959, after 140 years of British rule. On 30th May 1959, in the first elections under a newly-drafted Constitution which provided for a parliamentary system of Government, headed by a Cabinet of Ministers, the

Above: A new statue of Sir Stamford Raffles, unveiled in 1972, on the bank of Singapore River.

Left page: A mythological lion of Hindu origin from Indonesia, after which Singapore may have been named in the 14th Century.

Below: Singapore River, from a painting by E.A. Porcher, about 1843-47. Government Hill (later Fort Canning) is in the background.

People's Action Party (PAP) won 43 seats out of the 51 available.

In 1961 the concept of the Federation of Malaysia was proposed by the Prime Minister of the Federation of Malaya. In a Referendum in September 1962 the people of Singapore, by a 73 per cent vote, consented to the union; and the new Federation of Malaysia came into being just a year later, with Singapore one of the constituent states, thus gaining total freedom from colonial rule. The Union proved, however, to be a brief interlude. Conflicts of interest between the predominantly Malay Malaya and the predominantly Chinese Singapore proved too numerous and difficult. On 9th August 1965, by mutual agreement, Singapore was separated from Malaysia to become a fully-independent and sovereign nation. On 22nd December of the same year, it became a Republic with a President at its head.

Although the conduct of parliamentary business and the powers of the legislature are governed largely by rules adapted from those of the House of Commons at Westminster and from the British Constitutional model, the Government of Singapore today is, in practice, a one-party authority. Due to the unpopularity of some political parties and the unwillingness of other opposing factions to work within the system, the People's Action Party and its moderate Prime Minister, Mr Lee Kuan Yew, have continued to govern without serious rivalry from any quarter. In the 1968 General Elections, the PAP won all 58 seats in the Assembly, polling 65,812 of 77,984 votes cast, an enviable record of a people's faith and confidence.

As Mr Rajaratnam, Minister for Foreign Affairs subsequently stated: "The people are more interested in what is good government than in having an opposition".

And good government, most Singaporeans would agree, is what they have. With one of the highest living standards in Asia, the average citizen is enjoying the dual benefits of sound economy and efficient, progressive administration.

INSTANT ASIA

Sightseeing venues in the city include the famous Van Kleef Aquarium, the Botanic Gardens, the National Museum where prints of old Singapore provide fascinating comparison with the city today, and the original settlements like "Little India" in Serangoon Road, Arab Street, and Chinatown with its vital, vibrant market life. It is estimated that some million tourists have viewed the priceless jade collection at the House of Jade in Nassim Road.

On this tiny tropical island are to be found some 500 Chinese temples ranging from ancestral shrines to awesome monasteries. Amidst the profusion of hundreds of thousands of high-rise housing flats are the weird dragon eaves, onion-shaped domes of mosques, sculptured roofs of Hindu temples and the steeples of churches that could have come from an English hamlet.

From the vantage point of Mount Faber, one can view the Inner and Outer Roads of the spectacular Singapore Harbour, Sentosa, which is now being developed into a tourist resort and the islands of the Indonesian Rhio archipelago beyond. Going further out of the city there is Haw Par Villa or Tiger Balm Gardens—a colourful plastercast pageant of Chinese mythology. It is immediately meaningful to children who come, open-mouthed and wide-eyed, absorbed in the total atmosphere of fantasy. Adults cannot help but be awed by the tremendous amount of work put into it. From the Tiger Balm Gardens it is a short drive to the 20-hectare Jurong Bird Park, probably the largest of its kind in the world. It displays some 8,000 birds of about 350 different species.

THE FASCINATION OF SINGAPORE lies in its unique juxtaposition of "pace, race and cultures". The oriental splendour of the Chinese Chamber of Commerce, a Mogul restaurant, the American Embassy and an Armenian church, all face each other at a single road junction.

In addition to the traveller seeking to sample Asia in miniature, Singapore's strategic position in the East and her numerous, top-class hotels make her the natural choice of businessmen and convention organisers. The Island is linked to the world by more than 200 shipping lines and 25 international airlines. Its airport, which accommodates Jumbo Jets, is one of the most modern in Asia. It is the hub of the South-east Asian scene, being only three hours' flight from Manila, two hours from Bangkok, one and a half from Djakarta and 45 minutes from Kuala Lumpur.

Top left: Raffles Place combines modern garden layout with early Colonial architecture.

Lower left: The Scarlet Ibis is a special attraction at Jurong Bird Park.

Above: The Dragon Dance is traditional on Chinese Festival Days.

Below: Night time in Chinatown, and nearby one of innumerable out-door cafes where genuine Chinese food is a constant lure.

Another 'must' on the tourists' agenda is the Mandai Orchid Garden. This four-hectare Garden is of international repute and prides itself on rearing its own hybrids. There are some half million plants with over 300 varieties in the Garden. The orchid's long life span enables visitors to despatch sprays of them to almost any part of the world.

Although she has taken giant strides toward industrialising, Singapore is still primarily what she started out to be—a free port, a great emporium of the Orient. On Raffles Place there are the large European-style department stores, Chinese arcades, Indian jewellery shops and stores selling curios, antiques, novelties, arts and crafts, From here to Collyer Quay stretches the bargain hunter's bonanza, Change Alley. Singapore has created a paradise for the tourist who wants a duty-free camera or transistor or high-precision watch. Shopkeepers remain astoundingly courteous as visitors turn their shops inside out comparing prices invariably to discover the Japanese, Swiss and German products are cheaper than in their countries of origin.

Singapore has been described as one of the world's greatest eating houses. Its the Island's cosmopolitan character that has made it a gourmet's paradise—a melting pot into which have flowed the food cultures of Asia and the occidental world.

Kobe beefsteaks imported from Japan are of a high quality and other national specialities include Russian, Kashmiri, American, Korean, Swiss, French, Italian and Dutch. The best Chinese restaurants offer Peking cuisine, where duck is so roasted that the crisp outer skin is served as a separate course, as well as Szechuan, Cantonese, Teochew and Hokkien dishes.

Increasingly popular too are the restaurants that have mushroomed along the East Coast, specialising in seafood which is freshly caught and superbly prepared—chillie crabs, broiled lobsters, steamed fish, sizzling prawns, abalone in oyster sauce, stewed mussels, real turtle soup—music to the gourmet's ears. From Satay served at roadside stalls to the Continental cuisine and succulent Chinese dishes of lavish restaurants, eating-out Singapore Style is one of the essences of Instant Asia.

ART AND CULTURE

The diversity of racial threads in the tapestry of Singaporean society produces a range of many-patterned forms which is truly intriguing. Although the colonial rule produced little original art, the four main cultures—Chinese, Malay, Indian and English—burgeoned within their own distinct communities. In post war times, the island's adopted and native arts have flourished to a remarkable degree. English and Malay verse, Tamil plays and short stories, Chinese film scripts—all have thrived in the new climate of cross-cultural respect. Richard Tan, a Singapore Chinese, and an admired master of classical Indian dancing, typifies this new spirit of polycultural pioneering. Established Singapore writers also reflect it, among the prominent ones being Edwin Thumboo, Goh Sin Tub, Lim Thean Soo, Oliver Seet and Harun Aminurrashid.

Visual arts such as painting, batik, sculpture, ceramics and calligraphy have also flourished, incorporating the fecund imagery of traditional batik painting with the disciplined solids of 20th Century abstract.

Seah Kim Joo in batiks, and Sunyee in both Chinese and Western techniques, are two top names. The Art Museum of the University of Singapore has a good collection of South-east Asian art, including modern Singaporean art, sculpture, ceramics and the minor arts of former ages.

Singaporean theatre, dance and music thrive in all their separate manifestations.

The National Theatre has done much to stimulate appreciation of these arts and at present comprises a classical orchestra, a choir and a Chinese orchestra, and has plans to found Malay, Chinese and English dramatic companies. Chinese opera in all of its grandiose, stylised symmetry remains a popular spectacle but multi-lingual films, a small but growing number of which are now produced in Singapore, are the star attraction, being viewed by nearly 600,000 people every week. Both Radio and Television Singapore which have done much to encourage the arts, devote special time each day to the needs and interests of each community.

FESTIVALS

Another aspect of the unique multi-racial character of Singapore, the festival life of the Republic, is varied and hectic and rarely a month goes by without some major celebration. At Thaipusam, Hindus carry their temple deity through the streets in decorated chariots while the more devoted adherents drive skewers through their cheeks. Chinese New Year is just as colourful and is celebrated with much exuberance. It is a time for feasts, man-manoeuvred dragons and visiting relatives. Hari Raya Puasa is a big day for Muslims, for it marks the end of Ramadan, a month of fasting and penance. It is celebrated with prayers, followed by a trooping forth of the people in their various national dress. At Cheng Ming, the Chinese display their legendary reverence and regard for their dead, visiting ornately decorated tombs to pray and ask their ancestors for help on the earthly plane and thousands of Chinese burn incence, candles and joss papers and make sacrificial offerings of food.

EDUCATION—A GIANT TASK

In Singapore, as in all developing countries today, educating the people is a herculean task. In addition to the ills inherited from the colonial era, the system has to cope with an extremely large student population.

But, in spite of these and other problems, the present Government has created a system which is being rapidly acclaimed one of the best in Asia. Primary education is free to all Singaporean children from the ages of six to fourteen, and assistance is given to poor families by means of bursaries and other devices. Study loans and scholarships, too, are provided for secondary, university and technical students.

In 1969 the Government spent S$170 million on education, or 15 per cent of total budget expenditure.

Singapore's multi-racial, internationally-oriented society has its firmest base in its education system. All students, whether

Above: Interior of an ornate Temple depicting Chinese deities.

Top of page: One of the many Chinese temples for which Singapore is famous.

Top, opposite page: One of the most important events in Singapore is the celebration of National Day when many groups take part in a great parade.

Right: A devout priest praying for his people.

attending Government or Aided Schools, must learn a second language; English or another of the more generally spoken.

In order to promote the declared objective of Singapore as a nation rich in skilled managers, technicians and craftsmen, facilities for technical education have been extended and improved, practical workshops have been added to schools and the syllabus has been adapted to meet the country's real needs. In 1968, before the system was completely re-vamped, only 14 per cent of the nation's secondary school students were enrolled in technical or vocational courses; now at least one out of three students is pursuing these studies.

Tertiary education, too, is expanding. The University of Singapore, which teaches in English, offers degree courses in most academic and scientific disciplines. There are faculties of law, medicine, engineering, dentistry and architecture, and schools of education, accountancy and business administration. The Nanyang University is the second of Singapore's universities. It was founded in 1953 and its first students enrolled in 1956. A three years' course at any of the colleges—arts, science and commerce—provides a general degree, and a further course may bring an honours degree. There are two centres for the study of languages and computers. A college of Graduate Studies, comprising Institutes of Asian Studies, Natural Science, Mathematics and Business Studies has been set up. In 1972, the student body exceeded 2,000 and there were some 150 lecturers and professional teachers.

SOLVING THE HOUSING PROBLEM

Public housing in Singapore has had a profound impact on the physical and social environment. In place of what were once slums, dilapidated sheds and squatter areas, have sprung up imposing blocks of Housing Board flats. Squatters who formerly lived in dreary conditions now enjoy a better and brighter life in high-rise, low-cost flats which provide all the essential comforts of modern living. Although the community solidarity of the slums can give way to the alienation of encapsulated living, the evils of turn-of-the-century shop-houses with sixteen families sharing one kitchen and bathroom are missed by no-one!

Formed in 1960 to replace the former Singapore Improvement Trust when the present Government was elected to office, the Housing and Development Board has completed more than 100,000 units in its eleven years of operation. The Republic is thus among the very few developing countries to measure up to the housing target set by the United Nations Committee on building, housing and planning—ten new dwelling units per 1,000 population during the development decade of the 'sixties.

Today a flat is completed every 36 minutes and efforts are still being made to increase the pace so as to keep up with the demands and rising expectations of the people. About one-third of Singapore's population are now living in Housing Board flats, and a "Home Ownership" scheme is operating which permits increasingly large numbers in the lower income groups to purchase their own apartments. Most flats are let out at low rentals from S$20 to S$60 monthly, depending on the size of the unit.

Housing estates on the periphery of the city include the first satellite town, Queenstown, which now has more than 20,000 units housing over 110,000 people, and the second and even larger development, Toa Payoh. The 'neighbourhood principle' is incorporated into the layout of these estates whereby markets, shopping centres and primary schools are provided within the neighbourhood, each of which houses about 1,000 to 5,000 families. Where more than three neighbourhoods are close by, provision is made for a town centre with banks, a post office, departmental stores and theatres.

SPORT

More than 40 different outdoor and indoor sports are played in Singapore. Being an island, Singapore is a natural home for water-sports of which swimming, water-skiing, skin-diving, yachting and fishing are the most popular. Changi, Loyang and Pasir Ris are the best-known beaches, but many prefer to take a boat out to the smaller islands and islets to enjoy the seclusion of these tropical paradises.

Singapore's Bukit Timah Race Course is among the very finest in Asia, with excellently appointed grandstands for both members and the public. Many Australian-bred horses race there and jockeys from all over Asia and Australasia make Singapore racing colourful and ultra-competitive.

A huge sports complex is under construction in Kallang Park and the first phase, the National Stadium, has just been completed at a cost of S$17 million. It offers facilities for athletics, rugby, football and hockey and for such events as tattoos, rallies and open-air concerts. .It initially provides accommodation for 50,000 spectators with room to extend to 100,000. Two major international sporting events take place annually on the island: the Singapore Grand Prix, held during Easter, and the Pesta Sukan or Sports Festival, held during August to coincide with the Republic's National Day.

TRENDS IN DEVELOPMENT

During the latter half of the 'sixties, Singapore's economy began to adapt to her changing status in South-east Asia. Not the least problems to be faced were the upsurge in unemployment and the loss of foreign exchange resulting from the British military withdrawal from the island. (It was estimated that the British forces spent about S$400 million a year in the Republic.) Added to these, the post war 'baby-boom'-inflated labour force, increasing by over 16,000 annually, began to place added strains on the economy's ability to fruitfully employ and maintain the population, and despite birth control measures, this pattern continued to predominate into the 'seventies.

Between 1968 and 1969 however, the Gross Domestic Product rose by more than 13.5 per cent, and although entrepôt trade still continues to be a vital factor in the overall stimulation of development, today manufacture is contributing equally to the prosperity of the nation. Secondary industries such as oil-refining and shipbuilding and repairing, which have sprung up around the Port of Singapore and the industrial town of Jurong, have assumed a major significance in the overall economic picture. Tax and export incentives have induced both foreign and domestic investment—vital factors in the long-term development programme of the Republic. But of even greater significance is the sense of security engendered by a stable Government with a positive policy of economic expansion.

Agriculture and fisheries constitute less than 5 per cent of economic activity in the Republic, but as the result of new intensive methods, the production of poultry, pigs and eggs has increased considerably. These commodities are now exported, and deep-sea fishing is being scientifically developed in order to exploit the excellent waters near the island.

MANUFACTURING INDUSTRIES

The decisive advantages of Singapore as a manufacturing and distribution centre are well known and accepted overseas. Despite a lack of natural resources—even the bulk of the island's water and food supply is brought from outside—the Republic is superior to other Asian countries in three major respects: its favourable geographic position, its excellent infrastructure and its highly literate, highly urbanised and highly adaptable population.

It is only in the last decade, however, that sophisticated export industries have come to Singapore. Previously, processing industries such as tin smelting and latex making, a few consumer industries such as furniture and soft drink manufacture—the weight of whose finished products made import expensive—and service-orientated industries such as printing, publishing and tailoring, were the only real secondary activities pursued intensively. In 1957, manufacturing provided one-sixth of employment and one-eighth of the Gross Domestic Product (GDP). Since 1960, when the Government first drew up its economic development plan making industrialisation a cardinal feature, industrial production has expanded annually by more than 20 per cent. Factories have grown from around 500 in 1960 to some 1,800 in 1972: their output and value have increased sevenfold; and their employment figures have quadrupled.

How was this achieved? The answer lies in tax and export incentives. By fulfilling certain flexible conditions firms involved in pioneering manufacturing ventures during the 'sixties were able to enjoy freedom from taxes for periods of up to fifteen years, freedom from import duties on necessary machinery and equipment, and to enjoy temporary protective tariffs on the products they made. These new freedoms and tariff advantages have enabled manufacturers to enter the 1970's with a confidence of success completely lacking only a decade ago.

JURONG TOWN

Since the early days of the Republic's industrialisation, the Government has become more selective, but although its incentives now have limits, American, British, Japanese, Hong Kong, Malaysian, Taiwanese and Australian investors still vie for space in the island's industrial areas.

Jurong, a town specially created for industry, is synonymous with Singapore's dramatic drive to industrialisation and is taken as a model for development by other Asian states. Once called "Goh's Folly", after the Republic's Finance Minister Mr. Goh Keng Swee, who initiated its creation, Jurong is now the industrial showpiece of Singapore and an effective vindication of Government economic planning.

The town, planned with the help of World Bank experts, covers 4,200 acres of fully-developed area, with 1,100 more under development: it is served by a 3,000 feet deep-water wharf and 1,260 feet of coastal and lighter wharves. Twelve miles of railway link Jurong to the Singapore-Malaysia railway network; and it has 25 miles of metalled roads, a watermain capacity of 30 million gallons of fresh water daily and a

Right: Singapore's Prime Minister, Mr. Lee Kuan Yew escorting the Prime Minister of Australia, the Rt. Hon. William McMahon from his plane on arrival at Singapore in June 1972.

Left: Singapore's Supreme Court is an imposing and dramatic sight at night time.

Below, opposite page: To cope with the rapidly growing demand for housing the Government is building huge housing complexes incorporating shopping facilities, parks and gardens adjacent to home units and flats.

plant capable of supplying 10 million gallons of high quality industrial water. Power is available at 22,000 volts, and, when the Jurong Power Station is fully operational in 1973, it will have a capacity of 480 megawatts. Jurong has 4,615 housing units, and 3,000 under construction of which 1,700 are near completion; there are also luxury executive flats, a modern supermarket, banks, a swimming pool and a large top-class restaurant.

By the beginning of 1972 there were 270 factories in production and more being built. The wide range of goods currently manufactured in Jurong include metal products, heavy transport equipment, petroleum, building materials, electrical parts, chemicals and pharmaceuticals, rubber and leather, pulp and paper, textiles, garments and food products. Cameras, optical goods, marine diesel engines, telephones, record changers, television sets and even production equipment for one world-wide group's factories abroad—are now being produced.

INTERNATIONAL RELATIONS

From the penthouses and revolving restaurants of Singapore's tallest buildings the neighbouring islands of Indonesia and Malaysia can be seen. Malaysia in particular has much in common with the Island Republic: a common history, a five-power defence programme, freely interchangeable currency, a Stock Exchange, and a major newspaper—"The Straits Times".

In spite of the problems that still occasionally bedevil the neighbours, Singapore continues to explore all practical means of co-operation with the mainland.

The strains of the *Konfrontasi* period of 1963-1965 have necessarily affected relationships with Indonesia, but the policy of the Suharto Government which seeks to maximise foreign investment and exchange has encouraged Singapore to search out spheres of mutual interest and benefit with her giant (in population terms) neighbour.

Apart from these two nations, with the Philippines, Thailand and the rest of non-Communist Asia (all members of ASEAN since its formation in 1967), Singapore is creating closer links through trade, and economic and cultural relations. This progressive policy is also extending to the Pacific nations to the south and east, primarily Australia and New Zealand.

Australia has already invested large sums in the development of Singaporean industry and tourism.

In June 1972, close political ties were strengthened by the visit of the Australian Prime Minister, The Rt. Hon. William McMahon, C.H., M.P., on his tour embracing Indonesia, Singapore and Malaysia.

His meetings with the Prime Minister of Singapore, Mr. Lee Kuan Yew, were friendly and constructive. The main subject of discussion was the five-power defence agreement between Australia, New Zealand, Britain, Singapore and Malaysia. In his speech to the Singapore Press Club, Mr. McMahon made firm reference to "a continuing relevance and importance of the physical presence of our forces in Singapore and Malaysia".

Earlier at a dinner in honour of the visiting Prime Minister, Mr. Lee stated frankly that Singapore's progress was continuing at least in part due "to the quiet understanding and support of our friends". Moreover he said, "there is no reason why we should not make further progress in regional co-operation and consolidate the present stability of the region".

THE FUTURE

Despite setbacks during the 'sixties and early 'seventies, the resilient Singapore economy seems to have begun an era in which the economic forethought of a decade will begin to bear fruit. Gold and foreign exchange reserves totalling about S$760 million and foreign assets exceeding S$2,400 million will provide admirable shock-absorbers if any unforeseen financial buffettings are to come. Problems still likely to be faced include: unemployment, the provision of necessary capital for development, a lack of local entrepreneurship, the need for greater technological expertise and the finding of alternative means of filling the foreign exchange gap left by the British withdrawal. On the other hand, a sound base has already been established for the solution of these problems and for a continued growth in real living standards. As officials of the World Bank reported, "in 1968 Singapore entered a new phase of accelerated growth with boom conditions in private investment and a decline in unemployment, buoyancy of government revenues, the emergence of an overall surplus of savings over investments and a significant building up of foreign reserves". Although some adverse conditions were expected to affect growth in the early 'seventies, "the maintenance of a GNP growth of perhaps 5 per cent at the trough seems feasible".

IN THE EARLY DAYS of the present century the Chinese community of Malaya decided it was time to form a bank of their own. Before that time the territory was served by banking institutions established by the British and other foreign investors. The growth of shipping and commerce and expansion of the Malayan tin and rubber industries, in which the Chinese were becoming more and more involved, convinced them that the preservation of their identity demanded a more personal control of their financial interests.

Between 1900 and 1920 several Chinese banks were founded and from the amalgamation of three of the most influential of these bodies emerged the Oversea-Chinese Banking Corporation which today is one of the largest banking institutions in Asia. Its Head Office is in Singapore where it heads the list of the top hundred companies of the Republic and Malaysia.

The consolidated assets of the OCBC—as it is now more popularly known—total more than S$1,511 million and at the end of 1971 it recorded a net profit of S$11.6 million (after tax provisions and allocations to inner reserves), on a paid up share capital of S$60 million. It held S$58.9 million in reserves.

The birth of the Oversea-Chinese Banking Corporation in 1932 and its subsequent growth are well described by Tan Sri Tan Chin Tuan, the dynamic Chairman of the Bank. "It was a terrible time for the whole world. Everything was collapsing because of the Depression. Firms were going bankrupt and thousands of people were out of work. There was almost complete commercial stagnation. The records of the time show that the price of rubber fell to just over one US cent a pound, against the US$1.75 which the happily prosperous growers were getting 20 years before, in the golden days of the pre-war boom. But while stagnation was widespread, it was not total.

"The local Chinese banks were very small and not very strong. At the time, all the really big business—the old trading companies, the big rubber plantations and the shipping interests and so forth—was handled by the local branches of the foreign banks. You very seldom used to see a Chinese at the counters. The system in those days was that they had to go to a "comprador" who acted as an agent between the Chinese customer and the bank officials. There were very few who had direct dealings with the manager. It gave the compradors a great deal of power, and they often charged very high rates of commission for their services."

But this same comprador system gave three local Chinese banks a strong advantage when, towards the end of the Depression in 1932, they decided to put an end to the cut-throat competition which threatened to ruin them all, and merge their interests. The three were the Chinese Commercial Bank, which was established in 1912, the Ho Hong Bank, established in 1917, and the Oversea-Chinese Bank established in 1919. As one large and potentially powerful organisation instead of three relatively small institutions, the Oversea-Chinese Banking Corporation Limited, which they formed was in an unrivalled position to attract the loyalty and support of both the local and foreign-based Chinese communities.

In 1932, however, the funds available to the new Bank restricted its scope to local development. Paid up capital amounted to just over US$3.3 million and total assets to just over US$12.8 million. The net profit for the first twelve months was US$209,000 but no dividend was declared. Three years later, total assets had staggered up to US$15.3 million and the net profit to just over US$300,000 with a dividend of $2\frac{1}{2}$ per cent.

1936 was an unpropitious year. The branches which the Bank had opened in China were swallowed up by the Japanese who were avidly expanding their interests. Notwithstanding this setback, however, the Corporation's assets steadily rose till in 1940 they stood at US$26.4 million. Net profit was US$514,000 and encouraging

OVERSEA-CHINESE BANKING CORPORATION LIMITED

though it was, soon came to an end, for in that year the Japanese invading army began rolling down through Malaysia. Wherever it was possible, the Bank's branches and their staffs were pulled back behind the "impregnable" fortifications of Singapore. When the Japanese swarmed across the Causeway, to all intents and purposes, the Bank ceased to exist.

But the situation was not entirely hopeless. Many of the Bank's officers had managed to escape from enemy-occupied territory and several, led by Tan Sri Tan, were evacuated to India before the fall of Singapore. In Bombay they set up a small office from which they continued to control the activities of branches in regions which had not been overrun, and so guarded what remained of the Bank's precious foreign assets. They also made plans for their return to Singapore which eventually took place as soon as the Allied armies marched back into Malaya in 1945.

In addition to the widespread misery and chaos caused during the Occupation, 12 per cent of the Bank's staff had died. Records had all been destroyed and the organisation was almost non-existent. But the foundations still remained, and on them the Bank began to build again.

By 1946 assets had risen to US$43 million and profits passed the US million dollar mark for the first time—although it was considered best, in the circumstances, that no dividend be paid that year. From then on there was no looking back and the Bank has maintained an average growth rate of around US$10 million a year ever since; dividends often as high as 20 per cent.

Over the years, the Bank's traditionally close association with the Chinese community has paid off handsomely. Small and struggling enterprises which it helped to finance in the early days have grown to a substantial size as Singapore has flourished, and they remain faithful customers. But while the Bank continues to keep an eye open for soundly based local companies which have prospects for development, it keeps the other eye firmly fixed on possibilities created by the new needs of the commercial and industrial communities.

In addition to a network of branches in Singapore and Malaysia and two in China, the OCBC now has offices in Hong Kong—both on the Island and on the mainland at Kowloon—and in London, as well as representatives in every one of the world's principal cities. Apart from handling all the normal services of a clearing bank the OCBC is expanding into the wider fields of industrial financing and merchant banking, and it was well to the fore at the beginning of the thriving Asian dollar market. In the fast moving field of foreign exchange business, the OCBC is rapidly acquiring the reputation of being the International Bank of the East.

The OCBC has always been a solid institution: "Now", says the Chairman, "We are adding dynamism to solidness."

In 1970 the Bank launched First Oversea Credit Ltd., a leasing and industrial financing company formed in partnership with the First National City Bank. It carries out all such specialist activities as discounting book debts and financing building, plant and transport and it is also able to capitalise on local expertise and the corresponding ability to mobilise finance to produce the best of both worlds. The same philosophy lay behind the creation of Singapore International Merchant Banks Ltd., a consortium formed by the Crown Agents, Continental Illinois National Bank of Chicago, Alexanders Discount Co. and the OCBC, to underwrite issues, assemble complicated packages for financing new ventures, provide investment management and all the other services not normally handled in a clearing bank's operations. But the new ventures are only the latest in more than a score of other subsidiaries incorporated in Singapore, Malaysia, Hong Kong and the UK and which include such enterprises as Associated Investments and Securities, the Building Society of Malaya, Eastern Realty Co., Regal Holdings, Select Securities Ltd., Ho Hong Steamship Co.

As well as spreading outward, the Bank is now also growing upward. The old China Building—an extravagant combination of Chinese and Western architecture—which had served as the OCBC's headquarters since 1932 is now gone. The Bank is currently housed in unpretentious temporary quarters in Upper Pickering Street, Singapore, but on the old China Building site in Chulia Street, a prestigious skyscraper is being erected: the new OCBC Centre. Soaring to 52 storeys it will comprise more than 700,000 square feet of built-up area; it is to be completed in the mid-1970's. The centre will be manned by highly qualified banking and business personnel and will be a landmark in the heart of Singapore's busiest commercial area. In Orchard Road the Bank has just completed building another giant, a US$7 million, 25-storey Specialists' Centre.

All this progress does not mean that the Bank intends to favour the big firm clients, and overlook the needs of the more humble customer with perhaps nothing more than a small personal account. "We do not forget that the Bank only managed to grow through the support of the ordinary depositor", says Tan Sri Tan. "We try very hard not to give the impression that we are an impersonal Corporation and we go to great pains to bring home to our staff that courtesy is absolutely essential at all times. One of our strong points as an institution is that many local people often feel more comfortable with us..."

The OCBC has, in fact, maintained its personal touch. By this means it has won the faith and confidence of its many customers throughout South-east Asia, both big and small. Its 40 years of experience will enable it to meet the challenges of the decades ahead.

Opposite page: An Artist's Impression of the 52-storey OCBC Centre—OCBC's new headquarters now under construction in the heart of Singapore's commercial centre. It will provide 500,000 sq feet of prime office space.

Left:
The OCBC Specialists' Centre as it is viewed from Somerset Road, Singapore.

ADVENTURE was the spirit that moved the early British trading companies to sail the oceans on voyages of discovery and search for rare silks, aromatic spices, sandalwood, copra, pearls and other treasures. Much of the lure was in the Far East and often the trade winds carried the ships to uncharted, sometimes hostile, islands and even to the little known primeval jungle-covered peninsula known as Malaya

Reports of vast timber forests and alluvial tin led to the landing of settlers at the southern extremity, at a place named Singapura centuries before by Sang Nila Utama a prince of the Sri Vijaya Empire in the neighbouring island, Sumatra. Whilst searching for a place to found a city of his own, he saw a strange and beautifully furred animal he was told was a lion. He called the spot Singapura—the lion city.

Later came Sir Stamford Raffles in 1819 and proclamation of Singapore as a new colony under Britain followed five years afterwards.

By 1880 Singapore was well established as a busy outpost at the gateway to South-east Asia and the Pacific and enterprising traders—Chinese, Malays, Indians and Europeans—had already laid the foundations of the thriving metropolis it is today.

As the population grew and the demand for the necessities of life increased enthusiastic citizens ventured into fields of manufacture.

John Fraser and David Neave were two Britons who had already established a local printing office. They were aware that large sums of money were going into the coffers of overseas manufacturers, a surprising proportion being for the export of aerated waters to Singapore. This signified a steady local demand and they decided to build a factory to supply the home market. So the Singapore & Straits Aerated Water Company was formed. By 1885, two years after commencement, the partners were employing a staff of 20, including office personnel and factory workers.

Two years later an expert, with wide experience in London and Edinburgh, was brought out to superintend the factory and by 1890 the production of BEVERAGES was big business. Soda water, seltzer water, potass water, lemonade, tonic water, ginger ale and ginger beer were produced until 1898 when the enterprise had overreached its capacity. The partners decided to expand and in so doing afford the people of Singapore the opportunity to participate in the expansion. Thus the Singapore & Straits Printing Office and the Singapore & Straits Aerated Water Company were combined in a public company titled Fraser & Neave, whose ramifications now extend beyond Singapore and throughout Malaysia; to Malacca, Kuala Lumpur, Seremban, Kota Bharu, Telok Anson, Taiping, Alor Star, Butterworth, Ipoh, Johore Bahru and Penang. Farther still to Djakarta and Surabaja in Indonesia. From these places F & N distribute their products which now include the international favourites Seven-up, Coca-Cola, Fanta and Sunkist and a health drink Seletaris bottled at a new plant set up at Sembawang in 1967.

In 1966 the company ventured for the first time into eastern Malaysia and built a factory at Kuching, Sarawak. In 1971 another was added to the long chain at Kota Kinabalu, Sabah.

Thinking beyond the scope of aerated waters F & N entered into an agreement with the famous Dutch brewers, Heineken of Holland. Together they formed Malayan Breweries Ltd. in 1931 and so "Tiger" was born, to become one of the best known beers throughout South-east Asia. Heineken provided the technical knowledge and the F & N Company became managing agents and distributors.

In 1938 Tiger beer won an international award in competition with beers from all parts of the Commonwealth. To this venture was added the acquired Archipelago Brewery Co. Ltd. of Singapore in 1941 with its no less popular Anchor Beer and in 1955 the South Pacific Brewery in New Guinea also came within the fold. A year later the Leopard Brewery at Hastings, New Zealand, was purchased.

The first brewery in Malaysia was built at Sungei Besi, Kuala Lumpur in 1961 and Fraser & Neave made a multi-million dollar investment of it.

New CONTAINERS have had to be developed to cope with the changing times and the bottling and canning plants at Singapore, Kuala Lumpur, Bangkok and West Malaysia are the most modern of their kind. A subsidiary making P.V.C. containers has operated in Singapore since 1967 and in West Malaysia since 1969.

SINGAPORE A.B.C.

The trend of many large organisations in the world today is to expand into different fields of production and marketing. This policy of **DIVERSIFICATION** was extended to the Fraser & Neave group in 1961 when they embarked upon a major joint-venture with one of the biggest food manufacturing companies of the U.S.A. in setting up a $9 million sweetened condensed milk plant in Petaling Jaya, Kuala Lumpur. Built on a 9-acre site, it was the first of its kind to be established in Southeast Asia. Another American milk company was brought in, in 1966 and the Petaling Jaya factory was extended to incorporate the manufacture of evaporated milk and the making of cans. At Jurong in Singapore a second milk plant was built in 1968 at a cost of $1.8 million. This centre produces sweetened condensed milk, instant milk powder and liquid milk aseptically packed.

Left: The headquarters and aerated water factory of Fraser and Neave Pte. Ltd., Singapore.

Below: Two familiar sights in Singapore; an F & N soft drinks transport vehicle, and Anderson Bridge over Singapore River. The Bridge was completed in 1910 and named after the Governor of the Colony.

Right: "Tiger" and "Anchor" beers and other popular F & N beverages are good ambassadors for Singapore.

The diversification programme was further expanded when a fifty per cent shareholding in the Singapore Plywood Company was acquired in 1969, F & N becoming the managers and sales agents.

With its continually increasing activities F & N have had to look for markets far afield and their brands and trade marks are now to be found throughout Asia, in the Middle East, Africa, Europe and across the Pacific to the west coast of America.

From its tiny twenty-staff factory of 1883 the organisation now employs more than 3,500 in its aerated water factories, its breweries and bottling plants and other subsidiaries in Singapore and Malaysia and through its many products the Republic of Singapore is becoming widely and favourably known.

TELLING THE WORLD OF ASIA

CUNEIFORM WRITING

ORIGINAL PICTOGRAPH	PICTOGRAPH IN POSITION OF LATER CUNEIFORM	EARLY BABYLONIAN	ASSYRIAN	ORIGINAL OR DERIVED MEANING
				OX
				SUN DAY
				GRAIN

Cunieform script was the first system of writing devised by the Sumerians 3000 years ago.

Below:
The front page of the "Singapore Chronicle" December 9, 1824.

The written word was probably invented of necessity. The need to keep records of goods travelling to and from inland villages and the larger towns prompted the Sumerians of southern Mesopotamia to devise a writing system more than 3,000 years B.C. It was called cuneiform script, a style adapted to the special limitations of the Sumerian wedge-shaped writing stick.

Before the Sumerian, there were probably various other methods of accounting—other peoples, like the North American Indians, had probably used strings of shells, or strings and knots in various colours, like the Peruvian Incas.

The dim mists of prehistory were not entirely impenetrable, for the walls of caves in France, for example, still glow with crude paintings and hand impressions left by Paleolithic man. Some of them perhaps vaguely express a story, an idea or a magic spell, a plan to hunt and kill bison for the tribal food.

The Sumerian system spread from Egypt and by 2,000 B.C. it reached Crete in the Aegean, the birthplace of the classical Greek and Roman civilisations. A few centuries later, it had influenced the Hittite script of Anatolia.

There are seven known systems of early writing—Proto-Elamite, Proto-Indic and Cretan, Sumerian, Egyptian, Hittite and Chinese. The first three have never been deciphered despite the efforts of palaeographers.

Most writing seems to have developed in three stages: first, drawings to represent

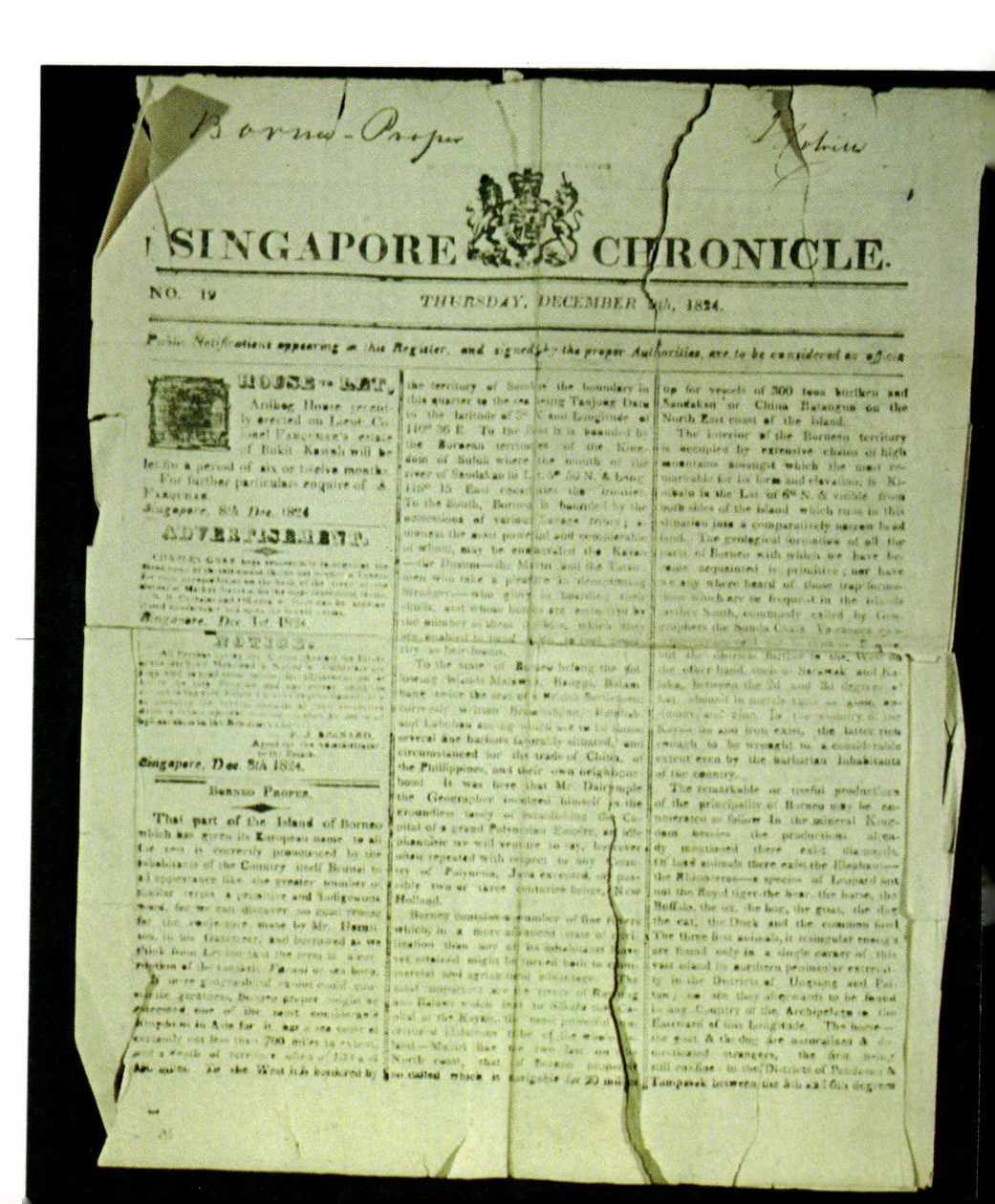

An impression of Singapore from the Esplanade, by Captain Bethune, at the time when Singapore's first newspaper, the "Chronicle" came into being.

specific objects, then pictures as memory aids—for example, a white hawk symbolising a man known as White Hawk—and finally signs representing the elements of language. Egyptian hieroglyphs, which first made an appearance somewhere about 3000 years B.C. were mainly in the form of animals, birds and inanimate objects. They were not intended to represent actual subjects depicted, but consonants in words.

Before 1800 A.D. nobody had been able to decipher hieroglyphs. But the discovery of the Rosetta stone, written in hieroglyphs, demotic—a later cursive sophistication of hieroglyphs of about 400-100 B.C.—and Greek, provided a key. It was largely due to the studies of this stone by Jean Francois Champollion, a French scholar, that hieroglyphs were finally unlocked.

The Chinese form of writing in characters is a particularly complex script. The first written Chinese was discovered on bones and tortoise shells of the Shang period, 1766-1123 B.C., the chosen mediums for recording divine oracles predicting the fate of the rice crop and so on. In the Chou period, 1122 to 256 B.C., the writing was transferred to bronze and stone. It was in the Chin period, when the first Emperor ruled from 221 to 207 B.C., that the "small seal" characters were standardised and since then Chinese script has undergone very little change.

Although it must have originated from Mesopotamia in some way, Chinese writing is markedly different. It is complex in that it is sometimes ideographic—depicting an idea: sometimes logographic—pictures standing in for words; and sometimes pictographic—pictures representing the objects they depict. It is also used independently from language as a visual art form, rather as "hip" poets have used "poesie concrete" in the twentieth century.

But records and methods of communication remained limited until about 1440, when Johann Gutenberg developed a process of printing. The earliest known printed piece was a Japanese Buddhist charm in an edition of one million copies, about 768-770 A.D. Early Japanese and Chinese printers, however, had shown little interest in exploring the technique for they found it difficult to adapt to their complex script. The first steam-powered flat-bed cylinder press was developed in 1814 by Frederick Konig, a German, for the Times newspaper of London. It made 1,100 impressions an hour. The first rotary press, built in 1866, increased the speed to 2,500 an hour. Today the written word is spread by the press to every corner of the world.

Singapore, a mere appendage to Malaya, a staging point for pirates, remained unremarked for centuries, its history obscure and scarcely worth recording in the annals of the times.

The seventh-century Buddhist Sri Vijaya Empire of Sumatra called it "Land below the wind".

In 1819 Sir Thomas Stamford Raffles, who had acquired the island for Britain, wrote to a friend: "You will probably have to consult the map in order to ascertain from what part of the world this letter is dated. Refer to the extremity of the Malay Peninsula.."

It was not until the advent of the Singapore Chronicle in 1824 that the real fabric of colonial life—the dressy parties, the snobbery, the escapades of an almost 90 percent male community, the insulting arrogance of "Mother India", ship arrivals and tiger attacks,—became known to the rest of the world.

Singapore had three newspapers even before its first bank was established—quite remarkable for an almost wholly commerce-orientated community.

The first issue of the Chronicle had to go to Bengal for approval before publication. Right up to 1835, the "Gagging Act" demanded that papers published in Singapore be submitted to the authorities for approval before being issued. The Act was repealed in 1835 and the Singapore Free Press was aptly christened on its founding in the same year; by 1837 the new paper had killed the Chronicle. Newspaper restrictions were reintroduced in 1857 when the Indian Mutiny broke out, but Singapore demonstrated its independence with a public protest against this move. Censorship was abrogated in the following year.

Then, with this cheery greeting, "Good morning to you, kind reader!," Editor Robert Carr Woods brought out the first issue of the Straits Times and Journal of Commerce in 1845, an eight-page weekly priced at "half a Spanish dollar".

The Bombay Times commented on the new paper: "Nothing perhaps could be better adapted for the country of Singapore where, as everybody knows, the people are only half civilised".

For the first 50 years the paper's daily circulation was less than 200 copies, produced on a hand press in a warehouse. Editors took on sundry extra jobs—Woods himself was Attorney General—and some were "characters" like Arnot Reid who, in 1889, after an editorial argument with local brokers, faced them out with a revolver and a large Sikh policeman.

Many papers came and went, including those in other language streams like the Tamil Singai Nesan, the Chinese Lat Pau and Seng Poh and the Malay Jawi Peranakan. The longest surviving of these is the Utusan Melayu, founded in 1911, and still being published.

After a disastrous fire in 1869, the Straits Times was reduced to assets worth only $40—scarcely worth auctioning. Typical of its spirit, however, the very next day the paper printed an attack on the fire brigade! In the 1930's the existence of the Straits Times was threatened by the Malayan Tribune which had been founded in 1915—notwithstanding the fact that the Times had acquired South-east Asia's only rotary press and had taken over other papers such as the Free Press and the Pinang Gazette. The new 27 years old General Manager, Alfred Charles Simmons—now Chairman of the Company—an ex-Pinang Gazette

Right:
Printing a top quality publication in the offset section of Times Printers.

Below:
A display of books printed by Times Printers at their printing works in Thomson Road, Singapore.

man, shrewdly persuaded the Straits Times directors to drop the paper's price from 10 to 5 cents, on a par with the Tribune. Within a year the circulation jumped from 6,000 to 15,000 and for the first time Asian readers were in the majority.

The Japanese-run Syonan Shimbun replaced the Straits Times during the Occupation of 1942-45. But when Malaya was liberated newspapermen rushed from the privations of internment to print the paper only two days after Mountbatten's landing, bearing the headline "Singapore is British again!"

Today, Straits Times Sdn. Bhd. dominates English Language communications in Singapore. It owns ten subsidiaries, among which is Times Printers, a major printing works with modern Web-offset printing facilities.

From an initial newspaper with a purely local readership of some 200 copies, the Straits Times has a daily circulation in Singapore of over 115,000 and is supplemented by 13 periodicals, all with wide distributions throughout South-east Asia.

Its printing plant is one of the most up-to-date in this part of the world, and its high standard of workmanship brings orders for the printing of top quality books from most Asian countries and even as far off as Australia.

Singapore itself has become a major communications centre for news and cable agencies and for international shipping and air lines. Its $14 million earth satellite station keeps it in intimate touch with every corner of the globe. The now flourishing Republic is a very far cry from that "ulu" backwoods once sneered at by the Bombay Times.

SINGAPORE—CONTAINER PORT

THE PORT OF SINGAPORE has now joined the ranks of the world's major shipping ports. With the official opening of its Container Port at East Lagoon on 23rd June 1972, Singapore established herself as a vital link in the chain of container ports throughout the world.

The Port of Singapore Authority (PSA) first conceived the idea of developing a Container Port in 1966. Subsequently, when a loan was granted by the World Bank for Development and Re-construction, work on the Container Port was commenced in February 1969.

The PSA Container Complex in its entirety consists of two main berths and one feeder berth on 60 acres (25 hectares) of land. The feeder berth, 700 feet long (213 metres) with 34 feet low water ordinary spring tide (10.34 metres) has been operational since October 1970. The two main berths of 2,250 ft. (685.80 metres) with 44 ft. (13.41 metres) LWOST will be extended by 750 ft. (228.60 metres) so as to allow three large container vessels to berth at the wharves at the same time. The first main container berth was completed at the end of 1971; the second will be operational by the end of 1972.

The entrance to the container berths is open harbour and container ships measuring 1,000 ft. (304.80 metres) or more can berth at the wharves. The turning basin is located south of the container berths.

A sheet-piled diaphragm breakwater shelters the lagoon from the north-east monsoon.

Bunkering facilities are available at the wharves. Marine diesel oil and fresh water are also available.

The yard covers an area of 25.36 acres (10.26 hectares) and in it more than 6,000 containers can be stacked two high. About 40 acres are available for immediate expansion and more land will be made available should the need arise for a more extensive area.

Three large freight stations covering 225,000 sq. ft. (20,902.50 sq. m.) are available at the Container Port.

The equipment available for handling containers includes three 35 ton (35.56 tonnes) container quay cranes, eight van carriers (30.488 tonnes), four semi-trailers, four prime movers, eight industrial tractors, 28 industrial trailers and 60 forklifts.

The Container Port will be operated on a three shift system on a common user basis.

This is an aerial view of the PSA Container Port. In the foreground, construction work on the extension to the Container Berths is in progress. When completed, 3,000 feet (914 metres) of wharves will be able to accommodate 3 large container ships at any time.

The *Nihon*, the first purpose-built container ship to call at the Container Port, is alongside the container berth.

In the background is a view of the 3 mile (4.8 Km) stretch of conventional wharves for ocean-going vessels. Extensive deep-water anchorages are also available to ships.

There is a daily average of 180 ships in Port waters. In 1971, 155.9 million net registered tonnage of shipping was recorded. Singapore has grown into a major petroleum port. Four of the world's large oil companies operate refineries in Singapore. During 1971, 48.1 million freight tons of cargo passed through the Port and of this total, 37.5 million tons was mineral-oil-in-bulk.

IN ITS EARLIER DAYS the town of Singapore was an obscure trading port and rated little in importance until the Portuguese began to settle along the coast of Malaya during the 14th Century. It became a minor principality about 1600 A.D. but gradually faded through lack of interest and for the next two centuries it made no impact on trading, even with neighbouring lands. It was only after the South China Sea was cleared of pirates and their predatory junks that peace was established in the coastal towns of the region; and peace brought trade and commerce.

From the time when Sir Stamford Raffles arrived in January 1819 and established a British trading post on the island near the mouth of the Kallang River, Singapore began to assume a new significance in the world of commerce. Large ships anchored in the harbour and discharged their cargoes onto sampans and lighters, to be carried to godowns on the wharves of Singapore River. There the goods were stored and new merchandise was loaded and transferred to the waiting vessels for transport to the markets of the seven seas.

Today the Port of Singapore is the fourth busiest in the world. There are more than 38,000 ship-calls annually and port facilities handle more than 45 million tons of cargoes.

Modern refineries and fast growing industrial complexes continue to increase port and ancillary activities.

In December 1968 the national shipping line of Singapore was incorporated under the title Neptune Orient Lines Limited. It began activities in May 1969 with an authorised capital of S$100 million to operate modern cargo liners between Singapore, Malaysia, Hong Kong, London and northern European ports. Cargoes of rubber, tin, timber, spices, produce and other commodities were shipped from Singapore and Malaysia and textiles, machinery, electrical and electronic goods, canned foods and toys from Japan and Hong Kong. On the return voyage the ships carried machinery, general consumer and luxury goods for the local and entrepôt markets, and special heavy cargoes for Singapore's industrial projects. The ships also carried up to twelve passengers when the occasion arose.

In the first year the fleet consisted of four modern motorships performing twelve round voyages between the Far East and U.K.-North Continent; and one tanker and one dry cargo ship for world-wide chartering. In 1970 five more modern

OVER THE SEAS IN SHIPS

motor vessels were acquired, four for Australia trade and the fifth to help improve the Far East-Europe trade. During 1970 two specialised combination carriers of 14,000 tons and 23-knots speed were ordered in Finland and two Freedom-type ships in Singapore's own Jurong Shipyard. One supertanker was ordered to be built in partnership with a Hong Kong company.

In 1971 contracts were given for two specialised product tankers. Also ordered were two car/bulk carriers and two more Freedom ships at Jurong as partnership ventures.

NOL ships are largely manned by Singapore officers and entirely by Singapore crews.

The Company trains its own deck and engineer cadets (Neptune Beryl is a cadet ship) and general purpose crews with a view to efficient manning of automated ships having sophisticated navigation, machinery and electrical equipment.

Neptune Orient have adopted a unique nomenclature for the ships of their fleet—the names of precious stones for dry cargo ships and constellations for tankers.

The interests of Neptune Orient have extended to all the oceans and the Company's burgee with its seven blue waves and a red trident can be seen in many parts of the world. Experienced port agents represent Neptune in the United Kingdom, North Continental countries, Poland, Scandinavia, Mediterranean ports, European hinterland, Switzerland, Panama, Hawaii, Hong Kong, Japan, People's Republic of China, Australia, New Zealand, the U.S.A., Canada, India, Pakistan, the Persian Gulf, the Red Sea, Sri Lanka East, West and North Africa, Indonesia and Malaysia.

NEPTUNE ORIENT LINES FLEET

Vessel	Type	Joins Fleet	Engagement
* 1. Neptune-World	233,200 Supertanker	April 73	Charter for world-wide trading.
* 2. Newbuilding I	33,200 Car/bulk carrier	1Q/74	—do—
* 3. Newbuilding II	33,200 Car/bulk carrier	2Q/74	—do—
† 4. Newbuilding III	14,800 Freedom type	1Q/73	—do—
† 5. Newbuilding IV	14,800 Freedom type	2Q/73	—do—
6. Neptune Ruby	14,800 Freedom type	3Q/72	—do—
7. Neptune Cyprine	14,800 Freedom type	4Q/72	—do—
8. Neptune Aries	25,700 Specialised product tanker	1Q/74	—do—
9. Neptune Orion	25,700 Specialised product tanker	2Q/74	—do—
10. Neptune Taurus	20,580 Crude tanker	In service	—do—
11. Neptune Garnet	9,280	In service	—do—
12. Neptune Emerald	23 knots Combination carriers, 200 containers, side-ports, latex tanks.	4Q/72	Nos. 12—18 inclusive operating on liner trade between Yokohama, Kobe, Otaru, Hong Kong Singapore, Malaysia, Mediterranean, Las Palmas, UK, Europe, and Scandinavian ports. Modern motorships with large refrigerated spaces, cranes to handle cargo, trading between S'pore, Malaysia, Thailand, & Australian ports, Tasmania & N. Zealand.
13. Neptune Sapphire		1Q/73	
14. Neptune Amethyst	19 knots	In service	
15. Neptune Aquamarine	19 knots	In service	
16. Neptune Zircon	19 knots	In service	
17. Neptune Topaz	19 knots	In service	
18. Neptune Amber	19 knots	In service	
19. Neptune Beryl	15 knots	In service	
20. Neptune Jasper	15 knots	In service	
21. Neptune Agate	15 knots	In service	
22. Neptune Jade	14 knots	In service	

* First three ships under joint ownership with World-wide (Shipping) Ltd. of Hong Kong.
† Fourth and fifth ships under joint ownership with Jurong Shipyard Ltd. of Singapore, "K" Line of Japan, and Bank of Tokyo.

Above left:
"Neptune Sapphire"
and sistership "Neptune Emerald"
will maintain a fast liner service
between Far East,
Mediterranean, United Kingdom,
European and Scandinavian ports.

Left:
"Neptune Zircon"
using her own Stulcken derrick
to raise a 150-ton lift—
"stand from under!"

Right:
The 233,200-ton supertanker,
"Neptune-World".

Below:
SIA hostesses not only uphold the Airlines reputation for happy, efficient service; they are able ambassadresses for Singapore.

Right:
Among the many centres of interest in Singapore are the beautifully designed Botanic Gardens.

THE NEW FLAG CARRIER of the Republic of Singapore is Singapore Airlines, successor to the former dual national service, MSA. For 25 years MSA had built up a reputation second to none in the world of commercial aviation, representing both the Governments of Singapore and Malaysia. In its last year of operation it earned a pre-tax profit of S$55 million—a tribute to the efficiency of those at the helm and tangible proof of the confidence placed in it by the flying public.

With the rapid development of its neighbouring countries the impracticability of a joint national airline became obvious and by mutual agreement MSA ceased to be and SIA and MAS were born. On 30th September 1972, the new-look jets of Singapore Airlines took to the skies. Most of the international routes operated by Malaysia-Singapore Airlines, its all Boeing fleet, management expertise and the majority of its 6,300 staff, have been inherited by Singapore Airlines. The Head Office Building and the highly sophisticated push-button airline computer system (KRISCOM), which began operations in June 1972 have also been inherited by SIA.

The history of Singapore Airline's predecessors is an intriguing exercise in name-changes. Commencing operations in 1947 as a domestic carrier known as Malayan Airways, it was renamed Malaysian Airways in 1963 to reflect the political changes

Right:
The international air routes of Singapore Airlines.

Opposite page:
A new SIA jet airliner in its smart new colour scheme and logo.

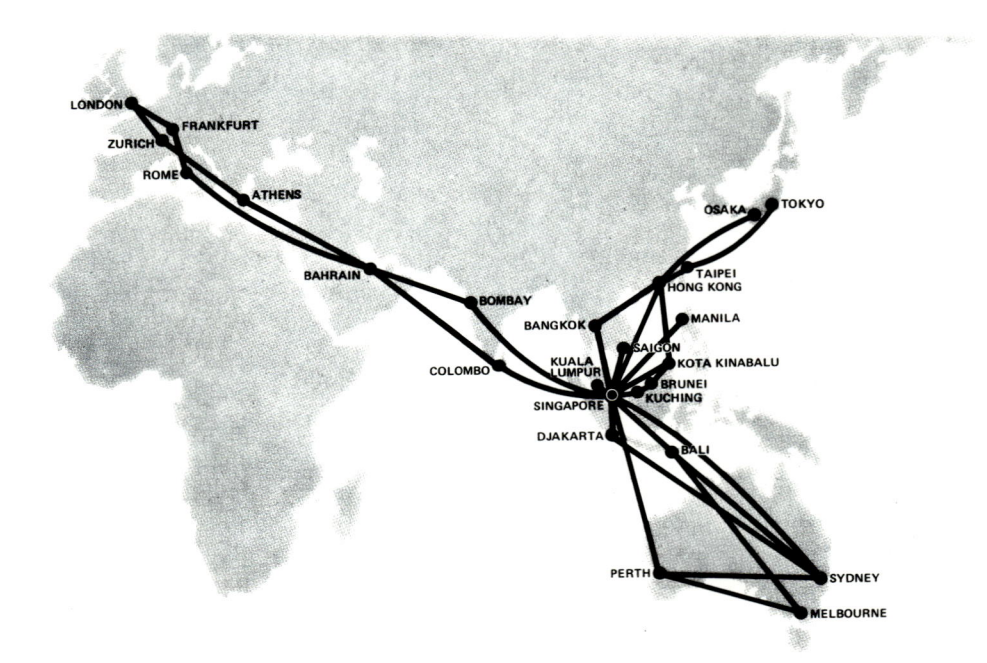

542

SINGAPORE AIRLINES—A NEW BIRD ON THE WING

of the time. In 1967, the airline again underwent a change in name to Malaysia-Singapore Airlines and in the ensuing period of five years it set the fastest pace of development in its history. As MSA it extended its international network, carried more passengers and established one of the most outstanding on-time records in the aviation industry.

Singapore Airlines serves London, Rome, Bahrain, Bombay, Colombo, Athens, Zurich, Frankfurt, Osaka, Tokyo, Hong Kong, Bangkok, Singapore, Djakarta, Perth, Melbourne, Sydney, Saigon, Manila and Brunei. With the exception of the Hong Kong and Kowloon offices, which will be shared with Malaysian Airline System, all other overseas offices have been taken over by the Singapore flag carrier. In Asia its offices are located in Malaysia, Thailand, Hong Kong, Japan, Indonesia, Brunei, India, Sri Lanka, South Vietnam, Khmer Republic, the Philippines and Taiwan.

In the Middle East there is an office in Bahrain, and in Europe offices are in the United Kingdom, Italy, Germany and Switzerland. In the America's, Singapore Airlines has taken over the former MSA offices in Canada, Mexico and the United States. All existing offices in Australia are now occupied by the newly-registered Airline.

The Singapore Airlines fleet, comprising at present five Boeing 707's and five Boeing 737's will be supplemented by three more Boeing 707's before the end of the current year.

Following the conversion of Singapore Airport to take 'Jumbo Jets', SIA has also placed an order for the purchase of two Boeing 747-200 aircraft at a cost of S$185.25 million (U.S.$65 million), including spares and ground equipment. These two aircraft will be placed in service in October 1973, initially for use on the Australia, and Tokyo route and possibly used on the London route.

The Airlines has further taken an option on two more Boeing 747 aircraft for delivery during or before 1974. It is forecast that a total of twelve Boeing Jumbo Jets will be needed by Singapore Airlines during the ensuing ten years.

Each Singapore Airlines' Jumbo will have a seating capacity of 349 with 24 in first-class and 325 in economy. There will be an upper-deck lounge seating 16 passengers and a main deck lounge to accommodate another 6. The aircraft may be converted to an all-economy class configuration of 500 seats. It will carry a maximum load of 60 tons and have a cargo capacity of 6,190 cubic feet. The range of the new aircraft will be 6,100 miles and its cruising speed, 600 m.p.h.

SIA will be the third Asian airline, after Japan Airlines and Air India, to introduce the Boeing 747 into service. In the next eighteen months its fleet will have doubled its present seating capacity.

A massive programme is being drawn up for the training of flight crews, engineers and other personnel in Singapore and the U.S.A. in anticipation of the delivery of the Company's new aircraft.

SERVICE IS THE KEY: The modern sophistication of Singapore Airlines is reflected in the smart livery worn by its flight crews and ground personnel. Its official colours are rich yellow and midnight blue and its logo—a stylised version of a bird— symbolises flight. Both the colours and the logo were adopted on the recommendation of Walter Landor Associates of San Francisco, the well-known creators of Airline images.

But an airline needs more substance than just a 'good image'. Mr. Lee Kuan Yew, Prime Minister of Singapore, has said: "I believe no magic set of initials, no logo, can sell to more than the first few, something which is not good...To improve efficiency of organisation, promptness of service, these must be our constant aims". This statement of plain facts will be the future policy of the Republic of Singapore's new Airline.

543

SOJOURN IN SINGAPORE

THE FUTURE of Singapore is viewed with a confidence that even a decade ago would have seemed wildly optimistic.

From an ancient entrepôt of intrigues and mysteries and more recently a dependent State of relatively minor industrial importance, it has emerged as an independent Republic already exercising an influence among the greater trading nations of the world.

Singapore still retains its aura of mystery and exotic living; the River is still crowded with tongkangs and other small water craft; from the tiny stalls in Koek Road are still wafted the aroma of every Chinese dish imaginable and in Change Alley, the keenest bargains in the East are to be found—for those who are good at bargaining — watches, jewellery, transistors, cameras; the list is endless.

The travelling markets still line the busy down-town sidewalks of Orchard Road every Wednesday, appearing out of nowhere at sunset and vanishing at midnight to reappear at some new sites every evening, until the following week. Their brightly lit stalls offer—sometimes at ridiculously low prices—everything from batiks to jade bracelets, from bananas and mangoes to silks and bamboo table settings.

What is new in this Eastern paradise is the number of modern hotels, bringing gracious living to the hundreds of thousands of visitors—tourists, businessmen and their wives and families pouring in from jets and ocean liners from every part of the world.

Only a few years ago Orchard Road, one of the principal arterial highways from the Harbour and the centre of the city, was a long stretch of small buildings and open spaces. Today it is one of the busiest roads in Asia, a continuous stream of traffic to the shops and to the big modern hotels centred there; and of the hotels the best known are the Goodwood Group.

HOTEL MALAYSIA SINGAPORE. Lying back in a setting of stately homes and gardens and fronted by a huge multi-streamed fountain is the Malaysia, a typical high ranking executive hotel. It has been the temporary home of many international celebrities, presidents, heads of state and prime ministers.

Highlighting its vast lobby is a giant batik mural designed for the hotel by one of Singapore's most noted batik painters.

The Hotel Malaysia Singapore is built in a spectacular architectural style and all its principal features conform—its Golden Lotus traditional Chinese restaurant; its continental Rajah Room gourmet restaurant of brilliant orange batik decor; its subdued, atmospherically-lit Orchard Bar where gaily saronged girls serve the evening cocktails; the top floor Supper Club where sophisticated cabaret acts entertain from 10 p.m. till dawn; The Pub discotheque where five bands interchange their rhythmic beats; and the great Convention Hall where 1,000 delegates may sit in comfort.

The Malaysia, designed for high standard accommodation, has 350 rooms, suites, cabanas and sumptuously furnished V.I.P. apartments. Like the three other hotels that make up the Goodwood Group, the Malaysia has an imposing arcade where almost everything can be purchased in endless variety from rows of intriguing little shops. There is a large first floor swimming pool for guests.

THE GOODWOOD PARK. A contrast to the sophisticated living of the Malaysia is the Goodwood Park Hotel, the parent of the Group. Like the rest of its family it is located in the fashionable suburb of Tanglin, a few minutes' ride by taxi to the main shopping centres and sightseeing places of interest.

In colonial days it was an exclusive German club, a majestic mansion standing in an almost isolated part of the island. One of its features was a noble Teutonic tower that became a landmark in Singapore Town from the time it was built soon after the turn of the century. At the close of World War II the club was converted into a luxury hotel and named Goodwood Park. The tower has been retained as a distinctive feature but the main building has been reconstructed, enlarged and extended to embrace several modern wings over an area of almost fifteen acres of landscaped lawns and gardens. There is the "Park Lane" and a two-storeyed octagonal shaped "Annexe" to house the Petroleum Club and basement carpark. The Club has a bar room exclusively for men but the ladies may join them in the richly furnished dining room.

The Hotel has many interesting features and one is unique—the Gordon Grill and Highland Bar, decorated and furnished in an authentic atmosphere of the Scottish Highlands. Most of the foods are imported from Scotland: Black Angus beef, river trout, salmon and haggis piped in by the traditional piper. The house-made Athol Brose brings visions of sparkling dew on purple heather. The waiters and waitresses are uniformed in Gordon Tartan. Continental cuisine and local specialities are served table d'hôte and à la carte at "Le Cafe" dining room; "L'Espresso" terrace cafe, nearby one of the three pools, provides refreshments for the swimmers. On Sunday evenings there is a poolside barbecue.

The "Mayfair" is a private wing and, separated from the rest of the Hotel, it encloses its own swimming pool and gardens interspersed with lounging chairs and shady umbrellas. There are three sumptuous new suites, each differently designed, differently furnished in bright colour harmonies and each on a different floor.

Left page: A typical street scene in Singapore: North Bridge Road in an off-peak period.

Above: The Goodwood Group of Hotels created the Ming Court in the elegance of the Ming Dynasty. It is an imposing landmark at the top of Orchard Road where it sweeps into Tanglin Road, the new fast developing commercial centre.

Left: Hotel Malaysia Singapore assumes a festive air after dusk when the fountain's multicoloured streams jet into the midnight blue sky.

MING COURT. A distinct contrast in living atmosphere is the most recent acquisition of the Goodwood Group, Ming Court Hotel, redolent of the oriental splendour of the Ming Dynasty. The architectural design of unusual elegance has been sustained throughout the building, the many restaurants and lounges, the shopping arcades and even the 350 bedrooms, air-conditioned to the prevalent tropical climate of Singapore, suggesting the luxurious living of the 14th Century Chinese War Lords.

There is the Genghis Grill for the finest European foods and specialising in its own charcoal broiled dishes; the Jade Lounge with its bar and private booths for intimate tête à tête; the Peacock Room Chinese restaurant where Chinese foods may be ordered in intriguing variety; the "swimming pool in the sky" on the fifth-storey forefront of the eighteen-storey building, the focal point of a lush and verdant garden; and the Barbarella, a space-age discotheque designed for the 21st Century teen- and young-ager with world famous dance bands.

Every Wednesday evening the Pagoda Poolside by the "swimming pool in the sky" turns Polynesian in gay abandon. The waiters and waitresses don bright Hawaiian shirts and sarongs, complete with leis; multi-coloured lights cast a happy radiance on outdoor grills where whole lambs, chickens, steaks and chops are barbecued to a golden turn.

For private parties, conventions and seminars the mezzanine floor houses the Fuji Room, the Polynesian Room and the Peacock Room. They have seating capacities of 50 to 450 and for cocktails can accommodate 100 to 800 guests.

LADYHILL. Many V.I.P. family groups visiting Singapore prefer a restful atmosphere for their holiday and this is found in the Ladyhill Hotel. Of contemporary Swiss architecture this interesting auberge stands in a quiet country-estate woodland setting, just off Orchard Road, about three minutes from Ming Court. Many of its elegantly designed suites have individual balconies overlooking the garden swimming pool. Ladyhill is known for the excellent Swiss cuisine of its restaurant "Le Chalet" where food and imported wines are served in Swiss cottage style. This is the main dining room with broad beams crisscrossing the rafters and ledges gleaming with antique beaten copper ware. Swiss insignia decorate the panelled walls and fondues are a favoured speciality. Quaint street signs on the private lanes that wind around the buildings and gardens point the way to the beauty salon, coffee shop, sauna bath and news stand.

The coffee shop juts out over the swimming pool and a covered terrace allows dripping wet swimmers to mingle with dry customers who prefer their snacks al fresco. Over the coffee shop is the Mauve Room, an ideal setting for private cocktails or small conferences.

MING CENTRE. Quite apart from the Hotels is "Ming Centre" on Clemenceau Avenue which houses a bevy of exclusive boutiques, tiny coffee shops and music stores grouped around a fountain in a covered patio; a cool and restful haven for the tired shopper. It also holds one of Singapore's most exotic theatre-nightclub restaurants, the "Marco Polo". Here the excellent Chinese and European foods are served with accompanying beverages by hostesses gowned in the long flowing robes of old Cathay's imperial courts. There are two nightly performances of international reviews and acts from Paris, London, Sydney, New York and San Francisco.

Down on the first floor is a long hall resplendent in Ming Dynasty red and gold decor. This is the Ming Palace Chinese restaurant which opens daily for "tim sum", when pert Chinese girls push trolleys filled with small dishes of Chinese delicacies. It can seat 100 easily but artistic screens roll up to provide privacy for small parties of 10 or more.

With the advent of the Jumbo jets and more frequent air services Singapore is becoming a popular venue for conventions and seminars and most of the top standard hotels are able to accommodate and cater for attendances numbering from a few hundred up to well over 1,000. The Goodwood Group falls into this category.

Left: Comfort and elegance by the pool of Ladyhill.

Right: This aerial shows Goodwood Park; Mayfair wing and hexagonal Petroleum Club on the left; the three swimming pools, and another new wing in the right mid-distance.

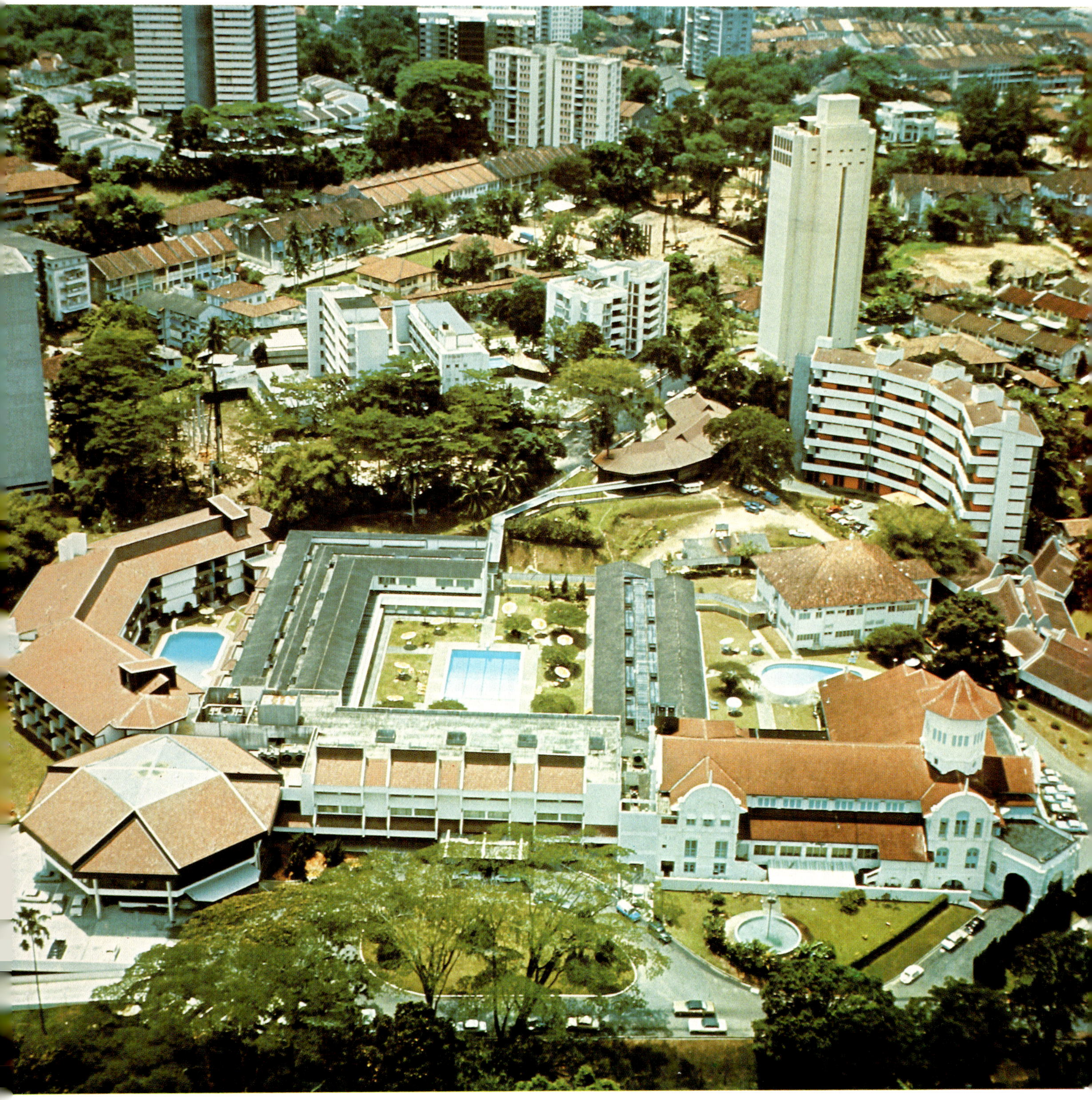

Shangri-La is one of the most sumptuous hotels in Asia. The picture on the right shows its front elevation in Orange Grove Road. Above is the comfortable lobby which features a sunken cocktail lounge.
Below: The Shangri-La's 34-metre free-form swimming pool and kiddies' paddling pool are set midst a palm tree oasis.

SHANGRI-LA

Those who are familiar with the story of "Lost Horizon" will remember the mythical city called Shangri-La where perfect peace and harmony ruled for ever and age stood still. This is the theme of Singapore's Shangri-La, one of the most fascinating of the many ultra-modern hotels to be built in South-east Asia in recent years.

Shangri-La is a 25-storeyed luxury hotel managed by the Western International Hotels of Seattle, U.S.A. It is located in Orange Grove Road in the midst of $12\frac{1}{2}$ acres of lush landscaped tropical vegetation within a few minutes' walking distance of the fashionable business and shopping centre of Orchard Road. Ten thousand trees and ornamental shrubs housed in nurseries and greeneries for special care have been planted like a miniature forest over the area. The grounds encompass a three-hole golf course, two swimming pools, sun decks, tennis courts, croquet lawns, and tropical fruit tree-lined walks leading to an interesting waterfall.

This is a fit setting for the palatial building of unusual design which holds so much that appeals to the sophisticated traveller of the 'seventies. Shangri-la possesses 520 richly appointed guest rooms and spacious suites with private lanais, oversized beds, radios, television, refrigerators, electric clocks, direct-dial telephones and modern airconditioning; its unique dining salons, restaurants and cocktail lounges; and for the businessman, there are twelve convention rooms providing translation facilities enabling those attending to listen to discussions interpreted in a variety of languages. There is one major convention room capable of seating up to 1,400 people with a mezzanine containing cubicles for the Press and translators. A unique system of under floor wiring enables any delegate to move about the room and remain tuned to the interpreter translating into his own tongue.

The ground level hotel lobby exudes an air of elegant sophistication, towering marble columns, sparkling chandeliers and panoramic garden views creating an atmosphere of quiet welcome.

There are five restaurants, each specialising in its own Continental or Asiatic cuisine and furnished in national decors correct in minute detail.

The Shang Palace was modelled from a Chinese courtyard to please the Oriental gourmet. In it are served all manner of Cantonese dishes and there are cosy pavilions with softly tuned music for special parties. There is a coffee lounge serving the croquet lawns and Lobby Court.

Another coffee shop, located on the ground floor of the hotel, has an unusual feature—large aviaries of varieties of exotic birds. It is open 24 hours a day. For the younger at heart the Four Seas Discotheque in nautical decor of Viking Ships, Spanish Galleons, gondolas and Chinese junks has everything in music to suit the prevailing mood.

High above from the Tiara Lounge on the 25th floor is a sweeping panoramic view of the island city, the Malaysian mainland and nearby Indonesian islands. This is a favoured meeting place where friends may gather in the cool of the evening for a quiet drink, to watch the myriad lights of Singapore blink and beckon and begin another night of eager expectation in the enchanting mystic East.

SINGAPURA INTER-CONTINENTAL

One of the longest established and more popular of Singapore's modern hotels is the Singapura, a member of the internationally known Inter-Continental family. Only a few years ago it stood in solitary majesty at the north end of Orchard Road but today it is surrounded by gardens and other buildings—the commercial hub of the busiest thoroughfare in Singapore. The Singapura has 193 comfortable airconditioned guest rooms and suites and, being somewhat smaller than many of the huge hotel complexes in vogue today, its staff give more personalised attention to their guests. Among the top-standard facilities available are the large open-air swimming pool with its snack bar and eventide mini-barbecue, from which sizzling satay is served by exotic, sarong-clad Malay girls. Local residents will agree that the Sentosa is one of the most frequented restaurants, where excellent Continental, Mexican and Chinese foods are always to be enjoyed. The Pebble Bar and 24-hours-service Coffee Shop are popular features. All other facilities considered essential at the present day are to be found in the shopping arcade, drug store, hairdressing salons and F.N.C.B. bank branch.

The Singapura Inter-Continental Hotel faces Orchard Road,
one of Singapore's busiest highways.
The swimming pool
is a cool oasis at which visitors
congregate for sunbaking
and in the evening for
a satay party.

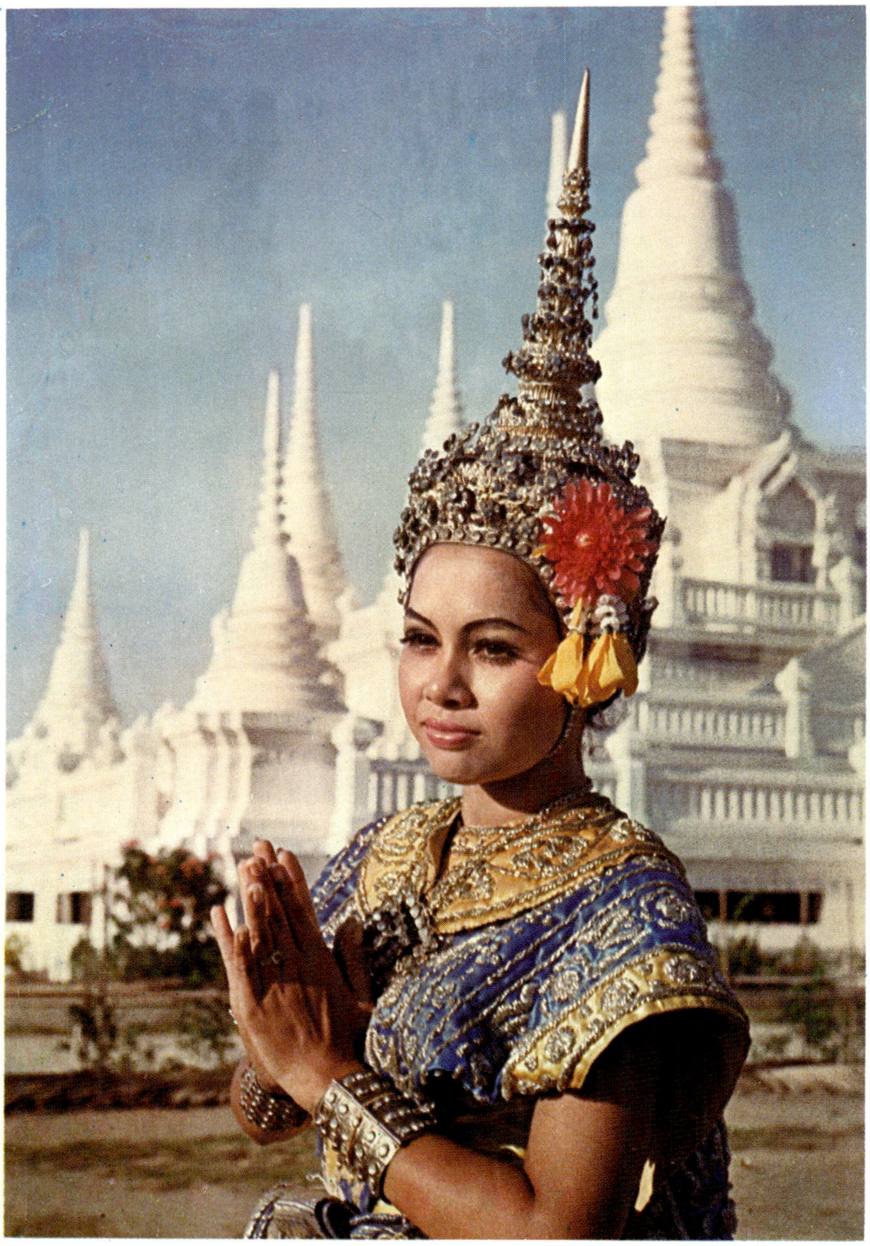

Kingdom of
THAILAND

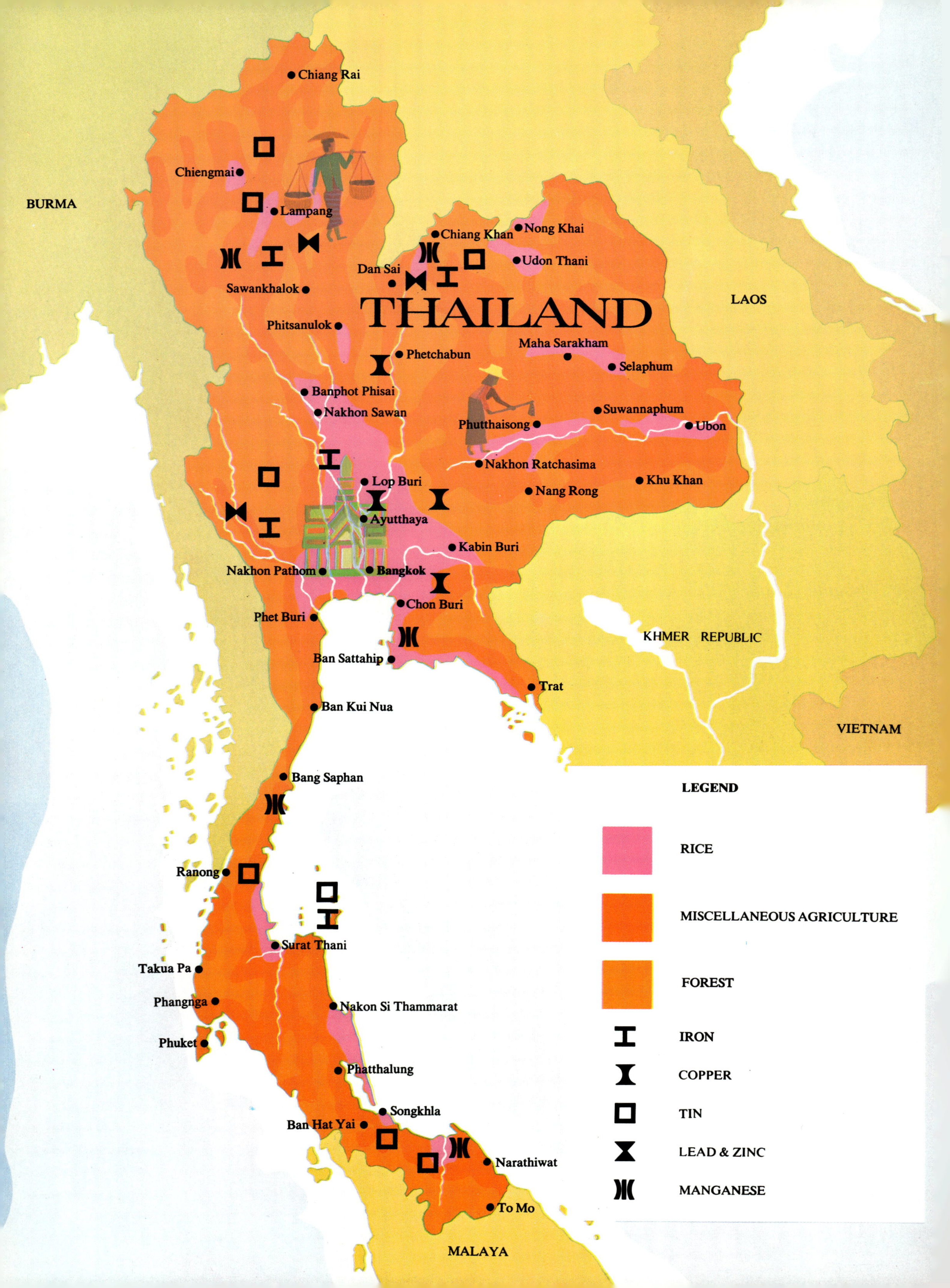
THAILAND
BURMA
LAOS
KHMER REPUBLIC
VIETNAM
MALAYA
Chiang Rai
Chiengmai
Lampang
Sawankhalok
Phitsanulok
Chiang Khan
Nong Khai
Udon Thani
Dan Sai
Phetchabun
Maha Sarakham
Selaphum
Banphot Phisai
Nakhon Sawan
Suwannaphum
Phutthaisong
Ubon
Nakhon Ratchasima
Lop Buri
Khu Khan
Nang Rong
Ayutthaya
Kabin Buri
Nakhon Pathom
Bangkok
Chon Buri
Phet Buri
Ban Sattahip
Trat
Ban Kui Nua
Bang Saphan
Ranong
Surat Thani
Takua Pa
Phangnga
Nakon Si Thammarat
Phuket
Phatthalung
Songkhla
Ban Hat Yai
Narathiwat
To Mo
LEGEND
RICE
MISCELLANEOUS AGRICULTURE
FOREST
IRON
COPPER
TIN
LEAD & ZINC
MANGANESE

The Royal Barge is a magnificent sight, propelled by oarsmen, gliding down the river past the Royal Palace.

Thailand

LOCATION:
On the Gulf of Thailand, bordered by Malaysia, Burma, Laos and the Khmer Republic (Cambodia).

AREA:
200,000 square miles (approximately).

LENGTH:
Slightly exceeding 1,000 miles.

WIDTH:
The greatest width is in the region of 480 miles.

POPULATION:
In 1972 the population was approximately 35 million.

ANNUAL RATE OF INCREASE:
Approximately 3 per cent per annum.

CAPITAL CITY:
Bangkok has a current population of about 3 million.

CLIMATE:
Monsoonal. Conditions from May to September, — south-west monsoon, — are rainy throughout. During October to February the north-east monsoon persists and milder tropical temperatures prevail. From March to April high temperatures are typical of the pre-monsoon. The average year-round temperature is 80°F and the average annual rainfall 73 inches.

RELIGION:
Ninety-three per cent of the people are Buddhist, the official State religion. Four per cent are Muslim living mainly in the deep South. The remaining three per cent comprise people of other faiths.

Land of Smiles

THE FIRST INHABITANTS to establish a kingdom in Thailand were not the Thai, but the Mon and Khmer. The Khmer were particularly powerful, and from the 9th Century A.D. they had established an empire, including the Chao Phya Valley, which later became the central structure of the Thai nation.

In the course of time the power of the Khmer was successfully challenged by the Thai, who established their capital at Sukotai, in the north of the country, about 1280 A.D. Although small bands of Thai had been trickling south from their homeland in southern China for some centuries prior to the establishment of Sukotai, their numbers were insignificant. The migration of much larger groups began when the all-conquering Kublai Khan imposed his rule over the Thai of southern China and ended their previously autonomous regime.

Sukotai has been called "the cradle of Thai civilisation". The achievements of the first king of the dynasty, Ramkhamhaeng, are recounted to this day in verse and song.

Ramkhamhaeng, who ruled from 1283 to 1317, was a very powerful monarch, heading a large army and exercising considerable diplomatic talent. But he was also a patron of the arts and was responsible for the formulation of the Thai alphabet, which remains largely unchanged to the present time. While he and his successors reigned, close links were forged with Sinhalese, variously called Hinayana or Theravada, Buddhism, which has been the main influence on religious thought in Thailand.

At the height of their power, the Sukotai Kings ruled over an area of country which included most of present-day Thailand and parts of Burma, the Khmer Republic (Cambodia) and Malaysia. In time, however, they crumbled before more powerful rival Thai Kingdoms and resurgent Burmese and Khmer forces. By 1500 A.D. a new dynasty founded by King Ramatibodi at Ayutthaya, just north of the present capital Bangkok, was the power in the land. The Kings of Ayutthaya reigned until 1767 when the city was sacked by the Burmese. Despite this severe setback, the Thai mustered sufficient forces to rout a Burmese army attempting in the following year to reoccupy Ayutthaya. The general responsible for the defeat of the Burmese, Phya Tak Sin, was crowned king. He abandoned the ruined capital, Ayutthaya, and established himself and his court at Thon Buri, at the mouth of the Chao Phya river, just across the stream from modern Bangkok. The capital was moved to Bangkok in 1782 on the accession of Chao Phya Chakri, who ruled as Rama I and founded the present Chakri dynasty.

The Kings of the Chakri dynasty paved the way for the emergence of Thailand as a modern state. The achievements of two kings, Rama IV (Mongkut) who ruled from 1851, and Rama V (Chulalongkorn) who succeeded him in 1868, were most outstanding. Unlike previous Thai monarchs, who were insulated from their subjects, surrounded by jealous officials and hemmed in by elaborate protocol, Mongkut and Chulalongkorn studied and travelled widely before acceding to the throne. They thus acquired a breadth of vision and range of contacts which had been denied to their predecessors. Pilgrimages during years as novice monks gave them unprecedented insight into the lives of their subjects.

Chulalongkorn, building on the foundations established by Mongkut, accomplished a number of remarkable transformations. He opened the door to Western trade, while being careful to maintain the autonomy of his nation: by skilful diplomacy he managed to retain his country's independence at a time when the rest of South-east Asia was falling under the domination of one or other of the colonial nations. Slavery was abolished, royal protocol relaxed, the financial structure of the country placed on a modern basis, provincial administration converted from a system of feudal privileges to an efficient, centralised organisation run by paid government servants, the administration of justice was reformed, education brought up to date and transport facilities improved. Many of these reforms were achieved with the assistance of foreign advisers of several nationalities.

The monarchy was perhaps ultimately a victim of its own modernising impulses, for in 1932 the King was deposed in a bloodless coup led by a group of military and civil officials. Although the success of the coup was partly due to the indecisiveness of King Rama VII, and to a mood of despondency —a product of the Great Depression— which had settled over the country, it was largely a consequence of the developing competence of the bureaucratic elite, the frustration many civil servants felt under the constraining hand of the King, and an infusion of Western democratic ideals.

The leaders of the "Revolutionary Government" established a quasi-parliamentary constitution, and then invited the King to continue ruling as a constitutional monarch on the British model. The populace as a whole were little influenced by the shift of power in the capital. Elections were held, but few bothered to vote and many of the parliamentary representatives were, as a consequence, appointed rather than elected by popular vote.

Two leaders emerged with sizeable followings in the struggle for power which occured after the 1932 coup. They were Pibun Songkram—who had the support of the armed forces—and Pridi Panomyong, a practising lawyer whose followers were drawn from the civilian sector of the administration. Pibun became Prime Minister in 1938, subsequently pursuing a strongly pro-Japanese foreign policy. While the Japanese army rampaged through neighbouring countries during World War II, Thailand escaped devastation, although she was forced to sacrifice a good deal of her autonomy to the Japanese authorities.

Pibun's support for the Japanese cause was his downfall. During the occupation, Pridi organised a strong resistance movement, maintained contact with allied governments and harassed the Japanese forces. At the end of the war, Pibun was forced to step down and Pridi became the new Prime Minister.

He effectively restored the country to order and took measures to revive the administrative and financial functions of the government, which had been thrown into chaos by the years of Japanese occupation.

Pridi may have ruled for many years had an unfortunate event not occurred: in 1946 the young King Ananda died from a bullet wound in the head. Whether his death was due to accident, murder or suicide was never clearly established, but playing upon the passions aroused by the event, Pibun openly alleged that Pridi was responsible for the King's death and won sufficient support to lead a coup in which Pridi was overthrown. Pridi was forced to flee into exile.

Pibun remained as Prime Minister for ten years. His fall from grace followed an uncharacteristic and ill-starred experiment in democracy. He declared that free elections would be held but in so doing alienated the army which forcibly deposed him.

Despite the fall of Pridi, the elections were held in 1957. Campaigning was very vigorous, but after the polls had been taken, some of the disappointed candidates alleged that there had been irregularities in the running of the election. Rioting broke out in Bangkok, and in the ensuing chaos a powerful army official, Sarit Thanarat seized the reins of government from the hands of the elected representatives.

Sarit ruled with a firm hand, enjoying virtually absolute power. Although after his death in 1963 it became clear that his personal fortune, misappropriated from the state coffers, amounted to more than $20,000,000, he at least brought back some of the country's former stability, pursued a progressive economic policy and directed the construction of dams, roads and irrigation facilities.

Since 1963 Field-Marshal Thanom Kittikachorn has been head of state, although many observers claim that his deputy, Prapass Charusathira, is the real power.

Under Thanom, municipal elections were held in 1967 and a new Constitution promulgated soon afterwards. The new Constitution provided for a Lower House of elected members, and elections were held in 1969. The Lower House remained, however, little more than a consultative body and had little real legislative power.

Thailand's location has placed it in a difficult position in relation to the warring

Left:
The Emerald Buddha Temple at Bangkok is one of many examples of imaginative Thai architectural art.

Above:
A Sukotai Buddha, radiating a serenity and ancient wisdom, even felt by non-Buddhists.

powers in Indo-China. As in the colonial era, and during the time of Japanese hegemony, the policy of the Government had been to maintain national autonomy while avoiding the devastation of war on Thai soil. In maintaining this position, the exigencies of the 1960's and 1970's tested Thai diplomatic skills to the utmost. Fearing Chinese and Vietnamese expansion—both of these peoples are traditional enemies of the Thai—the Americans were permitted to construct massive bases on Thai soil, and Thanom's government committed Thai troops to Vietnam to lend support to the U.S.A. forces.

The admission of the People's Republic of China to the United Nations in October 1971 precipitated a change in the Government of Thailand. On 17th November a revolutionary party headed by the Prime Minister, Field-Marshal Thanom Kittikachorn staged a coup, seized power and proclaimed martial law throughout the kingdom. The country's Constitution was suspended and Parliament dissolved. Thanom was reported to have issued a statement that the current world situation and the increasing threat to the national security required prompt action, which is not possible through due process of law under the present Constitution. The Prime Minister and other leaders of the new party reported to King Bhumibol on the necessity for the takeover and pledged itself to uphold the monarchy. Under the terms of the martial law, political gatherings of more than five people were prohibited, and all radio and television panel discussions, debates and public speaking activities by education bodies and other associations were suspended. General Post Office and telephone facilities were placed under guard.

Government ministries continued to function normally, but control was taken from the Ministers and transferred to the permanent Under-Secretaries. The new Ministerial heads were summoned before Field-Marshal Thanom and preparations were made for proclaiming an interim Constitution legalising the new military law. They were told that it was planned to set up a suitable Cabinet in due course, but that there would be no Parliament or Legislative Council in the meantime. All the former political parties were therefore banned.

Throughout the coup, although tanks were moved on some of the streets of Bangkok and around Parliament House, there was no violence and Thanom Kittikachorn achieved a bloodless victory.

The Constitution of the Kingdom of Thailand prior to November 1971 was enacted on 20th June 1968. It had a preamble which read:

"Enacted on the 20th day of June, B.E. 2511 Being the 23rd year of the present reign.

May there be virtue. Today is the tenth day of the waning moon in the seventh month of the year of the Monkey under the Lunar calendar, being Thursday, the twentieth of June under the Solar calendar, in the 2511th year of the Buddhist era."

As the years of the Buddhist era are 543 in advance of the Gregorian calendar, the year 1972 A.D. (Anno Domini) is the year B.E. (Buddhist era) 2515.

The 1968 Constitution was the culmination of a process of modernisation of Thailand's law and administration initiated by King Chulalongkorn, "the beloved monarch", who succeeded the monk-king, King Mongkut, to the throne in 1868. Constitutional monarchy was, however, not introduced until 1932, when a group of young civilians and army officers forced King Prajuadhipok (Rama VII) to grant a new Constitution.

More than 85 per cent of the Thai people live on the land, which has always been fertile and sufficient to provide adequate food for the population. This fact helps to explain why constitutional reforms should have been precipitated by an educated, mainly city-dwelling elite. Even though systems of rural slavery and forced labour existed in former centuries, there have been no peasant wars recorded throughout Thai history.

The Head of State is His Majesty King Bhumibol Adulyadej. Field-Marshal Thanom Kittikachorn was leader of the Saha Pracha Thai (United Thai People's Party), under whose leadership the 1968 Constitution was promulgated. Prior to 1968, government had been exercised by an Assembly created under an Interim Constitution brought into force by the Revolutionary Party headed by Field-Marshal Sarit Thanarat which, in December 1958, had seized power from the National Assembly that had been elected following the collapse of the regime of Field-Marshal Pibun Songkram in 1957.

Elections were held under the new Constitution in February 1969 and 219 Members were elected to the House of Representatives for a four-year term on a system of proportional representation for each province based on population figures. There was a Senate—whose members were limited to three-quarters of the number of members in the House of Representatives—appointed by the King for a term of six years.

The Senate and the House of Representatives of 162 members comprised the National Assembly, the legislative body.

Governors are appointed by the King to administer the 72 provinces of Thailand according to the laws and policies of the National Assembly. The provinces vary considerably in size and population, the province of Bangkok having the largest population and Ranong the smallest, with only 43,000. District officers responsible to the Governor of each province are appointed by the Ministry of the Interior.

Urban areas are divided into municipalities with locally-elected councils. In each rural village a head man (Puyaiban) is elected.

Areas comprising a number of villages have a chief head man (Kamnan) elected by the Puyaiban from among their own members. Locally elected leaders represent their people and work with the government officers who are responsible for their district.

CULTURES

Just as some of the cultures of Europe are closely related to one another, the Thai are a part of a cultural "family" which is distributed far beyond the frontiers of Thailand. This "family" comprises the Tai (literally means free) peoples, all of whom speak related languages and have similar customs. Members of the Tai group may be found as far apart as the war-torn lands of Vietnam, the denuded hills of southern China, and the deep forests of Burma. In Burma the Shan, in Laos the Lao and in north Vietnam the Black Thai all fall into the Tai category.

The Thai are the Tai peoples who live within the boundaries of Thailand. Within the nation three main Tai groups may be found —the Siamese in the Central Plain and around Bangkok; the Lao in the north-east, and the Khon Muang in the north. There are also some Shan in the northern valleys and hills. Dialectical differences are greater between some Tai peoples than between others: a Siamese could make himself understood to a Khon Muang, but may experience rather more difficulty in his attempts to communicate with a Shan. Broad cultural continuities arise to a large degree from the fact that all Tai peoples are adherents to the Buddhist faith.

In a rather different category are the hill tribes who live in the uplands of the north. They are not Buddhists and speak tongues which are not related to the Tai languages.

Another alien ethnic group—the Malay—live in the southernmost provinces of Thailand. The presence of the Malay should be evident even to the casual traveller: travelling south, Muslim mosques replace Buddhist temples to an increasing degree, and pedicab passengers are elevated above the seat of the driver. Unlike the Muslims, the Buddhists of the north are not offended by the driver's seat being on the same level as the passenger's head.

There are also Chinese in Thailand, although in proportion to the dominant ethnic group they are fewer than in Malaysia or Indonesia. Most Chinese live in Bangkok where they are active in commerce. According to the 1960 Census, 94 per cent of the population were ethnic Thai (including Siamese, Khon Muang and Lao); 4 per cent were Malay and 1.8 per cent were Chinese. The hill tribes were not included in the enumeration at all.

Right:
Thai sculpture on the Temple of the Dawn.

Below left:
A Buddhist monk contemplates a row of golden garudas outside the Temple of the Golden Buddha. The garuda or eagle is a divine symbol of the sky in Hindu mythology.

Thailand has been fortunate in having broad homogeneity in culture, language and religion. None of the bitter conflicts between different ethnic groups, which have rent the fabric of society in Indonesia and Malaysia at different times have occurred in Thailand. The non-Thai groups are small, and the Thai have a ready capacity for assimilating people of other cultures. Many Chinese, Malays and hill tribesmen have become "Thai", and people like the Mon, who inhabited part of Thailand when the Thai first moved into the country from the north over a millennium ago, have been almost totally absorbed.

EDUCATION

A network of educational institutions, covering much of the country, has contributed to a literacy rate which is higher than any other South-east Asian nation except Singapore. According to the 1966 UN Statistical Yearbook, all but 14 per cent of the population over the age of fifteen is literate. Government-run schools with standardised teacher training, curriculi and examination standards are replacing the traditional temple schools run by Buddhist monks. Education is compulsory for a period of seven years, but truancy laws are not uniformly enforced.

Although elementary schools are to be found in all but the smallest and most remote lowland villages, facilities for secondary education are, on the whole, limited to the large market towns and villages. It is thus not always easy for a village boy or girl to reach the level of education which would enable him to move to a skilled occupation, or to enter the civil service.

According to Education Department statistics, more than 50,000 students were enrolled in institutions of higher education in 1965. The original universities, Chulalongkorn and Thammasart Universities in Bangkok, have recently been supplemented by schools of medicine, agriculture, education and fine arts. In accordance with a policy of decentralisation, provincial universities have been established over the last decade at Chiang Mai in the north, Songkla in the south and Khonkaen in the north-east. Thai universities are not, however, of world standard, partly because traditional attitudes of respect, bordering on reverence, towards teachers inhibit independent enquiry among students, and partly because training in foreign languages—few text books have been written in Thai or translated from English and other languages—has not been developed at secondary level.

There are few channels for post graduate training and most Thai seeking advanced courses have to enrol at overseas tertiary institutions.

THE ARTS

Religious themes predominate in Thai art. The refinement of the art of Buddhist statuary is perhaps one of the greatest achievements of Thai craftsmen. Every devout household, shop or office, and every temple contains at least one bronze Buddha image before which daily offerings are placed. The images range from crude village-made Buddhas to the highly refined statues, sometimes of great antiquity, which are to be found in the famous temples and rich households of the country.

The main influence upon Thai statuary has come from India. The positions in which the Buddha appears in the images are highly conventionalised, and the aim of the artisan is to perfect the existing form, rather than to create a work of art which is entirely different to all others. Some of the best images radiate a sense of spirituality and serenity which conveys itself to the beholder, irrespective of his religious faith.

Many students of Buddhist art agree that the form reached its pinnacle of refinement in the Sukotai period, although other authorities have equal regard for the broader featured Buddhas of the U'Thong period, during which a fusion of the Thai and Cambodian styles occurred. After the U'Thong period, and up to the present day, the form has suffered some degeneration, and a tendency to over ornamentation has detracted from the essential religiosity of the earlier periods. At its best, the art of the Buddha in Thailand is comparable to the highest achievements of Indian craftsmen.

In contrast to the simple, clean lines of the traditional Buddha images, the decorative wood carvings and paintings of Thailand present a riot of colour and ornamentation, a testimony to a religion which has an optimistic view of the world, and of human nature. The wood carvings, which can be seen in their full glory in the temples of Bangkok and some of the provincial towns, range from representations of the fantastic creatures of the Ramakien—the Thai version of the Hindu Ramayana myths—to free flowing and complex designs representing in highly abstract forms subjects ranging from clouds to bulls' testes.

The latter, which grace the front architraves of many houses in the north, are believed to ensure the fertility of all residents. Unfortunately, with the availability of materials like plastics and plaster, and owing to the increasing scarcity of teak—the timber traditionally used for such work—the technique of wood carving is rapidly becoming a lost art and survives largely to produce items for the tourist trade.

Furthermore, little traditional graphic art survives, for the humid, tropical climate of Thailand causes rapid deterioration of cloth and paper, upon which the pictures were usually painted. Contemporary graphic art thrives in Bangkok, where artists are making efforts—not always successfully—to fuse traditional representational styles with the free abstract forms of present-day Western art.

Interest in the dance is widespread in Thailand. The visitor to Bangkok can see classical performances—which are an intrinsic part of dramatic enactments of episodes from the Ramakien—performed

Above: The floating market, the native fruit and vegetable vendors plying their produce from their small craft in a Bangkok klong (canal).

Left: The Thais are experts at making umbrellas, from the typical orange coloured utilitarian types to beautiful hand painted silken sun-shades.

Below: The Chakri Building of the Grand Palace.

Opposite page: The elephant is used extensively in heavy work, particularly in rolling teak logs from the forest to a nearby river for transport or floating to a timber mill.

by elaborately costumed players from the University of Fine Arts. As the Buddha image is stylised, so are the movements of the classical dance: the art of the performer lies in refining the form to the best of his ability.

A much more earthy dance, enjoyed by Thais from all parts of the nation and from all strata of society is the *ramwong*, a dance which is performed by graceful movements of the hands accompanied by bobbing motions of the body. The dance, in which both men and women participate, is sensuous, and can be quite suggestive.

In rural areas, local players enact dramas on domestic themes which may be either sentimental or humorous and bawdy. In the latter genre, puns and double entendres and clever ad-libbing by actors encouraged by enthusiastic audiences abound.

MODERNISATION TRENDS

Foreign cultural influences appear in many forms in Bangkok. Over the past ten or twenty years American and Japanese influences have replaced those which formerly came from the European countries.

Today, the shops are full of consumer goods, modern concrete buildings abound, elaborate cinemas screen the latest American and European films and the streets are full of new cars and motor cycles, mostly of Japanese origin. But despite such evidence of prosperity, Bangkok shares the malaises of modern urban life which afflict many

Western cities. Once Bangkok was known as the "Venice of South-east Asia" owing to the fact that its *klongs*, or canals, which intersected the city, provided the major avenues for transport. In former times laden barges and long narrow passenger vessels, propelled by oarsmen, plied the tree-lined canals. Today most of the waterways have been filled in, and most of the trees felled to make way for modern road transport. Traffic fills the streets to a point approaching chaos and the noise level, owing primarily to the open exhaust, two-stroke engined taxis which proliferate, is deafening. Apart from traffic snarls, Bangkok has a massive problem of sewerage disposal, and municipal authorities are unable to cope with the demand for water supplies and electricity. Further, a sizeable proportion of the population earns low wages and lives in exceedingly poor conditions. Many of the people constituting this section of the population have recently migrated from rural areas: the phenomenon of a wage earning, urbanised proletariat is new to rural Thailand.

Bangkok is, for all this, a tremendously vital and stimulating place to live in, or to visit. It conveys the impression of being a city with a vast and fascinating hinterland.

In fact Bangkok is the intersection of a far flung transport network: domestic airlines link the city with the provinces of the north, south and north-east of the nation; international flights link Thailand with most of the neighbouring countries including Vietnam, Laos, Khmer Republic (Cambodia) and Burma. Rail links radiating from Bangkok reach to Penang in the south, Chiang Mai in the north, and the Khmer Republic frontier in the east.

A number of international agencies which operate in South-east Asia have their headquarters in Bangkok. The Economic Commission for Asia and the Far East (ECAFE), an organisation of the United Nations, and the South-east Asia Treaty Organisation (SEATO) are among the most important of these. Bangkok also has a diplomatic community which is probably the largest and most widely representative to be found in any South-east Asian capital.

TOURISM
Tourism has also been a significant earner of foreign exchange. In 1969 tourists, mostly Americans and Japanese, spent US$85 million in Thailand. Nevertheless, many of the hotel facilities in Bangkok, constructed to cater for an influx of guests during the 1966 Asian Games, are under-utilised. The Tourist Organisation of Thailand hopes that its present vigorous publi-city campaign will increase the flow of tourists.

In most respects, then, Thailand's economy has performed well over the last decade with an average annual growth rate of 8 per cent between 1960 and 1969. However, the dampening of U.S. expenditure in the area will entail some quite radical replanning.

As far as future development is concerned, there is a great deal of potential for expansion in the agricultural sector of the economy, but increased production can only follow heavy application of money and effort by Government agencies. Any gains in the agricultural field will, however, be lost unless steps are taken to curtail the present high rate of population increase. Birth control policies have yet to be instituted, despite the efforts of economic planners and public health authorities to convince conservative government leaders of the wisdom of such moves. Meanwhile, in the industrial sector, redirection of resources currently employed in providing ancillary services for U.S. forces will present a considerable problem, but it is possible that many of these enterprises—particularly in the constructional field—will be able to cater for local needs and may even be able to earn export income. In sum, Thailand faces an inevitable decline in its foreign reserves, but there is no reason to believe that appropriate adjustments cannot be made.

ENTERTAINMENT AND NIGHT LIFE
In this field Bangkok boasts a range of establishments seldom surpassed in South-east Asia. The development of nightclubs and restaurants has been partially prompted by the large numbers of Americans in the country, yet the Thai are a pleasure loving people who prefer to entertain one another outside rather than in their homes, so there has never been a shortage of such facilities in Bangkok or in the larger towns.

A great many restaurants serve Thai food in Bangkok and in provincial areas. Thai food has a character all its own, more closely related to the cuisine of Malaya and Indonesia than to the Chinese. Some dishes are bland, but most are generously spiced with red hot chillies, so the uninitiated are advised to proceed with care.

Restaurants serving indigenous foods range from roadside stalls offering noodle dishes and fried rice to elaborate places catering for tourists and charging very high prices.

It is a good idea to choose a restaurant somewhere between these two extremes, and to ask the waiter for help with the menu.

A spicy Thai meal should be finished off with some local fresh fruit, of which there is a great range, including varieties completely foreign to the average Westerner.

Most memorable is the durian, a large spiky fruit which contains soft creamy flesh. To many the durian is an acquired taste, and its peculiar character and strong odour led one writer to remark that the sensation of durian eating was rather like "eating blanc mange in a toilet". In texture and flavour the durian is rather like a piquant camembert cheese.

There are a great many European restaurants in Bangkok, some of which are of world standard. Cuisine ranges from Mexican, to French and Danish, many establishments being run by expatriate Europeans.

Some are attached to the larger hotels like the Siam Inter-Continental, Erawan, President and Dusithani but it is well worth visiting some of the smaller, independent eateries like The Two Vikings, serving Scandinavian food, Chez Suzanne featuring French cuisine and the Nipa Hut, which specialises in Mexican delicacies. Liquor is expensive, and one can easily pay $8 for a bottle of fairly commonplace French or Australian wine. The local beer is good and cheap, but Mekong, the whisky manufactured by the government liquor monopoly, is strange to palates familiar with Scotch or Bourbon.

There are a great many nightclubs in Bangkok. The best of them are expensive, but they present floor shows by top internationally known artists. Other clubs cater for Thais and although Europeans are welcome many find the invariably gloomy lighting and Thai popular music, played at ear-splitting levels, not to their taste. Most bars and nightclubs have hostesses who will entertain the single male visitor, but patrons need have no qualms about taking a female companion to most of the establishments recommended in the tourist brochures.

559

WHEN IT WAS PROPOSED to build the Inter-Continental Hotel in Bangkok, Her Royal Highness the Princess Mother permitted 26 acres of the Srapatum Palace grounds to be used on condition that a large area be devoted to lawns and gardens.

With due regard to Her Royal Highness' request, the Siam Inter-Continental was designed as a typical Thai-motif hotel of exotic beauty in a similarly beautiful, landscaped tropical garden. This unique conception followed the Inter-Continental format of hotels adapted to local traditional architecture.

The Siam Inter-Continental is actually two buildings, one essentially Thai in appearance and the other a modern-style annexe. The elaborate undulating roof of the central building extends upwards in a series of receding tiers, and cantilevers support it over the broad poolside terraces like a giant ceremonial umbrella.

The interior of the hotel tells a story of Thai creativeness and craftsmanship. Motifs such as the Flame, the fight between the serpent Naga and the Monkey God, and the Royal Hunt for the mythical jewelled leopard are as old as Siam itself. Each guest room is distinctively furnished and carpeted in native materials. The lavish use of rich, colourful Thai silk, gold leaf, mirror mosaic, brass, carved wood and beading is in the centuries old tradition of the Kingdom.

Under the Inter-Continental's one continuous roof are all the services and comforts expected of a top ranking hotel: air-conditioning, around-the-clock room service, laundry and valet services and exclusive jewellery and souvenir shops and boutiques. In the annexe arcade are hair-

Above: Siamese dancers are seen performing on the hotel lawns.

Left: Visitors basking in the sun at the poolside.

HOTEL SIAM INTER-CONTINENTAL

dressing salons, a barber shop, an airline office, travel agency and shopping bazaar.

Thai food may be very hot, laced with chilli pepper, or rich but piquant, flavoured with rare spices and dashes of lemon grass and lime juice. The Inter-Continental's waiters in its three main restaurants advise newcomers as to the combinations most suitable to the uninitiated palate. The Golden Palms Coffee Shop with its informality and unusual decor, offers a wide selection of American and European specialities plus a choice of Thai dishes; also a Coffee Shop menu for the person who is interested in simple cuisine. The Talay Thong is a typical Thai inn, specialising in the sea food which is so abundantly available in Thailand. This is an informal restaurant where service is simple and cooking is in typical Thai fashion, suitable to all types of palates. The third restaurant is the Terrace Room where the daily buffet luncheon menus are changed every six weeks.

On Wednesdays and Sundays at The Terrace Room the Siam Inter-Continental holds its Thai Nights, when Thai dancing is performed by the hotel's own employees to the accompaniment of Thai music.

The Naga Bar, with its richness in decor and informality in atmosphere, is the ideal rendezvous for relaxation and enjoyment of evening cocktails. A resident pianist whiles away the pleasant hours with soft music. At the rear of the main building are green lawns and beautiful, landscaped gardens, through which flows a picturesque winding canal; there, also, is a miniature zoo.

The swimming pool is set in the centre of the two bedroom-wings of the main building. It has a tropical-awninged refreshment bar and shady palm trees amid which are scattered lounge chairs for the bathers. At the rear of the pool there is a garden sanctuary for native fauna surrounding a miniature lake. Seats are dotted here and there among the frangipani and other flowering trees, and one may walk the rose-bush and hibiscus-lined paths or sit at rest, listening to bird calls and the chattering of monkeys.

For those who prefer the more exciting night life, the Siam Inter-Continental offers one of Bangkok's most swinging nightclubs —the Safari—where guests are served drinks in a jungle atmosphere by white hunter girls whose beauty is unrivalled in this exotic land.

All this goes to make up one of the most complete hotel complexes on the South-east Asian scene.

The picture above
shows the distinctive Thai architecture of the Hotel Siam Inter-Continental in its miniature lakeside setting.

Left:
A corner of the popular
Naga Bar.

Left:
As in all Asian countries rice is the major crop. This rice field is typical of those described in the accompanying story "Life of a Thai."

Below:
Five and six-year-old children learn the Thai and Roman alphabets under the tuition of a young monk at a temple school in the village of Bangpakong.

Opposite page:
Chab sets off in his ox-drawn cart soon after dawn, to work on the neighbouring farm.

LIFE OF A THAI

Chab is a young man living in Thailand on the shores of the Gulf of Thailand overlooking the sea that reaches out to Borneo and Malaya. His village is rather unsophisticated and uncomfortable but he loves it because it is a peaceful one.

Chab gets up early every morning. This does not indicate that he is more diligent than any other man in the village but there is an inevitable task waiting to be done. It is his duty to fetch water from a nearby well.

Since there is only one well in the village everybody uses it and the ones who go there very early will have the clearest water. Some of the old people have told him that in the big towns there is running water and Chab thinks that it would be very good for him to have a river passing through his village like many others have. But he has to be content. He was born here and he loves it. Moreover he has the large sea instead of the river.

When he comes back from the well the breakfast will probably be ready for all members of the family. He used to think that there were no cooks superior to his his mother, even though he knew that all women in the village knew how to cook.

Chab remembers that four or five years ago, when he was a schoolboy, after he finished breakfast he had to hurry to go to school. The school was three miles from the house so he had to have lunch prepared at home and wrapped for him. Now he has finished the primary school. But he did not further his studies. He is the only son in the family so the responsibility for cultivating the rice fields falls upon him.

Chab is not a stupid boy and he hoped to be a teacher because a teacher is normally regarded as an important and intelligent person in the village. Everyone knows and respects teachers. Chab dreamed of studying in Bangkok, the capital of Thailand, which seemed a paradise on earth for the villagers like him and his neighbours. His teacher told him that in Bangkok there were many schools, cinemas, wide roads, buses and cars and big hotels. Chab was very surprised to learn this because his little village had no such things. He told himself that he must go to Bangkok one day.

As this season is not for sowing grain nor for harvest, Chab and his family are rather free. They spend their time making some utensils or anything necessary for religious days. Buddhism is their religion and although they are not a religious family they all go to the temple when there is an important religious day. They offer their food to the priests and this is what they call "making an offering". They do not know for certain that this act is witnessed and recorded; all they know is that making an offering makes them happy with a peaceful heart. However, they do believe in the "round of birth and death" and to make sure the next life will be better than the present one they must make an offering and do good to all people.

The temple is the centre of the village so a religious day is a chance for them to meet many of their friends and relatives.

It is generally believed that once in his life every man should be a priest or monk because to be a monk is a high and important event. Normally a man will enter priesthood at the age of 21. He will stay at the monastery more or less for three months. There he will study the teaching of Buddha and control his behaviour as well as he can.

He has only two meals a day, breakfast and lunch, and he must go to town and beg for them. After being a monk he will be regarded as a perfect man and a mature one. Chab is now twenty years old and he is waiting to be a monk. He used to think that every man in every village should become a monk. He knows now that he was wrong. His teacher has told him that life in big towns has changed and is rather different from his own. Chab tries to understand it. But in fact he does not understand. And he will not understand until he becomes a monk and studies the teaching of Buddha that seems to say, "All things must change, prepare yourselves to be better".

SPORTS

The major international sports do not have a wide following, but there are indigenous sports which are played over much of Thailand. The Thai are enthusiastic gamblers, and all over the country punters place bets on fighting cocks, fighting fish and boxing matches. The Thai form of boxing is of some interest to the visitor, for blows may be struck with the feet as well as the fists. In former times sharp objects were attached to gloves and foot bindings, allowing the combatants to inflict serious injury on one another. Today, no longer with these potentially lethal attachments, matches are held to the accompaniment of traditional music in rings ranging from the national stadium in Bangkok to makeshift structures in rural village squares. Given the following that boxing has, it is scarcely surprising that Thailand has produced a number of conventional boxers of world renown.

Other international sports are played by residents of Bangkok and some of the larger towns. Golf is played on fine courses by businessmen and high ranking civil servants with a fervour which is almost Japanese or American in intensity. Yachting is a sport recently adopted, having received a boost from the active participation and patronage of King Bhumibol. Team sports are not generally popular among the individualistic Thai, but some, particularly soccer and basketball, have attracted many supporters in the universities and colleges.

Apart from the field of boxing, few Thai sportsmen have made their mark on the international scene, undoubtedly because most sports have only recently been introduced. Nevertheless, in recent Asian Games involving participants from all South-east Asian countries—the Thai have been successful in a wide range of events.

ECONOMY

Yet Bangkok does not reflect the reality which is the rest of Thailand. True, it is a city of more than 3 million people, but it is the only real city in a nation of about 35 million. The next largest town is Chiang Mai, in the far north, which has a population under 100,000. Nevertheless, the development of the provincial towns reflects, on a smaller scale, the mushrooming of Bangkok itself. In Chiang Mai, Khon Kaen and a half dozen other towns the phenomena of rapid population growth through migration from rural districts: booming shopping centres stocked with manufactured goods ranging from electronic equipment and motor cars, to clothing and enamel cooking utensils; heavy motor traffic and leisure facilities such as bowling alleys, nightclubs and cinemas—all these are in evidence.

In rural areas, which are becoming increasingly accessible to provincial towns by networks of roads serviced by gaudily decorated, privately owned buses and trucks, one finds that the agricultural technology has not changed very much.

Fields are still ploughed by water buffaloes, rice paddies are still irrigated by primitive systems of canals and dykes, while most labour is performed without mechanical assistance. Yet the demand by rural dwellers for modern consumer goods, for commodities like motor cycles, radios and manufactured clothing, has recently increased to a significant degree. To finance the purchase of such goods, farmers have sought new avenues for gaining cash income. During the dry season, when agricultural pursuits demand little time, many work as wage labourers, although in some areas opportunities for cash employment are limited. Others have turned away from traditional preoccupations with rice cultivation toward the production of cash

563

Above: Thai boxing is a rugged sport.

Below: A stone cutter in the town of Ang Sila, near the Gulf of Thailand.

Opposite page: Ships of the world bring essential commodities to the port of Bangkok and take away their cargoes of rice and other products of Thailand.

ported. Most rice is shipped to India and Hong Kong, as well as other neighbouring countries.

While exports of rice are declining, other commodities—rubber, maize, tin and tapioca—are being shipped abroad in increasing quantities. While rice is shipped to other Asian nations, rubber, maize, tapioca and tin are most frequently exported to the developed nations of the West.

Without doubt the economy of Thailand has been boosted by enormous American spending in the country. Air bases have been established for operations over Vietnam, and until late 1969 large numbers of U.S. troops stayed in Bangkok while on leave from the battle zones of Vietnam.

Many local enterprises have developed to provide services for the U.S. forces. These have ranged all the way from bars and nightclubs to cement producers and construction companies. Foreign exchange earnings through U.S. military spending are estimated to be in the $200 to $300 million bracket per annum. This comprises about one-third of the value of commodity exports, which totalled US$687 million a year between 1966-70.

DEVELOPMENT OF INDUSTRY

One needs to travel only a short distance in Thailand to become aware that the majority of the population are engaged in rural occupations. Travelling north by train across the vast Chao Phya River basin, one passes through an almost unbroken sea of rice and subsidiary crops. According to 1966 figures compiled by the United Nations, 82 per cent of the population was then engaged in agricultural work, a proportion higher than any other South-east Asian nation with the probable exceptions of Burma and Indonesia.

Despite these impressions and statistics, the manufacturing sector has grown rapidly in recent years. Its contribution to the gross domestic product over the past ten years has increased at an annual average rate of 11 per cent. In 1969 manufacturing activities contributed 14.6 per cent to the State's gross domestic product.

Most of the manufactured goods produced in Thailand come from small backyard businesses—the 481,000 workers employed in this field operated in no less than 164,000 factories, an average of only 2.9 employees per enterprise. This characteristic is particularly striking in the textile field, which accounted for a third of the entire work force of Thailand's manufacturing industry.

Although textiles—particularly the famed Thai silks and cottons—ceramics and wooden goods are manufactured by techniques of great antiquity, there has recently been considerable progress in more modern fields. Among the most important of these have been the manufacture of construction materials—cement, bricks, tiles and steel formwork. A sizeable proportion of the cement produced in Thailand is exported to other South-east Asian countries. A number of factories producing consumer goods ranging from soap and clothing to electronic goods and motor cars have been established in the Bangkok area.

crops such as tobacco, peanuts and commercial vegetables—always in demand.

There is, then, little doubt that the economy of Thailand is booming. But the questions then arise, how did the boom come about? How is it sustained, and will it last? Since most of the consumer goods which stock the stores are imported, a healthy reserve of foreign currency is essential to Thailand. Traditionally the nation has been a rice surplus producer, with rice exports providing the greater proportion of the foreign exchange. Recently, however, a rapidly growing population has been consuming an increasing proportion of local rice production. Thus in 1966, rice earned the equivalent of US$192 million in foreign exchange, yet in 1970 it earned only the equivalent of US$121 million. In the 1930's up to 50 per cent of the total rice produced was exported; in 1970 only 12 per cent was ex-

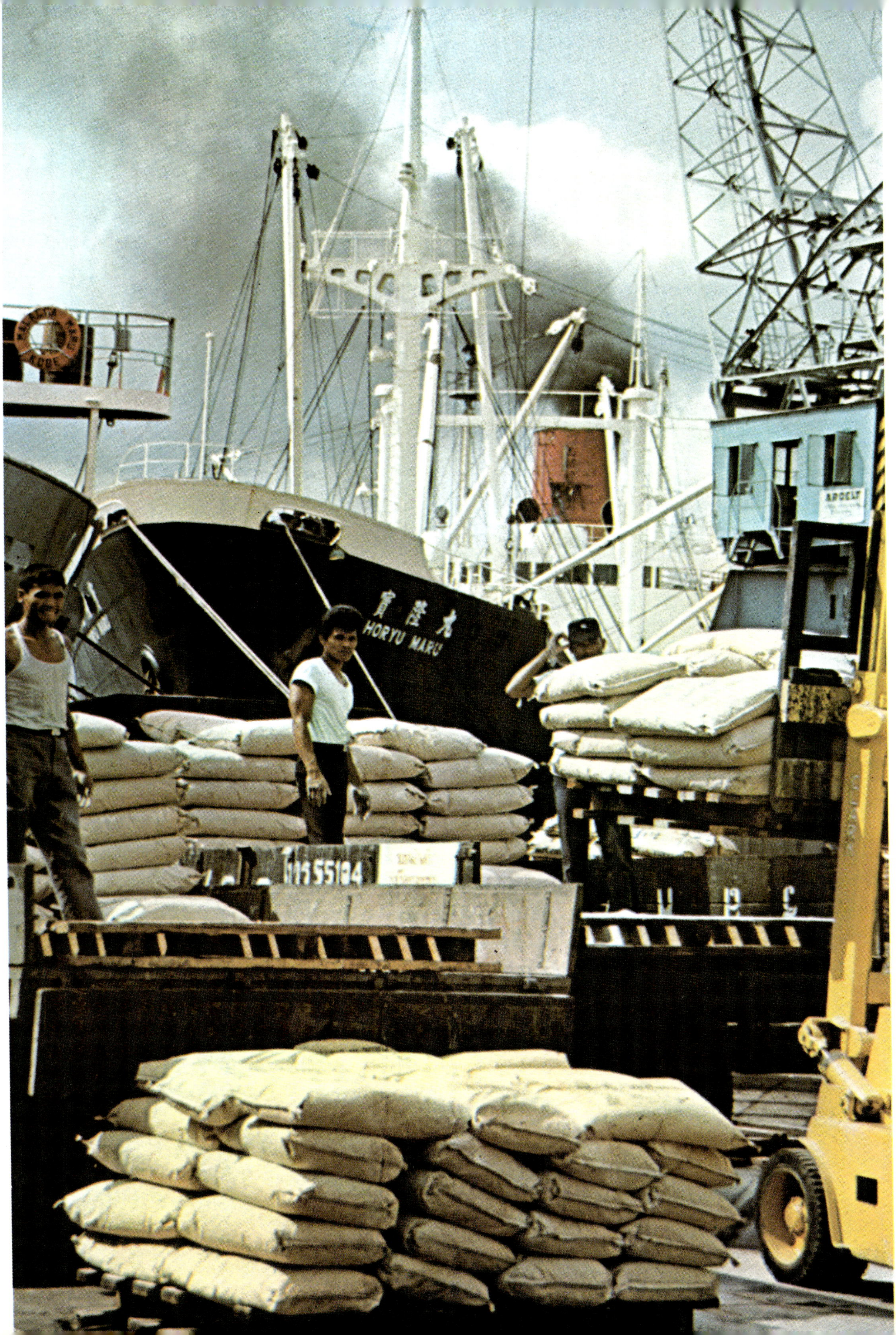
HORYU MARU

THE FIRST BANK to operate in Thailand was the foreign controlled Hong Kong and Shanghai Banking Corporation. It was established in 1888 and was followed in the next decade by two other foreign banking concerns, The Chartered Bank of Britain and the French Banque De L'Indochine. It was not until 1906 that Thailand got its first own locally founded bank. That was the Siam Commercial Bank, set up jointly by members of the Thai Royal Family and local businessmen.

After that, many banks were opened but only three survived the disastrous depression years of the 1930's. Lack of banking experience and the general economic climate of that period led to the downfall of the majority of the earlier banking ventures.

The Siam Commercial Bank, the Wang Lee Chan Bank founded in 1933, and the Bank of Asia established in 1939, were the only ones that managed to struggle through this lean time. Most of Thailand's present day banks date from the 1940's.

Today, banking in Thailand has emerged from its fragile infancy, and at the beginning of 1972 there were 29 banking groups operating throughout the country, sixteen local and thirteen foreign.

In the last few years there has been a dramatic rise in the status of Thai banking which has mirrored the expansion and growth of the country's economy and its developing sophistication. Basically, Thailand has always had an agrarian outlook, with 80 per cent of the people earning their living off the land. The Government is now trying to change this restricted way of life by the establishment of major manufacturing industries. The banks are in the forefront of this movement. They are the primary sources of finance for the building of factories, purchasing modern plant and machinery and they handle the salaries and wages of staffs, technicians and workers. Without the backing of banks, a developing nation can make little progress. The banks encourage the people to deposit their savings, and by so doing, earn interest on their money. In turn, the banks lend the invested funds to industrial concerns, and so help their country to develop its potentials. This provides more jobs and builds up a steady, stable economy.

As commercial banking is so essential to the growth and prosperity of Thailand, a way had to be found to convince the people of the wisdom of saving at least a portion of their earnings. Thus, in 1962, the current Commercial Banking Act came into force. It established a maximum ceiling rate of 8 per cent interest for a one year deposit. This was recently reduced to 7 per cent, but it is still higher than the maximum rate of 5 per cent prior to 1962. Over the last three years deposits in Thai banks have increased at an average of more than 20 per cent per annum, and a good deal of credit for this boost is due to the new rates of interest. The banks can now lend a substantially larger amount of money each year and so stimulate a more rapid economic growth.

Today the banking community is granting a very large proportion of its loans for the development of Thailand's export-import trade. 25 per cent of available funds is allocated for internal and foreign trade; 17 per cent for wholesale and retail trading; 13 per cent for personal loans and 8 per cent for construction. Only 4 per cent of loans is granted to the farmer, even though agriculture is still Thailand's most vital enterprise, with over three-quarters of the population employed on the land.

In order to channel more financial resources to the farmer, the Bangkok Bank Limited launched its agricultural credit programme in 1962. In fact it was the first banking institution to provide easy terms for the repayment of loans made to the man on the land. Others have since followed suit, especially as the result of the Government's Rural Development Programmes.

When most of the local banks were forced to close down in the 1930's, the Government introduced a specific law to govern the business of banking. This was called the Act for the Control of the Business of Banking B.E. 2480. (1937 A.D.). After World War II when banks again began to

566

COMMERCIAL BANKING IN THAILAND

flourish, the Commercial Banking Act B.E. 2488 (1945) was introduced to enforce stricter controls. This Act was particularly significant in that it empowered the Bank of Thailand (established in 1942) to act in a supervisory capacity over commercial banking practices. It still performs this function. In the years following World War II, local Thai banks gained precedence over foreign banks which, until the war, were in a dominant position. Today, locally incorporated banks far surpass the foreign institutions in terms of deposits, volume and types of transactions. Foreign banking companies now mainly serve foreign investors in the export-import trade and in hotel and industrial projects. However, recent trends seem to indicate that in the years ahead the numbers of depositors are likely to fall off. Already every area in Thailand, even remote areas, have easy access to bank branches. Competition for new depositors is running at fever-pitch, and officials will soon be looking for new methods of attracting more customers, for instance, by providing them with small, free services and lending money on less stringent terms of repayment.

At the end of 1971 there were 669 commercial bank branches throughout Thailand. There were also 14 overseas branches, all the latter belonging to the Bangkok Bank Limited, Thailand's largest and only international bank. With a staff of over 5,900 people, the Bangkok Bank has 90 branches throughout Thailand, 46 in the provinces, 44 in the City of Bangkok and Thon Buri. In 1954, this Bank opened its first overseas branch, in Hong Kong. Today it has branches in London, Singapore, Kuala Lumpur, Djakarta, Saigon, Taipei, Tokyo and Osaka. It also has its own agency office in New York.

The Bangkok Bank Limited works with Thailand's future very much in mind. It regards itself as a pacesetter in the country as evidenced by the computer system it has installed to facilitate accounting. The Bangkok Bank is the only banking organisation in Thailand which uses such a computer. It has laid down a policy of keeping ahead in staff efficiency and giving assistance to projects aimed at social development. It also gives regular donations to relief organisations and for medical and educational purposes. This has set an example with other banks, and several major Thai industrial concerns have followed.

It has already been mentioned that the Bank pioneered easy loan repayments for farmers. It currently offers advice on fertilisers, pest control, soil conservation and mechanisation. This is given to the farmers by the Bank's own staff of trained agronomists. This benevolence towards the man on the land has as its motive, helping him get increased yields from his crops and thus enabling him to save more money, which may well be deposited in its vaults.

At present most of the finance for industrialisation comes from Thailand's local commercial banks and to a smaller degree from the foreign banks. Armed with growing resources, they finance a wide range of activities from manufacturing to the construction of multi-purpose dams and highways. In this way, they set the foundations for the future prosperity of Thailand.

Top left page: Head Office of the Bangkok Bank, located at 3-9 Suapa Road, Bangkok.

Far left: The lobby at Head Office of the Bangkok Bank where customers may deposit their savings and earnings and withdraw the money they require for the family's weekly needs.

Below: The Bangkok Bank was the first bank in Thailand to use electronic data processing techniques. This picture shows the Computer Centre.

Right: Commercial Banks in Thailand have played important roles in providing assistance to importers and exporters. A scene at the Port of Bangkok.

INDUSTRIAL GIANTS OF THAILAND

DURING the years of his reign—1851 to 1865—King Mongkut opened Thailand to the West by signing a treaty with Britain, thus establishing friendship and paving the way for mutual trade. King Chulalongkorn (1868-1910) established a modern postal system and instituted reforms in provincial administration. In 1913 King Rama VI, with a view toward wider social and economic development, decreed that Thailand should have its own cement industry controlled and operated by Thais. These were some of the stones in the foundations of a future modern State, fitting itself to compete with the other nations of the world. Under King Rama VI, the Siam Cement Company was formed, the forerunner of what was later to become the Siam Cement Group, now the largest corporate enterprise in Thailand. For 60 years it has wielded a powerful influence in the economy of the country, a monument to the wisdom and foresight of King Rama VI.

In recent decades cement has become the basis of all construction; in modern concrete and steel commercial buildings, in concrete roads and in the great dams storing life-essential water for teeming millions throughout the world. When the Siam Cement Company was formed, Danish machinery and Danish technical advice helped to get production started and by 1915 its output reached 20,000 tons. From then onwards the Company's output of cement steadily increased until the Board decided in 1935 that the opportunity had arrived to diversify its activities and form into a Group.

The first affiliate, The Siam Fibre-Cement Company, was established in 1938 for the purpose of reducing Thailand's dependence on imported asbestos cement products, thus expanding the local base of Thailand's fledgling building materials industry. A small plant was set up at Bangsue—the site of the first cement works—for the manufacture of a popular type of asbestos cement roofing sheets known as "Roman tiles". Successive stages of expansion brought into production small and medium dimension drainage pipes, various building accessories, corrugated and flat roofing sheets and low-pressure asbestos cement pipes.

Although operations slowed down during World War II the Government became interested in establishing an iron and steel industry in Thailand. It offered the Siam Cement Company the concession for iron ore deposits discovered at Khao Thap Kwai, 70 kilometres north of Ta Luang, and in 1942 another member was added to the Group with the formation of The Siam Iron and Steel Company (SISCO). The project began as an experiment, as an extension of the cement plant's activities. The surge of development that followed the declaration of Peace gave the Company its chance to expand and a steel plant was set up in Ta Luang in 1946. For the next twenty years development continued at a steady pace. In 1966 a high pressure asbestos cement plant was set up and its capacity was doubled within twelve months. New plants at Thung Song in 1968 and Saraburi in 1970 helped to swell the asbestos cement output to 420,000 tons of roofing materials, flat sheets and sidings and 45,000 tons of high-pressure and low-pressure asbestos cement pipes.

The iron and steel venture had succeeded so well, that in 1966 a separate company was formed and a mammoth programme of expansion was begun.

The original facilities of smelting, steelmaking and a foundry had a total production capacity of 30,000 tons a year. Late in 1969 a large new rolling mill, a 30-ton electric arc furnace, a continuous casting machine and a wire drawing plant were installed, giving an annual rolling capacity of 165,000 tons of reinforcing bars, wire rods and shapes including 7,500 tons per year of high tensile wire for pre-stressed concrete. The foundry capacity has since been increased to 10,000 tons per year. The final stage of development is due to take place in the seventies—another 30-ton electric arc furnace will be added to increase the annual production of billets to 120,000 tons. With a new smelting plant, SISCO will become the first modern integrated iron and steel works in Thailand.

In its continual search for new fields of operation, in 1971 the Group commenced production of glass-reinforced polyester sheets ("Glasolit"), PVC plastic pipes ("D-Plast") and high quality fireproof ceiling panels ("Asbestolux").

Up to 1952 one of the Company's principal interests had been the manufacture of housing materials. In that year it established a subsidiary designed to supply most of the requirements of the general construction industry. Called Concrete Products and Aggregate Company (CPAC), this unit now makes nearly 250 products, notably "Sakrete", a pre-mixed packaged concrete requiring only the addition of water; and "Monier", a high quality coloured roof tile; and "Rocla", a spun concrete pipe of very large diameter and unusual length for application in major hydraulic engineering projects.

An interesting technique was recently developed by the Company's engineers, a special type of foundation called the "Prepak Pile", designed particularly for construction work in areas of high-density building, such as in the city of Bangkok. This does away with conventional pile driving: the earth is first augered and concrete is extruded *in situ* without noise and disturbance to nearby residents.

The Company's contributions to the industrial development of Thailand, particularly in the field of construction, are indicated in its current capacity: 40,000 cubic metres of pre-stressed concrete piles, bridge girders, beams and telephone poles, 13,000 cubic metres of ordinary and reinforced concrete pipes; 4 million concrete blocks; 500,000 cubic metres of ready-mixed concrete and 450,000 tons of aggregate. Cement production has reached a capacity of 3 million tons with the potential of an even greater output.

In order to market the Group's products more efficiently the Construction Material Marketing Company was formed and registered in 1962. CMMC maintains a network of over 300 dealers throughout Thailand and employs a large pool of qualified architects and engineers to provide an efficient technical service for its customers, a unique facility initiated by this company. In a three-storied Building Centre on Paholyothin Road in Bangkok a large selection of construction materials available in Thailand are on permanent display for the benefit of local consumers and overseas buyers.

Left: A general view of the Siam Cement Group's fourth, and newest factory at Kaeng Koi, Saraburi.

Above: An electric arc furnace at the Siam Iron and Steel Company's factory, Ta Luang.

THAI OIL

THAILAND, like so many other Asian countries, has found itself on the horns of an economic and social dilemma. Heavily dependent upon agricultural exports for foreign exchange, with 75 per cent of her population still deriving income from the land, she must find a place for herself in a world of fast expanding technology—a world that is continually forcing its standards to greater heights.

Short cuts to industrialisation have become necessary and this was apparent even at the beginning of the 1960's when a far-seeing Thai industrialist, Chow Chowkwanyun, established the Thai Oil Refinery Co. Ltd. (TORC) in 1961. Fuel power is essential to any modern industrial nation but its importation frequently exercises a heavy drain on foreign reserves. Chow contended that a local oil refinery was the answer and his enterprise has been the means of saving the Thai Government US$20 million in foreign exchange.

TORC has a capacity to handle just over 3 million tons (65,000 barrels) of crude oil per day and to the present time supplies about 50 per cent of the country's requirements in petroleum products. With an investment of about US$100 million it has become the largest industrial enterprise in Thailand and is owned entirely by private shareholders. It is estimated that by 1975 the current demand will have increased to 9 million tons and the TORC refineries will need to treble their output to meet demands. Apart from its very real contribution to Thailand's economic development, TORC is also performing a vital function in raising the levels of management and technological skills of Thai nationals. In this it has the benefit of long term agreements with its associates, the Royal Dutch-Shell Group, through which it is provided with technical know-how as well as raw materials.

The modern oil refinery is an essential factor in the sophisticated and complex science of petrochemicals. In 1967 Chow Chowkwanyun proposed the establishment of a petrochemical industry as a means of meeting domestic and regional demand for such products as polyethylene, polypropylene, vinyl chloride resin and polystyrene. Such a project, he claimed, could save Thailand US$140 million in foreign exchange by the development of the first phase during the first ten years of operation. By the establishment and operation of such an industry, in addition to its refinery, the Thai Oil Refinery Co. Ltd. is making a unique contribution to the nation's development, giving to the rural population some of the benefits and advantages of a modern industrial state.

THE THAI PETROCHEMICAL PROJECT

DURING THE PAST DECADE the petrochemical industry has become a major project in all developed and developing countries.

In Thailand the Government has approved the installation of one of the biggest plants in southern Asia and by 1974-1975 it is expected to come on stream.

The enterprise is being spearheaded by the Thai Petrochemical Company, a joint venture in which the Royal Dutch-Shell Group and Thai interests headed by Mr Chow Chowkwanyun have equal shareholdings. The project includes a naptha cracker with a capacity of about 200,000 tons of ethylene per annum and the various downstream industries for manufacturing petrochemical products such as low and high density polyethylene, polypropylene, polystyrene, P.V.C., alkylbenzene and D.M.T.

The downstream industries are being promoted mainly by companies belonging to major Japanese Groups such as Mitsubishi, Mitsui and Teijin, the products of their plants being intended primarily for consumption in the Thai market. Petrochemicals consumption in Thailand is relatively very high and when completed the Thai project is expected to surpass any other of its kind in the sub-continent.

The Above picture gives an idea of the complexity of the petrochemical industry and is based on a view of a plant in Japan, operated by one of the Japanese companies associated with the Thai project. The plant of the Thai Oil Refinery Company Ltd. is shown on the left page.

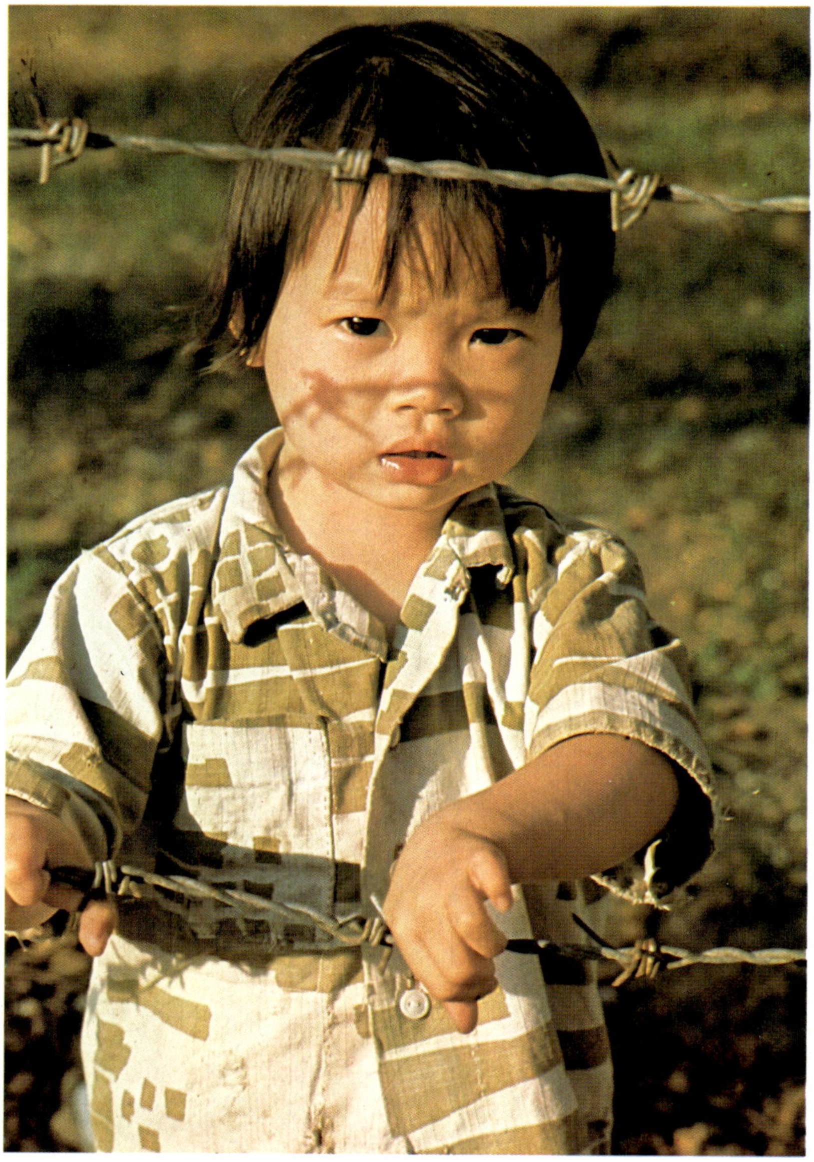

Republic of VIETNAM

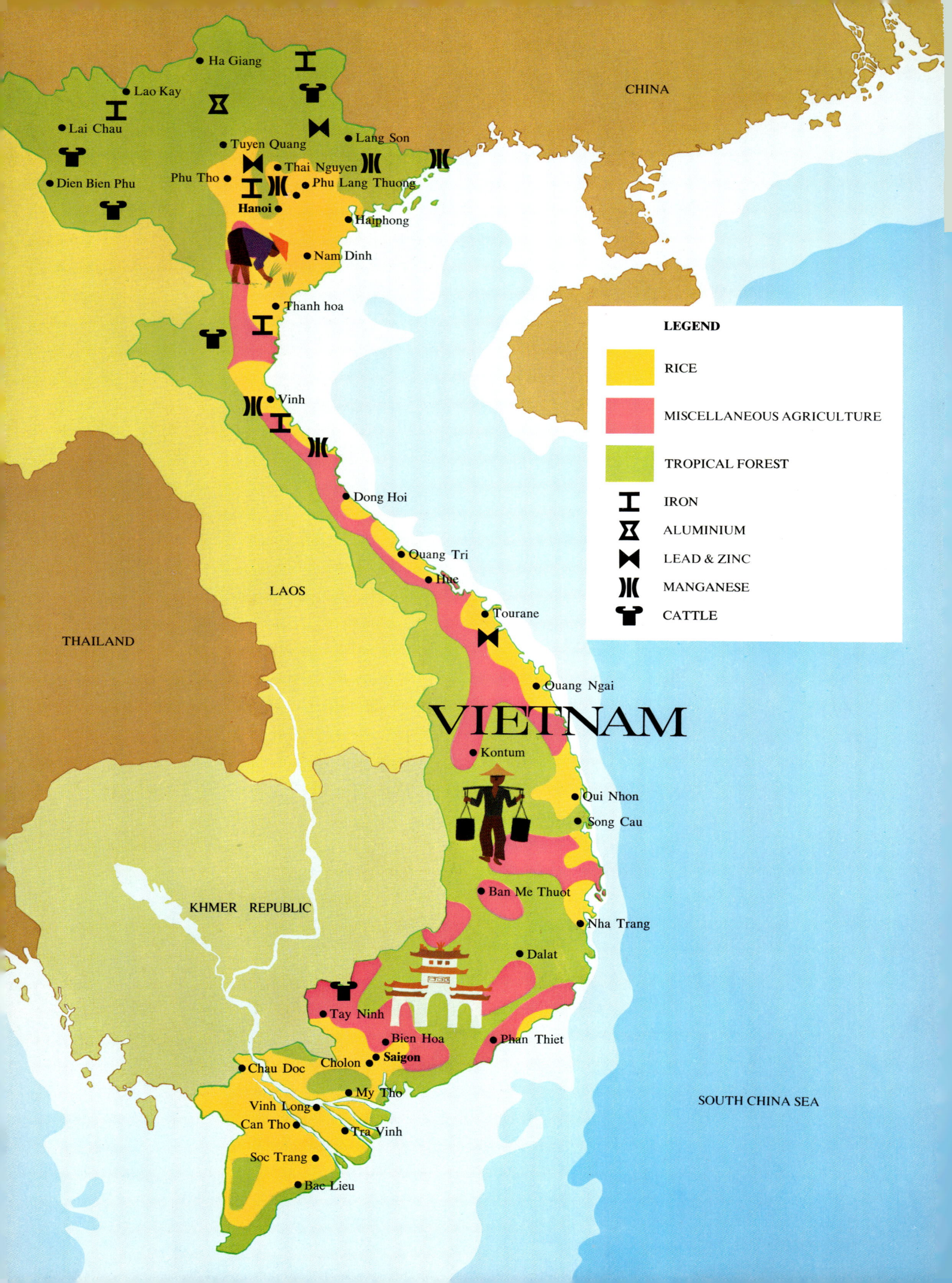

VIETNAM

LEGEND

- 🟨 RICE
- 🟥 MISCELLANEOUS AGRICULTURE
- 🟩 TROPICAL FOREST
- IRON
- ALUMINIUM
- LEAD & ZINC
- MANGANESE
- CATTLE

CHINA

LAOS

THAILAND

KHMER REPUBLIC

SOUTH CHINA SEA

- Ha Giang
- Lao Kay
- Lai Chau
- Dien Bien Phu
- Tuyen Quang
- Lang Son
- Phu Tho
- Thai Nguyen
- Phu Lang Thuong
- Hanoi
- Haiphong
- Nam Dinh
- Thanh hoa
- Vinh
- Dong Hoi
- Quang Tri
- Hue
- Tourane
- Quang Ngai
- Kontum
- Qui Nhon
- Song Cau
- Ban Me Thuot
- Nha Trang
- Dalat
- Tay Ninh
- Bien Hoa
- Phan Thiet
- Chau Doc
- Cholon
- Saigon
- My Tho
- Vinh Long
- Can Tho
- Tra Vinh
- Soc Trang
- Bac Lieu

Dragons guard the entrance to the National Museum at Saigon.

Vietnam

AREA:
Total Area: 128,401 square miles; South Vietnam: 67,108 square miles.

LENGTH:
Total north to south: approximately 900 miles; South Vietnam: 475 miles.

AVERAGE WIDTH:
100 miles

LOCATION:
Between 9° and 23° north latitude and 102° and 109° east longitude. Bounded on the north by China, on the east and south by the Gulf of Tonking and the South China Sea, and on the west by Cambodia and Laos. The border between North and South Korea agreed upon lies along the seventeenth parallel and is marked by the Ben Hoi river.

CLIMATE:
Tropical Monsoon—equatorial in the south, milder in the north. Hottest months are from May to October. January temperatures average around 70°F; August temperatures average in the mid to high 80'sF.

RAINFALL:
Summer monsoon brings the heaviest falls. Saigon averages 80" annually; Hue: 116".

TOPOGRAPHY:
The north is dominated by deltas and mountains, the latter representing the end of the Chinese Foldings. The long coastline of central Vietnam is backed by a series of alluvial plains fronting the Annamite mountain chain, the most important being Thanh Hoa and Vinh in the north, Hue in the middle and Qui Nhon in the south. The southern zone is notable for the alluvial deposits of the Mekong: in the east, the Saigon river and its tributaries drain a group of hills and constitute a system distinct from that of the Mekong. The coast is flat and muddy.

RACIAL GROUPS:
Vietnamese: 87 per cent: Chinese: 8 per cent; Cambodians and Laos: 2 per cent; others: 3 per cent.

RELIGIONS:
Buddhism, Taoism, Confucianism, Catholicism, Hao Nao, Caodaism, Ancestor Worship and Animism.

LANGUAGE:
Vietnamese is monosyllabic. It can be written in Chinese characters or in the romanised quoc ngu alphabet.

NATURAL RESOURCES:
Forests, fisheries, water-power, gold, molybdenum, phosphates and some low grade coal.

AGRICULTURE AND THE WORKFORCE:
Mainly rice and vegetable growing in the deltas; rubber, tobacco, copra, peanuts, sugarcane, pepper, cassava and sweet potatoes. The Man and the Meo occupy the highest ground, raising livestock and growing maize and opium. The Moi—a Vietnamese epithet for savage—are descendants of early Indonesians. Living in the mountains, they till the land, pick fruit, fish and hunt. The Chinese are traditionally traders and merchants, although the Vietnamese are quickly becoming the major force in the nation's commerce.

POPULATION:
Average density: 350 people per square mile.

Vietnamese girls wearing graceful flowing costumes of white silk pantaloons under a long tunic split at both sides. They are on their way to attend school.

MEANING "BEYOND THE SOUTH" and synonomous with Annam, which means "Quiet South", the term Vietnam officially dates from 1801. In its older, reverse form of Nam-Viet, it designates an ethnic branch of southern China to which the Vietnamese are traditionally said to belong. The forerunner of today's Vietnamese first settled the Red River delta—the area near Hanoi —where, by turning the marshes into paddy fields, a steady growth of population was made possible. This remote period, about 2,200 years ago, still haunts the national memory as a source of legends. On this plain dwelt the mythical princes of Hongbang—still commemorated at present-day Phutho—and it is during this period that the magic union of a dragon and a fairy commenced the line from which, the folk tales say, the Vietnamese descended.

In those days, the delta of the Red River, covered with swampy woods and inhabited by wild animals, was smaller than it is today. And the ancients lived as the Vietnamese mountain people do at present, chewing betel and decorating their bodies with tatoos.

During the 3rd Century B.C., Vietnam was conquered by China of the Han, who ruled until the 10th Century and laid the foundations of Vietnamese culture, although uprisings led by numerous heroes of independence mark the period. Autonomy was achieved after the success of Khuc Thua Dru in 906 A.D. and Nago Quyen, 938 A.D., although stability was not achieved until towards the end of the Kinh Dynasty which was replaced by that of the early Le in 980. Even after its independence, Vietnam fought against the Chinese army of the Sung, from 961-993 A.D., and battled the Indian-influenced Kingdom of Champa, which then occupied today's central Vietnam. The generals who emerged victorious from these battles often founded dynasties and are still hailed as popular heroes in many temples. With surprising repetition, later Vietnamese won battles against the redoubtable army of Genghis Khan.

City by city, the Vietnamese slowly conquered Champa and the Kingdom of Khmers and, in 1672, took Saigon which had formerly belonged to Cambodia. Despite violent rivalry between the northern Trinh and southern Nguyen clans, unification of Vietnam was finally completed in 1801 by the Emperor Gia Long of Nguyen with the help of the French. He saw Vietnam established from the Chinese border to Camau, with a 1,500-mile coastline, encompassing a linguistically and culturally homogeneous nation, its social structure based on agricultural life and its family structure welded by Confucian ethics.

Marco Polo in 1280, the Portuguese in the 16th Century, the Dutch in the 17th and later the English and French—all spoke favourably of the country's wealth, and several traded profitably in Vietnam's spices, silks, woods and metals. With the merchants came missionaries. Catholicism at first well received, was later persecuted, but by the end of the 17th Century, its faithful numbered several hundred thousand and the Church was firmly established. French intervention in Vietnam's domestic affairs and control of her foreign policy was initiated by the treaty of 1876, firmly established in the treaty of 1884 and was not to be ended until the Geneva Convention of 1954. The war of independence leading to the defeat of the French forces at Dien Bien Phu in May 1954 was conducted in the name of all the Vietnamese people by the Vietminh, a nationalist party formed on Chinese territory during World War II, under the leadership of Ho Chi-Minh. When the Geneva Convention divided Vietnam into two, near the 17th parallel of latitude, north of Hue, the Vietminh assumed control of the northern half. The Communist party, the Lao Dong, held the key industries and exercised control, via a hierarchy of committees, elected from an approved list of candidates.

South Vietnam, however, presented no such consolidated front. Bao Dai, the Chief of State, was a remote authority. Prime Ministers came and went. And the real power was divided between religious sects—Cao-Daists, Hao Hao and Bin Xuyen—and the generals of the new army.

The Land beyond the South

In July 1957 Pham Van Dong, Chairman of the Council of Ministers of North Vietnam, wrote to Ngo Dinh Diem, then President of South Vietnam, suggesting re-unification as set out in the Geneva agreement. Ngo, however, would not examine the subject unless South Vietnam received a guarantee that the Communists' supreme motive in re-unification was not imperialism. Later that year Ngo went to the United States for talks with President Eisenhower and to address Congress. Up until then all United States aid to South Vietnam was non-military—in 1956-57 this amounted to US$226 million—but, from that time onwards, slowly but inevitably, America found herself drawn increasingly deeper into the Indo-China War.

In the first half of 1965, American troops in the country numbered 25,000. By the middle of 1969 the American military strength had risen to only slightly less than 550,000, but from then onwards a steady withdrawal took effect, with "Vietnamisation" of combat forces the immediate goal. This policy was speeded up in 1970 as South Vietnam's forces had grown to over a million men an increase of 40 per cent over 1968, the year of general mobilisation. By summer 1971 the South Vietnam High Command assumed responsibility for all ground combat operations and official opinion was that the South could achieve victory over the North by 1973, despite the withdrawal of all allied forces—Australian, New Zealand, Thai, South Korean and Filipino—with only a residual United States force remaining.

Indeed, as 1971 drew to a close, it was the deteriorating economy that commanded increasing attention, prices continuing to climb and the inflationary spiral continuing to skyrocket through increases to military and civil service pay. In 1969 imports exceeded exports by 40 to 1. The piastre, the monetary unit, declined from its official market price of 80 to US$1 to an unofficial price of over 130 piastres to the dollar. The cost of living index, based on an index of 100 for 1963, went up to 580 in June 1970. Inevitably, economic difficulties fanned political discontent. Demonstrations by disabled veterans living on fixed incomes were common. They were joined by other anti-Government factions, particularly students and Buddhists.

But there were a number of encouraging signs that some of the war-engendered problems were being addressed with various measures of success. Vu Quoc Thuc, the Minister of State for Development, forecast that the national rate of production would be increased by 52 per cent in the 1970's to an equivalent of more than US$600 million annually. He also said the Government anticipated that rice production would reach 9.2 million tons a year by 1980, of which 1.5 million would be for export.

In August 1970 South Vietnamese voters cast their ballots for 30 members of the National Senate, one half the total body. Approximately 65 per cent of the eligible exercised their franchises. In October the same year, President Nguyen Van Thieu ran alone in an election when two other Presidential candidates withdrew after allegation of rigging. He was returned by a comfortable majority, despite severe criticism of his handling of the situation, both in the country and abroad. The victory confirmed him in power, endorsed his policies in the face of continuing American withdrawal and held out the promise of some political stability while his Government got to grips with its major problems.

For North Vietnam, the war situation changed suddenly and radically in early 1970, following the downfall of Prince Norodom Sihanouk in Cambodia. Traditional sanctuaries along the Cambodian border were destroyed, the Ho Chi Minh trail was disrupted and the fighting strength of the country was diminished. But the President, Ton Duc Thang, and the Premier, Pham Van Dong, in their public utterances, continued to maintain a firm line. Indeed, in August 1970 Hanoi's forces launched what Saigon described as "the heaviest artillery attacks in more than a year", along the demilitarised zone and the Laotian border.

Peace talks in Paris continued throughout 1971, but there was no progress. Hanoi found it unacceptable that United States withdrawals were tied to progress in building up the combat efficiency of the Saigon Government's army and reduction in the level of Communist military activity while the United States refused to withdraw on Communist terms.

As 1971 ended, there were hopes that peace would come to Vietnam as one of the results of President Nixon's visit to China in the spring of 1972. The country as a whole can be said to be tired of the war, though the Vietnamese realise that their history stands as a proof that they have always fought against overwhelming odds, have always persevered, and have never allowed adversity to suppress or disfigure the national spirit.

One of their great poets, Pham Ngo Lao, long ago, put it like this:

"My lance in hand, for years I have waged war across the kingdom, leading my valiant troops to battle, with untamed courage. To be worthy of the name, a man must pursue glory through the mightiest exploits. And, until he has succeeded, he should be ashamed to listen to the stories of the Heroes of the past".

LIFE IN SAIGON

Saigon, the capital of South Vietnam, used to be described as "the Paris of the Orient", but the end of French influence has caused some of the Gallic flavour also to retreat. Yet enough lingers in the air to give the city a remarkable individuality despite the inevitable encroachments of the war.

There are double rows of trees along fine boulevards, with public gardens, cafes, and open-air tables under colourful shades where the elite sip *aperitifs* and watch the passing parade.

Before the French conquest, Saigon, then known as Gai-dinh-thanh, was the capital of Lower Cochin-China, which consisted of six southern provinces of the Annamese empire, and constituted a viceroyalty under the government of a *kinhluoc*. The French captured it in 1859, and it was part of the territory ceded in 1862. During the Indo-Chinese war of 1946-54, the city was a centre for refugees.

With its wooden houses, its hedges alive with bamboo, its lakes of lotus, trees flaming with scarlet blossom, pagodas decorated with unicorns and dragons, its rice fields deep in water, the Vietnamese countryside around Saigon offers the most varied and picturesque of scenes.

There is the peasant labouring in his rice field, his plough drawn by a large black buffalo. He can be seen in the monsoon rain, latania-cloaked, sowing his paddy seed. Or, his face burned by the sun, body bathed in sweat, harvesting the rich crop of rice as the fruit of his labours.

In the summer he goes about almost naked. In winter his only garb is a tunic and trousers of blue vegetable-dyed cotton, with a hat and a cloak of palm leaves. On high days and holidays, he bedecks himself in a black turban, white trousers, and a long silken tunic.

Every day, throughout the year, he rises at cockcrow, wakes his wife and children, and the whole family takes up the daily round. The mother sets the rice to cook in a bowl made of dried earth. The children help her start the fire and wash the vegetables, while the father occupies himself with his tools, repairs the harrows and the ploughs, yokes the oxen and the buffalo. To the crow of the cock, the barking of dogs, the lowing of the cows, and the sound of bird calls, life begins each day in the Vietnamese village, as it does all over Southeast Asia.

The Vietnamese peasant works almost without ceasing throughout the seasons, resting only during the *Tet*, or the first days of the year, when he finds the time for household repairs, calls on friends, or works in the garden.

His emotional life revolves round his love for his wife and children. It consists also in exchanges of betel with the young women of the villages, in those poetic commonplaces which he addresses to his pretty neighbours.

The education of the Vietnamese peasant and his children comes through proverbs and popular songs, legends that are passed down from generation to generation, and which have a basis of popular wisdom. Vietnam, like all countries with an old civilisation, possesses a popular literature of great richness, largely composed of songs, and the most beautiful songs are those of love. In Vietnam, when a young man has the good fortune to meet a beautiful girl who attracts him, he offers a piece of betel and this enchanting song:

Since we meet each other here,
please accept a piece of betel,
A mere nothing,
but a form of introduction.
It is nothing,
a little piece of betel,
But it could forever unite
two beings in love.
In chewing betel one confides,
One weighs the pros and cons,
Chewing betel cherishes friendship
and prepares the way for love.

Among the sophisticated elements of the population, this idyllic intermingling of the betel with romance belongs to the past. The educated insist on ridding the peasantry of its dependence on the betel, and education is spreading. Statistics for 1967-68, the only available at the time of writing, show that there were 2,023,893 primary pupils under 34,066 teachers. Secondary pupils numbered 499,419 under 13,338 teachers and vocational pupils totalled 10,873 under 585 teachers. 3,118 teachers were undergoing training. Vietnamese taking higher studies numbered more than 33,930 under 914 lecturers.

Hanoi, the capital of North Vietnam, used to be the capital of Tonkin, on the right bank of the Red River, 80 miles from the Gulf of Tonkin. Beautiful Petit Lao separates the attractive former European quarter from the crowded districts stretching to the north-east.

The pagoda of the Great Buddha used to be a great tourist attraction. There is a regular launch service to Haiphong, and vessels up to 9 feet in draught can reach Hanoi when it is high water.

The city, the seat of numerous public and private bodies, is the transportation hub of northern Indo-China, and modern highways radiate to different points.

PREPARING FOR THE TET

TET, the Vietnamese Lunar New Year, usually happens a month after 31st December. With the passing of the years its celebration has been gradually changed, but the preparation for it almost remains the same. Even though the country is being torn mercilessly by the war and even though the cease-fire lasts not more than a couple of days during the solemn festival, nevertheless from the country to the city men, women, children, rich or poor are anxious to celebrate the anniversary.

It should be the most joyful day of the year because everybody has the opportunity to relax, visit the cemetery, pay respect to ancestors and visit relatives. In other respects its preparation for months before causes a lot of annoyances not only for the poor but also for the richest.

In the country, after the crops are brought to the barn, the landlord allows his farmhands to retire and sometimes gives them some bonuses, not in cash but in gifts such as the all important commodity, paddy rice. Here the atmosphere is not as feverish as in the city but, all the same, the people go about their preparations with much devotion and quiet ardour. The poor peasant, who during the year has been exhausted by his labour, now has to work even harder in the last days of the year in order to afford the new clothes and commodities his family needs to enjoy the TET.

All the flowers in the garden and fruit trees in the orchard are looked after with great care day and night. Approximately a week before the TET all the crops are rushed to the village market as well as to town. However, the best fruit remain as gifts for his relatives or neighbours and as offerings to ancestors.

The activity seems more vivacious in the evening. As it becomes darker, here and there, flickering lights appear from the thatched houses of the village. If we passed by one of them we would hear a hum like the buzz of a swarm of bees whose nest is broken. It is the chatting of the whole family who, gathering under the yellowish light of a kerosene lamp, are making the Banh Chung or Banh Tet, a kind of rice

A typical street scene in Saigon with people cooking on the sidewalk. Their food is mainly sun-dried fish, soup, and green vegetables flavoured with spices.

Opposite page:
The high cost of motor cars in Vietnam makes them prohibitive for the average citizen. The popular middle class vehicle is the motor cycle; hundreds of them jam the parking areas in Saigon.

cake filled with green peas and rolled in the leaves of banana trees. They have to keep awake and actually enjoy looking after it because the boiling goes on almost the whole night long.

This making of Banh Chung is the symbol of filial duty from children towards their parents. According to a myth, when the 16th Hung Vuong Emperor felt that he was dying, he called his children to his bed and asked them to prove their fidelity towards him, before he decided to whom to bequeath his throne. Thanks to his Banh Chung, the youngest prince became the heir because his cake was made of rice, the diamond of God, and had a square shape, representing the Earth. Ever since this rice cake has symbolised the duty of children to look on their parents as God.

Nowadays the people use the cake as a delicacy and as an offering to ancestors at TET and they are available at markets and shops for a week before the festival.

TET is also a great opportunity for the peasant to open his purse with pleasure, because during the year he has no time to think of himself. The tailors' and shoemakers' shops are bursting with clients although the prices are sometimes exorbitant. It is the time these tradesmen sit up all night doing their work.

After receiving the biggest possible amount of money for their goods, mothers and daughters bring back from the village or town market provisions, cakes, sweets or jams, for they will be able to enjoy at least three days of TET.

Fresh paint is applied to the houses. Old thatched roofs are recovered with new straw. Mud walls receive a new coat of white lime. Inside, the furniture, the ancestral altar particularly, is tended with care and sometimes polished again. Rich or poor, each one is trying to give his home a new face. The peasant believes with the new year he should have a new life, better and happier. Therefore he does not like to keep anything which has a link with the old year and its vestiges are wiped out.

In any case, the preparation for TET in the country is not so hectic as in town. In Saigon for instance, the bustle begins a month beforehand. Clerks in private firms, in addition to their wages for December, receive a bonus of a month's wages and are allowed to borrow another month's salary in advance. Public servants usually receive only an allowance of 4,000 piastres which is scarcely enough to prepare for TET.

The preparation is easily perceived around Saigon's Central Market. Rows of kiosks are quickly built around it where all kinds of goods, from inexpensive to valuable articles, are sold. Along Le Loi Boulevard in Saigon and Dong Khanh Boulevard in Cholon, bazaars have displays on the pavement. The vendors shout and scream at a high pitch, sometimes with microphones, to attract the crowds. Masses of vehicles jam the streets and pedestrians can hardly find a way through the sea of people. The Vietnamese love the beauty of flowers. No wonder then that the Nguyen Hue Boulevard instantly becomes a flower market where cars are prohibited for two weeks before TET. There we can find all sorts of flowers, both natural and artificial. Even for home decoration an extravagant purchaser may dare to pay 30,000 piastres for a branch of flowers from the peach tree. At the same time, hordes of beautiful girls stroll with their dainty mincing steps, just like "talking spring flowers". Every family, rich or poor, usually buys some watermelons for ornamentation on the altar, a pot of flowers, meat, cakes, jam, sweet lotus seeds and dry watermelon seeds as provisions for the celebrations. It creates a good opportunity for the pawn shops to receive a lot of clients, because the poor do not have any hesitation in borrowing money or putting their things in pawn to pay for TET preparations, even though from then onwards they will probably plunge even deeper into debt.

At present TET lasts not more than three days but everybody has to spend months for its preparation. Therefore the ecstasy of enjoying the TET sometimes changes its meaning and becomes only the relaxation of those strenuous days of overwork before the New Year Day. It is not without justification that some people have said that, if TET were abolished, they could live with ease and in peace.

580

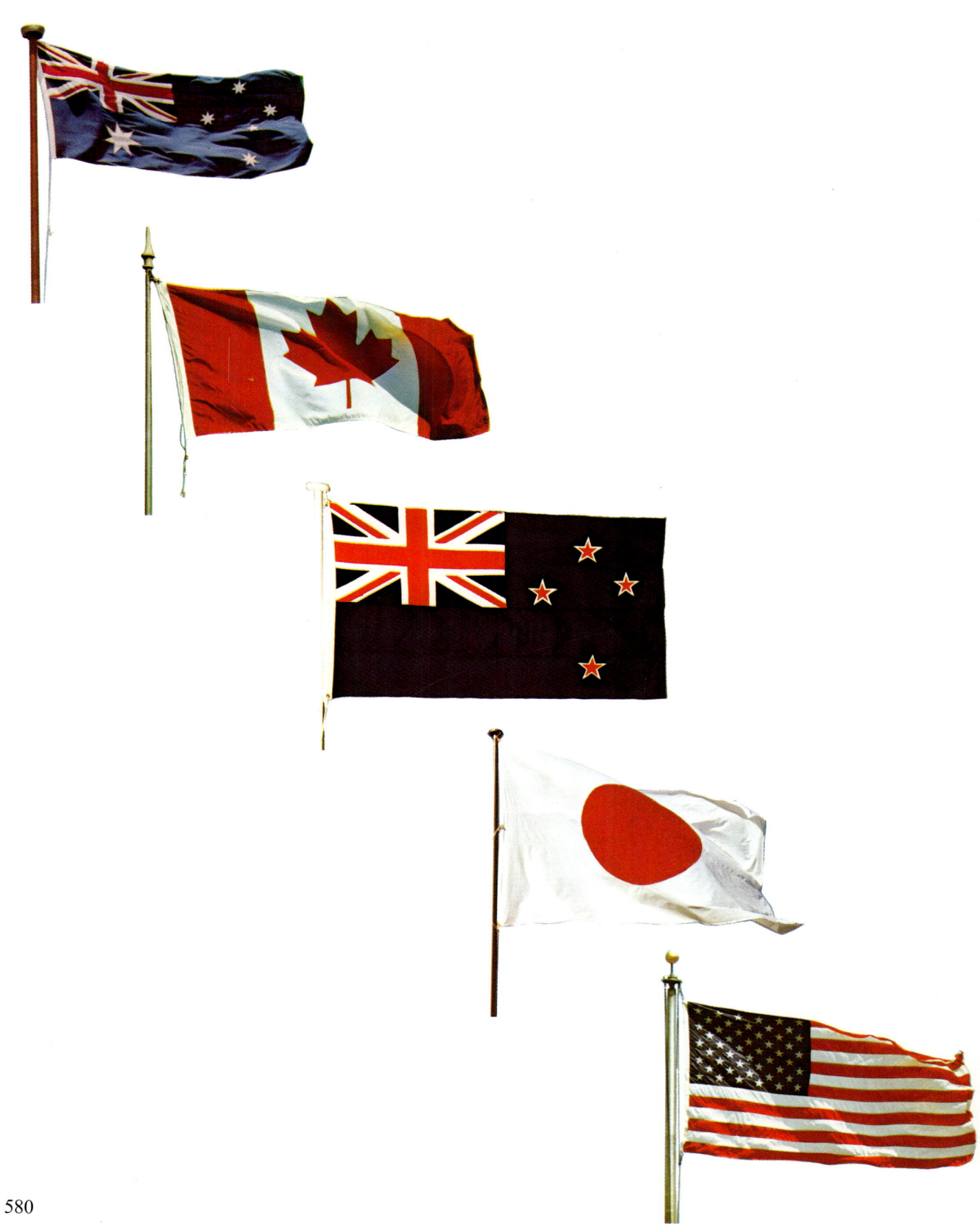

PACIFIC BASIN ECONOMIC COUNCIL

Pacific Basin Co-operation

BUSINESS CO-OPERATION between the nations of the world has long been a vital factor in the development of closer trading relations. Until the end of World War II individual companies accepted this as their responsibility but the post war period and the inevitable problems of rehabilitation have brought about a new phenomenon—the forming of Business Co-operation Committees.

Since 1960 when the first of these Committees was created, between Australia and Japan, others have been formed and are growing in strength and influence. As a medium for forging close ties between private enterprises of different countries, this plan is unique and clearly effective. Far reaching results have flowed from the meetings of the most distinguished of these co-operation bodies, the Pacific Basin Economic Council, a five-nation multilateral forum founded in 1967 by senior businessmen from Australia, Japan, the United States, Canada and New Zealand. PBEC, as it is termed, is the natural corollary of Australia's lead to the rest of the world in 1961 with the formation of the bilateral Australia-Japan Business Co-operation Committee.

Both PBEC and the A-JBCC are proof of the tangible and intangible benefits of person-to-person contact between leading businessmen of different countries. Initially participation in PBEC was limited to members from the five nations but the concept was not that of a "rich man's club" between them. Rather the idea was that at a later stage participation would be opened to other emerging countries, and today guest observers from the developing nations of the Pacific Basin are attending its conferences.

PBEC speaks with authority on specific projects for manufacturing, primary industry, mining, banking and commercial interests at annual conferences held each year on a rotational basis in the countries of member nations. It researches in depth a broad range of problems and topics, from tariff and non-tariff barriers, from two-way trade to joint ventures.

Although PBEC and its constituent National Committees maintain liaison with many governments and international agencies, the organisation operates entirely under private auspices. While members are organised in five separate national groups, they participate in PBEC as individuals. They seek to share the problems and the opportunities for peaceful enterprise in a changing world.

PBEC held its first meeting in Sydney, Australia in 1968, its second in San Francisco, U.S.A. in 1969, its third in Kyoto, Japan in 1970. Its fourth conference in Vancouver, Canada in 1971 drew 272 official delegates and non-member observers. It is a prime example of what private co-operation can achieve in a variety of areas so vital to the mutually beneficial development of commercial links in this era of fast-growing international interdependence.

Human resources development plays an integral part in PBEC's attack on the two principal handicaps to economic growth of the Pacific Basin region: lack of capital for equipment to lift productivity and lack of technical and managerial skills and experience to organise industrial operations. It was PBEC that led, for example, to the formation of the Private Investment Company for Asia (PICA)—a US$20 million regional joint investment company to facilitate capital investment in Asia. Its main sources of funds are companies from the private sectors of the five advanced nations of the area. PBEC is examining proposals to co-operate with PICA in the development of technical training in Indonesia, and, at the same time, assist PICA's development in that region.

During April-May 1971 businessmen of the five member nations collaborated to hold a 16-day Ocean Seminar to help train middle management executives. Twenty-seven executives, sponsored by their firms, spent five days at the East West Centre of Hawaii, before joining the Seminar ship S.S. "Wilson" to continue

The Hon. Sir Edward Warren
K.C.M.G., K.B.E., M.S.M., O.M.S.T.,
R.S.G.C., M.L.C.

study of a broad range of subjects as the liner made for San Francisco. Participants then attended the 4th General Meeting of PBEC in Vancouver.

One outstanding benefit derived from this meeting was that future leaders of their Companies got to know each other, to understand each other's thinking, and to cut through racial and national differences.

PBEC resolved at its Canada meeting to make concerted efforts to persuade individual governments to explore both multilateral and bilateral avenues, with a purpose to reducing or eliminating the non-tariff barriers on international trade.

Transportation—the need to improve services—is another key facet to PBEC's extensive role in accelerating the development of natural resources, trade and economic growth. It is confident that, as a sequel to its representations, greater importance will be given in future foreign aid programmes to the provision of improved harbours, airports, rail, road and harbour transfer facilities.

PBEC's influence is reflected in the Japanese Government's policy to allocate more than US$4 million in the 1971-72 fiscal year towards research and practical aid to developing countries through the intermediary of their International Development Centre, International Co-operation Chamber and Advisory Group to Indonesia.

It was PBEC's dedication and enthusiasm—its realistic approach to problems—

that led to the creation early in 1970 of the Australia-Korea Business Co-operation Council. Its second joint meeting was held in Seoul in October 1971.

PBEC's terms of reference are wide. Its covenant, adopted at its First General Meeting, maintains that the Council will engage in the following multilateral activities:

(A) 1. Expansion of trade; 2. Facilitation of exchange of capital and industrial technologies; 3. Promotion of tourism; 4. Conducting joint studies, exchanging relevant economic information and clarification of economic problems; 5. Promotion of cultural and scientific exchange.

(B) Co-operation with the developing countries in their efforts to achieve self-sustaining economic growth including, for example:

1. Promotion of capital and technological co-operation and agriculture, mining and other industrial fields; 2. Promotion of trade in the products of the developing countries; 3. Promotion of cultural and scientific exchange; 4. Promotion of tourism.

PBEC represents a grouping of countries whose populations and combined gross national products easily outstrip those of the European Economic Community. But early in its planning there was agreement that PBEC would not be aimed at establishing a Pacific free trade area. As there was no basis for liberalising capital and labour movements between the five nations, it was considered that it would be extremely difficult to establish a relationship along "common market" lines.

The view was held that the five Pacific nations were constituted differently from the nations of the European Economic Community and that the formation of a Pacific Basin common market type of body would not produce the same benefits to the member countries as those achieved in Europe. But there was agreement that, with the increasing world emphasis on regional trading blocs, the advanced nations of the Pacific area should attempt, even in a small way, some type of multilateral international co-operation that would best serve their own future development and the advancement of the lesser developed countries in the region.

PBEC's objectives are not grandiose. Nor are they theoretical. They are attainable, worthwhile goals. Developing nations are realising that a utilisation of the combined skills of the members of the PBEC can be mutually beneficial.

International tourism is a key plank in PBEC's programme for progress and development because of its role as an earner of foreign exchange for many specific countries. It will urge national tourist organisations of all Pacific Area Travel Association areas to co-operate with PATA and other international bodies in an effort to produce Pacific travel statistics in a standardised, comparable form.

Members feel that where total removal of travel restrictions is not possible then member governments should—where appropriate—urgently consider modifying and ameliorating existing restrictions, so that movements of tourism from one country to another will not be hindered.

At a conference of the five national committees held at Honolulu during October-November 1971 the objectives of PBEC were further amplified.

PBEC speaks for more than 400 leading companies in the five member countries and in its dedication to promoting trade and closer economic ties between its members and the developing nations, a draft of guide lines for improving investment opportunities in the Pacific Basin was submitted.

The viability of an international investment code also had been assessed. The members, aware of the importance of private overseas investment in economic development, are convinced that something must be done to counter the deterioration of the investment climate throughout the world.

In pledging their support for a Pacific Basin Charter, each of the five national committees of PBEC undertook to review the draft plan submitted by the United States Committee, before it is put to a collective vote in New Zealand in 1972. The U.S. Committee also suggested that the Pacific Basin Charter project might be followed in due course by a study of the concept of "World Corporations" with particular reference to the Pacific Basin. The basic idea is to study ways and means of stimulating multi-national joint ventures in the Pacific area.

It was agreed that private training schemes for middle-management and technicians from developing countries would be considered in Wellington. Already the Australian Committee has initiated two training schemes in negotiations with the Australian Government. It is seeking the full co-operation of its 54 Australian members' firms to help place Government sponsored trainees from Pacific Basin countries in industry in Australia and to provide twelve months' practical experience for overseas graduates—mostly from Colombo Plan countries.

PBEC's Transport Committee has been studying Pacific cargo flows in an attempt to rationalise shipping services and to eliminate a ballast leg from some voyages.

To cope with the world-wide problem of pollution PBEC proposes moving in Wellington for the establishment of its 6th Committee—one on environment. Japan's delegates will propose the setting up of a Pacific centre to deal with environment standards, control, costs, and preventive technology.

The Natural Resources Committee of PBEC is listing present and planned sources of anti-pollution information in member countries for consideration.

At Wellington PBEC will again throw open its international meeting to chosen observers from some developing countries of the Pacific Basin. The Steering Committee in Honolulu agreed to invite observers from Hong Kong, Indonesia, Philippines, South Korea, South Vietnam, Singapore, Taiwan, Fiji, Thailand and Malaysia. An observer will also be invited from PICA.

More than 250 business leaders from the five member nations of PBEC have agreed to attend the 1972 conference at the Victoria University in Wellington.

As PBEC consolidates it will develop its "aid through trade" concept and step up joint researches and expansion of resources of the Pacific area—the largest in the world. Its challenges are exciting and potentially rewarding in an area of great diversity, an area that is perhaps the most retarded in the trend towards regionalisation.

PBEC will continue to gather strength through full communication of thought and genuine understanding as it reaches out to help countries of the Pacific Basin.

At the opening of the Australia-Japan Business Co-operation Committee Conference at Kyoto on 5th April 1972, it was announced that the Emperor of Japan had conferred upon Sir Edward Warren the Order of the Sacred Treasure 1st Class. This was the first time that this Order—one of the highest of all Japanese honours— had ever been awarded to a non-Japanese.

The Hon. Sir Edward Warren, K.C.M.G., K.B.E., M.S.M., O.M.S.T., R.S.G.C., M.L.C.
President of the Pacific Basin Economic Council

AUSTRALIA'S ROLE IN ASIAN DEVELOPMENT

THERE IS NO AREA of the world in greater need of economic aid than South and South-east Asia. The World Bank has been active in bringing aid to the countries of the region and in 1965 member countries of the United Nations Economic Commission for Asia and the Far East (ECAFE) created the Asian Development Bank; but the main vehicle for assistance to this vast region for the past two decades has been the Colombo Plan. Australian initiative helped to create this Plan at the Commonwealth Foreign Ministers Conference in Colombo in January 1950, when the Australian delegation was led by Sir Percy Spender. Ever since its inception, all but a very small proportion of Australia's bilateral aid for Southern and South-east Asian countries has been provided from funds recorded in reports as "Colombo Plan Aid". However all bilateral assistance to the area is reported to the Colombo Plan Consultative Committee as part of Australia's effort and may be collectively considered as aid within the general framework of the Plan.

The Colombo Plan is not a plan in the sense of a blueprint for economic development. There is no overall programming; no central fund. Co-operation between member countries is the essential factor by which the efficient working of the Plan is assured. All aid is negotiated between the two countries involved, the recipient and donor. The donor provides aid only at the request and according to the needs of the recipient.

The aims of the Plan are simple and are described by Lester B. Pearson, former Prime Minister of Canada; "Our main efforts will have to continue to be directed to the age-old tasks of irrigating and enriching the land, cutting the timber, bringing up the ore from below the ground, improving the means of transport, generating energy from all available sources, building up sound and productive industries and combating disease". The Colombo Plan has been one of the most successful schemes in furthering these efforts. Structurally it consists of an annual ministerial meeting of a Consultative Committee—the senior policy making body—whose task it is to review economic development in the region, the Colombo Plan Council for Technical Co-operation which meets regularly in Colombo to co-ordinate and promote technical assistance in the region, and the Colombo Plan Bureau in Colombo which maintains records and disseminates information.

ORIGINS. The Colombo Conference of Commonwealth Foreign Ministers in January 1950 established a Consultative Committee, the original seven members of which—Australia, Canada, Ceylon, India, New Zealand, Pakistan and the United Kingdom—together with the then associated territories of Malaya and British Borneo, took part in the first meeting of the Consultative Committee in May 1950. They decided that the Asian members should prepare development plans for a six-year period from 1st July 1951 and set up arrangements for a technical co-operation scheme designed to provide training, technical experts and equipment in an effort to build up the basic skills essential for development. The Colombo Plan came into being effectively from 1st July 1951.

Since that time membership has grown to 24: Afghanistan, Australia, Bhutan, Britain, Burma, Canada, Ceylon, India, Indonesia, Iran, Japan, Khmer Republic, Republic of Korea, Laos, Malaysia, Republic of Maldives, Nepal, New Zealand, Pakistan, Philippines, Singapore, Thailand, United States of America and the Republic of Vietnam.

FORMS OF AID. Australian aid to the Colombo Plan countries can be divided roughly into two basic categories, capital aid and technical assistance. Capital aid covers funds for development projects, the supply of commodities including food grains, fertilisers and consumer goods, and specialised equipment including machinery, farm and laboratory equipment and transport vehicles. These types of aid help to build up the basic economic infrastructure necessary for development. Technical assistance covers all aspects of training, including provision of technical experts, facilities for study for trainees and students, and supply of equipment for training and research.

Capital aid projects have absorbed the greater part of the aid given. Thus, much effort has gone into roads, bridges and dams, railways, communications networks, and afterwards, into modernising agriculture, establishing secondary industries and adequate health facilities.

Two major examples of capital aid projects are the Mekong River Development Project in Indo-China and the Indus Basin Development Project in Pakistan. Australia is one of several donor countries which contribute expertise and capital for these projects.

A modern economy needs people who have technical skills. Technical assistance from all donors between 1950 and 1969 to Southern and South-east Asian countries under the Colombo Plan totalled US$1,369 million. Of this amount, 18 per cent was spent on 65,544 students, 49 per cent on 12,989 experts and 33 per cent on technical and research equipment.

The Colombo Plan is a co-operative effort in which every member country is willing

Left:
Irrigation has proved
a boon to Philippine farmers.
Scientific advice and funds provided
by P.B.E.C. countries have made
such fine crops as this
possible.

Opposite page:
Through the Colombo Plan,
Australia is contributing
substantially to the education of
South-east Asian children. This picture,
as a typical example,
was taken at a school
at Vuyyuru, India.

to help. But the bulk of aid is provided by the main group of donor countries comprising Australia, Britain, Canada, Japan, New Zealand, and the United States. Together these countries have given capital aid and technical assistance of nearly US$30 billion.

AUSTRALIA'S AID TO COLOMBO PLAN COUNTRIES. Australia has been a strong supporter of the Colombo Plan since its inception. Apart from aid to the Territory of Papua New Guinea more than 90 per cent of all Australian aid given on a bilateral basis has been to countries in South and South-east Asia. Up to June 1971 this amounted to more than $A340 million and the rate has been increasing during the last ten years. In 1970-71, expenditure on Colombo Plan aid was approximately $A40 million.

Indonesia is at present the largest recipient of Australian Colombo Plan aid. From $A1,500,000 in 1965-66 it has expanded to $A15,500,000 in 1970-71. Over the whole period of the Plan, however, the major recipient of Australian aid has been India. Australian expenditure to 31st December 1970 in the form of capital aid, technical assistance, food and other aid, totalled $A319,774,000, divided among the following Asian countries: Afghanistan, Bhutan, Brunei, Burma, Ceylon, India, Indonesia, Iran, Khmer Republic, Korea, Laos, Malaysia, Maldive Islands, Nepal, Pakistan, Philippines, Singapore, Thailand and Vietnam.

TECHNICAL SKILLS. By December 1970, over 10,000 students from South and South-east Asia had received awards for study or training in Australia.

They came from almost all countries in the region and studied and trained in many different fields. Agriculture and food production were the most popular courses of study. Other important fields of training have included engineering, science, education, medicine and public health and public administration. Over the years the Department of Foreign Affairs has acquired wide experience in arranging short intensive training courses in such fields as trade promotion, rural broadcasting, customs administration, road and bridge design, conservation, and aspects of agriculture.

Australia has provided education for about 30,000 private students from South and South-east Asia over the last twenty years. These students pay fees but the full cost of their education is an indirect form of aid from the Australian people whose taxes support the universities and schools. Australia also provides awards for students from one Colombo Plan country to study in a second member country other than Australia.

Australia is sending experts and teachers to the developing countries of South and South-east Asia. They supervise afforestation programmes in Nepal, direct the installation of communications networks in Pakistan, Indonesia and Malaysia, advise on road building in Thailand and Sabah, assist in education programmes, particularly the teaching of English, in many countries. Over 1,800 visits have been made to Asia by Australian experts and advisers in the twenty years since 1951, about 130 during the year 1970-71.

In 1970 a new scheme was established to encourage co-operation between Australian universities and universities in Indonesia, Malaysia and Singapore. Called the Australian/Asian University Aid and Co-operation Scheme, it provides fellowships for research and staff training in Australia, travel awards for Australian staff to work in universities in Indonesia, Malaysia and Singapore and also provides for gifts of books and laboratory equipment. In 1970-71 about $A138,000 was allocated to the scheme.

FOREIGN EXCHANGE SUPPORT. In certain circumstances an effective form of aid is by direct support of a recipient country's balance of payments. Foreign exchange is given to the recipient country and this is used to import material for economic development. For example, with other major donor countries, Australia has provided foreign exchange under the Devisa Kredit (DK) system to enable Indonesia to import Australian goods. (Devisa Kredit used to be known as Bonus Export (BE) Aid). Trucks, aluminium sheeting, chemicals, tinplate and farming equipment have been bought by Indonesia under this system. In 1970-71 about $A5.2 million of the $A15,500,000 aid to Indonesia was in this form.

By June 1971, Australia had allocated about $A4,300,000 to Laos through the Foreign Exchange Operations Fund set up in 1963. This fund is part of an economic stabilisation plan for Laos drawn up by the International Monetary Fund. Its purpose is to maintain a stable foreign exchange rate for the Laotian kip and to restrain inflationary trends, and it permits the Laotian Government to incur a budgetary deficit so that it can carry out essential programmes.

FOOD AID. Australia has provided food in the form of grains to help feed people living in areas struck by drought and natural disaster or otherwise unable to provide enough food for their own needs.

Food aid is not simply a hand out: it is an effective method of enabling developing countries to divert foreign exchange from the purchase of food to their development programmes. In the past, Australia made large gifts of food within the framework of the Colombo Plan, mainly to Ceylon, India and Pakistan. During the 1960's gifts of wheat to India were greatly increased because of severe droughts in the sub-continent. Since 1967-68 Australia has been a signatory to the Food Aid Convention of the International Grains Agreement. Under this convention, developed countries agreed to provide annually 4,5000,000 tons of wheat as food aid up to 30th June 1971, of which Australia's contribution was 225,000 metric tons of grains annually, valued at about $A12 million. In 1971 the International Grains Agreement was succeeded by the International Wheat Agreement which also embraces a Food Aid Convention. Australia again accepted a commitment to provide 225,000 metric tons of grains annually for the three years' period commencing 1st July 1971.

PROJECTS. Australia has undertaken a wide variety of aid projects of which the following are examples:

Road Construction in Thailand. The first of these was a network of feeder roads at Khon Kaen in north-east Thailand from 1962 to 1966. It involved the building of 105 miles of all weather roads and 33 miles of access roads. The Australian contribution to the project, which was managed by the Snowy Mountains Hydro-Electric Authority, came to the amount of $3,600,000 whilst the Thai Government provided $A2,600,000. Australia supplied heavy equipment, and 39 experts, including engineers, supervisors, instructors, geologists and accountants, to participate in the project over the course of four years. The Thai Highways Department supplied buildings, material, staff and labour.

One of the aims of the project was to train Thais in all aspects of roadbuilding and maintenance. During the life of the project 40 Thai engineers, 160 operators, 80 mechanics and 30 supervisors received onsite training and others were trained in Australia.

A further joint project, begun in 1966 and completed in 1970, was the construction of the Tak-Mae Sod Highway, a 53-mile stretch of the Asian Highway through mountainous terrain in north-western Thailand. Australia contributed about $A11 million or about one-third of the total cost. Another section of the main East-West Highway in Thailand between Lomsak and Chumpae is being constructed with Australian assistance. Road construction in southern Thailand began in January 1971.

Mekong Basin Project. Australia is contributing an estimated $A1.9 million to the Prek Thnot project in the Khmer Republic which is part of the overall Mekong Basin Development. The project is supported by twelve donor countries at an estimated cost of $20 million. Australia is making available the Snowy Mountains Engineering Corporation for the survey, design and supervision of the construction of the storage dam, diversion weir, hydro-electric power station of 18 megawatts capacity, and irrigation facilities which make up the project. In addition it has pledged $A564,000 in cash to the Nam Ngum hydro-electric and irrigation project in Laos, which is also part of the Mekong Basin Development.

AUSTRALIA'S TOTAL AID. Australia is involved with other international organisations concerning aid to developing countries: the Asian Development Bank, the United Nations and its specialised agencies, the Economic Commission for Asia and the Far East (ECAFE) and the World Bank and its various consultative groups. In 1966 Australia joined the Development Assistance Committee (DAC) of the Organisation for Economic Co-operation and Development (OECD) in order to develop closer relations with Western aid donors.

Australia's cumulative expenditure to 30th June 1970 was $A1451.6 million, consisting of $A317.2 million bilateral aid, $A206.0 multilateral aid, and $A928.4 million to Papua New Guinea. Estimates for the fiscal year 1970-71 provided for a total of $A186 million.

About two-thirds of Australia's aid expenditure goes to Papua New Guinea where the Commonwealth has the primary responsibility for economic development.

In recent years between 7 and 10 per cent of official aid has been given annually to the major multilateral aid agencies of which Australia is a member. 20 to 25 per cent is bilateral aid of which nine-tenths goes to Colombo Plan countries. All Australian aid is by direct grant. Leaving Papua New Guinea aside, assistance provided under Australia's bilateral and multilateral programmes expanded from $A29,400,000 in 1964-65 to nearly $A50,000,000 in 1969-70, an increase of over 70 per cent in a period of five years.

VOLUNTARY AID. Australia's official aid is supplemented by a significant contribution from voluntary organisations. The Australian Council of Overseas Aid, formed in 1965, is the main co-ordinating agency for 30 non-governmental bodies concerned with international development.

The Council estimates that in the calendar year 1969 the value of voluntary aid from Australian sources was more than $A13,000,000. The number of volunteers sponsored by member organisations of the Council serving in overseas countries in 1969 was 245.

TWENTY YEARS OF AUSTRALIAN AID. Twenty years is too short a time to bring about a complete change in the welfare of 1,000 million people. However, a substantial contribution has been made to the progress of social and economic development of Asia by donor countries such as Australia, through bilateral assistance and the multilateral aid agencies.

The effectiveness of aid for development depends substantially on the level of contributions of all donor countries, particularly the larger economic powers who are able to contribute more. Australia's contribution to development aid is part of the total effort and her record as a donor country has been a good one. For several years she has ranked third among all western donors in official aid expressed as a percentage of Gross National Product. In 1970 this was 0.59 per cent.

NEW ZEALAND AND PBEC

WITH THE INCREASING attention being focused on the Pacific Basin, its people and emerging countries, the multi-national Pacific Basin Economic Council promises to assume a new and more important role in the future. The entry of Britain into the European Economic Community has accentuated this and as far as New Zealand is concerned a steady upsurge in interest can be detected through an increasing awareness of PBEC.

New Zealand's participation in PBEC is sponsored by four national organisations: the Bankers' Association, the Associated Chambers of Commerce of New Zealand, the Federated Farmers of New Zealand and the New Zealand Manufacturers' Federation. These sponsors have secured a place for New Zealand in debating important issues which affect, or will affect, the development of trade and human relations in the vast and vital area of the Pacific Basin.

The New Zealand Committee has adopted the following seven point plan in pursuit of the overall objects of the Pacific Basin Economic Council:

a) To combine with other member nations in achieving the aims and objectives of the Pacific Basin Economic Council as defined in Article A of the PBEC Covenant confirmed at the annual general meeting in San Francisco;

b) To constitute the membership of the New Zealand Committee and Executive so as to ensure that full recognition is made of PBEC's role as a private enterprise organisation;

c) To make special efforts to obtain better access to world markets for New Zealand exports and, in particular, agricultural products;

d) To promote and increase trading opportunities for New Zealand abroad by means of mutual co-operation, development and technical assistance;

e) To encourage New Zealand participation in investment programmes in the Pacific Basin both within and outside the Private Investment Company for Asia;

f) To encourage and promote tourist business in general and, in particular, among countries in the Pacific Basin;

g) To foster actively the above objectives in a way which will encourage participation by major New Zealand companies and organisations in activities in the Pacific Basin.

Article A of the PBEC Covenant referred to in (a) above reads as follows:

1. To promote economic collaboration among the member countries, including expansion of trade, exchange of capital and industrial technology, promotion of tourism, joint studies, exchange of economic information, clarification of economic problems and promotion of cultural and scientific pursuits.

2. To co-operate with the developing countries in their efforts to achieve self sustaining economic growth including, for example, the promotion of capital and technology in agriculture, mining and other industrial fields, the expansion of trade in products of the developing countries, the development of cultural and scientific exchange and the promotion of tourism.

In particular the New Zealand Committee has maintained an active interest in the progress of the recently established University of the South Pacific in Fiji. Recognising that a prime need exists for lower and middle management training in the area before solid progress can be made, the New Zealand Committee is maintaining a close liaison with the New Zealand Government which has already made available to the University the land and buildings which once comprised the Royal New Zealand Air Force base at Laucala Bay. Further plans to assist the University are being studied by the Government at the present time.

As an example of the multi-national co-operation becoming evident in PBEC it is of interest to note that the Canadian Government in 1970 made a splendid contribution to the University in cash, equipment and provision of qualified staff to the value of NZ$250,000.

This year PBEC celebrated its fifth birthday when the annual conference was held in Wellington during May. A Central Planning Executive was established in 1971 and through the various functions it has organised New Zealand looks forward to renewing acquaintance with top executives from the world of commerce in Japan, Australia, Canada and the U.S.A.

To quote the late Theodore Roosevelt:
"The greatest of all the seas and the last to be used on a large scale by civilised man bids fair to become, in its turn, the first in importance."

An agricultural instructor with a class of New Zealand and Colombo Plan students, at a trial testing of corn varieties at Lincoln College, Christchurch.

THE NATION BUILDERS

IN THE PRESENT century the world has seen a complete metamorphosis of the pattern of life. From the relatively primitive, civilisation has moved to the highly sophisticated. The house of the ordinary man has become a home with every accessory and facility for comfortable living the architect can devise. Commercial and industrial buildings of skyscraping heights and massive proportions have been created with interior decors and modern amenities to attract and interest office staffs and factory workers.

On desert wastes vast mining complexes have arisen. In remote mountain ranges hydro-electric power stations have been constructed, providing light and power for new towns; mighty rivers divert into reservoirs for the irrigation of parched, desolate plains, transforming them into lush pasture lands.

These have been accomplished in a few short decades and in the 1970's the race to achievement has almost reached fever pitch. Nearly every country is undergoing development to a major or minor degree and in no part of the world is activity more in evidence than in the Pacific Basin regions.

The driving force behind this phenomenon are the Nation Builders, mammoth international corporations with the resources, equipment and technical know-how to make the most apparently impossible constructional projects feasible.

The year 1890 saw the birth of one such body, now the sixth biggest construction corporation in the world. It took place in Oshkosh, Wisconsin in the U.S.A. when John Simon (Si), Ralph and Casper Fluor founded the Fluor Brothers Construction Company with a capital of only US$100. Originally a skilled carpenter in the tiny Swiss village of Saas, Si migrated to the States to join his brothers who had already established themselves as construction engineers. Their first commissions were to build paper mills, saw mills and ice houses for logging companies in Wisconsin.

For 24 years the partnership prospered and then Si decided to move to California where he and his wife and five children settled in Santa Ana. Si started a construction firm of his own. Many office and bank buildings built by Si Fluor in his early days in California are still standing as monuments to his craftsmanship.

One of Si's major attributes—his integrity and his principle of scrupulously fair dealing with all his clients—is still reflected in the organisation that bears his name today. One of his early achievements was the patenting of a method of pre-casting concrete which proved so highly successful that in Southern California's disastrous earthquake in March 1933 none of his buildings were demaged.

In 1915 the Fluor family received their first contract for the oil and gas industry when the Southern Counties Gas Company hired them to build meter shops and an office building. Then came the California oil strikes of 1919 and Fluor was commissioned to construct a compressor station for the Industrial Fuel Supply Company, pumping natural gas to cities in Southern California. From compressors Si progressed to water cooler systems and he designed and built his first "Buddha" tower at Signal Hill, California; it had a cooling capacity of 1,000 gallons a minute. The demand for this plant made it necessary to add a new factory at Compton. As the oil boom extended Fluor went into refinery and natural gasoline plant construction.

In 1924, when the family was incorporated as Fluor Construction Company with a capital investment of US$100,000, Si was named President and his four sons were appointed to the Board of Directors. Si Junior was Assistant General Manager to his eldest brother Pete. At that time the firm had 100 employees.

In September 1929, only a month before the Wall Street Market crash, the company reincorporated as The Fluor Corporation Ltd. The following year brought the opportunity to extend operations beyond California when the mid-continent of the U.S.A. began its oil and gas boom. Fluor opened an office in Kansas City to handle a big project involving the building of compressor stations on a pipeline between Panhandle, Texas, and Indianapolis, Indiana. This was virtually the beginning of the Fluor construction work-force that developed into the vast organisation it is today.

From the Panhandle pipeline came a US $100,000 refining unit for the Shell Oil Company at Wood River, Illinois, and in

Some projects completed by the Fluor organisation:

Chin-Shui Natural Gas Processing Plant for the Chinese Petroleum Corporation, Taiwan, Republic of China.

Below: A 20,000 B/D refinery constructed for the Mobil Refining Company at Singapore.

1933 the first overseas venture began with the erection of cooling towers for an oil refinery at Bahrein Island in the Persian Gulf.

During the Depression of the 1930's the Fluor Company was hard pressed to avoid a total collapse but the family drew on their own personal fortunes to avoid a complete shut down.

When World War II seemed certain to envelop the U.S.A. Fluor gambled that their services would be in greater demand than ever. They bought property in East Los Angeles—now the City of Commerce —and there established the company's headquarters where it still remains today. By 1940 vast quantities of high-octane gasoline were needed for the armed forces and Fluor was commissioned to design and install a sulphuric acid alkylation plant for Sinclair Oil Company at its Richfield refinery in Watson, California. This was the first of many similar projects carried out by Fluor in the next four years during which America became directly involved in hostilities. In that period almost one-third of all

Above: The Island Bend Dam under construction by Fluor—one of the major projects of the Snowy Mountains Hydro-Electric Scheme, Australia.

year. A Gasoline Division was formed at Houston, Texas—the forerunner of today's Houston Division. A major construction for the Arabian American Oil Company in Saudi Arabia gave the company invaluable experience in planning and executing foreign projects. In the U.K. an affiliation agreement was arranged with Head Wrightson for cooling tower sales and service.

In 1949 the Fluor Corporation of Canada was established as a subsidiary and in 1950 for the first time projects were undertaken for the U.S. Government involving gasoline and power plants and the construction of a large materials Testing Reactor for the Atomic Energy Commission in Arco, Idaho.

With the outbreak of the Korean War there were immediate demands for increased output of vital petroleum products and Fluor's experience in this field placed it in an advantageous position. On the death of Pete Fluor, Si Jnr. became President in 1952 and under his guidance the company expanded overseas and entered an era of diversification, especially into the fields of multiple construction. At this time also Pete's son J. Robert Fluor was elected to the Board. Later he succeeded his uncle Si and became Chairman and Chief Executive Officer, a position he still holds today.

During the early 1950's Fluor obtained contracts for refining complexes in San Juan, Puerto Rico and for the U.S. Air Force at Dhahran Air Base in Saudi Arabia. During the 1950's Fluor established branches and formed joint associations in France, Britain, other European countries and the Middle East and extended further representations in the U.S.A., Canada and South America but important as these developments were the highlight of all its activities was the purchase of the worldwide heavy construction assets of Utah Construction & Mining Company of San Francisco on 25th July 1969.

the 100-octane gasoline plants erected in the States were built by Fluor and the Research Division earlier established was worked under abnormal pressure to evolve new techniques.

Si Senior died in 1944 and with Pete as President the sons carried on the traditions so well founded by their father. The following year Fluor handled a refinery expansion in Canada for the Shell Oil Company of British Columbia. In South America a contract was secured to build a natural gasoline plant for the Compania Consolidada de Petroleo of Venezuela. In 1946 the most significant job in the firm's history was undertaken—the construction of a grass-roots refinery for the Carter Oil Company at Billings, Montana—which established Fluor as a major engineer-constructor in this field. 1948 was a vital

Above: Kingsway Bridge and overpass crossing the Yarra River, Melbourne, Australia.

Right: Interior of the Manapouri Hydro-Electric complex, about 100 miles from Invercargill, New Zealand.

Early in 1950 Fluor came to Australia to build the Big Eildon Dam in Victoria and thus laid the foundations of one of the dominant influences in engineering construction in this fast developing land. Since then Fluor Australia Pty. Ltd. has been established to continue the work already begun as a division of Utah. Its engineers have gone out to the very edges of the continent to start up mines in Western Australia, to drive tunnels for the great Snowy Mountains Hydro-Electric Scheme, to build factories, refineries, power stations, bridges and safe ports for shipping. Fluor Australia has extended its operations to New Zealand where it built the Manapouri tail race tunnel and hydro-electric complex, to the Pacific Islands and many parts of South-east Asia. At Bougainville Island in a joint venture it has constructed plant for the copper mines of Conzinc Riotinto; in New Guinea and New Caledonia it has carried out constructional feasibility tests; it has built fertiliser plants in South Korea and acid plants in India; it has designed and constructed petroleum complexes in Singapore and Malaysia and built the Yankee Dam in Thailand. In Taiwan Fluor has built petroleum plant for the Government's Chinese Petroleum Corporation and completed military installations in Vietnam.

With almost unlimited mineral resources being uncovered in many parts of Australia Fluor will play a dominant part in future development not only of mining projects but in the establishment of new communities. Today Fluor Corporation Ltd. is big business and one of the really great Nation Builders. Its annual completed contracts total over US$400 million plus a backlog of work in hand worth more than US$600 million. Its enterprises reach to nineteen countries and construction workers and office staffs number more than 20,000; a far cry from Si Fluor's little firm that began 80 years ago with a capital of US$100.

Right: One of three off-shore oil rigs constructed by Fluor. The picture shows it standing on a monopod platform in Cook Island, Alaska.

Opposite page:
The imposing Main Office
of The Chartered Bank in Singapore
is reminiscent of earlier colonial days.

Below:
The development of the steel industry
in Thailand has been strongly supported
by The Chartered Bank.

Below right:
The tea industry
is the most important contributor
to the national wealth
of Sri Lanka (Ceylon).

BRITISH OVERSEAS BANKS

THE IMPORTANCE OF TRADE to the Orient can scarcely be exaggerated, for today as in the past it represents the key to the prosperity of the region as a whole.

Throughout the 19th Century and for some years thereafter, tea, rubber, jute, tin and other staples were sold to the United Kingdom, from which in return were bought textiles and other manufactured goods. Boosted by a massive inflow of British capital, this bilateral trade brought benefits to both areas: the United Kingdom obtained the raw materials necessary to keep its factories in production, while the Orient received a range of goods which have brought better living standards to many of its inhabitants.

However, since the end of World War II this pattern has undergone substantial changes. In its determination to boost export earnings the region has penetrated a whole new range of markets including the United States of America, the Continent of Europe, Japan and the Soviet bloc. Moreover, a number of individual territories within the region have now reached a stage in their development in which they can trade among themselves.

Inevitably the relationship between the United Kingdom and the Orient has been weakened in the process, though substantial trade and investment still flows between the two.

From its earliest days, The Chartered Bank—one of a group of London-based financial institutions which have come to be known as the British overseas banks—has specialised in the finance of overseas trade. And with more than 100 years of experience to its credit, it has become an expert in this field.

Founded in the United Kingdom by Royal Charter in 1853, the first branch was opened in Calcutta in 1858 to be followed five days later by the second in Bombay. Thereafter the bank moved steadily eastwards, so that, by the beginning of the present century, branches had been established in Ceylon, Burma, Thailand, Singapore, Malaysia, Indonesia, the Philippines, Japan, Hong Kong and China. Their geographical expansion was no accident, but the result of a conscious decision to keep up with British overseas trade as it penetrated this hitherto largely unknown region. Subsequently the same branches were to serve as channels for British capital, at first seeking outlets in plantations and mining and later in industry and commerce.

Once its organisation had been extended to cover virtually the whole of the Orient, The Chartered Bank began to look more closely at the West. In 1902 a branch was opened in New York, to be followed two years later by another in Hamburg. After World War II, its business was developed further, by establishing, in 1964, a wholly-owned subsidiary, The Chartered Bank of London, in San Francisco and by setting up the Anglo Nordic Bank in Zurich in 1969 and the European and Overseas Trading Bank in Rotterdam in 1970—both of the latter in conjunction with other banking interests.

Essentially, the developing nations of the world were not neglected; the Middle East became an important area of business from 1957 onwards through the acquisition of the Eastern Bank Limited, a British bank with strong connections in the Lebanon and the Gulf States. Subsequently, its branch system was absorbed into The Chartered Bank network.

As a result of this territorial diversification, The Chartered Bank today ranks as a major international organisation with branches, subsidiaries, or associates in nearly all the major centres of the world. Yet strong business connections in the West, stimulated by a highly successful entry into the Euro-currency market, have in no way over-shadowed the operations of The Chartered Bank in those countries in the Orient where it first started and where by now it has become an accepted part of the local environment.

Apart from financing trade, The Chartered Bank has also developed a range of services to meet the banking needs of the man in the street. Here it seeks not to encroach upon the activities of the indigenous banks but rather to supplement them in the common objective of encouraging small savers and spreading the banking habit; ample scope exists for both parties in the environment of rapid and sustained growth common to the region as a whole. To this end, like the indigenous banks, it offers the depositor current and savings accounts at various rates, together with loans on convenient terms for consumer durables, for house improvements and other needs of the community.

As well as catering for the everyday needs of the individual, The Chartered Bank offers comprehensive facilities to that increasingly important member of the business environment—the manufacturer of local products.

Although the close relationship between the United Kingdom and the East was beneficial to both over the long-term, it did possess a weakness: the fortunes of those countries relying upon commodities could vary quite sharply from year to year, according to whether prices in the West were high or low.

Today, throughout the whole region, industrialisation is receiving every form of official encouragement, to broaden the base of the economy as well as to generate new jobs, stimulate government revenue and offer fresh sources of earnings by means of new export markets.

Although Singapore, Malaysia, Thailand and others have already made substantial strides in this direction, their efforts continue unabated. The booming demand for finance which has arisen in the wake of industrial growth is being met by The Chartered Bank in four main ways: firstly, branches offer short-term finance in the form of a loan or overdraft to the factory owner who, for example, may wish to release funds tied up in stocks. Secondly, the bank itself has subscribed capital to a variety of government and semi-government institutions offering long-term finance to the manufacturer; thus The Chartered Bank is a shareholder in Malaysian Industrial Development Finance Berhad in Kuala Lumpur, the Development Bank of Singapore Limited and the Industrial Finance Corporation of Thailand.

Although such institutions have not been established in Hong Kong, the growth of this thriving industrial centre has in no way suffered; for in their absence, The Chartered Bank and other commercial banks adapted themselves to meet both long and short-term financial needs. Thirdly, the initiative has been seized to set up specialist merchant banking institutions in those centres, where industry is assuming a degree of sophistication and complexity hitherto found only in Western countries of the world.

Chartered Merchant Bankers Limited in Singapore, Chartered Merchant Bankers Malaysia Berhad in Kuala Lumpur and Schroders and Chartered Limited in Hong Kong have all been established to offer services covering all aspects of long-term finance. These services include arrangements to raise fresh capital in the form of new issues, debentures and loan stock, with underwriting if required, advice on mergers and acquisitions, and investment management. Similar institutions are likely to be set up in other areas as appropriate. For the three established to date, The Chartered Bank has combined with a leading London merchant bank to unite local business acumen with the expertise of the City of London. Finally, The Chartered Bank together with certain other licensed banks in Singapore, are opening up a fresh source of finance for regional business through their operations in the fast growing Asian dollar market.

In all their operations branches conform to the prudent and well-tried standards of commercial banking in the United Kingdom. In some areas the authorities have requested The Chartered Bank to advise on the establishment of a central bank, a monetary authority or sometimes a money market.

Such advice is freely given, for it has long been policy to promote the financial well-being of the region in every way possible.

Outside its purely financial services, The Chartered Bank is well placed to offer general business information and economic intelligence extending over all those parts of the world covered by its organisation. Thus its branches in the Orient can give customers the background to markets in the industrialised countries, while in the West they publicise the scope for investment throughout Asia. Frequently staff brief customers on important local factors such as exchange control, taxation and, most important, the generous investment incentives offered by host governments to those establishing businesses in their industrial sectors. When channelled through branches in Djakarta, this service can be of particular benefit to a potentially rich country like Indonesia, which urgently needs foreign capital for reconstruction and development after the disruption of the Sukarno regime. At the same time introductions can be arranged to potential importers and exporters on the other side of the world. Branch managers often find themselves in a position to influence the decisions of their customers; and as a group their efforts have done much to stimulate business between East and West. As an employer The Chartered Bank has always recruited staff from local communities and given them a thorough training in the many skills and techniques of commercial banking. Those who show particular promise are brought back to the United Kingdom for further training to equip them for more senior positions at a later stage. As a measure of its progress in this direction, today, out of a total staff of just over 9,100, only about 250 are British expatriates. It is not only the business of the Organisation which is international.

In October 1970 the terms of a merger between The Chartered Bank and another British overseas bank, the Standard Bank Limited, were agreed; as a result both became wholly-owned subsidiaries of a holding company, Standard and Chartered Banking Group Limited. Because to a large extent the business of the new part-

Opposite page: Rubber,
one of the most important industries
of Malaysia. The picture shows
latex flowing from a rubber tree
as the tapper carries out her routine
task soon after sunrise.

Right:
The Bank's Main Office
in Kuala Lumpur is a modern building
in keeping with the advanced
architectural pattern of
the expanding capital.

Below:
The machine is replacing traditional
farming methods throughout South-east
Asia and The Chartered Bank helps
in many ways to improve the harvest
of staple crops;
for example, this small cultivator
in Indonesia.

ner is based on the African continent and that of The Chartered Bank on the Orient, the two organisations serve to complement each other, with little or no overlap in their respective branch systems.

At a time when size is of growing importance for international operations, The Chartered Bank is backed by substantially greater resources as it stands poised to take full advantage of the developments throughout the Orient in the 1970's. With the vast mineral wealth of Australia coming to the surface, Japan expected to overcome the temporary problems of late 1971 and achieve still greater prosperity, and with trading links among the countries on the Pacific Rim likely to intensify, the next decade looks full of promise for the whole region.

For The Chartered Bank and other major banking organisations of the world operating in this area it could be a period as exciting as any in past history.

CANADIAN INVOLVEMENT

FOR MANY YEARS Canadian private enterprise, the Government and individuals have taken an active interest in the development of Asian countries. They have injected well over $C1.1 billion in funds, technical assistance and personal effort into the viability of regional projects.

Most of this has been contributed through the medium of the Colombo Plan. Through Canada's media, universities and libraries, the average Canadian has acquired a new appreciation of Asia—the histories, cultures and present-day problems of its countries and their inhabitants.

From commercial self-interest to religious idealism, Canadian businessmen, missionaries, teachers, traders and tourists for more than a century have contributed to the expansion and stabilisation of Asian economies and to the social welfare and education of the area's peoples. In addition, Canada's steadily increasing imports from Asia are providing developing countries with a growing market and much-needed foreign exchange. Since 1958, this market has expanded 306 per cent, compared with a world increase of only 138 per cent. Asian countries are also importing more and more Canadian capital goods, and technical services from fields in which Canada has developed considerable expertise, in order to aid industrialisation and the building of infrastructure.

Canadian businesses also are investing more heavily in Asia, particularly in industries such as tourism.

Today there are about 900 Canadian Roman Catholic and 600 Protestant missionaries in Asia; they are particularly active in Japan, the Philippines, Taiwan, Korea, Hong Kong and Indonesia. In addition to their religious duties, these men and women have established schools, hospitals and model farms; they teach in universities, they instruct peasants and primitive tribes in the less accessible parts of South-east Asia in hygiene, child-care and nutrition; they write scholarly books and papers on Asian society and generally care for the unwanted peoples of the region—the lepers, criminals, refugees, starved, sick and insane.

The air passenger services across the Pacific have increased by 21 per cent per annum in the past five years, compared with a world rate of 15 per cent. Canada's air link with Asia, Canadian Pacific Airlines, now jets four times weekly to Tokyo, three times weekly to Hong Kong, once weekly to Sydney via Fiji and new and more frequent services are to be scheduled in the near future.

While currently accounting for only about 5 per cent of visitor receipts, the Pacific is the fastest growing tourist area in the world. Receipts are growing at a rate of 16 per cent and individual travellers at a rate of 20 per cent. These figures indicate the growing demand for more top-standard hotels and motels, restaurants, recreation facilities and modern shops in the tourist centres of Asia. A Canadian mission to the area in the spring of 1969 investigated some sixteen multi-million dollar tourist developments in which it is expected that Canadian investors will participate. Another facet of Canadian tourist operations in Asia is the Canadian Government Travel Bureau which maintains offices in Tokyo and Sydney.

Although Canadian newspapers mostly rely on American press services, a greater number than ever before are appointing correspondents to cover the Far East from Hong Kong or Tokyo. The Canadian Broadcasting Corporation has a full-time representative based in Hong Kong who is responsible for radio and television coverage of Asia, from Japan to Indonesia.

As Hong Kong, Japan, Australia and other countries of the region now have satellite ground stations, it is possible to transmit television news reports instantly to Canada. The National Film Board has supplemented its purely local themes by films portraying Canadian aid and other activities in Asia, and the occasional interpretive study. The current exchange of film directors between the NFB and the Australian Commonwealth Film Unit may result in some joint studies of problems of economic and social development and education. Greater collaboration with other Asian countries is envisaged, directed towards the mutual appreciation of cultural values and understanding of social changes. This will be achieved through systematic circulation of films for schools, educational television, and joint production of films. Canadian public and university libraries are also offering increasing facilities to enable the public to be aware of Asia.

Asian studies programmes are being developed at home and Asians are encouraged to study at Canadian universities. The Universities of British Columbia and Toronto have established studies programmes to the Master of Arts Degree level, backed by adequate staffs and libraries. Chinese languages are taught at Saskatchewan, Guelph, Windsor and McGill Universities Japanese at UBC, Toronto and Victoria.

In 1968-69, there were 4,870 Pacific country students studying in Canada: about 30 per cent of all foreign students. Some were financed by Canadian International Development Agency (CIDA) grants under the Colombo Plan, a small number were on Commonwealth Scholarships but most were privately financed. The question of the Asian 'brain-drain' has been raised in a number of international conferences as well as in Canada. To assist Asia overcome its shortage of educated technical, and scientific and humanitarian personnel, CIDA requires those obtaining a Training Award to sign an undertaking to return to their home country at the end of their course of study or training. Many Asian governments also require their candidates to sign bonds or contracts before receiving their travel documents.

Canada's involvement in Asian development leans heavily on trade, for it is through trade that Asia can acquire the goods and services she lacks and in return dispose of the goods and services which she can provide. Canada's exports to and imports from the area are increasing at a much faster rate than those with any other region.

Canada's exports to Asia vary with the demands of the various countries: industrial raw materials and forest products for Japan and Korea; wheat for China; secondary raw materials and foods for other South-east Asian countries and manufactures and food products for Australia.

Sales to Japan will continue to dominate the Canadian export picture but there is increasing scope for Canadian capital goods and technical services; these are the relatively new fields that have opened up through the widespread concern to industrialise and to develop infrastructural sufficiency.

The 1968 import of $C640 million from Asian and Australasian sources accounted for 5.25 per cent of Canada's import needs and ranked the area as Canada's third most important source of supply. Canada's import trade with the Pacific is generally more varied than its export trade and thus it provides a valuable and growing market for Asian goods. In the case of Japan, the dominant trading partner, imports were spread over a thousand statistical categories, but 78 accounted for more than $C11 million each, mainly textiles and intensive manufactures, such as automotives and electronics. China and Southeast Asia are sources of textiles and light manufactures but Malaysia and Singapore also provide significant quantities to the value of $C13 million. 344 categories in 1968 were listed for imports from Australia,

IN THE DEVELOPMENT OF ASIA

of which nine represented values over $C1 million and these involved vegetable food products, meat and wool. Alumina imports were worth $C6 million.

THE COLOMBO PLAN. Two decades have passed since Canada first entered the field of foreign aid as a founding member of the Colombo Plan—now its major single avenue of contribution to the developing world. The bulk of Canadian economic assistance to Asia is granted under direct partnership agreements between Canada and the individual governments concerned, but significant allocations are also channelled through multilateral international and regional institutions and agencies. Of these, the Canadian commitment to the Asian Development Bank, of which Canada is a charter member, is becoming a major investment. An initial US$25 million allocated to the Bank's capitalisation in 1966 was supplemented by an additional US$25 million given to the Bank's Special Fund in 1968 to provide development loans on concessional terms.

Canada's bilateral assistance programme in South and South-east Asia has been largely concentrated in those fields where Canadian technological experience has been of special value: the construction of power plants, hydro-electric installations such as the Idikki Dam in India, transmission lines and transportation facilities, the provision of locomotives, medical and fisheries equipment. A new literacy centre was opened in 1971 in Hyderabad, India, and other recent projects have included the building of an atomic reactor at Trombay, India, a trade school in Kuala Lumpur, the furnishing of radio equipment for a hospital in Gombak, Malaysia, the establishment of Montfort Boys' School in Malaysia, a broadcasting centre in Kuala Lumpur, and the initiation of a sawmill workers' training scheme in Kuching, Malaysia.

Canada has also co-operated with the Asian Institute of Technology in Bangkok.

Forestry surveys and feasibility studies have recently been conducted by Canadian timber experts at Pahang Tengarra, Malaysia.

Above: C.I.D.A. President Paul Gérin-Lajoie and an Indian Government official on a tour of Trombay Reactor in April 1971.

Below: The Asian Institute of Technology at Bangkok.

Of growing importance to developing countries is the need for commodities, foodstuffs and other "non-project" assistance. Canadian industrial raw materials such as aluminium, zinc, lead, copper, asbestos, woodpulp and tallow have been supplied under the commodity assistance programme to offset the effect of severe shortage of foreign exchange on domestic productive capacity. These "maintenance" imports have become an important element of the aid programme, especially in India and Pakistan. In many cases, Canada provides fertilizers, pesticides and sulphur designed to improve agricultural production. Over the last twenty years the number of teachers and advisers sent to South-east Asia, and trainees brought to Canada under the Colombo Plan has been continuously increased.

CANADA'S NEW POLICIES FOR ASIAN DEVELOPMENT. In 1960 the increasing complexity of aid administration led to the formation of the External Aid Office. In 1968 its name was changed to the Canadian International Development Agency, which reflected the new sophistication of Canada's aid plans: a shift from the "no-policy" position of the 1950's with its lively anti-Communist instinct and its vision of a free multi-racial Commonwealth, to a more realistic and complex plan for the development of the poorer countries of the world.

In 1969 Canada's total contributions to international aid were in excess of $350 million, extended in an effective, co-ordinated form to the continents of Asia, Africa and Latin America for development in the truest sense of partnership. This involved, for example, the development of new ways of applying existing technologies to meet the particular needs of the less-developed countries.

This is an area in which Canada has been able to play an important role and for this purpose a bill was passed in 1970 establishing the International Development Research Centre of Canada, supported by a Government grant of a minimum of $30 million over the ensuing five years.

Functions of the Centre include supporting and undertaking research into problems involved in the development of economically-deprived regions, particularly in respect of the needs of the peoples of these regions. They also include facilities to enable the developing countries to build up their own scientific and technological resources.

In June 1970 the Canadian Government made public its White Paper on Canadian foreign policy which notes six vital policy themes for the future: the fostering of economic growth; safeguarding sovereignty and independence; working for peace and security; promoting social justice; enhancing the quality of life; and ensuring a harmonious natural environment. Specifically, Canada increased its international assistance by $60 million in 1971-72 from the previous year's allocation of $364 million.

In spite of this substantial aid in terms of money spent, Canada has not been a leading aid-giver but, by taking the initiative in researching more effective ways of helping individual Asian societies to achieve self-perpetuating growth, Canada has been a world leader. As the 1950 report of the Colombo Plan stated: "In a world racked by schism and confusion, it is doubtful whether free men can long afford to leave undeveloped and imprisoned in poverty the human resources of the countries of South and South-east Asia which could help so greatly, not only to restore the world's prosperity but also to redress its confusion and enrich the lives of all men everywhere."

Opposite page:
The Idikki Dam, India, under construction.

Above:
A forestry survey being carried out in Pahang Tengarra, Malaysia.

A class in rice cultivation techniques at Maharashtra, India, conducted as one of Japan's foreign aid projects.

JAPAN is sincerely committed to providing economic assistance to the developing countries of the world in the belief that neither its own prosperity nor the welfare of the world can be ensured without economic development and political stability in these countries.

Japan, as the only highly developed and industrialised nation of Asia, is fully cognizant of its responsibilities in assisting in the economic progress of the emerging countries, and realises that the world expects it to contribute substantially to this end.

Aware also that there remains room for improvement in both the quality and quantity of its economic aid, Japan is resolved to continue its efforts in degrees commensurate with its own economic growth.

The following facts and figures demonstrate Japan's sincerity in its aims:

VOLUME OF AID. In 1970, Japan's overseas economic assistance amounted to US$1,824 million, showing a remarkable increase of 44.4 per cent over 1969.

This meant that the ratio of Japan's foreign aid to the nation's Gross National Product (GNP) rose from 0.76 per cent in 1969 to 0.93 in 1970.

Japan thus came much closer to the goal of spending one per cent of its GNP in foreign aid by 1975, towards which it had pledged itself to the Ministerial Council of the Organisation for Economic Co-operation and Development (OECD) and other organisations.

Japan's foreign aid had increased so greatly in recent years that by 1968 it had become the world's fourth largest aid donor, ranking after the United States, the Federal Republic of Germany and France and outstripping the United Kingdom, which ranked fifth.

With its attitude towards overseas economic co-operation becoming more positive every year, Japan's rank among the major aid donors will probably rise even higher in the future.

Since Japan joined the Colombo Plan in 1954, it has annually increased its foreign economic aid, especially to newly developing countries in South-east Asia.

With the rapid growth of her own national economy during the last decade, Japan's foreign aid increased from US$200 million from 1960 to 1964 to US$400 million in 1965 and to the US$600 million level in 1966.

In 1967 the annual total rose further to US$797.5 million, in 1968 to US$1,049.3 million, in 1969 to US$1,263.1 million and finally in 1970 to US$1,824 million dollars, representing a threefold jump in four years.

FORM OF ASSISTANCE. Japan's economic assistance in 1970 consisted of US$458 million in "official development assistance", US$693.6 million in "other official flows" and US$672.3 million in "private flows", all showing substantial gains over the previous year.

Official development assistance showed a relatively small rise of 5.1 per cent, primarily because war reparations payments, which used to carry weight in bilateral grants, are drawing to a close and therefore sharply decreased.

Of the US$458 million official development assistance bilateral grants accounted for US$121.2 million, which was further broken down into US$99.6 million in non-repayable financial aid and US$21.6 million in technical co-operation.

The non-repayable financial aid included food under the Kennedy Round Arrangements to Indonesia, Laos, Ceylon and other countries, a contribution to the Foreign Exchange Operation Fund of Laos, assis-

JAPAN'S ECONOMIC AID TO DEVELOPING NATIONS

tance for the relief of refugees in Vietnam, and reparations payments to the Philippines and Indonesia. (Reparations payments to Indonesia ended in 1970, while those to the Philippines are to be completed in 1975).

Bilateral loans have so far accounted for the major portion of Japan's official development assistance. In 1970, they came to some US$250 million, contributed to Indonesia, the Republic of Korea, India, Pakistan and other countries, including refinancing and rescheduling of debts previously incurred.

OTHER FINANCIAL AIDS. Capital subscriptions and contributions to multilateral agencies amounted to US$86.5 million including contributions to the United Nations Development Programme (UNDP) and the United Nations International Children's Emergency Fund (UNICEF) and subscriptions to the Asian Development Bank (ADB) and the International Development Association (IDA)

Other official flows totalling US$693.6 million showed a jump of 84.6 per cent over the preceding year. This sum covered export credits, direct investment financing, Bank of Japan loans to the International Bank for Reconstruction and Development (World Bank), and others.

Lastly, private flows, aggregating US$672.3 million, represented an increase of 48.8 per cent over the previous year. They included, among others, export credits and direct investment.

TECHNICAL ASSISTANCE. Japan gives technical assistance to the developing countries, particularly those of South-east Asia, knowing that it is in a favourable position to do so.

Aid in this sector consists of the following measures:

1. Acceptance of trainees from abroad: During 1970 Japan received 1,660 technical trainees from abroad, including 1,211 from Asia, 233 from the Middle and Near East and Africa, 213 from Central and South America, and three from other regions. The grand total of these trainees during the past sixteen years (since 1954) reached 14,149.

2. Dispatch of Japanese experts: 241 Japanese experts in various fields of industry and science were sent to developing countries during 1970 (excluding those covered in categories 6,7,8,9, and 10 as follow.) 148 went to Asia, 65 to the Middle and Near East and Africa and 28 to Central and South America.

In 1970 also, ten experts were sent to the Economic Commission for Asia and the Far East (ECAFE), the South-east Asia Fishery Development Centre, the Asian Development Bank and other international agencies. During the past sixteen years no less than 2,516 such Japanese advisory experts visited these organisations.

3. Dispatch of Youth Corps: Agreements were concluded with thirteen countries, including Zambia and Uganda in 1970, on the dispatch of Japanese Overseas Co-operation Youth Corps Volunteers.

During that year 218 of these volunteers were sent abroad, including 139 to Asia, 66 to the Middle and Near East and Africa, and 13 to Central and South America. Since the inception of this system in 1965 943 Japanese Youth Corps Volunteers have gone abroad.

4. Provision of machinery and equipment: Industrial machinery and equipment worth US$440,000 has been provided in twenty-five instances to eighteen countries of Asia, the Middle and Near East, Africa and Central and South America.

These included ceramics training equipment for Thailand's Ministry of Industry, public water service equipment for Pakistan's Capital Development Public Corporation, well-drilling equipment for Ethiopia's Ministry of Water Resources, equipment for university-level civil engineering instruction for Nigeria, and minerals assaying equipment for Bolivia's Geological Survey Institute.

5. Technical Co-operation Centre: Japan has established 31 technical co-operation centres in eighteen countries, including the Telecommunications Research Centre established in Iran in 1971.

With an outlay of nearly US$2 million Japan continued to operate the Cottage Industry Centre in the Philippines, the Telecommunications Centre in Mexico, the Prototype Production Centre in Singapore, the Small-Scale Industry Centre in Kenya, the Textiles Manufacturing Centre in Ghana, the Vocational Training Centre in Uganda and the Fisheries Centre in Indonesia.

Japan continues to send experts and equipment to those centres whose management has been transferred to the governments of the country in which they are located.

6. Development surveys: Japanese experts have conducted surveys for 30 different development projects at a cost of some US$1.2 million, including 22 in Asia, six in the Middle and Near East and Africa and two in Central and South America.

In addition, blueprints were prepared by Japanese experts for an airport expansion project in Laos, a port construction project in Malaysia and a Japanese garden construction project in Singapore.

7. Medical assistance: Medical assistance to developing countries is one of the pillars of Japan's foreign aid programme. Japanese medical experts are at work in nineteen countries in a total of 41 medical co-operation projects.

Japan has spent about US$10 million for overseas medical aid since 1966 and has allocated a further US$2.4 million in the 1971-72 budget.

Medical and health problems are being solved, such as shortage of physicians, inadequate hospital and clinical facilities, lack of medicines, malnutrition and ignorance of public hygiene.

Japanese co-operation in these fields, as in others, consists of three elements: dispatch of experts, supply of equipment and materials and acceptance of trainees.

For the Choray Hospital in the Republic of Vietnam a building has been donated as a ward for brain surgery and Japanese medical specialists have given help and advice.

Since 1967 Japan has dispatched fifty medical experts to Thailand and accepted 26 Thai trainees. It has also furnished all the necessary equipment and materials in connection with Thailand's five-year programme for the establishment of its National Cancer Centre.

Since 1968 Japan has been co-operating in the Republic of Korea's anti-parasite campaign to exterminate roundworms among school children. Ten Japanese experts have been sent and 34 Korean trainees have been received in Japan in connection with this project.

Japan has provided hospitals in Korea with US$300,000 worth of equipment, including automobiles, microscopes and pharmaceuticals for combating filaria. To Laos, Japan has sent two doctors and two nurses to work at Thangone Clinic near Vientiane while providing equipment and materials necessary for its establishment.

In Ghana, Japanese experts are assisting in research and training in basic medicine. Japan provided equipment and materials worth US$200,000, including an electronic microscope, to the Ghana University where three Japanese medical and technical experts are at work.

Meanwhile, Japanese agencies are studying details of the proposed Asian Medical Organisation as an international body charged with the task of education, training,

Right: The great Da Nhim Earth Dam, completed in January 1965, as part of Japan's reparations payments to Vietnam.

Below: Fenchuganj Chemical Fertiliser Plant built by Japan in East Pakistan (now Bangladesh) has an annual production capacity of 108,000 tons of urea. It was delivered to the Pakistani authorities in April 1962. This plant, along with another at Ghorasal, is boosting food production.

research and information exchange in medical science and treatment to elevate standards in the Asian region particularly.

8. Agricultural assistance: As agriculture occupies an important place in the economy of many developing countries, particularly of South-east Asia, Japan places special emphasis on agricultural assistance in its overall foreign aid programme.

As a nation rich in experience and technical knowledge in the cultivation of rice and other farm products, Japan is keen to extend to its neighbours as much co-operation as possible in their efforts to raise their own agricultural standards.

Japan dispatched experts and provided machinery and equipment for a number of overseas agricultural developmental projects at a total cost of some US$1.9 million in 1970. Among them were the staple food production increase project in Western Java, Indonesia, the rice cultivation development project in the Philippines, the sericultural industry development project in Thailand, and a general farm production increase project in Ceylon, all of which had been continued since 1969.

In addition, five new projects were initiated during 1971 in the Republic of Vietnam, Laos, India, Indonesia and Malaysia, including those for the establishment of a faculty of agriculture within a South Vietnamese university and mechanisation of rice production in Malaysia.

9. Primary product development co-operation: Japan provides assistance in disseminating new industrial and agricultural techniques and know-how to countries where their lack constitutes a major limiting factor in the national economy.

In 1970 experts and equipment were sent to help organise mass cultivation of maize in Eastern Java, Indonesia and Cambodia, and to promote production of oil seeds, such as soya beans, in Thailand. Japan also dispatched teams of agricultural specialists to Thailand and Indonesia for preliminary surveys on large-scale maize production projects.

A budgetary outlay of about US$444,000 was made for this type of assistance during the year.

10. Science and agriculture education assistance: The Japanese Ministry of Education has dispatched experts in school science education to Thailand, Malaysia, Indonesia and Ceylon, as well as an expert in agricultural education to Iran, while providing teaching materials and equipment to these countries.

Keynote: Japan's positive foreign aid policy was recently keynoted by its Government leaders in the following manner:

At the Fourth Ministerial Conference for the Economic Development of South-east Asia held in Bangkok, the then Japanese Foreign Minister, Mr. Kiichi Aichi, stated, "The coming decade will present great opportunities to countries both in and out of the South-east Asian region. According to a tentative estimate, if Japan would maintain the fast economic growth of the past several years, her Gross National Product around 1980 might well reach the level of 500 billion dollars.

In this case, since Japan intends actively to pursue overseas economic co-operation commensurate with such growth of her national economy, the volume of her economic co-operation will achieve a very high level.

And since a major portion thereof will be directed toward Asia, the magnitude of economic co-operation which will then be extended to South-east Asia from Japan and developed countries outside the region will be such as to exceed levels that we can conceive at present."

At the Second Annual Meeting of the Board of Governors of the Asian Development Bank, the then Japanese Finance Minister, Mr. Takeo Fukuda, emphasised the importance of the economic development of Asia, stating, in part, "Our assistance to Asia amounted in 1968 to over five hundred million dollars. I should like to continue our best endeavours for further increase in our aid to Asian countries, and it is my desire to double the present flow of our aid to the Asian region within the coming five years, our economic resources permitting."

PARTNERSHIP PACIFIC

Operations under way at Panguna,
Bougainville Island,
where the copper concentrator
will be the largest
in the world.
Picturesque mountain scenery
and modern engineering
dominate the approach
across the rugged
Crown Prince Range
to the heart of
Bougainville Copper Pty. Limited's
operations at
Panguna.

THE DISCOVERY of Australia's economic wealth in minerals and other natural resources has paved the way for a dramatic increase in the operations of merchant banks in Australia. In spite of Australia's abundance of raw materials, the shortage of local capital has hampered the country's plans for growth and development.

Merchant banks have been attracted to Australia for obvious reasons. Australia's potential, with its natural wealth and booming industrial activity, is tremendous. The country's mineral and ore resources alone have staggering potential. These natural assets and industry based upon them are Australia's future.

But the future needs financing. Natural resource and industrial development ventures need financial assistance on a scope unavailable from the Australian domestic money market.

Merchant banks raising capital abroad are able to meet these extensive requirements. Partnership Pacific Limited is one of the leading merchant banks in Australia. It is sponsored by The Bank of America, N.T. and S.A., the largest bank in the world; the Bank of New South Wales; and The Bank of Tokyo Ltd., the principal foreign exchange bank of Japan. Thus it is backed by the expertise of three of the world's great banking institutions.

With this support, Partnership Pacific is able to operate in the much-needed, medium-term loan market. The activities of the organisation are centred on assisting development of basic industry and natural resources throughout Australia and in adjacent areas.

Large amounts have been marshalled and channelled to major mining undertakings, pastoral and agricultural development schemes and into the secondary industry sector. A substantial portion of Partnership Pacific's total funds employed is raised in the overseas financial centres of the world.

Partnership Pacific Limited is confident of Australia's future and the future of the nearby countries of the Pacific. This Company's support of sound natural resource and industrial ventures in the area is providing a secure base for the further growth and progress considered vital for optimum development of the Pacific region in the years ahead.

THE ASIAN BROADCASTING UNION

ONE OF ASIA'S greatest needs in its almost endless programme of development is the improvement, in the widest possible sense, of its systems of communications. Monsoons, periodical typhoons and other interferences to air and surface travel so prevalent in Asia, disruptions by wars and political upheavals, have made the relaying of information from one region to another almost entirely dependent upon radio and television.

Since the usage of these modes of communication has become international, untold benefits have been brought to millions of people, keeping them abreast of the times, improving their education and spreading greater knowledge in the fields of agriculture and other industries. Traditional and modern music and drama are brought to far-spread audiences; awareness of international and domestic happenings is no longer confined to cities and large towns but is even radioed to small jungle villages and desert camps. By these means the peoples of Asia are being brought closer to each other and to the rest of the world.

Fifteen years ago a professional, non-political organisation was set up to advise and assist in the development and improvement of broadcasting media throughout Asia; it was called The Asian Broadcasting Union (ABU). Its functions included the presentation of news and fair and unbiased comments on world happenings; the promotion of education and culture; the encouragement of religious tolerance and international understanding and respect for human rights and dignity.

Since that time the ABU's operations have been expanded to cover not only Asia but also the Pacific area west of the 170th parallel of longitude which passes through the Bering Straits.

The history of the ABU began in 1957, when the Japan Broadcasting Corporation (NHK) invited other Asian Broadcasters to Tokyo for the first Asian Broadcasters' Conference. Further meetings were convened in Tokyo in 1958 and 1960, and programme exchanges and other activities were so successful that a formal Union was proposed as a basis for the promotion of wider mutual interests.

At the Fourth Asian Broadcasters' Conference held in Kuala Lumpur in 1962, sixteen broadcasting organizations from Australia, Taiwan, India, Indonesia, Japan, Korea, Laos, Malaysia, New Zealand, Pakistan, the Philippines, Saudi Arabia, Thailand, Turkey, the United Arab Republic and South Vietnam agreed to establish the Union. Next year at Seoul, draft statutes were adopted, formally establishing the Asian Broadcasting Union as from July 1964, with eleven of the original sixteen as its inaugural members.

At its First General Assembly in 1964, the body elected Mr. Yoshinori Maeda, the President of NHK, as its President, a position he still continues to hold. In 1965, Sir Charles Moses, C.B.E., former General Manager of the Australian Broadcasting Commission, was appointed Secretary-General. A small, full-time Secretariat was set up at the ABU headquarters in Tokyo and the Secretary-General's administrative office was based in Sydney.

At its first meeting, the Union decided to work for the establishment of a broadcasting training institute in Asia and its perseverance has been rewarded by a unanimous decision to set up the school in Kuala Lumpur by 1975. From its inception the ABU has been officially linked with UNESCO, the UN agencies, ITU and FAO, and has co-operated with them in establishing workshops and organising seminars in various parts of the region it serves.

The ABU has been helped by the Ford Foundation with a grant of US$200,000, spread over five years, to enable it to become firmly established; the Friedrich-Ebert Foundation (West Germany), the Asia Foundation (USA), and the Edward E. Ford Foundation (USA) have also supported the Union with substantial funds. The ABU has always been keen to collaborate with other broadcasting bodies and it took the initiative in 1968 in arranging the first ever international meeting of the world's broadcasting unions.

In 1971, the ABU played a leading part in two very important seminars: one for broadcast news editors was held in Tokyo, where fourteen European and North American participants discussed common problems with 29 representatives of the Asian-Pacific region; the other, in Singapore, having the 1972 Olympics in Munich and Sapporo in mind, was for sports commentators—26 from Asia and six from West Germany.

The ABU's plans for 1972 include a seminar on programmes for young people in which it will be assisted by UNESCO and the Prix Jeunesse Foundation of West Germany; a seminar on broadcasting in the public interest; and a further meeting of news executives. For 1972 also, the Union has listed a third series of educational films for school children in primary and secondary grades. They will deal with the Pacific Islands, the two earlier series having covered Malaysia, Singapore and Brunei; and Iran and Afghanistan.

By October 1971, membership of the ABU had risen to 58, including 39 members from Asia and the Pacific area, eight from Europe, eight from North America and three from Africa—those from outside the region being associate members.

The activities of the ABU reach two-fifths of the way around the world—from Turkey to Tonga, from Korea to New Zealand—and represent many cultures, languages, religions and political creeds. The Union is a noteworthy example of professionals working in harmony for the raising of standards and for the mutual benefit of all peoples of the world.

THE U.S.A. IN ASIA

THE BASIC THEME in the drama of current Asian development is agriculture. Until food production can match demand and until the farmer can accumulate investment capital and command spending-power, secondary industry will continue to play a relatively minor role in most countries of the region. Underlining and compounding inefficient agriculture and infant-industrialisation is first and foremost the population explosion and secondarily, in degrees which vary from country to country, the problems of infrastructure, land-reform, education, underemployment, nutrition, urban renewal, the 'brain-drain', lack of applied research, finance and the conservation of the environment and balanced utilisation of resources. The future prosperity of individual Asian nations and the future stability of the region as a whole will depend on the effectiveness of solutions planned in these critical areas.

Through international, regional and national organisations such as the Colombo Plan, ECAFE, SEATO, U.S. AID and others, the world has shown, since World War II, increasing concern with the welfare of the developing countries of Asia. By far the largest donor of aid—in money, equipment, low interest loans, technical advice and personnel,—is the United States of America.

Since the inauguration of the Colombo Plan in January 1950, the original donor nations—the United Kingdom, Canada, Australia and New Zealand, have expanded to admit the United States and Japan, and the three original recipients—India, Pakistan and Ceylon, have increased to eighteen—including all South and South-east Asia except North Vietnam, as well as Japan, the Philippines, Iran and the Republic of Korea.

Of approximately US$34,000 million contributed by the donor countries in carrying out Colombo Plan projects or training programmes to June 1971, the United States had provided 87 per cent. Since it began carrying out its Asian foreign aid operations under the Colombo Plan in 1951, the U.S. has supplied about US$28,000 million in aid to the Plan's recipient numbers, about one-third of which has gone to India. In the last decade almost half of all U.S. foreign aid has gone to Colombo Plan countries.

As well as supplying technical advice, direct aid and student-exchange programmes, donor countries of the Plan are also the top priority markets for exports from recipient nations. These exports provide much-needed foreign exchange. Total U.S. imports from Plan recipients have been about US$1,500 million annually, compared with US$3,000 million in U.S. exports to the area. Much of the U.S. export total, however, has been under concessional arrangements, whereas U.S. imports from the area have been cash purchases. American imports of light manufactures have been increasing as have U.S. exports of farm products and complex machinery to the area.

Two decades under the Colombo Plan have brought population control, hydroelectricity, roads and bridges, advances in farming, commerce and construction, plus a large corps of foreign-trained technologists to South and South-east Asia. American financial assistance through the Plan has made workable what twenty years ago was thought mere idealism.

Much of the U.S. aid to Asia has been accounted for in massive shipments of wheat and other agricultural commodities, and by consignments of industrial equipment financed through loans repayable in dollars. The United States has also been the major contributor to programmes to boost food production and improve technical knowledge of agriculture, mainly through the work of the Agency for International Development, U.S. AID. Some examples of specific U.S. AID operations are summarised briefly below:

Many of the 2,000 American Peace Corps members working in India, Nepal, Thailand, Malaysia, the Philippines and South Korea teach better methods of farming and planning.

Thousands of recipient country technicians—fertiliser specialists, nutritionists and others—have studied in the United States for periods ranging from several weeks to six months.

An exchange programme for farm families has helped on a limited scale to update Asian farming methods. Under this programme American couples go to India, Pakistan or the Philippines to live with farm families for six weeks, and farmers from these countries come to live for six weeks with American farmers.

Currently the United States has about US$4,000 million in local currencies deposited in banks or on loan to governments and private firms in South and South-east Asia. They were generated by concessional sales of wheat and other agricultural commodities and are U.S. owned. These funds are used for such beneficial purposes as lending to governments for financing economic or rural development projects; to lend to private businesses for projects that contribute to overall economic developments; and to finance road construction.

Private American foundations have worked extensively in the development of the new high-yielding varieties of wheat and rice.

U.S. Government programmes have helped in the distribution to Asia of the rice varieties developed in the International Rice Research Institute (IRRI) in the Philippines. New 'miracle' strains developed at IRRI, notably IR-5 and IR-8, have doubled the yield potential of the crop and have left many former subsistence farms with surpluses. In 1968 about 10 per cent of the riceland of India and 25 per cent of that in Pakistan was planted with these varieties. South Vietnam has also made very substantial progress towards self-sufficiency through the use of these new strains.

High-yielding varieties of wheat developed in Mexico and used extensively in India and Pakistan are now spreading to Afghanistan, Iran, Nepal and other Asian countries—partly through the efforts of American farm specialists. The harvest of wheat in India and Pakistan in the spring of 1971 reached 28 million tons, almost double the production in 1966.

Factors which contribute to Asian malnutrition and agricultural inefficiency are the limited range of crops grown in many countries; the landlord-tenant system of land tenure, rural unemployment during the slack season; and lack of adequate roads, farm machinery, irrigation, pesticides and credit. Through its various agencies, particularly U.S. AID, the United States has set up schemes and projects designed to provide solutions to these problems. Brief outlines of some of these programmes are set out below:

Through its financial support of the multi-national Asian Vegetable Research and Development Centre in Taiwan, the United States is encouraging applied research into crop diversification, particularly vegetable cultivation.

One reason this Centre is starting out with high hopes is that diversification of land use has already seen success in various corners of Asia—such as Pampango Province in the Philippines, where farmers are planting second and third crops of vegetables and fruits, in addition to raising poultry. In many places, town governments are co-operating with U.S. AID personnel, to assist farmers. In Minalin, Pampanga, for example, the local authorities are promoting the scientific raising of poultry. At various times, Filipino farms receiving technical advice and seeds

Many millions of dollars have been contributed by the U.S.A. to finance the building of modern roads to replace inadequate tracks. New road projects frequently give employment to whole families. Remote rural villages are given new access to markets.

from U.S. AID grow crops as diverse as rice, corn, eggplant, squash, tomatoes, beans, mangoes, papayas and guavas.

In Vietnam, with the help of American money and technical knowledge, the Government has initiated a three-pronged attack on inefficient agriculture. New high-yield strains of rice have been introduced, land has been re-distributed to former tenant farmers and a bank has been established to grant low interest loans to farmers.

Until the International Rice Research Institute's strains of 'miracle' rice were introduced, Vietnam's rice yield averaged around 2 tons per hectare. The new varieties average 5 tons per hectare and sometimes as high as 16 tons. Some farmers call the new strains "Honda" rice, because they are using the profits from the bumper crops to buy motorcycles.

The second reform measure undertaken by the Government of South Vietnam is the redeeding of land to those tenants who formerly farmed it. Between 1969 and 1970, 150,000 hectares were redistributed through this scheme. Eventually, the Government will transfer 1 million hectares from absentee ownership to 800,000 families who till the soil. Landlords are adequately compensated for the loss of their land and the United States has pledged US$40 million for this purpose over the next three years. It has been proved by experience in Taiwan that the small landholders created by this programme will have a vested interest in improving and protecting their holdings and will play a personal role in developing national prosperity.

Capital is usually hard to accumulate on a small farm, in Asia or anywhere. Not until a farmer gets money, or its equivalent credit, can he invest in the machinery needed for modern, efficient farming. The provision of this capital through low interest loans is the third step in the Vietnam Government's programme to revitalise agriculture. The agency for these loans, the Agricultural Development Bank, was founded in 1967 and funded by initial capitalisation and loans from the Central Government and a Government of Vietnam -U.S. AID counterpart fund. The Bank, as the knowledge of low interest rates spreads, frees increasing numbers of small farmers each year from the usurious yoke of traditional moneylenders. In 1969, the Bank granted the equivalent of US$40 million in loans to nearly 90,000 farming and fishing families in all 44 provinces of South Vietnam.

Another problem common to the developing countries of Asia is the shift of population from rural to urban areas. During the slack season between crops, farmers leave the land to find work in the cities and rarely return to this sector of the economy which badly needs them. With the help of the United States Agency for International Development, South Korea has found one solution to this problem which is working: farmers are given jobs near their homes on projects essential to the development of the rural economy—the building of new roads, irrigation canals, dikes for land reclamation, sewage systems, reforestation and erosion control, fisheries, bridges, reservoirs and scores of other much-needed activities.

Founded in 1964, this joint U.S.-Korean scheme is called the Provincial Comprehensive Development Programme (PCDP).

What follows is a brief outline of how the programme works: Needy farmers, including widows with children to support, are hired to work on PCDP projects in their neighbourhood. The South Korean Government supervises and pays the workers cash wages. U.S. AID contributes a daily food allowance to each worker in the form of flour. The most remarkable thing about this project is that it tackles almost every aspect of the "rural problem" at the same time: it builds infrastructure, instills a spirit of self-help among the people and gives food and jobs to the needy and unemployed.

The most serious, and, in many Asian countries, the most widespread form of malnutrition is the deficiency of high-quality protein in the diet. A major source of Asia's high-grade protein is fish. The mapping of the area's fish resources, the conservation of some species and areas and the exploitation of others, and the effective use of fish, particularly the little utilised, oily varieties, as high protein food—these are some of the problems now concerning marine biologists and food technologists.

One of the most successful examples of regional co-operation in South-east Asia is the Regional Marine Biological Centre at the University of Singapore, sponsored by UNESCO and financially supported by many nations, including the United States. This Centre is actively engaged in the study of currents in the Pacific Ocean and the China Sea and the results of its research have already enabled Filipino and Thai fishermen to direct their boats to more productive grounds. Another source of data on the distribution of fish comes from American satellites equipped with infra-red sensors so sensitive they can distinguish silt-bearing fresh water from the salt water which surrounds it.

Temperature changes in currents of one degree centigrade—an increment which can make a great deal of difference in the location of various species of fish—can be located by National Aeronautics and Space Administration (NASA) satellites.

Although the answer to Asia's protein needs may be more usually discussed in terms of increased production, research is now being carried out in areas relating to the most economical form in which to supply these needs. One of the cheapest is fish powder concentrate, FPC, a fine, lightly-coloured, almost tasteless powder that can be added to bread, baby-foods, beverages, noodles and other foods to improve the quality and quantity of their protein. The United States National Marine Fisheries Services, leaders in fish protein research, have now produced a powder from the little-utilised fish, hake, which can be sold for 25-30 U.S. cents per half kilogramme Based on these estimates, 10 grammes of FPC which is regarded as a sufficient amount daily to supplement low-quality diets, would cost slightly more than one half a U.S. cent. On an equivalent protein basis, FPC is less than half the cost of dry skim milk and more than 20 times cheaper than steak, making it the cheapest source of protein in the world.

Many scientists are now confident that FPC can make a significant contribution to the world-wide need for high-quality protein. For years, scientists have been studying how FPC can best be produced and utilised. Now, plants are being built and large quantities of FPC are becoming available. Although not a cure-all or the total answer to the enormous and complex task of feeding Asia nutritiously, FPC will make a major contribution to the improvement of human diets in Asia and elsewhere.

Although the vital problems of agriculture and food production have required a great share of United State's aid to Asia, the U.S. continues to support many educational and cultural projects in the area. Summarised below are some of these programmes:

One of the most effective ways of gaining an understanding of a people is through study of their language and culture. Both Americans and Thais are gaining an appreciation of each other's way of life through the Bi-National Centre in Bangkok. Founded by the American University Alumni Association and supported by cash grants from the U.S. Government through its Information Service (USIS), the Centre is quickly becoming the hub of Bangkok's cultural life. It sponsors Thai teacher training seminars and workshops, Thai language classes for Americans residing in the capital, English classes for Thais, lectures and exhibits on Thai and American life and arts, classical and pop concerts and a 30,000 volume library and reading room. Every year more students apply for the English language classes. In 1971 alone, over 8,000 businessmen, government officials, military personnel, university and high school students and housewives studied together in the Bangkok Bi-National Centre and its fifteen provincial branches.

Another educational project to which America gives support is the Asian Institute of Technology, which was founded in 1959 by the South-east Asia Treaty Organisation, SEATO. Now completely independent from SEATO, the Institute, a graduate school of engineering, continues to receive financial aid from several countries, including the United States.

For the student, whether from Pakistan, the Philippines, Thailand, Malaysia, Hong Kong or Indonesia, tuition, transport to the school's headquarters in Bangkok, living expenses — everything is free.

Courses are in engineering relating to structures, hydraulics, transportation, public health, soil and foundations. New courses are planned in mechanical, electrical and possibly industrial and chemical engineering. 150 students are currently enrolled but an enormous graduate school is planned which will cater for about 1,000 students.

It is staggering to realise that at least two-thirds of Asian students who study in America fail to return to their homelands. The Asian Institute, with the aid of the United States of America and other contributing countries, has already done much towards halting or at least de-accelerating this wasteful 'brain-drain'. Over 90 per cent of the Institute's students go back to their own country to live and work.

On the level of secondary education in Asia, the United States has built and equipped many new high schools. An example of this sort of project is the Fa-Ngum High School in Vientiane, the capital of Laos. Fa-Ngum High School is the model for a number of high schools to be built in Laos with U.S. AID. It is providing a stimulating modern education for young Lao who will some day be at the helm of their nation's government, agriculture and industry. The first high school in the country to teach in the Lao language, it has been established by the Lao Government in partnership with U.S. AID, in order to combine an academic and vocational approach to education best suited to the country's needs. It is also hoped that the school will help provide the technical elite which will be required as local industry grows. Field trips, industrial arts, home economics and science laboratories, karate and judo instruction, guest speakers—including, recently a Lao authority on classical dancing, an agricultural expert and a Japanese flower arranger—these are all part of the Fa-Ngum educational environment, an atmosphere designed to stimulate and broaden young minds.

Today, in the survival battle of the international market, a country cannot prosper unless she can make new or better-quality products. Hence, the need for industrial technology, developed through intensive applied research. This need is particularly relevant to most countries of Asia which must capture markets in competition with nations who have established reputations, built up over many years of research and development.

With the help of joint U.S.-Korean finance, a non-profit institution called the Korea Institute of Science and Technology (KIST) is today making major contributions to South Korea's technological and industrial success. The first centre of its kind in Asia, KIST is regarded as a model for other developing countries. Founded in 1966, KIST was modelled after America's famous Batelle Memorial Institute in Columbus, Ohio, one of the world's top research institutes. KIST became fully operational in October 1969, yet for three years prior to that, unfinished though it was, the Institute completed an enormous amount of vital research for the Korean Government and private industry in some 17 fields, including food technology, computer utilisation, electronics, petro-chemicals, transportation and mining.

Essentially, the Institute is an applied-research centre. Applied-research—as opposed to pure research, is the type done at the request of a company or government department. For example: a company is making a bathtub and they cannot get the white material to stick to the metal. They approach KIST and ask for a solution to their dilemma. The Institute then assigns scientists who probe deeply into the problem, and conduct tests. They then report back to the company: "This is your problem. Here is the most economic solution".

KIST also supplies Government and industry with a computer service—the largest and most modern in Korea. Any firm or institution, unable to afford to buy their own computer, may rent KISTS's data processing unit on rates of hire based on the time requirements of their project.

The cost of KIST research projects are expected to reach over US$3.5 million in 1972. Hydrodynamics, titanium oxide, food preservation, lubricants and corro-

The U.S.A. has prepared an incredible programme for space exploration during the 1970's and 1980's —space stations in orbit, shuttle services to the Moon, a manned landing on Mars —thus gleaning scientific knowledge to solve human problems on Earth.

sion—these are some of the phenomena currently researched by KIST. Patents have already been applied for twelve products developed at the Institute.

One reason for Asia's lack of industrial development is the poor transport, roads and communications through much of the region. Today, the U.S. is financing several projects designed to improve the infrastructure and thus gain speedier trade and easier access to raw materials.

The first of these is the major road building programme now being undertaken in Malaysia and described in the Malaysia Chapter in this book.

Another U.S. financed project designed to expedite trade is the streamlining of procedures used at the Port of Saigon. Five years ago, the Port was so jammed with undelivered goods and idle ships waiting for berths that frustrated importers joked ruefully that they could walk across the Saigon River without wetting their feet.

Today, after the virtual completion of the project, vessels from every corner of the earth make their way from the South China Sea to their berths without delay.

Cargo now pours from the ships' holds at a rate averaging 5 million tons a year.

At any time, day or night, from a dozen to more than three dozen, vessels may be discharging cargoes simultaneously.

Some specific actions which sparked the Port's renaissance were:

The construction, with finance supplied by U.S. AID and the Vietnam Government, of new facilities for handling military cargoes as well as medical and food supplies vital to the nation.

With the help of U.S. AID, the importation of modern U.S. cargo handling equipment—forklifts, cranes, warehouse tractors and trailers, which permitted speedy offloading and in-transit storage.

Re-training of longshoremen, many of them women, to use this new equipment in a palletisation system for handling cargoes.

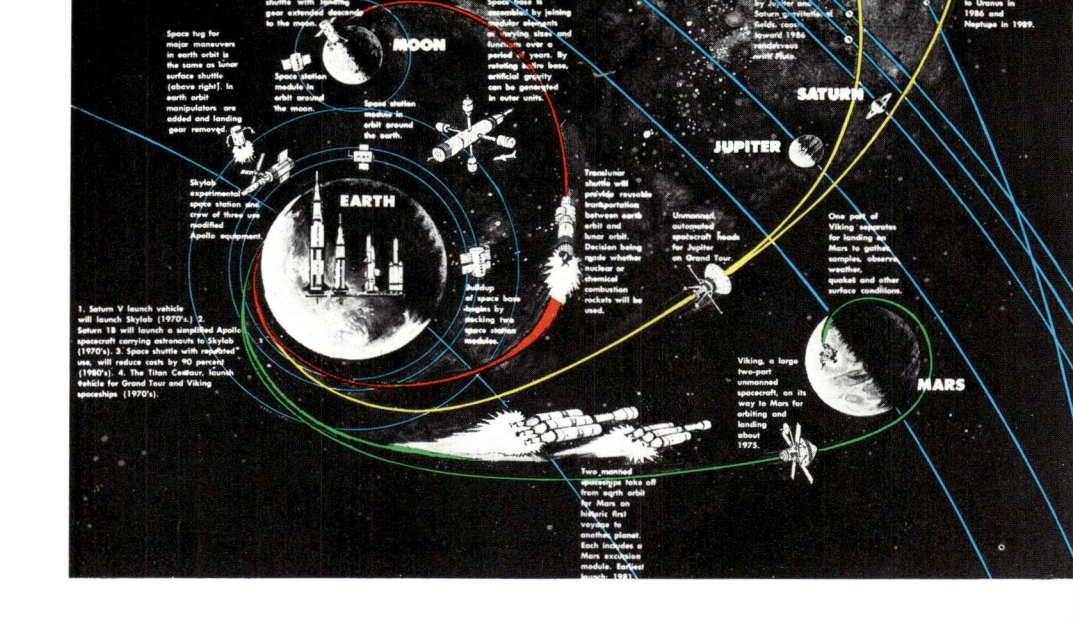

Adoption of a joint American-Vietnamese accountability system for aid grant imports that cut delivery losses between ships and warehouses to a fraction of 1 per cent.

Another of these projects concerns communications. A new satellite communications earth station has been built in Indonesia, linking the nation into a global satellite network, which provides improved international telephone, telegraph and television communications. This project has been undertaken by the Indonesian Government with the help of the American giant, International Telephone and Telegraph Corporation, ITT, which has built, equipped and agreed to operate the station for the next twenty years on a profit-sharing basis. The entire scheme has been made possible by the co-operation of U.S. AID which insured ITT's loan, thus making the investment possibility more attractive to the private financiers who backed the project.

Both in government and academic circles there has been a great interest in the United Nations Conference of the Human Environment to be held in 1972. The three themes of the conference—human settlements, management of natural resources and pollution control—are all of immediate interest to developing countries.

Many Asian countries are now beginning to realise that investment in pollution control and effective planning for preservation of the environment is not, in an overall economic sense, expensive. Such investment can lead to improved overall productivity by lowering the social costs such as health services and increasing the productivity of such industries as fishing.

In their contacts with Asian governments U.S. AID has encouraged bilateral research on the long-term effects of developmentary schemes. For example, there is a project in the Philippines to increase the agricultural productivity of the area around Laguna de Bay, a lake near Manila that is partially open to the sea. The damming of the outlet would result in a fresh water supply for agriculture, industry and the many settlements about the lake.

However, such damming might have unwanted secondary effects, such as preventing the flushing action of the sea, and the waters running into the lake would carry fertilisers from the farms as well as human waste. This increased nutritional load could lead to an explosion of water weeds or to eutrophication, the rapid growth of algae—both of which would kill off the rich fish population of the lake.

Currently, the development project is being examined by a team of experts to determine how best to meet the agricultural development needs of the region and preserve the fishing resources of the lake.

CONCLUSION. The United States of America has played an increasing role in the development of Asia since the end of World War II. Today, its projects—from the Bi-National Centre in Bangkok to the satellite communications earth station in Indonesia—play interlocking parts in a drama of vital importance to the future of mankind—the spreading of technology and a reasonable standard of living to over half the world's population. As United States President, Richard Nixon said in a radio address in February, 1971:

"A new Asia is emerging. The old enmities of World War II are dead or dying. Asian states are stronger and are joining together in vigorous regional groupings...

In the way they work together, and in the way we co-operate with their relationship, is the key to permanent peace in that area —and the Far East, the scene of such painful legacy of the recent past, can become an example of peace and stability in the future."

The Publishers gratefully acknowledge the valuable co-operation of the following Governments, Government bodies and private enterprise organisations in providing text and pictures and in various other ways making the publication of this volume possible.

AUSTRALIA
Prime Minister's Department
Department of Foreign Affairs
Department of Trade and Industry
Department of Immigration
Department of External Territories
Department of Primary Industry
Australian Wheat Board
Australian Wool Board
Australian Mining Industry Council
Snowy Mountains Hydro-Electric Authority
Qantas Airways Ltd.
Associated Chambers of Manufactures
Broken Hill Proprietary Company Limited
Colonial Sugar Refinery Co. Ltd.
Conzinc Riotinto of Australia
F & T Industries Ltd.
Fluor Australia Pty. Ltd.
General Motors-Holdens Pty. Ltd.
Hamersley Holdings Ltd.
ICI Australia Limited
NSW Department of Tourism
Oliver Shaul & Associates Pty. Ltd., Sydney
Overseas Telecommunications Com. (Aust.)
Pacific Basin Economic Council
Southern Cross Inter-Continental Hotel, Melbourne
Summit Restaurant, Sydney
Asian Broadcasting Union
Partnership Pacific Pty. Ltd.
The Chartered Bank Ltd.

BANGLADESH
Ministry of Information & Broadcasting,

BRUNEI
State of Brunei, Department of Broadcasting and Information

BURMA
Embassy of the Union of Burma, Canberra

CANADA
High Commission for Canada, Canberra

CHINA, Republic of
Government Information Office
Chinese Embassy, Canberra
Tourism Bureau, Ministry of Communications
China Airlines
First Commercial Bank of Taiwan
Taiwan Aluminium Corporation
Taiwan Shipbuilding Corporation
Taiwan Petroleum Corporation
Taiwan Power Corporation
Taiwan Sugar Corporation

HONG KONG
Hong Kong Government Information Services
Hong Kong Tourist Association
Cathay Pacific Airways Ltd.
The Hong Kong and Shanghai Banking Corp.
Wheelock Marden & Co. Ltd.
The Hong Kong & Shanghai Hotels Ltd.
Cable & Wireless Ltd.
Dodwell & Co. Ltd.
Asia Dairy Industries (Hong Kong) Ltd.
Graphic Communication Ltd.

INDONESIA
Dept. of Information, Govt. of Indonesia
Indonesia Foreign Languages Institute
P. N. Pertamina
Hotel Bali Beach Inter-Continental
Hotel Indonesia Inter-Continental
P.T. Australia—Indonesia Milk Industries

INDIA
Republic of India, Department of External Affairs, Foreign Ministry
High Commission of India, Canberra
State Trading Corporation of India Ltd.
Birla Bombay Pvt. Ltd., Bombay.
Minerals & Metals Trading Corp. of India.
Tata Industries Pvt. Ltd., Bombay
The Cotton Textiles Export Promotion Council
Bombay Dyeing & Manufg. Co. Ltd., Bombay
Ulka Advertising Pvt. Ltd., Bombay

JAPAN
The Japanese Embassy, Canberra,
The Japanese Consulate-General, Sydney
The Tokyo Chamber of Commerce
Nippon Steel Corporation
Mitsubishi Shoji Kaisha Ltd.
Mitsui & Co. Ltd.
Sumitomo Shoji Kaisha Ltd.
Japan Air Lines
Marubeni Corporation
C. Itoh & Co. Ltd.
Nissho-Iwai Co. Ltd.
Nissan Motor Co. Ltd.
Hitachi Ltd.
Tokyo Shibaura Electric Co. Ltd.
The Bank of Tokyo Ltd.
Kanematsu-Gosho Ltd.
Nippon Yusen Kabushiki Kaisha
Yamashita Shinnihon Steamship Co. Ltd.
Dodwell Marketing & Industry Consultants
Tokyo Boeki Ltd.
Japan National Tourist Organisation
Hotel Keio Plaza Inter-Continental
Nihon Keizaisha Advertising Ltd.

KOREA
Embassy of the Republic of Korea, Canberra
Ministry of Culture & Information

KHMER REPUBLIC, Cambodia
Embassy of the Khmer Republic, Canberra

LAOS
The Royal Lao Embassy, Bangkok, Thailand

MALAYSIA
Federal Department of Information, Ministry of Foreign Affairs
Department of Tourism
Malaysian Airline System
Penang Port Commission
Port Klang Authority
The Tin Industry (Research & Devt.) Board
Dunlop Malaysian Industries Berhad
Selangor Pewter Co. Sdn. Bhd.

NEPAL
Royal Nepalese Consulate General, Sydney

NEW ZEALAND
New Zealand High Commission, Canberra
New Zealand National Tourist & Publicity Dept.
New Zealand Broadcasting Corporation.
Inter-Continental Hotel Auckland.

PAKISTAN
Government of Islamic Republic of Pakistan Ministry of Inf. & National Affairs
Embassy of Pakistan, Canberra
Dawood Corporation
Pakistan International Airlines Corporation
Pakistan Tourism Development Corp. Ltd.
Hotel Inter-Continental, Karachi

THE PHILIPPINES
Department of Foreign Affairs
Embassy of the Philippines, Canberra, A.C.T.
Board of Travel and Tourist Industry
National Science Development Board
Philippine Air Lines
Philippine National Bank
A. Soriano y Cia
San Miguel Corporation
Manila Electric Co. (Meralco)
Atlas Mining Corporation
Philips Industrial Development Inc
Hotel Inter-Continental Manila

SINGAPORE
Republic of Singapore, Ministry of Culture
Singapore Tourist Promotion Board
Singapore Airlines
Straits Times Press (Malaysia) Berhad
Neptune Orient Lines Ltd.
Fraser & Neave (Singapore) Pte. Ltd.
The Port of Singapore Authority
Goodwood Hotels Corp. Pte. Ltd.
Shangri-La Hotel
Hotel Singapura Inter-Continental
Oversea-Chinese Banking Corporation Ltd.

SRI LANKA (Ceylon)
High Commission of Sri Lanka, Canberra,

THAILAND
Ministry of Foreign Affairs
The Royal Thai Embassy, Canberra, A.C.T.
Bangkok Bank Ltd.
The Construction Material Marketing Co. Ltd.
Thai Petrochemical Company Ltd.
Thai Oil Corporation
South-east Asian Ministers of Education Sec.
Hotel Siam Inter-Continental
Tourist Organisation of Thailand

UNITED STATES OF AMERICA
Embassy of the U.S.A. Canberra.
United States Information Service, Sydney

UNITED NATIONS
United Nations Information Centre, Sydney

VIETNAM
Embassy of the Republic of Vietnam, Canberra

The Publishers also gratefully acknowledge those responsible, in addition to those mentioned above, for contributing special material.

Art and Maps
The late Gert Sellheim (jacket design).
Bruce Watson
Harry Rogers
Victor Galbraith
Hagley & Hoyle.

Martin Bright (portraits of the Rt. Hon. William McMahon CH.MP. and the Hon. Sir Edward Warren).

Photographs
Mrs. B.J. Mander-Jones
Steve Vidler
Colin S. Freestone, B. Ec., Dip. Ed., Dip. Ind.
Mrs. Margaret Davis
Arthur M. Davis
Victor Minca
The Asia Magazine Ltd.
Photographic Library of Australia

S.E.A.M.E.S.
U.N.E.S.C.O.
Max Dupain and Associates
Department of Main Roads N.S.W.
Australian Tourist Commission
Aust. Department of External Territories
New South Wales Government Tourist Bureau
Ceylon Tea Bureau
Australian News and Information Bureau
Tourist Organisation of Thailand
Hong Kong Government Information Services
National Library Australia
Cathay Advertising, Kuala Lumpur

Special Editorials and Texts
Peter Hinton, M.A., Prof. Anthrop. (Univ. Sydney)
Colin S. Freestone, B.Ec., Dip. Ed., Dip. Ind.
M.S. Ahmad, Director Asian Highway

Peter Moss, Hong Kong
Brian Walsh, Sydney
Kapto Sonoto, Executive Board Chairman Foreign Language Publishing Inst. Djakarta
Marah Joenoes, Director Public Relations Pertamina.
Prabhat Chuenprasit, Bangkok.
Hong Kong Tourist Association
Dr. R.E. Precians, Macquarie University, Sydney
Christine Deer, Macquarie University, Sydney
M. Shimada, Japanese Consulate-General, Sydney
Roy O. Daniel, Ministry of Culture, Singapore.
V.D.P. Pillai, Ministry Foreign Aff. Malaysia
Ting Wei-tung, Director China News, Taiwan
Dr. Alfredo T. Morales, Asian Inst. for Teacher Educators, Philippines
Prof. Salvador P. Lopez, Pres. Univ. Philippines

THE FOLLOWING AUSTRALIAN ORGANISATIONS
have joined together in a co-operative effort to generate
a better, more tolerant and mutually beneficial understanding
among the nations of the world. The publication of
this book is a notable step towards
achieving their objectives.

AUSTRALIAN DAIRY PRODUCE BOARD
A. P. Beatty Esq.
Chairman

AUSTRALIAN GAS LIGHT CO.
Sir William W. Pettingell, C.B.E., B.Sc.
General Manager

AUSTRALIAN MEAT BOARD
Col. M. H. McArthur, O.B.E.
Chairman

BANK OF NEW SOUTH WALES
Sir John Cadwallader, K. T.
President

COAL & ALLIED (SALES) PTY. LTD.
The Hon. Sir Edward Warren, K.C.M.G., K.B.E.,
M.S.M., O.M.S.T., R.S.G.C., M.L.C.
Chairman

DAVID JONES LIMITED
Charles B. Lloyd Jones Esq.
Chairman

LAPORTE (AUSTRALIA) LIMITED
J. Maddock Esq.
Chairman

THE MUTUAL LIFE & CITIZENS' ASSURANCE
COMPANY LIMITED
A. F. Deer Esq., B.A., LL.B., B.Ec.
General Manager

P & O LINES OF AUSTRALIA PTY. LTD.
R. T. M. Rose Esq.
Chairman

PEKO-WALLSEND LIMITED
John S. Proud Esq.
Chairman

PHILIPS INDUSTRIES LTD.
H. D. Huyer Esq.
Chairman

PENFOLD WINES PTY. LTD.
J. Penfold-Hyland Esq., O.B.E.
Chairman

PROUDS PTY. LTD.
George Proud Esq.
Chairman

TRANS-AUSTRALIA AIRLINES
Air Chief Marshall Sir Frederick Scherger, K.B.E.,
C.B., D.S.O., A.F.C.,
Chairman

ALBERTO DA CRUZ a Senior Information Officer of the Hong Kong Government, formerly taught English in a Hong Kong school. He was a newspaper Features Editor and News Editor, author of an English text book for Chinese students and wrote a novel on the Opium War of the 1840's. His "History of the Asian Nations" and "Asian Gods and Creeds" are interesting chapters appearing in this book.

DEREK GWYN DAVIES M.A., a London born Welshman, was an Open Exhibitionist at Jesus College, Cambridge. He joined Reuters and was later appointed British Vice-Consul in Hanoi, North Vietnam in 1957 and then second Secretary at the British Embassy in Vienna (1959-61). In 1962 he joined the Far Eastern Economic Review, becoming editor in 1964. "The Economic Explosion" is his contribution to this book.

DICK WILSON whose contribution to this book is "The Mighty Mekong Project," is a noted author and journalist specialising in Asian affairs. Educated at Oxford and the University of California, he won the Magsaysay Award for Journalism and Literature in 1964. He has been a frequent contributor to leading British and Asian journals.

W. J. WEEDEN, O.B.E., M.A., Dip.Ed., was Senior Assistant Secretary to the Commonwealth Department of Education and Science until his recent retirement. He was Chairman of the Australian National Advisory Committee for UNESCO, and on eleven occasions a member of the Australian delegation to UNESCO General Conferences. His "UNESCO in Asia" appears in our opening chapters.

JAMES WADE author of the Korea Chapter of this book, is an American journalist and musician who came to Korea as a member of the U.S. Army in 1954. He has written three books and contributed innumerable articles for journals in most English speaking countries. His opera, "The Martyred", with a Korean theme, had a successful premiere in the South Korean capital during 1970.

PURA SANTILLAN-CASTRENCE Ph.C. B.S., M.S., M.A., Ph.D. is a former Ambassador of the Philippines, a senior officer of the Dept. of Foreign Affairs and holder of several Professorships at the University of The Philippines and Centro Escolar University. Named "Most Outstanding Filipino Woman Writer in English" in 1949 and "Most Distinguished Writer" in 1957. She co-ordinated the Philippines Chapter of this book.

CLIVE TURNBULL has written innumerable articles on Australian life. Author of many books, his most recent is "Australia: A Concise History", published by Thomas and Hudson. He edited "Hammond Innes Introduces Australia", a symposium published by Andre Deutsch in late 1971. His informative segment "The Wakening Land" introduces the Australia Chapter of this book.

S. AMJAD ALI C.I.S. is Deputy Director of Films and Publications in the Pakistan Ministry of Information and National Affairs. He is a noted author and was responsible for the general text and pictures for the Pakistan Chapter. He is editor of the well known journal "Pakistan Quarterly" and regularly contributes to official publications such as "Focus on Pakistan".

Authors

IN THE compilation of "The World and South-east Asia" many writers from the Asian and Pacific regions were called upon. They made significant contributions, in some cases in the form of special articles, and in others in the co-ordination of editorial material for specific chapters. Brief biographical notes of the more prominent of these writers are recorded on these pages.

THE RT. HON. A. A. CALWELL P.C., K.C.G.S., LL.B.(hon.), M.P. For more than 40 years, Mr. Calwell has been one of Australia's most colourful and able politicians. For seven years he was Leader of the Federal Opposition and during that time he became a Privy Councillor. In 1964 he received a Papal Knighthood (Knight Commander of the Order of St. Gregory the Great with Grand Silver Star). Mr. Calwell's fine work in planning and implementing Australia's Immigration Policy has earned him immortality in the annals of the country's history. His article "A Migrant Nation" appears in the Australia Chapter of this book.

INDEX TO ARTICLES

	Page
FOREWORD	
The Rt. Hon. William McMahon C.H., M.P. Prime Minister of Australia	5
PREFACE	7
CONTENTS	8
HISTORY OF THE ASIAN NATIONS	10
THE ECONOMIC EXPLOSION	26
UNESCO IN ASIA	42
THE SIGNIFICANCE OF SEAMEO	46
THE MIGHTY MEKONG PROJECT	50
THE ASIAN HIGHWAY	56
ASIAN GODS AND CREEDS	62
THE NOMAD TRIBES OF ASIA	68
KINGDOM OF BHUTAN	72
Map of Bhutan	74
Statistics	75
Valleys of Seclusion	76
SULTANATE OF BRUNEI	80
Sir Omar Ali Saifuddin Mosque	82
Map of Sumatra, Java and Borneo 1651	84
Statistics	85
An Eastern Sultanate	86
Life in Brunei	87
The Brunei People. Brunei Oil. Health.	89
Education. Social Services.	90
Banking and Finance	90
UNION OF BURMA	92
Map of Burma	94
Statistics	95
The Road to Mandalay	96
REPUBLIC OF SRI LANKA	100
Map of Ceylon	102
Statistics	103
The Resplendent Island	104
Cultural Heritage	105
Economic Structure	105
A Farmer in Ceylon	107
Colombo. Sports and Recreations.	109
Education. The Future.	109
REPUBLIC OF CHINA	110
Map of Taiwan	112
Statistics	113
The Island of Taiwan	116
"Wen"	118
Population Control	120
The Education System	120
The Political System	121

	Page
Taiwan is for the Tourist	122
Banking in Taiwan	126
Manufacture. Foreign Trade.	129
Taiwan Shipbuilding	130
Chemical Fertilisers	131
Taiwan Aluminium	131
Development of Electric Power	132
Chinese Petroleum	133
Agriculture	134
Technical Co-operation	135
The Sugar Industry	136
Communications	137
China Airlines	138
Television in Taiwan	140
Radio	141
COMMONWEALTH OF AUSTRALIA	142
Map of Australia	144
Central Australia Scene	146
The Wakening Land	148
Papua New Guinea Looks to Its Neighbours	154
A Migrant Nation	156
Australia—The Modern Mecca	158
Summit Talk	160
The Land of "The Southern Cross"	162
The Banking Scene	164
Australian Retailing	166
Natural Gas—Its Multiple Uses	168
Australian Opals and other Gemstones	170
Safeguarding Prosperity	173
Communications Gateway for South-east Asia	174
Sea, Land, and Air	175
Go North-West, Young Man!	176
Australia's Air Networks	178
The Maritime Revolution	180
The Growth of Industry	182
Australia as a World Trader	183
Australia's Automotive Innovator	184
Australian Technology Helps Asian Industry	186
Enterprise in Industry	188
The World of Electronics	190
Industrial Chemicals in the Modern World	192
Chemical Technology and Know-How	194
Makers of Modern Living	196
Australia's Physical Environment	198
Rural Industries	198
Australia's Wool in Asia's Future.	202

	Page
Proteins for the People of Asia	206
Australian wheat	209
Australian Sugar	210
Wine For the Orient	212
Meat for Asia's Millions	214
The Snowy Mountains Scheme	216
Australian Mining	218
The Significance of Coal in the Future of Asia	220
Mineral Diversities	222
Shaping a Continent	224
Iron Ore Country	226
Systems of Government	227
HONG KONG	228
Map of Hong Kong	230
The Boat Races	232
Hong Kong Story	234
The Switch to Industry	235
The Population Pressure	236
The System of Government	238
Cultures—Old and New	239
Changing Attitudes	241
The Family of Wing-Kun	242
The Hongkong and Shanghai Banking Corporation	244
The House of Heavenly Prosperity	248
Cables and Wireless Links Asia with the Rest of the World	250
The Hongs of Hong Kong	252
Seeing Hong Kong	256
History in the Making	259
The Air-World of Asia	262
REPUBLIC OF INDIA	264
This Ancient Land	266
Map of India	267
History in Perspective	268
The Government of India	270
Population Problems	270
Education. The Social Melieu.	270
Architecture and Sculpture	272
Painting. Dance	272
Music. Sports and Games.	273
Growth of Industry	274
The Economy. Export Markets	274
The Birlas of Bombay	276
India's Cotton Textiles	280
The State Trading Corporation of India	282
India's Woven Miracles	284
Mining and Minerals	286
Communications	287
Tata's Realm	288

	Page		Page		Page
International Co-operation	289	KINGDOM OF LAOS	392	A Filipino Farmer's Family	494
What of India's Future	289	Map of Laos	394	The Filipinos	494
India—Made for the Tourist	290	Statistics	395	Education Systems	495
KINGDOM OF SIKKIM	292	Kingdom of a Million Elephants	396	Economy	496
REPUBLIC OF INDONESIA	294	Conflict of Ideologies	398	The Government	497
Map of Indonesia. Statistics	296	The Economy	398	The Many Worlds of the Philippines	498
The Peoples of Indonesia	298	Customs Festivals and Arts	399	The Philippine Economy	502
The World's Largest Archipelago	300	FEDERATION OF MALAYSIA	400	Mineral Resources	502
Climatic Conditions	302	Map of Malaysia. Statistics	402	The Significance of Copper	502
Natural Resources	302	A Nation Emerging	404	National Science Development	504
Resource Utilisation	302	Realisation of Malaysia	405	The Philippine National Bank in Economic Progress	506
Agriculture. Manufacturing	303	The Country and its People	405	The Story of San Miguel	508
Oil in the Indonesian Economy	304	The Language. Religions. Festivals	405	Electric Power for National Development	510
Indonesia's Indomilk	308	The System of Government	406	Shaping a New Foreign Policy	512
The Family of Shamsuddin	310	The Installation	406	Electronics in the Philippines	513
City Life	312	Social Development	406	Hotel Inter-Continental Manila	514
A Tourists' Dream	313	Malaysia—Exotic Symbol of the Orient	407	To the Philippines with PAL	516
Handicrafts	314	Malaysian Art	411	REPUBLIC OF SINGAPORE	518
Economic Development	314	Dance and Drama	411	Map of Singapore	520
Rising Society	316	Games and Pastimes. Sports	411	Singapura—Lion City	524
Hotel Indonesia	318	The Federated States of Malaysia	412	Instant Asia	526
Bali Beach	319	Malaysian Railways	414	Art and Culture. Festivals	528
JAPAN	320	Air, Sea and Land Services	414	Education—A Giant Task	528
Map of Japan	322	East-west Highway Project	414	Solving the Housing Problem	529
Cherry Blossom Time	324	Communications	415	Sport. Trends in Development	530
A Country Called Japan	326	Port Klang	415	Manufacturing Industries	530
Who are the Japanese?	326	Port of Penang	416	Jurong Town	530
Living in Japan	328	MAS—Malaysian Airline System	418	International Relations	531
Japan's Democracy	328	The Malaysian Economy	420	The Future	531
Art and Culture	329	Rubber in Malaysia	421	The Overseas Chinese Banking Corpn.	532
The Education System	330	Straits tin	422	Singapore A.B.C.	534
An Urban Family at Home	332	Other Malaysian Minerals	425	Telling the World of Asia	536
Japan at Play	334	The Story of Selangor Pewter	426	Singapore—Container Port	539
Japan's Newest, Most Luxurious Hotel	334	KINGDOM OF NEPAL	428	Over the Seas in Ships	540
Foreign Exchange—Mainspring of Japan's Overseas Trade	336	Map of Nepal	430	Singapore Airlines—A New Bird on the Wing	542
An Industrious People	338	Statistics	431	Sojourn in Singapore	544
Growth of Industry	339	Kingdom in the Snows	432	Shangri-La	548
The Meiji Restoration and the Economic Miracle	340	The People and Life in Nepal	434	Singapura Inter-Continental	549
Industrial Unity Japanese Style	342	NEW ZEALAND	436	KINGDOM OF THAILAND	550
Steel—Blueprint of Success	344	Map of New Zealand	438	Map of Thailand	552
The Japanese Car	346	The Discovery of New Zealand	440	Statistics	553
Machinery—Image of New Japan	348	Government. The Ombudsman	440	Land of Smiles	554
The Electrical Goods Industry of Japan	350	Administration	440	Cultures	556
Japan in the World of Commerce	352	Public Services	441	Education. The Arts	557
Foreign Trade	354	Living in New Zealand	442	Modernisation Trends	558
Diversification in Commerce	354	Trade and Industry	444	Tourism	559
Trading with the Giants	356	Television and Radio in New Zealand	446	Entertainment and Night Life	559
Total Business	357	High Living in the Pacific Crossroads	447	Hotel Siam Inter-Continental	560
The Big Ten	358	ISLAMIC REPUBLIC OF PAKISTAN	448	Life of a Thai	562
The Trading House System	360	Map of Pakistan	450	Sports. Economy	563
Merchant Adventurers—World Traders	362	The Nature of Pakistan	451	Development of Industry	564
Transport	364	Background to History	452	Commercial Banking in Thailand	566
The Post War Growth of Civil Aviation	364	The People	455	Industrial Giants of Thailand	568
Japan's Merchant Marine	366	The Culture of Pakistan	456	Thai Oil	570
Agriculture	368	Education in Pakistan	458	The Thai Petrochemical Project	571
Fisheries	369	The Cities of Pakistan	460	REPUBLIC OF VIETNAM	572
Unique Tourist Land	370	The East Pakistan Crisis	462	Map of Vietnam	574
KHMER REPUBLIC (Cambodia)	372	The Nation's Economy	464	Statistics	575
Map of Khmer Republic	374	Agriculture	464	The Land Beyond the South	576
Statistics	375	Water and Power	466	Life in Saigon	577
A New-Born Republic	376	Good Living in Karachi	467	Preparing for the Tet	578
Primary Industry	377	On the Threshold of the Himalayas	468	THE PACIFIC BASIN	580
The Economy	378	Pakistan's National Airline	470	Pacific Basin Co-operation	582
The Lure of Angkor Wat	378	The Dawoods of Pakistan	472	Australia's Role in Asian Development	586
Military and Economic Aid	378	The Role of Pakistan	476	New Zealand and PBEC	589
Phnom Penh and its People	378	PEOPLE'S REPUBLIC OF BANGLADESH	478	The Nation Builders	590
Life in a Khmer Farming Community	379	Map of Bangladesh	480	British Overseas Banks	594
REPUBLIC OF KOREA	380	Young Nation, Old Country	482	Canadian Involvement in the Development of Asia	598
Map of Korea	382	The Land and the Living	483	Japan's Economic Aid to Developing Countries	602
New Horizons for an Ancient Nation	383	The Economy	484	Partnership Pacific	606
Land of the Morning Calm	384	Industry. Agriculture	485	The Asian Broadcasting Union	607
The Arts, Literature and Music	386	Natural Resources. Transport	485	The U.S.A. in Asia	608
South Korean Economy	386	REPUBLIC OF THE PHILIPPINES	486	ACKNOWLEDGEMENTS	612
Seeing Korea. National Sports	387	Map of the Philippines	488	AUTHORS	614
A modern Family in Korea	388	Facts about the Philippines	489	INDEX	615
Government	391	Whence Came the Filipino?	490		
		The Cultural Heritage	492		